SQL-99 Complete, Really

Peter Gulutzan and Trudy Pelzer

R&D Books
Lawrence, Kansas 66046

R&D Books
Miller Freeman, Inc.
1601 W. 23rd Street, Suite 200
Lawrence, KS 66046
USA

Designations used by companies to distinguish their products are often claimed as trademarks. In all instances where R&D is aware of a trademark claim, the product name appears in initial capital letters, in all capital letters, or in accordance with the vendor's capitalization preference. Readers should contact the appropriate companies for more complete information on trademarks and trademark registrations. All trademarks and registered trademarks in this book are the property of their respective holders.

The programs in this book are presented for instructional value. The programs have been carefully tested, but are not guaranteed for any particular purpose. The publisher does not offer any warranties and does not guarantee the accuracy, adequacy, or completeness of any information herein and is not responsible for any errors or omissions. The publisher assumes no liability for damages resulting from the use of the information in this book or for any infringement of the intellectual property rights of third parties that would result from the use of this information.

Cover art created by Robert Ward.

Distributed in the U.S. and Canada by:
Publishers Group West
P.O. Box 8843
Emeryville, CA 94662
ISBN: 0-87930-568-1

Trademarks

Access:	Microsoft Corp.
DB2:	International Business Machines Corp.
dBASE IV:	Inprise Corporation
Delphi:	Inprise Corporation
Informix:	Informix Corporation
Ingres:	Computer Associates International Inc.
Java:	Sun Microsystems, Inc.
Ocelot, OCELOT DBMS:	Ocelot Computer Services Inc.
Oracle:	Oracle Corp.
Paradox:	Inprise Corporation
SQL Server:	Sybase, Inc.
SQL/DS:	International Business Machines Corp.
Unicode:	Unicode, Inc.
Windows, Windows95, WindowsNT, SQL Server:	Microsoft Corp.

All trademarks (those above and any others mentioned in this book) are the property of their respective owners.

Table of Contents

Appendices on the CD-ROM

Preface

If you've ever used a relational database product, chances are that you're already familiar with SQL — the internationally-accepted standard programming language for databases which is supported by the vast majority of relational database management system (DBMS) products available today. You may also have noticed that, despite the large number of "reference" works that claim to describe standard SQL, not a single one provides a complete, accurate, and example-filled description of the entire SQL Standard. This book was written to fill that void.

Who Should Read this Book?

This book will be valuable to anyone who works with a DBMS that supports SQL. While our emphasis is on programming with SQL, you do not need to be a programmer to learn SQL from our examples. We do assume you know something about Windows and something about C, but our main concern is that you are interested in using "ANSI Standard SQL" in your projects. This is both a beginner's and an advanced-user's book. Our hope is that a beginner will be able to avoid the traditional "for beginners" books which, sadly, contain so much drivel that it is impossible to advance from them without re-learning everything.

Your Windows knowledge needn't be extensive, as we won't be getting into the details of the Windows Application Programming Interface (API). We'll touch only on things that occur in all versions of Windows, and occasionally analogize with Windows concepts and terms.

As for C, we assume you can read simple C programs, even if your favourite programming language is something else. We want to show you examples of SQL as it's used in programming projects — that is, in company with a "host language" — and C seemed the convenient choice. All example programs provided are short.

What's In It?

World's Longest SQL Poem (for obvious reasons)

All the snake-oil peddlers say, there's a fast and easy way,
To get your SQL program up and running,
But they're silent re the traps, that cause subtly buggy apps,
For to catch the unaware a chasm's yawning!

Date-arithmetic exceptions, auto-rollbacked disconnections,
Bit precisions, overflows, collate coercions,
And how NULL affects your summing, for to keep your DB humming,
You must know what happens in all vendors' versions!

Should this field be DOUBLE PRECISION?
Will logic rules soon see revision?
By the ANSI:Databases sub-committee?
When you DROP should you CASCADE?
How are NATURAL joins made?
Re UNIQUE-keys matching check the nitty-gritty!

Yeah the true and standard facts, you'll avoid those later hacks
That make Structured Query Language such a bore,
You'll find tips and charts aplenty, in this one-thousand-and-twenty
Four page volume (with an index) and yet more!

Author anon (also for obvious reasons)

This book describes the SQL syntax a DBMS must support to comply with the International Organization for Standardization (ISO) document ISO/IEC 9075:1999 Database Language SQL, also adopted as the American National Standards Institute (ANSI) document X3.135-1999 Database Language SQL — familiarly known as SQL3, standard SQL or ANSI SQL. We will use the more familiar terms "SQL" or "SQL3" to describe standard-conforming SQL in this book, rather than the formal term SQL-99.

It's true that some features discussed in this book aren't in <fill in your DBMS name here>. That's no reason to ignore them, because sooner or later they will be there, due to pressure on serious vendors to adhere to the SQL Standard.

Why Read It?

You need to know SQL, so you've been looking for an accurate reference work that describes the entire SQL Standard by way of examples. This is that book.

How much of what you need to know is in this book? Well, it's impossible for a single book to contain everything you need. We guarantee that the coverage is complete for the SQL language itself and is adequate for subjects that closely relate to SQL. Let's express "what you *will* know" as a percentage of "what you *should* know," with an assumption that you're an "average" person.

SQL3 Standard "foundation"	90%
Earlier ANSI and ISO Standards	100%
SQL/CLI	100%
Embedded SQL and host languages	40%
Object orientation (UDTs)	20%
Relational database theory	10%
Design	10%
Quirks of specific vendors' dialects	5%

"Complete" does not mean that everything which could be said about SQL will be said here. SQL is big. More exactly, it means that we will never refer you to further published material saying "the details are in the official standard document" or "further discussion is outside the scope of this book."

Further Information

When you look at our Table of Contents, you'll see that this book includes several Appendices, but only on the accompanying CD-ROM, to keep the book from becoming too unwieldy. Of the Appendix files, we especially recommend Appendix F, the Glossary (`appF.html` on the CD-ROM). It provides definitions for all the SQL technical terms we use.

1

Chapter 1

Introduction

SQL-99 (more commonly still called, "SQL3," the term we'll use throughout this book) will soon be the current internationally-accepted standard for the database programming language called SQL. The SQL Standard — a complicated monster consisting of over 2,100 pages of definitions, syntax, and usage rules — describes the required syntax and the rules that must be followed to generate the required result when the syntax is executed by a standard-conforming DBMS. (This compares to less than 150 pages required to describe the Standard's earlier version, SQL-89.) This book was written to describe standard-conforming SQL.

How To Read This Book

In this book, we've used the same descriptive terminology you'd find in the SQL Standard. You can check the meaning of unfamiliar terms in the glossary on the CD-ROM. To make it easier for you to follow our discussion, we use these notation conventions throughout:

- Words with special meaning in SQL are shown capitalized, e.g., Table.
- Words within angle brackets have specific definitions in SQL. See the appropriate syntax diagram for that definition.
- Direct SQL requires all SQL statements to be terminated with a semicolon. This book does not include the terminator in SQL syntax diagrams, but does include it in SQL statement examples.

Everything we describe is as mandated by the SQL Standard explicitly, unless the discussion starts with the notation: [OCELOT Implementation]. We use this notation to describe the conventions followed by THE OCELOT DBMS; the DBMS you'll find on the CD-ROM that comes with the book. Despite this, everything described as an [OCELOT Implementation] is legitimate SQL; it does not contradict the SQL mandate. Rather, it describes OCELOT's SQL implementation for the many areas where the SQL Standard specifies the matter is "implementation-defined" or "implementation-dependent." These are areas to note because there is no Standard-specified definition; requirements and responses will vary from one DBMS to another. Discussion of these areas starts with the notation: [NON-PORTABLE].

You may initially skip over paragraphs which begin with the notation: [Obscure Rule]. They describe details which will probably be unclear upon first reading and which are normally not utilized in typical installations.

How to Read SQL Syntax

We have used the following common variant of BNF notation for the SQL syntax diagrams in this book:

< > Angle brackets surround the names of syntactic elements. The brackets are not part of the syntax; do not include them in your SQL statement.

::= The definition operator separates the syntactic element being defined from its definition. Read the definition from left to right.

[ ] Square brackets surround optional syntax. You may choose whether or not to omit such syntax when forming an SQL statement. The brackets are not part of the syntax; do not include them in your SQL statement.

{ } Braces surround mandatory syntax groupings. You must include the entire grouping when forming an SQL statement. The braces are not part of the syntax; do not include them in your SQL statement.

| The vertical bar separates groups of syntactic elements. You must choose one of the elements when forming an SQL statement. The vertical bar is not part of the syntax; do not include it in your SQL statement.

... An ellipsis following a syntactic element indicates that the syntax is repeatable. You may include the element as often as you wish when forming an SQL statement. The ellipsis is not part of the syntax; do not include it in your SQL statement.

Blank spaces (whether single or multiple spaces and/or line breaks) separate syntactic elements.

All other characters in a definition stand for themselves.

We also follow these notation conventions:

- Words written in uppercase letters are SQL <keyword>s. You must write them exactly as shown when forming an SQL statement, except that you have the choice of writing them in either uppercase or lowercase letters.

- Words written in lowercase letters represent syntactic categories. You must replace them with actual <identifier>s or <literal>s when forming an SQL statement.
- Parentheses that appear in a syntax diagram are part of the syntax. You must include them when forming an SQL statement.

Thus, as in the following simplified example of an SQL syntax diagram:

```
CREATE TABLE <Table name> (
     <Column name> {INTEGER | CHARACTER(5)} )
```

- The words CREATE and TABLE are SQL <keyword>s and must be included without changes in a CREATE TABLE statement.
- The words <Table name> and <Column name> are syntactic categories and must be replaced with an actual <Table name> and <Column name>, respectively, in a CREATE TABLE statement. The angle brackets around Table name and Column name indicate these terms are defined with a syntax diagram somewhere in this book.
- The parentheses are part of the syntax and must be included exactly where shown in a CREATE TABLE statement.
- The braces and vertical bar after the <Column name> indicate that either one of the SQL <keyword>s INTEGER or CHARACTER(5) must be included without changes in a CREATE TABLE statement.

Based on this example, the following two SQL statements are the only valid uses of the syntax.

```
CREATE TABLE A_Table_Name (
     a_column_name INTEGER);

CREATE TABLE A_Table_Name (
     a_column_name CHARACTER(5));
```

What is SQL?

SQL (originally, Structured Query Language) is an internationally-recognized programming language for defining and maintaining relational databases.

Initially developed by IBM in the late 1970's, SQL caught on in the database world as vendors, realizing the many advantages of the relational approach to database management, began to develop commercial products based on those principles. Because SQL was the language most commonly supported by the new products, it soon became the *de facto* standard for relational database products.

The popularity of SQL further increased when the language became an official standard in October of 1986, with ANSI's (the American National Standards Institute) release of ANSI document X3.135-1986 "Database Language SQL." This first SQL Standard, SQL-86, became internationally accepted in 1987 when the International Organization for Standardization (ISO) — a worldwide federation of national standards bodies — adopted the ANSI document as well.

SQL-86 was updated and enhanced in 1989. ANSI X3.168-1989 "Database Language — Embedded SQL" became official in April of 1989. ANSI X3.135-1989 "Database Language

— SQL with Integrity Enhancement" followed in October of 1989 and SQL-89 became the new standard for DBMSs to follow. Then in August of 1992, another update, SQL-92, was released jointly by ISO and ANSI as ISO/IEC 9075:1992 "Database Language SQL." (Soon after, SQL-92 was adopted as a [United States] Federal Information Processing Standard. FIPS PUB 127-2 "Database Language SQL" also specified helpfully what the US government required for some of the features the SQL-92 Standard said were to be "implementation-defined.") This will be followed by the next version of the Standard, SQL3, expected to be released in early 1999 as ISO/IEC 9075:1999 "Information Technology — Database Languages — SQL." This brings us to current times and the writing of this book.

SQL Conformance

The complete SQL Standard consists of five interrelated documents. Additional parts, five in number so far, describing related features will be added sometime in the future. This book describes only the first five parts, Standard SQL3, which consists of these documents.

Part 1: SQL/Framework (ISO/IEC 9075-1, approximately 100 pages) defines the fundamental concepts on which SQL is based, as well as specifying the general requirements for SQL conformance. All parts of the Standard are dependent on SQL/Framework.

Part 2: SQL/Foundation (ISO/IEC 9075-2, approximately 1,050 pages) defines the fundamental syntax and operations of SQL. All parts of the Standard, except for SQL/Framework, are dependent on SQL/Foundation.

Part 3: SQL/Call-Level Interface, or CLI (ISO/IEC 9075-3, approximately 514 pages) defines an application programming interface to SQL. No part of the Standard is dependent on SQL/CLI.

Part 4: SQL/Persistent Stored Modules, or PSM (ISO/IEC 9075-4, approximately 193 pages) defines both the control structures that define SQL Routines and the Modules that may contain SQL Routines. No part of the Standard is dependent on SQL/PSM.

Part 5: SQL/Host Language Bindings (ISO/IEC 9075-5, approximately 270 pages) defines methods for embedding SQL statements in application programs written in a standard programming language. No part of the Standard is dependent on SQL/Bindings.

Minimal Conformance

The SQL3 Standard identifies two levels of SQL conformance which a DBMS may claim: Core SQL support and enhanced SQL support. (Conformance levels for SQL applications are also given; we ignore these in this book.) In order to claim conformance with the SQL Standard, a DBMS must support all of the following:

1. All features defined in SQL/Framework including an SQL Object Identifier that states the level of conformance being claimed as well as all Core SQL features defined in SQL/Foundation — see Appendix B "SQL Taxonomy" (`appB.html` on the CD-ROM) for these

requirements. A Core SQL DBMS does not have to support any of the features defined in the other parts of the Standard.

2. At least one of the following two binding styles:
   - The SQL-client Module binding style (defined in SQL/Foundation) for at least one host language.
   - The Embedded SQL binding style (defined in SQL/Bindings) for at least one host language.

In order to claim conformance, a DBMS must state whether or not the SQL-client Module binding style is supported and, if so, which of the host languages (Ada, C, COBOL, Fortran, MUMPS, Pascal, and PL/I) are supported. If applicable, the DBMS must also state which of these <keyword>s (`ADA`, `C`, `COBOL`, `FORTRAN`, `MUMPS`, `PASCAL`, `PLI` and `SQL`) may be specified for the `LANGUAGE` clause in an <external body reference>. A DBMS which supports `MUMPS` goes beyond Core SQL conformance.

<SQL Object Identifier>

[Obscure Rule] applies for this section.

The SQL Object Identifier identifies the characteristics of an SQL DBMS to other entities in an open systems environment. (The same information is available to SQL data users in the `INFORMATION_SCHEMA.SQL_LANGUAGES` View.) Listing 1.1 shows the required syntax for the SQL Object Identifier.

Listing 1.1 Required syntax for the SQL Object Identifier

```
<SQL Object Identifier> ::= <SQL provenance> <SQL variant>
    <SQL provenance> ::= <arc1> <arc2> <arc3>
        <arc1> ::= iso | 1 | iso(1)
        <arc2> ::= standard | 0 | standard(0)
        <arc3> ::= 9075
    <SQL variant> ::= <SQL edition> <SQL conformance>
    <SQL edition> ::= <1987> | <1989> | <1992> | <1999>
        <1987> ::= 0 | edition1987(0)
        <1989> ::= <1989 base> <1989 package>
             <1989 base> ::= 1 | edition1989(1)
             <1989 package> ::= <integrity no> | <integrity yes>
                  <integrity no> ::= 0 | IntegrityNo(0)
                  <integrity yes> ::= 1 | IntegrityYes(1)
        <1992> ::= 2 | edition1992(2)
        <1999> ::= 3 | edition1999(3)
    <SQL conformance> ::= <level> | <parts>
        <level> ::= <low> | <intermediate> | <high>
             <low> ::= 0 | Low(0)
             <intermediate> ::= 1 | Intermediate(1)
             <high> ::= 2 | High(2)
       <parts> ::= <Part 3> <Part 4> <Part 5> <Part 6> <Part 7> <Part 8> <Part 9>
<Part 10>
                 <Part n> ::= <Part n no> | <Part n yes>
                     <Part n no> ::= 0 | Part-nNo(0)
                     <Part n yes> ::= !! per ISO/IEC 9075-n
```

The SQL Object Identifier's <SQL provenance> identifies the Standards document that governs the DBMS's SQL conformance, i.e., "iso standard 9075." The <SQL variant> identifies the version of the SQL Standard that is supported.

The SQL Object Identifier's <SQL conformance> identifies the conformance level being claimed for that version of the Standard. There are four options.

1. If <SQL edition> is <1992>, the version of the Standard supported is SQL-92 and the Object Identifier must state which <level> of <SQL conformance> is claimed. A <level> of <low> means Entry SQL is supported, a <level> of <intermediate> means Intermediate SQL is supported, and a <level> of <high> means Full SQL is supported. A DBMS may claim a <high> <SQL conformance> only if SQL-92 is supported.
2. If <SQL edition> is <1987>, the version of the Standard supported is SQL-86. If <SQL edition> is <1989>, the version of the Standard supported is SQL-89. In both of these cases, the Object Identifier must state which <level> of <SQL conformance> is claimed. A

<level> of <low> means Level 1 SQL is supported and a <level> of <intermediate> means Level 2 SQL is supported.

3. If <SQL edition> is <1989>, an additional conformance claim must be made. A <1989 package> value of <integrity yes> means that the features defined in ANSI X3.135-1989 "Database Language — SQL with Integrity Enhancement" are supported by the DBMS. A <1989 package> value of <integrity no> means that the integrity enhancement features are not supported.
4. If <SQL edition> is <1999>, the version of the Standard supported is SQL3 with Core SQL conformance claimed. In this case, the Object Identifier must also state the DBMS's <SQL conformance> for each <part> of the Standard. A <Part n yes> value for any part means that the DBMS fully supports that part of the Standard. A <Part n no> value means that part of the Standard is not fully supported.

Enhanced Conformance

In order to claim enhanced conformance with the SQL Standard, a DBMS must also (*a*) fully support one or more of Parts 3 and up of the Standard and/or one or more additional "packages" of SQL features (identified below by their "Feature ID" values from Appendix B "SQL Taxonomy" on the CD-ROM) and (*b*) provide an SQL Flagger.

[Obscure Rule] applies for the rest of this section.

SQL Packages

The SQL Standard specifies seven SQL packages which may be supported by a DBMS claiming enhanced SQL conformance. They are as follows:

1. **Enhanced datetime facilities package** — To claim conformance with the "enhanced datetime facilities" SQL package, a DBMS must also support:
   - Feature ID F052 Interval data type.
   - Feature ID F411 Time zone specification.
   - Feature ID F551 Full datetime.
   - Feature ID T161 Optional interval qualifier.
2. **Enhanced integrity management package** — To claim conformance with the "enhanced integrity management" SQL package, a DBMS must also support:
   - Feature ID F521 Assertions.
   - Feature ID E142 Referential delete actions.
   - Feature ID F701 Referential update actions.
   - Feature ID F491 Constraint management.
   - Feature ID F671 Subqueries in CHECK constraints.
   - Feature ID T211 Triggers.
   - Feature ID T212 FOR EACH STATEMENT triggers.
   - Feature ID T191 Referential action RESTRICT.

3. **OLAP facilities package** — To claim conformance with the "OLAP facilities" SQL package, a DBMS must also support:
   - Feature ID T431 CUBE and ROLLUP.
   - Feature ID F302 INTERSECT table operator.
   - Feature ID F641 Row and table constructors.
   - Feature ID F401 FULL OUTER JOIN.
   - Feature ID F471 Scalar subquery values.
4. **PSM package** — To claim conformance with the "PSM" SQL package, a DBMS must also support:
   - Feature ID P01 Stored Modules (<SQL-server Module definition>).
   - Feature ID P02 Computational completeness.
   - Feature ID P03 INFORMATION_SCHEMA views.
5. **CLI package** — To claim conformance with the "CLI" SQL package, a DBMS must also support:
   - Feature ID C01 SQL/CLI.
6. **Basic object support package** — To claim conformance with the "basic object support" SQL package, a DBMS must also support:
   - Feature ID T322 Overloading of SQL-invoked functions and SQL-invoked procedures.
   - Feature ID O021 Basic user-defined types, including single inheritance.
   - Feature ID O041 Reference types.
   - Feature ID O051 CREATE TABLE of type.
   - Feature ID O091 Basic array support.
   - Feature ID O092 Arrays of UDTs.
   - Feature ID O094 Arrays of reference types.
   - Feature ID O121 Dereference operation.
   - Feature ID O131 Reference operation.
   - Feature ID O141 Attribute and field reference.
   - Feature ID O171 Array expressions.
   - Feature ID O191 Basic SQL routines on user-defined types, including dynamic dispatch.
   - Feature ID O201 SQL routine on arrays.
   - Feature ID O232 Array locators.
7. **Enhanced object support package** — To claim conformance with the "enhanced object support" SQL package, a DBMS must also support:
   - Feature ID O022 Enhanced user-defined types, including constructor option, attribute defaults, multiple inheritance and ordering clause.
   - Feature ID O061 ALTER TABLE, ADD named row type.
   - Feature ID O071 SQL-paths in function and type name resolution.
   - Feature ID O081 Subtables.
   - Feature ID O111 ONLY in query expressions (to restrict subtable search).

- Feature ID O151 Type predicate.
- Feature ID O161 <subtype treatment>.
- Feature ID O192 SQL routines on user-defined types, including identity functions and generalized expressions.
- Feature ID O211 User-defined cast functions.
- Feature ID O231 UDT locators.

SQL Flagger

An SQL Flagger is a facility that identifies SQL language extensions or processing alternatives. It must be provided by a DBMS claiming enhanced SQL conformance. The Flagger's purpose is to help you produce portable SQL code. This is necessary because the SQL Standard allows conforming DBMSs to provide options for processing operations that the Standard doesn't address (e.g., a `CREATE INDEX` statement). It also allows DBMSs to provide options for processing standard-defined SQL in a non-conforming manner, provided that the non-conforming results are returned only when you explicitly request them. Your DBMS's Flagger must identify all the non-standard syntax, features, and options supported, but it only has to do a static check of SQL syntax; the Standard doesn't require a Flagger to detect extensions that cannot be determined until runtime.

An SQL Flagger has to provide one or more of these "level of flagging" options to identify SQL language that violates a given subset of SQL:

- Core SQL Flagging — flags non-conforming Core SQL features.
- Part SQL Flagging — flags non-conforming enhanced SQL features.
- Package SQL Flagging — flags non-conforming package SQL features.

A Flagger also has to provide one or more of these "extent of checking" options:

- Syntax Only — only the SQL language presented is analyzed; the Flagger checks for syntax violations without accessing `INFORMATION_SCHEMA` so it doesn't necessarily detect violations that depend on the <data type> of syntactic elements.
- Catalog Lookup — the SQL language and the metadata is analyzed; the Flagger checks for both syntax and access violations (except for access violations that deal with Privileges).

Summary

In order to claim conformance with the SQL Standard, a DBMS must state four things:

1. Level of conformance supported for a given version of the Standard.
2. Binding style(s) supported.
3. Host language(s) supported.
4. The DBMS's definitions for all "elements and actions" the Standard specifies are implementation-defined. (Decisions made for the Standard's implementation-dependent features don't have to be documented.)

SQL Statement Classes

The SQL Standard groups the Core SQL statements into seven classes, according to their function. These classes are as follows:

1. **SQL-Schema statements** — create, alter, and drop Schemas and Schema Objects, so they may have a persistent effect on Schemas. The SQL-Schema statements are: CREATE SCHEMA, DROP SCHEMA, CREATE DOMAIN, ALTER DOMAIN, DROP DOMAIN, CREATE TABLE, ALTER TABLE, DROP TABLE, CREATE VIEW, DROP VIEW, CREATE ASSERTION, DROP ASSERTION, CREATE CHARACTER SET, DROP CHARACTER SET, CREATE COLLATION, DROP COLLATION, CREATE TRANSLATION, DROP TRANSLATION, CREATE TRIGGER, DROP TRIGGER, CREATE TYPE, DROP TYPE, CREATE ORDERING, DROP ORDERING, CREATE TRANSFORM, DROP TRANSFORM, CREATE PROCEDURE, CREATE FUNCTION, CREATE METHOD, DROP SPECIFIC ROUTINE, DROP SPECIFIC FUNCTION, DROP SPECIFIC PROCEDURE, CREATE ROLE, GRANT, REVOKE and DROP ROLE.
2. **SQL-data statements** — perform queries, insert, update, and delete operations, so they may have a persistent effect on SQL-data. The SQL-data statements are: DECLARE TABLE, DECLARE CURSOR, OPEN, CLOSE, FETCH, SELECT, FREE LOCATOR, HOLD LOCATOR and the SQL-data change statements INSERT, UPDATE and DELETE.
3. **SQL-transaction statements** — set parameters for transactions, as well as starting and ending transactions, so (except for the COMMIT statement) they have no effect that lasts after the SQL-session ends. The SQL-transaction statements are: START TRANSACTION, SET TRANSACTION, SET CONSTRAINTS, COMMIT, ROLLBACK, SAVEPOINT and RELEASE SAVEPOINT.
4. **SQL-control statements** — control the execution of a set of SQL statements and have no effect that lasts after the SQL-session ends. The SQL-control statements are: CALL and RETURN.
5. **SQL-Connection statements** — start and end Connections and allow an SQL-client to switch from a session with one SQL-server to a session with another, so they have no effect that lasts after the SQL-session ends. The SQL-Connection statements are: CONNECT, SET CONNECTION, and DISCONNECT.
6. **SQL-session statements** — set certain default values and other parameters for an SQL-session, so they have no effect that lasts after the SQL-session ends. The SQL-session statements are: SET TIME ZONE, SET ROLE, SET SESSION AUTHORIZATION and SET SESSION CHARACTERISTICS.
7. **SQL-diagnostics statements** — get diagnostics from the diagnostics area and signal exceptions in SQL routines, so they have no effect that lasts after the SQL-session ends. The SQL-diagnostics statement is: GET DIAGNOSTICS.

Transaction-initiating SQL Statements

If there is no current transaction, these SQL statements will begin one: (*a*) any SQL-Schema statement, (*b*) the SQL-transaction statements COMMIT and ROLLBACK (if they specify AND CHAIN), (*c*) the SQL-data statements OPEN, CLOSE, FETCH, SELECT, INSERT, UPDATE, DELETE, FREE LOCATOR and HOLD LOCATOR or (*d*) START TRANSACTION. The SQL-control statement RETURN will also begin a transaction if it causes the evaluation of a <subquery> when there is no current transaction. No other SQL statement will begin a transaction.

Which SQL Statements Can You Use?

Even if it conforms to the SQL Standard, your DBMS may not support all of the SQL statements described in this book because different SQL statements may be prepared and executed in different ways. Thus, the set of SQL statements supported by a DBMS depends on the binding style it supports. The options are as follows.

- SQL Module Language binding style — where both static and dynamic SQL statements are prepared when the Module is created and executed when the procedure that contains them is called.
- Embedded SQL Syntax binding style — where both static and dynamic SQL statements are prepared when the host language program is precompiled and executed when the host language program is run.
- Direct SQL Invocation binding style — where static SQL statements are effectively prepared immediately prior to execution.

SQL Rule Evaluation Order

The precedence of operators in an SQL statement is sometimes specified explicitly by the SQL Standard. Where this is the case, you'll find a note to that effect in our description of the operator in question. It is also possible to force a specific expression evaluation order by using parentheses in your SQL statements. Where the precedence of an SQL statement's operators is pre-determined (either by the Standard or by parentheses), those operators are effectively performed in the order specified by that precedence. Often, the Standard is silent on the subject of precedence. In cases where the precedence of operators in an SQL statement is not specifically determined either by the rules stated in the Standard or by parentheses within the SQL statement, evaluation of expressions is effectively performed from left to right.

2

Chapter 2

General Concepts

A *database system* can be described as essentially nothing more than a computerized record-keeping system. A *database*, then, is simply a collection of structured data files and any associated indexes. The user of such a system must be able to add, insert, retrieve, update, and delete data and files as necessary. Although the SQL Standard doesn't actually define the nebulous concept "database," SQL provides all of these functions and more.

In this chapter, we'll briefly discuss SQL's fundamental concepts — how the language fits into its overall environment, the data Objects you can expect to work with, and how SQL-data and SQL statements are structured. Then, in subsequent chapters, we'll revisit each of these areas in greater detail.

Set Theory

Georg Cantor was a German.
He invented Set Theory.
He was committed to a mental institution.
He died in 1918.

We can explain the preceding statements using Georg Cantor's own theory: a *set* is any collection of definite distinguishable things. We can conceive of the set as a whole, and in fact, we often do. For example, we speak of "the Germans" (a set) and can rephrase our first statement as "Georg Cantor was a member (or element) of the set of Germans." By rephrasing, we emphasize the collection of individual things over the individual things themselves. That much is intuitive. But Cantor was careful in his choice of words. By "distinguishable" (or distinct), he meant that in looking at any two things which fit in the set, we must be able to decide whether they are different. By "definite," he meant that if we know what the set is and we know what the thing is, we can decide whether the thing is a member of the set. Therefore, to know what a set "is," it is sufficient to know what the members are.

Here are a few examples. The "Germans" set also included Kaiser Wilhelm. However, it can be proved from historical records that Cantor was not a pseudonym or alias that the Kaiser used while off duty — therefore, the two members are distinguishable. At the same time, we know that there were several million other Germans, also distinguishable, and we could define the set by taking a census of all the Germans. There might be some difficulty deciding the individual question "What is a German?", but once that was done, there would be no difficulty deciding the collective question "What are the Germans?". Therefore, the members define the set, i.e., the members are definite.

The census we spoke of is possible because the Germans were a finite set (a fact which would have bored Cantor because he developed his theory to explain various gradations of infinity). We could enumerate the set thus:

```
{Georg Cantor, Kaiser Wilhelm, ...}
```

In this enumeration, we used braces to indicate "we are enumerating a set" and an ellipsis to indicate "and so on" — that is, the list could go on but we felt it unnecessary to continue for the sake of our exposition. These are standard conventions and we will use braces and ellipses again.

Enumeration is unwieldy for large sets, so let us revisit the question "What is a German?" by taking the bounds stated in the song "Deutschland Ueber Alles" — a German is a person living between the Maas, the Memel, the Esch, and the Belt (four bodies of water which now lie respectively in Holland, Russia, Austria, and Denmark). In Cantor's terms, that formula expresses a defining property. It is either true or it is false. If it is true, the person is in the set. If it is false, the person is outside the set.

Without stating the defining property in advance, the German census-takers would be unable to put together their forms and plan their information collection. The objective, though, is to produce an enumeration of all Germans. In computer terminology, we call the definition the *database design* and the enumeration the *database* itself. The "Germans" set can be broken up into several subsets such as:

```
{Berliners, Frankfurters, Hamburgers, ...}
```

These subsets are also sets with defining properties (city of residence) and presumably, with members — but that is not necessary. For example, the set of Germans who live in the Rhine River is an empty set, i.e., it has no members, but it is still a set. The implicit breaking-up that happens when we ask "Among the Germans which ones are Frankfurters?" is an example of a set operation. A *set operation* is something we do with sets that results in the production of more sets.

Relations

First, let's consider a binary relation — that is, a relation between two things. The things don't have to be of the same type; all we are concerned with is that they have some type of bond and that they be in order. Getting back to our hero... there is a relationship between Georg Cantor and the concept Set Theory (he invented it). There is also a relationship between Kaiser Wilhelm and World War I (he started it). We could use our braces notation to enumerate this:

```
{ (Georg Cantor, Set Theory), (Kaiser Wilhelm, World War I) }
```

but it looks clearer when diagrammed as a two-dimensional table:

NAME	ACTIVITY
Georg Cantor	Set Theory
Kaiser Wilhelm	World War I

There are some points to note about this diagram.

1. The table shows ordered pairs — we couldn't reverse them because Set Theory didn't invent Georg Cantor and World War I didn't cause Kaiser Wilhelm — the relationship between the NAME and ACTIVITY values is directional. Note, however, that the word "ordered" refers only to the horizontal order in the illustration — across the relation. We don't care which member of the set is listed first.
2. The table shows binary pairs — there is no space on the line for marking Georg Cantor's other achievements. Under "What did he do?" we can only express one thing. So, ordered means ordered, and pair means pair.

So what, precisely, is the "relation" here? Well, it's the whole thing. The *relationship* is the set of all the ordered pairs and the ordering itself (i.e., how part A relates to part B). What we have in the preceding diagram is a picture of a *relation* and nothing but a relation.

This relation is a set. It has members. The members define the set. However, the members are no longer "elements," but ordered pairs. There's no reason to limit ourselves to ordered pairs though. That's just the simplest relation, the *binary relation*, which is sometimes called "a relation of degree 2" (because there are two columns). We could have relations of degree 3, degree 4, degree 5, degree 6, degree 7, and so on, i.e., relations which are not binary but triple, quadruple, pentuple, sextuple, septuple... Did you notice how after a while all the words ended in "-tuple"? That's why the general term for a relation with *n* elements is *n-tuple*. Here is a relation of degree 4 showing all the information we have so far.

NAME	ACTIVITY	RESIDENCE	DATE_OF_DEATH
Georg Cantor	Set Theory	Mental Institution	1918
Kaiser Wilhelm	World War I	Imperial Palace	????

...

Some differences now appear between the words Cantor used ("set theory terminology") and the words we use ("database terminology"). The line:

```
{Georg Cantor, Set Theory,Mental Institution, 1918}
```

would be one tuple to Cantor, but in SQL, we prefer the word *row*. Or, to be precise, the *row value* is the four-element:

```
{Georg Cantor,Set Theory,Mental Institution, 1918}
```

and the row is the box that holds that information. (We don't usually need to be so precise in ordinary discussion.) Meanwhile, going down rather than across, Cantor would say that we have four attributes, labeled NAME, ACTIVITY, RESIDENCE, and DATE_OF_DEATH. But in SQL, we prefer the word *column* instead and we call each element going down (such as 'Georg Cantor' or 'Kaiser Wilhelm') a *column value*.

Here's a quick summary. Moving across the relation are tuples (but don't use that word) or rows. Moving up-and-down the relation are attributes (but don't use that word) or columns. The contents of a row is a row value. The intersection of a row and a column is a column value. The column value is "atomic" — it has only one element. There is always exactly one column value in each atomic box that is formed by the intersection of a row with a column.

Incidentally, in the diagram we used an ellipsis once more to mean "and so on" — there are more Germans in the set. We also used the symbol "????" for the column value of "When did he die?" for Kaiser Wilhelm. This is not a standard symbol; there is no standard way of expressing the fact that not only do we not know when Kaiser Wilhelm died (i.e., value is Unknown), but we're not even sure that he's dead (i.e., category is Not Applicable). This is not a problem for Set Theory but it is a problem in practice and we'll return to it later. When we do, we'll call the "????" a NULL or null value.

And there we have it. A relation is an ordered *n*-tuple set with all members having the same degree, which is representable as a table of rows and columns. It really does seem appropriate that we should know what a relation is because (we trust the following is not an unpleasant surprise) SQL is a relational database management system, and that means the database is made of relations. To quote the Kellogg's Rice Krispies™ commercial, "What the heck did you *think* they were made of?"

Admittedly, when anything looks that obvious, it must be a lie. And it is. Relational databases are actually made of tables rather than relations. What's the difference? Well, with a table we can have two Georg Cantors. This clearly breaks Cantor's "distinguishable" rule and it's quite a big break; we all know that the famous "Set Of Integers" doesn't go

```
{1,1,1,1,1,2,2,2,2,2,3,3,3,3,3,...}
```

By definition, a set has no duplicates. A relation is a set, so a relation has no duplicates. But a table can have duplicates. This is a concession to practicalities, since we know that duplicate data happens in the "real world." However, if our database contains two Georg Cantors who really are the same person, then we have an error — while if it contains two Georg Cantors whom we can't distinguish from one another, then we have a design flaw. The long and the short of it all is (*a*) a relational database consists of tables, (*b*) a table is not a relation, but the only difference between the two is that a table may have rows with duplicate row values, (*c*) you should get rid of duplicates regardless, therefore (*d*) all relational databases should consist of relations. (By the way, a table is sometimes called a *multiset* to distinguish it from a regular set. You'll see the word multiset in some Microsoft publications.)

Set Operations

Since SQL operates on sets, there must be such things as "set operations" that SQL can perform. In fact, SQL borrows all the standard operations from Set Theory textbooks, along with the terminology. Mercifully, it does not also borrow the notation. So to describe the set operations in this book, we've been able to use some English-looking terms which, in fact, have fairly precise meanings in Set Theory and some English-looking terms which, in fact, are SQL words for our notation. In the following quick introduction, we will describe a sequence of set operations. A *sequence*, also known as a *series*, is an ordered set. The order that we'll follow is the order of execution of the clauses of the most famous of SQL statement types: the query or SELECT statement.

Identity

The easiest operation is to take a copy of the table we started with:

NAME	ACTIVITY
Georg Cantor	Set Theory
Kaiser Wilhelm	World War I

The SQL for this is:

```
... FROM Germans ...
```

Because this is the first time we've said something "in SQL," we'll regard it as our equivalent of the famous "hello world" — so, some introductions are in order. We've used the ellipsis before. As usual, it means "and so on," so you can see that there's some stuff both before and after FROM Germans that we're not going to spell out just here. We need the ellipses to indicate that we're not illustrating a whole statement, merely one clause called the FROM clause. The word FROM is an SQL keyword and the word Germans is an SQL Table name. So, the FROM clause takes the Germans table and ends up with a result table that is the same as the Germans table.

Product

In the history of the world, there have been four great Mathematicians:

{Al-Khwarezm, Georg Cantor, Leonhard Euler, Rene Descartes}

If we put that side-by-side with our original Germans set, we get:

MATHEMATICIANS	GERMANS
Al-Khwarezm	Georg Cantor
Georg Cantor	Kaiser Wilhelm
Leonhard Euler	
Rene Descartes	

The Cartesian product operation yields the set of all pairs (x,y) such that x is a member of some set X and y is a member of some set Y. The result of GERMANS [Cartesian Product] MATHEMATICIANS is the following binary relation.

CARTESIAN_PRODUCT

GERMANS.NAME	MATHEMATICIANS.NAME
Al-Khwarezm	Georg Cantor
Georg Cantor	Georg Cantor
Leonhard Euler	Georg Cantor
Rene Descartes	Georg Cantor
Al-Khwarezm	Kaiser Wilhelm
Georg Cantor	Kaiser Wilhelm
Leonhard Euler	Kaiser Wilhelm
Rene Descartes	Kaiser Wilhelm

You must not object that Al-Khwarezm is unrelated to Kaiser Wilhelm because the spirit of a Cartesian-product relation is that everything relates to everything. The table above is a relation — it's mathematically valid (even if it doesn't seem to make any sense!). There are several ways to express this operation in SQL. The classic style is:

```
   ... FROM Germans, Mathematicians ...
```

That is, within a FROM clause the expression "table-name-1, table-name-2" means "yield a table which is the Cartesian product of table-name-1 and table-name-2."

Search Condition

In our Cartesian product relation, there is something special about the row:

```
(Georg Cantor, Georg Cantor)
```

That row, and that row only, has two column values that are the same. This is significant because the columns are defined in a meaningful way; one 'Georg Cantor' is the name of a German, while the other 'Georg Cantor' is the name of a mathematician. Therefore, Georg Cantor must be the only person who is both a German and a mathematician. (This assumes that names are unique.) And again, there is an SQL way to say this:

```
... FROM  Germans, Mathematicians
    WHERE Germans.name = Mathematicians.name ...
```

We now have two clauses in our example. The FROM clause exploded the tables into a Cartesian product relation. The WHERE clause reduces the result to a subset of that relation. The result subset is also a relation — it contains only those rows where this condition is TRUE: "the name equals the name." (This is known as a *search condition* in official SQL vocabulary.) Now we have this result:

CARTESIAN_PRODUCTS	
GERMANS.NAME	MATHEMATICIANS.NAME
Georg Cantor	Georg Cantor

So, the WHERE clause contains a search condition, takes as input the (table) result of the FROM clause, and produces as output a table which contains only those rows where the search condition is TRUE.

Join

In this example so far, the FROM clause contained two table names and the WHERE clause contained a comparison between columns from each table. This two-step process is usually called a *join*. In modern SQL, there are several ways to ask for a join. We have started with the oldest and best-known way because it best illustrates that a typical join is two separate operations.

Projection

Our result table now has one row with two columns and the value in each column is 'Georg Cantor' — but we only need one column to answer the question "Who is German *and* a mathematician?". If you think of the earlier search condition as being an operation which picks out certain rows, it's easy to get to the next step. A *projection* is a complementary operation which picks out certain columns. In SQL, we just list the columns we want:

```
SELECT Germans.name
FROM   Germans, Mathematicians
WHERE  Germans.name = Mathematicians.name ...
```

The column reference after the keyword SELECT is called a *select list*. We now have a result table that looks like this:

CARTESIAN_PRODUCT
GERMANS.NAME
Georg Cantor

So, the select list does a projection on the table produced by the WHERE clause. The result is (as always) a table. The words SELECT Germans.name FROM Germans, Mathematicians WHERE Germans.name = Mathematicians.name constitute a valid and complete SQL statement. Specifically, this sort of statement is called a *query*, presumably because it translates a question (in this case, "What Germans are mathematicians?"). It's also commonly called the SELECT statement.

Other Set Operations

SQL also handles the standard set operations intersect, union, and except. The following is an example of each: two example tables (the "input"), one result table (the "output"), and the SQL statement that makes it happen. To make the examples short, we've used unrealistically small examples with one column per table and no `WHERE` clauses. But don't worry about syntactical details or the exact workings of the operations — that comes later. You understand enough so far if you grasp that some well-known set operations can be expressed in SQL and work on tables.

Inputs		SQL query	Outputs
INTEGERS_1 COLUMN_1 5 4 13	INTEGERS_2 COLUMN_1 33 14 4	SELECT column_1 FROM Integers_1 INTERSECT SELECT column_1 FROM Integers_2	INTEGERS_3 COLUMN_1 4
STRINGS_1 COLUMN_1 Spain Greece Yugoslavia	STRINGS_2 COLUMN_1 Italy Denmark Belgium	SELECT column_1 FROM Strings_1 UNION SELECT column_1 FROM Strings_2	STRINGS_3 COLUMN_1 Spain Greece Italy Denmark Yugoslavia Belgium
DECIMALS_1 COLUMN_1 5.32 4.17 13.99	DECIMALS_2 COLUMN_1 33.08 14.00 4.17	SELECT column_1 FROM Decimals_1 EXCEPT SELECT column_1 FROM Decimals_2	DECIMALS_3 COLUMN_1 5.32 13.99

Therefore God Exists

Leonhard Euler is famed for his remark that "(a + b)**n/n = X, therefore God exists," which shows that any argument looks imposing if you use lots of math symbols. SQL does the opposite. It has a solid base on a mathematical theory, but the operations of Set Theory are hidden behind a somewhat English-like sentence structure. The result is, on balance, for the good. Most SQL beginners have an easy time grasping the concepts behind `WHERE` clauses or select lists, while they might have a less easy time with the dense polysymbolic notation of standard Set Theory. Unfortunately, the SQL language hides the operations so well that the following frequent delusions arise:

1. SQL is a "nonprocedural" language. Perhaps people get this idea from the fact that any operation on a set should affect all set members simultaneously. But the set operations themselves are ordered. One step follows another.
2. A whole SQL query operates on the tables in the `FROM` clause. This mode of thinking causes people to make certain common errors which could be avoided if they kept in mind

the truth; that each set operation produces a new, nameless, "virtual" table and passes it on. (Well, perhaps we should add "conceptually" — there will be hundreds of times in this book that we could add "conceptually" because your DBMS may do internal things in some out-of-order sequence, provided the method doesn't affect the results. That is not our present concern. What we must know from the outset is how a human being is supposed to view the operations.)

Coming away from this chapter, you only need to know that SQL has a specialized vocabulary which to a large extent arises from Set Theory and that SQL operations happen on tables. You should regard this as background information. This book takes a bottom-up approach, starting with the smallest units (the column and row values) so it will be several chapters before we reach the top and begin to emphasize the sets once more.

Recap: The Relational Model

A relational database is one which appears to be nothing more than a collection of tables. The model it is based on has three major aspects: the structure, the manipulation, and the integrity of data.

In the relational model, data are logically presented in two-dimensional tables made up of columns and rows. The rows of a table consist of a collection of values that describe an entity; for example, an employee. The columns of a table consist of a collection of similar data among rows; e.g., employee surnames. Operations on the data are simplified by the fact that a table's rows are unordered. The intersection of a row and a column contains individual data items called *values*. Values are always atomic; that is, each position in a table may contain only one datum.

Data manipulation is provided by a set of algebraic or calculus operators.

Data integrity is provided by two rules. Entity integrity requires that every value in the primary key of a table must be a unique, non-null data value. Referential integrity requires that every value in a foreign key must either equal some value of its related primary key or it must be NULL.

Design of a Relational Database

One of the main advantages of the relational model of database design is that it is based on a foundation of formal mathematical theory that allows its concepts to be defined and examined with great precision.

Remember that a relation is (essentially) a two-dimensional table consisting of horizontal rows and vertical columns. The advantage of this form is that almost everyone is familiar with data presented as a simple table. The relational model stipulates that no two rows in the table (relation) may be identical; there must be some combination of columns, called a *key*, whose values will uniquely identify each row.

As an example of the model's capabilities, we will design a structure for a personnel database which contains the following information: the name of each employee, the programming languages the employee is familiar with, the number of years the employee has used each language, the employee's title, the employee's length of service with the company, the employee's hourly rate of pay, the current projects to which the employee is assigned, and the manager of each of these projects.

The following PERSONNEL_1 table shows a sample of the data that might be stored in such a database, along with one possible structure.

PERSONNEL_1

NAME	LANG	YRS_USE	TITLE	YRS_EXP	PAY	PROJECT	MGR
Marvin	Cobol Fortran	3 2	Sr. Prog.	4	25.00	Payroll A/R	Smith Jones
Brown	Cobol Basic Ada	2 1 3	Sr. Prog.	3	24.00	Inventory	Norman
Norman	Cobol SQL	4 2	Prj. Mgr.	2	35.00	Inventory	Norman
James	SQL Pascal	1 3	Sys. Ana.	2	29.00	A/R Datcomm	Jones Harvey
Jones	Cobol Pascal SQL Basic	1 5 2 9	Prj. Mgr.	8	42.00	A/R	Jones

Each employee in this table has a unique name, so NAME may be used as the table's key. In practice, of course, there may be more than one way to construct a key — social security numbers or employee numbers are other values that might be used to uniquely identify an employee. Using this structure, any request of the form, "Tell me something about employee E," is easily answered. However, it isn't as simple to respond to such requests as, "Which employees can use language L?"; "Who is the manager of project P?"; "Display all employees assigned to project P"; or "Change the manager of project P to employee E." But through a process known as *normalization*, the organization of the data in PERSONNEL_1 can be changed so that it can be used more flexibly.

The first step in normalizing the design is based on the relational rule that each column of a table may take on only a single, non-repeating (atomic) value for each row of the table. Looking at PERSONNEL_1, it's easy to see that the columns LANG, YRS_USE, PROJECT, and MGR violate this rule because an employee may know more than one programming language and may be assigned to more than one project at a time. By duplicating the non-repeating values of NAME, TITLE, YRS_EXP, and PAY for each combination of values for the repeating groups, the entire table can be represented in *first normal form*. The PERSONNEL_2 table shown below is in first normal form.

PERSONNEL_2

NAME	LANG	YRS_USE	TITLE	YRS_EXP	PAY	PROJECT	MGR
Marvin	Cobol	3	Sr. Prog.	4	25.00	Payroll	Smith
Marvin	Fortran	2	Sr. Prog.	4	25.00	A/R	Jones

Brown	Cobol	2	Sr. Prog.	3	24.00	Inventory	Norman
Brown	Basic	1	Sr. Prog.	3	24.00	Inventory	Norman
Brown	Ada	3	Sr. Prog.	3	24.00	Inventory	Norman
Norman	Cobol	4	Prj. Mgr.	2	35.00	Inventory	Norman
Norman	SQL	2	Prj. Mgr.	2	35.00	Inventory	Norman
James	SQL	1	Sys. Ana.	2	29.00	A/R	Jones
James	Pascal	3	Sys. Ana.	2	29.00	Datcomm	Harvey
Jones	Cobol	1	Prj. Mgr.	8	42.00	A/R	Jones
Jones	Pascal	5	Prj. Mgr.	8	42.00	A/R	Jones
Jones	SQL	2	Prj. Mgr.	8	42.00	A/R	Jones
Jones	Basic	9	Prj. Mgr.	8	42.00	A/R	Jones

We can now see that NAME is no longer sufficient to uniquely identify a row of PERSONNEL_2 because multiple rows may be present for an employee who knows more than one language or is assigned to more than one project. One solution is to create a new key from a combination of columns. NAME, LANG, and PROJECT combined would be such a key, as those three values together uniquely identify a single row.

PERSONNEL_2 appears to be a step backward in our design. Not only does it require more space to present the data, but responding to requests such as, "Change employee E's title to T"; "Add the assignment of employee E to project P"; or "Make employee E the manager of project P" is now more difficult. This problem is addressed by the remaining normalization steps, which are based on the concept of dependence and the relational rule that in every row of a table, each column must be dependent on every part of the key.

If, for each row, the value of a column C1 uniquely determines the value of a column C2, then C2 is functionally dependent on C1. If the value in C1 limits the possible values in C2 to a specific set, then C2 is set dependent on C1. For example, because each employee has only one title, we may say that NAME determines TITLE and that TITLE is functionally dependent on NAME. PROJECT is set dependent on NAME, since each employee is assigned to a specific set of projects.

The columns TITLE, YRS_EXP, and PAY are not dependent on the entire key (NAME, LANG, PROJECT) of PERSONNEL_2 — they are dependent on NAME alone. To solve this, we must create a new table containing only NAME, TITLE, YRS_EXP, and PAY. The key for this table, called EMPLOYEES, will be NAME. Of the remaining columns, YRS_USE is determined by both NAME and

LANG and therefore cannot be part of EMPLOYEES. Another table, called LANGUAGES, must be formed by these three columns. LANGUAGES will have a key formed by a combination of the columns NAME and LANG. Because the table contains the NAME column as well, it is still possible to associate an employee's language experience with his employee data.

Splitting a table in this way prevents the experience part of the database from having columns that are dependent on only part of the table's key. A first normal form relation (atomic values in each portion of the table) that also has no partial key dependence is said to be in *second normal form.* The following tables, EMPLOYEES and LANGUAGES, are in second normal form.

EMPLOYEES

NAME	TITLE	YRS_EXP	PAY
Marvin	Sr. Prog.	4	25.00
Brown	Sr. Prog.	3	24.00
Norman	Prj. Mgr.	2	35.00
James	Sys. Ana.	2	29.00
Jones	Prj. Mgr.	8	42.00

LANGUAGES

NAME	LANG	YRS_USE
Marvin	Cobol	3
Marvin	Fortran	2
Brown	Cobol	2
Brown	Basic	1
Brown	Ada	3
Norman	Cobol	4
Norman	SQL	2
James	SQL	1
James	Pascal	3
Jones	Cobol	1
Jones	Pascal	5
Jones	SQL	2
Jones	Basic	9

The situation with project assignments is slightly different. We have already noted that an employee name determines the set of projects on which that employee works. This is independent of the languages used by the employee. This means that a table containing PROJECT should not have LANG in its key. However, the project name uniquely determines the project manager. MGR is transitively dependent on NAME, because NAME determines a set of values for PROJECT and PROJECT functionally determines MGR. To complete our design, we should remove any transitive dependencies, according to the relational rule that in every row of a table, all columns must depend directly on the key, without any transitive dependencies through other columns. A second normal form relation that has no transitive dependence is said to be in *third normal form.*

Because each project has only one manager, we can form a PROJECTS table with the columns PROJECT and MGR. PROJECTS' key will be PROJECT. Note that MGR could also be a key if each employee managed only one project. Finally, since each employee works on one or more projects, we will create a fourth table, called ASSIGNMENTS, using the columns NAME and PROJECT. This table forms the association between the EMPLOYEES and PROJECTS tables and is "all key," i.e., it has no additional dependent columns because the only thing dependent on both NAME and PROJECT is the fact that they are associated. Here are the third normal form tables.

PROJECTS

PROJECT	MGR
Payroll	Smith
A/R	Jones
Inventory	Norman
Datcomm	Harvey

ASSIGNMENTS

NAME	PROJECT
Marvin	Payroll
Marvin	A/R
Brown	Inventory
Norman	Inventory
James	A/R
James	Datcomm
Jones	A/R

At this point, our design is complete. All tables are in third normal form and requests such as those listed earlier can easily be dealt with.

Here are some tips for good database design:

- Don't use an existing database as the basis for a new database structure — you don't want to inadvertently duplicate awkward or inconsistent table definitions.
- Make sure that each table represents just one subject — that is, either one object or one event. This avoids unnecessary duplication of data.
- Define a primary key for every table — not only will it uniquely identify a row value, you'll use it to join tables. A primary key should have these characteristics: its value must be unique and "known not nullable," and its value should consist of the minimum number of columns to guarantee uniqueness.

- Don't define any multi-value columns — that is, don't use the `ROW` or `ARRAY` <data type>s.
- Implement data integrity; define unique keys and foreign keys for your tables.

The SQL-environment

The SQL Standard says that all SQL operations are executed within an SQL-environment. An SQL-environment has six components.

1. One SQL-agent responsible for causing the execution of SQL statements. It is usually an application program that calls one or more externally-invoked procedures in an SQL-client Module.
2. One SQL-implementation; a database management system (DBMS) that executes SQL statements. Your SQL-agent considers your DBMS to have two components: (*a*) one SQL-client to which the SQL-agent is bound and (*b*) one or more SQL-servers to manage your SQL-data. (SQL-data consists of the descriptions of all the SQL Objects, plus all the data values you can access with your DBMS.) The SQL-client is the part of your DBMS that establishes connections to the SQL-servers; it maintains a diagnostics area and other state data that relate to the interactions between the DBMS and the SQL-agent. Each SQL-server has three responsibilities: (*a*) it manages the SQL-session taking place over the SQL-Connection between itself and the SQL-client, (*b*) it executes SQL statements received from the SQL-client, receiving and sending data as required, and (*c*) it maintains the state of the SQL-session, including the <AuthorizationID> and certain session defaults. The method of communication between the SQL-client and the SQL-server(s) is implementation-defined, but the Standard does specify how an SQL-agent will communicate with your DBMS (*see* SQL Binding Styles).
3. Zero or more SQL-client Modules each containing zero or more externally-invoked procedures. SQL-client Modules are programming modules — exactly one is associated with an SQL-agent at any time.
4. Zero or more <AuthorizationID>s. An SQL <AuthorizationID> or authorization identifier represents a user of SQL-data.
5. Zero or more Catalogs.
6. Zero or more sites (e.g., Base tables) that contain SQL-data.

In short, an SQL-environment can be thought of as a specific operation of a DBMS on the collection of Catalogs (that contain SQL-data) within a specified SQL-server by all the users (that is, all persons and programs) that have authority to access the SQL-server during the time the DBMS is operating.

SQL Objects

The SQL Standard describes the concepts on which SQL is based in terms of Objects, such as Tables. Each SQL Object is defined in terms of the characteristics (e.g., its name) that describe it — the Standard calls this the Object's *descriptor.* Some Objects are dependent on other Objects, e.g., a Column is dependent on the Table it belongs to. If an Object is dropped (i.e., destroyed), then every Object dependent on it is also dropped.

Cluster

An SQL Cluster is the group of Catalogs available to an SQL-session at any point in time; that is, it contains all the SQL-data you may access through a given SQL-server. Clusters are created and dropped using implementation-defined methods. The Objects that belong to a Cluster are known as *Cluster Objects*; that is, they depend on some Cluster. Every Cluster Object has a name that must be unique (among Objects of its name class) within the Cluster it belongs to. The Cluster Object name classes are:

- <AuthorizationID>s
- Catalogs

<AuthorizationID>

An SQL <AuthorizationID> is a character string which identifies a user and the set of Privileges belonging to that user. (A user is either an actual person or an application program that has access to SQL-data.) An SQL Role is a set of zero or more role authorizations. A role authorization allows a given <AuthorizationID> to use every Privilege granted to that Role. <AuthorizationID>s are dependent on some Cluster; they are created, dropped, and mapped to real users using implementation-defined methods. Roles are dependent on some Schema and are created and dropped with the `CREATE ROLE` and `DROP ROLE` statements.

Privilege

An SQL Privilege authorizes a particular <AuthorizationID> to execute a given operation, either `DELETE`, `EXECUTE`, `INSERT`, `REFERENCES`, `SELECT`, `TRIGGER`, `UNDER`, `UPDATE`, or `USAGE` on a given Schema Object. It may also allow the grantee to pass the Privilege on to others. Privileges, dependent on some <AuthorizationID>, are created and assigned to <AuthorizationID>s with the `GRANT` statement and are dropped and removed with the `REVOKE` statement.

Catalog

An SQL Catalog is a named group of Schemas, one of which must be an Ur-Schema named `INFORMATION_SCHEMA`. (The `INFORMATION_SCHEMA` Schema is a set of Views and Domains that contain the descriptions of all the SQL-data belonging to that Catalog.) Catalogs are dependent on some Cluster and are created and dropped using implementation-defined methods.

Schema

An SQL Schema is a named group of SQL-data that is owned by a particular <AuthorizationID>. Schemas are dependent on some Catalog and are created, altered, and dropped using the SQL-Schema statements. The Objects that may belong to a Schema are known as *Schema Objects*; that is, they depend on some Schema. Every Schema Object has a name that must be unique (among Objects of its name class) within the Schema it belongs to. The Schema Object name classes are:

- Base tables and Views
- Domains and UDTs
- Constraints and Assertions

- Character sets
- Collations
- Translations
- Triggers
- SQL-server Modules
- SQL-invoked routines

Table

An SQL Table is a named set of rows — an ordered row of one or more <Column name>s together with zero or more unordered rows of data values. Tables store data about a specific entity; each row of the Table describes a single occurrence of that entity. The SQL Standard defines three types of Tables: Base tables, Views, and derived tables. Tables are dependent on some Schema or some Module. Base tables are created, altered, and dropped with the `CREATE TABLE`, `ALTER TABLE`, and `DROP TABLE` statements, Views are created and dropped with the `CREATE VIEW` and `DROP VIEW` statements, and derived tables are created when you execute a query.

Column

An SQL Column is a named component of a Table — a set of similar data values that describe the same attribute of an entity. A Column's values all belong to the same <data type> or to the same Domain and may vary over time. A Column value is the smallest unit of data that can be selected from, or updated for, a Table. Columns are dependent on some Table and are created, altered, and dropped with Column definition clauses in the `CREATE TABLE` and `ALTER TABLE` statements.

Domain and UDT

An SQL Domain and an SQL UDT, or user-defined type, are both named <data type>s that identify a set of valid data values. Their characteristics are defined by users and their purpose is to constrain the values that can be stored as SQL-data. Domains are dependent on some Schema and are created, altered, and dropped with the `CREATE DOMAIN`, `ALTER DOMAIN` and `DROP DOMAIN` statements. UDTs are dependent on some Schema or some Module and are created, altered, and dropped with the `CREATE TYPE`, `ALTER TYPE`, and `DROP TYPE` statements.

Constraint and Assertion

An SQL Constraint and an SQL Assertion are both named rules that identify sets of valid data values. They constrain the allowable data values for Columns, Domains, and Tables and are defined with two checking characteristics: a deferral mode (either `DEFERRABLE` or `NOT DEFERRABLE`) and a constraint check time (either `DEFERRED` or `IMMEDIATE`). Constraints are dependent on some Table or some Domain and are created and dropped with Constraint clauses in the `CREATE TABLE`, `ALTER TABLE`, `CREATE DOMAIN` and `ALTER DOMAIN` statements. Assertions are dependent on some Schema and are created and dropped with the `CREATE ASSERTION` and `DROP ASSERTION` statements.

Character Set

An SQL Character set is a named group of characters (the *character repertoire*) combined with that repertoire's Form-of-use or coding scheme — the usually one-to-one mapping scheme between each character in the repertoire and a set of internal codes (usually 8-bit values) that give the characters' order in the repertoire and define how the characters are encoded as numbers. Every Character set must contain a space character that is equivalent to the Unicode character U+0020. Character sets are dependent on some Schema and are created and dropped with the `CREATE CHARACTER SET` and `DROP CHARACTER SET` statements. Every Character set has a default Collation.

Collation

An SQL Collation is a named set of rules that describes a collating sequence. Each Collation is defined for exactly one Character set and is used to determine the results of comparisons between character strings based on that Character set. All Character sets have a default Collation. Additional Collations may also be created for any Character set, so for any character string comparison, there are one or more Collations that may be invoked by the `COLLATE` function. Collations are dependent on some Schema and are created and dropped with the `CREATE COLLATION` and `DROP COLLATION` statements.

Translation

An SQL Translation is a named set of rules that maps characters from a source Character set to characters in a target Character set for conversion purposes. For any pair of Character sets, there are zero or more Translations that may be invoked by the `TRANSLATE` function. Translations are dependent on some Schema and are created and dropped with the `CREATE TRANSLATION` and `DROP TRANSLATION` statements.

Trigger

An SQL Trigger is a named rule that is associated with a single Base table. Each Trigger defines a trigger event specifying which action — either `INSERT`, `DELETE`, or `UPDATE` — on the Table will cause the triggered actions, a trigger action time specifying whether the triggered action is to be taken before or after the trigger event, and one or more triggered actions (the action to take when the Trigger is fired or invoked). Triggers are dependent on some Schema and are created and dropped with the `CREATE TRIGGER` and `DROP TRIGGER` statements.

Module

An SQL Module is an optionally-named group of SQL statements that is treated as a unit of an application program. Such programs use SQL statements to carry out database operations instead of routines written in the host language. There are three kinds of SQL Modules: (*a*) an SQL-client Module contains SQL procedures that are invoked by a host language and is defined with the `MODULE` statement, (*b*) an SQL-session Module contains only SQL statements prepared in that SQL-session and is usually an implicit Module (that is, its presence isn't obvious to the user), and (*c*) an SQL-server Module (the SQL/PSM type) is dependent on some Schema, contains only SQL-invoked routines and is created, altered, and dropped with the CREATE MODULE, ALTER MODULE, and DROP MODULE statements.

SQL-invoked Routine

An SQL-invoked routine is a function or a procedure that can be invoked from SQL. An SQL-invoked function is invoked by a routine invocation in some value expression, while an SQL-invoked procedure is a procedure invoked with the CALL statement. SQL-invoked routines are dependent either directly on some Schema or on some Module and are created and dropped with the CREATE PROCEDURE, DECLARE PROCEDURE, CREATE FUNCTION, CREATE METHOD, DROP SPECIFIC ROUTINE, DROP SPECIFIC FUNCTION, and DROP SPECIFIC PROCEDURE statements.

SQL Data Types

Every data value belongs to some SQL <data type>. The logical representation of a data value is known as a <literal>. SQL supports three sorts of <data type>s: predefined <data type>s, constructed <data type>s, and <user-defined data type>s or UDTs — all of which may be used to define a set of valid data values. The predefined <data type>s are all scalar types; they contain atomic values (i.e., values that are not composed of sets of values of other <data type>s). The constructed <data type>s are mostly composite types; they contain array values (i.e., values that are composed of sets of values, each of a declared predefined <data type>). The UDTs are composite types. Their values and attributes are totally user-defined.

Each host language supported by the SQL Standard has its own data types. These are distinct from SQL <data type>s, though they often have similar names. The Standard includes instructions on how to map SQL <data type>s to host language data types.

SQL-data values are either non-null values or the null value. The *null value* is a special implementation-dependent value that can be assigned to any SQL <data type>. It is used to represent "value unknown" or "value inapplicable" and is distinct from all non-null values. The null value is often denoted by the <keyword> NULL.

Predefined <data type>s

SQL's predefined scalar <data type>s are identified by these <keyword>s: INTEGER, SMALLINT, NUMERIC, DECIMAL, FLOAT, REAL, DOUBLE PRECISION, BIT, BIT VARYING, BINARY LARGE OBJECT, CHARACTER, CHARACTER VARYING, NATIONAL CHARACTER, NATIONAL CHARACTER VARYING, CHARACTER LARGE OBJECT, NATIONAL CHARACTER LARGE OBJECT, DATE, TIME, TIME WITH TIME ZONE, TIMESTAMP, TIMESTAMP WITH TIME ZONE, INTERVAL, and BOOLEAN.

Number <data type>s

A numeric value is either an exact numeric (integer or decimal) number or an approximate numeric (floating point) number. The numeric <data type>s INTEGER (or INT), SMALLINT, NUMERIC, DECIMAL (or DEC), FLOAT, REAL, and DOUBLE PRECISION store numbers inserted in either exact numeric form (e.g., 75, –6.2) or approximate numeric form (e.g., 1.256E–4, –1.03E+5). INT and SMALLINT are exact numeric types with a predefined precision and a scale of zero; NUMERIC and DECIMAL are exact numeric types with definable precisions and scales; FLOAT is an approximate numeric type with a definable precision; and REAL and

DOUBLE PRECISION are approximate numeric types with predefined precisions. All numbers are mutually assignable and mutually comparable. Assignment and comparison are performed in the familiar, algebraic manner. The following SQL operations involve numbers: addition and unary plus, subtraction and unary minus, multiplication, division, assignment, comparison, ABS, BETWEEN, BIT_LENGTH, CARDINALITY, CHAR_LENGTH, DISTINCT, EXISTS, EXTRACT, FOR ALL, FOR SOME, IN, IS NULL, MATCH, MOD, OCTET_LENGTH, POSITION, and UNIQUE.

Bit String <data types>s

A bit string value is any sequence of bits or hexits. The bit string <data type>s BIT and BIT VARYING store bit string values inserted in either binary form (any sequence of zero or more 0-bits or 1-bits) or hexadecimal form (any sequence of zero or more 0-hexits, 1-hexits, 2-hexits, 3-hexits, 4-hexits, 5-hexits, 6-hexits, 7-hexits, 8-hexits, 9-hexits, A-hexits, B-hexits, C- hexits, D-hexits, E-hexits, or F-hexits). BIT has a definable fixed length; BIT VARYING has a definable variable length. All bit strings are mutually assignable and mutually comparable. Assignment of a bit string is performed bit-by-bit beginning with the source's most significant bit. For comparison purposes, a 0-bit is less than a 1-bit. The following SQL operations involve bit strings: concatenation, assignment, comparison, BETWEEN, BIT_LENGTH, CHAR_LENGTH, DISTINCT, EXISTS, FOR ALL, FOR SOME, IN, IS NULL, MATCH, OCTET_LENGTH, POSITION, SUBSTRING, and UNIQUE.

Binary String <data types>s

A binary string value is any sequence of octets that aren't associated with a Character set. The binary string <data type> BINARY LARGE OBJECT (BLOB) stores binary string values inserted in hexadecimal form. BLOB has a definable variable length. All binary strings are mutually assignable and mutually comparable. Assignment of a binary string is performed octet-by-octet beginning with the source's most significant octet. Comparison is supported only for equality. The following SQL operations involve binary strings: concatenation, assignment, comparison, BIT_LENGTH, CHAR_LENGTH, EXISTS, FOR ALL, FOR SOME, IS NULL, LIKE, OCTET_LENGTH, OVERLAY, POSITION, SUBSTRING, and TRIM.

Character String <data type>s

A character string value is any sequence of characters that belong to a given Character set. The character string <data type>s CHARACTER (CHAR), CHARACTER VARYING (VARCHAR), NATIONAL CHARACTER (NCHAR), and NATIONAL CHARACTER VARYING (NCHAR VARYING) store character strings, while the character string <data type>s CHARACTER LARGE OBJECT (CLOB) and NATIONAL CHARACTER LARGE OBJECT (NCLOB) store large object character strings. CHAR and NCHAR have a definable fixed length; VARCHAR, NCHAR VARYING, CLOB, and NCLOB have a definable variable length. CHAR, VARCHAR, and CLOB have a definable Character set; NCHAR, NCHAR VARYING, and NCLOB have a predefined Character set. All of the character string <data type>s have a definable Collation or collating sequence. All character strings that belong to the same Character set are mutually assignable and mutually comparable if they have the same Collation. Assignment of a character string is performed character-by-character beginning with the source's first character. The result of a character string comparison is determined by the rules of the Collation used for the comparison. The following SQL operations involve character strings: concatenation, assignment, comparison, BETWEEN, BIT_LENGTH, CHAR_LENGTH,

CONVERT, DISTINCT, EXISTS, FOR ALL, FOR SOME, IN, IS NULL, LIKE, LOWER, MATCH, OCTET_LENGTH, OVERLAY, POSITION, SIMILAR, SUBSTRING, TRANSLATE, TRIM, UNIQUE, and UPPER.

Temporal <data type>s

A temporal value is a date, a time, a timestamp, or an interval of time. The temporal <data type> DATE stores dates, TIME and TIME WITH TIME ZONE store times, TIMESTAMP and TIMESTAMP WITH TIME ZONE store timestamps, and INTERVAL stores intervals. DATE has a predefined precision; TIME, TIME WITH TIME ZONE, TIMESTAMP, and TIMESTAMP WITH TIME ZONE have definable fractional seconds precisions. There are two classes of INTERVAL. The first, *year-month intervals*, has a definable precision that includes some contiguous combination of the YEAR and MONTH datetime fields. The second, *day-time intervals*, has a definable precision that includes some contiguous combination of the DAY, HOUR, MINUTE, and SECOND datetime fields. TIME WITH TIME ZONE values are (and TIMESTAMP WITH TIME ZONE values include) times that are maintained in Universal Coordinated Time (UTC) — with a portion of the value representing a time zone offset. The time zone offset is an interval that specifies the difference between UTC and the actual date and time in the value's time zone. All temporal values of the same type are mutually assignable and mutually comparable; the results must follow the usual rules for temporal values according to the Gregorian calendar and the 24-hour clock. The following SQL operations involve temporal values: addition, subtraction, multiplication, division, assignment, comparison, ABS, BETWEEN, CURRENT_DATE, CURRENT_TIME, CURRENT_TIMESTAMP, DISTINCT, EXISTS, EXTRACT, FOR ALL, FOR SOME, IN, IS NULL, LOCALTIME, LOCALTIMESTAMP, MATCH, OVERLAPS, and UNIQUE.

Boolean <data type>s

A boolean value is a truth value; either TRUE, FALSE, or UNKNOWN. (The truth value UNKNOWN is sometimes represented by the null value.) The boolean <data type> BOOLEAN stores truth values. All truth values are mutually assignable and mutually comparable. TRUE and FALSE may be assigned to any boolean target; UNKNOWN may only be assigned if the boolean target allows NULLs. For comparison purposes, TRUE is greater than FALSE. The following SQL operations involve boolean values: AND, IS, NOT, OR, and the results of any predicate or search condition.

Constructed <data types>

An SQL constructed <data type> is either a <reference type>, a <row type>, or a <collection type>. A <reference type> is a scalar constructed <data type> identified by the <keyword> REF. A <row type> is a composite constructed <data type> identified by the <keyword> ROW. A <collection type> is a composite constructed <data type> identified by the <keyword> ARRAY.

<reference type>s

A reference value points to some row of a referenceable Base table (that is, a Base table that has a "with REF value" property).

<row type>s

A <row type> is a sequence of one or more (Field, <data type>) pairs. A value of a <row type> consists of one value for each of its Fields.

<collection type>s

A <collection type> is a composite data value that consists of zero or more elements of a specified <data type> known as the *element type* — that is, in SQL3, a <collection type> is an array.

User-defined Types

The SQL user-defined types (UDTs) are Schema Objects that can be defined by a standard, by a DBMS, or by an SQL application. UDTs have no corresponding <literal>s.

Data Type Conversions

SQL allows for implicit <data type> conversion in expressions and in `FETCH`, `SELECT`, `INSERT`, `DELETE`, and `UPDATE` operations. Explicit <data type> conversions may be performed with the `CAST` operator.

Sites

As defined in the SQL Standard, a *site* is "a place that holds an instance of a value of a specified <data type>." A site has a defined degree of persistence — if it exists until deliberately destroyed, it is a persistent site; if it ceases to exist at the end of an SQL statement, SQL transaction, or SQL-session, it is a temporary site; if it exists only to hold an argument or returned value, it is a transient site. The principal kind of persistent or temporary site is a Base table. Some sites may be referenced by their names (e.g., Base tables and SQL variables) or by a `REF` value. A site occupied by an element of an array may be referenced by its element number.

The instance at a site can be changed in two ways: by assignment or by mutation. *Assignment* is an operation that replaces the value at a site (the "target") with a new value (the "source"). *Mutation* is an operation that changes the value of some attribute of an instance at a site whose <data type> is a UDT. Neither assignment nor mutation has any effect on the reference value of a site, if any.

Every site has a nullability characteristic which indicates whether it may contain the null value (is "possibly nullable") or not (is "known not nullable"). Only the Columns of Base tables may be constrained to be "known not nullable," but the characteristic is inheritable.

Locators

An embedded host language variable, host parameter, SQL parameter, external routine, or the value returned by an external function may all be specified to be a Locator. The purpose of a Locator is to allow very large data values to be operated on without transferring the entire value to and from your application program.

A Locator is not SQL-data; instead, it is an SQL-session Object that can be used to reference a specific value. The SQL Standard defines three types of Locators: the large object (LOB) Locator, the UDT Locator, and the array Locator. A LOB Locator is either (*a*) a `BLOB` Locator (its value identifies a binary large object), (*b*) a `CLOB` Locator (its value identifies a character large object), or (*c*) an `NCLOB` Locator (its value identifies a national character large object). A UDT Locator identifies a value of a given user-defined type. An array Locator identifies a value of a given array.

SQL Language Elements

The SQL Standard has numerous rules for such basic issues as what makes a legal name and how to put together SQL syntax. The starting point for these rules is knowing what the basic scalar language elements are. The SQL basic scalar language elements are defined in the set of <SQL language character>s.

<SQL language character>

According to the SQL Standard, the syntactic element <SQL language character> defines "the terminal symbols of the SQL language and the elements of strings." In other words, you'll use <SQL language character>s to write SQL syntax or <token>s. <SQL language character>s are case insensitive; that is, uppercase and lowercase simple Latin letters are interchangeable so that, to a SQL parser, these three words are exactly alike:

```
SELECT
select
Select
```

The set of <SQL language character>s contains:

- The uppercase simple Latin letters A to Z.
- The lowercase simple Latin letters a to z.
- The digits 0 to 9.
- The set of <SQL special character>s.

<SQL special character>

The set of <SQL special character>s is part of the set of <SQL language character>s and contains:

	The space character
(	The left parenthesis
)	The right parenthesis
"	The double quote mark
'	The single quote mark
%	The percent sign
&	The ampersand
*	The asterisk or multiplication sign
/	The solidus or division sign
+	The plus sign
-	The minus sign or dash
,	The comma
.	The period

:	The colon
;	The semicolon
<	The less than operator
>	The greater than operator
?	The question mark
[	The left bracket
]	The right bracket
_	The underscore
|	The vertical bar
=	The equals operator
{	The left brace
}	The right brace
^	The circumflex

<token>

A <token> is either a <literal>, a <keyword>, an <identifier>, or an <SQL special character> or symbol — that is, a <token> is a group of characters that is recognized as a single unit by a SQL parser. For example, there are a total of 7 <token>s (`SELECT`, `a`, +, `5`, `FROM`, `t`, and ;) in the following SQL statement.

```
SELECT a+5 FROM t;
```

In SQL, <token>s are grouped into two types: <nondelimiter token>s and <delimiter token>s. The difference between them lies in the fact that, while any <token> may be followed by a <separator>, a <nondelimiter token> must be followed either by a <separator> or a <delimiter token>.

A <nondelimiter token> is an <unsigned numeric literal>, a <national character string literal>, a <bit string literal>, a <hex string literal>, a <keyword>, or a <regular identifier>. A <delimiter token> is a <character string literal>, a <date literal>, a <time literal>, a <timestamp literal>, an <interval literal>, a <delimited identifier>, an <SQL special character>, or one of these symbols:

<>	The not equals operator
>=	The greater than or equals operator
<=	The less than or equals operator
||	The concatenation operator
??(	The left trigraph
??)	The right trigraph
->	The right arrow
=>	The keyword parameter tag

For example, the <keyword> <token> `SELECT` may be followed either by a <separator> (usually a space) or by an <SQL special character>. Thus, both of the following are examples of legal SQL syntax.

```
SELECT column_1
```

is legal syntax because a space separates the <token> `SELECT` from the <token> `column_1`.

```
SELECT*
```

is legal syntax because, although no space separates the <token> `SELECT` from the <token> *, the asterisk is identified as a separate <token> because it is an <SQL special character>.

A <token> may not include any <separator>s unless it is a <character string literal>, a <bit string literal>, a <hex string literal>, a <timestamp literal>, an <interval literal>, or a <delimited identifier>.

<separator>

[Obscure Rule] applies to this entire section.

Your SQL parser must know where one <token> ends and another begins. To do so, it recognizes white space, a newline character, a simple comment, and a bracketed comment as <separator>s.

White space is usually just one or more spaces, but it can also consist of any consecutive sequence of these Unicode characters:

U+0009	Horizontal Tab
U+000A	Line Feed
U+000B	Vertical Tabulation
U+000C	Form Feed
U+000D	Carriage Return
U+0020	Space
U+00A0	No-Break Space
U+2000	En Quad
U+2001	Em Quad
U+2002	En Space
U+2003	Em Space
U+2004	Three-Per-Em Space
U+2005	Four-Per-Em Space
U+2006	Six-Per-Em Space
U+2007	Figure Space
U+2008	Punctuation Space
U+2009	Thin Space
U+200A	Hair Space
U+200B	Zero Width Space

U+200C	Zero Width Non-Joiner
U+200D	Zero Width Joiner
U+200E	Left-To-Right Mark
U+200F	Right-To-Left Mark
U+3000	Ideographic Space
U+2028	Line Separator
U+2029	Paragraph Separator
U+FEFF	Zero Width No-Break Space

[NON-PORTABLE] A newline character marks the end of a line. It is non-standard because the SQL Standard requires implementors to define which white space character(s) will be recognized as end-of-line indicators by their parsers. [OCELOT Implementation] The OCELOT DBMS that comes with this book recognizes carriage returns and line feeds as newline characters.

A simple comment begins with two or more consecutive dashes, contains any number of characters (including spaces and more dashes), and ends with a newline character. For example, these two SQL statements are both followed by a simple comment.

```
SELECT a+5 FROM t;      -- this is a simple comment
SELECT a+5 FROM t;      --- this is a simple comment too
```

A bracketed comment is a C-style comment. It begins with /*, ends with */, and contains any number of characters including zero or more <separator>s. For example, this SQL statement is followed by a bracketed comment.

```
SELECT a+5 FROM t;     /* this is a bracketed comment that contains a carriage
return */
```

If you want to restrict your code to Core SQL, don't use bracketed comments.

<literal>

A <literal> is a <token> that represents a non-null data value. SQL values are normally atomic — they cannot be subdivided — and are either non-null values or the null value. The null value isn't represented by a <literal>. Instead, the <keyword> `NULL` is used whenever it's necessary to indicate that the null value is represented.

[NON-PORTABLE] The logical representation of the null value is non-standard because the SQL Standard requires implementors to define that character used to display the null value. [OCELOT Implementation] The OCELOT DBMS that comes with this book displays a question mark to represent the null value.

In SQL, a <literal> is either a signed <numeric literal> (for example, +52.6), an unsigned <numeric literal> (for example, 15), or a general literal. An unsigned literal is thus either an unsigned <numeric literal> or a general literal. A general literal is one of the following:

- A <bit string literal>, for example, `B'1011'`
- A <hex string literal>, for example, `X'4A'`
- A <binary string literal>, for example, `X'44AF'`

- A <character string literal>, for example, `'hello'`
- A <national character string literal>, for example, `N'hello'`
- A <date literal>, for example, `DATE '1997-07-15'`
- A <time literal>, for example,
```
TIME '19:30:20'
TIME '19:30:20.05'
TIME '19:30:20+03:00'
```
- A <timestamp literal>, for example,
```
TIMESTAMP '1997-07-15 19:30:20'
TIMESTAMP '1997-07-15 19:30:20.05'
TIMESTAMP '1997-07-15 19:30:20.05-10:30'
```
- A <year–month literal>, for example,
```
INTERVAL '20' YEAR
INTERVAL '10' MONTH
INTERVAL '20-10' YEAR TO MONTH
```
- A <day–time literal>, for example,
```
INTERVAL -'20' DAY
INTERVAL '-10' HOUR
INTERVAL '15' MINUTE
INTERVAL '10' SECOND
INTERVAL '20 10:15:10' DAY TO SECOND
```
- A <boolean literal>, either `TRUE`, `FALSE`, or `UNKNOWN`.

<keyword>

A <keyword> is a word that has a special meaning for the SQL parser. There are two types of SQL <keyword>s: reserved <keyword>s and non-reserved <keyword>s. *Reserved* <keyword>s may not be used as <regular identifier>s. *Non-reserved* <keyword>s are not so restricted, but it's probably not a good idea to use them as <regular identifier>s anyway.

A <keyword> is case insensitive because all its characters are part of the set of <SQL language character>s. That is, uppercase and lowercase letters within a <keyword> are interchangeable; for example, these three <keyword>s are exactly alike to a SQL parser:

```
SELECT
select
Select
```

The Set of Reserved <keyword>s

ABSOLUTE
ACTION
ADD
ADMIN
AFTER
AGGREGATE
ALIAS
ALL
ALLOCATE
ALTER
AND
ANY
ARE
ARRAY
AS
ASC
ASSERTION
AT
AUTHORIZATION
BEFORE
BEGIN
BINARY
BIT
BLOB
BOOLEAN
BOTH
BREADTH
BY
CALL
CASCADE
CASCADED
CASE
CAST
CATALOG
CHAR
CHARACTER
CHECK
CLASS
CLOB
CLOSE
COLLATE
COLLATION
COLUMN
COMMIT
COMPLETION
CONDITION
CONNECT
CONNECTION
CONSTRAINT
COSTRAINTS
CONSTRUCTOR
CONTAINS
CONTINUE
CORRESPONDING
CREATE
CROSS
CUBE
CURRENT
CURRENT_DATE
CURRENT_PATH
CURRENT_ROLE
CURRENT_TIME
CURRENT_TIMESTAMP
CURRENT_USER
CURSOR
CYCLE
DATA
DATALINK
DATE
DAY
DEALLOCATE
DEC
DECIMAL
DECLARE
DEFAULT
DEFERRABLE
DEFERRED
DELETE
DEPTH
DEREF
DESC
DESCRIBE
DESCRIPTOR
DESTROY
DESTRUCTOR
DETERMINISTIC
DICTIONARY
DIAGNOSTICS
DISCONNECT
DISTINCT
DO
DOMAIN
DOUBLE
DROP
DYNAMIC
EACH
ELSE
ELSEIF
END
END-EXEC
EQUALS
ESCAPE
EVERY
EXCEPT
EXCEPTION
EXEC
EXECUTE
EXIT
EXPAND
EXPANDING
EXTERNAL
FALSE
FETCH
FIRST
FLOAT
FOR
FOREIGN
FOUND
FROM
FREE

FULL	LANGUAGE	OF	REF
FUNCTION	LARGE	OFF	REFERENCES
GENERAL	LAST	OLD	REFERENCING
GET	LATERAL	ON	RELATIVE
GLOBAL	LEADING	ONLY	REPEAT
GO	LEAVE	OPEN	RESIGNAL
GOTO	LEFT	OPERATION	RESTRICT
GRANT	LESS	OPTION	RESULT
GROUP	LEVEL	OR	RETURN
GROUPING	LIKE	ORDER	RETURNS
HANDLER	LIMIT	ORDINALITY	REVOKE
HAVING	LOCAL	OUT	RIGHT
HASH	LOCALTIME	OUTER	ROLE
HOST	LOCALTIMESTAMP	OUTPUT	ROLLBACK
HOUR	LOCATOR	PAD	ROLLUP
IDENTITY	LOOP	PARAMETER	ROUTINE
IF	MATCH	PARAMETERS	ROW
IGNORE	MEETS	PARTIAL	ROWS
IMMEDIATE	MINUTE	PATH	SAVEPOINT
IN	MODIFIES	PERIOD	SCHEMA
INDICATOR	MODIFY	POSTFIX	SCROLL
INITIALIZE	MODULE	PRECEDES	SEARCH
INITIALLY	MONTH	PRECISION	SECOND
INNER	NAMES	PREFIX	SECTION
INOUT	NATIONAL	PREORDER	SELECT
INPUT	NATURAL	PREPARE	SEQUENCE
INSERT	NCHAR	PRESERVE	SESSION
INT	NCLOB	PRIMARY	SESSION_USER
INTEGER	NEW	PRIOR	SET
INTERSECT	NEXT	PRIVILEGES	SETS
INTERVAL	NO	PROCEDURE	SIGNAL
INTO	NONE	PUBLIC	SIZE
IS	NORMALIZE	READ	SMALLINT
ISOLATION	NOT	READS	SOME
ITERATE	NULL	REAL	SPACE
JOIN	NUMERIC	RECURSIVE	SPECIFIC
KEY	OBJECT	REDO	SPECIFICTYPE

SQL
SQLEXCEPTION
SQLSTATE
SQLWARNING
START
STATE
STATIC
STRUCURE
SUCCEEDS
SYSTEM_USER
TABLE
TEMPORARY
TERMINATE
THAN
THEN
TIME
TIMESTAMP
TIMEZONE_HOUR
TIMEZONE_MINUTE
TO
TRAILING
TRANSACTION
TRANSLATION
TREAT
TRIGGER
TRUE
UNDER
UNDO
UNION
UNIQUE
UNKNOWN
UNTIL
UPDATE
USAGE
USER
USING
VALUE
VALUES
VARCHAR
VARIABLE
VARYING
VIEW
WHEN
WHENEVER
WHERE
WHILE
WITH
WITHOUT
WORK
WRITE
YEAR
ZONE

Note: SQL-92 and SQL3 both added a considerable number of words to the set of SQL reserved <keyword>s. The Standard acknowledges this and — as an aid to users — suggests that you include either a digit or an underline character in your <regular identifier>s and avoid names that begin with CURRENT_, SESSION_, SYSTEM_, or TIMEZONE_ and those that end with _LENGTH to avoid conflicts with reserved <keyword>s added in future revisions.

The Set of Non-reserved <keyword>s

ABS
ADA
ASENSITIVE
ASSIGNMENT
ASYMMETRIC
ATOMIC
AVG
BETWEEN
BIT_LENGTH
BITVAR
BLOCKED
C
CARDINALITY
CATALOG_NAME
CHAIN
CHAR_LENGTH
CHARACTER_LENGTH
CHARACTER_SET_CATALOG
CHARACTER_SET_NAME
CHARACTER_SET_SCHEMA
CHECKED
CLASS_ORIGIN
COALESCE
COBOL
COLLATION_CATALOG
COLLATION_NAME
COLLATION_SCHEMA
COLUMN_NAME
COMMAND_FUNCTION
COMMAND_FUNCTION_CODE
COMMITTED
CONCATENATE
CONDITION_NUMBER
CONNECTION_NAME
CONSTRAINT_CATALOG
CONSTRAINT_NAME
CONSTRAINT_SCHEMA
CONTAINS
CONTROL
CONVERT
COUNT
CURSOR_NAME
DATETIME_INTERVAL_CODE
DATETIME_INTERVAL_PRECISION
DB
DISPATCH
DLCOMMENT
DLFILESIZE

DLFILESIZEEXACT
DLLINKTYPE
DLURLCOMPLETE
DLURLPATH
DLURLPATHONLY
DLURLSCHEMA
DLURLSERVER
DLVALUE
DYNAMIC_FUNCTION
DYNAMIC_FUNCTION_CODE
EXISTING
EXISTS
EXTRACT
FILE
FINAL
FORTRAN
GENERATED
HOLD
INFIX
INSENSITIVE
INSTANTIABLE
INTEGRITY
KEY_MEMBER
KEY_TYPE
LENGTH
LINK
LOWER
MAX
MIN
MESSAGE_LENGTH
MESSAGE_OCTET_LENGTH
MESSAGE_TEXT
METHOD
MOD
MORE
MUMPS
NAME
NULLABLE
NUMBER
NULLIF
OCTET_LENGTH
OPTIONS
OVERLAPS
OVERLAY
OVERRIDING
PASCAL
PARAMETER_MODE
PARAMETER_ORDINAL_POSITION
PARAMETER_SPECIFIC_CATALOG
PARAMETER_SPECIFIC_NAME
PARAMETER_SPECIFIC_SCHEMA
PERMISSION
PLI
POSITION
RECOVERY
REPEATABLE
RESTORE
RETURNED_LENGTH
RETURNED_OCTET_LENGTH
RETURNED_SQLSTATE
ROUTINE_CATALOG
ROUTINE_NAME
ROUTINE_SCHEMA
ROW_COUNT
ROW_TYPE_CATALOG
ROW_TYPE_SCHEMA
ROW_TYPE_NAME
SCALE
SCHEMA_NAME
SELECTIVE
SELF
SENSITIVE
SERIALIZABLE
SERVER_NAME
SIMPLE
SOURCE
SPECIFIC_NAME
SIMILAR
STRUCTURE
SUBLIST
SUBSTRING
SUM
STYLE
SUBCLASS_ORIGIN
SYMMETRIC
SYSTEM
TABLE_NAME
TRANSACTIONS_COMMITTED
TRANSACTIONS_ROLLED_BACK
TRANSACTION_ACTIVE
TRANSFORM
TRANSLATE
TRIGGER_CATALOG
TRIGGER_SCHEMA
TRIGGER_NAME
TRIM
TYPE
UNCOMMITTED
UNLINK
UNNAMED
UPPER
USER_DEFINED_TYPE_CATALOG
USER_DEFINED_TYPE_NAME
USER_DEFINED_TYPE_SCHEMA
YES

The SQL Standard allows implementations to define more reserved words for their own DBMSs. Here are some words that are reserved in some dialect of one of the major vendors (e.g., Oracle, Sybase, Microsoft). You may be able to use these words as <regular identifier>s, but if you do so, you will lose portability.

ABORT
ACCEPT
ANALYZE
ARCHIVELOG
ARRAY
ASSIGN
ASYNCH
ATTRIBUTES
AUDIT
BACKUP
BINARY_INTEGER
BODY
CACHE
CHAR_BASE
CLUSTER
CLUSTERS
COLAUTH
COLUMNS
COMPRESS
CONSTANT
CRASH
CURVAL
DATA_BASE
DATABASE
DBA
DEBUGOFF
DEBUGON
DEFINITION
DELAY
DELTA
DICTIONARY
DIGITS
DISPLACEMENT
DISPOSE
ELEMENT
ENTRY
EXCEPTION_INIT
FACTOR
FORM
FREELISTS
GENERIC
IDENTIFIED
IGNORE
INCLUDE
INDEX
INDEXES
INFILE
INSTEAD
INSTANCE
LIMITED
LIST
MAXEEXTENTS
MINUS
MLSLABEL
MODE
NEW
NEW_TABLE
NEXTVAL
NOCOMPRESS
NONE
NUMBER
NUMBER_BASE
OFF
OID
OLD_TABLE
OPERATOR
OPERATORS
OTHERS
PACKAGE
PARTITION
PCTFREE
PENDANT
POSITIVE
PRAGMA
PREORDERED
PRIVATE
PROTECTED
RAISE
RANGE
RAW
RECORD
RELEASE
REM
RENAME
REPLACE
RESOURCE
REUSE
REVERSE
ROWID
ROWLABEL
ROWNUM
ROWTYPE
RUN
SEPARATE
SEQUENCE
SQLCA
SQLCODE
SQLERRM
SQLWARNING
STATEMENT
STDDEV
SUBTYPE
SYMBOL
TABAUTH
TABLES
TASK
TERM
TEST
THERE
TUPLE
USE
VARCHAR2
VARIANCE
VIEWS
VIRTUAL
VISIBLE
WAIT
XOR

<identifier>

An <identifier> (a <token> that names an SQL Object) is a character string, up to 128 characters long, from one Character set. Within a `CREATE SCHEMA` statement, an <identifier> that doesn't include an explicit <Schema name> names an Object that belongs to the Schema you're creating. In any other SQL statement, an <identifier> that doesn't include an explicit <Schema name> names an Object that belongs to the Schema named in the `SCHEMA` clause (or if there is no `SCHEMA` clause, in the `AUTHORIZATION` clause) of the `MODULE` statement that defines the Module you're running. SQL recognizes three types of <identifier>s: the <regular identifier>, the <SQL language identifier>, and the <delimited identifier>.

<regular identifier>

The required syntax for a <regular identifier> is:

```
<regular identifier> ::=
Object name
```

A <regular identifier> is a character string, up to 128 characters long, that consists only of letters, digits, and underscore characters. It must begin with a letter.

[Obscure Rule] We usually think of a "letter" as one of the simple Latin letters, but in fact — depending on the Character set being used — a "letter" can also be an accented character, a character in a non-Latin alphabet, or a syllable or ideograph; i.e., it can be any character with the Unicode alphabetic property or ideographic property. The "letter" that begins a <regular identifier> may not have the Unicode combining property; the letters following it may, with the proviso that these characters are not legal anywhere in a <regular identifier>:

U+06DD	Arabic End of Ayah
U+06DE	Arabic Start of Rub El Hizb
U+20DD	Combining Enclosing Circle
U+20DE	Combining Enclosing Square
U+20DF	Combining Enclosing Diamond
U+20E0	Combining Enclosing Circle Backslash

Depending on the Character set in use, you may also use these characters in a <regular identifier>, as long as they're not used as the <identifier>'s first character:

U+00B7	Middle Dot
U+02D0	Modifier Letter Triangular Colon
U+20D1	Modifier Letter Half Triangular Colon
U+0640	Arabic Tatweel
U+0E46	Thai Character Maiyamok
U+0EC6	Lao Ko La
U+3005	Ideographic Iteration Mark
U+3031 to U+3035 inclusive	Variations of Vertical Kana Repeat Mark
U+309B to U+309E inclusive	Variations of Combining Katakana-Hiragana Sound Mark and Hiragana Iteration Mark
U+30FC to U+30FE inclusive	Variations of Katakana-Hiragana Prolonged Sound Mark and Katakana Iteration Mark
U+FF70	Halfwidth Katakana-Hiragana Prolonged Sound Mark
U+FF9E	Halfwidth Katakana Voiced Sound Mark

U+FF9F	Halfwidth Katakana Semi-voiced Sound Mark
U+200C	Zero Width Non-Joiner
U+200D	Zero Width Joiner
U+200E	Left-To-Right Mark
U+200F	Right-To-Left Mark
U+202A	Left-To-Right Embedding
U+202B	Right-To-Left Embedding
U+202C	Pop Directional Formatting
U+202D	Left-To-Right Override
U+202E	Right-To-Left Override
U+206A	Inhibit Symmetric Swapping
U+206B	Activate Symmetric Swapping
U+206C	Inhibit Arabic Form Shaping
U+206D	Activate Arabic Form Shaping
U+206E	National Digit Shapes
U+206F	Nominal Digit Shapes
U+FEFF	Zero-Width No-Break Space
U+203F	Undertie
U+2040	Character Tie
U+FE33	Presentation Form for Vertical Low Line
U+FE34	Presentation Form for Vertical Wavy Low Line
U+FE4D	Dashed Low Line
U+FE4E	Centreline Low Line
U+FE4F	Wavy Low Line
U+FF3F	Fullwidth Low Line

A <regular identifier> is case insensitive. That is, uppercase and lowercase letters within a <regular identifier> are interchangeable; for example, these three <regular identifier>s are exactly alike to a SQL parser:

```
SAMS_TABLE
sams_table
Sams_Table
```

SQL doesn't allow a reserved <keyword> to be used as a <regular identifier>. When comparing a <regular identifier> and a reserved <keyword> to check for equality, your DBMS will replace the lowercase letters in each with their uppercase equivalents and assume that both belong to the `SQL_TEXT` Character set. In fact, your DBMS will replace all lowercase letters in a <regular identifier> with their uppercase equivalents prior to any comparison and prior to storing the <identifier> either in a Catalog's `INFORMATION_SCHEMA` or a diagnostics area.

Here are some examples of <regular identifier>s:

TABLE_1	a <regular identifier>
OCELOT_COMPUTER_SERVICES	another <regular identifier>
DATE_	a <regular identifier> that looks like a reserved <keyword>
MÜLLER_DATEI	a <regular identifier> that doesn't exclusively use simple Latin letters

If you want to restrict your code to Core SQL, make sure your <regular identifier>s are no more than 18 characters long.

<SQL language identifier>

The required syntax for a <SQL language identifier> is:

```
<SQL language identifier>  ::=
Object name
```

An <SQL language identifier> is a <regular identifier> that consists only of simple Latin letters, digits, and underscore characters. It must begin with a simple Latin letter. Here are two examples of <SQL language identifier>s:

```
TABLE_1
BOB_SCHEMA
```

<delimited identifier>

The required syntax for a <delimited identifier> is:

```
<delimited identifier> ::=
"Object name"
```

A <delimited identifier> is a character string, up to 128 characters long, surrounded by a pair of double quote marks. (The delimiting double quotes aren't part of the <identifier>, so they're not included in the calculation of its size.) Two consecutive double quotes within the character string (i.e., "") represent one double quote mark; together, they count as one character when calculating the size of the <identifier>.

A <delimited identifier> is case sensitive. That is, uppercase and lowercase letters within a <delimited identifier> are *not* interchangeable; for example, to a SQL parser, these three <delimited identifier>s

```
"SAMS_TABLE"
"sams_table"
"Sams_Table"
```

represent three different names. Your DBMS will not replace lowercase letters in a <delimited identifier> with their uppercase equivalents prior to any comparison or storage operation.

Here are some examples of <delimited identifier>s:

`"table#1"`	a <delimited identifier> that uses lowercase letters and a special character
`"OCELOT Computer Services"`	a <delimited identifier> that includes spaces
`"DATE"`	a <delimited identifier> that looks like a reserved <keyword>

If you want to restrict your code to Core SQL, make sure your <delimited identifier>s are no more than 18 characters long.

<identifier> Equivalence

Two <regular identifier>s are the same if they consist of the same characters. Your DBMS assumes the relevant Character set is `SQL_TEXT` when comparing them.

A <regular identifier> and a <delimited identifier> are the same if the <regular identifier> consists of the same characters that make up the body (i.e., the string of characters inside the double quote marks) of the <delimited identifier>. Two <delimited identifier>s are the same if their bodies consist of the same characters. Your DBMS assumes the relevant Character set is `SQL_TEXT` with a case sensitive Collation when comparing <regular identifier>s to <delimited identifier>s and <delimited identifier>s to one another.

Because of the difference in case sensitivity between <regular identifier>s and <delimited identifier>s, these two <regular identifier>s are the same:

```
P_TABLE
p_table
```

and both are equal to this <delimited identifier>:

```
"P_TABLE"
```

but neither are equal to this <delimited identifier>:

```
"p_table"
```

For another example, consider this group of <identifier>s:

1. `"E"`	A <delimited (uppercase) identifier>.
2. `"e"`	A <delimited (lowercase) identifier>.
3. `E`	A <regular identifier>.
4. `e`	A <regular identifier>.
5. `ë`	A <regular identifier>.

Because delimiting double quotes are not themselves part of an <identifier>, the <delimited identifier> `"E"` is the same as the <regular identifier> `E`, i.e., examples 1 and 3 are the same name. Because lowercase letters in a <regular identifier> are mapped to uppercase letters before comparison and storage, examples 3 and 4 are the same name and they're also the same name as example 1. Because lowercase letters in a <delimited identifier> are not mapped to uppercase letters at any time, example 2 is not the same name as example 4. Because there is no mapping of accented characters in an <identifier>, example 5 is not the same name as any of the others, but `ë` is a letter and so qualifies as a <regular identifier>. (This example assumes that the MS-Windows encoding scheme — the one that Microsoft calls "ANSI" — is in use. This is not always the case; the choice of possible Character sets is broad.)

Qualification of <identifier>s

All SQL Objects have names which are some combination of <regular identifier>s, <delimited identifier>s, or <SQL language identifier>s in an appropriate hierarchy of qualification. The top of the hierarchy is [SQL-server name.], an implicit name, therefore never specified. Then comes [<Catalog name>.] which is the first level of the hierarchy that can be explicitly stated. The next level is [<Schema name>.], then comes [the name of an Object], and (if the Object is a Table) the final level of the hierarchy is <.Column name>. The entire qualification hierarchy always exists but is not necessarily visible; the Standard contains rules by which high-level parts of the combination may be omitted and their values assumed by default.

3

Chapter 3

Numbers

In SQL, a number (i.e., any signed or unsigned combination of the digits 0 to 9) is either an exact numeric value or an approximate numeric value. A numeric value may be a <literal>, the value of a parameter or a host language variable, or the result of any expression or argument (including a possibly qualified <Column name>) that evaluates to a number.

Exact numeric values have a precision and a scale. The precision is a positive integer that determines the number of significant digits. The scale is a non-negative integer that specifies the number of digits to the right of the value's decimal point. Exact numeric values are stored in one of the four exact numeric <data type>s: `INTEGER`, `SMALLINT`, `NUMERIC`, or `DECIMAL`.

Approximate numeric values, or floating-point numbers, have two parts: a signed decimal number (the *mantissa*) and a signed integer (the *exponent*). The exponent specifies the magnitude of the mantissa, so the value of such a number is the mantissa raised to the power of the exponent. Approximate numeric values also have a precision; a positive integer that specifies the number of significant digits in the mantissa. Approximate numeric values are stored in one of the three approximate numeric <data type>s: `FLOAT`, `REAL`, or `DOUBLE PRECISION`.

Numeric <literal>s

A <numeric literal> is any number in one of two categories: the exact numeric integers and decimal numbers or the approximate numeric floating-point numbers.

<exact numeric literal>

An <exact numeric literal> is either an integer or a decimal number and its <data type> is exact numeric DECIMAL, though it is compatible with the INTEGER, SMALLINT, DECIMAL, NUMERIC, REAL, FLOAT, and DOUBLE PRECISION <data type>s. The <literal>'s precision is the number of digits it contains and its scale is the number of digits to the right of its decimal point. A valid integer <literal> is a signed or unsigned decimal integer with an implicit scale of zero, e.g., –65 or 476.

A valid decimal <literal> is a signed or unsigned decimal integer with an explicit scale (that can nevertheless default to zero), e.g., 65 or –819.3 or .67 or –.02.

<approximate numeric literal>

An <approximate numeric literal> is a floating-point number and its <data type> is approximate numeric FLOAT, though it is compatible with the INTEGER, SMALLINT, DECIMAL, NUMERIC, REAL, FLOAT, and DOUBLE PRECISION <data type>s. The <literal>'s precision is the precision of its mantissa and its numeric value is the product of its mantissa raised to the power of its exponent. A valid <approximate numeric literal> is a floating-point number consisting of a possibly signed decimal number (the mantissa) and a signed integer (the exponent) separated by the uppercase letter "E," e.g., –1.27982E+5 or .465E–7.

Here are some equivalent <literal>s in exact and in exponential notation:

Exact	REAL	DOUBLE PRECISION
.000000000000001	1.0000000E-15	1.00000000000000E-015
-0.1	-1.0000000E-01	-1.00000000000000E-001
1	1.0000000E+00	1.00000000000000E+000
+10	1.0000000E+01	1.00000000000000E+001
1000000000000000	1.0000000E+15	1.00000000000000E+015

In this example, we've shown the real and double precision numbers in a *normalized* form — with one digit before the decimal point. This is not mandatory, but strongly recommended. We also show a fixed number of digits after the decimal point so that maximum sizes will be apparent; in fact, leading zeros and signs as well as post-decimal zeros, are all optional. The one thing that is not optional is the letter "E" — always uppercase.

Numeric <data type>s

A numeric <data type> is defined by a descriptor that contains four pieces of information:

1. The <data type>'s name; either INTEGER, SMALLINT, NUMERIC, DECIMAL, FLOAT, REAL, or DOUBLE PRECISION.
2. The <data type>'s precision.
3. The <data type>'s scale (for exact numeric types).
4. Whether the <data type>'s precision and scale are expressed in decimal or binary terms.

INTEGER

The required syntax for an INTEGER <data type> specification is as follows.

```
INTEGER <data type> ::=
INTEGER
```

INTEGER may be abbreviated as INT; it defines a set of possibly signed whole numbers that have a scale of zero.

[NON-PORTABLE] INT's precision must be greater than or equal to the precision of SMALLINT but is non-standard because the SQL Standard requires implementors to define INT's precision. FIPS says that INT should have a precision of at least 9 decimal digits. [OCELOT Implementation] The OCELOT DBMS that comes with this book defines INT as a 32-bit, signed binary numeric, i.e., INT corresponds to the C long int data type. Thus, INT defines a set of values that are possibly signed whole numbers with a precision of 31 bits and a scale of zero, e.g., –6500 or 476673.

[NON-PORTABLE] INT's radix must be the same as the radix chosen for SMALLINT but is non-standard because the SQL Standard requires implementors to define whether INT and SMALLINT have a binary radix or a decimal radix. [OCELOT Implementation] The OCELOT DBMS that comes with this book defines INT and SMALLINT with a binary radix, i.e., 2. This gives INT a valid range of –2,147,483,647 to +2,147,483,647.

SMALLINT

The required syntax for a SMALLINT <data type> specification is as follows.

```
SMALLINT <data type> ::=
SMALLINT
```

SMALLINT defines a set of possibly signed whole numbers that have a scale of zero.

[NON-PORTABLE] SMALLINT's precision must be less than or equal to the precision of INT but is non-standard because the SQL Standard requires implementors to define SMALLINT's precision. FIPS says that SMALLINT should have a precision of at least 4 decimal digits. [OCELOT Implementation] The OCELOT DBMS that comes with this book defines SMALLINT as a 16-bit signed binary numeric, i.e., SMALLINT corresponds to the C int data type. Thus, SMALLINT defines a set of values that are possibly signed whole numbers with a precision of 15 bits and a scale of zero, e.g., –65 or 476.

[NON-PORTABLE] SMALLINT's radix must be the same as the radix chosen for INT but is non-standard because the SQL Standard requires implementors to define whether SMALLINT and INT have a binary radix or a decimal radix. [OCELOT Implementation] The OCELOT DBMS that comes with this book defines SMALLINT and INT with a binary radix, i.e., 2. This gives SMALLINT a range of –32,767 to +32,767.

NUMERIC

The required syntax for a NUMERIC <data type> specification is as follows.

```
NUMERIC <data type> ::=
NUMERIC [ (precision[,scale]) ]
```

NUMERIC is a fixed-point numeric with a decimal precision and decimal scale that are equal to the explicit precision and the explicit scale given; it defines a set of values that are possibly signed decimal numbers with an optionally defined precision and optionally defined scale, e.g., 65.73 or .6 or –819.3 or –.25.

The optional precision, if specified, is an unsigned integer that defines the maximum precision of acceptable values. The minimum precision is 1.

[NON-PORTABLE] The default precision and the maximum precision for NUMERIC are non-standard because the SQL Standard requires implementors to define NUMERIC's default and maximum precisions. Typically, the maximum precision is 15 (the FIPS requirement) but it may be as high as 38 (the DB2 maximum). [OCELOT Implementation] The OCELOT DBMS that comes with this book allows the precision of NUMERIC to range from 1 to 38, with a default precision of 1. For example, this <data type> specification defines a set of values that may range from –9999 to +9999 (4 digits defined):

```
NUMERIC(4)
```

and these two equivalent <data type> specifications define a set of values that may range from –9 to +9 (1 digit defined or default):

```
NUMERIC(1)
NUMERIC
```

The optional scale, if specified, is an unsigned integer, greater than or equal to zero, that defines the maximum number of digits which may follow the decimal point. It must be less than the precision and defaults to zero if omitted. You may define a scale for NUMERIC only if you also define a precision; if no precision is defined, the scale must default to zero.

[NON-PORTABLE] The maximum scale for NUMERIC must always be less than the defined precision but is non-standard because the SQL Standard requires implementors to define NUMERIC's maximum scale. [OCELOT Implementation] The OCELOT DBMS that comes with this book allows you to define a scale ranging from 1 to 38 for NUMERIC. For example, this <data type> specification defines a set of values that may range from –999.9 to +999.9 (3 digits before the decimal point and 1 digit after the decimal point, for a total of 4 digits):

```
NUMERIC(4,1)
```

DECIMAL

The required syntax for a DECIMAL <data type> specification is as follows.

```
DECIMAL <data type> ::=
DECIMAL [ (precision[,scale]) ]
```

DECIMAL may be abbreviated as DEC and is a fixed-point numeric with a decimal scale that is equal to the explicit scale given; it defines a set of values that are possibly signed decimal numbers with an optionally-defined precision and optionally-defined scale, e.g., 65.73 or .6 or –819.3 or –.25.

The optional precision, if specified, is an unsigned integer that defines the maximum precision of acceptable values. DEC's decimal precision must be at least equal to the precision you define — compare to COBOL, which allows PIC S9(3) COMP–1 but might allot a full-word PIC S9(5) for internal storage. The minimum precision is 1.

[NON-PORTABLE] The default precision, maximum precision, and exact precision for DEC are non-standard because the SQL Standard requires implementors to define DEC's default, maximum, and exact precisions. Typically, the maximum precision is 15 (the FIPS requirement); it may be as high as 38 (the DB2 maximum). [OCELOT Implementation] The OCELOT DBMS that comes with this book allows the precision of DEC to range from 1 to 38, with a default precision of 1. DEC's decimal precision is equal to the precision you define, i.e., OCELOT treats DEC and NUMERIC as synonyms. For example, this <data type> specification defines a set of values that may range from –9999 to +9999 (4 digits defined):

```
DEC(4)
```

and these two equivalent <data type> specifications define a set of values that may range from –9 to +9 (1 digit defined or default):

```
DEC(1)
DECIMAL
```

The optional scale, if specified, is an unsigned integer, greater than or equal to zero, that defines the maximum number of digits which may follow the decimal point. It must be less than the precision and defaults to zero if omitted. You may define a scale for DEC only if you also define a precision; if no precision is defined, the scale must default to zero.

[NON-PORTABLE] The maximum scale for DEC must always be less than the defined precision but is non-standard because the SQL Standard requires implementors to define DEC's maximum scale. [OCELOT Implementation] The OCELOT DBMS that comes with this book allows you to define a scale ranging from 1 to 38 for DEC. For example, this <data type> specification defines a set of values that may range from –999.9 to +999.9 (3 digits before the decimal point and 1 digit after the decimal point, for a total of 4 digits):

```
DEC(4,1)
```

FLOAT

The required syntax for a FLOAT <data type> specification is as follows.

```
FLOAT <data type> ::=
FLOAT [ (precision) ]
```

FLOAT is a floating-point numeric with a binary precision; it defines a set of values that are possibly signed floating-point numbers.

The optional precision, if specified, is an unsigned integer that defines the maximum number of bits (including the hidden bit) in the mantissa. FLOAT's binary precision must be at least equal to the precision you define. The minimum precision is 1.

[NON-PORTABLE] The default precision, maximum precision, and binary precision for FLOAT are non-standard because the SQL Standard requires implementors to define FLOAT's default, maximum, and exact precisions. FIPS says that FLOAT should have a binary precision of at least 20. [OCELOT Implementation] The OCELOT DBMS that comes with this book allows the precision of FLOAT to range from 1 to 53, with a default precision of 53. Thus, FLOAT defines a set of values that are possibly signed floating-point numbers with this format:

```
[sign]+digit+period+ up to 14 digits+E+[sign]+ up to 3 digits
```

For example, –1.27982E+015 or .465E–007. The IEEE Standard for Binary Floating-Point Arithmetic (IEEE Standard 754–1985) specifies two usual mantissa sizes: 24 and 53. OCELOT supports both; regardless of the actual precision specified for FLOAT, there are really only two possible results. If you define FLOAT with a precision that is less than or equal to 24, the actual binary precision will equal 24 bits in the mantissa. For example, these two <data type> specifications are equivalent; they both define a set of floating-point values whose mantissa may range up to a precision of 24 bits:

```
FLOAT(12)
FLOAT(24)
```

If you define FLOAT with a precision between 25 and 53, the actual binary precision will equal 53 bits in the mantissa. For example, these three <data type> specifications are equivalent; they all define a set of floating-point values whose mantissa may range up to a precision of 53 bits:

```
FLOAT
FLOAT(27)
FLOAT(53)
```

[NON-PORTABLE] The minimum exponent and the maximum exponent for FLOAT values are non-standard because the SQL Standard requires implementors to define FLOAT's minimum and maximum exponents. [OCELOT Implementation] The OCELOT DBMS that comes with this book allows you to use numbers with exponents ranging from –038 to +038 for FLOAT.

REAL

The required syntax for a REAL <data type> specification is as follows.

```
REAL <data type> ::=
REAL
```

REAL is a floating-point numeric with a binary precision, i.e., REAL defines a set of values that are possibly signed floating-point numbers.

[NON-PORTABLE] The binary precision of REAL must be less than the precision defined for DOUBLE PRECISION but is non-standard because the SQL Standard requires implementors to define REAL's exact precision. [OCELOT Implementation] The OCELOT DBMS that comes with this book treats REAL as equivalent to FLOAT(24). Thus, REAL defines a set of values that are possibly signed floating-point numbers with this format:

```
[sign]+digit+period+up to 6 digits+E+[sign]+ up to 2 digits
```

For example, –1.27982E+15 or .465E–07.

[NON-PORTABLE] The minimum exponent and the maximum exponent for REAL values are non-standard because the SQL Standard requires implementors to define REAL's minimum and maximum exponents. [OCELOT Implementation] The OCELOT DBMS that comes with this book allows you to use numbers with exponents ranging from –38 to +38 for REAL.

DOUBLE PRECISION

The required syntax for a DOUBLE PRECISION <data type> specification is as follows.

```
DOUBLE PRECISION <data type> ::=
DOUBLE PRECISION
```

DOUBLE PRECISION is a floating-point numeric with a binary precision, i.e., DOUBLE PRECISION defines a set of values that are possibly signed floating-point numbers.

[NON-PORTABLE] The binary precision of DOUBLE PRECISION must be greater than the precision defined for REAL but is non-standard because the SQL Standard requires implementors to define DOUBLE PRECISION's exact precision. FIPS says that DOUBLE PRECISION should have a binary precision of at least 30. [OCELOT Implementation] The OCELOT DBMS that comes with this book treats DOUBLE PRECISION as equivalent to FLOAT(53). Thus, DOUBLE PRECISION defines a set of values that are possibly signed floating-point numbers with this format:

```
[sign]+digit+period+up to 14 digits+E+[sign]+up to 3 digits
```

For example, -1.27982E+015 or .465E-007.

[NON-PORTABLE] The minimum exponent and the maximum exponent for DOUBLE PRECISION values are non-standard because the SQL Standard requires implementors to define DOUBLE PRECISION's minimum and maximum exponents. [OCELOT Implementation] The OCELOT DBMS that comes with this book allows you to use numbers with exponents ranging from -038 to +038 for DOUBLE PRECISION.

WARNING: Throughout this section, we've shown examples of <numeric literal>s that *conform to* the various SQL <data type>s we're describing. It is important to remember that your DBMS doesn't see them that way. To an SQL DBMS, <exact numeric literal>s have a DECIMAL <data type> and <approximate numeric literal>s have a FLOAT <data type>.

Now that we've described SQL's numeric <data type>s, let's look at some example SQL statements that put them to use.

These SQL statements make a Table with four exact numeric Columns, insert a row, then search for any number less than -1:

```
CREATE TABLE Exact_Examples (
     occurrence_decimal DECIMAL(5),
     occurrence_numeric NUMERIC(7,2),
     occurrence_integer INTEGER,
     occurrence_smallint SMALLINT);
INSERT INTO Exact_Examples (
     occurrence_decimal,
     occurrence_numeric,
     occurrence_integer,
     occurrence_smallint)
     VALUES (12345, 12345, 12345, 12345);
SELECT occurrence_decimal,
       occurrence_numeric,
       occurrence_integer,
       occurrence_smallint
 FROM  Exact_Examples
 WHERE occurrence_decimal < -1;
```

These SQL statements make a Table with three approximate numeric Columns, insert a row, then search for any number less than 50,000:

```
CREATE TABLE Approximate_Examples (
    occurrence_float FLOAT(53),
    occurrence_real REAL,
    occurrence_double DOUBLE PRECISION);
INSERT INTO Approximate_Examples (
    occurrence_float,
    occurrence_real,
    occurrence_double)
    VALUES (5E+2, 5E+2, 5E+2);
SELECT occurrence_float,
       occurrence_real,
       occurrence_double
FROM   Approximate_Examples
WHERE  occurrence_float < 5E+4;
```

IEEE Binary Floats

According to the IEEE Standard for Binary Floating-Point Arithmetic, "single-" and "double-precision" numbers are defined as follows.

PRECISION	SIGN [BITS]	EXPONENT [BITS]	MANTISSA [BITS]*	EXPONENT [DECIMAL]	RANGE [DECIMAL]
Single	1	8	24	–38 to +35	7 digits
Double	1	11	53	–304 to +308	15 digits

* The most significant mantissa bit is assumed to be 1. It is not stored.

You'd find the same specification in, say, an Intel FPU reference text or a C++ manual. But we found discrepancies when looking through documents for Java (where the exponent range is between –35 and +38), Delphi (where the exponent range is between –45 and +38 for single-precision and between –324 and +308 for double-precision), and FIPS SQL (where the `FLOAT` exponent+size are 9+47 and the `REAL` exponent+size are 7+23). So for portability reasons, it would be a good idea to avoid the extremes of the IEEE range.

Most DBMSs support IEEE float formats because FIPS requires that the decimal ranges be supported and because the DBMS code itself is written in a language that supports IEEE floats. But never does an official SQL standard tell vendors "how to store the data." So it might be that your DBMS actually uses the IEEE sizes or it might be that your DBMS actually stores float decimal literals (as xBase does) and processes with base-10 arithmetic. If so, the following information doesn't apply to you.

[Obscure Information] applies for the rest of this section.

Binary Floats are not exact. The danger with these numbers is easy to observe in a simple arithmetic exercise.

1. Represent the number one-third (1/3) in decimal. The maximum number of post-decimal digits (the scale) is large but not infinite. Result is 0.333333.
2. Take the sum of three occurrences of this number. Result is 0.333333 + 0.333333 + 0.333333 = 0.999999.
3. Note that the number is wrong (three thirds should equal 1). Increase the scale. Try again. You'll never get the correct result because you can't accurately represent 1/3 as a decimal fraction.

Now consider what would happen if your number was decimal, e.g., one-hundredth (1/100). Try to represent that number as a binary fraction. If you have 16 binary digits (a 16-bit "word"), there are only 2^{16} discrete values you can represent, so you are dealing in dividends which are sixty-five-thousand-five-hundred-and-thirty-sixths. The closest number to 1/100 is thus 655/65536, i.e., you have to store 655 in your word. This is a bit small. (Actually 655/65536 is closer to 0.09945, so our error is about one part in a thousand.) In other words, you cannot represent 1/100 as a binary fraction. Worse, if you now convert back to decimal, you will probably get 1/100 again (the smart computer rounds up) so you won't see the inaccuracy. Now consider the result of this SQL code:

```
SUM(column_containing_the_fractional_value_one_hundredth)
```

If your Table has 1,000 rows then the conversion to binary happens 1,000 times — cumulating the inaccuracy each time — and the conversion back to decimal happens only once when the final `SUM` is returned. Rounding won't save you because the result, 99.45, is good to the nearest hundredth. And you won't check the result in your head. Yet the result is "wrong."

In theory, this arithmetic exercise is not a "floating-point" problem. We introduced the inaccuracy by converting a decimal fraction to binary. Both fixed-point and floating-point binary fractions have the same danger of inaccuracy because the danger lies in the fact that we're dealing with binary numbers — not in the fact that we're dealing with floating-point numbers. So, in theory, the same "wrong" result could be returned for a `DECIMAL` Column or a `NUMERIC` Column. In practice, though, the better SQL DBMSs won't use binary fractions for `DECIMAL` or `NUMERIC` values. Instead, like COBOL with PIC 9V99, they actually store an integer with an implied decimal point — so the number 1/100 is, internally, 1. No conversion occurs because an integral number of hundredths are being stored, rather than a fraction.

TIP: Because of this, both money and interest ought to be `DECIMAL` or `NUMERIC` for all financial transactions. The frequency of definitions like:

```
CREATE TABLE Table_1 (salary FLOAT);
```

is a mistake; justified only by the fact that in C or Pascal, it's normal to define big or non-integer variables as floating-point.

Numeric Operations

A number is compatible with, and comparable to, all other numbers — that is, all numbers are mutually comparable and mutually assignable. Numbers may not be directly compared with, or directly assigned to, any other <data type> class though implicit type conversions can occur in expressions, SELECTs, INSERTs, DELETEs, and UPDATEs. Explicit numeric type conversions can be forced with the CAST operator.

CAST

In SQL, CAST is a scalar operator that converts a given scalar value to a given scalar <data type>. The required syntax for the CAST operator is as follows.

```
CAST (<cast operand> AS <cast target>)
   <cast operand> ::= scalar_expression
   <cast target> ::= <Domain name> | <data type>
```

The CAST operator converts values of a source <data type> into values of a target <data type> where each <data type> is an SQL pre-defined <data type> (data conversions between UDTs are done with a user-defined cast). The source <data type> (or <cast operand>) can be any expression that evaluates to a single value. The target <data type> (or <cast target>) is either an SQL predefined <data type> specification or the name of a Domain whose defined <data type> is your target <data type>. If you use CAST (... AS <Domain name>), your current <AuthorizationID> must have the USAGE Privilege on that Domain.

It isn't, of course, possible to convert the values of every <data type> into the values of every other <data type>. For numbers, the rules are:

- CAST (NULL AS <data type>) and CAST (numeric_source_is_a_null_value AS <data type>) both result in NULL.
- You can CAST an exact numeric source to these targets: exact numeric, approximate numeric, fixed length character string, variable length character string, CLOB, and NCLOB. You can also CAST an exact numeric source to an interval target, provided the target contains only one datetime field. That is, you can CAST an integer to INTERVAL YEAR or to INTERVAL MONTH, but you can't CAST it to INTERVAL YEAR TO MONTH. You can CAST an exact numeric source to a UDT target or a <reference type> target if a user-defined cast exists for this purpose and your current <AuthorizationID> has the EXECUTE Privilege on that user-defined cast.
- You can CAST an approximate numeric source to these targets: exact numeric, approximate numeric, fixed length character string, variable length character string, CLOB, and NCLOB. You can also CAST an approximate numeric source to a UDT target or a <reference type> target if a user-defined cast exists for this purpose and your current <AuthorizationID> has the EXECUTE Privilege on that user-defined cast.

When you CAST an exact numeric value or an approximate numeric value to an exact numeric target, e.g., CAST (25 AS INTEGER), CAST (1.47E-5 AS DECIMAL(9,7)), or when you CAST an exact numeric value or an approximate numeric value to an approximate numeric target, e.g., CAST (25 AS FLOAT), CAST (1.47E-5 AS DOUBLE PRECISION) — your DBMS checks whether the source is a valid value for the target's <data type> or if a valid value (one that doesn't lose any leading significant digits) can be obtained from the source by rounding or truncation. If so, then the source is converted to that target value. If neither of these are true, the CAST will fail; your DBMS will return the SQLSTATE error 22003 "data exception-numeric value out of range."

[NON-PORTABLE] If your source value is not a valid value for your target <data type>, then the value CAST is non-standard because the SQL Standard requires implementors to define whether the DBMS will round or will truncate to obtain a valid target value. [OCELOT Implementation] The OCELOT DBMS that comes with this book truncates to obtain a valid target value.

When you CAST an exact numeric value or an approximate numeric value to a fixed length character string target, your DBMS converts the number to the shortest string that represents that number, i.e.,

```
CAST (25 AS CHAR(2)) results in the character string '25'
CAST (1.47E-5 AS CHAR(8)) results in the character string '.0000147'
CAST (-25 AS CHAR(3)) results in the character string '-25'
CAST (+25 AS CHAR(3)) results in the character string '25'
CAST (025 AS CHAR(3)) results in the character string '25'
CAST (25. AS CHAR(3)) results in the character string '25'
CAST (25.0 AS CHAR(4)) results in the character string '25'
...
```

If the length of the result equals the fixed length of the target, then the source is CAST to that result. If the length of the result is shorter than the fixed length of the target, then the source is CAST to that result, padded on the right with however many spaces are needed to make the lengths the same. If the length of the result is longer than the fixed length of the target, the CAST will fail; your DBMS will return the SQLSTATE error 22001 "data exception-string data, right truncation." And if the result contains any characters that don't belong to the target's Character set, the CAST will also fail; your DBMS will return the SQLSTATE error 22018 "data exception-invalid character value for cast."

NOTE: If your approximate numeric source value is zero, the CAST result is the character string '0E0'.

When you CAST an exact numeric value or an approximate numeric value to a variable length character string target, a CLOB target, or an NCLOB target, your DBMS converts the number to the shortest string that represents that number. As with fixed length target, it strips off leading plus signs, leading zeros, and any insignificant decimal signs and trailing zeros. If the length of the result is less than or equals the maximum length of the target, then the source is CAST to that result. If the length of the result is longer than the maximum length of the target, the CAST will fail; your DBMS will return the SQLSTATE error 22001 "data exception-string data, right truncation." And if the result contains any characters that don't belong to the target's Character set, the CAST will also fail; your DBMS will return the SQLSTATE error 22018 "data exception-invalid character value for cast."

[Obscure Rule] The result of a CAST to a character string target has the COERCIBLE coercibility attribute; its Collation is the default Collation for the target's Character set.

When you CAST an exact numeric value to an interval target, your DBMS converts it to the value of the interval's single datetime field represented by that number, i.e., CAST (25 AS INTERVAL YEAR) results in an interval of 25 years. If the number you're casting is too large for the precision of the target, as in CAST (500 AS INTERVAL HOUR(2)) — the CAST will fail; your DBMS will return the SQLSTATE error 22015 "data exception-interval field overflow."

When you CAST an exact numeric value or an approximate numeric value to a UDT or a <reference type> target, your DBMS invokes the user-defined cast routine with the source value as the routine's argument. The CAST result is the value returned by the user-defined cast.

If you want to restrict your code to Core SQL, don't use <Domain name> as a CAST target; CAST only to a <data type>.

Assignment

In SQL, when an exact numeric or an approximate numeric value is assigned to an exact numeric target, the source is first converted to an exact numeric value with the precision and scale of the target. When an exact numeric or an approximate numeric value is assigned to an approximate numeric target, the source is first converted to an approximate numeric value with the precision of the target. In either case, if the assignment would result in the loss of any of the source value's most significant digits, the assignment will fail; your DBMS will return the SQLSTATE error 22003 "data exception-numeric value out of range."

[NON-PORTABLE] If the assignment of a numeric value would result in the loss of any of the source value's least significant digits, the result is non-standard because the SQL Standard requires implementors to define the result using either of two options: (*a*) your DBMS may truncate to fit the target and then make the assignment or (*b*) your DBMS may round to fit the target and then make the assignment. [OCELOT Implementation] The OCELOT DBMS that comes with this book truncates to fit the target.

[Obscure Rule] Since only SQL accepts null values, when a null value is taken from SQL-data to be assigned to a numeric target, your target's value is not changed. Instead, your DBMS will set the target's indicator parameter to –1 to indicate that an assignment of the null value was attempted. If your target doesn't have an indicator parameter, the assignment will fail; your DBMS will return the SQLSTATE error 22002 "data exception-null value, no indicator parameter." Going the other way, there are two ways to assign a null value to an SQL-data target. Within SQL, you can use the <keyword> NULL in an INSERT or an UPDATE statement to indicate that the target should be set to NULL; that is, if your source is NULL, your DBMS will set your target to NULL. Outside of SQL, if your source has an indicator parameter that is set to –1, your DBMS will set your target to NULL (regardless of the value of the source). An indicator parameter with a value less than –1 will cause an error; your DBMS will return the SQLSTATE error 22010 "data exception-invalid indicator parameter value." We'll talk more about indicator parameters in our chapters on SQL binding styles.

As an example, assume that you have an INTEGER Column and need to assign a non-integer value to it. The result will depend not only on what the source value is, but also on whether your DBMS uses rounding or truncation to turn it into an integer. The following table displays the choices (note that "rounding toward zero" is really truncating).

Source value	Rounding toward +infinity	Rounding toward –infinity	Rounding toward zero	Rounding toward nearest
1.5	2	1	1	2
–1.5	1	–2	–1	–2
etc.				

Most DBMSs use truncation but the following SQL statements show how to force the rounding method you prefer:

```
-- rounding toward positive infinity
CASE numeric_expression - CAST (numeric_expression AS INTEGER)
    WHEN > 0 numeric_expression+1
    WHEN < 0 numeric_expression-1
    ELSE numeric_expression
END

-- rounding toward negative infinity
CASE numeric_expression
   WHEN > 0 CAST (numeric_expression AS INTEGER)
    WHEN < 0 CAST (0 - (ABS(numeric_expression) + 0.5) AS INTEGER))
   ELSE numeric_expression
END

-- rounding toward zero
CAST (numeric_expression AS INTEGER)

-- rounding toward nearest
CAST (numeric_expression + 0.5 AS INTEGER)
```

Comparison

SQL provides the usual scalar comparison operators, = and <> and < and <= and > and >=, to perform operations on numbers. All of them will be familiar; there are equivalent operators in other computer languages. Numbers are compared in the usual manner. If any of the comparands are `NULL`, the result of the operation is `UNKNOWN`. For example:

```
97 = 105.2
```

returns `FALSE`.

```
97 <> {result is NULL}
```

returns `UNKNOWN`.

SQL also provides three quantifiers — `ALL`, `SOME`, `ANY` — which you can use along with a comparison operator to compare a value with the collection of values returned by a <table subquery>. Place the quantifier after the comparison operator, immediately before the <table subquery>. For example:

```
SELECT decimal_column
FROM   Table_1
WHERE  decimal_column < ALL (
   SELECT integer_column
   FROM   Table_2);
```

`ALL` returns `TRUE` either (*a*) if the collection is an empty set, i.e., if it contains zero rows or (*b*) if the comparison operator returns `TRUE` for every value in the collection. `ALL` returns `FALSE` if the comparison operator returns `FALSE` for at least one value in the collection.

`SOME` and `ANY` are synonyms. They return `TRUE` if the comparison operator returns `TRUE` for at least one value in the collection. They return `FALSE` either (*a*) if the collection is an empty set or (*b*) if the comparison operator returns `FALSE` for every value in the collection. The search condition `= ANY (collection)` is equivalent to `IN (collection)`.

Other Operations

With SQL, you have several other operations that you can perform on numbers or on other values to get a numeric result.

Arithmetic

SQL provides the usual scalar arithmetic operators, `+` and `-` and `*` and `/` , to perform operations on numbers. All of them will be familiar; there are equivalent operators in other computer languages. If any of the operands are `NULL`, the result of the operation is also `NULL`.

Monadic + and monadic – When used alone, `+` and `-` change the sign of an operand, e.g., a <literal> or a Column instance or a host variable. For example:

```
SELECT -5, -(-occurrence_decimal)
FROM   Exact_Examples
WHERE  occurrence_integer = +5;
```

NOTE: Because two dashes, i.e., `--` mean "comment start" in SQL, our example of a double negative has to be `-(-occurrence_decimal)` rather than `--occurrence_decimal`.

Dyadic + and dyadic – and dyadic * and dyadic / When used between two operands, + and - and * and / stand for add and subtract and multiply and divide, respectively, and return results according to the usual rules. For example:

```
SELECT occurrence_integer + 5, (occurrence_integer * 7) / 2
FROM   Exact_Examples
WHERE  occurrence_integer < (:host_variable - 7);
```

Precedence Dyadic * and / have priority over dyadic + and -, but monadic + and - have top priority. It's good style to use parentheses for any expressions with different operators.

Errors The two common arithmetic exception conditions are:

```
SQLSTATE 22003 — data exception - numeric value out of range
SQLSTATE 22012 — data exception - division by zero
```

The following is a snippet of an embedded SQL program that checks for overflow after executing a statement that contains addition.

```
EXEC SQL UPDATE Exact_Examples
         SET    occurrence_smallint = occurrence_decimal + 1;
if (strcmp(sqlstate,"22003")
printf("Overflow! Operation cancelled ...\n");
```

Error checks should follow every execution of an SQL statement, but imagine that the `Exact_Examples` Table has a million rows. To avoid the situation where, after chugging through 999,999 rows, your application collapses on the last one with "`Overflow! Operation cancelled ...`", try this code:

```
EXEC SQL UPDATE Exact_Examples
         SET    occurrence_smallint =
         CASE
           WHEN occurrence_smallint = 32767 THEN 0
           ELSE occurrence_smallint = occurrence_smallint + 1
         END;
```

TIP: `CASE` expressions are good for taking error-abating actions in advance.

TIP: SQL has no low-level debugging features, so sometimes you will need to force an error somewhere in a complex expression to be sure it is actually being executed. For this purpose, insert code that would cause a numeric overflow.

Mixing Numeric <data type>s

As we said earlier, all numbers — any <data type>, exact or approximate — are compatible. That means that you can mix them together in any numeric expression, which leads to the question: what comes out when you do mix them? That is, what is the <data type>, precision, and scale of the result? The SQL Standard says that the following are the results you will get:

[NON-PORTABLE] An exact numeric value added to, subtracted from, multiplied by, or divided by an exact numeric value yields an exact numeric value with a precision that is non-standard because the SQL Standard requires implementors to define the precision of the result. For all these operations, if the result of the operation can't be exactly represented with the correct precision and scale, the operation will fail; your DBMS will return the `SQLSTATE error 22003` "`data exception-numeric value out of range.`" [OCELOT Implementation] The OCELOT DBMS that comes with this book gives the result the same <data type> and precision as the most precise operand, e.g., for an operation with `SMALLINT` and `INT` operands, the result is an `INT`.

An exact numeric value added to or subtracted from an exact numeric value yields a result with a scale size that matches the scale of the operand with the largest scale, e.g., for an operation with `DECIMAL(6,2)` and `INT` operands, the result has a scale of 2.

An exact numeric value multiplied by an exact numeric value yields a result with a scale size that is the sum of the scales of the operands, e.g., for an operation with `DECIMAL(6,2)` and `NUMERIC(10,4)` operands, the result has a scale of 6.

[NON-PORTABLE] An exact numeric value divided by an exact numeric value yields a result with a scale size that is non-standard because the SQL Standard requires implementors to define the scale of the result. [OCELOT Implementation] The OCELOT DBMS that comes with this book gives the result a scale size that matches the scale of the operand with the largest scale, e.g., for an operation with `DECIMAL(6,2)` and `NUMERIC(10,4)` operands, the result has a scale of 4.

[NON-PORTABLE] An approximate numeric value added to, subtracted from, multiplied by, or divided by an approximate numeric value yields an approximate numeric value with a precision that is non-standard because the SQL Standard requires implementors to define the precision of the result. If the exponent of the result doesn't fall within the DBMS's supported exponent range, the operation will fail; your DBMS will return the `SQLSTATE error 22003` "`data exception-numeric value out of range.`" [OCELOT Implementation] The OCELOT DBMS that comes with this book gives the result the same <data type> and precision as the most precise operand, e.g., for an operation with `REAL` and `DOUBLE PRECISION` operands, the result is a `DOUBLE PRECISION`.

[NON-PORTABLE] An approximate numeric value added to, subtracted from, multiplied by, or divided by an exact numeric value (or vice versa) yields an approximate numeric value with a precision that is non-standard because the SQL Standard requires implementors to define the precision of the result. [OCELOT Implementation] The OCELOT DBMS that comes with this book gives the result the same <data type> and precision as the most precise operand, e.g., for an operation with `INT` and `DOUBLE PRECISION` operands, the result is a `DOUBLE PRECISION`.

In other words, the Standard always evades the big question, "What's the result precision?" To put this into perspective, consider a DBMS faced with a tough operation: add 1 to a Column which is defined as `DECIMAL(5)`. Because the Column might already contain the value 99999, adding 1 might yield 100000 — a `DECIMAL(6)` value. For such cases, the DBMS must decide what to do before executing because the application program, which will receive the result, must know the size in advance. The DBMS has two choices:

- Let it grow. The result is `DECIMAL(6)` if the operation is addition and slightly more if the operation is multiplication. This choice has the advantage that it eliminates "overflow" errors. But there are still undefined areas. What happens if the `DECIMAL` precision is already at the maximum? What happens if the operation adds 1 to a `SMALLINT` — does the <data type> upgrade to `INTEGER` so that the increased precision is valid?
- Chop it. The result is `DECIMAL(5)` regardless. This risks failure on even the most innocuous operations but it's a simple rule to follow: output precision = input precision. Programmers can understand it.

These choices are not mutually exclusive and your DBMS might make different decisions for different operations.

TIP: Before you divide, decide how many digits should follow the decimal point in the result. The number will almost certainly be greater than the number you start with. For instance, 12/5 (dividing scale-0 integers) yields 2.4 (a scale-1 decimal number) ...you hope. Your DBMS may increase the scale automatically but the Standard doesn't say it must. To force the result, use the following SQL code:

```
CAST (12 AS DECIMAL(3,1))/5   -- yields 2.4.
```

Incidentally, there are several bad ways to cast. This SQL code:

```
CAST ((12/5) AS DECIMAL(3,1))
```

will yield 2.0 if your DBMS doesn't increase the scale automatically — be sure to `CAST` the source, not the result. This SQL code:

```
CAST (12 AS DECIMAL(2,1))/5
```

will cause an error — be sure your source value fits in the `CAST` target.

Floating-point Arithmetic

If you want fast and complex floating-point arithmetic, buy a good Fortran compiler; SQL can't handle the fancy stuff. In particular,

- SQL lacks useful functions which in other languages are built-in, e.g., the ability to detect NaN (Not a Number).
- SQL vendors are only obliged to define and to accept IEEE numbers. They can do arithmetic without paying any attention to the IEEE standard at all. In particular, some vendors may use the same routines for approximate numerics as they use for exact numerics, and exact is slower.

Still, you can do the basic arithmetic functions — add, subtract, divide, multiply, compare — provided you take sensible precautions.

Comparing Two Floating-point Numbers for Equality Think of the inexact result produced when 1/100 was converted to a binary fraction. Because of this, the following SQL code:

```
... WHERE float_column = 1.0E+1
```

will fail if, e.g., the value of `float_column` was originally produced by summing 1/100 one hundred times. To get the "approximately right" answer, compare the absolute difference between the two numbers against a constant, e.g., with this SQL code:

```
... WHERE ABS(float_column - 1.0E+1) < :epsilon
```

To choose a value for epsilon, remember that the accuracy of floating- point numbers varies — by definition — according to magnitude. For example, between 1.0 and 2.0 there are about 8 million numbers, but between 1023.0 and 1024.0 there are only about 8 thousand numbers (assuming IEEE single-precision standards). In this example, since the comparison is for equality, we know that `float_column` must be about the same magnitude as the <literal> `1.0E+1`, therefore a reasonable value for epsilon is 1/8000000 or 1.25E–7. When you don't know one of the comparands in advance, start with a value for epsilon that's half as large, multiply it by the sum of the comparands (thus changing its magnitude to the comparands' magnitude), and then compare with the following SQL code:

```
... WHERE ABS(float_column_1 - float_column_2) <
          (ABS(float_column_1 + float_column_2) * :epsilon/2)
```

Subtraction We did the following operation with an IEEE-compatible compiler: 1234.567 – 1234.000. The result was 0.5670166.

Both inputs are single-precision floating-point numbers (7 digits precision), accurate to the third decimal place. Unfortunately, so is the output. Although the subtraction decreased the magnitude, causing the decimal place to shift right, the accuracy was unaffected; the extra digits after 0.567 are spurious precision. If a subtraction causes a drop in magnitude, spurious precision is likely. (This is often called the "insignificant digits" problem and applies to addition too, if operands can have negative signs.)

TIP: Eliminate insignificant digits using two `CAST`s. In this example, we know the input, so we could clear everything after the result's third decimal place with the SQL code below.

```
CAST (CAST ((1.234567E+04 - 1.234000E+04) AS DEC(8,3)) AS REAL)
```

Here, by casting to `DEC(8,3)` we first change the result 0.5670166 to 0.567. The second `CAST` casts this back to `REAL`, with a subsequent result of 0.5670000. Casting is a straightforward way to strip — unfortunately, it's only useful if you know a lot about the data.

TIP: If an SQL statement does both addition and subtraction, parenthesize so that the addition happens first — this makes a drop in magnitude less likely to occur. For example, change this SQL statement:

```
UPDATE Approximate_Examples
SET    occurrence_real = occurrence_real - :host_variable + 1.1E+01;
```

to this SQL statement:

```
UPDATE Approximate_Examples
SET    occurrence_real = occurrence_real - (:host_variable + 1.1E+01);
```

By the way, don't just transpose the operands. Order of expression evaluation varies.

Division When doing floating-point division, keep in mind that there is such a thing as "negative zero" and there are floating-point numbers which are so small that you'll get an exception when you divide by them, even though they don't exactly equal zero. This makes it a little harder to test for "division by zero" errors in advance.

Scalar Operations

SQL provides ten scalar operations that return a number: the <case expression>, the <cast specification>, the <position expression>, the three <length expression>s, the <extract expression>, the <cardinality expression>, the <absolute value expression>, and the <modulus expression>. Only the last two also operate exclusively on numbers; these are described below. We'll discuss the rest in other chapters. For now, just remember that they evaluate to a number and can therefore be used anywhere in an SQL statement that a number could be used.

<absolute value expression>

The required syntax for an <absolute value expression> is as follows.

```
<absolute value expression> ::=
 ABS(numeric_argument)
```

`ABS` operates on an argument that evaluates to a number. It strips a negative sign (if it's present) from the argument and returns a non-negative number whose <data type> is the same as the argument's <data type>, e.g., `ABS(-17)` returns `17`, `ABS(17)` returns `17`, and `ABS(0)` returns `0`. If the argument is `NULL`, `ABS` returns `NULL`.

If the result of `ABS` is a number that doesn't fit into the argument's <data type> range, the function will fail; your DBMS will return the `SQLSTATE error 22003 "data exception-numeric value out of range."`

ABS is new to SQL with SQL3 and is also supported by ODBC. If your DBMS doesn't support ABS, you can simulate it with this SQL statement:

```
CASE
   WHEN ... < 0 THEN ... * -1
   ELSE ...
END
```

If your DBMS doesn't support CASE, you can still get an absolute value of a number with the following arithmetic expression:

```
(number * number) / number
```

[Obscure Rule] ABS can also operate on an interval. We've ignored this option for now — look for it in Chapter 8 "Temporal Values."

<modulus expression>

The required syntax for a <modulus expression> is as follows.

```
<modulus expression> ::=
MOD(dividend_argument,divisor_argument)
```

MOD operates on two arguments, both of which must evaluate to an exact numeric integer. It divides the first number by the second number and returns the operation's remainder as a non-negative exact numeric integer whose <data type> is the same as the divisor_argument's <data type>, e.g., MOD(35,4) returns 3 and MOD(32,4) returns 0. If either argument is NULL, MOD returns NULL. If the divisor_argument is zero, the function will fail; your DBMS will return the SQLSTATE error 22012 "data exception-division by zero."

MOD is new to SQL with SQL3. In the Standard, MOD stands for "modulus" but the result of this function is not actually a modulus — it is a remainder achieved "by means of a modulus."

Set Functions

SQL provides five set functions that return a number: COUNT(*), COUNT, AVG, SUM, and GROUPING. All but COUNT(*) also operate on numbers (COUNT(*) operates on rows), as do the set functions MAX and MIN. Because none of these operate exclusively with numeric arguments, we won't discuss them here; look for them in Chapter 33 "Searching with Groups."

Predicates

In addition to the comparison operators, SQL provides eight other predicates that operate on numbers: the <between predicate>, the <in predicate>, the <null predicate>, the <exists predicate>, the <unique predicate>, the <match predicate>, the <quantified predicate>, and the <distinct predicate>. Each will return a boolean value; either TRUE, FALSE, or UNKNOWN. None of these operate strictly on numbers, so we won't discuss them here. Look for them in Chapter 29 "Simple Search Conditions."

Choosing the Right <data type>

When you're defining a <data type> specification, think about whether you really need a numeric <data type> for the expected data. Don't just ask, "Are the values always bunches of digits?" For example, phone numbers are digits but if you define a DECIMAL <data type> for them you might lose a valuable piece of information — whether a leading zero is significant. Identification numbers are digits but if you define a DECIMAL <data type> for them, you might have trouble calculating the check digit which is usually based on a substring extraction. Instead, consider the question, "Will I ever need to do standard arithmetic operations on the data?" If the answer is "no," use a string <data type> rather than a numeric type.

If the answer is "yes," then consider which numeric type to choose by answering the question, "Are the values going to be seen by users or by programs written in other computer languages?" If the former, it's a lot easier to explain to a user looking at a blank six-position field on a screen, "you can type in a number between –99999 and +99999" instead of "you can type in a number between –32767 and +32767." If the latter, pick the numeric type that's closest to the variable type that the other computer language will use. You can also follow this short decision tree:

```
IF (values might be huge (> 1 trillion) or tiny (< 1 trillionth)
  /* you need an approximate numeric <data type> */
  IF (your host program uses C "float" or Delphi "Single")
  AND(7 digit precision is satisfactory)
    /* you need a REAL <data type> */
  IF (your host program uses C or Delphi "double")
  AND(15 digit precision is satisfactory)
    /* you need a DOUBLE PRECISION <data type> */
ELSE (if values are not huge or tiny)
  /* you need an exact numeric <data type> - the usual case */
  IF (your host program uses C "short int" or Delphi "SmallInt" */
        /* you need a SMALLINT <data type> */
  IF (your host program uses C "int" or Delphi "Longint" */
        /* you need an INTEGER <data type> */
  ELSE
        /* you don't need an exact match with host-language
           variables */
               IF (you are accustomed to the word NUMERIC because
                   Oracle uses it)
                      /* you need a NUMERIC <data type> */
               ELSE
                      /* you need a DECIMAL <data type> */
```

Once you've gone through the decision tree, calculate the required precision and scale by looking at all expected values.

Dialects

The "typical" SQL DBMS supports most of the standard numeric data types, but often uses preferred local names. Here are some lists of local types derived from vendor manuals. The correlation with the leftmost ("Standard") column is sometimes imprecise. "ODBC" is not a DBMS but a spec.

Standard	Oracle	DB2	Sybase	ODBC
SMALLINT	NUMBER	SMALLINT	SMALLINT	SMALLINT
INTEGER	NUMBER	INTEGER	INT	INTEGER
DECIMAL	NUMBER	DECIMAL	MONEY	DECIMAL
NUMERIC	NUMBER	NUMERIC	MONEY	NUMERIC
REAL	NUMBER	REAL	FLOAT	REAL
FLOAT	NUMBER	FLOAT	FLOAT	FLOAT
DOUBLE PRECISION	NUMBER	DOUBLE PRECISION	FLOAT	DOUBLE PRECISION

Other commonly-seen numeric data types include TINYINT (8-bit signed integer), BIGINT (64-bit signed integer), and SERIAL (integer that goes up by 1 for each new inserted row).

The SQL Library

Before we finish discussing numbers, it's time to add something to our "SQL library." To be worthy of addition to the SQL library, a routine must (*a*) be good clean SQL, (*b*) be callable from C and Delphi, (*c*) be actually useful in C and Delphi because it does something that those languages can't, and (*d*) have nothing at all do with "databases" — it should be available for use just like any general function library.

Our addition to the SQL library for this chapter will be a calculator. It won't match C and Delphi for floating-point arithmetic, but it will give more exact answers.

Function: `SQL_calculator(lp_calculation, lp_result, lp_error)`

Pass: An arithmetic expression in the string `lp_calculation`. The string may contain any combination of numeric <literal>s (in valid SQL form), the operators `+ - * / MOD ABS` and parentheses.

Return: `lp_result`: Result of expression (a string containing a number).
`lp_error`: `SQLSTATE` and error message, if expression was invalid.

Example: Try passing the expression: (1.000001 + 1.999990) * 11000 to our calculator. Our proc gives the correct result: 33000.0000000. The compilers we tested gave the wrong result: 32999.9901000. (Remember that in SQL all the <literal>s in this expression are `DECIMAL`, not floating-point, <literal>s.)

4

Chapter 4

Bit Strings

In SQL, a bit string is either a binary bit string or a hexadecimal bit string. Binary bit strings are arbitrary sequences of zero or more binary digits (bits), each having a value of 0 or 1 and a length of 1 bit. Hexadecimal bit strings are arbitrary sequences of zero or more hexadecimal digits (hexits). A hexit is either (*a*) any of the digits 0 through 9 or (*b*) any of the letters A through F (uppercase or lowercase allowed) and is four bits long (0, 1, 2, 3, 4, 5, 6, 7, 8, 9, A, B, C, D, E, and F are interpreted as 0000, 0001, 0010, 0011, 0100, 0101, 0110, 0111, 1000, 1001, 1010, 1011, 1100, 1101, 1110, and 1111 respectively). A bit string value may be a <literal>, the value of a parameter or a host language variable, or the result of any expression or argument (including a possibly qualified <Column name>) that evaluates to a bit string.

A bit string has a length — a non-negative integer equal to the number of bits in the string. Bits in a bit string are numbered from left to right, beginning with 1 (the most significant bit). Bit strings are stored in either of the two bit string <data type>s: `BIT` or `BIT VARYING`.

<bit string literal>s

A <bit string literal> is either a binary <bit string literal> or a hexadecimal <bit string literal>.

Binary <bit string literal>

A binary <bit string literal> is the letter "B" (uppercase mandatory) followed by a string of zero or more bits inside a pair of single quote marks. Its <data type> is fixed length `BIT`, though it is compatible with both the `BIT` and the `BIT VARYING` <data type>s. The <literal>'s length is the number of bits inside the quote marks; the delimiting single quotes aren't part of the <literal>, so they're not included in the calculation of the <bit string literal>'s size. Here are some examples of binary <bit string literal>s:

```
B'00010110'
B'1101'
```

Hexadecimal <bit string literal>

A hexadecimal <bit string literal> is the letter "X" (uppercase mandatory) followed by a string of zero or more hexits inside a pair of single quote marks. Its <data type> is fixed length `BIT`, though it is compatible with both the `BIT` and the `BIT VARYING` <data type>s. The <literal>'s length is four times the number of hexits inside the quote marks; the delimiting single quotes are not part of the <literal>, therefore they are not included in the calculation of the <bit string literal>'s size. Here are some examples of hexadecimal <bit string literal>s:

```
X'49FE'
X'a31d'
```

[Obscure Rule] SQL allows you to break a long <bit string literal> up into two or more smaller <bit string literal>s, split by a <separator> that includes a newline character. When it sees such a <literal>, your DBMS will ignore the <separator> and treat the multiple strings as a single <literal>. For example, these two <bit string literal>s are equivalent:

```
   B'00001111'
  '01101100'
  B'0000111101101100'
```

(In the first example, there is a carriage return newline <separator> between `1111'` and `'0110`.)

These two <bit string literal>s are also equivalent:

```
X'09AF'
'ab42'
X'09afAB42'
```

If you want to restrict your code to Core SQL, do not use either binary or hexadecimal <bit string literal>s.

Bit string <data type>s

A bit string <data type> is defined by a descriptor that contains two pieces of information.

1. The <data type>'s name; either `BIT` or `BIT VARYING`.
2. The <data type>'s length in bits.

BIT

The required syntax for a `BIT` <data type> specification is as follows.

```
BIT <data type> ::=
BIT [ (length) ]
```

`BIT` is a fixed length bit string exactly "length" bits long; it defines a set of bit string values that are any correctly sized string of bits, e.g., 10110001.

The optional length, if specified, is an unsigned integer that defines the fixed length of acceptable values. The minimum length and the default length are both 1. For example, these two <data type> specifications are equivalent; both define a set of bit string values that must be exactly 1 bit long:

```
BIT
BIT(1)
```

[NON-PORTABLE] The maximum length for BIT is non-standard because the SQL Standard requires implementors to define BIT's maximum length. [OCELOT Implementation] The OCELOT DBMS that comes with this book allows the length of BIT to range from 1 to 32,768 (i.e., 4096*8 bits).

TIP: Always specify a bit length which is divisible by 8.

When operating on a BIT <data type>, you can use either binary <bit string literal>s or hexadecimal <bit string literal>s. For example, these two <literal>s represent the same bit value:

```
X'44'
B'01000100'
```

TIP: Use hexadecimal <bit string literal>s rather than binary <bit string literal>s whenever bit length is divisible by 4.

If you want to restrict your code to Core SQL, don't define any BIT <data type>s.

BIT VARYING

The required syntax for a BIT VARYING <data type> specification is as follows.

```
BIT VARYING <data type> ::=
BIT VARYING (length)
```

BIT VARYING is a variable length bit string up to "length" bits long; it defines a set of bit string values that are any correctly sized string of bits, e.g., 10110001.

The mandatory length is an unsigned integer greater than or equal to 1. It defines the maximum length of acceptable values in the BIT VARYING field. For example, this <data type> specification defines a set of bit string values that may be anywhere from 0 to 16 bits long:

```
BIT VARYING(16)
```

(Zero length bit strings can be stored in a BIT VARYING field.)

[NON-PORTABLE] The maximum length for BIT VARYING is non-standard because the SQL Standard requires implementors to define BIT VARYING's maximum length. [OCELOT Implementation] The OCELOT DBMS that comes with this book allows the length of BIT VARYING to range from 1 to 32,768 (i.e., 4,096*8 bits).

When operating on a `BIT VARYING` <data type>, you can use either binary <bit string literal>s or hexadecimal <bit string literal>s. For example, these two <literal>s represent the same bit value:

```
X'44'
B'01000100'
```

TIP: Use hexadecimal <bit string literal>s rather than binary <bit string literal>s whenever bit length is divisible by 4.

If you want to restrict your code to Core SQL, don't define any `BIT VARYING` <data type>s.

Now that we've described SQL's bit <data type>s, let's look at some example SQL statements that put them to use.

These SQL statements make a Table with two bit Columns, insert two rows, then search for any bit string equal to 01000100:

```
CREATE TABLE Bit_Examples (
      occurrence_bit BIT(8),
      occurrence_bitvarying BIT VARYING(8));

INSERT INTO Bit_Examples (
      occurrence_bit,
      occurrence_bitvarying)
      VALUES (B'11110000',X'4D');

INSERT INTO Bit_Examples (
      occurrence_bit,
      occurrence_bitvarying)
      VALUES (X'a9',B'01011010');

SELECT occurrence_bit,
       occurrence_bitvarying
FROM   Bit_Examples
WHERE  occurrence_bitvarying = X'44';

SELECT occurrence_bit,
       occurrence_bitvarying
FROM   Bit_Examples
WHERE  occurrence_bit = B'01000100';
```

Bit Operations

A bit string is compatible with, and comparable to, all other bit strings — that is, all bit strings are mutually comparable and mutually assignable. Bit strings may not be directly compared with, or directly assigned to, any other <data type> class though implicit type conversions can occur in expression SELECTs, INSERTs, DELETEs, and UPDATEs. Explicit bit string type conversions can be forced with the CAST operator.

CAST

In SQL, CAST is a scalar operator that converts a given scalar value to a given scalar <data type>. The required syntax for the CAST operator is as follows.

```
CAST (<cast operand> AS <cast target>)
   <cast operand> ::= scalar_expression
   <cast target> ::= <Domain name> | <data type>
```

The CAST operator converts values of a source <data type> into values of a target <data type>, where each <data type> is an SQL pre-defined <data type> (data conversions between UDTs are done with a user-defined cast). The source <data type> (or <cast operand>) can be any expression that evaluates to a single value. The target <data type> (or <cast target>) is either an SQL predefined <data type> specification or the name of a Domain whose defined <data type> is your target <data type>. If you use CAST (... AS <Domain name>), your current <AuthorizationID> must have the USAGE Privilege on that Domain.

It isn't, of course, possible to convert the values of every <data type> into the values of every other <data type>. For bit strings, the rules are:

- CAST (NULL AS <data type>) and CAST (bit_string_source_is_a_null_value AS <data type>) both result in NULL.
- You can CAST a fixed length or variable length bit string source to these targets: fixed length character string, variable length character string, CLOB, NCLOB, fixed length bit string, and variable length bit string. You can also CAST a fixed length or variable length bit string source to a UDT target or a <reference type> target if a user-defined cast exists for this purpose and your current <AuthorizationID> has the EXECUTE Privilege on that user-defined cast.

When you CAST a bit string to a UDT or a <reference type> target, your DBMS invokes the user-defined cast routine with the source value as the routine's argument. The CAST result is the value returned by the user-defined cast.

When you CAST a fixed length bit string or a variable length bit string to a fixed length bit string target and the bit length of the source value *equals* the fixed bit length of the target, the CAST result is the source bit string. When you CAST a fixed length bit string or a variable length bit string to a fixed length bit string target and the bit length of the source value is *less than* the fixed bit length of the target, the CAST result is the source bit string, padded on the least significant end with as many 0-bits as required to make the lengths match. When you CAST a fixed length bit string or a variable length bit string to a fixed length bit string target and the bit length of the source value is *greater than* the fixed bit length of the target, the CAST result is as much of the source bit string as will fit into the target — in this case, your DBMS will return the SQLSTATE warning 01004 "warning-string data, right truncation."

When you CAST a fixed length bit string or a variable length bit string to a variable length bit string target and the bit length of the source value is *less than* or *equals* the maximum bit length of the target, the CAST result is the source bit string. When you CAST a fixed length bit string or a variable length bit string to a variable length bit string target and the bit length of the source value is *greater than* the maximum bit length of the target, the CAST result is as much of the source bit string as will fit into the target — in this case, your DBMS will return the SQLSTATE warning 01004 "warning-string data, right truncation."

When you CAST a fixed length or a variable length bit string to a fixed length character string target, a variable length character string target, a CLOB target, or an NCLOB target — your DBMS first determines whether the source value needs to be padded. If the remainder from the result of the source's bit length divided by the smallest bit length of any character in the target's character set is not zero, then your DBMS will append a number of 0-bits to the least significant end of the source value — the number of 0-bits to append is determined by calculating the difference between the bit length of the smallest character and the remainder — and then return the SQLSTATE warning 01008 "warning-implicit zero-bit padding." The result of the CAST is the string of characters that results from the conversion of the bit string's bits into characters that belong to the target's Character set.

NOTE: If the length of the CAST result is *less than* the length of the (possibly padded) source string, your DBMS will return the SQLSTATE warning 01004 "warning-string data, right truncation." If the length of the CAST result is *greater than* the length of the source string, your DBMS will return the SQLSTATE warning 01008 "warning-implicit zero-bit padding."

Let's look more closely at what happens when you CAST a bit string to a character string. First of all, it's important to remember that character strings have a "form-of-use encoding" — it comes from the string's Character set. As an example, assume that the Character set for a CAST target <data type> is Unicode, where every character is 16 bits long. According to the Unicode standard, the code for the letter 'C' is 0043 hexadecimal (that is, the binary number 0000000001000011) and the code for the letter 'D' is 0044 hexadecimal (that is, the binary number 0000000001000100). Now, when you CAST from a bit string to a Unicode character string, you're instructing your DBMS to take the binary numbers that make up your bit string and convert them into the Unicode coded character values — so CAST(X'00430044' AS CHAR(2) CHARACTER SET UNICODE) will result in 'CD' and CAST(B'0000000001000011' AS CHAR(1) CHARACTER SET UNICODE) will result in 'C'. If your CAST is of a short bit string to a longer fixed length character string, 0-bits are padded on the right of the source to bring it to the proper length — so CAST(B'00000000010001' AS CHAR(2) CHARACTER SET UNICODE) will result in 'D\0' (we use the symbol \0 here to represent a 16-bit character with all bits zero).

[Obscure Rule] The result of a CAST to a character string target has the COERCIBLE coercibility attribute; its Collation is the default Collation for the target's Character set.

If you want to restrict your code to Core SQL, don't use <Domain name> as a CAST target; CAST only to a <data type>.

Assignment

In SQL, when a bit string is assigned to a bit string target, the assignment is done one bit at a time from left to right — that is, the source value's most significant bit is assigned to the target's most significant bit, then the source's next bit is assigned to the target's next bit, and so on.

When a bit string is taken from SQL-data to be assigned to a fixed length bit string target and the source is *shorter* than the target, the source is padded (on the right) with 0-bits until it matches the target's size. In this case, your DBMS will return the `SQLSTATE warning 01008 "warning-implicit zero-bit padding."` If the source is *longer* than the target, the source is truncated to fit the target. In this case, your DBMS will return the `SQLSTATE warning 01004 "warning-string data, right truncation."` When a bit string is taken from SQL-data to be assigned to a variable length bit string target, the size of the target is first set either to the size of the source or to its own maximum length, whichever is less. The source may then be truncated, if necessary, to match the size of the target. In this case, your DBMS will return the `SQLSTATE warning 01004 "warning-string data, right truncation."`

[Obscure Rule] Because only SQL accepts null values, if your source is `NULL`, then your target's value is not changed. Instead, your DBMS will set its indicator parameter to –1 to indicate that an assignment of the null value was attempted. If your target doesn't have an indicator parameter, the assignment will fail; your DBMS will return the `SQLSTATE error 22002 "data exception-null value, no indicator parameter."` If your source is a non-null value that fits into your target, your DBMS will set the target's indicator parameter (if any) to zero. If your source is longer than your target, your DBMS will set your target's indicator parameter to the length of the source. That is, if your source is 12 bits long and your target can accept only 10 bits, your DBMS will set the target's indicator parameter to 12, to indicate that 2 bits were lost on assignment. If the source's length is too big to be assigned to the indicator, the assignment will fail; your DBMS will return the `SQLSTATE error 22022 "data exception-indicator overflow."` We'll talk more about indicator parameters in Chapters 39, 40, and 52 on SQL binding styles.

When a bit string is assigned to a fixed length SQL-data bit string target and the source is shorter than the target, the assignment will fail; your DBMS will return the `SQLSTATE error 22026 "data exception-string data, length mismatch."` If the source is larger than the target, the assignment will also fail; your DBMS will return the `SQLSTATE error 22001 "data exception-string data, right truncation."` When a bit string is assigned to a variable length SQL-data bit string target, the size of the target is first set either to the size of the source or to its own maximum length, whichever is less. If the source is larger than the target, the assignment will fail; your DBMS will return the `SQLSTATE error 22001 "data exception-string data, right truncation."`

[Obscure Rule] There are two ways to assign a null value to an SQL-data target. Within SQL, you can use the <keyword> `NULL` in an `INSERT` or an `UPDATE` statement to indicate that the target should be set to `NULL`. That is, if your source is `NULL`, your DBMS will set your target to `NULL`. Outside of SQL, if your source has an indicator parameter that is set to –1, your DBMS will set your target to `NULL` (regardless of the value of the source). An indicator parameter with a value less than –1 will cause an error; your DBMS will return the `SQLSTATE error 22010 "data exception-invalid indicator parameter value."`

Comparison

SQL provides the usual scalar comparison operators, = and <> and < and <= and > and >=, to perform operations on bit strings. All of them will be familiar; there are equivalent operators in other computer languages. If any of the comparands are NULL, the result of the operation is UNKNOWN. For example:

```
B'0011' = B'0011'
```

returns TRUE.

```
B'0011' = {result is NULL}
```

returns UNKNOWN.

SQL also provides three quantifiers — ALL, SOME, ANY — which you can use along with a comparison operator to compare a value with the collection of values returned by a <table subquery>. Place the quantifier after the comparison operator, immediately before the <table subquery>, for example:

```
SELECT bit_column
FROM   Table_1
WHERE  bit_column < ALL (
   SELECT bit_column
   FROM   Table_2);
```

ALL returns TRUE either (*a*) if the collection is an empty set, i.e., if it contains zero rows or (*b*) if the comparison operator returns TRUE for every value in the collection. ALL returns FALSE if the comparison operator returns FALSE for at least one value in the collection.

SOME and ANY are synonyms. They return TRUE if the comparison operator returns TRUE for at least one value in the collection. They return FALSE either (*a*) if the collection is an empty set or (*b*) if the comparison operator returns FALSE for every value in the collection. The search condition = ANY (collection) is equivalent to IN (collection).

When a bit string is compared to another bit string, the comparison is done one bit at a time from left to right — that is, the first comparand's most significant bit is compared to the second comparand's most significant bit, then the next two bits are compared, and so on. A 0-bit is considered to be less than a 1-bit.

Bit strings of equal length are compared bit-by-bit until equality is either determined or not. Two bit strings, BIT_ARGUMENT_1 and BIT_ARGUMENT_2, are equal if (*a*) they have the same length and (*b*) each bit within BIT_ARGUMENT_1 compares as equal to the corresponding bit in BIT_ARGUMENT_2.

Bit strings of unequal length are compared bit-by-bit only after the longer comparand has been truncated to the length of the shorter comparand. Equivalence is determined as usual except that if the shorter comparand compares as equal to the substring of the longer comparand that matches its size, then the shorter bit string is considered to be less than the longer bit string — even if the remainder of the longer comparand consists only of 0-bits. That is, BIT_ARGUMENT_1 is less than BIT_ARGUMENT_2 if (*a*) the length of BIT_ARGUMENT_1 is less than the length of BIT_ARGUMENT_2 and (*b*) each bit within BIT_ARGUMENT_1 compares as equal to the corresponding bit in BIT_ARGUMENT_2. For example, the result of a comparison of these two bit strings:

```
B'101'
B'1010'
```

is that the first (shorter) bit string is less than the second (longer) bit string.

Other Operations

With SQL, you have several other operations that you can perform on bit strings, or on other values to get a bit string result.

Concatenation

The required syntax for a bit string concatenation is as follows.

```
bit concatenation ::=
bit_string_operand_1 || bit_string_operand_2
```

The concatenation operator operates on two operands, each of which must evaluate to a bit string. It joins the strings together in the order given and returns a bit string with a length equal to the sum of the lengths of its operands. If either of the operands is NULL, the result of the operation is also NULL. The following are two examples of bit string concatenations.

```
B'0000' || B'0011'     -- returns 00000011
bit_column || B'0011' -- returns bit_column's value followed by 0011
```

[Obscure Rule] If both operands are fixed length bit strings, the concatenation result is a fixed length bit string with a length *equal* to the sum of the lengths of the operands — this length may not exceed the maximum allowed for a fixed length bit string. If either operand is a variable length bit string and the sum of their lengths is *not greater than* the maximum allowed length for a variable length bit string, the concatenation result is a variable length bit string with a length equal to the sum of the lengths of the operands. If the sum of the operands' lengths is *greater than* the maximum allowed, but the extra bits are all 0-bits, the concatenation result is a variable length bit string with a length equal to the maximum allowed length. If the sum of the operands' lengths is greater than the maximum allowed and the extra bits are not all 0-bits, the concatenation will fail; your DBMS will return the SQLSTATE error 22001 "data exception-string data, right truncation."

If you want to restrict your code to Core SQL, don't use the concatenation operator with bit strings.

Scalar Operations

SQL provides three scalar operations that return a bit string: the <case expression>, the <cast specification>, and the <bit substring function>. It also provides four scalar functions that operate on bit strings, returning a number: the <bit position expression>, the <bit length expression>, the <char length expression>, and the <octet length expression>. All but the first two are described below (we've already talked about casting bit strings). We'll discuss the <case expression> in Chapter 29 "Simple Search Conditions"; for now, just remember that CASE can evaluate to a bit string and can therefore be used anywhere in an SQL statement that a bit string could be used.

<bit substring function>

The required syntax for a <bit substring function> is as follows.

```
<bit substring function> ::=
SUBSTRING (
      bit_argument
      FROM start_argument
      [ FOR length_argument ])
```

SUBSTRING operates on three arguments: the first must evaluate to a bit string, the other two must evaluate to exact numeric integers. It extracts a substring from bit_argument and returns a variable length bit string with a maximum length that equals the fixed length, or maximum variable length, of the bit argument (as applicable). If any of the arguments are NULL, SUBSTRING returns NULL.

The start_argument is a number that marks the first bit you want to extract from bit_argument. If SUBSTRING includes the (optional) FOR clause, length_argument is the total number of bits you want to extract. If you omit the FOR clause, SUBSTRING will begin at start_argument and extract all the rest of the bits in bit_argument. The following are some examples of SUBSTRING:

```
SUBSTRING(B'10001100' FROM 5)        -- returns 1100
SUBSTRING(B'10001100' FROM 5 FOR 3)  -- returns 110
SUBSTRING(bit_column FROM 1 FOR 4)    -- returns the first four bits of
                                      the value in BIT_COLUMN
```

If length_argument is negative, your DBMS will return the SQLSTATE error 22011 "data exception-substring error." If start_argument is greater than the length of bit_argument, or if (start_argument + length_argument) is less than one, SUBSTRING returns a zero-length bit string. If start_argument is negative, or if (start_argument + length_argument) is greater than the length of bit_argument, that's okay — the DBMS just ignores any bits before the start of bit_argument or after the end of bit_argument.

[Obscure Rule] SUBSTRING can also operate on a character string and a BLOB. We've ignored these options for now — look for them in Chapter 7 "Character Strings," and Chapter 5 "Binary Strings."

If you want to restrict your code to Core SQL, don't use SUBSTRING with bit strings.

<bit position expression>

The required syntax for a <bit position expression> is as follows.

```
<bit position expression> ::=
POSITION (
      bit_argument_1
      IN bit_argument_2)
```

POSITION operates on two arguments, both of which must evaluate to a bit string. It determines the first bit position (if any) at which bit_argument_1 is found in bit_argument_2 and returns this as an exact numeric integer. If either of the arguments are NULL, POSITION returns

NULL. If bit_argument_1 is a zero-length bit string, POSITION returns one. If bit_argument_1 is not found in bit_argument_2, POSITION returns zero. Here is an example:

```
POSITION(B'1011' IN B'001101011011')
-- returns 9
```

[NON-PORTABLE] The precision of POSITION's result is non-standard because the SQL Standard requires implementors to define the result's precision. [OCELOT Implementation] The OCELOT DBMS that comes with this book gives the result of POSITION an INTEGER <data type>.

[Obscure Rule] POSITION can also operate on a character string and a BLOB. We've ignored these options for now — look for them in Chapter 7 "Character Strings," and Chapter 5 "Binary Strings."

If you want to restrict your code to Core SQL, don't use POSITION with bit strings.

<bit length expression>

The required syntax for a <bit length expression> is as follows.

```
<bit length expression> ::=
BIT_LENGTH (bit_argument)
```

BIT_LENGTH operates on an argument that evaluates to a bit string. It determines the length of the argument, in bits, and returns this as an exact numeric integer, e.g., BIT_LENGTH(B'10110011') returns 8 and BIT_LENGTH(X'4AD9') returns 16. If the argument is NULL, BIT_LENGTH returns NULL.

[NON-PORTABLE] The precision of BIT_LENGTH's result is non-standard because the SQL Standard requires implementors to define the result's precision. [OCELOT Implementation] The OCELOT DBMS that comes with this book gives the result of BIT_LENGTH an INTEGER <data type>.

[Obscure Rule] BIT_LENGTH can also operate on a character string and a BLOB. We've ignored these options for now — look for them in Chapter 7 "Character Strings," and Chapter 5 "Binary Strings."

<char length expression>

The required syntax for a <char length expression> is as follows.

```
<char length expression> ::=
 {CHAR_LENGTH | CHARACTER_LENGTH} (bit_argument)
```

CHAR_LENGTH (or CHARACTER_LENGTH) operates on an argument that evaluates to a bit string. It determines the length of the argument in octets and returns this as an exact numeric integer, e.g., CHAR_LENGTH(B'10110011') returns 1 and CHAR_LENGTH(X'4AD92') returns 3. (The octet length of a string is the bit length divided by 8, rounded up.) If the argument is NULL, CHAR_LENGTH returns NULL.

[NON-PORTABLE] The precision of CHAR_LENGTH's result is non-standard because the SQL Standard requires implementors to define the result's precision. [OCELOT Implementation] The OCELOT DBMS that comes with this book gives the result of CHAR_LENGTH an INTEGER <data type>.

[Obscure Rule] CHAR_LENGTH can also operate on a character string and a BLOB. We've ignored these options for now — look for them in Chapter 7 "Character Strings," and Chapter 5 "Binary Strings."

<octet length expression>

The required syntax for an <octet length expression> is as follows.

```
<octet length expression> ::=
OCTET_LENGTH (bit_argument)
```

OCTET_LENGTH operates on an argument that evaluates to a bit string. It determines the length of the argument in octets and returns this as an exact numeric integer, e.g., OCTET_LENGTH(B'10110011') returns 1 and OCTET_LENGTH(X'4AD92') returns 3. (The octet length of a string is the bit length divided by 8, rounded up.) If the argument is NULL, OCTET_LENGTH returns NULL.

[NON-PORTABLE] The precision of OCTET_LENGTH's result is non-standard because the SQL Standard requires implementors to define the result's precision. [OCELOT Implementation] The OCELOT DBMS that comes with this book gives the result of OCTET_LENGTH an INTEGER <data type>.

[Obscure Rule] OCTET_LENGTH can also operate on a character string and a BLOB. We've ignored these options for now — look for them in Chapter 7 "Character Strings," and Chapter 5 "Binary Strings."

Set Functions

SQL provides four set functions that operate on bit strings: COUNT, MAX, MIN, and GROUPING. Since none of these operate exclusively with bit string arguments, we won't discuss them here. Look for them in Chapter 33 on "Searching with Groups."

Predicates

In addition to the comparison operators, SQL provides eight other predicates that operate on bit strings: the <between predicate>, the <in predicate>, the <null predicate>, the <exists predicate>, the <unique predicate>, the <match predicate>, the <quantified predicate>, and the <distinct predicate>. Each will return a boolean value; either TRUE, FALSE, or UNKNOWN. None of these operate strictly on bit strings, so we won't discuss them here. Look for them in Chapter 29 "Simple Search Conditions."

5

Chapter 5

Binary Strings

In SQL, a binary string (or `BLOB`) is any arbitrary sequence of zero or more octets that isn't associated with either a Character set or a Collation. A `BLOB` value may be a <literal>, the value of a parameter or a host language variable, or the result of any expression or argument (including a possibly qualified <Column name>) that evaluates to a binary string. `BLOB`s represent an unknown lump of binary data; the typical use of a `BLOB` <data type> is to store an image.

Octets in a `BLOB` are numbered from left to right beginning with 1 (the most significant octet). `BLOB`s are stored in the binary string <data type> `BLOB`.

<BLOB literal>s

A <BLOB literal> is the letter "X" (uppercase mandatory) followed by a string of zero or more hexits inside a pair of single quote marks. A *hexit* is either (*a*) any of the digits 0 through 9 or (*b*) any of the letters A through F (uppercase or lowercase allowed) and is four bits long — 0, 1, 2, 3, 4, 5, 6, 7, 8, 9, A, B, C, D, E, and F are interpreted as 0000, 0001, 0010, 0011, 0100, 0101, 0110, 0111, 1000, 1001, 1010, 1011, 1100, 1101, 1110, and 1111 respectively. Its <data type> is variable length `BLOB`. The <literal>'s length is four times the number of hexits inside the quote marks; the delimiting single quotes are not part of the <literal>, therefore they are not included in the calculation of the <BLOB literal>'s size. Here are some examples of <BLOB literal>s:

```
X'49FE'
X'a31d'
```

[Obscure Rule] A long <BLOB literal> may be broken up into two or more smaller <BLOB literal>s, split by a <separator> that must include a newline character. When such a <literal> is encountered, your DBMS will ignore the <separator> and treat the multiple strings as a single <literal>. For example, these two <BLOB literal>s are equivalent:

```
X'49FE'
'A31D'
X'49FEA31D'
```

(In the first example, there is a carriage return newline <separator> between `FE'` and `'A3`.)

BLOB <data type>s

A `BLOB` <data type> is defined by a descriptor that contains two pieces of information:

1. The <data type>'s name: `BINARY LARGE OBJECT`.
2. The <data type>'s maximum length in octets.

BLOB

The required syntax for a `BINARY LARGE OBJECT` <data type> specification is as follows.

```
BINARY LARGE OBJECT <data type> ::=
{ BINARY LARGE OBJECT | BLOB } [ (length) ]
```

`BINARY LARGE OBJECT` may be abbreviated as `BLOB` and is a variable length binary string up to "length" octets long. It defines a set of binary string values that are any correctly sized string of octets that are not associated with a Character set or a Collation. For example, these <BLOB literal>s:

```
X'49FE'
X'178FA3A8'
```

are both valid values for the following <data type> specification:

```
BLOB(8)
```

The optional length, if specified, is an unsigned integer, greater than or equal to one, possibly followed by a letter code (either "K," "M," or "G"). It defines the maximum octet length of acceptable values in the `BLOB` field.

- If the length *n* is not followed by a letter code, the `BLOB` may hold up to *n* octets.
- The length may include the letter code "K" (kilobyte), "M" (megabyte), or "G" (gigabyte). If the length is defined as *nK*, the `BLOB` may hold up to *n*1024* octets. If the length is defined as *nM*, the `BLOB` may hold up to *n*1,048,576* octets. If the length is defined as *nG*, the `BLOB` may hold up to *n*1,073,741,824* octets.

For example, this <data type> specification defines a set of binary string values that may range from zero to 20 octets:

```
BLOB(20)
```

(Zero length binary strings can be stored in a `BLOB` field.)

This <data type> specification defines a set of binary string values that may range from zero to 2048 octets:

```
BLOB(2K)
```

This <data type> specification defines a set of binary string values that may range from zero to 2,097,152 octets:

```
BLOB(2M)
```

And this <data type> specification defines a set of binary string values that may range from zero to 2,147,483,648 octets:

```
BLOB(2G)
```

[NON-PORTABLE] The default length and the maximum length for BLOB are non-standard because the SQL Standard requires implementors to define BLOB's default and maximum lengths. [OCELOT Implementation] The OCELOT DBMS that comes with this book allows the length of BLOB to range from 1 to 4K and sets the default length of a BLOB <data type> to 1K. For example, these two <data type> specifications are equivalent; both define a set of binary string values that may range from zero to 1024 octets:

```
BLOB
BLOB(1K)
```

Now that we've described SQL's BLOB <data type>, let's look at some example SQL statements that put it to use.

These SQL statements make a Table with one binary string Column, insert a row, then search for any binary string equal to the bit string 01000100:

```
CREATE TABLE Binary_Examples (
      occurrence_binary BLOB(2K));

INSERT INTO Binary_Examples (
      occurrence_binary)
      VALUES (X'4D');

SELECT occurrence_binary
FROM   Binary_Examples
WHERE  occurrence_binary = X'44';
```

BLOB Operations

A BLOB is compatible with, and comparable to, all other BLOBs — that is, all BLOBs are mutually assignable and mutually comparable. BLOBs may not be directly compared with, or directly assigned to, any other <data type> class though implicit type conversions can sometimes occur in expressions, SELECTs, INSERTs, DELETEs, and UPDATEs. Explicit BLOB conversions can be forced with the CAST operator.

CAST

In SQL, CAST is a scalar operator that converts a given scalar value to a given scalar <data type>. The required syntax for the CAST operator is as follows.

```
CAST (<cast operand> AS <cast target>)
   <cast operand> ::= scalar_expression
   <cast target> ::= <Domain name> | <data type>
```

The CAST operator converts values of a source <data type> into values of a target <data type>, where each <data type> is an SQL pre-defined <data type> (data conversions between UDTs are done with a user-defined cast). The source <data type> (or <cast operand>) can be any expression that evaluates to a single value. The target <data type> (or <cast target>) is either an SQL predefined <data type> specification or the name of a Domain whose defined <data type> is your target <data type>. If you use CAST (... AS <Domain name>), your current <AuthorizationID> must have the USAGE Privilege on that Domain.

It isn't, of course, possible to convert the values of every <data type> into the values of every other <data type>. For BLOBs, the rules are:

- CAST (NULL AS <data type>) and CAST (blob_source_is_a_null_value AS <data type>) both result in NULL.
- You can CAST a BLOB source to a BLOB target. You can also CAST a BLOB source to a UDT target or a <reference type> target if a user-defined cast exists for this purpose and your current <AuthorizationID> has the EXECUTE Privilege on that user-defined cast.

When you CAST a BLOB to a BLOB target, if the octet length of the source value is *less than* or *equals* the maximum octet length of the target, the result of the CAST is the source BLOB value. If the octet length of the source value is *greater than* the maximum octet length of the target, the result of the CAST is as much of the source BLOB value as will fit into the target — in this case, your DBMS will return the SQLSTATE warning 01004 "warning-string data, right truncation."

When you CAST a BLOB to a UDT or a <reference type> target, your DBMS invokes the user-defined cast routine with the source value as the routine's argument. The CAST result is the value returned by the user-defined cast.

If you want to restrict your code to Core SQL, (*a*) don't use <Domain name> as a CAST target; CAST only to a <data type> and (*b*) don't use CAST to convert any BLOB value to another <data type>.

Assignment

In SQL, when a BLOB is assigned to a binary string target, the assignment is done one octet at a time from left to right — that is, the source value's most significant octet is assigned to the target's most significant octet, then the source's next octet is assigned to the target's next octet, and so on.

When a BLOB is taken from SQL-data to be assigned to a binary string target, the size of the target is first set either to the size of the source or to its own maximum length, whichever is less. If the source is longer than the target, the source is truncated to fit the target. In this case, your DBMS will return the SQLSTATE warning 01004 "warning-string data, right truncation."

Here are some examples of the result you'll get when you move a BLOB from your database to a host language program (assume your host language variable has a variable size of 2 octets):

```
source X'5550' yields a target value of 5550
source X'55' yields a target value of 55
source X'555500' yields a target value of 5555 and SQLSTATE 01004
source X'555555' yields a target value of 5555 and SQLSTATE 01004
```

[Obscure Rule] Since only SQL accepts null values, if your source is NULL, then your target's value is not changed. Instead, your DBMS will set its indicator parameter to –1 to indicate that an assignment of the null value was attempted. If your target doesn't have an indicator parameter, the assignment will fail; your DBMS will return the SQLSTATE error 22002 "data exception-null value, no indicator parameter." If your source is a non-null value that fits into your target, your DBMS will set the target's indicator parameter (if any) to zero. If your source is longer than your target, your DBMS will set your target's indicator parameter to the length of the source. That is, if your source is 12 octets long and your target can accept only 10 octets, your DBMS will set the target's indicator parameter to 12, to indicate that 2 octets were lost on assignment. If the source's length is too big to be assigned to the indicator, the assignment will fail; your DBMS will return the SQLSTATE error 22022 "data exception-indicator overflow." We'll talk more about indicator parameters in Chapters 39, 40, and 52 on SQL binding styles.

When a binary string is assigned to an SQL-data BLOB target, the size of the target is first set either to the size of the source or to its own maximum length, whichever is less. If the source is larger than the target, but the extra octets are all 0-octets, the source's significant octet value is assigned to the target. If the source is larger than the target and the extra octets are not all 0-octets, the assignment will fail; your DBMS will return the SQLSTATE error 22001 "data exception-string data, right truncation."

Here are some examples of the result you'll get when you assign a binary string to your SQL database (assume your target is defined as BLOB(2)):

```
source X'5550' yields a target value of 5550
source X'55' yields a target value of 55
source X'555500' yields a target of 5555
source X'555555' yields no change to target; assignment fails
with SQLSTATE 22001
```

[Obscure Rule] There are two ways to assign a null value to an SQL-data target. Within SQL, you can use the <keyword> NULL in an INSERT or an UPDATE statement to indicate that the target should be set to NULL; that is, if your source is NULL, your DBMS will set your target to NULL. Outside of SQL, if your source has an indicator parameter that is set to –1, your DBMS will set your target to NULL (regardless of the value of the source). An indicator parameter with a value less than –1 will cause an error; your DBMS will return the SQLSTATE error 22010 "data exception-invalid indicator parameter value."

Comparison

SQL provides only two scalar comparison operators, = and <>, to perform operations on BLOBs. These will be familiar; there are equivalent operators in other computer languages. If any of the comparands are NULL, the result of the operation is UNKNOWN. For example:

```
X'A3D0' = X'A3D0'
```

returns TRUE.

```
X'A3D0' <> {result is NULL}
```

returns UNKNOWN.

When a BLOB is compared to another BLOB, the comparison is done one octet at a time from left to right — that is, the first comparand's most significant octet is compared to the second comparand's most significant octet, then the next two octets are compared, and so on.

Two BLOBs, blob_argument_1 and blob_argument_2, are equal if (*a*) they have the same length and (*b*) each octet within blob_argument_1 compares as equal to the corresponding octet in blob_argument_2.

If you want to restrict your code to Core SQL, don't use BLOBs in comparisons.

Other Operations

With SQL, you have several other operations that you can perform on BLOBs.

Concatenation

The required syntax for a BLOB concatenation is as follows.

```
BLOB concatenation ::=
BLOB operand_1 || BLOB operand_2
```

The concatenation operator operates on two operands, each of which must evaluate to a BLOB. It joins the binary strings together in the order given and returns a BLOB with a length equal to the sum of the lengths of its operands. If either of the operands is NULL, the result of the operation is also NULL. Here are two examples of BLOB concatenations:

```
X'0000' || X'0011'     -- returns 00000011
blob_column || X'0011' -- returns blob_column's value followed by 0011
```

[Obscure Rule] If the sum of the lengths of a BLOB concatenation's operands is not greater than the maximum allowed length for a BLOB, the concatenation result is a BLOB with a length equal to the sum of the lengths of the operands. If the sum of the operands' lengths is greater than the maximum allowed but the extra octets are all 0-octets, the concatenation result is a BLOB with a length equal to the maximum allowed length. If the sum of the operands' lengths is greater than the maximum allowed and the extra octets are not all 0-octets, the concatenation will fail; your DBMS will return the SQLSTATE error 22001 "data exception-string data, right truncation."

If you want to restrict your code to Core SQL, don't use the concatenation operator with BLOBs.

Scalar Operations

SQL provides five scalar operations that return a BLOB: the <case expression>, the <cast specification>, the <BLOB substring function>, the <BLOB overlay function>, and the <BLOB trim function>. It also provides four scalar functions that operate on BLOBs, returning a number: the <BLOB position expression>, the <bit length expression>, the <char length expression>, and the <octet length expression>. All but the first two are described below (we've already talked about casting binary strings). We'll discuss the <case expression> in Chapter 29 "Simple Search Conditions"; for now, just remember that CASE can evaluate to a binary string and can therefore be used anywhere in an SQL statement that a binary string could be used.

<BLOB substring function>

The required syntax for a <BLOB substring function> is as follows.

```
<BLOB substring function> ::=
SUBSTRING (blob_argument
   FROM start_argument [ FOR length_argument ])
```

SUBSTRING operates on three arguments: the first must evaluate to a BLOB, the other two must evaluate to exact numeric integers. It extracts a substring from blob_argument and returns a BLOB with a maximum length that equals the maximum length of the BLOB argument. If any of the arguments are NULL, SUBSTRING returns NULL.

The start_argument is a number that marks the first octet you want to extract from blob_argument. If SUBSTRING includes the (optional) FOR clause, length_argument is the total number of octets you want to extract. If you omit the FOR clause, SUBSTRING will begin at start_argument and extract all the rest of the octets from blob_argument. Here are some examples of SUBSTRING:

```
SUBSTRING(X'1049FE2996D54AB7' FROM 5)        -- returns 96D54AB7
SUBSTRING(X'1049FE2996D54AB7' FROM 5 FOR 3)  -- returns 96D54A
SUBSTRING(blob_column FROM 1 FOR 4)          -- returns the first
                                                four octets of the
                                                value in BLOB_COLUMN
```

If length_argument is negative, your DBMS will return SQLSTATE error 22011 "data exception-substring error." If start_argument is greater than the length of blob_argument, or if (start_argument + length_argument) is less than one, SUBSTRING returns a zero-length binary string. If start_argument is negative, or if (start_argument + length_argument) is greater than the length of blob_argument, that's okay — the DBMS just ignores any octets before the start of blob_argument or after the end of blob_argument.

[Obscure Rule] SUBSTRING can also operate on a bit string and a character string. We've ignored these options for now — look for them in Chapter 4 "Bit Strings" and Chapter 7 "Character Strings."

If you want to restrict your code to Core SQL, don't use SUBSTRING with BLOBs.

<BLOB overlay function>

The required syntax for a <BLOB overlay function> is as follows.

```
<BLOB overlay function> ::=
OVERLAY (blob_argument_1 PLACING blob_argument_2
   FROM start_argument [ FOR length_argument ])
```

OVERLAY operates on four arguments: the first two must evaluate to BLOBs, the other two must evaluate to exact numeric integers. It extracts a substring from blob_argument_1, replacing it with blob_argument_2, and returns the resulting BLOB. If any of the arguments are NULL, OVERLAY returns NULL.

The start_argument is a number that marks the first octet you want to replace in blob_argument_1. If OVERLAY includes the (optional) FOR clause, length_argument is the total number of octets you want to replace. Thus, start_argument and length_argument identify the portion of `blob_argument_1` that you want to replace, while `blob_argument_2` is what you want to replace with. If you omit the `FOR` clause, then `length_argument` defaults to the length of `blob_argument_2`. Here are some examples of `OVERLAY`:

```
OVERLAY(X'ABCDE' PLACING X'01' FROM 2)
-- returns A01DE
OVERLAY(X'DEF' PLACING X'01234' FROM 2 FOR 3)
-- returns D01234
OVERLAY(X'DEFABCD' PLACING X'01234' FROM 2 FOR 3)
-- returns D01234BCD
```

[Obscure Rule] `OVERLAY` can also operate on a character string. We've ignored this option for now — look for it in Chapter 7 "Character Strings."

<BLOB trim function>

The required syntax for a <BLOB trim function> is as follows.

```
<BLOB trim function> ::=
TRIM ( [ [ { LEADING | TRAILING | BOTH } ]
      [ blob_argument_1 ] FROM ]
      blob_argument_2)
```

`TRIM` operates on two arguments, each of which must evaluate to `BLOB`s. It strips all leading, all trailing, or both leading and trailing trim octets from `blob_argument_2` and returns the resulting `BLOB`. If any of the arguments are `NULL`, `TRIM` returns `NULL`.

The trim specification is either `LEADING`, i.e., trim all leading trim octets, `TRAILING`, i.e., trim all trailing trim octets, or `BOTH`, i.e., trim all leading and all trailing trim octets. If this clause is omitted, `TRIM` defaults to `BOTH`. For example, these two `TRIM` functions are equivalent; they both strip away all leading and all trailing zero-octets:

```
TRIM(X'00' FROM blob_column)
TRIM(BOTH X'00' FROM blob_column)
```

`blob_argument_1` defines the trim octet; the octet that should be stripped away by the `TRIM` function. If `blob_argument_1` is omitted, `TRIM` strips zero-octets away. For example, these two `TRIM` functions are equivalent; they both strip away all trailing zero-octets:

```
TRIM(TRAILING FROM blob_column)
TRIM(TRAILING X'00' FROM blob_column)
```

These two `TRIM` functions are also equivalent; they both strip away all leading zero-octets:

```
TRIM(LEADING FROM blob_column)
TRIM(LEADING X'00' FROM blob_column)
```

These two TRIM functions are equivalent; they both strip away all leading and all trailing zero-octets:

```
TRIM(blob_column)
TRIM(BOTH X'00' FROM blob_column)
```

If the length of blob_argument_1 is not one octet, TRIM will fail; your DBMS will return the SQLSTATE error 22027 "data exception-trim error."

[Obscure Rule] TRIM can also operate on a character string. We've ignored this option for now — look for it in Chapter 7 "Character Strings."

<BLOB position expression>

The required syntax for a <BLOB position expression> is as follows.

```
<BLOB position expression> ::=
POSITION (blob_argument_1 IN blob_argument_2)
```

POSITION operates on two arguments, both of which must evaluate to a BLOB. It determines the first octet position (if any) at which blob_argument_1 is found in blob_argument_2 and returns this as an exact numeric integer. If either argument is NULL, POSITION returns NULL. If blob_argument_1 is a zero-length binary string, POSITION returns one. If blob_argument_1 is not found in blob_argument_2, POSITION returns zero. Here is an example:

```
POSITION(X'3D' IN X'AF923DA7')
-- returns 5
```

[NON-PORTABLE] The precision of POSITION's result is non-standard because the SQL Standard requires implementors to define the result's precision. [OCELOT Implementation] The OCELOT DBMS that comes with this book gives the result of POSITION an INTEGER <data type>.

[Obscure Rule] POSITION can also operate on a bit string and a character string. We've ignored these options for now — look for them in Chapter 4 "Bit Strings" and Chapter 7 "Character Strings."

<bit length expression>

The required syntax for a <bit length expression> is as follows.

```
<bit length expression> ::=
BIT_LENGTH (blob_argument)
```

BIT_LENGTH operates on an argument that evaluates to a BLOB. It determines the length of the argument, in bits, and returns this as an exact numeric integer, e.g., BIT_LENGTH(X'4AD9') returns 16. If the argument is NULL, BIT_LENGTH returns NULL.

[NON-PORTABLE] The precision of BIT_LENGTH's result is non-standard because the SQL Standard requires implementors to define the result's precision. [OCELOT Implementation] The OCELOT DBMS that comes with this book gives the result of BIT_LENGTH an INTEGER <data type>.

[Obscure Rule] BIT_LENGTH can also operate on a bit string and a character string. We've ignored these options for now — look for them in Chapter 4 "Bit Strings" and Chapter 7 "Character Strings."

<char length expression>

The required syntax for a <char length expression> is as follows.

```
<char length expression> ::=
{CHAR_LENGTH | CHARACTER_LENGTH} (blob_argument)
```

CHAR_LENGTH (or CHARACTER_LENGTH) operates on an argument that evaluates to a BLOB. It determines the length of the argument in octets and returns this as an exact numeric integer, e.g., CHAR_LENGTH(X'4AD9') returns 2. (The octet length of a string is the bit length divided by 8, rounded up.) If the argument is NULL, CHAR_LENGTH returns NULL.

[NON-PORTABLE] The precision of CHAR_LENGTH's result is non-standard because the SQL Standard requires implementors to define the result's precision. [OCELOT Implementation] The OCELOT DBMS that comes with this book gives the result of CHAR_LENGTH an INTEGER <data type>.

[Obscure Rule] CHAR_LENGTH can also operate on a bit string and a character string. We've ignored these options for now — look for them in Chapter 4 "Bit Strings" and Chapter 7 "Character Strings."

<octet length expression>

The required syntax for an <octet length expression> is as follows.

```
<octet length expression> ::=
OCTET_LENGTH (blob_argument)
```

OCTET_LENGTH operates on an argument that evaluates to a BLOB. It determines the length of the argument in octets and returns this as an exact numeric integer, e.g., OCTET_LENGTH(X'4AD9') returns 2. (The octet length of a string is the bit length divided by 8, rounded up.) If the argument is NULL, OCTET_LENGTH returns NULL.

[NON-PORTABLE] The precision of OCTET_LENGTH's result is non-standard because the SQL Standard requires implementors to define the result's precision. [OCELOT Implementation] The OCELOT DBMS that comes with this book gives the result of OCTET_LENGTH an INTEGER <data type>.

[Obscure Rule] OCTET_LENGTH can also operate on a bit string and a character string. We've ignored these options for now — look for them in Chapter 4 "Bit Strings" and Chapter 7 "Character Strings."

Set Functions

SQL provides two set functions that operate on binary strings: COUNT and GROUPING. Since none of these operate exclusively with binary string arguments, we won't discuss them here; look for them in Chapter 33 "Searching with Groups."

Predicates

In addition to the = and <> comparison operators, SQL provides four other predicates that operate on BLOBs: the <like predicate>, the <null predicate>, the <exists predicate>, and the

<quantified predicate>. Each will return a boolean value: either TRUE, FALSE, or UNKNOWN. Only the <like predicate> operates strictly on string values; we'll discuss it here. Look for the rest in Chapter 29 "Simple Search Conditions."

<like predicate>

The required syntax for a <like predicate> is as follows.

```
<like predicate> ::=
blob_argument [ NOT ] LIKE pattern [ ESCAPE escape_octet ]
```

LIKE is a predicate that operates on three operands that evaluate to BLOBs; it searches for values that contain a given pattern. NOT LIKE is the converse and lets you search for values that don't contain a given pattern. The blob_argument is the binary string you're searching within, the pattern is the pattern you're searching for, and the optional escape_octet is an octet that tells your DBMS to treat a metaoctet in the pattern as itself (rather than as a metaoctet). If blob_argument contains the pattern, LIKE returns TRUE and NOT LIKE returns FALSE. If blob_argument does not contain the pattern, LIKE returns FALSE and NOT LIKE returns TRUE. If any of the operands are NULL, LIKE and NOT LIKE return UNKNOWN.

The pattern you specify in pattern may contain any combination of regular octets and metaoctets. Any single octet in pattern that is not a metaoctet or the escape_octet represents itself in the pattern. For example, the following predicate:

```
blob_column LIKE X'A3'
```

is TRUE for the octet represented by 'A3'.

Special significance is attached to metaoctets in a pattern. The metaoctets are equivalent to the _ and % characters. That is, an underscore metaoctet has the same bit pattern as an underscore character in the SQL_TEXT Character set and a percent metaoctet has the same bit pattern as a percent sign in the SQL_TEXT Character set. (In practice, the bit pattern for _ will be X'5F' and the bit pattern for % will be X'25'. These values correspond to the encodings used in all the ISO character sets.)

If the predicate doesn't include an ESCAPE clause, the metaoctets are interpreted as follows:

- An underscore metaoctet means "any single octet." For example, this predicate:

  ```
  blob_column LIKE X'AA5FCC'
  ```

  is TRUE for X'AA00CC', X'AAAACC', X'AABBCC', X'AA66CC' and so on.
- A percent metaoctet means "any string of zero or more octets." For example, this predicate:

  ```
  blob_column LIKE X'AA25CC'
  ```

  is TRUE for X'AACC', X'AA00CC', X'AABBCC', X'AA66CC', X'AA6666CC' and so on.

If you want to search for an octet that would normally be interpreted as a metaoctet, you must use the optional ESCAPE clause. To do so,

- Pick an octet that you won't need in the pattern and designate it as your escape octet.
- In the pattern, use your escape octet followed immediately by the metaoctet, to designate the metaoctet as an octet you want to search for. For example:

  ```
  ... LIKE X'BB25'
  ```

  (without an ESCAPE clause) means "like the octet BB followed by anything at all," while

  ```
  ... LIKE X'BBFF25' ESCAPE X'FF'
  ```

means "like the octet BB followed by the octet 25" (because 25 is preceded by the escape octet, it has no special significance in this pattern). Your escape octet can also be followed by itself in the pattern, if you want to search for the escape octet. For example:

```
... LIKE X'BBFFFF' ESCAPE X'FF'
```

means "like the octet BB followed by the octet FF" (because FF is preceded by the escape octet, it has no special significance in this pattern).

The `escape_octet` must be exactly one octet long. If it isn't, `[NOT] LIKE` will fail; your DBMS will return the `SQLSTATE error 2200D "data exception-invalid escape octet."` If `escape_octet` is the underscore metaoctet or the percent metaoctet and that metaoctet is used once only in your pattern or if `escape_octet` is used without being followed by a metaoctet (or by itself) in your pattern, `[NOT] LIKE` will fail; your DBMS will return the `SQLSTATE error 22025 "data exception-invalid escape sequence."` For example, these two predicates will both result in `SQLSTATE 22025`:

```
LIKE X'BB25BB' ESCAPE X'25'
LIKE X'BBFFBB' ESCAPE X'FF'
```

For the purposes of `[NOT] LIKE`, a substring of `blob_argument` is a sequence of zero or more contiguous octets where each octet belongs to exactly one such substring. A substring specifier of `pattern` is either (*a*) the underscore metaoctet, an arbitrary octet specifier, (*b*) the percent metaoctet, an arbitrary string specifier, (*c*) `escape_octet` followed by the underscore metaoctet or the percent metaoctet or the escape octet, or (*d*) any other single octet. If `blob_argument` and `pattern` both have a length of zero, `LIKE` returns `TRUE`. `LIKE` also returns `TRUE` if `pattern` is found in `blob_argument`. That is, `LIKE` returns `TRUE` only if the number of substrings in `blob_argument` equals the number of substring specifiers in `pattern` and the following conditions are also met:

- If the pattern's *n*-th substring specifier is the underscore metaoctet, then the argument's *n*-th substring must be any single octet.
- If the pattern's *n*-th substring specifier is the percent metaoctet, then the argument's *n*-th substring must be any sequence of zero or more octets.
- If the pattern's *n*-th substring specifier is any other octet, then the argument's *n*-th substring must have the same length and bit pattern as that substring specifier.

[Obscure Rule] `[NOT] LIKE` can also operate on character strings. We've ignored this option for now — look for it in Chapter 7 "Character Strings."

If you want to restrict your code to Core SQL, don't use the `[NOT] LIKE` predicate with `BLOB`s.

6

Chapter 6

Characters

"Now we know our Alphabet all the way from A to Z[ed]"
(Grade 1 Tune)

"Now we know our ABC all the way from A to Z[ee]"
(same, USA variant)

If you remember one of the above jingles, you've probably got a few things to unlearn before you can use SQL character strings properly. Many people think that the alphabet is something from grade 1; that they know it already. If you fall into this category, be patient with us. By the end of this chapter, you'll understand why we feel it's necessary to devote so much space to what appears to be a fairly simple topic.

Before we can begin to address the question, "What does SQL do with characters?," we first have to ask, "What should it do?" That's why this book has two chapters on characters and character strings. The first one (Chapter 6) explains what characters are, what the important character sets are, and how to relate or switch — the universal things. The following chapter (Chapter 7) gets into what the database solutions are. After you've read this chapter, you'll see why the "solutions" are varied, random, and wrong.

What is a Character?

Consider two vertical bars with a horizontal bar between them: H. This H is a glyph. To us, this glyph is a symbol — it's the letter "Aitch" and it appears in English words. Thus, a "letter" is a combination of a glyph and a meaning. (The importance of this will become apparent as you go through this chapter.) We know that H is the eighth letter of an alphabet. Or —

in SQL terms — H is the eighth symbol in a character repertoire. While an alphabet is a familiar example of a character repertoire, any computer will also support a repertoire containing digits, punctuators, and special characters as well as glyphless (non-printing) characters such as the \0 which terminates strings in C.

However, no computer can handle the letter H by itself. It can only handle numbers, so we have a convention that the letter H will be represented by some number, such as 72. If we all agree that "72 is the code for H, 74 is the code for J ..." and so on for every character in the repertoire, we can make a computer character set. Every character set has two parts: a character repertoire and an agreement on how the repertoire's characters will be encoded as numbers. (The SQL Standard calls the encoding scheme itself a *Form-of-use*.)

Internationally, there are many character sets and many names for them. When using SQL, you'll be concerned mainly with the ones that the International Organization for Standardization (ISO) has published standards for.

- ISO 646 (1965) also known as US-ASCII, DIN 66003, etc.
- ISO 8859-1 (1985) also known as LATIN 1 and Windows Code Page 1252.
- ISO 8859-2 (1987) also known as LATIN 2 and Windows Code Page 1250.
- ... and several others which we'll describe as we go along.

The numeric codes between 0 and 127 have the same meaning in every ISO standard; differences exist only for codes greater than 127. In each standard, the codes between 0 and 127 include punctuation, digits, special characters, and (what's most important for this discussion) — the uppercase letters A to Z (for example, the code for H is indeed 72), and the lowercase letters a to z. Thus, all character sets start with Latin.

Latin

Cicero never saw a W or a lowercase j, but medieval and modern Latin have 26 letters, each of which has two forms: uppercase and lowercase. These are the simple Latin letters:

```
ABCDEFGHIJKLMNOPQRSTUVWXYZ      -- simple uppercase Latin letters
abcdefghijklmnopqrstuvwxyz      -- simple lowercase Latin letters
```

These letters appear in all standard computer character sets including 7-bit ASCII and EBCDIC. They even appear in character sets for languages which don't use Latin. For instance, character sets used in Russia (such as KOI8R or ISO 8859-5) contain all the Latin letters with the same codes as 7-bit ASCII; the Russian Cyrillic letters follow the Latin letters.

Because they are universal, the Latin letters are vital for computer languages. In SQL, all <keyword>s and Standard-generated <regular identifier>s (or names) are made with Latin letters (though they may also contain digits and the underscore character).

The letters of the Latin alphabet are in alphabetic order. That might sound... well, "Duh"...but it helps to point out the most fundamental point about a collation or collating sequence — namely, that a collation represents a fixed order and that order is known to most members of the general public. They expect to see words and names sorted that way (though they don't expect A to sort before a — that's a computer thing).

English

English uses the Latin alphabet but adds rules when sorting. To set the scene for the complexities that follow, here are the rules for English sorting. (We'll naìvely pretend that when we write à l'anglaise, we don't need even a soupçon of those pesky "accented letters" for names like El Niño — we'll look at English only. All examples come from *The Concise Oxford Dictionary Of Current English*.)

Preprocess (Map to Simple Latin Uppercase Letters)

Preprocessing involves (*a*) stripping accents off all accented characters, e.g., Ò becomes O, (*b*) eliminating all special characters such as hyphen or space or apostrophe or dot, and (*c*) changing ligatures such as Æ to double-characters such as AE.

Sort

Use the alphabetical order: ABCDEFGHIJKLMNOPQRSTUVWXYZ

Tiebreakers

- Tiebreakers apply only if two words are otherwise equal.
- If a special character (such as a hyphen or apostrophe) was stripped in the preprocess stage, the word containing it *follows*. For example: "cant" before "can't" before "Cant." and "recollect" before "re-collect" and "nones" before "non est" and "francophone" before "franc tireur".
- If a word contained an accented character, it *follows*. For example: "lame" before "lamé."
- If a word contains a capital letter, it *doesn't matter.* For example: "Negus" before "negus," "AR" before "Ar" — but, "dan" before "Dan," "ma" before "MA." (We acknowledge that some people believe it does matter; we report only what actually happens.)

About 50% of English-world phone books have additional rules:

- Mc and Mac appear before M (sometimes M' does too, but only in Ireland). For example: "McDonald" before "Macdonald" before "Maastricht."
- Ste and St appear as if they were spelled "Saint." For example: "St John" before "Saan Stores Limited."
- In these cases, we effectively combine a group of letters into one and place the result in the hidden interstices between O and M, or between R and S. It looks odd, but many languages have two-letter combinations (called *digraphs*) which fit between primary letters of the alphabet.

From all this, we see that English sorting involves, in addition to the basic A-to-Z stuff, several special collation rules — including mapping, ligatures ("one character maps to two"), tiebreaking, and digraphs ("two characters map to one"). Nobody makes a fuss about English because the special cases are rare. But special cases in non-English languages are not rare at all — they are the norm, so it's the non-English collation rules that get the attention.

French

French words have:

a or e with Grave accent	ès à
a or e with Acute accent	Chrétien résumé
a or i or o with Circumflex	hôte côte
c with Cedilla	soupçon ça
i or e or o with Diaeresis	naïf coöpërant

In simple cases, the French sorting rules are like the English rules.

- Accented characters map to their Latin uppercase equivalents ("résumé" comes after "rester" but before "retard").
- Words with accented characters come after words with none ("à" comes after "a" — but that's only a tiebreaker; "à" comes before "abbé."

Then things get complicated.

- For words with multiple accented characters, the word with the last accented character *follows*. For example: "pêche" before "péché."
- France and French Canada don't capitalize accented letters the same way. In France, the uppercase of the word "résumé" is "RESUME" — there are no capital letters with accents, which is why the old PC-DOS Character set (IBM extended ASCII) could dispense with the letters É, Ó, etc. But French Canadians capitalize the word "résumé" and keep the accents: "RÉSUMÉ."

This shows us that we have more characters, another collation rule, and conflicting ideas for changing lowercase to uppercase.

German

German words have:

a or o or u with umlaut	Mädchen östlich Führer
sharp S or Eszet	bißchen

Sharp S's similarity to a Greek Beta is just coincidence; it is really a ligature which maps to "ss." This is the only character in any Latin alphabet which is always lowercase.

There are three ways to sort characters with umlauts, depending on the German-speaking country and the application.

1. In the German DIN-1 official standard, Ä = A and Ö = O and Ü = U. That is, accented characters map to unaccented equivalents. This is the standard used for dictionaries, book indexes, or any lists of words. Thus, Führer = Fuhrer.
2. In the German DIN-2 official standard, Ä = AE and Ö = OE and Ü = UE. That is, accented characters map to unaccented character plus E. This is the standard used for phone books, voter lists, or any lists of names in Germany. Thus, Göbbels = Goebbels and Düsseldorf = Duesseldorf.

3. In the Austrian unofficial standard, Ä > AZ and Ö > OZ and Ü > UZ. That is, each accented character is treated as a separate letter between A and B or O and P or U and V. This is the standard used for lists of names in Austria. Thus, Müller > Mzilikaze.

The Swiss use DIN-1 for all sorting.

The German tiebreaker rules are: unaccented before accented (this rule is universal), Eszet before umlaut, and umlaut before any other accent. The following table shows three lists sorted according to DIN-1 (Zürich phone book), DIN-2 (Berlin phone book), and Austrian collation (Vienna phone book).

DIN-1	DIN-2	Austrian
Moeller	Moeller	Moeller
Moffat	Möller	Moffat
Möller	Moffat	Morse
Morse	Morse	Möller
Möse	Möse	Möse
Motler	Motler	Motler

At this point, you may be wondering what happens if you click "use German collating sequence" on some Windows dialog box. Well, Microsoft seems to prefer DIN-1, but the point is: if you just click, you'll get a Microsoft choice which is wrong at least half the time. As we said at the beginning of this chapter; you have to know what the problem is before you know what the solutions are worth.

Spanish

Spanish words have:

tilde over n	cañon
acute accent over a u o i	corazón

Some circles (such as the Spanish-speaking community in the United States) use the English style rules to sort Spanish words; all accented characters map to their simple Latin equivalents, period. However, the following list and discussion on Spanish collation refers to the traditional rules which apply in most situations.

- CH comes between C and D
- LL comes between L and M
- N comes before Ñ

NOTE: From now on, we'll use the formula "<x> follows <y>" to mean "<x> is treated as a separate letter which follows <y> in the alphabet," as in: CH follows C.

The Spanish CH and LL digraphs are truly separate letters. They get separate headings in the dictionaries and the Spanish alphabet really has 28 letters:
a b c ch d e f g h i j k l ll m n ñ o p q r s t u v x y z

Here is an example of a sorted Spanish list:

calza
calle
cantor
cañon
culto
che

Dutch, Italian, Portuguese, Basque, and Catalan

These languages present no special problems. Dutch does have one digraph, IJ, which is sometimes used for Y but it is acceptable to use the letters IJ and sort with the digraph IJ. Acute accents are common in Portuguese, grave accents in Italian; however, they all map to simple Latin letters and there are no special collation rules.

Welsh

CH follows C. FF follows F. LL follows L. PH follows P. RH follows R. TH follows T.

Nordic

The Scandinavian alphabets have a common history and a few similar features, the most notable of which is their tendency to add letters at the end of the alphabet (after Z).

Central Europe

So far, we've discussed eleven alphabets and collations without having to change the standard computer character set. Every one of the symbols in the alphabets we've discussed appears in ISO 8859-1, usually called the LATIN 1 character set. They also appear in ISO 8859-1's most famous derivative, Windows code page 1252, which is the default code page on computers in North America and in all European countries west of a line drawn through Finland, Germany, Austria, and Italy. We are now going to cross that line and briefly discuss ISO 8859-2, usually called the LATIN 2 character set (or in Windows, code page 1250).

The Central European character set supports languages that use Latin-based characters with macrons, slashes, haceks, ogoneks, breves, bars, and carons. Many of these do not map to a simple Latin letter when sorting.

The many extra letters created by adding these marks to the simple Latin letters made it impossible to fit them all into the 8-bit LATIN 1 character set, because there can only be a maximum of 256 different symbols in an 8-bit set. (In fact, LATIN 1 actually provides fewer than 256 characters because `0x00` to `0x1f` and `0x7f` to `0x9f` are reserved for control "characters.") Therefore, the most convenient thing to do was group the Latin-based East European character sets together into LATIN 2.

There has been lots of confusion in the past and several national character set encodings are still in common use, so it's a bit idealistic to write as if the ISO standards were already universal; however, there's no other useful assumption that a small shop can make.

Baltic

The Baltic countries have alphabets containing yet more characters, culminating in the world's longest Latin-based alphabet — Latvian. Again, the addition of the extra letters made it necessary to set up another 8-bit character set. This one is ISO 8859-4, usually called the BALTIC character set (or in Windows, code page 1257). The Baltic collations are the only ones in which the simple Latin letters do not follow what we usually think of as alphabetic order.

Turkish

The Turkish character set is defined by ISO 8859-9, usually called the LATIN 5 character set (or in Windows, code page 1254). There is an irritating capitalization problem in Turkish (irritating to us, that is; we assume it doesn't bother the Turks much): the capital of i is a dotted capital "I" and the capital of ı is I. Because of this single character, it is impossible to capitalize simple-Latin-letter strings without being sure that the strings are not written in Turkish.

Cyrillic

The main Cyrillic character sets can be represented by a single Windows code page — 1251, a derivative of ISO 8859-5. In Ukrainian, the soft sign appears at the end of the alphabet instead of in the position (between YERU and E) used by other Cyrillic languages. This affects the order of a few words, so two collations are necessary for completeness: a Ukrainian collation and a generalized-Cyrillic (Bulgarian Russian Serbian) collation which differs only with respect to the position of this one letter.

NOTE: The Cyrillic letters А В Е І Ј К М Н О Р С Ѕ Т У Х are only similar to Latin letters in one respect: their appearance. Remember that we defined a character as "a combination of a glyph and a meaning." This is why. Similarity doesn't mean equivalence. These Cyrillic letters have codes of their own; they never map to Latin letters.

Greek

Greek is the oldest European character set and contains a few archaic features (for example, breath marks) which don't really indicate anything nowadays. On the other hand, we'd just as often want to use the Greek letters for classical texts as for modern Greek. So it's good that they're all found in ISO 8859-7, usually called the GREEK character set (or in Windows, code page 1253).

The Rest of the World

We have now described all the alphabets of Europe and given you some idea of their collation quirks. We think that's the minimum requirement for a book that mentions character sets. We also think that it's the maximum! With some relief, we note that other alphabets and other writing systems (syllabaries, hieroglyphs, etc.) are unavailable on a typically-configured computer in "the western world," so we won't talk about them in any detail. Three other systems deserve mention though.

Arabic Each character is displayable in several different forms — depending on whether it is alone, or is the first, middle, or last character in a word. Thus, search and sort features are needed that can recognize multiple encodings of the same symbol.

Chinese There are at least 13,000 different signs which are implemented with double byte character sets (usually "BIG5" in Taiwan, or "GB" in Red China). Ideally, the arrangement is that characters are sorted phonetically (Level 1) or according to radical and number of strokes (Level 2).

Japanese Several systems are in simultaneous use. For example, the word for "water" can be a single character (Kanji), two characters (Hiragana), two characters (Katakana), or four Latin letters (Romaji). The double character sets are usually encoded using escape characters. That saves space but makes it impossible to determine a text's length or find its *n*th letter without starting at the front and working through the text.

What's In It for Me?

Now that you've read this far, you know everything you'll need to write your own Serbian Sort or make party chat about the relative utility of 8-bit-code subsets. Of course, you're a high-level programmer — you haven't got any intention of doing either. Instead, you're going to want to ask:

1. Is it safe to regard character sets and collations as black boxes, for which you only need to know what the inputs are without worrying about the process or the outputs?
2. Are my OS and DBMS vendors aware of the problems and do they handle all cases correctly?

The answers (we hope you got this — if not, read the chapter again):

1. No.
2. No.

If you got both answers right, congratulations — you've understood the problem. In the next chapter, we'll look at how an SQL implementation solves it, but first we'll look at the Character sets that you can expect your DBMS to provide.

Predefined Character Sets

In SQL, a Character set may be a Character set defined by a national or international standard, by your DBMS, or by a user of SQL-data.

Standard-defined Character sets consist of a set of characters predefined by some standards body and have a default Collation that is the order of the characters in the relevant standard. The default Collation has the PAD SPACE characteristic. The SQL Standard requires a DBMS to support, at a minimum, these standard-defined Character sets: SQL_CHARACTER, GRAPHIC_IRV (also called ASCII_GRAPHIC), LATIN1, ISO8BIT (also called ASCII_FULL), and UNICODE (also called ISO10646).

Implementation-defined Character sets consist of a set of characters predefined by your DBMS and have a default Collation that is also defined by your DBMS. The default Collation may have either the PAD SPACE characteristic or the NO PAD characteristic. The SQL Standard requires a DBMS to support, at a minimum, the implementation-defined Character set SQL_TEXT.

SQL_CHARACTER

The SQL_CHARACTER Character set is an 8-bit Character set that consists of the 83 <SQL language character>s. These are found in codepage 1252.

SQL_CHARACTER characters and their codepage 1252 Form-of-use codes

decimal code 032	<space>
decimal code 034	" <double quote>
decimal code 037	% <percent>
decimal code 038	& <ampersand>
decimal code 039	' <single quote>
decimal code 040	(<left parenthesis>
decimal code 041	) <right parenthesis>
decimal code 042	* <asterisk>
decimal code 043	+ <plus sign>
decimal code 044	, <comma>
decimal code 045	- <minus sign>
decimal code 046	. <period>
decimal code 047	/ <solidus>
decimal code 048	0
decimal code 049	1
decimal code 050	2
decimal code 051	3
decimal code 052	4
decimal code 053	5
decimal code 054	6
decimal code 055	7
decimal code 056	8
decimal code 057	9

SQL_CHARACTER characters and their codepage 1252 Form-of-use codes

decimal code 058	: <colon>
decimal code 059	; <semicolon>
decimal code 060	< <less than operator>
decimal code 061	= <equals operator>
decimal code 062	> <greater than operator>
decimal code 063	? <question mark>
decimal code 065	A
decimal code 066	B
decimal code 067	C
decimal code 068	D
decimal code 069	E
decimal code 070	F
decimal code 071	G
decimal code 072	H
decimal code 073	I
decimal code 074	J
decimal code 075	K
decimal code 076	L
decimal code 077	M
decimal code 078	N
decimal code 079	O
decimal code 080	P
decimal code 081	Q
decimal code 082	R
decimal code 083	S
decimal code 084	T
decimal code 085	U
decimal code 086	V
decimal code 087	W
decimal code 088	X
decimal code 089	Y
decimal code 090	Z
decimal code 095	_ <underscore>
decimal code 097	a
decimal code 098	b
decimal code 099	c
decimal code 100	d

SQL_CHARACTER characters and their codepage 1252 Form-of-use codes

decimal code 101	e
decimal code 102	f
decimal code 103	g
decimal code 104	h
decimal code 105	i
decimal code 106	j
decimal code 107	k
decimal code 108	l
decimal code 109	m
decimal code 110	n
decimal code 111	o
decimal code 112	p
decimal code 113	q
decimal code 114	r
decimal code 115	s
decimal code 116	t
decimal code 117	u
decimal code 118	v
decimal code 119	w
decimal code 120	x
decimal code 121	y
decimal code 122	z
decimal code 124		<vertical bar>

[NON-PORTABLE] The default Collation for the SQL_CHARACTER Character set is non-standard because the SQL Standard requires implementors to define SQL_CHARACTER's default Collation. Most DBMSs will sort the characters of SQL_CHARACTER in the decimal order shown above. [OCELOT Implementation] The OCELOT DBMS that comes with this book has a default Collation (called SQL_CHARACTER) for the SQL_CHARACTER Character set that sorts the characters in their codepage 1252 decimal order.

GRAPHIC_IRV and ASCII_GRAPHIC

The GRAPHIC_IRV Character set (ASCII_GRAPHIC is a synonym) is an 8-bit Character set that consists of 95 characters; all of the SQL_CHARACTER characters plus an additional 12 characters from codepage 1252. The default Collation for the GRAPHIC_IRV Character set sorts the characters in their codepage 1252 decimal order.

GRAPHIC_IRV characters and their codepage 1252 Form-of-use codes (in default Collation order)

decimal code 032	<space>
decimal code 033	! <exclamation mark>
decimal code 034	" <double quote>
decimal code 035	# <number sign>
decimal code 036	$ <dollar sign>
decimal code 037	% <percent>
decimal code 038	& <ampersand>
decimal code 039	' <single quote>
decimal code 040	(<left parenthesis>
decimal code 041	) <right parenthesis>
decimal code 042	* <asterisk>
decimal code 043	+ <plus sign>
decimal code 044	, <comma>
decimal code 045	- <minus sign>
decimal code 046	. <period>
decimal code 047	/ <solidus>
decimal code 048	0
decimal code 049	1
decimal code 050	2
decimal code 051	3
decimal code 052	4
decimal code 053	5
decimal code 054	6
decimal code 055	7
decimal code 056	8
decimal code 057	9
decimal code 058	: <colon>
decimal code 059	; <semicolon>
decimal code 060	< <less than operator>
decimal code 061	= <equals operator>
decimal code 062	> <greater than operator>
decimal code 063	? <question mark>
decimal code 064	@ <commercial at sign>
decimal code 065	A
decimal code 066	B
decimal code 067	C

GRAPHIC_IRV characters and their codepage 1252 Form-of-use codes (in default Collation order)

decimal code 068	D
decimal code 069	E
decimal code 070	F
decimal code 071	G
decimal code 072	H
decimal code 073	I
decimal code 074	J
decimal code 075	K
decimal code 076	L
decimal code 077	M
decimal code 078	N
decimal code 079	O
decimal code 080	P
decimal code 081	Q
decimal code 082	R
decimal code 083	S
decimal code 084	T
decimal code 085	U
decimal code 086	V
decimal code 087	W
decimal code 088	X
decimal code 089	Y
decimal code 090	Z
decimal code 091	[<left square bracket>
decimal code 092	\ <backslash>
decimal code 093	] <right square bracket>
decimal code 094	^ <circumflex accent mark>
decimal code 095	_ <underscore>
decimal code 096	` <grave accent mark>
decimal code 097	a
decimal code 098	b
decimal code 099	c
decimal code 100	d
decimal code 101	e
decimal code 102	f
decimal code 103	g

GRAPHIC_IRV characters and their codepage 1252 Form-of-use codes (in default Collation order)

decimal code 104	h
decimal code 105	i
decimal code 106	j
decimal code 107	k
decimal code 108	l
decimal code 109	m
decimal code 110	n
decimal code 111	o
decimal code 112	p
decimal code 113	q
decimal code 114	r
decimal code 115	s
decimal code 116	t
decimal code 117	u
decimal code 118	v
decimal code 119	w
decimal code 120	x
decimal code 121	y
decimal code 122	z
decimal code 123	{ <left brace>
decimal code 124	| <vertical bar>
decimal code 125	} <right brace>
decimal code 126	~ <tilde>

[NON-PORTABLE] The default Collation for the GRAPHIC_IRV Character set has a non-standard name because the SQL Standard requires implementors to define what a legal <Collation name> is. [OCELOT Implementation] The OCELOT DBMS that comes with this book has a default Collation called GRAPHIC_IRV for the GRAPHIC_IRV Character set.

LATIN1

The LATIN1 Character set is an 8-bit Character set that consists of all the characters commonly used in Danish, Dutch, English, Faeroese, Finnish, French, German, Icelandic, Irish, Italian, Norwegian, Portuguese, Spanish, and Swedish — a total of 191 characters: all of the GRAPHIC_IRV characters plus an additional 96 characters from codepage 1252. The default Collation for the LATIN1 Character set sorts the characters in their codepage 1252 decimal order.

Additional LATIN1 characters and their codepage 1252 Form-of-use codes (in default Collation order)

decimal code 160	<no-break space>
decimal code 161	¡ <inverted exclamation mark>
decimal code 162	¢ <cent sign>
decimal code 163	£ <pound sign>
decimal code 164	¤ <currency sign>
decimal code 165	¥ <yen sign>
decimal code 166	¦ <broken bar>
decimal code 167	§ <section sign>
decimal code 168	¨ <diaeresis>
decimal code 169	© <copyright sign>
decimal code 170	ª <feminine ordinal indicator>
decimal code 171	“ <left angle quotation mark>
decimal code 172	¬ <not sign>
decimal code 173	- <soft hyphen>
decimal code 174	® <registered trade mark sign>
decimal code 175	¯ <macron>
decimal code 176	° <degree sign>
decimal code 177	± <plus-minus sign>
decimal code 178	² <superscript two>
decimal code 179	³ <superscript three>
decimal code 180	´ <acute accent>
decimal code 181	µ <micro sign>
decimal code 182	¶ <pilcrow sign>
decimal code 183	· <middle dot>
decimal code 184	¸ <cedilla>
decimal code 185	¹ <superscript one>
decimal code 186	º <masculine ordinal indicator>
decimal code 187	” <right angle quotation mark>
decimal code 188	¼ <fraction one quarter>
decimal code 189	½ <fraction one half>
decimal code 190	¾ <fraction three quarters>
decimal code 191	¿ <inverted question mark>
decimal code 192	À <A accent grave>
decimal code 193	Á <A acute accent>
decimal code 194	Â <A circumflex>

Additional LATIN1 characters and their codepage 1252 Form-of-use codes (in default Collation order)

decimal code 195	Ã <A tilde>
decimal code 196	Ä <A diaeresis>
decimal code 197	Å <A circle>
decimal code 198	Æ <AE ligature>
decimal code 199	Ç <C cedilla>
decimal code 200	È <E accent grave>
decimal code 201	É <E acute accent>
decimal code 202	Ê <E circumflex>
decimal code 203	Ë <E diaeresis>
decimal code 204	Ì <I accent grave>
decimal code 205	Í <I acute accent>
decimal code 206	Î <I circumflex>
decimal code 207	Ï <I diaeresis>
decimal code 208	Ð <Icelandic ETH>
decimal code 209	Ñ <N tilde>
decimal code 210	Ò <O accent grave>
decimal code 211	Ó <O acute accent>
decimal code 212	Ô <O circumflex>
decimal code 213	Õ <O tilde>
decimal code 214	Ö <O diaeresis>
decimal code 215	× <multiplication sign>
decimal code 216	Ø <O stroke>
decimal code 217	Ù <U accent grave>
decimal code 218	Ú <U acute accent>
decimal code 219	Û <U circumflex>
decimal code 220	Ü <U diaeresis>
decimal code 221	Ý <Y acute accent>
decimal code 222	Þ <THORN>
decimal code 223	ß <sharp s>
decimal code 224	à <a accent grave>
decimal code 225	á <a acute accent>
decimal code 226	â <a circumflex>
decimal code 227	ã <a tilde>
decimal code 228	ä <a diaeresis>
decimal code 229	å <a circle>
decimal code 230	æ <ae ligature>

Additional LATIN1 characters and their codepage 1252 Form-of-use codes (in default Collation order)

decimal code 231	ç <c cedilla>
decimal code 232	è <e accent grave>
decimal code 233	é <e acute accent>
decimal code 234	ê <e circumflex>
decimal code 235	ë <e diaeresis>
decimal code 236	ì <i accent grave>
decimal code 237	í <i acute accent>
decimal code 238	î <i circumflex>
decimal code 239	ï <i diaeresis>
decimal code 240	ð <Icelandic eth>
decimal code 241	ñ <n tilde>
decimal code 242	ò <o accent grave>
decimal code 243	ó <o acute accent>
decimal code 244	ô <o circumflex>
decimal code 245	õ <o tilde>
decimal code 246	ö <o diaeresis>
decimal code 247	÷ <division sign>
decimal code 248	ø <o stroke>
decimal code 249	ù <u accent grave>
decimal code 250	ú <u acute accent>
decimal code 251	û <u circumflex>
decimal code 252	ü <u diaeresis>
decimal code 253	ý <y acute accent>
decimal code 254	þ <thorn>
decimal code 255	ÿ <y diaeresis>

[NON-PORTABLE] The default Collation for the LATIN1 Character set has a non-standard name because the SQL Standard requires implementors to define what a legal <Collation name> is. [OCELOT Implementation] The OCELOT DBMS that comes with this book has a default Collation called LATIN1 for the LATIN1 Character set.

ISO8BIT and ASCII_FULL

The ISO8BIT Character set (ASCII_FULL is a synonym) is an 8-bit Character set that consists of 256 characters: all of the LATIN1 characters plus the rest of the characters (including control characters and graphic characters) from codepage 1252. The default Collation for the ISO8BIT Character set sorts the characters in their codepage 1252 decimal order.

ISO8BIT characters and their codepage 1252 Form-of-use codes (in default Collation order

decimal code 000	control character; not displayed
decimal code 001	control character; not displayed
decimal code 002	control character; not displayed
decimal code 003	control character; not displayed
decimal code 004	control character; not displayed
decimal code 005	control character; not displayed
decimal code 006	control character; not displayed
decimal code 007	control character; not displayed
decimal code 008	control character; not displayed
decimal code 009	control character; not displayed
decimal code 010	control character; not displayed
decimal code 011	control character; not displayed
decimal code 012	control character; not displayed
decimal code 013	control character; not displayed
decimal code 014	control character; not displayed
decimal code 015	control character; not displayed
decimal code 016	control character; not displayed
decimal code 017	control character; not displayed
decimal code 018	control character; not displayed
decimal code 019	control character; not displayed
decimal code 020	control character; not displayed
decimal code 021	control character; not displayed
decimal code 022	control character; not displayed
decimal code 023	control character; not displayed
decimal code 024	control character; not displayed
decimal code 025	control character; not displayed
decimal code 026	control character; not displayed
decimal code 027	control character; not displayed
decimal code 028	control character; not displayed
decimal code 029	control character; not displayed
decimal code 030	control character; not displayed
decimal code 031	control character; not displayed
decimal codes 032 through 126, from LATIN1	
decimal code 127	control character; not displayed
decimal code 128	control character; not displayed
decimal code 129	control character; not displayed
decimal code 130	control character; not displayed

ISO8BIT characters and their codepage 1252 Form-of-use codes (in default Collation order

decimal code 131	control character; not displayed
decimal code 132	control character; not displayed
decimal code 133	control character; not displayed
decimal code 134	control character; not displayed
decimal code 135	control character; not displayed
decimal code 136	control character; not displayed
decimal code 137	control character; not displayed
decimal code 138	control character; not displayed
decimal code 139	control character; not displayed
decimal code 140	control character; not displayed
decimal code 141	control character; not displayed
decimal code 142	control character; not displayed
decimal code 143	control character; not displayed
decimal code 144	control character; not displayed
decimal code 145	control character; not displayed
decimal code 146	control character; not displayed
decimal code 147	control character; not displayed
decimal code 148	control character; not displayed
decimal code 149	control character; not displayed
decimal code 150	control character; not displayed
decimal code 151	control character; not displayed
decimal code 152	control character; not displayed
decimal code 153	control character; not displayed
decimal code 154	control character; not displayed
decimal code 155	control character; not displayed
decimal code 156	control character; not displayed
decimal code 157	control character; not displayed
decimal code 158	control character; not displayed
decimal code 159	control character; not displayed
decimal codes 160 through 256, from LATIN1	

[NON-PORTABLE] The default Collation for the ISO8BIT Character set has a non-standard name because the SQL Standard requires implementors to define what a legal <Collation name> is. [OCELOT Implementation] The OCELOT DBMS that comes with this book has a default Collation called ISO8BIT for the ISO8BIT Character set.

UNICODE and ISO10646

The UNICODE Character set (ISO10646 is a synonym) is a 16-bit Character set that consists of every character represented by the Unicode specification (specifically, by The Unicode Standard Version 2.1). Since there are 38,887 characters in this set, we won't include a list in this book. It suffices to say that the UNICODE Character set includes all of the ISO8BIT characters, plus many others. The default Collation for the UNICODE Character set sorts the characters in their Unicode Form-of-use code order.

[NON-PORTABLE] The default Collation for the UNICODE Character set has a non-standard name because the SQL Standard requires implementors to define what a legal <Collation name> is. [OCELOT Implementation] The OCELOT DBMS that comes with this book has a default Collation called SQL_TEXT for the UNICODE Character set.

SQL_TEXT

The SQL Standard requires every DBMS to provide an Ur-Character set named SQL_TEXT. The complete set of SQL_TEXT characters is implementation-defined but SQL_TEXT must contain every <SQL language character> plus every other character that the DBMS supports. That is, SQL_TEXT (at a minimum) includes all of the UNICODE characters and is therefore at least a 16-bit Character set.

[NON-PORTABLE] The default Collation for the SQL_TEXT Character set must be called SQL_TEXT too, but is otherwise non-standard because the SQL Standard requires implementors to define the default Collation and Form-of-use of SQL_TEXT. [OCELOT Implementation] The OCELOT DBMS that comes with this book sorts the characters of SQL_TEXT in their Unicode Form-of-use code order.

There are some curious consequences to making SQL_TEXT (and UNICODE) a 16-bit, rather than an 8-bit Character set.

The consequences are the result of the fact that all <identifier>s and other character strings in INFORMATION_SCHEMA, all <SQL-server name>s, all <Connection name>s, all <AuthorizationID>s, and the results of many functions (e.g., USER, CURRENT_USER, SESSION_USER, SYSTEM_USER) are SQL_TEXT character strings.

SQL_TEXT, however, is normally not the default Character set (the default Character set is almost always an 8-bit Character set) — and SQL specifically prohibits comparisons between strings that belong to different Character sets. The rules require that, for such comparisons, one string be translated to the other string's Character set first — see the TRANSLATE function in Chapter 7, "Character Strings."

So, will you have special trouble when you want to display INFORMATION_SCHEMA strings, <AuthorizationID>s, <SQL-server name>s, <Connection name>s, or the like? There are two possibilities, and the answer is usually "No" to both.

Possibility 1

Consider the following SQL statements:

```
SELECT TABLE_NAME FROM INFORMATION_SCHEMA.TABLES;
SELECT SESSION_USER FROM INFORMATION_SCHEMA.TABLES;
```

The SQL Standard allows a DBMS to decide whether there should be an automatic translation from SQL_TEXT to the default Character set when an SQL statement assigns an

SQL_TEXT string to a host language variable or parameter. In such cases, most DBMSs do the automatic translation for you, e.g., the OCELOT DBMS that comes with this book does. So, to display the result of a SELECT from INFORMATION_SCHEMA or the result from a function that returns an SQL_TEXT string, you won't need to do anything special. It won't normally be necessary to use the TRANSLATE function to translate the retrieved values from 16-bit SQL_TEXT characters into 8-bit, readable format or vice versa. Just write your SQL statement as if the Character set difference doesn't exist. (In the example above, by the way, the ASCII <identifier> TABLE_NAME would also be automatically converted to an SQL_TEXT string by your DBMS before the search was done.)

Possibility 2

Consider this SQL statement:

```
SELECT TABLE_NAME
FROM   INFORMATION_SCHEMA.TABLES
WHERE  TABLE_NAME = 'ocelot';
```

The SQL Standard does not allow a DBMS to decide whether there should be an automatic translation from SQL_TEXT to the default Character set when an SQL statement involves a comparison between an SQL_TEXT string and a default Character set string. But the rules do allow a DBMS to provide a predefined Translation for this purpose. In such cases, most DBMSs will use this option to do an automatic translation for you, e.g., the OCELOT DBMS that comes with this book does. So, to compare SQL_TEXT strings with default Character set strings, you won't need to do anything special. It won't normally be necessary to use the TRANSLATE function to translate the retrieved values from 16-bit SQL_TEXT characters into 8-bit, readable format or vice versa. Just write your SQL statement as if the Character set difference doesn't exist.

A second consequence of the fact that SQL_TEXT is 16-bit and the default Character set is usually 8-bit involves the use of <AuthorizationID>s, <SQL-server name>s, and <Connection name>s. Although <AuthorizationID>s, <SQL-server name>s, and <Connection name>s are stored as 16-bit SQL_TEXT strings, the SQL-Connection arguments in the CONNECT statement are inevitably 8-bit strings because ASCII is used to type them. If, however, these same arguments are assigned to host language variables or parameters, you will see them as 16-bit strings. Therefore, when you have an expression like

```
... WHERE <AuthorizationID> = 'x' ...
```

you know that the <character string literal> 'x' is a 16-bit string because <AuthorizationID>s are SQL_TEXT strings. But the same <literal> in a CONNECT statement, e.g.,

```
CONNECT TO 'x';
```

has to be an 8-bit string because it is typed in ASCII.

One last comment, about parsing SQL_TEXT strings. Consider the following expression, which concatenates a character string with a value from a Column:

```
... _INFORMATION_SCHEMA.SQL_TEXT 'A ' || column_1
```

The default Character set for an SQL statement is usually an 8-bit Character set but the string 'A' in this example is explicitly introduced as 16-bit SQL_TEXT. Thus, what appears to be two 8-bit characters, A and <space>, is in fact, one 16-bit character — the Unicode value 4120h.

Parsing of SQL statements is always based on 8-bit values regardless of the Character set of a string, so your DBMS will consider the SQL_TEXT string 'A' to begin after the first single quote mark and end before the second single quote mark; i.e., although the characters inside the single quotes are 16-bit, the delimiting single quote marks themselves are 8-bit. Thus, when the parser reaches the second single quote mark, it knows that the string is over — despite the fact that in 16-bit, a single quote mark character has not yet been found.

7

Chapter 7

Character Strings

In SQL, a character string is any sequence of zero or more alphanumeric characters that belong to a given Character set. A *Character set* is a named character repertoire that includes a Form-of-use encoding scheme which defines how the repertoire's characters are encoded as numbers. The SQL Standard defines several standard Character sets that your DBMS must support. A *character string value* may be: a <literal>, an <identifier>, the value of a parameter or a host language variable, or the result of any expression or argument that evaluates to a character string. All character strings belong to some Character set and are governed by the rules of some Collation during comparisons. A *Collation* is a named collating sequence. Character strings that belong to the same Character set are compatible.

A character string has a length — a non-negative integer equal to the number of characters in the string. Characters in a character string are numbered from left to right beginning with 1. A Character string also has a coercibility attribute; this helps your DBMS determine which Collation to use for a comparison that doesn't provide an explicit `COLLATE` clause. The coercibility attribute can be either `COERCIBLE`, `EXPLICIT`, `IMPLICIT`, or `NO COLLATION`. (A coercibility attribute of `COERCIBLE`, `EXPLICIT`, or `IMPLICIT` means the string has a current default Collation. A coercibility attribute of `NO COLLATION` means the string does not have a current default Collation.) Character strings are stored in either of the six character string <data type>s: `CHARACTER`, `CHARACTER VARYING`, `CHARACTER LARGE OBJECT`, `NATIONAL CHARACTER`, `NATIONAL CHARACTER VARYING`, or `NATIONAL CHARACTER LARGE OBJECT`.

Character String <literal>s

An SQL <character string literal> has five parts.

1. Its value — the sequence of characters that make up the <literal>.
2. Its length — the number of characters that make up the <literal>.
3. The name of the Character set that the <literal> belongs to.
4. The name of the <literal>'s default Collation. (This is the Collation that may be used to compare the <literal> with another character string in the absence of an explicit COLLATE clause.)
5. The <literal>'s coercibility attribute — normally COERCIBLE, but can be EXPLICIT. (The coercibility attribute helps your DBMS determine which Collation to use for a comparison that doesn't provide an explicit COLLATE clause.)

A <character string literal> is either a <character string literal> or a national <character string literal>.

<character string literal>

The required syntax for a <character string literal> is as follows.

```
<character string literal> ::=
[ _<Character set name> ]'string' [ COLLATE <Collation name> ]
```

A <character string literal> is a string of zero or more alphanumeric characters inside a pair of single quote marks. The string's characters must all belong to the same Character set. Its <data type> is fixed length CHARACTER, though it is compatible with the CHARACTER, CHARACTER VARYING, CHARACTER LARGE OBJECT, NATIONAL CHARACTER, NATIONAL CHARACTER VARYING, and NATIONAL CHARACTER LARGE OBJECT <data type>s. The <literal>'s length is the number of characters inside the quote marks; the delimiting single quotes aren't part of the <literal>, so they're not included in the calculation of the <character string literal>'s size. Two consecutive single quotes within a character string (i.e., '') represent one single quote mark; together, they count as one character when calculating the size of the <literal>. Here is an example of a <character string literal>:

```
'This is a <character string literal>'
```

[Obscure Rule] The optional Character set specification — an underscore character immediately preceding a <Character set name> (no space is allowed between them) — names the Character set to which the <literal> belongs. Your current <AuthorizationID> must have the USAGE Privilege for that Character set. For example, this <character string literal>:

```
_LATIN1'Hello'
```

belongs to the LATIN1 Character set. Note: For qualified names, the underscore character always precedes the highest level of explicit qualification in the <Character set name>. If you omit the Character set specification, the characters in the <literal> must belong to the Character set of the SQL-client Module that contains the <literal>. Here are two examples of a <character string literal>:

```
'This is a string in the default Character set'
_LATIN1'This is a string in the LATIN1 Character set'
```

[Obscure Rule] A <character string literal> normally has a coercibility attribute of COERCIBLE and a default Collation that is the Collation defined for its Character set — See "Character Strings and Collations" on page 159. The optional COLLATE clause names the <literal>'s EXPLICIT Collation for an operation. The Collation named must be a Collation defined for the relevant Character set, but you may specify a default Collation for a <literal> that is different from the default Collation of its Character set. If you're using COLLATE in an SQL-Schema statement, then the <AuthorizationID> that owns the containing Schema must have the USAGE Privilege on <Collation name>. If you're using COLLATE in any other SQL statement, then your current <AuthorizationID> must have the USAGE Privilege on <Collation name>. Here are four more examples of a <character string literal>:

```
'This string in the default Character set will use the default Character set''s
Collation'
_LATIN1'This in the LATIN1 Character set will use LATIN1''s Collation'
'This string in the default Character set will use a Collation named
MY.COLLATION_1' COLLATE my.collation_1
_LATIN1'This string in the LATIN1 Character set will use a Collation named
MY.COLLATION_1' COLLATE my.collation_1
```

[Obscure Rule] SQL allows you to break a long <character string literal> into two or more smaller <character string literal>s, split by a <separator> that includes a newline character. When it sees such a <literal>, your DBMS will ignore the <separator> and treat the multiple strings as a single <literal>. For example, here are two equivalent <character string literal>s:

```
'This is part of a string'
' and this is the other part'

'This is part of a string and this is the other part'
```

(In the first example, there is a carriage return newline <separator> between string' and ' and.)

If you want to restrict your code to Core SQL, don't add a Character set specification to <character string literal>s, don't add a COLLATE clause to <character string literal>s, and don't split long <character string literal>s into smaller strings.

<national character string literal>

The required syntax for a <national character string literal> is as follows.

```
<national character string literal> ::=
N'string' [ COLLATE <Collation name> ]
```

A <national character string literal> is a <character string literal> preceded by the letter N; it is a synonym for a <character string literal> that belongs to a predefined "national" Character set. Its <data type> is fixed length NATIONAL CHARACTER, though it is compatible with the CHARACTER, CHARACTER VARYING, CHARACTER LARGE OBJECT, NATIONAL CHARACTER, NATIONAL CHARACTER VARYING, and NATIONAL CHARACTER LARGE OBJECT <data type>s.

Other than the fact that you may not add a Character set specification to a <national character string literal> because N'string' implies the same national Character set used for NCHAR, NCHAR VARYING, and NCLOB <data type>s, the specifications for the two types of <character string literal>s are the same. Here are two examples of a <national character string literal>:

```
N'This string in the national Character set will use the national Character
set''s Collation'
N'This string in the national Character set will use a Collation named
MY.COLLATION_1' COLLATE my.collation_1
```

[NON-PORTABLE] The national Character set used by <national character string literal>s and the NCHAR, NCHAR VARYING, and NCLOB <data type>s is non-standard because the SQL Standard requires implementors to define a national Character set. [OCELOT Implementation] The OCELOT DBMS that comes with this book defines the national Character set to be ISO8BIT. For example, here are two equivalent <character string literal>s:

```
N'Hello there'
_ISO8BIT'Hello there'
```

If you want to restrict your code to Core SQL, don't use <national character string literal>s.

Character String <data type>s

A character string <data type> is defined by a descriptor that contains five pieces of information.

1. The <data type>'s name — either CHARACTER, CHARACTER VARYING, CHARACTER LARGE OBJECT, NATIONAL CHARACTER, NATIONAL CHARACTER VARYING, or NATIONAL CHARACTER LARGE OBJECT.
2. The <data type>'s fixed length or maximum length (as applicable).
3. The name of the Character set that the <data type>'s set of valid values belongs to. (An operation that attempts to make a character string <data type> contain a character that does not belong to its Character set will fail; your DBMS will return the SQLSTATE error 22021 "data exception-character not in repertoire.")
4. The name of the <data type>'s default Collation. (This is the Collation that may be used to compare the <data type>'s values in the absence of an explicit COLLATE clause.)
5. The <data type>'s coercibility attribute — normally IMPLICIT, but can be EXPLICIT. (The coercibility attribute helps your DBMS determine which Collation to use for a comparison that doesn't provide an explicit COLLATE clause.)

CHARACTER

The required syntax for a CHARACTER <data type> specification is as follows.

```
CHARACTER <data type> ::=
CHARACTER [ (length) ]
[ CHARACTER SET <Character set name> ]
[ COLLATE <Collation name> ]
```

CHARACTER may be abbreviated as CHAR and is a fixed length alphanumeric string exactly "length" characters long. It defines a set of character string values that belong to a given Character set. For example, the <character string literal>:

```
'BOB'
```

is a valid value for the <data type> specification:

```
CHAR(3)
```

The optional length (if specified) is an unsigned, positive integer that defines the exact length, in characters, of acceptable values. The minimum length and the default length are both 1. For example, these two <data type> specifications:

```
CHAR
CHAR(1)
```

both define a set of character string values that are exactly one character long.

[NON-PORTABLE] The maximum length for CHAR is non-standard because the SQL Standard requires implementors to define CHAR's maximum length. FIPS says that CHAR should have a maximum length of at least 1,000 characters. [OCELOT Implementation] The OCELOT DBMS that comes with this book allows you to define a length ranging from 1 to 4,096 for CHAR.

[Obscure Rule] The optional CHARACTER SET clause names the Character set that the <data type>'s values belong to. Your current <AuthorizationID> must have the USAGE Privilege for that Character set. For example, the <data type> specification:

```
CHAR(15) CHARACTER SET LATIN1
```

defines a set of character string values, exactly 15 characters long, that belongs to the LATIN1 Character set. If you omit the CHARACTER SET clause when specifying a character string <data type> in a <Column definition> or a CREATE DOMAIN statement, the <data type>'s Character set is the Character set named in the DEFAULT CHARACTER SET clause of the CREATE SCHEMA statement that defines the Schema in which the <data type> is defined. For example, consider the following SQL statement which creates a Schema that has a default Character set of LATIN1:

```
CREATE SCHEMA schema_example
   DEFAULT CHARACTER SET INFORMATION_SCHEMA.LATIN1;
```

Based on this definition, the <data type> specification in this SQL statement defines a set of character string values, exactly 15 characters long, that belong to the LATIN1 Character set:

```
CREATE TABLE schema_example.Table_1 (
   column_1 CHAR(15));
```

[NON-PORTABLE] If you omit the CHARACTER SET clause when specifying a character string <data type> anywhere other than in a <Column definition> or a CREATE DOMAIN statement, the <data type>'s Character set is non-standard because the SQL Standard requires implementors to define a default Character set for such situations. [OCELOT Implementation] The OCELOT DBMS that comes with this book defines ISO8BIT as the default Character set for such situations.

[Obscure Rule] A CHAR <data type> has a coercibility attribute of IMPLICIT. The optional COLLATE clause defines the <data type>'s default Collation. The Collation named must be a Collation defined for the relevant Character set, but you may define a Column, Field, or Domain with a default Collation that is different from the default Collation of its Character set. If you're using COLLATE in an SQL-Schema statement, then the <AuthorizationID> that owns the containing Schema must have the USAGE Privilege on <Collation name>. If you're using COLLATE in any other SQL statement, then your current <AuthorizationID> must have the USAGE Privilege on <Collation name>. For example, the following two <data type> specifications:

```
CHAR(15) COLLATE my.collation_1
CHAR(15) CHARACTER SET my.charset_1 COLLATE my.collation_1
```

both define a set of character string values exactly 15 characters long. The first example defines the <data type>'s Character set to be the default Character set. The second example defines the <data type>'s Character set to be a Character set named my.charset_1. Both examples define the <data type>'s default Collation to be a Collation named my.collation_1. If you omit the COLLATE clause, the <data type> is defined as if its Character set's default Collation was explicitly specified — See "Character Strings and Collations" on page 159.

If you want to restrict your code to Core SQL, don't use the CHARACTER SET clause or the COLLATE clause for CHAR <data type> specifications.

NATIONAL CHARACTER

The required syntax for a NATIONAL CHARACTER <data type> specification is as follows.

```
NATIONAL CHARACTER <data type> ::=
NATIONAL CHARACTER [ (length) ] [ COLLATE <Collation name> ]
```

NATIONAL CHARACTER may be abbreviated as NATIONAL CHAR or as NCHAR. NCHAR is a synonym for a CHAR <data type> that belongs to a predefined "national" Character set.

Other than the fact that you may not add a CHARACTER SET clause to an NCHAR <data type> specification because NCHAR implies the same national Character set used for <national character string literal>s and NCHAR VARYING and NCLOB <data type>s, the specifications for the NCHAR and CHAR <data type>s are the same. Here are two examples of an NCHAR <data type> specification:

```
NCHAR(10)
-- uses the national Character set's Collation
NCHAR(10) COLLATE my.collation_1
-- uses a Collation named MY.COLLATION_1
```

[NON-PORTABLE] The national Character set used by <national character string literal>s and the NCHAR, NCHAR VARYING, and NCLOB <data type>s is non-standard because the SQL Standard requires implementors to define a national Character set. [OCELOT Implementation] The OCELOT DBMS that comes with this book defines the national Character set to be ISO8BIT. For example, these two <data type> specifications both define the same set of valid values:

```
NCHAR(10)
CHAR(10) CHARACTER SET ISO8BIT
```

If you want to restrict your code to Core SQL, don't use the NCHAR <data type>.

CHARACTER VARYING

The required syntax for a CHARACTER VARYING <data type> specification is as follows.

```
CHARACTER VARYING <data type> ::=
CHARACTER VARYING (length)
[ CHARACTER SET <Character set name> ]
[ COLLATE <Collation name> ]
```

CHARACTER VARYING may be abbreviated as CHAR VARYING or as VARCHAR and is a variable length alphanumeric string from zero to "length" characters long. It defines a set of character string values that belong to a given Character set. For example, the following three <character string literal>s:

```
'BOB'
'BOBBY'
'ROBERT'
```

are all valid values for this <data type> specification:

```
VARCHAR(6)
```

The mandatory length specification is an unsigned, positive integer that defines the maximum length, in characters, of acceptable values. The minimum length is 1.

[NON-PORTABLE] The maximum length for VARCHAR is non-standard because the SQL Standard requires implementors to define VARCHAR's maximum length. FIPS says that VARCHAR should have a maximum length of at least 1,000 characters. [OCELOT Implementation] The OCELOT DBMS that comes with this book allows you to define a length ranging from 1 to 4,096 for VARCHAR.

[Obscure Rule] The optional CHARACTER SET clause names the Character set that the <data type>'s values belong to — see the remarks under the "CHARACTER" section. For example, the <data type> specification:

```
VARCHAR(15) CHARACTER SET LATIN1
```

defines a set of character string values, 0 to 15 characters long, that belong to the LATIN1 Character set. (Zero length strings may be stored in a VARCHAR field.)

[Obscure Rule] A VARCHAR <data type> has a coercibility attribute of IMPLICIT. The optional COLLATE clause defines the <data type>'s default Collation — see the remarks under the "CHARACTER" section. For example, these two <data type> specifications:

```
VARCHAR(15) COLLATE my.collation_1
VARCHAR(15) CHARACTER SET my.charset_1 COLLATE my.collation_1
```

both define a set of character string values, 0 to 15 characters long, that have a default Collation called my.collation_1.

If you want to restrict your code to Core SQL, don't use the CHARACTER SET clause or the COLLATE clause for VARCHAR <data type> specifications.

NATIONAL CHARACTER VARYING

The required syntax for a NATIONAL CHARACTER VARYING <data type> specification is as follows.

```
NATIONAL CHARACTER VARYING <data type> ::=
NATIONAL CHARACTER VARYING (length) [ COLLATE <Collation name> ]
```

NATIONAL CHARACTER VARYING may be abbreviated as NATIONAL CHAR VARYING or as NCHAR VARYING. NCHAR VARYING is a synonym for a VARCHAR <data type> that belongs to a predefined "national" Character set.

Other than the fact that you may not add a CHARACTER SET clause to an NCHAR VARYING <data type> specification because NCHAR VARYING implies the same national Character set used for <national character string literal>s and NCHAR and NCLOB <data type>s, the specifications for the NCHAR VARYING and VARCHAR <data type>s are the same. Here are two examples of an NCHAR VARYING <data type> specification:

```
NCHAR VARYING(10)
-- uses the national Character set's Collation
NCHAR VARYING(10) COLLATE my.collation_1
-- uses a Collation named MY.COLLATION_1
```

[NON-PORTABLE] The national Character set used by <national character string literal>s and the NCHAR, NCHAR VARYING, and NCLOB <data type>s is non-standard because the SQL Standard requires implementors to define a national Character set. [OCELOT Implementation] The OCELOT DBMS that comes with this book defines the national Character set to be ISO8BIT. For example, these two <data type> specifications both define the same set of valid values:

```
NCHAR VARYING(10)
VARCHAR(10) CHARACTER SET ISO8BIT
```

If you want to restrict your code to Core SQL, don't use the NCHAR VARYING <data type>.

CHARACTER LARGE OBJECT

The required syntax for a CHARACTER LARGE OBJECT <data type> specification is as follows.

```
CHARACTER LARGE OBJECT <data type> ::=
{CHARACTER LARGE OBJECT | CLOB} [ (length) ]
[ CHARACTER SET <Character set name> ]
[ COLLATE <Collation name> ]
```

CHARACTER LARGE OBJECT may be abbreviated as CHAR LARGE OBJECT or as CLOB and is a variable length alphanumeric string from zero to "length" characters long. It defines a set of large object character string values that belong to a given Character set. For example, the following three <character string literal>s:

```
'BOB'
'BOBBY'
'ROBERT'
```

are all valid values for the <data type> specification:

```
CLOB(6)
```

The optional length, if specified, is an unsigned integer, greater than or equal to one, possibly followed by a letter code (either "K", "M", or "G"). It defines the maximum character length of acceptable values in the CLOB field.

- If the length *n* is not followed by a letter code, the CLOB may hold up to *n* characters.
- The length may include the letter code "K" (kilobyte), "M" (megabyte), or "G" (gigabyte). If the length is defined as *nk*, the CLOB may hold up to *n*1024* characters. If the length is defined as *nM*, the CLOB may hold up to *n*1,048,576* characters. If the length is defined as *nG*, the CLOB may hold up to *n*1,073,741,824* characters.

For example, the following <data type> specification defines a set of large object character string values that may range from zero to 20 characters.

```
CLOB(20)
```

(Zero length large object character strings can be stored in a CLOB field.)

This <data type> specification defines a set of large object character string values that may range from zero to 2048 characters:

```
CLOB(2K)
```

This <data type> specification defines a set of large object character string values that may range from zero to 2,097,152 characters:

```
CLOB(2M)
```

And this <data type> specification defines a set of large object character string values that may range from zero to 2,147,483,648 characters:

```
CLOB(2G)
```

[NON-PORTABLE] The default length and the maximum length for CLOB are non-standard because the SQL Standard requires implementors to define CLOB's default and maximum lengths. [OCELOT Implementation] The OCELOT DBMS that comes with this book allows the length of CLOB to range from 1 to 4K and sets the default length of a CLOB <data type> to

1K. For example, the following two <data type> specifications are equivalent; both define a set of large object character string values that may range from zero to 1024 characters:

```
CLOB
CLOB(1K)
```

[Obscure Rule] The optional CHARACTER SET clause names the Character set that the <data type>'s values belong to; see the remarks under the "CHARACTER" section. For example, the <data type> specification:

```
CLOB(5M) CHARACTER SET LATIN1
```

defines a set of large object character string values, 0 to 5,242,880 characters long, that belong to the LATIN1 Character set.

[Obscure Rule] A CLOB <data type> has a coercibility attribute of IMPLICIT. The optional COLLATE clause defines the <data type>'s default Collation; see the remarks under the "CHARACTER" section. For example, these two <data type> specifications:

```
CLOB(3G) COLLATE my.collation_1
CLOB(3G) CHARACTER SET my.charset_1 COLLATE my.collation_1
```

both define a set of large object character string values, 0 to 3,221,225,472 characters long, that have a default Collation called my.collation_1.

If you want to restrict your code to Core SQL, don't use the CHARACTER SET clause or the COLLATE clause for CLOB <data type> specifications.

NATIONAL CHARACTER LARGE OBJECT

The required syntax for a NATIONAL CHARACTER LARGE OBJECT <data type> specification is as follows.

```
NATIONAL CHARACTER LARGE OBJECT <data type> ::=
NATIONAL CHARACTER LARGE OBJECT [ (length) ][ COLLATE <Collation name> ]
```

NATIONAL CHARACTER LARGE OBJECT may be abbreviated as NCHAR LARGE OBJECT or as NCLOB. NCLOB is a synonym for a CLOB <data type> that belongs to a predefined "national" Character set.

Other than the fact that you may not add a CHARACTER SET clause to an NCLOB <data type> specification because NCLOB implies the same national Character set used for <national character string literal>s and NCHAR and NCHAR VARYING <data type>s, the specifications for the NCLOB and CLOB <data type>s are the same. Here are two examples of an NCLOB <data type> specification:

```
NCLOB(2K)
-- uses the national Character set's Collation
NCLOB(2K) COLLATE my.collation_1
-- uses a Collation named MY.COLLATION_1
```

[NON-PORTABLE] The national Character set used by <national character string literal>s and the NCHAR, NCHAR VARYING, and NCLOB <data type>s is non-standard because the SQL Standard requires implementors to define a national Character set. [OCELOT Implementation] The OCELOT DBMS that comes with this book defines the national Character set to be ISO8BIT. For example, these two <data type> specifications both define the same set of valid values:

```
NCLOB(1G)
CLOB(1G) CHARACTER SET ISO8BIT
```

If you want to restrict your code to Core SQL, don't use the NCLOB <data type>.

Now that we've described SQL's character string <data type>s, let's look at some example SQL statements that put them to use.

These SQL statements make a Table with six fixed length character string Columns, insert a row, then search for any string greater than 'hi'.

```
CREATE TABLE Fixed_Char_Examples (
      occurrence_char_1 CHAR(2),
      occurrence_char_2 CHAR(2) CHARACTER SET LATIN1,
      occurrence_char_3 CHAR(2) COLLATE my.collation_1,
      occurrence_char_4 CHAR(2) CHARACTER SET LATIN1 COLLATE my.collation_1,
      occurrence_nchar_1 NCHAR(2),
      occurrence_nchar_2 NCHAR(2) COLLATE my.collation_1);

INSERT INTO Fixed_Char_Examples (
      occurrence_char_1,
      occurrence_char_2,
      occurrence_char_3,
      occurrence_char_4,
      occurrence_nchar_1,
      occurrence_nchar_2)
      VALUES ('mm','mm','mm','mm','mm','mm');

SELECT occurrence_char_1,
       occurrence_char_2,
       occurrence_char_3,
       occurrence_char_4,
       occurrence_nchar_1,
       occurrence_nchar_2
FROM   Fixed_Char_Examples
WHERE  occurrence_char_4 > 'hi';
```

```
SELECT occurrence_char_1,
       occurrence_char_2,
       occurrence_char_3,
       occurrence_char_4,
       occurrence_nchar_1,
       occurrence_nchar_2
FROM   Fixed_Char_Examples
WHERE  occurrence_nchar_2 > N'hi';
```

The following SQL statements make a Table with six variable length character string Columns, insert a row, then search for any string not equal to 'hi'.

```
CREATE TABLE Varying_Char_Examples (
      occurrence_varchar_1 VARCHAR(5),
      occurrence_varchar_2 VARCHAR(5) CHARACTER SET LATIN1,
      occurrence_varchar_3 VARCHAR(5) COLLATE my.collation_1,
      occurrence_varchar_4 VARCHAR(5) CHARACTER SET LATIN1
                COLLATE my.collation_1,
      occurrence_nvchar_1 NCHAR VARYING(5),
      occurrence_nvchar_2 NCHAR VARYING(5) COLLATE my.collation_1);

INSERT INTO Varying_Char_Examples (
      occurrence_varchar_1,
      occurrence_varchar_2,
      occurrence_varchar_3,
      occurrence_varchar_4,
      occurrence_nvchar_1,
      occurrence_nvchar_2)
      VALUES ('mm','mm','mm','mm','mm','mm');

SELECT occurrence_varchar_1,
       occurrence_varchar_2,
       occurrence_varchar_3,
       occurrence_varchar_4,
       occurrence_nvchar_1,
       occurrence_nvchar_2
FROM   Varying_Char_Examples
WHERE  occurrence_varchar_4 <> 'hi';
```

```
SELECT occurrence_varchar_1,
       occurrence_varchar_2,
       occurrence_varchar_3,
       occurrence_varchar_4,
       occurrence_nvchar_1,
       occurrence_nvchar_2
FROM   Varying_Char_Examples
WHERE  occurrence_nvchar_2 <> N'hi';
```

The following SQL statements make a Table with six large object character string Columns, insert a row, then search for any string equal to 'hi'.

```
CREATE TABLE Large_Char_Examples (
   occurrence_clob_1 CLOB(10),
   occurrence_clob_2 CLOB(10K) CHARACTER SET LATIN1,
   occurrence_clob_3 CLOB(10M) COLLATE my.collation_1,
   occurrence_clob_4 CLOB(10G) CHARACTER SET LATIN1 COLLATE my.collation_1,
   occurrence_nclob_1 NCLOB(2K),
   occurrence_nclob_2 NCLOB COLLATE my.collation_1);

INSERT INTO Large_Char_Examples (
      occurrence_clob_1,
      occurrence_clob_2,
      occurrence_clob_3,
      occurrence_clob_4,
      occurrence_nclob_1,
      occurrence_nclob_2)
      VALUES ('mm','mm','mm','mm','mm','mm');

SELECT occurrence_clob_1,
       occurrence_clob_2,
       occurrence_clob_3,
       occurrence_clob_4,
       occurrence_nclob_1,
       occurrence_nclob_2
FROM   Large_Char_Examples
WHERE  occurrence_clob_4 = 'hi';
```

```
SELECT occurrence_clob_1,
       occurrence_clob_2,
       occurrence_clob_3,
       occurrence_clob_4,
       occurrence_nclob_1,
       occurrence_nclob_2
FROM   Large_Char_Examples
WHERE  occurrence_nclob_2 = N'hi';
```

Character String Operations

A character string is compatible with, and comparable to, all other character strings from the same Character set — that is, character strings are mutually comparable and mutually assignable as long as they belong to the same Character set. Character strings may not be directly compared with, or directly assigned to, any other <data type> class, though implicit type conversions can occur in expressions, SELECTs, INSERTs, DELETEs, and UPDATEs. Explicit character string type conversions can be forced with the CAST operator.

CAST

In SQL, CAST is a scalar operator that converts a given scalar value to a given scalar <data type>. The required syntax for the CAST operator is as follows.

```
CAST (<cast operand> AS <cast target>)
<cast operand> ::= scalar_expression
<cast target> ::= <Domain name> | <data type>
```

The CAST operator converts values of a source <data type> into values of a target <data type>, where each <data type> is an SQL pre-defined <data type> (data conversions between UDTs are done with a user-defined cast). The source <data type> (or <cast operand>) can be any expression that evaluates to a single value. The target <data type> (or <cast target>) is either an SQL predefined <data type> specification or the name of a Domain whose defined <data type> is your target <data type>. (If you use CAST (... AS <Domain name>) your current <AuthorizationID> must have the USAGE Privilege on that Domain.)

It isn't, of course, possible to convert the values of every <data type> into the values of every other <data type>. For character strings, the rules are:

- CAST (NULL AS <data type>) and CAST (character_string_source_is_a_null_value AS <data type>) both result in NULL.
- You can CAST a fixed length or variable length character string or a CLOB or NCLOB source to these targets:
  - exact numeric
  - approximate numeric
  - fixed length character string (if source and target belong to the same Character set)
  - variable length character string (if source and target belong to the same Character set)

- CLOB (if source and target belong to the same Character set)
- NCLOB (if source and target belong to the same Character set)
- fixed length bit string
- variable length bit string
- date
- time
- timestamp
- year-month interval
- day-time interval
- boolean.

You can also CAST a fixed length or variable length character string or a CLOB or NCLOB source to a UDT target or a <reference type> target if a user-defined cast exists for this purpose and your current <AuthorizationID> has the EXECUTE Privilege on that user-defined cast.

When you CAST a character string to an exact numeric target or an approximate numeric target, your DBMS strips any leading or trailing spaces from the source and converts the remaining string — which must be the character representation of a number — to that number. For example, CAST ('-25' AS SMALLINT) results in a SMALLINT value of –25. If your source string doesn't represent a number, the CAST will fail; your DBMS will return the SQLSTATE error 22018 "data exception-invalid character value for cast."

When you CAST a character string to a fixed length character string target, a variable length character string target, a CLOB target, or an NCLOB target, both source and target must belong to the same Character set. The result has the COERCIBLE coercibility attribute and the Collation of the result is the default Collation of the target's Character set.

- For fixed length character string targets, if the length of the source *equals* the fixed length of the target, the result of the CAST is the source string. If the length of the source is *shorter* than the fixed length of the target, the result of the CAST is the source string padded on the right with however many spaces are required to make the lengths match. If the length of the source is *longer* than the fixed length of the target, the result of the CAST is a character string that contains as much of the source string as possible. In this case, if the truncated characters are not all spaces, your DBMS will return the SQLSTATE warning 01004 "warning-string data, right truncation."
- For variable length character string or CLOB or NCLOB targets, if the length of the source is *less than or equals* the maximum length of the target, the result of the CAST is the source string. If the length of the source is *longer* than the maximum length of the target, the result of the CAST is a character string that contains as much of the source string as possible. In this case, if the truncated characters are not all spaces, your DBMS will return the SQLSTATE warning 01004 "warning-string data, right truncation."

When you CAST a character string to a fixed length bit string or a variable length bit string target, the result is the character string converted to a string of bits. That is, when you CAST a character string (which has a "Form-of-use encoding") to a bit string (which has no encoding), you get the bits that make up the characters in the source string. For example, assume the source character string for a CAST belongs to the ISO8BIT Character set. In this Character set, the code for the letter 'A' is 41 hexadecimal (the binary number 01000001) and the code for the letter 'B' is 42 hexadecimal (the binary number 01000010) — so CAST ('AB' TO BIT(16)) will result in B'0100000101000010'.

- For fixed length bit string targets, if the bit length of the converted source string *equals* the fixed bit length of the target, the result of the CAST is the converted source string. If the converted source value's bit length is *larger* than the fixed bit length of the target, the result of the CAST is a bit string that contains as much of the converted source string as possible. In this case, if the truncated bits are not all 0-bits, your DBMS will return the SQLSTATE warning 01004 "warning-string data, right truncation." If the converted source value's bit length is *less than* the fixed bit length of the target, the result of the CAST is the converted bit string, padded on the least significant end with as many 0-bits as required to make the lengths match. In this case, your DBMS will return the SQLSTATE warning 01008 "warning-implicit zero-bit padding."
- For variable length bit string targets, if the bit length of the converted source string is *less than or equals* the maximum bit length of the target, the result of the CAST is the converted source string. If the converted source value's bit length is *larger* than the maximum bit length of the target, the result of the CAST is a bit string that contains as much of the converted source string as possible. In this case, if the truncated bits are not all 0-bits, your DBMS will return the SQLSTATE warning 01004 "warning-string data, right truncation."

When you CAST a character string to a date target, your DBMS strips any leading or trailing spaces from the source and converts the remaining string — which must be the character representation of a valid date — to that date. If your source string doesn't represent a valid date, the CAST will fail; your DBMS will return the SQLSTATE error 22007 "data exception-invalid datetime format."

When you CAST a character string to a time target, your DBMS strips any leading or trailing spaces from the source and converts the remaining string — which must be the character representation of a valid time — to that time. If your source string doesn't represent a valid time, the CAST will fail; your DBMS will return the SQLSTATE error 22007 "data exception-invalid datetime format." If your source string isn't a string that could represent any time (even an invalid one), the CAST will also fail; your DBMS will return the SQLSTATE error 22018 "data exception-invalid character value for cast."

When you CAST a character string to a timestamp target, your DBMS strips any leading or trailing spaces from the source and converts the remaining string — which must be the character representation of a valid timestamp — to that timestamp. If your source string doesn't represent a valid timestamp, the CAST will fail; your DBMS will return the SQLSTATE error 22007 "data exception-invalid datetime format." If your source string isn't a string that could represent any timestamp (even an invalid one), the CAST will also fail; your DBMS will return the SQLSTATE error 22018 "data exception-invalid character value for cast."

When you CAST a character string to an interval target, your DBMS strips any leading or trailing spaces from the source and converts the remaining string — which must be the character representation of a valid interval for the target — to that interval. If your source string doesn't represent a valid interval for the target, the CAST will fail; your DBMS will return the SQLSTATE error 22XXX "data exception-invalid interval format" (the SQL committee had not determined the SQLSTATE subcode for this error at the time of printing). If your source string isn't a string that could represent any interval (even an invalid one for the target), the

CAST will also fail; your DBMS will return the SQLSTATE error 22007 "data exception-invalid datetime format."

When you CAST a character string to a boolean target, your DBMS strips any leading or trailing spaces from the source and converts the remaining string — which must be the character representation of one of the truth values TRUE, FALSE, or UNKNOWN — to that truth value. If your source string doesn't represent a truth value, the CAST will fail; your DBMS will return the SQLSTATE error 22018 "data exception-invalid character value for cast."

When you CAST a character string to a UDT or a <reference type> target, your DBMS invokes the user-defined cast routine, with the source value as the routine's argument. The CAST result is the value returned by the user- defined cast.

Here are some examples of CAST operations with character string source operands:

```
CAST (N'The rain in Spain' AS CHAR(18))
-- result is the string 'The rain in Spain '
CAST (' 050.00 ' AS DECIMAL(3,1))
-- result is the number 50.0
CAST ('1997-04-04' AS DATE)
-- result is the date DATE '1997-04-04'
CAST ('FALSE' AS BOOLEAN)
-- result is the truth value FALSE
```

If you want to restrict your code to Core SQL, (*a*) don't use <Domain name> as a CAST target; CAST only to a <data type> and (*b*) don't use CAST to convert any CLOB or NCLOB values to another <data type>.

Assignment

SQL allows you to assign only compatible character strings — that is, character strings are mutually assignable only if the source string and the target string belong to the same Character set. If you need to assign a character string to a target that belongs to a different Character set, use the TRANSLATE function to translate the source into an equivalent string that belongs to the target's Character set.

In SQL, when a character string is assigned to a character string target, the assignment is done one character at a time, from left to right.

When a character string is taken from SQL-data to be assigned to a fixed length character string target and the source is *shorter* than the target, the source is padded (on the right) with spaces until it matches the target's size. If the source is *longer* than the target, the source is truncated to fit the target. In this case, your DBMS will return the SQLSTATE warning 01004 "warning-string data, right truncation." When a character string is taken from SQL-data to be assigned to a variable length character string or CLOB target, the size of the target is first set either to the size of the source or to its own maximum length, whichever is less. The source may then be truncated, if necessary, to match the size of the target. In this case, your DBMS will return the SQLSTATE warning 01004 "warning-string data, right truncation."

[Obscure Rule] Since only SQL accepts null values, if your source is NULL, then your target's value is not changed. Instead, your DBMS will set its indicator parameter to –1, to indicate that an assignment of the null value was attempted. If your target doesn't have an indicator parameter, the assignment will fail; your DBMS will return the SQLSTATE error 22002 "data exception-null value, no indicator parameter." If your source is a non-null value that fits into your target, your DBMS will set the target's indicator parameter (if any) to zero. If your source is longer than your target, your DBMS will set your target's indicator parameter to the length of the source; that is, if your source is 12 characters long and your target can accept only 10 characters, your DBMS will set the target's indicator parameter to 12, to indicate that 2 characters were lost on assignment. If the source's length is too big to be assigned to the indicator, the assignment will fail; your DBMS will return the SQLSTATE error 22022 "data exception-indicator overflow." We'll talk more about indicator parameters in Chapters 39, 40, and 52 on SQL binding styles.

When a character string is assigned to a fixed length SQL-data character string target and the source is *shorter* than the target, the source is padded (on the right) with spaces until it matches the target's size. If the source is *larger* than the target, but the extra characters are all spaces, the source's significant character string value is assigned to the target. If the source is *larger* than the target and the extra characters are *not* all spaces, the assignment will fail; your DBMS will return the SQLSTATE error 22001 "data exception-string data, right truncation." When a character string is assigned to a variable length SQL-data character string or CLOB target, the size of the target is first set either to the size of the source or to its own maximum length, whichever is less. If the source is *larger* than the target, but the extra characters are all spaces, the source's significant character string value is assigned to the target. If the source is *larger* than the target and the extra characters are *not* all spaces, the assignment will fail; your DBMS will return the SQLSTATE error 22001 "data exception-string data, right truncation."

[Obscure Rule] There are two ways to assign a null value to an SQL-data target. Within SQL, you can use the <keyword> NULL in an INSERT or an UPDATE statement to indicate that the target should be set to NULL; that is, if your source is NULL, your DBMS will set your target to NULL. Outside of SQL, if your source has an indicator parameter that is set to –1, your DBMS will set your target to NULL (regardless of the value of the source). An indicator parameter with a value less than –1 will cause an error; your DBMS will return the SQLSTATE error 22010 "data exception-invalid indicator parameter value."

Comparison

SQL provides the usual scalar comparison operators, = and <> and < and <= and > and >=, to perform operations on CHAR, VARCHAR, NCHAR, and NCHAR VARYING character strings but provides only the = and <> operators to perform operations on CLOB and NCLOB character strings. All of them will be familiar; there are equivalent operators in other computer languages. If any of the comparands are NULL, the result of the operation is UNKNOWN. For example:

```
'hello' < 'zebra'
```

returns TRUE.

```
'hello' > {result is NULL}
```

returns UNKNOWN.

SQL also provides three quantifiers — ALL, SOME, ANY — which you can use along with a comparison operator to compare a CHAR, VARCHAR, NCHAR, or NCHAR VARYING value with the collection of values returned by a <table subquery>. (You can't use quantifiers in CLOB or

NCLOB comparisons.) Place the quantifier after the comparison operator, immediately before the <table subquery>. For example:

```
SELECT char_column
FROM   Table_1
WHERE  char_column = ALL (
  SELECT char_column
  FROM   Table_2);
```

ALL returns TRUE either (*a*) if the collection is an empty set, i.e., if it contains zero rows or (*b*) if the comparison operator returns TRUE for every value in the collection. ALL returns FALSE if the comparison operator returns FALSE for at least one value in the collection.

SOME and ANY are synonyms. They return TRUE if the comparison operator returns TRUE for at least one value in the collection. They return FALSE either (*a*) if the collection is an empty set or (*b*) if the comparison operator returns FALSE for every value in the collection. The search condition = ANY (collection) is equivalent to IN (collection).

SQL allows you to compare character strings only if (*a*) they belong to the same Character set and (*b*) have, or can be coerced into having, the same Collation for the comparison — that is, character strings are mutually comparable only if both their Character sets and their Collations are the same. The result of the comparison is determined by the rules of the relevant Collation. Because of this, two strings with different lengths may, or may not, compare as equal.

Although a comparison involves two character strings, both of which have a default Collation, only one of the Collations can be used to govern the result of the comparison. So, when you (*a*) compare character strings that have different current default Collations and (*b*) don't explicitly specify a Collation for the comparison, your DBMS will use the coercibility attribute of each string to choose the relevant Collation.

A <Column name>, <Column reference>, or other character string value that includes a COLLATE clause has a coercibility attribute of EXPLICIT — its Collation is the Collation named. If a <Column name> or <Column reference> doesn't include a COLLATE clause, it has a coercibility attribute of IMPLICIT — its Collation is the Collation specified when the Column was created (see the <data type> definitions). If any other character string value (e.g., a host variable or a <literal>) doesn't include a COLLATE clause, it normally has a coercibility attribute of COERCIBLE — its Collation is the default Collation for its Character set. Sometimes a character string value is the result of an expression that joins strings with different Collations (e.g., a concatenation operation that doesn't include a COLLATE clause). These character strings have a coercibility attribute of NO COLLATION.

After determining the coercibility attribute of each character string in a comparison, your DBMS will choose the relevant Collation using these rules:

- Strings with COERCIBLE coercibility may be compared to strings with any coercibility attribute except NO COLLATION. If both comparands have COERCIBLE coercibility, the relevant Collation is the default Collation of their mutual Character set. If one comparand has COERCIBLE coercibility and the other has EXPLICIT coercibility, the relevant Collation is the EXPLICIT Collation. If one comparand has COERCIBLE coercibility and the other has IMPLICIT coercibility, the relevant Collation is the IMPLICIT Collation.

- Strings with EXPLICIT coercibility may be compared to strings with any coercibility attribute. If one comparand has EXPLICIT coercibility and the other has COERCIBLE, IMPLICIT, or NO COLLATION coercibility, the relevant Collation is the EXPLICIT Collation. If both comparands have EXPLICIT coercibility, they must also have the same Collation. The relevant Collation is their mutual EXPLICIT Collation.
- Strings with IMPLICIT coercibility may be compared to strings with any coercibility attribute except NO COLLATION. If one comparand has IMPLICIT coercibility and the other has COERCIBLE coercibility, the relevant Collation is the IMPLICIT Collation. If one comparand has IMPLICIT coercibility and the other has EXPLICIT coercibility, the relevant Collation is the EXPLICIT Collation. If both comparands have IMPLICIT coercibility, they must also have the same Collation. The relevant Collation is their mutual IMPLICIT Collation.
- Strings with NO COLLATION coercibility may only be compared to strings with a coercibility attribute of EXPLICIT. The relevant Collation is the EXPLICIT Collation.

When you compare character strings that have different lengths, the result also depends on whether the relevant Collation has the PAD SPACE attribute or the NO PAD attribute. If the relevant Collation has the PAD SPACE attribute, your DBMS will extend the shorter character string to the length of the larger string (by padding it on the right with spaces) before comparing the strings. If the relevant Collation has the NO PAD attribute, then — all other things being equal — the longer string will evaluate as greater than the shorter string. That is, with a NO PAD Collation, the result of these rules is that a shorter comparand which is equal to the same-length substring of a larger comparand will evaluate as less than the larger comparand — even if the remainder of the larger string consists only of spaces or control characters. For example, a comparison of these two <literal>s:

```
'BOB'
'BOB      '
```

would result in the first <literal> being evaluated as equal to the second with a PAD SPACE Collation and as less than the second with a NO PAD Collation (assuming that the Collations both use the familiar Latin collating rules).

Here's another example of the difference between the PAD SPACE and the NO PAD attributes for Collations.

```
CREATE TABLE Table_1 (
   char_column CHAR(5));

INSERT INTO Table_1 (char_column)
VALUES ('A');
```

In this example, the string actually inserted is five characters long, i.e.,

```
'A    '
```

Thus, with a PAD SPACE Collation, this predicate is TRUE:

```
   ... WHERE char_column = 'A'
```

and with a NO PAD Collation, the same predicate is FALSE.

To summarize, SQL doesn't allow character strings to be compared unless they belong to the same Character set and have the same Collation for the comparison. You may explicitly specify the relevant Character set or allow it to default to an implicit Character set chosen by your DBMS. You may also explicitly specify the relevant Collation by adding a `COLLATE` clause to your expression; this will override the expression's default collating sequence. If you omit the `COLLATE` clause, your DBMS will choose the relevant Collation for you — for more information, see "Character Strings and Collations" on page 159.

If you want to restrict your code to Core SQL, don't use `CLOB`s or `NCLOB`s in comparisons.

Other Operations

With SQL, you have a wide range of operations that you can perform on character strings or on other values to get a character string result.

Concatenation

The required syntax for a character string concatenation is as follows.

```
character concatenation ::=
character_string_operand_1 || character_string_operand_2
[ COLLATE <Collation name> ]
```

The concatenation operator operates on two operands, each of which must evaluate to character strings belonging to the same Character set. It joins the strings together in the order given and returns a character string with a length equal to the sum of the lengths of its operands. If either of the operands is `NULL`, the result of the operation is also `NULL`. Here are two examples of character string concatenations:

```
'hello' || ' bob'
-- returns hello bob

char_column || 'hello'
-- returns CHAR_COLUMN's value followed by hello
```

[Obscure Rule] If both operands are fixed length character strings, the concatenation result is a fixed length character string with a length equal to the sum of the lengths of the operands — this length may not exceed the maximum allowed for a fixed length character string.

[Obscure Rule] If either operand is a variable length character string and the sum of their lengths is not greater than the maximum allowed length for a variable length character string, the concatenation result is a variable length character string with a length equal to the sum of the lengths of the operands. If the sum of the operands' lengths is greater than the maximum allowed, but the extra characters are all spaces, the concatenation result is a variable length character string with a length equal to the maximum allowed length. If the sum of the operands' lengths is greater than the maximum allowed, and the extra characters are not all spaces, the concatenation will fail; your DBMS will return the `SQLSTATE error 22001` "`data exception-string data, right truncation.`"

[Obscure Rule] The result of a character string concatenation normally has a coercibility attribute and Collation determined by Table 7.2, "Collating sequences and coercibility rules for dyadic operations," (see page 161), but you can use the optional `COLLATE` clause to force

EXPLICIT coercibility with a specific Collation. The Collation named must be a Collation defined for the relevant Character set. If you're using COLLATE in an SQL-Schema statement, then the <AuthorizationID> that owns the containing Schema must have the USAGE Privilege on <Collation name>. If you're using COLLATE in any other SQL statement, then your current <AuthorizationID> must have the USAGE Privilege on <Collation name>. For example,

```
'hello' || 'bob' COLLATE my.collation_1
```

specifies that the result of the concatenation should use a Collation named my.collation_1.

If you want to restrict your code to Core SQL, don't use the concatenation operator with CLOBs or NCLOBs and don't use the COLLATE clause to force an EXPLICIT Collation for any character string concatenation.

Scalar Operations

SQL provides eleven scalar operations that return a character string: the <case expression>, the <cast specification>, the <char substring function>, the <char overlay function>, the <char trim function>, the <fold function>, the <character translation function>, the <form-of-use conversion function>, the <regular expression substring function>, the <specific type function>, and the <niladic user function>. It also provides four scalar functions that operate on character strings, returning a number: the <char position expression>, the <bit length expression>, the <char length expression>, and the <octet length expression>. We'll discuss all but the <specific type function>, the <niladic user function>, the <case expression>, and the <cast specification> here. We've already talked about casting character strings; look for the rest in other chapters. For now, just remember that they all evaluate to a character string and can therefore be used anywhere in SQL that a character string could be used.

<char substring function>

The required syntax for a <char substring function> is as follows.

```
<char substring function> ::=
 SUBSTRING (character_string_argument
    FROM start_argument [ FOR length_argument ]
    [ COLLATE <Collation name> ])
```

SUBSTRING operates on three arguments: the first must evaluate to a character string, the other two must evaluate to exact numeric integers. It extracts a substring from character_string_argument and returns a variable length character string with a maximum length that equals the fixed length or maximum variable length (as applicable) of the character string argument. If any of the arguments are NULL, SUBSTRING returns NULL.

The start_argument is a number that marks the first character you want to extract from character_string_argument. If SUBSTRING includes the (optional) FOR clause, length_argument is the total number of characters you want to extract. If you omit the FOR clause, SUBSTRING will begin at start_argument and extract all the rest of the characters in character_string_argument. Here are some examples of SUBSTRING.

```
SUBSTRING('epiphany' FROM 5)
-- returns hany

SUBSTRING('epiphany' FROM 5 FOR 3)
-- returns han

SUBSTRING(char_column FROM 1 FOR 4)
-- returns the first four characters of the value in CHAR_COLUMN

... WHERE SUBSTRING (char_column FROM 3 FOR 1) = 'A'
-- returns TRUE if the third character of the value in CHAR_COLUMN is the let-
ter A
```

If length_argument is negative, your DBMS will return SQLSTATE error 22011 "data exception-substring error." If start_argument is greater than the length of character_string_argument, or if (start_argument + length_argument) is less than one, SUBSTRING returns a zero-length character string. If start_argument is negative, or if (start_argument + length_argument) is greater than the length of character_string_argument, that's okay — the DBMS just ignores any characters before the start of character_string_argument or after the end of character_string_argument. Note that

```
SUBSTRING('abc' FROM -2 FOR 4)
```

is legal SQL syntax, but pointless because it won't return the "expected" result. The SQL Standard requires SUBSTRING to return 'a' for this operation — not 'ab'.

[Obscure Rule] The result of SUBSTRING belongs to the same Character set that its string argument does. It normally has a coercibility attribute and Collation determined by Table 7.1, "Collating sequences and coercibility rules for monadic operations," (see page 160), where character_string_argument is the monadic operator, but you can use the optional COLLATE clause to force EXPLICIT coercibility with a specific Collation. The Collation named must be a Collation defined for the relevant Character set. If you're using COLLATE in an SQL-Schema statement, then the <AuthorizationID> that owns the containing Schema must have the USAGE Privilege on <Collation name>. If you're using COLLATE in any other SQL statement, then your current <AuthorizationID> must have the USAGE Privilege on <Collation name>. For example,

```
SUBSTRING(char_column FROM 1 FOR 4) COLLATE my.collation_1
```

specifies that the result of SUBSTRING should use a Collation named my.collation_1.

[Obscure Rule] SUBSTRING can also operate on a bit string and a BLOB. We've ignored these options for now — look for them in Chapters 4 and 5 on bit strings and BLOBs.

If you want to restrict your code to Core SQL, don't use SUBSTRING with NCLOBs and don't use the COLLATE clause to force an EXPLICIT Collation for any SUBSTRING operation.

<char overlay function>

The required syntax for a <char overlay function> is as follows.

```
<character overlay function> ::=
OVERLAY (character_string_argument_1
PLACING character_string_argument_2
FROM start_argument [ FOR length_argument ]
[ COLLATE <Collation name> ])
```

OVERLAY operates on four arguments: the first two must evaluate to character strings belonging to the same Character set, the other two must evaluate to exact numeric integers. It extracts a substring from character_string_argument_1, replacing it with character_string_argument_2, and returns the resulting character string. If any of the arguments are NULL, OVERLAY returns NULL.

The start_argument is a number that marks the first character you want to replace in character_string_argument_1. If OVERLAY includes the (optional) FOR clause, length_argument is the total number of characters you want to replace. Thus, start_argument and length_argument identify the portion of character_string_argument_1 you want to replace, while character_string_argument_2 is what you want to replace with. If you omit the FOR clause, then length_argument defaults to the length of character_string_argument_2. Here are some examples of OVERLAY:

```
OVERLAY('epiphany' PLACING 'no' FROM 5)
-- returns epipnony

OVERLAY('epiphany' PLACING 'no' FROM 5 FOR 3)
-- returns epipnoy
```

[Obscure Rule] The result of OVERLAY belongs to the same Character set that its arguments do. It normally has a coercibility attribute and Collation determined by Table 7.2, "Collating sequences and coercibility rules for dyadic operations," (see page 161), but you can use the optional COLLATE clause to force EXPLICIT coercibility with a specific Collation. The Collation named must be a Collation defined for the relevant Character set. If you're using COLLATE in an SQL-Schema statement, then the <AuthorizationID> that owns the containing Schema must have the USAGE Privilege on <Collation name>. If you're using COLLATE in any other SQL statement, then your current <AuthorizationID> must have the USAGE Privilege on <Collation name>. For example,

```
OVERLAY('epiphany' PLACING 'no' FROM 5) COLLATE my.collation_1
```

specifies that the result of OVERLAY should use a Collation named my.collation_1.

[Obscure Rule] OVERLAY can also operate on a BLOB. We've ignored this option for now — look for it in Chapter 5 "Binary Strings."

If you want to restrict your code to Core SQL, don't use OVERLAY with character strings.

<char trim function>

The required syntax for a <char trim function> is as follows.

```
<char trim function> ::=
TRIM ([ [ {LEADING | TRAILING | BOTH} ] [ character_string_argument_1 ]
FROM ] character_string_argument_2
[ COLLATE <Collation name> ])
```

TRIM operates on two arguments, each of which must evaluate to character strings that belong to the same Character set and have the same Collation for the operation. It strips all leading, all trailing, or both leading and trailing trim characters from character_string_argument_2 and returns the resulting variable length character string. The result has a maximum length that equals the fixed length or maximum variable length (as applicable) of character_string_argument_2. If any of the arguments are NULL, TRIM returns NULL.

The trim specification is either LEADING (i.e., trim all leading trim characters), TRAILING (i.e., trim all trailing trim characters) or BOTH (i.e., trim all leading and all trailing trim characters). If this clause is omitted, TRIM defaults to BOTH. For example, these two TRIM functions are equivalent — they both strip away all leading and all trailing letters A:

```
TRIM('A' FROM char_column)
TRIM(BOTH 'A' FROM char_column)
```

The character_string_argument_1 defines the trim character — the character that should be stripped away by the TRIM function. If character_string_argument_1 is omitted, TRIM strips spaces away. For example, these two TRIM functions are equivalent — they both strip away all trailing spaces:

```
TRIM(TRAILING FROM char_column)
TRIM(TRAILING ' ' FROM char_column)
```

These two TRIM functions are equivalent — they both strip away all leading spaces:

```
TRIM(LEADING FROM char_column)
TRIM(LEADING ' ' FROM char_column)
```

These two TRIM functions are equivalent — they both strip away all leading and all trailing spaces:

```
TRIM(char_column)
TRIM(BOTH ' ' FROM char_column)
```

If the length of character_string_argument_1 is not one character, TRIM will fail; your DBMS will return the SQLSTATE error 22027 "data exception-trim error."

[Obscure Rule] The result of TRIM belongs to the same Character set that its arguments do. It normally has a coercibility attribute and Collation determined by Table 7.1, "Collating sequences and coercibility rules for monadic operations," (see page 160), where character_string_argument_2 is the monadic operand, but you can use the optional COLLATE clause to force EXPLICIT coercibility with a specific Collation. The Collation named must be a Collation defined for the relevant Character set. If you're using COLLATE in an SQL-Schema statement, then the <AuthorizationID> that owns the containing Schema must have the USAGE Privilege on <Collation name>. If you're using COLLATE in any other SQL statement, then your current <AuthorizationID> must have the USAGE Privilege on <Collation name>. For example,

```
TRIM(BOTH '' FROM char_column) COLLATE my.collation_1
```

specifies that the result of TRIM should use a Collation named my.collation_1.

[Obscure Rule] TRIM can also operate on a BLOB. We've ignored this option for now — look for more in Chapter 5, "Binary Strings."

If you want to restrict your code to Core SQL, don't use TRIM with NCLOBs and don't use the COLLATE clause to force an EXPLICIT Collation for any TRIM operation.

<fold function>

The required syntax for a <fold function> is as follows.

```
<fold function> ::=
{ UPPER | LOWER } (character_string_argument [ COLLATE <Collation name> ])
```

UPPER and LOWER operate on an argument that evaluates to a character string. UPPER converts every lowercase letter in character_string_argument to its corresponding uppercase equivalent, while LOWER converts every uppercase letter in character_string_argument to its corresponding lowercase equivalent. Any character that has no upper- or lowercase equivalent (as applicable) remains unchanged. The conversion reflects the normal rules for letters of the simple Latin 26-letter alphabet — that is, abcdefghijklmnopqrstuvwxyz converts to and from ABCDEFGHIJKLMNOPQRSTUVWXYZ — but it also reflects the normal rules for the accented letters in character_string_argument's Character set, e.g., ö converts to and from Ö.

Both UPPER and LOWER return a character string with a length that equals the fixed length or maximum variable length (as applicable) of character_string_argument. If the character string argument is NULL, UPPER and LOWER return NULL. Here are some examples:

```
UPPER('E. E. Cummings')
-- returns E. E. CUMMINGS

LOWER('E. E. Cummings')
-- returns e. e. cummings

UPPER(LOWER('E. E. Cummings'))
-- returns E. E. CUMMINGS
```

In the last example, UPPER and LOWER do not cancel each other out; the output string is not the same as the input string. Such information loss occurs because fold functions don't affect characters which are already in the right case.

TIP: A string which contains no letters will be the same after UPPER and LOWER, so if you need to test whether a character string contains letters do this:

```
SELECT character_column
FROM   Table_Of_Character_Strings
WHERE  UPPER(character_column) <> LOWER(character_column);
```

Such a query will find '1a 2' but will not find '1$ 2'; thus you can use fold functions to filter out strings which contain letters.

[Obscure Rule] The result of UPPER and LOWER is a fixed length string if character_string_argument is a fixed length string and a variable length string if character_string_argument is a variable length string. In either case, the result belongs to the same Character set that the argument does. It normally has a coercibility attribute and Collation determined by Table 7.1, "Collating sequences and coercibility rules for monadic operations," (see page 160), but you can use the optional COLLATE clause to force EXPLICIT coercibility with a specific Collation. The Collation named must be a Collation defined for the relevant Character set. If you're using COLLATE in an SQL-Schema statement, then the <AuthorizationID> that owns the containing Schema must have the USAGE Privilege on <Collation name>. If you're using COLLATE in any other SQL statement, then your current <AuthorizationID> must have the USAGE Privilege on <Collation name>. For example,

```
UPPER('hello') COLLATE my.collation_1
```

specifies that the result of UPPER should use a Collation named my.collation and

```
LOWER('HELLO') COLLATE my.collation_1
```

specifies that the result of LOWER should use a Collation named my.collation_1.

If you want to restrict your code to Core SQL, don't use the COLLATE clause to force an EXPLICIT Collation for any UPPER or LOWER operation.

<character translation function>

The required syntax for a <character translation function> is as follows.

```
<character translation function> ::=
TRANSLATE (character_string_argument USING <Translation name>
   [ COLLATE <Collation name> ])
```

TRANSLATE operates on an argument that evaluates to a character string. It converts every character in character_string_argument to its corresponding equivalent in another Character set (by changing each character according to some many-to-one or one-to-one mapping) and returns a variable length character string that belongs to the target Character set defined for <Translation name>. If the character string argument is NULL, TRANSLATE returns NULL. Here is an example of TRANSLATE:

```
TRANSLATE('hello' USING my.translation_1)
-- returns a string, equivalent to hello, that belongs to the target Character
set defined for a Translation called MY.TRANSLATION_1
```

(Translations are defined using the CREATE TRANSLATION statement.)

If you're using TRANSLATE in an SQL-Schema statement, then the <AuthorizationID> that owns the containing Schema must have the USAGE Privilege on <Translation name>. If you're using TRANSLATE in any other SQL statement, then your current <AuthorizationID> must have the USAGE Privilege on <Translation name>.

[Obscure Rule] The result of TRANSLATE normally has a coercibility attribute of IMPLICIT and uses the default Collation of the Translation's target Character set, but you can use the optional COLLATE clause to force EXPLICIT coercibility with a specific Collation. The Collation named must be a Collation defined for the target Character set. If you're using COLLATE in an SQL-Schema statement, then the <AuthorizationID> that owns the containing Schema must have the USAGE Privilege on <Collation name>. If you're using COLLATE in any other SQL statement, then your current <AuthorizationID> must have the USAGE Privilege on <Collation name>. For example,

```
TRANSLATE('hello' USING my.translation_1) COLLATE my.collation_1
```

specifies that the result of TRANSLATE should use a Collation named my.collation_1.

If you want to restrict your code to Core SQL, don't use TRANSLATE.

<form-of-use conversion function>

The required syntax for a <form-of-use conversion function> is as follows.

```
<form-of-use conversion function> ::=
CONVERT (character_string_argument USING <Form-of-use conversion name>
[ COLLATE <Collation name> ])
```

CONVERT operates on an argument that evaluates to a character string. It converts every character in character_string_argument to its corresponding equivalent using another Form-of-use and returns the resulting variable length character string. If the character string argument is NULL, CONVERT returns NULL. The following is an example of CONVERT:

```
CONVERT('hello' USING INFORMATION_SCHEMA.new_form)
-- returns a string, equivalent to hello, whose characters are encoded using a
Form-of-use called NEW_FORM
```

A Form-of-use is a character repertoire's encoding scheme — the one-to-one mapping scheme between each character in the repertoire and a set of internal codes (usually 8-bit values) that define how the repertoire's characters are encoded as numbers. (These codes are also used to specify the order of the characters within the repertoire.) Supported Forms-of-use are all predefined by your DBMS and thus belong to INFORMATION_SCHEMA. SQL provides no ability to define your own Forms-of-use.

CONVERT's purpose is to allow you to transfer character strings between SQL-data and your host application, therefore you may only use the function in certain places. When transferring SQL-data to the host, CONVERT is legal only as part of a <select sublist>. For example,

```
SELECT CONVERT(char_column USING INFORMATION_SCHEMA.new_form)
FROM   Table_1
WHERE  char_column = 'hello';
```

When transferring host values into SQL-data, use CONVERT to change any host parameter. For example,

```
INSERT INTO Table_1 (char_column)
VALUES (CONVERT(:char_parameter USING INFORMATION_SCHEMA.new_form));
```

TIP: You might want to use CONVERT to change a character string's encoding scheme from 8-bit to 16-bit.

[NON-PORTABLE] Whether you can use CONVERT or not is non-standard because the SQL Standard requires implementors to define all Forms-of-use supported, but has no requirement that a DBMS must support any Form-of-use at all. However, you can use TRANSLATE to provide an equivalent operation. [OCELOT Implementation] The OCELOT DBMS that comes with this book does not provide support for any Form-of-use.

[Obscure Rule] The result of CONVERT belongs to a Character set that consists of the same character repertoire as that of its argument's Character set, but with a different Form-of-use encoding. It normally has a coercibility attribute of IMPLICIT and uses the default Collation of its Character set, but you can use the optional COLLATE clause to force EXPLICIT coercibility with a specific Collation. The Collation named must be a Collation defined for the target Character set. If you're using COLLATE in an SQL-Schema statement, then the <AuthorizationID> that owns the containing Schema must have the USAGE Privilege on <Collation name>. If you're using COLLATE in any other SQL statement, then your current <AuthorizationID> must have the USAGE Privilege on <Collation name>. For example,

```
CONVERT('hello' USING INFORMATION_SCHEMA.new_form) COLLATE my.collation_1
```

specifies that the result of CONVERT should use a Collation named my.collation_1.

If you want to restrict your code to Core SQL, don't use CONVERT.

<regular expression substring function>

The required syntax for a <regular expression substring function> is as follows.

```
<regular expression substring function> ::=
SUBSTRING (character_string_argument FROM pattern FOR escape_character
[ COLLATE <Collation name> ])
```

SUBSTRING operates on three arguments, all of which evaluate to character strings that belong to the same Character set. It extracts a substring based on pattern from character_string_argument and returns a variable length character string with a maximum length that equals the fixed length or maximum variable length (as applicable) of character_string_argument. Both pattern and escape_character must be regular expressions (see our discussion of the SIMILAR predicate) and escape_character must be exactly one character long. If any of the arguments are NULL, SUBSTRING returns NULL.

The pattern shows the substring you want to extract from character_string_argument. It's actually a triple pattern; it must consist of three regular expressions, the middle of which is a tagged regular expression (a regular expression that is delimited by escape_character immediately followed by a double quote sign). For example, if your escape character is ?, then pattern must contain ?" exactly two times, as in:

```
'The rain?"%?"Spain'
```

The three parts of pattern — start pattern ?"middle pattern?" end pattern — must match character_string_argument's start, middle and end, that is, the expression:

```
'character_string_argument' SIMILAR TO 'pattern'
```

must be TRUE if the "escape <double quote>" markers are stripped from the pattern. If that's not the case — that is, if the start or end patterns aren't in the string — SUBSTRING returns NULL. Otherwise the result of SUBSTRING is character_string_argument's middle string which corresponds to the middle pattern. Thus, for the SUBSTRING function,

```
SUBSTRING('The rain in Spain' FROM 'The rain?"%?"Spain' FOR '?')
```

the result is ' in ' — that is, the return from SUBSTRING is the string of characters which appears between the start pattern ('The rain') and the end pattern ('Spain').

[Obscure Rule] The result of SUBSTRING belongs to the same Character set as its string arguments. It normally has a coercibility attribute and Collation determined by Table 7.1, "Collating sequences and coercibility rules for monadic operations," (see page 160), where character_string_argument is the monadic operator, but you can use the optional COLLATE clause to force EXPLICIT coercibility with a specific Collation. The Collation named must be a Collation defined for the relevant Character set. If you're using COLLATE in an SQL-Schema statement, then the <AuthorizationID> that owns the containing Schema must have the USAGE Privilege on <Collation name>. If you're using COLLATE in any other SQL statement, then your current <AuthorizationID> must have the USAGE Privilege on <Collation name>. For example:

```
SUBSTRING(char_column FROM 'hi/"[b-o]/"by' FOR '/') COLLATE my.collation_1
```

specifies that the result of SUBSTRING should use a Collation named my.collation_1.

If you want to restrict your code to Core SQL, don't use the <regular expression substring function> form of SUBSTRING.

<char position expression>

The required syntax for a <char position expression> is as follows.

```
<char position expression> ::=
POSITION (character_string_argument_1 IN character_string_argument_2)
```

POSITION operates on two arguments, each of which must evaluate to character strings that belong to the same Character set. It determines the first character position (if any) at which character_string_argument_1 is found in character_string_argument_2 and returns this as an exact numeric integer. If either of the arguments are NULL, POSITION returns NULL. If character_string_argument_1 is a zero-length character string, POSITION returns one. If character_string_argument_1 is not found in character_string_argument_2, POSITION returns zero. Here are some examples of POSITION:

```
POSITION('is' IN 'mistake')
-- returns 2

POSITION('yy' IN 'mistake')
-- returns 0

POSITION('' IN 'mistake')
-- returns 1
```

[NON-PORTABLE] The precision of POSITION's result is non-standard because the SQL Standard requires implementors to define the result's precision. [OCELOT Implementation] The OCELOT DBMS that comes with this book gives the result of POSITION an INTEGER <data type>.

[Obscure Rule] POSITION can also operate on a bit string and a BLOB. We've ignored these options for now — look for them in Chapter 4 "Bit Strings," and Chapter 5 "Binary Strings."

If you want to restrict your code to Core SQL, don't use POSITION with character strings.

<bit length expression>

The required syntax for a <bit length expression> is as follows.

```
<bit length expression> ::=
BIT_LENGTH (character_string_argument)
```

BIT_LENGTH operates on an argument that evaluates to a character string. It determines the length of the argument, in bits, and returns this as an exact numeric integer, e.g., BIT_LENGTH('hello') returns 40 (assuming that an 8-bit Character set is in use). If the argument is NULL, BIT_LENGTH returns NULL.

TIP: The length of a character string argument depends on the Character set it belongs to. Most Character sets are 8-bit sets, so BIT_LENGTH would return 8 for each character in your argument. But if you're using Unicode, remember that BIT_LENGTH will allot 16 bits for each character.

TIP: BIT_LENGTH will return the total length of your character string argument — including any trailing (or leading) spaces. If you're looking for the length of the significant value only, use TRIM with BIT_LENGTH. For example:

```
BIT_LENGTH('hello   ')
-- returns 64; the length of hello followed by 3 spaces
BIT_LENGTH(TRIM('hello   '))
-- returns 40; the length of hello
```

[NON-PORTABLE] The precision of BIT_LENGTH's result is non-standard because the SQL Standard requires implementors to define the result's precision. [OCELOT Implementation] The OCELOT DBMS that comes with this book gives the result of BIT_LENGTH an INTEGER <data type>.

[Obscure Rule] BIT_LENGTH can also operate on a bit string and a BLOB. We've ignored these options for now — look for them in Chapter 4 "Bit Strings," and Chapter 5 "Binary Strings."

If you want to restrict your code to Core SQL, don't use BIT_LENGTH with NCLOBs.

<char length expression>

The required syntax for a <char length expression> is as follows.

```
<char length expression> ::=
{CHAR_LENGTH | CHARACTER_LENGTH} (character_string_argument)
```

CHAR_LENGTH (or CHARACTER_LENGTH) operates on an argument that evaluates to a character string. It determines the length of the argument, in characters, and returns this as an exact numeric integer, e.g., CHAR_LENGTH('hello') returns 5. If the argument is NULL, CHAR_LENGTH returns NULL.

TIP: CHAR_LENGTH will return the total length of your character string argument — including any trailing (or leading) spaces. If you're looking for the length of the significant value only, use TRIM with CHAR_LENGTH. For example:

```
CHAR_LENGTH('hello   ')
-- returns 8; the length of hello followed by 3 spaces
CHAR_LENGTH(TRIM('hello   '))
-- returns 5; the length of hello
```

TIP: CHAR_LENGTH returns the number of Latin letters in your character string argument. For example, if your argument is 'Chorizo' and you're using a Spanish Collation, the second character is 'h' — it is not 'o' despite the digraph, because CHAR_LENGTH doesn't care about the Collation. Thus,

```
CHAR_LENGTH('Chorizo') COLLATE my.spanish_collation
```

returns 7, not 6.

[NON-PORTABLE] The precision of CHAR_LENGTH's result is non-standard because the SQL Standard requires implementors to define the result's precision. [OCELOT Implementation] The OCELOT DBMS that comes with this book gives the result of CHAR_LENGTH an INTEGER <data type>.

[Obscure Rule] CHAR_LENGTH can also operate on a bit string and a BLOB. We've ignored these options for now — look for them in Chapter 4 "Bit Strings," and Chapter 5 "Binary Strings."

If you want to restrict your code to Core SQL, don't use CHAR_LENGTH with NCLOBs.

<octet length expression>

The required syntax for an <octet length expression> is as follows.

```
<octet length expression> ::=
OCTET_LENGTH (character_string_argument)
```

OCTET_LENGTH operates on an argument that evaluates to a character string. It determines the length of the argument, in octets, and returns this as an exact numeric integer, e.g., OCTET_LENGTH('hello') returns 5 (assuming that an 8-bit Character set is in use; the octet length of a string is the bit length divided by 8, rounded up.) If the argument is NULL, OCTET_LENGTH returns NULL.

TIP: The length of a character string argument depends on the Character set to which it belongs. Most Character sets are 8-bit sets, so OCTET_LENGTH would return 1 for each character in your argument. But if you're using Unicode, remember that OCTET_LENGTH will allot 2 octets for each character.

TIP: OCTET_LENGTH will return the total length of your character string argument — including any trailing (or leading) spaces. If you're looking for the length of the significant value only, use TRIM with OCTET_LENGTH. For example:

```
OCTET_LENGTH('hello   ')
-- returns 8; the length of hello followed by 3 spaces
OCTET_LENGTH(TRIM('hello   '))
-- returns 5; the length of hello
```

[NON-PORTABLE] The precision of OCTET_LENGTH's result is non-standard because the SQL Standard requires implementors to define the result's precision. [OCELOT Implementation] The OCELOT DBMS that comes with this book gives the result of OCTET_LENGTH an INTEGER <data type>.

[Obscure Rule] OCTET_LENGTH can also operate on a bit string and a BLOB. We've ignored these options for now — look for them in Chapter 4 "Bit Strings," and Chapter 5 "Binary Strings."

If you want to restrict your code to Core SQL, don't use OCTET_LENGTH with NCLOBs.

Set Functions

SQL provides four set functions that operate on CHAR, VARCHAR, NCHAR, and NCHAR VARYING character strings: COUNT, MAX, MIN, and GROUPING. SQL also provides two set functions that operate on CLOB and NCLOB character strings: COUNT and GROUPING. Since none of these operate exclusively with character string arguments, we won't discuss them here; look for them in Chapter 33 "Searching with Groups."

Predicates

In addition to the comparison operators, SQL provides ten other predicates that operate on CHAR, VARCHAR, NCHAR, and NCHAR VARYING character strings: the <like predicate>, the <similar predicate>, the <between predicate>, the <in predicate>, the <null predicate>, the <exists predicate>, the <unique predicate>, the <match predicate>, the <quantified predicate>, and the <distinct predicate>. SQL also provides five predicates that operate on CLOB and NCLOB character strings: the <like predicate>, the <similar predicate>, the <null predicate>, the <exists predicate>, and the <quantified predicate>. Each will return a boolean value; either TRUE, FALSE, or UNKNOWN. Only the <like predicate> and the <similar predicate> operate strictly on strings; we'll discuss them here. Look for the rest in Chapter 29 "Simple Search Conditions."

<like predicate>

The required syntax for a <like predicate> is as follows.

```
<like predicate> ::=
character_string_argument [ NOT ] LIKE pattern [ ESCAPE escape_character ]
```

LIKE is a predicate that operates on three operands that evaluate to character strings belonging to the same Character set — it searches for values that contain a given pattern. NOT LIKE is the converse and lets you search for values that don't contain a given pattern. The character_string_argument is the character string you're searching within, the pattern is the pattern you're searching for, and the optional escape_character is a character that tells your DBMS to treat a metacharacter in the pattern as itself (rather than as a metacharacter). If character_string_argument contains the pattern, LIKE returns TRUE and NOT LIKE returns FALSE. If character_string_argument does not contain the pattern, LIKE returns FALSE and NOT LIKE returns TRUE. If any of the operands are NULL, LIKE and NOT LIKE return UNKNOWN.

The pattern you specify in pattern may contain any combination of regular characters and metacharacters. Any single character in pattern that is not a metacharacter or the escape_character represents itself in the pattern. For example, the predicate:

```
char_column LIKE 'A'
```

is TRUE for 'A'.

Special significance is attached to metacharacters in a pattern. The metacharacters are: _ and %. If the predicate doesn't include an ESCAPE clause, the metacharacters are interpreted as follows:

- _ An underscore character means "any single character." For example, the predicate:

  ```
  char_column LIKE 'A_C'
  ```

  is TRUE for 'A C', 'AAC', 'ABC', 'A#C', and so on.
- % A percent sign means "any string of zero or more characters." For example, the predicate:

  ```
  char_column LIKE 'A%C'
  ```

  is TRUE for 'AC', 'A C', 'AxC', 'AxxxxxxxxC', and so on.

If you want to search for a character that would normally be interpreted as a metacharacter, you must use the optional ESCAPE clause. To do so,

1. Pick a character that you won't need in the pattern and designate it as your escape character.
2. In the pattern, use your escape character followed immediately by the metacharacter, to designate the metacharacter as a character you want to search for. For example,

   ```
   ... LIKE 'B$%'
   ```

   (without an ESCAPE clause) means "like the letter B followed by a dollar sign followed by anything at all," while,

   ```
   ... LIKE 'B$?%' ESCAPE '?'
   ```

   means "like the letter B followed by a dollar sign followed by a percent sign" (since % is preceded by the escape character it has no special significance in this pattern). Your escape character can also be followed by itself in the pattern, if you want to search for the escape character. For example,

   ```
   ... LIKE 'B$??' ESCAPE '?'
   ```

   means "like the letter B followed by a dollar sign followed by a question mark" (since ? is preceded by the escape character it has no special significance in this pattern). Your best choice for an escape character is an SQL special character which isn't a [NOT] LIKE metacharacter. We suggest the question mark.

The escape_character must be exactly one character long. If it isn't, [NOT] LIKE will fail; your DBMS will return the SQLSTATE error 22019 "data exception-invalid escape character." If escape_character is _ or % and that metacharacter is used only once in your pattern, or if escape_character is used without being followed by a metacharacter (or by itself) in your pattern, [NOT] LIKE will fail; your DBMS will return the SQLSTATE error 22025 "data exception-invalid escape sequence." For example, this predicate will result in SQLSTATE 22025:

```
LIKE 'B%B' ESCAPE '%'
```

For the purposes of [NOT] LIKE, a substring of character_string_argument is a sequence of zero or more contiguous characters where each character belongs to exactly one such substring (this includes any trailing spaces in the argument). A substring specifier of pattern is either (*a*) _: an arbitrary character specifier, (*b*) %: an arbitrary string specifier, (*c*) escape_character followed by _ or % or escape_character, or (*d*) any other single character. If character_string_argument and pattern are both variable length character strings with a length of zero, LIKE returns TRUE. LIKE also returns TRUE if pattern is found in character_string_argument. That is, LIKE returns TRUE only if the number of substrings in character_string_argument equals the number of substring specifiers in pattern and the following conditions are also met:

- If the pattern's *n*-th substring specifier is _, then the argument's *n*-th substring must be any single character.
- If the pattern's *n*-th substring specifier is %, then the argument's *n*-th substring must be any sequence of zero or more characters.
- If the pattern's *n*-th substring specifier is any other character, then the argument's *n*-th substring must be equal (in length and character representation) to that substring specifier — without trailing spaces being added to the argument. Note that this means if the pattern is found in the argument, but the lengths don't match, LIKE returns FALSE. For example, these four predicates all return TRUE:

```
'bob' LIKE 'b_b'
'bob' LIKE 'b%b'
'bob   ' LIKE 'b_b   '
'bob   ' LIKE 'b%b   '
```

But the following two predicates return FALSE because of the trailing spaces in character_string_argument that aren't found in pattern:

```
'bob   ' LIKE 'b_b'
'bob   ' LIKE 'b%b'
```

And these two predicates return FALSE because of the trailing spaces in pattern that aren't found in character_string_argument:

```
'bob' LIKE 'b_b   '
'bob' LIKE 'b%b   '
```

Note that this is only a problem with fixed length character string arguments. Here's a more complete example:

```
CREATE TABLE Test_Stuffs (
   column_1 CHAR(4));

INSERT INTO Test_Stuffs (column_1)
VALUES ('ABC');
-- actually inserts 'ABC ' (four characters)

SELECT *
FROM   Test_Stuffs
WHERE  column_1 = 'ABC';
-- works because comparisons will pad the shorter argument (assuming the rele-
vant Collation has the PAD SPACE attribute) so the test is WHERE 'ABC ' = 'ABC '

SELECT *
FROM   Test_Stuffs
WHERE  column_1 LIKE '%C';
-- fails because LIKE never pads the shorter argument, no matter what Collation
is used, so the test is "find a value of any length that ends in C" — and 'ABC '
ends in a space, not in C
```

To get around this, use `TRIM` to get rid of trailing spaces in your `character_string_argument`, like this:

```
SELECT *
FROM   Test_Stuffs
WHERE  TRIM (TRAILING FROM column_1) LIKE '%C';
```

[Obscure Rule] The result of `[NOT] LIKE` belongs to the same Character set as its operands. If you omit the `ESCAPE` clause, then it has a Collation determined by Table 7.3, "Collating sequences used for comparisons," (see page 162), where `character_string_argument` is comparand 1 and `pattern` is comparand 2. If you include the `ESCAPE` clause, then it also has a Collation determined by Table 7.3 where

- comparand 1 is determined by Table 7.2 on page 161 where `character_string_argument` is operand 1 and `pattern` is operand 2.
- comparand 2 is `escape_character`.

[Obscure Rule] `[NOT] LIKE` can also operate on `BLOB`s. We've ignored this option for now — look for it in Chapter 5 "Binary Strings."

If you want to restrict your code to Core SQL, don't use the `[NOT] LIKE` predicate with `CLOB`s or `NCLOB`s and when you do use `[NOT] LIKE`, make sure your `character_string_argument` is a <Column reference> and that your `pattern` and your `escape_character` are both <value specification>s.

<similar predicate>

The required syntax for a <similar predicate> is as follows.

```
<similar predicate> ::=
character_string_argument [ NOT ] SIMILAR TO pattern
[ ESCAPE escape_character ]
```

SIMILAR is a predicate that operates on three operands that evaluate to character strings belonging to the same Character set. It works much like Unix's grep; it searches for values that contain a given pattern. NOT SIMILAR is the converse and lets you search for values that don't contain a given pattern. The character_string_argument is the character string you're searching within, the pattern is the pattern you're searching for, and the optional escape_character is a character that tells your DBMS to treat a metacharacter in the pattern as itself (rather than as a metacharacter). If character_string_argument contains the pattern, SIMILAR returns TRUE and NOT SIMILAR returns FALSE. If character_string_argument does not contain the pattern, SIMILAR returns FALSE and NOT SIMILAR returns TRUE. If any of the operands are NULL, SIMILAR and NOT SIMILAR return UNKNOWN.

The pattern you specify in pattern must be a regular expression — a sequence of ordinary characters combined with some special characters (or metacharacters). It may contain character ranges, repetitions, and combinations. Any single character in pattern that is not a metacharacter or the escape_character represents itself in the pattern. For example, this predicate,

```
char_column SIMILAR TO 'A'
```

is TRUE for 'A'.

Special significance is attached to metacharacters in a pattern. The metacharacters are: _ and % and * and + and | and (and) and [and] and ^ and - and :. If the predicate doesn't include an ESCAPE clause, the metacharacters are interpreted as follows:

- _ An underscore character means "any single character." For example, this predicate,

  ```
  char_column SIMILAR TO 'A_C'
  ```

  is TRUE for 'A C', 'AAC', 'ABC', 'A#C' and so on.
- % A percent sign means "any string of zero or more characters." For example, this predicate,

  ```
  char_column SIMILAR TO 'A%C'
  ```

  is TRUE for 'AC', 'A C', 'AxC', 'AxxxxxxxxC' and so on.
- * An asterisk means "preceding repeats indefinitely" (from zero to infinity times). For example, this predicate,

  ```
  char_column SIMILAR TO 'A*'
  ```

  is TRUE for '', 'A', 'AA', 'AAA', 'AAAA' and so on.
- + A plus sign means "preceding repeats indefinitely" (from one to infinity times). For example, this predicate,

  ```
  char_column SIMILAR TO 'A+'
  ```

  is TRUE for 'A', 'AA', 'AAA', 'AAAA' and so on.
- [ ] Brackets are used for character enumeration in the pattern. There are two ways to enumerate: as a simple list or with a minus sign, with the result that a match is made with any one of the characters inside the brackets. For example, the predicate,

```
char_column SIMILAR TO '[A]'
```

is TRUE for 'A'. The predicate,

```
char_column SIMILAR TO '[AQZ]'
```

is TRUE for 'A' or 'Q' or 'Z'. The predicate,

```
char_column SIMILAR TO '[A-E]'
```

is TRUE for 'A' or 'B' or 'C' or 'D' or 'E'. And the predicate,

```
char_column SIMILAR TO '[A-EQ-S]'
```

is TRUE for 'A' or 'B' or 'C' or 'D' or 'E' or 'Q' or 'R' or 'S'.

- [^] A circumflex inside enumerating brackets means negative enumeration. The options are the same as for ordinary enumeration, with a negated meaning. For example, the predicate,

```
char_column SIMILAR TO '[^A-C]'
```

is TRUE for anything not equal to 'A' or to 'B' or to 'C'. The predicate,

```
char_column SIMILAR TO '[^AQZ]'
```

is TRUE for anything not equal to 'A' or 'Q' or 'Z'. And the predicate,

```
'ABCDE' SIMILAR TO '%[^C-F]'
```

is FALSE because the last character in the character string argument must not be 'C' or 'D' or 'E' or 'F'.

- [: :] Brackets containing colons surrounding one of ALPHA, UPPER, LOWER, DIGIT, or ALNUM are used for set enumeration in the pattern. For example, the predicate,

```
char_column SIMILAR TO '[:ALPHA:]'
```

is TRUE for values of char_column that are equal to any simple Latin letter, i.e., to any of ABCDEFGHIJKLMNOPQRSTUVWXYZabcdefghijklmnopqrstuvwxyz. This predicate,

```
char_column SIMILAR TO '[:UPPER:]'
```

is TRUE for values of char_column that are equal to any simple Latin uppercase letter, i.e., to any of ABCDEFGHIJKLMNOPQRSTUVWXYZ. The predicate,

```
char_column SIMILAR TO '[:LOWER:]'
```

is TRUE for values of char_column that are equal to any simple Latin lowercase letter, i.e., to any of abcdefghijklmnopqrstuvwxyz. The predicate,

```
char_column SIMILAR TO '[:DIGIT:]'
```

is TRUE for values of char_column that are equal to any digit, i.e., to any of 0123456789. And the predicate,

```
char_column SIMILAR TO '[:ALNUM:]'
```

is TRUE for values of char_column that are equal to any simple Latin letter or to any digit, i.e., to any of ABCDEFGHIJKLMNOPQRSTUVWXYZabcdefghijklmnopqrstuvwxyz0123456789.

- | The vertical bar means "the logical OR of the first and second expressions." For example, the predicate,

```
char_column SIMILAR TO '[A-C]|[:DIGIT:]'
```

is TRUE for any of ABC0123456789. The | operator has a lower priority than * and + have.

- || The concatenation operator means "concatenate one element from first expression with one element from second expression." For example, the predicate,

```
char_column SIMILAR TO '[A-C]||[:DIGIT:]'
```

is TRUE for: 'A0', 'A1', 'A2', 'A3', 'A4', 'A5', 'A6', 'A7', 'A8', 'A9', 'B0', 'B1', 'B2', 'B3', 'B4', 'B5', 'B6', 'B7', 'B8', 'B9', 'C0', 'C1', 'C2', 'C3', 'C4', 'C5', 'C6', 'C7', 'C8', and 'C9'.

- ( ) Parentheses in a pattern force the order of evaluation, in the usual way. For example, the predicate,

  ```
  char_column SIMILAR TO '[:UPPER:]|([:DIGIT:][:DIGIT:])'
  ```

  is TRUE for any single uppercase letter or for any two digits.

- If pattern is not a valid pattern, [NOT] SIMILAR will fail; your DBMS will return the SQLSTATE error 2201B "data exception-invalid regular expression." Here are two examples of invalid patterns:

  ```
  '^[:UPER:]'
  '[:abc:]'
  ```

If you want to search for a character that would normally be interpreted as a metacharacter, you must use the optional ESCAPE clause. To do so:

1. Pick a character that you won't need in the pattern and designate it as your escape character.
2. In the pattern, use your escape character followed immediately by the metacharacter, to designate it as a character you want to search for. For example,

   ```
   ... SIMILAR TO 'B$%'
   ```

   (without an ESCAPE clause) means "similar to the letter B followed by a dollar sign followed by anything at all," while,

   ```
   ... SIMILAR TO 'B$?%' ESCAPE '?'
   ```

   means "similar to the letter B followed by a dollar sign followed by a percent sign" (since % is preceded by the escape character it has no special significance in this pattern). Your escape character can also be followed by itself in the pattern, if you want to search for the escape character. For example,

   ```
   ... SIMILAR TO 'B$??' ESCAPE '?'
   ```

   means "similar to the letter B followed by a dollar sign followed by a question mark" (since ? is preceded by the escape character it has no special significance in this pattern). Your best choice for an escape character is an SQL special character which isn't a [NOT] SIMILAR metacharacter. We suggest the question mark.

The escape_character must be exactly one character long. If it isn't, [NOT] SIMILAR will fail; your DBMS will return the SQLSTATE error 22019 "data exception-invalid escape character." If escape_character is [or] or (or) or | or ^ or - or + or * or _ or % and that metacharacter is used once only in your pattern or if escape_character is used without being followed by a metacharacter (or itself) in your pattern, [NOT] SIMILAR will fail; your DBMS will return the SQLSTATE error 2200C "data exception-invalid use of escape character." For example, this predicate will result in SQLSTATE 2200C:

```
SIMILAR TO 'B?B' ESCAPE '?'
```

If escape_character is a colon and your pattern contains that metacharacter surrounding one of ALPHA, UPPER, LOWER, DIGIT, or ALNUM, [NOT] SIMILAR will fail; your DBMS will return the SQLSTATE error 2200B "data exception-escape character conflict."

[Obscure Rule] The result of `[NOT] SIMILAR` belongs to the same Character set as its operands. If you omit the `ESCAPE` clause, then it has a Collation determined by Table 7.3, "Collating sequences used for comparisons," (see page 162), where `character_string_argument` is comparand 1 and `pattern` is comparand 2. If you include the `ESCAPE` clause, then it also has a Collation determined by Table 7.3 where

- comparand 1 is determined by Table 7.2 on page 161 where `character_string_argument` is operand 1 and `pattern` is operand 2.
- comparand 2 is `escape_character`.

If you want to restrict your code to Core SQL, don't use the `[NOT] SIMILAR` predicate.

Common Checks

Although `[NOT] SIMILAR` is not terribly useful in `WHERE` clauses (it's too inefficient), it is great for `CHECK` clauses. Here are some real-world examples of strings which have rigid format specifications. `[NOT] SIMILAR` is appropriate for making sure the strings meet the specifications.

Postal Codes These strings must be "letter digit letter space digit letter digit" — and the letters must be uppercase simple Latin letters, e.g., `'T5E 1G7'`, `'V1K 4K0'`. To make sure your data fits these requirements, use a simple Domain Constraint:

```
ALTER DOMAIN postal_code
ADD CONSTRAINT postal_code_specs
CHECK (VALUE SIMILAR TO
  '[:UPPER:][:DIGIT:][:UPPER:] [:DIGIT:][:UPPER:][:DIGIT:]');
```

Periodic Table Symbols These strings are either a single uppercase simple Latin letter (e.g., 'H', 'O') or one uppercase and one lowercase letter (e.g., 'Al', 'Fe'). To make sure your data fits these requirements, use another simple Domain Constraint:

```
CREATE DOMAIN periodic_table_element CHAR(2)
CHECK (VALUE SIMILAR TO '[A-Z]|([A-Z][a-z])');
```

North American Telephone Numbers These strings must be "digit digit digit minus-sign digit digit digit digit" — optionally preceded by "left-parenthesis digit digit digit right-parenthesis," e.g., '498-1234' or '(604)498-1234'. This is a hard one; the string includes both an optional format and a special character that needs "escaping." To make sure your data fits these requirements, use a Table Constraint:

```
CREATE TABLE Table_1 (
phone_number CHAR(13),
CHECK (phone_number SIMILAR TO
  '([:DIGIT:][:DIGIT:][:DIGIT:]?-[:DIGIT:][:DIGIT:][:DIGIT:][:DIGIT:])
   |
   (?([:DIGIT:][:DIGIT:][:DIGIT:]?)[:DIGIT:][:DIGIT:][:DIGIT:]?-
   [:DIGIT:][:DIGIT:][:DIGIT:][:DIGIT:])' ESCAPE '?');
```

(This example is shown on multiple lines for clarity; in reality the string may not contain carriage returns, nor would the "pattern.")

[NOT] LIKE or [NOT] SIMILAR?

[NOT] LIKE and [NOT] SIMILAR are both pattern-matching predicates. You should continue to use [NOT] LIKE if the pattern contains only _ and % metacharacters. Although [NOT] SIMILAR can use these metacharacters too, there is no advantage in using an SQL3 expression when an SQL-92 expression will do. For more complex patterns, your choice is between [NOT] SIMILAR and nothing. When you make the switchover, remember that there are subtle differences between [NOT] SIMILAR and [NOT] LIKE, in the way that collating sequences are handled (which affects which characters are regarded as "equal" and whether there are pad spaces at the end of a string).

Character Strings and Character Sets

[Obscure Rule] applies for this entire section.

In the last chapter, we made the observation that a computer character set has two parts: a character repertoire and an agreement on how the repertoire's characters will be encoded as numbers. SQL has a similar rule — an SQL Character set is a combination of two things:

1. A character repertoire — the set of characters that belong to the Character set.
2. A Form-of-use — the repertoire's encoding scheme; the one-to-one mapping scheme between each character in the repertoire and a set of internal codes (usually 8-bit values) that define how the repertoire's characters are encoded as numbers. (These codes are also used to specify the order of the characters within the repertoire.)

All SQL character strings belong to some Character set. Whenever you're working with an SQL character string, you may either specify the Character set to which it belongs, or allow it to belong to a default Character set chosen by your DBMS. (To simplify matters, we recommend that you always follow the latter course. This will ensure that you get standard results across SQL-sessions.)

To explicitly specify a Character set for a character string, add a CHARACTER SET clause to a <data type> specification and/or _<Character set name> to a <literal>, as shown in the appropriate syntax diagrams in this chapter. Your current <AuthorizationID> must have the USAGE Privilege for the Character set named.

If you choose not to specify a Character set for a character string, the current default Character set is implicit. Your DBMS will choose the current default Character set using these rules:

1. A character string <data type> specification (in CREATE SCHEMA, CREATE TABLE, CREATE DOMAIN, ALTER TABLE, and ALTER DOMAIN) that doesn't include an explicit CHARACTER SET clause is treated as if the default Character set of the Schema that the <data type> is defined in was explicitly named in the <data type> specification.

[NON-PORTABLE] In any operation other than defining a Domain, defining a Column, or defining a Field (e.g., in a CAST operation), a character string <data type> specification that doesn't include a CHARACTER SET clause will be treated as if it belongs to a Character set that is non-standard because the SQL Standard requires implementors to define the operation's default Character set. [OCELOT Implementation] The OCELOT DBMS that comes with this book uses `ISO8BIT` — the DBMS's initial default Character set — as the default Character set for such operations.

2. Any other character string value that doesn't include an explicit Character set specification must either consist only of <SQL language character>s or the value's Character set defaults to (*a*) the default Character set of the Schema, if it's found in a `CREATE SCHEMA` statement, (*b*) the default Character set of the SQL-session, if it's found in a dynamic SQL statement, or (*c*) the default Character set of the Module you're running, if it's found in any other SQL statement in a Module.

Every Character set has at least one Collation — its default Collation. You may define additional Collations for any Character set.

If you want to restrict your code to Core SQL, don't explicitly define the Character set in which any character string belongs — always allow it to belong to the default Character set.

Character Strings and Collations

[Obscure Rule] applies for this entire section.

A Collation, or collating sequence, is a set of rules that determines the result when character strings are compared. The result of any character string comparison thus depends on the Collation used — we'll call this the *relevant Collation*. Different Collations might result in different comparison results for the same two strings, e.g., a case-sensitive Collation will determine that the letter "A" and the letter "a" are not equal, but a case-insensitive Collation will determine that "A" and "a" are equal.

Whenever you're comparing an SQL character string, you may either specify the relevant Collation, or allow the comparison to be governed by a default Collation chosen by your DBMS. (To simplify matters, we recommend that you always follow the latter course. This will ensure that you get standard results across SQL-sessions.)

To explicitly specify a Collation for a comparison, add a `COLLATE` clause to your character string, as shown in the appropriate syntax diagrams in this chapter. The Collation you name must either (*a*) be the default Collation for the relevant Character set or (*b*) be defined as a Collation for the relevant Character set by some `CREATE COLLATION` statement. If you're using `COLLATE` in an SQL-Schema statement, then the <AuthorizationID> that owns the containing Schema must have the `USAGE` Privilege on <Collation name>. If you're using `COLLATE` in any other SQL statement, then your current <AuthorizationID> must have the `USAGE` Privilege on <Collation name>.

If you choose not to specify a Collation for a comparison, the current default Collation is implicit. Your DBMS will choose the current default Collation for a character string using the following rules.

First, to choose a character string's default Collation:

- If a character string <data type> specification doesn't include a `COLLATE` clause but does include a `CHARACTER SET` clause, the default Collation for that <data type>'s values is the default Collation of the Character set named.
- If any other character string value doesn't include a `COLLATE` clause, the default Collation for that value is the default Collation of the value's Character set.

Second, to choose one of the comparand's default Collations for the comparison:

- Expressions that involve only non-Columns (i.e., a <literal>, host language variable, parameter, or expression result) are compared using the default Collation for the character string values' mutual Character set.
- Expressions that involve both Columns (i.e., <Column name>s or <Column reference>s) and non-Columns are compared using the Column(s)' mutual default Collation. If you want to compare values from multiple Columns with different default Collations, you must include a `COLLATE` clause in your expression.

Table 7.1 shows how the collating sequence and coercibility attribute are determined for the result of a monadic operation.

Table 7.1 Collating sequences and coercibility rules for monadic operations

OPERAND'S COERCIBILITY ATTRIBUTE	OPERAND'S COLLATION	RESULT'S COERCIBILITY ATTRIBUTE	RESULT'S COLLATION
Coercible	Default	Coercible	Default
Implicit	X	Implicit	X
No Collation	None	No Collation	None
Explicit	X	Explicit	X

Table 7.2 shows how the collating sequence and coercibility attribute are determined for the result of a dyadic operation.

Table 7.2 Collating sequences and coercibility rules for dyadic operations

OPERAND_1'S COERCIBILITY ATTRIBUTE	OPERAND_1'S COLLATION	OPERAND_2'S COERCIBILTY ATTRIBUTE	OPERAND_2'S COLLATION	RESULT'S COERCIBILITY ATTRIBUTE	RESULT'S COLLATION
Coercible	Default	Coercible	Default	Coercible	Default
Coercible	Default	Implicit	X	Implicit	X
Coercible	Default	No Collation	None	No Collation	None
Coercible	Default	Explicit	X	Explicit	X
Implicit	X	Coercible	Default	Implicit	X
Implicit	X	Implicit	X	Implicit	X
Implicit	X	Implicit	Y<>X	No Collation	None
Implicit	X	No Collation	None	No Collation	None
Implicit	X	Explicit	Y	Explicit	Y
No Collation	None	Coercible	Default	No Collation	None
No Collation	None	Implicit	X	No Collation	None
No Collation	None	No Collation	None	No Collation	None
No Collation	None	Explicit	X	Explicit	X
Explicit	X	Coercible	Default	Explicit	X
Explicit	X	Implicit	Y	Explicit	X
Explicit	X	No Collation	None	Explicit	X
Explicit	X	Explicit	X	Explicit	X
Explicit	X	Explicit	Y<>X	invalid syntax	

Table 7.3 shows how the collating sequence is determined for a particular comparison.

Table 7.3 Collating sequences used for comparisons

COMPARAND_1'S COERCIBILITY ATTRIBUTE	COMPARAND_1'S COLLATION	COMPARAND_2'S COERCIBILITY ATTRIBUTE	COMPARAND_2'S COLLATION	COLLATION USED FOR COMPARISON
Coercible	Default	Coercible	Default	Default
Coercible	Default	Implicit	X	X
Coercible	Default	No Collation	None	invalid syntax
Coercible	Default	Explicit	X	X
Implicit	X	Coercible	Default	X
Implicit	X	Implicit	X	X
Implicit	X	Implicit	Y<>X	invalid syntax
Implicit	X	No Collation	None	invalid syntax
Implicit	X	Explicit	Y	Y
No Collation	None	Coercible	Default	invalid syntax
No Collation	None	Implicit	X	invalid syntax
No Collation	None	No Collation	None	invalid syntax
No Collation	None	Explicit	X	X
Explicit	X	Coercible	Default	X
Explicit	X	Implicit	Y	X
Explicit	X	No Collation	None	X
Explicit	X	Explicit	X	X
Explicit	X	Explicit	Y<>X	invalid syntax

Note: For expressions involving more than two comparands, the collating sequence is effectively determined on a cumulative basis; the result for the first two comparands becomes `comparand_1` for the next comparison, the result for this becomes `comparand_1` for the comparison after that, and so on.

Dialects

The "typical" SQL DBMS supports most of the standard character data types, but often uses preferred local names. For example, Oracle has a 2,000-byte maximum (2,048 for Oracle Lite) for the `CHAR` <data type> and offers a (non-standard) LONG VARCHAR type to define larger character string fields.

Sybase allows for a large variety of Character sets, with only one "group" (Character set) allowed at a time. Baltic languages are in the East European group (8859-2) though it doesn't seem possible to get a correct result in this case. Collations supported are: English+French+German (all together!), Spanish, Hungarian, Russian — then everything else is binary. Sybase does not support SQL `CHARACTER SET`s, `COLLATION`s, or `TRANSLATION`s, nor does it support `CONVERT` — to convert you need an offline utility. It does provide some Unicode support.

8

Chapter 8

Temporal Values

In SQL, a *temporal value* is either a datetime (i.e., a date, a clock time, or a timestamp) or an interval (i.e., a span of time). They consist of a contiguous subset of one or more of the datetime fields (in order of significance): YEAR, MONTH, DAY, HOUR, MINUTE, SECOND, TIMEZONE_HOUR, and TIMEZONE_MINUTE. A temporal value may be a <literal>, the value of a parameter or a host language variable, or the result of any expression or argument (including a possibly qualified <Column name>) that evaluates to a date, a time, a timestamp, or an interval. Temporal values must obey the familiar rules for dates and times, i.e., those of the Gregorian calendar and the 24-hour clock.

Datetimes are either dates, times, or timestamps. Dates are stored in the DATE <data type>, times are stored in either the TIME or the TIME WITH TIME ZONE <data type>s, and timestamps are stored in either the TIMESTAMP or the TIMESTAMP WITH TIME ZONE <data type>s.

Intervals are either year–month intervals (spans of time involving years and/or months) or day–time intervals (spans of time involving days and/or hours and/or minutes and/or seconds and/or fractions of a second). They include a qualifier which specifies which of the datetime fields are represented in the interval. All interval values are signed. Intervals are stored in the INTERVAL <data type>.

Some Preliminaries

Before we talk about datetimes and intervals, there is some necessary background to go through. We provide most of this information mainly for reference purposes though. If you decide not to read it thoroughly right now, you'll still understand most of what follows. However, we will be referring to these concepts throughout this chapter.

[Obscure Rule] applies for the rest of this section.

The Gregorian Calendar

The SQL Standard says that all dates must be valid "according to the Gregorian calendar." Most people know the main rules:

- Thirty days hath September, April, June, and November, all the rest have thirty-one, except (the rhyme scheme starts to fail here) February which has 28 days, or 29 in a leap year.
- A leap year occurs every four years.

These first two rules are the rules of the Julian Calendar. Pope Gregory XIII added this exception in 1582:

- A leap year does not occur at the end of a century, except every 400 years, i.e., 1700, 1800, 1900, 2100, 2200, and 2300 are not leap years.

In a majority of practical situations, it's only necessary to know what the Gregorian calendar is and that SQL enforces it. A minority of practical cases, however, involve historians or astronomers. For these cases, let's clear out the wrong ideas about the calendar rules and about the Julian-to-Gregorian transition.

The Julian calendar took effect starting January 1, 45 BC. (It is a nice coincidence that January 1 was the year-start in 45 BC and in our time; we ignore the variations that happened between then and now.) There was some confusion and fiddling until 4 AD (which was not a leap year) but after that, the first two rules held firmly: a leap year every 4 years, with the average "Julian year" being 365.25000 days long. (We now consider the correct period for a year as 365.24220 days, decreasing by about 0.5 seconds per century. The difference, 000.00780 days, is statable as 3 days every 400 years.)

The result meant that by the 1500s, the spring equinox was on March 11th. This violated Church teaching, particularly the finding of the 4th-Century Council of Nicaea, which made clear that the spring equinox is March 21st. To solve the problem, Pope Gregory XIII had to do two things: shift the calendar forward 10 days and change the rules, so that there would no longer be an overestimate of 3 days every 400 years. He therefore decreed that the day after Thursday, October 4th, 1582 should be Friday, October 15th, 1582. The decree took effect immediately in the Papal States and Iberia, after a short delay in France, and by 1700 in most German Protestant states and Scandinavia (though Sweden went back and forth). England held out until 1752 (by which time the discrepancy was 11 days, from September 3rd to September 14th). Japan went Gregorian in 1873, with the proviso that Year #1 is based on the Emperor's reign rather than Christ's birth. China changed in 1911, Russia in 1918, and Greece in 1923. Even among Moslem countries, the only non-fully-gregorianized significant holdout, there has been a breakaway: Turkey, which converted in 1927.

As we said earlier, the switch to the Gregorian calendar doesn't affect most of us — but it has caused some problems for groups like historians and astronomers who use SQL.

The first problem is that SQL allows dates like `DATE '1582-10-14'` — even though, according to Pope Gregory, there was no such date. Also, any Gregorian date before October 3rd, 1582 is what the Oxford Concise Dictionary calls "*prolepsis*: ...representation of thing as existing before it actually does or did so." (When Americans observed Washington's birthday on February 22nd, they were proleptic; he was born on February 11 OS where the initials

"OS" stand for "Old Style," i.e., Julian.) Going the other way, into the future, there will certainly have to be more tweaking because the Pope's rules do not remove all drift.

The second problem is that, although it serves many purposes well, the Gregorian calendar is inevitably non-decimal. It would be simpler to begin with a fixed moment far in the past — noon on January 1st, 4713 BC, for example — and count how many million days have elapsed since then, with no regard for higher units or any calendar rules. This is the system of "Julian days." Since a Julian day is expressible as a `DECIMAL`, there is no need for a separate data type for such values. Some ephemerides tables use Julian days, so if your project involves astronomy look for a DBMS that can convert a Julian day to a (proleptic Gregorian) `DATE`. Standard SQL DBMSs can't because they may only allow for dates starting with 0001 AD.

Leap Seconds

The earth's revolutions are getting shorter; it goes round the sun about 0.5 seconds faster than it did in 1900. We point this out for the sake of people who define "1 year" as "1 earth revolution period" — that kind of year is getting shorter, but the other kind, the "civil year," isn't. Here's why.

The earth's rotations are getting longer; it turns on its axis about 0.04 seconds slower than it did in 1900. A bit of the slowdown is due to tidal friction but mostly we're looking at an irregular and unpredictable fluctuation — indeed, for all we know, the rotation may get faster in future. We point this out for the sake of people who define "1 day" as "the average period between two sunrises" which is closely linked to the earth's rotation period. You can keep that definition, but you should see that such a shifty period cannot be the standard in a precise measurement system.

The resonance of a caesium-133 atom is getting neither shorter nor longer. Its electrons change spin (relative to the nucleus) at a constant frequency. So the International System of Units bases its definition of a "second" on a caesium clock, thus: "the duration of 9,192,631,770 periods of the radiation corresponding to [the shift between parallel and anti-parallel electron spin] of the caesium-133 atom." The official second is this atomic second and since 1972, we have defined a day as 60560524 atomic seconds.

At one instant, the standard day was the same as the day-derived-from-rotation. But since the latter fluctuates, the two figures won't stay in synch. Yet we must synch them, else the number of days in a year would change fractionally with each revolution. The solution: when the atomic-second time gains/loses relative to the from-rotation time, add/drop 1 or 2 seconds in the last second of the last day of a month. In practice, it has always been necessary to add and the change has always been on June 30th or December 31st. Since we are adding to the year, the term *leap second* is good by analogy.

The day-derived-from-rotation time is known as "Universal Time 1" (UT1); corrected for polar wobble, it is used for celestial navigation. The day-based-purely-on-atomic-clock time is known as "International Atomic Time" (TAI); it represents the consensus of several caesium clocks as monitored by a standards bureau in France. The atomic-but-synched-with-UT1-by-leap-seconds time is "Co-ordinated Universal Time" (UTC). It is this last time, UTC, which matters for time signals, for SQL, and for us. Do not confuse UTC with the old standard "Greenwich Mean Time" (GMT) — GMT was a variant of UT1 that used a different method to correct for fluctuations. Beware of two prevalent but false opinions: that years are not getting longer (they are), or that UTC is a renaming of GMT (it is not). The distinctions are tiny, but any program which uses leap seconds or fractional seconds is getting into magnitudes which are smaller than those tiny distinctions.

Knowing what leap seconds are, we can move at last to their use in SQL:

- First, the Standard requires a DBMS to extend the range of seconds-field values to "less than 62" (rather than "less than 60") and thus, account for up to 2 positive leap seconds. (There is a GOTCHA here: leap seconds should always be for the last minute of a day, as in `TIME '23:59:60'`, but the Standard allows erroneous values like `TIME '12:34:60'`.)
- Second, because of leap seconds, it isn't possible to tell whether `TIME '23:59:58'` is two seconds before midnight, one second before midnight (leap seconds can be negative, though it has never happened), or as much as four seconds before midnight. The information is simply not present in the syntax of a `TIME` expression, nor derivable from any Table. Thus, arithmetic with carrying has uncertainty. Not surprisingly, the SQL Standard states that any expressions which involve leap-seconded `TIME`s will show implementation-defined results.

Time Zones

In 330 BC, a lunar eclipse was seen at Arbela around 3 AM and in Carthage around midnight. The ancient Greeks knew how eclipses worked so this was one proof that the earth was round (other proofs were that the sun got higher in the sky as one travelled south and that one could still see ships' masts after their hulls disappeared below the horizon). In our terms, Aristotle and Company were seeing that our anchor point of midnight — the halfway point between dusk and dawn — must change with longitude.

Nowadays, we mark the world off into *time zones* with one time zone equal to about 15 degrees of longitude. Time zones are political divisions that allow us to use the convention that all locations in a time zone have the same time, known as *local time*. Thus, although times and timestamps are supposed to represent an absolute time of day (times) and an absolute time of a specific day (timestamps), they can have ambiguous meanings when an SQL-environment spans multiple time zones. The SQL Standard tries to cater both to users who have only local dealings and thus care only about local time and to users who operate across time zones. It does this by providing a <time zone interval> option for time and timestamp values. A value without a <time zone interval> (e.g., a `TIME` or `TIMESTAMP` <data type>) may represent local time or UTC time, while a value with a <time zone interval> (e.g., a `TIME WITH TIME ZONE` or `TIMESTAMP WITH TIME ZONE` <data type>) always represents the UTC time. Unless your SQL-environment spans multiple time zones and you have a need for "real time" database operations, the entire matter of time zones probably won't concern you. In that case, be sure to define your time and timestamp fields with the `TIME` and `TIMESTAMP` <data type>s; don't use the `TIME WITH TIME ZONE` or the `TIMESTAMP WITH TIME ZONE` <data type>s at all. If, however, "real time" operations are vital, you may want to define time and timestamp fields with the `TIME WITH TIME ZONE` and `TIMESTAMP WITH TIME ZONE` <data type>s.

<time zone interval>

The required syntax for a <time zone interval> is as follows.

```
<time zone interval> ::=
   {+ | -} HH:MM
```

A <time zone interval> specifies a time or timestamp value's time zone offset from UTC. It has a <data type> of `INTERVAL HOUR TO MINUTE`.

`HH` is 2 digits (ranging from 0 to 13) representing the number of hours (called `TIMEZONE_HOUR`s) in the time zone offset and `MM` is 2 digits (ranging from 0 to 59) representing the number of additional minutes (called `TIMEZONE_MINUTE`s) in the time zone offset. For example, the following represents a <time zone interval> of 3 hours:

```
+3:00
```

A <time zone interval>'s mandatory sign — either + (plus) or - (minus) — indicates whether the time zone offset is added to or subtracted from the UTC time to obtain the local time. The valid range of <time zone interval>s is from –12:59 to +13:00. Any operation that attempts to specify a <time zone interval> that is not within this range will fail; your DBMS will return the `SQLSTATE error 22009` "`data exception-invalid time zone displacement value.`"

A time or timestamp value that doesn't include a <time zone interval> represents a time in the SQL-session's current default time zone, that is, it represents a local time. A time or timestamp value that does include a <time zone interval> represents a time in the specified time zone.

If you want to restrict your code to Core SQL, don't use <time zone interval>s.

Time Zone Example

Time zones start at zero longitude (the Prime Meridian) which goes through Greenwich, Britain. The time zones West Of Greenwich ("Wogs") are behind UTC because the earth rotates from west to east. Therefore, when it's 12:00 UTC, it's only 8:30 AM in Newfoundland and even earlier as we go west from there. The time zones East Of Greenwich ("Eogs") are ahead of UTC, so when it's 12:00 UTC, it's already 5:30 PM in Delhi, India and even later as we go east from there. Consider this timeline:

+8:00	+5:00	+0:00	–2:00	–5:30
Vancouver	Detroit	Greenwich	Moscow	Delhi

The numbers on the timeline indicate the time zones' offsets from UTC in hours and minutes. (The math is somewhat counterintuitive, since the SQL Standard requires you to subtract the offset from the local time to calculate UTC.) A time zone's offset from UTC is its <time zone interval>.

As an example, consider an SQL-environment with three installations: one in Vancouver, Canada (with a default time zone offset of +8:00), one in London, England (with a default time zone offset of +0:00), and one in Delhi, India (with a default time zone offset of –5:30). All three installations have access to this Table:

```
CREATE TABLE Time_Examples (
   Time_Local TIMESTAMP,
   Time_With_Time_Zone TIMESTAMP WITH TIME ZONE);
```

A user at the London installation adds the following row to the Table.

```
INSERT INTO Time_Examples (Time_Local, Time_With_Time_Zone)
VALUES (TIMESTAMP '1995-07-15 07:30', TIMESTAMP '1995-07-15 07:30');
```

Now, to a user at the Vancouver installation, this moment in time is equivalent to a local timestamp of '1995-07-14 23:30' (Vancouver time is 8 hours earlier than London time) and to a user at the Delhi installation, the same moment in time is equivalent to a local timestamp of '1995-07-15 13:00' (Delhi time is 5.5 hours after London time). So, despite the fact that "1995-07-15 07:30", "1995-07-14 23:30", and "1995-07-15 13:00" look like three different values, in this case, they all represent the same absolute moment in time. If each user now does a SELECT on the Table, this is the result they'll see:

TIME_LOCAL	TIME_WITH_TIME_ZONE	
1995-07-15 07:30:00	1995-07-14 23:30:30-8:00	-- in Vancouver
1995-07-15 07:30:00	1995-07-15 07:30:00+0:00	-- in London
1995-07-15 07:30:00	1995-07-15 13:00:00+5:30	-- in Delhi

Note that the value in the TIME_LOCAL Column stays the same regardless of the installation; a time or timestamp without a <time zone interval> always means "local time" unless the application requires it to take on a time zone offset. The value in the TIME_WITH_TIME_ZONE Column, however, changes with the installation — this is because the <timestamp literal> was forced to take on the default time zone offset at each installation. In this example, the UTC time is equal to the London local time of '1995-07-15 07:30', i.e., when the London user selects from the Table, the display reads:

```
'1995-07-15 07:30+00:00'
```

to show that the local time is the same as the UTC time; that is, it must be offset by 0 hours and 0 minutes to a UTC time of:

```
'1995-07-15 07:30'
```

When the Vancouver user does the same SELECT, however, the display reads:

```
'1995-07-14 23:30-08:00'
```

to show that the local time is 8 hours less than the UTC time; that is, it must be offset by 8 hours and 0 minutes to a UTC time of:

```
'1995-07-15 07:30'
```

And when the Delhi user does the same SELECT, the display reads:

```
'1995-07-15 13:00+05:30'
```

to show that the local time is 5.5 hours greater than the UTC time; that is, it must be offset –5 hours and 30 minutes to a UTC time of:

```
'1995-07-15 07:30'
```

Time Zone Offset Arithmetic

Earlier we said that time zone offset arithmetic is somewhat counterintuitive — here's a more detailed explanation. Recall that a time zone offset is the difference between local time and UTC time — say, for example, 4 hours. Then,

- In the case of a time zone that is 4 hours earlier than UTC (e.g., 12:00 local is 16:00 UTC), the time zone offset is –04:00 (i.e., local time is 4 hours less than UTC time).
- In the case of a time zone that is 4 hours later than UTC (e.g., 16:00 UTC is 20:00 local), the time zone offset is +04:00 (i.e., local time is 4 hours plus UTC time).

The rule: to get the UTC value, subtract the time zone offset from the time or timestamp. Thus, a local time of '12:00-04:00' evaluates to UTC 16:00 (add the 4 hours, you're subtracting a negative) and a local time of '20:00+04:00' evaluates to UTC 16:00 (subtract the 4 hours).

Temporal <literal>s

A temporal <literal> is any temporal value in one of two categories: datetimes and intervals.

Datetime <literal>s

A datetime <literal> is either a <date literal>, a <time literal>, or a <timestamp literal>. Datetime <literal>s must obey the familiar rules for dates and times, i.e., those of the Gregorian calendar and the 24-hour clock.

<date literal>

A <date literal> represents a date in the Gregorian calendar. The required syntax for a <date literal> is as follows.

```
<date literal> ::=
DATE 'yyyy-mm-dd'
```

yyyy is 4 digits (ranging from 1 to 9999) representing a YEAR, mm is 2 digits (ranging from 1 to 12) representing a MONTH in the specified year, and dd is 2 digits (ranging from 1 to 31, depending on the month) representing a DAY of the specified month. For example, this <date literal> represents July 15, 1997:

```
DATE '1997-07-15'
```

The valid range of dates is from DATE '0001-01-01' (January 1, 1 AD) to DATE '9999-12-31' (December 31, 9999 AD).

A <date literal>'s <data type> is DATE.

<time literal>

A <time literal> represents a time of day. The required syntax for a <time literal> is as follows.

```
<time literal> ::=
TIME 'hh:mm:ss[.[nnnnnn]][ <time zone interval> ]'
```

hh is 2 digits (ranging from 0 to 23) representing an HOUR on a 24 hour clock, mm is 2 digits (ranging from 0 to 59) representing a MINUTE within the specified hour, and ss is 2 digits (ranging from 0 to 61) representing a SECOND within the specified minute (SQL allows for the addition of up to 2 "leap" seconds in a valid time). For example, this <time literal> represents 1:35:16 PM:

```
TIME '13:35:16'
```

The optional .nnnnnn, if specified, is a period followed by an unsigned integer and represents a fraction of a second within the specified second — this is the time value's *fractional seconds precision*. The minimum fractional seconds precision and the default fractional seconds precision are both zero. For example, these three <time literal>s all represent 1:35:16 PM:

```
TIME '13:35:16'
TIME '13:35:16.'
TIME '13:35:16.00'
```

The following <time literal> represents 1:35:16 and one-hundredth of a second PM:

```
TIME '13:35:16.01'
```

[NON-PORTABLE] The valid range of times must include, at a minimum, all times from `TIME '00:00:00'` to `TIME '23:59:61.999999'` but is non-standard because the SQL Standard requires implementors to define the maximum fractional seconds precision for time values. [OCELOT Implementation] The OCELOT DBMS that comes with this book allows <time literal>s to have a fractional seconds precision up to 6 digits long. This allows you to deal with times ranging from whole seconds to millionths of a second.

[Obscure Rule] A <time literal> may include a <time zone interval> to specify the value's time zone offset. A <time literal> without a <time zone interval> represents a time in the SQL-session's current default time zone, that is, it represents a local time. A <time literal> that includes a <time zone interval> represents a time in the specified time zone. For example, this <time literal> represents 12:35 and 16.5 seconds AM with a time zone offset of 3 hours and 15 minutes (UTC 09:20:16.5):

```
TIME '12:35:16.5+03:15'
```

The following <time literal> represents the local time 12:35 and 16.5 seconds AM:

```
TIME '12:35:16.5'
```

A <time literal> without a <time zone interval> has a <data type> of `TIME(fractional seconds precision)` though it is compatible with the `TIME` and `TIME WITH TIME ZONE` <data type>s. For example, the <literal>:

```
TIME '13:35:16'
```

has a <data type> of `TIME` and the <literal>:

```
TIME '13:35:16.01'
```

has a <data type> of `TIME(2)`.

[Obscure Rule] A <time literal> with a <time zone interval> has a <data type> of `TIME(fractional seconds precision) WITH TIME ZONE` though it is compatible with the `TIME` and `TIME WITH TIME ZONE` <data type>s. For example, the <literal>:

```
TIME '13:35:16.5+10:30'
```

has a <data type> of `TIME(1) WITH TIME ZONE`.

If you want to restrict your code to Core SQL, don't add a fractional seconds precision or a <time zone interval> to your time values.

<timestamp literal>

A <timestamp literal> represents a time of a given day. The required syntax for a <timestamp literal> is as follows.

```
<timestamp literal> ::=
TIMESTAMP 'date value <space> time value'
```

that is,

```
TIMESTAMP 'yyyy-mm-dd hh:mm:ss[.[nnnnnn]][ <time zone interval> ]'
```

As with dates, yyyy is 4 digits representing a YEAR, mm is 2 digits representing a MONTH in the specified year, and dd is 2 digits representing a DAY of the specified month. As with times, hh is 2 digits representing an HOUR within the specified day, mm is 2 digits representing a MINUTE within the specified hour, ss is 2 digits representing a SECOND within the specified minute, and the optional .nnnnnn represents a fraction of a second within the specified second. For example, this <timestamp literal> represents 1:35:16 PM on July 15, 1997:

```
TIMESTAMP '1997-07-15 13:35:16'
```

The following <timestamp literal> represents 1:35:16 and one-hundredth of a second PM on July 15, 1997:

```
TIMESTAMP '1997-07-15 13:35:16.01'
```

[NON-PORTABLE] The valid range of timestamps must include, at a minimum, all timestamps from TIMESTAMP '0001-01-01 00:00:00' to TIMESTAMP '9999-12-31 23:59:61.999999' but is non-standard because the SQL Standard requires implementors to define the maximum fractional seconds precision for timestamp values. [OCELOT Implementation] The OCELOT DBMS that comes with this book allows <timestamp literal>s to have a fractional seconds precision up to 6 digits long. This allows you to deal with timestamps whose time values range from whole seconds to millionths of a second.

[Obscure Rule] A <timestamp literal> may include a <time zone interval>. As with times, a <timestamp literal> without a <time zone interval> represents a local timestamp, while a <timestamp literal> that includes a <time zone interval> represents a timestamp in the specified time zone. A <timestamp literal> without a <time zone interval> has a <data type> of TIMESTAMP(fractional seconds precision), though it is compatible with the TIMESTAMP and TIMESTAMP WITH TIME ZONE <data type>s. For example, this <literal>:

```
TIMESTAMP '1997-07-15 13:35:16'
```

has a <data type> of TIMESTAMP and this <literal>:

```
TIMESTAMP '1997-07-15 13:35:16.01'
```

has a <data type> of TIMESTAMP(2).

[Obscure Rule] A <timestamp literal> with a <time zone interval> has a <data type> of TIMESTAMP(fractional seconds precision) WITH TIME ZONE though it is compatible with the TIMESTAMP and TIMESTAMP WITH TIME ZONE <data type>s. For example, the <literal>:

```
TIMESTAMP '1997-07-15 13:35:16.5+10:30'
```

has a <data type> of TIMESTAMP(1) WITH TIME ZONE.

If you want to restrict your code to Core SQL, don't add a fractional seconds precision greater than 6 digits or a <time zone interval> to your timestamp values.

Interval <literal>s

An <interval literal> is either a <year–month interval literal> or a <day–time interval literal>. The type of interval is determined by the <interval qualifier> that is part of the <interval literal>.

<interval qualifier>

An <interval qualifier> defines the type (or precision) of an interval. The required syntax for an <interval qualifier> is as follows.

```
<interval qualifier> ::=
start_datetime [ TO end_datetime ]

   start_datetime ::=
   YEAR [ (leading precision) ] |
   MONTH [ (leading precision) ] |
   DAY [ (leading precision) ] |
   HOUR [ (leading precision) ] |
   MINUTE [ (leading precision) ] |
   SECOND [ (leading precision [ ,fractional seconds precision ]) ]

end_datetime ::=
   YEAR |
   MONTH |
   DAY |
   HOUR |
   MINUTE |
   SECOND [ (fractional seconds precision) ]
```

Both start_datetime and end_datetime may be either: YEAR, MONTH, DAY, HOUR, MINUTE, or SECOND — providing that start_datetime is not less significant than end_datetime. If start_datetime is YEAR, then end_datetime must either be YEAR, MONTH, or it must be omitted. If start_datetime is MONTH, then end_datetime must either be MONTH or it must be omitted. If start_datetime is SECOND, then end_datetime must either be SECOND with a fractional seconds precision less than start_datetime's fractional seconds precision or it must be omitted.

The optional start_datetime leading precision, if specified, is an unsigned integer that defines the maximum number of digits allowed in the start_datetime value. For example, the start_datetime:

```
MONTH(1)
```

means that the month value may range from 0 to 9 months (up to 1 digit). The minimum start_datetime precision is 1. The default start_datetime precision is 2. For example, these two <interval qualifier>s both describe an interval that may contain from 0 to 99 seconds:

```
SECOND
SECOND(2)
```

[NON-PORTABLE] The maximum start_datetime leading precision may not be less than 2 digits but is non-standard because the SQL Standard requires implementors to define an <interval qualifier>'s maximum leading precision. [OCELOT Implementation] The OCELOT DBMS that comes with this book allows the leading precision of YEAR to range from 1 to 4 digits and allows the leading precision of MONTH, DAY, HOUR, MINUTE, and SECOND to range from 0 to 2 digits.

An <interval qualifier>'s `start_datetime` has a precision as specified. All other datetime fields in the interval, except for `SECOND`, have an implied precision of 2 digits. The implied precision for `SECOND` is 2 digits before the decimal point and a number of digits equal to the fractional seconds precision after the decimal point. In all cases, the non-leading fields are constrained by the familiar rules for dates and times; months within years may range from zero to 11, hours within days may range from zero to 23, minutes within hours may range from zero to 59, and seconds within minutes may range from zero to 59.*9n* (where .*9n* represents the number of digits defined for the fractional seconds precision).

The optional fractional seconds precision for a `start_datetime` or an `end_datetime` of `SECOND`, if specified, is an unsigned integer that defines the number of digits in the `SECOND` value's fractional seconds portion. For example, the `start_datetime`:

```
SECOND(2,3)
```

means that the seconds value may range from 0 to 99.999 seconds (up to 2 digits for the seconds value, followed by up to 3 digits for the fractional seconds value). The `end_datetime`:

```
TO SECOND(3)
```

means that the seconds value may range from 0 to 59.999 seconds. (Note that `end_datetime` may never have an explicit leading precision, even for `SECOND`.) The minimum fractional seconds precision is 0. The default fractional seconds precision is 6. For example, these two `start_datetimes` both describe an interval that may contain from 0 to 99 seconds:

```
SECOND(2)
SECOND(2,0)
```

These two `start_datetimes` both describe an interval that may contain from 0 to 99.999999 seconds:

```
SECOND
SECOND(2,6)
```

The following `end_datetime` describes an interval that may contain from 0 to 59 seconds:

```
TO SECOND(0)
```

And these two `end_datetimes` both describe an interval that may contain from 0 to 59.999999 seconds:

```
TO SECOND
TO SECOND(6)
```

[NON-PORTABLE] The maximum fractional seconds precision for an <interval qualifier>'s `start_datetime` or `end_datetime` of `SECOND` may not be less than 6 digits but is non-standard because the SQL Standard requires implementors to define an <interval qualifier>'s maximum fractional seconds precision. [OCELOT Implementation] The OCELOT DBMS that comes with this book allows the fractional seconds precision of `SECOND` to range from 0 to 6 digits.

[Obscure Rule] Of two `start_datetimes` that are the same except for their leading precision, the one with the higher precision is treated as more significant. Of two `end_datetime` values with a <data type> of `SECOND` that are the same except for their fractional seconds precision, the one with the larger fractional seconds precision is treated as more significant. This may become relevant during assignments, comparisons, and type conversions.

This <interval qualifier> means that the `YEAR` value for the interval may be any 3 digit number, i.e., the `YEAR` value may range from 0 to 999 years:

```
YEAR(3)
```

Examples of <interval qualifier>s

YEAR	YEAR may range from 0 to 99
YEAR(4) TO MONTH	YEAR may range from 0 to 9999, MONTH may range from 0 to 11
SECOND	SECOND may range from 0 to 99
SECOND(1)	SECOND may range from 0 to 9
SECOND(1,3)	SECOND may range from 0.000 to 9.999
HOUR TO SECOND	HOUR may range from 0 to 99, SECOND may range from 0.000000 to 59.999999
HOUR TO SECOND(3)	HOUR may range from 0 to 99, SECOND may range from 0.000 to 59.999

If you want to restrict your code to Core SQL, don't use <interval qualifier>s.

<interval literal>

An <interval literal> represents a span of time and is either a <year–month literal> or a <day–time literal>.

<year–month literal>

The required syntax for a <year–month literal> is as follows.

```
<year-month literal> ::=
INTERVAL [ {+ | -} ]'yy' <interval qualifier> |
INTERVAL [ {+ | -} ]'[ yy- ] mm' <interval qualifier>
```

A <year–month literal> includes either YEAR, MONTH, or both. It may not include the datetime fields DAY, HOUR, MINUTE, or SECOND. Its <data type> is INTERVAL with a matching <interval qualifier>.

The optional sign specifies whether this is a positive interval or a negative interval. If you omit the sign, it defaults to +, a positive interval. A negative <interval literal> can be written in one of two ways. For example, for the interval "minus (5 years 5 months)," you could write either:

```
INTERVAL -'05-05' YEAR TO MONTH
```

or

```
INTERVAL '-05-05' YEAR TO MONTH
```

that is, the minus sign can be either outside or inside the interval string. In fact, it can even be both, e.g.,

```
-'-05-05' YEAR TO MONTH
```

which is a double negative and therefore a positive interval, "plus (5 years 5 months)."

TIP: Use the second form. If you're going to be passing intervals as parameters, get used to the idea that the sign can be part of the string.

yy is 1 or more digits representing a number of YEARs and mm is 1 or more digits representing a number of MONTHs. There are three types of <year–month literal>s. For ease of reading, the following examples mostly exclude the use of explicit leading precisions.

This <year–month literal> has a <data type> of INTERVAL YEAR and represents a time span of four years:

```
INTERVAL '4' YEAR
```

These two <year–month literal>s have a <data type> of INTERVAL MONTH and both represent a negative time span of fifty months:

```
INTERVAL -'50' MONTH
INTERVAL '-50' MONTH
```

(Note the sign, which may be written outside the single quotes delimiting the month value or within the quotes.)

This <year–month literal> has a <data type> of INTERVAL YEAR TO MONTH and represents a time span of four hundred years and 6 months:

```
INTERVAL '400-03' YEAR(3) TO MONTH
```

(Note the minus sign between the year value and the month value.)

<day–time literal>

The required syntax for a <day–time literal> is as follows.

```
<day-time literal> ::=
INTERVAL [ {+ | -} ]'dd [ <space>hh [ :mm [ :ss [.nn]]]]' <interval qualifier>
INTERVAL [ {+ | -} ]'hh [ :mm [ :ss [ .nn ]]]' <interval qualifier>
INTERVAL [ {+ | -} ]'mm [ :ss [ .nn ]]' <interval qualifier>
INTERVAL [ {+ | -} ]'ss [ .nn ]' <interval qualifier>
```

A <day–time literal> includes either DAY, HOUR, MINUTE, SECOND, or some contiguous subset of these fields. It may not include the datetime fields YEAR or MONTH. Its <data type> is INTERVAL with a matching <interval qualifier>.

The optional sign specifies whether this is a positive interval or a negative interval. If you omit the sign, it defaults to +, a positive interval. A negative <interval literal> can be written with the sign inside or outside the string — see "<year–month literal>" on page 174

dd is 1 or more digits representing a number of DAYs, hh is 1 or more digits representing a number of HOURs, mm is 1 or more digits representing a number of MINUTEs, ss is 1 or more digits representing a number of SECONDs, and .nn is 1 or more digits representing a number of fractions of a SECOND. There are ten types of <day–time literal>s. For ease of reading, the following examples mostly exclude the use of explicit leading precisions and fractional seconds precisions.

This <day–time literal> has a <data type> of INTERVAL DAY and represents a time span of 94 days:

```
INTERVAL '94' DAY
```

The following <day–time literal> has a <data type> of INTERVAL HOUR and represents a time span of 35 hours:

```
INTERVAL '35' HOUR(2)
```

This <day–time literal> has a <data type> of `INTERVAL MINUTE` and represents a time span of 20 minutes:

```
INTERVAL '20' MINUTE
```

The following <day–time literal> has a <data type> of `INTERVAL SECOND` and represents a time span of 77 seconds (or 77.000000 seconds):

```
INTERVAL '77' SECOND(2)
```

This <day–time literal> has a <data type> of `INTERVAL SECOND` and represents a time span of 142.999 seconds:

```
INTERVAL '142.999' SECOND(3,3)
```

This <day–time literal> has a <data type> of `INTERVAL DAY TO HOUR` and represents a time span of forty days and 23 hours:

```
INTERVAL '40 23' DAY(2) TO HOUR
```

(Note the space between the day value and the hour value.)

This <day–time literal> has a <data type> of `INTERVAL DAY TO MINUTE` and represents a time span of 45 days, 23 hours, and 16 minutes:

```
INTERVAL '45 23:16' DAY TO MINUTE
```

(Note the colon between the hour value and the minute value.)

The following <day–time literal> has a <data type> of `INTERVAL DAY TO SECOND` and represents a time span of 45 days, 23 hours, 16 minutes, and 15 seconds:

```
INTERVAL '45 23:16:15' DAY TO SECOND(0)
```

(Note the colon between the minute value and the second value.)

This <day–time literal> has a <data type> of `INTERVAL DAY TO SECOND` and represents a time span of 45 days, 23 hours, 16 minutes, and 15.25 seconds:

```
INTERVAL '45 23:16:15.25' DAY TO SECOND(2)
```

(Note the decimal point between the second value and the fractional second value.)

The following <day–time literal> has a <data type> of `INTERVAL HOUR TO MINUTE` and represents a time span of 23 hours and 16 minutes:

```
INTERVAL '23:16' HOUR TO MINUTE
```

This <day–time literal> has a <data type> of `INTERVAL HOUR TO SECOND` and represents a time span of 23 hours, 16 minutes, and 15.25 seconds:

```
INTERVAL '23:16:15.25' HOUR TO SECOND(2)
```

This <day–time literal> has a <data type> of `INTERVAL MINUTE TO SECOND` and represents a time span of 16 minutes and 15.25 seconds:

```
INTERVAL '16:15.25' MINUTE TO SECOND(2)
```

If you want to restrict your code to Core SQL, don't use <interval literal>s.

Temporal <data type>s

A temporal <data type> is either a datetime <data type> or an interval <data type>.

Datetime <data type>s

A datetime <data type> is defined by a descriptor that contains two pieces of information:

1. The <data type>'s name — either `DATE`, `TIME`, `TIME WITH TIME ZONE`, `TIMESTAMP`, or `TIMESTAMP WITH TIME ZONE`.

2. The <data type>'s fractional seconds precision (for TIME, TIME WITH TIME ZONE, TIMESTAMP, and TIMESTAMP WITH TIME ZONE types).

DATE

The required syntax for a DATE <data type> specification is as follows.

```
DATE <data type> ::=
DATE
```

DATE combines the datetime fields YEAR, MONTH, and DAY; it defines a set of correctly formed values that represent any valid Gregorian calendar date between '0001-01-01' and '9999-12-31' (i.e., between January 1, 1 AD and December 31, 9999 AD). It has a length of 10 positions.

DATE expects dates to have the following form:

yyyy-mm-dd

e.g., the following date represents July 15, 1994:

1994-07-15

Any operation that attempts to make a DATE <data type> contain a YEAR value that is either less than 1 or greater than 9999 will fail; the DBMS will return the SQLSTATE error 22007 "data exception-invalid datetime format."

Here is an example of DATE:

```
CREATE TABLE date_table_1 (
   start_date DATE);

INSERT INTO date_table_1 (start_date)
VALUES (DATE '1996-01-01');
```

TIME

The required syntax for a TIME <data type> specification is as follows.

```
TIME <data type> ::=
TIME [ (fractional seconds precision) ] [ WITHOUT TIME ZONE ]
```

TIME (or TIME WITHOUT TIME ZONE) combines the datetime fields HOUR, MINUTE, and SECOND; it defines a set of correctly formed values that represent any valid time of day (based on a 24 hour clock) between '00:00:00' and (at a minimum) '23:59:61.999999'. (The SQL Standard requires DBMSs to allow for the addition of up to 2 "leap" seconds in a valid time.) TIME has a length of at least 8 positions.

The optional fractional seconds precision, if specified, is an unsigned integer that specifies the number of digits following the decimal point in the SECOND datetime field. The minimum fractional seconds precision and the default fractional seconds precision are both zero. For example, these two <data type> specifications both define a set of times with a fractional seconds precision of zero digits:

```
TIME
-- would contain values like 13:30:22

TIME(0)
-- would also contain values like 13:30:22
```

The following <data type> specification defines a set of times with a fractional seconds precision of two digits, i.e., of one-hundredth of a second:

```
TIME(2)    -- would contain values like 13:30:22.05
```

[NON-PORTABLE] The maximum fractional seconds precision for `TIME` (*a*) may not be less than 6 digits and (*b*) must be equal to the maximum allowed for the `TIME WITH TIME ZONE`, `TIMESTAMP`, and `TIMESTAMP WITH TIME ZONE` <data type>s but is non-standard because the SQL Standard requires implementors to define `TIME`'s maximum fractional seconds precision. [OCELOT Implementation] The OCELOT DBMS that comes with this book allows the fractional seconds precision of `TIME` to range from 0 to 6 digits.

`TIME` expects times to have the following form:

`hh:mm:ss[.nnnnnn]`

e.g., these two times both represent half past one, plus 22 seconds, PM:

`13:30:22`
`13:30:22.00`

and this time represents half past one, plus 22 and one-tenth seconds, PM:

`13:30:22.10`

The actual length of a `TIME` depends on the fractional seconds precision. These two <data type> specifications have a length of 8 positions:

`TIME`
`TIME(0)`

The following <data type> specification has a length of 10 positions:

```
TIME(1)    -- 8 plus decimal point plus 1 digit in fractional seconds precision
```

This <data type> specification has a length of 15 positions:

`TIME(6)`

[Obscure Rule] `TIME` has a time zone offset equal to the current default time zone offset of the SQL-session — it represents a local time.

Here is an example of `TIME`:

```
CREATE TABLE time_table_1 (
   start_time_1 TIME,
   start_time_2 TIME(2));

INSERT INTO time_table_1 (start_time_1, start_time_2)
VALUES (TIME '14:14:14', TIME '14:14:14.00');
```

```
INSERT INTO time_table_1 (start_time_1, start_time_2)
VALUES (TIME '15:15:15.', TIME '15:15:15.10');

INSERT INTO time_table_1 (start_time_1, start_time_2)
VALUES (TIME '16:16:16.00', TIME '16:16:16.05');
```

If you want to restrict your code to Core SQL, don't define your `TIME` <data type>s with a fractional seconds precision and don't add the optional noise words `WITHOUT TIME ZONE` — use only `TIME`, never `TIME(x) WITHOUT TIME ZONE`.

TIME WITH TIME ZONE

[Obscure Rule] applies for this entire section.

The required syntax for a `TIME WITH TIME ZONE` <data type> specification is as follows.

```
TIME WITH TIME ZONE <data type> ::=
TIME [ (fractional seconds precision) ] WITH TIME ZONE
```

`TIME WITH TIME ZONE` combines the datetime fields `HOUR`, `MINUTE`, `SECOND`, `TIMEZONE_HOUR`, and `TIMEZONE_MINUTE`; it defines a set of correctly formed values that represent any valid time of day (based on a 24-hour clock) between `'00:00:00'` and (at a minimum) `'23:59:61.999999'` with a time zone offset that must be between `'-12:59'` and `'+13:00'`. (The SQL Standard requires DBMSs to allow for the addition of up to 2 "leap" seconds in a valid time.) `TIME WITH TIME ZONE` has a length of at least 14 positions.

As with `TIME`, the optional fractional seconds precision for `TIME WITH TIME ZONE` specifies the number of digits following the decimal point in the `SECOND` datetime field. The minimum fractional seconds precision and the default fractional seconds precision are both zero.

[NON-PORTABLE] The maximum fractional seconds precision for `TIME WITH TIME ZONE` (*a*) may not be less than 6 digits and (*b*) must be equal to the maximum allowed for the `TIME`, `TIMESTAMP`, and `TIMESTAMP WITH TIME ZONE` <data type>s but is non-standard because the SQL Standard requires implementors to define `TIME WITH TIME ZONE`'s maximum fractional seconds precision. [OCELOT Implementation] The OCELOT DBMS that comes with this book allows the fractional seconds precision of `TIME WITH TIME ZONE` to range from 0 to 6 digits.

`TIME WITH TIME ZONE` expects times to have the following form:

```
hh:mm:ss[.nnnnnn ][{+|-}HH:MM ]
```

e.g., the following time represents "half past one, plus 22 seconds, PM" with a time zone offset of 2 and a half hours:

```
13:30:22+02:30
```

The actual length of a `TIME WITH TIME ZONE` depends on the fractional seconds precision. These two <data type> specifications have a length of 14 positions:

```
TIME WITH TIME ZONE
TIME(0) WITH TIME ZONE
```

This <data type> specification has a length of 16 positions:

```
TIME(1) WITH TIME ZONE     -- 14 plus decimal point plus 1 digit in fractional
                              seconds precision
```

This <data type> specification has a length of 21 positions:

```
TIME(6) WITH TIME ZONE
```

[Obscure Rule] TIME WITH TIME ZONE has a time zone offset equal to the <time zone interval> specified for a given time value — it represents a time in the given time zone. If the <time zone interval> is omitted from a given time value, TIME WITH TIME ZONE has a time zone offset equal to the default time zone offset of the SQL-session — it represents a local time. The default time zone offset is the <time zone interval> specified in the most recent SET TIME ZONE statement issued during the SQL-session. If you haven't issued a SET TIME ZONE statement, the default time zone offset is your DBMS's initial default time zone offset.

[NON-PORTABLE] The default time zone offset is non-standard because the SQL Standard requires implementors to define the initial default time zone offset for an SQL-session. [OCELOT Implementation] The OCELOT DBMS that comes with this book sets the SQL-session's initial default time zone offset to INTERVAL '+00:00' HOUR TO MINUTE — this represents UTC.

Here is an example of TIME WITH TIME ZONE:

```
CREATE TABLE time_table_2 (
   start_time_1 TIME WITH TIME ZONE,
   start_time_2 TIME(2) WITH TIME ZONE);

INSERT INTO time_table_2 (start_time_1, start_time_2)
VALUES (TIME '14:14:14+03:00', TIME '14:14:14.00+03:00');

INSERT INTO time_table_2 (start_time_1, start_time_2)
VALUES (TIME '15:15:15.-03:00', TIME '15:15:15.10-03:00');

INSERT INTO time_table_2 (start_time_1, start_time_2)
VALUES (TIME '16:16:16.00+03:30', TIME '16:16:16.05+03:30');
```

If you want to restrict your code to Core SQL, don't use TIME WITH TIME ZONE <data type>s.

TIMESTAMP

The required syntax for a TIMESTAMP <data type> specification is as follows.

```
TIMESTAMP <data type> ::=
TIMESTAMP [ (fractional seconds precision) ][ WITHOUT TIME ZONE ]
```

TIMESTAMP (or TIMESTAMP WITHOUT TIME ZONE) combines the datetime fields YEAR, MONTH, DAY, HOUR, MINUTE, and SECOND — it defines a set of correctly formed values that represent any valid Gregorian calendar date between '0001-01-01' and '9999-12-31' (i.e., between January 1, 1 AD and December 31, 9999 AD) combined with any valid time of day (based on a 24 hour clock) between '00:00:00' and (at a minimum) '23:59:61.999999'. (The SQL Standard requires DBMSs to allow for the addition of up to 2 "leap" seconds in a valid time.) TIMESTAMP has a length of at least 19 positions.

The optional fractional seconds precision, if specified, is an unsigned integer that specifies the number of digits following the decimal point in the SECOND datetime field. The minimum fractional seconds precision is zero. The default fractional seconds precision is 6. For example, this <data type> specification defines a set of timestamps with a fractional seconds precision of zero digits:

```
TIMESTAMP(0)
-- would contain values like '1994-07-15 13:30:22'
```

The following two <data type> specifications both define a set of timestamps with a fractional seconds precision of 6 digits, i.e., of one-millionth of a second:

```
TIMESTAMP
-- would contain values like '1994-07-15 13:30:22.999999'

TIMESTAMP(6)
-- would also contain values like '1994-07-15 13:30:22.999999'
```

[NON-PORTABLE] The maximum fractional seconds precision for TIMESTAMP (*a*) may not be less than 6 digits and (*b*) must be equal to the maximum allowed for the TIME, TIME WITH TIME ZONE, and TIMESTAMP WITH TIME ZONE <data type>s but is non-standard because the SQL Standard requires implementors to define TIMESTAMP's maximum fractional seconds precision. [OCELOT Implementation] The OCELOT DBMS that comes with this book allows the fractional seconds precision of TIMESTAMP to range from 0 to 6 digits.

Any operation that attempts to make a TIMESTAMP <data type> contain a YEAR value that is either less than 1 or greater than 9999 will fail; the DBMS will return the SQLSTATE error 22007 "data exception-invalid datetime format."

TIMESTAMP expects timestamps to have the following form:

```
yyyy-mm-dd hh:mm:ss[.nnnnnn]
```

e.g., these two timestamps both represent half past one, plus 22 seconds, PM on July 15, 1994:

```
1994-07-15 13:30:22
1994-07-15 13:30:22.00
```

and this timestamp represents half past one, plus 22 and one-tenth seconds, PM on July 15, 1994:

```
1994-07-15 13:30:22.10
```

Note the mandatory space between the date portion and the time portion of the timestamps.

The actual length of a TIMESTAMP depends on the fractional seconds precision. This <data type> specification has a length of 19 positions:

```
TIMESTAMP(0)
```

This <data type> specification has a length of 21 positions:

```
TIMESTAMP(1)    -- 19 plus decimal point plus 1 digit in fractional seconds
                   precision
```

The following two <data type> specifications both have a length of 26 positions:

```
TIMESTAMP
TIMESTAMP(6)
```

[Obscure Rule] TIMESTAMP has a time zone offset equal to the current default time zone offset of the SQL-session; it represents a local timestamp.

Here is an example of TIMESTAMP:

```
CREATE TABLE timestamp_table_1 (
   start_timestamp_1 TIMESTAMP,
   start_timestamp_2 TIMESTAMP(2));
```

```
INSERT INTO timestamp_table_1 (start_timestamp_1, start_timestamp_2)
VALUES (
   TIMESTAMP '1997-04-01 14:14:14.999999',
   TIMESTAMP '1994-07-15 15:15:15.15');
```

If you want to restrict your code to Core SQL, don't define your TIMESTAMP <data type>s with a fractional seconds precision other than 0 or 6 and don't add the optional noise words WITHOUT TIME ZONE; use only TIMESTAMP, TIMESTAMP(0), or TIMESTAMP(6) — never TIMESTAMP(x) WITHOUT TIME ZONE.

TIP: Consider using a TIMESTAMP to store time-of-day values if you plan on doing time arithmetic, e.g., TIMESTAMP '1000-01-01 13:45:00' instead of TIME '13:45:00'. Although this wastes space on a meaningless date value, your time arithmetic will be more meaningful, since any "carries" or "borrows" will show up in the results.

TIMESTAMP WITH TIME ZONE

[Obscure Rule] applies for this entire section.

The required syntax for a TIMESTAMP WITH TIME ZONE <data type> specification is as follows.

```
TIMESTAMP WITH TIME ZONE <data type> ::=
TIMESTAMP [ (fractional seconds precision) ] WITH TIME ZONE
```

TIMESTAMP WITH TIME ZONE combines the datetime fields YEAR, MONTH, DAY, HOUR, MINUTE, SECOND, TIMEZONE_HOUR, and TIMEZONE_MINUTE; it defines a set of correctly formed values that represent any valid Gregorian calendar date between '0001-01-01' and '9999-12-31' (i.e., between January 1, 1 AD and December 31, 9999 AD) combined with any valid time of day (based on a 24-hour clock) between '00:00:00' and (at a minimum) '23:59:61.999999' with a time zone offset that must be between '-12:59' and '+13:00'. (The SQL Standard requires

DBMSs to allow for the addition of up to 2 "leap" seconds in a valid time.) TIMESTAMP WITH TIME ZONE has a length of at least 25 positions.

As with TIMESTAMP, the optional fractional seconds precision for TIMESTAMP WITH TIME ZONE specifies the number of digits following the decimal point in the SECOND datetime field. The minimum fractional seconds precision is zero. The default fractional seconds precision is 6.

[NON-PORTABLE] The maximum fractional seconds precision for TIMESTAMP WITH TIME ZONE *(a)* may not be less than 6 digits and *(b)* must be equal to the maximum allowed for the TIME, TIME WITH TIME ZONE, and TIMESTAMP <data type>s but is non-standard because the SQL Standard requires implementors to define TIMESTAMP WITH TIME ZONE's maximum fractional seconds precision. [OCELOT Implementation] The OCELOT DBMS that comes with this book allows the fractional seconds precision of TIMESTAMP WITH TIME ZONE to range from 0 to 6 digits.

Any operation that attempts to make a TIMESTAMP WITH TIME ZONE <data type> contain a YEAR value that is either less than 1 or greater than 9999 will fail; the DBMS will return the SQLSTATE error 22007 "data exception-invalid datetime format."

TIMESTAMP WITH TIME ZONE expects timestamps to have the following form:

```
yyyy-mm-dd hh:mm:ss[.nnnnnn ][{+|-}HH:MM ]
```

e.g., the following timestamps all represent half past one, plus 22 seconds, PM on July 15, 1994 with a time zone offset of 2 and a half hours:

```
1994-07-15 13:30:22+02:30
1994-07-15 13:30:22.+02:30
1994-07-15 13:30:22.00+02:30
```

The actual length of a TIMESTAMP WITH TIME ZONE depends on the fractional seconds precision. This <data type> specification has a length of 25 positions:

```
TIMESTAMP(0) WITH TIME ZONE
```

This <data type> specification has a length of 27 positions:

```
TIMESTAMP(1) WITH TIME ZONE     -- 25 plus decimal point plus 1 digit in
                                   fractional seconds precision
```

These two <data type> specifications both have a length of 32 positions:

```
TIMESTAMP WITH TIME ZONE
TIMESTAMP(6) WITH TIME ZONE
```

[Obscure Rule] TIMESTAMP WITH TIME ZONE has a time zone offset equal to the <time zone interval> specified for a given timestamp value; it represents a timestamp in the given time zone. If the <time zone interval> is omitted from a given timestamp value, TIMESTAMP WITH TIME ZONE has a time zone offset equal to the default time zone offset of the SQL-session; it represents a local timestamp. The default time zone offset is the <time zone interval> specified in the most recent SET TIME ZONE statement issued during the SQL-session. If you haven't issued a SET TIME ZONE statement, the default time zone offset is your DBMS's initial default time zone offset.

[NON-PORTABLE] The default time zone offset is non-standard because the SQL Standard requires implementors to define the initial default time zone offset for an SQL-session. [OCELOT Implementation] The OCELOT DBMS that comes with this book sets the SQL-session's initial default time zone offset to INTERVAL '+00:00' HOUR TO MINUTE — this represents UTC.

Here is an example of TIMESTAMP WITH TIME ZONE:

```
CREATE TABLE timestamp_table_2 (
   start_timestamp_1 TIMESTAMP WITH TIME ZONE,
   start_timestamp_2 TIMESTAMP(2) WITH TIME ZONE);

INSERT INTO timestamp_table_2 (start_timestamp_1, start_timestamp_2)
VALUES (
   TIMESTAMP '1997-04-01 14:14:14.999999-03:00',
   TIMESTAMP '1994-07-15 14:14:14.35+02:15');
```

If you want to restrict your code to Core SQL, don't use TIMESTAMP WITH TIME ZONE <data type>s.

Interval <data type>s

An interval <data type> is defined by a descriptor that contains two pieces of information:

1. The <data type>'s name — INTERVAL.
2. The <data type>'s <interval qualifier> which specifies the type of interval and the precision of the interval's set of valid values.

INTERVAL

The required syntax for an INTERVAL <data type> specification is as follows.

```
INTERVAL <data type> ::=
INTERVAL <interval qualifier>
```

INTERVAL is a span of time; it defines a set of correctly formed values that represent any span of time compatible with the <interval qualifier>. It combines the datetime fields YEAR and/or MONTH if it is a year–month interval. It combines the datetime fields DAY and/or HOUR and/or MINUTE and/or SECOND if it is a day–time interval. INTERVAL has a length of at least 1 position.

A year–month INTERVAL combines one or more of the datetime fields YEAR and MONTH in the <interval qualifier>. The possible definitions are thus:

```
INTERVAL YEAR [ (leading precision) ]
INTERVAL MONTH [ (leading precision) ]
INTERVAL YEAR [ (leading precision) ] TO MONTH
```

The leading precision, if specified, is as described in "<interval qualifier>" on page 172. The values of the start_datetime field are constrained only by the leading precision of that field. The month value in INTERVAL YEAR TO MONTH represents an additional number of months (within years) and can thus range only from 0 to 11.

INTERVAL YEAR expects intervals to have the following form:

```
'y[...]'
```

e.g., '20' represents a span of 20 years. INTERVAL YEAR has a length of "leading precision" positions. For example, this <data type> specification has a length of 4 positions:

```
INTERVAL YEAR(4)
```

INTERVAL MONTH expects intervals to have the following form:

'm[...]'

e.g., '15' represents a span of 15 months. INTERVAL MONTH has a length of "leading precision" positions. For example, this <data type> specification has a length of 2 positions:

INTERVAL MONTH

(The default precision is 2 digits.)

INTERVAL YEAR TO MONTH expects intervals to have the following form:

'y[...]-mm'

e.g., '20-03' represents a span of 20 years plus 3 months. INTERVAL YEAR TO MONTH has a length of "leading precision" plus 3 positions. For example, this <data type> specification has a length of 5 positions:

INTERVAL YEAR TO MONTH

A day–time INTERVAL combines one or more of the datetime fields DAY, HOUR, MINUTE, and SECOND in the <interval qualifier>. The possible definitions are thus:

```
INTERVAL DAY [ (leading precision) ]
INTERVAL HOUR [ (leading precision) ]
INTERVAL MINUTE [ (leading precision) ]
INTERVAL SECOND [ (leading precision [ ,fractional seconds
                    precision ]) ]
INTERVAL DAY [ (leading precision) ] TO HOUR
INTERVAL DAY [ (leading precision) ] TO MINUTE
INTERVAL DAY [ (leading precision) ] TO SECOND [ (fractional seconds
                 precision) ]
INTERVAL HOUR [ (leading precision) ] TO MINUTE
INTERVAL HOUR [ (leading precision) ] TO SECOND [ (fractional seconds
                  precision) ]
INTERVAL MINUTE [ (leading precision) ] TO SECOND [ (fractional seconds
                    precision) ]
```

The leading precision, if specified, is as described in "<interval qualifier>" on page 172. The values of the start_datetime field are constrained only by the leading precision of that field. The hour value in INTERVAL DAY TO HOUR, INTERVAL DAY TO MINUTE, and INTERVAL DAY TO SECOND represents an additional number of hours (within days) and can thus range only from 0 to 23. The minute value in INTERVAL DAY TO MINUTE, INTERVAL DAY TO SECOND, INTERVAL HOUR TO MINUTE, and INTERVAL HOUR TO SECOND represents an additional number of minutes (within hours) and can thus range only from 0 to 59. The seconds value in INTERVAL DAY TO SECOND, INTERVAL HOUR TO SECOND, and INTERVAL MINUTE TO SECOND represents an additional number of seconds and fractions of a second (within minutes) and can thus range only from 0 to 59.9n (where .9n represents the number of digits defined for the fractional seconds precision). The fractional seconds precision, if specified, is as described in <interval qualifier>.

INTERVAL DAY expects intervals to have the following form:

'd[...]'

e.g., '1' represents a span of 1 day. INTERVAL DAY has a length of "leading precision" positions. For example, this <data type> specification has a length of 2 positions:

INTERVAL DAY

(The default precision is 2 digits.)

`INTERVAL HOUR` expects intervals to have the following form:

```
'h[...]'
```

e.g., `'15'` represents a span of 15 hours. `INTERVAL HOUR` has a length of "leading precision" positions. For example, this <data type> specification has a length of 2 positions:

```
INTERVAL HOUR
```

`INTERVAL MINUTE` expects intervals to have the following form:

```
'm[...]'
```

e.g., `'75'` represents a span of 75 minutes. `INTERVAL MINUTE` has a length of "leading precision" positions. For example, this <data type> specification has a length of 2 positions:

```
INTERVAL MINUTE
```

`INTERVAL SECOND` expects intervals to have the following form:

```
's[...[.n...]]'
```

e.g., `'1'` represents a span of 1 second, `'20'` and `'20.0'` both represent a span of 20 seconds and `'20.5'` represents a span of 20.5 seconds. `INTERVAL SECOND` has a length of "leading precision" plus "fractional seconds precision" positions. For example, this <data type> specification has a length of 2 positions:

```
INTERVAL SECOND(0)
```

These two <data type> specifications both have a length of 9 positions:

```
INTERVAL SECOND
INTERVAL SECOND(6)
```

(The default fractional seconds precision is 6 digits. A fractional seconds precision greater than zero includes one position for the decimal point.)

`INTERVAL DAY TO HOUR` expects intervals to have the following form:

```
'd[...] h[...]'
```

e.g., `'1 1'` represents a span of 1 day plus 1 hour and `'20 10'` represents a span of 20 days plus 10 hours. (Note the mandatory space between the days portion and the hours portion of the interval.) `INTERVAL DAY TO HOUR` has a length of "leading precision" plus 3 positions. For example, the following <data type> specification has a length of 5 positions:

```
INTERVAL DAY TO HOUR
```

`INTERVAL DAY TO MINUTE` expects intervals to have the following form:

```
'd[...] h[...]:m[...]'
```

e.g., `'1 1:1'` represents a span of 1 day, 1 hour plus 1 minute and `'20 10:15'` represents a span of 20 days, 10 hours plus 15 minutes. (Note the mandatory colon between the hours portion and the minutes portion of the interval.) `INTERVAL DAY TO MINUTE` has a length of "leading precision" plus 6 positions. For example, this <data type> specification has a length of 8 positions:

```
INTERVAL DAY TO MINUTE
```

`INTERVAL DAY TO SECOND` expects intervals to have the following form:

```
'd[...] h[...]:m[...]:s[...[.n...]]'
```

e.g., `'1 1:1:1'` and `'01 01:01:01.00'` both represent a span of 1 day, 1 hour, 1 minute plus 1 second and `'20 10:15:20.5'` represents a span of 20 days, 10 hours, 15 minutes plus 20.5 seconds. (Note the mandatory colon between the minutes portion and the seconds portion of the interval.) `INTERVAL DAY TO SECOND` has a length of "leading precision" plus "fractional seconds precision" plus 9 positions. For example, this <data type> specification has a length of 11 positions:

```
INTERVAL DAY TO SECOND(0)
```

These two <data type> specifications both have a length of 18 positions:

```
INTERVAL DAY TO SECOND
INTERVAL DAY TO SECOND(6)
```

`INTERVAL HOUR TO MINUTE` expects intervals to have the following form:

```
'h[...]:m[...]'
```

e.g., `'10:15'` represents a span of 10 hours plus 15 minutes. `INTERVAL HOUR TO MINUTE` has a length of "leading precision" plus 3 positions. For example, this <data type> specification has a length of 5 positions:

```
INTERVAL HOUR TO MINUTE
```

`INTERVAL HOUR TO SECOND` expects intervals to have the following form:

```
'h[...]:m[...]:s[...[.n...]]'
```

e.g., `'10:15:20.5'` represents a span of 10 hours, 15 minutes plus 20.5 seconds. `INTERVAL HOUR TO SECOND` has a length of "leading precision" plus "fractional seconds precision" plus 6 positions. For example, this <data type> specification has a length of 8 positions:

```
INTERVAL HOUR TO SECOND(0)
```

These two <data type> specifications both have a length of 15 positions:

```
INTERVAL HOUR TO SECOND
INTERVAL HOUR TO SECOND(6)
```

`INTERVAL MINUTE TO SECOND` expects intervals to have the following form:

```
'm[...]:s[...[.n...]]'
```

e.g., `'15:20.5'` represents a span of 15 minutes plus 20.5 seconds and `'14:15'` represents a span of 14 minutes plus 15 seconds. `INTERVAL MINUTE TO SECOND` has a length of "leading precision" plus "fractional seconds precision" plus 3 positions. For example, this <data type> specification has a length of 5 positions:

```
INTERVAL MINUTE TO SECOND(0)
```

These two <data type> specifications both have a length of 12 positions:

```
INTERVAL MINUTE TO SECOND
INTERVAL MINUTE TO SECOND(6)
```

Here is an example of `INTERVAL`:

```
CREATE interval_table (
   interval_column_1 INTERVAL YEAR(3) TO MONTH,
   interval_column_2 INTERVAL DAY TO MINUTE,
   interval_column_3 INTERVAL MINUTE TO SECOND(4));
```

```
INSERT INTO interval_table (
   interval_column_1,
   interval_column_2,
   interval_column_3)
VALUES (
   INTERVAL '150-01' YEAR(3) TO MONTH,
   INTERVAL '-36 22:30' DAY TO MINUTE,
   INTERVAL -'15:22.0001' MINUTE TO SECOND(4));
```

If you want to restrict your code to Core SQL, don't use the `INTERVAL` <data type>.

Now that we've described SQL's datetime <data type>s, let's look at some example SQL statements that put them to use.

These SQL statements make a Table with a date Column, insert a row, then search for any date after January 2nd, 2000:

```
CREATE TABLE Date_Examples (
   occurrence_date DATE);

INSERT INTO Date_Examples (occurrence_date)
VALUES (DATE '2001-02-28');

SELECT occurrence_date
FROM   Date_Examples
WHERE  occurrence_date > DATE '2000-01-02';
```

These SQL statements make a Table with two time-of-day Columns, insert a row, then search for any time before 8:30 PM:

```
CREATE TABLE Time_Examples (
   occurrence_time TIME,
   occurrence_time_zone TIME WITH TIME ZONE);

INSERT INTO Time_Examples (occurrence_time, occurrence_time_zone)
VALUES (TIME '12:00:00', TIME '12:00:00+3:00');

SELECT occurrence_time, occurrence_time_zone
FROM   Time_Examples
WHERE  occurrence_time < TIME '20:30:00';
```

These SQL statements make a Table with two timestamp Columns, insert a row, then search for any timestamp equal to January 2nd, 2000 at 1 second past midnight:

```
CREATE TABLE Timestamp_Examples (
   occurrence_timestamp TIMESTAMP,
   occurrence_timestamp_zone TIMESTAMP WITH TIME ZONE);

INSERT INTO Timestamp_Examples (
   occurrence_timestamp,
   occurrence_timestamp_zone)
VALUES (
   TIMESTAMP '2001-02-28 16:00:00',
   TIMESTAMP '2001-02-28 16:00:00+0:00');

SELECT occurrence_timestamp, occurrence_timestamp_zone
FROM   Timestamp_Examples
WHERE  occurrence_timestamp_zone = TIMESTAMP '2000-01-02 00:00:01';
```

These SQL statements make a Table with two year–month interval Columns, insert a row, then search for any interval that is less than or equal to 37 months:

```
CREATE TABLE YInterval_Examples (
   occurrence_interval_1 INTERVAL YEAR,
   occurrence_interval_2 INTERVAL YEAR TO MONTH);

INSERT INTO YInterval_Examples (
   occurrence_interval_1,
   occurrence_interval_2)
VALUES (
   INTERVAL '3' YEAR,
   INTERVAL '02-10' YEAR TO MONTH);

SELECT occurrence_interval_1, occurrence_interval_2
FROM   YInterval_Examples
WHERE  occurrence_interval_1 <= INTERVAL '37' MONTH;
```

These SQL statements make a Table with two day–time interval Columns, insert two rows, then search for any interval that doesn't equal 30 seconds:

```
CREATE TABLE DInterval_Examples (
   occurrence_interval_1 INTERVAL SECOND,
   occurrence_interval_2 INTERVAL SECOND(2,4));
```

```
INSERT INTO DInterval_Examples (
   occurrence_interval_1,
   occurrence_interval_2)
VALUES (
   INTERVAL '25.000005' SECOND,
   INTERVAL '25.0001' SECOND);

INSERT INTO DInterval_Examples (
   occurrence_interval_1,
   occurrence_interval_2)
VALUES (
   INTERVAL '22' SECOND,
   INTERVAL '22' SECOND);

SELECT occurrence_interval_1, occurrence_interval_2
FROM   DInterval_Examples
WHERE  occurrence_interval_1 <> INTERVAL '30' SECOND;
```

Temporal Operations

A temporal value is only compatible with, and comparable to, a matching temporal value; that is, only temporal values of the same type, that also consist of matching datetime fields, are mutually comparable and mutually assignable. Thus, (*a*) dates are comparable and assignable only to dates, (*b*) times are comparable and assignable only to times, (*c*) timestamps are comparable and assignable only to timestamps, (*d*) year–month intervals are comparable and assignable only to year–month intervals, and (*e*) day–time intervals are comparable and assignable only to day–time intervals. Temporal values may not be directly compared with, or directly assigned to, non-compatible datetimes or intervals or to any other <data type> class, though implicit type conversions can occur in expressions, SELECTs, INSERTs, DELETEs, and UPDATEs. Explicit temporal type conversions can be forced with the CAST operator.

CAST

In SQL, CAST is a scalar operator that converts a given scalar value to a given scalar <data type>. The required syntax for the CAST operator is as follows.

```
CAST (<cast operand> AS <cast target>)
   <cast operand> ::= scalar_expression
   <cast target> ::= <Domain name> | <data type>
```

The CAST operator converts values of a source <data type> into values of a target <data type>, where each <data type> is an SQL pre-defined <data type> (data conversions between UDTs are done with a user-defined cast). The source <data type> (or <cast operand>) can be any expression that evaluates to a single value. The target <data type> (or <cast target>) is either an SQL predefined <data type> specification or the name of a Domain whose defined

<data type> your target <data type>. (If you use CAST (... AS <Domain name>), your current <AuthorizationID> must have the USAGE Privilege on that Domain.)

It isn't, of course, possible to convert the values of every <data type> into the values of every other <data type>. For temporal values, the rules are:

- CAST (NULL AS <data type>) and CAST (temporal_source_is_a_null_value AS <data type>) both result in NULL.
- You can CAST a date source to these targets: fixed length character string, variable length character string, CLOB, NCLOB, date, and timestamp. You can also CAST a date source to a UDT target or a <reference type> target if a user-defined cast exists for this purpose and your current <AuthorizationID> has the EXECUTE Privilege on that user-defined cast.
- You can CAST a time source to these targets: fixed length character string, variable length character string, CLOB, NCLOB, time, and timestamp. You can also CAST a time source to a UDT target or a <reference type> target if a user-defined cast exists for this purpose and your current <AuthorizationID> has the EXECUTE Privilege on that user-defined cast.
- You can CAST a timestamp source to these targets: fixed length character string, variable length character string, CLOB, NCLOB, date, time, and timestamp. You can also CAST a timestamp source to a UDT target or a <reference type> target if a user-defined cast exists for this purpose and your current <AuthorizationID> has the EXECUTE Privilege on that user-defined cast.
- You can CAST a year–month interval source to these targets: fixed length character string, variable length character string, CLOB, NCLOB, and year–month interval. You can CAST a day–time interval source to these targets: fixed length character string, variable length character string, CLOB, NCLOB, and day–time interval. You can also CAST an interval source to an exact numeric target, provided the source contains only one datetime field — that is, you can CAST an INTERVAL YEAR to an integer or an INTERVAL MONTH to an integer, but you can't CAST an INTERVAL YEAR TO MONTH to an integer. You can CAST an interval source to a UDT target or a <reference type> target if a user-defined cast exists for this purpose and your current <AuthorizationID> has the EXECUTE Privilege on that user-defined cast.

When you CAST any temporal value to a fixed length character string, variable length character string, CLOB or NCLOB target, your DBMS converts the source value to the shortest possible character string that can express the source value (for example, CAST (DATE '1994-07-15' AS CHAR(10)) results in the character string '1994-07-15').

- For fixed length character string targets, if the length of the converted source value *equals* the fixed length of the target, then the result is the converted source value. If the length of the result is *shorter* than the fixed length of the target, then the result is the converted source value, padded on the right with however many spaces are needed to make the lengths the same. If the length of the result is *longer* than the fixed length of the target, the CAST will fail; your DBMS will return the SQLSTATE error 22001 "data exception-string data, right truncation." And if the result contains any characters that don't belong to the target's Character set, the CAST will also fail; your DBMS will return the SQLSTATE error 22018 "data exception-invalid character value for cast."
- For variable length character string, CLOB, or NCLOB targets, if the length of the converted source value is *less than* or *equals* the maximum length of the target, then the result is the converted source value. If the length of the result is *longer* than the maximum length of the target, the CAST will fail; your DBMS will return the SQLSTATE error 22001 "data exception-string data, right truncation." And if the result contains any characters

that don't belong to the target's Character set, the CAST will also fail; your DBMS will return the SQLSTATE error 22018 "data exception-invalid character value for cast."

- [Obscure Rule] The result of a CAST to a character string target has the COERCIBLE coercibility attribute; its Collation is the default Collation for the target's Character set.

When you CAST any temporal value to a UDT or a <reference type> target, your DBMS invokes the user-defined cast routine with the source value as the routine's argument. The CAST result is the value returned by the user-defined cast.

When you CAST any datetime value to a temporal target, the rules are as follows.

CAST (DATE AS temporal)

- When you CAST a date to a date target, the result is the source date.
- When you CAST a date to a timestamp target, the result is a timestamp whose date portion is the same as the source date and whose time portion is zero (that is, CAST (DATE '1994-07-15' AS TIMESTAMP) results in TIMESTAMP '1994-07-15 00:00:00.000000').

CAST (TIME AS temporal)

- When you CAST a time to a time target or a time with time zone to a time with time zone target, the result is the source time.
- When you CAST a time to a time with time zone target, the result is the source time converted to UTC.
- When you CAST a time with time zone to a time target, the result is the source time converted to the local time.
- When you CAST a time to a timestamp target or a time with time zone to a timestamp with time zone target, the result is a timestamp whose date portion is the value of CURRENT_DATE and whose time portion is the same as the source time (that is, CAST (TIME '10:10:10.01' AS TIMESTAMP) results in TIMESTAMP '1994-07-15 10:10:10.010000' if today's date is July 15, 1994).
- When you CAST a time to a timestamp with time zone target, the result is a timestamp whose date portion is the value of CURRENT_DATE and whose time portion is the same as the source time converted to UTC.
- When you CAST a time with time zone to a timestamp target, the result is a timestamp whose date portion is the value of CURRENT_DATE and whose time portion is the same as the source time converted to the local time.

CAST (TIMESTAMP AS temporal)

- When you CAST a timestamp to a date target, the result is the date portion of the timestamp. For example,
  CAST (TIMESTAMP '1994-07-15 10:10:10.010000' AS DATE)
  results in DATE '1994-07-15'. When you CAST a timestamp with time zone to a date target, the result is the date portion of the timestamp, adjusted by the time zone offset if required.
- When you CAST a timestamp to a time target or a timestamp with time zone to a time with time zone target, the result is the time portion of the timestamp. For example, CAST (TIMESTAMP '1994-07-15 10:10:10.010000+02:30' AS TIME WITH TIME ZONE) results in TIME '10:10:10.010000+02:30'.

- When you CAST a timestamp to a time with time zone target, the result is the time portion of the timestamp converted to UTC.
- When you CAST a timestamp with time zone to a time target, the result is the time portion of the timestamp converted to the local time.
- When you CAST a timestamp to a timestamp target or a timestamp with time zone to a timestamp with time zone target, the result is the source timestamp.
- When you CAST a timestamp to a timestamp with time zone target, the result is the source timestamp, with both its date and time portions converted to UTC.
- When you CAST a timestamp with time zone to a timestamp target, the result is the source timestamp, with both its date and time portions converted to the local time.

When you CAST any interval to a numeric target or temporal target, the rules are as follows:

- When you CAST an interval to an exact numeric target, your interval has to be for one datetime field only. The result of the CAST is the numeric value of that datetime field. For example, CAST ('100' INTERVAL YEAR(3) AS SMALLINT) results in a SMALLINT value of 100. (Note: if the numeric value of your interval can't be represented as a target value without losing any leading significant digits, the CAST will fail; your DBMS will return the SQLSTATE error 22003 "data exception-numeric value out of range.")
- When you CAST a year–month interval to a year–month interval target or a day–time interval to a day–time interval target, if both source and target have the same <interval qualifier> then the result of the CAST is the source interval.
- When you CAST a year–month interval to a year–month interval target or a day–time interval to a day–time interval target, if the source and target have different <interval qualifier>s, then the result of the CAST is the source interval converted to its equivalent in units of the target interval. For example, CAST ('3' INTERVAL YEAR TO INTERVAL MONTH) results in INTERVAL '36' MONTH and CAST ('62' INTERVAL MINUTE AS INTERVAL HOUR TO MINUTE) results in INTERVAL '01:02' HOUR TO MINUTE. (Note: if the CAST would result in the loss of precision of the most significant datetime field of the converted source value, the CAST will fail; your DBMS will return the SQLSTATE error 22015 "data exception-interval field overflow.")

If you want to restrict your code to Core SQL, don't use <Domain name> as a CAST target — CAST only to a <data type>.

Assignment

In SQL, temporal values must be compatible to be assigned to one another — that is, the source and the target must either (*a*) both be dates, (*b*) both be times (with or without time zone), (*c*) both be timestamps (with or without time zone), (*d*) both be year–month intervals, or (*e*) both be day–time intervals.

[Obscure Rule] Since only SQL accepts null values, if your source is NULL and your target is not an SQL-data target, then your target's value is not changed. Instead, your DBMS will set the target's indicator parameter to –1, to indicate that an assignment of the null value was attempted. If your target doesn't have an indicator parameter, the assignment will fail; your DBMS will return the SQLSTATE error 22002 "data exception-null value, no indicator parameter." Going the other way, there are two ways to assign a null value to an SQL-data target. Within SQL, you can use the <keyword> `NULL` in an `INSERT` or an `UPDATE` statement to indicate that the target should be set to `NULL`; that is, if your source is `NULL`, your DBMS will set your target to `NULL`. Outside of SQL, if your source has an indicator parameter that is set to –1, your DBMS will set your target to `NULL` (regardless of the value of the source). An indicator parameter with a value less than –1 will cause an error; your DBMS will return the `SQLSTATE error 22010 "data exception-invalid indicator parameter value."` We'll talk more about indicator parameters in Chapters 39, 40, and 52 on SQL binding styles.

Datetime Assignment

When you assign a datetime to a datetime target, your DBMS checks whether the source is a valid value for the target's <data type> (or if a valid value can be obtained from the source by rounding). If so, then the target is set to that value. If neither of these are true, the assignment will fail; your DBMS will return the `SQLSTATE error 22008 "data exception-datetime field overflow."`

`DATE` assignment is straightforward, since all dates have the same form.

[Obscure Rule] `TIME`, `TIME WITH TIME ZONE`, `TIMESTAMP`, and `TIMESTAMP WITH TIME ZONE` assignment is somewhat more complicated, due to the possibility that only one of the source and target may include a <time zone interval>. If this is the case, your DBMS will effectively replace the source value with the result obtained by:

```
CAST (source TO target)
```

This means that if you're assigning a datetime without time zone source value to a datetime `WITH TIME ZONE` target, your DBMS will *(a)* assume the source is a local time value, *(b)* subtract the default SQL-session time zone offset from the source to convert to the source's UTC equivalent, and then *(c)* assign the UTC result with resulting time zone offset to the target. If you're assigning a datetime `WITH TIME ZONE` source value to a datetime without time zone target, your DBMS will *(a)* assume the source is a UTC time value, *(b)* add the source's time zone offset to the source to convert to the source's local time equivalent, and then *(c)* assign the local time result without a time zone offset to the target.

Interval Assignment

When you assign an interval to an interval target, your DBMS checks whether the source is a valid value for the target's <data type> (or if a valid value can be obtained from the source by rounding or truncation). If so, then the target is set to that value. If neither of these are true, the assignment will fail; your DBMS will return the `SQLSTATE error 22015 "data exception-interval field overflow."`

[NON-PORTABLE] If your source value is not a valid value for your interval target's <data type>, then the value assigned to the target is non-standard because the SQL Standard requires implementors to define whether the DBMS will round or will truncate the source to obtain a valid value. [OCELOT Implementation] The OCELOT DBMS that comes with this book truncates the interval source to obtain a valid value for the target.

Assignment of year–month intervals to other year–month intervals or of day–time intervals to other day–time intervals is straightforward — providing both target and source have the same <interval qualifier>. That is, for example, if both year–month intervals are `INTERVAL YEAR`, or both are `INTERVAL MONTH`, or both are `INTERVAL YEAR TO MONTH`, assignment is straightforward because all intervals with the same <interval qualifier> have the same form.

If, however, the <interval qualifier>s of the source and target do not match exactly, then your DBMS will effectively convert both to the same precision before the operation is carried out. The conversion is done either by a simple mathematical process or by extending one of the intervals at its most significant and/or at its least significant end, with an appropriate datetime field set (initially) to zero. Thus, for example:

- If you assign `INTERVAL '3' YEAR` to an `INTERVAL YEAR TO MONTH` target, your DBMS will extend the source at its least significant end by attaching a zero `MONTH` field. The source effectively becomes `INTERVAL '3-00' YEAR TO MONTH` and assignment becomes straightforward.
- If you assign `INTERVAL '13' MONTH` to an `INTERVAL YEAR TO MONTH` target, your DBMS will extend the source at its most significant end by attaching a zero `YEAR` field. The source effectively becomes `INTERVAL '0-13' YEAR TO MONTH`. Since a `MONTH` field may not be more than 11 months in a year–month interval, the source is further adjusted to `INTERVAL '1-01' YEAR TO MONTH` (1 year and 1 month equals 13 months) and assignment becomes straightforward.
- If you assign `INTERVAL '3' YEAR` to an `INTERVAL MONTH` target, your DBMS converts the source to an `INTERVAL MONTH` value by multiplying the year value by 12. The source effectively becomes `INTERVAL '36' MONTH` and assignment becomes straightforward.
- If you assign `INTERVAL '3-01' YEAR TO MONTH` to an `INTERVAL MONTH` target, your DBMS converts the source to an `INTERVAL MONTH` value by multiplying the year value by 12 and adding the number of months to the result. The source effectively becomes `INTERVAL '37' MONTH` and assignment becomes straightforward.
- If you assign `INTERVAL '24' MONTH` to an `INTERVAL YEAR` target, your DBMS converts the source to an `INTERVAL YEAR` value by dividing the month value by 12. The source effectively becomes `INTERVAL '2' YEAR` and assignment becomes straightforward. If, however, the source's month value is not evenly divisible by 12 (e.g., a source of `INTERVAL '37' MONTH` being assigned to an `INTERVAL YEAR` target), the assignment will fail so that no information is lost; your DBMS will return the `SQLSTATE error 22015 "data exception-interval field overflow."`
- If you assign `INTERVAL '2-00' YEAR TO MONTH` to an `INTERVAL YEAR` target, your DBMS converts the source to an `INTERVAL YEAR` value by assigning the source's year value to the target, that is, the source effectively becomes `INTERVAL '2' YEAR`, and assignment becomes straightforward. If, however, the source's month value is not equal to zero (e.g., a source of `INTERVAL '2-05' YEAR TO MONTH` being assigned to an `INTERVAL YEAR` target), the assignment will fail so that no information is lost; your DBMS will return the `SQLSTATE error 22015 "data exception-interval field overflow."`
- The same considerations apply for assignments of day–time intervals that don't have the same <interval qualifier>.

Comparison

SQL provides the usual scalar comparison operators, = and <> and < and <= and > and >= , to perform operations on temporal values. All of them will be familiar; there are equivalent operators in other computer languages. If any of the comparands are `NULL`, the result of the operation is `UNKNOWN`. For example:

```
DATE '1997-07-15' = DATE '1997-08-01'
```

returns FALSE.

```
DATE '1997-07-15' = {result is NULL}
```

returns UNKNOWN.

SQL also provides three quantifiers —ALL, SOME, ANY — which you can use along with a comparison operator to compare a value with the collection of values returned by a <table subquery>. Place the quantifier after the comparison operator, immediately before the <table subquery>. For example:

```
SELECT date_column
FROM   Table_1
WHERE  date_column < ALL (
   SELECT date_column
   FROM   Table_2);
```

ALL returns TRUE either (*a*) if the collection is an empty set (i.e., if it contains zero rows) or (*b*) if the comparison operator returns TRUE for every value in the collection. ALL returns FALSE if the comparison operator returns FALSE for at least one value in the collection.

SOME and ANY are synonyms. They return TRUE if the comparison operator returns TRUE for at least one value in the collection. They return FALSE either (*a*) if the collection is an empty set or (*b*) if the comparison operator returns FALSE for every value in the collection. (The search condition = ANY (collection) is equivalent to IN (collection).)

Temporal values must be compatible to be compared with one another — that is, the source and the target must either (*a*) both be dates, (*b*) both be times (with or without time zone), (*c*) both be timestamps (with or without time zone), (*d*) both be year–month intervals, or (*e*) both be day–time intervals. The results of temporal comparisons are governed by the familiar rules for dates and times, i.e., those of the Gregorian calendar and the 24-hour clock.

Datetime Comparison

[Obscure Rule] When you compare two datetime values, the result is determined according to the interval obtained when your comparands are subtracted from one another. If you're comparing times or timestamps with different <time zone interval>s, your DBMS will ignore the value of the time zone offset for the comparison.

Interval Comparison

[Obscure Rule] When you compare two interval values, your DBMS will effectively convert both comparands to the same precision, in the least-significant common datetime unit, before the operation is carried out. For example, for this comparison:

```
INTERVAL '2-05' YEAR TO MONTH = INTERVAL '3' YEAR
```

both comparands are first converted to INTERVAL MONTH, making the actual comparison:

```
INTERVAL '29' MONTH = INTERVAL '36' MONTH
```

The result, of course, is FALSE.

Other Operations

With SQL, you have several other operations that you can perform on temporal values to get a temporal result.

Arithmetic

SQL provides the usual scalar arithmetic operators, + and - and * and / , to perform operations on temporal values. All of them will be familiar; there are equivalent operators in other computer languages. Arithmetic operations on temporal values are governed by the familiar rules for dates and times and yield valid datetimes or intervals according to the Gregorian calendar and the 24-hour clock. If any of the operands are `NULL`, the result of the operation is also `NULL`.

SQL doesn't allow you to do arithmetic on every possible combination of datetime and interval operands. Here are the valid possibilities and the <data type> of the result:

Date + Interval and Interval + Date both yield Date
Date – Interval yields Date
Date – Date yields Interval
Time + Interval and Interval + Time both yield Time
Time – Interval yields Time
Timestamp + Interval and Interval + Timestamp both yield Timestamp
Timestamp – Interval yields Timestamp
year–month Interval + year–month Interval yields year–month Interval
day–time Interval + day–time Interval yields day–time Interval
year–month Interval – year–month Interval yields year–month Interval
day–time Interval – day–time Interval yields day–time Interval
Time – Time yields Interval
Timestamp – Timestamp yields Interval
Interval * Number and Number * Interval both yield Interval
Interval / Number yields Interval

In each of these cases, the operands can be any argument that evaluates to the specified <data type>.

The rules for temporal arithmetic can be explained with this analogy. When you subtract the `INTEGER` value 123456 from 123557, you get another `INTEGER` value: –101. So, when you subtract `TIME '12:34:56'` from `TIME '12:35:57'`, should you get the `TIME` value: `'-00:01:01'`? Well, no — there's no such thing as a negative time-of-day so SQL's `TIME` <data type> can't hold this value.

Regardless, some people are of the opinion that it looks right to represent the result as <negative> zero hours : one minute : one second. After all, the result is still a time, although it is reasonable to distinguish "time as an elapsed duration" from "time as a moment in the time scale."

Other people don't believe that the "negative time value" looks correct. They feel that (time minus time) should result in an `INTEGER` — the number of elapsed seconds, 61. While there are still several DBMSs which follow this line, they aren't SQL DBMSs — the SQL Standard states that operations like (datetime minus datetime) yield an `INTERVAL`, which can be signed.

Our analogy would make us expect "date intervals" along these lines:

1994-03-02	1994-01-31
–1994-01-31	+0000-01-02
0000-01-02	1994-03-02

but SQL considers these calculations to be illegal because year–month intervals are not compatible with day–time intervals. That is, in SQL temporal arithmetic, you cannot carry from the days field to the months field, nor borrow from the months field to the days field. There is a way to get around what we call "The Day–Month Arithmetic Barrier" — but first we'll look at the interval combinations that are encouraged by the Standard.

As stated earlier, the year–month intervals are compatible with each other, so this is legal:

```
INTERVAL '00' YEAR + INTERVAL '00' MONTH
```

The result is `INTERVAL '00-00' YEAR TO MONTH`.

The day–time intervals are also compatible with each other, so this is legal:

```
INTERVAL '00:00' HOUR TO MINUTE +
INTERVAL '00:00' MINUTE  TO SECOND
```

The result is `INTERVAL '00:00:00' HOUR TO SECOND`.

Since year–month intervals and day–time intervals are not compatible, the following is illegal:

```
INTERVAL '00' MONTH + INTERVAL '01' DAY
```

(From this, it is apparent that the Standard's words "`INTERVAL` <data type>" are misleading. For all practical purposes we really have two <data types> that are not compatible with one another.)

The 1998 movie *Titanic* was billed as a "2 hour 74 minute" movie. This is legitimate if there is no law that says "when number of minutes is greater than or equal to 60, carry into the hours column." However, SQL won't allow <interval literal>s like:

```
INTERVAL '02:74' HOUR TO MINUTE
```

because, according to the SQL Standard, interval fields must follow "the natural rules for intervals" — and these rules are (*a*) there are no more than 60 seconds in a minute, (*b*) there are no more than 60 minutes in an hour, (*c*) there are no more than 24 hours in a day, and (*d*) there are no more than 12 months in a year. This is not to say, though, that the result of temporal *arithmetic* operations should look odd — as with assignment and comparison, your DBMS will normalize the result to maintain the integrity of its datetime <data type>. For year–month intervals, it carries: (`if month>=12 carry to year`). For the day–time intervals, it also carries: (`if second>=60 carry to minute`), (`if minute>=60 carry to hour`), (`if hour>=24 carry to day`). Because the result is normalized, the expression:

```
INTERVAL '02' HOUR + INTERVAL '74' MINUTE
```

yields:

```
INTERVAL '03:14' HOUR TO MINUTE
```

Here, then, is the syntax allowed for temporal expressions:

```
datetime expression ::=
datetime value [ AT {LOCAL | TIME ZONE <time zone interval} ] |
interval expression + datetime value [ AT {LOCAL | TIME ZONE <time
        zone interval} ] |
datetime value [ AT {LOCAL | TIME ZONE <time zone interval} ] +
                interval term |
datetime value [ AT {LOCAL | TIME ZONE <time zone interval} ] -
                interval term

interval expression ::=
interval term |
interval expression + interval term |
interval expression - interval term |
(datetime expression - datetime value [ AT {LOCAL | TIME ZONE <time
         zone interval} ]) <interval qualifier>

   interval term ::=
   [ + | - ] interval value |
   [ + | - ] interval value * number |
   [ + | - ] interval value / number |
   number * [ + | - ] interval value
```

Datetime expressions may only contain values of the same type. A datetime expression involving dates evaluates to a date. A datetime expression involving times evaluates to a time. A datetime expression involving timestamps evaluates to a timestamp. The optional AT LOCAL or AT TIME ZONE clause is valid only for datetime values that evaluate to times or to timestamps. The first case — e.g., TIME '10:15:00' AT LOCAL — means you want the time value to be adjusted to the current default time zone offset for the SQL-session; this is the default situation. The second case — e.g., TIMESTAMP '1994-07-15 14:00:00' AT TIME ZONE INTERVAL '-04:00' HOUR TO MINUTE — means you want the timestamp value to be adjusted to the time zone offset you've specified. The result <data type> is TIME WITH TIME ZONE or TIMESTAMP WITH TIME ZONE, as applicable. If <time zone interval> is NULL, the result of the operation is also NULL.

Interval expressions may only contain values of the same type. An interval expression involving year–month intervals evaluates to a year–month interval. An interval expression involving day–time intervals evaluates to a day–time interval.

All temporal arithmetic depends on the concept of the interval; a span of time expressed in calendar or clock units (as appropriate). Intervals may only be used with datetime and/or interval expressions that involve at least one compatible datetime field. For example, this is a legal expression:

```
start_date + INTERVAL '2' MONTH
```

because a date and the specified interval have the MONTH field in common. This is not a legal expression:

```
start_date + (INTERVAL '2' MONTH + INTERVAL '1' DAY)
```

because the interval expression inside the parentheses would have to be evaluated first, and the two intervals have no datetime fields in common.

These rules apply for date arithmetic:

1. If one operand evaluates to a date, the other operand must evaluate to a date, an INTERVAL YEAR, an INTERVAL MONTH, an INTERVAL YEAR TO MONTH, or an INTERVAL DAY.
2. You can't add two dates. You can only add a date and an interval.
3. You can subtract a date from a date and you can subtract an interval from a date. You can't subtract a date from an interval.
4. Date expressions are evaluated according to the rules for valid Gregorian calendar dates. If the result is an invalid date, the expression will fail; your DBMS will return the SQLSTATE error 22008 "data exception-datetime field overflow."
5. Remember that if your interval operand is a year–month interval, there is no carry from the date operand's DAY field. Thus while this expression:

   ```
   DATE '1997-07-31' + INTERVAL '1' MONTH
   ```

   returns DATE '1997-08-31' as expected, the result of the expression:

   ```
   DATE '1997-10-31' + INTERVAL '1' MONTH
   ```

   is an error. There is no DAY field carry, so the result evaluates to DATE '1997-11-31' — an invalid date.

These rules apply for time arithmetic:

1. If one operand evaluates to a time, the other operand must evaluate to a time, an INTERVAL DAY, an INTERVAL HOUR, an INTERVAL MINUTE, an INTERVAL SECOND, an INTERVAL DAY TO HOUR, an INTERVAL DAY TO MINUTE, an INTERVAL DAY TO SECOND, an INTERVAL HOUR TO MINUTE, an INTERVAL HOUR TO SECOND, or an INTERVAL MINUTE TO SECOND.
2. You can't add two times. You can only add a time and an interval.
3. You can subtract a time from a time and you can subtract an interval from a time. You can't subtract a time from an interval.
4. Time expressions are evaluated modulo 24 — that is:

   ```
   TIME '19:00:00' + INTERVAL '9' HOUR
   ```

   returns TIME '04:00:00'. If the result is an invalid time, the expression will fail; your DBMS will return the SQLSTATE error 22008 "data exception-datetime field overflow."
5. The result of an operation between operands containing a SECONDs value has a fractional seconds precision that is the greater of the operands' fractional seconds precisions.
6. [Obscure Rule] Arithmetic operations involving a time and an interval preserve the time operand's <time zone interval>. If your operand is a time without time zone, then the current default time zone offset is assumed.

These rules apply for timestamp arithmetic:

1. If one operand evaluates to a timestamp, the other operand must evaluate to a timestamp, an `INTERVAL YEAR`, an `INTERVAL MONTH`, an `INTERVAL YEAR TO MONTH`, an `INTERVAL DAY`, an `INTERVAL HOUR`, an `INTERVAL MINUTE`, an `INTERVAL SECOND`, an `INTERVAL DAY TO HOUR`, an `INTERVAL DAY TO MINUTE`, an `INTERVAL DAY TO SECOND`, an `INTERVAL HOUR TO MINUTE`, an `INTERVAL HOUR TO SECOND`, or an `INTERVAL MINUTE TO SECOND`.
2. You can't add two timestamps. You can only add a timestamp and an interval.
3. You can subtract a timestamp from a timestamp and you can subtract an interval from a timestamp. You can't subtract a timestamp from an interval.
4. Timestamp expressions are evaluated according to the rules for valid Gregorian calendar dates. This means that, unlike time expressions, timestamp expressions are not evaluated modulo 24 because `HOUR`s will carry to/from `DAY`s. Thus, the result of the expression:

   ```
   TIMESTAMP '1997-07-15 19:00:00' + INTERVAL '9' HOUR
   ```

   is `TIMESTAMP '1997-07-16 04:00:00'`. If the result of a timestamp expression is an invalid timestamp, the expression will fail; your DBMS will return the `SQLSTATE error 22008` "`data exception-datetime field overflow.`"
5. The result of an operation between operands containing a `SECOND`s value has a fractional seconds precision that is the greater of the operands' fractional seconds precisions.
6. [Obscure Rule] Arithmetic operations involving a timestamp and an interval preserve the timestamp operand's <time zone interval>. If your operand is a timestamp without time zone, then the current default time zone offset is assumed.

   These additional rules apply for `INTERVAL` arithmetic:

1. If one operand evaluates to a year–month interval, the other operand must evaluate to a year–month interval, a date, or a timestamp. If one operand evaluates to a day–time interval, the other operand must evaluate to a day–time interval, a date, a time, or a timestamp.
2. You can add two intervals of the same type.
3. You can subtract two intervals of the same type.
4. You can multiply an interval with a number or a number with an interval.
5. You can divide an interval by a number. You can't divide a number by an interval.
6. The result of an operation between interval operands containing a `SECOND`s value has a fractional seconds precision that is the greater of the operands' fractional seconds precisions.
7. Interval expressions that result in invalid intervals will fail; your DBMS will return the `SQLSTATE error 22015` "`data exception-interval field overflow.`"

If you want to restrict your code to Core SQL, don't add or subtract datetime expressions, don't add the optional `AT LOCAL/AT TIME ZONE` clause to any time or timestamp value and don't use interval expressions at all.

Coming back to the problem of subtracting two dates, we can see that the following expression:

```
DATE '1994-03-02' - DATE '1994-01-31'
```

is impossible on the face of it, because it would yield a nonexistent year–month–day interval. The converse is also true — the expression:

```
DATE '1994-01-31' + INTERVAL '00-01-02' YEAR TO DAY
```

will return a syntax error. All, however, is not lost. When subtracting these dates, you can force the result with the syntax (datetime expression – datetime value) <interval qualifier>, where the result is determined by the least significant datetime field in <interval qualifier>. For example, if you want to know the difference between the two dates in years, use:

```
(DATE '1994-03-02' - DATE '1994-01-31') YEAR
```

which results in `INTERVAL '00' YEAR`. (The least significant datetime field in the interval is `YEAR`, and 1994-1994 is zero.) If you want to know the difference between the two dates in months, use:

```
(DATE '1994-03-02' - DATE '1994-01-31') MONTH
```

which results in `INTERVAL '02' MONTH`. (Note that this is not the "intuitive" answer one might expect! The least significant field in the interval is `MONTH`, and `((1994*12 months)+ 3 months)-((1994*12 months)+ 1 month)` is two, so even though we can see that the difference between the dates is not a full two months, the correct SQL result is two.) If you want to know the difference between the two dates in years and months, use:

```
(DATE '1994-03-02' - DATE '1994-01-31') YEAR TO MONTH
```

which results in `INTERVAL '00-01' YEAR TO MONTH`. If you want to know the difference between the two dates in days, use:

```
(DATE '1994-03-02' - DATE '1994-01-31') DAY
```

which results in `INTERVAL '30' DAY`. (The least significant field in the interval is `DAY` and (61 days – 31 days) is 30.)

A runaway serf must hide in a town for a year and a day to gain freedom. If he runs away on March 12 1346, when can he party? SQL doesn't allow the expression:

```
DATE '1346-03-12' + (INTERVAL '1' YEAR + INTERVAL '1' DAY)
```

because the two interval types can't combine. But they each go well with a date, so:

```
(DATE '1346-03-12' + INTERVAL '1' YEAR) + INTERVAL '1' DAY
```

yields `DATE '1347-03-13'`. (The parentheses here are optional, because calculation is left-to-right.)

Errors

The four common arithmetic exception conditions are as follows.

`SQLSTATE 22007`	data exception — invalid datetime format e.g., returned for this result: `DATE '1994-02-30'`
`SQLSTATE 22008`	data exception — datetime field overflow e.g., returned for this expression: `DATE '9999-01-01' + INTERVAL '1-00' YEAR TO MONTH`
`SQLSTATE 22015`	data exception — interval field overflow e.g., returned for this result: `INTERVAL '999-11' YEAR TO MONTH` (too many digits in leading field)
`SQLSTATE 22009`	data exception — invalid time zone displacement value e.g., returned for this result: `TIME '02:00:00+14:00'`

Scalar Operations

SQL provides nine scalar operations that return a temporal value: the <case expression>, the <cast specification>, the current date value function, the current time value function, the current timestamp value function, the current local time value function, and the current local timestamp value function (we'll call these last five the *niladic datetime functions*), the <extract expression>, and the <interval absolute value function>. We'll discuss all but the <case expression> and the <cast specification> here. We've already talked about casting temporal values; look for the <case expression> in Chapter 29 "Simple Search Conditions." For now, just remember that CASE can evaluate to a temporal value and can therefore be used anywhere in SQL that a temporal value could be used.

Niladic Datetime Functions

The required syntax for a niladic datetime function is:

```
niladic datetime function ::=
CURRENT_DATE |
CURRENT_TIME [ (fractional seconds precision) ] |
CURRENT_TIMESTAMP [ (fractional seconds precision) ] |
LOCALTIME [ (fractional seconds precision) ] |
LOCALTIMESTAMP [ (fractional seconds precision) ]
```

CURRENT_DATE is a niladic datetime function with a result <data type> of DATE. It returns "today" — that is, the current date. Here is an example of CURRENT_DATE:

```
...WHERE date_column = CURRENT_DATE
```

CURRENT_TIME is a niladic datetime function with a result <data type> of TIME WITH TIME ZONE. It returns "now" — that is, the current time, with a time zone offset equal to the SQL-session default time zone offset. The default time zone offset is the <time zone interval> specified in the most recent SET TIME ZONE statement issued during the SQL-session. If you haven't issued a SET TIME ZONE statement, the default time zone offset is your DBMS's initial default time zone offset.

[NON-PORTABLE] The default time zone offset is non-standard because the SQL Standard requires implementors to define the initial default time zone offset for an SQL-session. [OCELOT Implementation] The OCELOT DBMS that comes with this book sets the SQL-session's initial default time zone offset to INTERVAL +'00:00' HOUR TO MINUTE — this represents UTC.

Here is an example of CURRENT_TIME:

```
...WHERE time_column <> CURRENT_TIME
```

As with the TIME WITH TIME ZONE <data type>, the optional fractional seconds precision, if specified, is an unsigned integer that specifies the number of digits following the decimal point in the SECONDs field of CURRENT_TIME's result.

CURRENT_TIMESTAMP is a niladic datetime function with a result <data type> of TIMESTAMP WITH TIME ZONE. It returns "now" — that is, the current time "today," with a time zone offset equal to the SQL-session default time zone offset. As with the TIMESTAMP WITH TIME ZONE <data type>, the optional fractional seconds precision, if specified, is an unsigned integer that specifies the number of digits following the decimal point in the SECONDs field of CURRENT_TIMESTAMP's result. Here is an example of CURRENT_TIMESTAMP:

```
...WHERE timestamp_column > CURRENT_TIMESTAMP
```

LOCALTIME is a niladic datetime function with a result <data type> of TIME. It returns "now-here" — that is, the current local time, with no time zone offset. As with the TIME <data type>, the optional fractional seconds precision, if specified, is an unsigned integer that specifies the number of digits following the decimal point in the SECONDs field of LOCALTIME's result. The result of LOCALTIME is obtained by casting CURRENT_TIME's result — i.e.,

```
LOCALTIME = CAST (CURRENT_TIME AS TIME)
```

or, if fractional seconds precision is specified:

```
LOCALTIME(precision) = CAST (CURRENT_TIME(precision) AS TIME(precision))
```

Here is an example of LOCALTIME:

```
...WHERE time_column < LOCALTIME
```

LOCALTIMESTAMP is a niladic datetime function with a result <data type> of TIMESTAMP. It returns "now-here" — that is, the current local time "today," with no time zone offset. As with the TIMESTAMP <data type>, the optional fractional seconds precision, if specified, is an unsigned integer that specifies the number of digits following the decimal point in the SECONDs field of LOCALTIMESTAMP's result. The result of LOCALTIMESTAMP is obtained by casting CURRENT_TIMESTAMP's result — i.e.,

```
LOCALTIMESTAMP = CAST (CURRENT_TIMESTAMP AS TIMESTAMP)
```

or, if fractional seconds precision is specified:

```
LOCALTIMESTAMP(precision) = CAST (CURRENT_TIMESTAMP(precision) AS
TIMESTAMP(precision))
```

Here is an example of LOCALTIMESTAMP:

```
...WHERE timestamp_column >= LOCALTIMESTAMP
```

All niladic datetime functions in an SQL statement are effectively evaluated at the same time; that is, all references to CURRENT_DATE, CURRENT_TIME, CURRENT_TIMESTAMP, LOCALTIME, or LOCALTIMESTAMP in a single SQL statement will return their respective values based on a single clock reading. CURRENT_DATE, CURRENT_TIMESTAMP, and LOCALTIMESTAMP will therefore always return the same date, and CURRENT_TIME, CURRENT_TIMESTAMP, LOCALTIME, and LOCALTIMESTAMP will always return the same effective time when used within the same SQL statement.

[NON-PORTABLE] The timing of the clock reading for the evaluation of these functions is non-standard because the SQL Standard requires implementors to define when the clock is read. The choices are to read the clock at the beginning of a transaction, at the end of a transaction, or somewhere in-between. [OCELOT Implementation] The OCELOT DBMS that comes with this book reads the clock immediately prior to performing any operations based on a niladic datetime function.

If you want to restrict your code to Core SQL, don't use CURRENT_TIME or CURRENT_TIMESTAMP, don't specify a fractional seconds precision for LOCALTIME, and don't specify a fractional seconds precision for LOCALTIMESTAMP other than zero or 6.

NOTE: The CURRENT_TIME and CURRENT_TIMESTAMP functions differ in SQL-92 and SQL3. In SQL-92, CURRENT_TIME and CURRENT_TIMESTAMP return the current local time and their <data type>s are TIME and TIMESTAMP (*without* time zone). In SQL3, the functions that return the current local time are LOCALTIME and LOCALTIMESTAMP. CURRENT_TIME and CURRENT_TIMESTAMP now return values with a <data type> of TIME WITH TIME ZONE and TIMESTAMP WITH TIME ZONE (that is, *with* a time zone offset) and are not part of Core SQL.

<extract expression>

The required syntax for an <extract expression> is as follows.

```
<extract expression> ::=
EXTRACT(datetime_field FROM temporal_argument)
```

EXTRACT operates on an argument that evaluates to a date, a time, a timestamp, or an interval. It extracts the numeric value of datetime_field from temporal_argument and returns it as an exact numeric value. If the argument is NULL, EXTRACT returns NULL.

The datetime_field may be any one of: YEAR, MONTH, DAY, HOUR, MINUTE, SECOND, TIMEZONE_HOUR, or TIMEZONE_MINUTE. If datetime_field is TIMEZONE_HOUR or TIMEZONE_MINUTE, temporal_argument must evaluate to a TIME WITH TIME ZONE value or a TIMESTAMP WITH TIME ZONE value.

For any datetime_field other than SECOND, EXTRACT returns an integer. For a datetime_field of SECOND, EXTRACT returns a decimal number. For example:

```
EXTRACT (MINUTE FROM INTERVAL '-05:01:22.01' HOUR TO SECOND)
```

returns the integer –1 (when temporal_argument is a negative interval, the result will be a negative number).

```
EXTRACT (SECOND FROM INTERVAL '-05:01:22.01' HOUR TO SECOND)
```

returns the decimal number –22.01.

[NON-PORTABLE] The precision of EXTRACT's result is non-standard because the SQL Standard requires implementors to define the result's precision and (if applicable) the result's scale. (The scale defined must be at least large enough to accept the full size of the argument's fractional seconds precision.) [OCELOT Implementation] The OCELOT DBMS that comes with this book gives the result of EXTRACT an INTEGER <data type> for all datetime_fields other than SECOND. It gives the result of EXTRACT a DECIMAL(8,2) <data type> for a datetime_field of SECOND.

Here is an SQL statement which extracts the YEAR field from a timestamp:

```
SELECT EXTRACT(YEAR FROM occurrence_timestamp)
FROM   Timestamp_Examples;
```

The result is the integer 2001.

If you want to restrict your code to Core SQL, don't use EXTRACT.

<interval absolute value function>

The required syntax for an <interval absolute value function> is as follows.

```
<interval absolute value function> ::=
 ABS (interval_argument)
```

ABS operates on an argument that evaluates to an interval. It strips a negative sign (if it's present) from the argument and returns a non-negative interval whose <data type> is the same as the argument's <data type>, e.g., ABS(INTERVAL '-05' YEAR) returns INTERVAL '5' YEAR, ABS(INTERVAL '05' YEAR) returns INTERVAL '05' YEAR, and ABS(INTERVAL '00' YEAR) returns INTERVAL '00' YEAR. If the argument is NULL, ABS returns NULL.

[Obscure Rule] ABS can also operate on a number. We've ignored this option for now — look for it in Chapter 3 "Numbers."

If you want to restrict your code to Core SQL, don't use ABS with an interval argument.

Set Functions

SQL provides four set functions that operate on datetime values: COUNT, MAX, MIN, and GROUPING. SQL also provides six set functions that operate on intervals: COUNT, MAX, MIN, SUM, AVG, and GROUPING. Since none of these operate exclusively with temporal arguments, we won't discuss them here; look for them in Chapter 33 "Searching with Groups."

Predicates

In addition to the comparison operators, SQL provides nine other predicates that operate on temporal values: the <overlaps predicate>, the <between predicate>, the <in predicate>, the <null predicate>, the <exists predicate>, the <unique predicate>, the <match predicate>, the <quantified predicate>, and the <distinct predicate>. Each will return a boolean value; either TRUE, FALSE, or UNKNOWN. Only the first predicate operates strictly on temporal values; we'll discuss it here. Look for the rest in Chapter 29 "Simple Search Conditions."

<overlaps predicate>

The required syntax for an <overlaps predicate> is:

```
<overlaps predicate> ::=
(datetime_argument_1, temporal_argument_1)
OVERLAPS
(datetime_argument_2, temporal_argument_2)
```

OVERLAPS is a predicate that operates on two operands that evaluate to a span of time. It compares either a pair of datetimes, or a datetime and an interval, to test whether the two chronological periods overlap in time. It returns TRUE if they do, FALSE if they don't, and UNKNOWN if the result can't be determined because of NULL arguments.

Each OVERLAPS operand is a parenthesized pair of temporal arguments separated by a comma. (This is a special case of a <row value expression>). The first part of each operand must evaluate either to a date, a time, or a timestamp. The second part of each operand must either (*a*) evaluate to the same datetime <data type> as the first part or (*b*) evaluate to an interval that contains only the same datetime fields as the first part. Each operand represents a chronological span of time, as either "start to end" or "start and interval." The possible argument combinations as follows.

- (date,date) OVERLAPS (date,date)
- (date,date) OVERLAPS (date,interval of years or months or days)
- (date,interval of years or months or days) OVERLAPS (date,date)
- (date,interval of years or months or days) OVERLAPS (date,interval of years or months or days)
- (time,time) OVERLAPS (time,time)
- (time,time) OVERLAPS (time,interval of hours or minutes or seconds)
- (time,interval of hours or minutes or seconds) OVERLAPS (time,time)
- (time,interval of hours or minutes or seconds) OVERLAPS (time,interval of hours or minutes or seconds)
- (timestamp,timestamp) OVERLAPS (timestamp,timestamp)
- (timestamp,timestamp) OVERLAPS (timestamp,interval of years or months or days or hours or minutes or seconds)
- (timestamp,interval of years or months or days or hours or minutes or seconds) OVERLAPS (timestamp,timestamp)
- (timestamp,interval of years or months or days or hours or minutes or seconds) OVERLAPS (timestamp,interval of years or months or days or hours or minutes or seconds)

Here is an example of a search condition using OVERLAPS:

```
(DATE '1994-01-01',DATE '1994-05-01') OVERLAPS
(DATE '1993-07-01',DATE '1994-03-01')
```

The example is asking whether the two temporal periods overlap as in this diagram:

```
                January 1 1994                              May 1 1994
                ***********************************************
                ^                     ^
July 1 1993                         March 1 1994
**********************************************
```

The diagram shows us that there is an overlap — the search condition result is TRUE. In this example, both OVERLAPS operands are "start to end" argument pairs; they're both of the same <data type>. Here is an equivalent example, using "start and interval" argument pairs instead:

```
(DATE '1994-01-01',INTERVAL '05' MONTH) OVERLAPS
(DATE '1993-07-01',INTERVAL '08' MONTH)
```

(The INTERVAL argument must be compatible with the datetime <data type>, so that the operation "datetime + interval" will be possible. This is how OVERLAPS determines the "end" argument.)

OVERLAPS is really a comparison operation whose result is determined by this equivalent search condition (the OVERLAPS datetime_argument_1 is first_start, temporal_argument_1 is first_end, datetime_argument_2 is second_start, and temporal_argument_2 is second_end):

```
(first_start > second_start AND
   (first_start < second_end OR first_end < second_end))
OR
(second_start > first_start AND
   (second_start < first_end OR second_end < first_end))
OR
(first_start = second_start AND
   (first_end <> second_end OR first_end = second_end))
```

If the second argument of a pair is smaller than the first (i.e., if the end point is earlier in time than the start point) or if the first argument of a pair is NULL, OVERLAPS switches them around. For example, if the search condition contains:

```
(DATE '1994-01-01',DATE '1993-05-01') OVERLAPS
(DATE '1993-07-01',DATE '1994-03-01')
```

the expression your DBMS will actually evaluate is:

```
(DATE '1993-05-01',DATE '1994-01-01') OVERLAPS
(DATE '1993-07-01',DATE '1994-03-01')
```

which evaluates to TRUE; the periods overlap. If the search condition contains:

```
(NULL,DATE '1994-05-01') OVERLAPS
(DATE '1993-07-01',DATE '1994-03-01')
```

the expression your DBMS will actually evaluate is:

```
(DATE '1994-05-01',NULL) OVERLAPS
(DATE '1993-07-01',DATE '1994-03-01')
```

which evaluates to UNKNOWN. However, this search condition evaluates to TRUE, despite the NULL argument:

```
(DATE '1994-07-01',INTERVAL '06' MONTH) OVERLAPS
(DATE '1994-08-01',NULL)
```

If you want to restrict your code to Core SQL, don't use the OVERLAPS predicate.

Dialects

The "typical" SQL DBMS supports date, time, and timestamp data types but interval (as a separate data type) is not common yet. The majority of SQL DBMSs can't handle time zones, fractional seconds, or leap seconds. For example, the Oracle DATE data type is typically a timestamp (i.e., it includes both a date portion and a time portion, despite the name) with no fractional seconds, formatted as DD-MON-YY (e.g., 06-JAN-97). Valid dates fall into the range January 1 4713 BC to December 31 4712 AD. Intervals are expressed only as integers, representing number of days. The Oracle SYSDATE function returns the current date and the current time.

ODBC has several datetime functions; most are replaceable with standard SQL3. Here are the different names to expect:

Standard	ODBC
CURRENT_DATE	CURDATE
LOCALTIME	CURTIME
LOCALTIMESTAMP	NOW
EXTRACT(MONTH ...	MONTH
(EXTRACT(MONTH...)/4	QUARTER
EXTRACT(DAY ...	DAYOFMONTH
not supported	DAYOFWEEK
not supported	DAYOFYEAR
EXTRACT(HOUR ...	HOUR
EXTRACT(MINUTE ...	MINUTE
EXTRACT(SECOND ...	SECOND

The SQL Library

Before we finish discussing temporal values, it's time to add something to our SQL library. To be worthy of addition to the SQL library, a routine must (*a*) be good clean SQL, (*b*) be callable from C and Delphi, (*c*) be actually useful in C and Delphi because it does something that those languages can't, and (*d*) have nothing at all do with "databases" — it should be available for use just like any general function library.

Our addition to the SQL library for this chapter will check dates for SQL validity. Here it is.

```
/* proleptic test -- test whether the DBMS uses a proleptic calendar
   Pass:   Nothing
   Return: 0 DBMS uses standard SQL with proleptic Gregorian calendar
           1 DBMS uses standard SQL with corrected Gregorian calendar
           2 DBMS uses Julian calendar
           3 DBMS has deviant date calculator
           4 DBMS does not understand standard SQL syntax */
int proleptic_test (void *)
{
  SQLExecDirect(...,
  "SELECT ... WHERE DATE '2000-02-28' + '2' DAY = DATE '2000-03-01'",
  ...);
  if (return_code == syntax_error) return (4);
  if (number_of_rows_returned == 0) return (3);
```

```
  SQLExecDirect(...,
  "SELECT ... WHERE DATE '1900-02-28' + '2' DAY = DATE '1900-03-02'",
  ...);
  if (return_code == syntax_error) return (4);
  if (number_of_rows_returned == 0) return (2);

  SQLExecDirect(...,
  "SELECT ... WHERE DATE '1582-10-04' + '1' DAY = DATE '1582-10-15'",
  ...);
  if (return_code == syntax_error) return (3);
  if (number_of_rows_returned == 0) return (0);
  return (1); }

/* date_valid_test -- test whether a date is valid
   Pass:   A string containing a date in the format yyyy-mm-dd
   Return: 0 date is valid
          <0 date is not valid
          >0 date is valid but a warning was set */
int date_valid_test (char *szdate)
{
  char tmp[128];
  strcpy(tmp,"VALUES (DATE '");
  strcat(tmp,szdate);
  strcat(tmp,"')");
  return (SQLExecDirect(...,tmp,...)); }
```

9

Chapter 9

Boolean Values

In SQL, a Boolean value — either TRUE, FALSE, or UNKNOWN — is a truth value. A Boolean value may be a <literal>, the value of a parameter or a host language variable, or the result of any expression or argument (including a possibly qualified <Column name>, or the result of an SQL predicate or search condition) that evaluates to a truth value. Boolean values are stored in the Boolean <data type>: BOOLEAN.

<Boolean literal>s

A <Boolean literal> is one of these three words:

```
TRUE
FALSE
UNKNOWN
```

Its <data type> is BOOLEAN. A <Boolean literal> of TRUE represents the truth value TRUE, a <Boolean literal> of FALSE represents the truth value FALSE, and a <Boolean literal> of UNKNOWN represents the truth value UNKNOWN.

If you want to restrict your code to Core SQL, don't use <Boolean literal>s.

Boolean <data type>s

A Boolean <data type> is defined by a descriptor that contains one piece of information — the <data type>'s name: BOOLEAN.

BOOLEAN

The required syntax for a BOOLEAN <data type> specification is as follows.

```
BOOLEAN <data type> ::=
BOOLEAN
```

BOOLEAN defines a set of truth values: either TRUE, FALSE, or UNKNOWN.

The SQL Standard doesn't differentiate between BOOLEAN's null value (that is, UNKNOWN) and the UNKNOWN truth value that is returned by an SQL predicate, search condition, or any argument or expression that returns a Boolean value — it allows both to be used interchangeably to mean the same thing. Warning: by saying that UNKNOWN and NULL are the same thing, one is saying that the answers "I don't know" and "I know that the data is missing" are the same thing. The drafters of the SQL Standard apparently forgot the distinction, and they have been justly criticized for this error.

If you want to restrict your code to Core SQL, don't define any BOOLEAN <data type>s.

Now that we've described SQL's Boolean <data type>, let's look at some example SQL statements that put it to use.

These SQL statements make a Table with three Boolean Columns, insert a row, then search for a pair of equal Column values:

```
CREATE TABLE Logicals (
   boolean_1 BOOLEAN,
   boolean_2 BOOLEAN,
   boolean_3 BOOLEAN);

INSERT INTO Logicals (
   boolean_1,
   boolean_2,
   boolean_3)
VALUES (TRUE,FALSE,UNKNOWN);

SELECT boolean_1
FROM   Logicals
WHERE  boolean_1 = boolean_3;
```

Boolean Operations

A Boolean value is compatible with, and comparable to, all other Boolean values and all SQL truth values (for example, the truth values returned by an SQL predicate) — that is, all truth values are mutually comparable and mutually assignable. Truth values may not be directly compared with, or directly assigned to, any other <data type> class, though implicit type conversions can occur in expressions, SELECTs, INSERTs, DELETEs, and UPDATEs. Explicit truth value type conversions can be forced with the CAST operator.

CAST

In SQL, CAST is a scalar operator that converts a given scalar value to a given scalar <data type>. The required syntax for the CAST operator is as follows

```
CAST (<cast operand> AS <cast target>)
   <cast operand> ::= scalar_expression
   <cast target> ::= <Domain name> | <data type>
```

The CAST operator converts values of a source <data type> into values of a target <data type> where each <data type> is an SQL pre-defined <data type> (data conversions between UDTs are done with a user-defined cast). The source <data type> (or <cast operand>) can be any expression that evaluates to a single value. The target <data type> (or <cast target>) is either an SQL predefined <data type> specification or the name of a Domain whose defined <data type> is your target <data type>. (If you use CAST (... AS <Domain name>), your current <AuthorizationID> must have the USAGE Privilege on that Domain.)

It isn't, of course, possible to convert the values of every <data type> into the values of every other <data type>. For Boolean values, the rules are:

- CAST (NULL AS <data type>) and CAST (Boolean_source_is_a_null_value AS <data type>) both result in NULL.
- You can CAST a Boolean source to these targets: fixed length character string, variable length character string, CLOB, NCLOB, and Boolean. You can also CAST a Boolean source to a UDT target or a <reference type> target if a user-defined cast exists for this purpose and your current <AuthorizationID> has the EXECUTE Privilege on that user-defined cast.

When you CAST a Boolean value to a Boolean target, the result of the CAST is the source value.

When you CAST a Boolean value to a fixed length character string target, there are four possibilities:

1. The source value is TRUE and the fixed length of the target is at least four characters. In this case, the result of the CAST is 'TRUE', padded on the right with spaces if necessary to make it the exact fixed length of the target.
2. The source value is FALSE and the fixed length of the target is at least five characters. In this case, the result of the CAST is 'FALSE', padded on the right with spaces if necessary to make it the exact fixed length of the target.
3. The source value is UNKNOWN. As already stated, the result of the CAST is NULL.
4. The fixed length of the target is less than the length of the source value. In this case, the CAST will fail; your DBMS will return the SQLSTATE error 22018 "data exception-invalid character value for cast."

When you CAST a Boolean value to a variable length character string, CLOB, or NCLOB target, there are four possibilities:

1. The source value is TRUE and the maximum length of the target is at least four characters. In this case, the result of the CAST is 'TRUE'.
2. The source value is FALSE and the fixed length of the target is at least five characters. In this case, the result of the CAST is 'FALSE'.

3. The source value is UNKNOWN. As already stated, the result of the CAST is NULL.
4. The maximum length of the target is less than the length of the source value. In this case, the CAST will fail; your DBMS will return the SQLSTATE error 22018 "data exception-invalid character value for cast."

[Obscure Rule] The result of a CAST to a character string target has the COERCIBLE coercibility attribute; its Collation is the default Collation for the target's Character set.

When you CAST a Boolean value to a UDT or a <reference type> target, your DBMS invokes the user-defined cast routine with the source value as the routine's argument. The CAST result is the value returned by the user-defined cast.

If you want to restrict your code to Core SQL, don't use <Domain name> as a CAST target — CAST only to a <data type>.

Assignment

In SQL, the TRUE and FALSE truth values may be assigned to any Boolean target and the UNKNOWN truth value may be assigned to any Boolean target that isn't constrained by a NOT NULL Constraint.

Comparison

SQL provides the usual scalar comparison operators, = and <> and < and <= and > and >=, to perform operations on truth values. All of them will be familiar; there are equivalent operators in other computer languages. In SQL, TRUE is greater than FALSE. If any of the comparands are the UNKNOWN truth value or are NULL, the result of the operation is UNKNOWN. For example:

```
TRUE = {result is FALSE}
```

returns FALSE.

```
TRUE <> {result is NULL}
```

returns UNKNOWN.

SQL also provides three quantifiers — ALL, SOME, ANY — which you can use along with a comparison operator to compare a truth value with the collection of truth values returned by a <table subquery>. Place the quantifier after the comparison operator, immediately before the <table subquery>. For example:

```
SELECT occurrence_boolean
FROM   Boolean_Example
WHERE  occurrence_boolean = ALL (
   SELECT char_column
   FROM   Table_1
   WHERE  char_column LIKE '%e');
```

ALL returns TRUE either (*a*) if the collection is an empty set (i.e., if it contains zero rows) or (*b*) if the comparison operator returns TRUE for every value in the collection. ALL returns FALSE if the comparison operator returns FALSE for at least one value in the collection.

SOME and ANY are synonyms. They return TRUE if the comparison operator returns TRUE for at least one value in the collection. They return FALSE either (*a*) if the collection is an empty set or (*b*) if the comparison operator returns FALSE for every value in the collection. (The search condition = ANY (collection) is equivalent to IN (collection).)

Other Operations

With SQL, you have several other operations that you can perform on truth values or on other values to get a truth value result.

Boolean Operators

SQL provides the usual scalar Boolean operators — AND and OR and NOT and IS — to perform operations on Boolean operands. Each returns a Boolean result, or truth value. All of them will be familiar; there are equivalent operators in other computer languages. If any operand is the UNKNOWN truth value or is NULL, the result of the operation is UNKNOWN. Here is the syntax allowed for Boolean expressions:

```
<boolean value expression> ::=
<boolean term> |
<boolean value expression> OR <boolean term>

   <boolean term> ::=
   [ NOT ] <boolean test> |
   <boolean term> AND [ NOT ] <boolean test>

      <boolean test> ::=
      boolean_argument [ IS [ NOT ] {TRUE | FALSE | UNKNOWN} ]
```

A Boolean expression operates on one or more operands that evaluate to a truth value — that is, the boolean_argument shown in this syntax diagram is either a <Boolean literal>, the value of a parameter or a host language variable, or the result of any expression or argument (including a possibly qualified <Column name> or — most often — the result of an SQL predicate or search condition) that evaluates to a truth value. The result is also a truth value derived by applying the given Boolean operator(s) to the boolean_argument result.

IS is a monadic Boolean operator. It tests for a condition: is the result of the expression TRUE, is it FALSE, or is it UNKNOWN? You use the <Boolean test> to influence a search condition result, since its effect is to change a Boolean value (which is TRUE or FALSE or UNKNOWN) to either TRUE or FALSE. For example, consider these SQL statements which create a Table that contains four rows:

```
CREATE TABLE Boolean_Test (
   column_1 SMALLINT);

INSERT INTO Boolean_Test (column_1)
VALUES (5);
```

```
INSERT INTO Boolean_Test (column_1)
VALUES (NULL);

INSERT INTO Boolean_Test (column_1)
VALUES (0);

INSERT INTO Boolean_Test (column_1)
VALUES (10);
```

Row 1 of the Table BOOLEAN_TEST contains 5, row 2 contains NULL, row 3 contains 0, and row 4 contains 10. Normally, of course, a search for equality doesn't find NULLs — so the result of this SQL statement:

```
SELECT column_1
FROM   Boolean_Test
WHERE  column_1 = 5;
```

is row 1 and the result of this SQL statement:

```
SELECT column_1
FROM   Boolean_Test
WHERE  column_1 <> 5;
```

is row 3 and row 4. If you add a <Boolean test> though, you can override the comparison's usual result. Thus, the result of this SQL statement:

```
SELECT column_1
FROM   Boolean_Test
WHERE  (column_1 = 5 IS UNKNOWN);
```

is row 2 — it returns the rows where the search condition is UNKNOWN, rather than the rows where it is TRUE. The result of this SQL statement:

```
SELECT column_1
FROM   Boolean_Test
WHERE (column_1 = 5 IS FALSE);
```

is row 3 and row 4 — it returns only the rows where the search condition is FALSE. The result of this SQL statement:

```
SELECT column_1
FROM   Boolean_Test
WHERE (column_1 = 5 IS TRUE);
```

is row 1 — it returns the rows where the search condition is TRUE. Since this is the same result you'd get without the <Boolean test>, adding it is redundant. Finally, the result of this SQL statement:

```
SELECT column_1
FROM   Boolean_Test
WHERE (column_1 = 5 IS NOT FALSE);
```

is row 1 and row 2 — it returns the rows where the search condition is either TRUE or UNKNOWN. Table 9.1 shows how the result of a Boolean IS operation is determined.

Table 9.1 Truth values for the Boolean IS operator

If a Boolean value is:	...and the operator is:	...then the result is:
TRUE	IS TRUE	TRUE
TRUE	IS FALSE	FALSE
TRUE	IS UNKNOWN	FALSE
FALSE	IS TRUE	FALSE
FALSE	IS FALSE	TRUE
FALSE	IS UNKNOWN	FALSE
UNKNOWN	IS TRUE	FALSE
UNKNOWN	IS FALSE	FALSE
UNKNOWN	IS UNKNOWN	TRUE
TRUE	IS NOT TRUE	FALSE
TRUE	IS NOT FALSE	TRUE
TRUE	IS NOT UNKNOWN	TRUE
FALSE	IS NOT TRUE	TRUE
FALSE	IS NOT FALSE	FALSE
FALSE	IS NOT UNKNOWN	TRUE
UNKNOWN	IS NOT TRUE	TRUE
UNKNOWN	IS NOT FALSE	TRUE
UNKNOWN	IS NOT UNKNOWN	FALSE

NOT is a monadic Boolean operator. It negates the result of a Boolean expression (except in the case of NULLs) — that is:

- NOT (TRUE) returns FALSE.
- NOT (FALSE) returns TRUE.
- NOT (UNKNOWN) returns UNKNOWN.

AND is a dyadic Boolean operator. It increases the number of conditions that must be met by a value to be included in a search; the result is TRUE only if both conditions are TRUE. For example, the result of this SQL statement:

```
SELECT column_1
FROM   Boolean_Test
WHERE (column_1 > 0 AND column_1 < 10);
```

is row 1. Table 9.2 shows how the result of a Boolean AND operation is determined.

Table 9.2 Truth for the Boolean AND operator

If the first Boolean value is:	... and the second Boolean value is:	... then the result is:
TRUE	TRUE	TRUE
TRUE	FALSE	FALSE
TRUE	UNKNOWN	UNKNOWN
FALSE	TRUE	FALSE
FALSE	FALSE	FALSE
FALSE	UNKNOWN	FALSE
UNKNOWN	TRUE	UNKNOWN
UNKNOWN	FALSE	FALSE
UNKNOWN	UNKNOWN	UNKNOWN

OR is a dyadic Boolean operator. It decreases the number of conditions that must be met by a value to be included in a search — the result is TRUE if either condition is TRUE. For example, the result of this SQL statement:

```
SELECT column_1
FROM   Boolean_Test
WHERE (column_1 > 0 OR column_1 < 10);
```

is row 1 and row 3. Table 9.3 shows how the result of a Boolean OR operation is determined.

Table 9.3 Truth values for the Boolean OR operator

If the first Boolean value is:	... and the second Boolean value is:	... then the result is:
TRUE	TRUE	TRUE
TRUE	FALSE	TRUE
TRUE	UNKNOWN	TRUE
FALSE	TRUE	TRUE
FALSE	FALSE	FALSE

If the first Boolean value is:	... and the second Boolean value is:	... then the result is:
FALSE	UNKNOWN	UNKNOWN
UNKNOWN	TRUE	TRUE
UNKNOWN	FALSE	UNKNOWN
UNKNOWN	UNKNOWN	UNKNOWN

The precedence of the Boolean operators and their effect on Boolean values is as follows:

Precedence	Operator	Effect on Boolean value(s)
1.	IS	overrides normal result
2.	NOT	negates result
3.	AND	combines, with logical AND
4.	OR	combines, with logical inclusive OR

The precedence shown determines evaluation order, unless you use parentheses to force a different order. Although SQL's three-valued logic can complicate things if we use contrived and unlikely examples, the normal situation is straightforward for any speaker of a human tongue. When we hear the English expression, "Martians are vicious and dishonest but not stupid," we know we could search them with the SQL expression `x = 'vicious' AND x = 'dishonest' AND x <> 'stupid'`. The correct application of the Boolean operators turns out to be an intuitive calculation for most people. The most common error is to forget operator precedence and that can be corrected easily — always use parentheses if the search condition contains two different Boolean operators.

If you want to restrict your code to Core SQL, don't use the optional truth value Boolean test (i.e., don't use the constructs `boolean_argument IS TRUE`, `boolean_argument IS FALSE`, or `boolean_argument IS UNKNOWN`) and don't use `boolean_argument` unless it's an SQL predicate or it's enclosed in parentheses.

Scalar Operations

SQL provides no scalar functions that return or operate on a Boolean value.

Set Functions

SQL provides seven set functions that operate on Booleans: `EVERY`, `ANY`, `SOME`, `COUNT`, `MAX`, `MIN`, and `GROUPING`. We'll discuss them all in Chapter 33 "Searching with Groups."

Predicates

Every SQL predicate returns a Boolean value. Because none of them operate strictly on truth values, we won't discuss them here. Look for them in Chapter 29 "Simple Search Conditions" and chapters on the various other <data type>s.

10

Chapter 10

Collection Types

[Obscure Rule] applies for this entire chapter.

In SQL, a <collection type> is an array — a composite constructed SQL <data type>.

Collection <data type>s

A <collection type> is defined by a descriptor that contains three pieces of information:

1. The <data type>'s name: ARRAY.
2. The maximum number of elements in the array.
3. The array's element <data type> specification.

ARRAY

The required syntax for a <collection type> specification is as follows.

```
<collection type> ::=
<data type> <array specification>

   <array specification> ::=
   ARRAY[unsigned integer] | ARRAY??(unsigned integer??)
```

A <collection type> specification defines an array — it consists of an element <data type> specification followed by an indication of the array's maximum element size. For example, both of the following <collection type> specifications define an array of up to ten numbers, all of which must fall into the range supported by SQL's SMALLINT <data type>:

```
SMALLINT ARRAY[10]
SMALLINT ARRAY??(10??)
```

A <collection type> may not specify, either directly or indirectly (e.g., via a Domain), a <data type> of REF or ARRAY. All other SQL <data type>s are supported.

It is important to note that the square brackets in the <collection type>'s syntax diagrams should not be read as if they are BNF brackets — that is, they don't mean that ARRAY can optionally be followed by an integer. Instead, you use either square brackets or trigraphs to delimit the integer that specifies the size of the array. We'll use square brackets in the rest of our examples.

An array is an ordered collection of elements. There are some similarities between SQL ARRAYs and C or Pascal arrays, but there are also some significant differences: (*a*) SQL ARRAYs are only "vectors," so an array of an array is not supported and (*b*) SQL ARRAYs are variable size; the specification defines an array's maximum size rather than its exact size. In earlier SQL versions, there was no support for ARRAYs. In part, this lack of support was due to a well-known principle of database design, the rule of first normal form, "A field (a column/row intersection) may have only one atomic value." If rows contain arrays, they violate this principle, so a well-designed database doesn't define arrays all over the place.

[Obscure Rule] A <collection type> is a subtype of a <data type> if (*a*) both are arrays and (*b*) the element <data type> of the first array is a subtype of the element <data type> of the second array.

ARRAY **<element reference>**

An <element reference> returns an element of an array. The required syntax for an <element reference> is as follows.

```
<element reference> ::=
array_argument[numeric_argument] |
array_argument??(numeric_argument??)
```

An <element reference> allows you to access a specific element of an array. It operates on two arguments: the first must evaluate to an array and the second must evaluate to an integer. (The integer refers to the ordinal position of the element in the array: the first element in an array is element number 1, the second element is element number 2, and so on.) If either portion of an element reference is NULL, that element is also NULL. Here are two equivalent examples of an <element reference>:

```
array_column[4]
array_column??(4??)
```

In each case, the reference would return the fourth element of the array.

If numeric_argument is a negative number, or if it is greater than the number of elements in the array, the <element reference> will fail; your DBMS will return the SQLSTATE error 2202E "data exception-array element error."

<array value constructor>

An <array value constructor> is used to construct an array. The required syntax for an <array value constructor> is as follows.

```
<array value constructor> ::=
ARRAY[element_expression [ {,element_expression}... ]] |
ARRAY??(element_expression [ {,element_expression}... ]??)
```

An <array value constructor> allows you to assign values to the elements of an array. An `element_expression` may be any expression that evaluates to a scalar value with a <data type> that is assignable to the array's element <data type>. The result is an array whose *n*-th element value is the value of the *n*-th `element_expression` you specify. Here are two equivalent examples of an <array value constructor>:

```
ARRAY['hello','bob','and','sally']
ARRAY??('hello','bob','and','sally'??)
```

These examples both construct an array with four elements. The first element has a value of `'hello'`, the second has a value of `'bob'`, the third has a value of `'and'`, and the fourth has a value of `'sally'`. Both <array value constructor>s would be valid for this <collection type> specification:

```
VARCHAR(5) ARRAY[4]
```

An <array value constructor> serves the same purpose for an array as a <literal> does for a predefined <data type>. It has the same format as the <collection type>'s `ARRAY` specification — that is, `ARRAY[ ]` or `ARRAY??( ??)` — but instead of a number inside the size delimiters, it contains comma-delimited values of the correct <data type>. These are called *array elements* in SQL, though in other languages, an instance of an array is called an "occurrence." For example, if your <collection type> specification is:

```
INT ARRAY[3]
```

a valid <array value constructor> would be:

```
ARRAY[20,10,52]
```

And if your <collection type> specification is:

```
BIT(4) ARRAY[3]
```

a valid <array value constructor> would be:

```
ARRAY[B'1011',B'0011',B'0110']
```

The number of elements in an <array value constructor> may vary from zero elements (for example `ARRAY[]`, an empty specification) to any number of elements up to the array's maximum size.

If you want to restrict your code to Core SQL, don't define any `ARRAY` <data type>s and don't use any of SQL's array syntax.

Collection Operations

An array is compatible with, and comparable to, any array with a compatible element <data type> — that is, arrays are mutually comparable and mutually assignable only if their element <data type>s are mutually comparable and mutually assignable. Arrays may not be directly compared with, or directly assigned to, any other <data type> class though implicit type conversions can occur in expressions, SELECTs, INSERTs, DELETEs, and UPDATEs. Explicit array type conversions can be forced with the CAST operator.

CAST

In SQL, CAST is a scalar operator that converts a given scalar value to a given scalar <data type>. The required syntax for the CAST operator is as follows.

```
CAST (<cast operand> AS <cast target>)
   <cast operand> ::= scalar_expression
   <cast target> ::= <Domain name> | <data type>
```

The CAST operator converts values of a source <data type> into values of a target <data type>, where each array element <data type> is an SQL pre-defined <data type> (data conversions between UDTs are done with a user-defined cast). The source <data type> (or <cast operand>) can be any expression that evaluates to a single value. The target <data type> (or <cast target>) is either an SQL predefined <data type> specification or the name of a Domain whose defined <data type> is your target <data type>. (If you use CAST (... AS <Domain name>), your current <AuthorizationID> must have the USAGE Privilege on that Domain.)

It isn't, of course, possible to convert the values of every <data type> into the values of every other <data type>. For <collection type>s, the rules are:

- CAST (NULL AS <data type>) and CAST (array_source_is_a_null_value AS <data type>) both result in NULL.
- You can CAST a <collection type> source only to a <collection type> target whose element <data type> is an appropriate CAST target for the source's element <data type>.

When you CAST an array to an array target, you're actually asking your DBMS to CAST the values of the source elements' <data type> to the target elements' <data type>, so the CAST implied therein must be a legal CAST. (See our descriptions of CAST for each predefined SQL <data type>.) Your source may be an empty array — that is, <cast operand> may be ARRAY[] or ARRAY??(??). In this case, the result of the CAST is an empty array whose element <data type> is the target element <data type>. Otherwise, the result of the CAST is an array with the same number of elements as the source and the target element <data type>.

Assignment

In SQL, when an array is assigned to an array target, the assignment is done one element at a time — that is, the source's first element is assigned to the target's first element, the source's next element is assigned to the target's next element, and so on. Two arrays are assignable if their element <data type>s are mutually assignable.

When an array is taken from SQL-data to be assigned to an array target, if the number of elements in the source array *equals* the maximum number of elements in the target array, assignment is straightforward — the value of each element of the source is assigned to the corresponding element of the target. If the maximum number of elements in the target array is *less than* the number of elements in the source array, then assignment of as many of the source element values to the target elements as is possible occurs and your DBMS will return the `SQLSTATE` `warning 0102F` "`warning-array data, right truncation.`" If the maximum number of elements in the target array is *greater than* the number of elements in the source array, then assignment of each of the source element values to the target elements occurs and the size of the target for that row becomes the number of elements assigned. (Note: this doesn't mean that the maximum size of the target for other assignments lessens.)

[Obscure Rule] Because only SQL accepts null values, if your source is `NULL`, then your target's value is not changed. Instead, your DBMS will set its indicator parameter to –1, to indicate that an assignment of the null value was attempted. If your target doesn't have an indicator parameter, the assignment will fail; your DBMS will return the `SQLSTATE` `error 22002` "`data exception-null value, no indicator parameter.`" We'll talk more about indicator parameters in Chapters 39, 40, and 52 on SQL binding styles.

When an array is assigned to an SQL-data array target, if the number of elements in the source array *equals* the maximum number of elements in the target array, assignment is straightforward — the value of each element of the source is assigned to the corresponding element of the target. If the maximum number of elements in the target array is *less than* the number of elements in the source array, but the extra source elements are all `NULL`, then the value of each non-null element of the source is assigned to the corresponding element of the target. If the maximum number of elements in the target array is *less than* the number of elements in the source array and the extra source elements are not all `NULL`, the assignment will fail; your DBMS will return the `SQLSTATE` `error 2202F` "`data exception-array data, right truncation.`" If the maximum number of elements in the target array is *greater than* the number of elements in the source array, then assignment of each of the source element values to the target elements occurs and the size of the target for that row becomes the number of elements assigned. (Note: once again, this doesn't mean that the maximum size of the target for other assignments lessens.)

[Obscure Rule] There are two ways to assign a null value to an SQL-data target. Within SQL, you can use the <keyword> `NULL` in an `INSERT` or an `UPDATE` statement to indicate that the target should be set to `NULL`; that is, if your source is `NULL`, your DBMS will set your target to `NULL`. Outside of SQL, if your source has an indicator parameter that is set to –1, your DBMS will set your target to `NULL` (regardless of the value of the source). An indicator parameter with a value less than –1 will cause an error; your DBMS will return the `SQLSTATE` `error 22010` "`data exception-invalid indicator parameter value.`"

Comparison

SQL provides only two scalar comparison operators, = and <>, to perform operations on arrays. Both will be familiar; there are equivalent operators in other computer languages. Two arrays are comparable if their element <data type>s are mutually comparable. During comparison, the elements of the comparands are compared pairwise in element order — that is, the first element of the first array is compared to the first element of the second array, the second element of the first array is compared to the second element of the second array, and so on. The two arrays are equal if (*a*) they both have the same number of elements and (*b*) each pair of elements is equal. The arrays are not equal if (*a*) they do not have the same number of elements or (*b*) at least one pair of elements is not equal. If either comparand is NULL, or if at least one element is NULL and all non-null element pairs are equal, the result of the operation is UNKNOWN. For example:

```
ARRAY[1] <> ARRAY[2]
```

returns TRUE and:

```
array_column = {array result is NULL}
```

returns UNKNOWN.

But:

```
ARRAY[1,NULL] = ARRAY[1]
```

returns FALSE because the number of elements is not equal.

Other Operations

With SQL, you have several other operations that you can perform on <collection type>s.

Scalar Operations

SQL provides two scalar operations that return a <collection type> — the <array concatenation function> and the <cardinality expression>.

<array concatenation function>

The required syntax for an <array concatenation function> is as follows.

```
<array concatenation function> ::=
CONCATENATE(array_argument_1 { , | WITH } array_argument_2)
```

CONCATENATE operates on two operands, each of which must evaluate to an array. It joins the arrays together in the order given and returns an array value that consists of every element of array_argument_1 followed by every element of array_argument_2. If either operand is NULL, CONCATENATE returns NULL. For this function, you can use either a comma or the <keyword> WITH to separate your operands. Here are two equivalent examples of array concatenations:

```
CONCATENATE(array_column,ARRAY['element_1','element_2'])
CONCATENATE(array_column WITH ARRAY['element_1','element_2'])
```

[Obscure Rule] There are various details about the precise characteristics of the elements in the result array; if you're interested, see "Rules of Aggregation," in our description of the CASE expression in Chapter 29 "Simple Search Conditions."

If you want to restrict your code to Core SQL, don't use CONCATENATE.

<cardinality expression>

The required syntax for a <cardinality expression> is as follows.

```
<cardinality expression> ::=
CARDINALITY (array_argument)
```

CARDINALITY operates on an argument that evaluates to an array. It counts the number of elements in the array and returns this as an exact numeric integer. If the argument is NULL, CARDINALITY returns NULL. Here is an example:

```
CARDINALITY(ARRAY[10,20,30,40])
--returns 4
```

[NON-PORTABLE] The precision of CARDINALITY's result is non-standard because the SQL Standard requires implementors to define the result's precision. [OCELOT Implementation] The OCELOT DBMS that comes with this book gives the result of CARDINALITY an INTEGER <data type>.

If you want to restrict your code to Core SQL, don't use CARDINALITY.

Set Functions

SQL provides two set functions that operate on a <collection type>: COUNT and GROUPING. Since none of these operate exclusively with array arguments, we won't discuss them here; look for them in Chapter 33 "Searching with Groups."

Predicates

In addition to the comparison operators, SQL provides four other predicates that operate on arrays: the <null predicate>, the <exists predicate>, the <quantified predicate>, and the <distinct predicate>. Each will return a boolean value: either TRUE, FALSE, or UNKNOWN. None of these operate strictly on arrays, so we won't discuss them here. Look for them in Chapter 29 "Simple Search Conditions."

Comprehensive Example

Now that we've described SQL's <collection type>, let's look at some example SQL statements that put it to use.

For our example, we've chosen a street address — a plausible choice for an array because its subdivisions ("lines") are not meaningful, e.g., we don't require that the fourth line of a street address contain a city name. Here is an SQL statement that creates a Table with three Columns, the third of which is an array:

```
CREATE TABLE Mailouts (
   given_name CHAR(5),
   surname CHAR(5),
   street_address CHAR(20) ARRAY[5]);
```

In this Table definition, ARRAY[5] indicates that the street_address Column is an array which occurs up to 5 times.

The following SQL statement adds a row to the Mailouts Table:

```
INSERT INTO TABLE Mailouts (
  given_name,
  surname,
  street_address)
VALUES (
  'Jean',                                 -- given_name
  'Boyer',                                -- surname
  ARRAY['line#1','line#2','line#3']);     -- street_address
```

In this INSERT statement, ARRAY['line#1','line#2','line#3'] is an <array value constructor> that specifies the values for the first three elements of the street_address Column array. The two possible remaining elements are not provided with values, so they aren't constructed for this row.

An element of an ARRAY can be updated using an <element reference>. For example, this SQL statement would change the rows in the Mailouts Table by updating the second element of every street_address value:

```
UPDATE Mailouts SET
  street_address[2] = 'line#2 after update';
```

This example uses a <character string literal> to change the value of street_address's second element. (Remember that the <data type> of each array element is CHAR(20), so any assignment of a compatible character string value would be accepted.) The result is that the second array element contains the string 'line#2 after update' and the other elements are unchanged. We could have achieved the same result by assigning an <array value constructor> to the street_address Column as a whole, as in this example:

```
UPDATE Mailouts SET
   street_address = ARRAY['line#1','line #2 after update','line#3'];
```

NOTE: If you assign a 2-element <array value constructor> to a 3-element array, the result is a 2-element array — not a 3-element array with the final element unchanged. That is, if the previous example was:

```
UPDATE Mailouts SET
   street_address = ARRAY['line#1','line #2 after update'];
```

the result in the street_address Column would be 'line#1','line #2 after update' rather than 'line#1','line #2 after update','line#3'.

TIP: To avoid "array element error," ensure all occurrences of an array are fixed size — pad with NULLs if necessary.

Both of the previous examples updated the value of an existing array element. It's also possible to place a value into an element that hasn't been constructed for the row yet. For example, the SQL statement:

```
UPDATE Mailouts SET
   street_address[5] = 'line#5';
```

has a two-fold effect — as the UPDATE explicitly requires, it creates element number five for the row, placing the string 'line#5' into it and it creates element number four for the row, placing the null value into it (because the UPDATE statement doesn't provide an explicit value for the fourth element and since the fifth element can't exist unless the first four also exist).

Here is an example of a query on the Mailouts Table:

```
SELECT given_name, surname, street_address
FROM   Mailouts
WHERE  street_address <> ARRAY[];
```

In this SELECT statement, the street_address Column is being referred to as a whole in both the <select list> and the WHERE clause. We could have also used an <element reference> (e.g., street_address[3]) in either clause to refer to a specific element of the Column. (This is true in most situations.) Our sample query searches for all rows of the Mailouts Table where street_address is not an empty array; TRUE for the row we inserted earlier.

This SQL statement uses CONCATENATE to query the Mailouts Table:

```
SELECT CONCATENATE(street_address WITH ARRAY['line#4','line#5'])
FROM   Mailouts;
```

In this example, we've used CONCATENATE to join the elements of two arrays — one array-Column reference and one <array value constructor>. The result is an array containing five elements; three from the street_address Column and two from the <array value constructor>, in that order. Each element of the result is a CHAR string.

Illegal Operations

SQL places a number of restrictions on where you may validly use arrays. These are worth pointing out, since most of the language is orthogonal in this respect.

- You may not use arrays in a JOIN Column list, as a grouping Column, or in a Constraint definition (for UNIQUE or PRIMARY KEY or FOREIGN KEY Constraints). Constraints are illegal in most predicates and can't contain REFs or ARRAYs.
- Be very careful with <element reference>s — the fact that an array is defined as ARRAY[5] does not guarantee that array element [4] exists. Above all, it is a mistake to assume that an <element reference> is allowed wherever a <Column reference> is allowed — SQL's rules aren't there to help you break the rules of database design.

11

Chapter 11

Row Types

[Obscure Rule] applies for this entire chapter.

In SQL, a <row type> is a row of data; a composite constructed SQL <data type>. A row in a Table is an instance of a <row type> and every row of the same Table has the same type — the intent is to provide a <data type> that can represent the rows of a Table so that complete rows can be stored in variables, passed as arguments to routines, and returned by functions.

Row <data type>s

A <row type> is defined by a descriptor that contains three pieces of information:

1. The <data type>'s name: `ROW`.
2. The <data type>'s degree: the number of Fields that belong to the row.
3. A descriptor for every Field that belongs to the row. The Field descriptor contains: the name of the Field, the Field's ordinal position in the <row type>, the Field's <data type> and nullability attribute, the Field's Character set and default Collation (for character string <data type>s), and the Field's <reference scope check> (for <reference type>s).

ROW

The required syntax for a <row type> specification is as follows.

```
<row type> ::=
ROW (<Field definition> [ {,<Field definition>}... ])

   <Field definition> ::=
   <Field name> <data type>
      [ <reference scope check> ]
      [ COLLATE <Collation name> ]
```

A <row type> specification defines a row of data — it consists of a sequence of one or more parenthesized {<Field name>,<data type>} pairs, known as Fields. The degree of a row is the number of Fields it contains. A value of a row consists of one value for each of its Fields while a value of a Field is a value of the Field's <data type>. Each Field in a row must have a unique name. Here is an example of a <row type> specification:

```
ROW (field_1 INT, field_2 DATE, field_3 INTERVAL(4) YEAR)
```

A <Field name> identifies a Field and is either a <regular identifier> or a <delimited identifier> that is unique (for all Fields and Columns) within the Table it belongs to. You define a Field's <data type> by putting a <data type> specification after <Field name>. The <data type> of a Field can be any type — in particular, it can itself be a <row type>. Here is an example of a <row type> specification; it defines a row with one Field (called `field_1`) whose defined <data type> is `DATE`:

```
ROW (field_1 DATE)
```

[Obscure Rule] If the <data type> of a Field is `CHAR`, `VARCHAR`, or `CLOB`, the Character set in which the Field's values must belong is determined as follows:

- If the <Field definition> contains a <data type> specification that includes a `CHARACTER SET` clause, the Field's Character set is the Character set named. Your current <AuthorizationID> must have the `USAGE` Privilege on that Character set.
- If the <Field definition> does not include a <data type> specification but the Field is based on a Domain whose definition includes a `CHARACTER SET` clause, the Field's Character set is the Character set named.
- If the <Field definition> does not include any `CHARACTER SET` clause at all — either through a <data type> specification or through a Domain definition — the Field's Character set is the Character set named in the `DEFAULT CHARACTER SET` clause of the `CREATE SCHEMA` statement that defines the Schema in which the Field belongs.

For example, the effect of this SQL statement:

```
CREATE SCHEMA bob AUTHORIZATION bob
 DEFAULT CHARACTER SET LATIN1
  CREATE TABLE Table_1 (
    column_1 ROW(
       field_1 CHAR(10),
       field_2 INT));
```

is to create a Table in Schema bob. The Table has a Column with a ROW <data type> containing two Fields. The character string Field's set of valid values are fixed length character strings exactly 10 characters long, all of whose characters must be found in the INFORMATION_SCHEMA.LATIN1 Character set — the Schema's default Character set. The effect of the following SQL statement:

```
CREATE SCHEMA bob AUTHORIZATION bob
 DEFAULT CHARACTER SET LATIN1
  CREATE TABLE Table_1 (
    column_1 ROW(
       field_1 CHAR(10) CHARACTER SET SQL_CHARACTER,
       field_2 INT));
```

is to create the same Table with one difference. This time, the character string Field's values must consist only of characters found in the INFORMATION_SCHEMA.SQL_CHARACTER Character set — the explicit Character set specification in CREATE TABLE constrains the Field's set of values. The Schema's default Character set does not.

[Obscure Rule] If the <data type> of a Field is CHAR, VARCHAR, CLOB, NCHAR, NCHAR VARYING, or NCLOB, and your <Field definition> does not include a COLLATE clause, the Field has a coercibility attribute of COERCIBLE — but if your <Field definition> includes a COLLATE clause, the Field has a coercibility attribute of IMPLICIT. In either case, the Field's default Collation is determined as follows:

- If the <Field definition> includes a COLLATE clause, the Field's default Collation is the Collation named. Your current <AuthorizationID> must have the USAGE Privilege on that Collation.
- If the <Field definition> does not include a COLLATE clause but does contain a <data type> specification that includes a COLLATE clause, the Field's default Collation is the Collation named. Your current <AuthorizationID> must have the USAGE Privilege on that Collation.
- If the <Field definition> does not include a COLLATE clause, but the Field is based on a Domain whose definition includes a COLLATE clause, the Field's default Collation is the Collation named.
- If the <Field definition> does not include any COLLATE clause at all — either explicitly, through a <data type> specification, or through a Domain definition — the Field's default Collation is the default Collation of the Field's Character set.

[Obscure Rule] If the <data type> of a Field is REF(UDT), your current <AuthorizationID> must have the USAGE Privilege on that UDT. If the <data type> of a Field includes REF with a <scope clause>, your <Field definition> must also include this <reference scope check> clause: REFERENCES ARE [NOT] CHECKED ON DELETE NO ACTION — to indicate whether references are to be checked or not. Do not add a <reference scope check> clause under any other circumstances.

- If a Field is defined with REFERENCES ARE CHECKED and a <scope clause> is included in the <Field definition>, then there is an implied DEFERRABLE INITIALLY IMMEDIATE Constraint on the Field. This Constraint checks that the Field's values are also found in the corresponding Field of the system-generated Column of the Table named in the <scope clause>.
- If the <data type> of a Field in a row is a UDT, then the current <AuthorizationID> must have the USAGE Privilege on that UDT.
- A <row type> is a subtype of a <data type> if (*a*) both are <row type>s with the same degree and (*b*) for every pair of corresponding <Field definition>s, the <Field name>s are the same and the <data type> of the Field in the first <row type> is a subtype of the <data type> of the Field in the second <row type>.

<row reference>

A <row reference> returns a row. The required syntax for a <row reference> is as follows.

```
<row reference> ::=
ROW {<Table name> | <query name> | <Correlation name>}
```

A row of data values belonging to a Table (or a query result which is also a Table) is also considered to be a <row type>. In a Table, each Column of a data row corresponds to a Field of the <row type> — the Column and Field have the same ordinal positions in the Table and <row type>, respectively. A <row reference> allows you to access a specific row of a Table or a query result. Here is an example of a <row reference> that would return a row of a Table named Table_1:

```
ROW(Table_1)
```

<Field reference>

A <Field reference> returns a Field of a row. The required syntax for a <Field reference> is as follows.

```
<Field reference> ::=
row_argument.<Field name>
```

A <Field reference> allows you to access a specific Field of a row. It operates on two arguments: the first must evaluate to a <row type> and the second must be the name of a Field belonging to that row. If the value of row_argument is NULL, then the specified Field is also NULL. If row_argument has a non-null value, the value of the Field reference is the value of the specified Field in row_argument. Here is an example of a <Field reference> that would return the value of a Field named Field_1 that belongs to a row of Table_1:

```
ROW(Table_1).field_1
```

<row value constructor>

A <row value constructor> is used to construct a row of data. The required syntax for a <row value constructor> is as follows.

```
<row value constructor> ::=
element_expression |
[ ROW ] (element_expression [ {,element_expression}... ]) |
( <query expression> )

   element_expression ::=
   element_expression |
   NULL |
   ARRAY[] |
   ARRAY??(??) |
   DEFAULT
```

A <row value constructor> allows you to assign values to the Fields of a row using either a list of element_expressions or the result of a subquery. An element_expression may be any expression that evaluates to a scalar value with a <data type> that is assignable to the corresponding Field's <data type>. A subquery — (<query expression>) — is discussed in Chapter 31 "Searching with Subqueries." The result is a row whose *n*-th Field value is the value of the *n*-th element_expression (or whose value is the value of the subquery) you specify. If your element_expression is NULL, the corresponding Field is assigned the null value. If your element_expression is ARRAY[] or ARRAY??(??), the corresponding Field is assigned an empty array. If your element_expression is DEFAULT, the corresponding Field is assigned its default value. Here is an example of a <row value constructor>:

```
ROW ('hello',567,DATE '1994-07-15',NULL,DEFAULT,ARRAY[])
```

This example constructs a row with six Fields. The first Field has a character string value of 'hello', the second has a numeric value of 567, the third has a date value of '1994-07-15', the fourth has a null value, the fifth has a value that is the fifth Field's default value, and the sixth has a value that is an empty array. This <row value constructor> would be valid for this <row type> specification:

```
ROW (
  field_1 CHAR(5),
  field_2 SMALLINT,
  field_3 DATE,
  field_4 BIT(4),
  field_5 VARCHAR(2) DEFAULT 'hi',
  field_6 INT ARRAY[4])
```

A <row value constructor> serves the same purpose for a row as a <literal> does for a predefined <data type>. It has the same format as the <row type>'s ROW specification — that is, ROW() — but instead of a series of <Field definition>s inside the size delimiters, it contains comma-delimited values of the correct <data type> for each Field. For example, if your <row type> specification is:

```
ROW (field_1 INT, field_2 CHAR(5), field_3 BIT(4))
```

a valid <row value constructor> would be:

```
ROW(20,'hello',B'1011')
```

If you construct a row with a subquery, the row takes on the <data type> of the subquery's result. An empty subquery result constructs a one-Field row whose value is NULL. A non-empty subquery result constructs a one-Field row whose value is the subquery result.

If you want to restrict your code to Core SQL, (*a*) don't use the ROW <data type> or <row reference>s and <Field reference>s and when using a <row value constructor>, (*b*) don't use ARRAY[] or ARRAY??(??) as an element_expression, (*c*) don't construct a row with more than one Field, (*d*) don't use the ROW <keyword> in front of your element_expression, and (*e*) don't use a subquery to construct your row.

Row Operations

A row is compatible with, and comparable to, any row with compatible Fields — that is, rows are mutually comparable and mutually assignable only if they have the same number of Fields and each corresponding pair of Fields is mutually comparable and mutually assignable. Rows may not be directly compared with, or directly assigned to, any other <data type> class, though implicit type conversions of their Fields can occur in expressions, SELECTs, INSERTs, DELETEs, and UPDATEs. Explicit row type conversions are not possible.

Assignment

In SQL, when a <row type> is assigned to a <row type> target, the assignment is done one Field at a time — that is, the source's first Field value is assigned to the target's first Field, the source's second Field value is assigned to the target's second Field, and so on. Assignment of a <row type> to another <row type> is possible only if (*a*) both <row type>s have the same number of Fields and (*b*) each corresponding pair of Fields have <data type>s that are mutually assignable.

[Obscure Rule] Because only SQL accepts null values, if your source is `NULL`, then your target's value is not changed. Instead, your DBMS will set its indicator parameter to –1 to indicate that an assignment of the null value was attempted. If your target doesn't have an indicator parameter, the assignment will fail; your DBMS will return the `SQLSTATE error 22002` "`data exception-null value, no indicator parameter.`" Going the other way, there are two ways to assign a null value to an SQL-data target. Within SQL, you can use the <keyword> `NULL` in an `INSERT` or an `UPDATE` statement to indicate that the target should be set to `NULL`; that is, if your source is `NULL`, your DBMS will set your target to `NULL`. Outside of SQL, if your source has an indicator parameter that is set to –1, your DBMS will set your target to `NULL` (regardless of the value of the source). (An indicator parameter with a value less than –1 will cause an error; your DBMS will return the `SQLSTATE error 22010` "`data exception-invalid indicator parameter value.`") We'll talk more about indicator parameters in Chapters 39, 40, and 52 on SQL binding styles.

Comparison

SQL provides the usual scalar comparison operators, = and <> and < and <= and > and >= , to perform operations on rows. All of them will be familiar; there are equivalent operators in other computer languages. Two rows are comparable if (*a*) both have the same number of Fields and (*b*) each corresponding pair of Fields have <data type>s that are mutually comparable. Comparison is between pairs of Fields in corresponding ordinal positions — that is, the first Field of the first row is compared to the first Field of the second row, the second Field of the first row is compared to the second Field of the second row, and so on. If either comparand is `NULL`, the result of the operation is `UNKNOWN`.

The result of a <row type> comparison depends on two things: (*a*) the comparison operator and (*b*) whether any Field is `NULL`. The order of comparison is:

- If the comparison operator is = or <>: First the Field pairs which don't include `NULL`s, then the pairs which do.
- If the comparison operator is anything other than = or <>: Field pairs from left to right. Comparison stops when the result is unequal or `UNKNOWN`, or when there are no more Fields. The result of the row comparison is the result of the last Field pair comparison.

  Here are the possibilities.

1. Comparison operator is =. The row comparison is (*a*) `TRUE` if the comparison is `TRUE` for every pair of Fields, (*b*) `FALSE` if any non-null pair is not equal, and (*c*) `UNKNOWN` if at least one Field is `NULL` and all non-null pairs are equal. For example:

```
ROW(1,1,1) = ROW(1,1,1)          -- returns TRUE
ROW(1,1,1) = ROW(1,2,1)          -- returns FALSE
ROW(1,NULL,1) = ROW(2,2,1)       -- returns FALSE
ROW(1,NULL,1) = ROW(1,2,1)       -- returns UNKNOWN
```

2. Comparison operator is <>. The row comparison is (*a*) TRUE if any non-null pair is not equal, (*b*) FALSE if the comparison is FALSE for every pair of Fields, and (*c*) UNKNOWN if at least one Field is NULL and all non-null pairs are equal. For example:

```
ROW(1,1,1) <> ROW(1,2,1)              -- returns TRUE
ROW(2,NULL,2) <> ROW(2,2,1)           -- returns TRUE
ROW(2,2,1) <> ROW(2,2,1)              -- returns FALSE
ROW(1,NULL,1) <> ROW(1,2,1)           -- returns UNKNOWN
```

3. Comparison operator is anything other than = or <>. The row comparison is (*a*) TRUE if the comparison is TRUE for at least one pair of Fields and every pair *before* the TRUE result is equal, (*b*) FALSE if the comparison is FALSE for at least one pair of Fields and every pair *before* the FALSE result is equal, and (*c*) UNKNOWN if the comparison is UNKNOWN for at least one pair of Fields and every pair *before* the UNKNOWN result is equal. Comparison stops as soon as any of these results (TRUE, FALSE, or UNKNOWN) is established. For example:

```
ROW(1,1,1) < ROW(1,2,0)                   -- returns TRUE
ROW(1,NULL,1) < ROW(2,NULL,0)             -- returns TRUE
ROW(1,1,1) < ROW(1,1,1)                   -- returns FALSE
ROW(3,NULL,1) < ROW(2,NULL,0)             -- returns FALSE
ROW(1,NULL,1) < ROW(1,2,0)                -- returns UNKNOWN
ROW(NULL,1,1) < ROW(2,1,0)                -- returns UNKNOWN
```

SQL also provides three quantifiers — ALL, SOME, ANY — which you can use along with a comparison operator to compare a row value with the collection of values returned by a <table subquery>. Place the quantifier after the comparison operator, immediately before the <table subquery>. For example:

```
SELECT row_column
FROM   Table_1
WHERE  row_column < ALL (
   SELECT row_column
   FROM   Table_2);
```

ALL returns TRUE either (*a*) if the collection is an empty set (i.e., if it contains zero rows) or (*b*) if the comparison operator returns TRUE for every value in the collection. ALL returns FALSE if the comparison operator returns FALSE for at least one value in the collection.

SOME and ANY are synonyms. They return TRUE if the comparison operator returns TRUE for at least one value in the collection. They return FALSE either (*a*) if the collection is an empty set or (*b*) if the comparison operator returns FALSE for every value in the collection. The search condition = ANY (collection) is equivalent to IN (collection).

Other Operations

With SQL, you have several other operations that you can perform on <row type>s.

Scalar Operations

All of SQL's scalar functions return a row with one Field — its value is the result of the function. We discuss the scalar functions in our other <data type> chapters and won't repeat the information here.

Set Functions

SQL provides two set functions that operate on a <row type>: COUNT and GROUPING. Since neither of these operate exclusively with row arguments, we won't discuss them here; look for them in Chapter 33 "Searching with Groups."

Predicates

In addition to the comparison operators, SQL provides twelve other predicates that operate on rows: the <between predicate>, the <in predicate>, the <like predicate>, the <null predicate>, the <exists predicate>, the <unique predicate>, the <match predicate>, the <overlaps predicate>, the <similar predicate>, the <quantified predicate>, the <distinct predicate>, and the <type predicate>. Each will return a boolean value: either TRUE, FALSE, or UNKNOWN. Look for the <like predicate> and the <similar predicate> in Chapter 7 "Character Strings," the <overlaps predicate> in Chapter 8 "Temporal Values," the <null predicate> in Chapter 13 "NULLs," the <type predicate> in Chapter 27 "User-Defined Types," and the rest in Chapter 29 "Simple Search Conditions," and Chapter 31 "Searching with Subqueries."

Comprehensive Example

Now that we've described SQL's <row type>, let's look at some example SQL statements that put it to use.

Here is an SQL statement that creates a Table with three Columns, the third of which is a <row type>:

```
CREATE TABLE Lineage (
  name CHAR(5),
  status CHAR(10),
  last_litter ROW(dog CHAR(5),mated DATE,pups SMALLINT));
```

In this Table definition, ROW(...) indicates that the last_litter Column is a <row type> with three Fields.

The following SQL statement adds a row to the Lineage Table:

```
INSERT INTO TABLE Lineage (
  name,
  status,
  last_litter)
VALUES (
  'Spot',                              -- name
  'Field Dog',                         -- status
  ROW('Fido',DATE '1994-07-15',6));    -- last_litter
```

In this INSERT statement, ROW('Fido',DATE '1994-07-15',6) is a <row value constructor> that specifies the values for the three Fields of the last_litter Column <row type>.

A Field of a <row type> can be updated using a <Field reference>. For example, this SQL statement would change the rows in the Lineage Table by updating the third Field of every last_litter value:

```
UPDATE Lineage SET
  last_litter.pups = 5;
```

This example uses a <numeric literal> to change the value of last_litter's third Field. The result is that the third Field contains the number 5 and the other Fields are unchanged. We could have achieved the same result by assigning a <row value constructor> to the last_litter Column as a whole, as in this example:

```
UPDATE Lineage SET
  last_litter = ROW('Fido',DATE '1994-07-15',5);
```

Here is an example of a query on the Lineage Table:

```
SELECT name, status, last_litter
FROM   Lineage
WHERE  last_litter.dog = 'Fido';
```

In this SELECT statement, the last_litter Column is referred to as a whole in the <select list>, but only the value of its first Field is referred to in the WHERE clause. The result is the entire row we inserted earlier.

12

Chapter 12

Reference Types

[Obscure Rule] applies for this entire chapter.

In SQL, a <reference type> is a pointer; a scalar constructed SQL <data type>. It points to a row of a Base table that has the *with REF value* property — that is, a <reference type> points to a UDT value. Unless you are familiar with Object-Oriented Programming, this chapter will probably not be fully comprehensible until you have read Chapter 27 "User-Defined Types."

Reference <data type>s

A <reference type> is defined by a descriptor that contains three pieces of information:

1. The <data type>'s name: REF.
2. The name of the UDT that the <reference type> is based on. (The UDT is known as the referenced type.)
3. The scope of the <reference type>; the name of the Table that makes up the <reference type>'s scope.

REF

The required syntax for a <reference type> specification is as follows.

```
<reference type> ::=
REF (<UDT name>)
  [ SCOPE <Table name> [<reference scope check>] ]
```

```
<reference scope check> ::=
REFERENCES ARE [NOT] CHECKED
[ ON DELETE
   {CASCADE | SET NULL | SET DEFAULT | RESTRICT | NO ACTION} ]
```

A <reference type> specification defines a pointer; its value is a value that references some site. (A site either does or does not have a REF value.) For example, this REF specification defines a <reference type> based on a UDT (the "referenced type") called my_udt:

```
REF(my_udt)
```

As already mentioned, a REF is a pointer. The value in a REF cloumn "refers" to a row in a Base table that has the *with REF value* property (this is known as a *typed table*). The row that the REF value points to contains a value of the UDT that the REF Column is based on.

If you're putting a REF specification in an SQL-Schema statement, the <AuthorizationID> that owns the containing Schema must have the USAGE Privilege on <UDT name>. If you're putting a REF specification in any other SQL statement, then your current <AuthorizationID> must have the USAGE Privilege on <UDT name>.

For each site that has a REF value and is defined to hold a value of the referenced UDT, there is exactly one REF value — at any time, it is distinct from the REF value of any other site in your SQL-environment. The <data type> of the REF value is REF(UDT).

[NON-PORTABLE] The data type and size of a REF value in an application program must be some number of octets but is non-standard because the SQL Standard requires implementors to define the octet-length of a REF value.

A REF value might have a scope; it determines the effect of a dereference operator on that value. A REF value's scope is a typed Table and consists of every row in that Table. The optional SCOPE clause of a <reference type> specification identifies REF's scope. The Table named in the SCOPE clause must be a referenceable Table with a structured type that is the same as the structured type of the UDT that REF is based on. Here is an example:

```
CREATE TABLE Table_1 (
   column_1 SMALLINT,
   column_2 REF(my_udt) SCOPE Table_2);
```

If you omit the SCOPE clause, the scope defaults to the Table that owns the Column you're defining.

If a REF specification with a SCOPE clause is part of a <Field definition>, it must include this <reference scope check>: REFERENCES ARE [NOT] CHECKED ON DELETE NO ACTION. If a REF specification with a SCOPE clause is part of a <Column definition>, it must include a <reference scope check> with or without the optional ON DELETE sub-clause. The <reference scope check> clause may not be used under any other circumstances.

A <reference type> is a subtype of a <data type> if (*a*) both are <reference type>s and (*b*) the UDT referenced by the first <reference type> is a subtype of the UDT referenced by the second <reference type>.

If you want to restrict your code to Core SQL, don't use the REF <data type>.

Reference Operations

A <reference type> is compatible with, and comparable to, all other <reference type>s of the same referenced type — that is, <reference type>s are mutually comparable and mutually assignable if they are based on the same UDT supertype.

CAST

In SQL, CAST is a scalar operator that converts a given scalar value to a given scalar <data type>. CAST, however, can't be used with <reference type>s. To cast REF values, you'll have to use a user-defined cast.

It isn't, of course, possible to convert the values of every <data type> into the values of every other <data type>. You can cast a <reference type> source to a UDT target and to any SQL predefined <data type> target (except for <collection type>s and <row type>s) provided that a user-defined cast exists for this purpose and your current <AuthorizationID> has the EXECUTE Privilege on that user-defined cast. When you cast a <reference type> to any legal target, your DBMS invokes the user-defined cast routine with the source value as the routine's argument. The cast result is the value returned by the user-defined cast.

Assignment

In SQL, when a <reference type> is assigned to a <reference type> target, the assignment is straightforward — however, assignment is possible only if your source's UDT is a subtype of the UDT of your target.

[Obscure Rule] Since only SQL accepts null values, if your source is NULL, then your target's value is not changed. Instead, your DBMS will set its indicator parameter to –1 to indicate that an assignment of the null value was attempted. If your target doesn't have an indicator parameter, the assignment will fail; your DBMS will return the SQLSTATE error 22002 "data exception-null value, no indicator parameter." Going the other way, there are two ways to assign a null value to an SQL-data target. Within SQL, you can use the <keyword> NULL in an INSERT or an UPDATE statement to indicate that the target should be set to NULL; that is, if your source is NULL, your DBMS will set your target to NULL. Outside of SQL, if your source has an indicator parameter that is set to –1, your DBMS will set your target to NULL (regardless of the value of the source). (An indicator parameter with a value less than –1 will cause an error; your DBMS will return the SQLSTATE error 22010 "data exception-invalid indicator parameter value.") We'll talk more about indicator parameters in Chapters 39, 40, and 52 on SQL binding styles.

Comparison

SQL provides only two scalar comparison operators, = and <> , to perform operations on <reference type>s. Both will be familiar; there are equivalent operators in other computer languages. Two REF values are comparable if they're both based on the same UDT supertype. If either comparand is NULL, the result of the operation is UNKNOWN.

Other Operations

With SQL, you have several other operations that you can perform on <reference type>s.

Scalar Operations

SQL provides two scalar operations that operate on or return a <reference type>: the <dereference operation> and the <reference resolution>.

<dereference operation>

The required syntax for a <dereference operation> is as follows.

```
<dereference operation> ::=
reference_argument -> <Attribute name>
```

The <dereference operation> operates on two operands — the first must evaluate to a <reference type> that has a non-empty scope and the second must be the name of an Attribute of the <reference type>'s UDT. The <dereference operation> allows you to access a Column of the row identified by a REF value; it returns a result whose <data type> is the <data type> of <Attribute name> and whose value is the value of the system-generated Column of the Table in the <reference type>'s scope (where the system-generated Column is equal to reference_argument). That is, given a REF value, the <dereference operation> returns the value at the site referenced by that REF value. If the REF value doesn't identify a site (perhaps because the site it once identified has been destroyed), the <dereference operation> returns NULL.

If you want to restrict your code to Core SQL, don't use the <dereference operation>.

<reference resolution>

The required syntax for a <reference resolution> is as follows.

```
<reference resolution> ::=
DEREF (reference_argument)
```

DEREF operates on any expression that evaluates to a <reference type> that has a non-empty scope. It returns the value referenced by a REF value. Your current <AuthorizationID> must have the SELECT WITH HIERARCHY Privilege on reference_argument's scope Table.

If you want to restrict your code to Core SQL, don't use DEREF.

Set Functions

SQL provides two set functions that operate on a <reference type>: COUNT and GROUPING. Because neither of these operate exclusively with REF arguments, we won't discuss them here — look for them in Chapter 33 "Searching with Groups."

Predicates

In addition to the = and <> comparison operators, SQL provides seven other predicates that operate on <reference type>s: the <in predicate>, the <null predicate>, the <exists predicate>, the <unique predicate>, the <match predicate>, the <quantified predicate>, and the <distinct predicate>. Each will return a boolean value: either TRUE, FALSE, or UNKNOWN. Because none of them operates strictly on <reference type>s, we won't discuss them here. Look for them in Chapter 29 "Simple Search Conditions."

13

Chapter 13

NULLs

"The problem isn't what they don't know. It's what they do know that ain't so."
— Ronald Reagan

Suppose we make a list of US presidents from memory:

YEAR OF ELECTION	NAME
?	Fillmore
1860	Lincoln
?	Johnson
1880	?
1952	Eisenhower
1980	Reagan

We have no idea when Fillmore was elected. We know that somebody was elected in 1880 (Americans hold elections every four years), but we can't remember who. As for Johnson (the Andrew, not the Lyndon) he wasn't elected; he just took over for awhile after Lincoln's assassination. Now let's "query" this list:

- How many presidents are there? Either 5 or 6 (it depends, maybe the guy elected in 1880 was Fillmore).
- Is Lincoln the first president? Probably. The best answer would be "yes."

- Was Eisenhower elected in 1880? Probably not. But suppose he was elected once in 1880 and then again in 1952? Our list doesn't tell us.

At this point, you might be thinking that we have a bad "database." But technically we don't; none of the data is "bad." This is what a bad database looks like:

YEAR OF ELECTION	NAME
0000	Fillmore
1860	Lincoln
9999	Johnson
1880	(unknown)
1952	Eisenhower
1980	Reagan

Here, where we previously had question marks, we've filled in some "default" values: 0000 means "don't know," 9999 means "not applicable," (unknown) means "don't know." Now if we query our list, we get some certain answers:

- How many presidents are there? Obviously 6.
- Is Lincoln the first president? No — Fillmore's date (0000) is less than Lincoln's (1860).
- Was Eisenhower elected in 1880? No — 'Eisenhower' is not equal to '(unknown)'.

Now *that's* a bad database. The problem is that our "default" values have no special significance to our DBMS, so it applied its regular operators and spewed out definite-looking answers. But it was actually right the first time; there *are* no definite answers and a good DBMS would reflect that.

This example teaches us three things: (*a*) that Ronald Reagan was a sage, (*b*) that some data can be "unknown" (a data collection failure) or "not applicable" (a database definition anomaly), and (*c*) that it's better to admit the deficiencies in a way that the DBMS can account for. This is unpleasant and mathematically unsound, but it's what we've got.

Representing Missing Data with NULL

Those missing values that we represented with question marks in our list are what SQL calls NULLs. The NULL value is an amorphous thing, but it does have certain properties which we will now enumerate.

1. NULL is a value. Oh, it's true that it *represents* missing data but that doesn't mean that it *is missing* data — you can put NULL into Columns and you can take it out again. Those operations are only possible with values, therefore NULL is a value.
2. NULL belongs to a Domain. We know that because all values belong to Domains. Therefore, whatever the missing value is in our YEAR Column, it must be an integer — just like all the other values in that Column. And whatever the missing value is in our NAME Column, it must be a character string — just like all the other values in that Column. We might not know what its <data type> is by looking at it, but every NULL does have a <data type> — and every <data type> has a null value.

3. As we stressed when describing each <data type>, whenever you compare NULL with another value, even another NULL, you cannot say whether it is "less than" or "greater than" or "equal to" that other value. There are some times, though, when your DBMS might simply ignore NULLs, or pretend that NULL equals NULL, because in some contexts it won't matter.
4. NULL cannot be represented by a <literal>. Take, for instance, the SMALLINT <data type>. SMALLINT stands for the scale-zero (integral) values between -32,767 and +32,767. Can you use any of those values to mean NULL? No — because if you did, you would have a number that is less than or greater than or equal to another number in the same set. That is what you're trying to avoid.
5. The null value is designated by the keyword NULL in some SQL contexts. Since NULL is, strictly speaking, a <specification> rather than a <literal>, you can use NULL to denote the null value in SQL statements but you can't use it everywhere that a <literal> is allowed. For example, you can't do this:

```
SELECT NULL FROM Widgets;
```

because your DBMS wouldn't be able to guess the <data type>.

The Meaning of NULL

"The cat is neither alive nor dead."

— Erwin Schrödinger

Pay close attention to what these two definitions *don't* say:

- NULL — An SQL keyword. Used for specifying missing (absent) values for any <data type>.
- UNKNOWN — An SQL keyword. One of three values in a truth table (the other two are TRUE and FALSE). A value in a Boolean <data type>.

There is no suggestion that NULL and UNKNOWN are synonyms (except as values for <data type> BOOLEAN). Ordinarily, the two <keyword>s are used in different contexts, although they have a close association with each other (because the usual result of comparing something with NULL is the truth value UNKNOWN).

Speaking informally, we can say that a value is NULL "because it's unknown." But there are several possible reasons for a datum to be missing, including nuances of unknownness and including a quite distinct reason — inapplicability. Different people distinguish different reasons for nullness but we believe that all the reasons can be squeezed into two large groups. In order of importance, they are:

Group 1 — the NULL / UNKNOWN group. The particular reason might be displayed or explained as "secret," "figure not available," "to be announced," "impossible to calculate," "partly unknown," "uncertain," or "pending." The assumption behind all these words is: there is a value and the entity possesses the value, but we can't say precisely what the value is right now.

Group 2 — the NULL / NOT APPLICABLE group. The particular reason might be displayed or explained as "undefined," "moot," "quantum uncertain," "irrelevant," "none," or "n/a." The assumption behind all these words is: there is a value, but the entity does not possess the value. Warning: if you have lots of NULL / NOT APPLICABLE values, that might signal a flaw in your database design. Most commonly, there is a broken linkage as in:

```
Table: Books
   Column: Date_Due
```

The Date_Due is properly an attribute of the book's transaction status (only); therefore for all books which are not out, the Date_Due has to be NULL.

The distinction between "unknown" and "not applicable" is an old one. Here is ISO's suggested coding scheme for sex:

0 =	UNKNOWN
1 =	MALE
2 =	FEMALE
9 =	NOT APPLICABLE

So much for what NULL means — it's a representation of a value that's missing, either because we don't know it or because it doesn't apply. We can help this definition along if we delimit things NULL doesn't mean.

- NULL doesn't mean NaN (Not a Number). NaN means the value is outside the numeric Domain and we've already shown that NULLs are in the Domain. Therefore, NULL does not mean NaN or anything similar such as the result of overflow, the result of underflow, a date that's not representable with the Gregorian calendar, the square root of –1... in short, an illegitimate value is not a null value. There is no way to store an illegitimate value, but there is a way to store NULL.
- NULL doesn't mean zero. It's confusing that C manuals say that NULL is zero but there is no reason to worry about that. Back in Al-Khwarezm's day, there was much hullaballoo over the number zero — the objection being "how can there be a number which is no number?"
- NULL doesn't mean '' (empty string). This has often been used in the past for "unknown"s — but we can't let that confuse us.

Three-Valued Logic

Most logical systems rest on two values: is/isn't, yes/no, 0/1, TRUE/FALSE. SQL's system is more like: is/isn't/could-be, yes/no/maybe, 0/1/?, TRUE/FALSE/UNKNOWN. The UNKNOWN truth value will generally result from a comparison that involves a null value. SQL's three-valued logical system is a departure from the tried-and-true paths of other programming languages. We will encounter some tricky features and surprises.

The original rule is that any comparison returns the UNKNOWN truth value if one of the operands is NULL. The combinatory rules can most easily be shown with truth tables; see Chapter 9 "Boolean Values," if you need to refresh your memory.

Predicates

We've already said that NULL can't be used with a regular comparison predicate: WHERE X = NULL and WHERE X <> NULL are both illegal SQL constructs. There's a logical reason for this.

The expression `X = NULL` has a `NULL` operand, therefore (that's the rule!) the result of the expression is always `UNKNOWN`. SQL does, however, support a predicate that will return `TRUE` when `X` is `NULL` and `FALSE` when `X` is not `NULL`; this is the <null predicate>.

<null predicate>

The required syntax for a <null predicate> is as follows.

```
<null predicate> ::=
expression IS [NOT] NULL
```

A <null predicate> tests a value to see whether it is `NULL` and returns either `TRUE` or `FALSE`. `IS NULL` searches for null values. `IS NOT NULL` searches for non-null values. The predicate's expression argument can be any expression which evaluates to either a single value or a row.

`IS NULL` is `TRUE` if every value resulting from `expression` is `NULL`. `IS NOT NULL` is `TRUE` if no value resulting from `expression` is `NULL`. This is straightforward if the expression is a scalar value like a <Column name>. If there's a null value in the Column, then `<Column name> IS NULL` is `TRUE` and `<Column name> IS NOT NULL` is `FALSE`. If the expression results in a row value, then things are less straightforward. Certainly, if `x` and `y` are both `NULL`, then `(x,y) IS NULL` is `TRUE` and `(x,y) IS NOT NULL` is `FALSE`. And if neither `x` nor `y` are `NULL`, then `(x,y) IS NULL` is `FALSE` and `(x,y) IS NOT NULL` is `TRUE`. So far so good. The surprise is that if only one of `x` and `y` is `NULL`, then `(x,y) IS NULL` is `FALSE` and `(x,y) IS NOT NULL` is also `FALSE`.

Nullability

There are times when you'll want to ensure that a null value can't be put in a Column. The obvious case is when it's a primary key; in our example at the beginning of this chapter, the '?' symbol makes no sense for a `NAME` — first, because then we can't tell how many distinct presidents there are for sure and second, because then there's no real value for what's supposed to be the identifying piece of information. To force *non nullability* for a value, you can use a `NOT NULL` Constraint when defining the Object to which that value will be assigned.

There are some who argue that a `NOT NULL` Constraint should be used as a matter of course. We'd rather think that it's a matter of choice. But anyway, `NOT NULL` is a common <Column Constraint>. We'll discuss it in our chapter on Constraints and Assertions. For now, just keep in mind that all Columns have a nullability characteristic of either "possibly nullable" or "known not nullable" — it determines (*a*) whether an attempt to `INSERT` the null value into the Column will fail and (*b*) whether a `SELECT` from the Column can ever return the null value. The "possibly nullable" characteristic allows both; the "known not nullable" characteristic disallows both.

If you're a programmer, it's useful to know whether a Column is possibly nullable because that will tell you whether `NULL` indicators are needed in your code. A Column's nullability characteristic is "possibly nullable" unless one of these situations apply:

1. A Column's nullability characteristic is "known not nullable" if a non-deferrable Constraint/Assertion on the Column evaluates to `Column IS NOT NULL` or if the Column is based on a Domain and a non-deferrable Constraint/Assertion on that Domain evaluates to `VALUE IS NOT NULL`.

2. A Column's nullability characteristic is "known not nullable" if a non-deferrable Constraint on the Column is a PRIMARY KEY Constraint.

The Duplicate Loophole

"Identification for duplicate removal is at a lower level of detail than equality testing in the evaluation of retrieval conditions. Hence it is possible to adopt a different rule."

— E.F. Codd

Here is a syllogism based on some of the things we've said so far:

1. Two values are equal if an equality comparison (=) returns TRUE.
2. If either value is NULL, an equality comparison returns UNKNOWN.
3. Therefore a null value is never equal to a null value.
   Well, we've said those things several times and we won't go back on them. But we will introduce a teensy loophole:
4. However, a null value is a duplicate of a null value.

That is, while we'll never say that NULL equals NULL, we will say that NULL duplicates NULL. And it goes without saying that, as well, two values are duplicates if they are equal. There are several operations that this loophole will affect. Specifically:

GROUP BY — If you GROUP BY column_5 and every column_5 value is NULL, you end up with only one group.

DISTINCT — If the values before a DISTINCT operation are the set {7,33,NULL,15,7,NULL}, then the values afterwards are the set {7,33,NULL,15}.

UNION — As with DISTINCT, if the values before a UNION operation are the set {7,33,NULL,15,7,NULL}, then the values afterwards are the set {7,33,NULL,15}.

EXCEPT — As with DISTINCT, if the values before an EXCEPT operation are the set {7,33,NULL,15,7,NULL}, then the values afterwards are the set {7,33,NULL,15}.

INTERSECT — As with DISTINCT, if the values before an INTERSECT operation are the set {7,33,NULL,15,7,NULL}, then the values afterwards are the set {7,33,NULL,15}.

Fun with NULLs

There are many operations which are affected by the presence of NULLs. Our choice has been to describe the exceptional situation when we describe the operation. So this is just a quick summary; for full effects read the appropriate section in another chapter.

NULL Specification

The NULL specification can be used as if it's a <literal> in these situations only:

- In an UPDATE ... SET clause, to specify a "value" to assign to a Column, i.e., UPDATE ... SET ... = NULL

- In an INSERT ... VALUES clause, to specify a "value" to assign to a Column, i.e., INSERT ... VALUES(NULL)
- To specify a default "value" for a Column or Domain, i.e., DEFAULT NULL
- To specify a FOREIGN KEY Constraint rule, i.e., ON UPDATE SET NULL, ON DELETE SET NULL
- As a CAST source, i.e., CAST (NULL AS ...)
- As a CASE result, i.e., CASE ... THEN NULL ... END, CASE ... ELSE NULL END
- In a row or Table constructor

Set Functions

NULLs are ignored during most set functions and an appropriate warning is issued (null value eliminated).

Searches

WHERE clauses and HAVING clauses are "satisfied" if the result of the search condition is TRUE. Since WHERE rejects both UNKNOWN and FALSE, the expression WHERE column_1 = column_1 is functionally equivalent to WHERE column_1 IS NOT NULL.

Constraints

A CHECK Constraint is "satisfied" (not violated) if the result of the search condition is either TRUE or UNKNOWN. Notice the difference here between "what satisfies a search" and "what satisfies a Constraint."

Scalar Operators and Functions

The rule for almost any operator or function is that if a significant operand is NULL, the result of the whole operation is NULL. For example, 5 + [null-value] returns NULL and UPPER([null-value]) returns NULL. Not only that, but a NULL trumps a zero — [null-value] / 0 returns NULL (not a division-by-zero error) and 0 * [null-value] returns NULL (not zero). The only exceptions to this rule are the COALESCE and NULLIF functions (see CASE expression in our chapter on simple search conditions) which are specifically designed to convert null values.

Sorts

For the ORDER BY clause, NULLs are considered to be either higher than all non-null values or lower than all non-null values (it's implementation-defined, so will vary from DBMS to DBMS).

UNIQUE Predicate

NULLs cannot equal anything else, so they can't stop UNIQUE from being TRUE. For example, a series of rows containing {1,NULL,2,NULL,3} is UNIQUE. UNIQUE never returns UNKNOWN.

<reference type>s

If a REF value involves no site, perhaps because the site has been destroyed, NULL is returned.

SQL/CLI

In our chapters on the Call Level Interface, you'll notice that many functions return blank (or zero) when the situation screams for a NULL return. You'll just have to get used to inconsistencies.

Problems For Optimizers

If you were to write a DBMS optimizer, you'd want to take advantage of certain *transformation rules*. Usually these rules depend on two-valued logic, for instance the idea that everything is "either A or not-A." We will give only one example, which we think is the most famous one.

The Transitivity Rule states: IF A = B AND B = C THEN A = C. Therefore, a DBMS should detect situations of this nature:

```
SELECT ...
FROM   t1,t2
WHERE  (t1.column1 = t2.column1 AND t2.column2 = 5);
```

and — because the join (t1.column1 = t2.column1) might be expensive — consider replacing the query with this apparently equivalent (and valid) one:

```
SELECT ...
FROM   t1,t2
WHERE (t1.column1 = 5 AND t2.column2 = 5);
```

However, if the DBMS encounters the similar-looking SQL statement:

```
SELECT ...
FROM   t1,t2
WHERE (t1.column1 = t2.column1 AND
       t2.column2 = 5) IS NOT FALSE;
```

the transform will not be valid. If t2.column2 is NULL, then there will be a difference between what the original query returns as opposed to what the "transformed" query would return (UNKNOWN versus FALSE). Therefore a major optimization becomes too dangerous to try. This is not usually a serious worry because the usual query involves a WHERE alone, which means that UNKNOWNs are filtered out the same way that FALSEs are. But occasionally you'll help your optimizer by ensuring that Columns which will be used in complex queries are always not nullable.

Nulloclasts vs. Nullodules

If you know any Byzantine history at all, you know about the hundred year struggle between the Iconoclasts ("smashers of icons") and the Iconodules ("slaves of icons"). It is disgusting to use a metaphor for that struggle — by referring to Nulloclasts ("NULL smashers") and Nullodules ("NULL slaves") — because NULL is a Latin word while -clast and -dule are Greek suffixes. It's a good metaphor though.

The Nulloclast Position

The champion on this side is C. J. Date, possibly the best known database pundit, and author of several books which contain zero howling errors (a remarkable feat in this field). Here are selected quotes from C. J. Date's *An Introduction to Database Systems*, sixth edition:

> "... in our opinion, NULLs — and the entire theory of three-valued logic on which they are based — are *fundamentally misguided* ..."
>
> "... it is our general opinion that NULLs are such a bad idea that it is not worth wrecking the whole relational model over them, just because some suitable target tuple sometimes does not exist for some particular foreign key ..."
>
> "... NULLs and [three-valued logic] *undermine* the entire foundation of the relational model."
>
> "... SQL manages to introduce a number of *additional flaws*, over and above the flaws that are inherent in three-valued logic per se..."
>
> "Our recommendation to DBMS users would thus be to ignore the vendor's [three-valued logic] support entirely, and to use a disciplined 'default values' scheme instead (thereby staying firmly in two-valued logic)."

(Incidentally, Date — and sure he is an honourable man — specifically decries some of the things we've said here:

- We used the term "null value" — and an absence of value is not a value.
- We said that nulls are in Domains — and that leads to logical complications; all attribute integrity checks would succeed, for instance, because null is part of the Domain.)

The Nullodule Position

The defenders include E. F. Codd, the founder of relational theory. (In fact Mr. Codd favours the idea that there should be more than one NULL class, and therefore a four-valued logic.) But we will just quote from Jim Melton, editor of the SQL Standard:

> "Some notable database personalities have strongly urged the SQL standards committee to abandon the notion of NULL values in favour of default values."

But — summarizing here — in practice, we don't worry that in the expression x = 5, x is a "different kind of thing" than 5 because we know that x *represents* an integer value. And by the way, after a series of back-and-forth persecutions, a few revolts, and several thousand deaths — the Iconodules won.

14

Chapter 14

SQL Clusters

The SQL Standard describes the concepts on which SQL is based in terms of Objects, such as Tables. Each SQL Object is defined in terms of the characteristics (e.g., its name) that describe it; the Standard calls this the Object's *descriptor.* Some Objects are dependent on other Objects, e.g., a Column is dependent on the Table to which it belongs. If an Object is dropped (i.e., destroyed), then every Object dependent on it is also dropped. The diagram on the following page shows the main SQL Object hierarchy illustrating, for example, that a Cluster can contain one or more Catalogs; Catalogs can contain one or more Schemas; Schemas can contain one or more Domains, Tables, Character sets, etc.

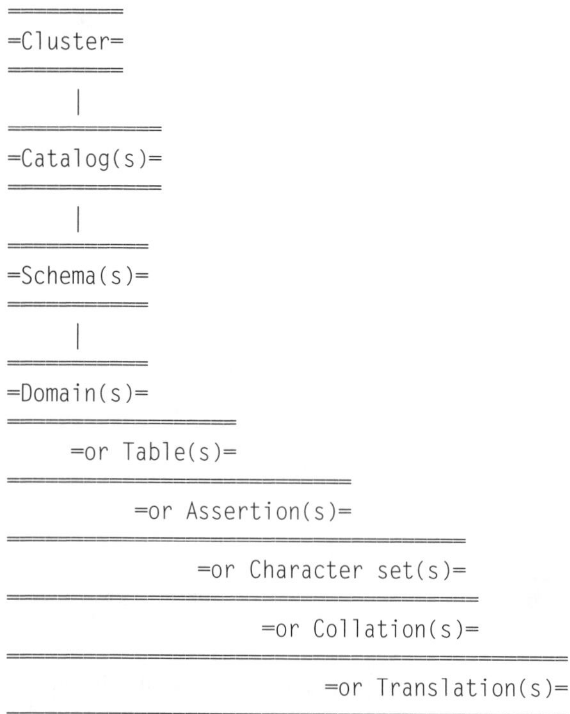

(There are several other SQL Objects; this diagram shows only the major ones.)

In this chapter, we'll describe SQL Clusters in detail, and show you the syntax to use to create, alter, and destroy them.

Cluster

An SQL Cluster is the group of Catalogs available to an SQL-session at any point in time; that is, it contains all the SQL-data you may access through a given SQL-server. The Objects that belong to a Cluster are known as Cluster Objects; that is, they depend on some Cluster. Every Cluster Object has a name that must be unique (among Objects of its name class) within the Cluster to which it belongs. The Cluster Object name class is: Catalogs.

A Cluster may consist of zero or more Catalogs. The Cluster's name implicitly qualifies the names of the Objects that belong to it and cannot be explicitly stated. Three SQL statements relate to Clusters: `CONNECT`, `SET CONNECTION`, and `DISCONNECT`.

[NON-PORTABLE] SQL does not include any CREATE CLUSTER, OPEN CLUSTER, ADD TO CLUSTER, or DROP CLUSTER statements. The method you'll use to access a Cluster with your DBMS is thus non-standard because the SQL Standard requires implementors to define the physical aspects of a Cluster, whether any Catalog can be part of more than one Cluster at a time, how a Cluster comes into being, how it may be accessed, and how it may be destroyed.

[OCELOT Implementation] applies for the rest of this chapter.

The OCELOT DBMS that comes with this book considers a Cluster to be a directory on your storage device, e.g., this would represent a Cluster on an MS-DOS hard drive:

```
C:\CLUSTER
```

Each Cluster directory contains two files and zero or more subdirectories. The first file, called CLUSTER, contains the current definition of all the lower-level SQL Objects contained within the Catalogs that make up the Cluster. The second file, called CLUSTER.BAK, contains the definitions as they were prior to the last COMMIT statement issued during an SQL-session. Any subdirectories in the Cluster directory represent SQL Catalogs. OCELOT does not allow a Catalog to be part of multiple Clusters.

OCELOT's method of creating and connecting to Clusters depends on the way you choose to begin an SQL session.

- If the first SQL statement in your SQL-session is a CONNECT statement, the DBMS will search for a CLUSTER file on a directory whose name matches the CONNECT statement's <SQL-server name>. If a CLUSTER file is found on the correct directory, the file will be opened. If the correct directory is found but there is no CLUSTER file on it, a CLUSTER file will be created on that directory and then opened. If no directory with the correct name is found, the directory will be created, then a CLUSTER file will be created on that directory and opened.
- If the first SQL statement in your SQL-session is not a CONNECT statement, the DBMS will open a CLUSTER file on a directory named OCELOT.

To drop a Cluster, simply delete the CLUSTER file from your storage device.

Cluster Names

An <SQL-server name> identifies a Cluster. The required syntax for an <SQL-server name> is as follows.

```
<SQL-server name> ::=
string
```

An <SQL-server name> has a maximum length of 128 octets and is either a <character string literal>, the name of a host character string parameter, or a reference to an SQL character string parameter that conforms to the rules for an <identifier>.

[NON-PORTABLE] An <SQL-server name> must be unique (for all Clusters) within an SQL-environment, but is non-standard because the SQL Standard requires implementors to define what an <SQL-server name> may be and to which Character set it belongs. [OCELOT Implementation] The OCELOT DBMS that comes with this book defines an <SQL-server name> as any <identifier> belonging to the SQL_TEXT Character set that also follows the rules for a directory name on the operating system in use; generally it may include [drive:] and \upper-level name.

Here are some examples of possible <SQL-server name>s:

```
'CLUSTER_1'
-- an <SQL-server name> that is a <character string literal>
```

```
:CLUSTER_1
-- an <SQL-server name> that is a host parameter name

CLUSTER_1
-- an <SQL-server name> that is an SQL parameter name
```

15

Chapter 15

AuthorizationIDs

In this chapter, we'll describe <AuthorizationID>s in detail and show you the syntax to use to create, alter, and destroy them.

<AuthorizationID>

We use the non-standard term <AuthorizationID> to mean a named bundle of Privileges, which is either a User or a Role. Users and Roles can be distinguished as follows:

- A User is either an actual person or an application program that has access to SQL-data. Users are outside Schemas. If an <AuthorizationID> is a User, the methods used to create, drop, and map it to actual persons/application programs are implementation-defined.
- A Role generally refers to a title or a set of duties within an organization. Roles are inside Schemas. If an <AuthorizationID> is a Role, it is created and dropped using standard SQL statements.

All <AuthorizationID>s must be unique within the SQL-environment.

The Objects that may belong to a User or a Role are called *Privileges*; they depend on some <AuthorizationID>. An <AuthorizationID> may have the use of zero or more Privileges.

User

A User is either an actual person or an application program that has access to SQL-data.

[NON-PORTABLE] SQL does not include any CREATE USER, MAP USER, or DROP USER statements. The methods you'll use with your DBMS to create and drop Users and to identify the real-life user an <AuthorizationID> represents are non-standard because the SQL Standard requires implementors to define how a User comes into being, how it may be destroyed, how it maps to users of SQL-data, and what constitutes a valid <AuthorizationID>. [OCELOT Implementation] The OCELOT DBMS that comes with this book "creates" a User automatically when its identifier is used in a `CONNECT` statement, a `CREATE SCHEMA` statement, a `MODULE` statement, a `SET SESSION AUTHORIZATION` statement, or a `GRANT` statement. Users are "dropped" if they own no Objects and all their Privileges have been revoked.

Role

Large organizations may have hordes of users with the same Privileges on the same Objects. For instance, circulation assistants are all allowed to do the circulation process. In SQL-92, the solutions were unsatisfactory:

- If each circulation assistant had a different <AuthorizationID>, then there were too many Objects in the Catalog and granting/revoking was a major chore.
- If all circulation assistants had the same <AuthorizationID>, some other method had to be devised so that one could distinguish which assistant really did what.

In SQL3, there is a major improvement — Roles. An SQL Role is a named bundle of zero or more Privileges. Granting a Role to an <AuthorizationID> allows that <AuthorizationID> to use every Privilege granted to that Role. There is a many-to-many relationship between Users and Roles; a User may be granted the use of many Roles and the use of the same Role may be granted to many Users. The use of a Role may also be granted to another Role.

Types of <AuthorizationID>

An <AuthorizationID> is defined by a descriptor that contains three pieces of information:

1. The <identifier> that is the name of the <AuthorizationID>.
2. Whether the <AuthorizationID> is a User or a Role.
3. A Privilege descriptor for every Privilege granted to the <AuthorizationID>. At any point in time, an <AuthorizationID> has the use of every Privilege granted to `PUBLIC`, every Privilege directly granted to that <AuthorizationID>, and every Privilege granted to every Role that has been granted to that <AuthorizationID>. (Because a Role may be granted to another Role, all dependent Role Privileges are also available to the <AuthorizationID>.)

   The SQL Standard identifies six types of <AuthorizationID>s:

- The *SQL-session <AuthorizationID>* is the <User name> for an SQL-session. Initially, it is the User that started a given SQL-session and is determined from the `USER` clause of the `CONNECT` statement. The SQL-session <AuthorizationID> may never be `NULL` — if the `CONNECT...USER` clause names a Role instead of a User, the SQL-session <AuthorizationID> is set to a default value by your DBMS. You can change the SQL-session <AuthorizationID> with the `SET SESSION AUTHORIZATION` statement. The user function `SESSION_USER` returns the value of the current SQL-session <AuthorizationID>.
- The context of an SQL-session includes its *current User* and its *current Role* — together, they determine the Privileges available to execute SQL statements in the SQL-session and one of them is always the "current <AuthorizationID>." Either one of current User or

current Role may be NULL at any time, but they may not both be NULL at the same time — the non-null <identifier> is the SQL-session's current <AuthorizationID>. At the beginning of every SQL-session, the current User is set to the value of the SQL-session <AuthorizationID> and the current Role is set to the Role that started the SQL-session. (The current Role is determined from the CONNECT statement; if CONNECT...USER specifies a <Role name>, that Role becomes the current Role; otherwise, the current Role is NULL.) You can change the current Role with the SET ROLE statement. The equivalent user functions CURRENT_USER and USER return the value of the current User <AuthorizationID>. The user function CURRENT_ROLE returns the value of the current Role <AuthorizationID>.

- The *Module <AuthorizationID>* is the owner of a given Module and is the current <AuthorizationID> when the Module's SQL procedures are executed. The Module <AuthorizationID> may either be specifically identified (in the MODULE statement) or it will default to the current SQL-session <AuthorizationID>.
- The *Schema <AuthorizationID>* is the owner of a given Schema and may either be specifically identified (in the CREATE SCHEMA statement) or it will default to the current Module <AuthorizationID>, if there is one. If the Module you're running doesn't have an explicit owner either, the Schema <AuthorizationID> defaults to the current SQL-session <AuthorizationID>.
- The *current <AuthorizationID>* is the <AuthorizationID> whose Privileges are checked prior to the execution of an SQL statement. If the current <AuthorizationID> doesn't have the required Privilege to perform an operation on SQL-data, the SQL statement will fail. For direct SQL, the SQL-session <AuthorizationID> is always the current <AuthorizationID>.

To create a Role and grant its use to the current <AuthorizationID>, use the CREATE ROLE statement. To destroy a Role, use the DROP ROLE statement. To grant Privileges to a User or a Role, or to grant the use of a Role to an <AuthorizationID>, use the GRANT statement. To revoke Privileges from a User or a Role, or to revoke the use of a Role from an <AuthorizationID>, use the REVOKE statement or the DROP ROLE statement. To change the current SQL-session <AuthorizationID>, use the SET SESSION AUTHORIZATION statement. And to change the current Role, use the SET ROLE statement.

If you want to restrict your code to Core SQL, don't use Roles at all.

<AuthorizationID> Names

An <AuthorizationID> name is either a <User name> or a <Role name>. The required syntax for an <AuthorizationID> name is as follows.

```
<AuthorizationID> name ::=
string
```

An <AuthorizationID> name is a <regular identifier> or a <delimited identifier>, no more than 128 characters long, that is unique (for all Users and Roles) within the SQL-environment. Typically, an <AuthorizationID> name is a Christian name (e.g., BOB or SAM, identifying a User) or a department name (e.g., DOCUMENTATION, identifying a Role) and most often, has a one-to-one relationship to some person (i.e., each person has only one <AuthorizationID> name).

The <regular identifier> — PUBLIC — is a valid <AuthorizationID> only in the GRANT statement and the REVOKE statement. PUBLIC is the SQL special grantee, used as an "all-purpose" grantee, to enable system-wide Privileges to be granted to and/or revoked from all current and future <AuthorizationID>s with a single SQL statement. Every <AuthorizationID> always has the use of every Privilege granted to PUBLIC. The <delimited identifier> — "PUBLIC" — is never a valid <AuthorizationID>.

The <delimited identifier> — "_SYSTEM" — is a valid <AuthorizationID> only when you're looking at INFORMATION_SCHEMA. "_SYSTEM" is the SQL special grantor, used (by your DBMS) as an "all-purpose" grantor, to enable Object-wide Privileges to be granted to an <AuthorizationID> that creates an Object, or to revoke cascading, system-wide Privileges from an <AuthorizationID> that drops an Object. (In the case of a DROP, "_SYSTEM" is also the grantee that revokes all related Privileges from all other <AuthorizationID>s.)

[NON-PORTABLE] Except for the cases (PUBLIC, "PUBLIC", and "_SYSTEM") noted earlier, what your DBMS will recognize as a valid <AuthorizationID> name is non-standard because the SQL Standard requires implementors to define a valid <AuthorizationID> name. [OCELOT Implementation] The OCELOT DBMS that comes with this book will accept any SQL_TEXT <identifier> as an <AuthorizationID> name.

CREATE ROLE Statement

The CREATE ROLE statement defines a new Role. The required syntax for the CREATE ROLE statement is as follows.

```
CREATE ROLE <Role name> [ WITH ADMIN <grantor> ]

   <grantor> ::= CURRENT_USER | CURRENT_ROLE
```

The CREATE ROLE statement specifically defines an <AuthorizationID> to be a Role rather than a User; this is necessary because otherwise your DBMS could mistake <Role name> for a <User name> which appears in similar contexts. <Role name> is an <AuthorizationID> name that is unique within your SQL-environment and CREATE ROLE automatically grants the use of the new Role to the current <AuthorizationID> WITH ADMIN OPTION (that is, the current <AuthorizationID> gets the use of the new Role and may pass this use on to others).

[NON-PORTABLE] Whether you can use CREATE ROLE is non-standard because the SQL Standard requires implementors to define what Privilege (if any) is needed to execute CREATE ROLE.

The optional WITH ADMIN clause decides which <AuthorizationID> (either the current User or the current Role) gets the use of this Role; CURRENT_USER is the <AuthorizationID> name of the current User and CURRENT_ROLE is the <AuthorizationID> name of the current Role. If you omit the clause, it defaults to WITH ADMIN CURRENT_USER — but if CURRENT_USER is NULL, the clause defaults to WITH ADMIN CURRENT_ROLE. If you specify WITH ADMIN CURRENT_USER and the current <AuthorizationID> is a <Role name>, or if you specify WITH ADMIN CURRENT_ROLE and the current <Role name> is NULL, the CREATE ROLE statement will fail; your DBMS will return the SQLSTATE error 0L000 "invalid grantor." Here are two examples:

```
CREATE ROLE my_schema.assistants_role WITH ADMIN CURRENT_USER;
-- creates a Role, identified by the <AuthorizationID> ASSISTANTS_ROLE, for the
current User

CREATE ROLE my_schema.assistants_role WITH ADMIN CURRENT_ROLE;
-- creates a Role, identified by the <AuthorizationID> ASSISTANTS_ROLE, for the
current Role
```

If you want to restrict your code to Core SQL, don't use the CREATE ROLE statement.

Privilege

An SQL Privilege allows an <AuthorizationID> to perform a given action on a specific Table, Column, Domain, Character set, Collation, Translation, Trigger, SQL-invoked routine, or UDT. Privileges are dependent on some <AuthorizationID>, are created and granted with the GRANT statement, and are destroyed with the REVOKE statement and the DROP ROLE statement. A Privilege is defined by a descriptor that contains six pieces of information:

1. The name of the Object on which the Privilege acts.
2. The <AuthorizationID> that granted the Privilege.
3. The <AuthorizationID> that may use the Privilege.
4. The action (either INSERT, UPDATE, DELETE, SELECT, REFERENCES, USAGE, UNDER, TRIGGER, or EXECUTE) that may be taken on the specified Object.
5. Whether the Privilege is grantable by the grantee.
6. Whether the Privilege also applies to subtables in a hierarchy (for SELECT only).

<privileges>

The required syntax for a Privilege specification is as follows.

```
<privileges> ::=
<object privileges> ON <Object name>

   <Object name> ::=
   [ TABLE ] <Table name> |
   DOMAIN <Domain name>  |
   CHARACTER SET <Character set name> |
   COLLATION <Collation name> |
   TRANSLATION <Translation name> |
   TYPE {<UDT name> | typed <Table name>} |
   <specific routine designator>
```

```
<object privileges> ::=
ALL PRIVILEGES |
<action> [ {,<action>}... ]

   <action> ::=
   DELETE |
   SELECT [ (<Column name> [ {,<Column name>} ... ]) ] |
   INSERT [ (<Column name> [ {,<Column name>} ... ]) ] |
   UPDATE [ (<Column name> [ {,<Column name>} ... ]) ] |
   REFERENCES [ (<Column name> [ {,<Column name>} ... ]) ] |
   TRIGGER |
   UNDER |
   USAGE |
   EXECUTE
```

The Privilege specification specifies one or more Privileges for a specific Object. Not all Privileges are valid for every Object.

`ALL PRIVILEGES` is shorthand; it means every Privilege the grantor has on "<Object name>." If "<Object name>" identifies a temporary Table, `ALL PRIVILEGES` is the only valid Privilege specification. Here's an example:

```
ALL PRIVILEGES ON TABLE Table_1
```

In theory, you could substitute `ALL PRIVILEGES` for `USAGE` or `EXECUTE`, but there's never a good reason to do so. Traditionally, `ALL PRIVILEGES` substitutes for the combination of Table Privileges: `SELECT`, `INSERT`, `UPDATE`, `DELETE`, and perhaps `TRIGGER` or `REFERENCES`. The closest analogous construct is the * in "`SELECT * ...`". And similar objections to using it apply:

- You can't tell by reading the SQL code what Privileges are, in fact, being granted.
- Because `ALL PRIVILEGES` is shorthand, it might mean something different the next time you use it (because somebody might have, in the interim, granted additional Privileges to the <AuthorizationID>).
- If the <AuthorizationID> has only one Privilege, you will not notice that all the other potentially applicable Privileges are not being granted.

You should prefer to be explicit about what you're granting; if you depend on a complex system of defaults, you'll miss something. These considerations don't apply to temporary Tables because, for them, `ALL PRIVILEGES` really does mean all of: `SELECT`, `INSERT`, `UPDATE`, `DELETE`, `TRIGGER`, `REFERENCES`.

A `SELECT`, `INSERT`, `UPDATE`, `REFERENCES`, `DELETE`, or `TRIGGER` Privilege is called a *Table Privilege*; it allows the specified action on the entire Table named in the Privilege's descriptor — including on any Columns that are subsequently added to that Table. You may not grant the `TRIGGER` Table Privilege on anything but a Base table. You may not grant the other Table Privileges on a declared `LOCAL TEMPORARY` Table or on any other Object. Note that the <keyword>

TABLE is noise; it may be omitted from the Privilege specification. Here are two equivalent examples:

```
DELETE ON TABLE Table_1
DELETE ON Table_1
```

Both of these Privilege specifications define a Privilege that deletes rows from TABLE_1. Here's an example of a Privilege specification that defines a Privilege that selects values from every Column of TABLE_1:

```
SELECT ON TABLE Table_1
```

And here's an example of a Privilege specification that defines a Privilege that enables a Trigger to operate on every Column of TABLE_1:

```
TRIGGER ON TABLE Table_1
```

A SELECT(<Column name> list), INSERT(<Column name> list), UPDATE(<Column name> list), or REFERENCES(<Column name> list) is called a *Column Privilege*; it allows the specified action only on the Columns actually named when the Privilege is granted. You may not grant Column Privileges on the Columns of a declared LOCAL TEMPORARY Table or on any other Object. Here are two equivalent examples:

```
UPDATE(column_1,column_3) ON TABLE Table_1
UPDATE(column_1,column_3) ON Table_1
```

Both of these Privilege specifications define a Privilege that updates the values of TABLE_1.COLUMN_1 and TABLE_1.COLUMN_3. Here's an example of a Privilege specification that defines a Privilege that inserts values into TABLE_1.COLUMN_2:

```
INSERT(column_2) ON TABLE Table_1
```

And here's an example of a Privilege specification that defines a Privilege that enables TABLE_1.COLUMN_3 to be named in a Constraint or Assertion definition:

```
REFERENCES(column_3) ON TABLE Table_1
```

Every Privilege you have on a Table that is the basis for an updatable View is also granted to you on that View. For example, if you have the INSERT and SELECT Privileges on a Table and create an updatable View based on that Table, you will also have the INSERT and SELECT Privileges on the View. If your Table Privileges are grantable Privileges, your Privileges on the View will also be grantable.

An UNDER Privilege may either apply to a structured type or it may apply to a typed Table. An UNDER Privilege on a UDT allows the creation of subtypes; an UNDER Privilege on a typed Table allows the creation of subtables. You may not grant an UNDER Privilege on any other Object. Here's an example:

```
UNDER ON TYPE bob.bob_udt
```

A USAGE Privilege allows the use of the Domain, UDT, Character set, Collation, or Translation named in the Privilege's descriptor. You may not grant a USAGE Privilege on any other Object. Here's two examples:

```
USAGE ON DOMAIN domain_1
USAGE ON CHARACTER SET bob.charset_1
```

When a Catalog is "created," your DBMS grants the USAGE Privilege on all INFORMATION_SCHEMA Character sets, Collations, and Translations to PUBLIC WITH GRANT OPTION so you always have the use of those Objects. If for some reason you should ever create a new character-related Object, do the same — there is no point being secretive here.

An EXECUTE Privilege allows the SQL-invoked routine named in the Privilege's descriptor to be executed. You may not grant an EXECUTE Privilege on any other Object. Here's an example:

```
EXECUTE ON SPECIFIC ROUTINE some_routine
```

(We define <specific routine designator> in Chapter 25 "SQL-Invoked Routines.")

Note that if two Privileges are identical except that one is a grantable Privilege and the other is not, the grantable Privilege takes precedence and both Privileges are set to grantable Privileges. Similarly, if two otherwise identical Privileges indicate one has the WITH HIERARCHY OPTION and the other does not, the first takes precedence. Your DBMS will then eliminate the redundant duplicate Privilege.

If you want to restrict your code to Core SQL, don't specify the UNDER Privilege, don't specify the SELECT Privilege as a Column Privilege (i.e., with a <Column name> list), and don't specify the INSERT Privilege as a Column Privilege.

GRANT Statement

The GRANT statement defines both Privilege grants and Role authorizations and so has two different syntaxes. The first is identified as the <grant privilege statement> and the second as the <grant role statement>.

<grant privilege statement>

The required syntax for the <grant privilege statement> form of the GRANT statement is as follows.

```
<grant privilege statement> ::=
GRANT <privileges> TO <grantee> [ {,<grantee>}... ]
[ WITH HIERARCHY OPTION ] [ WITH GRANT OPTION ]
[ FROM <grantor> ]

   <grantee> ::= PUBLIC | <AuthorizationID>
   <grantor> ::= CURRENT_USER | CURRENT_ROLE
```

The <grant privilege statement> grants one or more Privileges on a given Object to one or more grantees, including (possibly) PUBLIC. The grantor of the Privileges must, of course, hold those Privileges as grantable Privileges.

We've already shown you the syntax for the <privileges> Privilege specification; it's used exactly that way in this form of the GRANT statement. Here are some examples:

```
GRANT SELECT ON TABLE Table_1 TO PUBLIC;
GRANT INSERT(column_1,column_5) ON Table_1 TO sam;
GRANT ALL PRIVILEGES ON TABLE Table_1 TO PUBLIC, bob, sam;
GRANT USAGE ON DOMAIN domain_1 TO bob;
GRANT EXECUTE ON SPECIFIC ROUTINE some_routine TO sam;
```

If your <grantee> is PUBLIC, you're granting the Privilege to a list of <grantee>s that contains all of the <AuthorizationID>s in the SQL-environment — now and in the future. If your <grantee> is one or more <AuthorizationID>s, you're granting the Privilege only to those <AuthorizationID>s. (Remember that an <AuthorizationID> may be either a User or a Role.)

The optional WITH HIERARCHY OPTION clause may apply only to a SELECT Table Privilege that is granted on a typed Table. When you use this option, you are granting the SELECT Privilege not only on the Table named, but also on all of that Table's subtables.

The optional FROM clause names the grantor of the Privileges; CURRENT_USER is the <AuthorizationID> of the current user and CURRENT_ROLE is the <AuthorizationID> of the current Role. If you omit the clause, it defaults to FROM CURRENT_USER — but if CURRENT_USER is NULL, the clause defaults to FROM CURRENT_ROLE. If you specify FROM CURRENT_USER and the current <AuthorizationID> is a <Role name>, or if you specify FROM CURRENT_ROLE and the current <Role name> is NULL, the GRANT statement will fail; your DBMS will return the SQLSTATE error 0L000 "invalid grantor." Here are two examples:

```
GRANT UPDATE(column_1,column_5) ON Table_1 TO sam FROM CURRENT_USER;
GRANT DELETE ON Table_1 TO PUBLIC FROM CURRENT_ROLE;
```

The optional WITH GRANT OPTION clause defines a grantable Privilege; one that the grantee may, in turn, grant to other <AuthorizationID>s. If you omit the clause, the grantee will not be able to pass the Privilege on to others. Here are two examples:

```
GRANT REFERENCES(column_4,column_5) ON Table_1 TO bob,sam
      WITH GRANT OPTION FROM CURRENT_USER;
GRANT TRIGGER Table_1 TO PUBLIC
      WITH GRANT OPTION FROM CURRENT_ROLE;
```

If the GRANT statement isn't able to successfully create a Privilege descriptor for every one of its Privilege specifications, your DBMS will return the SQLSTATE warning 01007 "warning-privilege not granted."

If you want to restrict your code to Core SQL, don't use the FROM <grantor> clause or the WITH HIERARCHY OPTION with the GRANT statement.

<grant role statement>

The required syntax for the <grant role statement> form of the GRANT statement is as follows.

```
<grant role statement> ::=
GRANT <Role name> [ {,<Role name>}... ] TO <grantee> [ {,<grantee>}... ]
[ WITH ADMIN OPTION ]
[ FROM <grantor> ]

   <grantee> ::= PUBLIC | <AuthorizationID>
   <grantor> ::= CURRENT_USER | CURRENT_ROLE
```

The <grant role statement> grants the use of one or more Roles to one or more grantees, including (possibly) PUBLIC. The grantor of the Roles must, of course, hold those Roles as grantable Roles (that is, WITH ADMIN OPTION).

If your <grantee> is PUBLIC, you're granting the use of <Role name> to a list of <grantee>s that contains all of the <AuthorizationID>s in the SQL-environment — now and in the future. If your <grantee> is one or more <AuthorizationID>s, you're granting the use of the Role only to those <AuthorizationID>s. Keep in mind that an <AuthorizationID> may be either a User or a Role — this means you can grant the use of a Role not only to a User, but to another Role. Be careful with this last option; SQL doesn't allow you to grant the use of a Role to a Role that already has the use of that Role — that is, no cycles of Role grants are allowed. Note that if two Role grants are identical except that one is a grantable Role and the other is not, the grantable Role takes precedence and both Roles are set to grantable Roles. Your DBMS will then eliminate the redundant duplicate Role grant.

The optional FROM clause names the grantor of the Roles; CURRENT_USER is the <AuthorizationID> of the current user and CURRENT_ROLE is the <AuthorizationID> of the current Role. If you omit the clause, it defaults to FROM CURRENT_USER — but if CURRENT_USER is NULL, the clause defaults to FROM CURRENT_ROLE. If you specify FROM CURRENT_USER and the current <AuthorizationID> is a <Role name>, or if you specify FROM CURRENT_ROLE and the current <Role name> is NULL, the GRANT statement will fail; your DBMS will return the SQLSTATE error 0L000 "invalid grantor." For example, in this SQL statement, the current user is granting the use of the ASSISTANTS_ROLE Role to every <AuthorizationID>:

```
GRANT assistants_role TO PUBLIC FROM CURRENT_USER;
```

In the following SQL statement, the current Role is granting the use of the ASSISTANTS_ROLE and the BOSSES_ROLE Role to the bob and joe <AuthorizationID>s:

```
GRANT assistants_role, bosses_role TO bob, joe FROM CURRENT_ROLE;
```

The optional WITH ADMIN OPTION clause defines a grantable Role; one that the grantee may, in turn, grant the use of to other <AuthorizationID>s. If you omit the clause, the grantee will not be able to pass the use of the Role on to others. Here are two examples:

```
GRANT assistants_role TO PUBLIC WITH ADMIN OPTION FROM CURRENT_USER;

GRANT assistants_role, bosses_role TO bob, joe
  WITH ADMIN OPTION FROM CURRENT_ROLE;
```

If you want to restrict your code to Core SQL, don't use the <grant role statement> form of the GRANT statement and don't grant any grantable Privileges on your Objects to other users — Core SQL only allows the owner of an Object to hold a grantable Privilege.

Data Control

You need explicit permission to perform any action on any SQL Object. SQL's security system is discretionary (meaning that your rights vary depending on the action and on the Object). If you try to violate security, what usually happens is an error message. It's not a sophisticated system, but there is some complexity when we get into details and definitions. Here's a simple GRANT statement:

```
GRANT INSERT                          -- action
ON   Books                            -- Object
TO   joe;                             -- user
```

After this SQL statement is executed, the user named joe will be able to use the INSERT statement on the Table named Books. SQL's security system boils down to this: you can let people access data with GRANT statements or you can refuse to do so. The combination {action plus Object} is a Privilege. The action is usually a verb, the Object is usually a Table, and the user is usually a person.

Action and Object

What action is possible depends on the Object. Here is a chart of the Object types which can be in GRANT statements and the applicable actions for them:

OBJECT	ACTION(S)
Base table	SELECT, INSERT, UPDATE, DELETE, TRIGGER, REFERENCES
View	SELECT, INSERT, UPDATE, DELETE, REFERENCES
Column	SELECT, INSERT, UPDATE, REFERENCES
Domain	USAGE
Character Set	USAGE
Collation	USAGE
Translation	USAGE
SQL-invoked routine	EXECUTE
UDT	UNDER

Except for USAGE and UNDER, the GRANT actions correspond to verbs that are used in SQL statements, for example:

```
UPDATE Integer_Tables SET
   integer_1 = CAST('1' AS INFORMATION_SCHEMA.CARDINAL_NUMBER);
```

For this SQL statement to be possible, the current <AuthorizationID> must have the following Privileges:

- The UPDATE Privilege on Table INTEGER_TABLES and/or the UPDATE Privilege on Column INTEGER_TABLES.INTEGER_1.
- The USAGE Privilege on Domain INFORMATION_SCHEMA.CARDINAL_NUMBER.

User/Role

It's important to remember that Users are outside the "database" — the effect is that <User name>s are unqualified names, that there are no CREATE USER / DROP USER statements in standard SQL, and that some important questions depend on your operating system. An easy way to appreciate this is to remember that "joe" is still "joe" even if you switch to a different Schema in a different Catalog. By contrast, a Role is inside the database (it's a Schema Object). Regardless, both Users and Roles are <AuthorizationID>s. Other points about <AuthorizationID>s:

- All DBMS operations are done on behalf of some <AuthorizationID>.
- All Objects are owned by some <AuthorizationID>.
- <AuthorizationID>s refer to real-world entities like people ("Sam Brown," "Joe") or jobs ("VP Marketing," "Tellers") or departments ("Acquisitions," "Front Office") or robots ("Consolidate Report program," "Internet spider"). DBMSs can't distinguish between these categories.

In a security context, we're concerned with the entity's authorization to ask for certain acts to be performed. That's where the GRANT statement comes in.

Owners

Consider this SQL statement:

```
CREATE SCHEMA Sally_Schema AUTHORIZATION Sally
   CREATE TABLE Sally_Dates (date_1 DATE, date_2 DATE);
```

(The question, "Who may execute a CREATE SCHEMA statement?" is a tough one. It's implementor-defined, which might mean "anybody at all," but more likely means "some special database administrator who exists when you first install the DBMS." Though the question is important, it rarely is going to come up.)

In this example, a Role named Sally is the owner of SALLY_SCHEMA. Therefore, by definition, Sally is the owner of all Objects within that Schema — right now, this includes Table SALLY_DATES and the Columns DATE_1 and DATE_2.

TRAP: You'll often hear that the "owner of a Table" is "the <AuthorizationID> who created the Table." Technically, that's wrong. Suppose another User/Role (Joe) was able to create a Table and store it in Sally's Schema:

```
CREATE TABLE Sally_Schema.Joe_Dates (
     date_1 DATE, date_2 DATE);
```

Joe is the creator of Table JOE_DATES — but the owner is Sally, because Sally owns the Schema. The distinction between creators and owners is trivial for SQL-92 users because it is illegal to create Objects in a Schema that you don't own. It is legal in SQL3 though — so don't let old definitions mix you up.

As the Schema owner, Sally now has the power to CREATE, ALTER, or DROP all Objects in the Schema. Sally alone has this power — she cannot delegate it — so a Schema owner's CREATE/ALTER/DROP power is a right, not a Privilege. This power exists, but we will not trouble with it further because it does not involve the GRANT statement.

Sally also has a full set of all Privileges that apply for each Object in her Schema. For example, Sally has the USAGE Privilege for all of her Schema's Domains, Character sets, Collations, and Translations and she has SELECT, UPDATE, INSERT, DELETE, REFERENCES, and TRIGGER Table Privileges for all of her Schema's Base tables. Sally's set of Privileges stems automatically from her ownership of the Schema. Technically, it is considered that she was "granted" these powers by a pseudo-user named "_SYSTEM", but for practical purposes she is the ultimate authority. She cannot lose her right to do these operations. She can, however, pass on any or all of her Privileges to any other user. This ability is called the GRANT OPTION, because Sally has the option of granting the Privileges she holds. Sally also may pass on the grant option itself.

GRANTs on Tables

Let's follow what a DBMS does with a GRANT statement, using a series of examples based on SALLY_SCHEMA. Here's a GRANT statement for that Schema (assume Sally is the current <AuthorizationID>):

```
GRANT SELECT, INSERT ON Sally_Dates TO joe WITH GRANT OPTION;
```

Given this SQL statement, a DBMS acts as follows:

- It determines that Sally owns the Schema — therefore she has a full set of Privileges on Table SALLY_DATES. There is no need to find a Privilege descriptor to see whether she may grant Privileges.
- It determines that Joe does not exist, so it silently creates a user named Joe. Even if Joe has not made his existence known before, that would be no reason to believe he does not exist. [We're making some assumptions here for the sake of the example. This would be the usual case, but your DBMS might require you to execute some form of (non-standard) CREATE USER statement or it may have some operating-system dependent check on whether Joe exists.]
- It creates these six new Privilege descriptors:

GRANTOR	GRANTEE	OBJECT	NAME	ACTION	GRANT_OPTION
Sally	Joe	Table	Sally_Dates	SELECT	YES
Sally	Joe	Table	Sally_Dates	INSERT	YES
Sally	Joe	Column	date_1	SELECT	YES
Sally	Joe	Column	date_1	INSERT	YES

GRANTOR	GRANTEE	OBJECT	NAME	ACTION	GRANT_OPTION
Sally	Joe	Column	date_2	SELECT	YES
Sally	Joe	Column	date_2	INSERT	YES

The four "Column Privilege" descriptors may surprise you a bit since the GRANT statement syntax doesn't include COLUMN as an Object. But since it does allow Column Privileges to be defined, the effect is that a GRANT on a Table creates, not only a Privilege descriptor for that Table, but also a Privilege descriptor for every applicable Column of that Table.

Now, suppose that time passes and the current <AuthorizationID> becomes Joe who executes this GRANT statement:

```
GRANT INSERT, UPDATE ON Sally_Dates TO Sam;
```

Given this SQL statement, a DBMS acts as follows:

- It determines that Joe does not own the Schema, so it looks through the Privilege descriptors to see if there are any where grantee = 'Joe', Object = 'Table', Name = 'Sally_Dates', and grant_option = YES. It finds INSERT Privileges but it does not find UPDATE Privileges, so it returns the SQLSTATE warning 01007 "warning-privilege not granted" and it creates these three new Privilege descriptors:

GRANTOR	GRANTEE	OBJECT	NAME	ACTION	GRANT_OPTION
Joe	Sam	Table	Sally_Dates	INSERT	NO
Joe	Sam	Column	date_1	INSERT	NO
Joe	Sam	Column	date_2	INSERT	NO

More time passes and Sally is once again the current <AuthorizationID>. She does the following:

```
GRANT INSERT ON Sally_Dates TO Sam;
GRANT INSERT(date_1) ON Sally_Dates TO bob;
```

Given these SQL statements, a DBMS acts as follows:

- Once again it sees that Sally owns the Schema and so has full Privileges, all grantable.
- It creates these five new Privilege descriptors:

GRANTOR	GRANTEE	OBJECT	NAME	ACTION	GRANT_OPTION
Sally	Sam	Table	Sally_Dates	INSERT	NO
Sally	Sam	Column	date_1	INSERT	NO
Sally	Sam	Column	date_2	INSERT	NO
Sally	Bob	Table	Sally_Dates	INSERT	NO
Sally	Bob	Column	date_1	INSERT	NO

These Privilege descriptors for Sam are not duplicates of the ones that were created earlier when Joe granted Sam the same Privileges, therefore the DBMS makes new Privilege descriptors. Later, however, Sally repeats this GRANT:

```
GRANT INSERT ON Sally_Dates TO Sam;
```

In this final case, nothing happens; there are already Privilege descriptors with the same {grantor, grantee, Object, name, action} and duplicates will not be added to INFORMATION_SCHEMA. Your DBMS will return "okay" after creating zero new rows.

A related example — trivial, but worth making because older SQL books describe it incorrectly — concerns the question, "What if the last example had contained the WITH GRANT OPTION clause?" In that case, the grant_option field for the last two Privilege descriptors would have been changed from NO to YES.

In the end, we have fourteen new Privilege descriptors. Sally has the same powers of ownership as before, Joe can INSERT INTO Sally_Dates or SELECT FROM Sally_Dates, Sam can INSERT INTO Sally_Dates, and Bob can INSERT INTO Sally_Dates.date_1. Joe's Privileges are WITH GRANT OPTION, Sam's and Bob's are not. We have been at some pains to show that the result is both Table and Column Privilege descriptors and no two Privilege descriptors can be exact duplicates. There can, however, be considerable overlap as is seen by the fact that Sam has two sets of INSERT Privileges on the same Object — one with grantor=Sally and the other with grantor=Joe.

TRAP: It is a delusion to believe that Bob may now execute the SQL statement:

```
INSERT INTO Sally_Dates (date_1) VALUES (CURRENT_DATE);
```

because to do this, Bob needs the INSERT Privilege for both Column DATE_1 and Column DATE_2 — INSERT statements create whole rows. So it's useless to "GRANT INSERT(Column-list)" unless (*a*) you expect that somebody else will grant access on the other Columns or (*b*) your (Column-list) contains the names of all Columns in the Table, but you don't want to just "GRANT INSERT ON <Table name>" because that would give access not only to all Columns currently in the Table, but to all Columns which will ever be in the Table (including Columns added by future ALTER TABLE statements).

If Sally does the following:

```
GRANT UPDATE(date_1) ON Sally_Dates TO Sam;
```

the effect is that Sam can do this:

```
UPDATE Sally_Dates SET date_1 = DATE '1994-07-15';
```

but Sam can't do this:

```
UPDATE Sally_Dates SET date_2 = DATE '1994-07-15';
```

There are times when such fine-tuning of controls is desirable. If Sally does the following:

```
GRANT SELECT(date_1) ON Sally_Dates TO Sam;
```

the effect is that Sam can do this:

```
SELECT date_1 FROM Sally_Dates;
SELECT COUNT(*) FROM Sally_Dates;
```

but he can't specifically SELECT the second Column.

TRAP: If SELECT(Column-list) Privileges are granted, the recipients should avoid using "SELECT * ...". The "SELECT * ..." statement will suddenly cease to work for them if new Columns are added to the Table.

We would never recommend by-Column granting without first looking at the alternative — granting on a View.

GRANTs on Views

By definition, a View is a Table. So the considerations specific to "GRANTs on Views" have nothing to do with syntax — the syntax is the same as for any Table — but with the effect. Specifically, let's see what would occur if Joe owns a View of Table SALLY_DATES.

To make the example possible, we have to start by giving Joe his own Schema. It's convenient to make Joe's View at the same time. Here's the SQL statement to do it:

```
CREATE SCHEMA Joe_Schema AUTHORIZATION Joe
   CREATE VIEW Joe_Views AS
      SELECT date_1,date_2 FROM Sally_Schema.Sally_Dates;
```

To do this, Joe will need the SELECT Privilege on the Columns of Table SALLY_DATES in SALLY_SCHEMA — we gave these to him earlier. Naturally, the rules don't let Joe gain new Privileges by owning a View. He can DROP this View (that's his power as an owner and he can SELECT FROM or INSERT INTO this View (those are the grantable Privileges he holds on SALLY_DATES) — and that's all. He cannot do this:

```
UPDATE Joe_Views SET date_1 = CURRENT_DATE;
```

because UPDATE is not a Privilege he holds on SALLY_DATES, and ultimately, an UPDATE on the View will UPDATE the Table. Now assume that Joe creates another View:

```
CREATE VIEW Joe_Views_2 AS
   SELECT date_1 FROM Joe_Views WHERE date_1 > DATE '1994-01-03';
```

and then does a GRANT to Sam:

```
GRANT INSERT, SELECT ON Joe_Views_2 TO Sam;
```

...a beautiful example of why Views are useful for security systems. Here, Joe has restricted Sam's access not only to a particular Column of a Table, but to particular rows of that Table. He has done more than is possible with by-Column granting — and he has done it cleanly.

GRANTs on Procedures

The sad news is that the most useful GRANT of all is one that hardly anyone can use yet. It depends on the existence of procedures, which are an SQL3 Object. Only GRANTs on procedures can bring us real-word examples like the following one.

Think of a bank. Tellers in the bank do not have Privileges on Tables or on Columns within Tables. If we give them UPDATE Privileges on customer accounts, they'll be able to do anything at all to the accounts (too dangerous); if we don't, they won't be able to do anything at all (too restrictive). What everyone — managers, tellers, and customers — wants is a Privilege that allows a specific combination of operations. For example, let Joe transfer money — that is, let him withdraw from one account and deposit to another account provided that the total of the transaction balances out to $0.00. You could define this situation in a program using syntax like this:

```
CREATE PROCEDURE Transfer_Procedure
  ... INSERT
  ... UPDATE
  ... CHECK
  ... CASE
  ...;
```

And then you could allow Joe to use the procedure with:

```
GRANT EXECUTE ON Transfer_Procedure TO Joe;
```

Almost always, restricting based on an SQL verb (INSERT / UPDATE / DELETE) is vague. Administrators of non-imaginary institutions would prefer finer tuning; they want to restrict actions based on entire SQL statements or, more often, on combinations of SQL statements. Since procedure granting will give them that, eventually they'll throw away the old grants on Tables / Columns / Views and GRANT EXECUTE will become the norm.

Constraints

If a user names a Column within a Constraint or Assertion definition, that means he/she/it REFERENCES the Column. (Don't be misled by the appearance of the <keyword> REFERENCES in FOREIGN KEY Constraint definitions; in this context we're talking about any kind of Constraint. And don't be misled by the appearance of the <keyword> SELECT inside some complex CHECK Constraints; the action here is REFERENCES so the SELECT Privilege is irrelevant for Constraints.) Here's an example — Sally (who owns the Table SALLY_DATES) may issue this GRANT statement:

```
GRANT REFERENCES ON Sally_Dates TO Joe;
```

This means that Joe can now create a Constraint or Assertion that uses the Columns of SALLY_DATES — for example:

```
CREATE ASSERTION joe_constraint CHECK (
   Joe_Views.date_1 <> DATE '1999-12-31');
```

Not only does this Assertion limit the values of JOE_VIEWS, it also limits the values of SALLY_DATES, because that is the Table on which the View is based. Obviously, Joe should not be able to set limits on Sally's data unless she specifically allows him to — thus, the REFERENCES Privilege.

REVOKE Statement

By the time we finish setting up a Catalog and granting appropriate Privileges to our users, we probably have several thousand Privilege descriptors in INFORMATION_SCHEMA — more than the count for all other Schema Objects combined. Maintaining them is made easier by the fact that when an Object is dropped, the DBMS will silently destroy all associated Privilege descriptors. That leaves only the problem, "How do we adjust for the occasional necessity to remove a Privilege descriptor due to a change in status of a particular User (or Role)?" The problem does not occur frequently, but can be mightily cumbersome; the SQL Standard devotes about 40 pages to it. We have managed to simplify the description somewhat, by focusing on the two "essentials" of the process:

1. We are trying to reverse the effects of a GRANT statement, using a REVOKE statement — the clauses of which have almost the same syntax as GRANT's clauses.
2. We are actually deleting Privilege descriptor rows from INFORMATION_SCHEMA.

The REVOKE statement destroys both Privilege descriptors and Role authorizations and so has two different syntaxes. The first is identified as the <revoke privilege statement> and the second as the <revoke role statement>. The required syntax for the REVOKE statement is as follows.

```
<revoke privilege statement> ::=
REVOKE [ {GRANT OPTION FOR | HIERARCHY OPTION FOR}  ]
<privileges> FROM <grantee> [ {,<grantee>}... ]
[ FROM {CURRENT_USER | CURRENT_ROLE} ] {RESTRICT | CASCADE}

<revoke role statement> ::=
REVOKE [ ADMIN OPTION FOR ] <Role name> [ {,<Role name>}... ]
FROM <grantee> [ {,<grantee>}... ]
[ FROM {CURRENT_USER | CURRENT_ROLE} ]
{RESTRICT | CASCADE}

   <grantee> ::= PUBLIC | <AuthorizationID>
```

The <revoke privilege statement> revokes one or more Privileges on a given Object from one or more grantees including (possibly) PUBLIC, while the <revoke role statement> revokes the use of one or more Roles from one or more grantees. Only the grantor of the Privileges (or the Roles) may revoke them.

We've already shown you the syntax for the <privileges> Privilege specification; it's used exactly that way in the <revoke privilege statement> form of the REVOKE statement. Here are some examples:

```
REVOKE SELECT ON TABLE Table_1 FROM PUBLIC CASCADE;
REVOKE INSERT(column_1,column_5) ON Table_1 FROM sam CASCADE;
REVOKE ALL PRIVILEGES ON TABLE Table_1 FROM PUBLIC CASCADE;
REVOKE USAGE ON DOMAIN domain_1 FROM bob CASCADE;
REVOKE EXECUTE ON SPECIFIC ROUTINE some_routine FROM sam CASCADE;
```

And here's an example of the <revoke role statement> form of REVOKE:

```
REVOKE assistants_role FROM PUBLIC CASCADE;
```

In both cases, if your <grantee> is PUBLIC, you're revoking the Privilege (or the use of the Role) from a list of <grantee>s that contains all of the <AuthorizationID>s in the SQL-environment. If your <grantee> is one or more <AuthorizationID>s, you're revoking the Privilege (or the use of the Role) only from those <AuthorizationID>s. (Remember that an <AuthorizationID> may be either a User or a Role.)

Remember that, for Tables, GRANT creates Privilege descriptors for both the Table and its Columns. Well, when you REVOKE a Table Privilege, all by-Column Privileges for that Table disappear too. The effect is a bit strange; when you revoke a Table Privilege, you lose the Column Privilege (even if it was granted separately) and when you revoke a Column Privilege, you lose that Column Privilege — even if it resulted from a Table Privilege GRANT.

The optional FROM clause names the grantor of the Privileges or the Role you're revoking; CURRENT_USER is the <AuthorizationID> of the current User and CURRENT_ROLE is the <AuthorizationID> of the current Role. If you omit the clause, it defaults to FROM CURRENT_USER — but if CURRENT_USER is NULL, the clause defaults to FROM CURRENT_ROLE. If you specify FROM CURRENT_USER and the current <AuthorizationID> is a <Role name>, or if you specify FROM CURRENT_ROLE and the current <Role name> is NULL, the REVOKE statement will fail; your DBMS will return the SQLSTATE error 0L000 "invalid grantor." Here are two examples:

```
REVOKE UPDATE ON Table_1 FROM sam FROM CURRENT_USER CASCADE;
-- revokes the UPDATE Privilege on TABLE_1 from Sam only if the
current User granted that Privilege in the first place

REVOKE assistants_role FROM PUBLIC FROM CURRENT_ROLE CASCADE;
-- revokes the use of the ASSISTANTS_ROLE Role from PUBLIC only if the current
Role granted the use of that Role in the first place
```

The optional HIERARCHY OPTION FOR clause (applicable only to the <revoke privilege statement>) allows you to revoke only the WITH HIERARCHY OPTION from the specified SELECT Privilege.

The optional GRANT OPTION FOR (<revoke privilege statement>) and ADMIN OPTION FOR (<revoke role statement>) clauses allow you to revoke only the grantability of a Privilege or a Role. For example, consider these SQL statements:

```
GRANT UPDATE ON TABLE Table_1 TO sam WITH GRANT OPTION;
REVOKE GRANT OPTION FOR UPDATE ON Table_1 FROM sam CASCADE;
```

The first SQL statement allows Sam to update TABLE_1 and to pass this Privilege on to others. The second SQL statement revokes the latter ability; Sam can still update TABLE_1, but may no longer pass the Privilege on. Here's another example:

```
GRANT assistants_role TO bob WITH ADMIN OPTION;
REVOKE ADMIN OPTION FOR assistants_role FROM bob CASCADE;
```

The first SQL statement allows Bob to use all of the Privileges belonging to the ASSISTANTS_ROLE Role and to pass the use of this Role on to others. The second SQL statement revokes the latter ability; Bob can still use the Role's Privileges, but may no longer pass that use on.

The GRANT/ADMIN option clauses have another effect. Suppose that a user holds a Privilege on a Table WITH GRANT OPTION, and does so, also with GRANT OPTION. The second user can now do the same for a third user, and so on — for example:

```
GRANT DELETE ON TABLE Sally_Dates TO joe WITH GRANT OPTION;
-- assume Sally does this

GRANT DELETE ON TABLE Sally_Dates TO sam WITH GRANT OPTION;
-- assume Joe does this

GRANT DELETE ON TABLE Sally_Dates TO bob WITH GRANT OPTION;
-- assume Sam does this
```

What should happen if Sally now does the following?

```
REVOKE DELETE ON TABLE Sally_Dates FROM joe;
```

Here, we've deliberately left off RESTRICT/CASCADE for the sake of the example, so let's assume that the SQL statement works — Joe no longer has the DELETE Privilege on SALLY_DATES. The Privileges handed down from Joe to Sam, and from Sam to Bob, are now called "abandoned Privileges"; they are dependent on Joe's DELETE Privilege — and Joe doesn't have it any more. This is where the RESTRICT/CASCADE <keyword>s come in.

- If your REVOKE statement specifies CASCADE, the REVOKE succeeds — and it cascades down to revoke any Privileges that would otherwise be abandoned. In our example, that means both Sam and Bob would no longer have the DELETE Privilege on SALLY_DATES either.
- If your REVOKE statement specifies RESTRICT, the REVOKE succeeds only if the Privilege being revoked has no dependent Privileges. In our example, that means the REVOKE statement would fail.

The same holds true for revoking the use of a Role.

Objects can also become "abandoned" when a Privilege or the use of a Role is revoked. For example, remember that Joe holds the SELECT Privilege on SALLY_DATES and, with this, was able to create his View, JOE_VIEWS. Now suppose Sally does this:

```
REVOKE SELECT ON Sally_Dates FROM joe CASCADE;
```

The effect is that, not only does Joe lose his ability to SELECT from SALLY_DATES, but that JOE_VIEWS is dropped! The reason is that, in effect, JOE_VIEWS is nothing but a SELECT that Joe does from SALLY_DATES, and because such SELECTs are no longer allowed, the View may no longer exist. If, on the other hand, Sally does the following:

```
REVOKE SELECT ON Sally_Dates FROM joe RESTRICT;
```

the effect is that the REVOKE statement fails; Sally may not revoke Joe's ability to SELECT from SALLY_DATES because this would mean that JOE_VIEWS would be abandoned — and this is not allowed. The same holds true for any Object that anyone was able to create only because they held some required Privilege (or were able to use a Role that held that Privilege) — if REVOKE...RESTRICT is used, the statement will fail but if REVOKE...CASCADE is used, the statement will not only revoke but drop all Objects that would otherwise be abandoned.

If the REVOKE statement isn't able to find a Privilege descriptor for every one of its Privilege specifications, your DBMS will return the SQLSTATE warning 01006 "warning-privilege not revoked."

If you want to restrict your code to Core SQL, don't use the <revoke role statement> form of the REVOKE statement and don't use REVOKE...CASCADE or the GRANT OPTION FOR or HIERARCHY OPTION FOR clauses. Also, when revoking, make sure that your current <AuthorizationID> is the owner of the Schema that owns the Object you're revoking Privileges for.

DROP ROLE Statement

The DROP ROLE statement destroys a Role. The required syntax for the DROP ROLE statement is as follows.

```
DROP ROLE <Role name>
```

The <Role name> must identify an existing Role for which an enabled <AuthorizationID> has the WITH ADMIN OPTION. That is, only an <AuthorizationID> with the WITH ADMIN OPTION on a Role may drop it. The effect of DROP ROLE <Role name>, e.g.,

```
DROP ROLE assistants_role;
```

is that the Role named ASSISTANTS_ROLE will be destroyed and that your DBMS will also do this for every <AuthorizationID> that was granted use of the Role:

```
REVOKE assistants_role FROM <AuthorizationID> RESTRICT;
```

If you want to restrict your code to Core SQL, don't use the DROP ROLE statement.

What Privileges Do I Have?

Earlier in this chapter, we said that every Privilege is defined by a descriptor stored in INFORMATION_SCHEMA. You can thus find out what Privileges you have by querying the appropriate Views therein (see Chapter 16 "SQL Catalogs.") Each "Privilege descriptor" View includes Columns for grantor, grantee, Object, <Object name>, and is_grantable — the basic

Privilege description stuff. You might think that this makes things fairly straightforward — but take note! There is deep trickiness implied by simple sounding questions like, "May Joe SELECT from SALLY_DATES?"

The first trickiness is that it is not enough to look for "Grantee = 'Joe'". Joe may have a Privilege due to his ROLE and at any rate, Joe is a member of the PUBLIC. So when searching for Joe's Privileges, the conditions should include "Grantee = 'PUBLIC' and Grantee = 'whatever Role Joe may be able to use'."

The second trickiness is that it is not enough to look for "Object = 'Sally_Dates'" in the TABLE_PRIVILEGES View. Joe may have a Privilege on only one Column, so you have to search the COLUMN_PRIVILEGES View too. And even if you find that Joe does have the SELECT Privilege, that might not be enough — he might also need separate USAGE Privileges for the UDT, the Character set, and the Collation associated with each Column in the Table. And even if you find that Joe doesn't have the SELECT Privilege, the answer may be insufficient — he might have the SELECT Privilege on a View of the Table or he might be able to get all the data he needs using a procedure.

TIP: Explain these trickinesses to other users at your site, then ask them to observe these limits:

- Number of by-Column GRANTs = 0
- Number of Roles = 1 (not including PUBLIC)
- Number of Views = 1 per Table
- Number of USAGE GRANTs = 1 (i.e., one GRANT only, to PUBLIC)

Violating the Security System

Each of the following scenarios depends on a "hole" in the Standard SQL security wall. Perhaps the vendor of your particular DBMS hasn't plugged the hole. What fun it would be to find out ...

If you have the SELECT Privilege WITH GRANT OPTION on a single Table: Suppose the grantor of your Privilege is Sally. Why not reciprocate and GRANT your Privilege back to her? The advantage is that if Sally tries to revoke your Privilege later and forgets to say CASCADE, she will fail because there is now a chain of Privilege descriptors, terminating with her.

If your database is stored on a local microcomputer: The DBMS can't block your access to the file — usually its only line of defense is encryption or proprietary formatting (Microsoft Access and dBASE IV use variations of this defense). If you know what the Table and Column names are, you can go to another computer and make a database with the same structure but different data. Then copy your file over the legitimate one. This is a *cuckoo's egg* violation.

If your database is stored on a distant server: There's still a chance that the client receives complete row copies for local filtering. Start a long query, then turn your computer off. Start it up again and look for temporary unclosed files, probably in the \windows\temp directory.

Here is a security hole that is opened up by the REFERENCES Privilege: Sally creates a Table —

```
CREATE TABLE Sally_1 (column1 SMALLINT);
```

Sally lets Joe reference her Table —

```
GRANT REFERENCES ON Sally_1 TO joe;
```

Joe creates a Table —

```
CREATE TABLE Joe_1 (column_1 INT REFERENCES Sally_1);
```

Joe lets Sam update his Table —

```
GRANT UPDATE ON Joe_1 to Sam;
```

Now, even though Sam has no Privileges at all on Sally's Table, he can find out what's in it! All he has to do is:

```
UPDATE Joe_Schema.Joe_1 SET
   column_1 = :x;
```

in a loop, for x = all possible SMALLINT values. If, and only if, UPDATE succeeds, then the value of x is in Sally's Table.

User Functions

The SQL Standard defines four types of <AuthorizationID>s whose values can be obtained through the use of the scalar user functions USER, CURRENT_USER, SESSION_USER, SYSTEM_USER, and CURRENT_ROLE; each returns an SQL_TEXT character string whose value represents an <AuthorizationID>.

[NON-PORTABLE] The result of a user function is non-standard because the SQL Standard requires implementors to define whether the result string is fixed length or variable length and the result string's fixed length or maximum length (as applicable). [OCELOT Implementation] The OCELOT DBMS that comes with this book has each user function return a variable length SQL_TEXT string. The result has a maximum length of 128 characters.

The required syntax for a user function is as follows.

```
user function ::=
USER |
CURRENT_USER |
SESSION_USER |
SYSTEM_USER |
CURRENT_ROLE
```

A user function returns an SQL_TEXT character string with the COERCIBLE coercibility attribute.

CURRENT_USER returns the <AuthorizationID> name of the current User. This is either the User specified in the CONNECT statement that began the SQL-session (assuming it was a User and not a Role that began the session) or a default <AuthorizationID> set by your DBMS. CURRENT_USER will be NULL if the current <AuthorizationID> is a <Role name>. USER is a synonym for CURRENT_USER that may be used in Core SQL.

CURRENT_ROLE returns the <AuthorizationID> name of the current Role. This is either the Role specified in the CONNECT statement that began the SQL-session (assuming it was a Role and not a User that began the session; otherwise NULL) or the Role specified in the most recent SET ROLE statement issued for the SQL-session. CURRENT_ROLE will be NULL if the current <AuthorizationID> is a User rather than a Role.

SESSION_USER returns the <AuthorizationID> name of the SQL-session user. This is either the User specified in the CONNECT statement that began the SQL-session (assuming it was a User and not a Role that began the session; otherwise a default <AuthorizationID> set by your DBMS) or the User specified in the most recent SET SESSION AUTHORIZATION statement issued for the SQL-session. In most cases, the SQL-session <AuthorizationID> is the same as the current <AuthorizationID>.

[NON-PORTABLE] SYSTEM_USER returns an <AuthorizationID> name that represents the operating system user who executed the SQL-client Module that contains the SYSTEM_USER function call and is thus non-standard because the SQL Standard requires implementors to define their system user. [OCELOT Implementation] The OCELOT DBMS that comes with this book has a SYSTEM_USER called OCELOT.

The current <AuthorizationID> is the User or Role against which Privilege checking is done to see whether an SQL operation is allowable. For example, prior to executing this SQL statement:

```
SELECT * FROM Table_1;
```

your DBMS will check to see that the current <AuthorizationID> has the SELECT Privilege on that Table. If the current <AuthorizationID> has the Privilege, the SELECT is performed. If the current <AuthorizationID> does not have the Privilege, the SELECT is disallowed.

The SQL-session <AuthorizationID> is the <AuthorizationID> that is used as the default <AuthorizationID> whenever an SQL operation which requires an <AuthorizationID> is not provided with an explicit <AuthorizationID> specification. For example, when executing this SQL statement:

```
CREATE SCHEMA bob;
```

your DBMS effectively executes this SQL statement:

```
CREATE SCHEMA bob AUTHORIZATION SESSION_USER;
```

If you want to restrict your code to Core SQL, don't use CURRENT_USER, SESSION_USER, SYSTEM_USER, or CURRENT_ROLE.

Dialects

Many vendors have added their own Privileges to the SQL Standard's set. For example:

- IBM's DB2 has a SYSADM (system administrator) who can CREATE and DROP in any Schema and who can create Schemas (one of the implementor-defined areas in the Standard). Several other vendors also have similar "super user" Privileges which are not associated with any particular Object.
- Sybase has a CONNECT Privilege; other vendors allow connection by anyone, but new users can't do anything without further Privileges.
- The most popular non-standard Privilege is GRANT ALTER (which sometimes allows users to both alter and drop Tables).
- DBMSs which allow non-standard Objects allow non-standard Privileges to go with them; thus GRANT INDEX is common and DB2 also has access controls for tablespaces and indexspaces (which are somewhat like "files").

On the other hand, older DBMSs may fail to support the REFERENCES Privilege. They allow Constraints to be defined by anyone who has the appropriate SELECT Privileges instead.

A few SQL3 features are already fairly common. Sybase, Microsoft SQL Server, and Informix allow "GRANT SELECT (Column-name list) ...". Oracle has had a CREATE ROLE statement since version 7.0; Sybase and Microsoft SQL Server also allow Roles but they use non-standard terms and syntax.

As for syntax — the majority of DBMSs will let you specify more than just one "Object" in both GRANT and REVOKE statements. This leads to ambiguities — what is "GRANT UPDATE(column1) ON Tables_1, Tables_2" supposed to do? And is it proper if the different Objects are in different Catalogs? And what if different Privileges apply for different Objects? You're on safer ground if you just ignore this sort of enhancement.

The biggest variations involve the ways that the DBMS can identify and acknowledge users. If your operating system has a list of valid users and passwords (something you'll notice if you have to "log in" to your computer), then your DBMS can get the user by querying the OS (Ingres, Informix, and DB2 do this). Alternatively, or in addition, your DBMS might require you to supply both a user ID and a password when you CONNECT (Oracle and Sybase do this). In the former case, the user's name is probably limited to as few as eight characters because the OS has more restrictions than the DBMS does. In the latter case, there is probably a non-standard CREATE USER statement and a "user" Object stored inside the database.

Finally, you will see some DBMSs skimping on their obligation to store Privilege descriptors for owners. A quick glance at the INFORMATION_SCHEMA.COLUMN_PRIVILEGES View should tell you whether your DBMS is one of these.

16

Chapter 16

SQL Catalogs

In this chapter, we'll describe SQL Catalogs in detail and show you the syntax to use to create, alter, and destroy them.

Catalog

A Cluster may contain zero or more Catalogs. An *SQL Catalog* is a named group of Schemas, one of which must be an Ur-Schema named `INFORMATION_SCHEMA`. (The `INFORMATION_SCHEMA` Schema is a set of Views and Domains that contain the descriptions of all the SQL-data belonging to that Catalog.) Catalogs are dependent on some Cluster — the <Catalog name> must be unique within the Cluster the Catalog belongs to — and are created and dropped using implementation-defined methods.

Schemas are known as *Catalog Objects* and, as already stated, a Catalog may consist of one or more Schemas. The Catalog's name qualifies the names of the Schemas that belong to it and can either be explicitly stated or a default name will be supplied by your DBMS.

[NON-PORTABLE] SQL does not include any CREATE CATALOG, OPEN CATALOG, or DROP CATALOG statements. The method you'll use to access a Catalog with your DBMS is thus non-standard because the SQL Standard requires implementors to define how a Catalog comes into being, how it may be accessed, and how it may be destroyed.

[OCELOT Implementation] applies for the rest of this section.

The OCELOT DBMS that comes with this book considers a Catalog to be either a directory on your storage device (not necessarily the same device used to store the enclosing Cluster) or a subdirectory within the Cluster directory, e.g., either of these following would represent a Catalog:

```
C:\CATALOG
C:\CLUSTER\CATALOG
```

OCELOT's method of creating and connecting to Catalogs depends on the way you choose to begin an SQL session.

- When you run a Module defined with a MODULE statement that includes an explicit <Catalog name> in the SCHEMA clause or AUTHORIZATION clause, the DBMS will search, on the default Cluster directory, for a subdirectory with a name that matches that <Catalog name>. If the subdirectory can't be found, the DBMS will search for a directory with the same name. If the directory can't be found, it will be created and opened.
- If the MODULE statement doesn't provide an explicit <Catalog name> or if you're not running a Module, the DBMS will open a subdirectory or directory named OCELOT.

Catalog Names

A <Catalog name> identifies a Catalog and is never explicitly qualified with the name of the SQL-server (or Cluster) it belongs to. The required syntax for a <Catalog name> is as follows.

```
<Catalog name> ::=
string
```

[NON-PORTABLE] A <Catalog name> is a <regular identifier> or <delimited identifier> that is unique (for all Catalogs) within the Cluster it belongs to, but is non-standard because the SQL Standard requires implementors to define what a <Catalog name> may be. [OCELOT Implementation] The OCELOT DBMS that comes with this book requires a <Catalog name> to follow the rules for a directory name or a subdirectory name on the operating system in use; generally it may include [drive:] and [\upper-level name(s)] and \name. The <SQL-server name> which implicitly qualifies an OCELOT <Catalog name> identifies the Cluster that the Catalog belongs to and is the same as the <SQL-server name> argument of the most recent CONNECT TO statement issued for the SQL-session during which the Catalog was created. Here is an example of a possible <Catalog name>:

```
CATALOG_1
```

If you want to restrict your code to Core SQL, don't use explicit <Catalog name>s.

The Information Schema

Every Catalog in your SQL-environment contains a Schema called INFORMATION_SCHEMA; it contains a series of Views, Assertions, and Domains — together, they allow you to look at (but not change) the description of every Object that belongs to the Catalog as though it was regular SQL-data. The SELECT Privilege is granted to PUBLIC WITH GRANT OPTION on every View in INFORMATION_SCHEMA; the intent is that you will only be able to see those rows that describe Objects on which you have Privileges. The USAGE Privilege is also granted to PUBLIC WITH GRANT OPTION on every Domain in INFORMATION_SCHEMA.

INFORMATION_SCHEMA also contains the definition of every built-in SQL function, that is, every function that you can use as part of SQL (for example: ABS, CHAR_LENGTH, CARDINALITY, etc.). The EXECUTE Privilege is granted to PUBLIC on each one.

NOTE: The INFORMATION_SCHEMA Views are based on the Tables of an Ur-Schema called DEFINITION_SCHEMA, but the Standard doesn't require it to actually exist — its purpose is merely to provide a data model to support INFORMATION_SCHEMA. If DEFINITION_SCHEMA did exist though, its Base tables would describe all the Objects and SQL-data available to an SQL-server at any time — that is, DEFINITION_SCHEMA would describe an SQL Cluster.

[NON-PORTABLE] The total number of Views in INFORMATION_SCHEMA, and their exact definition, is non-standard because the SQL Standard allows implementors to add additional Views, as well as to add additional Columns to the Standard-defined Views, to describe additional, implementation-defined features. However, minus one exception, the View descriptions that follow must all be supported by your SQL DBMS.

In SQL, INFORMATION_SCHEMA is the Schema that contains the Information Schema Tables, Assertions, and Domains. It is considered to have been created by a CREATE SCHEMA statement that includes an AUTHORIZATION clause showing an <AuthorizationID> of INFORMATION_SCHEMA. A Standard INFORMATION_SCHEMA contains one Base table, one Assertion, four Domains, and 56 Views. Their descriptions follow.

INFORMATION_SCHEMA Base Tables

INFORMATION_SCHEMA.INFORMATION_SCHEMA_CATALOG_NAME
Definition:

```
CREATE TABLE INFORMATION_SCHEMA_CATALOG_NAME (
   CATALOG_NAME SQL_IDENTIFIER,
   CONSTRAINT INFORMATION_SCHEMA_CATALOG_NAME_PRIMARY_KEY
      PRIMARY KEY (CATALOG_NAME),
   CONSTRAINT INFORMATION_SCHEMA_CATALOG_NAME_CHECK
      CHECK (
         (SELECT COUNT(*) FROM INFORMATION_SCHEMA_CATALOG_NAME)=1))
```

The INFORMATION_SCHEMA_CATALOG_NAME Base table identifies the Catalog that contains this Information Schema; the CATALOG_NAME Column contains the name of the relevant Catalog.

INFORMATION_SCHEMA Assertions

INFORMATION_SCHEMA.INFORMATION_SCHEMA_CATALOG_NAME_CARDINALITY
Definition:

```
CREATE ASSERTION INFORMATION_SCHEMA_CATALOG_NAME_CARDINALITY
      CHECK (1=(SELECT COUNT(*) FROM INFORMATION_SCHEMA_CATALOG_NAME))
```

The INFORMATION_SCHEMA_CATALOG_NAME_CARDINALITY Assertion ensures that there is exactly one row in the INFORMATION_SCHEMA_CATALOG_NAME Table.

INFORMATION_SCHEMA Domains

INFORMATION_SCHEMA.CARDINAL_NUMBER
Definition:

```
CREATE DOMAIN CARDINAL_NUMBER AS INTEGER
      CONSTRAINT CARDINAL_NUMBER_DOMAIN_CHECK
            CHECK (VALUE >= 0)
```

The set of CARDINAL_NUMBER values includes all non-negative numbers that are less than your DBMS's defined maximum for INTEGER values. (Note: This is probably an error in the Standard — CARDINAL_NUMBER should include all non-negative numbers that are less than or equal to your DBMS's defined maximum for INTEGER values.)

INFORMATION_SCHEMA.CHARACTER_DATA
Definition:

```
CREATE DOMAIN CHARACTER_DATA AS CHARACTER VARYING(ML)
      CHARACTER SET SQL_TEXT
```

The set of CHARACTER_DATA values includes all character strings, from zero to ML characters long, that belong to the SQL_TEXT Character set. (ML is replaced by your DBMS's defined maximum length for a variable-length character string.)

INFORMATION_SCHEMA.SQL_IDENTIFIER
Definition:

```
CREATE DOMAIN SQL_IDENTIFIER AS CHARACTER VARYING(L)
      CHARACTER SET SQL_TEXT
```

The set of SQL_IDENTIFIER values includes all character strings, from one to L characters long, that are valid <regular identifier>s and <delimited identifier> bodies. (L is replaced by your DBMS's defined maximum length for a <regular identifier> and <delimited identifier> body.

INFORMATION_SCHEMA.TIME_STAMP
Definition:

```
CREATE DOMAIN TIME_STAMP AS TIMESTAMP(2) DEFAULT CURRENT_TIMESTAMP(2)
```

The set of TIME_STAMP values includes an SQL timestamp value.

INFORMATION_SCHEMA Views

INFORMATION_SCHEMA.ADMINISTRABLE_ROLE_AUTHORIZATIONS

This View has the following Columns:

Name	Domain	Nullable?
GRANTEE	SQL_IDENTIFIER	no
ROLE_NAME	SQL_IDENTIFIER	no
IS_GRANTABLE	CHARACTER_DATA	no

ADMINISTRABLE_ROLE_AUTHORIZATIONS shows the role authorizations that the current user may grant to others.

- GRANTEE and ROLE_NAME uniquely identify a role authorization which the current user may use.
- IS_GRANTABLE is 'YES' (the role authorization is grantable).

If you want to restrict your code to Core SQL, do not reference INFORMATION_SCHEMA.ADMINISTRABLE_ROLE_AUTHORIZATIONS.

INFORMATION_SCHEMA.APPLICABLE_ROLES

This View has the following Columns:

Name	Domain	Nullable?
GRANTEE	SQL_IDENTIFIER	no
ROLE_NAME	SQL_IDENTIFIER	no
IS_GRANTABLE	CHARACTER_DATA	no

APPLICABLE_ROLES shows the role authorizations that the current user may use.

- GRANTEE and ROLE_NAME uniquely identify a role authorization that the current user may use.
- IS_GRANTABLE is either 'YES' (the role authorization is grantable) or 'NO' (the role authorization is not grantable).

If you want to restrict your code to Core SQL, do not reference INFORMATION_SCHEMA.APPLICABLE_ROLES.

INFORMATION_SCHEMA.ASSERTIONS
This View has the following Columns:

Name	Domain	Nullable?
CONSTRAINT_CATALOG	SQL_IDENTIFIER	no
CONSTRAINT_SCHEMA	SQL_IDENTIFIER	no
CONSTRAINT_NAME	SQL_IDENTIFIER	no
IS_DEFERRABLE	CHARACTER_DATA	no
INITIALLY_DEFERRED	CHARACTER_DATA	no

ASSERTIONS shows the Assertions in this Catalog that are owned by the current user.

- CONSTRAINT_CATALOG, CONSTRAINT_SCHEMA, CONSTRAINT_NAME uniquely identify an Assertion owned by the current user.
- IS_DEFERRABLE is either 'YES' (the Assertion is DEFERRABLE) or 'NO' (the Assertion is NOT DEFERRABLE).
- INITIALLY_DEFERRED is either 'YES' (the Assertion is INITIALLY DEFERRED) or 'NO' (the Assertion is INITIALLY IMMEDIATE).

If you want to restrict your code to Core SQL, do not reference INFORMATION_SCHEMA.ASSERTIONS.

INFORMATION_SCHEMA.ATTRIBUTES
This View has the following Columns:

Name	Domain	Nullable?
UDT_CATALOG	SQL_IDENTIFIER	no
UDT_SCHEMA	SQL_IDENTIFIER	no
UDT_NAME	SQL_IDENTIFIER	no
ATTRIBUTE_NAME	SQL_IDENTIFIER	no
ORDINAL_POSITION	CARDINAL_NUMBER	no
COLUMN_DEFAULT	CHARACTER_DATA	yes
IS_NULLABLE	CHARACTER_DATA	no
DATA_TYPE	CHARACTER_DATA	no
CHARACTER_MAXIMUM_LENGTH	CARDINAL_NUMBER	yes
CHARACTER_OCTET_LENGTH	CARDINAL_NUMBER	yes
NUMERIC_PRECISION	CARDINAL_NUMBER	yes
NUMERIC_PRECISION_RADIX	CARDINAL_NUMBER	yes
NUMERIC_SCALE	CARDINAL_NUMBER	yes
DATETIME_PRECISION	CARDINAL_NUMBER	yes
INTERVAL_TYPE	CHARACTER_DATA	yes
INTERVAL_PRECISION	CARDINAL_NUMBER	yes
CHARACTER_SET_CATALOG	SQL_IDENTIFIER	yes

Name	Domain	Nullable?
CHARACTER_SET_SCHEMA	SQL_IDENTIFIER	yes
CHARACTER_SET_NAME	SQL_IDENTIFIER	yes
COLLATION_CATALOG	SQL_IDENTIFIER	yes
COLLATION_SCHEMA	SQL_IDENTIFIER	yes
COLLATION_NAME	SQL_IDENTIFIER	yes
DOMAIN_CATALOG	SQL_IDENTIFIER	yes
DOMAIN_SCHEMA	SQL_IDENTIFIER	yes
DOMAIN_NAME	SQL_IDENTIFIER	yes
USER_DEFINED_TYPE_CATALOG	CHARACTER_DATA	yes
USER_DEFINED_TYPE_SCHEMA	CHARACTER_DATA	yes
USER_DEFINED_TYPE_NAME	CHARACTER_DATA	yes
CHECK_REFERENCES	CHARACTER_DATA	yes
CHECK_ACTION	CHARACTER_DATA	yes

ATTRIBUTES shows the Attributes of UDTs in this Catalog on which the current user has Privileges.

- UDT_CATALOG, UDT_SCHEMA, UDT_NAME, ATTRIBUTE_NAME uniquely identify an Attribute on which the current user has Privileges.
- ORDINAL_POSITION is the position of the Attribute in its UDT. The first Attribute has ordinal position 1, the second Attribute has ordinal position 2, etc. Warning: the position can change if ALTER TYPE is used to drop an Attribute.
- COLUMN_DEFAULT shows the Attribute's default value (presumably the DBMS will CAST the value to a character value if it must). It will be NULL if the Attribute was defined without a DEFAULT clause (and presumably if it was defined with DEFAULT NULL). COLUMN_DEFAULT will be 'TRUNCATED' if the default value was too long to be stored.
- IS_NULLABLE is either 'YES' (the Attribute is possibly nullable) or 'NO' (the Attribute is known not nullable).
- DATA_TYPE shows the Attribute's <data type>: either 'BINARY LARGE OBJECT', 'BIT', 'BIT VARYING', 'CHARACTER', 'CHARACTER VARYING', 'CHARACTER LARGE OBJECT', 'INTEGER', 'SMALLINT', 'NUMERIC', 'DECIMAL', 'REAL', 'DOUBLE PRECISION', 'FLOAT', 'DATE', 'TIME', 'TIME WITH TIME ZONE', 'TIMESTAMP', 'TIMESTAMP WITH TIME ZONE', 'INTERVAL', 'BOOLEAN', 'USER-DEFINED TYPE' — or something else, such as an implementation-defined data type.
- CHARACTER_MAXIMUM_LENGTH shows the Attribute's maximum length in characters (for 'CHARACTER', 'CHARACTER VARYING', 'CHARACTER LARGE OBJECT') or in bits (for 'BIT', 'BIT VARYING', 'BINARY LARGE OBJECT'). For other <data type>s, CHARACTER_MAXIMUM_LENGTH is NULL.
- CHARACTER_OCTET_LENGTH shows the Attribute's maximum length in octets (for 'CHARACTER', 'CHARACTER VARYING', 'CHARACTER LARGE OBJECT', 'BIT', 'BIT VARYING', 'BINARY LARGE OBJECT'). For other <data type>s, CHARACTER_OCTET_LENGTH is NULL.

- NUMERIC_PRECISION shows the Attribute's precision (for 'INTEGER', 'SMALLINT', 'NUMERIC', 'DECIMAL', 'REAL', 'FLOAT', 'DOUBLE PRECISION', 'DATE', 'TIME', 'TIMESTAMP', 'TIME WITH TIME ZONE', 'TIMESTAMP WITH TIME ZONE', 'INTERVAL'). For other <data type>s, NUMERIC_PRECISION is NULL.
- NUMERIC_PRECISION_RADIX is either 2 or 10, depending on your DBMS (for 'INTEGER', 'SMALLINT', 'DATE', 'TIME', 'TIMESTAMP', 'TIME WITH TIME ZONE', 'TIMESTAMP WITH TIME ZONE', 'INTERVAL'), 10 (for 'NUMERIC', 'DECIMAL'), 2 (for 'REAL', 'FLOAT', 'DOUBLE PRECISION'). For other <data type>s, NUMERIC_PRECISION_RADIX is NULL.
- NUMERIC_SCALE is either 0 (for 'INTEGER', 'SMALLINT') or shows the Attribute's scale (for 'NUMERIC', 'DECIMAL'). For other <data type>s, NUMERIC_SCALE is NULL.
- DATETIME_PRECISION shows the Attribute's fractional-seconds precision (for 'TIME', 'TIMESTAMP', 'TIME WITH TIME ZONE', 'TIMESTAMP WITH TIME ZONE', 'INTERVAL'). For other <data type>s, DATETIME_PRECISION is NULL.
- INTERVAL_TYPE shows the Attribute's interval type (for 'INTERVAL'): either 'YEAR', 'MONTH', 'DAY', 'HOUR', 'MINUTE', 'SECOND', 'YEAR TO MONTH', 'DAY TO HOUR', 'DAY TO MINUTE', 'DAY TO SECOND', 'HOUR TO MINUTE', 'HOUR TO SECOND', 'MINUTE TO SECOND'. For other <data type>s, INTERVAL_TYPE is NULL.
- INTERVAL_PRECISION shows the Attribute's precision for the interval leading field (for 'INTERVAL'). For other <data type>s, INTERVAL_PRECISION is NULL.
- CHARACTER_SET_CATALOG, CHARACTER_SET_SCHEMA, CHARACTER_SET_NAME uniquely identify the Character set the Attribute values belong to (for 'CHARACTER', 'CHARACTER VARYING', 'CHARACTER LARGE OBJECT'). For other <data type>s, these fields are NULL.
- COLLATION_CATALOG, COLLATION_SCHEMA, COLLATION_NAME uniquely identify the Attribute's default Collation (for 'CHARACTER', 'CHARACTER VARYING', 'CHARACTER LARGE OBJECT'). For other <data type>s, these fields are NULL.
- DOMAIN_CATALOG, DOMAIN_SCHEMA, DOMAIN_NAME uniquely identify the Domain that the Attribute depends on. If no Domain was used in the Attribute definition, these fields are NULL.
- USER_DEFINED_TYPE_CATALOG, USER_DEFINED_TYPE_SCHEMA, USER_DEFINED_TYPE_NAME uniquely identify the UDT which is the Attribute's data type (if any); otherwise, these fields are NULL.
- CHECK_REFERENCES is NULL if the Attribute's <data type> is not a reference type. Otherwise, CHECK_REFERENCES is 'YES' (reference values are checked) or 'NO' (reference values are not checked).
- CHECK_ACTION is NULL if the Attribute's <data type> is not a reference type. Otherwise, CHECK_ACTION is 'NO ACTION' (<reference scope check action> is NO ACTION).

If you want to restrict your code to Core SQL, do not reference INFORMATION_SCHEMA.ATTRIBUTES.

INFORMATION_SCHEMA.CHARACTER_SETS

This View has the following Columns:

Name	Domain	Nullable?
CHARACTER_SET_CATALOG	SQL_IDENTIFIER	no
CHARACTER_SET_SCHEMA	SQL_IDENTIFIER	no
CHARACTER_SET_NAME	SQL_IDENTIFIER	no
FORM_OF_USE	SQL_IDENTIFIER	no
NUMBER_OF_CHARACTERS	CARDINAL_NUMBER	no
DEFAULT_COLLATE_CATALOG	SQL_IDENTIFIER	no
DEFAULT_COLLATE_SCHEMA	SQL_IDENTIFIER	no
DEFAULT_COLLATE_NAME	SQL_IDENTIFIER	no

CHARACTER_SETS shows the Character sets in this Catalog on which the current user has Privileges.

- CHARACTER_SET_CATALOG, CHARACTER_SET_SCHEMA, CHARACTER_SET_NAME uniquely identify a Character set that the current user may use.
- FORM_OF_USE is a zero-length string. (Note: This may be an error in the Standard. FORM_OF_USE should probably name the Form-of-use for the Character set.)
- NUMBER_OF_CHARACTERS is a zero-length string. (Note: This is an error in the Standard. NUMBER_OF_CHARACTERS must be a number and therefore should probably show the number of characters in the Character set.)
- DEFAULT_COLLATE_CATALOG, DEFAULT_COLLATE_SCHEMA, DEFAULT_COLLATE_NAME uniquely identify the Character set's default Collation.

INFORMATION_SCHEMA.CHECK_CONSTRAINTS
This View has the following Columns:

Name	Domain	Nullable?
CONSTRAINT_CATALOG	SQL_IDENTIFIER	no
CONSTRAINT_SCHEMA	SQL_IDENTIFIER	no
CONSTRAINT_NAME	SQL_IDENTIFIER	no
CHECK_CLAUSE	CHARACTER_DATA	yes

CHECK_CONSTRAINTS shows the CHECK Constraints in this Catalog that are owned by the current user. (This category includes the user's Domain Constraints, Assertions and some Table Constraints.)

- CONSTRAINT_CATALOG, CONSTRAINT_SCHEMA, CONSTRAINT_NAME uniquely identify a CHECK Constraint owned by the current user.
- CHECK_CLAUSE shows the Constraint's CHECK clause in full. It will be NULL if the CHECK clause was too long to be stored.

INFORMATION_SCHEMA.COLLATIONS
This View has the following Columns:

Name	Domain	Nullable?
COLLATION_CATALOG	SQL_IDENTIFIER	no
COLLATION_SCHEMA	SQL_IDENTIFIER	no
COLLATION_NAME	SQL_IDENTIFIER	no
CHARACTER_SET_CATALOG	SQL_IDENTIFIER	no
CHARACTER_SET_SCHEMA	SQL_IDENTIFIER	no
CHARACTER_SET_NAME	SQL_IDENTIFIER	no
PAD_ATTRIBUTE	CHARACTER_DATA	no
COLLATION_TYPE	CHARACTER_DATA	no
COLLATION_DEFINITION	CHARACTER_DATA	no
COLLATION_DICTIONARY	CHARACTER_DATA	no

COLLATIONS shows the Collations in this Catalog on which the current user has Privileges.

- COLLATION_CATALOG, COLLATION_SCHEMA, COLLATION_NAME uniquely identify a Collation that the current user may use.
- CHARACTER_SET_CATALOG, CHARACTER_SET_SCHEMA, CHARACTER_SET_NAME uniquely identify the Character set for the Collation.
- PAD_ATTRIBUTE is either 'NO PAD' (the Collation has the NO PAD attribute) or 'SPACE' (the Collation has the PAD SPACE attribute).
- COLLATION_TYPE, COLLATION_DEFINITION, and COLLATION_DICTIONARY are zero-length strings. To date, the Standard makes no use of these fields.

If you want to restrict your code to Core SQL, do not reference INFORMATION_SCHEMA.COLLATIONS.

INFORMATION_SCHEMA.COLUMNS
This View has the following Columns:

Name	Domain	Nullable?
TABLE_CATALOG	SQL_IDENTIFIER	no
TABLE_SCHEMA	SQL_IDENTIFIER	no
TABLE_NAME	SQL_IDENTIFIER	no
COLUMN_NAME	SQL_IDENTIFIER	no
ORDINAL_POSITION	CARDINAL_NUMBER	no
COLUMN_DEFAULT	CHARACTER_DATA	yes
IS_NULLABLE	CHARACTER_DATA	no
DATA_TYPE	CHARACTER_DATA	no
CHARACTER_MAXIMUM_LENGTH	CARDINAL_NUMBER	yes
CHARACTER_OCTET_LENGTH	CARDINAL_NUMBER	yes

Name	Domain	Nullable?
NUMERIC_PRECISION	CARDINAL_NUMBER	yes
NUMERIC_PRECISION_RADIX	CARDINAL_NUMBER	yes
NUMERIC_SCALE	CARDINAL_NUMBER	yes
DATETIME_PRECISION	CARDINAL_NUMBER	yes
INTERVAL_TYPE	CHARACTER_DATA	yes
INTERVAL_PRECISION	CARDINAL_NUMBER	yes
CHARACTER_SET_CATALOG	SQL_IDENTIFIER	yes
CHARACTER_SET_SCHEMA	SQL_IDENTIFIER	yes
CHARACTER_SET_NAME	SQL_IDENTIFIER	yes
COLLATION_CATALOG	SQL_IDENTIFIER	yes
COLLATION_SCHEMA	SQL_IDENTIFIER	yes
COLLATION_NAME	SQL_IDENTIFIER	yes
DOMAIN_CATALOG	SQL_IDENTIFIER	yes
DOMAIN_SCHEMA	SQL_IDENTIFIER	yes
DOMAIN_NAME	SQL_IDENTIFIER	yes
USER_DEFINED_TYPE_CATALOG	SQL_IDENTIFIER	yes
USER_DEFINED_TYPE_SCHEMA	SQL_IDENTIFIER	yes
USER_DEFINED_TYPE_NAME	SQL_IDENTIFIER	yes
SCOPE_CATALOG	SQL_IDENTIFIER	yes
SCOPE_SCHEMA	SQL_IDENTIFIER	yes
SCOPE_NAME	SQL_IDENTIFIER	yes
IS_SELF_REFERENCING	CHARACTER_DATA	no
CHECK_REFERENCES	CHARACTER_DATA	yes
CHECK_ACTION	CHARACTER_DATA	yes

COLUMNS shows the Columns in this Catalog on which the current user has Privileges.

- TABLE_CATALOG, TABLE_SCHEMA, TABLE_NAME, COLUMN_NAME uniquely identify a Column that the current user may use.
- ORDINAL_POSITION shows the position of the Column in its Table; the first Column has ordinal position 1, the second Column has ordinal position 2, etc. Warning: the position can change if ALTER TABLE is used to add or drop a Column.
- COLUMN_DEFAULT shows the Column's default value (presumably the DBMS will CAST the value to a character string if it must). It will be NULL if the Column was defined without a DEFAULT clause (and presumably if it was defined with DEFAULT NULL) or if the Column's default value comes only from a Domain. COLUMN_DEFAULT will be 'TRUNCATED' if the default value was too long to be stored.
- IS_NULLABLE is either 'YES' (the Column is possibly nullable) or 'NO' (the Column is known not nullable).

- DATA_TYPE shows the Column's <data type>: either 'BINARY LARGE OBJECT', 'BIT', 'BIT VARYING', 'CHARACTER', 'CHARACTER VARYING', 'CHARACTER LARGE OBJECT', 'INTEGER', 'SMALLINT', 'NUMERIC', 'DECIMAL', 'REAL', 'DOUBLE PRECISION', 'FLOAT', 'DATE', 'TIME', 'TIME WITH TIME ZONE', 'TIMESTAMP', 'TIMESTAMP WITH TIME ZONE', 'INTERVAL', 'BOOLEAN', 'USER-DEFINED TYPE' — or something else, such as an implementation-defined data type.
- CHARACTER_MAXIMUM_LENGTH shows the Column's maximum length in characters (for 'CHARACTER', 'CHARACTER VARYING', 'CHARACTER LARGE OBJECT') or in bits (for 'BIT', 'BIT VARYING', 'BINARY LARGE OBJECT'). For other <data type>s, CHARACTER_MAXIMUM_LENGTH is NULL.
- CHARACTER_OCTET_LENGTH shows the Column's maximum length in octets (for 'CHARACTER', 'CHARACTER VARYING', 'CHARACTER LARGE OBJECT', 'BIT', 'BIT VARYING', 'BINARY LARGE OBJECT'). For other <data type>s, CHARACTER_OCTET_LENGTH is NULL.
- NUMERIC_PRECISION shows the Column's precision (for 'INTEGER', 'SMALLINT', 'NUMERIC', 'DECIMAL', 'REAL', 'FLOAT', 'DOUBLE PRECISION', 'DATE', 'TIME', 'TIMESTAMP', 'TIME WITH TIME ZONE', 'TIMESTAMP WITH TIME ZONE', 'INTERVAL'). For other <data type>s, NUMERIC_PRECISION is NULL.
- NUMERIC_PRECISION_RADIX is either 2 or 10, depending on your DBMS (for 'INTEGER', 'SMALLINT', 'DATE', 'TIME', 'TIMESTAMP', 'TIME WITH TIME ZONE', 'TIMESTAMP WITH TIME ZONE', 'INTERVAL'), 10 (for 'NUMERIC', 'DECIMAL'), 2 (for 'REAL', 'FLOAT', 'DOUBLE PRECISION'). For other <data type>s, NUMERIC_PRECISION_RADIX is NULL.
- NUMERIC_SCALE is either 0 (for 'INTEGER', 'SMALLINT') or shows the Column's scale (for 'NUMERIC', 'DECIMAL'). For other <data type>s, NUMERIC_SCALE is NULL.
- DATETIME_PRECISION shows the Column's fractional-seconds precision (for 'TIME', 'TIMESTAMP', 'TIME WITH TIME ZONE', 'TIMESTAMP WITH TIME ZONE', 'INTERVAL'). For other <data type>s, DATETIME_PRECISION is NULL.
- INTERVAL_TYPE shows the Column's interval type (for 'INTERVAL'); either 'YEAR', 'MONTH', 'DAY', 'HOUR', 'MINUTE', 'SECOND', 'YEAR TO MONTH', 'DAY TO HOUR', 'DAY TO MINUTE', 'DAY TO SECOND', 'HOUR TO MINUTE', 'HOUR TO SECOND', 'MINUTE TO SECOND'. For other <data type>s, INTERVAL_TYPE is NULL.
- INTERVAL_PRECISION shows the Column's precision for the interval leading field (for 'INTERVAL'). For other <data type>s, INTERVAL_PRECISION is NULL.
- CHARACTER_SET_CATALOG, CHARACTER_SET_SCHEMA, CHARACTER_SET_NAME uniquely identify the Character set the Column values belong to (for 'CHARACTER', 'CHARACTER VARYING', 'CHARACTER LARGE OBJECT'). For other <data type>s, these fields are NULL.
- COLLATION_CATALOG, COLLATION_SCHEMA, COLLATION_NAME uniquely identify the Column's default Collation (for 'CHARACTER', 'CHARACTER VARYING', 'CHARACTER LARGE OBJECT'). For other <data type>s, these fields are NULL.
- DOMAIN_CATALOG, DOMAIN_SCHEMA, DOMAIN_NAME uniquely identify the Domain on which the Column depends. If no Domain was used in the Column definition, these fields are NULL.
- USER_DEFINED_TYPE_CATALOG, USER_DEFINED_TYPE_SCHEMA, USER_DEFINED_TYPE_NAME uniquely identify the UDT that the Column depends on. If the Column doesn't use a UDT, these fields are NULL.

- SCOPE_CATALOG, SCOPE_SCHEMA, SCOPE_NAME uniquely identify the Column's scope Table. If the Column has no scope, these fields are NULL.
- IS_SELF_REFERENCING is either 'YES' (the column is self-referencing) or 'NO' (the column is not self-referencing).
- CHECK_REFERENCES is NULL if the Column is part of a View or if its <data type> is not a reference type. Otherwise, CHECK_REFERENCES is 'YES' (reference values are checked) or 'NO' (reference values are not checked).
- CHECK_ACTION is NULL if the Column is part of a View or if its <data type> is not a reference type. Otherwise, CHECK_ACTION is 'RESTRICT' (<reference scope check action> is RESTRICT) or 'SET NULL' (<reference scope check action> is SET NULL).

INFORMATION_SCHEMA.COLUMN_DOMAIN_USAGE
This View has the following Columns:

Name	Domain	Nullable?
DOMAIN_CATALOG	SQL_IDENTIFIER	no
DOMAIN_SCHEMA	SQL_IDENTIFIER	no
DOMAIN_NAME	SQL_IDENTIFIER	no
TABLE_CATALOG	SQL_IDENTIFIER	no
TABLE_SCHEMA	SQL_IDENTIFIER	no
TABLE_NAME	SQL_IDENTIFIER	no
COLUMN_NAME	SQL_IDENTIFIER	no

COLUMN_DOMAIN_USAGE shows the Columns that depend on Domains in this Catalog, where the Domains are owned by the current user.

- DOMAIN_CATALOG, DOMAIN_SCHEMA, DOMAIN_NAME uniquely identify a Domain owned by the current user.
- TABLE_CATALOG, TABLE_SCHEMA, TABLE_NAME, COLUMN_NAME uniquely identify a Column that depends on the Domain.

If you want to restrict your code to Core SQL, do not reference INFORMATION_SCHEMA.COLUMN_DOMAIN_USAGE.

INFORMATION_SCHEMA.COLUMN_PRIVILEGES
This View has the following Columns:

Name	Domain	Nullable?
GRANTOR	SQL_IDENTIFIER	no
GRANTEE	SQL_IDENTIFIER	no
TABLE_CATALOG	SQL_IDENTIFIER	no
TABLE_SCHEMA	SQL_IDENTIFIER	no
TABLE_NAME	SQL_IDENTIFIER	no
COLUMN_NAME	SQL_IDENTIFIER	no

Name	Domain	Nullable?
PRIVILEGE_TYPE	CHARACTER_DATA	no
IS_GRANTABLE	CHARACTER_DATA	no

COLUMN_PRIVILEGES shows the Privileges on Columns belonging to Tables in this Catalog, where the Privileges are either available to, or granted by, the current user.

- GRANTOR shows the <AuthorizationID> who granted the Privilege.
- GRANTEE shows the <AuthorizationID> who may use the Privilege. By definition, if GRANTOR isn't CURRENT_USER, then GRANTEE is either CURRENT_USER or 'PUBLIC'.
- TABLE_CATALOG, TABLE_SCHEMA, TABLE_NAME, COLUMN_NAME uniquely identify a Column belonging to a Table in this Catalog.
- PRIVILEGE_TYPE shows the Privilege granted; either 'INSERT', 'UPDATE', 'REFERENCES', 'SELECT'.
- IS_GRANTABLE is either 'YES' (Privilege was granted WITH GRANT OPTION) or 'NO' (Privilege was not granted WITH GRANT OPTION).

If you want to restrict your code to Core SQL, do not reference INFORMATION_SCHEMA.COLUMN_PRIVILEGES.

INFORMATION_SCHEMA.COLUMN_USER_DEFINED_TYPE_USAGE

This View has the following Columns:

Name	Domain	Nullable?
USER_DEFINED_TYPE_CATALOG	SQL_IDENTIFIER	no
USER_DEFINED_TYPE_SCHEMA	SQL_IDENTIFIER	no
USER_DEFINED_TYPE_NAME	SQL_IDENTIFIER	no
TABLE_CATALOG	SQL_IDENTIFIER	no
TABLE_SCHEMA	SQL_IDENTIFIER	no
TABLE_NAME	SQL_IDENTIFIER	no
COLUMN_NAME	SQL_IDENTIFIER	no

COLUMN_USER_DEFINED_TYPE_USAGE shows the Columns that depend on a UDT in this Catalog, where the UDT is owned by the current user.

- USER_DEFINED_TYPE_CATALOG, USER_DEFINED_TYPE_SCHEMA, USER_DEFINED_TYPE_NAME uniquely identify a UDT that belongs to the current user.
- TABLE_CATALOG, TABLE_SCHEMA, TABLE_NAME, COLUMN_NAME uniquely identify a Column that depends on the UDT.

If you want to restrict your code to Core SQL, do not reference INFORMATION_SCHEMA.COLUMN_USER_DEFINED_TYPE_USAGE.

INFORMATION_SCHEMA.CONSTRAINT_COLUMN_USAGE

This View has the following Columns:

Name	Domain	Nullable?
TABLE_CATALOG	SQL_IDENTIFIER	no
TABLE_SCHEMA	SQL_IDENTIFIER	no
TABLE_NAME	SQL_IDENTIFIER	no
COLUMN_NAME	SQL_IDENTIFIER	no
CONSTRAINT_CATALOG	SQL_IDENTIFIER	no
CONSTRAINT_SCHEMA	SQL_IDENTIFIER	no
CONSTRAINT_NAME	SQL_IDENTIFIER	no

CONSTRAINT_COLUMN_USAGE shows the Columns used by any Constraint or Assertion in this Catalog, where the Constraint or Assertion is owned by the current user.

- TABLE_CATALOG, TABLE_SCHEMA, TABLE_NAME, COLUMN_NAME uniquely identify a Column that appears in a Constraint/Assertion.
- CONSTRAINT_CATALOG, CONSTRAINT_SCHEMA, CONSTRAINT_NAME uniquely identify the Constraint/Assertion that uses the Column. The Constraint/Assertion is owned by the current user.

If you want to restrict your code to Core SQL, do not reference INFORMATION_SCHEMA.CONSTRAINT_COLUMN_USAGE.

INFORMATION_SCHEMA.CONSTRAINT_TABLE_USAGE

This View has the following Columns:

Name	Domain	Nullable?
TABLE_CATALOG	SQL_IDENTIFIER	no
TABLE_SCHEMA	SQL_IDENTIFIER	no
TABLE_NAME	SQL_IDENTIFIER	no
CONSTRAINT_CATALOG	SQL_IDENTIFIER	no
CONSTRAINT_SCHEMA	SQL_IDENTIFIER	no
CONSTRAINT_NAME	SQL_IDENTIFIER	no

CONSTRAINT_TABLE_USAGE shows the Tables used by any Constraint or Assertion in this Catalog, where the Constraint or Assertion is owned by the current user.

- TABLE_CATALOG, TABLE_SCHEMA, TABLE_NAME uniquely identify a Table that appears in a Constraint/Assertion.
- CONSTRAINT_CATALOG, CONSTRAINT_SCHEMA, CONSTRAINT_NAME uniquely identify the Constraint/Assertion that uses the Table. The Constraint/Assertion is owned by the current user.

If you want to restrict your code to Core SQL, do not reference INFORMATION_SCHEMA.CONSTRAINT_TABLE_USAGE.

INFORMATION_SCHEMA.DIRECT_SUPERTABLES
This View has the following Columns:

Name	Domain	Nullable?
TABLE_CATALOG	SQL_IDENTIFIER	no
TABLE_SCHEMA	SQL_IDENTIFIER	no
TABLE_NAME	SQL_IDENTIFIER	no
SUPERTABLE_NAME	SQL_IDENTIFIER	no

DIRECT_SUPERTABLES shows the direct subtables in this Catalog that are related to a supertable, where the subtables are owned by the current user.

- TABLE_CATALOG, TABLE_SCHEMA, TABLE_NAME uniquely identify a Table owned by the current user.
- SUPERTABLE_NAME identifies the related supertable for the Table.

If you want to restrict your code to Core SQL, do not reference INFORMATION_SCHEMA.DIRECT_SUPERTABLES.

INFORMATION_SCHEMA.DIRECT_SUPERTYPES
This View has the following Columns:

Name	Domain	Nullable?
USER_DEFINED_TYPE_CATALOG	SQL_IDENTIFIER	no
USER_DEFINED_TYPE_SCHEMA	SQL_IDENTIFIER	no
USER_DEFINED_TYPE_NAME	SQL_IDENTIFIER	no
SUPERTYPE_CATALOG	SQL_IDENTIFIER	no
SUPERTYPE_SCHEMA	SQL_IDENTIFIER	no
SUPERTYPE_NAME	SQL_IDENTIFIER	no

DIRECT_SUPERTYPES shows the direct subtypes in this Catalog that are related to a supertype, where the subtypes are owned by the current user.

- USER_DEFINED_TYPE_CATALOG, USER_DEFINED_TYPE_SCHEMA, USER_DEFINED_TYPE_NAME uniquely identify a UDT owned by the current user.
- SUPERTYPE_CATALOG, SUPERTYPE_SCHEMA, SUPERTYPE_NAME uniquely identify the related supertype for the UDT.

If you want to restrict your code to Core SQL, do not reference INFORMATION_SCHEMA.DIRECT_SUPERTYPES.

INFORMATION_SCHEMA.DOMAINS
This View has the following Columns:

Name	Domain	Nullable?
DOMAIN_CATALOG	SQL_IDENTIFIER	no
DOMAIN_SCHEMA	SQL_IDENTIFIER	no

Name	Domain	Nullable?
DOMAIN_NAME	SQL_IDENTIFIER	no
DATA_TYPE	CHARACTER_DATA	no
CHARACTER_MAXIMUM_LENGTH	CARDINAL_NUMBER	yes
CHARACTER_OCTET_LENGTH	CARDINAL_NUMBER	yes
COLLATION_CATALOG	SQL_IDENTIFIER	yes
COLLATION_SCHEMA	SQL_IDENTIFIER	yes
COLLATION_NAME	SQL_IDENTIFIER	yes
CHARACTER_SET_CATALOG	SQL_IDENTIFIER	yes
CHARACTER_SET_SCHEMA	SQL_IDENTIFIER	yes
CHARACTER_SET_NAME	SQL_IDENTIFIER	yes
NUMERIC_PRECISION	CARDINAL_NUMBER	yes
NUMERIC_PRECISION_RADIX	CARDINAL_NUMBER	yes
NUMERIC_SCALE	CARDINAL_NUMBER	yes
DATETIME_PRECISION	CARDINAL_NUMBER	yes
INTERVAL_TYPE	CHARACTER_DATA	yes
INTERVAL_PRECISION	CARDINAL_NUMBER	yes
DOMAIN_DEFAULT	CHARACTER_DATA	yes
USER_DEFINED_TYPE_CATALOG	SQL_IDENTIFIER	yes
USER_DEFINED_TYPE_SCHEMA	SQL_IDENTIFIER	yes
USER_DEFINED_TYPE_NAME	SQL_IDENTIFIER	yes
SCOPE_CATALOG	SQL_IDENTIFIER	yes
SCOPE_SCHEMA	SQL_IDENTIFIER	yes
SCOPE_NAME	SQL_IDENTIFIER	yes

DOMAINS shows the Domains in this Catalog on which the current user has Privileges.

- DOMAIN_CATALOG, DOMAIN_SCHEMA, DOMAIN_NAME uniquely identify a Domain that the current user may use, either because of a USAGE Privilege directly on the Domain or because of a Privilege on any Column that depends on the Domain.
- DATA_TYPE shows the Domain's <data type>: either 'BINARY LARGE OBJECT', 'BIT', 'BIT VARYING', 'CHARACTER', 'CHARACTER VARYING', 'CHARACTER LARGE OBJECT', 'INTEGER', 'SMALLINT', 'NUMERIC', 'DECIMAL', 'REAL', 'DOUBLE PRECISION', 'FLOAT', 'DATE', 'TIME', 'TIME WITH TIME ZONE', 'TIMESTAMP', 'TIMESTAMP WITH TIME ZONE', 'INTERVAL', 'BOOLEAN', 'USER-DEFINED TYPE' — or something else, such as an implementation-defined data type.
- CHARACTER_MAXIMUM_LENGTH shows the Domain's maximum length in characters (for 'CHARACTER', 'CHARACTER VARYING', 'CHARACTER LARGE OBJECT') or in bits (for 'BIT', 'BIT VARYING', 'BINARY LARGE OBJECT'). For other <data type>s, CHARACTER_MAXIMUM_LENGTH is NULL.

- CHARACTER_OCTET_LENGTH shows the Domain's maximum length in octets (for 'CHARACTER', 'CHARACTER VARYING', 'CHARACTER LARGE OBJECT', 'BIT', 'BIT VARYING', 'BINARY LARGE OBJECT'). For other <data type>s, CHARACTER_OCTET_LENGTH is NULL.
- COLLATION_CATALOG, COLLATION_SCHEMA, COLLATION_NAME uniquely identify the Domain's default Collation (for 'CHARACTER', 'CHARACTER VARYING', 'CHARACTER LARGE OBJECT'). For other <data type>s, these fields are NULL.
- CHARACTER_SET_CATALOG, CHARACTER_SET_SCHEMA, CHARACTER_SET_NAME uniquely identify the Character set the Domain values belong to (for 'CHARACTER', 'CHARACTER VARYING', 'CHARACTER LARGE OBJECT'). For other <data type>s, these fields are NULL.
- NUMERIC_PRECISION shows the Domain's precision (for 'INTEGER', 'SMALLINT', 'NUMERIC', 'DECIMAL', 'REAL', 'FLOAT', 'DOUBLE PRECISION', 'DATE', 'TIME', 'TIMESTAMP', 'TIME WITH TIME ZONE', 'TIMESTAMP WITH TIME ZONE', 'INTERVAL'). For other <data type>s, NUMERIC_PRECISION is NULL.
- NUMERIC_PRECISION_RADIX is either 2 or 10, depending on your DBMS (for 'INTEGER', 'SMALLINT', 'DATE', 'TIME', 'TIMESTAMP', 'TIME WITH TIME ZONE', 'TIMESTAMP WITH TIME ZONE', 'INTERVAL'), 10 (for 'NUMERIC', 'DECIMAL'), 2 (for 'REAL', 'FLOAT', 'DOUBLE PRECISION'). For other <data type>s, NUMERIC_PRECISION_RADIX is NULL.
- NUMERIC_SCALE is either 0 (for 'INTEGER', 'SMALLINT') or shows the Domain's scale (for 'NUMERIC', 'DECIMAL'). For other <data type>s, NUMERIC_SCALE is NULL.
- DATETIME_PRECISION shows the Domain's fractional-seconds precision (for 'TIME', 'TIMESTAMP', 'TIME WITH TIME ZONE', 'TIMESTAMP WITH TIME ZONE', 'INTERVAL'). For other <data type>s, DATETIME_PRECISION is NULL.
- INTERVAL_TYPE shows the Domain's interval type (for 'INTERVAL'); either 'YEAR', 'MONTH', 'DAY', 'HOUR', 'MINUTE', 'SECOND', 'YEAR TO MONTH', 'DAY TO HOUR', 'DAY TO MINUTE', 'DAY TO SECOND', 'HOUR TO MINUTE', 'HOUR TO SECOND', 'MINUTE TO SECOND'. For other <data type>s, INTERVAL_TYPE is NULL.
- INTERVAL_PRECISION shows the Domain's precision for the interval leading field (for 'INTERVAL'). For other <data type>s, INTERVAL_PRECISION is NULL.
- DOMAIN_DEFAULT shows the Domain's default value (presumably the DBMS will CAST the value to a character string if it must). It will be NULL if the Domain was defined without a DEFAULT clause (and presumably if it was defined with DEFAULT NULL). DOMAIN_DEFAULT will be 'TRUNCATED' if the default value was too long to be stored.
- USER_DEFINED_TYPE_CATALOG, USER_DEFINED_TYPE_SCHEMA, USER_DEFINED_TYPE_NAME uniquely identify the UDT that the Domain depends on. If the Domain doesn't use a UDT, these fields are NULL.
- SCOPE_CATALOG, SCOPE_SCHEMA, SCOPE_NAME uniquely identify the Domain's scope Table. If the Domain has no scope, these fields are NULL.

If you want to restrict your code to Core SQL, do not reference INFORMATION_SCHEMA.DOMAINS.

INFORMATION_SCHEMA.DOMAIN_CONSTRAINTS
This View has the following Columns:

Name	Domain	Nullable?
CONSTRAINT_CATALOG	SQL_IDENTIFIER	no
CONSTRAINT_SCHEMA	SQL_IDENTIFIER	no
CONSTRAINT_NAME	SQL_IDENTIFIER	no
DOMAIN_CATALOG	SQL_IDENTIFIER	no
DOMAIN_SCHEMA	SQL_IDENTIFIER	no
DOMAIN_NAME	SQL_IDENTIFIER	no
IS_DEFERRABLE	CHARACTER_DATA	no
INITIALLY_DEFERRED	CHARACTER_DATA	no

DOMAIN_CONSTRAINTS shows the Domain Constraints (i.e., the Constraints defined on Domains in this Catalog) that are owned by the current user.

- CONSTRAINT_CATALOG, CONSTRAINT_SCHEMA, CONSTRAINT_NAME uniquely identify a Domain Constraint owned by the current user.
- DOMAIN_CATALOG, DOMAIN_SCHEMA, DOMAIN_NAME uniquely identify the Domain that uses the Constraint.
- IS_DEFERRABLE is either 'YES' (the Constraint is DEFERRABLE) or 'NO' (the Constraint is NOT DEFERRABLE).
- INITIALLY_DEFERRED is either 'YES' (the Constraint is INITIALLY DEFERRED) or 'NO' (the Constraint is INITIALLY IMMEDIATE).

If you want to restrict your code to Core SQL, do not reference INFORMATION_SCHEMA.DOMAIN_CONSTRAINTS.

INFORMATION_SCHEMA.DOMAIN_USER_DEFINED_TYPE_USAGE
This View has the following Columns:

Name	Domain	Nullable?
USER_DEFINED_TYPE_CATALOG	SQL_IDENTIFIER	no
USER_DEFINED_TYPE_SCHEMA	SQL_IDENTIFIER	no
USER_DEFINED_TYPE_NAME	SQL_IDENTIFIER	no
DOMAIN_CATALOG	SQL_IDENTIFIER	no
DOMAIN_SCHEMA	SQL_IDENTIFIER	no
DOMAIN_NAME	SQL_IDENTIFIER	no

DOMAIN_USER_DEFINED_TYPE_USAGE shows the Domains that depend on UDTs in this Catalog, where the UDT is owned by the current user.

- USER_DEFINED_TYPE_CATALOG, USER_DEFINED_TYPE_SCHEMA, USER_DEFINED_TYPE_NAME uniquely identify a UDT owned by the current user.
- DOMAIN_CATALOG, DOMAIN_SCHEMA, DOMAIN_NAME uniquely identify a Domain that uses the UDT.

If you want to restrict your code to Core SQL, do not reference INFORMATION_SCHEMA.DOMAIN_USER_DEFINED_TYPE_USAGE.

INFORMATION_SCHEMA.ENABLED_ROLES
This View has the following Columns:

Name	Domain	Nullable?
ROLE_NAME	SQL_IDENTIFIER	no

ENABLED_ROLES shows the enabled roles for the current SQL-session.

- ROLE_NAME uniquely identifies an enabled Role.

If you want to restrict your code to Core SQL, do not reference INFORMATION_SCHEMA.ENABLED_ROLES.

INFORMATION_SCHEMA.KEY_COLUMN_USAGE
This View has the following Columns:

Name	Domain	Nullable?
CONSTRAINT_CATALOG	SQL_IDENTIFIER	no
CONSTRAINT_SCHEMA	SQL_IDENTIFIER	no
CONSTRAINT_NAME	SQL_IDENTIFIER	no
TABLE_CATALOG	SQL_IDENTIFIER	no
TABLE_SCHEMA	SQL_IDENTIFIER	no
TABLE_NAME	SQL_IDENTIFIER	no
COLUMN_NAME	SQL_IDENTIFIER	no
ORDINAL_POSITION	CARDINAL_NUMBER	no

KEY_COLUMN_USAGE shows the Columns in this Catalog that are keys in Constraints owned by the current user.

- CONSTRAINT_CATALOG, CONSTRAINT_SCHEMA, CONSTRAINT_NAME uniquely identify a Constraint owned by the current user.
- TABLE_CATALOG, TABLE_SCHEMA, TABLE_NAME, COLUMN_NAME uniquely identify a Column that is a key in the Constraint.
- ORDINAL_POSITION is the position of the Column within the Constraint.

If you want to restrict your code to Core SQL, do not reference INFORMATION_SCHEMA.KEY_COLUMN_USAGE.

INFORMATION_SCHEMA.METHOD_SPECIFICATIONS
This View has the following Columns:

Name	Domain	Nullable?
USER_DEFINED_TYPE_CATALOG	SQL_IDENTIFIER	no
USER_DEFINED_TYPE_SCHEMA	SQL_IDENTIFIER	no
USER_DEFINED_TYPE_NAME	SQL_IDENTIFIER	no

METHOD_CATALOG	SQL_IDENTIFIER	no
METHOD_SCHEMA	SQL_IDENTIFIER	no
METHOD_NAME	SQL_IDENTIFIER	no
IS_STATIC	CHARACTER_DATA	yes
DATA_TYPE	CHARACTER_DATA	no
CHARACTER_MAXIMUM_LENGTH	CARDINAL_NUMBER	yes
CHARACTER_OCTET_LENGTH	CARDINAL_NUMBER	yes
COLLATION_CATALOG	SQL_IDENTIFIER	yes
COLLATION_SCHEMA	SQL_IDENTIFIER	yes
COLLATION_NAME	SQL_IDENTIFIER	yes
NUMERIC_PRECISION	CARDINAL_NUMBER	yes
NUMERIC_PRECISION_RADIX	CARDINAL_NUMBER	yes
NUMERIC_SCALE	CARDINAL_NUMBER	yes
DATETIME_PRECISION	CARDINAL_NUMBER	yes
INTERVAL_TYPE	CHARACTER_DATA	yes
INTERVAL_PRECISION	CARDINAL_NUMBER	yes
RETURN_USER_DEFINED_TYPE_CATALOG	SQL_IDENTIFIER	yes
RETURN_USER_DEFINED_TYPE_SCHEMA	SQL_IDENTIFIER	yes
RETURN_USER_DEFINED_TYPE_NAME	SQL_IDENTIFIER	yes
SCOPE_CATALOG	SQL_IDENTIFIER	yes
SCOPE_SCHEMA	SQL_IDENTIFIER	yes
SCOPE_NAME	SQL_IDENTIFIER	yes
METHOD_LANGUAGE	CHARACTER_DATA	yes
PARAMETER_STYLE	CHARACTER_DATA	yes
IS_DETERMINISTIC	CHARACTER_DATA	yes
SQL_DATA_ACCESS	CHARACTER_DATA	yes
IS_NULL_CALL	CHARACTER_DATA	yes
METHOD_SPECIFICATION_CREATED	TIME_STAMP	yes
METHOD_SPECIFICATION_LAST_ALTERED	TIME_STAMP	yes

METHOD_SPECIFICATIONS shows the SQL-invoked routines in this Catalog on which the current user has Privileges.

- USER_DEFINED_TYPE_CATALOG, USER_DEFINED_TYPE_SCHEMA, USER_DEFINED_TYPE_NAME, METHOD_CATALOG, METHOD_SCHEMA, METHOD_NAME uniquely identify an SQL-invoked routine that the current user may use.
- IS_STATIC is either 'YES' (the routine is defined with STATIC DISPATCH) or 'NO' (the routine is not defined with STATIC_DISPATCH).
- DATA_TYPE shows the routine's result <data type>: either 'BINARY LARGE OBJECT', 'BIT', 'BIT VARYING', 'CHARACTER', 'CHARACTER VARYING', 'CHARACTER LARGE OBJECT', 'INTEGER',

'SMALLINT', 'NUMERIC', 'DECIMAL', 'REAL', 'DOUBLE PRECISION', 'FLOAT', 'DATE', 'TIME', 'TIME WITH TIME ZONE', 'TIMESTAMP', 'TIMESTAMP WITH TIME ZONE', 'INTERVAL', 'BOOLEAN', 'USER-DEFINED TYPE' — or something else, such as an implementation-defined data type.

- CHARACTER_MAXIMUM_LENGTH shows the routine's result maximum length in characters (for 'CHARACTER', 'CHARACTER VARYING', 'CHARACTER LARGE OBJECT') or in bits (for 'BIT', 'BIT VARYING', 'BINARY LARGE OBJECT'). For other <data type>s, CHARACTER_MAXIMUM_LENGTH is NULL.
- CHARACTER_OCTET_LENGTH shows the routine's result maximum length in octets (for 'CHARACTER', 'CHARACTER VARYING', 'CHARACTER LARGE OBJECT', 'BIT', 'BIT VARYING', 'BINARY LARGE OBJECT'). For other <data type>s, CHARACTER_OCTET_LENGTH is NULL.
- COLLATION_CATALOG, COLLATION_SCHEMA, COLLATION_NAME uniquely identify the routine's result default Collation (for 'CHARACTER', 'CHARACTER VARYING', 'CHARACTER LARGE OBJECT'). For other <data type>s, these fields are NULL.
- NUMERIC_PRECISION shows the routine's result precision (for 'INTEGER', 'SMALLINT', 'NUMERIC', 'DECIMAL', 'REAL', 'FLOAT', 'DOUBLE PRECISION', 'DATE', 'TIME', 'TIMESTAMP', 'TIME WITH TIME ZONE', 'TIMESTAMP WITH TIME ZONE', 'INTERVAL'). For other <data type>s, NUMERIC_PRECISION is NULL.
- NUMERIC_PRECISION_RADIX is either 2 or 10, depending on your DBMS (for 'INTEGER', 'SMALLINT', 'DATE', 'TIME', 'TIMESTAMP', 'TIME WITH TIME ZONE', 'TIMESTAMP WITH TIME ZONE', 'INTERVAL'), 10 (for 'NUMERIC', 'DECIMAL'), 2 (for 'REAL', 'FLOAT', 'DOUBLE PRECISION'). For other <data type>s, NUMERIC_PRECISION_RADIX is NULL.
- NUMERIC_SCALE is either 0 (for 'INTEGER', 'SMALLINT') or shows the routine's result scale (for 'NUMERIC', 'DECIMAL'). For other <data type>s, NUMERIC_SCALE is NULL.
- DATETIME_PRECISION shows the routine's result fractional-seconds precision (for 'TIME', 'TIMESTAMP', 'TIME WITH TIME ZONE', 'TIMESTAMP WITH TIME ZONE', 'INTERVAL'). For other <data type>s, DATETIME_PRECISION is NULL.
- INTERVAL_TYPE shows the routine's result interval type (for 'INTERVAL'); either 'YEAR', 'MONTH', 'DAY', 'HOUR', 'MINUTE', 'SECOND', 'YEAR TO MONTH', 'DAY TO HOUR', 'DAY TO MINUTE', 'DAY TO SECOND', 'HOUR TO MINUTE', 'HOUR TO SECOND', 'MINUTE TO SECOND'. For other <data type>s, INTERVAL_TYPE is NULL.
- INTERVAL_PRECISION shows the routine's result precision for the interval leading field (for 'INTERVAL'). For other <data type>s, INTERVAL_PRECISION is NULL.
- RETURN_USER_DEFINED_TYPE_CATALOG, RETURN_USER_DEFINED_TYPE_SCHEMA, RETURN_USER_DEFINED_TYPE_NAME uniquely identify a UDT that the routine uses. If no UDT is used, these fields are NULL.
- SCOPE_CATALOG, SCOPE_SCHEMA, SCOPE_NAME uniquely identify the routine's scope. If the routine has no scope, these fields are NULL.
- METHOD_LANGUAGE shows the language the routine is written in: either 'SQL', 'ADA', 'C', 'COBOL', 'FORTRAN', 'MUMPS', 'PASCAL', 'PLI'.
- If METHOD_LANGUAGE is 'SQL', then PARAMETER_STYLE is NULL. If METHOD_LANGUAGE is any other language, then PARAMETER_STYLE is either 'SQL' (the method specifies PARAMETER STYLE SQL), or 'GENERAL' (the method specifies PARAMETER STYLE GENERAL).

- If METHOD_LANGUAGE is 'SQL', then IS_DETERMINISTIC is NULL. If METHOD_LANGUAGE is any other language, then IS_DETERMINISTIC is either 'YES' (the method is deterministic), or 'NO' (the method is possibly not deterministic).
- SQL_DATA_ACCESS is either 'NONE' (the SQL-invoked routine does not possibly contain SQL), 'CONTAINS' (the SQL-invoked routine possibly contains SQL), 'READS' (the SQL-invoked routine possibly reads SQL-data), or 'MODIFIES' (the SQL-invoked routine possibly modifies SQL-data).
- IS_NULL_CALL is either 'YES' (the SQL-invoked routine is a null-call function) or 'NO' (the SQL-invoked routine is not a null-call function).
- METHOD_SPECIFICATION_CREATED shows the CURRENT_TIMESTAMP from the time the SQL-invoked method was created.
- METHOD_SPECIFICATION_LAST_ALTERED shows the CURRENT_TIMESTAMP from the time the SQL-invoked method was last altered. (This will be the same as the METHOD_SPECIFICATION_CREATED value if the routine hasn't been altered.)

If you want to restrict your code to Core SQL, do not reference INFORMATION_SCHEMA.METHOD_SPECIFICATIONS.

INFORMATION_SCHEMA.METHOD_SPECIFICATION_PARAMETERS

This View has the following Columns:

Name	Domain	Nullable?
USER_DEFINED_TYPE_CATALOG	SQL_IDENTIFIER	no
USER_DEFINED_TYPE_SCHEMA	SQL_IDENTIFIER	no
USER_DEFINED_TYPE_NAME	SQL_IDENTIFIER	no
METHOD_CATALOG	SQL_IDENTIFIER	no
METHOD_SCHEMA	SQL_IDENTIFIER	no
METHOD_NAME	SQL_IDENTIFIER	no
ORDINAL_POSITION	CARDINAL_NUMBER	no
PARAMETER_MODE	CHARACTER_DATA	yes
IS_RESULT	CHARACTER_DATA	yes
AS_LOCATOR	CHARACTER_DATA	yes
PARAMETER_NAME	SQL_IDENTIFIER	yes
DATA_TYPE	CHARACTER_DATA	no
CHARACTER_MAXIMUM_LENGTH	CARDINAL_NUMBER	yes
CHARACTER_OCTET_LENGTH	CARDINAL_NUMBER	yes
COLLATION_CATALOG	SQL_IDENTIFIER	yes
COLLATION_SCHEMA	SQL_IDENTIFIER	yes
COLLATION_NAME	SQL_IDENTIFIER	yes
CHARACTER_SET_CATALOG	SQL_IDENTIFIER	no
CHARACTER_SET_SCHEMA	SQL_IDENTIFIER	no

Name	Domain	Nullable?
CHARACTER_SET_NAME	SQL_IDENTIFIER	no
NUMERIC_PRECISION	CARDINAL_NUMBER	yes
NUMERIC_PRECISION_RADIX	CARDINAL_NUMBER	yes
NUMERIC_SCALE	CARDINAL_NUMBER	yes
DATETIME_PRECISION	CARDINAL_NUMBER	yes
INTERVAL_TYPE	CHARACTER_DATA	yes
INTERVAL_PRECISION	CARDINAL_NUMBER	yes
USER_DEFINED_TYPE_CATALOG	SQL_IDENTIFIER	yes
USER_DEFINED_TYPE_SCHEMA	SQL_IDENTIFIER	yes
USER_DEFINED_TYPE_NAME	SQL_IDENTIFIER	yes
SCOPE_CATALOG	SQL_IDENTIFIER	yes
SCOPE_SCHEMA	SQL_IDENTIFIER	yes
SCOPE_NAME	SQL_IDENTIFIER	yes

METHOD_SPECIFICATION_PARAMETERS shows the parameters of the SQL-invoked methods in this Catalog on which the current user has Privileges.

- USER_DEFINED_TYPE_CATALOG, USER_DEFINED_TYPE_SCHEMA, USER_DEFINED_TYPE_NAME uniquely identify the UDT that a parameter is associated with.
- METHOD_CATALOG, METHOD_SCHEMA, METHOD_NAME uniquely identify the SQL-invoked method that contains the parameter.
- ORDINAL_POSITION shows the ordinal position of the parameter in its SQL-invoked method.
- PARAMETER_MODE is either 'IN' (the parameter is an input parameter), 'OUT' (the parameter is an output parameter), or 'INOUT' (the parameter is both an input and an output parameter).
- IS_RESULT is either 'YES' (the parameter is the RESULT parameter of a type-preserving function) or 'NO' (the parameter is not the RESULT parameter of a type-preserving function).
- AS_LOCATOR is either 'YES' (the parameter is passed AS LOCATOR) or 'NO' (the parameter is not passed AS LOCATOR).
- PARAMETER_NAME is the name of the parameter, if it was specified when the SQL-invoked routine was created. Otherwise, PARAMETER_NAME is NULL.
- DATA_TYPE shows the parameter's <data type>: either 'BINARY LARGE OBJECT', 'BIT', 'BIT VARYING', 'CHARACTER', 'CHARACTER VARYING', 'CHARACTER LARGE OBJECT', 'INTEGER', 'SMALLINT', 'NUMERIC', 'DECIMAL', 'REAL', 'DOUBLE PRECISION', 'FLOAT', 'DATE', 'TIME', 'TIME WITH TIME ZONE', 'TIMESTAMP', 'TIMESTAMP WITH TIME ZONE', 'INTERVAL', 'BOOLEAN', 'USER-DEFINED TYPE' — or something else, such as an implementation-defined data type.
- CHARACTER_MAXIMUM_LENGTH shows the parameter's maximum length in characters (for 'CHARACTER', 'CHARACTER VARYING', 'CHARACTER LARGE OBJECT') or in bits (for 'BIT',

'BIT VARYING', 'BINARY LARGE OBJECT'). For other <data type>s, CHARACTER_MAXIMUM_LENGTH is NULL.

- CHARACTER_OCTET_LENGTH shows the parameter's maximum length in octets (for 'CHARACTER', 'CHARACTER VARYING', 'CHARACTER LARGE OBJECT', 'BIT', 'BIT VARYING', 'BINARY LARGE OBJECT'). For other <data type>s, CHARACTER_OCTET_LENGTH is NULL.
- COLLATION_CATALOG, COLLATION_SCHEMA, COLLATION_NAME uniquely identify the parameter's default Collation (for 'CHARACTER', 'CHARACTER VARYING', 'CHARACTER LARGE OBJECT'). For other <data type>s, these fields are NULL.
- CHARACTER_SET_CATALOG, CHARACTER_SET_SCHEMA, CHARACTER_SET_NAME uniquely identify the Character set on which the parameter's default Collation is defined.
- NUMERIC_PRECISION shows the parameter's precision (for 'INTEGER', 'SMALLINT', 'NUMERIC', 'DECIMAL', 'REAL', 'FLOAT', 'DOUBLE PRECISION', 'DATE', 'TIME', 'TIMESTAMP', 'TIME WITH TIME ZONE', 'TIMESTAMP WITH TIME ZONE', 'INTERVAL'). For other <data type>s, NUMERIC_PRECISION is NULL.
- NUMERIC_PRECISION_RADIX is either 2 or 10, depending on your DBMS (for 'INTEGER', 'SMALLINT', 'DATE', 'TIME', 'TIMESTAMP', 'TIME WITH TIME ZONE', 'TIMESTAMP WITH TIME ZONE', 'INTERVAL'), 10 (for 'NUMERIC', 'DECIMAL'), 2 (for 'REAL', 'FLOAT', 'DOUBLE PRECISION'). For other <data type>s, NUMERIC_PRECISION_RADIX is NULL.
- NUMERIC_SCALE is either 0 (for 'INTEGER', 'SMALLINT') or shows the parameter's scale (for 'NUMERIC', 'DECIMAL'). For other <data type>s, NUMERIC_SCALE is NULL.
- DATETIME_PRECISION shows the parameter's fractional-seconds precision (for 'TIME', 'TIMESTAMP', 'TIME WITH TIME ZONE', 'TIMESTAMP WITH TIME ZONE', 'INTERVAL'). For other <data type>s, DATETIME_PRECISION is NULL.
- INTERVAL_TYPE shows the parameter's interval type (for 'INTERVAL'); either 'YEAR', 'MONTH', 'DAY', 'HOUR', 'MINUTE', 'SECOND', 'YEAR TO MONTH', 'DAY TO HOUR', 'DAY TO MINUTE', 'DAY TO SECOND', 'HOUR TO MINUTE', 'HOUR TO SECOND', 'MINUTE TO SECOND'. For other <data type>s, INTERVAL_TYPE is NULL.
- INTERVAL_PRECISION shows the parameter's precision for the interval leading field (for 'INTERVAL'). For other <data type>s, INTERVAL_PRECISION is NULL.
- USER_DEFINED_TYPE_CATALOG, USER_DEFINED_TYPE_SCHEMA, USER_DEFINED_TYPE_NAME uniquely identify the UDT that the parameter uses. If no UDT is used, these fields are NULL.
- SCOPE_CATALOG, SCOPE_SCHEMA, SCOPE_NAME uniquely identify the parameter's scope. If the parameter has no scope, these fields are NULL.

If you want to restrict your code to Core SQL, do not reference INFORMATION_SCHEMA.METHOD_SPECIFICATION_PARAMETERS.

INFORMATION_SCHEMA.PARAMETERS

This View has the following Columns:

Name	Domain	Nullable?
SPECIFIC_CATALOG	SQL_IDENTIFIER	no
SPECIFIC_SCHEMA	SQL_IDENTIFIER	no
SPECIFIC_NAME	SQL_IDENTIFIER	no

Name	Domain	Nullable?
ORDINAL_POSITION	CARDINAL_NUMBER	no
PARAMETER_MODE	CHARACTER_DATA	yes
IS_RESULT	CHARACTER_DATA	yes
AS_LOCATOR	CHARACTER_DATA	yes
PARAMETER_NAME	SQL_IDENTIFIER	yes
DATA_TYPE	CHARACTER_DATA	no
CHARACTER_MAXIMUM_LENGTH	CARDINAL_NUMBER	yes
CHARACTER_OCTET_LENGTH	CARDINAL_NUMBER	yes
COLLATION_CATALOG	SQL_IDENTIFIER	yes
COLLATION_SCHEMA	SQL_IDENTIFIER	yes
COLLATION_NAME	SQL_IDENTIFIER	yes
CHARACTER_SET_CATALOG	SQL_IDENTIFIER	no
CHARACTER_SET_SCHEMA	SQL_IDENTIFIER	no
CHARACTER_SET_NAME	SQL_IDENTIFIER	no
NUMERIC_PRECISION	CARDINAL_NUMBER	yes
NUMERIC_PRECISION_RADIX	CARDINAL_NUMBER	yes
NUMERIC_SCALE	CARDINAL_NUMBER	yes
DATETIME_PRECISION	CARDINAL_NUMBER	yes
INTERVAL_TYPE	CHARACTER_DATA	yes
INTERVAL_PRECISION	CARDINAL_NUMBER	yes
USER_DEFINED_TYPE_CATALOG	SQL_IDENTIFIER	yes
USER_DEFINED_TYPE_SCHEMA	SQL_IDENTIFIER	yes
USER_DEFINED_TYPE_NAME	SQL_IDENTIFIER	yes
SCOPE_CATALOG	SQL_IDENTIFIER	yes
SCOPE_SCHEMA	SQL_IDENTIFIER	yes
SCOPE_NAME	SQL_IDENTIFIER	yes

PARAMETERS shows the parameters of the SQL-invoked routines in this Catalog on which the current user has Privileges.

- SPECIFIC_CATALOG, SPECIFIC_SCHEMA, SPECIFIC_NAME uniquely identify the SQL-invoked routine that contains the parameter being described.
- ORDINAL_POSITION shows the ordinal position of the parameter in its SQL-invoked routine.
- PARAMETER_MODE is either 'IN' (the parameter is an input parameter), 'OUT' (the parameter is an output parameter), or 'INOUT' (the parameter is both an input and an output parameter).

- IS_RESULT is either 'YES' (the parameter is the RESULT parameter of a type-preserving function) or 'NO' (the parameter is not the RESULT parameter of a type-preserving function).
- AS_LOCATOR is either 'YES' (the parameter is passed AS LOCATOR) or 'NO' (the parameter is not passed AS LOCATOR).
- PARAMETER_NAME is the name of the parameter, if it was specified when the SQL-invoked routine was created. Otherwise, PARAMETER_NAME is NULL.
- DATA_TYPE shows the parameter's <data type>: either 'BINARY LARGE OBJECT', 'BIT', 'BIT VARYING', 'CHARACTER', 'CHARACTER VARYING', 'CHARACTER LARGE OBJECT', 'INTEGER', 'SMALLINT', 'NUMERIC', 'DECIMAL', 'REAL', 'DOUBLE PRECISION', 'FLOAT', 'DATE', 'TIME', 'TIME WITH TIME ZONE', 'TIMESTAMP', 'TIMESTAMP WITH TIME ZONE', 'INTERVAL', 'BOOLEAN', 'USER-DEFINED TYPE' — or something else, such as an implementation-defined data type.
- CHARACTER_MAXIMUM_LENGTH shows the parameter's maximum length in characters (for 'CHARACTER', 'CHARACTER VARYING', 'CHARACTER LARGE OBJECT') or in bits (for 'BIT', 'BIT VARYING', 'BINARY LARGE OBJECT'). For other <data type>s, CHARACTER_MAXIMUM_LENGTH is NULL.
- CHARACTER_OCTET_LENGTH shows the parameter's maximum length in octets (for 'CHARACTER', 'CHARACTER VARYING', 'CHARACTER LARGE OBJECT', 'BIT', 'BIT VARYING', 'BINARY LARGE OBJECT'). For other <data type>s, CHARACTER_OCTET_LENGTH is NULL.
- COLLATION_CATALOG, COLLATION_SCHEMA, COLLATION_NAME uniquely identify the parameter's default Collation (for 'CHARACTER', 'CHARACTER VARYING', 'CHARACTER LARGE OBJECT'). For other <data type>s, these fields are NULL.
- CHARACTER_SET_CATALOG, CHARACTER_SET_SCHEMA, CHARACTER_SET_NAME uniquely identify the Character set on which the parameter's default Collation is defined.
- NUMERIC_PRECISION shows the parameter's precision (for 'INTEGER', 'SMALLINT', 'NUMERIC', 'DECIMAL', 'REAL', 'FLOAT', 'DOUBLE PRECISION', 'DATE', 'TIME TIMESTAMP', 'TIME WITH TIME ZONE', 'TIMESTAMP WITH TIME ZONE', 'INTERVAL'). For other <data type>s, NUMERIC_PRECISION is NULL.
- NUMERIC_PRECISION_RADIX is either 2 or 10, depending on your DBMS (for 'INTEGER', 'SMALLINT', 'DATE', 'TIME', 'TIMESTAMP', 'TIME WITH TIME ZONE', 'TIMESTAMP WITH TIME ZONE', 'INTERVAL'), 10 (for 'NUMERIC', 'DECIMAL'), 2 (for 'REAL', 'FLOAT', 'DOUBLE PRECISION'). For other <data type>s, NUMERIC_PRECISION_RADIX is NULL.
- NUMERIC_SCALE is either 0 (for 'INTEGER', 'SMALLINT') or shows the parameter's scale (for 'NUMERIC', 'DECIMAL'). For other <data type>s, NUMERIC_SCALE is NULL.
- DATETIME_PRECISION shows the parameter's fractional-seconds precision (for 'TIME', 'TIMESTAMP', 'TIME WITH TIME ZONE', 'TIMESTAMP WITH TIME ZONE', 'INTERVAL'). For other <data type>s, DATETIME_PRECISION is NULL.
- INTERVAL_TYPE shows the parameter's interval type (for 'INTERVAL'); either 'YEAR', 'MONTH', 'DAY', 'HOUR', 'MINUTE', 'SECOND', 'YEAR TO MONTH', 'DAY TO HOUR', 'DAY TO MINUTE', 'DAY TO SECOND', 'HOUR TO MINUTE', 'HOUR TO SECOND', 'MINUTE TO SECOND'. For other <data type>s, INTERVAL_TYPE is NULL.
- INTERVAL_PRECISION shows the parameter's precision for the interval leading field (for 'INTERVAL'). For other <data type>s, INTERVAL_PRECISION is NULL.

- USER_DEFINED_TYPE_CATALOG, USER_DEFINED_TYPE_SCHEMA, USER_DEFINED_TYPE_NAME uniquely identify the UDT that the parameter uses. If no UDT is used, these fields are NULL.
- SCOPE_CATALOG, SCOPE_SCHEMA, SCOPE_NAME uniquely identify the parameter's scope. If the parameter has no scope, these fields are NULL.

INFORMATION_SCHEMA.REFERENTIAL_CONSTRAINTS
This View has the following Columns:

Name	Domain	Nullable?
CONSTRAINT_CATALOG	SQL_IDENTIFIER	no
CONSTRAINT_SCHEMA	SQL_IDENTIFIER	no
CONSTRAINT_NAME	SQL_IDENTIFIER	no
UNIQUE_CONSTRAINT_CATALOG	SQL_IDENTIFIER	no
UNIQUE_CONSTRAINT_SCHEMA	SQL_IDENTIFIER	no
UNIQUE_CONSTRAINT_NAME	SQL_IDENTIFIER	no
MATCH_OPTION	CHARACTER_DATA	no
UPDATE_RULE	CHARACTER_DATA	no
DELETE_RULE	CHARACTER_DATA	no

REFERENTIAL_CONSTRAINTS shows the FOREIGN KEY Constraints in this Catalog, where the Constraints are owned by the current user.

- CONSTRAINT_CATALOG, CONSTRAINT_SCHEMA, CONSTRAINT_NAME uniquely identify a FOREIGN KEY Constraint owned by the current user.
- UNIQUE_CONSTRAINT_CATALOG, CONSTRAINT_SCHEMA, UNIQUE_CONSTRAINT_NAME uniquely identify the UNIQUE Constraint or PRIMARY KEY Constraint that contains the key which this FOREIGN KEY Constraint references.
- MATCH_OPTION will be one of: 'NONE' (no match type defined), 'PARTIAL' (match type of PARTIAL defined), or 'FULL' (match type of FULL defined).
- UPDATE_RULE shows the referential action that will take place on UPDATE; either 'CASCADE' (referential action of CASCADE defined), 'SET NULL' (referential action of SET NULL defined), 'SET DEFAULT' (referential action of SET DEFAULT defined), 'RESTRICT' (referential action of RESTRICT defined), or 'NO ACTION' (referential action of NO ACTION defined).
- DELETE_RULE shows the referential action that will take place on DELETE; either 'CASCADE' (referential action of CASCADE defined), 'SET NULL' (referential action of SET NULL defined), 'SET DEFAULT' (referential action of SET DEFAULT defined), 'RESTRICT' (referential action of RESTRICT defined), or 'NO ACTION' (referential action of NO ACTION defined).

INFORMATION_SCHEMA.ROLE_COLUMN_GRANTS
This View has the following Columns:

Name	Domain	Nullable?
GRANTOR	SQL_IDENTIFIER	no
GRANTEE	SQL_IDENTIFIER	no

Name	Domain	Nullable?
TABLE_CATALOG	SQL_IDENTIFIER	no
TABLE_SCHEMA	SQL_IDENTIFIER	no
TABLE_NAME	SQL_IDENTIFIER	no
COLUMN_NAME	SQL_IDENTIFIER	no
PRIVILEGE_TYPE	CHARACTER_DATA	no

ROLE_COLUMN_GRANTS shows the Privileges on Columns in this Catalog that currently enabled Roles may use.

- GRANTOR shows the <AuthorizationID> who granted this Privilege.
- GRANTEE shows the Role <AuthorizationID> that may use the Privilege.
- TABLE_CATALOG, TABLE_SCHEMA, TABLE_NAME, COLUMN_NAME uniquely identify the Column to which the Privilege applies.
- PRIVILEGE_TYPE shows the Privilege granted; either 'INSERT', 'UPDATE', 'REFERENCES', or 'SELECT'.

If you want to restrict your code to Core SQL, do not reference INFORMATION_SCHEMA.ROLE_COLUMN_GRANTS.

INFORMATION_SCHEMA.ROLE_ROUTINE_GRANTS

This View has the following Columns:

Name	Domain	Nullable?
GRANTOR	SQL_IDENTIFIER	no
GRANTEE	SQL_IDENTIFIER	no
SPECIFIC_CATALOG	SQL_IDENTIFIER	no
SPECIFIC_SCHEMA	SQL_IDENTIFIER	no
SPECIFIC_NAME	SQL_IDENTIFIER	no
PRIVILEGE_TYPE	CHARACTER_DATA	no
IS_GRANTABLE	CHARACTER_DATA	no

ROLE_ROUTINE_GRANTS shows the Privileges on SQL-invoked routines in this Catalog that currently enabled Roles may use.

- GRANTOR shows the <AuthorizationID> who granted this EXECUTE Privilege.
- GRANTEE shows the Role <AuthorizationID> that may use the Privilege.
- SPECIFIC_CATALOG, SPECIFIC_SCHEMA, SPECIFIC_NAME uniquely identify the SQL-invoked routine to which the Privilege applies.
- PRIVILEGE_TYPE shows the Privilege granted: 'EXECUTE'.
- IS_GRANTABLE is either 'YES' (Privilege was granted WITH GRANT OPTION) or 'NO' (Privilege was not granted WITH GRANT OPTION).

If you want to restrict your code to Core SQL, do not reference INFORMATION_SCHEMA.ROLE_ROUTINE_GRANTS.

INFORMATION_SCHEMA.ROLE_TABLE_GRANTS
This View has the following Columns:

Name	Domain	Nullable?
GRANTOR	SQL_IDENTIFIER	no
GRANTEE	SQL_IDENTIFIER	no
TABLE_CATALOG	SQL_IDENTIFIER	no
TABLE_SCHEMA	SQL_IDENTIFIER	no
TABLE_NAME	SQL_IDENTIFIER	no
PRIVILEGE_TYPE	CHARACTER_DATA	no

ROLE_TABLE_GRANTS shows the Privileges on Tables in this Catalog that currently enabled Roles may use.

- GRANTOR shows the <AuthorizationID> who granted this Privilege.
- GRANTEE shows the Role <AuthorizationID> that may use the Privilege.
- TABLE_CATALOG, TABLE_SCHEMA, TABLE_NAME uniquely identify the Table to which the Privilege applies.
- PRIVILEGE_TYPE shows the Privilege granted: either 'DELETE', 'INSERT', 'UPDATE', 'REFERENCES', 'TRIGGER', or 'SELECT'.

If you want to restrict your code to Core SQL, do not reference INFORMATION_SCHEMA.ROLE_TABLE_GRANTS.

INFORMATION_SCHEMA.ROLE_USAGE_GRANTS
This View has the following Columns:

Name	Domain	Nullable?
GRANTOR	SQL_IDENTIFIER	no
GRANTEE	SQL_IDENTIFIER	no
OBJECT_CATALOG	SQL_IDENTIFIER	no
OBJECT_SCHEMA	SQL_IDENTIFIER	no
OBJECT_NAME	SQL_IDENTIFIER	no
OBJECT_TYPE	CHARACTER_DATA	no
IS_GRANTABLE	CHARACTER_DATA	no

ROLE_USAGE_GRANTS shows the USAGE Privileges on Objects in this Catalog that currently enabled Roles may use.

- GRANTOR shows the <AuthorizationID> who granted this Privilege.
- GRANTEE shows the Role <AuthorizationID> that may use the Privilege.
- OBJECT_CATALOG, OBJECT_SCHEMA, OBJECT_NAME, OBJECT_TYPE uniquely identify the Object — either a Domain, Character set, Collation, or Translation — that the Role may use.
- IS_GRANTABLE is either 'YES' (Privilege was granted WITH GRANT OPTION) or 'NO' (Privilege was not granted WITH GRANT OPTION).

If you want to restrict your code to Core SQL, do not reference INFORMATION_SCHEMA.ROLE_USAGE_GRANTS.

INFORMATION_SCHEMA.ROLE_USER_DEFINED_TYPE_GRANTS

This View has the following Columns:

Name	Domain	Nullable?
GRANTOR	SQL_IDENTIFIER	no
GRANTEE	SQL_IDENTIFIER	no
USER_DEFINED_TYPE_CATALOG	SQL_IDENTIFIER	no
USER_DEFINED_TYPE_SCHEMA	SQL_IDENTIFIER	no
USER_DEFINED_TYPE_NAME	SQL_IDENTIFIER	no
PRIVILEGE_TYPE	CHARACTER_DATA	no
IS_GRANTABLE	CHARACTER_DATA	no

ROLE_USER_DEFINED_TYPE_GRANTS shows the Privileges on UDTs in this Catalog that currently enabled Roles may use.

- GRANTOR shows the <AuthorizationID> who granted this Privilege.
- GRANTEE shows the Role <AuthorizationID> that may use the Privilege.
- USER_DEFINED_TYPE_CATALOG, USER_DEFINED_TYPE_SCHEMA, USER_DEFINED_TYPE_NAME uniquely identify the UDT the Role may use.
- PRIVILEGE_TYPE shows the Privilege granted: 'TYPE USAGE'.
- IS_GRANTABLE is either 'YES' (Privilege was granted WITH GRANT OPTION) or 'NO' (Privilege was not granted WITH GRANT OPTION).

If you want to restrict your code to Core SQL, do not reference INFORMATION_SCHEMA.ROLE_USER_DEFINED_TYPE_GRANTS.

INFORMATION_SCHEMA.ROUTINES

This View has the following Columns:

Name	Domain	Nullable?
SPECIFIC_CATALOG	SQL_IDENTIFIER	no
SPECIFIC_SCHEMA	SQL_IDENTIFIER	no
SPECIFIC_NAME	SQL_IDENTIFIER	no
ROUTINE_CATALOG	SQL_IDENTIFIER	yes
ROUTINE_SCHEMA	SQL_IDENTIFIER	yes
ROUTINE_NAME	SQL_IDENTIFIER	yes
ROUTINE_TYPE	CHARACTER_DATA	no
MODULE_CATALOG	SQL_IDENTIFIER	yes
MODULE_SCHEMA	SQL_IDENTIFIER	yes
MODULE_NAME	SQL_IDENTIFIER	yes

Name	Domain	Nullable?
USER_DEFINED_TYPE_CATALOG	SQL_IDENTIFIER	yes
USER_DEFINED_TYPE_SCHEMA	SQL_IDENTIFIER	yes
USER_DEFINED_TYPE_NAME	SQL_IDENTIFIER	yes
DATA_TYPE	CHARACTER_DATA	no
CHARACTER_MAXIMUM_LENGTH	CARDINAL_NUMBER	yes
CHARACTER_OCTET_LENGTH	CARDINAL_NUMBER	yes
COLLATION_CATALOG	SQL_IDENTIFIER	yes
COLLATION_SCHEMA	SQL_IDENTIFIER	yes
COLLATION_NAME	SQL_IDENTIFIER	yes
NUMERIC_PRECISION	CARDINAL_NUMBER	yes
NUMERIC_PRECISION_RADIX	CARDINAL_NUMBER	yes
NUMERIC_SCALE	CARDINAL_NUMBER	yes
DATETIME_PRECISION	CARDINAL_NUMBER	yes
INTERVAL_TYPE	CHARACTER_DATA	yes
INTERVAL_PRECISION	CARDINAL_NUMBER	yes
TYPE_USER_DEFINED_TYPE_CATALOG	SQL_IDENTIFIER	yes
TYPE_USER_DEFINED_TYPE_SCHEMA	SQL_IDENTIFIER	yes
TYPE_USER_DEFINED_TYPE_NAME	SQL_IDENTIFIER	yes
SCOPE_CATALOG	SQL_IDENTIFIER	yes
SCOPE_SCHEMA	SQL_IDENTIFIER	yes
SCOPE_NAME	SQL_IDENTIFIER	yes
ROUTINE_BODY	CHARACTER_DATA	no
ROUTINE_DEFINITION	CHARACTER_DATA	yes
EXTERNAL_NAME	SQL_IDENTIFIER	yes
EXTERNAL_LANGUAGE	CHARACTER_DATA	yes
PARAMETER_STYLE	CHARACTER_DATA	yes
IS_DETERMINISTIC	CHARACTER_DATA	yes
SQL_DATA_ACCESS	CHARACTER_DATA	no
SQL_PATH	CHARACTER_DATA	yes
SCHEMA_LEVEL_ROUTINE	CHARACTER_DATA	yes
MAX_DYNAMIC_RESULT_SETS	CARDINAL_NUMBER	yes
IS_USER_DEFINED_CAST	CHARACTER_DATA	no
IS_IMPLICITLY_INVOCABLE	CHARACTER_DATA	yes
ROUTINE_CREATED	TIME_STAMP	yes
ROUTINE_LAST_ALTERED	TIME_STAMP	yes

ROUTINES shows the SQL-invoked routines in this Catalog on which the current user has Privileges.

- SPECIFIC_CATALOG, SPECIFIC_SCHEMA, SPECIFIC_NAME, ROUTINE_CATALOG, ROUTINE_SCHEMA, ROUTINE_NAME uniquely identify an SQL-invoked routine on which the current user has Privileges. Among the routines in this View, you will find all the functions which your DBMS defined in advance; the SQL built-in functions, e.g., ABS, BIT_LENGTH, CHARACTER_LENGTH, CHAR_LENGTH, LOWER, MOD, OCTET_LENGTH, POSITION, SUBSTRING, UPPER.
- ROUTINE_TYPE is either 'PROCEDURE' (the SQL-invoked routine is an SQL-invoked procedure), 'FUNCTION' (the SQL-invoked routine is an SQL-invoked function that is not an SQL-invoked method), or 'METHOD' (the SQL-invoked routine is an SQL-invoked method).
- MODULE_CATALOG, MODULE_SCHEMA, MODULE_NAME are all NULL.
- USER_DEFINED_TYPE_CATALOG, USER_DEFINED_TYPE_SCHEMA, USER_DEFINED_TYPE_NAME uniquely identify the UDT that this SQL-invoked routine is a method of. If the routine is not defined as a method of a UDT, these fields are NULL.
- DATA_TYPE shows the routine's result <data type>: either 'BINARY LARGE OBJECT', 'BIT', 'BIT VARYING', 'CHARACTER', 'CHARACTER VARYING', 'CHARACTER LARGE OBJECT', 'INTEGER', 'SMALLINT', 'NUMERIC', 'DECIMAL', 'REAL', 'DOUBLE PRECISION', 'FLOAT', 'DATE', 'TIME', 'TIME WITH TIME ZONE', 'TIMESTAMP', 'TIMESTAMP WITH TIME ZONE', 'INTERVAL', 'BOOLEAN', 'USER-DEFINED TYPE' — or something else, such as an implementation-defined data type.
- CHARACTER_MAXIMUM_LENGTH shows the routine's result maximum length in characters (for 'CHARACTER', 'CHARACTER VARYING', 'CHARACTER LARGE OBJECT') or in bits (for 'BIT', 'BIT VARYING', 'BINARY LARGE OBJECT'). For other <data type>s, CHARACTER_MAXIMUM_LENGTH is NULL.
- CHARACTER_OCTET_LENGTH shows the routine's result maximum length in octets (for 'CHARACTER', 'CHARACTER VARYING', 'CHARACTER LARGE OBJECT', 'BIT', 'BIT VARYING', 'BINARY LARGE OBJECT'). For other <data type>s, CHARACTER_OCTET_LENGTH is NULL.
- COLLATION_CATALOG, COLLATION_SCHEMA, COLLATION_NAME uniquely identify the routine's result default Collation (for 'CHARACTER', 'CHARACTER VARYING', 'CHARACTER LARGE OBJECT'). For other <data type>s, these fields are NULL.
- NUMERIC_PRECISION shows the routine's result precision (for 'INTEGER', 'SMALLINT', 'NUMERIC', 'DECIMAL', 'REAL', 'FLOAT', 'DOUBLE PRECISION', 'DATE', 'TIME', TIMESTAMP', 'TIME WITH TIME ZONE', 'TIMESTAMP WITH TIME ZONE', 'INTERVAL'). For other <data type>s, NUMERIC_PRECISION is NULL.
- NUMERIC_PRECISION_RADIX is either 2 or 10, depending on your DBMS (for 'INTEGER', 'SMALLINT', 'DATE', 'TIME', 'TIMESTAMP', 'TIME WITH TIME ZONE', 'TIMESTAMP WITH TIME ZONE', 'INTERVAL'), 10 (for 'NUMERIC', 'DECIMAL'), 2 (for 'REAL', 'FLOAT', 'DOUBLE PRECISION'). For other <data type>s, NUMERIC_PRECISION_RADIX is NULL.
- NUMERIC_SCALE is either 0 (for 'INTEGER', 'SMALLINT') or shows the routine's result scale (for 'NUMERIC', 'DECIMAL'). For other <data type>s, NUMERIC_SCALE is NULL.
- DATETIME_PRECISION shows the routine's result fractional-seconds precision (for 'TIME', 'TIMESTAMP', 'TIME WITH TIME ZONE', 'TIMESTAMP WITH TIME ZONE', 'INTERVAL'). For other <data type>s, DATETIME_PRECISION is NULL.

- INTERVAL_TYPE shows the routine's result interval type (for 'INTERVAL'): either 'YEAR', 'MONTH', 'DAY', 'HOUR', 'MINUTE', 'SECOND', 'YEAR TO MONTH', 'DAY TO HOUR', 'DAY TO MINUTE', 'DAY TO SECOND', 'HOUR TO MINUTE', 'HOUR TO SECOND', 'MINUTE TO SECOND'. For other <data type>s, INTERVAL_TYPE is NULL.
- INTERVAL_PRECISION shows the routine's result precision for the interval leading field (for 'INTERVAL'). For other <data type>s, INTERVAL_PRECISION is NULL.
- TYPE_USER_DEFINED_TYPE_CATALOG, TYPE_USER_DEFINED_TYPE_SCHEMA, TYPE_USER_DEFINED_TYPE_NAME uniquely identify a UDT that the routine uses. If no UDT is used, these fields are NULL.
- SCOPE_CATALOG, SCOPE_SCHEMA, SCOPE_NAME uniquely identify the routine's scope. If the routine has no scope, these fields are NULL.
- ROUTINE_BODY is either 'SQL' (the SQL-invoked routine is an SQL routine) or 'EXTERNAL' (the SQL-invoked routine is an external routine).
- If this SQL-invoked routine is an SQL routine that is not part of an SQL-server Module definition, ROUTINE_DEFINITION shows the routine body. If the routine body was too big to be stored, or if this is not an SQL routine that doesn't belong to an SQL-server Module definition, ROUTINE_DEFINITION is NULL.
- If this SQL-invoked routine is an external routine (i.e., ROUTINE_BODY is 'EXTERNAL'), EXTERNAL_NAME shows its external name. If ROUTINE_BODY is 'SQL', EXTERNAL_NAME is NULL.
- If this SQL-invoked routine is an external routine (i.e., ROUTINE_BODY is 'EXTERNAL'), EXTERNAL_LANGUAGE shows the language it's written in: either 'ADA', 'C', 'COBOL', 'FORTRAN', 'MUMPS', 'PASCAL', or 'PLI'. If ROUTINE_BODY is 'SQL', EXTERNAL_LANGUAGE is NULL.
- If this SQL-invoked routine is an external routine (i.e., ROUTINE_BODY is 'EXTERNAL'), PARAMETER_STYLE shows its SQL parameter passing style: either 'SQL' or 'GENERAL'. If ROUTINE_BODY is 'SQL', PARAMETER_STYLE is NULL.
- If this SQL-invoked routine is an external routine (i.e., ROUTINE_BODY is 'EXTERNAL'), IS_DETERMINISTIC is either 'YES' (routine was defined as DETERMINISTIC), or 'NO' (routine was not defined as DETERMINISTIC). If ROUTINE_BODY is 'SQL', IS_DETERMINISTIC is NULL.
- SQL_DATA_ACCESS is either 'NONE' (the SQL-invoked routine does not possibly contain SQL), 'CONTAINS' (the SQL-invoked routine possibly contains SQL), 'READS' (the SQL-invoked routine possibly reads SQL-data), or 'MODIFIES' (the SQL-invoked routine possibly modifies SQL-data).
- If this SQL-invoked routine is an SQL routine, SQL_PATH shows the SQL-path of the Schema that contains it. Otherwise, SQL_PATH is NULL.
- SCHEMA_LEVEL_ROUTINE is either 'YES' (this is a Schema-level routine) or 'NO' (this is not a Schema-level routine).
- If this is an SQL-invoked procedure that was defined by an SQL-invoked routine containing a <maximum dynamic result sets> clause in its definition, MAX_DYNAMIC_RESULT_SETS shows that value. Otherwise, MAX_DYNAMIC_RESULT_SETS is zero.
- IS_USER_DEFINED_CAST is either 'YES' (the routine is a user-defined cast) or 'NO' (the routine is not a user-defined cast).

- IS_IMPLICITLY_INVOCABLE is either 'YES' (the routine can be implicitly invoked) or 'NO' (the routine cannot be implicitly invoked) or NULL (the routine is not a user-defined cast).
- ROUTINE_CREATED shows the CURRENT_TIMESTAMP from the time this SQL-invoked routine was created.
- ROUTINE_LAST_ALTERED shows the CURRENT_TIMESTAMP from the time this SQL-invoked routine was last altered. (This will be the same as the ROUTINE_CREATED value if the routine hasn't been altered.)

INFORMATION_SCHEMA.ROUTINE_COLUMN_USAGE
This View has the following Columns:

Name	Domain	Nullable?
SPECIFIC_CATALOG	SQL_IDENTIFIER	no
SPECIFIC_SCHEMA	SQL_IDENTIFIER	no
SPECIFIC_NAME	SQL_IDENTIFIER	no
ROUTINE_CATALOG	SQL_IDENTIFIER	yes
ROUTINE_SCHEMA	SQL_IDENTIFIER	yes
ROUTINE_NAME	SQL_IDENTIFIER	yes
TABLE_CATALOG	SQL_IDENTIFIER	no
TABLE_SCHEMA	SQL_IDENTIFIER	no
TABLE_NAME	SQL_IDENTIFIER	no
COLUMN_NAME	SQL_IDENTIFIER	no

ROUTINE_COLUMN_USAGE shows the Columns on which SQL-invoked routines in this Catalog depend, where the Columns are owned by the current user.

- SPECIFIC_CATALOG, SPECIFIC_SCHEMA, SPECIFIC_NAME, ROUTINE_CATALOG, ROUTINE_SCHEMA, ROUTINE_NAME uniquely identify an SQL-invoked routine.
- TABLE_CATALOG, TABLE_SCHEMA, TABLE_NAME, COLUMN_NAME uniquely identify a Column that is owned by the current user and upon which this routine depends.

If you want to restrict your code to Core SQL, do not reference INFORMATION_SCHEMA.ROUTINE_COLUMN_USAGE.

INFORMATION_SCHEMA.ROUTINE_PRIVILEGES
This View has the following Columns:

Name	Domain	Nullable?
GRANTOR	SQL_IDENTIFIER	no
GRANTEE	SQL_IDENTIFIER	no
SPECIFIC_CATALOG	SQL_IDENTIFIER	no
SPECIFIC_SCHEMA	SQL_IDENTIFIER	no
SPECIFIC_NAME	SQL_IDENTIFIER	no
ROUTINE_CATALOG	SQL_IDENTIFIER	yes

Name	Domain	Nullable?
ROUTINE_SCHEMA	SQL_IDENTIFIER	yes
ROUTINE_NAME	SQL_IDENTIFIER	yes
PRIVILEGE_TYPE	CHARACTER_DATA	no
IS_GRANTABLE	CHARACTER_DATA	no

ROUTINE_PRIVILEGES shows the Privileges on SQL-invoked routines in this Catalog, where the Privileges are either available to, or granted by, the current user.

- GRANTOR shows the <AuthorizationID> who granted the Privilege.
- GRANTEE shows the <AuthorizationID> who may use the Privilege. By definition, if GRANTOR isn't CURRENT_USER, then GRANTEE is either CURRENT_USER or 'PUBLIC'.
- SPECIFIC_CATALOG, SPECIFIC_SCHEMA, SPECIFIC_NAME, ROUTINE_CATALOG, ROUTINE_SCHEMA, ROUTINE_NAME uniquely identify the SQL-invoked routine that this Privilege applies to.
- PRIVILEGE_TYPE shows the Privilege granted: 'EXECUTE'.
- IS_GRANTABLE is either 'YES' (Privilege was granted WITH GRANT OPTION) or 'NO' (Privilege was not granted WITH GRANT OPTION).

INFORMATION_SCHEMA.ROUTINE_TABLE_USAGE

This View has the following Columns:

Name	Domain	Nullable?
SPECIFIC_CATALOG	SQL_IDENTIFIER	no
SPECIFIC_SCHEMA	SQL_IDENTIFIER	no
SPECIFIC_NAME	SQL_IDENTIFIER	no
ROUTINE_CATALOG	SQL_IDENTIFIER	yes
ROUTINE_SCHEMA	SQL_IDENTIFIER	yes
ROUTINE_NAME	SQL_IDENTIFIER	yes
TABLE_CATALOG	SQL_IDENTIFIER	no
TABLE_SCHEMA	SQL_IDENTIFIER	no
TABLE_NAME	SQL_IDENTIFIER	no

ROUTINE_TABLE_USAGE shows the Tables on which SQL-invoked routines in this Catalog depend, where the Tables are owned by the current user.

- SPECIFIC_CATALOG, SPECIFIC_SCHEMA, SPECIFIC_NAME, ROUTINE_CATALOG, ROUTINE_SCHEMA, ROUTINE_NAME uniquely identify an SQL-invoked routine in this Catalog.
- TABLE_CATALOG, TABLE_SCHEMA, TABLE_NAME uniquely identify a Table that is owned by the current user and upon which this routine depends.

If you want to restrict your code to Core SQL, do not reference INFORMATION_SCHEMA.ROUTINE_TABLE_USAGE.

INFORMATION_SCHEMA.SCHEMATA

This View has the following Columns:

Name	Domain	Nullable?
CATALOG_NAME	SQL_IDENTIFIER	no
SCHEMA_NAME	SQL_IDENTIFIER	no
SCHEMA_OWNER	SQL_IDENTIFIER	no
DEFAULT_CHARACTER_SET_CATALOG	SQL_IDENTIFIER	no
DEFAULT_CHARACTER_SET_SCHEMA	SQL_IDENTIFIER	no
DEFAULT_CHARACTER_SET_NAME	SQL_IDENTIFIER	no
SQL_PATH	CHARACTER_DATA	yes

SCHEMATA shows the Schemas in this Catalog that are owned by the current user.

- CATALOG_NAME, SCHEMA_NAME uniquely identify a Schema owned by the user.
- SCHEMA_OWNER shows the current user <AuthorizationID>. This was the Schema owner specified in the Schema definition.
- DEFAULT_CHARACTER_SET_CATALOG, DEFAULT_CHARACTER_SET_SCHEMA, DEFAULT_CHARACTER_SET_NAME uniquely identify the Character set that was specified by a DEFAULT CHARACTER SET clause in the Schema definition. This is the default Character set for the Columns and Domains belonging to this Schema.
- SQL_PATH shows the contents of the Schema definition's PATH clause, if there was one. If PATH was omitted or if its value was too large to be stored SQL_PATH is NULL.

INFORMATION_SCHEMA.SQL_FEATURES

This View has the following Columns:

Name	Domain	Nullable?
FEATURE_ID	CHARACTER_DATA	no
FEATURE_NAME	CHARACTER_DATA	no
SUB_FEATURE_ID	CHARACTER_DATA	no
SUB_FEATURE_NAME	CHARACTER_DATA	no
IS_SUPPORTED	CHARACTER_DATA	no
IS_VERIFIED_BY	CHARACTER_DATA	yes
FEATURE_COMMENTS	CHARACTER_DATA	yes

SQL_FEATURES shows all the SQL Standard-defined features and subfeatures (see Appendix B, "SQL Taxonomy" on the CD-ROM for a list of these) and marks the ones your DBMS supports.

- FEATURE_ID, SUB_FEATURE_ID uniquely identify an SQL feature or subfeature. If SUB_FEATURE_ID is zero, this is a feature; otherwise this is a subfeature.
- FEATURE_NAME is the name assigned to the feature by the Standard.
- SUB_FEATURE_NAME is the name assigned to the subfeature by the Standard. If SUB_FEATURE_NAME is a zero-length string, this is a feature; otherwise this is a subfeature.

- IS_SUPPORTED is either 'YES' (the DBMS fully supports this feature/subfeature) or 'NO' (the DBMS doesn't fully support this feature/subfeature). Note: if IS_SUPPORTED is 'YES' for a feature, then it must also be 'YES' for every subfeature of that feature.
- If your DBMS has had its conformance claim for this feature/subfeature independently tested, IS_VERIFIED_BY identifies the conformance test used to verify the claim. If no such verification exists, IS_VERIFIED_BY is NULL. (Note: if IS_SUPPORTED is 'NO' or NULL, IS_VERIFIED_BY must be NULL.)
- FEATURE_COMMENTS is either NULL or shows any implementor's comments that are pertinent to this feature/subfeature.

If you want to restrict your code to Core SQL, do not reference INFORMATION_SCHEMA.SQL_FEATURES.

INFORMATION_SCHEMA.SQL_IMPLEMENTATION_INFO
This View has the following Columns:

Name	Domain	Nullable?
IMPLEMENTATION_INFO_ID	CHARACTER_DATA	no
IMPLEMENTATION_INFO_NAME	CHARACTER_DATA	no
INTEGER_VALUE	CARDINAL_NUMBER	yes
CHARACTER_VALUE	CHARACTER_DATA	yes
IMPLEMENTATION_INFO_COMMENTS	CHARACTER_DATA	yes

SQL_IMPLEMENTATION_INFO lists all the information items that the SQL Standard states are "implementation-defined" and shows your DBMS's defined value for each one.

- IMPLEMENTATION_INFO_ID uniquely identifies an implementation-defined information item.
- IMPLEMENTATION_INFO_NAME shows the name for this IMPLEMENTATION_INFO_ID.
- INTEGER_VALUE and CHARACTER_VALUE show your DBMS's defined value for this item. Depending on the item's type, one field will contain a value and the other will be NULL. If INTEGER_VALUE is zero, or CHARACTER_VALUE is a zero-length string, then your DBMS's value for this item is not known. If both fields are NULL, then the value for this item is not applicable for your DBMS, probably because the feature is not supported.
- IMPLEMENTATION_INFO_COMMENTS is either NULL or shows any implementor's comments that are pertinent to this item.

If you want to restrict your code to Core SQL, do not reference INFORMATION_SCHEMA.SQL_IMPLEMENTATION_INFO.

INFORMATION_SCHEMA.SQL_PACKAGES
This View has the following Columns:

Name	Domain	Nullable?
FEATURE_ID	CHARACTER_DATA	no
FEATURE_NAME	CHARACTER_DATA	no
IS_SUPPORTED	CHARACTER_DATA	no

Name	Domain	Nullable?
IS_VERIFIED_BY	CHARACTER_DATA	yes
FEATURE_COMMENTS	CHARACTER_DATA	yes

SQL_PACKAGES shows all the features that make up an SQL Standard-defined SQL package (see Chapter 1 "Introduction" for a list of these) and marks the ones your DBMS supports.

- FEATURE_ID uniquely identifies an SQL feature that is part of a package.
- FEATURE_NAME is the name assigned to the feature by the Standard.
- IS_SUPPORTED is either 'YES' (the DBMS fully supports this feature) or 'NO' (the DBMS doesn't fully support this feature).
- If your DBMS has had its conformance claim for this feature independently tested, IS_VERIFIED_BY identifies the conformance test used to verify the claim. If no such verification exists, IS_VERIFIED_BY is NULL. (Note: if IS_SUPPORTED is 'NO' or NULL, IS_VERIFIED_BY must be NULL.)
- FEATURE_COMMENTS is either NULL or shows any implementor's comments that are pertinent to this feature.

If you want to restrict your code to Core SQL, do not reference INFORMATION_SCHEMA.SQL_PACKAGES.

INFORMATION_SCHEMA.SQL_SIZING

This View has the following Columns:

Name	Domain	Nullable?
SIZING_ID	CARDINAL_NUMBER	no
SIZING_NAME	CHARACTER_DATA	no
SUPPORTED_VALUE	CARDINAL_NUMBER	yes
SIZING_COMMENTS	CHARACTER_DATA	yes

SQL_SIZING lists all the sizing items defined in the SQL Standard and shows the size supported by your DBMS for each one.

- SIZING_ID uniquely identifies a sizing item defined in the SQL Standard.
- SIZING_NAME shows the name for this SIZING_ID.
- SUPPORTED_VALUE shows the maximum size your DBMS supports for this item. If SUPPORTED_VALUE is NULL, then your DBMS doesn't support any features that use this item. If SUPPORTED_VALUE is zero, then your DBMS either doesn't place a limit on this item or can't determine the item's limit.
- SIZING_COMMENTS is either NULL or shows any implementor's comments that are pertinent to this item.

If you want to restrict your code to Core SQL, do not reference INFORMATION_SCHEMA.SQL_SIZING.

INFORMATION_SCHEMA.SQL_SIZING_PROFILES
This View has the following Columns:

Name	Domain	Nullable?
SIZING_ID	CARDINAL_NUMBER	no
SIZING_NAME	CHARACTER_DATA	no
PROFILE_ID	CHARACTER_DATA	no
REQUIRED_VALUE	CARDINAL_NUMBER	yes
SIZING_PROFILES_COMMENTS	CHARACTER_DATA	yes

SQL_SIZING_PROFILES lists all the sizing items defined in the SQL Standard and shows the size required by one or more profiles of the Standard.

- SIZING_ID, PROFILE_ID uniquely identify a sizing item for a given profile.
- SIZING_NAME is the name for this SIZING_ID.
- REQUIRED_VALUE shows the minimum size that this profile requires for this item. If REQUIRED_VALUE is NULL, then the item isn't used by any features supported by this profile. If REQUIRED_VALUE is zero, then this profile doesn't set a limit for the item.
- SIZING_PROFILES_COMMENTS is either NULL, or shows any implementor's comments that are pertinent to this item within this profile.

If you want to restrict your code to Core SQL, do not reference INFORMATION_SCHEMA.SQL_SIZING_PROFILES.

INFORMATION_SCHEMA.SQL_LANGUAGES
This View has the following Columns:

Name	Domain	Nullable?
SQL_LANGUAGE_SOURCE	CHARACTER_DATA	no
SQL_LANGUAGE_YEAR	CHARACTER_DATA	no
SQL_LANGUAGE_CONFORMANCE	CHARACTER_DATA	no
SQL_LANGUAGE_INTEGRITY	CHARACTER_DATA	yes
SQL_LANGUAGE_IMPLEMENTATION	CHARACTER_DATA	yes
SQL_LANGUAGE_BINDING_STYLE	CHARACTER_DATA	no
SQL_LANGUAGE_PROGRAMMING_LANGUAGE	CHARACTER_DATA	yes

SQL_LANGUAGES shows the SQL conformance levels, options, and dialects supported by your DBMS.

- SQL_LANGUAGE_SOURCE shows the name of the source of your DBMS's SQL language definition. For SQL defined by the SQL Standard, this is 'ISO 9075'. If your DBMS supports some other version of SQL, SQL_LANGUAGE_SOURCE must show some implementation-defined value, as must all of the Columns in this View. We'll ignore this possibility when discussing the rest of the Columns.
- SQL_LANGUAGE_YEAR shows the year that the supported version of the SQL Standard was approved: either '1987', '1989', '1992', or '1999'. It may not be NULL.

- SQL_LANGUAGE_CONFORMANCE shows the level of SQL Standard conformance your DBMS claims: for '1987' and '1989', either '1' or '2'; for '1992', either 'ENTRY', 'INTERMEDIATE', or 'FULL' and for '1999', 'CORE'. It may not be NULL.
- SQL_LANGUAGE_INTEGRITY shows whether the 1989 SQL Standard integrity features are fully supported by your DBMS: for '1989', either 'YES' (SQL-89 integrity features fully supported) or 'NO' (SQL-89 integrity features not fully supported); it may not be NULL. For '1987', '1992', and '1999' SQL_LANGUAGE_INTEGRITY must be NULL.
- SQL_LANGUAGE_IMPLEMENTATION is NULL if SQL_LANGUAGE_SOURCE is 'ISO 9075'. If your DBMS supports some other version of SQL, SQL_LANGUAGE_IMPLEMENTATION shows some implementation-defined value.
- SQL_LANGUAGE_BINDING_STYLE shows the binding style supported by your DBMS: either 'MODULE' (SQL-client Module support), 'EMBEDDED' (embedded SQL support), or 'DIRECT' (direct SQL invocation support). It may not be NULL. Note: if your DBMS supports more than one binding style, there will be a separate row in the View for each one.
- SQL_LANGUAGE_PROGRAMMING_LANGUAGE shows the host language supported by your DBMS for this binding style: (*a*) for 'DIRECT', this Column is NULL; (*b*) for '1987' and '1989' and either 'EMBEDDED' or 'MODULE', either 'COBOL', 'FORTRAN', 'PASCAL', or 'PLI' and (*c*) for '1992' and '1999' and either 'EMBEDDED' or 'MODULE', either 'ADA', 'C', 'COBOL', 'FORTRAN', 'MUMPS', 'PASCAL', or 'PLI'. Note: if your DBMS supports more than one host language for this binding style, there will be a separate row in the View for each one.

INFORMATION_SCHEMA.TABLES

This View has the following Columns:

Name	Domain	Nullable?
TABLE_CATALOG	SQL_IDENTIFIER	no
TABLE_SCHEMA	SQL_IDENTIFIER	no
TABLE_NAME	SQL_IDENTIFIER	no
TABLE_TYPE	CHARACTER_DATA	no
SELF_REFERENCING_COLUMN_NAME	SQL_IDENTIFIER	yes
REFERENCE_GENERATION	CHARACTER_DATA	yes

TABLES shows the Tables (i.e., Base tables and Views) in this Catalog on which the current user has Privileges.

- TABLE_CATALOG, TABLE_SCHEMA, TABLE_NAME uniquely identify a Table which the current user may use — i.e., CURRENT_USER (or PUBLIC) has any Privilege on the Table or on any Column of the Table.
- TABLE_TYPE is either: 'BASE TABLE' (for a persistent Base table), 'VIEW' (for a View), 'LOCAL TEMPORARY' (for a local temporary Table), or 'GLOBAL TEMPORARY' (for a global temporary Table). Note: instead of 'BASE TABLE' some DBMSs will return 'TABLE' because (for some reason or other) Delphi expects 'TABLE' here.
- SELF_REFERENCING_COLUMN_NAME shows the name of the Table's self-referencing Column. If the Table has no self-referencing Column, this field is NULL.

- REFERENCE_GENERATION is either 'SYSTEM GENERATED' (reference types are system generated) or 'USER GENERATED' (reference types are user generated) or 'DERIVED' (reference types are derived from corresponding Columns) or NULL (reference types don't apply to this Table).

INFORMATION_SCHEMA.TABLE_CONSTRAINTS
This View has the following Columns:

Name	Domain	Nullable?
CONSTRAINT_CATALOG	SQL_IDENTIFIER	no
CONSTRAINT_SCHEMA	SQL_IDENTIFIER	no
CONSTRAINT_NAME	SQL_IDENTIFIER	no
TABLE_CATALOG	SQL_IDENTIFIER	no
TABLE_SCHEMA	SQL_IDENTIFIER	no
TABLE_NAME	SQL_IDENTIFIER	no
CONSTRAINT_TYPE	CHARACTER_DATA	no
IS_DEFERRABLE	CHARACTER_DATA	no
INITIALLY_DEFERRED	CHARACTER_DATA	no

TABLE_CONSTRAINTS shows the Table Constraints in this Catalog, where the Constraints are owned by the current user.

- CONSTRAINT_CATALOG, CONSTRAINT_SCHEMA, CONSTRAINT_NAME uniquely identify a Constraint owned by the current user.
- TABLE_CATALOG, TABLE_SCHEMA, TABLE_NAME uniquely identify the Table to which this Constraint applies.
- CONSTRAINT_TYPE is either: 'UNIQUE', 'PRIMARY KEY', 'FOREIGN KEY', or 'CHECK'.
- IS_DEFERRABLE is either 'YES' (the Constraint is DEFERRABLE) or 'NO' (the Constraint is NOT DEFERRABLE).
- INITIALLY_DEFERRED is either 'YES' (the Constraint is INITIALLY DEFERRED) or 'NO' (the Constraint is INITIALLY IMMEDIATE).

INFORMATION_SCHEMA.TABLE_METHOD_PRIVILEGES
This View has the following Columns:

Name	Domain	Nullable?
GRANTOR	SQL_IDENTIFIER	no
GRANTEE	SQL_IDENTIFIER	no
TABLE_CATALOG	SQL_IDENTIFIER	no
TABLE_SCHEMA	SQL_IDENTIFIER	no
TABLE_NAME	SQL_IDENTIFIER	no
SPECIFIC_CATALOG	SQL_IDENTIFIER	no
SPECIFIC_SCHEMA	SQL_IDENTIFIER	no

Name	Domain	Nullable?
SPECIFIC_NAME	SQL_IDENTIFIER	no
IS_GRANTABLE	CHARACTER_DATA	no

TABLE_METHOD_PRIVILEGES shows the EXECUTE Privileges on methods in this Catalog, where the Privileges are either available to, or granted by, the current user.

- GRANTOR shows the <AuthorizationID> who granted the Privilege.
- GRANTEE shows the <AuthorizationID> who may use the Privilege. By definition, if GRANTOR isn't CURRENT_USER, then GRANTEE is either CURRENT_USER or 'PUBLIC'.
- TABLE_CATALOG, TABLE_SCHEMA, TABLE_NAME uniquely identify the typed Table for which the described method is defined. The Table must be in this Catalog.
- SPECIFIC_CATALOG, SPECIFIC_SCHEMA, SPECIFIC_NAME uniquely identify the method to which this Privilege applies.
- IS_GRANTABLE is either 'YES' (Privilege was granted WITH GRANT OPTION) or 'NO' (Privilege was not granted WITH GRANT OPTION).

If you want to restrict your code to Core SQL, do not reference INFORMATION_SCHEMA.TABLE_METHOD_PRIVILEGES.

INFORMATION_SCHEMA.TABLE_PRIVILEGES

This View has the following Columns:

Name	Domain	Nullable?
GRANTOR	SQL_IDENTIFIER	no
GRANTEE	SQL_IDENTIFIER	no
TABLE_CATALOG	SQL_IDENTIFIER	no
TABLE_SCHEMA	SQL_IDENTIFIER	no
TABLE_NAME	SQL_IDENTIFIER	no
PRIVILEGE_TYPE	CHARACTER_DATA	no
IS_GRANTABLE	CHARACTER_DATA	no
WITH_HIERARCHY	CHARACTER_DATA	yes

TABLE_PRIVILEGES shows the Privileges on Tables in this Catalog, where the Privileges are either available to, or granted by, the current user.

- GRANTOR shows the <AuthorizationID> who granted the Privilege.
- GRANTEE shows the <AuthorizationID> who may use the Privilege. By definition, if GRANTOR isn't CURRENT_USER, then GRANTEE is either CURRENT_USER or 'PUBLIC'.
- TABLE_CATALOG, TABLE_SCHEMA, TABLE_NAME uniquely identify a Table in this Catalog.
- PRIVILEGE_TYPE shows the Privilege granted: either 'INSERT', 'UPDATE', 'REFERENCES', 'DELETE', 'TRIGGER', or 'SELECT'.
- IS_GRANTABLE is either 'YES' (Privilege was granted WITH GRANT OPTION) or 'NO' (Privilege was not granted WITH GRANT OPTION).

- WITH_HIERARCHY is 'YES' (this is a SELECT Privilege granted WITH HIERARCHY OPTION) or 'NO' (this is a SELECT Privilege that was not granted WITH HIERARCHY OPTION) or NULL (this is not a SELECT Privilege).

If you want to restrict your code to Core SQL, do not reference INFORMATION_SCHEMA.TABLE_PRIVILEGES.

INFORMATION_SCHEMA.TRANSFORMS

This View has the following Columns:

Name	Domain	Nullable?
USER_DEFINED_TYPE_CATALOG	SQL_IDENTIFIER	no
USER_DEFINED_TYPE_SCHEMA	SQL_IDENTIFIER	no
USER_DEFINED_TYPE_NAME	SQL_IDENTIFIER	no
SPECIFIC_CATALOG	SQL_IDENTIFIER	yes
SPECIFIC_SCHEMA	SQL_IDENTIFIER	yes
SPECIFIC_NAME	SQL_IDENTIFIER	yes
GROUP_NAME	SQL_IDENTIFIER	no
TRANSFORM_TYPE	CHARACTER_DATA	no

TRANSFORMS shows the transforms on UDTs in this Catalog, where the transforms may be used by the current user.

- USER_DEFINED_TYPE_CATALOG, USER_DEFINED_TYPE_SCHEMA, USER_DEFINED_TYPE_NAME uniquely identify the UDT to which this transform applies.
- SPECIFIC_CATALOG, SPECIFIC_SCHEMA, SPECIFIC_NAME uniquely identify the SQL-invoked routine that acts as the transform function for this transform.
- GROUP_NAME is the name of the transform group.
- TRANSFORM_TYPE is either: 'TO SQL' (the transform is a to-sql function) or 'FROM SQL' (the transform is a from-sql function).

If you want to restrict your code to Core SQL, do not reference INFORMATION_SCHEMA.TRANSFORMS.

INFORMATION_SCHEMA.TRANSLATIONS

This View has the following Columns:

Name	Domain	Nullable?
TRANSLATION_CATALOG	SQL_IDENTIFIER	no
TRANSLATION_SCHEMA	SQL_IDENTIFIER	no
TRANSLATION_NAME	SQL_IDENTIFIER	no
SOURCE_CHARACTER_SET_CATALOG	SQL_IDENTIFIER	no
SOURCE_CHARACTER_SET_SCHEMA	SQL_IDENTIFIER	no
SOURCE_CHARACTER_SET_NAME	SQL_IDENTIFIER	no
TARGET_CHARACTER_SET_CATALOG	SQL_IDENTIFIER	no

Name	Domain	Nullable?
TARGET_CHARACTER_SET_SCHEMA	SQL_IDENTIFIER	no
TARGET_CHARACTER_SET_NAME	SQL_IDENTIFIER	no
TRANSLATION_DEFINITION	CHARACTER_DATA	no

TRANSLATIONS shows the Translations in this Catalog that the current user has Privileges on.

- TRANSLATION_CATALOG, TRANSLATION_SCHEMA, TRANSLATION_NAME uniquely identify a Translation that the current user may use.
- SOURCE_CHARACTER_SET_CATALOG, SOURCE_CHARACTER_SET_SCHEMA, SOURCE_CHARACTER_SET_NAME uniquely identify the Character set named in the FOR clause of the Translation definition.
- TARGET_CHARACTER_SET_CATALOG, TARGET_CHARACTER_SET_SCHEMA, TARGET_CHARACTER_SET_NAME uniquely identify the Character set named in the TO clause of the Translation definition.
- TRANSLATION_DEFINITION is a zero-length string. To date, the Standard makes no use of this field.

If you want to restrict your code to Core SQL, do not reference INFORMATION_SCHEMA.TRANSLATIONS.

INFORMATION_SCHEMA.TRIGGERED_UPDATE_COLUMNS

This View has the following Columns:

Name	Domain	Nullable?
TRIGGER_CATALOG	SQL_IDENTIFIER	no
TRIGGER_SCHEMA	SQL_IDENTIFIER	no
TRIGGER_NAME	SQL_IDENTIFIER	no
EVENT_OBJECT_CATALOG	SQL_IDENTIFIER	no
EVENT_OBJECT_SCHEMA	SQL_IDENTIFIER	no
EVENT_OBJECT_TABLE	SQL_IDENTIFIER	no
EVENT_OBJECT_COLUMN	SQL_IDENTIFIER	no

TRIGGERED_UPDATE_COLUMNS shows the Columns in this Catalog that are referenced by the explicit UPDATE trigger event Columns of a Trigger in this Catalog, where the Trigger is owned by the current user.

- TRIGGER_CATALOG, TRIGGER_SCHEMA, TRIGGER_NAME uniquely identify a Trigger with a trigger event of UPDATE. The Trigger is owned by the current user.
- EVENT_OBJECT_CATALOG, EVENT_OBJECT_SCHEMA, EVENT_OBJECT_TABLE, EVENT_OBJECT_COLUMN uniquely identify a Column that is affected by the Trigger.

INFORMATION_SCHEMA.TRIGGERS
This View has the following Columns:

Name	Domain	Nullable?
TRIGGER_CATALOG	SQL_IDENTIFIER	no
TRIGGER_SCHEMA	SQL_IDENTIFIER	no
TRIGGER_NAME	SQL_IDENTIFIER	no
EVENT_MANIPULATION	CHARACTER_DATA	yes
EVENT_OBJECT_CATALOG	SQL_IDENTIFIER	no
EVENT_OBJECT_SCHEMA	SQL_IDENTIFIER	no
EVENT_OBJECT_TABLE	SQL_IDENTIFIER	no
ACTION_ORDER	CARDINAL_NUMBER	no
ACTION_CONDITION	CHARACTER_DATA	yes
ACTION_STATEMENT	CHARACTER_DATA	no
ACTION_ORIENTATION	CHARACTER_DATA	yes
CONDITION_TIMING	CHARACTER_DATA	yes
CONDITION_REFERENCE_OLD_TABLE	SQL_IDENTIFIER	yes
CONDITION_REFERENCE_NEW_TABLE	SQL_IDENTIFIER	yes
TRIGGER_CREATED	TIME_STAMP	no

TRIGGERS shows the Triggers in this Catalog, where the Triggers are owned by the current user.

- TRIGGER_CATALOG, TRIGGER_SCHEMA, TRIGGER_NAME uniquely identify a Trigger that is owned by the current user.
- EVENT_MANIPULATION is either: 'INSERT' (the trigger event is INSERT), 'DELETE' (the trigger event is DELETE), or 'UPDATE' (the trigger event is UPDATE).
- EVENT_OBJECT_CATALOG, EVENT_OBJECT_SCHEMA, EVENT_OBJECT_TABLE uniquely identify the Table the Trigger acts on.
- ACTION_ORDER shows the ordinal position of the triggered action in the list of all Triggers on the same Table, where the Triggers have the same EVENT_MANIPULATION, CONDITION_TIMING, and ACTION_ORIENTATION values.
- ACTION_CONDITION shows the Trigger's search condition for its triggered action.
- ACTION_STATEMENT shows the Trigger's statement list for its triggered action.
- ACTION_ORIENTATION is either: 'ROW' (the trigger action is FOR EACH ROW) or 'STATEMENT' (the trigger action is FOR EACH STATEMENT).
- CONDITION_TIMING is either: 'BEFORE' (the trigger action time is BEFORE) or 'AFTER' (the trigger action time is AFTER).
- CONDITION_REFERENCE_OLD_TABLE shows the <old value correlation name> of the Trigger.
- CONDITION_REFERENCE_NEW_TABLE shows the <new value correlation name> of the Trigger.
- TRIGGER_CREATED shows the CURRENT_TIMESTAMP from the time the Trigger was created.

INFORMATION_SCHEMA.TRIGGER_COLUMN_USAGE
This View has the following Columns:

Name	Domain	Nullable?
TRIGGER_CATALOG	SQL_IDENTIFIER	no
TRIGGER_SCHEMA	SQL_IDENTIFIER	no
TRIGGER_NAME	SQL_IDENTIFIER	no
TABLE_CATALOG	SQL_IDENTIFIER	no
TABLE_SCHEMA	SQL_IDENTIFIER	no
TABLE_NAME	SQL_IDENTIFIER	no
COLUMN_NAME	SQL_IDENTIFIER	no

TRIGGER_COLUMN_USAGE shows the Columns on which Triggers in this Catalog depend, where the Triggers are owned by the current user.

- TRIGGER_CATALOG, TRIGGER_SCHEMA, TRIGGER_NAME uniquely identify a Trigger that is owned by the current user. The Trigger's trigger event is either 'INSERT' or 'DELETE'.
- TABLE_CATALOG, TABLE_SCHEMA, TABLE_NAME, COLUMN_NAME uniquely identify a Column that this Trigger depends on. The dependence is created by one of two things: either (*a*) this Column belongs to a Table named in the search condition of this Trigger's triggered action clause or (*b*) this Column, or the Table it belongs to, is referred to in a triggered SQL statement of this Trigger's definition.

If you want to restrict your code to Core SQL, do not reference INFORMATION_SCHEMA.TRIGGER_COLUMN_USAGE.

INFORMATION_SCHEMA.TRIGGER_TABLE_USAGE
This View has the following Columns:

Name	Domain	Nullable?
TRIGGER_CATALOG	SQL_IDENTIFIER	no
TRIGGER_SCHEMA	SQL_IDENTIFIER	no
TRIGGER_NAME	SQL_IDENTIFIER	no
TABLE_CATALOG	SQL_IDENTIFIER	no
TABLE_SCHEMA	SQL_IDENTIFIER	no
TABLE_NAME	SQL_IDENTIFIER	no

TRIGGER_TABLE_USAGE shows the Tables on which Triggers in this Catalog depend, where the Triggers are owned by the current user.

- TRIGGER_CATALOG, TRIGGER_SCHEMA, TRIGGER_NAME uniquely identify a Trigger that is owned by the current user.
- TABLE_CATALOG, TABLE_SCHEMA, TABLE_NAME uniquely identify a Table that this Trigger depends on. The dependence is created by one of two things: either (*a*) this Table is named in the search condition of this Trigger's triggered action clause or (*b*) this Table is referred to in a triggered SQL statement of this Trigger's definition.

If you want to restrict your code to Core SQL, do not reference INFORMATION_SCHEMA.TRIGGER_TABLE_USAGE.

INFORMATION_SCHEMA.TYPE_INFO

[NON-PORTABLE] The total number of Views in INFORMATION_SCHEMA is non-standard because the SQL Standard allows vendors to add additional Views to describe additional, implementation-defined features. [OCELOT Implementation] The OCELOT DBMS that comes with this book has one non- standard INFORMATION_SCHEMA View, called INFORMATION_SCHEMA.TYPE_INFO. The Standard defines TYPE_INFO as a temporary, make-believe Table — in order to make the CLI SQLGetTypeInfo Catalog function more comprehensible. We decided that, because TYPE_INFO is effectively a metadata Table, it makes sense to describe TYPE_INFO here rather than in our chapter on SQL/CLI Catalog functions. Though you can't simply select from TYPE_INFO with most DBMSs, you can select the same information using the CLI.

This View has the following Columns:

Name	Data Type	Nullable?
TYPE_NAME	VARCHAR(128)	no
DATA_TYPE	SMALLINT	no
COLUMN_SIZE	INTEGER	yes
LITERAL_PREFIX	VARCHAR(128)	yes
LITERAL_SUFFIX	VARCHAR(128)	yes
CREATE_PARAMS	VARCHAR(128)	yes
NULLABLE	SMALLINT	no
CASE_SENSITIVE	SMALLINT	no
SEARCHABLE	SMALLINT	no
UNSIGNED_ATTRIBUTE	SMALLINT	yes
FIXED_PREC_SCALE	SMALLINT	no
AUTO_UNIQUE_VALUE	SMALLINT	no
LOCAL_TYPE_NAME	VARCHAR(128)	yes
MINIMUM_SCALE	INTEGER	yes
MAXIMUM_SCALE	INTEGER	yes
SQL_DATA_TYPE	SMALLINT	no
SQL_DATETIME_SUB	SMALLINT	yes
NUM_PREC_RADIX	INTEGER	yes
INTERVAL_PRECISION	SMALLINT	yes

TYPE_INFO shows a description of every SQL predefined <data type> that the DBMS supports.

- TYPE_NAME shows the name of this <data type>, either: 'CHARACTER' (or 'CHAR'), 'NUMERIC', 'DECIMAL' (or 'DEC'), 'INTEGER' (or 'INT'), 'SMALLINT', 'FLOAT', 'REAL', 'DOUBLE PRECISION', 'CHARACTER VARYING' (or 'VARCHAR' or 'CHAR VARYING'), 'CLOB', 'CLOB LOCATOR',

'BIT', 'BIT VARYING', 'REF', 'DATE', 'TIME', 'TIMESTAMP', 'TIME WITH TIME ZONE', 'TIMESTAMP WITH TIME ZONE', 'INTERVAL YEAR', 'INTERVAL MONTH', 'INTERVAL DAY', 'INTERVAL HOUR', 'INTERVAL MINUTE', 'INTERVAL SECOND', 'INTERVAL YEAR TO MONTH', 'INTERVAL DAY TO HOUR', 'INTERVAL DAY TO MINUTE', 'INTERVAL DAY TO SECOND', 'INTERVAL HOUR TO MINUTE', 'INTERVAL HOUR TO SECOND' , 'INTERVAL MINUTE TO SECOND', 'BLOB', 'BLOB LOCATOR', 'ROW TYPE', 'ARRAY', 'ARRAY LOCATOR', 'BOOLEAN', 'USER-DEFINED TYPE', 'USER-DEFINED TYPE LOCATOR'. Most implementations give the name in uppercase and use the full name, e.g., 'DECIMAL' or 'INTEGER' rather than 'DEC' or 'INT'. Sometimes an SQL <data type> can map to several data types. For example, the 'NUMERIC' <data type> might also be called 'MONEY' or 'SERIAL'. In that case, it's implementation-defined whether TYPE_INFO will contain only one row or several rows to describe this <data type.

- DATA_TYPE shows the Concise Code Value for this <data type>. These values are as follows:
  - For 'CHARACTER' the code is: 1.
  - For 'NUMERIC' the code is: 2.
  - For 'DECIMAL' the code is: 3.
  - For 'INTEGER' the code is: 4.
  - For 'SMALLINT' the code is: 5.
  - For 'FLOAT' the code is: 6.
  - For 'REAL' the code is: 7.
  - For 'DOUBLE PRECISION' the code is: 8.
  - For 'CHARACTER VARYING' the code is: 12.
  - For 'BIT' the code is: 14.
  - For 'BIT VARYING' the code is: 15.
  - For 'BOOLEAN' the code is: 16.
  - For 'USER-DEFINED TYPE' the code is: 17.
  - For 'USER-DEFINED TYPE LOCATOR' the code is: 18.
  - For 'ROW TYPE' the code is: 19.
  - For 'REF' the code is: 20.
  - For 'BLOB' the code is: 30.
  - For 'BLOB LOCATOR' the code is: 31.
  - For 'CLOB' the code is: 40.
  - For 'CLOB LOCATOR' the code is: 41.
  - For 'ARRAY' the code is: 50.
  - For 'ARRAY LOCATOR' the code is: 51.
  - For 'DATE' the code is: 91.
  - For 'TIME' the code is: 92.
  - For 'TIMESTAMP' the code is: 93.
  - For 'TIME WITH TIME ZONE' the code is: 94.
  - For 'TIMESTAMP WITH TIME ZONE' the code is: 95.

- For 'INTERVAL YEAR' the code is: 101.
- For 'INTERVAL MONTH' the code is: 102.
- For 'INTERVAL DAY' the code is: 103.
- For 'INTERVAL HOUR' the code is: 104.
- For 'INTERVAL MINUTE' the code is: 105.
- For 'INTERVAL SECOND' the code is: 106.
- For 'INTERVAL YEAR TO MONTH' the code is: 107.
- For 'INTERVAL DAY TO HOUR' the code is: 108.
- For 'INTERVAL DAY TO MINUTE' the code is: 109.
- For 'INTERVAL DAY TO SECOND' the code is: 110.
- For 'INTERVAL HOUR TO MINUTE' the code is: 111.
- For 'INTERVAL HOUR TO SECOND' the code is: 112.
- For 'INTERVAL MINUTE TO SECOND' the code is: 113.

- COLUMN_SIZE shows the size of this <data type>, not including the size of the literal prefix or the literal suffix.
  - For 'CHARACTER', 'CHARACTER VARYING', and 'CLOB' the size is the maximum possible length in characters supported by the DBMS.
  - For 'NUMERIC', 'DECIMAL', 'INTEGER', 'SMALLINT', 'FLOAT', 'REAL', and 'DOUBLE PRECISION' the size is the maximum possible precision supported by the DBMS.
  - For 'BIT', 'BIT VARYING', and 'BLOB' the size is the maximum possible length in bits supported by the DBMS.
  - For 'DATE', 'TIME', 'TIMESTAMP', 'TIME WITH TIME ZONE', 'TIMESTAMP WITH TIME ZONE', and all the INTERVAL types the size is the maximum possible length in positions supported by the DBMS. 'DATE' is always 10; 'TIME' must be at least 15; 'TIMESTAMP' must be at least 26; 'TIME WITH TIME ZONE' must be at least 21; 'TIMESTAMP WITH TIME ZONE' must be at least 32; 'INTERVAL YEAR' must be at least 4; 'INTERVAL MONTH', 'INTERVAL DAY', 'INTERVAL HOUR', and 'INTERVAL MINUTE' must be at least 2; 'INTERVAL SECOND' must be at least 9; 'INTERVAL YEAR TO MONTH' must be at least 7; 'INTERVAL DAY TO HOUR', 'INTERVAL DAY TO MINUTE', and 'INTERVAL HOUR TO MINUTE' must be at least 5; 'INTERVAL DAY TO SECOND', 'INTERVAL HOUR TO SECOND', and 'INTERVAL MINUTE TO SECOND' must be at least 12.
  - For all other types the size is the null value.
- LITERAL_PREFIX shows the character string that must precede any literal of this <data type>. If no prefix string is required, LITERAL_PREFIX is NULL.
  - For 'CHARACTER', 'CHARACTER VARYING', and 'CLOB' the prefix is: ' (i.e., a single quote mark).
  - For 'BIT' and 'BIT VARYING' the prefix is: either X' or B'.
  - For 'BLOB' the prefix is X'.
  - For 'DATE' the prefix is: DATE '.
  - For 'TIME' and 'TIME WITH TIME ZONE' the prefix is: TIME '.
  - For 'TIMESTAMP' and 'TIMESTAMP WITH TIME ZONE' the prefix is: TIMESTAMP '.
  - For all the 'INTERVAL' types the prefix is: INTERVAL '.

  - For all other types the prefix is the null value.
- LITERAL_SUFFIX shows the character string that must follow any literal of this <data type>. If no suffix string is required, LITERAL_SUFFIX is NULL.
  - For 'CHARACTER', 'CHARACTER VARYING', 'CLOB', 'BIT', 'BIT VARYING', 'BLOB', 'DATE', 'TIME', 'TIME WITH TIME ZONE', 'TIMESTAMP', and 'TIMESTAMP WITH TIME ZONE' the suffix is: ' (i.e., a single quote mark).
  - For 'INTERVAL YEAR' the suffix is: ' YEAR.
  - For 'INTERVAL MONTH' the suffix is: ' MONTH.
  - For 'INTERVAL DAY' the suffix is: ' DAY.
  - For 'INTERVAL HOUR' the suffix is: ' HOUR.
  - For 'INTERVAL MINUTE' the suffix is: ' MINUTE.
  - For 'INTERVAL SECOND' the suffix is: ' SECOND.
  - For 'INTERVAL YEAR TO MONTH' the suffix is: ' YEAR TO MONTH.
  - For 'INTERVAL DAY TO HOUR' the suffix is: ' DAY TO HOUR.
  - For 'INTERVAL DAY TO MINUTE' the suffix is: ' DAY TO MINUTE.
  - For 'INTERVAL DAY TO SECOND' the suffix is: ' DAY TO SECOND.
  - For 'INTERVAL HOUR TO MINUTE' the suffix is: ' HOUR TO MINUTE.
  - For 'INTERVAL HOUR TO SECOND' the suffix is: ' HOUR TO SECOND.
  - For 'INTERVAL MINUTE TO SECOND' the suffix is: ' MINUTE TO SECOND.
  - For all other types the suffix is the null value.
- CREATE_PARAMS is a list of the names (in order, separated by commas) of size-related attributes which can be used in specifications for this <data type>. If no options exist for this <data type>, CREATE_PARAMS is NULL. The possible names are: 'LENGTH' (for length), 'PRECISION' (for numeric precision, interval leading field precision, and fractional seconds precision), or 'SCALE' (for numeric scale).
  - For 'CHARACTER', 'CHARACTER VARYING', 'CLOB', 'BIT', 'BIT VARYING', and 'BLOB', CREATE_PARAMS is 'LENGTH'.
  - For 'NUMERIC' and 'DECIMAL', CREATE_PARAMS is 'PRECISION,SCALE'.
  - For 'FLOAT', 'TIME', 'TIME WITH TIME ZONE', 'TIMESTAMP', and 'TIMESTAMP WITH TIME ZONE', CREATE_PARAMS is 'PRECISION'.
  - For 'INTERVAL YEAR', 'INTERVAL MONTH', 'INTERVAL DAY', 'INTERVAL HOUR', 'INTERVAL MINUTE', 'INTERVAL YEAR TO MONTH', 'INTERVAL DAY TO HOUR', 'INTERVAL DAY TO MINUTE', and 'INTERVAL HOUR TO MINUTE', CREATE_PARAMS is 'PRECISION'.
  - For 'INTERVAL SECOND', 'INTERVAL DAY TO SECOND', 'INTERVAL HOUR TO SECOND', and 'INTERVAL MINUTE TO SECOND', CREATE_PARAMS is 'PRECISION,PRECISION'.
  - For all other types, CREATE_PARAMS is the null value.
- NULLABLE shows whether this <data type> may contain NULLs. It is either: '0' ("false") if the <data type> may not contain NULLs, '1' ("true") if the <data type> might contain NULLs, or '2' ("nullable unknown") if it isn't known whether the <data type> might contain NULLs. In Standard SQL, NULLABLE is always '1' for all predefined <data type>s.
- CASE_SENSITIVE shows, for the 'CHARACTER', 'CHARACTER VARYING', and 'CLOB' <data type>s, whether the default collation of the <data type>'s repertoire is case sensitive. If this

is so, CASE_SENSITIVE is '1' ("true"). If this is not so, and for all other <data type>s, CASE_SENSITIVE is '0'.

- SEARCHABLE is comprised of two values and shows the type of predicates that values of this <data type> may be used with. If values based on this <data type> may be used with LIKE, the first value is: '1'; if they can't, the first value is: '0'. If values based on this <data type> may be used with ordinary predicates, the second value is: '2'; if they can't, the second value is: '0'. The two values are added together, thus SEARCHABLE is either: '0', '1', '2', or '3' for all <data type>s.
  - For 'CHARACTER', 'CHARACTER VARYING', 'CLOB', and 'BLOB', SEARCHABLE is: '3', i.e., '1' for 'works with LIKE' plus '2' for 'works with ordinary predicates'.
  - For all other predefined <data type>s, SEARCHABLE is: '2', i.e., '0' for 'doesn't work with LIKE' plus '2' for 'works with ordinary predicates'.
- UNSIGNED_ATTRIBUTE shows whether this <data type> is a signed type. It is either: '0' for a signed type, '1' for an unsigned type, or NULL for all non-numeric types.
  - For 'NUMERIC', 'DECIMAL', 'INTEGER', 'SMALLINT', 'FLOAT', 'REAL', 'DOUBLE PRECISION', and all the 'INTERVAL' types, UNSIGNED_ATTRIBUTE is: '0'.
  - For 'ARRAY LOCATOR', 'BLOB LOCATOR', 'CLOB LOCATOR', and 'USER-DEFINED TYPE LOCATOR', 'UNSIGNED_ATTRIBUTE' is: '1'.
  - For all other types, UNSIGNED_ATTRIBUTE is the null value.
- FIXED_PREC_SCALE shows whether this <data type> is an exact numeric type with a fixed precision and scale. It is: '1' ("true") for 'INTEGER' and 'SMALLINT' and '0' ("false") for all other <data type>s. (In Standard SQL, FIXED_PREC_SCALE is '0' for 'DECIMAL' and 'NUMERIC' because these <data type>s have user-specifiable precision and scale.)
- AUTO_UNIQUE_VALUE shows, for this <data type>, whether any new row is guaranteed to be unique when it is inserted; it is either: '0' ("false") or '1' ("true"). There is no Standard SQL <data type> like this — for all predefined SQL <data type>s, AUTO_UNIQUE_VALUE is: '0' — but many implementations have it, naming it something like 'SERIAL'. Watch out: just because it's unique when you INSERT, doesn't mean it remains unique after you UPDATE.
- [NON-PORTABLE] LOCAL_TYPE_NAME shows an implementation-defined "localized representation" of this <data type>'s TYPE_NAME value. This could mean that the Albanian term for 'CHARACTER VARYING' would appear here; your DBMS should output what would be appropriate in a dialog box. For Standard SQL names, LOCAL_TYPE_NAME and TYPE_NAME would usually be the same. [OCELOT Implementation] The OCELOT DBMS that comes with this book shows the same name in both the TYPE_NAME and the LOCAL_TYPE_NAME Columns for all <data type>s.
- MINIMUM_SCALE shows the minimum possible value of the scale (for <data type>s that have one) or the minimum possible value of a fractional seconds precision (for <data types> that have one). For <data type>s that have neither, MINIMUM_SCALE is NULL.
  - For 'NUMERIC', 'DECIMAL', 'INTEGER', 'SMALLINT', 'TIME', 'TIMESTAMP', 'TIME WITH TIME ZONE', 'TIMESTAMP WITH TIME ZONE', 'INTERVAL SECOND', 'INTERVAL DAY TO SECOND', 'INTERVAL HOUR TO SECOND', and 'INTERVAL MINUTE TO SECOND', MINIMUM_SCALE is: '0'.
  - For all other types, MINIMUM_SCALE is the null value.

- MAXIMUM_SCALE shows your DBMS's maximum possible value of the scale (for <data type>s that have one) or the maximum possible value of a fractional seconds precision (for <data types> that have one). For <data type>s that have neither, MAXIMUM_SCALE is NULL.
  - For 'INTEGER' and 'SMALLINT', MAXIMUM_SCALE is '0'.
  - [NON-PORTABLE] For 'NUMERIC', 'DECIMAL', 'TIME', 'TIMESTAMP', 'TIME WITH TIME ZONE', 'TIMESTAMP WITH TIME ZONE', 'INTERVAL SECOND', 'INTERVAL DAY TO SECOND', 'INTERVAL HOUR TO SECOND', and 'INTERVAL MINUTE TO SECOND', MAXIMUM_SCALE is implementation-defined. [OCELOT Implementation] The OCELOT DBMS that comes with this book shows these maximum scale values:
    - For 'NUMERIC' and 'DECIMAL', MAXIMUM_SCALE is '38'.
    - For 'TIME', 'TIMESTAMP', 'TIME WITH TIME ZONE', 'TIMESTAMP WITH TIME ZONE', 'INTERVAL SECOND', 'INTERVAL DAY TO SECOND', 'INTERVAL HOUR TO SECOND', and 'INTERVAL MINUTE TO SECOND', MAXIMUM_SCALE is '6'.
  - For all other types, MAXIMUM_SCALE is the null value.
- SQL_DATA_TYPE shows the SQL Data Type Code value. This will be the same as the DATA_TYPE value for all non-temporal <data type>s. There is a correspondence with the SQL_DESC_TYPE field of a descriptor.
  - For 'CHARACTER' the code is: '1'.
  - For 'NUMERIC' the code is: '2'.
  - For 'DECIMAL' the code is: '3'.
  - For 'INTEGER' the code is: '4'.
  - For 'SMALLINT' the code is: '5'.
  - For 'FLOAT' the code is: '6'.
  - For 'REAL' the code is: '7'.
  - For 'DOUBLE PRECISION' the code is: '8'.
  - For 'CHARACTER VARYING' the code is: '12'.
  - For 'BIT' the code is: '14'.
  - For 'BIT VARYING' the code is: '15'.
  - For 'REF' the code is: '20'.
  - For 'DATE', 'TIME', 'TIMESTAMP', 'TIME WITH TIME ZONE', and 'TIMESTAMP WITH TIME ZONE' the code is: '9'.
  - For all the 'INTERVAL' types the code is: '10'.
- SQL_DATETIME_SUB shows the SQL_DATA_TYPE subtype for the temporal <data type>s. For all the non-temporal <data type>s, this field is NULL.
  - For 'DATE' the code is: '1'.
  - For 'TIME' the code is: '2'.
  - For 'TIMESTAMP' the code is: '3'.
  - For 'TIME WITH TIME ZONE' the code is: '4'.
  - For 'TIMESTAMP WITH TIME ZONE' the code is: '5'.
  - For 'INTERVAL YEAR' the code is: '1'.
  - For 'INTERVAL MONTH' the code is: '2'.
  - For 'INTERVAL DAY' the code is: '3'.

  - For 'INTERVAL HOUR' the code is: '4'.
  - For 'INTERVAL MINUTE' the code is: '5'.
  - For 'INTERVAL SECOND' the code is: '6'.
  - For 'INTERVAL YEAR TO MONTH' the code is: '7'.
  - For 'INTERVAL DAY TO HOUR' the code is: '8'.
  - For 'INTERVAL DAY TO MINUTE' the code is: '9'.
  - For 'INTERVAL DAY TO SECOND' the code is: '10'.
  - For 'INTERVAL HOUR TO MINUTE' the code is: '11'.
  - For 'INTERVAL HOUR TO SECOND' the code is: '12'.
  - For 'INTERVAL MINUTE TO SECOND' the code is: '13'.
- NUM_PREC_RADIX shows your DBMS's radix of the precision for this <data type> (if there is one). If there is no precision, this field is NULL. For exact numeric <data type>s, the precision's radix will almost always be 10 (indeed for ODBC it must be 10), but some implementations declare that SMALLINT and INTEGER have binary radices, in which case COLUMN_SIZE would be respectively 15 and 31 (the number does not include the sign bit). For approximate numeric <data type>s, the precision's radix will usually be 2.
  - [NON-PORTABLE] For 'NUMERIC', 'DECIMAL', 'INTEGER', 'SMALLINT', 'FLOAT', 'REAL', and 'DOUBLE PRECISION', NUM_PREC_RADIX is implementation-defined. [OCELOT Implementation] The OCELOT DBMS that comes with this book shows these radix values:
    - For 'NUMERIC' and 'DECIMAL', NUM_PREC_RADIX is: '10'.
    - For 'INTEGER', 'SMALLINT', 'FLOAT', 'REAL', and 'DOUBLE PRECISION', NUM_PREC_RADIX is: '2'.
  - For all other types, NUM_PREC_RADIX is the null value.
- INTERVAL_PRECISION shows your DBMS's interval leading field precision for an INTERVAL <data type>. If this is not an INTERVAL, INTERVAL_PRECISION is NULL.
- [NON-PORTABLE] For all the 'INTERVAL' types, INTERVAL_PRECISION is implementation-defined. [OCELOT Implementation] The OCELOT DBMS that comes with this book shows these interval precision values:
  - For 'INTERVAL YEAR' and 'INTERVAL YEAR TO MONTH', INTERVAL_PRECISION is: '4'.
  - For all other 'INTERVAL' types, INTERVAL_PRECISION is: '2'.

INFORMATION_SCHEMA.USAGE_PRIVILEGES
This View has the following Columns:

Name	Domain	Nullable?
GRANTOR	SQL_IDENTIFIER	no
GRANTEE	SQL_IDENTIFIER	no
OBJECT_CATALOG	SQL_IDENTIFIER	no
OBJECT_SCHEMA	SQL_IDENTIFIER	no
OBJECT_NAME	SQL_IDENTIFIER	no
OBJECT_TYPE	CHARACTER_DATA	no

Name	Domain	Nullable?
PRIVILEGE_TYPE	CHARACTER_DATA	no
IS_GRANTABLE	CHARACTER_DATA	no

USAGE_PRIVILEGES shows the USAGE Privileges on Objects (i.e., Domains, Character sets, Collations, or Translations) in this Catalog, where the Privileges are either available to, or granted by, the current user.

- GRANTOR shows the <AuthorizationID> who granted the Privilege.
- GRANTEE shows the <AuthorizationID> who may use the Privilege. By definition, if GRANTOR isn't CURRENT_USER, then GRANTEE is either CURRENT_USER or 'PUBLIC'.
- OBJECT_CATALOG, OBJECT_SCHEMA, OBJECT_NAME, OBJECT_TYPE uniquely identify an Object in this Catalog. OBJECT_TYPE is either: 'DOMAIN', 'CHARACTER SET', 'COLLATION', or 'TRANSLATION'.
- PRIVILEGE_TYPE shows the Privilege granted: 'USAGE'.
- IS_GRANTABLE is either 'YES' (Privilege was granted WITH GRANT OPTION) or 'NO' (Privilege was not granted WITH GRANT OPTION).

If you want to restrict your code to Core SQL, do not reference INFORMATION_SCHEMA.USAGE_PRIVILEGES.

INFORMATION_SCHEMA.USER_DEFINED_TYPE_PRIVILEGES

This View has the following Columns:

Name	Domain	Nullable?
GRANTOR	SQL_IDENTIFIER	no
GRANTEE	SQL_IDENTIFIER	no
USER_DEFINED_TYPE_CATALOG	SQL_IDENTIFIER	no
USER_DEFINED_TYPE_SCHEMA	SQL_IDENTIFIER	no
USER_DEFINED_TYPE_NAME	SQL_IDENTIFIER	no
PRIVILEGE_TYPE	CHARACTER_DATA	no
IS_GRANTABLE	CHARACTER_DATA	no

USER_DEFINED_TYPE_PRIVILEGES shows the TYPE USAGE Privileges on UDTs in this Catalog, where the Privileges are either available to, or granted by, the current user.

- GRANTOR shows the <AuthorizationID> who granted the Privilege.
- GRANTEE shows the <AuthorizationID> who may use the Privilege. By definition, if GRANTOR isn't CURRENT_USER, then GRANTEE is either CURRENT_USER or 'PUBLIC'.
- USER_DEFINED_TYPE_CATALOG, USER_DEFINED_TYPE_SCHEMA, USER_DEFINED_TYPE_NAME uniquely identify a UDT in this Catalog.
- PRIVILEGE_TYPE shows the Privilege granted: 'TYPE USAGE'.
- IS_GRANTABLE is either 'YES' (Privilege was granted WITH GRANT OPTION) or 'NO' (Privilege was not granted WITH GRANT OPTION).

If you want to restrict your code to Core SQL, do not reference INFORMATION_SCHEMA.USER_DEFINED_TYPE_PRIVILEGES.

INFORMATION_SCHEMA.USER_DEFINED_TYPES
This View has the following Columns:

Name	Domain	Nullable?
USER_DEFINED_TYPE_CATALOG	SQL_IDENTIFIER	no
USER_DEFINED_TYPE_SCHEMA	SQL_IDENTIFIER	no
USER_DEFINED_TYPE_NAME	SQL_IDENTIFIER	no
CATEGORY	CHARACTER_DATA	no
IS_INSTANTIABLE	CHARACTER_DATA	no
IS_FINAL	CHARACTER_DATA	no
ORDERING_FORM	CHARACTER_DATA	no
ORDERING_CATEGORY	CHARACTER_DATA	no
ORDERING_ROUTINE_CATALOG	SQL_IDENTIFIER	yes
ORDERING_ROUTINE_SCHEMA	SQL_IDENTIFIER	yes
ORDERING_ROUTINE_NAME	SQL_IDENTIFIER	yes
REFERENCE_TYPE	CHARACTER_DATA	yes

USER_DEFINED_TYPES shows the UDTs in this Catalog that the current user has Privileges on.

- USER_DEFINED_TYPE_CATALOG, USER_DEFINED_TYPE_SCHEMA, USER_DEFINED_TYPE_NAME uniquely identify a UDT in this Catalog that the current user has Privileges on.
- CATEGORY is either 'STRUCTURED' (the UDT is a structured type) or 'DISTINCT' (the UDT is a distinct type).
- IS_INSTANTIABLE is either 'YES' (the UDT is instantiable) or 'NO' (the UDT is not instantiable).
- IS_FINAL is either 'YES' (the UDT may not have subtypes) or 'NO' (the UDT may have subtypes).
- ORDERING_FORM is either 'NONE' (UDT values can't be compared) or 'FULL' (UDT values can be compared for equality or for relative order) or 'EQUALS' (UDT values can be compared for equality only).
- ORDERING_CATEGORY is either 'RELATIVE' (UDT values can be compared with a relative routine) or 'HASH' (UDT values can be compared with a hash routine) or 'STATE' (UDT values can be compared with a state routine).
- ORDERING_ROUTINE_CATALOG, ORDERING_ROUTINE_SCHEMA, ORDERING_ROUTINE_NAME uniquely identify an ordering routine for this UDT.
- REFERENCE_TYPE is either 'SYSTEM GENERATED' (reference types are system generated) or 'USER GENERATED' (reference types are user generated) or 'DERIVED' (reference types are derived from corresponding Columns).

If you want to restrict your code to Core SQL, do not reference INFORMATION_SCHEMA.USER_DEFINED_TYPES.

INFORMATION_SCHEMA.VIEWS
This View has the following Columns:

Name	Domain	Nullable?
TABLE_CATALOG	SQL_IDENTIFIER	no
TABLE_SCHEMA	SQL_IDENTIFIER	no
TABLE_NAME	SQL_IDENTIFIER	no
VIEW_DEFINITION	CHARACTER_DATA	yes
CHECK_OPTION	CHARACTER_DATA	no
IS_UPDATABLE	CHARACTER_DATA	no

VIEWS shows the Views in this Catalog that the current user has Privileges on.

- TABLE_CATALOG, TABLE_SCHEMA, TABLE_NAME uniquely identify a View that the current user may use.
- VIEW_DEFINITION shows the query specification that defines the View. If the expression was too big to be stored, or if the current user doesn't own TABLE_SCHEMA, then VIEW_DEFINITION is NULL.
- CHECK_OPTION is either: 'CASCADED' (the View definition has a WITH CASCADED CHECK OPTION clause), 'LOCAL' (the View definition has a WITH LOCAL CHECK OPTION clause), or 'NONE' (the View definition has no CHECK OPTION clause).
- IS_UPDATABLE is either: 'YES' (the View definition simply contains an updatable query specification) or 'NO' (the View definition simply contains a query specification that isn't updatable). If IS_UPDATABLE is 'NO', then CHECK_OPTION must be 'NONE'.

INFORMATION_SCHEMA.VIEW_COLUMN_USAGE
This View has the following Columns:

Name	Domain	Nullable?
VIEW_CATALOG	SQL_IDENTIFIER	no
VIEW_SCHEMA	SQL_IDENTIFIER	no
VIEW_NAME	SQL_IDENTIFIER	no
TABLE_CATALOG	SQL_IDENTIFIER	no
TABLE_SCHEMA	SQL_IDENTIFIER	no
TABLE_NAME	SQL_IDENTIFIER	no
COLUMN_NAME	SQL_IDENTIFIER	no

VIEW_COLUMN_USAGE shows the Columns on which Views in this Catalog depend, where the Views are owned by the current user.

- VIEW_CATALOG, VIEW_SCHEMA, VIEW_NAME uniquely identify a View that is owned by the current user.
- TABLE_CATALOG, TABLE_SCHEMA, TABLE_NAME, COLUMN_NAME uniquely identify a Column which is (explicitly or implicitly) referred to in this View's query specification.

If you want to restrict your code to Core SQL, do not reference INFORMATION_SCHEMA.VIEW_COLUMN_USAGE.

INFORMATION_SCHEMA.VIEW_TABLE_USAGE
This View has the following Columns:

Name	Domain	Nullable?
VIEW_CATALOG	SQL_IDENTIFIER	no
VIEW_SCHEMA	SQL_IDENTIFIER	no
VIEW_NAME	SQL_IDENTIFIER	no
TABLE_CATALOG	SQL_IDENTIFIER	no
TABLE_SCHEMA	SQL_IDENTIFIER	no
TABLE_NAME	SQL_IDENTIFIER	no

VIEW_TABLE_USAGE shows the Tables on which Views in this Catalog depend, where the Views are owned by the current user.

- VIEW_CATALOG, VIEW_SCHEMA, VIEW_NAME uniquely identify a View that is owned by the current user.
- TABLE_CATALOG, TABLE_SCHEMA, TABLE_NAME uniquely identify a Table which is referred to in this View's query specification.

If you want to restrict your code to Core SQL, do not reference INFORMATION_SCHEMA.VIEW_TABLE_USAGE.

17

Chapter 17

SQL Schemas

The SQL Standard describes the concepts on which SQL is based in terms of Objects, such as Tables. Most of these Objects are Schema Objects; that is, they depend on some Schema. In this chapter, we'll describe SQL Schemas in detail and show you the syntax to use to create, alter, and destroy them.

Schema

A Catalog may contain one or more Schemas. An SQL Schema is a named group of SQL-data that is owned by a particular <AuthorizationID>. Schemas are dependent on some Catalog — the <Schema name> must be unique within the Catalog to which the Schema belongs — and are created, altered, and dropped using the SQL-Schema statements. The Objects that may belong to a Schema are known as Schema Objects; that is, they depend on some Schema. Every Schema Object has a name that must be unique (among Objects of its name class) within the Schema to which it belongs. The Schema Object name classes are:

- Base tables and Views.
- Domains and UDTs.
- Constraints and Assertions.
- Character sets.
- Collations.
- Translations.
- Triggers.

- SQL-server Modules.
- SQL-invoked routines.
- Roles.

A Schema may consist of zero or more of these Schema Objects. The Schema's name qualifies the names of the Objects that belong to it, and can either be explicitly stated, or a default name will be supplied by your DBMS.
A Schema is defined by a descriptor that contains five pieces of information:

1. The <Schema name> qualified by the <Catalog name> of the Catalog to which it belongs.
2. The <AuthorizationID> that owns the Schema and its Objects.
3. The name of the Schema's default Character set.
4. The specification that defines the path for the Schema's SQL-invoked routines.
5. A descriptor for every SQL Object that belongs to the Schema.

To create a Schema, use the `CREATE SCHEMA` statement. It specifies the enclosing Catalog; names the Schema; defines the Schema's default Character set, default path, and zero or more Schema Objects; and identifies the Schema's owner. To change an existing Schema, use the appropriate `CREATE` / `DROP` / `ALTER` / `GRANT` / `REVOKE` statements to adjust the Schema's Objects. To destroy a Schema, use the `DROP SCHEMA` statement.

There is a one-to-many association between Schemas and users; one <AuthorizationID> can own many Schemas. For compatibility with the ODBC qualifier structure (database.owner.object) though, we recommend that a <Schema name> be the same as the owning <AuthorizationID> and that each <AuthorizationID> be allowed to own only one Schema in a Cluster.

Schema Names

A <Schema name> identifies a Schema. The required syntax for a <Schema name> is as follows.

```
<Schema name> ::=
[ <Catalog name>. ] unqualified name
```

A <Schema name> is a <regular identifier> or a <delimited identifier> that is unique (for all Schemas) within the Catalog to which it belongs. The <Catalog name> which qualifies a <Schema name> names the Catalog to which the Schema belongs and can either be explicitly stated or a default will be supplied by your DBMS, as follows:

- If the unqualified <Schema name> is found in a Module, the default qualifier is the name of the Catalog identified in the `SCHEMA` clause or `AUTHORIZATION` clause of the `MODULE` statement that defines that Module.
- [NON-PORTABLE] If the `MODULE` statement doesn't provide an explicit <Catalog name>, or if the unqualified <Schema name> is not in a Module, the default <Catalog name> qualifier is non-standard because the SQL Standard requires implementors to define the default qualifier in such cases. Your DBMS will usually define its initial default <Catalog name> as the qualifier, but this is not required. [OCELOT Implementation] The OCELOT DBMS that comes with this book uses its initial default <Catalog name> (OCELOT) as the qualifier in such cases.

Here are some examples of <Schema name>s:

```
SCHEMA_1
-- a <Schema name>

CATALOG_1.SCHEMA_1
-- a qualified <Schema name>
```

Note that the <regular identifier> — DEFINITION_SCHEMA — may not be used as a <Schema name>.

CREATE SCHEMA Statement

The CREATE SCHEMA statement names a new Schema; defines the Schema's default Character set, default path, and zero or more Schema Objects; and identifies the Schema's owner. The required syntax for the CREATE SCHEMA statement is as follows.

```
CREATE SCHEMA <Schema name clause>
   [ DEFAULT CHARACTER SET <Character set name> ]
   [ PATH <Schema name> {,<Schema name>}... ]
   [ <Schema element list> ]

   <Schema name clause> ::=
   <Schema name> |
   AUTHORIZATION <AuthorizationID> |
   <Schema name> AUTHORIZATION <AuthorizationID>

     <Schema element list> ::=
      CREATE DOMAIN statement(s) |
      CREATE TABLE statement(s) |
      CREATE VIEW statement(s) |
      CREATE ASSERTION statement(s) |
      CREATE CHARACTER SET statement(s) |
      CREATE COLLATION statement(s) |
      CREATE TRANSLATION statement(s) |
      CREATE TRIGGER statement(s) |
      CREATE TYPE statement(s) |
      CREATE PROCEDURE statement(s) |
      CREATE FUNCTION statement(s) |
      CREATE ROLE statement(s) |
      GRANT statement(s)
```

CREATE SCHEMA defines a new Schema.

- The <Schema name clause> names the Schema and identifies the <AuthorizationID> that owns it. A <Schema name> that includes an explicit <Catalog name> qualifier belongs to the Catalog named. A <Schema name> that does not include an explicit <Catalog name> qualifier belongs to the SQL-session default Catalog. The <Schema name> must be unique within the Catalog that contains it.

The <Schema name clause> may contain either a <Schema name>, an AUTHORIZATION clause, or both. For example, this SQL statement creates a Schema named BOB, owned by <AuthorizationID> BOB:

```
CREATE SCHEMA bob AUTHORIZATION bob;
```

If <Schema name clause> doesn't include an explicit <Schema name>, the <Schema name> defaults to the value of the AUTHORIZATION clause's <AuthorizationID>. For example, this SQL statement also creates a Schema named BOB, owned by <AuthorizationID> BOB:

```
CREATE SCHEMA AUTHORIZATION bob;
```

If <Schema name clause> doesn't include an explicit AUTHORIZATION clause, the <AuthorizationID> that owns the Schema defaults to the <Module AuthorizationID> (or if there is no <Module AuthorizationID>, it defaults to the current SQL-session <AuthorizationID>). Note: The current <AuthorizationID> for the creation of a Schema is normally the <AuthorizationID> named in the AUTHORIZATION clause. If you omit the AUTHORIZATION clause, then the current <AuthorizationID> for the creation of the Schema is the SQL-session <AuthorizationID>.

TRAP: The <AuthorizationID> associated with CREATE SCHEMA does not become the current <AuthorizationID> for subsequent SQL statements, nor does the <Schema name> become the default Schema. Consider these three SQL statements:

```
CONNECT TO 'cluster_1' AS 'connection_1' USER 'bob';
-- establishes the SQL-session <AuthorizationID> to be BOB

CREATE SCHEMA sam AUTHORIZATION sam
   CREATE TABLE sam_1 (column1 INT);
-- creates a Schema named SAM, that contains one Table, both owned by <Authori-
zationID> SAM

INSERT INTO sam_1 VALUES (10);
-- fails because the Table can't be found
```

In this example, although the CREATE SCHEMA statement did create the Table we're trying to INSERT into, it did not change the default <AuthorizationID> from BOB to SAM, nor did it change the default Schema from BOB to SAM. Thus, the INSERT fails because the DBMS doesn't recognize a Table named SAM_1 associated with <AuthorizationID> BOB in Schema BOB.

The optional DEFAULT CHARACTER SET clause names the Schema's default Character set; the Character set assumed for all of this Schema's Column and Domain definitions when they don't include an explicit Character set specification. For example, all three of these SQL statements create a Schema that contains a Domain whose values must belong to the LATIN1 Character set:

```
CREATE SCHEMA bob AUTHORIZATION bob
      DEFAULT CHARACTER SET INFORMATION_SCHEMA.LATIN1
   CREATE DOMAIN char_domain AS CHAR(12)
      CHARACTER SET INFORMATION_SCHEMA.LATIN1;

CREATE SCHEMA bob AUTHORIZATION bob
      DEFAULT CHARACTER SET INFORMATION_SCHEMA.ISO8BIT
   CREATE DOMAIN char_domain AS CHAR(12)
      CHARACTER SET INFORMATION_SCHEMA.LATIN1;

CREATE SCHEMA bob AUTHORIZATION bob
      DEFAULT CHARACTER SET INFORMATION_SCHEMA.LATIN1
   CREATE DOMAIN char_domain AS CHAR(12);
```

(In the second example, the explicit CHARACTER SET clause in CREATE DOMAIN overrides the Schema's default Character set specification.)

[NON-PORTABLE] If CREATE SCHEMA doesn't include an explicit DEFAULT CHARACTER SET clause, the Schema's default Character set is non-standard because the SQL Standard requires implementors to define it. [OCELOT Implementation] The OCELOT DBMS that comes with this book always uses INFORMATION_SCHEMA.ISO8BIT as the default Character set.

The optional PATH clause names the Schema's default path; the path used to qualify unqualified <Routine name>s that identify <routine invocation>s that are part of this CREATE SCHEMA statement. You must include the name of the Schema being created in the PATH clause and if you include multiple names, all of the Schemas named must belong to the same Catalog.

[NON-PORTABLE] If CREATE SCHEMA doesn't include an explicit PATH clause, the Schema's path specification must include the new Schema's name, but is otherwise non-standard because the SQL Standard requires implementors to define a path specification for the Schema.

[NON-PORTABLE] Whether or not you may create a Schema is non-standard because the SQL Standard requires implementors to define what Privilege (if any) allows an <AuthorizationID> to execute CREATE SCHEMA. [OCELOT Implementation] The OCELOT DBMS that comes with this book allows any <AuthorizationID> to execute CREATE SCHEMA.

The only separator between the SQL statements that make up the <Schema element list> is white space. For example, this is a single SQL statement that creates a Schema:

```
CREATE SCHEMA sam AUTHORIZATION sam
      DEFAULT CHARACTER SET INFORMATION_SCHEMA.LATIN1
   CREATE DOMAIN dept_domain AS CHAR(3)
   CREATE TABLE department (dept dept_domain, name1 CHAR(10))
   CREATE TABLE employee (empname CHAR(20), dept dept_domain)
   GRANT SELECT ON department TO bob;
```

If you want to restrict your code to Core SQL, don't use a `DEFAULT CHARACTER SET` clause or a `PATH` clause in your `CREATE SCHEMA` statements and don't include any of the following in your <Schema element list>: `CREATE ASSERTION` statements, `CREATE CHARACTER SET` statements, `CREATE COLLATION` statements, `CREATE DOMAIN` statements, `CREATE TRANSLATION` statements, `CREATE TYPE` statements, `CREATE ROLE` statements, or `GRANT` statements to Roles.

DROP SCHEMA Statement

The `DROP SCHEMA` statement destroys an entire Schema. The required syntax for the `DROP SCHEMA` statement is as follows.

```
DROP SCHEMA <Schema name> {RESTRICT | CASCADE}
```

The <Schema name> must identify an existing Schema whose owner is either the current <AuthorizationID> or a Role that the current <AuthorizationID> may use. That is, only the <AuthorizationID> that owns the Schema may drop it.

The effect of `DROP SCHEMA` <Schema name> `RESTRICT`, e.g.,

```
DROP SCHEMA catalog_1.schema_1 RESTRICT;
```

is that the Schema named `CATALOG_1.SCHEMA_1` will be destroyed, providing that (*a*) it doesn't contain any Objects, (*b*) it isn't referred to in any SQL routine, and (*c*) it isn't referred to in the path specification of any other Schema. That is, `RESTRICT` ensures that only an empty Schema, on which nothing else depends, can be destroyed.

The effect of `DROP SCHEMA` <Schema name> `CASCADE`, e.g.,

```
DROP SCHEMA catalog_1.schema_1 CASCADE;
```

is that the Schema named `CATALOG_1.SCHEMA_1` will be destroyed — as will all of the Schema's Objects (with a `CASCADE` drop behaviour for Tables, Views, Domains, Collations, Roles, UDTs, and SQL-invoked routines), and any SQL routines (with a `CASCADE` drop behaviour) and path specifications that depend on this Schema.

If you want to restrict your code to Core SQL, don't use the `DROP SCHEMA` statement.

18

Chapter 18

SQL Tables and Views

In this chapter, we'll describe SQL Tables in detail and show you the syntax to use to create, alter, and destroy them.

A Schema may contain zero or more Tables. An SQL Table is a collection of rows; one header-row of <Column name>s and zero or more rows of data values. (We'll use the word *row* to mean a row of data values from now on; note that a row of a Table is an instance of an SQL <row type>.) Tables are dependent on some Schema — the <Table name> must be unique within the Schema to which the Table belongs — and are created, altered, and dropped using standard SQL statements. The Objects that may belong to a Table are Columns and Table Constraints; they depend on some Table. The number of Columns in a Table is the degree of the Table. The number of rows in a Table is the cardinality of the Table. An empty Table has a cardinality of zero.

Tables contain data (as atomic values at the intersection of each row and <Column name>) about a specific entity. Each row of the Table describes a single occurrence of that entity. Rows are the smallest unit of Table insertion and deletion. Table rows are unordered, but an order can be imposed on them during retrieval. Table Columns are ordered, from left to right — their ordinal position matches the ordinal position of the <Column definition> in the Table's definition.

SQL supports two types of Tables: the physically existent, named *Base table* and the derived, named *View*. We use the word *Table* to mean both Base tables and Views throughout this book. (SQL also supports the concept of unnamed derived tables — these are tables derived from a <query expression>, so we won't discuss them here.)

Base Table

A Base table is either a Schema Object (that is, its definition is part of a Schema definition) or a Module Object (that is, its definition is part of a Module definition). Schema Base tables are known as created Base tables and may be either persistent or temporary. Module Base tables are known as declared temporary Tables and may only be temporary.

There are two kinds of Schema Base tables: the persistent Base table and the temporary Base table.

A persistent Base table is autonomous; it exists in its own right — that is, physically-stored records that directly represent the Table actually exist on some data storage device. A persistent Base table contains rows of persistent SQL-data and can be accessed from multiple SQL-sessions. You create persistent Base tables with the `CREATE TABLE` statement.

A temporary Base table is an SQL-session-dependent Table; it can't be accessed from any other SQL-session. There are two types of temporary Base tables: the global temporary Base table (which can be accessed from any SQL-client Module in a single SQL-session) and the created local temporary Base table (which can be accessed only from the SQL-client Module that refers to it). Temporary Base tables are always empty when an SQL-session begins; their rows are all deleted either at the end of a transaction or at the end of the SQL-session (depending on the Table's definition). You create global temporary Base tables with `CREATE GLOBAL TEMPORARY TABLE` and created local temporary Base tables with `CREATE LOCAL TEMPORARY TABLE`.

There is one kind of Module Base table — the declared local temporary Base table.

- The declared local temporary Base table is a named Table defined (with the `DECLARE TABLE` statement) in an SQL-client Module. It is effectively materialized the first time it is referenced in an SQL-session and it persists until that SQL-session ends. A declared local temporary Base table can only be accessed by <externally-invoked procedure>s within the SQL-client Module that contains the Table's declaration. Temporary Base tables are always empty when an SQL-session begins and are always emptied when the SQL-session ends.

Subtables and Supertables

In SQL3, a Table can be defined as a direct subtable of a supertable, using the optional `CREATE TABLE ... UNDER` clause. This is an object/relational feature; for details, see Chapter 27 "User-Defined Types."

A Base table is defined by a descriptor that contains 13 pieces of information:

1. The <Table name> qualified by the <Schema name> of the Schema to which it belongs.
2. The Base table's type: either persistent Base table, global temporary Base table or created local temporary Base table (for Schema Base tables), or (only for Module Base tables) declared local temporary Base table.
3. The degree of the Table — the number of Columns that belong to the Table.
4. A descriptor for every Column that belongs to the Table.

5. A descriptor for every Constraint that belongs to the Table.
6. [Obscure Rule] The name of the structured type (if any) associated with the Table.
7. [Obscure Rule] Whether the Table's rows have the `REF VALUE` characteristic.
8. [Obscure Rule] The name of the Table's direct supertable, if any.
9. [Obscure Rule] A list (possibly empty) of the names of the Table's direct subtables.
10. [Obscure Rule] The Table's row type.
11. [Obscure Rule] A non-empty set of the Table's functional dependencies.
12. [Obscure Rule] A non-empty set of the Table's candidate keys.
13. [Obscure Rule] An identification of the Table's preferred candidate key (this may or may not be defined as the Table's `PRIMARY KEY`).

The data contained in a Base table is always updatable via the SQL statements `INSERT`, `UPDATE`, and `DELETE`. To create a Base table, use the `CREATE TABLE` statement (either as a stand-alone SQL statement or within a `CREATE SCHEMA` statement). `CREATE TABLE` specifies the enclosing Schema, names the Table, and defines the Table's Columns and Constraints. To change an existing Base table, use the `ALTER TABLE` statement. To destroy a Base table, use the `DROP TABLE` statement. To declare a temporary Table for a Module, use the `DECLARE TABLE` statement.

View

A *View* is a named, derived (or "virtual") Table; it doesn't physically exist, although its definition is persistent. Instead, a View is logically derived from one or more existing Tables and can be thought of as another way of looking at the presented data. Views are either updatable or read-only, depending on their definitions. A View is defined by a descriptor that contains ten pieces of information:

1. The <Table name> qualified by the <Schema name> of the Schema to which the View belongs.
2. The degree of the View; the number of Columns that are part of the View.
3. A descriptor for every Column that is part of the View.
4. The <query expression> that defines how the View is derived.
5. Whether or not the View is updatable.
6. Whether the View definition includes a `CHECK OPTION` clause and, if so, whether the clause is `CHECK OPTION CASCADED` or `CHECK OPTION LOCAL`.
7. [Obscure Rule] The name of the structured type (if any) associated with the View.
8. [Obscure Rule] Whether the View's rows have the `REF VALUE` characteristic.
9. [Obscure Rule] The name of the View's direct supertable, if any.
10. [Obscure Rule] A list (possibly empty) of the names of the Views's direct subtables.

Depending on the View's definition, the data shown through a View may be updatable via the SQL statements `INSERT`, `UPDATE`, and `DELETE`. To create a View, use the `CREATE VIEW` statement (either as a stand-alone SQL statement or within a `CREATE SCHEMA` statement). `CREATE VIEW` specifies the enclosing Schema, names the View and its Columns, and defines the <query expression> that determines how the View is derived and updated. To change an existing View, destroy and then redefine it. To destroy a View, use the `DROP VIEW` statement.

Table Names

A <Table name> identifies a Base table or a View. With an SQL statement, you can represent a Table with a <Correlation name> — usually to prevent ambiguity and to make your SQL statement easier to read.

<Table name>

The required syntax for a <Table name> is either:

```
<Table name> ::=
[ <Schema name>. ] unqualified name
```

or, for a declared LOCAL TEMPORARY Table only:

```
<Table name> ::=
[ MODULE. ] unqualified name
```

A <Table name> is a <regular identifier> or a <delimited identifier> that is unique (for all Base tables and Views) within the Schema to which it belongs. The <Schema name> that qualifies a <Table name> names the Schema to which the Table belongs and can either be explicitly stated or a default will be supplied by your DBMS, as follows:

- If a <Table name> in a CREATE SCHEMA statement isn't qualified, the default qualifier is the name of the Schema you're creating.
- If the unqualified <Table name> is found in any other SQL statement in a Module, the default qualifier is the name of the Schema identified in the SCHEMA clause or AUTHORIZATION clause of the MODULE statement which defines that Module.

Here are some examples of <Table name>s:

```
TABLE_1
-- a <Table name>

SCHEMA_1.TABLE_1
-- a simple qualified <Table name>

CATALOG_1.SCHEMA_1.TABLE_1
-- a fully qualified <Table name>

MODULE.TABLE_1
-- a declared LOCAL TEMPORARY <Table name>
```

<Correlation name>

A <Correlation name> (or alias) identifies a variable that ranges over some Table; that is, a variable whose only permitted values are the rows of a given Table. A <Correlation name> is evaluated as an alternate <Table name> and is normally used to prevent ambiguity in complex SQL statements. Once you've defined a <Correlation name> for a Table, you must use it to refer to that Table throughout the entire SQL statement — for example, whenever you would normally use the <Table name> to qualify a <Column name>, use the <Correlation name> instead. Because a <Correlation name> is associated with a Table only in the context in which you define it, you can use the same <Correlation name>, for any Table, in other SQL statements. The required syntax for a <Correlation name> is as follows.

```
<Correlation name> ::=
unqualified name
```

A <Correlation name> is a <regular identifier> or a <delimited identifier> that is unique within the Table it represents for the period of an SQL statement. The scope of a <Correlation name> is either a SELECT statement (or some other query form), a Trigger definition, or both (correlation scopes may be nested). Here is an example of a <Correlation name>:

```
CORRELATION_1
-- a <Correlation name>
```

The syntax required to define a <Correlation name> for a Table is as follows.

```
<Table reference> [ AS ] <Correlation name>
   [ (derived <Column name> [ {,derived <Column name> }... ]) ]
```

A <Table reference> is a reference to some Table — this is usually a named Table (that is, a Base table or a View) but could also be an unnamed Table (e.g., the result of a join, a subquery, or a query expression). Most often, a <Table reference> is just a <Table name> and we'll use only that form for now. Here are two equivalent examples (the <keyword> AS is noise and can be omitted):

```
SELECT First.column_1, Second.column_1
   FROM Table_1 AS First, Table_1 AS Second
   WHERE First.column_2 = Second.column_2;

SELECT First.column_1, Second.column_1
   FROM Table_1 First, Table_1 Second
   WHERE First.column_2 = Second.column_2;
```

These SQL statements execute a join of TABLE_1 with itself, over matching COLUMN_2 values. What the SELECTs are doing is looking at all possible pairs of TABLE_1 rows and retrieving the COLUMN_1 values from each row where the COLUMN_2 values are equal to one another. To do so, the DBMS must be able to refer to two rows of TABLE_1 at once — and this requires that it be able to distinguish between the two references. The <Correlation name> allows the DBMS to do this; it calls the one row FIRST, and the other row SECOND, just like the <Correlation name>s specified in the SQL statements. To further clarify the request, each <Column name> specified is qualified with the appropriate <Correlation name> so that the DBMS knows which Column belongs to which of the rows it's looking at.

Because a <Table reference> can also refer to an unnamed Table that results from a query, it's sometimes necessary (or at least useful) to be able to name the Columns of the <Table reference>

result. The optional derived <Column name> list with the AS <Correlation name> clause allows you to do this. Here's an example:

```
SELECT joined_col_1, joined_col_2
FROM   (Table_1 NATURAL JOIN Table_2) AS Joined_Table
       (joined_col_1, joined_col_2, joined_col_3, joined_col_4)
...
```

In this example, Table_1 NATURAL JOIN Table_2 is a <Table reference> that evaluates to the Table resulting from the NATURAL JOIN operation — and JOINED_TABLE is the <Correlation name> for that result. The Columns of JOINED_TABLE are explicitly given the names JOINED_COL_1, JOINED_COL_2, JOINED_COL_3, and JOINED_COL_4 — and these are the names that are used to refer to those Columns throughout the SQL statement. If you use this option, you must specify a unique, unqualified name for every Column of the result Table, even if you're never going to refer to some of the Columns again.

Column

A Table may contain one or more Columns. An SQL Column is a collection of similar data values that describe the same attribute of the entity that is fully described by the Table that owns the Column. Columns are dependent on some Table — the <Column name> must be unique within the Table to which the Column belongs — and are created, altered, and dropped using standard SQL statements. The Objects that may belong to a Column are Column Constraints; they depend on some Column.

Columns are ordered within the Table they belong to, from left to right — their ordinal position matches the ordinal position of the <Column definition> in the Table's definition. All Columns have a nullability characteristic; it determines (*a*) whether an attempt to INSERT the null value into the Column will fail and (*b*) whether a SELECT from the Column can ever return the null value. A Column's nullability characteristic is "possibly nullable" unless one of these situations apply:

- A Column's nullability characteristic is "known not nullable" if a non-deferrable Constraint/Assertion on the Column evaluates to Column IS NOT NULL or if the Column is based on a Domain and a non-deferrable Constraint/Assertion on that Domain evaluates to VALUE IS NOT NULL.
- A Column's nullability characteristic is "known not nullable" if a non-deferrable Constraint on the Column is a PRIMARY KEY Constraint.

A Column is defined by a descriptor that contains eight pieces of information:

1. The <Column name> qualified by the <Table name> of the Table it belongs to. (It is possible to have a Column with a default name, rather than a name you defined for it yourself. In this case, the Column's descriptor also indicates that the name is an implementation-dependent, or default, name.)
2. The ordinal position of the Column in its Table. (A Table may contain only one referenceable Column; it must be the first Column in the Table.)
3. The Column's <data type> specification, including its name, length, precision, and scale, as applicable (or, if the Column is based on a Domain, the <Domain name>).

4. The name of the Character set to which the Column's set of values must belong (for character string types).
5. The name of the Column's default Collation. (This is the Collation that may be used to compare a character string Column's values in the absence of an explicit `COLLATE` clause.)
6. [Obscure Rule] Whether or not the Column is a self-referencing Column (for `REF` types).
7. The Column's default value (if any).
8. The Column's nullability characteristic: either "known not nullable" or "possibly nullable."

To create a Column, use a <Column definition> in a `CREATE TABLE` or `ALTER TABLE` statement. To change or destroy an existing Column, use the `ALTER TABLE` statement.

Column Names

A <Column name> identifies a Column. The SQL Standard does not consider a <Column name> to be a qualified name but, in practice, <Column name>s are often qualified to prevent ambiguity in complex SQL statements. This practice is called a <Column reference>. A qualified <Column name> is not allowed in a <Column definition> — that is, a <Column reference> may not be used to identify a Column in a `CREATE TABLE` or an `ALTER TABLE` statement.

<Column name>

The required syntax for a <Column name> is as follows.

```
<Column name> ::=
unqualified name
```

A <Column name> is a <regular identifier> or a <delimited identifier> that is unique (for all Columns) within the Table to which it belongs. Here is an example of a <Column name>:

```
COLUMN_1
-- a <Column name>
```

<Column reference>

The required syntax for a <Column reference>, valid only outside of a <Column definition> is either:

```
<Column reference> ::=
[ Table specification. ] <Column name>

   Table specification ::=
   <Table name> |
   <Correlation name>
```

or, for a declared `LOCAL TEMPORARY` Table only:

```
<Column reference> ::=
MODULE.<Table name>.<Column name>
```

A <Column reference> is a <Column name> qualified by a Table specification, or by MODULE.<Table name>. The Table specification which qualifies a <Column name> identifies the Table to which the Column belongs and is either that Table's name or a <Correlation name> that identifies that Table. If you omit the Table specification from a <Column reference>, it will default to the <Table name> of the Table that owns the Column. Here are some examples of <Column reference>s:

```
TABLE_1.COLUMN_1
-- a <Column reference> with a <Table name>

CORRELATION_1.COLUMN_1
-- a <Column reference> with a <Correlation name>

MODULE.TABLE_1.COLUMN_1
-- a <Column reference> for a declared LOCAL TEMPORARY Table
```

CREATE TABLE Statement

The CREATE TABLE statement names a new Base table and defines the Table's Columns and Constraints. The required syntax for the CREATE TABLE statement is as follows.

```
CREATE [ {GLOBAL TEMPORARY | LOCAL TEMPORARY} ] TABLE <Table name>
   <table contents source>
   [ ON COMMIT {PRESERVE ROWS | DELETE ROWS} ]

   <table contents source> ::=
   (<table element list>) |
   OF <UDT name> [ UNDER <supertable name> ] [ (<table element list>) ]

   <table element list> ::=
   <table element> [ {,<table element>}... ]

      <table element> ::=
      <Column definition> |
      <Table Constraint> |
      LIKE <Table name> |
      <Column name> WITH OPTIONS <column option list> |
      REF IS <Column name>
             {SYSTEM GENERATED | USER GENERATED | DERIVED}

             <Table Constraint> ::=
             [ CONSTRAINT <Constraint name> ]
             Constraint_type
             [ <constraint attributes> ]
```

```
<column option list> ::=
[ <scope clause> ]
[ <default clause> ]
[ <Column Constraint>... ]
[ COLLATE <Collation name> ]
```

CREATE TABLE defines a new persistent Base table. CREATE GLOBAL TEMPORARY TABLE defines a new global temporary Base table. CREATE LOCAL TEMPORARY TABLE defines a new created local temporary Base table.

- The <Table name> identifies the Table and the Schema to which it belongs. A <Table name> that includes an explicit <Schema name> qualifier belongs to the Schema named. A <Table name> that does not include an explicit <Schema name> qualifier belongs to the SQL-session default Schema. The <Table name> must be unique (for all Base tables and Views) within the Schema that contains it.

If CREATE TABLE is part of a CREATE SCHEMA statement, the <Table name>, (if explicitly qualified) must include the <Schema name> of the Schema being created; that is, it isn't possible to create a Base table belonging to a different Schema from within CREATE SCHEMA. For example, this SQL statement will not return an error because the <Table name> will default to include the qualifying <Schema name>:

```
CREATE SCHEMA bob
   CREATE TABLE Table_1 (column_1 SMALLINT);
   -- creates a Table called BOB.TABLE_1 in Schema BOB
```

The following SQL statement will not return an error either because the <Table name> explicitly includes a qualifying <Schema name> that matches the name of the Schema being created:

```
CREATE SCHEMA bob
   CREATE TABLE bob.Table_1 (column_1 SMALLINT);
   -- creates a Table called BOB.TABLE_1 in Schema BOB
```

But this SQL statement will return an error because the <Table name> explicitly includes a qualifying <Schema name> that is different from the name of the Schema being created:

```
CREATE SCHEMA bob
   CREATE TABLE sam.Table_1 (column_1 SMALLINT);
  -- tries to create a Table belonging to Schema SAM inside Schema BOB; illegal
syntax
```

[Obscure Rule] In effect, a temporary Table does not exist until it is invoked during an SQL-session. Once invoked, it will only be visible to the SQL-session (or the Module) that invoked it — that is, the temporary Table will not be visible to other users. At the end of the SQL-session, all temporary Tables invoked during the SQL-session are dropped. Because temporary Tables are materialized only when invoked, the Schema they belong to is actually defined by your DBMS.

- If you're creating a temporary Table with CREATE GLOBAL TEMPORARY TABLE, the <Table name> may not be explicitly qualified. Because a global temporary Table is distinct within an SQL-session, the Schema it belongs to is a Schema determined by your DBMS — in effect, it fixes a qualifying <Schema name> for the Table based on the Schema in which the global temporary Table is defined, coupled with the DBMS's name for the SQL-session in which you invoke that Table.

- If you're creating a temporary Table with `CREATE LOCAL TEMPORARY TABLE`, the <Table name> may not be explicitly qualified. Because a local temporary Table is distinct within an SQL-client Module within an SQL-session, the Schema it belongs to is a Schema determined by your DBMS. In effect, it fixes a qualifying <Schema name> for the Table based on the Schema in which the global temporary Table is defined, coupled with the DBMS's name for the SQL-session in which you invoke that Table, coupled with the DBMS's name for the SQL-client Module that refers to that Table.

If `CREATE TABLE` is executed as a stand-alone SQL statement, the current <AuthorizationID> must either be the owner of the Schema to which this new Table belongs or the Schema's owner must be a Role that the current <AuthorizationID> may use. That is, only the owner of a Schema can create Tables for that Schema. In addition to creating a Table, `CREATE TABLE` also causes the SQL special grantor, `"_SYSTEM"`, to grant grantable `INSERT`, `SELECT`, `UPDATE`, `DELETE`, `TRIGGER`, and `REFERENCES` Privileges on the new Table, as well as grantable `SELECT`, `INSERT`, `UPDATE`, and `REFERENCES` Privileges on every Column in the new Table, to the Schema owner <AuthorizationID> (i.e., the <AuthorizationID creating the Table).

<table contents source clause>

The <table contents source> clause defines the structure of the Table's contents; it tells you what sort of data the Table contains. This clause is either a list of elements, such as Column and Table Constraint definitions, or an `OF` clause that defines the UDT structure that makes up the Table. Every <table element list> has to contain at least one <Column definition>.

[Obscure Rule] If `CREATE TABLE` includes the `OF` clause, then <UDT name> must identify a structured type. If the `OF` clause also includes the (optional) <table element list>, the list (*a*) may not contain a `LIKE` clause and (*b*) may contain only one <table element> that is a <Column definition>; it must define a Column with a `REF` <data type> that specifies `VALUES ARE SYSTEM GENERATED`. The optional `UNDER` sub-clause in the `OF` clause identifies the direct supertable of the Table being created, if any. The supertable named must belong to the same Schema that will contain this new Table. (The Schema owner <AuthorizationID> must have the `UNDER` Privilege on the supertable.) The new Table is a direct subtable of its direct supertable. (The effect of `CREATE TABLE` on the new Table's supertable is that its name is added to the list of direct subtables in the supertable's definition.) If you add the `UNDER` sub-clause to a `CREATE TABLE` statement: (*a*) the structured type identified by <UDT name> must be a direct subtype of the structured type of the direct supertable of the new Table, (*b*) your Table definition may not include a `PRIMARY KEY` Constraint, (*c*) the supertable of the new Table must include a `UNIQUE` Constraint that constrains a Column with a nullability characteristic of "known not nullable," and (*d*) the Schema owner's <AuthorizationID> is granted grantable `SELECT`, `UPDATE`, and `REFERENCES` Privileges for every inherited Column of the new Table. (The grantor of these Privileges is the SQL special grantor, `"_SYSTEM"`.) Note that if the direct supertable of the new Table is a referenceable Base table, then this new Table is also a referenceable Base table. In this case, your `OF` clause (if it contains a <table element list>) may not include a <Column definition>. If any <table element> contains a <scope clause> the Table referred to therein must be either (*a*) a persistent Table, if CREATE TABLE contains no <table scope>, (*b*) a GLOBAL TEMPORARY Base table if you're creating a GLOBAL TEMPORARY Base table, or (*c*) a created LOCAL TEMPORARY Base table if you're creating a LOCAL TEMPORARY Base table. For further details, refer to our chapter on User-defined Types.

The common form of CREATE TABLE uses a parenthesized <table element list> as its <table contents source> clause. A <table element> is either a <Column definition> (see "<Column definition>" on page 362), a <Table Constraint> (see Chapter 20 "SQL Constraints and Assertions"), a LIKE clause, or a <column options> clause. Multiple <table element>s must be separated by commas.

The effect of CREATE TABLE <Table name> (<Column definition>,<Column definition>), e.g.,

```
CREATE TABLE Table_1 (
   column_1 SMALLINT,
   column_2 DATE);
```

is to create a Table, called TABLE_1, that contains two Columns called COLUMN_1 and COLUMN_2. At least one Column must be defined in a <table element list>. The row type of the new Table is the set of pairs (<Column name>, <data type>) defined for the Table.

The effect of CREATE TABLE <Table name> (<Column definition>,<Table Constraint>), e.g.,

```
CREATE TABLE Table_1 (
   column_1 SMALLINT,
   CONSTRAINT constraint_1 PRIMARY KEY(column_1));
```

is to create a Table, called TABLE_1, that contains one Column called COLUMN_1, and one <Table Constraint> that defines COLUMN_1 as the Table's primary key. Zero or more <Table Constraint>s may be defined in a <table element list>. If the new Table is a temporary Base table, then all Tables referred to in the new Table's <Table Constraint>s must also be temporary Base tables.

The effect of CREATE TABLE <Table name> (LIKE <Table name>) is to create a Table whose <Column definitions>s are copied from another Table. In the LIKE clause, <Table name> identifies the Table whose <Column definition>s you want to copy into the new Table. For example, this SQL statement creates a Table in the usual manner:

```
CREATE TABLE Table_1 (
   column_1 SMALLINT,
   column_2 DATE,
   column_3 CHAR(8),
   CONSTRAINT constraint_1 CHECK (column_1 BETWEEN 50 AND 5000));
```

And the following SQL statement uses the LIKE clause to create another Table with the same <Column definition>s:

```
CREATE TABLE Table_2 (LIKE Table_1);
```

The result is a Table, called TABLE_2, whose structure will be exactly as if it had been defined with this SQL statement:

```
CREATE TABLE Table_2 (
   column_1 SMALLINT,
   column_2 DATE,
   column_3 CHAR(8));
```

Note that the <Table Constraint> from TABLE_1's definition is not recopied into TABLE_2's definition; the LIKE clause copies only <Column definition>s. However, because a <Column Constraint> is effectively replaced by a <Table Constraint> in a Table's definition, the LIKE clause also won't copy any <Column Constraint>s from the existing Table into the new Table. For example, for these two SQL statements,

```
CREATE TABLE Table_1 (
   column_1 SMALLINT NOT NULL,
   column_2 DATE,
   column_3 CHAR(8));

CREATE TABLE Table_2 (LIKE Table_1);
```

the result in the first case is a Table called TABLE_1 whose structure will be exactly as if it had been defined with the following SQL statement:

```
CREATE TABLE Table_1 (
   column_1 SMALLINT,
   column_2 DATE,
   column_3 CHAR(8)
   CONSTRAINT CHECK (column_1 IS NOT NULL));
```

and thus, the result in the second case is a Table called TABLE_2 whose structure will be exactly as if it had been defined with this SQL statement:

```
CREATE TABLE Table_2 (
   column_1 SMALLINT,
   column_2 DATE,
   column_3 CHAR(8));
```

If CREATE TABLE includes a LIKE clause, the current <AuthorizationID> must have the SELECT Privilege on the Table named.

The effect of CREATE TABLE <Table name> (<Column definition,<Column name> WITH OPTIONS <column option list>) is to create a Table containing one or more Columns whose definitions are further outlined by the <column option>(s) chosen.

Temporary Tables

If you're creating a temporary Table, you may also use the ON COMMIT clause to specify whether you want the Table to be emptied whenever a COMMIT statement is executed. If you omit the ON COMMIT clause from CREATE TEMPORARY TABLE, it defaults to ON COMMIT DELETE ROWS. For example, these two SQL statements are equivalent:

```
CREATE GLOBAL TEMPORARY TABLE Table_1 (
   column_1 SMALLINT);

CREATE GLOBAL TEMPORARY TABLE Table_1 (
   column_1 SMALLINT)
   ON COMMIT DELETE ROWS;
```

Based on this Table definition, the effect of these two SQL statements:

```
INSERT INTO Table_1 (column_1)
VALUES(10);

COMMIT;
```

is that TABLE_1 is first materialized and has data inserted into it, and then the rows are deleted. That is, at COMMIT time, your DBMS effectively executes this SQL statement:

```
DELETE FROM Table_1;
```

because the definition of TABLE_1 states that the Table is to be emptied at COMMIT. On the other hand, the effect of these three SQL statements:

```
CREATE GLOBAL TEMPORARY TABLE Table_1 (
   column_1 SMALLINT)
   ON COMMIT PRESERVE ROWS;

INSERT INTO Table_1 (column_1)
VALUES(10);

COMMIT;
```

is that TABLE_1 is created, materialized, and has data inserted into it and then the rows are committed. That is, at COMMIT time, your DBMS does not delete the rows, since TABLE_1's definition explicitly says not to. (The rows will, however, be deleted at the end of the SQL-session.)

If you want to restrict your code to Core SQL, don't create any temporary Base tables, don't use a LIKE clause as a <table element>, don't use an OF clause as a <table element>, and don't add a <column scope clause> to any CREATE TABLE statement.

<Column definition>

A <Column definition> is used to create or alter a Column of a Base table. Used in a CREATE TABLE or an ALTER TABLE statement, it names a Column and defines the Column's <data type>, default value and Constraints. The required syntax for a <Column definition> is:

```
<Column definition> ::=
unqualified <Column name> { <data type> | <Domain name> }
[ <reference scope check> ]
[ DEFAULT default value ]
[ <Column Constraint> list ]
[ COLLATE <Collation name> ]

   <Column Constraint> list ::=
   <Column Constraint> [ <Column Constraint> ]

      <Column Constraint> ::=
      [ CONSTRAINT <Constraint name> ]
      Constraint_type
      [ <constraint attributes> ]

   <reference scope check> ::=
   REFERENCES ARE [ NOT ] CHECKED
   [ ON DELETE <reference scope check action> ]

      <reference scope check action> ::= RESTRICT | SET NULL
```

A <Column definition> defines a new Column for a Base table. The <Column name> identifies the Column and the Table to which it belongs. A <Column name> in a <Column definition> may not be qualified; it belongs to the Table named in the enclosing CREATE TABLE or ALTER TABLE statement. The <Column name> must be unique within the Table that contains it.

<data type>

A Column must be defined to accept a certain type of data. This is done in one of two ways: you can either define a Column with a <data type> specification or you can define it as being based on a Domain. If you base a Column on a Domain, your current <AuthorizationID> must have the USAGE Privilege on that Domain. The Column's specified <data type> (or the <data type> of the Domain it is based on) constrains the values that can be accepted by the Column. The <data type> specification includes length, precision, and scale as applicable. Valid <data type>s are: INT, SMALLINT, NUMERIC(p,s), DECIMAL(p,s), FLOAT(p), REAL, DOUBLE PRECISION, BIT(l), BIT VARYING(l), BLOB(l), CHAR(l), NCHAR(l), VARCHAR(l), NCHAR VARYING(l), CLOB(l), NCLOB(l), DATE, TIME(p), TIME(p) WITH TIME ZONE, TIMESTAMP(p), TIMESTAMP(p) WITH TIME ZONE, INTERVAL <interval qualifier>, BOOLEAN, ARRAY, ROW, and REF.

The effect of the syntax CREATE TABLE <Table name> (<Column name> <data type>) is to define a Column with a <data type> specification. For example, this SQL statement creates a Table with a Column that has a <data type> of DECIMAL(9,2):

```
CREATE TABLE Table_1 (
column_1 DEC(9,2));
```

The effect of the syntax CREATE TABLE <Table name> (<Column name> <Domain name>) is to define a Column based on a Domain. For example, the effect of these SQL statements is also a Table with a Column that has a <data type> of DECIMAL(9,2):

```
CREATE DOMAIN domain_1 AS DEC(9,2);

CREATE TABLE Table_1 (
   column_1 domain_1);
```

[Obscure Rule] If the <data type> of a Column is CHAR, VARCHAR, or CLOB, the Character set that the Column's values must belong to is determined as follows:

- If the <Column definition> contains a <data type> specification that includes a CHARACTER SET clause, the Column's Character set is the Character set named. Your current <AuthorizationID> must have the USAGE Privilege on that Character set.
- If the <Column definition> does not include a <data type> specification, but the Column is based on a Domain whose definition includes a CHARACTER SET clause, the Column's Character set is the Character set named.
- If the <Column definition> does not include any CHARACTER SET clause at all — either through a <data type> specification or through a Domain definition — the Column's Character set is the Character set named in the DEFAULT CHARACTER SET clause of the CREATE SCHEMA statement that defines the Schema to which the Column belongs.

For example, the effect of these two SQL statements:

```
CREATE SCHEMA bob AUTHORIZATION bob
   DEFAULT CHARACTER SET INFORMATION_SCHEMA.LATIN1;

CREATE TABLE Table_1 (
   column_1 CHAR(10));
```

is to create a Table, with one Column, in Schema BOB. The Column's set of valid values are fixed length character strings, exactly 10 characters long, all of whose characters must be found in the INFORMATION_SCHEMA.LATIN1 Character set — the Schema's default Character set.

The effect of these two SQL statements:

```
CREATE SCHEMA bob AUTHORIZATION bob
   DEFAULT CHARACTER SET INFORMATION_SCHEMA.LATIN1;

CREATE TABLE Table_1 (
   column_1 CHAR(10) CHARACTER SET INFORMATION_SCHEMA.SQL_CHARACTER);
```

is to create the same Table with one difference; this time, its Column's values must consist only of characters found in the INFORMATION_SCHEMA.SQL_CHARACTER Character set — the explicit Character set specification in CREATE TABLE constrains the Column's set of values. The Schema's default Character set does not.

[Obscure Rule] If the <data type> of a Column is CHAR, VARCHAR, CLOB, NCHAR, NCHAR VARYING, or NCLOB, and your <Column definition> does not include a COLLATE clause, the Column has a coercibility attribute of COERCIBLE — but if your <Column definition> includes a COLLATE clause, the Column has a coercibility attribute of IMPLICIT. In either case, the Column's default Collation is determined as follows:

- If the <Column definition> includes a COLLATE clause, the Column's default Collation is the Collation named. Your current <AuthorizationID> must have the USAGE Privilege on that Collation.
- If the <Column definition> does not include a COLLATE clause, but does contain a <data type> specification that includes a COLLATE clause, the Column's default Collation is the Collation named. Your current <AuthorizationID> must have the USAGE Privilege on that Collation.
- If the <Column definition> does not include a COLLATE clause, but the Column is based on a Domain whose definition includes a COLLATE clause, the Column's default Collation is the Collation named.
- If the <Column definition> does not include any COLLATE clause at all — either explicitly, through a <data type> specification, or through a Domain definition — the Column's default Collation is the default Collation of the Column's Character set.

[Obscure Rule] If the <data type> of a Column is REF(UDT), your current <AuthorizationID> must have the USAGE Privilege on that UDT. If the <data type> of a Column includes REF with a <scope clause>, your <Column definition> must also include a <reference scope check> clause, to indicate whether references are to be checked or not (don't add a <reference scope check> clause under any other circumstances). In this case, you may also add the optional <reference scope check action> clause to indicate the action to be taken when the Column is the subject of a DELETE statement. If you omit the <reference scope check action> clause, it defaults to ON DELETE RESTRICT.

- If a Column is defined with REFERENCES ARE CHECKED and a <scope clause> is included in the <Column definition>, then there is an implied DEFERRABLE INITIALLY IMMEDIATE Constraint on the new Column which checks that the Column's values are also found in the system-generated Column of the Table named in the <scope clause>. In this case, if the <reference scope check action> is SET NULL then, prior to deleting any rows from the Table that owns this Column, your DBMS will *(a)* execute a SET CONSTRAINT statement that sets the implied Constraint's constraint check time to DEFERRED, *(b)* DELETE the rows as required, *(c)* set the value of the system-generated Column in the Table named in the <scope clause> to NULL, for each row that matched the deleted rows, and *(d)* execute a SET CONSTRAINT statement that sets the implied Constraint's constraint check time to IMMEDIATE.

DEFAULT Clause

The optional DEFAULT clause defines the Column's default value; the value to insert whenever this Column is the target of an INSERT statement that doesn't include an explicit value for it. The DEFAULT options are: DEFAULT <literal>, DEFAULT CURRENT_DATE, DEFAULT CURRENT_TIME(p), DEFAULT CURRENT_TIMESTAMP(p), DEFAULT LOCALTIME(p), DEFAULT LOCALTIMESTAMP(p), DEFAULT USER, DEFAULT CURRENT_USER, DEFAULT SESSION_USER, DEFAULT SYSTEM_USER, DEFAULT CURRENT_PATH, DEFAULT ARRAY[], DEFAULT ARRAY??(??), and DEFAULT NULL (see "<default clause>" on page 367). The DEFAULT clause is optional whether or not the Column is based on a Domain that has a defined default value, so a Column's default value is determined as follows:

- If a <Column definition> that contains a <data type> specification omits the DEFAULT clause, the Column has no default value.
- If a <Column definition> that contains a <data type> specification includes the DEFAULT clause, the Column's default value is the default value specified — that is, the syntax CREATE TABLE <Table name> (<Column name> DEFAULT default value) defines a Column with an explicit default value. For example, this SQL statement creates a Table with a Column whose default value is the <character string literal> 'bobby':

```
CREATE TABLE Table_1 (
   column_1 CHAR(5) DEFAULT 'bobby');
```

- If a Column is based on a Domain and the <Column definition> omits the DEFAULT clause, the Column's default value is the Domain's default value. If the Domain has no defined default value, then the Column has no default value either. For example, the effect of these two SQL statements is to define a Column whose default value is the <character string literal> 'bobby' — taken from the Domain that the Column is based on:

```
CREATE DOMAIN domain_1 AS
   CHAR(5) DEFAULT 'bobby';

CREATE TABLE Table_1 (
   column_1 domain_1);
```

If a Column is based on a Domain and the <Column definition> includes the DEFAULT clause, the Column's default value is the default value specified — even if the Domain has a defined default value. The <Column definition>'s DEFAULT clause always overrides any default value defined for the Domain that a Column is based on. For example, the effect of these two SQL statements is to define a Column whose default value is the <character string literal> 'bobby' — despite the fact that the Domain that the Column is based on has a default value that is the <character string literal> 'sammy':

```
CREATE DOMAIN domain_1 AS
   CHAR(5) DEFAULT 'sammy';

CREATE TABLE Table_1 (
   column_1 domain_1 DEFAULT 'bobby');
```

<Column Constraint>s

The optional <Column Constraint> list clause is used to define zero or more <Constraint>s on the Column; the Constraint rules will restrict the Column's set of valid values — see Chapter 20 "SQL Constraints and Assertions." (If the Column is based on a Domain, the Column's set of valid values is restricted by both the Domain's Constraints and the Column's Constraints.) All <Constraint name>s must be unique within the Schema that the Column belongs to. The syntax `CREATE TABLE <Table name> (<Column name> <data type> <Column Constraint>, <Column name> <Domain name> <Column Constraint>)` defines Columns whose definitions include a <Column Constraint>. Here is an example:

```
CREATE TABLE Table_1 (
   column_1 SMALLINT NOT NULL,
   column_2 domain_1 PRIMARY KEY NOT DEFERRABLE);
   -- column_1 excludes null values and column_2 is the Table's primary key
```

The syntax `CREATE TABLE <Table name> (<Column name> <data type> DEFAULT default value <Column Constraint>, <Column name> <Domain name> DEFAULT default value <Column Constraint>)` also defines Columns whose definitions include a <Column Constraint>. Here is an example:

```
CREATE TABLE Table _1 (
   column_1 SMALLINT DEFAULT 100
      CONSTRAINT constraint_1 PRIMARY KEY NOT DEFERRABLE,
   column_2 domain1 DEFAULT 'bobby'
      CONSTRAINT constraint_2 CHECK (column_2 IS NOT NULL);
   -- column_1 is the Table's primary key and column_2 excludes null values
```

A <Column Constraint> is valid only in a <Column definition> because, once defined, <Column Constraint>s logically become <Table Constraint>s of the Table to which the Column belongs. To change or drop a <Column Constraint>, or to add a <Column Constraint> to a Table once `CREATE TABLE` has been executed, use the `ALTER TABLE` statement.

If you want to restrict your code to Core SQL, don't add a `COLLATE` clause to your <Column definition>s, don't base your Columns on Domains, don't name your <Column Constraint>s, and don't define a <Column Constraint> with a <referential triggered action>.

<default clause>

A <default clause> defines the default value for a Column, a Domain, or an attribute of a UDT. The required syntax for a <default clause> is as follows.

```
<default clause> ::=
DEFAULT default value

   default value ::=
   <literal> |
   USER |
   CURRENT_USER |
   SESSION_USER |
   SYSTEM_USER |
   CURRENT_PATH |
   CURRENT_DATE |
   CURRENT_TIME[(p)] |
   CURRENT_TIMESTAMP[(p)] |
   LOCALTIME[(p)] |
   LOCALTIMESTAMP[(p)] |
   ARRAY[] |
   ARRAY??(??) |
   NULL
```

The default value of an Object is the data value that will be inserted into the Object whenever it is the target of an INSERT statement that does not provide an explicit data value for that Object. If the definition of an Object does not include a <default clause>, no default value is assigned to it — so when the Object is the target of an INSERT statement that does not provide an explicit data value for it, your DBMS will INSERT a null value. (If the Object doesn't allow nulls, the INSERT will, of course, fail.) The <data type> of a default value must match the Object's <data type> (i.e., the default value and the Object's <data type> must be mutually assignable).

- If the <data type> of an Object is a <reference type>, the <default clause> must be DEFAULT NULL.
- If the <data type> of an Object is a <collection type>, the <default clause> must be DEFAULT NULL or DEFAULT ARRAY[] or DEFAULT ARRAY??(??), or DEFAULT <literal>.

If a <default clause> is DEFAULT <literal>, the value represented by the <literal> is the target Object's default value. Here are some examples of <default clause>s with a <literal> as the default value:

```
CREATE DOMAIN domain_1 AS NCHAR(5) DEFAULT N'sammy';

CREATE TABLE Table_1 (column_1 VARCHAR(6) DEFAULT 'bob');
```

```
CREATE DOMAIN domain_1 AS BIT VARYING(4) DEFAULT B'0010';

CREATE TABLE Table_1 (column_1 BIT(16) DEFAULT X'4E2C');
   -- If the target Object has a BIT <data type> and the length of your <lit-
eral> is less than the defined length of the Object, your DBMS will return the
SQLSTATE warning 01008 "warning-implicit zero-bit padding."

CREATE DOMAIN domain_1 AS SMALLINT DEFAULT 100;

CREATE TABLE Table_1 (column_1 REAL DEFAULT 15000);

CREATE DOMAIN domain_1 AS DATE DEFAULT DATE '1994-07-15';

CREATE TABLE Table_1 (
   column_1 INTERVAL MONTH DEFAULT INTERVAL '03' MONTH);

CREATE DOMAIN domain_1 AS BOOLEAN DEFAULT FALSE;
```

If a <default clause> is DEFAULT USER, DEFAULT CURRENT_USER, DEFAULT SESSION_USER, or DEFAULT SYSTEM_USER, the value returned by the function is the target Object's default value. In this case, the target Object must have a character string <data type> with a defined length of at least 128 characters and must belong to the SQL_TEXT Character set. Here are some examples of <default clause>s with a <niladic user function> as the default value:

```
CREATE DOMAIN domain_1 AS
   CHAR(128) CHARACTER SET SQL_TEXT DEFAULT CURRENT_USER;

CREATE TABLE Table_1 (
   column_1 VARCHAR(256) CHARACTER SET SQL_TEXT DEFAULT SESSION_USER);
```

If a <default clause> is DEFAULT CURRENT_PATH, the value returned by the function is the target Object's default value. In this case, the target Object must have a character string <data type> with a defined length of at least 1,031 characters and must belong to the SQL_TEXT Character set. Here are some examples of <default clause>s with CURRENT_PATH as the default value:

```
CREATE DOMAIN domain_1 AS
   CHAR(1031) CHARACTER SET SQL_TEXT DEFAULT CURRENT_PATH;

CREATE TABLE Table_1 (
   column_1 VARCHAR(2000) CHARACTER SET SQL_TEXT
   DEFAULT CURRENT_PATH);
```

If a <default clause> is DEFAULT CURRENT_DATE, DEFAULT CURRENT_TIME[(p)], DEFAULT CURRENT_TIMESTAMP[(p)], DEFAULT LOCALTIME[(p)], or DEFAULT LOCALTIMESTAMP[(p)], the value returned by the function is the target Object's default value. In this case, the target Object must have a datetime <data type> that matches the function's <data type>. Here are some examples of <default clause>s with a <datetime value function> as the default value:

```
CREATE DOMAIN domain_1 AS
   DATE DEFAULT CURRENT_DATE;

CREATE TABLE Table_1 (
   column_1 TIME WITH TIME ZONE DEFAULT CURRENT_TIME);

CREATE DOMAIN domain_1 AS
   TIMESTAMP(4) DEFAULT CURRENT_TIMESTAMP(4);

CREATE TABLE Table_1 (
   column_1 TIME(4) DEFAULT LOCALTIME(4));
```

If a <default clause> is `DEFAULT ARRAY[]` or `DEFAULT ARRAY??(??)`, an empty array value is the target <collection type>'s default value. Here is an example of a <default clause> with an empty array as the default value:

```
CREATE DOMAIN domain_1 AS
   INT ARRAY[3] DEFAULT ARRAY[];
```

If a <default clause> is `DEFAULT NULL`, the null value is the target Object's default value. (The Object can't, of course, have a `NOT NULL` Constraint.) Here is an example of a <default clause> with a null value as the default value:

```
CREATE TABLE Table_1 (
   column_1 CHAR(15) DEFAULT NULL);
```

[Obscure Rule] If a <default clause> that is part of an SQL-Schema statement defines a default value that can't be represented in `INFORMATION_SCHEMA` without truncation, your DBMS will return the `SQLSTATE warning 0100B` "`warning-default value too long for information schema.`"

If you want to restrict your code to Core SQL, don't use `DEFAULT CURRENT_PATH` when defining a <default clause>.

ALTER TABLE Statement

The `ALTER TABLE` statement changes a Base table's definition. The required syntax for the `ALTER TABLE` statement is as follows.

```
ALTER TABLE <Table name> <alter table action>

   <alter table action> ::=
   ADD [ COLUMN ] <Column definition> |
   ALTER [ COLUMN ] <Column name> SET DEFAULT default value |
```

```
ALTER [ COLUMN ] <Column name> DROP DEFAULT |
ALTER [ COLUMN ] <Column name> ADD SCOPE <Table name> |
ALTER [ COLUMN ] <Column name> DROP SCOPE {RESTRICT | CASCADE} |
DROP [ COLUMN ] <Column name> {RESTRICT | CASCADE} |
ADD <Table Constraint> |
DROP CONSTRAINT <Constraint name> {RESTRICT | CASCADE}
```

The <Table name> must identify an existing Base table whose owner is either the current <AuthorizationID> or a Role that the current <AuthorizationID> may use. That is, only the <AuthorizationID> that owns the Table may alter it. `ALTER TABLE` can be used to change a persistent Base table, a `GLOBAL TEMPORARY` Base table, or a created `LOCAL TEMPORARY` Base table — but you can't use it to change a declared `LOCAL TEMPORARY` Base table.

ADD [COLUMN] Clause

The effect of `ALTER TABLE` <Table name> `ADD [COLUMN]` <Column definition>, e.g.,

```
ALTER TABLE Table_1 ADD COLUMN
column_1 SMALLINT DEFAULT 150
   CONSTRAINT constraint_1 NOT NULL NOT DEFERRABLE;
```

is that the Table named will increase in size by one Column; the Column defined by the <Column definition>. The <keyword> `COLUMN` in the `ADD [COLUMN]` clause is noise and can be omitted. For example, these two SQL statements are equivalent:

```
ALTER TABLE Table_1 ADD COLUMN
   column_1 SMALLINT DEFAULT 150;

ALTER TABLE Table_1 ADD
   column_1 SMALLINT DEFAULT 150;
```

Adding a new Column to a Table has a four-fold effect:

1. The degree (i.e., the number of Columns) of the Table is increased by 1; the new Column's ordinal position in the Table is the new degree of the Table.
2. Every <AuthorizationID> that has a `SELECT`, `UPDATE`, `INSERT`, or `REFERENCES` Privilege on the Table receives a matching set of Privileges on the new Column. The grantor of the new Privilege(s) is the same as the grantor of the previous Privileges(s) and so is the grantability of the new Privilege(s).
3. The value of the new Column for every existing row of the Table is set to its default value.
4. The Column is added to the Column list of every `UPDATE` Trigger event for all Triggers that act on the Table. However, adding a new Column to a Table has no effect on any existing View definition or Constraint definition that refers to the Table because implicit <Column name>s in these definitions are replaced by explicit <Column name>s the first time the View or Constraint is evaluated.

ALTER [COLUMN] ... SET DEFAULT Clause

The effect of ALTER TABLE <Table name> ALTER [COLUMN] <Column name> SET DEFAULT default value, e.g.,

```
ALTER TABLE Table_1 ALTER COLUMN
   column_1 SET DEFAULT 200;
```

is that the default value of the Column named will be changed. (You can use this version of ALTER TABLE either to add a default value to a <Column definition> or to change a Column's existing default value.) The <keyword> COLUMN in the ALTER [COLUMN] clause is noise and can be omitted. For example, these two SQL statements are equivalent:

```
ALTER TABLE Table_1 ALTER COLUMN
   column_1 SET DEFAULT CURRENT_TIME;

ALTER TABLE Table_1 ALTER
   column_1 SET DEFAULT CURRENT_TIME;
```

The ALTER [COLUMN] ... SET DEFAULT options are: DEFAULT <literal>, DEFAULT CURRENT_DATE, DEFAULT CURRENT_TIME(p), DEFAULT CURRENT_TIMESTAMP(p), DEFAULT LOCALTIME(p), DEFAULT LOCALTIMESTAMP(p), DEFAULT USER, DEFAULT CURRENT_USER, DEFAULT SESSION_USER, DEFAULT SYSTEM_USER, DEFAULT CURRENT_PATH, DEFAULT ARRAY[], DEFAULT ARRAY??(??), and DEFAULT NULL — See "<default clause>" on page 367.

ALTER [COLUMN] ... DROP DEFAULT Clause

The effect of ALTER TABLE <Table name> ALTER [COLUMN] <Column name> DROP DEFAULT, e.g.,

```
ALTER TABLE Table_1 ALTER COLUMN
   column_1 DROP DEFAULT;
```

is that the default value of the Column named will be removed from the <Column definition>. (You'll get a syntax error if the Column's definition doesn't include a default value.) The <keyword> COLUMN in the ALTER [COLUMN] clause is noise and can be omitted. For example, these two SQL statements are equivalent:

```
ALTER TABLE Table_1 ALTER COLUMN
   column_1 DROP DEFAULT;

ALTER TABLE Table_1 ALTER
   column_1 DROP DEFAULT;
```

ALTER [COLUMN] ... ADD SCOPE Clause

The effect of ALTER TABLE <Table name> ALTER [COLUMN] <Column name> ADD SCOPE <Table name>, e.g.,

```
ALTER TABLE Table_2 ALTER COLUMN
   column_1 ADD SCOPE Table_1;
```

is that a non-empty scope is added to the <Column definition> of the Column named. This version of ALTER TABLE can only be used (*a*) for Columns with a REF(UDT) <data type>, where the <reference type> descriptor includes an empty scope and (*b*) where the Column named is not the referenceable Column of its Table. (The Table named in the SCOPE clause must, of course, be a referenceable Base table whose structured type is the same as the structured type of the referenced UDT.) The <keyword> COLUMN in the ALTER [COLUMN] clause is noise and can be omitted. For example, these two SQL statements are equivalent:

```
ALTER TABLE Table_3 ALTER COLUMN
   column_1 ADD SCOPE Table_1;

ALTER TABLE Table_3 ALTER
   column_1 ADD SCOPE Table_1;
```

ALTER [COLUMN] ... DROP SCOPE Clause

The effect of ALTER TABLE <Table name> ALTER [COLUMN] <Column name> DROP SCOPE RESTRICT, e.g.,

```
ALTER TABLE Table_2 ALTER COLUMN
   column_1 DROP SCOPE RESTRICT;
```

is that the SCOPE clause in the definition of the Column named becomes empty, provided that no impacted dereference operation is contained in an SQL routine, in a View definition, in a Constraint or Assertion definition, or in the triggered action of a Trigger definition. (An impacted dereference operation is a <dereference operation> that operates on the Column named, a <method reference> that operates on the Column named, or a <reference resolution> that operates on the Column named.) That is, RESTRICT ensures that only a scope with no dependent Objects can be made empty. If the Column is operated on by any impacted dereference operation, ALTER TABLE ... DROP SCOPE RESTRICT will fail.

The effect of ALTER TABLE <Table name> ALTER [COLUMN] <Column name> DROP SCOPE CASCADE, e.g.,

```
ALTER TABLE Table_2 ALTER COLUMN
   column_1 DROP SCOPE CASCADE;
```

is that the SCOPE clause in the definition of the Column named becomes empty and that all Objects which contain an impacted dereference operation for the Column are also dropped, with the CASCADE drop behaviour (except for Assertions, where this is not applicable). This version of ALTER TABLE can only be used (*a*) for Columns with a REF(UDT) <data type>, where the <reference type> descriptor includes a SCOPE clause and (*b*) where the Column named is not the referenceable Column of its Table. The <keyword> COLUMN in the ALTER [COLUMN] clause is noise and can be omitted. For example, these two SQL statements are equivalent:

```
ALTER TABLE Table_2 ALTER COLUMN
   column_1 DROP SCOPE RESTRICT;

ALTER TABLE Table_2 ALTER
   column_1 DROP SCOPE RESTRICT;
```

DROP [COLUMN] Clause

The effect of ALTER TABLE <Table name> DROP [COLUMN] <Column name> RESTRICT, e.g.,

```
ALTER TABLE Table_1 DROP COLUMN
   column_1 RESTRICT;
```

is that the Column named is removed from the definition of the Table that owns it, provided that the Column is not referred to in any View definition, SQL routine, Trigger definition, or in any Constraint or Assertion definition (with one exception) — and, if the Column is the system-generated Column of its Table, provided that the Table is not named in any SCOPE clause. That is, RESTRICT ensures that only a Column with no dependent Objects can be destroyed. If the Column is used by any other Object, ALTER TABLE ... DROP COLUMN RESTRICT will fail. (Note: A Column referred to in a <Table Constraint> of the Table that owns the Column can be dropped despite the RESTRICT <keyword> if it is the only Column on which the <Table Constraint> operates.) The Column named may not be the only Column in its Table because a Table must always contain at least one Column. If the Table is a typed Base table, the Column named must be the Table's referenceable Column.

The effect of ALTER TABLE <Table name> DROP [COLUMN] <Column name> CASCADE, e.g.,

```
ALTER TABLE Table_1 DROP COLUMN
   column_1 CASCADE;
```

is that the Column named is removed from the definition of the Table that owns it and that all Objects which are dependent on the Column are also dropped. The <keyword> COLUMN in the DROP [COLUMN] clause is noise and can be omitted. For example, these two SQL statements are equivalent:

```
ALTER TABLE Table_1 DROP COLUMN
   column_1 RESTRICT;

ALTER TABLE Table_1 DROP
   column_1 RESTRICT;
```

Dropping a Column from a Table has a six-fold effect:

1. The degree (i.e., the number of Columns) of the Table is decreased by 1; the ordinal position of each Column that followed this Column in the Table's definition is adjusted accordingly.

2. The INSERT, UPDATE, SELECT, and REFERENCES Privileges on the Column are revoked (by the SQL special grantor, "_SYSTEM") from the <AuthorizationID> that owns the Column's Table with a CASCADE drop behaviour, so that the same Privileges are also revoked from all other <AuthorizationID>s.
3. Any Trigger whose definition explicitly includes the Column is dropped and any UPDATE Trigger whose definition includes the Column only implicitly is changed so that it no longer operates on that Column.
4. Any View, Constraint, Assertion, or SQL routine whose definition includes the Column is dropped with a CASCADE drop behaviour.
5. If the Column is the system-generated Column of its Table, the Table's definition is changed so that it no longer shows the Table to be a referenceable Base table and the Table is removed from every SCOPE clause that includes it.
6. The data in the Column is destroyed.

ADD <Table Constraint> Clause

The effect of ALTER TABLE <Table name> ADD <Table Constraint>, e.g.,

```
ALTER TABLE Table_1 ADD CONSTRAINT
   constraint_1 CHECK(column_1 IS NOT NULL) NOT DEFERRABLE;
```

is that one <Table Constraint> is added to the definition of the Table named — see the section "<Table Constraint> and <Column Constraint>" on page 408 in Chapter 20.

DROP CONSTRAINT Clause

The effect of ALTER TABLE <Table name> DROP CONSTRAINT <Constraint name> RESTRICT, e.g.,

```
ALTER TABLE Table_1 DROP CONSTRAINT constraint_1 RESTRICT;
```

is that the Constraint named is removed from the definition of the Table that owns it, provided that the Constraint is not used by any SQL routine and provided that no other Constraint and no View are dependent on the Constraint. (A FOREIGN KEY Constraint is dependent on the UNIQUE or PRIMARY KEY Constraint that names its referenced Columns and a View is dependent on a Constraint if (*a*) it's a grouped View that includes a Column which isn't also referred to in a set function and (*b*) if the Constraint is needed to conclude that there is a known functional dependency between the group and the Column named.) That is, RESTRICT ensures that only a Constraint with no dependent Objects can be dropped. If the Constraint is used by any other Object, ALTER TABLE ... DROP CONSTRAINT will fail.

The effect of ALTER TABLE <Table name> DROP CONSTRAINT <Constraint name> CASCADE, e.g.,

```
ALTER TABLE Table_1 DROP CONSTRAINT constraint_1 CASCADE;
```

is that the Constraint named is removed from the definition of the Table that owns it and that all dependent Constraints, Views, and SQL routines are also dropped with a CASCADE drop behaviour. (Note: If the dropped Constraint caused one or more Columns to have the "known not nullable" nullability characteristic, then the affected Columns' nullability characteristic becomes "possibly nullable" unless some other Constraint also constrains them to non-null values.)

If you want to restrict your code to Core SQL, don't use ALTER TABLE to drop a Column from a Table, to change a <Column definition> using any of the available options, to add a Constraint to a Table, or to drop a Constraint from a Table.

DROP TABLE Statement

The DROP TABLE statement destroys a Base table. The required syntax for the DROP TABLE statement is as follows.

```
DROP TABLE <Table name> {RESTRICT | CASCADE}
```

DROP TABLE destroys a Base table and its data. The <Table name> must identify an existing Base table whose owner is either the current <AuthorizationID> or a Role that the current <AuthorizationID> may use. That is, only the <AuthorizationID> that owns the Table may drop it. DROP TABLE can be used to drop a persistent Base table, a GLOBAL TEMPORARY Base table or a created LOCAL TEMPORARY Base table, but you can't use it to drop a declared LOCAL TEMPORARY Base table.

The effect of DROP TABLE <Table name> RESTRICT, e.g.,

```
DROP TABLE Table_1 RESTRICT;
```

is that the Table named is destroyed, provided that the Table *(a)* has no subtables, *(b)* is not referred to in any View definition, Assertion definition, Trigger definition, or SQL routine, *(c)* is not referred to in any <Table Constraint> that isn't owned by this Table, and *(d)* doesn't fall within the scope of any other Table or an SQL parameter. That is, RESTRICT ensures that only a Table with no dependent Objects can be destroyed. If the Table is used by any other Object, DROP TABLE ... RESTRICT will fail.

The effect of DROP TABLE <Table name> CASCADE, e.g.,

```
DROP TABLE Table_1 CASCADE;
```

is that the Table named is destroyed.

Successfully destroying a Table has a five-fold effect:

1. The Base table named (and all the data it contains) is destroyed.
2. All subtables of the Table are dropped with a CASCADE drop behaviour.
3. For the Table's supertable, all superrows of the Table's rows are deleted and the Table is removed from the supertable's list of direct subtables.
4. All Privileges held on the Table by the <AuthorizationID> that owns it are revoked (by the SQL special grantor, "_SYSTEM") with a CASCADE revoke behaviour, so that all Privileges held on the Table by any other <AuthorizationID> are also revoked.
5. All SQL routines, Views, Constraints, Assertions, and Triggers that depend on the Table are dropped with a CASCADE drop behaviour.

If you want to restrict your code to Core SQL, don't use the CASCADE drop behaviour for your DROP TABLE statements.

CREATE VIEW Statement

The CREATE VIEW statement names a new View and defines the query which, when evaluated, determines the rows of data that are shown in the View. The required syntax for the CREATE VIEW statement is as follows.

```
CREATE [ RECURSIVE ] VIEW <Table name>
[ (<Column name> [ {,<Column name>} ...) ] ] |
[ OF <UDT name> [ UNDER <supertable name> ]
     [ REF is <Column name>
             {SYSTEM GENERATED | USER GENERATED | DERIVED} ]
     [ <Column name> WITH OPTIONS SCOPE <Table name> ] ]
AS <query expression>
[ WITH [ {CASCADED | LOCAL} ] CHECK OPTION ]
```

CREATE VIEW defines a new derived Table, or View.

- The <Table name> identifies the View and the Schema that it belongs to. A <Table name> that includes an explicit <Schema name> qualifier belongs to the Schema named. A <Table name> that does not include an explicit <Schema name> qualifier belongs to the SQL-session default Schema. The <Table name> must be unique (for all Base tables and Views) within the Schema that contains it.

If CREATE VIEW is part of a CREATE SCHEMA statement, the <Table name> (if explicitly qualified) must include the <Schema name> of the Schema being created; i.e., it isn't possible to create a View belonging to a different Schema from within CREATE SCHEMA. For example, this SQL statement will not return an error because the <Table name> will default to include the qualifying <Schema name>:

```
CREATE SCHEMA bob
   CREATE TABLE Table_1 (column_1 SMALLINT, column_2 CHAR(5))
   CREATE VIEW View_1 (column_1) AS
      SELECT column_1 FROM Table_1;
   -- creates a View called BOB.VIEW_1 in Schema BOB
```

The following SQL statement will not return an error either because the <Table name> explicitly includes a qualifying <Schema name> that matches the name of the Schema being created:

```
CREATE SCHEMA bob
   CREATE TABLE bob.Table_1 (
      column_1 SMALLINT, column_2 CHAR(5))
   CREATE VIEW bob.View_1 (column_1) AS
      SELECT column_1 FROM bob.Table_1;
   -- creates a View called BOB.VIEW_1 in Schema BOB
```

But this SQL statement will return an error because the <Table name> explicitly includes a qualifying <Schema name> that is different from the name of the Schema being created:

```
CREATE SCHEMA bob
   CREATE TABLE Table_1 (column_1 SMALLINT, column_2 CHAR(5))
   CREATE VIEW sam.View_1 (column_1) AS
      SELECT column_1 FROM bob.Table_1;
   -- tries to create a View belonging to Schema SAM inside Schema BOB; illegal
syntax
```

Privileges

If CREATE VIEW is executed as a stand-alone SQL statement, the current <AuthorizationID> must either be the owner of the Schema to which this new View belongs or the Schema's owner must be a Role that the current <AuthorizationID> may use. That is, only the owner of a Schema can create Views for that Schema. The current <AuthorizationID> must also have the SELECT Privilege on every Column used in the View's query definition.

In addition to creating a View, CREATE VIEW also causes the SQL special grantor, "_SYSTEM", to grant Privileges on the View to the Schema owner <AuthorizationID> (that is, the <AuthorizationID creating the View). Your Privileges on a View stem from your Privileges on the underlying Tables that make up the View. That is, you get the same Privileges on a View that you hold on the Tables/Columns used in the View's query definition — with the proviso that if you have the UPDATE, INSERT, and/or DELETE Privileges on a Table and you're creating a non-updatable View, those Privileges will not cascade. So, when you create a View, "_SYSTEM" will grant you Table Privileges (any of INSERT, SELECT, UPDATE, DELETE, and REFERENCES that are applicable) on the new View, as well as Column Privileges (any of SELECT, INSERT, UPDATE, and REFERENCES that are applicable) on every Column of the new View. If your Privileges on the underlying Tables are grantable, your Privileges on the View will be too.

That is, Views are Tables, but when it comes to Privileges, there are some big differences between the things that happen for Base tables and the things that happen for Views. The main difference, understandable if you consider that operations on Views are ultimately operations on Base tables, is this: the mere fact that you own a View doesn't mean that you have ALL PRIVILEGES for that View. Usually you either "inherit" View Privileges (because you possess the Privilege on the underlying Table) or you get them explicitly (because someone GRANTs them to you). So:

- In order to create the View — you must have all Privileges necessary to perform the View's query on the underlying Tables.
- If you own the View — you have one automatic Privilege; you may destroy it using the DROP VIEW statement.
- If you have the SELECT Privilege on every Column that your View is based on, you get the SELECT Privilege on the View, so you may SELECT from the View. If all of your underlying SELECT Privileges are grantable, so is your SELECT Privilege on the View. You inherit REFERENCES Privileges in the same way; if you have the REFERENCES Privilege on every Column on which your View is based, you get the REFERENCES Privilege on the View, so you may use the View in an Assertion.

- You inherit INSERT, UPDATE, and DELETE Privileges in the same way, with a major exception; these Privileges cannot exist if the View is not updatable. That explains why, when you try to update a non-updatable View, the likely error is "Syntax error or access violation" — the ultimate cause is the non-updatability, but the immediate cause at update time is that you lack the appropriate Privilege.
- In addition to the inherited Privileges, you may hold Privileges which are explicitly granted to you. If you don't own the View, this is the only way to get Privileges on it — you do not hold any Privileges on a View you don't own merely because you own an underlying Table.
- If your Privilege on an underlying Table is revoked, your Privilege on the View you created using that Privilege is also revoked. This may cause the entire View to be destroyed.

<Column name> Clause

The optional parenthesized <Column name> clause of the CREATE VIEW statement explicitly names the View's Columns. (As is usual with Tables, each Column must have a name that is unique — for all Columns — within the View.) If you omit this clause, the View's Columns will inherit the names of the Columns on which they are based. For example, consider these two SQL statements:

```
CREATE TABLE Table_1 (column_1 SMALLINT, column_2 CHAR(5));

CREATE VIEW View_1 AS SELECT column_1 FROM Table_1;
```

Because the <Column name> clause is omitted, the View's Column will be named COLUMN_1 — just like the Column on which it's based. Here's another example:

```
CREATE TABLE Table_1 (column_1 SMALLINT, column_2 CHAR(5));

CREATE VIEW View_1 (view_column) AS
   SELECT column_1 FROM Table_1;
```

Because the <Column name> clause is included, the View's Column will be named VIEW_COLUMN — even though the Column on which it's based has a different name. Note that if you do use the <Column name> clause, you must provide a name for every one of the View's Columns — it isn't possible to name some and allow the others to default.

There are times when you may not omit the <Column name> clause. You must explicitly name a View's Columns if (*a*) any of the Columns are derived through the use of a set function, scalar function, <literal>, or expression, because none of these have a <Column name> which CREATE VIEW can inherit, (*b*) the same name would be inherited for more than one of the View's Columns, usually the case when the View is derived from a join of multiple Tables, or (*c*) when you're defining a RECURSIVE View. Here's an example that shows a View definition where the <Column name> clause is mandatory because the second and third Columns have no name to inherit:

```
CREATE VIEW View_1 (view_column_1, view_column_2, view_column_3) AS
   SELECT   column_1, column_1+25, 'explanation'
   FROM     Table_1;
```

Note, however, that this CREATE VIEW statement would give you the same result:

```
CREATE VIEW View_1 AS
   SELECT   column_1 AS view_column_1,
            column_1+25 AS view_column_2,
            'explanation' AS view_column_3
   FROM     Table_1;
```

that is, you can also use the AS <Column name> clause in the select list of your View query to provide explicit names for the View's Columns.

[Obscure Rule] If CREATE VIEW includes the OF clause in place of the <Column name> clause, then <UDT name> must identify a structured type. The rules are basically the same as those we've already outlined for the CREATE TABLE statement (see page 356) and we won't repeat them here.

AS **Clause**

The AS clause of the CREATE VIEW statement defines the query that determines the data you'll see each time you look at the View. At any point in time, a View's data consists of the rows that result if its query definition were evaluated. If the query is updatable, then your View is an updatable View. Normally, a "query" is a form of SELECT statement (it may also be VALUES or TABLE; we'll define "query" more thoroughly in a later chapter), so you can define a View using pretty well any combination of predicates and search conditions. There are, however, some restrictions:

- The query may not contain a host variable or SQL parameter reference.
- The query may not refer to any declared LOCAL TEMPORARY Tables.
- The query may not use an expression which would result in a View Column with a NO COLLATION coercibility attribute.
- The query may not include any references to the View you're defining unless you're explicitly defining a RECURSIVE View.

A View's Columns inherit their <data type> and other attributes and Constraints from the Columns on which they're based.

[Obscure Rule] If a View's query can't be represented in INFORMATION_SCHEMA without truncation, your DBMS will return the SQLSTATE warning 0100A "warning-query expression too long for information schema." If you define a View with a query that includes a GROUP BY and/or a HAVING clause that isn't in a subquery, the View is known as a *grouped View.*

Macros and Materializers

When materializing a View, your DBMS's problem is to transform the View's query definition into a query on the Base table(s) on which the View is based. There are two ways to do this.

The Macro, or Inline, View The DBMS sees from the View's query that View V is based on Base table T, so it simply replaces all occurrences of V with T, and all occurrences of V's <Column name>s with T's <Column name>s. Thus, for example:

```
SELECT V.column_1 FROM V WHERE V.column_2 = 7;
```

becomes:

```
SELECT T.column_1 FROM T WHERE T.column_2 = 7;
```

This is conceptually the same as the way that an assembler handles a macro, hence the name. A good DBMS will do the entire transformation during the prepare stage, outside the runtime path, so it is very unlikely that a View query will be measurably slower than a query on the underlying Table if a macro transform is possible. However, here's an example where it's not possible:

```
CREATE VIEW View_1 AS
   SELECT g, COUNT(*) AS g_count FROM Table_1 GROUP BY g;

SELECT AVG(g_count) FROM View_1 WHERE g_count = 5;
```

This SELECT statement can't work because the macro transform would evaluate to:

```
SELECT AVG(COUNT(*)) FROM Table_1 WHERE COUNT(*)=5 GROUP BY g;
```

and that's not legal SQL syntax.

The Materialized View The DBMS makes a hidden "temporary Base table" with the same definition as the Columns in the View and then populates the temporary Table using the View's query. Thus it would handle our difficult-to-do-with-a-macro View (previous example) like this:

```
CREATE LOCAL TEMPORARY TABLE Some_Table_Name (
   g_count INTEGER);

INSERT INTO g_count
   SELECT COUNT(*) FROM Table_1 GROUP BY g;
```

Now the transform is of the Table expression only, so:

```
SELECT AVG(g_count) FROM View_1 WHERE g_count = 5;
```

becomes:

```
SELECT AVG(g_count) FROM Some_Table_Name;
```

A materialized View is more flexible and is easier to implement than a macro View because the method of creation is always the same and because any query expression is transformable. On the negative side of the ledger, it usually takes extra time to populate the temporary Table; the DBMS is not just "selecting from Table A," it's "selecting from Table A and putting the results in Table B, then selecting from Table B." And, if we consider any operation other than SELECT or REFERENCE, we quickly see that the temporary Table is useless — for example, when we INSERT into a View we want the insertion to happen on the actual Table, not on some ephemeral ad-hoc copy of the actual Base table that disappears when we SELECT again. So, we expect that a good DBMS will use macro Views for simple queries and switch to materialized Views when the going gets rough.

Updatable Views

We have seen that, when we SELECT from a View, the DBMS will transform our request into some equivalent request which is a SELECT from the underlying Base table(s). Now, UPDATE or INSERT or DELETE operations ("updates" for short) must also involve a change to the underlying Base tables, otherwise they would be pointless. So, for updates on Views, your DBMS must reverse the transformation. This is often difficult or impossible. The SQL-92 rules for updatability are:

- The query must be a single SELECT... on a single Table, so Views are not updatable if the SELECT contains select functions (UNION, INTERSECT, EXCEPT, CORRESPONDING) or join operators (JOIN or joining commas as in FROM a,b,c). The query may also be TABLE <Table name> because TABLE <Table name> is, at bottom, a SELECT. Rule 1 is relaxed in SQL3 which has the big effect that you can update Views of joins.
- The select list may contain only <Column name>s and [AS name] clauses. Therefore, this SQL statement defines an updatable View:

```
CREATE VIEW View_1 AS SELECT a,b,c FROM Table_1;
```

  but these SQL statements do not:

```
CREATE VIEW View_1 AS SELECT a+5 FROM Table_1;

CREATE VIEW View_1 AS SELECT 'x' FROM Table_1;

CREATE VIEW View_1 AS SELECT a COLLATE polish FROM Table_1;
```

  (These are all theoretically updatable Views, but our main concern here is with what the SQL Standard regards as updatable.) Rule 2 is irritating because many arithmetic and string operations are in fact reversible — but the DBMS doesn't know it.
- There must be no implicit or explicit grouping, so the <keyword>s DISTINCT or GROUP BY or HAVING, or any set function, may not appear in the main query (though they may appear in that query's subqueries), nor may any subqueries be correlated subqueries (that is, they may not themselves refer to the Table named in the outer query). Rule 3 cannot be gotten around. For example, you can't change the average salary; you have to change the individual salaries (unless you're the Canadian Anti-Poverty Commission which once announced that "most Canadians make less than the average wage"). However, the rule is syntax-based — you might find that, in fact, DISTINCT is a no-op (i.e., the decision, "Is it distinct?" is a matter of syntax, not of fact).
- The query may not refer to the View being defined.

- If there are multiple levels of View (that is, Views of Views), the above rules must be followed at every level — that is, if the "single Table" in the query expression is not a Base table, it must be an updatable View. Sometimes, as a very general summation of these rules, people say "a View is updatable only if it represents a subset of the rows and Columns of a single Base table."

What actually happens when you update a View? Your DBMS performs the operation on the underlying Base table. For these two SQL statements:

```
DELETE FROM View_1;

UPDATE View_1 SET column_1 = value;
```

the operation transforms straightforwardly to:

```
DELETE FROM Table_1;

UPDATE Table_1 SET column_1 = value;
```

For INSERT operations, there is an additional problem if the View is based on only a subset of the Columns of the underlying Base table. In that case, the rest of the Base table's Columns all are set to their default value. For example:

```
CREATE TABLE Table_1 (
   column_1 SMALLINT DEFAULT 12,
   column_2 CHAR(5) DEFAULT 'hello');

CREATE VIEW View_1 (view_column) AS
   SELECT column_1 FROM Table_1;

INSERT INTO View_1 (view_column) VALUES (28);
```

The result of the INSERT operation on the View is:

```
INSERT INTO Table_1 (column_1, column_2)
   VALUES (28,'hello');
```

WITH CHECK OPTION Clause

Consider these two SQL statements:

```
CREATE VIEW View_1 (view_col_1, view_col_2) AS
   SELECT column_1,column_2 FROM Table_1 WHERE column_1 =5;

UPDATE View_1 SET view_col_1=4;
```

The View definition restricts it to those rows of TABLE_1 where COLUMN_1 has a value of 5 — but as soon as the UPDATE operation succeeds, there will be no such rows. To the user, the apparent effect is that all the rows of VIEW_1 "disappear" — as if they were deleted instead of updated. That is okay and legal, but doesn't it contradict the View idea? That is, if someone is restricted during SELECT to finding only those rows that match the condition column_1=5, why should he/she/it be allowed to UPDATE or INSERT rows that do not follow the same restriction?

The solution is to use the optional WITH CHECK OPTION clause in your updatable View definitions (it is valid only if you *are* defining an updatable View). Adjust the two SQL statements to:

```
CREATE VIEW View_1 (view_col_1, view_col_2) AS
   SELECT column_1,column_2 FROM Table_1 WHERE column_1 =5
   WITH CHECK OPTION;

UPDATE View_1 SET view_col_1=4;
```

and now the UPDATE statement will fail; your DBMS will return the SQLSTATE error 44000 "with check option violation." The effect of WITH CHECK OPTION is to say, "the WHERE clause defines what is in the View and you cannot go outside the bounds of that definition in any INSERT or UPDATE operation."

A View's CHECK OPTION is effectively a Constraint. That is, there is a similarity between the two definitions in this example:

```
-- Constraint on Base table
CREATE TABLE Table_1 (
   column_1 INT,
   CHECK (column_1<5000));

INSERT INTO Table_1 VALUES(6000);
-- results in error

-- Constraint on View
CREATE TABLE Table_1 (column_1 INT);

CREATE VIEW View_1 AS
   SELECT column_1 FROM Table_1  WHERE column_1<5000
   WITH CHECK OPTION;

INSERT INTO View_1 VALUES(6000);
-- results in error
```

If WITH CHECK OPTION is included in a View definition, then all INSERT and UPDATE operations on that View will be checked to ensure that every new row satisfies the View's query conditions. Such "View Constraints" are popular, probably because the CREATE VIEW statement has been around for a longer time than the Base table CHECK Constraint. There are a few downsides you should be aware of, though, if you use such View Constraints:

- You do not have the option of deferring Constraint checking. All checks happen at the end of the INSERT or UPDATE operation.

- It is somewhat easier to violate a View Constraint than a proper Table Constraint.
- In SQL3, the behaviour is different if NULLs are used (and therefore the result of the Constraint check is UNKNOWN rather than TRUE or FALSE). For the Base table insertion:

```
INSERT INTO Table_1 VALUES (NULL);
```

there is no Constraint violation and so the INSERT is allowed. But for the View insertion:

```
INSERT INTO View_1 VALUES (NULL);
```

there is a Constraint violation and the INSERT is not allowed.

Regardless of the reasons you use WITH CHECK OPTION — as a general constrainer or as an encapsulation enforcer — the View must obey the following rules:

- The WHERE clause must be "deterministic" (this only means that you can't use Columns which might change in value, such as one based on CURRENT_TIME). For a more complete explanation, see Chapter 20 "SQL Constraints and Assertions."
- The View must be updatable.

Suppose you create Views within Views within Views, for example:

```
CREATE TABLE Table_1 (
   column_1 INTEGER,
   column_2 INTEGER,
   column_3 INTEGER,
   column_4 INTEGER,
   column_5 INTEGER);

CREATE VIEW View_1 AS
   SELECT * FROM Table_1 WHERE column_1 <> 0;

CREATE VIEW View_2 AS
   SELECT * FROM View_1 WHERE column_2 <> 0
   WITH CASCADED CHECK OPTION;

CREATE VIEW View_3 AS
   SELECT * FROM View_2 WHERE column_3 <> 0;

CREATE VIEW View_4 AS
   SELECT * FROM View_3 WHERE column_4 <> 0
   WITH LOCAL CHECK OPTION;

CREATE VIEW View_5 AS
   SELECT * FROM View_4 WHERE column_5 <> 0;
```

JARGON: A Table used in the definition of another Table is an *immediately underlying* Table; thus Table TABLE_1 underlies View VIEW_1. Because VIEW_1 is then used in the definition of VIEW_2, we say that VIEW_1 immediately underlies VIEW_2 and that TABLE_1 indirectly underlies VIEW_2. Taken together, both TABLE_1 and VIEW_1 *generally underlie* VIEW_2; one indirectly and the other immediately.

Our example contains a variety of WITH CHECK OPTION clauses. To see what their effects are, we will try to do an INSERT for each of the Views. We begin with VIEW_1:

```
INSERT INTO View_1 VALUES (0,0,0,0,0);
```

This INSERT operation is legal; there is no check option in the View's definition, so the row is inserted into TABLE_1 despite the fact that we won't be able to see that effect by looking at VIEW_1.

Here's an INSERT into VIEW_2:

```
INSERT INTO View_2 VALUES (1,0,1,1,1);
```

This INSERT operation will fail; there is a check option saying that the second column may not be 0. No surprise there, but the following INSERT will fail too!

```
INSERT INTO View_2 VALUES (0,1,1,1,1);
```

When you define a View with WITH CASCADED CHECK OPTION (or with WITH CHECK OPTION; they mean the same thing because CASCADED is the default), then the check applies not only to the View you're updating, but to every View that underlies it — and VIEW_1 contains a condition that disallows zeros in COLUMN_1.

Here are two INSERTs into VIEW_3:

```
INSERT INTO View_3 VALUES (0,1,1,1,1);

INSERT INTO View_3 VALUES (1,0,1,1,1);
```

These INSERT operations will also fail; although VIEW_3 has no check option, its underlying Views do and so operations on VIEW_3 may not violate their conditions. But, since VIEW_3 has no check option of its own, the following INSERT is legal:

```
INSERT INTO View_3 VALUES (1,1,0,1,1);
```

because there is no check on VIEW_3 or on its underlying Views, that disallows zeros in COLUMN_3.

Now, here's an INSERT into VIEW_4:

```
INSERT INTO View_4 VALUES (0,0,0,1,1);
```

This INSERT operation is legal. For VIEW_4, there is only one check condition in effect — that COLUMN_4 may not be zero — and this condition is satisfied by the INSERT. VIEW_3's condition — that COLUMN_3 may not be zero — doesn't have to be satisfied because VIEW_4 was defined with WITH LOCAL CHECK OPTION. This means that, while VIEW_4's condition will be checked, the conditions of its immediately underlying View will only be checked if that View was defined with a WITH CHECK OPTION clause (which is not the case for VIEW_3). It also means that the conditions of its indirectly underlying Views (that is, of VIEW_1 and VIEW_2) won't be checked at all, regardless of their WITH CHECK OPTION definitions.

Finally, here's an INSERT into VIEW_5:

```
INSERT INTO View_5 VALUES (0,0,0,1,0);
```

Once again, this INSERT operation is legal; VIEW_5 has no WITH CHECK OPTION clause and so its condition is not checked. However, the View it's based on (VIEW_4) does have a WITH CHECK OPTION clause and so this INSERT statement will fail:

```
INSERT INTO View_5 VALUES (1,1,1,0,1);
```

because VIEW_4's condition is checked for any INSERT or UPDATE operation on VIEW_5. But, because VIEW_4 was defined with WITH LOCAL CHECK OPTION, the View immediately underlying VIEW_4 is the only other View whose conditions will be checked — and then only if that View was defined with a WITH CHECK OPTION clause. Thus, for this example, operations on VIEW_5 are affected only by the conditions set for VIEW_4 — COLUMN_1 may be zero, COLUMN_2 may be zero, and COLUMN_3 may be zero because the conditions for VIEW_1, VIEW_2, and VIEW_3 don't apply.

Our example is fairly complex because we mixed all the possibilities together. In real life, one avoids the complexity by declaring a company policy — always use WITH CASCADED CHECK OPTION.

RECURSIVE Views

Here is a contrived, illegal example of two Views that reference each other:

```
CREATE SCHEMA some_schema
   CREATE TABLE Table_1 (column_1 INTEGER)
   CREATE VIEW View_1 (view_1_col_1,view_1_col_2,view_1_col_3) AS
      SELECT column_1,view_2_col_1,'A' FROM Table_1,View_2
   CREATE VIEW View_2 (view_2_col_1,view_2_col_2,view_2_col_3) AS
      SELECT view_1_col_1,column_1,'B' FROM Table_1,View_1;
```

Although the definition of VIEW_1 is legal, the definition of VIEW_2 is not because it defines a recursive View; a View whose query refers to the View being defined — that is, because VIEW_2 is based on VIEW_1, and because VIEW_1 is based on VIEW_2, ultimately, VIEW_2 is based on itself. We used the CREATE SCHEMA statement for this example because, within CREATE SCHEMA, each Column in each View derives ultimately from either a Base table Column or a <literal>, so recursive Views are possible in theory. In reality, though, current DBMSs don't allow them and neither does the SQL-92 Standard. In SQL3, though, recursion is allowed provided it's explicit and provided that CREATE VIEW includes a <Column name> clause but no WITH CHECK OPTION clause. Thus, with SQL3 only, this SQL statement is possible:

```
CREATE SCHEMA some_schema
   CREATE TABLE Table_1 (column_1 INTEGER)
   CREATE VIEW View_1 (view_1_col_1,view_1_col_2,view_1_col_3) AS
      SELECT column_1,view_2_col_1,'A' FROM Table_1,View_2
   CREATE RECURSIVE VIEW View_2
      (view_2_col_1,view_2_col_2,view_2_col_3) AS
      SELECT view_1_col_1,column_1,'B' FROM Table_1,View_1;
```

If you want to restrict your code to Core SQL, don't define any RECURSIVE Views, don't use the EXCEPT, INTERSECT, or CORRESPONDING operators in your View queries, and don't use the optional CASCADED or LOCAL levels specification in your check clauses — always define Views only with WITH CHECK OPTION alone.

Getting More Out Of Views

A View's virtue is that it isn't the whole picture. Something is hidden. Hidden is good. In the following descriptions, which all show Views being put to some useful purpose, the same refrain could be sung each time, "Views Hide — Good."

One thing we'd like to hide, or abstract, is the retrieval method. For a mailing list, the method might look like this:

```
SELECT Customers.given,
       Customers.surname,
       Customers.city,
       Customers.address
FROM   Customers
UNION
SELECT Suppliers.given,
       Suppliers.surname,
       Suppliers.city,
       Suppliers.address
FROM   Suppliers;
```

Some people, sometimes, need to know that the mailing list is a union of data from two Tables. But when you print your list, all you really want to say is:

```
SELECT given, surname, city, address FROM Mailouts;
```

This is *not* a mere matter of "reducing keystrokes." The idea is to remove information which is not necessary for the task at hand.

Another thing we want to hide is details. For example, there are some people who only care about department-level sales figures, as opposed to individual sales. For them we want to say:

```
CREATE VIEW View_1 AS
    SELECT SUM(sales_amount), manager
    FROM Sales
    GROUP BY manager;
```

... and they can select whatever they like from VIEW_1 (which is an example of a *grouped View*).

The next thing we want to hide is secrets. We could grant PUBLIC access to some grouped Views or we could grant PUBLIC access to only certain Columns in certain Tables. In fact, granting on Column-subset Views is the normal way to do a by-Column GRANT (see Chapter 15 "AuthorizationIDs").

TIP: Make a one-row permanent Table with:

```
CREATE VIEW View_name AS VALUES (1,2,3);
```

To create one-row Tables which you never intend to update, this is more convenient than using the CREATE TABLE statement because you can forget about file storage. If your DBMS doesn't allow the use of the <keyword> VALUES for a View's <query expression>, make your View with a selection from a one-row Table in INFORMATION_SCHEMA, e.g.,

```
CREATE VIEW View_name AS
SELECT 1,2,3 FROM INFORMATION_SCHEMA.SQL_LANGUAGES;
```

DROP VIEW Statement

The DROP VIEW statement destroys a View. The required syntax for the DROP VIEW statement is as follows.

```
DROP VIEW <Table name> {RESTRICT | CASCADE}
```

DROP VIEW destroys a View, but does not destroy any data; the data in the underlying Tables will remain. The <Table name> must identify an existing View whose owner is either the current <AuthorizationID> or a Role that the current <AuthorizationID> may use. That is, only the <AuthorizationID> that owns the View may drop it.

The effect of DROP VIEW <Table name> RESTRICT, e.g.,

```
DROP VIEW View_1 RESTRICT;
```

is that the View named is destroyed, provided that the View is not referred to in any other View definition and is not referred to in any Constraint definition, Assertion definition, Trigger definition, or SQL routine. That is, RESTRICT ensures that only a View with no dependent Objects can be destroyed. If the View is used by any other Object, DROP VIEW ... RESTRICT will fail.

The effect of DROP VIEW <Table name> CASCADE, e.g.,

```
DROP VIEW View_1 CASCADE;
```

is that the View named is destroyed.

Successfully destroying a View has a three-fold effect:

1. The View named is destroyed.
2. All Privileges held on the View by the <AuthorizationID> that owns it are revoked (by the SQL special grantor, "_SYSTEM") with a CASCADE revoke behaviour, so that all Privileges held on the View by any other <AuthorizationID> are also revoked.
3. All SQL routines, Views, Constraints, Assertions, and Triggers that depend on the View are dropped with a CASCADE drop behaviour.

If you want to restrict your code to Core SQL, don't use the CASCADE drop behaviour for your DROP VIEW statements.

DECLARE TABLE Statement

The DECLARE TABLE statement names a new declared local temporary Base table and defines the Table's Columns and Constraints. The required syntax for the DECLARE TABLE statement is as follows.

```
DECLARE LOCAL TEMPORARY TABLE [ MODULE. ]<Table name>
   (<table element> [ {,<table element>}... ])
   [ ON COMMIT {PRESERVE ROWS | DELETE ROWS} ]

        <table element> ::=
        <Column definition> |
        <Table Constraint> |
        LIKE <Table name> |
        <Column name> WITH OPTIONS <column option list>
```

DECLARE LOCAL TEMPORARY TABLE defines a new declared local temporary Base table. You can only use this SQL statement within a MODULE statement. Declared temporary Tables aren't part of the Table metadata in INFORMATION_SCHEMA.

In effect, a declared local temporary Table does not exist until it is invoked by an SQL-client Module during an SQL-session. Once invoked, it will only be visible to the Module in which it is declared — it will not be visible to other users. At the end of the SQL-session, all declared temporary Tables invoked during the SQL-session are dropped.

- The <Table name> identifies the Table and the Module to which it belongs and must be unique (for all declared local temporary Base tables) within the Module that owns it. Because a declared local temporary Table is distinct within an SQL-client Module within an SQL-session, the Schema to which it belongs is a Schema determined by your DBMS, so don't add a qualifying <Schema name> when you declare a temporary Table. (In effect, your DBMS will fix a qualifying <Schema name> for a declared local temporary Table based on the DBMS's name for the SQL-session in which you invoke that Table, coupled with its name for the SQL-client Module that contains that Table's declaration.) Whenever you refer to a declared local temporary Table, you must preface the <Table name> with `MODULE`.

The <table element> clause defines the structure of the Table's contents; it tells you what sort of data the Table contains. This clause contains a list of table elements, such as Column and Table Constraint definitions, that are just like the elements we described for the `CREATE TABLE` statement — review that section on page 356 for detailed information. Every temporary Table declaration has to contain at least one <Column definition>. Here are two equivalent examples:

```
DECLARE LOCAL TEMPORARY TABLE MODULE.Table_1 (
   column_1 SMALLINT,
   column_2 DATE,
   column_3 VARCHAR(25),
   CONSTRAINT constraint_1 UNIQUE(column_1),
   CONSTRAINT constraint_2 CHECK(column_3 IS NOT NULL));

DECLARE LOCAL TEMPORARY TABLE Table_1 (
   column_1 SMALLINT,
   column_2 DATE,
   column_3 VARCHAR(25),
   CONSTRAINT constraint_1 UNIQUE(column_1),
   CONSTRAINT constraint_2 CHECK(column_3 IS NOT NULL));
```

When you declare a local temporary Table, you may use the `ON COMMIT` clause to specify whether you want the Table to be emptied whenever a `COMMIT` statement is executed. If you omit the `ON COMMIT` clause from `DECLARE LOCAL TEMPORARY TABLE`, it defaults to `ON COMMIT DELETE ROWS`. For example, these two SQL statements are equivalent:

```
DECLARE LOCAL TEMPORARY TABLE Table_1 (
   column_1 SMALLINT);

DECLARE LOCAL TEMPORARY TABLE Table_1 (
   column_1 SMALLINT)
   ON COMMIT DELETE ROWS;
```

Based on this Table declaration, the effect of the following two SQL statements:

```
INSERT INTO MODULE.Table_1 (column_1) VALUES(10);

COMMIT;
```

is that TABLE_1 is first materialized and has data inserted into it and then the rows are deleted. That is, at COMMIT time, your DBMS effectively executes this SQL statement:

```
DELETE FROM Table_1;
```

because the declaration of TABLE_1 states that the Table is to be emptied at COMMIT. On the other hand, the effect of these three SQL statements:

```
DECLARE LOCAL TEMPORARY TABLE Table_1 (
   column_1 SMALLINT)
   ON COMMIT PRESERVE ROWS;

INSERT INTO MODULE.Table_1 (column_1) VALUES(10);

COMMIT;
```

is that TABLE_1 is declared, materialized, and has data inserted into it and then the rows are committed. That is, at COMMIT time, your DBMS does not delete the rows because TABLE_1's declaration explicitly says not to. (The rows will, however, be deleted at the end of the SQL-session.)

In addition to declaring a Table, DECLARE LOCAL TEMPORARY TABLE also causes the SQL special grantor, "_SYSTEM", to grant non-grantable INSERT, SELECT, UPDATE, DELETE, and REFERENCES Privileges on the declared Table, as well as non-grantable SELECT, INSERT, UPDATE, and REFERENCES Privileges on every Column in the declared Table, to the current <AuthorizationID>. This ensures that the Table may be materialized, and operated on, by any <AuthorizationID> that can run the Module that contains the Table declaration.

If you want to restrict your code to Core SQL, don't use the DECLARE LOCAL TEMPORARY TABLE statement.

Dialects

Some vendors relax the rules on what may be an updatable View. For example, IBM's DB2 will let you DELETE from Views whose queries contain arithmetic expressions and will even let you UPDATE such Views provided you don't try to update the Column derived from the expression.

Although the Full-SQL syntax for the check option clause is WITH [{CASCADED|LOCAL}] CHECK OPTION, the majority of vendors only allow the optionless syntax WITH CHECK OPTION, which is all that's required for Core SQL. In general, the check option is always CASCADED (as required by the Standard), but there was a time when the default was LOCAL so some caution is necessary. Sometimes WITH CHECK OPTION may be illegal even though the View is updatable; for example IBM's DB2 once insisted that there could be no subqueries in the View definition.

19

Chapter 19

SQL Domains

In this chapter, we'll describe SQL Domains in detail and show you the syntax to use to create, alter, and destroy them.

Domain

A Schema may contain zero or more Domains. An SQL Domain is a named, user-defined set of valid values. Domains are dependent on some Schema — the <Domain name> must be unique within the Schema to which the Domain belongs (it may not be the same as any <UDT name> in its Schema either) — and are created, altered, and dropped using standard SQL statements. The Objects that may belong to a Domain are known as *Domain Constraints*; they depend on some Domain.

A Domain is defined by a descriptor that contains seven pieces of information:

1. The <Domain name> qualified by the <Schema name> of the Schema to which it belongs.
2. The Domain's SQL <data type> specification, including its name, length, precision, and scale (as applicable).
3. The name of the Character set to which the Domain's set of values must belong (for character string types).
4. The name of the Domain's default Collation. (This is the Collation that may be used to compare a character string Domain's values in the absence of an explicit `COLLATE` clause.)
5. Whether reference values must be checked and whether <reference scope check action> specifies `RESTRICT` or `SET NULL` (for `REF` types).
6. The Domain's default value (if any).

7. A descriptor for every Constraint that belongs to the Domain.

To create a Domain, use the `CREATE DOMAIN` statement (either as a stand-alone SQL statement or within a `CREATE SCHEMA` statement). `CREATE DOMAIN` specifies the enclosing Schema, names the Domain, and identifies the Domain's set of valid values. To change an existing Domain, use the `ALTER DOMAIN` statement. To destroy a Domain, use the `DROP DOMAIN` statement.

There is a one-to-many association between Domains and Columns; one Domain can be used to identify the set of valid values for multiple Columns.

Domain Names

A <Domain name> identifies a Domain. The required syntax for a <Domain name> is as follows.

```
<Domain name> ::=
[ <Schema name>. ] unqualified name
```

A <Domain name> is a <regular identifier> or a <delimited identifier> that is unique (for all Domains and UDTs) within the Schema to which it belongs. The <Schema name> which qualifies a <Domain name> names the Schema to which the Domain belongs and can either be explicitly stated or a default will be supplied by your DBMS as follows:

- If a <Domain name> in a `CREATE SCHEMA` statement isn't qualified, the default qualifier is the name of the Schema you're creating.
- If the unqualified <Domain name> is found in any other SQL statement in a Module, the default qualifier is the name of the Schema identified in the `SCHEMA` clause or `AUTHORIZATION` clause of the `MODULE` statement that defines that Module.

Here are some examples of <Domain name>s:

```
DOMAIN_1
-- a <Domain name>

SCHEMA_1.DOMAIN_1
-- a simple qualified <Domain name>

CATALOG_1.SCHEMA_1.DOMAIN_1
-- a fully qualified <Domain name>
```

`CREATE DOMAIN` Statement

The `CREATE DOMAIN` statement names a new Domain and defines the Domain's set of valid values. The required syntax for the `CREATE DOMAIN` statement is as follows.

```
CREATE DOMAIN <Domain name> [ AS ] <data type>
     [ DEFAULT default value ]
     [ <Domain Constraint> list ]
     [ COLLATE <Collation name> ]
```

```
<Domain constraint> list::=
<Domain Constraint> [ <Domain Constraint>... ]

    <Domain constraint> ::=
    [ CONSTRAINT <Constraint name> ]
    Constraint_type
    [ <constraint attributes> ]
```

CREATE DOMAIN defines a new Domain; a named set of valid data values that can be used — somewhat like a macro — to replace the <data type> specification in subsequent <Column definition>s.

- The <Domain name> identifies the Domain and the Schema to which it belongs. A <Domain name> that includes an explicit <Schema name> qualifier belongs to the Schema named. A <Domain name> that does not include an explicit <Schema name> qualifier belongs to the SQL-session default Schema. The <Domain name> must be unique (for all Domains and UDTs) within the Schema that contains it.

If CREATE DOMAIN is part of a CREATE SCHEMA statement, the <Domain name>, if explicitly qualified, must include the <Schema name> of the Schema being created; that is, it isn't possible to create a Domain belonging to a different Schema from within CREATE SCHEMA. For example, this SQL statement will not return an error because the <Domain name> will default to include the qualifying <Schema name>:

```
CREATE SCHEMA bob
   CREATE DOMAIN domain_1 AS SMALLINT;
-- creates a Domain called BOB.DOMAIN_1 in Schema BOB
```

The following SQL statement will not return an error either because the <Domain name> explicitly includes a qualifying <Schema name> that matches the name of the Schema being created:

```
CREATE SCHEMA bob
   CREATE DOMAIN bob.domain_1 AS SMALLINT;
-- creates a Domain called BOB.DOMAIN_1 in Schema BOB
```

But this SQL statement will return an error because the <Domain name> explicitly includes a qualifying <Schema name> that is different from the name of the Schema being created:

```
CREATE SCHEMA bob
   CREATE DOMAIN sam.domain_1 AS SMALLINT;
-- tries to create a Domain belonging to Schema SAM inside Schema BOB; illegal
syntax
```

Privileges

If CREATE DOMAIN is executed as a stand-alone SQL statement, the current <AuthorizationID> must either be the owner of the Schema to which this new Domain belongs or the

Schema's owner must be a Role that the current <AuthorizationID> may use. That is, only the owner of a Schema can create Domains for that Schema. In addition to creating a Domain, CREATE DOMAIN also causes the SQL special grantor, "_SYSTEM", to grant the USAGE Privilege on the new Domain to the Schema owner <AuthorizationID> (i.e., the <AuthorizationID creating the Domain). This USAGE Privilege will be grantable if (*a*) the grantee also has a grantable REFERENCES Privilege for each Column named in the Domain definition and (*b*) the grantee also has a grantable USAGE Privilege for each Domain, Collation, Character set, and Translation named in a <Domain Constraint> in the Domain definition.

<data type>

A Domain must be defined to accept a certain type of data. The Domain's <data type> specification constrains the values that can be accepted by the Domain. The <data type> specification includes length, precision, and scale as applicable. Valid <data type>s are: INT, SMALLINT, NUMERIC(p,s), DECIMAL(p,s), FLOAT(p), REAL, DOUBLE PRECISION, BIT(l), BIT VARYING(l), BLOB(l), CHAR(l), NCHAR(l), VARCHAR(l), NCHAR VARYING(l), CLOB(l), NCLOB(l), DATE, TIME(p), TIME(p) WITH TIME ZONE, TIMESTAMP(p), TIMESTAMP(p) WITH TIME ZONE, INTERVAL <interval qualifier>, BOOLEAN, ARRAY, ROW, and REF.

The <keyword> AS in the <data type> clause is noise and can be omitted. For example, these two SQL statements are equivalent:

```
CREATE DOMAIN domain_1 AS CHAR(10);

CREATE DOMAIN domain_1 CHAR(10);
```

[Obscure Rule] If the <data type> of a Domain is CHAR, VARCHAR, or CLOB, the Character set to which the Domain's values must belong is determined as follows:

- If your CREATE DOMAIN statement includes a CHARACTER SET clause, the Domain's Character set is the Character set named. Your current <AuthorizationID> must have the USAGE Privilege on that Character set.
- If your CREATE DOMAIN statement does not include a CHARACTER SET clause, the Domain's Character set is the Character set named in the DEFAULT CHARACTER SET clause of the CREATE SCHEMA statement that defines the Schema to which the Domain belongs.

For example, the effect of these two SQL statements:

```
CREATE SCHEMA bob AUTHORIZATION bob
   DEFAULT CHARACTER SET INFORMATION_SCHEMA.LATIN1;

CREATE DOMAIN domain_1 AS CHAR(10);
```

is to create a Domain in Schema BOB. The Domain's set of valid values are fixed length character strings, exactly 10 characters long, all of whose characters must be found in the

INFORMATION_SCHEMA.LATIN1 Character set — the Schema's default Character set. The effect of these two SQL statements:

```
CREATE SCHEMA bob AUTHORIZATION bob
   DEFAULT CHARACTER SET INFORMATION_SCHEMA.LATIN1;

CREATE DOMAIN domain_1 AS CHAR(10)
   CHARACTER SET INFORMATION_SCHEMA.SQL_CHARACTER;
```

is to create the same Domain with one difference; this time, its values must consist only of characters found in the INFORMATION_SCHEMA.SQL_CHARACTER Character set — the explicit Character set specification in CREATE DOMAIN constrains the Domain's set of values. The Schema's default Character set does not.

[Obscure Rule] If the <data type> of a Domain is CHAR, VARCHAR, CLOB, NCHAR, NCHAR VARYING, or NCLOB, and your CREATE DOMAIN statement does not include a COLLATE clause, the Domain has a coercibility attribute of COERCIBLE — but if your CREATE DOMAIN statement includes a COLLATE clause, the Domain has a coercibility attribute of IMPLICIT. In either case, the Domain's default Collation is determined as follows:

- If your CREATE DOMAIN statement includes a COLLATE clause, the Domain's default Collation is the Collation named. Your current <AuthorizationID> must have the USAGE Privilege on that Collation.
- If your CREATE DOMAIN statement does not include a COLLATE clause, the Domain's default Collation is the default Collation of the Domain's Character set.

[Obscure Rule] If the <data type> of a Domain is REF(UDT), your current <AuthorizationID> must have the USAGE Privilege on that UDT. If the <data type> of a Domain includes REF with a <scope clause>, your CREATE DOMAIN statement must also include a <reference scope check> clause to indicate whether references are to be checked or not (don't add a <reference scope check> clause under any other circumstances). In this case, you may also add the optional <reference scope check action> clause to indicate the action to be taken whenever a Column based on this Domain is the subject of a DELETE statement. If you omit the <reference scope check action> clause, it defaults to ON DELETE RESTRICT.

- If a Domain is defined with REFERENCES ARE CHECKED and a <scope clause> is included in the CREATE DOMAIN statement, then there is an implied DEFERRABLE INITIALLY IMMEDIATE Constraint on the new Domain which checks that the values of every Column based on the Domain are also found in the system-generated Column of the Table named in the <scope clause>. In this case, if the <reference scope check action> is SET NULL then, prior to deleting any rows from the Tables that own a Column based on this Domain, your DBMS will (*a*) execute a SET CONSTRAINT statement that sets the implied Constraint's constraint check time to DEFERRED, (*b*) DELETE the rows as required, (*c*) set the value of the system-generated Column in the Table named in the <scope clause> to NULL, for each row that matched the deleted rows, and (*d*) execute a SET CONSTRAINT statement that sets the implied Constraint's constraint check time to IMMEDIATE.

DEFAULT Clause

The optional DEFAULT clause defines the Domain's default value; the value to insert whenever a Column based on this Domain is the target of an INSERT statement that doesn't include an explicit value for that Column. The DEFAULT options are: DEFAULT <literal>, DEFAULT CURRENT_DATE, DEFAULT CURRENT_TIME(p), DEFAULT CURRENT_TIMESTAMP(p), DEFAULT LOCALTIME(p), DEFAULT LOCALTIMESTAMP(p), DEFAULT USER, DEFAULT CURRENT_USER, DEFAULT SESSION_USER, DEFAULT SYSTEM_USER, DEFAULT CURRENT_PATH, DEFAULT ARRAY[], DEFAULT ARRAY??(??), and DEFAULT NULL — see "<default clause>" on page 367 in Chapter 18 "SQL Tables and Views." For example, this SQL statement creates a Domain whose default value is the <character string literal> 'bobby':

```
CREATE DOMAIN domain_1 AS VARCHAR(15)
   DEFAULT 'bobby';
```

And this SQL statement creates a Domain whose default value is the value returned by the CURRENT_DATE function:

```
CREATE DOMAIN domain_1 AS DATE
   DEFAULT CURRENT_DATE;
```

<Domain Constraint>s

The optional <Domain Constraint> list clause of CREATE DOMAIN is used to define zero or more <Constraint>s on the Domain; the Constraint rules will restrict the Domain's set of valid values — see Chapter 20 "SQL Constraints and Assertions." The syntax CREATE DOMAIN <Domain name> AS <data type> DEFAULT default value <Domain Constraint> <Domain Constraint> defines a Domain whose definition includes two <Domain Constraint>s. Here is an example:

```
CREATE DOMAIN domain_1 AS SMALLINT
   DEFAULT 150
   CONSTRAINT constraint_1
      CHECK (VALUE IS NOT NULL) NOT DEFERRABLE
   CONSTRAINT constraint_2
      CHECK (VALUE BETWEEN -1000 AND 9999)
      DEFERRABLE INITIALLY IMMEDIATE;
```

In this example, DOMAIN_1 has a default value of 150 and is constrained to accept only integers that fall into SMALLINT's range. The Domain is further constrained (by CONSTRAINT_1) not to accept null values and (by CONSTRAINT_2) to accept only values between –1,000 and +9,999. Because a <Domain Constraint>'s search condition may not be recursive, this SQL statement will return an error because the <Domain Constraint> refers to the Domain to which it belongs:

```
CREATE DOMAIN domain_1 AS FLOAT
   CONSTRAINT constraint_1
       CHECK (CAST(VALUE AS domain_1) > 0) NOT DEFERRABLE;
```

If you want to restrict your code to Core SQL, don't use the CREATE DOMAIN statement.

ALTER DOMAIN Statement

The ALTER DOMAIN statement changes a Domain's definition. The required syntax for the ALTER DOMAIN statement is as follows.

```
ALTER DOMAIN <Domain name> <alter domain action>

   <alter domain action> ::=
   SET DEFAULT default value |
   DROP DEFAULT |
   ADD <Domain Constraint> |
   DROP CONSTRAINT <Constraint name>
```

The <Domain name> must identify an existing Domain whose owner is either the current <AuthorizationID> or a Role that the current <AuthorizationID> may use. That is, only the <AuthorizationID> that owns the Domain may alter it. Every Column that is based on the Domain will be affected by the change.

SET DEFAULT Clause

The effect of ALTER DOMAIN <Domain name> SET DEFAULT default value, e.g.,

```
ALTER DOMAIN domain_1 SET DEFAULT 200;
```

is that the default value of the Domain named will be changed. (You can use this version of ALTER DOMAIN either to add a default value to a Domain or to change a Domain's existing default value.) The ALTER DOMAIN ... SET DEFAULT options are: DEFAULT <literal>, DEFAULT CURRENT_DATE, DEFAULT CURRENT_TIME(p), DEFAULT CURRENT_TIMESTAMP(p), DEFAULT LOCALTIME(p), DEFAULT LOCALTIMESTAMP(p), DEFAULT USER, DEFAULT CURRENT_USER, DEFAULT SESSION_USER, DEFAULT SYSTEM_USER, DEFAULT CURRENT_PATH, DEFAULT ARRAY[], DEFAULT ARRAY??(??), and DEFAULT NULL — see "<default clause>" on page 367 in Chapter 18 "SQL Tables and Views."

DROP DEFAULT Clause

The effect of ALTER DOMAIN <Domain name> DROP DEFAULT, e.g.,

```
ALTER DOMAIN domain_1 DROP DEFAULT;
```

is that the default value of the Domain named will be removed from the Domain's definition. (You'll get a syntax error if the Domain's definition doesn't include a default value.) Before removing the default value from the Domain's definition, your DBMS will first check the definitions of every Column based on the Domain for a default value. If a dependent <Column definition> has no default value, your DBMS will add the Domain's default value to the <Column definition>. For example, the effect of this SQL statement:

```
ALTER domain_1 DROP DEFAULT;
```

is twofold. First, the definition of every Column dependent on DOMAIN_1 will be checked for a Column default value. If none is found, the default value from the Domain definition is added to the <Column definition> to ensure that the Column is not left without a default value for future insertions. The second effect is that the Domain's default value is removed from the definition of DOMAIN_1.

ADD <Domain Constraint> Clause

The effect of ALTER DOMAIN <Domain name> ADD <Domain Constraint>, e.g.,

```
ALTER DOMAIN domain_1 ADD CONSTRAINT constraint_1
   CHECK(VALUE IS NOT NULL) NOT DEFERRABLE;
```

is that one <Domain Constraint> is added to the definition of the Domain named — see "<Domain Constraint>" on page 408 in Chapter 20 "SQL Constraints and Assertions."

DROP CONSTRAINT Clause

The effect of ALTER DOMAIN <Domain name> DROP CONSTRAINT <Constraint name>, e.g.,

```
ALTER DOMAIN domain_1 DROP CONSTRAINT constraint_1;
```

is that the Constraint named is removed from the definition of the Domain that owns it. (Note: If the dropped Constraint caused one or more Columns to have the "known not nullable" nullability characteristic, then the affected Columns' nullability characteristic becomes "possibly nullable" unless some other Constraint also constrains them to non-null values.)

If you want to restrict your code to Core SQL, don't use the ALTER DOMAIN statement.

DROP DOMAIN Statement

The DROP DOMAIN statement destroys a Domain. The required syntax for the DROP DOMAIN statement is as follows.

```
DROP DOMAIN <Domain name> {RESTRICT | CASCADE}
```

The <Domain name> must identify an existing Domain whose owner is either the current <AuthorizationID> or a Role that the current <AuthorizationID> may use. That is, only the <AuthorizationID> that owns the Domain may drop it.

The effect of DROP DOMAIN <Domain name> RESTRICT, e.g.,

```
DROP DOMAIN domain_1 RESTRICT;
```

is that the Domain named is destroyed, provided that (*a*) no Columns are based on the Domain and (*b*) that the Domain isn't referred to in any View definition, Constraint or Assertion definition, or SQL routine. That is, RESTRICT ensures that only a Domain with no dependent Objects can be destroyed. If the Domain is used by any other Object, DROP DOMAIN ... RESTRICT will fail.

The effect of DROP DOMAIN <Domain name> CASCADE, e.g.,

```
DROP DOMAIN domain_1 CASCADE;
```

is that the Domain named is destroyed.

Successfully dropping a Domain has a five-fold effect:

1. The Domain named is destroyed.
2. All Privileges held on the Domain by the <AuthorizationID> that owns it are revoked (by the SQL special grantor, "_SYSTEM") with a CASCADE revoke behaviour, so that all Privileges held on the Domain by any other <AuthorizationID> are also revoked.
3. The definition of every Column based on the Domain is changed; the <Domain name> is removed and the Domain's <data type> specification is added. If the <Column definition> has no default value, the Domain's default value is added. If the <Column definition> has no COLLATE clause, the Domain's COLLATE clause is added, provided that the <AuthorizationID> has the USAGE Privilege on the Collation named.
4. The definition of every Table that owns a Column based on the Domain is changed; a <Table Constraint> that is equivalent to every applicable <Domain Constraint> is added, provided that the <AuthorizationID> has all the Privileges needed to add such <Table Constraint>s.
5. All SQL routines, Views and Constraints that depend on the Domain are dropped with a CASCADE drop behaviour.

   If you want to restrict your code to Core SQL, don't use the DROP DOMAIN statement.

Frequently-Used Numeric Domains

Any business needs to store "money" — usually a signed decimal with two fixed digits after the decimal point; and "interest" — usually an unsigned decimal with 3 digits after the decimal point. Some SQL DBMSs have special data types for business needs, but Standard SQL doesn't, so this is a good place to use a Domain. For example, these four SQL statements define and utilize two numeric Domains:

```
CREATE DOMAIN MONEY_ AS DECIMAL(8,2);

CREATE DOMAIN INTEREST_ AS DECIMAL(5,3);

ALTER DOMAIN INTEREST_ ADD CONSTRAINT constraint_1
   CHECK (VALUE >= 00.000);

CREATE TABLE Money_Examples (
   money_column_1 MONEY_,
   interest_column_1 INTEREST_,
   money_column_2 MONEY_,
   interest_column_2 INTEREST_);
```

In this example, the first two SQL statements create two Domains named MONEY_ and INTEREST_. The third SQL statement adds a Constraint to the INTEREST_ Domain; it must always have a value greater than or equal to zero. Lastly, the Domains are used in a CREATE TABLE statement — this saves a bit of typing, but more importantly, using the Domains makes it clear that money and interest fields are being defined — rather than merely vague, generic decimal fields.

SQL provides a predefined unsigned-integer Domain, called CARDINAL_NUMBER, that you could use on the theory that anything predefined is better than a roll-your-own. Because all predefined Objects belong to INFORMATION_SCHEMA, use a <Schema name> qualifier when making Columns with CARDINAL_NUMBER, for example:

```
ALTER TABLE Exact_Examples ADD COLUMN
   occurrence_cardinal INFORMATION_SCHEMA.CARDINAL_NUMBER;
```

This definition will cause the following SQL statement to fail because CARDINAL_NUMBER allows only unsigned numbers (that is, only numbers that are greater than or equal to zero):

```
UPDATE Exact_Examples SET
   occurrence_cardinal = -1;
```

But this SQL statement will work:

```
UPDATE Exact_Examples SET
   occurrence_cardinal = +1;
```

NOTE: Numbers in a CARDINAL_NUMBER Domain don't have the same range as C/Delphi "unsigned."

20

Chapter 20

SQL Constraints and Assertions

In this chapter, we'll describe SQL Constraints and SQL Assertions in detail and show you the syntax to use to create, alter, and destroy them.

Constraint

A Schema may contain zero or more integrity Constraints (an Assertion is just a special type of integrity Constraint; it is not necessarily dependent on a single Base table as are simple Constraints). An SQL Constraint is a named rule which helps define valid sets of values by putting limits on the results of `INSERT`, `UPDATE`, or `DELETE` operations performed on a Base table; an Assertion, by contrast, may define valid sets of values for individual rows of a Base table or for an entire Base table or it may define the set of valid values required to exist among a number of Base tables. Constraints are dependent on some Schema — the <Constraint name> must be unique within the Schema to which the Constraint belongs — and are created and dropped using standard SQL statements.

There are four Constraint variations — `UNIQUE` Constraints, `PRIMARY KEY` Constraints, `FOREIGN KEY` Constraints, and `CHECK` Constraints.

1. A `UNIQUE` Constraint defines one or more Columns of a Table as unique Columns; it is satisfied if no two rows in the Table have the same non-null values in the unique Columns.
2. A `PRIMARY KEY` Constraint is a `UNIQUE` Constraint that specifies `PRIMARY KEY`; it is satisfied if (*a*) no two rows in the Table have the same non-null values in the unique Columns and

(*b*) none of the primary key Columns are NULL. UNIQUE Constraints and PRIMARY KEY Constraints describe a Base table's candidate keys.

3. A FOREIGN KEY Constraint defines one or more Columns of a Table as referencing Columns whose values must match the values of some corresponding referenced Columns in a referenced Base table (the referenced Columns must be UNIQUE Columns for the referenced Table). It is satisfied if, for every row in the referencing Table, the values of the referencing Columns are equal to those of the corresponding referenced Columns in some row of the referenced Table. (If either Table contains NULLs, satisfaction of the FOREIGN KEY Constraint depends on the Constraint's match type.) FOREIGN KEY Constraints describe linkages between Base tables.
4. A CHECK Constraint defines a search condition; it is violated if the result of the condition is FALSE for any row of the Table. An Assertion is a CHECK Constraint that may operate on multiple Tables.

Non-Deterministic Constraints

A CHECK Constraint may not define a non-deterministic search condition — that is, any condition whose result may vary from time to time. Here is an example of an invalid CHECK Constraint:

```
CREATE TABLE Table_1 (
   column_1 DATE CHECK (column_1 = CURRENT_DATE);
```

This SQL statement would return an error because the CHECK Constraint's search condition is non-deterministic — because the value of CURRENT_DATE changes each time the function is called, your DBMS is not able to determine whether the Constraint has been violated or not. For another example, run this query twice, on the same database:

```
SELECT *
FROM   Table_1
WHERE  column_time = TIME '13:14:15';
```

You can be sure that the results will be the same both times. Now run this query twice:

```
SELECT *
FROM   Table_1
WHERE  column_time = CURRENT_TIME;
```

You can't be sure that the results will be the same both times because the current time is a value from outside your SQL environment, beyond the control of your DBMS. Now run this query twice:

```
SELECT 'a '
FROM   Table_1
UNION
SELECT 'A'
FROM   Table_1;
```

Once again, you can't be sure that the results will be the same both times. With most Collations (NO PAD and "case insensitive"), the <literal>s 'a ' and 'A' are equivalent — that is, they're equal to each other. But they're still not the same <literal>.

The point is that the only predictable queries are those which depend on SQL-data and defined rules. As soon as you start to use values which are outside SQL or which result from implementation-dependent answers to areas which the SQL Standard leaves undefined, you have a query which requires a nine-syllable term to describe: "possibly non-deterministic." Specifically, queries are possibly non-deterministic (and therefore not allowed in Constraints) if they depend on:

- A niladic function (CURRENT_DATE, CURRENT_TIME, CURRENT_TIMESTAMP, LOCALTIME, LOCALTIMESTAMP, USER, CURRENT_USER, SESSION_USER, SYSTEM_USER, CURRENT_PATH, CURRENT_ROLE).
- An operation which picks from multiple values that may be equivalent-but-not-the-same. Picky operations include: MIN, MAX, UNION (though UNION ALL is okay), INTERSECT, EXCEPT, DISTINCT, and grouping columns. Equivalent-but-not-the-same can be true for character strings and times and timestamps (in the latter cases the external factor that causes non-determinism is the time zone).
- A routine invocation which is based on a procedure in a host language or on parameters that are set by a host program.

No matter what type of Constraint you're defining, the main ideas are always the same.

1. You're describing a state which must not be FALSE. This means it can be either TRUE or UNKNOWN. (It can also be "temporarily FALSE" — your DBMS is supposed to allow bad data until constraint check time. Then, if it descries a FALSE condition, it must wipe the bad data out again, so it's equally correct to say "Constraint violation" and "attempted Constraint violation.") Evaluation of a Constraint is one of the areas where NULLs and three-valued logic play an important role.
2. A Constraint is an Object in a Schema — it is not a procedure. It is, rather, a revelation to the DBMS about what you want and what you don't want to see in your database.

Constraint Deferrability

All Constraints are defined with a deferral mode of either DEFERRABLE or NOT DEFERRABLE. A deferral mode of DEFERRABLE allows you to specify when you want your DBMS to check the Constraint for violation (the choices are at statement end or at transaction end). A deferral mode of NOT DEFERRABLE doesn't give you this option; your DBMS will check the Constraint for violation as soon as it finishes executing an SQL statement. Of course, not every SQL statement will cause your DBMS to check Constraints — the main statements that cause Constraint checking are INSERT, UPDATE, and DELETE (there is no Constraint checking for DROP statements). DELETE is slightly less important because whenever you get rid of a row, there is no longer any need to check whether that row violates a Constraint. Consider these SQL statements:

```
CREATE TABLE Table_1 (
   column_1 SMALLINT);

ALTER TABLE Table_1 ADD CONSTRAINT constraint_1
   UNIQUE (column_1) NOT DEFERRABLE;

INSERT INTO Table_1 (column_1)
VALUES (1);

INSERT INTO Table_1 (column_1)
VALUES (2);

UPDATE Table_1 SET
   column_1 = column_1 + 1;
```

Believe it or not, there are DBMSs alive today which will fail when they encounter this example's `UPDATE` statement. The reason is that they `UPDATE` one row at a time and perform the Constraint check immediately after doing each row (this is normally the case whenever a DBMS implements `UNIQUE` Constraints using a "unique index"). Therefore, as soon as `1+1 = 2` is done for the first row, there's a duplication — even though, if the DBMS would only proceed to do the next row, the duplication would disappear (it would end up with a `2` in the first row and a `3` in the second row). The fact is, there never is a need for the Constraint to be checked until the end of the `UPDATE` statement — nor does the SQL Standard allow for Constraint checking until that time.

Every Constraint is also defined with a persistent initial constraint check time that depends on its deferral mode; it is either `INITIALLY IMMEDIATE` or `INITIALLY DEFERRED`. A Constraint that is `NOT DEFERRABLE` always has an initial constraint check time of `INITIALLY IMMEDIATE`. A Constraint that is `DEFERRABLE` may have an initial constraint check time of either `INITIALLY IMMEDIATE` or `INITIALLY DEFERRED`. During a transaction, each Constraint also has a current constraint check time; its defined initial constraint check time is always the current constraint check time at the beginning of a transaction but you may change the check time for the period of the transaction (from `IMMEDIATE` to `DEFERRED` or vice versa) if the Constraint is `DEFERRABLE`.

- During a transaction, your DBMS will check every Constraint with a current constraint check time of `IMMEDIATE` for violation right after it executes an SQL statement — thus each such Constraint may be checked multiple times during a transaction.
- During a transaction, your DBMS will wait to check every Constraint with a current constraint check time of `DEFERRED` until the transaction ends — thus each such Constraint will be checked only once per transaction.

For each SQL-session, the current constraint check time of all Constraints is a property of that SQL-session.

To create a Constraint, use a <Table Constraint> definition or a <Column Constraint> definition in a CREATE TABLE or an ALTER TABLE statement or use a <Domain Constraint> definition in a CREATE DOMAIN or an ALTER DOMAIN statement or use the CREATE ASSERTION statement. To destroy a Constraint, use the ALTER TABLE, ALTER DOMAIN, or DROP ASSERTION statements. To change an existing Constraint, drop and then redefine it.

There is a one-to-many association between Base tables and <Table Constraint>s or <Column Constraint>s; one Base table may be constrained by the rules of many <Table Constraint>s and/or many <Column Constraint>s (each of which may help define only that Table's set of valid values). There is also a many-to-many association between Base tables and <Domain Constraint>s; multiple Base tables may contain one or more Columns that are based on the same Domain — and that Domain may be constrained by the rules of many <Domain Constraint>s. Finally, there is a many-to-many association between Base tables and Assertions; multiple Base tables may be constrained by the rules of one Assertion and one Base table may be constrained by the rules of many Assertions.

Constraint Names

A <Constraint name> identifies a Constraint or an Assertion. The required syntax for a <Constraint name> is as follows.

```
<Constraint name> ::=
[ <Schema name>. ] unqualified name
```

A <Constraint name> is a <regular identifier> or a <delimited identifier> that is unique (for all Constraints and Assertions) within the Schema to which it belongs. The <Schema name> that qualifies a <Constraint name> names the Schema to which the Constraint or Assertion belongs and can either be explicitly stated or a default will be supplied by your DBMS as follows:

- If a <Constraint name> in a CREATE SCHEMA statement isn't qualified, the default qualifier is the name of the Schema you're creating.
- If the unqualified <Constraint name> is found in any other SQL statement in a Module, the default qualifier is the name of the Schema identified in the SCHEMA clause or AUTHORIZATION clause of the MODULE statement which defines that Module.

Here are some examples of <Constraint name>s:

```
CONSTRAINT_1
-- a <Constraint name>

SCHEMA_1.CONSTRAINT_1
-- a simple qualified <Constraint name>

CATALOG_1.SCHEMA_1.CONSTRAINT_1
-- a fully qualified <Constraint name>
```

<Table Constraint> and <Column Constraint>

A Base table may be constrained by zero or more <Table Constraint>s; Constraints defined on one or more of its Columns in a `CREATE TABLE` or an `ALTER TABLE` statement. <Table Constraint>s are dependent on some Base table and therefore on some Schema — the <Constraint name> must be unique within the Schema to which the Constraint belongs. There are five kinds of <Table Constraint>s: `UNIQUE` Constraints, `PRIMARY KEY` Constraints, `FOREIGN KEY` Constraints, `CHECK` Constraints, and `NOT NULL` Constraints (which are really just a type of `CHECK` Constraint).

A <Column definition> (and therefore a Base table) may be constrained by zero or more <Column Constraint>s; Constraints defined on a single Column in a `CREATE TABLE` or an `ALTER TABLE` statement. A <Column Constraint> logically becomes a <Table Constraint> as soon as it is created. <Column Constraint>s are dependent on some Base table and therefore on some Schema — the <Constraint name> must be unique within the Schema to which the Constraint belongs. A <Column Constraint> may be any Constraint that can be a <Table Constraint>.

<Domain Constraint>

A Domain may be constrained by zero or more <Domain Constraint>s; Constraints defined in a `CREATE DOMAIN` or an `ALTER DOMAIN` statement. <Domain Constraint>s are dependent on some Domain and therefore on some Schema — the <Constraint name> must be unique within the Schema to which the Constraint belongs. All <Domain Constraint>s are `CHECK` Constraints whose search conditions are applied to all Columns based on the Domain and to all values cast to the Domain. The search condition may not be a recursive search condition (i.e., it may not refer, either directly or indirectly, to the Domain to which the <Domain Constraint> belongs) and it must use the <value specification> `VALUE`; that is, the only proper form for a <Domain Constraint>'s rule is:

```
CHECK (...VALUE...)
```

Three things wrong with the World Wide Web are:

1. Pages can be written in different styles and formats or just be garbage.
2. Pages can be duplicated.
3. Links can be broken (the notorious "URL not found" error).

If we could control the World Wide Web, we'd do what we could to stomp out each of those practices, in turn. Specifically, we'd add three basic kinds of Constraints. Well, we don't control the Web. But we do control databases, so we can use Constraints to stop bad data from getting into our Base tables. (There are other lines of defense against bad data — for example, the requirement that values correspond to a defined <data type>, the `WITH CHECK OPTION` requirement on a View, the SQL3 `TRIGGER` feature, and the procedures in your host language programs. We describe these defenses in other chapters.)

If it's possible, you should create your Constraints and associate them only with Base tables — that way, the process is clear to all users. You'll know where to look for information about the Constraints — they'll be associated with the Tables themselves in the `INFORMATION_SCHEMA`. And, after reading this chapter, you'll know what the specific (rather rigid) rules are — which reduces uncertainty, since specific and rigid rules are clear and well-understood rules. In any case, it is logically proper to associate a Constraint with a Table because a Table is a set of row values and a Constraint is a restriction (or description) of that set of values.

Constraint Descriptors

A `UNIQUE` Constraint is defined by a descriptor that contains five pieces of information:

1. The <Constraint name> qualified by the <Schema name> of the Schema to which it belongs.
2. The Constraint's deferral mode: either `DEFERRABLE` or `NOT DEFERRABLE`.
3. The Constraint's initial constraint check time: either `INITIALLY DEFERRED` or `INITIALLY IMMEDIATE`.
4. The Constraint's rule, the <keyword> `UNIQUE`, which forces the Table's set of valid values for one or more Columns to be unique.
5. The names and positions of the Columns that are required to contain only unique values.

A `PRIMARY KEY` Constraint is defined by a descriptor that contains five pieces of information:

1. The <Constraint name> qualified by the <Schema name> of the Schema to which it belongs.
2. The Constraint's deferral mode: either `DEFERRABLE` or `NOT DEFERRABLE`.
3. The Constraint's initial constraint check time: either `INITIALLY DEFERRED` or `INITIALLY IMMEDIATE`.
4. The Constraint's rule, the <keyword> phrase `PRIMARY KEY`, which forces the Table's set of valid values for one or more Columns to be unique and not `NULL`.
5. The names and positions of the Columns that are the Table's primary key and thus are required to contain only unique, non-null values. (A Table that has a primary key cannot have a proper supertable.)

A `FOREIGN KEY` Constraint is defined by a descriptor that contains nine pieces of information:

1. The <Constraint name> qualified by the <Schema name> of the Schema to which it belongs.
2. The Constraint's deferral mode: either `DEFERRABLE` or `NOT DEFERRABLE`.
3. The Constraint's initial constraint check time: either `INITIALLY DEFERRED` or `INITIALLY IMMEDIATE`.
4. The Constraint's rule, the <keyword> phrase `FOREIGN KEY`, which forces the Table's set of valid values for one or more Columns to match some corresponding Columns.
5. The names and positions of the referencing Column(s) that make up a foreign key for a Table.
6. The name of the Table that contains the referenced Column(s).
7. The names and positions of the referenced Column(s) in the referenced Table.
8. The Constraint's `MATCH` type (if any).
9. The Constraint's referential triggered actions (if any).

A NOT NULL Constraint is defined by a descriptor that contains four pieces of information:

1. The <Constraint name> qualified by the <Schema name> of the Schema to which it belongs.
2. The Constraint's deferral mode: either DEFERRABLE or NOT DEFERRABLE.
3. The Constraint's initial constraint check time: either INITIALLY DEFERRED or INITIALLY IMMEDIATE.
4. The Constraint's rule: CHECK (<Column name> IS NOT NULL).

A CHECK Constraint is defined by a descriptor that contains four pieces of information:

1. The <Constraint name> qualified by the <Schema name> of the Schema to which it belongs.
2. The Constraint's deferral mode: either DEFERRABLE or NOT DEFERRABLE.
3. The Constraint's initial constraint check time: either INITIALLY DEFERRED or INITIALLY IMMEDIATE.
4. The Constraint's rule, the <keyword> CHECK, followed by the parenthesized search condition that forces the Table's set of valid values for one or more Columns to be TRUE or UNKNOWN for the condition.

An Assertion is defined by a descriptor that contains four pieces of information:

1. The <Constraint name> qualified by the <Schema name> of the Schema to which it belongs.
2. The Constraint's deferral mode: either DEFERRABLE or NOT DEFERRABLE.
3. The Constraint's initial constraint check time: either INITIALLY DEFERRED or INITIALLY IMMEDIATE.
4. The Constraint's rule, the <keyword> CHECK, followed by the parenthesized search condition that forces the set of valid values for one or more Base Tables to be TRUE or UNKNOWN for the condition.

Constraint Definition

A Constraint definition creates a <Table Constraint>, a <Column Constraint>, or a <Domain Constraint>. Used in a CREATE TABLE, ALTER TABLE, CREATE DOMAIN, or ALTER DOMAIN statement, it names a Constraint and defines the Constraint's type, deferral mode, and constraint check time. The required syntax for a Constraint definition is as follows.

```
Constraint definition ::=
[ CONSTRAINT <Constraint name> ]
Constraint_type
[ <constraint attributes> ]

   Constraint_type ::=
   <Table Constraint> |
   <Column Constraint> |
   <Domain Constraint>
```

```
    <Table Constraint> ::=
    UNIQUE Constraint |
    PRIMARY KEY Constraint |
    FOREIGN KEY Constraint |
    CHECK Constraint

    <Column Constraint> ::=
    UNIQUE Constraint |
    PRIMARY KEY Constraint |
    FOREIGN KEY Constraint |
    NOT NULL Constraint |
    CHECK Constraint

    <Domain Constraint> ::=
    CHECK Constraint

<constraint attributes> ::=
<constraint check time> [ [ NOT ] DEFERRABLE ] |
[ NOT ] DEFERRABLE [ <constraint check time> ]

    <constraint check time> ::=
    INITIALLY DEFERRED | INITIALLY IMMEDIATE
```

A Constraint definition defines a new rule that will constrain a Base table's set of valid values.

<Constraint name>

All Constraints have names. The optional CONSTRAINT clause of a Constraint definition is used to provide an explicit name for a Constraint. If you omit the CONSTRAINT clause from a Constraint definition, your DBMS will provide a default <Constraint name> to identify the Constraint. For example, this SQL statement includes a Constraint definition that includes a CONSTRAINT clause:

```
ALTER TABLE Table_1 ADD CONSTRAINT constraint_1
   PRIMARY KEY(column_1);
```

(The name of the Constraint is CONSTRAINT_1.) The following SQL statement includes a Constraint definition that omits the CONSTRAINT clause:

```
CREATE TABLE Table_1 (
   column_1 SMALLINT PRIMARY KEY);
```

(The name of the Constraint is defined by your DBMS and is therefore non- standard, so we recommend that you explicitly name all of your Constraints.)

The <Constraint name> identifies the Constraint and the Schema to which it belongs. A <Constraint name> that includes an explicit <Schema name> qualifier belongs to the Schema named. A <Constraint name> that does not include an explicit <Schema name> qualifier belongs to the SQL-session default Schema. (In both cases, that Schema must, of course, own the Table or Domain for which the Constraint is defined.) The <Constraint name> must be unique (for all Constraints and Assertions) within the Schema that contains it. If `CREATE TABLE`, `ALTER TABLE`, `CREATE DOMAIN`, or `ALTER DOMAIN` are part of a `CREATE SCHEMA` statement, the <Constraint name> (if explicitly qualified) must include the <Schema name> of the Schema being created; that is, it isn't possible to create a Constraint belonging to a different Schema from within `CREATE SCHEMA`.

Types of Constraints

A <Table Constraint> defines a rule that limits the set of values for one or more Columns of a Base table.

A <Column Constraint> defines a rule that limits the set of values for one Column of a Base Table. You may define a <Column Constraint> only within a <Column definition>. Once created, a <Column Constraint> logically becomes a <Table Constraint> for the Table that owns the Column that the Constraint is defined for.

A <Domain Constraint> defines a rule that limits the set of values for every Column that is based on the Domain that the Constraint is defined for. One or more Columns from one or more Base tables may thus be affected by a <Domain Constraint>. A <Domain Constraint> is a `CHECK` Constraint that uses the <value specification> `VALUE`.

Deferral Mode

A Constraint definition may include a specification of the Constraint's deferral mode: either `DEFERRABLE` or `NOT DEFERRABLE`. A deferral mode of `NOT DEFERRABLE` means that your DBMS will check the Constraint for violation immediately after executing every SQL statement in a transaction. A deferral mode of `DEFERRABLE` means that your DBMS may defer checking the Constraint for violation until the end of the transaction. If you omit the deferral mode specification from a Constraint definition, the Constraint's deferral mode depends on its initial constraint check time; the deferral mode for an `INITIALLY DEFERRED` Constraint defaults to `DEFERRABLE` and the deferral mode for an `INITIALLY IMMEDIATE` Constraint defaults to `NOT DEFERRABLE`.

Constraint Check Time

A Constraint definition may also include a specification of the Constraint's initial constraint check time: either `INITIALLY DEFERRED` or `INITIALLY IMMEDIATE`. If you omit the constraint check time specification from a Constraint definition, the Constraint will have a constraint check time of `INITIALLY IMMEDIATE`.

If its initial constraint check time is `INITIALLY DEFERRED`, a Constraint's deferral mode must be `DEFERRABLE` and its constraint check time will be `DEFERRED` at the beginning of every transaction. You may use the `SET CONSTRAINTS` statement to change a `DEFERRABLE INITIALLY DEFERRED` Constraint's constraint check time for a transaction (this is the current constraint check time) to `IMMEDIATE`.

If its initial constraint check time is INITIALLY IMMEDIATE, a Constraint's deferral mode may be either DEFERRABLE or NOT DEFERRABLE and its constraint check time will be IMMEDIATE at the beginning of every transaction. You may use the SET CONSTRAINTS statement to change a DEFERRABLE INITIALLY IMMEDIATE Constraint's constraint check time for a transaction to DEFERRED but you may not use SET CONSTRAINTS on a NOT DEFERRABLE INITIALLY IMMEDIATE Constraint because such Constraints can't have their constraint check times changed.

Immediately after executing any SQL statement, your DBMS checks every Constraint with a current constraint check time of IMMEDIATE for violation, but does not check the Constraints with a current constraint check time of DEFERRED. At the end of a transaction, any Constraints with a current constraint check time of DEFERRED have it changed to IMMEDIATE — thus, your DBMS checks every Constraint for violation at the end of a transaction. When checked, if any Constraint is violated, the SQL statement that caused it to be checked will fail; your DBMS will return the SQLSTATE error 23000 "integrity constraint violation" unless the SQL statement that fails is a COMMIT statement. If COMMIT fails, your DBMS will return the SQLSTATE error 40002 "transaction rollback-integrity constraint violation." In either case, the status of all SQL-data remains as it was prior to the execution of the failed SQL statement.

TRAP: You're taking a huge risk when you use deferred Constraints, because you're not warned of any problems until COMMIT time. Remember that, at this point, instead of returning a message like, "sorry the Constraint's been violated" and giving you a chance to fix the problem, your DBMS will say, "sorry the Constraint's been violated" and ROLLBACKs the entire transaction! In other words, although you've asked for COMMIT, what you get is ROLLBACK. This is perhaps the only command in any programming language where, if you ask for *x*, you not only don't get *x*, you actually get the precise reverse of *x*! If you must use deferred Constraints, add this SQL statement to your transaction before you COMMIT:

```
SET CONSTRAINTS ALL IMMEDIATE;
```

The advantage of SET CONSTRAINTS ALL IMMEDIATE is that it won't ROLLBACK, so if you execute it before you COMMIT, you improve your chances of having something to commit.

Although it's usually best to check all Constraints for violation right after you've done an operation that might cause your data to be invalid, here's some reasons why you might want to defer Constraint checking:

- Because some invalid state might be true for a while (such as a transaction that temporarily throws everything out of balance), but you know that the situation will resolve itself by transaction end.
- Because you want to subvert or ignore Constraints until there is some reason to worry about them. For example, there might be some calculations that you want to perform on a "what if" basis and the only way to get them straight is by temporarily turning off the Constraint checking mechanism. Such "what if" calculations are normally ended with a ROLLBACK statement.

TRAP: There are some systems — the notorious example is the requirement for ODBC — which "auto-commit." This means that as soon as an SQL statement is finished, your helpful DBMS will automatically execute a COMMIT statement for you! As well as being a violation of the SQL Standard and making the ROLLBACK statement useless, this action destroys the basis on which we lay our deferred-Constraint plans.

Here is an example of an SQL statement that adds a NOT DEFERRABLE INITIALLY IMMEDIATE Constraint to a Table:

```
ALTER TABLE Table_1 ADD CONSTRAINT constraint_1
   CHECK (column_1 > 500) NOT DEFERRABLE INITIALLY IMMEDIATE;
```

The following SQL statement adds a DEFERRABLE INITIALLY IMMEDIATE Constraint to a Table:

```
ALTER TABLE Table_1 ADD CONSTRAINT constraint_1
   CHECK (column_1 > 500) DEFERRABLE INITIALLY IMMEDIATE;
```

This SQL statement adds a DEFERRABLE INITIALLY DEFERRED Constraint to a Table:

```
ALTER TABLE Table_1 ADD CONSTRAINT constraint_1
   CHECK (column_1 > 500) DEFERRABLE INITIALLY DEFERRED;
```

If you want to restrict your code to Core SQL, don't name your Constraints and don't add a <constraint attributes> clause to your Constraint definitions. (This means you'll be defining all Constraints as NOT DEFERRABLE INITIALLY IMMEDIATE.)

Constraint_type — UNIQUE Constraint

A UNIQUE Constraint is either a <Table Constraint> or a <Column Constraint> and defines a rule that constrains a unique key to non-duplicate values only. The required syntax for a UNIQUE Constraint is as follows.

```
UNIQUE <Table Constraint> ::=
[ CONSTRAINT <Constraint name> ]
UNIQUE (<Column name> [ {,<Column name>}... ]) | UNIQUE (VALUE)
[ <constraint attributes> ]

UNIQUE <Column Constraint> ::=
[ CONSTRAINT <Constraint name> ] UNIQUE
[ <constraint attributes> ]
```

A Base table may be constrained by zero or more UNIQUE Constraints, each specifying a rule that a group of one or more Columns (the unique key) may contain only unique values. You can't define a unique key with Columns that have a <data type> of BLOB, CLOB, NCLOB, or ARRAY. A unique key is also known as a candidate key of the Table. The main reasons you need candidate keys are (*a*) to get row-level addressing, (*b*) so that foreign keys can reference the candidate key, and (*c*) to prevent duplication (keyboard errors, etc.).

Each UNIQUE Constraint must name a set of Columns that is different from the set of Columns named by any other UNIQUE or PRIMARY KEY Constraint defined for the Table. If you use UNIQUE (VALUE) to define a UNIQUE Constraint, you're constraining the Table that owns the Constraint to have just that one UNIQUE Constraint and — because a PRIMARY KEY Constraint is a type of UNIQUE Constraint — you're also constraining that Table not to have any PRIMARY KEY Constraint. UNIQUE (VALUE) constrains the entire row of the Table to be unique from any other row.

Here are some examples of UNIQUE Constraint definitions:

```
CREATE TABLE Table_1 (
   column_1 SMALLINT,
   CONSTRAINT constraint_1 UNIQUE(column_1));
-- defines a UNIQUE <Table Constraint> in CREATE TABLE

CREATE TABLE Table_1 (
   column_1 SMALLINT
   CONSTRAINT constraint_1 UNIQUE DEFERRABLE INITIALLY DEFERRED,
   column_2 CHAR(5));
-- defines a UNIQUE <Column Constraint> in CREATE TABLE

ALTER TABLE Table_1 ADD CONSTRAINT constraint_2
   UNIQUE(column_1,column_2) DEFERRABLE INITIALLY DEFERRED;
-- defines a UNIQUE <Table Constraint> in ALTER TABLE
```

Once created, a UNIQUE <Column Constraint> logically becomes a UNIQUE <Table Constraint>. The <Column Constraint> in this SQL statement:

```
CREATE TABLE Table_1 (column_1 SMALLINT UNIQUE);
```

is therefore equivalent to the <Table Constraint> in this SQL statement:

```
CREATE TABLE Table_1 (
   column_1 SMALLINT,
   UNIQUE(column_1));
```

A UNIQUE Constraint makes it impossible to COMMIT any operation that would cause the unique key to contain any non-null duplicate values. (Multiple null values are allowed because the null value is never equal to anything, even another null value.) A UNIQUE Constraint is violated if its condition is FALSE for any row of the Table to which it belongs. Consider these SQL statements:

```
CREATE TABLE Table_1 (
   column_1 SMALLINT,
   column_2 VARCHAR(5),
   CONSTRAINT constraint_1
      UNIQUE(column_1,column_2) DEFERRABLE INITIALLY DEFERRED);
```

```
INSERT INTO Table_1 (column_1, column_2)
VALUES (1, 'hello');
```

For this example, CONSTRAINT_1 would be violated only if you tried to INSERT another {1, 'hello'} row into TABLE_1: a {1, 'bye'} row, a {2, 'hello'} row, a {null, 'hello'} row, a {1, null} row and a {null, null} row would all satisfy the Constraint.

If you want to restrict your code to Core SQL, don't use the UNIQUE(VALUE) form to define a UNIQUE Constraint and don't add a NOT NULL Constraint to any Column that is part of a unique key for a UNIQUE Constraint.

Constraint_type — PRIMARY KEY Constraint

A PRIMARY KEY Constraint is either a <Table Constraint> or a <Column Constraint> and defines a rule that constrains a unique key to non-duplicate, non-null values only. The required syntax for a PRIMARY KEY Constraint is as follows.

```
PRIMARY KEY <Table Constraint> ::=
[ CONSTRAINT <Constraint name> ]
PRIMARY KEY (<Column name> [ {,<Column name>}... ])
[ <constraint attributes> ]

PRIMARY KEY <Column Constraint> ::=
[ CONSTRAINT <Constraint name> ] PRIMARY KEY
[ <constraint attributes> ]
```

A Base table may be constrained by no more than one PRIMARY KEY Constraint, which specifies a rule that a group of one or more Columns is the Table's primary key. A primary key is the set of Columns in a Base table that (because they will be used as the main unique identifier for a row) must contain only unique and not null values. You can't define a primary key with Columns that have a <data type> of BLOB, CLOB, NCLOB, or ARRAY.

A Table's PRIMARY KEY Constraint must name a set of Columns that is different from the set of Columns named by any other UNIQUE Constraint defined for the Table. Which unique key should be the primary key for a Table? The criteria are:

- Simplicity, i.e., the key with the fewest Columns and smallest size.
- Permanence.
- Mnemonicity, i.e., the key that people will understand and remember.
- The key's use in other (e.g., foreign) Tables.

Here are some examples of PRIMARY KEY Constraint definitions:

```
CREATE TABLE Table_1 (
   column_1 SMALLINT,
   CONSTRAINT constraint_1 PRIMARY KEY(column_1) NOT DEFERRABLE;
-- defines a PRIMARY KEY <Table Constraint> in CREATE TABLE
```

```
CREATE TABLE Table_1 (
   column_1 SMALLINT CONSTRAINT constraint_1 PRIMARY KEY
            NOT DEFERRABLE,
   column_2 CHAR(5));
-- defines a PRIMARY KEY <Column Constraint> in CREATE TABLE

ALTER TABLE Table_2 ADD CONSTRAINT constraint_2
   PRIMARY KEY(column_1,column_2) NOT DEFERRABLE INITIALLY IMMEDIATE;
-- defines a PRIMARY KEY <Table Constraint> in ALTER TABLE
```

Once created, a PRIMARY KEY <Column Constraint> logically becomes a PRIMARY KEY <Table Constraint>. The <Column Constraint> in this SQL statement:

```
CREATE TABLE Table_1 (
   column_1 SMALLINT PRIMARY KEY);
```

is therefore equivalent to the <Table Constraint> in this SQL statement:

```
CREATE TABLE Table_1 (
   column_1 SMALLINT,
   PRIMARY KEY(column_1));
```

A PRIMARY KEY Constraint makes it impossible to COMMIT any operation that would cause the unique key to contain any NULLs or any duplicate values. A PRIMARY KEY Constraint is violated if its condition is FALSE for any row of the Table to which it belongs. Consider these SQL statements:

```
CREATE TABLE Table_1 (
   column_1 SMALLINT,
   column_2 VARCHAR(5),
   CONSTRAINT constraint_1 PRIMARY KEY(column_1,column_2)
              NOT DEFERRABLE );

INSERT INTO Table_1 (column_1, column_2)
VALUES (1, 'hello');
```

For this example, CONSTRAINT_1 would be violated if you tried to INSERT another {1, 'hello'} row into TABLE_1 or if you tried to insert a {null, 'hello'} row, a {1, null} row or a {null, null} into TABLE_1.

The uniqueness of a primary key helps guarantee the integrity of your data. Once you've defined a primary key for a Table, you're protected from simple errors like putting in the same person twice. More importantly (or at least equally importantly), you have the reflection of the "real world" fact that two things aren't alike in every respect — if they were, they'd form the same record. When you declare a primary key, you are hinting to your DBMS that the data in the key is relatively static. Many attributes of a Table are transient; an employee's salary, age, weight, title, evaluation, etc. But a primary key Column's values tend to be stable — we don't change people's names or our part numbers very often. A primary key identifier also comes in handy when you're splitting your data into two Tables. For example, consider an "Internet address." You might start off with this Table definition:

```
CREATE TABLE Table_1 (
   table_id VARCHAR(40),
   int_address VARCHAR(50));
```

This is fine as long as whoever is represented in the TABLE_ID Column only has one Internet address. But that person now gives you the Internet address used at work and perhaps at several other locations. Should you have a repeating Column (ARRAY) for this data? Well maybe, but the use of non-atomic values is still frowned on and deservedly has a bad rep — see Chapter 10 "Collection Types" for a discussion of the problem. The classic relational solution is to split your data into two Tables. For example:

```
CREATE TABLE Table_1 (
   table_id VARCHAR(40),
   CONSTRAINT constraint_1 PRIMARY KEY(table_id));
CREATE TABLE Table_2 (
   table_id VARCHAR(40),
   int_address VARCHAR(50),
   CONSTRAINT constraint_2 FOREIGN KEY(int_address)
              REFERENCES Table_1);
```

These definitions allow you to store as many Internet addresses for a single person as you want — a repeating group is possible in SQL, it's just an avoidance of first-normal form if you try to put it into one Table.

Constraint_type — FOREIGN KEY Constraint

A FOREIGN KEY Constraint is either a <Table Constraint> or a <Column Constraint> and defines a rule that constrains a foreign key to values that match only those values contained in a referenced unique key. The required syntax for a FOREIGN KEY Constraint is as follows.

```
FOREIGN KEY <Table Constraint> ::=
[ CONSTRAINT <Constraint name> ]
FOREIGN KEY (referencing <Column name> [ {,<Column name>}... ])
   REFERENCES referenced <Table name>
      [ (referenced <Column name> [ {,<Column name>}... ]) ]
   [ MATCH {FULL | PARTIAL | SIMPLE} ]
   [ <referential triggered action> ]
[ <constraint attributes> ]

      <referential triggered action> ::=
      ON UPDATE <action> [ ON DELETE <action> ] |
      ON DELETE <action> [ ON UPDATE <action> ]
```

```
        <action> ::=
        NO ACTION |
        CASCADE |
        RESTRICT |
        SET NULL |
        SET DEFAULT

FOREIGN KEY <Column Constraint> ::=
[ CONSTRAINT <Constraint name> ]
REFERENCES referenced <Table name>
     [ (referenced <Column name>) ]
   [ MATCH {FULL | PARTIAL | SIMPLE} ]
   [ <referential triggered action> ]
[ <constraint attributes> ]
```

A Base table may be constrained by zero or more FOREIGN KEY Constraints, which specify a rule that a group of one or more Columns of the Table may contain only those values found in a similar set of unique Columns belonging to (usually) another Table. You can't define a foreign key with Columns that have a <data type> of BLOB, CLOB, NCLOB, or ARRAY. Here are some examples of FOREIGN KEY Constraint definitions:

```
CREATE TABLE Table_2 (
   column_1 SMALLINT,
   CONSTRAINT constraint_1 FOREIGN KEY(column_1) REFERENCES Table_1
      NOT DEFERRABLE);
-- defines a FOREIGN KEY <Table Constraint> in CREATE TABLE

CREATE TABLE Table_2 (
   column_1 SMALLINT CONSTRAINT constraint_1
     REFERENCES Table_1 NOT DEFERRABLE,
   column_2 CHAR(5));
-- defines a FOREIGN KEY <Column Constraint> in CREATE TABLE

ALTER TABLE Table_2 ADD CONSTRAINT constraint_2
   FOREIGN KEY(column_1,column_2)
   REFERENCES Table_1(column_3,column_5)
      DEFERRABLE INITIALLY IMMEDIATE;
-- defines a FOREIGN KEY <Table Constraint> in ALTER TABLE
```

Once created, a FOREIGN KEY <Column Constraint> logically becomes a FOREIGN KEY <Table Constraint>. The <Column Constraint> in the following SQL statement:

```
CREATE TABLE Table_2 (
   column_1 SMALLINT REFERENCES Table_1);
```

is therefore equivalent to the <Table Constraint> in this SQL statement:

```
CREATE TABLE Table_2 (
   column_1 SMALLINT,
   FOREIGN KEY(column_1) REFERENCES Table_1);
```

The rationale for a foreign key: you can't have an employee in department D if there is no department D, you can't have a branch that produces Widgets if you don't have a product called a Widget, you can't locate an office in state = TY if there is no state named Tynnessee. A FOREIGN KEY Constraint forges a link between the referencing Table and the referenced Table; it makes it impossible to COMMIT any operation that would cause the foreign key to contain any values that are not found in the referenced unique key. (The referencing Table is the Table to which the FOREIGN KEY Constraint belongs; the foreign key itself is made up of one or more Columns of that Table — these are called the *referencing Columns*. The referenced Table is the Table that contains the unique key that the foreign key must match; the Columns that make up that unique key are called the referenced Columns. SQL allows the referencing Table and the referenced Table to be the same.) In the usual situation, illustrated in the previous examples (other actions can be specified), the Constraint makes it impossible to drop TABLE_1 (because TABLE_2 references it) or to delete or change a row in TABLE_1 so that TABLE_2 is left with unmatched referencing values, or to insert a row into TABLE_2 unless its referencing values are matched somewhere in TABLE_1. A FOREIGN KEY Constraint is violated if its condition is FALSE for any row of the Table to which it belongs. The result of the evaluation of the FOREIGN KEY Constraint condition depends on the presence of null values and the degree of matching specified for the Constraint — see the comments in "MATCH Clause" on page 422.

Referencing Columns

The FOREIGN KEY clause of a FOREIGN KEY <Table Constraint> definition names the referencing Columns; the group of one or more Columns that make up the foreign key (a Column may appear in the list only once). You may specify only unqualified <Column name>s in this clause.

Referenced Table and Columns

The REFERENCES clause of a FOREIGN KEY Constraint definition names the referenced Base table; the Base table that contains the referenced unique key. The Table types must match. If the Table that owns the FOREIGN KEY Constraint is a persistent Base table, the referenced Table must also be a persistent Base Table. If the referencing Table is a GLOBAL TEMPORARY Base table, the referenced Table must also be a GLOBAL TEMPORARY Base Table. If the referencing Table is a created LOCAL TEMPORARY Base table, the referenced Table must be either a GLOBAL TEMPORARY Base Table or a created LOCAL TEMPORARY Base table. If the referencing Table is a declared LOCAL TEMPORARY Base table, the referenced Table must be either a GLOBAL TEMPORARY Base Table, a created LOCAL TEMPORARY Base table, or a declared LOCAL TEMPORARY Base table. And if the referencing Table is any temporary Base table defined with an ON COMMIT DELETE ROWS clause, the referenced Table must also be a temporary Base Table defined with that clause.

The referenced Columns, optionally named in the REFERENCES clause of a FOREIGN KEY Constraint definition, are the group of one or more Columns that make up the referenced unique key (that is, the referenced Columns must be named in a NOT DEFERRABLE UNIQUE or NOT DEFERRABLE PRIMARY KEY Constraint that belongs to the referenced Table and may therefore appear in the list only once). You may specify only unqualified <Column name>s in this clause. The Columns in the foreign key must match the number of, and have a comparable <data type> with, the corresponding Columns in the referenced unique key. If you omit the referenced Columns list from a FOREIGN KEY Constraint definition, the referenced Table must be constrained by a NOT DEFERRABLE PRIMARY KEY Constraint; the primary key is also the referenced unique key.

Here are some more examples of FOREIGN KEY Constraint definitions:

```
CREATE TABLE Table_1 (
   column_1 SMALLINT,
   column_2 VARCHAR(4),
   CONSTRAINT c_1 PRIMARY KEY(column_1,column_2));

CREATE TABLE Table_2 (
   column_1 SMALLINT,
   column_2 VARCHAR(4),
   CONSTRAINT c_2 FOREIGN KEY(column_1,column_2) REFERENCES Table_1);
-- Here the referenced unique key defaults to Table_1's primary key

CREATE TABLE Table_1 (
   column_1 SMALLINT,
   column_2 VARCHAR(4),
   CONSTRAINT c_1 PRIMARY KEY(column_1,column_2));

CREATE TABLE Table_2 (
   column_1 SMALLINT,
   column_2 VARCHAR(4),
   CONSTRAINT c_2 FOREIGN KEY(column_1,column_2)
         REFERENCES Table_1(column_1,column_2));
-- Here the foreign key explicitly matches Table_1's primary key
```

```
CREATE TABLE Table_1 (
   column_1 SMALLINT,
   column_2 VARCHAR(4),
   column_3 DATE,
   CONSTRAINT constraint_1
      PRIMARY KEY(column_1,column_2) NOT DEFERRABLE,
   CONSTRAINT constraint_2
      UNIQUE(column3) NOT DEFERRABLE);

CREATE TABLE Table_2 (
   column_1 SMALLINT,
   column_2 VARCHAR(4),
   column_3 DATE,
   CONSTRAINT constraint_3
      FOREIGN KEY(column3) REFERENCES Table_1(column3));
-- Here the foreign key explicitly matches Table_1's unique key; this is manda-
tory because, if the referenced Column list were omitted, your DBMS would
attempt to match the foreign key (COLUMN_3) to Table_1's primary key
(COLUMN_1,COLUMN_2) and would fail.
```

Privileges

In order to create a FOREIGN KEY Constraint, the <AuthorizationID> that owns the referencing Table must be the current <AuthorizationID> and must have the REFERENCES Privilege on every referenced Column named.

MATCH Clause

The optional MATCH clause of a FOREIGN KEY Constraint definition specifies the degree of the required match between the values of the foreign key and the referenced unique key. There are three match options: MATCH SIMPLE, MATCH FULL, and MATCH PARTIAL. If you omit the MATCH clause, it defaults to MATCH SIMPLE. For example, these two SQL statements are equivalent:

```
CREATE TABLE Table_2 (
   column_1 SMALLINT CONSTRAINT constraint_1
       REFERENCES Table_1);

CREATE TABLE Table_2 (
   column_1 SMALLINT CONSTRAINT constraint_1
       REFERENCES Table_1 MATCH SIMPLE);
```

The MATCH option specified for a FOREIGN KEY Constraint has an effect only when your foreign key contains null values.

For MATCH SIMPLE, a FOREIGN KEY Constraint is satisfied if, for each row of the referencing Table, either (*a*) at least one of the foreign key Columns is NULL or (*b*) none of the foreign key Columns is NULL and the value of the entire foreign key equals the value of the entire unique key in at least one row of the referenced Table. For example, given a referenced Table with these two unique key rows:

```
{10,'tiny'} {20,'huge'}
```

these foreign key rows are valid for the referencing Table:

```
{10,'tiny'} -- because a matching unique key row exists
{NULL,'tiny'} {10,NULL} {NULL,'soso'} {30,NULL} -- because, in each case, one
foreign key Column is NULL
```

and this foreign key row is invalid:

```
{10,'huge'} -- because no matching unique key row exists
```

For MATCH FULL, a FOREIGN KEY Constraint is satisfied if, for each row of the referencing Table, either (*a*) every foreign key Column is NULL or (*b*) none of the foreign key Columns is NULL and the value of the entire foreign key equals the value of the entire unique key in at least one row of the referenced Table. (If you define a FOREIGN KEY Constraint with MATCH FULL and there is either (*a*) only one Column in the foreign key or (*b*) one or more Columns defined as NOT NULL in the foreign key, then the Constraint will have the same effect as if you had defined the Constraint with MATCH SIMPLE.) For example, given a referenced Table with these two unique key rows:

```
{10,'tiny'} {20,'huge'}
```

these foreign key rows are valid for the referencing Table:

```
{10,'tiny'} -- because a matching unique key row exists
{NULL,NULL} -- because the entire foreign key is NULL
```

and these foreign key rows are invalid:

```
{10,'huge'} -- because no matching unique key row exists
{NULL,'tiny'} {10,NULL} -- because, in each case, only some of the foreign key
is NULL
```

For MATCH PARTIAL, a FOREIGN KEY Constraint is satisfied if, for each row of the referencing Table, at least one foreign key Column is NULL and the values of the rest of the foreign key Columns equal the values of the corresponding unique key Columns in at least one row of the referenced Table. (If you define a FOREIGN KEY Constraint with MATCH PARTIAL and there is either (*a*) only one Column in the foreign key or (*b*) one or more Columns defined as NOT NULL in the foreign key, then the Constraint will have the same effect as if you had defined the Constraint with MATCH SIMPLE.) For example, given a referenced Table with these two unique key rows:

```
{10,'tiny'} {20,'huge'}
```

these foreign key rows are valid for the referencing Table:

```
{10,'tiny'} -- because a matching unique key row exists
{NULL,NULL} -- because the entire foreign key is NULL
{NULL,'tiny'} {10,NULL} {NULL,'huge'} {20,NULL} -- because, in each case, one foreign key Column is NULL but the other matches the corresponding unique Column in some row of the referenced Table
```

and these foreign key rows are invalid:

```
{10,'huge'} -- because no matching unique key row exists
{NULL,'big'} {30,NULL} -- because, although one foreign key Column is NULL, the other does not match the value of the corresponding unique Column in any row of the referenced Table
```

TIP: Use MATCH FULL or define all foreign key Columns with a NOT NULL Constraint.

Referential Action

What happens if you UPDATE a primary key? What happens if you DELETE a primary key? Neither should happen often, but if you must, remember that the rule for primary/foreign key relationships is in terms of database states, "no foreign key shall dangle." There are two ways to get rid of a dangling key: prevent it from happening in the first place or compensate if it does happen. You can do this by defining your FOREIGN KEY Constraints with one ON UPDATE clause and/or one ON DELETE clause, in any order. The optional ON UPDATE clause specifies the action you want your DBMS to take when an UPDATE operation on the referenced Table causes the FOREIGN KEY Constraint to be violated. The optional ON DELETE clause specifies the action you want your DBMS to take when a DELETE operation on the referenced Table causes the FOREIGN KEY Constraint to be violated. If you omit either clause, both default to ON UPDATE NO ACTION and ON DELETE NO ACTION. For example, these two SQL statements are equivalent:

```
CREATE TABLE Table_2 (
   column_1 SMALLINT CONSTRAINT constraint_1
      REFERENCES Table_1);

CREATE TABLE Table_2 (
   column_1 SMALLINT CONSTRAINT constraint_1
    REFERENCES Table_1
       ON UPDATE NO ACTION ON DELETE NO ACTION);
```

Besides NO ACTION, you may also specify these actions in the ON UPDATE and ON DELETE clauses: RESTRICT, CASCADE, SET NULL, and SET DEFAULT. To decide which to use, consider first what you would like to happen. Should you be prevented from leaving a dangling reference — or should you change the dangling reference too? (A *dangling reference* is a foreign key that doesn't point to a unique key any more and it isn't allowed in SQL.) If you do change the dangling reference, should you be changing to (*a*) the same value as the new unique key, (*b*) NULL, or (*c*) some other value? Or should the change be a deletion? All these options are available. The action taken by your DBMS in all cases depends on the definition of "matching rows" for the FOREIGN KEY Constraint; this, in turn, depends on the FOREIGN KEY Constraint's MATCH option.

For MATCH SIMPLE and MATCH FULL, given a row in the referenced Table, every row in your referencing Table that contains a foreign key whose value equals the value of that unique key, is a matching row. For MATCH PARTIAL, given a row in the referenced Table, every row in your referencing Table that contains a foreign key with at least one non-null Column whose value equals the value of that unique key, is a matching row — and a matching row that matches only one row of the referenced Table is a unique matching row.

- If you define a FOREIGN KEY Constraint with MATCH SIMPLE ON DELETE CASCADE or with MATCH FULL ON DELETE CASCADE, every time you DELETE rows from the referenced Table — your DBMS will also DELETE all matching rows from the referencing Table. If you define a FOREIGN KEY Constraint with MATCH PARTIAL ON DELETE CASCADE, every time you DELETE rows from the referenced Table — your DBMS will also DELETE all unique matching rows from the referencing Table.
- If you define a FOREIGN KEY Constraint with MATCH SIMPLE ON DELETE SET NULL or with MATCH FULL ON DELETE SET NULL, every time you DELETE rows from the referenced Table — your DBMS will also set the entire foreign key in every matching row of the referencing Table to NULL. If you define a FOREIGN KEY Constraint with MATCH PARTIAL ON DELETE SET NULL, every time you DELETE rows from the referenced Table — your DBMS will also set the entire foreign key in every unique matching row of the referencing Table to NULL.
- If you define a FOREIGN KEY Constraint with MATCH SIMPLE ON DELETE SET DEFAULT or with MATCH FULL ON DELETE SET DEFAULT, every time you DELETE rows from the referenced Table — your DBMS will also set each Column of the foreign key in every matching row of the referencing Table to its default value. If you define a FOREIGN KEY Constraint with MATCH PARTIAL ON DELETE SET DEFAULT, every time you DELETE rows from the referenced Table — your DBMS will also set each Column of the foreign key in every unique matching row of the referencing Table to its default value.
- If you define a FOREIGN KEY Constraint with MATCH SIMPLE ON DELETE RESTRICT or with MATCH FULL ON DELETE RESTRICT, every time you attempt to DELETE rows from the referenced Table — your DBMS will check for matching rows in the referencing Table. If you define a FOREIGN KEY Constraint with MATCH PARTIAL ON DELETE RESTRICT, every time you attempt to DELETE rows from the referenced Table — your DBMS will check for unique matching rows in the referencing Table. In either case, if any matching (or unique matching, as appropriate) rows exist, the operation will fail; your DBMS will return the SQLSTATE error 23001 "integrity constraint violation-restrict violation." A FOREIGN KEY Constraint defined with ON DELETE NO ACTION acts essentially the same as one defined with ON DELETE RESTRICT.
- If you define a FOREIGN KEY Constraint with MATCH SIMPLE ON UPDATE CASCADE or with MATCH FULL ON UPDATE CASCADE, every time you UPDATE a referenced Column — your DBMS will also UPDATE the corresponding foreign key Column in all matching rows of the referencing Table to the same value. If you define a FOREIGN KEY Constraint with MATCH PARTIAL ON UPDATE CASCADE, every time you UPDATE a referenced Column — your DBMS

will also UPDATE any corresponding non-null foreign key Column in every unique matching row of the referencing Table to the same value, provided that, for each referencing row changed, all rows of the referenced Table that considered that referencing row to be a matching row also have the same change made. If this isn't the case, the operation will fail; your DBMS will return the SQLSTATE error 27000 "triggered data change violation."

- If you define a FOREIGN KEY Constraint with MATCH SIMPLE ON UPDATE SET NULL, every time you UPDATE a referenced Column — your DBMS will also set the corresponding foreign key Column in all matching rows of the referencing Table to NULL. If you define a FOREIGN KEY Constraint with MATCH FULL ON UPDATE SET NULL, every time you UPDATE a referenced Column — your DBMS will also set the entire foreign key in every matching row of the referencing Table to NULL. If you define a FOREIGN KEY Constraint with MATCH PARTIAL ON UPDATE SET NULL, every time you UPDATE a referenced Column — your DBMS will also set any corresponding non-null foreign key Column in every unique matching row of the referencing Table to NULL.
- If you define a FOREIGN KEY Constraint with MATCH SIMPLE ON UPDATE SET DEFAULT or with MATCH FULL ON UPDATE SET DEFAULT, every time you UPDATE a referenced Column — your DBMS will also set the corresponding foreign key Column in all matching rows of the referencing Table to its default value. If you define a FOREIGN KEY Constraint with MATCH PARTIAL ON UPDATE SET DEFAULT, every time you UPDATE a referenced Column — your DBMS will also set any corresponding non-null foreign key Column in every unique matching row of the referencing Table to its default value.
- If you define a FOREIGN KEY Constraint with MATCH SIMPLE ON UPDATE RESTRICT or with MATCH FULL ON UPDATE RESTRICT, every time you attempt to UPDATE a referenced Column — your DBMS will check for matching rows in the referencing Table. If you define a FOREIGN KEY Constraint with MATCH PARTIAL ON UPDATE RESTRICT, every time you attempt to UPDATE a referenced Column — your DBMS will check for unique matching rows in the referencing Table. In either case, if any matching (or unique matching, as appropriate) rows exist, the operation will fail; your DBMS will return the SQLSTATE error 23001 "integrity constraint violation-restrict violation." A FOREIGN KEY Constraint defined with ON UPDATE NO ACTION acts essentially the same as one defined with ON UPDATE RESTRICT.

For an example of the NO ACTION/RESTRICT option, consider the following SQL statements:

```
CREATE TABLE Table_1 (
   column_1 SMALLINT DEFAULT 12,
      CONSTRAINT constraint_1 PRIMARY KEY(column_1) NOT DEFERRABLE);

CREATE TABLE Table_2 (
   column_1 SMALLINT DEFAULT 15,
      CONSTRAINT constraint_2 FOREIGN KEY(column_1) REFERENCES Table_1
         MATCH FULL
         ON UPDATE NO ACTION ON DELETE NO ACTION
         NOT DEFERRABLE);
```

```
INSERT INTO Table_1 VALUES(10);

INSERT INTO Table_1 VALUES(15);

INSERT INTO Table_2 VALUES(10);
```

For TABLE_1 and TABLE_2, the effect of each of the following SQL statements:

```
UPDATE Table_1 SET column_1=11 WHERE column_1=10;

UPDATE Table_2 SET column_1=11 where column_1=10;

INSERT INTO Table_2 VALUES(11);
```

is an error return, because the result in each case would be a value in TABLE_2.COLUMN_1 that does not match some value in TABLE_1.COLUMN_1.

NOTE: The action specified for the ON UPDATE clause has no effect on UPDATE operations or INSERT operations performed on the referencing Table. Thus, an INSERT operation that attempts to put a row into TABLE_2 or an UPDATE operation that attempts to change a row of TABLE_2, will always fail if the resulting value in TABLE_2.COLUMN_1 does not match some value of TABLE_1.COLUMN_1.

The effect of this SQL statement:

```
DELETE FROM Table_1 WHERE column_1=10;
```

is also an error return, because deleting the applicable row from TABLE_1 would leave TABLE_2 with a row containing a COLUMN_1 value that does not match any TABLE_1.COLUMN_1 value.

To summarize:

- When an UPDATE operation attempts to update a non-null value in a Column that is referenced in a FOREIGN KEY Constraint defined with ON UPDATE NO ACTION or ON UPDATE RESTRICT, the UPDATE fails, regardless of the MATCH option, if there are matching rows in the referencing Table.
- When a DELETE operation attempts to delete a row from a Table that is referenced in a FOREIGN KEY Constraint defined with ON DELETE NO ACTION or ON DELETE RESTRICT, the DELETE operation fails, regardless of the MATCH option, if there are matching rows in the referencing Table.

For an example of the CASCADE option, consider the following SQL statements:

```
CREATE TABLE Table_1 (
   column_1 SMALLINT DEFAULT 12,
      CONSTRAINT constraint_1 PRIMARY KEY(column_1) NOT DEFERRABLE);
```

```
CREATE TABLE Table_2 (
   column_1 SMALLINT DEFAULT 15,
      CONSTRAINT constraint_2 FOREIGN KEY(column_1) REFERENCES Table_1
         MATCH FULL
         ON UPDATE CASCADE ON DELETE CASCADE
         NOT DEFERRABLE);

INSERT INTO Table_1 VALUES(10);

INSERT INTO Table_1 VALUES(15);

INSERT INTO Table_2 VALUES(10);
```

For TABLE_1 and TABLE_2, the effect of the following SQL statement:

```
UPDATE Table_1 SET column_1=11 where column_1=10;
```

is that all values of TABLE_1.COLUMN_1 that are equal to 10 are set to 11, with the same effect cascading down; that is, all values in TABLE_2.COLUMN_1 that are equal to 10 are also set to 11. And the effect of this SQL statement:

```
DELETE FROM Table_1 WHERE column_1=10;
```

is that all applicable rows are deleted from TABLE_1, with the same effect cascading down; that is, all matching rows of TABLE_2 are also deleted.

To summarize:

- When an UPDATE operation attempts to update a non-null value in a Column that is referenced in a FOREIGN KEY Constraint defined with MATCH SIMPLE or MATCH FULL and ON UPDATE CASCADE, the referenced Column, and the corresponding referencing Column in all matching rows, are set to the new value. When an UPDATE operation attempts to update a non-null value in a Column that is referenced in a FOREIGN KEY Constraint defined with MATCH FULL and ON UPDATE CASCADE, the referenced Column, and the corresponding referencing Column in all unique matching rows where the referencing Column contains a non-null value, are set to the new value. Unique matching rows with a referencing Column that contains the null value are not updated.
- When a DELETE operation attempts to delete a row from a Table that is referenced in a FOREIGN KEY Constraint defined with MATCH SIMPLE or MATCH FULL and ON DELETE CASCADE, the applicable row, and all matching rows, are deleted. When a DELETE operation attempts to delete a row from a Table that is referenced in a FOREIGN KEY Constraint defined with MATCH PARTIAL and ON DELETE CASCADE, the applicable row, and all unique matching rows, are deleted.

For an example of the SET NULL option, consider the following SQL statements:

```
CREATE TABLE Table_1 (
   column_1 SMALLINT DEFAULT 12,
      CONSTRAINT constraint_1 PRIMARY KEY(column_1) NOT DEFERRABLE);

CREATE TABLE Table_2 (
   column_1 SMALLINT DEFAULT 15,
      CONSTRAINT constraint_2 FOREIGN KEY(column_1) REFERENCES Table_1
         MATCH FULL
         ON UPDATE SET NULL ON DELETE SET NULL
         NOT DEFERRABLE);

INSERT INTO Table_1 VALUES(10);

INSERT INTO Table_1 VALUES(15);

INSERT INTO Table_2 VALUES(10);
```

For TABLE_1 and TABLE_2, the effect of this SQL statement:

```
UPDATE Table_1 SET column_1=11 where column_1=10;
```

is that all values of TABLE_1.COLUMN_1 that are equal to 10 are set to 11, and that all values in TABLE_2.COLUMN_1 that are equal to 10 are set to the null value. (If TABLE_2.COLUMN_1 did not allow null values, the UPDATE statement would fail.) And the effect of this SQL statement:

```
DELETE FROM Table_1 WHERE column_1=10;
```

is that all applicable rows are deleted from TABLE_1 and that all values in TABLE_2.COLUMN_1 that are equal to 10 are set to the null value. (If TABLE_2.COLUMN_1 did not allow null values, the DELETE statement would fail.)

To summarize:

- When an UPDATE operation attempts to update a non-null value in a Column that is referenced in a FOREIGN KEY Constraint defined with MATCH SIMPLE and ON UPDATE SET NULL, the referenced Column is set to the new value and the corresponding referencing Column in all matching rows is set to the null value. When an UPDATE operation attempts to update a non-null value in a Column that is referenced in a FOREIGN KEY Constraint defined with MATCH FULL and ON UPDATE SET NULL, the referenced Column is set to the new value and every referencing Column (not just the corresponding Column) in all matching rows is set to the null value. When an UPDATE operation attempts to update a non-null value in a Column that is referenced in a FOREIGN KEY Constraint defined with MATCH PARTIAL and ON UPDATE SET NULL, the referenced Column is set to the new value and the corresponding referencing Column in all unique matching rows is set to the null value.
- When a DELETE operation attempts to delete a row from a Table that is referenced in a FOREIGN KEY Constraint defined with MATCH SIMPLE or MATCH FULL and ON DELETE SET NULL,

the applicable row is deleted and, for all matching rows, each referencing Column is set to the null value. When a DELETE operation attempts to delete a row from a Table that is referenced in a FOREIGN KEY Constraint defined with MATCH PARTIAL and ON DELETE SET NULL, the applicable row is deleted, and, for all unique matching rows, each referencing Column is set to the null value.

For an example of the SET DEFAULT option, consider the following SQL statements:

```
CREATE TABLE Table_1 (
   column_1 SMALLINT DEFAULT 12,
      CONSTRAINT constraint_1 PRIMARY KEY(column_1) NOT DEFERRABLE);

CREATE TABLE Table_2 (
   column_1 SMALLINT DEFAULT 15,
   CONSTRAINT constraint_2 FOREIGN KEY(column_1) REFERENCES Table_1
      MATCH FULL
      ON UPDATE SET DEFAULT ON DELETE SET DEFAULT
         NOT DEFERRABLE);

INSERT INTO Table_1 VALUES(10);

INSERT INTO Table_1 VALUES(15);

INSERT INTO Table_2 VALUES(10);
```

For TABLE_1 and TABLE_2, the effect of this SQL statement:

```
UPDATE Table_1 SET column_1=11 where column_1=10;
```

is that all values of TABLE_1.COLUMN_1 that are equal to 10 are set to 11, and that all values of TABLE_2.COLUMN_1 that are equal to 10 are set to COLUMN_1's default value, 15. (If no row existed where the value of TABLE_1.COLUMN_1 was 15, the UPDATE statement would fail.) And the effect of this SQL statement:

```
DELETE FROM Table_1 WHERE column_1=10;
```

is that all applicable rows are deleted from TABLE_1 and that all values in TABLE_2.COLUMN_1 that are equal to 10 are set to COLUMN_1's default value, 15. (If no row existed where the value of TABLE_1.COLUMN_1 was 15, the DELETE statement would fail.)

To summarize:

- When an UPDATE operation attempts to update a non-null value in a Column that is referenced in a FOREIGN KEY Constraint defined with MATCH SIMPLE or MATCH FULL and ON UPDATE SET DEFAULT, the referenced Column is set to the new value and the corresponding referencing Column in all matching rows is set to its default value. When an UPDATE operation attempts to update a non-null value in a Column that is referenced in a FOREIGN KEY Constraint defined with MATCH PARTIAL and ON UPDATE SET DEFAULT, the referenced Column is set to the new value and the corresponding referencing Column in all unique matching rows is set to its default value.

- When a DELETE operation attempts to delete a row from a Table that is referenced in a FOREIGN KEY Constraint defined with MATCH SIMPLE or MATCH FULL and ON DELETE SET DEFAULT, the applicable row is deleted, and, for all matching rows, each referencing Column is set to its default value. When a DELETE operation attempts to delete a row from a Table that is referenced in a FOREIGN KEY Constraint defined with MATCH PARTIAL and ON DELETE SET DEFAULT, the applicable row is deleted, and, for all unique matching rows, each referencing Column is set to its default value.

NOTE: It is not possible to update the same Column more than once in a single SQL statement. If such an operation is attempted, the statement will fail; your DBMS will return the SQLSTATE error 27000 "triggered data change violation."

NOTE: All rows that are to be deleted by an SQL statement are effectively deleted at the end of that statement's execution, prior to the checking of any integrity constraints.

If you want to restrict your code to Core SQL, don't define your FOREIGN KEY Constraints with a MATCH clause, an ON UPDATE clause, or an ON DELETE clause.

Constraint_type — NOT NULL Constraint

A NOT NULL Constraint is a <Column Constraint>, defining a rule that constrains a key to non-null values only. The required syntax for a NOT NULL Constraint is as follows.

```
NOT NULL <Column Constraint> ::=
[ CONSTRAINT <Constraint name> ] NOT NULL
[ <constraint attributes> ]
```

A Column may be constrained by no more than one NOT NULL Constraint, which specifies a rule that the Column may contain only non-null values. Here is an example of a NOT NULL Constraint definition:

```
CREATE TABLE Table_1 (
   column_1 SMALLINT
      DEFAULT 15
      CONSTRAINT constraint_1 NOT NULL
        DEFERRABLE INITIALLY IMMEDIATE);
-- defines a NOT NULL <Column Constraint> in CREATE TABLE
```

Once created, a NOT NULL <Column Constraint> logically becomes a CHECK <Table Constraint>. The <Column Constraint> in this SQL statement:

```
CREATE TABLE Table_1 (
   column_1 SMALLINT NOT NULL);
```

is therefore equivalent to the <Table Constraint> in the following SQL statement:

```
CREATE TABLE Table_1 (
   column_1 SMALLINT,
   CHECK (column_1 IS NOT NULL));
```

A NOT NULL Constraint makes it impossible to COMMIT any operation that would cause the Column to which it belongs to contain any NULLs. A NOT NULL Constraint is violated if it is FALSE for any row of the Table to which it belongs. Consider this SQL statement:

```
CREATE TABLE Table_1 (
   column_1 SMALLINT CONSTRAINT constraint_1 NOT NULL,
   column_2 VARCHAR(4));
```

For this example, CONSTRAINT_1 would be violated if you tried to make COLUMN_1 contain NULL.

Constraint_type — CHECK Constraint

A CHECK Constraint is either a <Table Constraint>, a <Column Constraint>, or a <Domain Constraint> and defines a rule that constrains the set of valid values for a Base table. The required syntax for a CHECK Constraint is as follows.

```
CHECK <Table Constraint> ::=
[ CONSTRAINT <Constraint name> ]
CHECK (search condition)
[ <constraint attributes> ]

CHECK <Column Constraint> ::=
[ CONSTRAINT <Constraint name> ]
CHECK (search condition)
[ <constraint attributes> ]

CHECK <Domain Constraint> ::=
[ CONSTRAINT <Constraint name> ]
CHECK (search condition)
[ <constraint attributes> ]
```

A Base table may be constrained by zero or more CHECK Constraints, which specify a rule that a group of one or more Columns of a Table may contain only those values that fall into the set defined by the rule — that is, a CHECK Constraint is satisfied if its search condition evaluates to TRUE or to UNKNOWN for all rows within its scope.

Here are some examples of CHECK Constraint definitions:

```
CREATE TABLE Table_1 (
   column_1 SMALLINT,
   CONSTRAINT constraint_1 CHECK(column_1<400) NOT DEFERRABLE);
-- defines a CHECK <Table Constraint> in CREATE TABLE

CREATE TABLE Table_1 (
   column_1 SMALLINT
      CONSTRAINT constraint_1 CHECK(column_1<400) NOT DEFERRABLE,
   column_2 CHAR(5));
-- defines a CHECK <Column Constraint> in CREATE TABLE

ALTER TABLE Table_2 ADD CONSTRAINT constraint_2
   CHECK(column_1>100 OR column_2='hello')
      NOT DEFERRABLE INITIALLY IMMEDIATE;
-- defines a CHECK <Table Constraint> in ALTER TABLE

CREATE DOMAIN domain_1 AS SMALLINT
   CONSTRAINT constraint_1 CHECK(VALUE IN (50,100,150))
      DEFERRABLE INITIALLY DEFERRABLE;
-- defines a CHECK <Domain Constraint> in CREATE DOMAIN

ALTER DOMAIN domain_1 ADD CONSTRAINT constraint_2
   CHECK(VALUE IS NOT NULL);
-- defines a CHECK <Domain Constraint> in ALTER DOMAIN
```

CHECK <Column Constraint>s may be defined only in a CREATE TABLE statement and must be for a single Column only. CHECK <Table Constraint>s may be defined in a CREATE TABLE or an ALTER TABLE statement and may be for one or more Columns. CHECK <Domain Constraint>s may be defined in a CREATE DOMAIN or an ALTER DOMAIN statement and must contain a search condition that uses the <value specification> VALUE (the <data type> of a given instance of VALUE is the <data type> of the Domain to which the <Domain Constraint> belongs). A <Domain Constraint>'s search condition may not be a recursive search condition (i.e., it may not refer, either directly or indirectly, to the Domain to which the <Domain Constraint> belongs).

Once created, a CHECK <Column Constraint> logically becomes a CHECK <Table Constraint>. The <Column Constraint> in the following SQL statement:

```
CREATE TABLE Table_1 (
   column_1 SMALLINT CHECK(column_1<400));
```

is therefore equivalent to the <Table Constraint> in this SQL statement:

```
CREATE TABLE Table_1 (
   column_1 SMALLINT,
   CHECK(column_1<400));
```

A CHECK Constraint's search condition may specify any conditional expression, subject to the following rules:

- The search condition may not contain (*a*) a <target specification> or (*b*) a set function (i.e., COUNT, AVG, MAX, MIN, or SUM) unless the set function is contained in a subquery or (*c*) any of these functions: CURRENT_PATH, CURRENT_USER, SESSION_USER, SYSTEM_USER, USER, CURRENT_DATE, CURRENT_TIME, CURRENT_TIMESTAMP, LOCALTIME, or LOCALTIMESTAMP, or (*d*) any query that is possibly non-deterministic, as defined earlier in this chapter.
- The search condition may not invoke a non-deterministic routine or a routine which possibly modifies SQL-data.
- If a CHECK Constraint belongs to a persistent Base table or to a Domain, its search condition may not refer to any temporary Tables.
- If a CHECK Constraint belongs to a GLOBAL TEMPORARY Base table, its search condition may refer only to GLOBAL TEMPORARY Base Tables. If a CHECK Constraint belongs to a created LOCAL TEMPORARY Base table, its search condition may refer only to GLOBAL TEMPORARY Base Tables or to created LOCAL TEMPORARY Base tables. If a CHECK Constraint belongs to a declared LOCAL TEMPORARY Base table, its search condition may not refer to any persistent Base Tables.
- If a CHECK Constraint belongs to a temporary Table defined with ON COMMIT PRESERVE ROWS, its search condition may not contain a subquery that refers to a temporary Table defined with ON COMMIT DELETE ROWS.

[Obscure Rule] If a CHECK Constraint's search condition can't be represented in INFORMATION_SCHEMA without truncation, your DBMS will return the SQLSTATE warning 01009 "warning-search condition too long for information schema."

Privileges

In order to create a CHECK Constraint, the <AuthorizationID> that owns the Schema to which the Constraint will belong must be the current <AuthorizationID> and must have the REFERENCES Privilege on every Column that is explicitly named in the CHECK Constraint's search condition. If the search condition doesn't explicitly name any Columns, the current <AuthorizationID> must have the REFERENCES Privilege on at least one Column of every Table referred to in the search condition.

A CHECK Constraint makes it impossible to COMMIT any operation that would cause the Constraint's search condition to evaluate to FALSE. (This means, of course, that if the condition evaluates to TRUE or to UNKNOWN, the Constraint is satisfied.) For example, the Constraint defined in this CREATE TABLE statement is violated if any row of TABLE_1 contains a COLUMN_1 value that is greater than 99:

```
CREATE TABLE Table_1 (
   column_1 SMALLINT,
   column_2 VARCHAR(4),
   CONSTRAINT constraint_1 CHECK(column_1<100) NOT DEFERRABLE);
```

This SQL statement would therefore violate CONSTRAINT_1:

```
INSERT INTO Table_1 (column_1) VALUES (105);
```

because a search condition that evaluates to FALSE violates the Constraint.

Both of these SQL statements, however, would satisfy CONSTRAINT_1:

```
INSERT INTO Table_1 (column_1) VALUES (-30);
-- a search condition that evaluates to TRUE satisfies the Constraint

INSERT INTO Table_1 (column_1) VALUES (NULL);
-- NULL is allowed; a search condition that evaluates to UNKNOWN
satisfies the Constraint
```

The first use of a CHECK <Table Constraint> is to restrict what range of values is allowed in a Column, for example:

```
ALTER TABLE Table_1 ADD CONSTRAINT constraint_1
   CHECK(column_1 BETWEEN 5 AND 9) NOT DEFERRABLE;
```

You'll often see Column values restrained like this; it's a feature in dialog boxes. The second use of a CHECK <Table Constraint> is to see that two Columns within the same Table agree with each other, for example:

```
ALTER TABLE Films ADD CONSTRAINT constraint_1
   CHECK(film_type <> 'Action' OR star = 'Stallone') NOT DEFERRABLE;
```

The third use is to find out whether some relation is true between a row in one Table, and a row in another Table or a different row in the same Table, for example:

```
ALTER TABLE Table_1 ADD CONSTRAINT constraint_1
   CHECK (column_1 > (SELECT MAX(column_2)) FROM Table_2) NOT DEFERRABLE;
```

This sort of thing was once illegal, but in modern variations of SQL, you'll see inter-table Constraint references on an occasional basis. The fourth use of a CHECK <Table Constraint> is documentary, for example:

```
ALTER TABLE Table_1 ADD CONSTRAINT comment_1
   CHECK ('this is a comment ...' IS NOT NULL)
      DEFERRABLE INITIALLY DEFERRED;
```

Most DBMSs allow comments to be added to the metadata some other way, so this final use is rare.

For <Domain Constraint>s, the general idea is that object *X* doesn't belong in type *Y* or, to put it positively: certain things go in certain classes. These two examples both express the theme "values based on this Domain must not be space":

```
CREATE DOMAIN domain_1 AS CHAR(1)
   CONSTRAINT constraint_1 CHECK (VALUE <> ' ');

CREATE DOMAIN domain_2 AS CHAR(1);

ALTER DOMAIN domain_2 ADD CONSTRAINT constraint_2
   CHECK (VALUE <> ' ');
```

In a <Domain Constraint>'s CHECK condition, the word VALUE is a placeholder; your DBMS replaces it with the appropriate <Column name> when checking the Constraint. The second of these two SQL statements would force a Constraint check:

```
CREATE TABLE Table_1 (
   column_1 domain_1,
   column_2 CHAR(10));
-- makes a Column based on DOMAIN_1

INSERT INTO Table_1
VALUES (' ',
        'bob');
-- fails; CONSTRAINT_1 stops it
```

A <Domain Constraint> applies to every Column that's defined on the Domain, now or in the future. This makes sense because it's rare that a Column is in a Domain all on its own — and if the name of a manager is subject to some Constraint (must be alphabetic, say), then surely the employees' names and spouses' names should be subject to the same Constraint. There's a case for suggesting that "data type checking" is just a vague form of "<Domain Constraint> checking"; the error messages are different, but the point is the same — you are restricted as to what you can put in.

If you want to restrict your code to Core SQL, don't use a subquery in a CHECK Constraint's search condition. Also, for Core SQL, the REFERENCES Privilege isn't needed to create a CHECK Constraint.

CREATE ASSERTION Statement

The CREATE ASSERTION statement names a new Constraint and defines the Constraint's deferral mode, initial constraint check time, and its CHECK search condition. The required syntax for the CREATE ASSERTION statement is as follows.

```
CREATE ASSERTION <Constraint name>
CHECK (search condition)
[ <constraint attributes> ]
```

CREATE ASSERTION defines a new rule that will constrain the set of valid values for one or more Base tables.

- The <Constraint name> identifies the Assertion and the Schema to which it belongs. A <Constraint name> that includes an explicit <Schema name> qualifier belongs to the Schema named. A <Constraint name> that does not include an explicit <Schema name> qualifier belongs to the SQL-session default Schema. (In both cases, that Schema must, of course, own the Tables for which the Assertion is defined.) The <Constraint name> must be unique (for all Constraints and Assertions) within the Schema that contains it.

If CREATE ASSERTION is part of a CREATE SCHEMA statement, the <Constraint name>, if explicitly qualified, must include the <Schema name> of the Schema being created; that is, it isn't possible to create an Assertion belonging to a different Schema from within CREATE SCHEMA. For example, this SQL statement will not return an error because the <Constraint name> will default to include the qualifying <Schema name>:

```
CREATE SCHEMA bob
   CREATE TABLE Table_1 (column_1 SMALLINT)
   CREATE ASSERTION constraint_1
      CHECK ((SELECT AVG(column_1) FROM Table_1) >40) NOT DEFERRABLE;
-- creates an Assertion called BOB.CONSTRAINT_1 in Schema BOB
```

The following SQL statement will not return an error either because the <Constraint name> explicitly includes a qualifying <Schema name> that matches the name of the Schema being created:

```
CREATE SCHEMA bob
   CREATE TABLE bob.Table_1 (column_1 SMALLINT)
   CREATE ASSERTION bob.constraint_1
      CHECK ((SELECT AVG(column_1) FROM Table_1) >40) NOT DEFERRABLE;
-- creates an Assertion called BOB.CONSTRAINT_1 in Schema BOB
```

But this SQL statement will return an error because the <Constraint name> explicitly includes a qualifying <Schema name> that is different from the name of the Schema being created:

```
CREATE SCHEMA bob
   CREATE TABLE Table_1 (column_1 SMALLINT)
   CREATE ASSERTION sam.constraint_1
      CHECK ((SELECT AVG(column_1) FROM Table_1) >40) NOT DEFERRABLE;
-- tries to create a Constraint belonging to Schema SAM inside Schema BOB;
illegal syntax
```

If CREATE ASSERTION is executed as a stand-alone SQL statement, the current <AuthorizationID> must either be the owner of the Schema to which this new Constraint belongs or the Schema's owner must be a Role that the current <AuthorizationID> may use. That is, only the owner of a Schema can create Constraints for that Schema.

An Assertion's CHECK search condition may specify any conditional expression (it will almost inevitably contain the <keyword> EXISTS, the <keyword> UNIQUE or a set function), subject to the following rules (note that these rules are slightly different from the rules given earlier for a CHECK Constraint's search condition):

- The search condition may not contain a <host parameter name>, an <SQL parameter name>, any of these functions: CURRENT_PATH, CURRENT_USER, SESSION_USER, SYSTEM_USER, USER, CURRENT_DATE, CURRENT_TIME, CURRENT_TIMESTAMP, LOCALTIME, or LOCALTIMESTAMP, or any query that is possibly non-deterministic, as defined earlier in this chapter.
- The search condition may not invoke a non-deterministic routine or a routine which possibly modifies SQL-data.
- The search condition may not refer to any temporary Tables.

[Obscure Rule] If an Assertion's CHECK search condition can't be represented in INFORMATION_SCHEMA without truncation, your DBMS will return the SQLSTATE warning 01009 "warning-search condition too long for information schema."

An Assertion makes it impossible to COMMIT any operation that would cause the Constraint's search condition to evaluate to FALSE. (This means, of course, that if the condition evaluates to TRUE or to UNKNOWN, the Constraint is satisfied.) Thus, for example, for these two SQL statements:

```
CREATE TABLE Table_1 (
   column_1 SMALLINT,
   column_2 VARCHAR(4));

CREATE ASSERTION constraint_1
   CHECK ((SELECT AVG(column_1) FROM Table_1) >40) NOT DEFERRABLE;
```

CONSTRAINT_1 is violated if the average of the TABLE_1.COLUMN_1 values is less than 41. Assume that TABLE_1 contains one row, where COLUMN_1 contains 42. This SQL statement would then violate CONSTRAINT_1:

```
INSERT INTO Table_1 (column_1) VALUES (38);
```

because a search condition that evaluates to FALSE violates the Constraint. Both of these SQL statements, however, would satisfy CONSTRAINT_1:

```
INSERT INTO Table_1 (column_1) VALUES (100);
-- a search condition that evaluates to TRUE satisfies the Constraint

INSERT INTO Table_1 (column_1) VALUES (NULL);
-- NULL is allowed; a search condition that evaluates to UNKNOWN satisfies the
Constraint
```

The <constraint attributes> clause of CREATE ASSERTION is as defined previously in "Constraint Definition" on page 410. If you omit the clause, the Constraint defaults to a NOT DEFERRABLE INITIALLY IMMEDIATE Constraint.

We've already said that an Assertion constrains Base tables. The reason they're not <Table Constraint>s — or the reason you'll sometimes want to use Assertions rather than <Table Constraint>s — lies in the difference between the way an Assertion is checked and the way a <Table Constraint> is checked. An Assertion is checked once, while a <Table Constraint> is checked once for each row in the Table. This difference doesn't affect efficiency; modern

DBMSs are capable of figuring out when they really need to check, so we note this only as a guide to what "effectively" happens. But consider what it means to you — assume a Constraint that, in English, is, "There must be at least one row in Table TABLE_1." If you try to implement this requirement as a <Table Constraint>, for example with this SQL statement:

```
ALTER TABLE Table_1 ADD CONSTRAINT constraint_1
   CHECK (0 <> (SELECT COUNT(*) FROM Table_1));
```

you'll find it won't work; because a <Table Constraint> is checked once "for each row" and there are no rows, the check never happens if you leave TABLE_1 empty. To make it work, create an Assertion to ensure the condition is checked at least once. For example:

```
CREATE ASSERTION constraint_1
   CHECK (0 <> (SELECT COUNT(*) FROM Table_1));
```

It's always a good idea to consider creating an Assertion when you see a SELECT condition. Here's another example; consider a Constraint that, in English, is, "We can only hold picnics if there's money." In this case, you could use this <Table Constraint> and it would work:

```
ALTER TABLE Picnics ADD CONSTRAINT constraint_1
   CHECK (EXISTS (SELECT * FROM Accounts WHERE balance > 0));
```

But CONSTRAINT_1, as defined, is misleading — the SQL statement suggests that there's a Constraint on the PICNICS Table. There is, of course, but there's a Constraint on the ACCOUNTS Table too and this isn't immediately clear. If you define the same condition with CREATE ASSERTION, you'll be signalling that there's more to it; for example:

```
CREATE ASSERTION Picnic_Account_Check
CHECK (NOT EXISTS (SELECT * FROM Picnics) OR
      EXISTS (SELECT * FROM Accounts WHERE balance > 0));
```

If you want to restrict your code to Core SQL, don't use the CREATE ASSERTION statement.

Interlocking References

An example of an interlocking reference is:

- Every Employee must be in a department.
- Every Department must have at least one employee.

This is an "interlock" problem because there must be a reference from the EMPLOYEES Table to the DEPARTMENTS Table, as well as a reference going the other way — from the DEPARTMENTS Table to the EMPLOYEES Table. Here are the Table definitions:

```
CREATE TABLE Employees (
   emp_id INT,
   dept_id INT,
   CONSTRAINT emp_constraint_1
         FOREIGN KEY (dept_id) REFERENCES Departments NOT DEFERRABLE);
```

```
CREATE TABLE Departments (
   dept_id INT,
   CONSTRAINT dept_constraint_1
      PRIMARY KEY (dept_id) NOT DEFERRABLE,
   CONSTRAINT dept_constraint_2
      CHECK (dept_id IN (SELECT dept_id FROM Employees))
             NOT DEFERRABLE;
-- this CHECK clause illustrates the normal way to make a "foreign
reference" to a "key" which is not unique or primary
```

In this example, the `CREATE TABLE Employees...` statement will return an error because it refers to the `DEPARTMENTS` Table before that Table has been created. Interchanging the statement order wouldn't help, because then the `CREATE TABLE Departments...` statement will return an error because it refers to the `EMPLOYEES` Table before that Table has been created. You could put both Table definitions inside a `CREATE SCHEMA` statement, but that isn't a general solution. To solve the problem, split the `CREATE TABLE` statements up like this:

```
CREATE TABLE Employees (
   emp_id INT,
   dept_id INT);

CREATE TABLE Departments (
   dept_id INT);

ALTER TABLE Departments ADD CONSTRAINT dept_constraint_1
   PRIMARY KEY (dept_id) NOT DEFERRABLE;

ALTER TABLE Employees ADD CONSTRAINT emps_constraint_1
   FOREIGN KEY (dept_id) REFERENCES Departments NOT DEFERRABLE;

ALTER TABLE Departments ADD CONSTRAINT dept_constraint_2
   CHECK (dept_id IN (SELECT dept_id FROM Employees))
         NOT DEFERRABLE;
```

Not only does this second attempt resolve the legalities, it also looks better; it's easier to read several short statements, rather than a few long statements. Anyway, with this method, there's no problem defining interlocked Tables. However, there's still a problem with putting data into them. For example, assuming no data exists in either Table, this SQL statement:

```
INSERT INTO Employees VALUES (1, 1);
```

will cause `EMPS_CONSTRAINT_1` to fail because there are no departments. And this SQL statement:

```
INSERT INTO Departments VALUES (1);
```

will cause `DEPT_CONSTRAINT_2` to fail because there are no employees.

There are three solutions to this problem.

Solution #1 Use SQL3 features. There are, in fact, a few ways to do this with SQL3 — the clearest would be to join the two Tables and update the join.

Solution #2 Take advantage of the fact that NULL matches anything. Begin with the assumption that the DEPARTMENTS Table is not empty, presumably because you used Solution #1 for some other department. Then execute these SQL statements:

```
INSERT INTO Employees VALUES (1, NULL);

INSERT INTO Departments VALUES (1);

UPDATE Employees SET dept_id = 1 WHERE emp_id = 1;
```

You can sometimes use NULL where you can't use anything else — so insert a NULL as a temporary placeholder, and replace it when both rows exist.

Solution #3 Change the initial setup so that all Constraints are deferred. For example:

```
CREATE TABLE Employees (
   emp_id INT,
   dept_id INT);

CREATE TABLE Departments (
   dept_id INT);

ALTER TABLE Departments ADD CONSTRAINT dept_constraint_1
   PRIMARY KEY (dept_id) NOT DEFERRABLE;

ALTER TABLE Employees ADD CONSTRAINT emps_constraint_1
   FOREIGN KEY (dept_id) REFERENCES Departments
      DEFERRABLE INITIALLY DEFERRED;

ALTER TABLE Departments ADD CONSTRAINT dept_constraint_2
   CHECK (dept_id IN (SELECT dept_id FROM Employees))
      DEFERRABLE INITIALLY DEFERRED;
```

This method causes the INSERT problem to disappear because no checks will occur at INSERT time. Thus, these INSERT statements would now work without returning an error:

```
INSERT INTO Departments VALUES (1);

INSERT INTO Employees VALUES (1, 1);

SET CONSTRAINTS ALL IMMEDIATE;
-- recommended once the INSERTs are done
```

We like Solution #3 best because it lacks dependence on SQL3-only features or on tricks.

Dropping Constraints

Dropping a Constraint is straightforward, providing that you know the <Constraint name> — that's why we recommend that you explicitly give every Constraint a name when you make it (even a `NOT NULL` Constraint). <Table Constraint>s and <Column Constraint>s are dropped using the `DROP CONSTRAINT` <Constraint name> clause of the `ALTER TABLE` statement, <Domain Constraint>s are dropped using the `DROP CONSTRAINT` <Constraint name> clause of the `ALTER DOMAIN` statement, and Assertions are dropped with the `DROP ASSERTION` statement.

DROP ASSERTION Statement

The `DROP ASSERTION` statement destroys an Assertion. The required syntax for the `DROP ASSERTION` statement is as follows.

```
DROP ASSERTION <Constraint name>
```

The <Constraint name> must identify an existing Assertion whose owner is either the current <AuthorizationID> or a Role that the current <AuthorizationID> may use. That is, only the <AuthorizationID> that owns the Schema may drop its Assertions. If <Constraint name> does not include an explicit <Schema name> qualifier, the Assertion must belong to the SQL-session default Schema.

The effect of `DROP ASSERTION` <Constraint name>, e.g.,

```
DROP ASSERTION constraint_1;
```

is that the Assertion named `CONSTRAINT_1` will be destroyed, providing that `CONSTRAINT_1` is not referred to in any SQL routine or in any Trigger. If the Assertion's `CHECK` search condition includes a `NOT NULL` condition that causes one or more Columns to have the "known not nullable" nullability characteristic, then the affected Columns' nullability characteristic becomes "possibly nullable" (unless some other Constraint also constrains them to non-null values).

If you want to restrict your code to Core SQL, don't use the `DROP ASSERTION` statement.

Dialects

In most DBMSs, it's common that the `UNIQUE` specification is not supported, but you'll often see a (non-SQL) CREATE UNIQUE INDEX statement that gives you the same functionality instead.

Some DBMSs reportedly don't support the `FOREIGN KEY` <Column Constraint> syntax, but do allow foreign keys to be defined as <Table Constraint>s.

21

Chapter 21

SQL Character Sets

[Obscure Rule] applies to this entire chapter.

In this chapter, we'll describe SQL Character sets in detail and show you the syntax to use to create, alter, and destroy them.

Character Set

A Schema may contain zero or more Character sets. As we explained in Chapter 7 "Character Strings," an *SQL Character set* is a combination of a character repertoire (a set of characters) and a Form-of-use (the repertoire's internal encoding scheme). Character sets are dependent on some Schema — the <Character set name> must be unique within the Schema to which the Character set belongs. User-defined Character sets are created and dropped using standard SQL statements.

In SQL, a Character set may be a Character set defined by a national or international standard, by your DBMS, or by a user of SQL-data.

Standard-defined Character sets consist of a set of characters predefined by some standards body and have a default Collation that is the order of the characters in the relevant standard. The default Collation has the `PAD SPACE` characteristic. The SQL Standard requires a DBMS to support, at a minimum, these standard-defined Character sets: `SQL_CHARACTER`, `GRAPHIC_IRV` (also called `ASCII_GRAPHIC`), `LATIN1`, `ISO8BIT` (also called `ASCII_FULL`), and `UNICODE` (also called `ISO10646`).

Implementation-defined Character sets consist of a set of characters predefined by your DBMS and have a default Collation that is also defined by your DBMS. The default Collation may have either the `PAD SPACE` characteristic or the `NO PAD` characteristic. The SQL Standard requires a DBMS to support, at a minimum, this implementation-defined Character set: SQL_TEXT.

[NON-PORTABLE] The complete set of predefined Character sets supported by a DBMS is non-standard because the SQL Standard allows implementors to include support for other Character sets, in addition to the required ones. [OCELOT Implementation] The OCELOT DBMS that comes with this book provides support for seven other predefined Character sets, based on commonly available MS-Windows codepages. They are:

CODEPAGE_0437	MS-DOS West European codepage 437
CODEPAGE_0850	MS-DOS International codepage 850
CODEPAGE_1250	MS-Windows Latin II codepage 1250
CODEPAGE_1251	MS-Windows Cyrillic codepage 1251
CODEPAGE_1253	MS-Windows Greek codepage 1253
CODEPAGE_1254	MS-Windows Turkish codepage 1254
CODEPAGE_1257	MS-Windows Baltic codepage 1257

The pre-defined Character sets provided by your DBMS belong to INFORMATION_SCHEMA (as do Collations defined by standards and Collations, Translations, and Form-of-use conversions defined by your DBMS). The SQL special grantee, PUBLIC, always has a USAGE Privilege on every predefined Character set provided by your DBMS. For details on the predefined Character sets, see Chapter 6 "Characters."

Every Character set has a default Collation; it specifies the rules that determine the results of comparisons in the absence of an explicit COLLATE clause.

A Character set is defined by a descriptor that contains three pieces of information:

1. The <Character set name> qualified by the <Schema name> of the Schema to which it belongs.
2. A list of the characters that belong to the Character set.
3. The name of the Character set's default Collation. (This may be the Form-of-use encoding scheme for the Character set's repertoire.)

User-defined Character sets may belong to any Schema owned by the creator. To create a Character set, use the CREATE CHARACTER SET statement (either as a stand-alone SQL statement or within a CREATE SCHEMA statement). CREATE CHARACTER SET specifies the enclosing Schema, names the Character set, and identifies the Character set's repertoire and default Collation. To destroy a Character set, use the DROP CHARACTER SET statement. To change an existing Character set, drop and then redefine it.

There is a one-to-many association between Character sets and Collations; one Character set can have many possible Collations defined for it, although only one can be its default Collation.

Character Set Names

A <Character set name> identifies a Character set. The required syntax for a <Character set name> is as follows.

```
<Character set name> ::=
[ <Schema name>. ] unqualified name
```

A <Character set name> is a <SQL language identifier> that is unique (for all Character sets) within the Schema to which it belongs. The <Schema name> which qualifies a <Character set name> names the Schema to which the Character set belongs and can either be explicitly stated or it will default to INFORMATION_SCHEMA; that is, an unqualified <Character set name> is always assumed to belong to INFORMATION_SCHEMA — even if a CREATE CHARACTER SET statement is part of a CREATE SCHEMA statement. (User-defined Character sets may not belong to INFORMATION_SCHEMA. Therefore, when defining, using, or dropping a user-defined Character set, always provide an explicit <Schema name> qualifier for the <Character set name>.)

Here are some examples of <Character set name>s:

```
LATIN1
-- a predefined <Character set name>

SCHEMA_1.CHARACTER_SET_1
-- a simple qualified user-defined <Character set name>

CATALOG_1.SCHEMA_1.CHARACTER_SET_1
-- a fully qualified user-defined <Character set name>
```

If you want to restrict your code to Core SQL, don't use any <Character set name>s.

CREATE CHARACTER SET Statement

The CREATE CHARACTER SET statement names a new user-defined Character set and specifies the Character set's repertoire and default Collation. The required syntax for the CREATE CHARACTER SET statement is as follows.

```
CREATE CHARACTER SET user-defined <Character set name> [ AS ]
      GET predefined <Character set name>
      [ COLLATE <Collation name> ]
```

CREATE CHARACTER SET defines a new user-defined Character set.

The user-defined <Character set name> identifies the new Character set and the Schema to which it belongs. A <Character set name> that includes an explicit <Schema name> qualifier belongs to the Schema named. A <Character set name> that does not include an explicit <Schema name> qualifier belongs to INFORMATION_SCHEMA. Because a user-defined Character set can't belong to INFORMATION_SCHEMA, always provide an explicit <Schema name> qualifier when you're creating a Character set.

If CREATE CHARACTER SET is part of a CREATE SCHEMA statement, the <Character set name> must include the <Schema name> of the Schema being created; that is, it isn't possible to create a Character set belonging to a different Schema from within CREATE SCHEMA. For example, this SQL statement will not return an error because the <Character set name> explicitly includes a qualifying <Schema name> that matches the name of the Schema being created:

```
CREATE SCHEMA bob
   CREATE CHARACTER SET bob.charset_1 AS GET LATIN1;
-- creates a Character set called BOB.CHARSET_1 in Schema BOB
```

But the following SQL statement will return an error because the <Character set name> explicitly includes a qualifying <Schema name> that is different from the name of the Schema being created:

```
CREATE SCHEMA bob
   CREATE CHARACTER SET sam.charset_1 AS GET LATIN1;
-- tries to create a Character set belonging to Schema SAM inside Schema BOB;
illegal syntax
```

If CREATE CHARACTER SET is executed as a stand-alone SQL statement, the current <AuthorizationID> must either be the owner of the Schema to which this new Character set belongs, or the Schema's owner must be a Role that the current <AuthorizationID> may use. That is, only the owner of a Schema can create Character sets for that Schema. In addition to creating a Character set, CREATE CHARACTER SET also causes the SQL special grantor, "_SYSTEM", to grant a grantable USAGE Privilege on the new Character set to the Schema owner <AuthorizationID> (that is, the <AuthorizationID creating the Character set).

A user-defined Character set must be defined as using the repertoire (and possibly the default Collation) of a predefined Character set provided by the DBMS; that is, you can't create a Character set based on another user-defined Character set. The GET clause of the CREATE CHARACTER SET statement names the predefined Character set that is the source for the new Character set. For example, this SQL statement:

```
CREATE CHARACTER SET bob.charset_1 AS GET LATIN1;
```

defines a new user-defined Character set, called BOB.CHARSET_1, in the Schema named BOB. Except for its name, the Character set BOB.CHARSET_1 will be exactly the same as the LATIN1 Character set — that is, it is not truly possible to "create" new Character sets; merely to rename (and possibly assign new default Collations for) them. The <keyword> AS in the GET clause is noise and can be omitted. For example, these two SQL statements are equivalent:

```
CREATE CHARACTER SET bob.charset_1 AS GET LATIN1;

CREATE CHARACTER SET bob.charset_1 GET LATIN1;
```

The optional COLLATE clause of the CREATE CHARACTER SET statement allows you to define a default Collation for your user-defined Character set that is different from the default Collation of its source Character set. Your current <AuthorizationID> must have the USAGE Privilege on the Collation named. Here is an example:

```
CREATE CHARACTER SET bob.charset_1 AS GET LATIN1
   COLLATE bob.collation_1;
```

This SQL statement defines a new user-defined Character set, called BOB.CHARSET_1. It contains the same characters as LATIN1 does, but is slightly different because its default Collation won't be LATIN1's default Collation — instead, its default Collation is a Collation named BOB.COLLATION_1.

If you want to restrict your code to Core SQL, don't use the CREATE CHARACTER SET statement.

DROP CHARACTER SET Statement

The DROP CHARACTER SET statement destroys a user-defined Character set. The required syntax for the DROP CHARACTER SET statement is as follows.

```
DROP CHARACTER SET <Character set name>
```

The <Character set name> must identify an existing Character set whose owner is either the current <AuthorizationID> or a Role that the current <AuthorizationID> may use. That is, only the <AuthorizationID> that owns the Character set may drop it and so it isn't possible to drop any of the predefined Character sets provided by your DBMS.

The effect of DROP CHARACTER SET <Character set name>, e.g.,

```
DROP CHARACTER SET bob.charset_1;
```

is that the user-defined Character set named BOB.CHARSET_1 is destroyed, provided that the Character set is not referred to in any View definition, Constraint or Assertion definition, Collation definition, Translation definition, or SQL routine. That is, DROP CHARACTER SET ensures that only a Character set with no dependent Objects can be destroyed. If the Character set is used by any other Object, DROP CHARACTER SET will fail.

If successful, DROP CHARACTER SET has a two-fold effect.

1. The Character set named is destroyed.
2. The USAGE Privilege held on the Character set by the <AuthorizationID> that owns it is revoked (by the SQL special grantor, "_SYSTEM") with a CASCADE revoke behaviour, so that the USAGE Privilege held on the Character set by any other <AuthorizationID> is also revoked.

If you want to restrict your code to Core SQL, don't use the DROP CHARACTER SET statement.

22

Chapter 22

SQL Collations

[Obscure Rule] applies to this entire chapter.

In this chapter, we'll describe SQL Collations in detail and show you the syntax to use to create, alter, and destroy them.

Collation

A Schema may contain zero or more Collations. An *SQL Collation* is a set of rules that determines the result when character strings are compared. Collations are dependent on some Schema — the <Collation name> must be unique within the Schema to which the Collation belongs. User-defined Collations are created and dropped using standard SQL statements.

In SQL, a Collation may be a Collation defined by a national or international standard, by your DBMS, or by a user of SQL-data.

Standard-defined Collations are collating sequences predefined for a character repertoire by some standards body. The SQL Standard requires a DBMS to provide a default Collation (based on the character repertoire order) for each of the standard-defined Character sets it supports. In each case, the default Collation has the `PAD SPACE` characteristic.

Implementation-defined Collations are collating sequences predefined for a character repertoire by your DBMS. These Collations may have either the `PAD SPACE` characteristic or the `NO PAD` characteristic. The SQL Standard requires a DBMS to provide a default Collation, called `SQL_TEXT`, for the `SQL_TEXT` Character set.

[NON-PORTABLE] The complete set of predefined Collations provided by a DBMS is non-standard because the SQL Standard allows implementors to include support for other Collations, in addition to the required ones. It also requires implementors (*a*) to define the names for the standard-defined and (except for SQL_TEXT) the implementation-defined Collations it provides and (*b*) to define the PAD characteristic for each implementation-defined Collation it provides. [OCELOT Implementation] The OCELOT DBMS that comes with this book provides an SQL_TEXT Collation that follows the order of the Unicode Form-of-use codes. The SQL_TEXT Collation has the PAD SPACE characteristic and is the default Collation for both the SQL_TEXT Character set and the UNICODE Character set. It also provides thirty-one other predefined Collations, all with the PAD SPACE characteristic. The default Collations are as follows:

SQL_CHARACTER	default Collation for Character set SQL_CHARACTER
GRAPHIC_IRV	default Collation for Character set GRAPHIC_IRV
LATIN1	default Collation for Character set LATIN1
ISO8BIT	default Collation for Character set ISO8BIT
CODEPAGE_0437	default Collation for Character set CODEPAGE_0437
CODEPAGE_0850	default Collation for Character set CODEPAGE_0850
CODEPAGE_1250	default Collation for Character set CODEPAGE_1250
CODEPAGE_1251	default Collation for Character set CODEPAGE_1251
CODEPAGE_1253	default Collation for Character set CODEPAGE_1253
CODEPAGE_1254	default Collation for Character set CODEPAGE_1254
CODEPAGE_1257	default Collation for Character set CODEPAGE_1257

The OCELOT DBMS allows pre-defined Collations to apply for any Character set (this is SQL-92; it's no longer legal in SQL3). The pre-defined Collations that apply for all Character sets are: ALBANIAN, AUSTRIAN, CROATIAN, CZECH, DUTCH, ESTONIAN, GERMAN, HUNGARIAN, LATVIAN, LITHUANIAN, NORDIC, POLISH, ROMANIAN, SLOVAK, SLOVENIAN, SPANISH, TURKISH, UKRAINIAN, WELSH, and CASE_INSENSITIVE. For other European languages there is no need for a special Collation — the repertoire order is sufficient.

The pre-defined Collations provided by your DBMS belong to INFORMATION_SCHEMA. The SQL special grantee, PUBLIC, always has a USAGE Privilege on every predefined Collation provided by your DBMS.

A Collation is defined by a descriptor that contains three pieces of information:

1. The <Collation name> qualified by the <Schema name> of the Schema to which it belongs.
2. The name of the Character set on which the Collation operates.
3. Whether the NO PAD or the PAD SPACE characteristic applies to the Collation.

User-defined Collations may belong to any Schema owned by the creator. To create a Collation, use the CREATE COLLATION statement (either as a stand-alone SQL statement or within a CREATE SCHEMA statement). CREATE COLLATION specifies the enclosing Schema, names the Collation, and defines the Collation's Character set and PAD characteristic. To destroy a Collation, use the DROP COLLATION statement. To change an existing Collation, drop and then redefine it.

There is a one-to-many association between Character sets and Collations; one Character set can have many possible Collations defined for it, although only one can be its default Collation.

The default Collation for a Character set is the Collation that will be used to compare characters belonging to that Character set in the absence of an explicit specification to the contrary and can either be a Collation defined for the Character set or the Form-of-use encoding scheme for that Character set's repertoire — that is, the default Collation for a Character set can be defined to be the order of the characters in the character repertoire. (For example, in the 7-bit ASCII character set, the decimal code for the letter `A` is `65` and the decimal code for the letter `B` is `66`. This is a happy coincidence; it allows your DBMS to discover that `'A'` is less than `'B'` by merely executing a CMP; a machine-code numeric comparison. And that's what is meant by "the order of the characters in the repertoire." Note that, because the decimal code for the letter `a` is `97`, it follows that `'A'` is less than `'a'` — that is, character repertoire order specifies a case-sensitive collating sequence.)

Collation Names

A <Collation name> identifies a Collation. The required syntax for a <Collation name> is as follows.

```
<Collation name> ::=
[ <Schema name>. ] unqualified name
```

A <Collation name> is a <regular identifier> or a <delimited identifier> that is unique (for all Collations) within the Schema to which it belongs. The <Schema name> which qualifies a <Collation name> names the Schema to which the Collation belongs and can either be explicitly stated or it will default to `INFORMATION_SCHEMA`; that is, an unqualified <Collation name> is always assumed to belong to `INFORMATION_SCHEMA` — even if a `CREATE COLLATION` statement is part of a `CREATE SCHEMA` statement. (User-defined Collations may not belong to `INFORMATION_SCHEMA`. Therefore, when defining, using, or dropping a user-defined Collation, always provide an explicit <Schema name> qualifier for the <Collation name>.)

Here are some examples of possible <Collation name>s:

```
SQL_TEXT
-- a predefined <Collation name>

SCHEMA_1.COLLATION_1
-- a simple qualified user-defined <Collation name>

CATALOG_1.SCHEMA_1.COLLATION_1
-- a fully qualified user-defined <Collation name>
```

Form-of-Use Conversion Names

A <Form-of-Use conversion name> identifies a character repertoire's encoding scheme — the one-to-one mapping scheme between each character in the repertoire and a set of internal codes (usually 8-bit values) that define how the repertoire's characters are encoded as numbers. These codes are also used to specify the order of the characters within the repertoire and so can be used to specify the default Collation for a Character set. Supported Forms-of-use are all predefined by your DBMS and thus belong to INFORMATION_SCHEMA. SQL provides no ability to define your own Forms-of-use. The required syntax for a <Form-of-use conversion name> is as follows.

```
<Form-of-use conversion name> ::=
[ INFORMATION_SCHEMA. ] unqualified name
```

A <Form-of-use conversion name> is a <regular identifier> or a <delimited identifier> that is unique (for all Forms-of-use) within INFORMATION_SCHEMA. The <Schema name> which qualifies a <Form-of-use conversion name> names the Schema to which the Form-of-use belongs and can either be explicitly stated or it will default to INFORMATION_SCHEMA; the only Schema that may own a Form-of-use.

Here are some examples of possible <Form-of-use conversion name>s:

```
FORM_1
-- a possible <Form-of-use conversion name>

INFORMATION_SCHEMA.FORM_1
-- a simple qualified possible <Form-of-use conversion name>

CATALOG_1.INFORMATION_SCHEMA.FORM_1
-- a fully qualified possible <Form-of-use conversion name>
```

[NON-PORTABLE] The Forms-of-use available for use are non-standard because the SQL Standard requires implementors to define which (if any) Forms-of-use they will explicitly provide. [OCELOT Implementation] The OCELOT DBMS that comes with this book provides no explicit Forms-of- use.

If you want to restrict your code to Core SQL, don't use any <Collation name>s or <Form-of-use conversion name>s.

CREATE COLLATION Statement

The CREATE COLLATION statement names a new user-defined Collation and specifies the Collation's PAD characteristic and the Character set that the Collation is for. The required syntax for the CREATE COLLATION statement is as follows.

```
CREATE COLLATION user-defined <Collation name>
      FOR <Character set name>
      FROM existing <Collation name> [ {NO PAD | PAD SPACE} ]
```

CREATE COLLATION defines a new user-defined Collation.

The user-defined <Collation name> identifies the new Collation and the Schema to which it belongs. A <Collation name> that includes an explicit <Schema name> qualifier belongs to the Schema named. A <Collation name> that does not include an explicit <Schema name> qualifier belongs to INFORMATION_SCHEMA. Because a user-defined Collation can't belong to

INFORMATION_SCHEMA, always provide an explicit <Schema name> qualifier when you're creating a Collation.

If CREATE COLLATION is part of a CREATE SCHEMA statement, the <Collation name> must include the <Schema name> of the Schema being created; that is, it isn't possible to create a Collation belonging to a different Schema from within CREATE SCHEMA. For example, this SQL statement will not return an error because the <Collation name> explicitly includes a qualifying <Schema name> that matches the name of the Schema being created:

```
CREATE SCHEMA bob
   CREATE COLLATION bob.collation_1 FOR bob.charset_1 FROM SQL_TEXT;
-- creates a Collation called BOB.COLLATION_1 in Schema BOB
```

But the following SQL statement will return an error because the <Collation name> explicitly includes a qualifying <Schema name> that is different from the name of the Schema being created:

```
CREATE SCHEMA bob
CREATE COLLATION sam.collation_1 FOR bob.charset_1 FROM SQL_TEXT;
-- tries to create a Collation belonging to Schema SAM inside Schema BOB; ille-
gal syntax
```

If CREATE COLLATION is executed as a stand-alone SQL statement, the current <AuthorizationID> must either be the owner of the Schema to which this new Collation belongs or the Schema's owner must be a Role that the current <AuthorizationID> may use. That is, only the owner of a Schema can create Collations for that Schema. In addition to creating a Collation, CREATE COLLATION also causes the SQL special grantor, "_SYSTEM", to grant the USAGE Privilege on the new Collation to the Schema owner <AuthorizationID> (that is, the <AuthorizationID creating the Collation). The Privilege is grantable if the <AuthorizationID> also has a grantable USAGE Privilege on the Collation named in the FROM clause of the CREATE COLLATION statement.

A user-defined Collation must be defined to operate on a Character set. The FOR clause of the CREATE COLLATION statement names that Character set. <Character set name> must be the name of an existing Character set for which the current <AuthorizationID> has the USAGE Privilege.

A user-defined Collation must also be defined as using the collating sequence of an existing Collation that is already defined for the Character set named in the FOR clause of the CREATE COLLATION statement. The FROM clause of the CREATE COLLATION statement names this Collation source. The existing <Collation name> must be the name of an existing Collation for which the current <AuthorizationID> has the USAGE Privilege. For example, this SQL statement:

```
CREATE COLLATION bob.collation_1 FOR bob.charset_1 FROM SQL_TEXT;
```

defines a new user-defined Collation, called BOB.COLLATION_1, in the Schema named BOB. Except for its name, the Collation BOB.COLLATION_1 will be exactly the same as the SQL_TEXT Collation — that is, it is not truly possible to "create" new Collations, merely to rename (and possibly assign a new PAD characteristic to) them. To define a new Collation, the CREATE COLLATION statement must use some pre-existing Collation as a Collation source

— and, ultimately, all Collations can only be based on some pre-defined Collation provided by your DBMS.

The optional PAD characteristic clause of the CREATE COLLATION statement allows you to define a PAD characteristic for your user-defined Collation that is different from the PAD characteristic of its source Collation. If you omit the PAD clause, your new Collation will have the same PAD characteristic as its source Collation does. For example, this SQL statement:

```
CREATE COLLATION bob.collation_1 FOR bob.charset_1 FROM SQL_TEXT;
```

defines a new user-defined Collation that will have the same PAD characteristic as Collation SQL_TEXT; that is, except for its name, BOB.COLLATION_1 is exactly like SQL_TEXT. This SQL statement:

```
CREATE COLLATION bob.collation_1 FOR bob.charset_1 FROM SQL_TEXT
   PAD SPACE;
```

defines a new user-defined Collation that will have the PAD SPACE characteristic. And this SQL statement:

```
CREATE COLLATION bob.collation_1 FOR bob.charset_1 FROM SQL_TEXT
   NO PAD;
```

defines a new user-defined Collation that will have the NO PAD characteristic.

A Collation's PAD characteristic affects the result when two strings of unequal size are compared. If the Collation in effect for a comparison has the PAD SPACE characteristic, the shorter string is padded with spaces (on the right) until it's the same length as the larger string; then the comparison is done. If the Collation in effect for a comparison has the NO PAD characteristic, the shorter string is padded with some other character before the comparison is done. In this case, the result is that the shorter comparand will evaluate as less than the longer comparand if they contain the same characters for their common length — for more information, see Chapter 7 "Character Strings."

If you want to restrict your code to Core SQL, don't use the CREATE COLLATION statement.

DROP COLLATION Statement

The DROP COLLATION statement destroys a user-defined Collation. The required syntax for the DROP COLLATION statement is as follows.

```
DROP COLLATION <Collation name> {RESTRICT | CASCADE}
```

The <Collation name> must identify an existing Collation whose owner is either the current <AuthorizationID> or a Role that the current <AuthorizationID> may use. That is, only the <AuthorizationID> that owns the Collation may drop it and so it isn't possible to drop any of the predefined Collations provided by your DBMS.

The effect of DROP COLLATION <Collation name> RESTRICT, e.g.,

```
DROP COLLATION bob.collation_1 RESTRICT;
```

is that the user-defined Collation named BOB.COLLATION_1 is destroyed, provided that the Collation is not referred to in any View definition, Constraint or Assertion definition, or SQL routine. That is, DROP COLLATION ensures that only a Collation with no dependent Views,

Constraints, Assertions, or SQL routines can be destroyed. If the Collation is used by any of these Objects, DROP COLLATION ... RESTRICT will fail.

The effect of DROP COLLATION <Collation name> CASCADE, e.g.,

```
DROP COLLATION bob.collation_1 CASCADE;
```

is that the user-defined Collation named BOB.COLLATION_1 is destroyed.

If successful, DROP COLLATION has a six-fold effect.

1. The Collation named is destroyed.
2. The USAGE Privilege held on the Collation by the <AuthorizationID> that owns it is revoked (by the SQL special grantor, "_SYSTEM") with a CASCADE revoke behaviour, so that the USAGE Privilege held on the Collation by any other <AuthorizationID> is also revoked.
3. The definition of any other Collation that named this Collation is amended, so that it no longer refers to it. The effect is that each Collation that was based on the dropped Collation will subsequently use the Form-of-use encoding scheme for the repertoire of its Character set as a collating sequence.
4. The definition of any Character set that named this Collation is amended, so that it no longer refers to it. The effect is that each Character set that used the dropped Collation as its default Collation will subsequently use the Form-of-use encoding scheme for its repertoire as a default Collation.
5. The definition of any Column, Domain, View, Constraint, or Assertion that named this Collation is amended, so that it no longer refers to it. The effect is that each Column or Domain that used the dropped Collation as its default Collation will subsequently use the default Collation of its Character set as a default Collation.
6. Every SQL routine that names this Collation is dropped with a CASCADE drop behaviour.

If you want to restrict your code to Core SQL, don't use the DROP COLLATION statement.

23

Chapter 23

SQL Translations

[Obscure Rule] applies to this entire chapter.

In this chapter, we'll describe SQL Translations in detail and show you the syntax to use to create, alter, and destroy them.

Translation

A Schema may contain zero or more Translations. An *SQL Translation* is a set of rules that maps the characters from a source Character set to the characters of a target Character set; effectively translating source strings into target strings. Any pair of Character sets may have zero or more Translations defined to translate strings belonging to one (the source Character set) into strings belonging to the other (the target Character set). Translations are dependent on some Schema — the <Translation name> must be unique within the Schema to which the Translation belongs. User-defined Translations are created and dropped using standard SQL statements.

In SQL, a Translation may be a Translation defined by a national or international standard, by your DBMS, or by a user of SQL-data.

Standard-defined Translations are translations predefined for two character repertoires by some standards body. Implementation-defined Translations are translations predefined for two Character sets by your DBMS. The pre-defined Translations provided by your DBMS belong to `INFORMATION_SCHEMA`. The SQL special grantee, `PUBLIC`, always has a `USAGE` Privilege on every predefined Translation provided by your DBMS.

[NON-PORTABLE] The set of predefined Translations provided by a DBMS is non-standard because the SQL Standard has no required Translations; it requires implementors to define any Translations supported. [OCELOT Implementation] The OCELOT DBMS that comes with this book provides a Translation named OCELOT. It translates SQL_TEXT strings to ISO8BIT strings.

A Translation is defined by a descriptor that contains four pieces of information:

1. The <Translation name> qualified by the <Schema name> of the Schema to which it belongs.
2. The name of the Translation's source Character set; the Character set from which it translates.
3. The name of the Translation's target Character set; the Character set to which it translates.
4. The mapping scheme for the Translation.

Two character strings may be compared or assigned to one another only if they both belong to the same Character set. The way to force a comparison or assignment between strings from different Character sets is to use the TRANSLATE function, which uses a Translation defined for the Character sets as an argument.

User-defined Translations may belong to any Schema owned by the creator. To create a Translation, use the CREATE TRANSLATION statement (either as a stand-alone SQL statement or within a CREATE SCHEMA statement). CREATE TRANSLATION specifies the enclosing Schema; names the Translation; and defines the Translation's source Character set, target Character set, and Translation source. To destroy a Translation, use the DROP TRANSLATION statement. To change an existing Translation, drop and then redefine it.

There is a one-to-many relationship between Translations and Character sets; a Translation may translate the characters of only one pair of Character sets, but a Character set can be named as either the source or the target for many different Translations.

Translation Names

A <Translation name> identifies a Translation. The required syntax for a <Translation name> is as follows.

```
<Translation name> ::=
[ <Schema name>. ] unqualified name
```

A <Translation name> is a <regular identifier> or a <delimited identifier> that is unique (for all Translations) within the Schema to which it belongs. The <Schema name> which qualifies a <Translation name> names the Schema to which the Translation belongs and can either be explicitly stated or it will default to INFORMATION_SCHEMA; that is, an unqualified <Translation name> is always assumed to belong to INFORMATION_SCHEMA — even if a CREATE TRANSLATION statement is part of a CREATE SCHEMA statement. (User-defined Translations may not belong to INFORMATION_SCHEMA. Therefore, when defining, using, or dropping a user-defined Translation, always provide an explicit <Schema name> qualifier for the <Translation name>.)

Here are some examples of possible <Translation name>s:

```
TRANSLATION_1
-- a <Translation name>

SCHEMA_1.TRANSLATION_1
-- a simple qualified <Translation name>

CATALOG_1.SCHEMA_1.TRANSLATION_1
-- a fully qualified <Translation name>
```

If you want to restrict your code to Core SQL, don't use any <Translation name>s.

CREATE TRANSLATION Statement

The CREATE TRANSLATION statement names a new user-defined Translation and specifies the Translation's source and target Character sets as well as the Translation's source. The required syntax for the CREATE TRANSLATION statement is as follows.

```
CREATE TRANSLATION user-defined <Translation name>
   FOR source <Character set name>
   TO target <Character set name>
   FROM <translation source>

   <translation source> ::=
   existing <Translation name> |
   <specific routine designator>
```

CREATE TRANSLATION defines a new user-defined Translation.

The user-defined <Translation name> identifies the new Translation and the Schema to which it belongs. A <Translation name> that includes an explicit <Schema name> qualifier belongs to the Schema named. A <Translation name> that does not include an explicit <Schema name> qualifier belongs to INFORMATION_SCHEMA. Because a user-defined Translation can't belong to INFORMATION_SCHEMA, always provide an explicit <Schema name> qualifier when you're creating a Translation.

If CREATE TRANSLATION is part of a CREATE SCHEMA statement, the <Translation name> must include the <Schema name> of the Schema being created; that is, it isn't possible to create a Translation belonging to a different Schema from within CREATE SCHEMA. For example, this SQL statement will not return an error because the <Translation name> explicitly includes a qualifying <Schema name> that matches the name of the Schema being created:

```
CREATE SCHEMA bob
   CREATE TRANSLATION bob.translation_1
      FOR SQL_CHARACTER TO LATIN1 FROM function_name;
-- creates a Translation called BOB.TRANSLATION_1 in Schema BOB
```

But the following SQL statement will return an error because the <Translation name> explicitly includes a qualifying <Schema name> that is different from the name of the Schema being created:

```
CREATE SCHEMA bob
   CREATE TRANSLATION sam.translation_1
      FOR SQL_CHARACTER TO LATIN1 FROM function_name;
-- tries to create a Translation belonging to Schema SAM inside Schema BOB;
illegal syntax
```

If CREATE TRANSLATION is executed as a stand-alone SQL statement, the current <AuthorizationID> must either be the owner of the Schema to which this new Translation belongs or the Schema's owner must be a Role that the current <AuthorizationID> may use. That is, only the owner of a Schema can create Translations for that Schema. In addition to creating a Translation, CREATE TRANSLATION also causes the SQL special grantor, "_SYSTEM", to grant the USAGE Privilege on the new Translation to the Schema owner <AuthorizationID> (that is, the <AuthorizationID creating the Translation). The Privilege is grantable if the <AuthorizationID> also has a grantable USAGE Privilege on both the Translation's source Character set and its target Character set.

A user-defined Translation must be defined to operate on a pair of Character sets. The FOR clause of the CREATE TRANSLATION statement names the source Character set; the TO clause names the target Character set. In each case, <Character set name> must be the name of an existing Character set for which the current <AuthorizationID> has the USAGE Privilege.

A user-defined Translation must also be defined as using a source mapping scheme; it defines the source and target Character sets' corresponding pairs of characters. The FROM clause of the CREATE TRANSLATION statement names this Translation source. If the FROM clause names some other Translation as the new Translation's source, the existing <Translation name> must be the name of an existing Translation for which the current <AuthorizationID> has the USAGE Privilege and whose source Character set and target Character set are the same as the source and target Character sets you're defining for the new Translation. For example, this SQL statement:

```
CREATE TRANSLATION bob.translation_2
   FOR SQL_CHARACTER TO LATIN1 FROM bob.translation_1;
```

defines a new user-defined Translation, called BOB.TRANSLATION_2, in the Schema named BOB. Except for its name, the Translation BOB.TRANSLATION_2 will be exactly the same as the BOB.TRANSLATION_1 Translation — that is, it is not truly possible to "create" new Translations with this format, merely to rename them. The other option for specifying a Translation source is to use a <specific routine designator> that names an SQL-invoked function for which the current <AuthorizationID> has the EXECUTE Privilege. The function named must (*a*) have one character string parameter whose Character set is this Translation's source Character set and (*b*) return a character string that belongs to this Translation's target Character set.

If you want to restrict your code to Core SQL, don't use the CREATE TRANSLATION statement.

DROP TRANSLATION Statement

The DROP TRANSLATION statement destroys a user-defined Translation. The required syntax for the DROP TRANSLATION statement is as follows.

```
DROP TRANSLATION <Translation name>
```

The <Translation name> must identify an existing Translation whose owner is either the current <AuthorizationID> or a Role that the current <AuthorizationID> may use. That is, only the <AuthorizationID> that owns the Translation may drop it and so it isn't possible to drop any of the predefined Translations provided by your DBMS.

The effect of DROP TRANSLATION <Translation name>, e.g.,

```
DROP TRANSLATION bob.translation_1;
```

is that the user-defined Translation named BOB.TRANSLATION_1 is destroyed, provided that the Translation is not referred to in any View definition; Constraint or Assertion definition; Collation definition; other Translation definition or SQL routine. That is, DROP TRANSLATION ensures that only a Translation with no dependent Objects can be destroyed. If the Translation is used by any other Object, DROP TRANSLATION will fail.

If successful, DROP TRANSLATION has a two-fold effect.

1. The Translation named is destroyed.
2. The USAGE Privilege held on the Translation by the <AuthorizationID> that owns it is revoked (by the SQL special grantor, "_SYSTEM") with a CASCADE revoke behaviour, so that the USAGE Privilege held on the Translation by any other <AuthorizationID> is also revoked.

If you want to restrict your code to Core SQL, don't use the DROP TRANSLATION statement.

24

Chapter 24

SQL Triggers

"If you press the SECOND dorsal fin-spine on a trigger fish, an amazing event occurs. The FIRST dorsal fin-spine goes down too."

— Applied Ichthyology

In this chapter, we'll describe SQL Triggers in detail and show you the syntax to use to create, alter, and destroy them.

Trigger

A Schema may contain zero or more Triggers. An *SQL Trigger* is a named chain reaction that you set off with an SQL-data change statement; it specifies a set of SQL statements that are to be executed (either once for each row or once for the whole triggering INSERT, DELETE, or UPDATE statement) either before or after rows are inserted into a Table, rows are deleted from a Table, or one or more Columns are updated in rows of a Table. Triggers are dependent on some Schema — the <Trigger name> must be unique within the Schema to which the Trigger belongs — and are created, altered, and dropped using standard SQL statements.

Triggers are similar to Constraints. (In fact, referential Constraints are now defined by the SQL Standard as merely a type of Trigger, although they don't share the same name-space.) What distinguishes a Trigger from a Constraint is flexibility; the Trigger body may contain actual SQL procedure statements that you define yourself. In effect, when you "create a Trigger on Table TABLE_1," you are saying "whenever (in the future) a specific sort of event occurs which changes Table TABLE_1, execute the following further SQL statements." For example, you could create a Trigger so that, whenever TABLE_1 is updated, a counter should be incremented in a summary Table.

Triggers are an SQL3 feature, but most DBMS vendors implemented them years ago. People use Triggers to enforce business rules, to maintain logs, or to substitute for Constraints (where the rules for Constraints are too restrictive).

A Trigger is defined by a descriptor that contains eight pieces of information:

1. The <Trigger name> qualified by the <Schema name> of the Schema to which it belongs.
2. The name of the Table whose data, when changed, will cause the Trigger to be activated. (This is called the Trigger's *subject Table*.)
3. The Trigger action time, which tells your DBMS when to execute the Trigger body (either BEFORE or AFTER the Trigger event).
4. The Trigger event, which tells your DBMS which data change statement (either INSERT, UPDATE, or DELETE), executed on the Trigger's Table, activates the Trigger.
5. The Trigger Column list for the Trigger event, as well as whether the list was explicitly or implicitly defined (for UPDATE Trigger events only).
6. Any old values <Correlation name>, new values <Correlation name>, old values Table alias, or new values Table alias defined for the Trigger.
7. The Trigger body; the SQL statements you want your DBMS to execute on the Trigger's Table when the Trigger is activated.
8. The Trigger's timestamp; when it was created.

To create a Trigger use the CREATE TRIGGER statement (either as a stand-alone SQL statement or within a CREATE SCHEMA statement). CREATE TRIGGER specifies the enclosing Schema, names the Trigger, and defines the Trigger's Table, action time, event, and body. To destroy a Trigger, use the DROP TRIGGER statement. To change an existing Trigger, drop and then redefine it.

Trigger Names

A <Trigger name> identifies a Trigger. The required syntax for a <Trigger name> is as follows.

```
<Trigger name> ::=
[ <Schema name>. ] unqualified name
```

A <Trigger name> is a <regular identifier> or a <delimited identifier> that is unique (for all Triggers) within the Schema to which it belongs. The <Schema name> that qualifies a <Trigger name> names the Schema to which the Trigger belongs and can either be explicitly stated or a default will be supplied by your DBMS, as follows:

- If a <Trigger name> in a CREATE SCHEMA statement isn't qualified, the default qualifier is the name of the Schema you're creating.
- If the unqualified <Trigger name> is found in any other SQL statement in a Module, the default qualifier is the name of the Schema identified in the SCHEMA clause or AUTHORIZATION clause of the MODULE statement which defines that Module.

Here are some examples of <Trigger name>s:

```
TRIGGER_1
-- a <Trigger name>

SCHEMA_1.TRIGGER_1
-- a simple qualified <Trigger name>

CATALOG_1.SCHEMA_1.TRIGGER_1
-- a fully qualified <Trigger name>
```

CREATE TRIGGER Statement

The CREATE TRIGGER statement names a new Trigger and defines the Trigger's Table, action time, event, and body. The required syntax for the CREATE TRIGGER statement is as follows.

```
CREATE TRIGGER <Trigger name>
{BEFORE | AFTER} <trigger event> ON <Table name>
[ REFERENCING <old or new values alias list> ]
<triggered action>

<trigger event> ::=
   INSERT |
   DELETE |
   UPDATE [ OF <trigger Column list> ]

      <trigger Column list> ::= <Column name> [ {,<Column name>} ... ]

   <old or new values alias list> ::=
   <old or new values alias>...

      <old or new values alias> ::=
      OLD [ ROW ] [ AS ] old values <Correlation name> |
      NEW [ ROW ] [ AS ] new values <Correlation name> |
      OLD TABLE [ AS ] <old values Table alias> |
      NEW TABLE [ AS ] <new values Table alias>

         <old values Table alias> ::= <identifier>

         <new values Table alias> ::= <identifier>
```

```
<triggered action> ::=
[ FOR EACH {ROW | STATEMENT} ] [ WHEN (search condition) ]
      <triggered SQL statement>

      <triggered SQL statement> ::=
      SQL statement |
      BEGIN ATOMIC {SQL statement;}... END
```

`CREATE TRIGGER` defines a new Trigger.

The <Trigger name> identifies the Trigger and the Schema to which it belongs. Typical <Trigger name>s include the Trigger event, e.g., `Employee_Update` or `After_Delete_From_Employee`. A <Trigger name> that includes an explicit <Schema name> qualifier belongs to the Schema named. A <Trigger name> that does not include an explicit <Schema name> qualifier belongs to the SQL-session default Schema. The <Trigger name> must be unique (for all Triggers) within the Schema that contains it.

If `CREATE TRIGGER` is part of a `CREATE SCHEMA` statement, the <Trigger name>, if explicitly qualified, must include the <Schema name> of the Schema being created; that is, it isn't possible to create a Trigger belonging to a different Schema from within `CREATE SCHEMA`. For example, this SQL statement will not return an error because the <Trigger name> will default to include the qualifying <Schema name>:

```
CREATE SCHEMA bob
   CREATE TABLE Table_1 (column_1 SMALLINT)
   CREATE TRIGGER Trigger_1 AFTER DELETE ON Table_1
      INSERT INTO Log_table VALUES ('deleted from Table_1');
-- creates a Trigger called BOB.TRIGGER_1 in Schema BOB
```

The following SQL statement will not return an error either because the <Trigger name> explicitly includes a qualifying <Schema name> that matches the name of the Schema being created:

```
CREATE SCHEMA bob
   CREATE TABLE bob.Table_1 (column_1 SMALLINT)
   CREATE TRIGGER bob.Trigger_1 AFTER DELETE ON Table_1
      INSERT INTO Log_table VALUES ('deleted from Table_1');
-- creates a Trigger called BOB.TRIGGER_1 in Schema BOB
```

But this SQL statement will return an error because the <Trigger name> explicitly includes a qualifying <Schema name> that is different from the name of the Schema being created:

```
CREATE SCHEMA bob
   CREATE TABLE bob.Table_1 (column_1 SMALLINT)
   CREATE TRIGGER sam.Trigger_1 AFTER DELETE ON bob.Table_1
      INSERT INTO Log_table VALUES ('deleted from Table_1');
-- tries to create a Trigger belonging to Schema SAM inside Schema BOB; illegal
syntax
```

If CREATE TRIGGER is executed as a stand-alone SQL statement, the current <AuthorizationID> must either be the owner of the Schema to which this new Trigger belongs or the Schema's owner must be a Role that the current <AuthorizationID> may use. That is, only the owner of a Schema can create Triggers for that Schema.

The CREATE TRIGGER statement's main parts are its Table, its event (the description of the SQL-data change statement that activates the Trigger), and its action (the SQL statements which are to be executed by the Trigger).

ON Clause

The ON clause of the CREATE TRIGGER statement names the Trigger's Table; the Base table that, when changed, may cause the Trigger to act. The Table must belong to the same Schema to which the Trigger will belong and the current <AuthorizationID> must have the TRIGGER Privilege on that Table. (You do not need a Privilege to "use" a Trigger. Triggers will be activated whenever you execute the appropriate SQL-data change statement on the Table, whether you want them or not.)

Trigger Action Time

The Trigger action time defines when you want the Trigger's action to be executed; it may be either BEFORE or AFTER. Trigger action time should be BEFORE if you want the Trigger action to occur before the Trigger event. It should be AFTER if you want the Trigger action to occur after the Trigger event.

Trigger Event

The Trigger event defines the SQL-data change statement whose execution (on the Trigger's Table) will activate the Trigger; it may be either INSERT, DELETE, or UPDATE. In the case of UPDATE only, you may add an optional subclause that lists the Trigger Columns; the Columns on which an UPDATE will activate the Trigger (UPDATE on Columns not in the list won't activate the Trigger). The Column list names some or all of the Trigger Table's Columns (each may appear in the list only once). If you omit this optional subclause, the effect is as if you included an OF clause that names every Column of the Trigger's Table. For example, given this Table definition:

```
CREATE TABLE Table_1 (column_1 SMALLINT, column_2 CHAR(5));
```

these two Trigger definitions are equivalent:

```
CREATE TRIGGER Trigger_1
   AFTER UPDATE ON Table_1
      INSERT INTO Log_table VALUES ('updated Table_1');

CREATE TRIGGER Trigger_1
   AFTER UPDATE OF column_1,column_2 ON Table_1
      INSERT INTO Log_table VALUES ('updated Table_1');
```

Here are two more Trigger definition examples:

```
CREATE TRIGGER Trigger_1
   AFTER INSERT ON Table_1
      INSERT INTO Log_table VALUES ('insert into Table_1');

CREATE TRIGGER Trigger_1
   AFTER DELETE ON Table_1
      INSERT INTO Log_table VALUES ('delete from Table_1');
```

REFERENCING Clause

The optional REFERENCING clause of the CREATE TRIGGER statement defines a list of one to four unique <Correlation name>s, or aliases; one name for the old row acted on by the Trigger and/or one name for the new row acted on by the Trigger and/or one name for the old Table acted on by the Trigger and/or one name for the new Table acted on by the Trigger (each may be specified once). The <keyword> AS in each alias option is noise and may be omitted. If neither ROW nor TABLE is specified, the default is ROW — for example, these four SQL statements are equivalent:

```
CREATE TRIGGER Trigger_1
   AFTER UPDATE ON Table_1 REFERENCING OLD ROW AS old_row_name
      FOR EACH ROW INSERT INTO Log_table VALUES ('updated Table_1');

CREATE TRIGGER Trigger_1
   AFTER UPDATE ON Table_1 REFERENCING OLD ROW old_row_name
      FOR EACH ROW INSERT INTO Log_table VALUES ('updated Table_1');

CREATE TRIGGER Trigger_1
   AFTER UPDATE ON Table_1 REFERENCING OLD AS old_row_name
      FOR EACH ROW INSERT INTO Log_table VALUES ('updated Table_1');

CREATE TRIGGER Trigger_1
   AFTER UPDATE ON Table_1 REFERENCING OLD old_row_name
      FOR EACH ROW INSERT INTO Log_table VALUES ('updated Table_1');
```

Your Trigger definition must include a REFERENCING clause if the Trigger action contains references to the Trigger's <Table name> or any of its <Column name>s. The OLD values are the values before the UPDATE/DELETE Trigger event (OLD ROW and OLD TABLE are not allowed if the Trigger event is INSERT) and the NEW values are the values after the UPDATE/INSERT Trigger event (NEW ROW and NEW TABLE are not allowed if the Trigger event is DELETE). If Trigger action time is BEFORE, a REFERENCING clause may not specify OLD TABLE or NEW TABLE. Here are some more REFERENCING clause examples:

```
... REFERENCING OLD ROW AS old_row

... REFERENCING OLD ROW AS old_row, NEW ROW AS new_row

... REFERENCING OLD Table AS old_table, NEW Table AS new_table
```

(A table alias is either a <regular identifier> or a <delimited identifier>.)

Every Trigger event has its own "execution context"; it includes the old row values and/or the new row values of the Trigger's Table. If the Trigger event is INSERT, then there are no old row values because no existing rows of a Table are affected by INSERT. If the Trigger event is DELETE, then there are no new row values because DELETE's action is to remove rows from a Table. If the Trigger event is UPDATE, then there are three row versions:

1. The actual row of data in the Trigger's Table.
2. The "old row values" copy of the actual row — often the same as version 1, but if there are two distinct UPDATE events then there might be a difference between version 1 and version 2. We'll call this the "old row" from now on. The set of all old rows is the "old Table."
3. The "new row values" copy of the actual row — it contains what the DBMS proposes to change the actual row to once the UPDATE statement's execution is completed. We'll call this the "new row" from now on. The set of all new rows is the "new Table." (Note: Even with a BEFORE Trigger, the "new row values" are known to the DBMS.)

A Trigger's execution context is important (indeed, it's mandatory) if you are going to refer to the Trigger's Table in the Trigger's action statements. It would usually be wrong to refer to Column COLUMN_1 of Table TABLE_1 with its <Column reference>, TABLE_1.COLUMN_1, because the <Column reference> refers to that Column in the actual Base table copy. What you really need to refer to is either the old row or the new row. The REFERENCING clause of the CREATE TRIGGER statement makes it possible to specify what context names you will use for referring to OLD ROW or NEW ROW in the Trigger action.

The execution context is "atomic" in the usual SQL sense of the word; if any action statements fail, then all action statements fail and so does the statement that caused the Trigger activation — your DBMS will return the SQLSTATE error 09000 "triggered action exception." In other words, the old row and the new row are simply destroyed and you're left with the same thing you started with — the actual row.

Trigger Action

The Trigger action defines the SQL statements you want the Trigger to execute when it is activated and has three parts: the action granularity, the action when condition, and the action body.

Action Granularity

The optional `FOR EACH` clause of the `CREATE TRIGGER` statement defines the Trigger action granularity; it may be either `FOR EACH STATEMENT` (the default) or `FOR EACH ROW`. The action granularity tells your DBMS how big the field of action is. For example, suppose you create a Trigger for `AFTER UPDATE OF column_1 ON Employees`, then do this:

```
UPDATE Employees SET column_1 = 5;
```

Assume that the `EMPLOYEES` Table has 1,000 rows. If action granularity is `FOR EACH STATEMENT`, the Trigger action will occur once (just for the statement). If action granularity is `FOR EACH ROW`, the Trigger action will occur 1,000 times (once for each row of the Trigger Table). As stated earlier, the default is `FOR EACH STATEMENT`, but "row" granularity is more common. In fact, if your Trigger definition contains a `REFERENCING` clause that includes either `OLD ROW` or `NEW ROW`, it must also include an action granularity clause of `FOR EACH ROW`.

Action When Condition

The optional `WHEN` clause of the `CREATE TRIGGER` statement defines the Trigger action when condition; it may be any parenthesized search condition. When the Trigger is activated, if the search condition is `TRUE`, the Trigger action will occur; if the search condition is `FALSE`, the Trigger action will not occur; and if the search condition is `UNKNOWN`, then apparently the Trigger action will not occur (the Standard document is unclear about this point; see the term "satisfies" in the Glossary on the CD-ROM). If you omit the `WHEN` clause from a Trigger definition, the Trigger action will occur as soon as the Trigger is activated.

Typically, you'd add a `WHEN` clause to your Trigger definition if the Trigger event definition is too general for your purposes. For example, the Trigger event might be "`UPDATE Employees`," but the Trigger action should occur only "`WHEN salary > 1000.00`." Such specificity only makes sense if the action granularity is `FOR EACH ROW`.

Action Body

The action body of the `CREATE TRIGGER` statement defines the Trigger action itself; the SQL statement(s) you want your DBMS to execute when the Trigger is activated. The action body may be either a single SQL statement or it may be a series of SQL statements, delimited by semicolons, with a `BEGIN ATOMIC ... END` subclause. Here are two examples of Trigger action bodies (the first shows an action body using a single SQL statement and the second shows an action body using multiple SQL statements):

```
... UPDATE Table_1

... BEGIN ATOMIC
      DELETE FROM Table_1;
      DELETE FROM Table_2;
      DELETE FROM Table_3;
    END
```

The Trigger action may not contain a host variable or an SQL parameter reference, nor may it contain a <triggered SQL statement> that is an SQL-transaction statement, an SQL-Connection statement, an SQL-Schema statement, or an SQL-session statement (see "SQL Statement Classes" on page 10 in Chapter 1). A variety of SQL statements are legal inside the Trigger body, though.

- If Trigger action time is `BEFORE`, the Trigger action may include these SQL statements: `DECLARE TABLE`, `DECLARE CURSOR`, `OPEN`, `CLOSE`, `FETCH`, `SELECT` (for a single row only), `FREE LOCATOR`, `HOLD LOCATOR`, `CALL`, `RETURN`, and `GET DIAGNOSTICS`. It may also name an SQL-invoked routine, as long as that routine isn't one that possibly modifies SQL-data.
- If Trigger action time is `AFTER`, the Trigger action may include all of the SQL statements allowed for `BEFORE` Triggers, plus: `INSERT`, `UPDATE`, and `DELETE`. It may also name any SQL-invoked routine.

Of the SQL statements available to you for a Trigger action — `OPEN`, `FETCH`, `CLOSE`, single-row `SELECT`, and `GET DIAGNOSTICS` are not very useful because it is forbidden to include host variables and parameters inside the action body of a Trigger definition. `INSERT`, `UPDATE`, and `DELETE` are much more useful; often a Trigger action body consists of just one such SQL-data change statement. (Remember, though, that you can't use them with a `BEFORE` Trigger.) SQL-invoked routines are useful too. In effect, a procedure in your host language program can be called by a Trigger — compare the various "callback" situations in the Windows API.

If you want to restrict your code to Core SQL, don't use the `CREATE TRIGGER` statement.

Activation of Triggers

In our discussion of the `CREATE TRIGGER` statement, we made this true, but imprecise statement, "When the Trigger event occurs, the Trigger is activated." Let's get more precise about the meaning of "when" and "activated."

The meaning of "when" depends on the Trigger action time (`BEFORE` or `AFTER`) and on the Trigger's priority relative to other Triggers or Constraints. For example, suppose we associate three Triggers and one Constraint with Table `TABLE_1`:

```
CREATE TRIGGER Trigger_1 AFTER UPDATE ON Table_1 ...;

CREATE TRIGGER Trigger_2 BEFORE UPDATE ON Table_1 ...;

CREATE TRIGGER Trigger_3 AFTER UPDATE ON Table_1 ...;

ALTER TABLE Table_1 ADD CONSTRAINT Constraint_1 ...;
```

What is the effect when an `UPDATE` on `TABLE_1` is executed? Because such an `UPDATE` is a Trigger event for `TABLE_1`, several things happen — in a rigid order of events.

- First, `TRIGGER_2` is activated. It's a `BEFORE` Trigger, so it's first. The DBMS executes `TRIGGER_2`'s action (if `TRIGGER_2`'s definition includes a `WHEN` clause; this happens only if the search condition is `TRUE`).
- Second, the DBMS updates `TABLE_1`. Trigger events follow `BEFORE` Trigger actions.
- Third, `CONSTRAINT_1` is checked. Constraint checks occur at end-of-statement.

- Fourth, TRIGGER_1 is activated. It's an AFTER Trigger, so it occurs after execution of the action statement — and after any Constraint checking associated with the action statement.
- Fifth, TRIGGER_3 is activated. It's another AFTER Trigger, and it follows TRIGGER_1 because it was created later (Triggers are timestamped so the DBMS knows the order in which Triggers were created — older Triggers have priority).

To sum it up, the order-of-execution for any Triggered SQL-data change statement is: (*1*) BEFORE Triggers, (*2*) SQL-data change statement itself, (*3*) Constraint checks on SQL-data change statement, (*4*) AFTER Triggers — and within that, old Triggers before young Triggers.

The meaning of "activated" means "the Trigger action happens." Remember that the Trigger action is defined by three separate clauses in the CREATE TRIGGER statement:

```
[FOR EACH {ROW|STATEMENT}]                -- granularity
[WHEN (search condition)]                 -- when condition
SQL statement |                           -- body
BEGIN ATOMIC {SQL statement;}... END
```

If Trigger action doesn't include "WHEN (search condition)" or if Trigger action does include "WHEN (search condition)" and the condition is TRUE, the DBMS decides that the Trigger action has happened. This specifically means that:

- If the action body is an SQL statement, the DBMS executes that SQL statement.
- Otherwise, the action body must be BEGIN ATOMIC ... END, and the DBMS executes all of the SQL statements that occur between the <keyword>s ATOMIC and END in the order that they are defined.

If any part of the Trigger action can't be executed successfully, that SQL statement will fail and so will the entire Trigger action and so will the Trigger event statement that caused the Trigger to activate; your DBMS will return the SQLSTATE error 09000 "triggered action exception." The result is that no change is made to the Trigger's Table or to any other Object that the Trigger might have affected.

Trigger Examples

The following four scenarios show the use of a Trigger in a real-life situation.

Trigger Example — Logging Deletions

Scenario: We want to keep a log file containing data from rows that have been deleted from the BOOKS Table. Here's a Trigger definition that accomplishes this:

```
CREATE TRIGGER Books_Delete
AFTER DELETE ON Books                   /* See note (a) */
   REFERENCING OLD ROW AS Old           /* See note (b) */
FOR EACH ROW                            /* See note (c) */
   INSERT INTO Books_Deleted_Log
      VALUES (Old.title);               /* See note (d) */
```

This Trigger copies the title of every book deleted from the BOOKS Table into a Table (the log) called BOOKS_DELETED_LOG.

Note (a): The Trigger action has to be AFTER because the Trigger action includes an SQL-data change statement.
Note (b): It is conventional to use the alias "Old" or "Old_Row" for the old row.
Note (c): No log will occur for a DELETE statement that affects zero rows.
Note (d): OLD is an alias for a single old row, so OLD.TITLE is the scalar value derived from the TITLE Column of that old row.

Trigger Example — Inserting Default Expressions

Scenario: When we add a client, we want the default value for HOME_TELEPHONE to be the same as the WORK_TELEPHONE number. The DEFAULT clause is no good for cases like this because "DEFAULT <Column name>" is not a legal option. Here's a Trigger definition that accomplishes this:

```
CREATE TRIGGER Clients_Insert
BEFORE INSERT ON Clients
   REFERENCING NEW ROW AS New
   FOR EACH ROW
      SET New.home_telephone =
         COALESCE(New.home_telephone,New.work_telephone);
```

(The SET statement causes the value on the right to be "assigned to" the target on the left; this is part of the "Persistent Stored Modules" feature package — see Chapter 26 "PSM; Not Just Persistent Stored Modules.")

With this Trigger in place, this SQL statement:

```
INSERT INTO Clients (work_telephone)
VALUES ('493-1125');
```

will insert a new row into CLIENTS that has '493-1125' in the HOME_TELEPHONE Column as well as in the WORK_TELEPHONE Column. This Trigger must be activated BEFORE the INSERT, but it is possible to see in advance what values the DBMS has tentatively assigned for the new row.

Trigger Example — Constraint Substitute

Scenario: The department's budget can't be changed after 5 pm. Here's a Trigger definition that accomplishes this — but it has some flaws:

```
CREATE TRIGGER Departments_Update
AFTER UPDATE OF budget ON Departments          /* first flaw */
WHEN (CURRENT_TIME > TIME '17:00:00')          /* second flaw */
   SELECT MAX(budget) / 0 FROM Departments;    /* third flaw */
```

Because this CREATE TRIGGER statement contains no action granularity clause, the default applies: FOR EACH STATEMENT. This means that if this SQL statement is executed:

```
UPDATE Departments SET budget = <value>;
```

the Trigger's SELECT action will be executed — and it will fail because it contains a division-by-zero expression. This, in turn, will cause the Trigger event — the UPDATE statement — to fail too, because execution context is atomic. (Actually there will be two errors. The main one will be "Triggered action exception" and the secondary one will be "Division by zero.") Therefore, this Trigger prevents anyone from updating DEPARTMENTS.BUDGET after 5 pm. Usually it works, but sometimes it doesn't work — it contains subtle flaws.

The first flaw is that an SQL statement like this:

```
UPDATE Departments SET budget = <value>, name = <value>;
```

might fail to activate the Trigger. In strict Standard SQL, a Trigger's explicit UPDATE Column list — which in this case is BUDGET — must exactly match the Columns in the UPDATE statement.

The second flaw is that the WHEN clause is non-deterministic. In a sense, that's the point of using a Trigger here rather than a Constraint; SQL doesn't allow non-deterministic expressions in a Constraint.

The third flaw is that this SQL statement:

```
UPDATE Departments SET budget = NULL;
```

will pass — it won't activate the Trigger because dividing a NULL value by zero is legal SQL syntax — and so the Trigger doesn't accomplish its purpose 100% of the time.

We're not saying that it's bad to use Triggers as Constraint substitutes. This example only shows that you should think hard about the possible consequences before using "tricks."

Trigger Example — Cascading Update

Scenario: The first time we elect Bob, we all get a 1% tax cut. On the other hand, every change in taxes will affect the national debt and cause Bob's popularity to drop. Here are two Trigger definitions that map this situation:

```
CREATE TRIGGER Prime_Minister_Update
AFTER UPDATE ON Prime_Ministers
   REFERENCING OLD ROW AS Old, NEW ROW AS New FOR EACH ROW
WHEN (New.name = 'Bob' AND New.name <> Old.name)
   UPDATE Taxpayers SET tax_payable = tax_payable * 0.99;
```

```
CREATE TRIGGER Taxpayer_Update
AFTER UPDATE ON Taxpayers
   REFERENCING OLD ROW AS Old, NEW ROW AS New FOR EACH ROW
BEGIN ATOMIC
   UPDATE National_Debt SET
      amount = amount + (New.payable - Old.payable);
   UPDATE Prime_Ministers SET
      approval_rating = approval_rating - 0.01;
END;
```

In this example, some updates of the PRIME_MINISTERS Table will cause an update of the TAXPAYERS Table and updates of TAXPAYERS will cause both an update of the NATIONAL_DEBT Table and of PRIME_MINISTERS. Shown as a diagram, with --> as a symbol for "causes possible UPDATE of," we have:

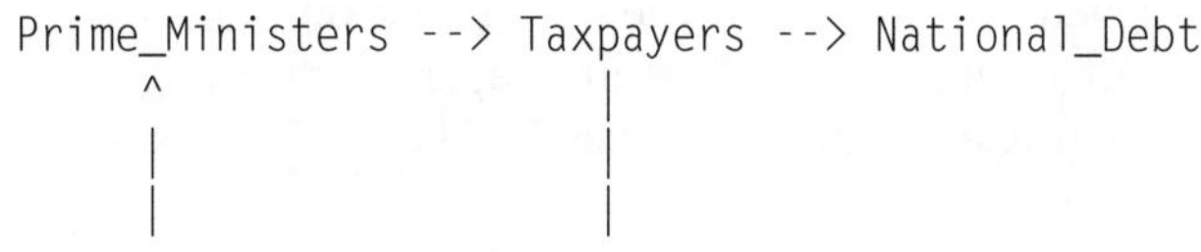

```
Prime_Ministers --> Taxpayers --> National_Debt
     ^                  |
     |                  |
     |                  |
     --------------------
```

There is an apparent cycle here, but the second UPDATE to PRIME_MINISTERS is for a different Column than the first, so the effects don't cascade forever. If we said "a change in the national debt will Trigger Bob's overthrow," then we would have a true cycle — that would be bad. Your DBMS is supposed to detect it if the same Column changes value twice in a cycle and cause the Trigger action (and the SQL data-change statement that activated the Trigger) to fail; it will return the SQLSTATE error 27000 "triggered data change violation."

Triggers versus Constraints

The essential idea of a Trigger is that if you change a Table, you cause a given set of SQL statements to be executed. This idea is good; it allows you to associate "rules" with Tables. And it can be efficient in a client-server environment because Trigger actions are pre-parsed and stored on the server. However, Triggers are not the only way to implement this idea. There are other ways to accomplish the same effect.

As one alternative, you could incorporate SQL statements in "method" procedures. This requires somewhat advanced knowledge; see Chapter 27 "User-Defined Types."

As another alternative, you could use a Constraint to declare what rules are most important. As we said earlier though, the advantage of using a Trigger, instead of a Constraint, is *flexibility*. You can use a wide variety of SQL statements in a Trigger, while the only things you can do with Constraints are integrity checks and foreign key options. But is flexibility a good thing? There are reasons why you should prefer the "rigidity" that Constraints imply:

- Your DBMS can recognize exactly what you're trying to accomplish and optimize accordingly.
- You know what the consequences are, because people thought them through when they devised the rigid syntax — so there's less chance of bugs.
- Constraints have been part of standard SQL for a long time, while Triggers have not been.

- Constraints are deferrable; Triggers aren't. Most experts appear to agree that you should use Constraints instead of Triggers if you can. Triggers are tricky.

DROP TRIGGER Statement

The DROP TRIGGER statement destroys a Trigger. The required syntax for the DROP TRIGGER statement is as follows.

```
DROP TRIGGER <Trigger name>
```

DROP TRIGGER destroys a Trigger. The <Trigger name> must identify an existing Trigger whose owner is either the current <AuthorizationID> or a Role that the current <AuthorizationID> may use. That is, only the <AuthorizationID> that owns the Trigger may drop it.

The effect of DROP TRIGGER <Table name>, e.g.,

```
DROP TRIGGER Trigger_1;
```

is that the Trigger named is destroyed; it will have no further effect on SQL-data. No other Objects are affected by DROP TRIGGER because no Objects are dependent on Triggers.

If you want to restrict your code to Core SQL, don't use the DROP TRIGGER statement.

Dialects

Triggers are not part of SQL-92 or the SQL3 Core SQL specifications but many DBMSs have had them for years — particularly "client-server" DBMSs. Because these DBMSs supported Triggers before SQL3 came out, they naturally differ from SQL3 and from each other. Here are some deviations we have noticed:

- There is no TRIGGER Privilege; only Table owners can create Triggers.
- A given Table can have only one BEFORE Trigger and one AFTER Trigger or can have only a limited number of Triggers (e.g., 12) in total.
- Trigger events are conglomerable, e.g., BEFORE INSERT OR UPDATE OF ....
- It is illegal to access the subject Table during the Trigger action, except through "new" and "old" row references. Such references must always be preceded by a colon (as if they're host variables).
- The WHEN clause is not supported.
- Assignments do not include the keyword SET and are legal only for Triggers.

25

Chapter 25

SQL-Invoked Routines

In this chapter, we'll describe SQL-invoked routines in detail and show you the syntax to use to create, alter, and destroy them.

Routine

A Schema may contain zero or more SQL-invoked routines. An *SQL-invoked routine* (or SQL routine) is the generic name for either a procedure (SQL-invoked procedure) or a function (SQL-invoked function). SQL routines are dependent on some Schema (they're also called *Schema-level routines*) and are created, altered, and dropped using standard SQL statements.

The concepts of "procedure" and "function" are the same in SQL as in other languages, so the ideas in this chapter will be old hat to any programmer. However, the syntax is all new; there was no standardized way to make SQL routines until SQL3. Actually there still isn't — it will take time before all vendors fall in line — but it's certainly time that everybody knows what routines are, according to the SQL Standard.

In SQL, a routine consists of at least three items: a <Routine name>, a set of parameter declarations, and a routine body. An SQL procedure is a routine that is invoked with a `CALL` statement; it may have input parameters, output parameters, and parameters that are both input parameters and output parameters. An SQL function is a routine that returns a value when invoked by a <routine invocation>; it has only input parameters, one of which may be defined as the result parameter (if you do this, the function is called a *type-preserving function* because the <data type> of the result is a subtype of the <data type> of the result parameter). A function can also be defined as an SQL-invoked method; it is invoked by a <method invocation> and its first parameter (called the subject parameter) must be a UDT.

The case for routines can be summarized by noting the following advantages.

Flexibility You can do even more with routines than you can with Constraints or Triggers and you can do them in a wider variety of scenarios.

Efficiency Quite often, it's possible to replace slow, generic SQL statements with painstakingly-optimized routines, especially "external routines" (i.e., routines written in languages other than SQL).

Cleanliness Routines let you avoid writing the same SQL code in two places.

Globalization Is your SQL code enforcing the rules of the whole business? Then it should be associated with the entire database. Procedures are particularly useful for specialized Privilege checking.

Sharing Routines are (usually) cached on the server and are (sometimes) accessible to all programmers. You needn't re-transmit and re-prepare every frequently-used code piece.

An SQL-invoked routine is defined by a descriptor that contains 18 pieces of information:

1. The not necessarily unique <Routine name> of the routine qualified by the <Schema name> of the Schema to which it belongs (or by `MODULE`).
2. The unique <specific name> of the routine qualified by the <Schema name> of the Schema to which it belongs.
3. The <external routine name> of the routine (for external routines).
4. The routine's <AuthorizationID>.
5. The routine's SQL-path.
6. The language the routine is written in.
7. A descriptor for every parameter in the routine. The parameter descriptor contains the <SQL parameter name> (if any); the parameter's <data type>; the ordinal position of the parameter in the routine body; and whether the parameter is an input parameter, an output parameter, or both.
8. Whether the routine is an SQL-invoked function or an SQL-invoked procedure and, in the first case, whether it is also an SQL-invoked method.
9. The maximum number of dynamic result sets (for procedures).
10. Whether the routine is deterministic or possibly non-deterministic.
11. Whether the routine possibly modifies SQL-data, possibly reads SQL-data, possibly contains SQL, or does not possibly contain SQL.
12. The <returns data type> of the routine and whether the return value is a locator (for functions).
13. Whether the routine is a type-preserving function or a mutator function.
14. The routine's result parameter (for type-preserving functions).
15. Whether the routine is a null-call routine (for functions).
16. The routine's creation timestamp; when it was created.

17. The routine's last-altered timestamp; when it was last changed.
18. The routine body of the routine; the SQL procedure statement that is executed when the routine is run (for SQL routines) or the host language statements that are executed when the routine is run (for external routines).

An SQL-invoked routine can be an SQL routine (a routine written in SQL) or an external routine (a routine written in a standard host language). Routines can, of course, also be externally-invoked routines, but in this chapter, we are concerned strictly with "Schema routines" — SQL-invoked routines that are stored in the database just like other Schema Objects (Tables, Domains, etc.). Our aim is to describe how routines are created and how they are "invoked" (i.e., called). The first part is the hard part.

To create an SQL-invoked routine, use the `CREATE PROCEDURE/FUNCTION/METHOD` statement (either as a stand-alone SQL statement or within a `CREATE SCHEMA` statement). `CREATE PROCEDURE/FUNCTION/METHOD` specifies the enclosing Schema, names the SQL-invoked routine, and defines the routine's body and routine characteristics. To destroy an SQL-invoked routine, use the `DROP ROUTINE/PROCEDURE/FUNCTION/METHOD` statement. To change an existing routine, use the `ALTER PROCEDURE` statement.

SQL-Invoked Routine Names

An SQL-invoked routine name is either a <Routine name> or a <specific name>; both identify an SQL-invoked routine. The required syntax for an SQL-invoked routine name is as follows.

```
<Routine name> ::=
[ <Schema name>. ] unqualified name |
[ MODULE. ] unqualified name

<specific name> ::=
[ <Schema name>. ] unqualified name
```

A <Routine name> and a <specific name> are both a <regular identifier> or a <delimited identifier>. The <Schema name> that qualifies a <Routine name> or a <specific name> names the Schema to which the SQL-invoked routine belongs and can either be explicitly stated or a default will be supplied by your DBMS, as follows:

- If a <Routine name> or a <specific name> in a `CREATE SCHEMA` statement isn't qualified, the default qualifier is the name of the Schema you're creating.
- If the unqualified <Routine name> or <specific name> is found in any other SQL statement in a Module, the default qualifier is the name of the Schema identified in the `SCHEMA` clause or `AUTHORIZATION` clause of the `MODULE` statement which defines that Module.

More than one SQL-invoked routine in a Schema may have the same <Routine name>. Your DBMS will determine which routine is being invoked as follows:

- Because procedures and functions are created with separate SQL statements, your DBMS can uniquely identify the type of multiple routines identified by the same <Routine name>.
- Two procedures in a Schema may have the same <Routine name> only if they don't also have the same number of parameters. Thus, your DBMS can uniquely identify one procedure from another by checking the parameters of each procedure with the same <Routine name>.

- Two functions in a Schema must have unique <specific name>s. Thus, your DBMS can uniquely identify one function from another by checking the <specific name> of each function with the same <Routine name>.

  Here are some examples of <Routine name>s:

```
ROUTINE_1
-- a <Routine name>

SCHEMA_1.ROUTINE_1
-- a simple qualified <Routine name>

CATALOG_1.SCHEMA_1.ROUTINE_1
-- a fully qualified <Routine name>

MODULE.ROUTINE_1
-- a local <Routine name>
```

SQL Parameter Names

An <SQL parameter name> identifies an SQL parameter. The required syntax for an <SQL parameter name> is as follows.

```
<SQL parameter name> ::= <identifier>
```

An <SQL parameter name> is a <regular identifier> or a <delimited identifier> that is unique (for all parameters) in the routine to which it belongs. Here are some examples of <SQL parameter name>s:

```
PARAMETER_1
-- a <regular identifier>

"PARAMETER_1's helper"
-- a <delimited identifier>
```

CREATE PROCEDURE/FUNCTION/METHOD Statement

The CREATE PROCEDURE/FUNCTION/METHOD statement names a new SQL-invoked procedure or function and defines the routine's SQL parameters, characteristics, and routine body. The required syntax for the CREATE PROCEDURE/FUNCTION/METHOD statement is as follows.

```
CREATE PROCEDURE <Routine name>
<SQL parameter declaration list>
<routine characteristics>
<routine body>
```

```
CREATE {<function specification> | <method specification>}
<routine body>

   <function specification> ::=
   FUNCTION <Routine name>
   <SQL parameter declaration list>
   <returns clause>
   <routine characteristics>
   STATIC DISPATCH

   <method specification> ::=
   <partial method specification> FOR <UDT name>
   [ SPECIFIC <specific name> ]

   <SQL parameter declaration list> ::=
   ([ <parameter declaration> [ {,<parameter declaration>}... ] ])

      <parameter declaration> ::=
      [ {IN | OUT | INOUT} ]
      [ <SQL parameter name> ]
      <data type> [ AS LOCATOR ]
      [ RESULT ]

<routine characteristics> ::=
[ <routine characteristic>... ]

   <routine characteristic> ::=
   LANGUAGE {ADA | C | COBOL | FORTRAN | MUMPS | PASCAL | PLI | SQL} |
   PARAMETER STYLE {SQL | GENERAL} |
   SPECIFIC <specific name> |
   {DETERMINISTIC | NOT DETERMINISTIC} |
   <SQL-data access indication> |
   {RETURN NULL ON NULL INPUT | CALL ON NULL INPUT) |
   DYNAMIC RESULT SETS unsigned integer

      <SQL-data access indication> ::=
      NO SQL |
      CONTAINS SQL |
      READS SQL DATA |
      MODIFIES SQL DATA
```

```
    <returns clause> ::=
    RETURNS <data type> [ AS LOCATOR ]
    [ CAST FROM <data type> [ AS LOCATOR ] ]

<routine body> ::=
<SQL routine body> |
<external body reference>

    <SQL routine body> ::= SQL procedure statement

    <external body reference> ::=
    EXTERNAL [ NAME <external routine name> ]
    [ PARAMETER STYLE {SQL | GENERAL} ]
    [ TRANSFORM GROUP <group name> ]
```

The `CREATE PROCEDURE/FUNCTION/METHOD` statement lets you define an SQL-invoked routine. Here's a simpler version of the required syntax:

```
{CREATE PROCEDURE | CREATE FUNCTION}
<Routine name>                           /* name of procedure or function */
([parameter [{,parameter}...]])           /* parameter declaration list */
[RETURNS <data type> <result cast>]                /* for function only */
                                   /* <routine characteristics> start */
[LANGUAGE {ADA|C|COBOL|FORTRAN|MUMPS|PASCAL|PLI|SQL}]      /*language */
[PARAMETER STYLE {SQL|GENERAL}]                       /* parameter style */
[SPECIFIC <specific name>]
[DETERMINISTIC|NOT DETERMINISTIC]    /* deterministic characteristic */
[NO SQL|CONTAINS SQL|READS SQL DATA|MODIFIES SQL DATA]      /* access */
[RETURN NULL ON NULL INPUT|CALL ON NULL INPUT]    /* null-call clause */
[DYNAMIC RESULT SETS unsigned integer]          /* for procedure only */
                                     /* <routine characteristics> end */
[STATIC DISPATCH]                                  /* for function only */
<routine body>
```

As you can see, our "simple" version isn't much simpler — there's lots of options! So what we'll do with this SQL statement is first give you a quick one-paragraph description of each clause, then we'll start with some examples of simple SQL routines and work our way up — piece-by-piece — to fairly complicated matters.

CREATE ... <Routine name> Clause

First of all, to create an SQL-invoked routine, the <keyword> phrase CREATE PROCEDURE or CREATE FUNCTION is the basic choice. Either way, you are creating a "routine." But there are two kinds of routines: "procedures" (which don't return values) and "functions" (which do return values). Your choice at this stage will determine how the routine is called later. CREATE PROCEDURE defines a new SQL-invoked procedure. CREATE FUNCTION defines a new SQL-invoked function.

The <Routine name> identifies the routine and the Schema to which it belongs — this is the name of the routine as it appears to SQL. The description of the routine is stored (as a Schema Object) in INFORMATION_SCHEMA, so <Routine name> has to follow the same rules as any other Schema Object name. A <Routine name> that includes an explicit <Schema name> qualifier belongs to the Schema named. A <Routine name> that does not include an explicit <Schema name> qualifier belongs to the SQL-session default Schema. However — an unusual point — <Routine name> does not have to be unique within its Schema; that is, two different routines in the same Schema may have the same <Routine name> because your DBMS will have other ways of uniquely identifying a routine (this easement of the usual rule is not allowed in Core SQL.)

If CREATE PROCEDURE/CREATE FUNCTION is part of a CREATE SCHEMA statement, the <Routine name>, if explicitly qualified, must include the <Schema name> of the Schema being created; that is, it isn't possible to create a routine belonging to a different Schema from within CREATE SCHEMA. The owner of a Schema always has the EXECUTE Privilege on every routine that belongs to that Schema. This Privilege is a grantable Privilege only if (*a*) the routine is an SQL routine and the Schema owner has a grantable Privilege for every part of the routine body or (*b*) the routine is an external routine.

Parameter Declaration List

A routine's parameter declaration list is a parenthesized, comma-delimited sequence of declarations taking the form "[IN | OUT | INOUT] [<parameter name>] <data type> ..." and so on. The purpose of a parameter declaration is to describe what values or addresses are being passed to the routine. The optional <parameter name> identifies a parameter and must be unique (for all parameters) in the routine to which it belongs. We'll discuss the details later when we've given you some examples. The parameter declaration list is mandatory, but it may be blank — for example: "()".

RETURNS Clause

The RETURNS clause — RETURNS <data type> <result cast> — is a mandatory clause if your SQL statement is CREATE FUNCTION. Usually this clause describes the <data type> of what the function returns, for example: RETURNS SMALLINT. Sometimes it is necessary to cast the result, for example: RETURNS CHAR(10) CAST FROM DATE.

Having described the initial mandatory parts of the routine specification, we can now give you a rough analogy for the C function declaration:

```
long function1 (param1 short);
```

In SQL, this is:

```
CREATE FUNCTION function1
   (IN param1 SMALLINT) RETURNS INTEGER ...
```

At this point, we need to emphasize that this example is a rough analogy. The SQL statement is executable (it is not a mere function declaration) and it is far from finished yet.

Routine Characteristics Clause

The routine characteristics clause defines certain characteristics of your routine. It may include zero or one specification of any (or all) of the eight optional characteristic specification subclauses, in any order.

LANGUAGE Subclause

The LANGUAGE subclause names the language the routine is written in. The official expectation is that the routine is written in one of the ISO "standard" languages: Ada, C, COBOL, FORTRAN, MUMPS, Pascal, PLI (note the spelling), or SQL. In practice, your DBMS probably won't support all of the standard languages (for example, MUMPS is often excluded); but it may support others (for example, BASIC or Java). If you omit the LANGUAGE subclause, the default is LANGUAGE SQL and your routine is an SQL routine. A routine written in any language other than SQL is an external routine to SQL.

PARAMETER STYLE Subclause

The PARAMETER STYLE subclause is only necessary for external routines and can be specified only once in a routine definition — you can only put it in either one of the <routine characteristics> clause or the <external body reference> clause. If you omit the PARAMETER STYLE subclause, the default is PARAMETER STYLE SQL. Again, we'll discuss parameter details when we have some examples to show you.

SPECIFIC Subclause

The SPECIFIC <specific name> subclause uniquely identifies the routine. Because your routine definition will already contain a <Routine name>, what would you need a <specific name> for? Well, it mostly relates to UDTs and we'll defer discussing routines for UDTs until Chapter 27.

Deterministic Characteristic Subclause

The DETERMINISTIC | NOT DETERMINISTIC subclause is important if you intend to include the routine in a Constraint because Constraint routines must be deterministic. If you omit the deterministic characteristic subclause, the default is NOT DETERMINISTIC (which actually means "possibly non-deterministic" — see Chapter 20 "SQL Constraints and Assertions"). A DETERMINISTIC function always returns the same value for a given list of SQL arguments. A DETERMINISTIC procedure always returns the same values in its SQL parameters for a given list of SQL arguments. A possibly NOT DETERMINISTIC routine might, at different times, return different results even though the SQL-data is the same. You may not specify DETERMINISTIC if the routine could return different results at different times.

SQL Data Access Indication Subclause

The NO SQL | CONTAINS SQL | READS SQL DATA | MODIFIES SQL DATA subclause specifies what sort of SQL statements are in the routine (if any). If your routine LANGUAGE subclause is LANGUAGE SQL, then the routine will certainly "contain" SQL statements but even an external LANGUAGE PASCAL routine can contain SQL/CLI functions or embedded SQL statements, so LANGUAGE PASCAL ... CONTAINS SQL is a valid specification. If a routine contains any SQL-data change statements (INSERT, UPDATE, and/or DELETE), its SQL data access subclause must state MODIFIES SQL DATA; otherwise if the routine contains any other SQL-data statements (e.g., SELECT or FETCH), the SQL data access subclause must state READS SQL DATA; otherwise if the routine contains any other SQL statements, the SQL data access subclause must state CONTAINS SQL; otherwise if the routine contains no SQL statements at all, the SQL data access subclause must state NO SQL. If you omit the SQL data access indication subclause, the default is CONTAINS SQL.

Null-Call Subclause

The RETURN NULL ON NULL INPUT | CALL ON NULL INPUT subclause is for functions written in a host language because a host language cannot handle NULLs. When the null-call subclause is RETURN NULL ON NULL INPUT, the routine is a "null-call" routine. If you call a null-call routine with any parameter set to the null value, the return is immediate; the function returns NULL. When the null-call subclause is CALL ON NULL INPUT and you call the routine with any parameter set to the null value, execution of the routine follows standard rules for operations with null values (e.g., comparisons of nulls to other values return UNKNOWN and so on). If you omit the null-call subclause, the default is CALL ON NULL INPUT.

DYNAMIC RESULT SETS Subclause

The DYNAMIC RESULT SETS subclause is legal only within a CREATE PROCEDURE statement. The "result sets" in question are query results and the concept here is that, within the routine, a certain number of Cursors (the unsigned integer) can be opened for the results. In other words, you can CALL a procedure which contains up to *n* OPEN (Cursor) statements and those Cursors will be visible after you return from the procedure. If you omit the DYNAMIC RESULT SETS subclause, the default is DYNAMIC RESULT SETS 0.

Remember that the "routine characteristics" subclauses may be defined in any order in a routine definition. The final two clauses must appear at the end of the SQL statement.

STATIC DISPATCH Clause

The optional STATIC DISPATCH clause is legal only within a CREATE FUNCTION statement. It must be specified for functions that are not also SQL-invoked methods and that contain parameters whose <data type> is either a <reference type>, a UDT, or an ARRAY whose element <data type> is either a <reference type> or a UDT.

<routine body>

The <routine body> is a mandatory part of a routine definition. For a LANGUAGE SQL routine, you'd put an SQL procedure statement here (it may be any SQL statement other than an SQL-Schema statement, an SQL-Connection statement, or an SQL-transaction statement).

For an external routine, you'd put an external interface description here. Clearly, the body of the routine is what really matters.

Routine Parameters

A routine's SQL parameter declaration list is a parenthesized, comma-delimited list of definitions for the routine's parameters. Here's the required syntax for a parameter definition in a CREATE PROCEDURE/CREATE FUNCTION statement again:

```
<parameter declaration> ::=
[ {IN | OUT | INOUT} ]                        /* parameter mode */
[ <SQL parameter name> ]
<data type> [ AS LOCATOR ]
[ RESULT ]
```

Parameter Mode

The optional [IN | OUT | INOUT] parameter mode specification is legal only within CREATE PROCEDURE statements. IN defines an input SQL parameter, OUT defines an output SQL parameter, and INOUT defines both an input SQL parameter and an output SQL parameter. (In SQL routines, the SQL parameters may not be named in a host variable or parameter specification in the routine body.) This is a directional specification. If you omit the parameter mode subclause, the default is IN.

<SQL parameter name>

The optional <SQL parameter name> is simply that — a name that you'll use if you refer to the parameter within the routine. If you're defining an SQL routine, this subclause is not optional; you must include an <SQL parameter name> for each of the routine's parameters. If you're defining an external routine, an <SQL parameter name> for each of its parameters is not mandatory because in an external routine you can use any name you like; the ordinal position of the parameter within the routine is what matters.

<data type>

The <data type> of a parameter is always an SQL <data type> and must be defined for every parameter. The value of an SQL parameter with a character string <data type> has IMPLICIT coercibility. At this time, we include the optional [AS LOCATOR] indicator here only for completeness; it's valid only when you're defining an external routine with a parameter whose <data type> is either BLOB, CLOB, NCLOB, ARRAY, or a UDT.

RESULT

The optional <keyword> RESULT is applicable only for UDTs and is noted here only for completeness at this time.

Here's an example of a parameter declaration list for a CREATE PROCEDURE statement:

```
CREATE PROCEDURE procedure_1 (
IN Apple CHAR(6), OUT Orange CHAR(6))
...
```

The list is legal only within a CREATE PROCEDURE statement because it contains IN and OUT declarations (within a CREATE FUNCTION statement, all parameters are assumed to be IN). The parameter named Apple is a 6-character input parameter; the parameter named Orange is a 6-character output parameter. Here's an example of a parameter declaration list for a CREATE FUNCTION statement:

```
CREATE FUNCTION function_1 (Apple CHAR(6))
...
```

Invoking Routines

Creating a routine is complex. Invoking a routine can be easy. The secret: don't use the same <Routine name> twice in the same Schema.

CALL Statement

The CALL statement invokes a procedure. The required syntax for the CALL statement is as follows.

```
CALL <Routine name> <SQL argument list>

   <SQL argument list> ::=
   ([ <SQL argument> [ {,<SQL argument>}... ] ])

      <SQL argument> ::=
      scalar_expression_argument |
      :<host parameter name> [ [ INDICATOR ]:<host parameter name> ]
```

The <Routine name> must identify an SQL-invoked procedure and the <SQL argument list> must correspond to that procedure's parameter declarations in both number and comparable <data type>. (A scalar_expression_argument is any expression which evaluates to a single value.) For example, for this procedure:

```
CREATE PROCEDURE procedure_1 (
IN in_param SMALLINT, OUT out_param SMALLINT
...
```

uses this CALL statement to invoke it:

```
CALL procedure_1(5,:variable name);
```

The SQL argument for an IN SQL parameter or an INOUT SQL parameter must be a scalar_expression_argument. The SQL argument for an OUT SQL parameter may be a host language variable.

Your current <AuthorizationID> must have the EXECUTE Privilege on a procedure to CALL it.

<routine invocation>

A <routine invocation> invokes a function. The required syntax for a <routine invocation> for functions is as follows.

```
<Routine name> <SQL argument list>

   <SQL argument list> ::=
   ([ <SQL argument> [ {,<SQL argument>}... ] ])

      <SQL argument> ::=
      scalar_expression_argument |
      scalar_expression_argument AS <UDT name>
```

The <Routine name> must identify an SQL-invoked function and the <SQL argument list> must correspond to that function's parameter declarations in both number and comparable <data type>. (A scalar_expression_argument is any expression which evaluates to a single value.) For example, for this function:

```
CREATE FUNCTION function_1 (in_param SMALLINT) ...;
```

uses this <routine invocation> to invoke it wherever it's legal to use a value expression:

```
function_1(5)
```

Here's an example:

```
INSERT INTO Table_1 VALUES (function_1(5));
```

Your current <AuthorizationID> must have the EXECUTE Privilege on a function to invoke it.

Routine Examples

Here are four examples of SQL-invoked routines that might be used in real-life situations.

Routine Example — Reset Procedure

Objective: Define and invoke a procedure which sets Column COLUMN_1, in Table TABLE_1, to zero for all rows. Here's a procedure definition to accomplish this:

```
CREATE PROCEDURE
   Reset_table_1                              /* Routine name */
   ()                                /* An empty parameter list */
   MODIFIES SQL DATA                        /* Data access clause */
   UPDATE Table_1 SET column_1 = 0;          /* The routine body */
```

To invoke RESET_TABLE_1, use this SQL statement:

```
CALL Reset_table_1();
```

When you invoke a routine, you're telling your DBMS to execute the routine body. For this example, this SQL statement:

```
CALL Reset_table_1();
```

has the same effect as this SQL statement:

```
UPDATE Table_1 SET column_1 = 0;
```

Details worth noting:

- It's fairly common for a <Routine name> to consist of a verb and an Object, as in this case. The style of routine definitions is still evolving.
- Even though there are no parameters, the parentheses which enclose the parameter declaration list are necessary, both during creation and during invocation.
- The SQL-data access clause — `MODIFIES SQL DATA` — is necessary in this case because the procedure contains the SQL-data change statement `UPDATE`. It's a good habit to specify the data access clause even when it is not necessary.

Routine Example — Constant Function

Objective: Define and invoke a function which returns the constant pi (π), as a `DECIMAL` value. Here's a function definition to accomplish this:

```
CREATE FUNCTION
   Pi                                               /* Routine name */
   ()                                      /* An empty parameter list */
   RETURNS DECIMAL(3,2)                 /* What the function returns */
   CONTAINS SQL                                /* Data access clause */
   RETURN 3.14;                                  /* The routine body */
```

To invoke `Pi`, use the <routine invocation> `Pi()` in an SQL statement, for example:

```
INSERT INTO Table_1 (decimal_column) VALUES (Pi());
```

In this example, the routine body contains a `RETURN` statement which is legal only within SQL functions. `RETURN` must specify some value (you can put any expression which evaluates to a single value here) with a <data type> that is assignable to the <data type> defined in the function definition's `RETURNS` clause. In this case, the function invocation in this SQL statement:

```
INSERT INTO Table_1 (decimal_column) VALUES (Pi());
```

has the same effect as this SQL statement:

```
INSERT INTO Table_1 (decimal_column) VALUES (3.14);
```

TIP: You can't define constants in SQL, but you can define constant functions. They help ensure that values like p (pi) are defined only once and are referenced by a name rather than a <literal>.

Routine Example — Subquery Function

Objective: Define and invoke a replacement for a frequently-used subquery. Here's a function definition to accomplish this:

```
CREATE FUNCTION
   Max_                              /* Routine name */
   ()                                /* An empty parameter list */
   RETURNS DATE                      /* What the function returns */
   CONTAINS SQL                      /* Data access clause */
   RETURN (                          /* The routine body */
      SELECT MAX(date_column)
      FROM   Table_1
      WHERE  smallint_column > 5);
```

To invoke MAX_, use the <routine invocation> Max_() in an SQL statement, for example:

```
SELECT * FROM Table_2 WHERE Column_1 < Max_();
```

The potential advantage with this example is that Max_() is easier to type than SELECT MAX(date_column) FROM Table_1 WHERE smallint_column > 5;. It's also safer — if a subquery is long and complex and used frequently, you'll reduce the chances of error by putting the subquery into a function.

A far less likely advantage is that the MAX_ routine is parsed and done only once. Although that sort of optimization is theoretically possible, there are some hidden dynamic variables that could change each time MAX_ is invoked (for example, the Schema that contains TABLE_1). One does not call functions like this for "efficiency" reasons.

Routine Example — Withdrawal Procedure

Objective: Perform a logged balanced withdrawal, like real banks do. Here's a procedure definition to accomplish this:

```
CREATE PROCEDURE
   Withdraw                              /* Routine name */
   (parameter_amount DECIMAL(6,2),      /* Parameter list */
   parameter_teller_id INTEGER,
   parameter_customer_id INTEGER)
   MODIFIES SQL DATA                    /* Data access clause */
   BEGIN ATOMIC                         /* Routine body */
      UPDATE Customers
         SET balance = balance - parameter_amount
         WHERE customer_id = parameter_customer_id;
      UPDATE Tellers
         SET cash_on_hand = cash_on_hand - parameter_amount
         WHERE teller_id = parameter_teller_id;
```

```
    INSERT INTO Transactions VALUES (
        parameter_customer_id,
        parameter_teller_id,
        parameter_amount);
END;
```

To invoke WITHDRAW, use a CALL statement that names the procedure and provides a value for each of its parameters, for example:

```
CALL Withdraw (15.33,44,90182);
```

Typical bank transactions always involve changes to multiple accounts (for the general ledger, the customer, and the teller), and are always logged. Therefore, in the real world, withdrawals are done via procedures. This example is translated from a procedure written in a host language (not SQL); however, the routine is really used in a real bank. Details worth noting:

- The parameters (all of which are IN SQL parameters) are simply referenced by name within the routine body.
- The routine body contains a compound SQL procedure statement (a sequence of SQL statements within a BEGIN ATOMIC ... END block). Correctly, compound SQL statements are only legal in Triggers or as part of the "Persistent Stored Modules" SQL package (see Chapter 26 "PSM; Not Just Persistent Stored Modules") — so this example shows the use of an extension to Standard Core SQL.

Routines are particularly applicable to Roles. For example, a bank teller might not have the Privilege to access a Table, but would have the Privilege to EXECUTE the WITHDRAW Procedure. Typically, one finds that when groups of employees are involved, the applicable Privilege is not an "access Privilege on a Table" but an "EXECUTE Privilege on a routine."

RETURN Statement

The RETURN statement returns a value from an SQL-invoked function. The required syntax for the RETURN statement is as follows.

```
RETURN <value expression> | NULL
```

The RETURN statement ends the execution of an SQL-invoked function, returning the function's result. The return can either be a <value expression> or, if the function's result is a null value, the <keyword> NULL.

External Routines

"Host calls DBMS: no story. DBMS calls host: story!"

— Journalist's man-bites-dog rule, slightly adapted

Because most applications involve two languages — SQL and the host — there are four possible routine interface situations:

1. Host invokes SQL — this is a common situation, discussed in our chapters on SQL/CLI and embedded SQL.
2. Host invokes host — this is also common, but none of our business; this is an SQL book.

3. SQL invokes SQL — this is the situation we've shown you in the examples so far; they've all been SQL routines.
4. SQL invokes host — this is not a common situation, but external routines are conceivably quite useful.

You can write Standard SQL routines in Ada, C, COBOL, Fortran, MUMPS, Pascal, or PL/1. If you do, the routine definition must include a LANGUAGE clause that names the host language you're using and its routine body would have to be a reference to an external routine instead of an SQL procedure statement. Here, once again, is the required syntax for an <external body reference> in a CREATE PROCEDURE/CREATE FUNCTION statement:

```
EXTERNAL
[ NAME <external routine name> ]
[ PARAMETER STYLE {SQL | GENERAL} ]
[ TRANSFORM GROUP <group name> ]
```

The <keyword> EXTERNAL tells your DBMS you're defining an external routine.

NAME Clause

The optional NAME clause specifies the routine's external name. If you omit the NAME clause, it will default to the routine's unqualified <Routine name>.

PARAMETER STYLE Clause

The optional PARAMETER STYLE clause determines whether some additional parameters will be passed automatically and has two options: SQL or GENERAL. If the specification is PARAMETER STYLE SQL, then automatic parameters (such as indicators) will be passed as well. If the specification is PARAMETER STYLE GENERAL, then there is no automatic parameter passing. If you omit the clause, the default is PARAMETER STYLE SQL. Remember not to use a parameter style clause here if there is already a parameter style clause in the main definition.

TRANSFORM GROUP Clause

The optional TRANSFORM GROUP <group name> clause is necessary only if the function is for transforming UDT values to host values or vice versa. If you omit the clause, the default is TRANSFORM GROUP DEFAULT.

Here's an example of an external routine that is an SQL-invoked procedure:

```
CREATE PROCEDURE
   Routine_1                  /* Routine name */
   ()                         /* empty parameter list */
   LANGUAGE C                 /* language clause */
   NO SQL                     /* C routine has no SQL calls */
   EXTERNAL                   /* routine body */
      NAME "wHoldPrivilegeTest";  /* actual name of the routine*/
```

Unfortunately, this information is not quite sufficient. In Windows, for example, we would also need to know the name of the DLL. So there has to be some non-standard extra stuff added to this routine which will be done at the implementation level.

External routines are necessary, or at least very useful, for these things:

Accessing the operating system For example, you can't call the Windows API from SQL, but you can create an external routine that does so. The ability to access the operating system is particularly useful for Privilege checks.

Translating data The traditional usage here is encryption/decryption. We'd also note that, if your DBMS produces error messages in English and you want them in Italian, this is a good place to intercept them.

Optimizing Because SQL is not famous for low-level efficiency, it's usually faster to write some routines in a compiled language or better yet in assembler (shameless plug — see our book *Optimizing C With Assembly Code*). Hashing and pattern matching would make good examples here.

External routines are not so wonderful if you're trying to write purely portable SQL applications. Also, their existence can confuse the DBMS's optimizer and even confuse application programmers. We suggest that you keep it simple; don't write external routines that call SQL.

If you want to restrict your code to Core SQL, don't use `LOCATOR` indicators, `DYNAMIC RESULT SETS` clauses, `TRANSFORM GROUP` clauses, or duplicate <Routine name>s when defining an SQL-invoked routine and don't define any SQL-invoked methods.

ALTER ROUTINE/PROCEDURE/FUNCTION/METHOD Statement

The `ALTER ROUTINE/PROCEDURE/FUNCTION/METHOD` statement lets you change an SQL-invoked routine. The required syntax for the `ALTER ROUTINE/PROCEDURE/FUNCTION/METHOD` statement is as follows.

```
ALTER <specific routine designator> <routine characteristics>
{CASCADE | RESTRICT}

      <specific routine designator> ::=
      ROUTINE <Routine name> [ <data type>s ] |
      PROCEDURE <Routine name> [ <data type>s ] |
      FUNCTION <Routine name> [ <data type>s ] |
      [ INSTANCE | STATIC ] METHOD <Routine name> [ <data type>s ] |
      SPECIFIC ROUTINE <Routine name> <specific name> |
      SPECIFIC PROCEDURE <Routine name> <specific name> |
      SPECIFIC FUNCTION <Routine name> <specific name>
```

```
<data type>s ::=
([ <data type> [ {,<data type>}... ] ])
```

ALTER ROUTINE/PROCEDURE/FUNCTION/METHOD changes an SQL-invoked routine. We showed you the syntax for the <routine characteristics> clause beginning on page 484, so here we'll just briefly list the characteristics which can be altered:

- LANGUAGE (either ADA, C, COBOL, FORTRAN, MUMPS, PASCAL, PLI, SQL).
- PARAMETER STYLE (either SQL or GENERAL).
- SQL-data access indication (either NO SQL, CONTAINS SQL, READS SQL DATA, MODIFIES SQL DATA).
- null-call clause (either RETURN NULL ON NULL INPUT or CALL ON NULL INPUT).
- DYNAMIC RESULTS SETS (followed by an unsigned integer).
- NAME <external routine name>.

Notice that <routine body> is not in the list; this ALTER statement doesn't let you change the actions the routine takes.

For example, suppose you want to change the name of a procedure's external (Pascal) routine, from whatever it used to be to Update_Test_In_C. The following SQL statement would accomplish this:

```
ALTER PROCEDURE Routine_1
NAME "Update_Test_In_C"
RESTRICT;
```

You shouldn't use ALTER ROUTINE/PROCEDURE/FUNCTION/METHOD if the routine is referenced by some other Object. But if you do, the RESTRICT <keyword> will cause the ALTER to fail. If the ALTER statement includes CASCADE rather than RESTRICT, the change will cascade down through all dependent routines.

DROP ROUTINE/PROCEDURE/FUNCTION/METHOD Statement

The DROP ROUTINE/PROCEDURE/FUNCTION/METHOD statement destroys an SQL-invoked procedure or function. The required syntax for the DROP ROUTINE/PROCEDURE/FUNCTION/METHOD statement is as follows.

```
DROP <specific routine designator> {RESTRICT | CASCADE}
```

DROP ROUTINE/PROCEDURE/FUNCTION/METHOD destroys an SQL-invoked routine. The <Routine name> must identify an existing SQL-invoked routine whose owner is either the current <AuthorizationID> or a Role that the current <AuthorizationID> may use. That is, only the <AuthorizationID> that owns the routine may drop it. If <Routine name> is not unique within the routine's Schema, then you must include a <data type> list that provides the <data type> of each of the routine's parameters — your DBMS will match this list to the parameter declaration lists of every routine called "<Routine name>" to find the one you want to drop.

If you remember to always give unique <Routine name>s to your routines, you'll avoid a great deal of potential difficulty.

We showed you the syntax for <specific routine designator> in our discussion of the ALTER ROUTINE... statement on page 493. DROP ROUTINE drops either an SQL-invoked function or an SQL-invoked procedure, so it's best to be more specific. DROP FUNCTION drops an SQL-invoked function, so <Routine name> must identify a function. DROP PROCEDURE drops an SQL-invoked procedure, so <Routine name> must identify a procedure. In no case may <Routine name> identify a routine that was created as part of a UDT definition.

The effect of DROP routine type <Routine name> RESTRICT, e.g.,

```
DROP ROUTINE routine_1 RESTRICT;

DROP FUNCTION function_1 RESTRICT;

DROP PROCEDURE procedure_1 RESTRICT;
```

is that the routine named is destroyed, provided that the routine is not invoked or used by any other routine or in a View definition, Constraint definition, Assertion definition, Trigger definition, Column definition, or Domain definition and provided that the routine is not a from-sql function or a to-sql function associated with an external routine. That is, RESTRICT ensures that only a routine with no dependent Objects can be destroyed. If the routine is used by any other Object, DROP ROUTINE/PROCEDURE/FUNCTION/METHOD ... RESTRICT will fail.

The effect of DROP routine type <Routine name> CASCADE, e.g.,

```
DROP ROUTINE routine_1 CASCADE;

DROP FUNCTION function_1 CASCADE;

DROP PROCEDURE procedure_1 CASCADE;
```

is that the routine named is destroyed.

Successfully destroying a routine has a three-fold effect:

1. The routine named is destroyed.
2. The EXECUTE Privilege held on the routine by the <AuthorizationID> that owns it is revoked (by the SQL special grantor, "_SYSTEM") with a CASCADE revoke behaviour, so that all EXECUTE Privileges held on the routine by any other <AuthorizationID> are also revoked.
3. All SQL routines, Views, Constraints, Assertions, Triggers, Columns, and Domains that depend on the routine are dropped with a CASCADE drop behaviour.

If you want to restrict your code to Core SQL, don't use the CASCADE drop behaviour for your DROP ROUTINE/FUNCTION/PROCEDURE statements.

Dialects

One way or another, DBMSs have been calling routines for several years. The oldest example we can think of is IBM DB2's EDITPROC and VALIDPROC functions, which were used to massage or verify input data and had to be written in 360/Assembler.

At the moment, a minority of DBMSs include support for "procedures" (not functions). The syntax for creation and invocation is essentially the same as what we've described in this chapter, but in all cases the details differ. For example, the ODBC document has a definition for procedures, an escape mechanism for calling them, and a specification of some CLI functions that depend on them (such as the `SQLProcedures` function). However, ODBC makes no attempt to specify the grammar for a `CREATE PROCEDURE` statement.

26

Chapter 26

PSM; Not Just Persistent Stored Modules

The initials *PSM* refer to the specifications of a document labelled "ISO/IEC 9075-4 Information Technology - Database Languages - SQL: Part 4: Persistent Stored Modules (SQL/PSM)." Part 4 is one of the standard SQL documents, but it is not essential — that is, it describes SQL features that are optional. A DBMS that complies with part 4 can claim "enhanced SQL conformance" (provided, of course, that it also fully supports Core SQL). We will use the phrase "essential SQL" to mean "SQL without PSM, as defined in Parts 1 and 2 of the SQL Standard." Unless you are a programmer familiar with SQL (particularly with embedded SQL or ODBC), this chapter will probably not be fully comprehensible until you have read Chapter 36 on SQL transactions, Chapter 39 on embedded SQL, and Chapters 40–51 on SQL/CLI.

In essential SQL, the concept of Modules — i.e., SQL-client Modules — is defined and used frequently (in effect, every type of SQL binding style conceptually uses Modules, at least implicitly). However, nobody implements them and nobody cares. What vendors have implemented and what programmers have used throughout SQL's history, is some variant of: (*a*) embedded SQL, (*b*) SQL/CLI, or (*c*) both. There has been no popular implementation of a complete SQL language which can do all the things that other programming languages offer.

For example, in essential SQL, there is no easy way to do the following things:

- Declare variables.
- Assign to variables.

- Control flow of execution with loops or if/then statements.
- Write complete program modules.

With PSM, there is a way to overcome those deficiencies — if they are deficiencies. Essentially, PSM is a package of extensions to the essential SQL specification. Because one important extension is the ability to create and destroy program modules, the package name is "Persistent Stored Modules." However, the other extensions — variable handling and program control — can be implemented independently. For example, some DBMSs allow "assignment" statements to be used within Triggers even though they have no support for persistent stored modules.

Persistent Stored Modules

In SQL, the word "persistent" is applied to Schema Objects that survive over SQL-sessions (as "persistent Base tables" do). And the sort of Modules we're talking about are indeed Schema Objects — they're stored in Schemas, just as Tables and Domains and other Schema Objects. (The actual storage is on the server and these Objects are sometimes called "SQL-server Modules," but their physical location is not important.)

It is, then, reasonable to think of a Persistent Stored Module as a [program] Module which is stored permanently within a Schema of an SQL "database." As with other Schema Objects, there are `CREATE`, `ALTER`, and `DROP` statements for creating, altering, and dropping Modules. In this chapter, we'll briefly describe these Modules and show you the syntax to use to create, alter, and destroy them.

A Schema may contain zero or more Modules. An SQL Module is a named group of SQL statements. Modules are dependent on some Schema — the <Module name> must be unique within the Schema to which the Module belongs — and are created, altered, and dropped using standard SQL statements. All Modules consist of various identifying elements (e.g., the Module name, the Module <AuthorizationID>, and an associated <Schema name> and <Character set name>) as well as the temporary Table declarations necessary to use the Module. In addition, a Module must contain one or more SQL procedures.

An SQL procedure is a named program procedure that will execute an SQL statement when it is called. It contains the list of parameter declarations necessary to execute the procedure and exactly one SQL statement. Procedures are called from Modules with a call statement that provides the procedure name and the necessary values for the parameters that are declared in the procedure. SQL procedures must reference parameters to pass values between the program and SQL-data. Because parameters must map to host language variables, they are not nullable unless they are coupled with an indicator parameter.

SQL provides a status parameter — `SQLSTATE` — whose value indicates whether or not an SQL statement was successfully executed. All procedures must contain an `SQLSTATE` declaration.

A Module is defined by a descriptor that contains six pieces of information:

1. The <Module name> qualified by the <Schema name> of the Schema to which it belongs.
2. The name of the Character set that is used to express the names of all Schema Objects mentioned in the Module's definition.
3. The Module's <AuthorizationID> — this is the <AuthorizationID> that owns the Module's Schema.

4. The list of <Schema name>s contained in the Module's path specification.
5. A descriptor for every declared local temporary Table defined in the Module.
6. A descriptor for every SQL-invoked routine contained in the Module.

To create a Module, use the CREATE MODULE statement (either as a stand-alone SQL statement or within a CREATE SCHEMA statement). CREATE MODULE specifies the enclosing Schema; names the Module; and identifies the Module's Character set, declared Tables, and routines. To change an existing Module, use the ALTER MODULE statement. To destroy a Module, use the DROP MODULE statement.

There is a one-to-many association between Schemas and Modules; one Schema can own multiple Modules.

Module Names

A <Module name> identifies a Module. The required syntax for a <Module name> is as follows.

```
<Module name> ::=
[ <Schema name>. ] unqualified name
```

A <Module name> is a <regular identifier> or a <delimited identifier> that is unique (for all Modules) within the Schema to which it belongs. The <Schema name> which qualifies a <Module name> names the Schema to which the Module belongs and can either be explicitly stated or a default will be supplied by your DBMS as follows:

- If a <Module name> in a CREATE SCHEMA statement isn't qualified, the default qualifier is the name of the Schema you're creating.
- If the unqualified <Module name> is found in any other SQL statement, the default qualifier is the name of the Schema identified in the SCHEMA clause or AUTHORIZATION clause of the CREATE MODULE statement that defines that Module.

Here are some examples of <Module name>s:

```
MODULE_1
-- a <Module name>

SCHEMA_1.MODULE_1
-- a simple qualified <Module name>

CATALOG_1.SCHEMA_1.MODULE_1
-- a fully qualified <Module name>
```

CREATE MODULE Statement

The CREATE MODULE statement creates an SQL-server Module; a Module that belongs to a Schema. The required syntax for the CREATE MODULE statement is as follows.

```
CREATE MODULE <Module name>
   [ NAMES ARE <Character set name> ]
   [ SCHEMA default <Schema name>]
   [ PATH <Schema name> [ {,<Schema name>}... ] ]
   [ DECLARE TABLE statement(s) ]
   <SQL-invoked routine>; ...
   END MODULE
```

CREATE MODULE defines a new SQL-server Module — don't get this mixed up with the simple MODULE statement that is part of essential SQL, it defines an SQL-client Module and although the two are similar, PSM statements won't work on anything but a PSM Module.

The <Module name> identifies the Module and the Schema to which it belongs. A <Module name> that includes an explicit <Schema name> qualifier belongs to the Schema named. A <Module name> that does not include an explicit <Schema name> qualifier belongs to the SQL-session default Schema. The <Module name> must be unique within the Schema that contains it.

If CREATE MODULE is part of a CREATE SCHEMA statement, the <Module name>, if explicitly qualified, must include the <Schema name> of the Schema being created; that is, it isn't possible to create a Module belonging to a different Schema from within CREATE SCHEMA.

The optional NAMES ARE clause provides the name of the Character set that is used to express the names of all Schema Objects mentioned in the Module's definition. If you omit the clause, the Module's Character set is the default Character set of the Schema to which it belongs.

The optional SCHEMA clause names the default Schema for the Module — that is, the name of the Schema that owns the Schema Objects referred to in the Module. If you omit the clause, the default <Schema name> is the name of the Schema that owns the Module.

The optional PATH clause names the Module's default path; the path used to qualify unqualified <Routine name>s that identify <routine invocation>s that are part of this CREATE MODULE statement. You must include the name of the Schema being created in the PATH clause and if you include multiple names, all of the Schemas named must belong to the same Catalog. If you omit the clause, your DBMS will give the Module a default path that includes the name of the Schema to which the Module belongs.

The Module can contain zero or more DECLARE TABLE statements, each declaring a local temporary Table that will only be visible to this Module.

The Module can contain one or more SQL-invoked routines — these do the Module's work. Here's a simple example:

```
CREATE MODULE Employees_Module              /* This begins and names the Module */
  DECLARE PROCEDURE Delete_Employees()               /* This is an SQL routine */
      MODIFIES SQL DATA
      DELETE FROM Employees;
  DECLARE PROCEDURE Update_Employees()               /* This is an SQL routine */
      MODIFIES SQL DATA
      UPDATE Employees SET col=NULL;
  DECLARE PROCEDURE Insert_Employees()               /* This is an SQL routine */
      MODIFIES SQL DATA
      INSERT INTO Employees VALUES (5);
END MODULE
```

If your memory stretches back to Chapter 25 "SQL-Invoked Routines," you'll recognize the PROCEDURE statements here — procedures and functions are part of essential SQL. What the CREATE MODULE statement allows you to do is construct a "package" of procedures, in the same way that a C implementation allows the construction of a library. Our example is a rather crude attempt to "package" the main SQL-data change statements that can happen with the EMPLOYEES Table. Note: The DECLARE <keyword> before PROCEDURE is optional.

ALTER MODULE Statement

The ALTER MODULE statement lets you change a Module's definition. The required syntax for the ALTER MODULE statement is as follows.

```
ALTER MODULE <Module name>
   {ADD | DROP} <Module contents> ...
```

ALTER MODULE changes an existing Module. <Module contents> can be a function, a procedure, or any of the other things that might be part of a Module (exceptions, handlers, variables, Cursors, declared Tables, and so on).

Here's an example of an ALTER MODULE statement:

```
ALTER MODULE Employees_Module
DROP PROCEDURE Insert_Employees;
```

After the execution of this ALTER MODULE statement, the EMPLOYEES_MODULE Module will have only two procedures left: Delete_Employees and Update_Employees.

DROP MODULE Statement

The DROP MODULE statement destroys an SQL-server Module. The required syntax for the DROP MODULE statement is as follows.

```
DROP MODULE <Module name> {RESTRICT | CASCADE}
```

The <Module name> must identify an existing Module whose owner is either the current <AuthorizationID> or a Role that the current <AuthorizationID> may use. That is, only the <AuthorizationID> that owns the Module may drop it.

The effect of DROP MODULE <Module name> RESTRICT, e.g.,

```
DROP MODULE module_1 RESTRICT;
```

is that the Module named is destroyed, provided that the Module doesn't contain the definition of an SQL-invoked routine that is invoked outside of the Module — i.e., in an SQL routine that isn't defined in this Module or in any View definition, Trigger definition, Constraint definition, or Assertion definition. That is, RESTRICT ensures that only a Module with no dependent Objects can be destroyed. If the Module is used by any other Object, DROP MODULE ... RESTRICT will fail.

The effect of DROP MODULE <Module name> CASCADE, e.g.,

```
DROP MODULE module_1 CASCADE;
```

is that the Module named is destroyed.

Successfully dropping a Module has a three-fold effect:

1. The Module named is destroyed.
2. All Privileges held on the Module by the <AuthorizationID> that owns it are revoked (by the SQL special grantor, "_SYSTEM") with a CASCADE revoke behaviour, so that all Privileges held on the Module by any other <AuthorizationID> are also revoked.
3. All SQL routines, Triggers, Views, and Constraints that depend on the Module are dropped with a CASCADE drop behaviour.

BEGIN ... END Compound Statement

Advance warning: BEGIN ... END has several optional clauses. We are going to start with the simplest form and examine the options in following sections.

In its simplest form, BEGIN ... END in SQL serves the same purpose as "begin...end" in Pascal or "{...}" in C. BEGIN ... END encloses a sequence of statements which are part of the same syntactical unit; a compound statement. The simplest required syntax is as follows.

```
BEGIN
   [ <SQL statement>; ... ]
END
```

Here's a simple example:

```
BEGIN
   INSERT INTO Table_1 VALUES (5);
   INSERT INTO Table_2 VALUES (6);
END
```

ATOMIC Statements

A slightly more complicated form of a compound statement has one extra optional clause: [NOT] ATOMIC. The required syntax is as follows.

```
BEGIN [ [ NOT ] ATOMIC ]    /* whether compound statement is atomic */
   [ <SQL statement>; ... ]
END
```

If ATOMIC is specified, the compound statement may not contain COMMIT or ROLLBACK. If you omit the clause, it defaults to NOT ATOMIC; the compound statement may contain COMMIT or ROLLBACK. Here's an example:

```
BEGIN ATOMIC
   INSERT INTO Table_1 VALUES (5);
   INSERT INTO Table_2 VALUES (6);
END
```

We've already discussed the idea that transactions are atomic and individual SQL statements are atomic. Compound SQL statements can be atomic too, provided that they are explicitly designated by the <keyword> ATOMIC. Thus, in the above example, if the first INSERT statement succeeds but the second INSERT statement fails, then the effect of the first INSERT is cancelled. It's as if there was a savepoint at the beginning of the compound statement and a ROLLBACK TO SAVEPOINT was executed when the second INSERT failed.

Variables

A slightly more complicated form of a compound statement has one more optional clause; a variable declaration list. The required syntax is as follows.

```
BEGIN [ [ NOT ] ATOMIC ]
   [ <variable declaration>; ... ]                /* variable-declaration list */
   [ <SQL statement>; ... ]
END

<variable declaration> ::=
DECLARE <SQL variable name> <data type> [ DEFAULT default value ]
```

Here's an example:

```
BEGIN ATOMIC
   DECLARE v1 CHAR(5);                                /* variable declaration */
   DECLARE v2,v3,v4 SMALLINT;                         /* variable declaration */
   DECLARE v5 DATE DEFAULT DATE '1993-01-01';         /* variable declaration */
   SELECT * INTO v1,v2,v3,v4 FROM Table_1;                       /* statement */
   INSERT INTO Table_2 VALUES (v1,v2,v3,v4,v5);                  /* statement */
END
```

TRAP: Don't get confused by the similarity to a <Column definition>. A variable definition can contain *only* a <data type> and (optionally) a `DEFAULT` clause. It cannot contain a <Domain name>, a <Constraint> or a `COLLATE` clause.

In our example we defined five variables: `v1`, `v2`, `v3`, `v4`, `v5`. `BEGIN` ... `END` defines a "local scope," which means that (*a*) these variable names have no meaning outside the compound statement, (*b*) the values in these variables are not saved when the compound statement ends, and (*c*) the values in these variables are not reset by execution of a `ROLLBACK` statement because variables are not part of the database.

The example uses the first four variables as targets in a singleton `SELECT` statement. It also uses all five variables as sources in an `INSERT` statement. Variables can be used in all sorts of <value expression>s. Variables are extremely useful for temporary storage and it's a wonder that most SQL implementations get along without them. The designers of SQL don't give us the option of using variables for persistent storage; we're supposed to use Base tables for that.

Assignment Statements

Assignment statements begin with the <keyword> `SET` — but don't call them "`SET` statements," to avoid confusion with non-PSM statements that also begin with `SET`. Assignment statements are syntactically similar to the `SET` clauses used in `UPDATE` statements. Here is the required syntax:

```
SET
<target>                    /* where the value goes to; usually a variable */
=
<source>                    /* where the value comes from; an expression */
```

In theory the <target> doesn't have to be a variable — it could be a parameter or a "host variable" — but normal programs will take the form "<variable> = <expression>." Here are some examples:

```
SET v2 = 5

SET v2 = (v2+7)/5

SET v2 = NULL

SET v2 = column_1
```

Cursors

A slightly more complicated form of a compound statement has one more optional clause; a Cursor declaration list. The required syntax is as follows.

```
BEGIN [ [ NOT ] ATOMIC ]
  [ <variable declaration>; ... ]
  [ DECLARE CURSOR statement; ... ]                    /* Cursor-declaration list */
  [ <SQL statement>; ... ]
END
```

The mechanics of Cursors are the same for PSM as they are for embedded SQL and for SQL/CLI. Here's an example:

```
BEGIN
  DECLARE v1 SMALLINT;                                 /* variable-declaration */
  DECLARE cc CURSOR FOR
     SELECT column_1 FROM Table_1;                     /* Cursor-declaration */
  OPEN cc;                                                      /* statement */
  FETCH cc INTO v1;                                             /* statement */
  CLOSE cc;                                                     /* statement */
  INSERT INTO Table_2 VALUES (v1);                              /* statement */
END
```

Objects that you declare in a compound statement have "local scope," so the <Cursor name> in this example — cc — can only be used by SQL statements within the BEGIN ... END. The example could be replaced with this SQL statement:

```
INSERT INTO Table_2 SELECT column_1 FROM Table_1;
```

if there is only one row in TABLE_1.

Conditions

A slightly more complicated form of a compound statement changes the optional variable declaration clause; instead of a variable declaration list, BEGIN ... END actually allows a variable or condition declaration list, so that you can declare conditions as well as variables. The required syntax is as follows.

```
BEGIN [ [ NOT ] ATOMIC ]
  [ <variable | condition declaration>; ... ]        /*variable-or-condition declaration list*/
  [ DECLARE CURSOR statement; ... ]
  [ <SQL statement>; ... ]
END

<condition declaration> ::=
   DECLARE <condition name> CONDITION [ FOR <sqlstate value> ]
```

Quick review: An SQLSTATE value is a 5-character status code string. Upon completion of any SQL statement, there will be a status code in SQLSTATE, which is the main diagnostic field. Typical values are '01006' (warning-privilege not revoked), '22012' (data exception-division by zero), and '42000' (syntax error or access violation). You'll find a complete list of SQLSTATE values in Chapter 47 "SQL/CLI: Diagnostic Functions."

Here's an example of the latest form of BEGIN ... END:

```
BEGIN ATOMIC
  DECLARE v1 SMALLINT;                                    /* variable-declaration */
  DECLARE warning_revoke CONDITION FOR '01006';           /*condition declaration*/
  DECLARE divide_by_zero CONDITION FOR '22012';           /*condition declaration*/
  DECLARE syntax_error CONDITION FOR '42000';             /*condition declaration*/
  DECLARE cc CURSOR FOR
    SELECT column_1 FROM Table_1;                         /* Cursor-declaration */
  OPEN cc;                                                /* statement */
  FETCH cc INTO v1;                                       /* statement */
  CLOSE cc;                                               /* statement */
  INSERT INTO Table_2 VALUES (v1);                        /* statement */
  INSERT INTO Table_1 VALUES (0);                         /* statement */
  INSERT INTO Table_2 VALUES (1);                         /* statement */
END
```

In this example, we have simply given condition names to three of the possible SQLSTATE values.

Handlers

A slightly more complicated form of a compound statement adds another optional clause; a handler declaration list. The required syntax is as follows.

```
BEGIN [ [ NOT ] ATOMIC ]
  [ <variable | condition declaration>; ... ]
  [ DECLARE CURSOR statement; ... ]
  [ <handler declaration>; ... ]                  /* handler-declaration list */
  [ <SQL statement>; ... ]
END

  <handler declaration> ::=
  DECLARE <handler type>
       HANDLER FOR <condition value list> <handler action>

     <handler type> ::= {CONTINUE | EXIT | UNDO }

     <handler action> ::= <SQL statement>
```

```
<condition value list> ::=
<condition value> [ {,<condition value>}... ]

        <condition value> ::=
        <sqlstate value>|
        <condition name>|
        SQLEXCEPTION |
        SQLWARNING |
        NOT FOUND
```

The following example contains three handlers. The first is for an SQLSTATE value, the second is for a condition name, and the third is for any warning (i.e., any SQLSTATE in class '01').

```
BEGIN
  DECLARE constraint_error CONDITION FOR '23000';   /* condition declaration */
  DECLARE v1 CHAR(5) DEFAULT 'Okay!';                 /* variable declaration */
  DECLARE CONTINUE HANDLER FOR '22003'                /* handler declaration */
     SET v1 = 'Ovflw';
  DECLARE CONTINUE HANDLER FOR constraint_error        /* handler declaration */
     SET v1 = 'c-err';
  DECLARE CONTINUE HANDLER FOR SQLWARNING             /* handler declaration */
     SET v1 = '?????';
  INSERT INTO Table_1 VALUES (99999);                           /* statement */
  INSERT INTO Table_2 VALUES (v1);                              /* statement */
END
```

To see the effect of these handlers, consider what will happen with the SQL statement:

```
INSERT INTO Table_1 VALUES (99999);
```

If this SQL statement fails due to overflow, then variable v1 gets 'Ovflw'; if it fails due to an integrity Constraint violation, then variable v1 gets 'c-err'; if it succeeds but there is some warning, then variable v1 gets '?????'. But, regardless, play continues because all the handlers are CONTINUE handlers. So the second INSERT statement will put in one of the values 'Ovflw', 'c-err', '?????', or 'Okay!' ('Okay!' is the default value for v1 so this is what goes in if the result of the first INSERT is success with no warnings).

What if exception '42000' happens? That would be an "unhandled exception" because we did not define a handler for exception '42000'. The result would be that the second INSERT is not attempted — the whole compound statement fails.

The following chart compares the exception-handling features of embedded SQL, the CLI, and the PSM.

	EMBEDDED SQL	CLI	PSM
method of declaration	EXEC SQL WHENEVER	none	handler-declaration
what happens	GOTO	N/A	any SQL statement
handles SQLNOTFOUND?	yes	N/A	yes
handles SQLERROR?	yes	N/A	yes
handles SQLWARNING?	yes	N/A	yes
handles specific status codes?	no	N/A	yes

Among the SQL statements that a handler can execute are two new special ones: the SIGNAL statement and the RESIGNAL statement. These SQL statements affect the diagnostics area.

Labels

We're still not done with the BEGIN ... END statement. The final form of a compound statement adds two more optional clauses: a beginning label and an end label. The required syntax for a compound statement is as follows.

```
[ <beginning_label>: ]
BEGIN [ [ NOT ] ATOMIC ]
  [ <variable | condition declaration>; ... ]
  [ DECLARE CURSOR statement; ... ]
  [ <handler declaration>; ...]
  [ <SQL statement>; ... ]
END [ <end_label> ]

  <beginning_label> ::= <identifier>

  <end_label> ::= <identifier>
```

If you add labels to your compound statement, they should be equivalent (if both are specified). Labels are useful as referents for various control statements, which we will discuss later. Here's an example:

```
full_blown_example:                                          /* beginning_label */
BEGIN ATOMIC                                      /* compound statement is atomic */
      DECLARE v1 INTEGER DEFAULT 0;                         /* variable declaration */
      DECLARE c1 CONDITION FOR '01000';                    /* condition declaration */
      DECLARE CONTINUE HANDLER FOR SQLERROR                  /* handler declaration */
```

```
        SET v1 = 1;                          /* assignment statement */
    INSERT INTO Table_1 VALUES (0);                      /* statement */
    INSERT INTO Table_2 VALUES (v1);                     /* statement */
END full_blown_example                                   /* end_label */
```

This is our final version of BEGIN ... END. It looks quite imposing. That's because *most syntactic items are local to the compound statement*. Therefore, everything is within the compound statement and by contrast, the Module definition is trivial.

SIGNAL Statement

The SIGNAL statement is used to clear the diagnostics area. The required syntax for the SIGNAL statement is as follows.

```
SIGNAL <condition name or sqlstate value>
  SET <signal information item list>

  <signal information item list> ::=
  <signal information item> [ {,<signal information item>}... ]

    <signal information item> ::=
    <condition information item name> = <simple value specification>
```

The SIGNAL statement clears every record in the diagnostics area. The end result is a record containing the passed condition name or SQLSTATE value. If you include the optional SET clause, your DBMS effectively executes:

```
RESIGNAL <signal information item list>;
```

Note: You'll find the list of <condition information item name>s in Chapter 39 "Embedded SQL Binding Style" — see the GET DIAGNOSTICS statement.

RESIGNAL Statement

The RESIGNAL statement is used to pass conditions on to another handler. The required syntax for the RESIGNAL statement is as follows.

```
RESIGNAL [ <condition name or sqlstate value> ]
  [ SET <signal information item list> ]
```

The RESIGNAL statement passes the given exception "up the line" to the next appropriate handler (because compound statements may be embedded in compound statements, this next appropriate handler will usually be in some outside context). The current diagnostics area remains unchanged, but — if the optional [<condition name or sqlstate value>] clause is specified — there will be one more diagnostics record containing this new value. If you include the optional SET clause, the <condition information item name> field in the first condition area in the diagnostics area is changed to the value indicated.

Program Control

Essential SQL has almost nothing that can control the program flow (except for the CALL and RETURN statements which are associated with SQL routines). By contrast, a DBMS with PSM support will allow eight control statements. Of these, seven are similar to statements which appear in other languages. The eighth, FOR, depends on Objects which are unique to the SQL environment. Here's a list of these statements:

- CASE — Switch depending on condition.
- IF — If (condition) do.
- ITERATE — Restart loop.
- LOOP — Do statement(s) repeatedly.
- LEAVE — Break out of a loop or block.
- WHILE — Repeat statement(s) as long as condition is true.
- REPEAT — Repeat statement(s) until condition is true.
- FOR — Cursor-based FETCH loop.

CASE Statement

The CASE statement is useful for switching between possible execution paths. There are two forms — one contains search conditions, the other contains value expressions. The required syntax for the CASE statement is as follows.

```
searched CASE statement ::=
CASE
  WHEN <search condition> THEN <statement>(s)
  [ WHEN <search condition> THEN <statement>(s) ... ]
  [ ELSE <statement>(s) ]
END CASE

simple CASE statement ::=
CASE <case value>
  WHEN <when value> THEN <statement>(s)
  [ WHEN <when value> THEN <statement>(s) ... ]
  [ ELSE <statement>(s) ]
END CASE
```

A "simple CASE statement" is merely a shorthand and may be replaced by a "searched CASE statement" which has the form: "CASE WHEN <when value> = <case value> ...". Thus, the following examples, showing a searched CASE statement on the left and a simple CASE statement on the right, are exactly equivalent:

```
CASE
  WHEN parameter_value = 15
   THEN INSERT INTO t VALUES (15);
  WHEN parameter_value = 17
   THEN INSERT INTO t VALUES (17);
  ELSE INSERT INTO t VALUES (0);
END CASE
```

```
CASE parameter_value
  WHEN 15
   THEN INSERT INTO t VALUES (15);
  WHEN 17
   THEN INSERT INTO t VALUES (17);
  ELSE INSERT INTO t VALUES (0);
END CASE
```

When executing a CASE statement, the DBMS goes through the WHEN clauses from top to bottom, looking for a TRUE condition. If it finds one, it executes the statement(s) after THEN and the CASE terminates. If it finds none, it executes the statements(s) after ELSE — or, if there is no ELSE, returns the SQLSTATE error 20000 "case not found for case statement." For the previous example, then, if the value of parameter_value is 5, then the DBMS will execute this SQL statement:

```
INSERT INTO t VALUES (0);
```

TRAP: The syntax for the CASE statement is somewhat different from the syntax for the SQL CASE expression (see Chapter 29 "Simple Search Conditions"). In particular, the CASE statement has no equivalent for the ELSE NULL clause and the terminator is END CASE rather than END.

IF Statement

The IF statement is useful for simple "if (x) then (do this)" situations. The required syntax for the IF statement is as follows.

```
IF <search condition> THEN <SQL statement>(s)
   ELSEIF <search condition> THEN <SQL statement>(s)
   ELSE <SQL statement>(s)
END IF
```

Here's an example:

```
IF
 5=5 THEN UPDATE Table_1 SET column_1 = column_1 + 1;
END IF
```

In this example, the search condition is TRUE, so the UPDATE statement will be executed. If the search condition had been FALSE or UNKNOWN, then the UPDATE statement would not have been executed.

LOOP Statement

The LOOP statement is useful for repeated execution of SQL statements. The required syntax for the LOOP statement is as follows.

```
[ <beginning_label>: ]
   LOOP
   <SQL statement>(s)
END LOOP [ <end_label> ]
```

The SQL statements between LOOP and END LOOP are repeated until the loop finishes. The <beginning_label> and the <end_label> must be equivalent, if you use them both. Here's an example:

```
LOOP
   SET x = x + 1;
END LOOP
```

This example shows an infinite loop. The usual way to exit from a loop is with the LEAVE statement.

LEAVE Statement

The LEAVE statement is useful for exiting a block or for exiting a loop. The required syntax for the LEAVE statement is as follows.

```
LEAVE <statement_label>
```

Here's an example:

```
beginning_label:
LOOP
  SET x = x + 1;
  IF x > 1000 THEN LEAVE beginning_label; END IF;
END LOOP beginning_label
```

In this example, the loop will be exited once the value of x passes 1,000.

WHILE Statement

The WHILE statement is useful for repeated execution of SQL statements, with a built-in equivalent to the LEAVE statement. The required syntax for the WHILE statement is as follows.

```
[ <beginning_label>: ]
WHILE <search condition> DO
   <SQL statement>(s)
END WHILE [ <end_label> ]
```

As long as the <search condition> is TRUE, the SQL statements between WHILE and END WHILE are repeatedly executed. The <beginning_label> and the <end_label> must be equivalent, if you use them both. Here's an example:

```
WHILE x <= 1000 DO
   SET x = x + 1;
END WHILE
```

This example will loop, incrementing x, until x <= 1000 is either FALSE or UNKNOWN. If the <search condition> is FALSE or UNKNOWN when the loop begins, then nothing happens.

REPEAT Statement

The REPEAT statement is much like the WHILE statement, except that the condition is tested *after* the execution of the SQL statement(s). The required syntax for the REPEAT statement is as follows.

```
[ <beginning_label>: ]
REPEAT
   <SQL statement>(s) UNTIL <search condition>
END REPEAT [ <end_label> ]
```

As long as the <search condition> is FALSE or UNKNOWN, the SQL statements between REPEAT and END REPEAT are repeatedly executed. The <beginning_label> and the <end_label> must be equivalent, if you use them both. Here's an example:

```
REPEAT
   DELETE FROM Table_1 WHERE column_1 = x;
   SET x = x + 1;
   UNTIL x > 5
END REPEAT
```

In this example, the UPDATE statement will be repeated until x is greater than 5 — that is, the loop will repeat until after the condition is TRUE.

TRAP: The example is an infinite loop if the initial value of x is NULL.

FOR Statement

The FOR statement is useful for simplified FETCH loops. Execution takes place for each row of a result set. The required syntax for the FOR statement is as follows.

```
[ <beginning_label>: ]
FOR <loop variable name> AS [ <Cursor name>
   [ {ASENSITIVE | INSENSITIVE | SENSITIVE} ] CURSOR FOR ]
   <query expression> [ ORDER BY clause ] [ updatability clause ]
```

```
DO
   <SQL statement>(s)
END FOR [ <end_label> ]
```

Here's an example:

```
FOR x AS Cursor_1 CURSOR FOR
   SELECT name, address_1, address_2 FROM Addresses
DO
   UPDATE Addresses SET address_1 = '' WHERE CURRENT OF Cursor_1;
END FOR
```

Effectively, a Cursor is opened when the loop begins, fetched for each row of the result set, and closed when the loop ends. In this example, the UPDATE statement is executed for each fetched row before the next iteration. SQL's FOR loop is different, in style and meaning, from FOR loops in other languages.

ITERATE Statement

The ITERATE statement is useful for "re-starting" — going back to the beginning of the list of statements inside a loop and proceeding with the next iteration of the loop. The required syntax for the ITERATE statement is as follows.

```
ITERATE <statement_label>
```

The ITERATE statement can appear only within an "iterated SQL statement" — that is, within LOOP, WHILE, REPEAT, or FOR. The <statement_label> must be the <beginning_label> of the iterated SQL statement. If the iteration condition for the iterated SQL statement is TRUE, or if the statement doesn't have an iteration condition, ITERATE causes the next iteration of the loop to start. If the iteration condition is FALSE or UNKNOWN, ITERATE causes the loop to end. Here's an example:

```
beginning_of_while:
WHILE (color_of_moon_in_june = 'blue') DO
   ...
   SET spot_remover = 'active';
   IF (birthday_test() IS UNKNOWN)
     THEN ITERATE beginning_of_while;
   END IF
   SET checkout_status = 0;
END WHILE
```

Should Everything be in SQL?

PSM is an extension package which makes SQL3 a reasonably complete language. There are still some things you can't do (such as disk or screen I/O), but anybody could write external-routine libraries which would plug the remaining gaps.

So what?

For several years, programmers have written applications in "host languages" and invoked SQL statements either via embedded SQL or via the CLI. By now there is an awful lot of legacy code in those host languages. It has to be expected, too, that there are good host-language optimizers out there — don't bother pitting C and SQL head-to-head with a "Sieve of Eratosthenes" benchmark. The SQL code would lose.

On the other hand, we could say that:

- Yes, SQL optimizers are inferior for low-level benchmarks, but they're better at the high level — and you'd be helping SQL optimizers if you could pass them groups of SQL statements rather than individual SQL statements.
- A lot of programming effort is spent solving the "impedance mismatch" problem — the fact that host languages don't store data the SQL way or process sets the SQL way or have the same ideas of access control. With Modules inside the SQL environment, DBMSs can act in a consistent way across platforms.
- Remote Data Access is feasible with SQL, but not with a host language.

In the end, the world's SQL developers will decide which arguments are the most convincing. At the moment, PSM is not (yet) the popular way to go.

Dialects

PSM's features are vaguely similar to Oracle's PL/SQL, which also has: `BEGIN` ... `END`, `LOOP`, `WHILE`, and (using different keywords) assignment statements and handlers. Informix SQL has a FOREACH statement which does the same thing as the standard `FOR` statement.

Even if a vendor does not support any form of PSM, you may find that some of the above-described features have been added individually into essential SQL. For example, a DBMS which fully supports SQL routines will probably allow compound statements too, in at least a limited way.

27

Chapter 27

User-Defined Types

[Obscure Rule] applies for this entire chapter.

SQL began life as a procedurally oriented language or — properly speaking — as a language with procedures that worked on sets. Nowadays the rage is for object-oriented languages — like C++ and Java. The popularity of object orientation ("OO" for short) has been so great, that some have attempted to supersede SQL with pure "OO DBMSs" (POET is an example). On the other hand, a great deal of time and trouble has been invested getting SQL to where it is today, so most users and experts have looked to a more moderate solution. Namely, extending SQL so that it can handle databases the OO way but without abandoning the current language. We'll call this hybrid *object/relational* or O/R for short.

The inspirations have come from languages like C++ and Object Pascal, which are extensions of C and Pascal. Those extended languages have been successful. It appears that there will be an equivalent success for the Object-Oriented SQL extensions once DBMS vendors implement them and users get acquainted with them.

We're not at that stage yet. What you're going to read about in this chapter is the very latest stuff, just accepted as part of the SQL Standard and still quite wet around the edges. Because that's so, we will depart from the usual chapter organization. The first parts of this chapter are merely a tutorial which (we hope) you'll find is fairly light reading, peppered with liberating slogans like "a type is a class" or "a row is an object." The middle parts of this chapter are more of a syntactical slog as we get into the details of `CREATE TYPE` and the various SQL statements associated with it; however, we have omitted some details which we think will not be part of real DBMS implementations for some years.

If you've ever used an object-oriented language, you'll find the concepts are familiar (which they're supposed to be — that's the point). However, you must start with a good recollection of the earlier chapters on <data type>s, procedures, and SQL syntax.

UDTs

Until now, all the SQL <data type>s we've described have predefined <data type>s, sometimes called "built-in" or "primitive" <data type>s — although some portions of them are definable by users (for example, the length of a `CHAR` <data type>), most of their inherent structure is already set. The O/R part of SQL, though, uses user-defined data types, or UDTs. UDTs are just as easy to use as predefined data types; however, they are a lot harder to set up.

Just consider some of the things which are already handled for you (programmed in the DBMS) if you use a predefined data type:

- There's a way of storing the data physically in a Table (this is the concept of *instantiation*, which we'll have some trouble with later).
- There are comparison operations for the <data type>s, so you can tell whether two values are the same or one is greater than the other (this is the concept of *ordering*).
- There are built-in operators for the <data type>s, for example, + is used to add to numbers together and produce another number (this is the concept of *methods* that change values of certain data types).
- There are cast operations so that values in one <data type> can be converted to another or interchanged with host language variables (this is the concept of *cast methods* and *transforms*).

With UDTs, you're on your own in all these cases. When you make a UDT, you're going to have to remember that all those things won't be there unless you put them there yourself.

However, when you do it, you'll end up with a <data type> that's just as good as the predefined types. You'll be able to use your new UDT wherever you could use a predefined type before.

A Schema may contain zero or more UDTs. An SQL UDT is a named, user-defined set of valid values. UDTs are dependent on some Schema — the <UDT name> must be unique within the Schema to which the UDT belongs (it may not be the same as any <Domain name> in its Schema either) — and are created, altered, and dropped using standard SQL statements. The Objects that may belong to a UDT are known as Attributes; they depend on some UDT.

A UDT can be either a distinct type — a UDT that is based on a single predefined <data type> or a structured type — a UDT that is based on a list of Attribute definitions.

A UDT is defined by a descriptor that contains twelve pieces of information:

1. The <UDT name> qualified by the <Schema name> of the Schema to which it belongs.
2. Whether the UDT is ordered.
3. The UDT's ordering form; either `EQUALS`, `FULL`, or `NONE`.
4. The UDT's ordering category; either `RELATIVE`, `HASH`, or `STATE`.
5. The <specific routine designator> that identifies the UDT's ordering function.
6. The name of the UDT's direct supertype, if any.
7. If the UDT is a distinct type, then the descriptor of the <data type> on which it's based; otherwise an Attribute descriptor for each of the UDT's Attributes.

8. The UDT's degree; the number of its Attributes.
9. Whether the UDT is instantiable or not instantiable.
10. Whether the UDT is final or not final.
11. The UDT's Transform descriptor.
12. If the UDT's definition includes a method signature list, a descriptor for each method signature named.

To create a UDT, use the CREATE TYPE statement (either as a stand-alone SQL statement or within a CREATE SCHEMA statement). CREATE TYPE specifies the enclosing Schema, names the UDT, and identifies the UDT's set of valid values. To destroy a UDT, use the DROP TYPE statement. None of SQL3's UDT syntax is Core SQL, so if you want to restrict your code to Core SQL, don't use UDTs.

UDT Names

A <UDT name> identifies a UDT. The required syntax for a <UDT name> is as follows.

```
<UDT name> ::=
[ <Schema name>. ] unqualified name
```

A <UDT name> is a <regular identifier> or a <delimited identifier> that is unique (for all Domains and UDTs) within the Schema to which it belongs. The <Schema name> which qualifies a <UDT name> names the Schema to which the UDT belongs and can either be explicitly stated or a default will be supplied by your DBMS as follows:

- If a <UDT name> in a CREATE SCHEMA statement isn't qualified, the default qualifier is the name of the Schema you're creating.
- If the unqualified <UDT name> is found in any other SQL statement in a Module, the default qualifier is the name of the Schema identified in the SCHEMA clause or AUTHORIZATION clause of the MODULE statement that defines that Module.

UDT Example

Here's an example of a UDT definition:

```
CREATE TYPE book_udt AS                    -- the UDT name will be book_udt
title CHAR(40),                            -- title is the first attribute
buying_price DECIMAL(9,2),       -- buying_price is the second attribute
selling_price DECIMAL(9,2)       -- selling_price is the third attribute
NOT FINAL                            -- this is a mandatory Finality Clause
METHOD profit() RETURNS DECIMAL(9,2);          -- a method, defined later
```

This CREATE TYPE statement results in a UDT named BOOK_UDT. The components of the UDT are three attributes (named TITLE, BUYING_PRICE, and SELLING_PRICE) and one method (named PROFIT).

1. The three name-and-data-type pairs title CHAR(40) and buying_price DECIMAL(9,2) and selling_price DECIMAL(9,2) are the UDT's Attribute definitions.

2. The words NOT FINAL matter only for subtyping, which we'll get to later. Briefly, though, if a UDT definition doesn't include an UNDER clause, the finality clause must specify NOT FINAL.
3. The clause METHOD profit () RETURNS DECIMAL (9,2) is a teaser. Like an Attribute, a "method" is a component of a UDT. However, this method — PROFIT — is actually a declaration that a function named PROFIT exists. This function isn't defined further in the UDT definition; there is a separate SQL statement for defining functions — CREATE METHOD. All we can see at this stage is that PROFIT has a name and a (predefined) <data type>, just as regular Attributes do. Some people would call PROFIT a "derived Attribute."

Columns Based on UDTs

Let us begin by making a Table, one of whose Columns is a UDT:

```
CREATE TABLE T (
   book_column book_udt,
   serial_number INTEGER);
```

You can use a UDT wherever the syntax requires <data type>. So far so good. Now let's INSERT a new row into the Table. This won't be so simple.

```
BEGIN                                      /* compound statement: start */
  DECLARE u book_udt;                   /* temporary variable declaration */
  SET u = book_udt();                            /* constructor function */
  SET u = u.title('The Compleat SQL');               /* mutator function */
  SET u = u.buying_price(10.00);                     /* mutator function */
  SET u = u.selling_price(20.00);                    /* mutator function */
  INSERT INTO T VALUES (u,1);         /* ordinary-looking SQL statement */
END;                                         /* compound statement: end */
```

To understand the above compound statement, you'll need to look closely at the declaration and the four function calls that precede the INSERT statement. They are simple things, but the terminology is fancy.

First: DECLARE u book_udt; is a declaration of a temporary variable named u. Nothing new about that (if you remember your PSM chapter), but it shows that variables too can be based on UDTs instead of predefined <data type>s.

Second: u = book_udt(); is a constructor function. The function we're calling is named BOOK_UDT, the same as the UDT. That's not a coincidence. The DBMS's job is to create a constructor function automatically. When the CREATE TYPE book_udt was executed, this SQL statement happened implicitly:

```
CREATE FUNCTION book_udt ()
RETURNS book_udt
...
RETURN V
```

In this `CREATE FUNCTION` statement, the `RETURN V`, is a value of type `book_udt`, with all Attribute instance values equal to their default! What does that mean? It means that when we call the `book_udt` function, the return is a "default value" of the `book_udt` type. That's useful, so it's good to know that the DBMS makes a constructor function for every UDT.

Third: `u.title('The Compleat SQL');` is a mutator function. The function we're calling is named `TITLE`, the same as the first Attribute in the UDT. Once again, this is not a coincidence. The DBMS's job is to create a mutator function automatically. When the `CREATE TYPE book_udt` was executed, this SQL statement also happened implicitly:

```
CREATE METHOD title
   (attribute CHAR(40))
      RETURNS book_udt
      SELF AS RESULT
      LANGUAGE SQL
      DETERMINISTIC
      CONTAINS SQL
      RETURN NULL ON NULL INPUT
```

This statement defines a "method" (or "method function") because it is a component of a UDT. To invoke the method, we just have to say "<udt instance>.<method name> (<new value>)" and the new value is a `CHAR(40)` string, which is compatible with the Attribute's definition. The reason that this method is called a mutator function is that it changes the value in the object instance. So now the title in `u` is `'The Compleat SQL'`.

You might wonder, "Why all the fuss?" If the whole point is to set `U.TITLE` to a value, why not just:

```
SET u.title = 'The Compleat SQL';      /* not a good idea! */
```

Using a `SET` statement like this would violate an object-oriented principle called "encapsulation," according to which the only access to Attributes is via their functions (methods) — so `SET` is not legal. If you're used to Windows programming, you'll see the benefits of encapsulation; nothing can access the storage except pre-approved routines which change if the storage method changes.

Fourth and Fifth: `u.buying_price(10.00);` and `u.selling_price(20.00);` are two more mutator functions. When the UDT was created, the DBMS made methods for `BUYING_PRICE` and for `SELLING_PRICE` too, just as it must do for every Attribute in a UDT.

The bottom line is: constructor functions are the ordinary way to make new instances of UDTs; mutator functions are the ordinary way to change Attributes in UDT instances. Using the constructor and the mutators, we have been able to set up a fully-initialized UDT instance — `u` — with the contents we want.

Sixth: `INSERT INTO T VALUES (u,1);` is dènouement. Clearly, it puts a value into Table `T`. What the value looks like, we have no idea; it's encapsulated. We do know, though, that what we put in was `{'The Compleat SQL', 10.00, 20.00}`. Insertion phase complete.

Let us now get something back out of the UDT. You've probably guessed already that we aren't going to just say:

```
SELECT book_column, serial_number
FROM   T;
```

To retrieve from a UDT, we need yet another function — the opposite of a mutator — to get the Attribute values out of `BOOK_COLUMN` into a representation that we can read. Such a function is called an *observer function* and, once again, the DBMS makes observer functions implicitly at the time that a UDT is created — one for each Attribute, like this:

```
CREATE METHOD title ()
   RETURNS CHAR(40)
   LANGUAGE SQL
   DETERMINISTIC
   CONTAINS SQL
   RETURN NULL ON NULL INPUT;
```

Because the observer method exists to help us get values out, we can use them in `SELECT` statements. To get all the values, we can use this SQL statement:

```
SELECT book_column.title(),
       book_column.buying_price(),
       book_column.selling_price()
FROM   T
WHERE  serial_number > 0;
```

In summary, these are the functions associated with our example UDT `BOOK_UDT`:

- One constructor function named `BOOK_UDT`.
- Three mutator functions named `TITLE`, `BUYING_PRICE`, and `SELLING_PRICE`.
- Three observer functions also named `TITLE`, `BUYING_PRICE`, and `SELLING_PRICE`. (Actually the above is only for the "default case," we'll worry about options later.) As the examples indicated, constructors and mutators and observers are all we need for simple storage and retrieval operations.

Routine Names and Signatures

One of the strengths of the Object/Relational system is that all the functions have the same name as the Attribute they're associated with, which makes them easy to remember. But at first there's a little confusion too! How do we tell them apart? If you look closely at these three references, you'll see the differences:

- `title` — the name of an Attribute.
- `title()` — the name of an observer method.
- `title('The Compleat SQL')` — the name of a mutator method.

The DBMS distinguishes between names the same way that you do. The first distinction is easy; if it's got parentheses after it, then it must be a routine name. The next distinction is that `title()` has no arguments, while `title('The Compleat SQL')` has one argument. That's the difference between an observer and a mutator. Let's express this latter distinction as a general set of rules.

Rule 1 It is legal for two routines to be "in the same name class" — that is, two routines with the same name may be in the same Schema.

Rule 2 Routines are distinguishable by their category. The four categories are "procedures," "functions," and two types of "method."

Rule 3 Routines in the same category are distinguishable by the count of parameters and the declared type of those parameters in their parameter list.

Because the name alone isn't enough, we have to come up with a different term to describe "what it is that distinguishes routines." The term that is in common use is "signature." The *signature* of a routine is the routine name plus the routine category plus the parameter-data-type list and it's what the DBMS uses when it needs to figure out what routine you're really trying to call.

Defining a Typed Table Based on a UDT

It's one thing to base Columns on UDTs. It's quite another thing to base Tables on UDTs. Tables based on UDTs are called "typed Tables" (or "referenceable Tables"). They are also called "the two-sided coin" because from one angle, typed Tables look like relations but from another angle they look like "instantiated classes" (to borrow a term from OO).

To make a typed Table, use the `REF` syntax: "`CREATE TABLE <Table name> OF <UDT name> ... REF IS <column name>`". For example:

```
CREATE TABLE Book
  OF book_udt REF IS self_referencing_column;
```

To execute this SQL statement, you must have the Privilege to create a Table — that is, you must be the Schema owner and you must have a `USAGE` privilege on the UDT. There are several options and there are some side effects but let us concentrate now on the OO significance; this instantiates the class.

As we said, "instantiated classes" are OO terminology. The OO equivalent for "user-defined type" is "class." In pure OO languages, creating a class (with its Attributes and methods) takes care of everything because classes are by default "instantiable" ("instantiable" is a short way to say "there can be instances of the class, namely objects based on the class definition").

This form of `CREATE TABLE` takes the Attribute definitions from a UDT and transfers them to <Column definition>s in a Table. Since `BOOK_UDT` has three Attributes — `TITLE`, `BUYING_PRICE`, `SELLING_PRICE` — the `BOOK` Table will have four Columns: <self-referencing column>, `TITLE`, `BUYING_PRICE`, `SELLING_PRICE`. Of these, only the first Column, <self-referencing column>, needs a bit of explanation.

A self-referencing Column is the equivalent of what in object-oriented terminology would be an "object identifier." All typed Tables have a self-referencing Column; that's why typed Tables are sometimes called "referenceable Tables." The point about this self-referencing Column is that it uniquely identifies a single row. Now, the row in the BOOK Table is going to be an instance of the "class" BOOK_UDT — which means a row is an object. So we'll be able to reference this object later, by referring to the value in its self-referencing Column. The name of the self-referencing Column is whatever we specify in the REF IS clause — in this case, SELF_REFERENCING_COLUMN.

There are several options for generation of self-referencing Column values. Theoretically, the best option is to derive the values from the Table's primary key. But in this phase of the discussion we'll just use the default option: SYSTEM GENERATED. In effect, with the default option, a self-referencing column is an arbitrary row identifier.

Treating a Typed Table as a Table

This is the heads side of our two-sided coin. Table BOOK is just a Table. Therefore, all these operations are legal:

```
INSERT INTO Book (title, buying_price, selling_price)
VALUES ('The compleat SQL',10.00,20.00);

UPDATE Book SET
  title = 'The Incompleat SQL';

SELECT selling_price - buying_price
FROM   Book
WHERE  title LIKE '%SQL%';
```

Notice that in the INSERT statement example, we did not trouble to specify a new value for SELF_REFERENCING_COLUMN. That is because the value is system-generated.

Now here is another operation — let us make a new Table which "references" the BOOK Table:

```
CREATE TABLE Book_chapter (
  book_ref_column REF(book),        /* a referencing Column */
  other_column CHAR(1024));         /* an ordinary Column */

INSERT INTO Book_chapter
  SELECT self_referencing_column, 'text for other column'
  FROM   Book
  WHERE  title = 'The Incompleat SQL';
```

We described the REF <data type> in Chapter 12 "Reference Types" and you can look up the details there for how REF is defined. Here, at last, is an actual use for the REF <data type>. The new row in BOOK_CHAPTER will contain a "reference" to a single row in BOOK. This is awfully similar to referencing a primary key row from a foreign key and in fact the

BOOK_CHAPTER's BOOK_REF_COLUMN can be made to have the paraphernalia of a foreign key, including ON DELETE or CASCADE options.

Treating a Typed Table as an Instantiable Class

This is the flip side of our two-sided coin. It is possible to refer to the UDT's Attributes as they are stored (instanced) in the typed Table, using references. For example:

```
book_udt_reference_value -> profit()
```

will invoke the PROFIT method on the underlying value in BOOK_UDT.

Further: if we have a "REF (book)" value to steer by, we can perform "navigational" tricks. For example, this expression is legal:

```
book_ref_column -> title
```

The result is the value in the TITLE Column of BOOK, for the row whose self-referencing Column is the value in the BOOK_REF_COLUMN of BOOK_CHAPTER.

Now, getting deeply into the object-oriented business, we arrive at the concepts of "subclasses" and "superclasses" — or, because we're using UDTs, "subtypes" and "supertypes." The concept is fairly easy to grasp if we remind ourselves that we are merely modelling the real world and in the real world the following statements are manifestly true:

- The BOOK_UDT type can be subdivided by topic — say, SCIENCE or HISTORY.
- The HISTORY type can be further subdivided into ANCIENT and MODERN, while the SCIENCE type can be further subdivided into PHYSICS and (following Lord Kelvin's famous dictum that "all science is either physics or stamp collecting") STAMP COLLECTING.

In other words, we can think of a "family of types," of which the proud single patriarch is BOOK_UDT (but we avoid the word patriarch and say "maximal supertype" instead). HISTORY and SCIENCE are subtypes of BOOK_UDT; therefore, by definition, BOOK_UDT is the supertype of HISTORY and SCIENCE. HISTORY, in turn, is the supertype of ANCIENT and MODERN, and so on.

The point of all this is: BOOK_UDT is a data type, so — like any data type — its specification includes a description of its representation and of the operations that can be performed on it. That description is applicable as well for HISTORY and for STAMP COLLECTING, unless we explicitly say otherwise; the subtype inherits the Attributes and methods of the supertype.

We could, of course, reflect some subtyping concept using purely relational operations (by joining a BOOK Table to a PHYSICS Table, for example). But the advantage of object orientation is that such operations are implicit in the definition. By declaring that a is a subtype of b, you are saying that a is automatically linked to b, so the linking process is practically invisible.

To make the above discussion concrete, here are some SQL statements that make subtypes. In these examples, the <keyword> UNDER means "as a subtype of."

```
CREATE TYPE history UNDER book_udt            NOT FINAL;
CREATE TYPE science UNDER book_udt            NOT FINAL;
CREATE TYPE modern UNDER history              NOT FINAL;
CREATE TYPE ancient UNDER history             NOT FINAL;
CREATE TYPE physics UNDER science             NOT FINAL;
CREATE TYPE stamp_collecting UNDER science    NOT FINAL;
```

Admittedly, these new types lack personality. We've kept it that way so that you can imagine for yourself what additional Attributes or methods you would want to add to the subtypes on top of the "inheritance" that they receive from the supertypes.

Finally, we can flip the coin over again and say, "if a type can have subtypes, surely the instantiation of a type can have instantiations of subtypes." In other words, Tables can have subtables:

```
CREATE TABLE History UNDER Book;
CREATE TABLE Science UNDER Book;
CREATE TABLE Ancient UNDER History;
CREATE TABLE Moderns UNDER History;
CREATE TABLE Physics UNDER Science;
CREATE TABLE Stamp_collecting UNDER Science;
```

Notice that the "subtables" and "supertables" defined are a family whose relationships match the relationships of the "subtypes" and "supertypes" on which they are based. In fact, that is a requirement.

Here endeth the tutorial.

CREATE TYPE Statement

The CREATE TYPE statement defines a UDT. The required syntax for the CREATE TYPE statement is as follows.

```
CREATE TYPE <UDT name>
[ UNDER <supertype UDT name> ]
[ AS {<predefined type> | <Attribute definition list>} ]
[ {INSTANTIABLE | NOT INSTANTIABLE} ]
{FINAL | NOT FINAL}
[ <reference type specification> ]
[ <cast option> ]
[ <method specification> [ {,<method specification> }... ] ]

   <Attribute definition list> ::=
   (<Attribute definition> [ {,<Attribute definition>}... ])

      <Attribute definition> ::=
      <Attribute name> { <data type> | <Domain name> }
      [ REFERENCES ARE [ NOT ] CHECKED [ ON DELETE
          {NO ACTION | CASCADE | RESTRICT | SET NULL | SET DEFAULT} ] ]
      [ DEFAULT default value ]
      [ COLLATE <Collation name> ]
```

```
<reference type specification> ::=
REF USING <predefined type> [ <ref cast option> ] |
REF <Attribute name> [ {,<Attribute name>} ... ] |
REF IS SYSTEM GENERATED

   <ref cast option> ::=
   [ CAST (SOURCE AS REF) WITH <cast-to-ref identifier> ]
   [ CAST (REF AS SOURCE) WITH <cast-to-type identifier> ]

<cast option> ::=
[ CAST (SOURCE AS DISTINCT) WITH <cast to distinct identifier> ]
[ CAST (DISTINCT AS SOURCE) WITH <cast to source identifier> ]

<method specification> ::=
<original method specification> |
OVERRIDING [ INSTANCE | STATIC ] <partial method specification>

   <original method specification> ::=
   [ INSTANCE | STATIC ] <partial method specification>
   [ SELF AS RESULT ] [ SELF AS LOCATOR ]
   [ LANGUAGE {ADA | C | COBOL | FORTRAN | MUMPS | PASCAL | PLI | SQL} ]
   [ PARAMETER STYLE {SQL | GENERAL} ]
   [ [ NOT ] DETERMINISTIC ]
   [ {NO SQL | CONTAINS SQL | READS SQL DATA | MODIFIES SQL DATA} ]
   [ {RETURN NULL ON NULL INPUT | CALL ON NULL INPUT} ]

   <partial method specification> ::=
   METHOD <routine name>
   (SQL parameter declaration list)
   RETURNS <data type>
```

CREATE TYPE defines a new UDT; a named set of valid data values.

- The <UDT name> identifies the UDT and the Schema to which it belongs. A <UDT name> that includes an explicit <Schema name> qualifier belongs to the Schema named. A <UDT name> that does not include an explicit <Schema name> qualifier belongs to the SQL-session default Schema. The <UDT name> must be unique (for all Domains and UDTs) within the Schema that contains it. If CREATE TYPE is part of a CREATE SCHEMA statement, the <UDT name> (if explicitly qualified) must include the <Schema name> of the Schema being created; that is, it isn't possible to create a UDT belonging to a different Schema from within CREATE SCHEMA.

There are actually three variants of CREATE TYPE, used in distinct ways:

Making structured types (garden variety UDTs)	Making structured types (subtype UDTs)	Making distinct types (not really truly UDTs)
CREATE TYPE <name>	CREATE TYPE <name>	CREATE TYPE <name>
AS <Attribute definitions>	UNDER <name>	AS <predefined type>
...	...	...
NOT FINAL	[NOT] FINAL	FINAL

If the representation clause is "AS <predefined data type>" — for example:

```
CREATE TYPE UDT_1 AS CHAR(15) FINAL
```

then this UDT is a distinct type. Usually when we talk about UDTs we mean the other kind of UDT — the structured type — because there's not much that one can do with a distinct type.

If you use a subtype clause — for example:

```
CREATE TYPE a UNDER b ...
```

you are making a new subtype under an existing supertype. The supertype must exist, it must be a structured type UDT that was defined as NOT FINAL and you must have the UNDER Privilege on it. Notice that there can be only one supertype; this means that SQL, like Java, has a "single inheritance" rule. Notice too that you can have both a subtype clause and an Attribute definition list in the same CREATE TYPE statement; this means that the subtype can have both inherited Attributes (Attributes taken from the supertype) and original Attributes (Attributes taken from the new definition, which follow the inherited Attributes).

If the representation is "... AS <Attribute list> ...", then each Attribute definition must look very much like a <Column definition> looks in a CREATE TABLE statement — for example:

```
attribute_1 CHAR(1000) CHARACTER SET ISO8BIT,
attribute_2 TIME DEFAULT TIME '12:00:00'
```

Constraints (such as NOT NULL) are illegal though. An <Attribute name> is an <identifier>; all <Attribute name>s must be unique within their UDT. The Attribute's <data type> may be a UDT, but cyclic references are illegal.

The Standard is contradictory about the instantiable clause. It's safe to assume that "instantiable," as in all OO languages, means "can be instantiated" (a "non-instantiable" or "abstract" UDT would have no instances but could have instantiable subtypes). Use of typed Tables is only possible if the type is instantiable.

In the finality clause, FINAL means (as in Java) that the new UDT may have no proper subtypes. That is, no further UDT may be created UNDER it. (There is a belief that the clause is for distinguishing distinct types from structured types. We don't believe that. We repeat that a distinct type is a UDT defined with "AS <predefined type>," all other UDTs are structured types.) If the CREATE TYPE statement contains any Attribute definitions, then NOT FINAL is mandatory. Otherwise either FINAL or NOT FINAL is mandatory.

The reference specification is either "user-generated" (REF USING), "derived" (REF <Attribute list>), or "system-generated" (REF IS SYSTEM GENERATED). With the default, REF

IS SYSTEM GENERATED, there is no further specification because values are implementation-dependent. With the main option, REF USING, there is a further specification; the <Attribute name> list. Because (as in pure relational systems) a row's uniqueness should depend on Column values, the <Attribute name>s here would be an indirect list of a "key value."

The cast option is legal only for distinct types. The cast's source and target <data type>s are the <predefined type> specified earlier in the CREATE TYPE statement and the name of the UDT, respectively.

A UDT's methods are defined in pretty well the same way as functions; indeed a method is a function, albeit a function which cannot live without its UDT and which is called in a slightly different way than a regular function. The default method characteristics are LANGUAGE SQL, PARAMETER STYLE SQL, NOT DETERMINISTIC, CONTAINS SQL, RETURN NULL ON NULL INPUT. (Note: Although the Standard says that NOT DETERMINISTIC is the default, it's hard to believe that this is the true intent.) The difference between an "overriding" and an "original" method is that an overriding method "overrides" an already-existing method with the same name, in some supertype. Method signatures must be distinct. Remember that, as noted in the tutorial section of this chapter, structured UDTs have implicitly-created methods; one constructor method for the UDT as a whole, *n* mutator methods (one for each Attribute), and *n* observer methods (one for each Attribute). As for distinct types — apparently no implicitly-created methods exist for them, but there may be a "transform" function for casting to/from host languages.

Distinct Types

The simplest way to make a UDT is with:

```
CREATE TYPE <UDT name> AS <predefined data type> FINAL;
```

which — because it has no Attribute list — is not a specification of a "structured type" with all the OO trimmings. Instead, UDTs made this way are called "distinct types." The main idea behind distinct types is that they constitute enforceable domains. For example, suppose we define two currency data types:

```
CREATE TYPE euro AS DECIMAL(8,2) FINAL;

CREATE TYPE mark AS DECIMAL(8,2) FINAL;
```

If we now attempt to pass a euro value to a mark target, we will fail — the distinct type provides us with a simple form of type checking that we cannot achieve using an SQL Domain.

Distinct types have methods just like structured types. However, they are limited in various ways. Usually, when we make generalized comments about object-orientation analogies — such as "UDTs are classes" — we have structured types in mind, not distinct types.

CREATE TABLE Statement

We've already shown you the CREATE TABLE statement in Chapter 18 "SQL Tables and Views." However, there are two options to add to that description now for Object/Relational Tables.

The first option has to do with the creation of typed Tables. Here's the syntax:

```
CREATE TABLE <Table name>
OF <UDT name>
...
[ REF IS <self-referencing Column name>
   {SYSTEM GENERATED | USER GENERATED | DERIVED} ]
```

In addition to the usual rules for Table creation, here are other rules to follow when you use this syntax:

- You must have the USAGE Privilege on <UDT name>.
- <UDT name> must specify a structured UDT.
- The optional REF clause may appear within the Table element list (that is, inside the parentheses along with the Column and Constraint definitions). The <self-referencing Column name> must be a valid and distinct <identifier>. The three options associated with "REF IS ..." are (like CREATE TYPE's REF clause) either "user-generated," "derived," or "system-generated." With the default — SYSTEM GENERATED — the Column values are implementation-dependent. With the main option — DERIVED — Column values come from the Table's primary key. A typed Table always has one self-referencing Column and its position within the Table is fixed; it is always the first Column in the Table. The "REF IS ..." clause only specifies a few details about the self-referencing Column. Note: typed Tables are known (sometimes) as "referenceable Tables" and (rarely) as "object UDTs."

The second option has to do with the creation of subtables. Here's the syntax:

```
CREATE TABLE <subtable name>
...
UNDER <supertable name>
...
```

In addition to the usual rules for Table creation, here are other rules to follow when you use this syntax:

- You must have the UNDER Privilege on <supertable name>.
- Both the subtable and the supertable must be typed Tables.
- The subtable/supertable relationship must mirror the subtype/supertype relationship. For example: if ty1 is a subtype of ty2, and ta1 is a typed Table based on ty1 and ta2 is a typed Table based on ty2, then it is legal to create ta1 UNDER ta2 — but it is not legal to create ta2 UNDER ta1.

CREATE CAST Statement

With UDTs, you'll need some way of assigning UDT values to predefined <data type> targets or vice versa. Further, if you have two distinct UDTs — say UDT1 and UDT2 — then you'll also need some way to assign values based on UDT1 to UDT2 targets or vice versa. This might all be complicated by the fact that subtypes contain their supertypes' Attributes which should imply a degree of mutual assignability. In sum, you need the ability to "cast" a UDT to or from another data type. The solution is to create a user-defined cast for the chosen

<data type>s with the CREATE CAST statement. The required syntax for the CREATE CAST statement is as follows.

```
CREATE CAST (<source type> AS <target type>)
WITH <specific routine designator>
[ AS ASSIGNMENT ]
```

A UDT value is assignable to a UDT target only if the source value is a subtype of the target UDT. There can be only one user-defined cast for any given combination of source and target types. Either <source type> or <target type> must be either UDT or REF but the other operand can be any <data type>. To execute CREATE CAST, you must be the owner of both the cast function (identified by <specific routine designator>) and the <target type> (if it is a UDT).

The <specific routine designator> is usually a signature — for example, "FUNCTION f (SMALLINT)" can be a <specific routine designator>. It is also possible to identify a routine using a specific name, which is a unique, possibly mangled, name that is usually assigned by the DBMS. The cast function identified by the <specific routine designator> must have the general form:

```
FUNCTION <name> (<source type>) RETURNS <target type>
... DETERMINISTIC
... { NO SQL | CONTAINS SQL }
...
```

AS ASSIGNMENT (which is not the default) means that the cast is "implicitly invocable" during assignment operations. That is, if x is UDT_1 and there is an implicitly-invocable cast, then this is a legal assignment:

```
x = 'F'
```

Otherwise, this is a legal assignment:

```
x = CAST ('F' AS UDT_1)
```

[Obscure Rule] An assignment might involve a choice between several possible "implicitly invocable" cast functions. The DBMS picks the one that fits these criteria:

- It's an implicitly-invocable cast function — i.e., it was mentioned with AS ASSIGNABLE.
- The cast function's result <data type> is the target's declared type.
- The cast function has one parameter and that parameter has a "declared type," and that declared type is in the "type precedence list" of the declared type of the source value. If there are two cast functions which meet all these requirements, the DBMS picks the one whose declared type is highest in the "type precedence list."

TIP: If you decide to make a user-defined cast for "a to b", be reciprocal; make a user-defined cast for "b to a" as well. Users expect all casts to be two-way.

TIP: For hierarchy's sake; if A1 is a supertype of A2 and B1 is a supertype of B2, then make casts from A1 to B1 and from A2 to B2 — not A1 to B2 nor A2 to B1. That is, cast from super to super and from sub to sub.

Here is a user-defined cast for the BOOK_UDT type which we used in earlier examples. The UDT has three Attributes (title CHAR(40), buying_price DECIMAL(9,2), selling_price DECIMAL(9,2)). Because each Attribute's type is either CHAR or castable to CHAR, we'll make a function which simply concatenates each Attribute into one big character string. Here's how:

```
CREATE FUNCTION f (book_udt) RETURNS CHAR(80)
  DETERMINISTIC CONTAINS SQL
  BEGIN
    DECLARE c CHAR(60);
    SET c = book_udt.title()
          ||
          CAST(book_udt.buying_price() AS char(20))
          ||
          CAST(book_udt.selling_price() AS char(20));
    RETURN (u);
END;
```

Now that we have a function, we can make a cast for the function:

```
CREATE CAST (book_udt AS CHAR(60))
WITH FUNCTION f (book_udt);
```

Now that we have a cast, we can use BOOK_UDT in a CAST expression:

```
SELECT CAST(book_udt AS CHAR(60))
FROM   Books;
```

Thus, we can design our own external representation of a UDT without worrying about its internal representation.

For distinct type UDTs only, the DBMS automatically creates two casts. For example, if you make this UDT:

```
CREATE TYPE longitude AS REAL FINAL;
```

the DBMS will make these two casts for it:

```
CREATE CAST (longitude AS REAL) ... AS ASSIGNMENT;
CREATE CAST (REAL AS longitude) ... AS ASSIGNMENT;
```

Now, suppose you have a variable lo of type LONGITUDE. Because of the automatic cast, it's legal to cast a <literal> to LONGITUDE, for example:

```
SET lo = CAST (33.59 AS longitude);
```

Not only that, though! The casts are AS ASSIGNMENT casts, so this SQL statement is also legal:

```
SET lo = 33.59;
```

The AS ASSIGNMENT feature, which got into the SQL Standard at a very late stage, is bound to confuse some people; they'll think that "distinct types" are just a way to rename predefined <data type>s. That would be a delusion. The reason that SET lo = 33.59; is legal is that there is an implicit cast (the DBMS makes it silently) which happens to be an implicitly-invoked cast (it contains an AS ASSIGNMENT clause).

TIP: Implicitly invocable casts are convenient but error-prone. If you don't want to allow loosely-typed phrases like money_column = 5.00, you should DROP the cast that the DBMS created and then explicitly make it again — but without specifying AS ASSIGNMENT in the definition.

CREATE ORDERING Statement

For UDT values, you'll need some way of knowing that "udt-value-1 is greater than udt-value-2" or less or equal. Otherwise you'll be unable to use UDTs in search conditions, in ORDER BY clauses, in GROUP BY clauses, or after the word DISTINCT. The solution is to create an ordering for the UDT with the CREATE ORDERING statement. The required syntax for the CREATE ORDERING statement is as follows.

```
CREATE ORDERING FOR <UDT name>
{EQUALS ONLY BY | ORDER FULL BY}
<ordering category>

   <ordering category> ::=
   RELATIVE WITH <specific routine designator> |
   HASH WITH <specific routine designator> |
   STATE [ <specific name> ]
```

A UDT value is comparable to another UDT value only if both UDTs are in the same subtype family. There can be only one ordering for a UDT. To execute CREATE ORDERING, you must be the owner of both the UDT and routine named in the <ordering category>. Because UDTs in the same type family are related, all orderings for UDTs within the same type family must all be defined either with EQUALS ONLY BY or with ORDER FULL BY.

A <specific routine designator> is usually a signature. For example, FUNCTION f (SMALLINT) can be a <specific routine designator>. It is also possible to identify a routine using a <specific name>; an additional routine name used to uniquely identify a routine. A routine's <specific name> is usually assigned by the DBMS. The ordering routine must be DETERMINISTIC and must not possibly modify SQL-data.

The <ordering category> "RELATIVE WITH <specific routine designator>" is legal only for maximal supertypes (i.e., types that have no proper supertypes of their own). RELATIVE WITH functions have two parameters (both are UDT types) and return an INTEGER.

The <ordering category> "HASH WITH <specific routine designator>" is legal for subtypes, but only if their supertypes are also defined with HASH WITH orderings. Typically, the <specific routine designator> named will identify an observer method for one of the UDT's Attributes. HASH WITH functions have one parameter (its type is UDT) and return a predefined <data type>.

The <ordering category> STATE is legal only for maximal supertypes. If you specify STATE, the DBMS implicitly creates a function named EQUALS. It is the duty of the EQUALS function to return TRUE if all Attribute values are equal.

Because the ordering routine is user-defined, it's impossible to say exactly what the various ordering categories imply. The following is a generalization:

- An EQUALS function returns TRUE if all values are equal; otherwise it returns FALSE. It never returns UNKNOWN.
- A RELATIVE function returns an integer value less than zero for less than values, returns zero for equal values, and returns an integer greater than zero for greater than values.
- A HASH function returns an absolute ordering within the predefined <data type>.

Here's an example of CREATE ORDERING:

```
CREATE ORDERING FOR book_udt
ORDER FULL BY HASH WITH
   FUNCTION title (book_udt);        /* observer function for title Attribute */
```

There is no need to create an ordering for a distinct type. As with casts, the DBMS implicitly does the following when CREATE TYPE is executed:

```
CREATE ORDERING FOR <UDT name>
ORDER FULL BY HASH WITH
   FUNCTION <Schema name>.<cast-to-source identifier> (<UDT name>);
```

Comparisons of distinct types work exactly the same way as comparisons of the predefined <data type>s on which they are based.

TIP: When you create a maximal supertype, make sure to execute a CREATE ORDERING statement for that type. When you create a subtype, the matter is less urgent because subtypes inherit from their supertypes.

Other Processes for Object/Relational Users

There are several other SQL statements and expressions which are useful, but not vital, when working with Object/Relational SQL. All of these statements are simply analogs of statements we have already seen; only the type of Schema Object is different. We therefore limit ourselves to noting their existence here, in the hope that you'll find the details to be intuitive.

ALTER TYPE Statement

The ALTER TYPE statement lets you change the definition of a UDT. The required syntax for the ALTER TYPE statement is as follows.

```
ALTER TYPE <UDT name> <alter type action>

      <alter type action> ::=
      ADD ATTRIBUTE <Attribute definition> |
      DROP ATTRIBUTE <Attribute name>
```

CREATE METHOD Statement

The CREATE METHOD statement lets you make a new method — it's actually a special form of the CREATE FUNCTION statement. The required syntax for the CREATE METHOD statement is as follows.

```
CREATE [ INSTANCE | STATIC ] METHOD <routine name>
(SQL parameter declaration list)
RETURNS <data type>
FOR <UDT name>
[ SPECIFIC <specific name> ]
<routine body>
```

(See Chapter 25 "SQL-Invoked Routines" for a definition of <routine body>.)

A method is a function which is associated with a UDT. Methods and functions can look quite different, even when they're the same thing. Consider these two examples:

```
CREATE FUNCTION f
(book_udt)
RETURNS FLOAT
```

```
CREATE METHOD f
()
RETURNS FLOAT
FOR book_udt
```

These examples — shorn of unnecessary detail — illustrate a confusing fact; the function and the method are the same thing! When you want to list a method's parameters, you should "augment" the parameter list by adding one parameter, called the "self" parameter, in ordinal position 1.

CREATE TRANSFORM Statement

The CREATE TRANSFORM statement lets you make a method that will be used in casting for host languages. The required syntax for the CREATE TRANSFORM statement is as follows.

```
CREATE {TRANSFORM | TRANSFORMS} FOR <UDT name>
<group name>
(<transform element> [ {,<transform element>} ... ])
```

```
<transform element> ::=
TO SQL WITH <specific routine designator> |
FROM SQL WITH <specific routine designator>
```

A *transform* is an SQL-invoked function that is automatically invoked when you transfer UDT values to and from a host language program. It identifies one or two functions — each identified by a <group name> (the name is either an <identifier> or the <keyword> DEFAULT).

The transform's TO SQL function casts a predefined <data type> value to a UDT value and gets invoked whenever a UDT value is passed to the DBMS by a host language program or external routine. The transform's FROM SQL function casts a UDT value to a predefined <data type> value and gets invoked whenever a UDT value is passed from the DBMS to a host language program or external routine.

DROP CAST Statement

The DROP CAST statement lets you destroy a user-defined cast. The required syntax for the DROP CAST statement is as follows.

```
DROP CAST (<source type> AS <target type>) {CASCADE | RESTRICT}
```

DROP ORDERING Statement

The DROP ORDERING statement lets you destroy an ordering for a UDT. The required syntax for the DROP ORDERING statement is as follows.

```
DROP ORDERING FOR <UDT name> {CASCADE | RESTRICT}
```

DROP TRANSFORM Statement

The DROP TRANSFORM statement lets you destroy a transform. The required syntax for the DROP TRANSFORM statement is as follows.

```
DROP TRANSFORM {ALL | <group name>} FOR <UDT name>
     {CASCADE | RESTRICT}
```

DROP TYPE Statement

The DROP TYPE statement lets you destroy a UDT. The required syntax for the DROP TYPE statement is as follows.

```
DROP TYPE <UDT name> {CASCADE | RESTRICT}
```

NEW Statement

The NEW statement lets you invoke a method on a newly-constructed value of a structured type. The required syntax for the NEW statement is as follows.

```
NEW <method invocation>
```

TREAT Statement

The TREAT statement lets you modify the declared type of a structured type expression to a type of one of its supertypes. The required syntax for the TREAT statement is as follows.

```
TREAT (<subtype expression> AS <target UDT>)
```

DEREF Function

The DEREF function (or <reference resolution>) lets you obtain the data value referenced by a <reference type>. The required syntax is as follows (for details, see Chapter 12 "Reference Types").

```
<reference resolution> ::=
DEREF (reference_argument)
```

SPECIFICTYPE Function

The SPECIFICTYPE function returns an SQL_TEXT character string containing the fully-qualified name of the UDT to which a given value belongs. The required syntax is as follows.

```
<specifictype function> ::=
SPECIFICTYPE (UDT value expression)
```

Dereference Operation

The <dereference operation> allows you to access a Column of the row identified by a REF value. The required syntax is as follows (for details, see Chapter 12 "Reference Types").

```
<dereference operation> ::=
reference_argument -> <Attribute name>
```

TYPE Predicate

The TYPE Predicate returns TRUE if a given value is within the set of values defined by a UDT (or by a list of UDTs which are all in the same subtype family). The required syntax is as follows.

```
<type predicate> ::=
<UDT value expression> IS [ NOT ] OF
([ ONLY ] <UDT-name-1> [ {,<UDT-name-2>} ... ])
```

Is Object/Relational Really Object-Oriented?

Is O/R really OO? Let's go through the features that are considered to be standard parts of an object-oriented specification and see whether SQL3 delivers them. (In this list, "UDT" means "UDTs which are structured types.")

Classes UDTs are classes. SQL3 vocabulary may include words like "type family" where most languages' vocabulary would have "class family," but the essential functionality is the same.

Encapsulation SQL3 keeps data representation separate from data access, but does not allow for PRIVATE and PUBLIC Attribute definitions — those are matters for `GRANT` and `REVOKE` to handle.

Extensibility It is possible to put together packages consisting of new type families, methods, and representations. Such packages exist today, although to a large extent — for efficiency reasons — the methods are external functions written in some other language.

Inheritance A UDT may be defined under another UDT. Subtypes inherit the methods and Attributes of their supertypes. Inheritance is single as in most pure object-oriented languages.

Instantiation SQL3's UDTs may be used in place of predefined <data type>s in SQL-data statements. Rows in typed Tables may be treated as objects complete with object identifiers.

Introspection SQL already has a clean way to find out what a database's structural components are: `INFORMATION_SCHEMA`. It should be no big deal to put wrappers around SQL statements that `SELECT` from `INFORMATION_SCHEMA`. Unfortunately, it is more likely that wrappers will instead be put around the unwieldy CLI Catalog functions (see Chapter 51 "SQL/CLI: Catalog Functions").

Polymorphism Multiple methods in a type family may have the same name. The DBMS will choose the specific method based on the signature. This is Java-like.

It should be admitted that, like any hybrid, SQL3 will look bad to purists on both sides. The relational theorists will note that SQL3's new features — especially self-referencing columns — allow for "pointer-chasing" demons which we thought were buried along with pre-SQL DBMSs. The object-oriented aficionados may decry the ease with which encapsulation can be broken, at least in appearance, by recourse to SQL-92 manipulation methods. From both directions, SQL3 will get flak as a chimera — a monster with a lion's head on a goat's body with a serpent's tail — which certainly betrays its origins as an animal designed by a committee.

All such criticisms are beside the point though. SQL3 was put together to meet certain needs which are urgent in the current market environment:

- To meld with object-oriented host languages, especially Java.
- To allow for multi-media extensions.
- To preempt the chaos which would result from non-standard vendor definitions or competition from pure OO DBMSs.

Given these goals, Object/Relational SQL3 is a reasonable development. We now wait to see whether users will find that it truly meets these urgent needs.

Dialects

Some SQL vendors have already introduced Object/Relational features. We give special note to the following vendors.

UniSQL A smaller group, which gained note in 1992 for being the first to introduce an Object/Relational SQL (though some O/R features can be traced all the way back to 1980s versions of DB2 and Ingres).

IBM Offers "relational extenders," which are packages containing UDTs, user-defined functions, triggers, and constraints. At the moment, IBM's "universal database" is probably the implementation which is closest to the SQL3 Object/Relational spec.

Informix Bought Illustra (one of the Object/Relational pioneers) and since then has won some praise for its DataBlades™ plug-ins which are described as data-type extensions — that is, Informix emphasizes the utility of defining your own data types, rather than the purported benefits of OO.

Oracle Oracle8's "cartridges" are another name for what we might call "class libraries" in pure OO contexts. So far, most cartridges have been multimedia packages, for example "Video cartridges" and "Spatial cartridges." For performance reasons, Oracle's Object/Relational features have not been popular among its users until recently.

And finally, watch Sun. The world is waiting to see the impact of JavaBlend™ which purportedly will merge Java with SQL3's Object/Relational extensions.

28

Chapter 28

Introduction to SQL-Data Operations

In this chapter, we'll describe some common SQL constructs. We'll be using these constructs in the following chapters to describe how operations on SQL-data work. [Obscure Rule] applies to everything we talk about here but the definitions are a necessary evil for understanding some of what lies ahead.

<value specification>

A <value specification> is a scalar expression that specifies either a <literal>, a host language variable parameter, or an SQL parameter as a source for a data value. The required syntax for a <value specification> is as follows.

```
<value specification> ::=
<literal> |
<general value specification>
```

```
<general value specification> ::=
<host parameter name> [ [ INDICATOR ] <host parameter name> ] |
<SQL parameter reference> |
<element reference> |
CURRENT_PATH |
CURRENT_ROLE |
CURRENT_USER |
SESSION_USER |
SYSTEM_USER |
USER |
VALUE

<simple value specification> ::=
<literal> |
<host parameter name> |
<SQL parameter reference>
```

A <value specification> specifies a value that is not selected from a Table — i.e., a <value specification> is either the value represented by a <literal>, the value represented by a host language variable, or the value represented by an SQL parameter. A <simple value specification> is either a <literal>, the value of a host language variable, or the value of an SQL parameter; it may not be the null value. If a <simple value specification> does evaluate to `NULL`, the SQL statement that contains it will fail; your DBMS will return the `SQLSTATE error 22004` "`data exception-null value not allowed.`"

A host parameter specification identifies a host parameter (or a host parameter and its indicator) in an SQL-client Module. If the indicator for a host parameter is set to a negative number, that means the value represented by the host parameter is `NULL`. If the indicator is set to any other number, that means the value represented by the host parameter is the current value of that host parameter. The required syntax for a <host parameter name> is as follows.

```
<host parameter name> ::=
:<identifier>
```

A <host parameter name> is a <regular identifier> or a <delimited identifier> preceded by a colon (for example, `:param_name`). The <identifier> identifies a host language parameter, so the name you choose must also, of course, be a valid parameter name in that host language. Each <identifier> that is a <host parameter name> must be declared in the SQL-client Module in which it will be used. The indicator for a host parameter has to be an integer type. We'll talk more about host parameters and variables in Chapters 39, 40, and 52 on binding styles.

An <SQL parameter reference> identifies a parameter of an SQL-invoked routine, so it can be the name of a function that returns only one value (for example, `CURRENT_ROLE`) or an <SQL parameter name>. (For the syntax of an <SQL parameter name>, see Chapter 25 "SQL-Invoked Routines.") The value represented by an <SQL parameter reference> is the current value of that SQL parameter.

An <element reference> identifies an element of an array; see Chapter 10 "Collection Types." The value represented by an <element reference> is the current value of that element in that particular array.

CURRENT_ROLE, CURRENT_USER, SESSION_USER, SYSTEM_USER, and USER all identify an <AuthorizationID>; see Chapter 15 "AuthorizationIDs." The value represented by any of these functions is the current value returned by that function; each returns an SQL_TEXT character string whose value represents an <AuthorizationID>.

CURRENT_PATH identifies a <Schema name> list that helps your DBMS track routines. In the list, both the <Schema name>s and their qualifying <Catalog name>s are <delimited identifier>s and multiple <Schema name>s are separated by commas.

[NON-PORTABLE] The result of CURRENT_PATH is non-standard because the SQL Standard requires implementors to define whether the result string is fixed length or variable length and the result string's fixed length or maximum length (as applicable).

[OCELOT Implementation] The OCELOT DBMS that comes with this book has CURRENT_PATH return a variable length SQL_TEXT string. The result has a maximum length of 128 octets.

VALUE identifies an instance of a data value and is usually used only in a Domain definition; see Chapter 19 "SQL Domains."

[Obscure Rule] If the <data type> of a <value specification> is character string, the character string it represents has a coercibility attribute of COERCIBLE.

If you want to restrict your code to Core SQL, don't use an <element reference> or CURRENT_PATH to specify a value.

<value expression>

A <value expression> is an expression that specifies a data value. In this book, we most often use the term scalar_expression to show you where a <value expression> is allowed in SQL syntax. The required syntax for a <value expression> is as follows.

```
<value expression> ::=
<numeric value expression> |
<string value expression> |
<datetime value expression> |
<interval value expression> |
<boolean value expression> |
<UDT value expression> |
<row value expression> |
<reference value expression> |
<collection value expression>
```

A <value expression> specifies a value that may or may not be selected from a Table — that is, it may be a <value specification> or it may be the result of an expression on SQL-data that returns a single number, character string, bit string, BLOB, date, time, timestamp, interval, Boolean value, UDT value, row of data, REF value, or array. The <data type> of a <value expression> is determined by the <data type> of the value to which it evaluates.

The following SQL constructs all qualify as <value expression>s; each can optionally include a Collation specification (i.e., `COLLATE` <Collation name>) to force a collating sequence for the value represented by the <value expression> provided that value's <data type> is character string:

- A <Column reference> — represents the value of that Column.
- A set function specification — represents the value returned by that function.
- A scalar subquery — represents the value returned by that subquery.
- A `CASE` expression — represents the value returned by that expression.
- A `CAST` specification — represents the value as `CAST` to the target <data type>.
- A `TREAT` result — represents the value as modified.
- A <dereference operation> — represents the value returned by that function.
- An <array value expression> — represents the value of that array.
- A <routine invocation> — represents the value returned by that routine.
- A <Field reference> — represents the value of that Field of a particular row.
- A <method invocation> and a <method reference> — represent the value returned by that method.

If you want to restrict your code to Core SQL, don't use a <value expression> that evaluates to a Boolean value, an array, an interval, or a `REF` value; don't use `TREAT`; and don't use the `COLLATE` clause to force a collating sequence for any value.

<row value constructor>

A <row value constructor> defines an ordered set of values that make up one row of data. The required syntax for a <row value constructor> is as follows.

```
<row value constructor> ::=
<value expression> |
(<value expression> [ {,<value expression>} ... ]) |
<row subquery>
```

A <row value constructor> constructs a row of data values in one of three possible ways:

1. By evaluating a single <value expression>, for example, the <character string literal> `'GOODBYE'`. In this case, the <value expression> may not be enclosed in parentheses. This rule is explicitly stated in the SQL Standard to resolve a syntactic ambiguity; in certain circumstances, the syntax: (<value expression>) is permitted.
2. By evaluating two or more comma-delimited <value expression>s enclosed in parentheses, for example: `('GOODBYE',10)`.
3. By evaluating a <row subquery>, for example:

```
... (SELECT column_2, column_5 FROM Table_2)
```

The <data type>s of the Column(s) of a <row value constructor> are the <data type>s of the <value expression>(s) or the Column(s) of the <row subquery> that make up the <row value constructor>. If a <row value constructor> is derived from a <row subquery>, then the degree (i.e., the number of Columns) of the <row value constructor> is the degree of the Table that results from the evaluation of the <row subquery>; otherwise, the degree of the <row value constructor> is the number of <value expression>s that make up the <row value constructor>.

In this case, if the number of rows returned by the <row subquery> is zero, the result is a single row containing null values for every Column of the <row subquery>. If the number of rows returned by the subquery is one, the result is that single row. (Note: a <row subquery> may not return more than one row.)

<target specification>

A <target specification> is a scalar expression that specifies a host language variable parameter, an SQL parameter, or a Column as the target for a data value. The required syntax for a <target specification> is as follows.

```
<target specification> ::=
<host parameter name> [ [ INDICATOR ] <host parameter name> ] |
<SQL parameter name> |
<Column reference>
```

A <target specification> specifies a place to put a value. Most often, this will be a <Column reference> (as in an `INSERT` statement) but you can also assign values to an output SQL parameter (see Chapter 25 "SQL-Invoked Routines") or to a variable in a host language program (see Chapters 39, 40, and 52 on binding styles). A <simple target specification> is either a host language variable, an output SQL parameter, or a "known not nullable" Column; it may not be the null value.

29

Chapter 29

Simple Search Conditions

We've come at last to the point where we can begin showing you the most important aspect of SQL — how to query your "database." In this chapter, we'll begin by describing simple search conditions.

Truth Values

In our chapter on the Boolean <data type>, we noted what SQL's truth values are: TRUE, FALSE, and UNKNOWN. But what are truth values for? There are four possible answers to that question:

1. To support conditional branches and loops, as in traditional programming languages. There are optional SQL3 constructs like "IF (condition is TRUE) THEN (perform this operation)." We discussed program control operations in Chapter 26 "PSM; Not Just Persistent Stored Modules."
2. To store in the database. For that, we have the BOOLEAN <data type>.
3. To support the CASE expression.
4. To support relational restriction.

It is answer #4 — "to support relational restriction" — that most people think of first. Commonly, they would use simple terms for the process — like "finding" or "searching" — because the essence of the affair is indeed simple — they just want to pick certain rows from a Table; say, the ones where the NAME Column contains Smith or the ones where the value in the SPENDING Column is greater than the value in the BUDGET Column. These are such simple questions that they seem trite, but they already illustrate some distinguishing features of SQL searching.

First of all, they show that rows are picked by content, not by address. Although most SQL packages have some option for selecting rows according to their position or ordinal location, the makers of relational theory did not intend that to be an important part of the search process.

Secondarily, they show that Column values must meet certain conditions (such as being equal or being greater). We can easily contrive exceptions to this statement; for example some searches do not involve Column values. But certainly the idea that "conditions must be met" is universal. For successful searching, you have to know how to conceive and specify these conditions.

As we said at the beginning, in this chapter we will concern ourselves only with the simpler conditional expressions which are necessary for searching. Before we do that, though, we'll briefly discuss the SQL statement that you will use with search conditions most often — the SELECT statement.

SELECT Statement

The SELECT statement retrieves data from one or more Tables. Here is the required syntax for a simple SELECT statement (or, as the SQL Standard calls it, a <query specification>):

```
SELECT [ DISTINCT | ALL ]
{Column expression [ AS name ]} [ ,... ] | *
FROM <Table reference> [ {,<Table reference>} ... ]
[ WHERE search condition ]
[ GROUP BY Columns [ HAVING condition ] ]
```

The SELECT statement queries your SQL-data; it returns a results Table derived from the Tables referred to in the FROM clause. The derivation of the result Table can be described as a sequence of operations in which the result of each operation is input for the next. The sequence of the operations is FROM, then WHERE, then GROUP BY, then HAVING, then the select list (that is, the list of Column expressions), and the descriptions of the clauses that follow appear in this order.

FROM Clause

The FROM clause supplies a list of <Table references> for the query. A <Table reference> is any expression which results in a Table but is usually just a <Table name> or a <Correlation name> that identifies a Table that contains SQL-data you want to query. <Column name>s throughout the SELECT statement must be unambiguous; that is, they must be qualified with a <Correlation name> if one was defined for the Table that owns them and with their <Table name> if SELECT is retrieving data from multiple Tables which have Columns with identical names. The required syntax for the FROM clause is as follows.

```
FROM <Table reference> [ {,<Table reference>} ... ]
```

Table Reference

Several times throughout this book, we make the comment that the result of an SQL query is a Table. To understand the entire syntax that you may use to formulate a query then, you'll have to start with what a Table is — and we've already shown you that a Table is a set of Columns and rows. Up until now, though, whenever we've talked about Tables, we've referred to them only with a <Table name>. Because the result of a query is a Table derived by evaluating that query, not all SQL Tables have an explicit <Table name> — so SQL allows you to refer to any Table using a <Table reference>. The required syntax for a <Table reference> is as follows.

```
<Table reference> ::=
[ ONLY ]{<Table name> | <query name>} [ [ AS ] <Correlation name>
   [ (<derived Column list>) ] ] |
<Table subquery> [ AS ] <Correlation name>
   [ (<derived Column list>) ] |
<joined Table> |
LATERAL (<query expression>) [ AS ] <Correlation name>
   [ (<derived Column list>) ]

   <derived Column list> ::=
   <Column name> [ {,<Column name> }... ]
```

A <Table reference> is simply a reference to some Table; this may be a reference to a named Table (that is, a <Table name> that identifies a Base table or a View) or a reference to a Table returned by a query. Thus there are five possible options for a <Table reference>:

1. It can refer to a Base table or a View using a <Table name>. The optional <keyword> `ONLY` in front of such a reference can only be used if the reference is to a typed Table. In that case, the <Table reference> refers to every row of the Table (or result Table), except for any rows that have a subrow in a proper subtable of that Table.
2. It can refer to a result Table using a <query name>.
3. It can refer to the result of a Table subquery.
4. It can refer to the result of a join of multiple Tables.
5. It can refer to a lateral Table; the result of a parenthesized <query expression> preceded by the <keyword> `LATERAL`.

In each case, you can optionally provide a <Correlation name> for the Table being referred to, as well as explicit names for each of the Columns belonging to the Table being referred to (the names specified must, of course, be unique for that reference).

If you want to restrict your code to Core SQL, don't use a <query name> to make up a <Table reference> and don't use the <keyword> `ONLY` to make up a <Table reference> that refers to a typed Table.

WHERE Clause

The optional WHERE clause is used to set the retrieval conditions for rows. Any rows that don't fall into the guidelines specified are eliminated from the results Table. The search conditions specified may include the arithmetic and Boolean operators, the SQL predicates (e.g., comparison, BETWEEN, LIKE), and the SQL scalar functions, as well as parentheses to set the desired evaluation order. The required syntax for the WHERE clause is as follows.

```
WHERE <search condition>
```

GROUP BY Clause

The optional GROUP BY clause logically rearranges the interim result returned by the WHERE clause into groups. The result is a set of rows where each common datum is gathered into one group. That is, within a group, all values of a grouping Column are the same value. For grouping, all NULLs are considered equal; they form one group. Because every row that contains a group contains the same value for that group, the name of a grouping Column can be used in a condition for the HAVING clause or to identify a result Column in the select list. We'll show you the required syntax for the GROUP BY clause in Chapter 33 "Searching with Groups."

HAVING Clause

The optional HAVING clause is used to set the retrieval conditions for groups. Any groups that don't fall into the guidelines specified are eliminated from the results Table. The search conditions specified may include the arithmetic and Boolean operators, the SQL predicates (e.g., comparison, BETWEEN, LIKE), and the SQL scalar functions, as well as parentheses to set the desired evaluation order. HAVING is normally applied to the interim result returned by the GROUP BY clause. If a SELECT statement doesn't include a GROUP BY clause, then HAVING treats all rows of the interim result as a single group. We'll show you the required syntax for the HAVING clause in Chapter 33 "Searching with Groups."

SELECT LIST Clause

The select list produces a final results Table by selecting only those Columns (or Column expressions) specified. The select list may include <Column name>s, <Column reference>s, Column expressions (that is, any expression which evaluates to a single Column, such as a scalar subquery), or an asterisk, as well as one of the <keyword>s DISTINCT or ALL. (The asterisk is a shorthand for a list of all the Columns of the Tables named in the FROM clause. The DISTINCT option ensures that duplicate rows are eliminated from the result. The ALL option, which is the default, ensures that duplicate rows are included in the result.) A Column expression can be a <literal>, a scalar function or some other expression derived from the Columns whose values you want to retrieve but may not include any expression that will evaluate to a Column with a BLOB, CLOB, or NCLOB <data type> if DISTINCT is specified. You can use the optional AS name clause to specify a name for a Column expression; it will be used to identify that result for the entire SELECT statement. The required syntax for a select list is as follows.

```
SELECT [ ALL | DISTINCT ] Column list

   Column list ::=
   expression [ [ AS ] <Column name> ] [ , ... ] |
   *
```

Let's try some SELECT examples on a small group of Tables. They look like this (a question mark in a Column represents a null value):

DEPARTMENT

DEPT	MANAGER	FUNCTION	CODE
A	SMITH A	ACCOUNTING	1
B	JONES B	INF SYSTEMS	2
C	BROWN C	CUST REL	3
D	BLACK D	OPERATIONS	4
E	GREEN E	SALES	5

EMPLOYEE

EMPNUM	DEPT	SURNAME	GNAME	ADDRESS
1	A	KOO	SARA	234 WEST
2	B	MARSH	JOHN	456 EAST
3	C	JONES	MABEL	567 NORTH
4	D	MORGAN	CHUCK	963 SOUTH
10	A	SMITH	ALICE	234 WEST
11	B	JONES	BOB	325 RIVER
20	E	FRANCIS	CHRIS	861 BERLIN
28	B	TURNER	LINDA	114 ROBIN
35	E	OLSEN	CAROL	555 RIVER
40	B	WARREN	NANCY	?

PAYROLL

EMPNUM	RATE	LOCATION	PAID	APPT
1	6.00	10TH FLOOR	1989-10-31	10:15:00
2	5.00	16TH FLOOR	1989-09-30	10:20:00
3	5.00	WAREHOUSE	1989-09-30	10:30:00
4	8.00	BASEMENT	1989-10-15	12:00:10
10	16.00	16TH FLOOR	1989-09-30	12:30:00

PAYROLL

11	16.00	16TH FLOOR	1989-10-15	13:15:10
20	9.00	WAREHOUSE	1989-10-15	14:00:00
28	?	16TH FLOOR	1989-09-15	14:10:00
35	9.00	10TH FLOOR	1989-10-31	14:20:00
40	16.00	10TH FLOOR	1989-10-31	14:35:07

Simple Retrieval

To find all departments with employees (retrieve a single Column from a Table), the following SQL statements are equivalent:

```
SELECT dept FROM Employee;
SELECT ALL dept FROM Employee;
SELECT Employee.dept FROM Employee;
SELECT ALL Employee.dept FROM Employee;
```

The first two examples use unqualified <Column name>s in the select list, while the last two use <Column reference>s (that is, <Column name>s qualified with their <Table name>s). Unless the lack of a qualifier makes a <Column name> ambiguous, the qualifier is unnecessary. The result in all cases is:

DEPT
A
B
C
D
A
B
E
B
E
B

Departments are duplicated in the result because `SELECT` doesn't eliminate them unless the `DISTINCT` option is used, as in these equivalent SQL statements:

```
SELECT DISTINCT dept FROM Employee;
SELECT DISTINCT Employee.dept FROM Employee;
```

The result in both cases is:

DEPT
A
B
C
D
E

To find the name of each department's manager (retrieve multiple Columns from one Table):

```
SELECT dept,manager FROM Department;
```

The result is:

DEPT	MANAGER
A	SMITH A
B	JONES B
C	BROWN C
D	BLACK D
E	GREEN E

To retrieve all Columns of one Table, these three SQL statements are equivalent:

```
SELECT empnum,rate,location,paid FROM Payroll;
SELECT * FROM Payroll;
SELECT Payroll.* FROM Payroll;
```

The result in all three cases is the entire PAYROLL Table. (An asterisk can be used as shorthand for "all Columns" and can be qualified just as a <Column name> can be.)

Qualified Retrieval

To find all employees working in department A (retrieve one Column which fulfills one search condition):

```
SELECT surname FROM Employee WHERE dept='A';
```

The result is:

SURNAME
KOO
SMITH

Remember that <character string literal>s must always be enclosed in single quotes.

To find department A employees with an employee number smaller than 10 (retrieve one Column fulfilling multiple search conditions):

```
SELECT surname FROM Employee
WHERE  dept='A' AND empnum<10;
```

The result is:

SURNAME
KOO

To find the full name of the department A employee whose employee number is 10 (retrieve multiple Columns fulfilling multiple conditions from a Table):

```
SELECT gname,surname FROM Employee
WHERE  dept='A' AND empnum=10;
```

The result is:

GNAME	SURNAME
ALICE	SMITH

Retrieval with a <literal>

To include a <literal> in a result:

```
SELECT empnum,
       'Hourly Rate=' AS hourly_rate,
       rate
FROM   Payroll
WHERE  empnum=1 OR empnum=10;
```

The result is:

EMPNUM	HOURLY_RATE	RATE
1	Hourly Rate=	6.00
10	Hourly Rate=	16.00

The second Column of the result is derived from the <character string literal> expression in the select list.

Retrieval with an Arithmetic Expression

To calculate an employee's daily pay from the hourly rate earned (retrieve multiple Columns from a Table with an arithmetic expression):

```
SELECT empnum,
       'Daily Rate=' AS comment,
       rate*8 AS daily_rate
FROM   Payroll
WHERE  empnum=1 OR empnum=10;
```

The result is:

EMPNUM	COMMENT	DAILY_RATE
1	Daily Rate=	48.00
10	Daily Rate=	128.00

The third Column of the result is derived from the arithmetic expression in the select list.

Retrieval with LIKE

To find all employees with surnames beginning with "M" (retrieve all values matching a simple string pattern):

```
SELECT empnum,surname FROM Employee
WHERE  surname LIKE 'M%' AND empnum<3;
```

The result is:

EMPNUM	SURNAME
2	MARSH

To find the departments whose manager's surname has the letter "R" as the second character:

```
SELECT dept,manager FROM Department
WHERE  surname LIKE '_R%';
```

The result is:

DEPT	MANAGER
C	BROWN C
E	GREEN E

To find all employees whose given name does not include the letter "A" (retrieve values which do not match a simple string pattern):

```
SELECT empnum,gname FROM Employee
WHERE  gname NOT LIKE '%A%';
```

The result is:

EMPNUM	GNAME
2	JOHN
4	CHUCK
11	BOB

(We discussed the LIKE predicate in Chapter 7 "Character Strings.")

Retrieval with SIMILAR

To find all employees whose location starts with 2 digits (retrieve all values matching a complicated string pattern):

```
SELECT empnum,location FROM Payroll
WHERE  location SIMILAR TO '[:DIGIT:][:DIGIT:]%';
```

The result is:

EMPNUM	LOCATION
1	10TH FLOOR
2	16TH FLOOR
10	16TH FLOOR
11	16TH FLOOR
28	16TH FLOOR
35	10TH FLOOR
40	10TH FLOOR

To find all employees whose location doesn't start with 2 digits (retrieve all values that don't match a complicated string pattern):

```
SELECT empnum,location FROM Payroll
WHERE  location NOT SIMILAR TO '[:DIGIT:][:DIGIT:]%';
```

The result is:

EMPNUM	LOCATION
3	WAREHOUSE
4	BASEMENT
20	WAREHOUSE

(We discussed the SIMILAR predicate in Chapter 7 "Character Strings.")

Retrieval with IS NULL

To find all employees with unknown addresses on file (retrieve all rows containing a null value):

```
SELECT empnum,surname,gname    FROM   Employee
WHERE  address IS NULL;
```

The result is:

EMPNUM	SURNAME	GNAME
40	WARREN	NANCY

To find the departments with known managers (retrieve all rows that don't contain null values):

```
SELECT manager FROM Department
WHERE  manager IS NOT NULL;
```

The result is:

MANAGER
SMITH A
JONES B
BROWN C
BLACK D
GREEN E

(We discussed the IS NULL predicate in Chapter 13 "NULLs.")

Retrieval with a Scalar Function

To concatenate an employee's first initial and surname:

```
SELECT empnum,
       SUBSTRING(gname FROM 1 FOR 1) || '. ' || surname AS fullname
FROM   Employee
WHERE  empnum=10;
```

The result is:

EMPNUM	FULLNAME
10	A. SMITH

To concatenate the values retrieved from a Column with a <literal>:

```
SELECT 'HELLO ' || gname AS greeting
FROM   Employee
WHERE  empnum=4;
```

The result is:

GREETING
HELLO CHUCK

To find the length of a Column value and a <literal>:

```
SELECT surname,
       CHAR_LENGTH(surname) AS surname_length,
       CHAR_LENGTH('MARY') AS literal_length
FROM   Employee
WHERE  dept='A';
```

The result is:

SURNAME	SURNAME_LENGTH	LITERAL_LENGTH
KOO	3	4
SMITH	5	4

(The CHAR_LENGTH function returns a character string's length inclusive of blanks and trailing zeros. This example assumes that SURNAME is a variable length Column.)

Retrieval using Date Arithmetic

To find the number of days since the last pay date (assume the current date is November 10, 1989):

```
SELECT paid,
       (DATE '1989-11-10' - paid) INTERVAL DAY AS last_paid
FROM   PAYROLL
WHERE  empnum=1;
```

The result is:

PAID	LAST_PAID
1989-10-31	10

To add three months and two days to the last pay date:

```
SELECT empnum,
       paid,
       ((paid + INTERVAL '3' MONTH) + INTERVAL '2' DAY) AS new_date
FROM   PAYROLL
WHERE  empnum=1;
```

The result is:

EMPNUM	PAID	NEW_DATE
1	1989-10-31	1990-02-02

Joins

The ability to join a Table to others is one of the most powerful features of SQL. A *join* is an operation in which data is retrieved from multiple Tables. Here are some examples.

To find all information available on all employees (retrieve a join of all Columns) the following SQL statements are equivalent:

```
SELECT Employee.*,Payroll.*
FROM   Employee,Payroll
WHERE  Employee.empnum=Payroll.empnum;

SELECT *
FROM   Employee,Payroll
WHERE  Employee.empnum=Payroll.empnum;
```

The result is the entire EMPLOYEE Table joined with the entire PAYROLL Table over their matching employee numbers; ten rows and ten columns in all. Note the <Column reference>s for the EMPNUM Column — necessary to avoid ambiguity. To eliminate duplicate Columns from the result, specific <Column reference>s (rather than *) must also be listed in the select list, as in this SQL statement:

```
SELECT Employee.empnum,dept,surname,rate,location
FROM   Employee,Payroll
WHERE  Employee.empnum=1 AND Employee.empnum=Payroll.empnum;
```

The result is:

EMPNUM	DEPT	SURNAME	RATE	LOCATION
1	A	KOO	6.00	10TH FLOOR

To find an employee's manager (retrieve one Column from multiple Tables):

```
SELECT surname,manager
FROM   Employee,Department
WHERE  empnum=28 AND Employee.dept=Department.dept;
```

The result is:

SURNAME	MANAGER
TURNER	JONES B

To find the pay rates and locations of all department A employees (join values fulfilling multiple conditions from multiple Tables):

```
SELECT Employee.*,Payroll.*
FROM   Employee,Payroll
WHERE  dept='A' AND Employee.empnum=Payroll.empnum;
```

The result is the `EMPLOYEE` Table joined with the `PAYROLL` Table, for all rows where the `DEPT` column contains `'A'`.

To find the department and payroll data for employee 35:

```
SELECT Employee.empnum,surname,Employee.dept,manager,rate
FROM   Employee,Department,Payroll
WHERE  Employee.empnum=35 AND
       Employee.empnum=Payroll.empnum AND
       Employee.dept=Department.dept;
```

The result is:

EMPNUM	SURNAME	DEPT	MANAGER	RATE
35	OLSEN	E	GREEN E	9.00

To find the manager and locations of department C's employees:

```
SELECT Department.dept,manager,location
FROM   Department,Payroll,Employee
WHERE  Department.dept='C' AND
       Department.dept=Employee.dept AND
       Employee.empnum=Payroll.empnum;
```

The result is:

DEPT	MANAGER	LOCATION
C	BROWN C	WAREHOUSE

Predicates

You'll have noticed by now that the fundamental SQL condition is the predicate. It states a condition whose result is either TRUE, FALSE, or UNKNOWN. An example of a predicate is the familiar expression:

Example #1: `x = 5`

Specifically, Example#1 is an example of a <comparison predicate>. Note that the predicate contains a single condition. This is not a predicate:

Example #2: `x = 5 AND y = 6`

because AND is a Boolean operator that combines two predicates. However, both Example #1 and Example #2 are examples of "search conditions," and we will get back to Boolean operators later on.

The one thing we can say about predicates in general is that they describe operations which take non-truth-value arguments and return truth-value results. The truth value might be TRUE or FALSE; for most predicates (but not all) the truth value might also be UNKNOWN.

Listed below are the fourteen SQL3 predicates, of which ten are SQL-92 predicates and seven are acceptable in Core SQL, and of which all but five may return any of TRUE, FALSE, or UNKNOWN (T,F,U).

STANDARD NAME	KEYWORDS OR SYMBOLS	SQL-92?	CORE?	TFU
<comparison predicate>	= > >= < <= <>	YES	YES	TFU
<quantified comparison predicate>	= > >= < <= <> ALL|ANY|SOME	YES	YES	TFU
<between predicate>	[NOT] BETWEEN	YES	YES	TFU
<in predicate>	[NOT] IN	YES	YES	TFU
<like predicate>	[NOT] LIKE	YES	YES	TFU
<null predicate>	IS [NOT] NULL	YES	YES	TF
<exists predicate>	[NOT] EXISTS	YES	YES	TF
<unique predicate>	[NOT] UNIQUE	YES		TF
<match predicate>	[NOT] MATCH	YES		TF
<overlaps predicate>	[NOT] OVERLAPS	YES		TFU
<similar predicate>	[NOT] SIMILAR TO			TFU
<quantified predicate>	FOR ALL|ANY|SOME			TFU
<distinct predicate>	IS DISTINCT FROM			TF
<type predicate>	IS [NOT] OF (type-list)			TFU

We already talked about the <like predicate> (Chapters 5 and 7), the <similar predicate> (Chapter 7), the <overlaps predicate> (Chapter 8), the <null predicate> (Chapter 13), and the <type predicate> (Chapter 27). We'll discuss the <comparison predicate>, the <between predicate>, and the <distinct predicate> here, but we'll defer discussion of the final six predicates to Chapter 31.

<comparison predicate>

The required syntax for a <comparison predicate> is as follows.

```
<comparison predicate> ::=
expression_1 comparison operator expression_2
```

A <comparison predicate> compares two values and returns either TRUE, FALSE, or UNKNOWN. (If either argument is NULL, the <comparison predicate> returns UNKNOWN.) There are six comparison operators. Listed below are their symbols, their official names, their converses (i.e., what the operator would be if the predicate was negated) and two examples of predicates which contain the symbol and are TRUE.

Symbol	Name	Examples of TRUE predicates	Negation
=	equals	1=1 X'1'=B'0001'	<>
>	greater than	1>0 DATE '2100-01-01'>CURRENT_DATE	<=
>=	greater than or equals	1>=0 CURRENT_TIME>=CURRENT_TIME	<
<	less than	1<2 TIME '01:01:01'<TIME '01:01:02'	>=
<=	less than or equals	1<=2 B'000000'<=B'000000'	>
<>	not equals	1<>2 'A'<>'B'	=

There is nothing about the SQL comparison operators which would surprise the experienced programmer, although the use of the symbol <> for "not equals" is worth noting. There are some old DBMSs which accept != instead, but only <> is acceptable in standard SQL. Most commonly, the first comparand is a <Column name> and the second is a <literal>, e.g.,

```
city = 'PARIS'   -- a Column/<literal> comparison
```

Some general rules:

- The two expression arguments must be "comparable." Generally, this is the case if they have comparable <data type>s; e.g., if both are numeric. If the comparands are rows, each corresponding pair of Fields must have comparable <data type>s. We discussed what is meant by a comparable <data type> in our chapters on each of the SQL predefined <data type>s; refer to those discussions for complete details.
- For BLOBs, CLOBs, NCLOBs, REFs, and ARRAYs, the only legal comparison operators are = and <>. There may also be some restrictions for UDTs.

It's remarkable to think that, in primitive DBMSs, the Column/<literal> comparison was pretty well all there was. But today we can get much fancier:

```
UPPER(city) = 'PARIS'
   -- an expression/<literal> comparison

spending >= budget
   -- a Column/Column comparison

'PARIS' = city
   -- a <literal>/Column comparison (not recommended)

column_1+5=column_2+7
   -- an expression/expression comparison
```

Finally, we could use row values instead of scalar values in our comparisons:

```
(column_1,column_2) = ('ADAMS',77)
   -- a row-value/row-value comparison
```

Use row-value comparisons sparingly, because some DBMSs won't support them.

<between predicate>

The required syntax for a <between predicate> is as follows.

```
<between predicate> ::=
expression_1 [ NOT ] BETWEEN [ ASYMMETRIC | SYMMETRIC ]
expression_2 AND expression_3
```

A <between predicate> compares a value to a range of values and returns either `TRUE`, `FALSE`, or `UNKNOWN`. (If any argument is `NULL`, the <between predicate> returns `UNKNOWN`.) `BETWEEN` searches for data in a specific range. `NOT BETWEEN` searches for data that do not fall into the range given.

Some general rules:

- The three expressions must be comparable. If the comparands are rows, they must be of the same degree and each corresponding pair of Fields must have comparable <data type>s.
- The <between predicate> can't be used with `BLOB`s, `CLOB`s, `NCLOB`s, `REF`s and `ARRAY`s.

The `ASYMMETRIC` <between predicate> is `TRUE` if the value of `expression_1` is greater than or equals the value of `expression_2` and the value of `expression_1` is less than or equals the value of `expression_3`. For example, these <between predicate>s are all `TRUE`:

```
1 BETWEEN 0 AND 2
'B' BETWEEN 'A' AND 'B'
CURRENT_TIME BETWEEN TIME '00:00:00.000000' AND TIME '23:59:59.999999'
```

NOT BETWEEN is simply the negation of BETWEEN so this predicate is also TRUE:

```
3 NOT BETWEEN 0 AND 2
```

By default, a <between predicate> is ASYMMETRIC.

The SYMMETRIC <between predicate> is TRUE either (*a*) if the value of expression_1 is greater than or equals the value of expression_2 and the value of expression_1 is less than or equals the value of expression_3 or (*b*) if the value of expression_1 is greater than or equals the value of expression_3 and the value of expression_1 is less than or equals the value of expression_2. For example, these <between predicate>s are both TRUE:

```
1 BETWEEN SYMMETRIC 2 AND 0
3 NOT BETWEEN SYMMETRIC 2 AND 0
```

The SYMMETRIC option is new to SQL with SQL3.

In short, BETWEEN is just a shorthand for a combination of >= and <= comparisons, so the same rules that apply for comparisons of specific <data type>s apply to BETWEEN as well.

Retrieval With BETWEEN

Here are two <between predicate> retrieval examples from the sample Tables shown at the beginning of this chapter. First, to find the names of the manager of departments A, B, and C (retrieve values that match any in a specified range):

```
SELECT dept,manager FROM Department
WHERE  dept BETWEEN 'A' AND 'C';
```

The result is:

DEPT	MANAGER
A	SMITH A
B	JONES B
C	BROWN C

To find the employee numbers of all employees whose pay rate is either less than 8.00 or greater than 16.00 (retrieve values not falling into a specified range):

```
SELECT empnum,rate FROM Payroll
WHERE  rate NOT BETWEEN 8 AND 16;
```

The result is:

EMPNUM	RATE
1	6.00
2	5.00
3	5.00

<distinct predicate>

The required syntax for a <distinct predicate> is as follows.

```
<distinct predicate> ::=
expression_1 IS DISTINCT FROM expression_2
```

A <distinct predicate> tests two values to see whether they are distinct and returns either TRUE or FALSE. The <distinct predicate> is new to SQL with SQL3.

The two expressions must be comparable. If the comparands are rows, they must be of the same degree and each corresponding pair of Fields must have comparable <data type>s.

The <distinct predicate> is TRUE if the value of expression_1 is not equal to the value of expression_2 — that is, IS DISTINCT FROM is the same as the <> <comparison predicate> in every way — except one. If expression_1 is NULL and expression_2 is NULL, this predicate returns UNKNOWN:

```
expression_1 <> expression_2
```

(all comparisons return UNKNOWN if either argument is NULL). On the other hand, this predicate will return FALSE:

```
expression_1 IS DISTINCT FROM expression_2
```

That is, two NULL values are not distinct from one other. And if expression_1 is NULL and expression_2 is non-null, this predicate returns UNKNOWN:

```
expression_1 <> expression_2
```

On the other hand, this predicate will return TRUE:

```
expression_1 IS DISTINCT FROM expression_2
```

That is, a NULL value is distinct from every non-null value. (For arrays, IS DISTINCT FROM tests each corresponding pair of array elements. If the arrays are empty, or if any element of the first array contains the same value as its corresponding element in the second array, or if both elements are NULL, IS DISTINCT FROM returns FALSE.) Except for the difference when NULLs are involved, IS DISTINCT FROM is just a shorthand for the <> comparison, so the same rules that apply for comparisons of specific <data type>s apply to IS DISTINCT FROM as well.

Retrieval With IS DISTINCT FROM

Here is a <distinct predicate> retrieval example from the sample Tables shown at the beginning of this chapter. To find the names of employees who don't live at 234 West (retrieve values that are distinct from a specified value):

```
SELECT gname,surname FROM Employee
WHERE  address IS DISTINCT FROM '234 West';
```

The result is:

GNAME	SURNAME
JOHN	MARSH
MABEL	JONES

GNAME	SURNAME
CHUCK	MORGAN
BOB	JONES
CHRIS	FRANCIS
LINDA	TURNER
CAROL	OLSEN
NANCY	WARREN

Note that the final row is included in the result despite the fact that Nancy Warren's address is unknown; that is, there is a null value in the ADDRESS Column for that employee.

If you want to restrict your code to Core SQL, don't use the <distinct predicate>.

Search Conditions

A search condition consists of one or more Boolean value expressions. A Boolean value is either TRUE or FALSE or UNKNOWN. In SQL-92, only a predicate can return TRUE, FALSE, or UNKNOWN and therefore all search conditions are predicates (or multiple predicates) with Boolean operators. In SQL3, the definition is broader because there is another source for Boolean values, namely <literal>s or Column values of <data type> BOOLEAN, therefore search conditions might also contain values of <data type> BOOLEAN.

Here are six examples of search conditions. The first two consist of a simple predicate and a simple Boolean, respectively. The other four are more complex.

```
x = 1
NOT x = 1
x = 1 AND y = 3
x = 1 OR y = 3
(boolean_column_1 OR boolean_column_2) IS FALSE
```

We discussed the Boolean operators in Chapter 9 "Boolean Values." Here's a quick recap.

- The IS [NOT] {TRUE | FALSE | UNKNOWN} Boolean operator is rarely seen. Its effect is to change a Boolean value (which is TRUE or FALSE or UNKNOWN) to either TRUE or FALSE. For example, given a search condition "(x = 5) IS UNKNOWN," if x is NULL then the predicate "x = 5" returns UNKNOWN, therefore the search condition as a whole is TRUE.
- The NOT Boolean operator reverses TRUEs and FALSEs, but leaves UNKNOWNs alone. There is a trap here; the search condition "NOT (x = 1)" differs slightly from "(x = 1) IS FALSE" (you can see why if you assume again that the value of x is NULL). In any case, "NOT (x = 1)" is a bad style choice because people have trouble reading Boolean operators. The better choice is "(x <> 1)".
- The AND Boolean operator combines two Boolean values; if both are TRUE, the result is TRUE. For example, this search condition is true: "5 > 0 AND 0 = 0 AND 0 <= 5". However, this search condition is false: "5 > 0 AND 0 = 0 AND 0 >= 5".
- The OR Boolean operator combines two Boolean values; if either one is TRUE, the result is TRUE.

Search Conditions in Clauses

Because an SQL3 search condition returns a Boolean value, it can be used in situations which would appear exotic/erroneous in SQL-92, for example:

```
SELECT (numeric_column=5)
FROM   Table_1
WHERE  boolean_column=(char_column LIKE 'A%');
```

But our immediate interest is not exotica. We want to look at some plain everyday clauses which contain search conditions as a matter of course. The interesting thing about these clauses is that they contain implicit Boolean operators. Here are the clauses and the implicit Boolean operators.

Clause	Implicit Boolean Operator
CHECK (in Constraint definition)	IS NOT FALSE
WHERE	IS TRUE
WHEN (in a CASE expression)	IS TRUE
ON (for joining)	IS TRUE
WHEN (in a Trigger definition)	("satisfies")
HAVING	IS TRUE

Notice that the implicit Boolean looks for TRUE in every case but one — we talked about the CHECK clause in Chapter 20 "SQL Constraints and Assertions" and noted that a condition that evaluates to UNKNOWN also satisfies a Constraint. Everywhere else though, although SQL has lots of rules for generating and manipulating UNKNOWN values, it normally throws them away in the final step of a search. So, if you want to see results which are either TRUE or UNKNOWN, you must force them through with this expression:

```
... WHERE (search condition) IS NOT FALSE
```

Because IS NOT FALSE is evaluated before WHERE, all UNKNOWNs are converted to TRUEs before the WHERE's implicit IS TRUE Boolean operator takes effect. (Actually, most people don't want to see results which are UNKNOWN, but forcing them through is handy if you want to simulate the effect of a CHECK Constraint search condition.)

There is also an implicit Boolean AND operator between clauses. For example, this SQL statement:

```
SELECT Table_1.*,
       Table_2.*
FROM   Table_1 INNER JOIN Table_2 ON Table_1.column_1 =
       Table_2.column_1
WHERE  Table_1.column_2 = 5;
```

is effectively the same as this SQL statement:

```
SELECT Table_1.*,
       Table_2.*
FROM   Table_1, Table_2
WHERE  Table_1.column_1 = Table_2.column_1 AND
       Table_1.column_2 = 5;
```

However, such a transformation ignores evaluation order. We'll get back to joins in a later chapter.

Some Example Searches

The main use of search conditions is to search. Let's try some examples on a small Table. This Table, which we'll call TEAMS, contains this data:

TEAMS

CITY	TEAM_NAME	STADIUM_CAPACITY	STANDING	REVENUE
Calgary	Stampeders	45,000	5	15,000,000.00
Edmonton	Eskimos	60,000	4	20,000,000.00
Hamilton	Tiger Cats	22,000	1	25,000,000.00
Montreal	Alouettes	18,000	3	30,000,000.00
Regina	Roughriders	31,000	6	35,000,000.00
Toronto	Argonauts	80,000	2	40,000,000.00
Vancouver	Lions	?	7	45,000,000.00
Winnipeg	Blue Bombers	31,000	8	50,000,000.00

- Question: What city is represented by the Blue Bombers?

  SQL query:

```
SELECT city
FROM   Teams
WHERE team_name = 'Blue Bombers';
```

  Answer: Winnipeg.

- Question: What teams, other than the Edmonton Eskimos, have stadia with a capacity of over 40,000?

  SQL query:

```
SELECT team_name
FROM   Teams
WHERE  (city<>'Edmonton' OR team_name<>'Eskimos') AND
       stadium_capacity > 40000;
```

  Answer: Calgary, Toronto.

- Question: What teams, other than the Edmonton Eskimos, might have stadia with a capacity of over 40,000?

  SQL query:

```
SELECT team_name
FROM   Teams
WHERE  (city<>'Edmonton' OR team_name<>'Eskimos') AND
       (stadium_capacity > 40000 ) IS NOT FALSE;
```

  Answer: Calgary, Toronto, Vancouver.

- Question: Show teams whose revenue per seat is more than $1,000, as well as teams which are in the top half of the standings.

  SQL query:

```
SELECT team_name
FROM   Teams
WHERE  revenue/stadium_capacity > 1000 OR standing > 4;
```

  Answer: Hamilton, Montreal, Regina, Winnipeg, Toronto, Edmonton.

- Question: Show all teams.

  SQL query:

```
SELECT *
FROM   Teams
WHERE  TRUE;
```

  Answer: Calgary, Edmonton, Hamilton, Montreal, Regina, Toronto, Vancouver, Winnipeg.

This SQL statement is the same as `SELECT * FROM Teams` and it shows an interesting SQL3 development. Whereas in SQL-92 it was necessary to express "always true" and "always false" with explicit literal expressions like `1 = 1` and `1 <> 2`, it's now possible to use a simple <Boolean literal>.

Here's a few more examples, this time from the sample Tables shown at the beginning of this chapter. First, to find the employees who are located in the basement or whose pay rate is between 5.00 and 6.00:

```
SELECT empnum,rate,location FROM Payroll
WHERE  location='BASEMENT' OR rate BETWEEN 5 AND 6;
```

The result is:

EMPNUM	RATE	LOCATION
1	6.00	10TH FLOOR
2	5.00	16TH FLOOR
3	5.00	WAREHOUSE
4	8.00	BASEMENT

To find the names of employees with employee numbers less than 10 who also work in Department B:

```
SELECT gname,surname FROM Employee
WHERE  dept='B' AND empnum<10;
```

The result is:

GNAME	SURNAME
JOHN	MARSH

SQL's <case expression>

The CASE expression is not a filtering operation, but it fits in this context because CASE specifies a conditional value; it takes a search condition as input and returns a scalar value. The required syntax for the <case expression> is as follows.

```
<case expression> ::= <case abbreviation> | <case specification>

   <case abbreviation> ::=
   NULLIF(<value expression> ,<value expression>) |
   COALESCE(<value expression> {,<value expression>}... )

   <case specification> ::= <simple case> | <searched case>

      <simple case> ::=
      CASE
         <value expression>
         {WHEN <value expression> THEN <result>}...
         [ ELSE <result> ]
      END

      <searched case> ::=
         CASE
         {WHEN <search condition> THEN <result>}...
         [ ELSE <result> ]
      END

      <result> ::= <value expression> | NULL
```

The <case abbreviation>s NULLIF and COALESCE are both shorthands for a simple CASE expression. For example, this expression:

```
NULLIF(value_1,value_2)
```

is equivalent to this expression:

```
CASE WHEN value_1=value_2 THEN NULL
   ELSE value_1
END
```

Use NULLIF when you have some special value instead of NULL, for example the displayable ? to represent a null value.

This expression:

```
COALESCE(value_1,value_2)
```

is equivalent to this expression:

```
CASE WHEN value_1 IS NOT NULL THEN value_1
   ELSE value_2
END
```

And an expression containing more than two COALESCE values is equivalent to a series of COALESCE expressions, which are, in turn, equivalent to a series of CASE conditions. For example, this expression:

```
COALESCE(value_1,value_2,value_3)
```

is equivalent to this expression:

```
CASE WHEN value_1 IS NOT NULL THEN value_1
   ELSE COALESCE(value_2,value_3)
END
```

A simple CASE expression operates on a <value expression>; any expression that returns a scalar value except for a routine that is possibly non-deterministic or that might modify SQL-data. The <data type> of this CASE operand must be comparable with the <data type> of the WHEN clause's <value expression> (because the simple CASE expression compares the two to see if they are equal) and with the ELSE clause's <result>. (If you omit the ELSE clause, it defaults to ELSE NULL.)

A searched CASE expression also operates on a <value expression> that must be comparable with the <data type> of the WHEN clause's operands and the <data type> of the ELSE clause's <result>. You may specify any appropriate search condition in a searched CASE expression's WHEN clause. Once again, the default ELSE clause is ELSE NULL.

Here are two equivalent examples of CASE expressions (the first example is a searched CASE, the second is a simple CASE).

```
CASE
   WHEN column_1 = 1 THEN 'one!'
   WHEN column_1 = 2 THEN 'two!'
   ELSE 'many'
END
```

```
CASE column_1
   WHEN 1 THEN 'one!'
   WHEN 2 THEN 'two!'
   ELSE 'many'
END
```

The searched CASE expression works as follows:

- Find the first WHEN clause whose search condition is TRUE. Return the value given in that WHEN clause's THEN sub-clause.
- If no WHEN search condition is TRUE, return the value given in the ELSE clause.
- All returnable values (in THEN clauses and in the ELSE clause) must have <data type>s that are comparable with the CASE operand.
- At least one of the THEN values must be non-null. For example, this expression is not legal:

```
CASE column_1
  WHEN 1 THEN NULL
   ELSE NULL
END
```

The simple CASE expression works the same way — simple CASE is merely a shorthand form of searched CASE, where each WHEN clause is taken to mean "WHEN case operand = when expression."

We prefer to use searched CASE expressions on stylistic grounds, but many people prefer simple CASE expressions because they're similar to Pascal's case or C's switch.

We will now repeat one of the questions that we asked in the previous section, about the TEAMS Table.

- Question: What city is represented by the Blue Bombers?

  SQL query:

```
SELECT CASE
         WHEN team_name = 'Blue Bombers' THEN city
         ELSE '*********'
       END AS city
FROM Teams;
```

Answer:
CITY
****
****
****
****
****
****
****
Winnipeg

The answer is the same, but with a lot of dross. It's possible to use CASE expressions this way as retrieval substitutes, but the more common applications are (*a*) to make up for SQL's lack of an enumerated <data type>, (*b*) to perform complicated if/then calculations, (*c*) for translation, and (*d*) to avoid exceptions. We find CASE expressions to be indispensable and it amazes us that in pre-SQL-92 DBMSs they didn't exist.

Rules of Aggregation

The THEN values in a CASE expression, as well as the results of set operations or arrays, are considered to be aggregations; that is, they have a <data type> that is determined by evaluating the <data type>s of each value in a set. The aggregation rules determine which <data type>s are compatible and what the <data type> of the result is. Stated in a very general way, the aggregation rules are "what's compatible for assignment is compatible for aggregation," "varying trumps fixed," and "long trumps short." More specifically:

- All numeric — INT, SMALLINT, NUMERIC, DECIMAL, FLOAT, REAL, DOUBLE PRECISION — values are compatible. If any aggregated value is approximate numeric, the result is approximate numeric; otherwise the result is exact numeric and the result's scale is the biggest scale of any of the aggregated values. For example, this expression:

```
CASE ...
  THEN CAST(x AS DECIMAL(9)) ...
  THEN CAST(y AS DECIMAL(5,3))
  ELSE NULL
END
```

  should return a result with a <data type> of DECIMAL(9,3). (Because some of the decisions here are implementation-defined, we say "should" — the only guaranteed facts are that the scale will be 3 and the <data type> will be some sort of exact numeric.)

- All BIT or BIT VARYING values are compatible. If any aggregated value is a BIT VARYING then the result is a BIT VARYING; otherwise the result is a BIT. The result's length is the length of the longest aggregated value. For example, if a Table was defined with "... column_1 BIT(5),column_2 BIT VARYING(4) ...", this expression:

```
CASE ... THEN column_1 ... ELSE column_2 END
```

  will return a result with a <data type> of BIT VARYING(5).

- All BLOB values are compatible.
- All CHAR, NCHAR, VARCHAR, NCHAR VARYING, CLOB, and NCLOB values are compatible, provided the Character set is the same. If any aggregated value is a CLOB then the result is a CLOB; otherwise if any value is a VARCHAR then the result is a VARCHAR; otherwise the result is a CHAR. The result's length is the length of the longest aggregated value. The result's Collation will depend on coercibility; see the appropriate tables in Chapter 7 "Character Strings." For example, this expression:

```
CASE ... THEN 'a' ... THEN 'abcd' ... ELSE 'abc' END
```

will return a result with a <data type> of CHAR(4) because <character string literal>s are fixed-length character strings and the size of the largest aggregated <literal> is 4 characters.

- All DATE values are compatible.
- All TIME and TIME WITH TIME ZONE values are compatible. If any aggregated value is TIME WITH TIME ZONE, the result is TIME WITH TIME ZONE; otherwise the result is TIME. The fractional seconds precision of the result is the largest fractional seconds precision of any of the aggregated values.
- All TIMESTAMP and TIMESTAMP WITH TIME ZONE values are compatible. If any aggregated value is TIMESTAMP WITH TIME ZONE, the result is TIMESTAMP WITH TIME ZONE; otherwise the result is TIMESTAMP. The fractional seconds precision of the result is the largest fractional seconds precision of any of the aggregated values.
- All year–month INTERVAL values are compatible. The datetime fields of the result are from the earliest to the latest fields in any aggregated value. For example, this expression:

```
CASE ... THEN INTERVAL '1' YEAR ... THEN INTERVAL '1' MONTH END
```

will return a result with a <data type> of INTERVAL YEAR TO MONTH.

- All day–time INTERVAL values are compatible. The datetime fields of the result are from the earliest to the latest fields in any aggregated value.
- All BOOLEAN values are compatible.
- All REF values of the same referenced type (UDT) are compatible.
- All UDT values whose most specific types have some common supertype are compatible.

If you want to restrict your code to Core SQL, don't use BLOBs, CLOBs, or NCLOBs in a CASE expression.

Dialects

The truth is, most vendors are just starting to get used to the SQL-92 search conditions, so don't depend heavily on these SQL3 features:

- BOOLEAN <data type>
- <distinct predicate>
- SYMMETRIC <between predicate>

You'll find even stricter limitations if you don't use a fairly powerful DBMS — there are some that don't support row-value comparisons, IS [NOT] {TRUE|FALSE|UNKNOWN} and the more difficult predicates (e.g., MATCH and OVERLAPS).

30

Chapter 30

Searching with Joins

It's France in the 1600s. René Descartes is playing cards with Madame du Barry. The game is War. Each player has a deck. René plays a card from the top of his deck. Madame du Barry plays a card from the top of her deck. If René's card has a higher value then Madame's, he wins the trick. If his card has a lower value, Madame wins the trick. In the case of a tie, each player throws down another card. They repeat this until one player has all the tricks or until René and Madame think of something more interesting to do (it's France in the 1600s).

In set theory, each trick is an ordered two-element pair. There are (52*52) possible first-round combinations. To honor Mr. Descartes, we call the set of all possible tricks the *Cartesian product* of the two original (deck) sets. Two valuable insights arise from playing the game:

1. Insight: What matters is the values on the cards. There are no threads connecting the queens in René's deck to the queens in Madame's deck. There are no notes on each card saying "I match the *n*th card from the top in the other deck." There are, in other words, no pointers — in the real world, we match based on values.
2. Insight: Slow, tedious meaninglessness. We recognize that there is always conceptually a Cartesian product, but we would like as quickly as possible to filter out the only interesting cases — the ties (the 52*4 cases where the cards' face values are equal).

The first insight is the basis of relational-database theory. The second is a warning that we want to minimize the undesirable consequences of joined Tables.

Joined Tables

The SQL definition for a joined Table: a Table derived from a Cartesian product, an inner join, an outer join, or a union join. The required syntax for a joined Table is as follows.

```
<joined Table> ::=
<Table reference> CROSS JOIN <Table reference> |
<Table reference> [ NATURAL ] [ <join type> ] JOIN <Table reference>
   [ <join specification> ] |
( <joined Table> )

   <join type> ::=
   INNER |
   {LEFT | RIGHT | FULL} [ OUTER ] |
   UNION

   <join specification> ::=
   ON <search condition> |
   USING (join <Column name> [ {,join <Column name>} ... ])
```

Basically, a joined Table is the result of some expression that represents an explicit join of two Tables, each of which is identified by a <Table reference> (the <Table reference> could itself be a joined Table but is usually just a <Table name> or a Table identified by a <Correlation name> and we'll use only that form for now). We'll use a library database with these Tables in all the examples of joins that follow. Here's our data:

BORROWERS

NAME	BORROWER_ID	PARENT
Paige	1	Barbara
Hayley	2	Barbara
Jaclyn	3	Christa
Christa	4	Edith
Barbara	5	Edith
Edith	6	NULL

CHECKOUTS

BORROWER_ID	BOOK_ID
1	1
2	2
2	3

BOOKS

CHECKOUT_DATE	BOOK_ID	TITLE
1999-04-27	1	The Borrowers
1999-04-28	2	The Unexpected Mrs. Pollifax
1999-04-29	3	The Hobbit
NULL	4	Friday

Our example database illustrates a very common Humans --> Transactions --> Objects framework, which appears in many businesses — (Customers --> Sales --> Products), (Clients --> Deposits_Withdrawals --> Accounts), (Workers --> Shifts --> Tasks) — so think of your own analogies for each example of a join situation that follows.

Cartesian-Filter Join

"List titles for all Books checked out on April 27."

Our answer to this question — the first of several answers — will use the traditional syntax, which is legal in all versions of SQL:

```
SELECT title
FROM   Books, Checkouts
WHERE  checkout_date = DATE '1999-04-27' AND
       Books.book_id = Checkouts.book_id;
```

In this SELECT statement, the words "FROM Books, Checkouts" tell the DBMS we want a Cartesian join of BOOKS and CHECKOUTS. That gives us four BOOKS/CHECKOUTS pairs. But the WHERE conditions filter out the unwanted pairs and leave us with only one.

When we think of both the WHERE clause conditions as "filters" that winnow the results from an imagined Cartesian BOOKS+CHECKOUTS Table, the two conditions both appear to be doing similar tasks. It appears natural that both conditions should be in the WHERE clause. Now, here is a niggle; it's not real. You are supposed to conceptualize that a Cartesian product is formed and then filtered, but — because the number of rows in a Cartesian product is always the number of rows in each individual Table multiplied by each other — its size rises geometrically as database size rises, so the DBMS will avoid it and quietly use a navigational trick instead ("first find a CHECKOUTS row where CHECKOUT_DATE = April 27, then take the BOOK_ID of that checkout and find BOOK_ID within BOOKS ...").

Efficiency of evaluation isn't the subject of this chapter though. Right now, we're only concerned with the fact that Cartesian products are a simplifying myth. Unfortunately, to programmers aware of the myth, it is obvious that the two conditions in the WHERE clause are not really the same sort of thing. One is a typical filter, but the other is a glue directive to the DBMS. It's not really a WHERE sort of condition at all.

Cartesian-Filter Join II — CROSS JOIN

As shown in our syntax diagram earlier, we could use the <keyword>s CROSS JOIN instead of a comma in the FROM clause to get the same result:

```
SELECT title
FROM   Books CROSS JOIN Checkouts
WHERE  checkout_date = DATE '1999-04-27' AND
       Books.book_id = Checkouts.book_id;
```

This is synonymous with the "... FROM Books, Checkouts ..." query (CROSS JOIN just means "Cartesian product") and it's too bad we didn't use English words instead of commas in the first place, but CROSS JOIN is relatively new (a SQL-92 introduction).

JOIN ... USING

We're still asking, "List titles for all Books checked out on April 27." This time we will use the modern syntax:

```
SELECT title
FROM   Books INNER JOIN Checkouts USING (book_id)
WHERE  checkout_date = DATE '1999-04-27';
```

For some years to come, the conventional syntax for joins (our first example) will still be the most popular. However, modern syntax (of which JOIN ... USING is the best example) is now seen frequently in tutorials and magazine articles, especially when Microsoft Access is the subject. In modern syntax, we acknowledge that joining conditions might look better in a clause of their own. The clause "USING (book_id)" replaces the traditional "WHERE ... Books.book_id = Checkouts.book_id". Thus, BOOK_ID is a reference to both BOOK_ID Columns — the one in the BOOKS Table and the one in the CHECKOUTS Table. It's not a piece of luck, you know, that we used the same <Column name> in both Tables — you should always use the same <Column name> when you anticipate joining over a pair of Columns.

NATURAL JOIN

The ultimate simplification of JOIN ... USING is to throw out the <Column name>s entirely and specify "wherever <Column name>s are the same in both Tables, join on them." Here's how:

```
SELECT title
FROM   Books NATURAL JOIN Checkouts
WHERE  checkout_date = DATE '1999-04-27';
```

A natural join is a join over matching Columns (Columns which have the same name in the Tables being joined). This is the ultimate step. It hides the join process from the user who gets the result. Perhaps, one could even change the join <Column name>s, or add new Columns, without having to change all SELECT statements which refer to the joined Tables. On the other hand, users of NATURAL JOIN have to be careful that all joinable Columns really do have the same name and that all non-joinable Columns don't. The casual-looking "Books

NATURAL JOIN Checkouts" is only possible when database naming conventions are formal and enforced.

In some places, the custom is to use NATURAL JOIN for only one class of situations — where one is joining a Table with a FOREIGN KEY Constraint to the Table that the foreign key REFERENCES. Such a join is, due to the way that primary/foreign keys work, always a "one-to-many" join (that is, there will always be only one row in TABLE_1 which is joined with between zero and infinity rows in TABLE_2).

JOIN ... ON

There is one more way to "List titles for books checked out on April 27":

```
SELECT title
FROM   Books INNER JOIN Checkouts
       ON Books.book_id = Checkouts.book_id
WHERE  checkout_date = DATE '1999-04-27';
```

With this syntax, the ON clause introduces a conditional expression for a join; it contains a conditional expression just like a WHERE clause does. Legally, you could take all the conditions out of the WHERE clause and put them in the ON clause, but that would flout the principle of the exercise, which is, "ON clauses should have joining conditions, WHERE clauses should have filtering conditions." Earlier we discussed why this syntax just looks better, to some people, than the conventional syntax. Later we'll discuss one situation where you *must* use ON rather than WHERE, but the current example is not one of those situations. The more immediate question is, "Why would we ever want to use ON rather than USING?" The immediate reply is, "Well, USING is only possible when you're joining over two Columns with the same name and when the relator is implicitly equality (=)." Joins can, of course, also be related using the other SQL comparison operators too.

Self-Joins

Here's a new question, "List parents with their children."

Among our library's borrowers are several children. Their parents also have cards (it's one of the conditions of membership for child borrowers). That is, there is a relationship between different rows of the same Table. When we have a query that bases itself on an intra-Table relationship, we must join the Table with itself — this is called a *self-join* and is one of the rare cases where SQL provides no alternative means of answering the query. Here's an example:

```
SELECT Parents.name,
       Children.name
FROM   Borrowers AS Parents,
       Borrowers AS Children
WHERE  Parents.name = Children.parent;
```

The result is:

NAME	NAME
Barbara	Paige
Barbara	Hayley
Christa	Jaclyn

In a self-join, by definition, all the Columns in the first Table have the same names as the Columns in the second Table. So we can't `SELECT name` ... or even `SELECT Borrowers.name` ... — such expressions are ambiguous. This is a case where we absolutely must use a <Correlation name> to explicitly identify each Table and each Column of a particular Table. Here, we've given one copy of the `BORROWERS` Table the <Correlation name> `PARENTS` and the other the <Correlation name> `CHILDREN`, so as to be able to distinguish between them.

Theta-Joins

A *theta-join* is any Cartesian product that's filtered by a condition which compares values from both Tables. That is, the general theta-join form is:

```
<Table_1.Column> relator <Table_2.Column>
```

where the relator is almost always "=", as in this example:

```
Sellers.seller_name = Sales.seller_name
```

This special case of theta-join — where the relation is equality — is called an *equijoin*. Although all relators are legal, the other kinds of theta-join are, in fact, rare.

In a typical programming life, you'll never encounter a lone, non-equijoin theta-join (or if you do, you're looking at some sort of an error). The common cases are always double theta-joins. The following is an example:

double theta: > combined with equijoin

"List identification numbers of borrowers who took out books on two different days."

To answer this request, we need to use a greater than operator, so this is an example of a general theta-join — but it's also an equijoin. Here are two ways of doing it (the first example uses the `WHERE` clause to set the conditions and the second example uses the `ON` clause for the same purpose):

```
-- <with WHERE>
SELECT DISTINCT Firsts.borrower_id
FROM   Checkouts Firsts, Checkouts Seconds
WHERE  Firsts.date > Seconds.date AND
       Firsts.borrower_id = Seconds.borrower_id;
```

```
--  <with ON>
SELECT DISTINCT Firsts.borrower_id
FROM Checkouts Firsts JOIN Checkouts Seconds
ON   (Firsts.borrower_id = Seconds.borrower_id) AND
     (Firsts.date > Seconds.date);
```

(Remember that the <keyword> AS is optional when you're defining a <Correlation name>.) The result is:

BORROWER_ID
2

TIP: For queries containing the word "different," consider whether a > will do. Queries with > are often a bit faster than queries with <>.

The double theta-join is, in practice, often associated with a self-join. Sometimes the relators are <= and >= (for instance, when we join over a floating-point number).

Bad Joins

"List all the borrowers whose names appear in a book title and the book titles."

```
SELECT Borrowers.name, Books.title
FROM   Borrowers INNER JOIN Titles
ON     POSITION(TRIM(Borrowers.name) IN Books.title) > 0;
```

The result is no rows found.

It might please 'Paige' to find her name on a book: 'The book of Paige ....' The syntax is technically legal. The reasons that we use this as a bad join example are:

- The Domain of BORROWERS.NAME is not the same as the Domain of BOOKS.TITLE and there are no Columns common to BORROWERS and BOOKS which would qualify for a NATURAL JOIN. Together, these two observations are always signs that a query is frivolous, if not downright erroneous.
- The joining expression contains a scalar function and has both Columns on the same side of the relator. Together, these two characteristics will choke every DBMS currently in existence.

Allow the query, of course. But, for critical and common situations, use only simple expressions, on related Tables, over similar Columns. Odd syntax is bad syntax.

Joins with Multiple Tables

"List titles and borrowers for books taken out on April 27."

The answer is straightforward — once you know two-Table joins you can also do three-Table joins:

```
SELECT DISTINCT Borrowers.name, Books.title
FROM   Borrowers, Checkouts, Books
WHERE  Borrowers.borrower_id = Checkouts.borrower_id AND
       Books.book_id = Checkouts.book_id AND
       Checkouts.checkout_date = DATE '1999-04-27';
```

The result is:

NAME	TITLE
Paige	The Borrowers

It should be possible in a 3-way join to follow a chain of links as a reading exercise. In this case, if we start with the first Table (BORROWERS), we can see that it's possible to go from there to CHECKOUTS (using the BORROWER_ID Column) and from CHECKOUTS to BOOKS (using the BOOK_ID Column). If there is no chain, think hard — maybe the query "goes Cartesian" during some intermediate stage.

TRAP: The next query looks like it does the same thing. In fact, though, it is an example of the most common mistake that can happen with multi-Table joins:

```
SELECT DISTINCT Borrowers.name, Books.title
FROM   Borrowers, Books
WHERE  Borrowers.borrower_id IN
   (SELECT borrower_id
    FROM   Checkouts
    WHERE  checkout_date = DATE '1999-04-27') AND
           Books.book_id IN
             (SELECT book_id
              FROM   Checkouts
              WHERE checkout_date = DATE '1999-04-27');
```

The error is in the assumption that "if A is linked to B and C is linked to B, then C is linked to A." That sounds like fundamental arithmetic (the Law Of Transitivity) — but it's wrong in this case because B is not a value — it is a set of values — and the IN predicate means "... linked to any one of (B) ...". When writing a multi-Table join, an intermediate link should be true "for all," not just "for any."

What about 4-Table, 5-Table, 6-Table joins? Yes, as long as you remember that adding a new Table adds time to your query geometrically. Eventually, you will run into a fixed limit for every DBMS. To conform with the US government's requirements (FIPS 127-2), an "intermediate level" SQL DBMS must be able to join at least 10 Tables. If you find yourself needing more than that, you might want to consider either (*a*) splitting up your query using temporary Tables or (*b*) combining two Tables into one ("denormalizing").

Avoiding Duplicates

"List names of borrowers who have taken out books."

To get the result, you can use any join syntax you like, provided you include DISTINCT in your select list. Here's an example:

```
SELECT DISTINCT name
FROM   Borrowers, Checkouts
WHERE  Borrowers.borrower_id = Checkouts.borrower_id;
```

The result is:

NAME
Paige
Hayley

Without DISTINCT, we would see 'Hayley' twice in the result, because Hayley took out two books. Any join can cause duplication unless both sides of the join are unique keys. So we are tempted to say, "Always use DISTINCT when you join" ... but that would be a false tip. True, you want to eliminate duplicates caused in this case by the join, but what if there are two Hayleys? That is, do you want to eliminate duplicates which were not caused by the join? Some people would answer, "Yes I do," and would add, "Duplicate information isn't real information anyway." We'll contrive an example then: (*a*) we want to hand out name cards to borrowers who took books out, so this list is going to a printer and (*b*) assume that there are two different 'Hayley's, one of whom took out two books. If we form a query using DISTINCT, we'll get too few 'Hayley' cards — but if we don't use DISTINCT we'll get too many 'Hayley' cards. For such situations, the real tip is: use a subquery, like this:

```
SELECT name
FROM   Borrowers
WHERE  borrower_id IN (SELECT borrower_id FROM Checkouts);
```

This query neither generates nor eliminates duplicates, so would be better. We'll talk more about subqueries in a later chapter.

Amusing story: There once was a vendor who secretly converted all subqueries into joins (the transform is fairly easy) and that vendor's DBMS produced spurious duplicate rows when subqueries were used. Instead of admitting this, that vendor's employees wrote an "SQL textbook" informing the public that false duplicates were a necessary evil of Standard SQL! The vendor is still around and sells thousands of copies a month.

OUTER JOIN

"List all books, along with the dates they were checked out and who borrowed them (if they're out)."

This query will give us the NATURAL JOIN of the BOOKS and CHECKOUTS Tables:

```
SELECT DISTINCT Books.title,
                Books.checkout_date,
                Checkouts.borrower_id
FROM   Books NATURAL JOIN Checkouts;
```

The result is:

TITLE	CHECKOUT_DATE	BORROWER_ID
The Borrowers	1999-04-27	1
The Unexpected Mrs. Pollifax	1999-04-28	2
The Hobbit	1999-04-29	2

There is one book missing from the list. At this point, most people will say, "What about 'Friday'? I realize it's not in the CHECKOUTS Table, but that very fact is important to me. It seems your join will always lose information unless both Tables have the same set of matching keys."

True — but there is a way around this. Let's give 'Friday' a checkout:

```
INSERT INTO Checkouts VALUES (NULL,4);
```

Now, when we do the NATURAL JOIN again, we get this result:

TITLE	CHECKOUT_DATE	BORROWER_ID
The Borrowers	1999-04-27	1
The Unexpected Mrs. Pollifax	1999-04-28	2
The Hobbit	1999-04-29	2
Friday	NULL	NULL

... and that's your answer. (Incidentally we inserted NULL in the BORROWER_ID Column because the book wasn't really checked out, so no one's ID could apply.)

"So, to band-aid your broken join you invent an ad-hoc CHECKOUTS row that matches. I can imagine what your idea of a general solution would be."

Exactly. The general solution would be imaginary rows. In fact, we don't really have to insert them all, we can just pretend they're there — and call what we're doing an OUTER JOIN.

"Okay."

But is it really okay? It's true that the OUTER JOIN has answered the example question; an OUTER JOIN will answer any question of the form "give me the join of Table A and Table B without losing information from Table A." So, sure it's okay, as long as we keep in mind that there's a band-aid involved. In particular — what is this NULL? Certainly it does not mean UNKNOWN. Remember, we're not uncertain what the BORROWER_ID is; on the contrary, we know perfectly well that there is no BORROWER_ID for 'Friday.'

SQL actually provides us with "official" syntax to express an OUTER JOIN request:

```
SELECT Books.title, Books.checkout_date, Checkouts.borrower_id
FROM   Checkouts RIGHT OUTER JOIN Books USING (book_id);
```

Our example is a "right" outer join because, although we have everything in the right (second) Table (which is BOOKS), there are implied NULLs in the left (first) Table (which is CHECKOUTS). In such cases, the <keyword> RIGHT is mandatory (although the <keyword> OUTER is optional). You must always use RIGHT [OUTER] JOIN in conjunction with a USING clause or an ON clause — though a query can certainly also include a WHERE clause, it should not contain the joining conditions.

Because there are RIGHT [OUTER] JOINs, there ought to be LEFT [OUTER] JOINs too and indeed there are. For instance, we could have made our query this way:

```
SELECT Books.title, Books.checkout_date, Checkouts.borrower_id
FROM   Books LEFT OUTER JOIN Checkouts USING (book_id);
```

There is also a FULL [OUTER] JOIN, for situations when there might be missing information from both joined Tables. This is rarely used.

To summarize: the basic idea behind an OUTER JOIN is that, where an INNER JOIN would lose rows because there is no row in one of the joined Tables that matches a row in the other Table, an OUTER JOIN includes such rows — with a NULL in the Column positions that would show values from some matching row, if a matching row existed. An INNER JOIN loses non-matching rows; an OUTER JOIN preserves them. For two Tables, a LEFT OUTER JOIN preserves non-matching rows from the first Table, a RIGHT OUTER JOIN preserves non-matching rows from the second Table, and a FULL OUTER JOIN preserves non-matching rows from both Tables.

Consider using OUTER JOIN if you worry that INNER JOIN would lose information that is really valuable. But if you use them a lot, that's too often. There are severe consequences to using outer joins unnecessarily:

OUTER JOIN **Downside #1 — Performance** Inner joins are always faster.

OUTER JOIN **Downside #2 — Syntax** Although all the major vendors are now able to handle the SQL-92 Standard syntax for outer joins, there is a bewildering variety of "outer join" syntaxes still in existence.

OUTER JOIN **Downside #3 — Three-way-join confusion** Let's face it, we're not bright enough to figure out what Table_1 LEFT JOIN Table_2 RIGHT JOIN Table_3 means. And it appears that not all vendors are bright either. Trying multiple outer joins with different DBMSs will give different results.

OUTER JOIN **Downside #4 — Nullability** You can't think "Column X was defined as NOT NULL so it will never be NULL" — any Column can be NULL if it's in an OUTER JOIN.

OUTER JOIN **Downside #5 — Confused** NULL We can't tell whether a NULL is due to an OUTER JOIN or was always there.

UNION JOIN

A UNION JOIN constructs a result Table that includes every Column of both Tables and every row of both Tables. Every Column position that has no value because it wasn't part of one or the other Table you're joining, gets a null value. Here's an example:

```
SELECT Checkouts UNION JOIN Books;
```

The result is:

BORROWER_ID	BOOK_ID	CHECKOUT_DATE	BOOK_ID	TITLE
1	1	NULL	NULL	NULL
2	2	NULL	NULL	NULL
2	3	NULL	NULL	NULL
NULL	NULL	1999-04-27	1	The Borrowers
NULL	NULL	1999-04-28	2	The Unexpected Mrs. Pollifax
NULL	NULL	1999-04-29	3	The Hobbit
NULL	NULL	NULL	4	Friday

Joined Tables aren't updatable in SQL-92. Usually, this means that a View which is based on a query that joins multiple Tables can't be the object of a DELETE, INSERT, or UPDATE statement.

But such Views might be updatable in SQL3. For example, a UNION JOIN is useful in SQL3 because it allows you to change the joined data. Consider a situation where you want to INSERT a row into a UNION JOIN of two Tables, where the first Table has five Columns and the second Table has six Columns (so the UNION JOIN has 11 Columns). There are three possible situations:

1. If the first 5 Columns of the new row are all NULL and any of the last six Columns are a non-null value, then the INSERT operation strips off the first 5 NULLs and puts the remaining new row into the second Table.
2. If any of the first 5 Columns of the new row are a non-null value and all of the last six Columns are NULL, then the INSERT operation strips off the last six NULLs and puts the remaining new row into the first Table.
3. If any of the first 5 Columns of the new row are a non-null value and any of the last six Columns are also a non-null value, then the INSERT operation will fail; your DBMS will return the SQLSTATE error 22014 "data exception-invalid update value."

Now consider a situation where you want to DELETE a row from the same UNION JOIN. This time, there are two possible situations:

1. If the row you want to DELETE was derived from the first Table (that is, the row contains only NULLs for every Column derived from the second Table), then the DELETE operation will remove that row from the first Table.
2. If the row you want to DELETE was derived from the second Table, then the DELETE operation will remove that row from the second Table.

Finally, consider a situation where you want to UPDATE a row from the same UNION JOIN. Once again, there are three possible situations:

1. If the row you want to UPDATE was derived from the first Table (and so the last six Columns of the row are NULL), then the UPDATE operation will change that row in the first Table.
2. If the row you want to UPDATE was derived from the second Table (and so the first five Columns of the row are NULL), then the UPDATE operation will change that row in the second Table.
3. If any of the first 5 Columns of the row you want to change are a non-null value and any of the last six Columns are also a non-null value, then the UPDATE operation will fail; your DBMS will return the SQLSTATE error 22014 "data exception-invalid update value."

Syntax Rules

Now that we've shown you an example of each type of join, here's a list of the formal syntax rules you'll have to follow when forming a join expression. First, we'll repeat the join syntax itself:

```
<joined Table> ::=
<Table reference> CROSS JOIN <Table reference> |
<Table reference> [ NATURAL ] [ <join type> ] JOIN <Table reference>
   [ <join specification> ] |
( <joined Table> )

   <join type> ::=
   INNER |
   {LEFT | RIGHT | FULL} [ OUTER ] |
   UNION

   <join specification> ::=
   ON <search condition> |
   USING (join <Column name> [ {,join <Column name>} ... ])
```

You can't join over BLOBs, CLOBs, NCLOBs, or ARRAYs, so don't name any Column with one of these <data type>s in a USING clause and don't expect a NATURAL JOIN to join over such Columns either.

If your join expression specifies NATURAL, it may not include either an ON clause or a USING clause; your DBMS will just search out the Columns with the same name and equal values in each Table. The common Columns must have mutually comparable <data type>s. For each pair of common Columns, only one Column will appear in the result. Because of this, when your SQL statement includes the join operator NATURAL, you may never qualify the common <Column name>(s) anywhere in the SQL statement.

If your join expression specifies UNION, it may not also specify NATURAL, nor may it include an ON clause or a USING clause; your DBMS will merely join every Column in each Table together, for all rows in both Tables.

If your join expression doesn't specify either NATURAL or UNION, then it must include either an ON clause or a USING clause, to tell your DBMS what the join conditions are. The USING clause provides the unqualified name of the common Column (or a list of names, if the Tables have multiple common Columns). Once again, for each pair of common Columns, only one Column will appear in the result, so any <Column name> that appears in a USING clause may never be qualified within the SQL statement that contains that USING clause. The ON clause provides the condition that must be met for joining the Tables so, within an SQL statement, common <Column name>s that appear in an ON clause may be qualified throughout that SQL statement.

If your join expression is "Table_1 NATURAL JOIN Table_2", the effect is the same as if you specified "Table_1 NATURAL INNER JOIN Table_2" — so non-matching rows won't be part of the result Table.

If you want to restrict your code to Core SQL, don't use CROSS JOIN, UNION JOIN, or NATURAL for any type of join and don't use FULL [OUTER] JOIN.

Retrieval using Joins

The ability to join a Table to others is one of the most powerful features of SQL. Here's some more examples of joins, using the sample database we defined in Chapter 29 "Simple Search Conditions." Remember that, to join Tables, the select list must contain the unambiguous names of the desired Columns and the ON, USING, or WHERE clause must specify the conditions which define the relationship between them. (The relationship is usually equality, but it need not be.) Also, of course, the Columns that specify the required join relationship must have comparable <data-type>s; that is, they must either both be numeric or both be character strings or both be dates, and so on. They do not always have to have the same name, but it is helpful in reading the query if they do.

To find all information available on all employees (retrieve a join of all Columns) the following SQL statements are equivalent:

```
SELECT Employee.*,Payroll.*
FROM   Employee,Payroll
WHERE  Employee.empnum=Payroll.empnum;

SELECT *
FROM   Employee,Payroll
WHERE  Employee.empnum=Payroll.empnum;

SELECT *
FROM   Employee NATURAL JOIN Payroll;

SELECT *
FROM   Employee JOIN Payroll USING(empnum);
```

```
SELECT *
FROM   Employee JOIN Payroll ON Employee.empnum=Payroll.empnum;
```

The result is the entire EMPLOYEE Table joined with the entire PAYROLL Table over their matching employee numbers; ten rows and ten columns in all. Note the <Column reference>s for the EMPNUM Column, to avoid ambiguity. To eliminate duplicate Columns from the result, specific <Column reference>s (rather than "*") must be put in the select list, as in these two equivalent SQL statements:

```
SELECT Employee.empnum,dept,surname,rate,location
FROM   Employee,Payroll
WHERE  Employee.empnum=1 and Employee.empnum=Payroll.empnum;

SELECT empnum,dept,surname,rate,location
FROM   Employee NATURAL JOIN Payroll
WHERE  empnum=1;
```

The result is:

EMPNUM	DEPT	SURNAME	RATE	LOCATION
1	A	KOO	6.00	10TH FLOOR

To find an employee's manager (retrieve one equivalent Column from multiple Tables):

```
SELECT surname,manager
FROM   Employee NATURAL JOIN Department
WHERE  empnum=28;
```

The result is:

SURNAME	MANAGER
TURNER	JONES B

To find the pay rates and locations of all department A employees (join values fulfilling multiple conditions from multiple Tables):

```
SELECT *
FROM   Employee NATURAL JOIN Payroll ON dept='A';
```

The result is the EMPLOYEE Table joined with the PAYROLL Table, for all rows where the DEPT Column contains an "A" in both Tables.

To find the department and payroll data for employee 35, here are two equivalent SQL statements:

```
SELECT Employee.empnum,surname,Employee.dept,manager,rate
FROM   Employee,Department,Payroll
WHERE  Employee.empnum=35 AND
       Employee.empnum=Payroll.empnum AND
       Employee.dept=Department.dept;

SELECT empnum,surname,dept,manager,rate
FROM   Department NATURAL JOIN Employee NATURAL JOIN Payroll
WHERE  empnum=35;
```

The result is:

EMPNUM	SURNAME	DEPT	MANAGER	RATE
35	OLSEN	E	GREEN E	9.00

Outer join results Tables are produced exactly the same way as inner join results are — with the exception that, in an outer join, rows are retrieved even when data in one of the Tables has no match in the other.

If a row in the first Table named has no match in the second Table and the outer join type is either a `LEFT JOIN` or a `FULL JOIN`, then a dummy row appears for the second Table. If a row in the second Table named has no match in the first Table and the outer join type is either a `RIGHT JOIN` or a `FULL JOIN`, then a dummy row appears for the first Table. In both cases, the Columns in a dummy row are all equal to their `DEFAULT` values.

For example, suppose `TABLE_1` has one Column and four rows, containing the values {`1,2,3,5`} and `TABLE_2` has one Column and four rows, containing the values {`2,4,5,7`}. An inner join query on the Tables would be:

```
SELECT Table_1.column_1 AS T1_column,
       Table_2.column_1 AS T2_column
FROM   Table_1 INNER JOIN Table_2
       ON Table_1.column_1 = Table_2.column_1;
```

The result is:

T1_COLUMN	T2_COLUMN
2	2
5	5

The values in either Table that have no match are not retrieved.

A left outer join query on the Tables would be:

```
SELECT Table_1.column_1 AS T1_column,
       Table_2.column_1 AS T2_column
FROM   Table_1 LEFT JOIN Table_2
       ON Table_1.column_1 = Table_2.column_1;
```

The result is:

T1_COLUMN	T2_COLUMN
1	NULL
2	2
3	NULL
5	5

The values in the first (left) Table that have no match are matched with a NULL (or default) value.

A right outer join query on the Tables would be:

```
SELECT Table_1.column_1 AS T1_column,
       Table_2.column_1 AS T2_column
FROM   Table_1 RIGHT JOIN Table_2
       ON Table_1.column_1 = Table_2.column_1;
```

The result is:

T1_COLUMN	T2_COLUMN
2	2
NULL	4
5	5
NULL	7

The values in the second (right) Table that have no match are matched with a NULL (or default) value.

A full outer join query on the Tables would be:

```
SELECT Table_1.column_1 AS T1_column,
       Table_2.column_1 AS T2_column
FROM   Table_1 FULL JOIN Table_2
       ON Table_1.column_1 = Table_2.column_1;
```

The result is:

T1_COLUMN	T2_COLUMN
1	NULL
2	2
3	NULL
NULL	4
5	5
NULL	7

The values in either Table that have no match are matched with a NULL (or default) value.

Dialects

Because "modern" syntax is relatively new to SQL, various products support different syntax for the types of joins we've illustrated here. For example:

- Oracle uses "WHERE Table_1.column (+) = Table_2.column" for a LEFT OUTER JOIN.
- For Microsoft SQL Server, the search condition for an OUTER JOIN must be an equals condition.

31

Chapter 31

Searching with Subqueries

A subquery is a parenthesized query enclosed within some outer SQL statement. Most queries are SELECTs, so this means that a subquery usually takes the form (SELECT ...), nested somewhere inside an expression. Queries return result sets, or Tables, and the values in such Tables can be used when the syntax of the outer expression calls for a value of the appropriate <data type>.

Subqueries make an SQL statement look structured and indeed it was the presence of subqueries that gave the original SQL its distinctive look (the letters SQL used to stand for "Structured Query Language"). Nowadays subqueries are less essential because there other ways (particularly joins and UNION/EXCEPT/INTERSECT operators) to reach the same ends. Nevertheless, they are important because they provide the following benefits:

- SQL statements with subqueries are readable. Most people, especially if they are familiar with the role of subordinate clauses in English, can figure that a subquery-containing SQL statement can be read "from the inside out" — that is, they can focus on the subquery's workings first and then on the separate analysis of the outer statement. Statements with joins, by contrast, must be read all at once.
- Certain types of problems can be stated more concisely and more efficiently with subqueries.

Subquery Syntax

A subquery is used to specify either a value (the scalar subquery, which returns one value), a row (the row subquery, which returns one row), or a Table (the Table subquery, which returns a result Table). The required syntax for a subquery is as follows.

```
<subquery> ::=
( <query expression> )
```

That is, a subquery is a parenthesized <query expression> — and the <query expression> is usually a SELECT statement. Here's an example:

```
SELECT                                         /* outer statement begins */
     Table_1.column_1,
     Table_1.column_2
FROM Table_1 WHERE Table_1.column_1 =
     (SELECT *                                 /* subquery begins */
      FROM   Table_2
      WHERE Table_2.column_1 = 5);
```

There are some restrictions regarding where subqueries can be used and what they may contain. In early SQL days, the restrictions were quite strict. For instance, the subquery had to be on the right side of a comparison operator within a WHERE clause, as in the previous example. Nowadays, the restrictions for an SQL subquery, in a fully-conformant DBMS environment, are mild:

- There can be no ORDER BY clause inside the subquery.
- The subquery's select list may not include any reference to a value that evaluates to a BLOB, CLOB, NCLOB, or ARRAY.
- A subquery may not be immediately enclosed within a set function, for example:

```
... AVG((SELECT column_1 FROM Table_1)) ...
```

is not legal syntax.

It is legal to nest subqueries within subqueries. The maximum level of nesting depends on your implementation because the Standard doesn't specify the number of levels of nesting that must be supported.

We said earlier that there are three types of subquery. They are distinguished from each other, not by their form — the general form of a subquery is always just "(<query expression>)" — but by the shape of their result; how many Columns and rows do they return?

- If a subquery can return exactly one Column and one row, it is a *scalar subquery.* The subquery:

```
... (SELECT MAX(Table_1.column_1) FROM Table_1) ...
```

would fit the bill, but usually it's not so easy to simply glance at a query and realize that it will return only one Column and one row.

- If a subquery can return more than one Column, but still exactly one row, it is a row subquery. A *row subquery* is just a generalized derivation of a scalar subquery used in some comparisons. Row subqueries are the least-frequently-seen type of subquery.
- If a subquery can return more than one Column and more than one row, it is a Table subquery. A *Table subquery* is another type of <Table reference> and can be used in an SQL statement wherever a <Table name> can be used — which isn't very often! However, there are some special search operators which are specifically designed to work with Table subqueries. Discussion of those search operators is an important part of this chapter.

Thus, the distinction between subquery types depends on the size of the select list and the number of rows returned. The three types of subquery are not utterly separate; a scalar subquery's definition is subsumed by a row subquery's definition, which is subsumed by a Table subquery's definition. (In fact, a one-Column Table subquery is such a common thing that some people regard it as a separate type which they call a "Column subquery.") Nevertheless, the potential distinction should be kept in mind. It's easy to get confused by assuming that everything which applies for one type, applies for the others as well. We will discuss scalar subqueries, row subqueries, and Table subqueries separately.

Scalar Subqueries

In general terms, a scalar subquery resembles a scalar function. Remember that a scalar function returns a single value, given an argument which is some sort of expression — well, a scalar subquery returns a single value, given an argument which is a <query expression>. Because that value must be a scalar value, a few aspects of scalar subqueries are simply logical consequences of their definitions:

- The <data type>, Collation, length, and all other significant attributes of the value are inherited from the attributes of the selected Column. For example, the result of the subquery:

```
... (SELECT 'abc' FROM Table_1) ...
```

  has a <data type> of `CHAR(3)`.
- It is an error if, at runtime, the DBMS discovers that a scalar subquery returns more than one row. If this is the case, the entire SQL statement will fail; your DBMS will return the `SQLSTATE error 21000 "cardinality violation."`

One thing that does *not* follow from the definition and, in fact, surprises some analysts, is the value returned when a scalar subquery returns zero rows. In this case, the result is `NULL`. For example, consider this SQL statement:

```
UPDATE Table_1 SET
   column_1 = (SELECT column_1 FROM Table_2 WHERE 1 = 2);
```

Because 1 is never equal to 2, the search condition in this subquery example will always be `FALSE` — so the subquery result is an empty set. In this case, the `UPDATE` operation assigns a null value to `COLUMN_1` in `TABLE_1`. This is a case where `NULL` obviously does not mean "unknown" or "not applicable" — it means "not there" — but no great harm results.

Here are some examples of scalar subqueries. You can tell that these must be scalar subqueries — not row subqueries or Table subqueries — because they are being used in places where only scalar values are legal.

```
-- scalar subquery in a select list
SELECT 'value is:',
       (SELECT column_1 FROM Table_1)
FROM   Table_2;

-- scalar subquery in an UPDATE ... SET clause
UPDATE Table_1 SET
   column_1 = (SELECT AVG(column_1) FROM Table_2);

-- scalar subquery in a comparison
SELECT column_3.column_1
FROM   Table_1
WHERE (SELECT MAX(column_1) FROM Table_1) =
      (SELECT MIN(column_1) FROM Table_2);

-- scalar subquery with arithmetic
INSERT INTO Table_1
VALUES (1 + (SELECT column_1 FROM Table_2));
```

Our third example of a scalar subquery shows its use in a `WHERE` clause. This is a traditional and common usage, as it used to be the only place a subquery could appear. These general observations apply if you're including a scalar subquery in a comparison:

- The "comparison" operator is not limited to the traditional operators; it can be pretty well any predicate, including `LIKE` or `BETWEEN`.
- The subquery can be on either side of the comparison operator. There can even be subqueries on both sides of the comparison operator.
- The subquery can be in an expression, along with arithmetic or scalar function operators.
- The subquery result will depend on the number of rows returned; one row is normal and gives a known result, two or more rows results in a "cardinality violation" error and zero rows results in the comparison predicate returning `UNKNOWN` because the subquery result value is `NULL`. We've repeated these general observations here because we want to emphasize that such observations apply only to scalar subqueries. None of them will apply when we discuss comparisons that involve Table subqueries.

Row Subqueries

Row subqueries are similar to scalar subqueries in the one fundamental respect — they may not return more than one row. If a row subquery returns two or more rows, the entire SQL statement will fail; your DBMS will return the `SQLSTATE error 21000 "cardinality violation."`

Row subqueries offer a slight convenience for comparison operations. For example, we can say:

```
SELECT *
FROM   Table_1
WHERE  (column_1,'X') = (SELECT column_1,column_2 FROM Table_2);
```

That is, we can compare two Column values using a single equals operator. This is more concise and probably more efficient than comparing twice with scalar subqueries, as in this equivalent example:

```
SELECT *
FROM   Table_1
WHERE  Table_1.column_1 = (SELECT Table_2.column_1 FROM Table_2) AND
       'X' = (SELECT Table_2.column_2 FROM Table_2);
```

A row subquery, then, is a form of row value expression — an expression that evaluates to one row. This construct can be used with every SQL predicate, not just basic comparison.

Table Subqueries

We now switch from talking about "one-row" subqueries, to talking about "multi-row" subqueries, or Table subqueries. This means, almost exclusively, subqueries that are used in comparison operations.

Quite often, a Table subquery looks like a scalar subquery, because — almost always — a single Column makes up the subquery's select list. You can distinguish a Table subquery from context, though; it will always be preceded by a special for-Table-subqueries-only operator, either <comparison_operator> `ALL`, <comparison_operator> `ANY` (or its synonym, <comparison_operator> `SOME`), `IN`, `EXISTS`, or `UNIQUE`.

Correlated Subqueries

A correlated subquery is a subquery that contains references to the values in Tables that are referred to in the outer statement (that is, the SQL statement in which the subquery is nested). These references are, in standard terminology, "outer references." One tends to find outer references in Table subqueries, although, in theory, there is nothing to restrict them to that role. Here's an example (for now, concentrate only on the syntax we're showing):

```
SELECT *
FROM   Table_1
WHERE  column_1 = ANY
       (SELECT column_1
        FROM   Table_2
        WHERE  column_2 = Table_1.column_2);
```

There are two things to note in this example:

First: The subquery's WHERE clause refers to Table_1.column_2, but TABLE_1 is not mentioned in the subquery's FROM clause. Instead, TABLE_1 is named in the outer query's FROM clause — this is the outer reference.

Second: Besides Table_1.column_2, the subquery's WHERE clause has another Column named COLUMN_2. This reference is to the COLUMN_2 that belongs to TABLE_2. We could have used the <Column reference> TABLE_2.COLUMN_2 for clarity, but this isn't necessary. By default, a <Column name> applies to the Table(s) in the nearest FROM clause — there is a scoping rule that says: Look in the local subquery first for resolution of <Column reference>s, then look outward, progressing if necessary through several levels of nesting, until the outermost query is reached.

Occasionally, the <Table name>s are the same in the subquery and in the outer statement. When this happens, it's the subquery analog of the self-join and so you'll need to define <Correlation name>s for the Tables. Here's an example:

```
SELECT *
FROM   Table_1 AS T_one_a
WHERE  column_1 = ANY
       (SELECT column_1
        FROM   Table_1 AS T_one_b
        WHERE T_one_b.column_2 = T_one_a.column_2);
```

Whenever a subquery contains an outer reference, it is correlated with the outer statement. That means your DBMS can't evaluate the subquery without feeding it values from outside the subquery. Correlation can be messy and some DBMSs handle it poorly. But sometimes there's no alternative.

Quantified Comparisons

In our chapters on the various <data type>s, we showed you which of them could be used in an expression that compared a value of that <data type> with the collection of values returned by a Table subquery. Here's a more detailed explanation of quantified comparisons using the quantifiers ALL, SOME, ANY.

ALL

The required syntax for an ALL quantified comparison is as follows.

```
scalar_expression comparison_operator ALL <Table subquery>
```

Here, scalar_expression may be any expression that evaluates to a single value and comparison_operator may be any one of: = or > or < or >= or <= or <>. ALL returns TRUE if the Table subquery returns zero rows or if the comparison operator returns TRUE for every row returned by the Table subquery. ALL returns FALSE if the comparison operator returns FALSE for at least one row returned by the Table subquery. Suppose that TABLE_1 has one Column, defined as DECIMAL(6,2). Here's what will happen, for different values in the rows of TABLE_1, for this expression:

```
... WHERE 1000.00 > ALL
     (SELECT column_1 FROM Table_1) ...
```

- If TABLE_1 contains the values {100.00, 200.00, 300.00}, the expression is TRUE; all of TABLE_1's values are less than 1000.00.
- If TABLE_1 contains the values {NULL, 2000.00, 300.00}, the expression is FALSE; one of TABLE_1's values is greater than 1000.00.
- If TABLE_1 contains the values {1000.00, 200.00, 300.00}, the expression is FALSE too; one of TABLE_1's values is equal to 1000.00.
- If TABLE_1 contains no values, the expression is TRUE; when the set is empty, ALL is TRUE.
- If TABLE_1 contains the values {100.00, NULL, 300.00}, the expression is UNKNOWN; when all non-null comparisons return TRUE, but there's a NULL, ALL is UNKNOWN.

ANY or SOME

The required syntax for an ANY or SOME quantified comparison is as follows.

```
scalar_expression comparison_operator ANY <Table subquery> |
scalar_expression comparison_operator SOME <Table subquery>
```

Once again, scalar_expression may be any expression that evaluates to a single value and comparison_operator may be any one of: = or > or < or >= or <= or <>. SOME and ANY are synonyms. They return TRUE if the comparison operator returns TRUE for at least one row returned by the Table subquery. They return FALSE if the Table subquery returns zero rows or if the comparison operator returns FALSE for every row returned by the Table subquery. Suppose, once again, that TABLE_1 has one Column, defined as DECIMAL(6,2). Here's what will happen, for different values in the rows of TABLE_1, for this expression:

```
... WHERE 1000.00 > ANY
     (SELECT column_1 FROM Table_1) ...
```

- If TABLE_1 contains the values {100.00, 200.00, 300.00}, the expression is TRUE; all of TABLE_1's values are less than 1000.00.
- If TABLE_1 contains the values {NULL, 2000.00, 300.00}, the expression is TRUE too; at least some of TABLE_1's values are less than 1000.00.
- If TABLE_1 contains no values, the expression is FALSE; when the set is empty, ANY is FALSE.
- If TABLE_1 contains the values {1000.00, 2000.00, 3000.00}, the expression is FALSE too; all of TABLE_1's values are greater than or equal to 1000.00.
- If TABLE_1 contains the values {1000.00, NULL, 3000.00}, the expression is UNKNOWN; when all non-null comparisons return FALSE, but there's a NULL, ANY is UNKNOWN.

There is a small trap when one considers the expression "... 1000.00 <> ANY (<subquery>) ...". Such an expression could be carelessly read as "... 1,000 is not equal to any subquery result ..." — that is, 1,000 is not equal to every row returned by the subquery. That is not the correct way to read such expressions because it leads to the English-language ambiguity that "any" can mean "every." There are three ways to avoid such ambiguities:

1. Don't use the ANY <keyword>. Use its synonym, SOME, instead.
2. When negatives are involved, replace ANY with ALL. Logic tells us that these transformations are possible:

```
expression <> ANY subquery -> expression = ALL subquery
NOT (expression = ANY subquery) -> expression <> ALL subquery
```

   as long as the subquery does not return an empty set.
3. Use a completely different syntax, for example, the EXISTS predicate, which we'll discuss later in this chapter.

Quantified Retrieval

Here's some examples of comparisons with subqueries using the sample database we defined in Chapter 29 "Simple Search Conditions." To find the records for the employees reporting to a manager named D. Black:

```
SELECT *
FROM   Employee
WHERE  dept =
   (SELECT dept FROM Department WHERE manager='BLACK D');
```

The result is:

EMPNUM	DEPT	SURNAME	GNAME	ADDRESS
4	D	MORGAN	CHUCK	963 SOUTH

Because there is only one possible row in the DEPARTMENT Table with a manager named BLACK D, the equals operator can be used in this subquery without a quantifier. If more than one value is possible, either ALL, ANY, or SOME is needed to quantify the comparison operator, as in this example:

```
SELECT manager
FROM   Department
WHERE  dept = ANY
       (SELECT dept FROM Employee WHERE empnum<3);
```

The result is:

MANAGER
SMITH A
JONES B

Predicates

In addition to quantified comparisons, SQL provides four other predicates that operate on the results of a Table subquery: the <in predicate>, the <exists predicate>, the <unique predicate>, and the <match predicate>. Each will return a boolean value: either TRUE, FALSE, or UNKNOWN.

<in predicate>

The required syntax for an <in predicate> is as follows.

```
<in predicate> ::=
row_expression [ NOT ] IN <in predicate value>

   <in predicate value> ::=
   <Table subquery> |
   (row_expression [ {,row_expression}... ])
```

An <in predicate> compares a value to a collection of values and returns either TRUE, FALSE, or UNKNOWN. (If any argument is NULL, the <in predicate> returns UNKNOWN.) IN searches for data that matches any one of a specified collection of values. NOT IN searches for data that doesn't match any of the values in the collection. Note the words we've used in this explanation; IN can be used to replace the quantified comparison "= ANY" — that is, these two expressions are equivalent:

```
... WHERE 'A' IN (SELECT column_1 FROM Table_1) ...
... WHERE 'A' = ANY (SELECT column_1 FROM Table_1) ...
```

This example shows one of the two variants of IN. The other variant is:

```
IN (<list of values>)
```

This syntax has nothing to do with subqueries, but while we're on the subject, these two expressions are also equivalent:

```
... WHERE column_1 IN ('A','B','C') ...
... WHERE column_1 = 'A' OR column_1 = 'B' OR column_1 = 'C' ...
```

With IN, all the expressions must be comparable. You can use [NOT] IN to compare one or more values to a collection; row_expression may be any expression which evaluates either to a single value or to a row of values.

The <in predicate> is TRUE if the value of row_expression is found within the <in predicate value>. For example, these <in predicate>s are both TRUE:

```
1 IN (1,2,3)
1 IN (SELECT column_1 FROM Table_1 where column_1 = 1)
```

NOT IN is simply the negation of IN so these predicates are also TRUE:

```
1 NOT IN (5,6,7)
1 NOT IN (SELECT column_1 FROM Table_1 where column_1 = 15)
```

In other words, the <in predicate> has two variants, both of which are merely shorthands for some other comparison syntax, so the same rules that apply for comparisons of specific <data type>s apply to IN as well. In both cases, IN appears to be more popular than the wordings it replaces.

If you want to restrict your code to Core SQL, make sure that all expressions in an <in value list> are either <literal>s, references to host variables or SQL parameters, <Field reference>s, or CURRENT_PATH, CURRENT_ROLE, CURRENT_USER, SESSION_USER, SYSTEM_USER, USER.

Retrieval with IN

Here's some examples of the <in predicate> using the sample database we defined in Chapter 29 "Simple Search Conditions." To find the addresses of the employees working in either department C or department D (retrieve values which match any of a list of specified values):

```
SELECT dept,empnum,address
FROM   Employee
WHERE  dept IN ('C','D');
```

The result is:

DEPT	EMPNUM	ADDRESS
C	3	567 NORTH
D	4	963 SOUTH

To find the employee numbers of the employees whose pay rate is not 5.00, 9.00, or 16.00 (retrieve values which do not match any of a specified list):

```
SELECT empnum
FROM   Payroll
WHERE  rate NOT IN (5,9,16);
```

The result is:

EMPNUM
1
4

To find the names of employees earning a rate of 8.00 (retrieve values which match any returned by a subquery):

```
SELECT surname
FROM   Employee
WHERE  empnum IN
   (SELECT empnum
   FROM   Payroll
   WHERE  rate=8);
```

The result is:

SURNAME
MORGAN

In this example, the subquery is first evaluated to find the payroll records with a rate of 8.00. The employee numbers of the result are then compared to the employee numbers of the EMPLOYEE Table to retrieve the surnames for the final result.

To find the employees located in the warehouse:

```
SELECT surname FROM Employee WHERE empnum IN
   (SELECT empnum FROM Payroll WHERE location='WAREHOUSE');
```

The result is:

SURNAME
JONES
FRANCIS

To find the names of the employees who report to A Smith:

```
SELECT gname,surname FROM Employee WHERE dept IN
   (SELECT dept FROM Department WHERE manager='SMITH A');
```

The result is:

GNAME	SURNAME
SARA	KOO
ALICE	SMITH

IN expressions can be nested. To find the manager of employees working in the warehouse:

```
SELECT manager FROM Department WHERE dept IN
   (SELECT dept FROM Employee WHERE empnum IN
      (SELECT empnum FROM Payroll WHERE location='WAREHOUSE'));
```

The result is:

MANAGER
BROWN C
GREEN E

To find the names of employees who don't work on the 10th floor (retrieve values which don't match any returned by a subquery):

```
SELECT gname,surname FROM Employees WHERE empnum IN
(SELECT empnum FROM Payroll WHERE location<>'10TH FLOOR');
```

The result is:

GNAME	SURNAME
JOHN	MARSH
MABEL	JONES
CHUCK	MORGAN
ALICE	SMITH
BOB	JONES
CHRIS	FRANCIS
LINDA	TURNER

<exists predicate>

The required syntax for an <exists predicate> is as follows.

```
<exists predicate> ::=
[ NOT ] EXISTS <Table subquery>
```

An <exists predicate> is a test for a non-empty set and returns either TRUE or FALSE. EXISTS is TRUE if the Table subquery returns at least one row; otherwise it is FALSE. NOT EXISTS is TRUE if the Table subquery returns zero rows; otherwise it is FALSE.

By tradition, the <Table subquery> following an <exists predicate> begins with SELECT *. In this case, the asterisk is not a shorthand for a list of Columns, it merely stands for "some Column." Unless you're using Core SQL, it doesn't actually matter what you put here — but in Core SQL, the Table subquery's select list must either be just an asterisk or it must evaluate to a single derived Column. Whatever you use, the result is the same; if the subquery returns any rows, EXISTS is TRUE — regardless of the number of Columns that the subquery result contains. Here's an example:

```
SELECT column_1
FROM   Table_1
WHERE  EXISTS (SELECT * FROM Table_2);
```

If there are any rows at all in TABLE_2, then the search condition is TRUE and all values of TABLE_1.COLUMN_1 will be selected. This is a rare example of a rather static subquery. Much more often, the Table subquery will be a correlated subquery.

If you use EXISTS, followed by a correlated subquery with a single outer reference, you are accomplishing the same thing as you would accomplish with a quantified ANY comparison. For example, here are two equivalent SQL statements:

```
-- query using "> ANY" and a simple subquery
SELECT *
FROM   Table_1
WHERE  column_1 > ANY
   (SELECT column_1
   FROM   Table_2
   WHERE  Table_2.column_2 = 5);

-- the same query, using EXISTS and a correlated subquery
SELECT *
FROM   Table_1
WHERE  EXISTS
   (SELECT *
   FROM   Table_2
   WHERE  Table_2.column_2 = 5 AND
          Table_1.column_1 > Table_2.column_1);
```

The EXISTS version of the request is more cumbersome, but it's a better choice if there are several items to compare between the outer statement and the subquery.

NOT EXISTS is merely the negation of EXISTS, but it deserves attention as a separate operator. The interesting case is a double-nested NOT EXISTS predicate, which can solve questions of the general form — find all the A's which are related to all of the B's. Logicians call these FORALL questions. An example of a FORALL question is, "List the students who are in a class for every course that the school offers." Expressed with a double-nested NOT EXISTS predicate, this question is answered with:

```
SELECT student_name
FROM   Students
WHERE  NOT EXISTS
   (SELECT *
   FROM   Courses
   WHERE  NOT EXISTS
      (SELECT *
      FROM   Classes
      WHERE  Classes.course_id = Courses.course_id AND
             Classes.student_id = Students.student_id));
```

In other words, "Look for the case where there exists no student where there exists no course where there exists a class for the course containing the student." We can't say that quickly three times, but it doesn't matter; you can use this example as a template for FORALL questions.

Retrieval with EXISTS

Here's some examples of the <exists predicate> using the sample database we defined in Chapter 29 "Simple Search Conditions." To find the names of employees earning a rate of 8.00 (retrieve a value only if some condition exists):

```
SELECT surname FROM Employee WHERE EXISTS
   (SELECT * FROM Payroll WHERE rate=8 AND empnum=Employee.Empnum);
```

The result is:

SURNAME
MORGAN

To find the employees located in the warehouse:

```
SELECT surname FROM Employee WHERE EXISTS
   (SELECT * FROM Payroll
    WHERE  location='WAREHOUSE' AND empnum=Employee.empnum);
```

The result is:

SURNAME
JONES
FRANCIS

EXISTS expressions can be nested. To find the managers of employees working in the warehouse:

```
SELECT MANAGER FROM Department WHERE EXISTS
   (SELECT * FROM Employee WHERE dept=Department.dept AND EXISTS
      (SELECT * FROM Payroll
       WHERE  location='WAREHOUSE' AND empnum=Employee.empnum));
```

The result is:

MANAGER
BROWN C
GREEN E

<unique predicate>

The required syntax for a <unique predicate> is as follows.

```
<unique predicate> ::=
[ NOT ] UNIQUE <Table subquery>
```

A <unique predicate> is a test for duplicate rows and returns either TRUE or FALSE. UNIQUE returns TRUE if the Table subquery returns zero rows or one row or if every row returned by the Table subquery is unique (that is, every row contains a different set of non-null values than every other row); otherwise it returns FALSE. NOT UNIQUE returns TRUE if any row returned by the Table subquery is an exact duplicate of another row; otherwise it returns FALSE. The <unique predicate> shouldn't be used if the Table subquery returns Columns with a <data type> of BLOB, CLOB, NCLOB, or ARRAY.

For an example of how UNIQUE works, suppose that TABLE_1 has one Column, defined as DECIMAL(6,2). Here's what will happen, for different values in the rows of TABLE_1, for this expression:

```
... WHERE UNIQUE (SELECT column_1 FROM Table_1) ...
```

- If TABLE_1 contains the values {100.00, 200.00, 300.00}, the expression is TRUE; all of TABLE_1's rows are different.
- If TABLE_1 contains only {100.00}, the expression is TRUE too; all of TABLE_1's rows are different because there is only one.
- If TABLE_1 contains no values, the expression is also TRUE; when the set is empty, UNIQUE is TRUE.
- If TABLE_1 contains the values {100.00, 2000.00, 100.00}, the expression is FALSE; at least two of TABLE_1's rows are the same.
- If TABLE_1 contains the values {100.00, NULL, 300.00}, the expression is TRUE; when NULLs are involved, UNIQUE ignores them and looks at the remaining values. In this case, all of TABLE_1's remaining rows are different.
- If TABLE_1 contains the values {100.00, NULL, 100.00}, the expression is FALSE; after eliminating NULLs, at least two of TABLE_1's remaining rows are the same.

The <unique predicate> was introduced to SQL with SQL-92 but is still not much used in application programs. Its main purpose is to expose the operation which the DBMS uses to handle UNIQUE Constraints. For example, in the following pair of SQL statements, the first is a UNIQUE Constraint definition and the second is a statement that the DBMS implicitly uses to enforce the Constraint:

```
   -- UNIQUE Constraint definition
ALTER TABLE Table_1 ADD CONSTRAINT unique_constraint
   UNIQUE(column_1);

-- implicitly-used enforcement statement
SELECT * FROM Table_1
WHERE  UNIQUE (SELECT column_1 FROM Table_1);
```

If you want to restrict your code to Core SQL, don't use the <unique predicate>.

<match predicate>

The required syntax for a <match predicate> is as follows.

```
<match predicate> ::=
row_expression MATCH [ UNIQUE ] [ SIMPLE | PARTIAL | FULL ]
<Table subquery>
```

A <match predicate> is a test for matching rows and returns either TRUE or FALSE. The row_expression can be any expression which evaluates to one row of values; this row must be comparable to the rows returned by the Table subquery — that is, row_expression and Table subquery must return rows with the same number of values and each pair of corresponding values must have comparable <data type>s. The <match predicate> can't be used if either row_expression or the Table subquery returns values with a <data type> of BLOB, CLOB, NCLOB, or ARRAY.

The <match predicate> has eight possible forms:

1. row_expression MATCH Table subquery
2. row_expression MATCH SIMPLE Table subquery
3. row_expression MATCH UNIQUE Table subquery
4. row_expression MATCH UNIQUE SIMPLE Table subquery
5. row_expression MATCH PARTIAL Table subquery
6. row_expression MATCH UNIQUE PARTIAL Table subquery
7. row_expression MATCH FULL Table subquery
8. row_expression MATCH UNIQUE FULL Table subquery

The first and second forms are equivalent, as are the third and fourth forms; if none of {SIMPLE | PARTIAL | UNIQUE} is specified, the default is SIMPLE.

The expression "row_expression MATCH SIMPLE Table subquery" is TRUE only in two cases:

1. It is TRUE if the result of row_expression contains at least one NULL — e.g., if row_expression evaluates to {100, NULL, 300}.
2. It is TRUE if the result of row_expression contains no NULLs and the Table subquery returns at least one row that is equal to row_expression.

The expression "row_expression MATCH UNIQUE SIMPLE Table subquery" is TRUE only in two cases:

1. It is TRUE if the result of row_expression contains at least one NULL.
2. It is TRUE if the result of row_expression contains no NULLs and the Table subquery returns exactly one row that is equal to row_expression.

The expression "row_expression MATCH PARTIAL Table subquery" is TRUE only in two cases:

1. It is TRUE if the result of row_expression contains only NULLs — e.g., if row_expression evaluates to {NULL, NULL, NULL}.
2. It is TRUE if the Table subquery returns at least one row whose values equal their corresponding non-null values in row_expression — e.g., if row_expression evaluates to {100,

NULL, 300}, at least one row returned by the subquery must be {100, <any value at all>, 300}.

The expression "row_expression MATCH UNIQUE PARTIAL Table subquery" is TRUE only in two cases:

1. It is TRUE if the result of row_expression contains only NULLs.
2. It is TRUE if the Table subquery returns exactly one row whose values equal their corresponding non-null values in row_expression.

The expression "row_expression MATCH FULL Table subquery" is TRUE only in two cases:

1. It is TRUE if the result of row_expression contains only NULLs.
2. It is TRUE if the result of row_expression contains no NULLs and the Table subquery returns at least one row that is equal to row_expression.

The expression "row_expression MATCH UNIQUE FULL Table subquery" is TRUE only in two cases:

1. It is TRUE if the result of row_expression contains only NULLs.
2. It is TRUE if the result of row_expression contains no NULLs and the Table subquery returns exactly one row that is equal to row_expression.

Assume a Table called TABLE_1, defined with three Columns and containing this data:

TABLE_1

COLUMN_1	COLUMN_2	COLUMN_3
10	10	10
10	10	10
10	NULL	10
10	10	20

Using TABLE_1, here are some examples of <match predicate> expressions, all of which are TRUE:

```
... WHERE ROW(10,NULL,10) MATCH SIMPLE
    (SELECT * FROM Table_1) ...
... WHERE ROW(10,10,10) MATCH SIMPLE
    (SELECT * FROM Table_1) ...
... WHERE ROW(10,NULL,10) MATCH UNIQUE SIMPLE
    (SELECT * FROM Table_1) ...
... WHERE ROW(NULL,NULL,NULL) MATCH PARTIAL
    (SELECT * FROM Table_1) ...
... WHERE ROW(10,NULL,10) MATCH PARTIAL
    (SELECT * FROM Table_1) ...
... WHERE ROW(NULL,NULL,NULL) MATCH UNIQUE PARTIAL
    (SELECT * FROM Table_1) ...
```

```
... WHERE ROW(NULL,NULL,NULL) MATCH FULL
    (SELECT * FROM Table_1) ...
... WHERE ROW(10,10,10) MATCH FULL
    (SELECT * FROM Table_1) ...
```

Still using TABLE_1, here are some examples of <match predicate> expressions, all of which are FALSE:

```
... WHERE ROW(10,10,10) MATCH UNIQUE SIMPLE
    (SELECT * FROM Table_1) ...
... WHERE ROW(10,NULL,10) MATCH UNIQUE PARTIAL
    (SELECT * FROM Table_1) ...
... WHERE ROW(10,NULL,10) MATCH FULL
    (SELECT * FROM Table_1) ...
... WHERE ROW(10,10,10) MATCH UNIQUE FULL
    (SELECT * FROM Table_1) ...
```

If you want to restrict your code to Core SQL, don't use the <match predicate>.

<quantified predicate>

The required syntax for a <quantified predicate> is as follows.

```
<quantified predicate> ::=
FOR ALL <Table reference> list (<search condition>) |
FOR ANY <Table reference> list (<search condition>) |
FOR SOME <Table reference> list (<search condition>)

   <Table reference> list ::=
   <Table reference> [ {,<Table reference>} ... ]
```

A <quantified predicate> is a three-valued comparison test; it takes the Cartesian product of "<Table reference> list," compares the resulting rows with the search condition specified and returns either TRUE, FALSE, or UNKNOWN. The <Table reference> list may contain one or more <Table name>s or expressions that evaluate to Tables. The <quantified predicate>s work the same way that the regular quantifiers do — that is:

- FOR ALL returns TRUE if the search condition is TRUE for every row of the result of "<Table reference> list," returns TRUE if the result of "<Table reference> list" is zero rows, returns FALSE if the search condition is FALSE for at least one row of the result of "<Table reference> list," and otherwise returns UNKNOWN.
- FOR ANY returns TRUE if the search condition is TRUE for at least one row of the result of "<Table reference> list," returns FALSE if the search condition is FALSE for every row of the result of "<Table reference> list," returns FALSE if the result of "<Table reference> list" is zero rows and otherwise returns UNKNOWN. (As usual, FOR SOME is a synonym for FOR ANY.)

Subqueries are good for answering many complex analytical questions, but they can be hard to understand. As a good example, consider the "double NOT EXISTS" method, which handles FORALL questions in an ugly manner. The SQL3 Standard tries to resolve this by introducing FOR ALL and FOR ANY — two new predicates, which work only with Tables. Syntactically, the quantified predicates don't have to involve subqueries. But there are times when they could be replacements for subqueries (particularly the confusing NOT EXISTS syntax). Here are some simple examples:

```
... FOR ALL
      (SELECT * FROM Employee AS Emps) (empnum>50)
```

evaluates to FALSE if there are no employees with employee numbers greater than 50.

```
... FOR ANY
      (SELECT * FROM Payroll AS Pay) (location='BASEMENT')
```

evaluates to TRUE if at least one employee works in the basement.

If you want to restrict your code to Core SQL, don't use the <quantified predicate>.

Joins versus Subqueries

Often, SQL statements containing subqueries can be re-formulated as statements containing joins or vice versa. The choice of which to use normally depends on taste or optimization considerations. There are some scenarios, though, which call for subqueries rather than joins:

- When you want duplicates, but not false duplicates. Suppose Table_1 has three rows — {1,1,2} — and Table_2 has two rows — {1,2,2}. If you need to list the rows in Table_1 which are also in Table_2, only this subquery-based SELECT statement will give the right answer (1,1,2):

```
SELECT Table_1.column_1
FROM   Table_1
WHERE  Table_1.column_1 IN
   (SELECT Table_2.column_1
    FROM   Table_2);
```

  This SQL statement won't work:

```
SELECT Table_1.column_1
FROM   Table_1,Table_2
WHERE  Table_1.column_1 = Table_2.column_1;
```

  because the result will be {1,1,2,2} — and the duplication of 2 is an error. This SQL statement won't work either:

```
SELECT DISTINCT Table_1.column_1
FROM   Table_1,Table_2
WHERE  Table_1.column_1 = Table_2.column_1;
```

  because the result will be {1,2} — and the removal of the duplicated 1 is an error too.

- When the outermost statement is not a query. The SQL statement:

```
UPDATE Table_1 SET column_1 = (SELECT column_1 FROM Table_2);
```

  can't be expressed using a join unless some rare SQL3 features are used.

- When the join is over an expression. The SQL statement:

```
SELECT * FROM Table_1
WHERE column_1 + 5 =
   (SELECT MAX(column_1) FROM Table_2);
```

  is hard to express with a join. In fact, the only way we can think of is this SQL statement:

```
SELECT Table_1.*
FROM   Table_1,
       (SELECT MAX(column_1) AS max_column_1 FROM Table_2) AS Table_2
WHERE  Table_1.column_1 + 5 = Table_2.max_column_1;
```

  which still involves a parenthesized query, so nothing is gained from the transformation.

- When you want to see the exception. For example, suppose the question is, "What books are longer than *Das Kapital*?" These two queries are effectively *almost* the same:

```
SELECT DISTINCT Bookcolumn_1.*
FROM   Books AS Bookcolumn_1 JOIN Books AS Bookcolumn_2
       USING(page_count)
WHERE  title = 'Das Kapital';

SELECT DISTINCT Bookcolumn_1.*
FROM   Books AS Bookcolumn_1
WHERE  Bookcolumn_1.page_count >
   (SELECT DISTINCT page_count
   FROM   Books AS Bookcolumn_2
   WHERE  title = 'Das Kapital');
```

  The difference between these two SQL statements is, if there are two editions of *Das Kapital* (with different page counts), then the self-join example will return the books which are longer than the shortest edition of *Das Kapital*. That might be the wrong answer because the original question didn't ask for "... longer than ANY book named *Das Kapital*" (it seems to contain a false assumption that there's only one edition).

Subquery Examples

The following examples are derived, with much editing, from an SQL application suite for a public library. They illustrate the most common situations where subqueries have proven to be useful tools.

When a query is on one Table, but requires a quick look at a Column in another Table — for example, "Show the number of books checked out for a particular patron." Here's a subquery that answers this:

```
SELECT COUNT(*) FROM Circulations WHERE patron_id = ANY
   (SELECT patron_id FROM Patrons WHERE Surname = 'Jones');
```

When detail and summary data are retrieved or compared in the same SQL statement — for example, "Set a report item to show the average cost of books." Here's a subquery that does this:

```
UPDATE Reports SET
   average_book_cost = (SELECT AVG(book_cost) FROM Books);
```

When a selection involves some calculation or complexity that has nothing to do with the contents of what is ultimately selected — for example, "Who has taken out books from either branch 9 or branch 10." Here's a subquery that answers this:

```
SELECT DISTINCT patron_id FROM Circulations WHERE book_copy_id = ANY
(SELECT book_copy_id FROM Book_Copies
 WHERE branch = 9 OR branch = 10);
```

Subquery Tips

Make sure your scalar subqueries return a maximum of one row. You can help by (*a*) using `DISTINCT` to remove duplicates, (*b*) selecting a value returned by a set-function, and (*c*) including a primary key among the selected Columns.

If your DBMS won't support row subqueries, you can still avoid repeating the same subquery twice. For example, replace a construct like this:

```
SELECT * FROM Table_1 WHERE smallint_column_1 =
   (SELECT smallint_column_1 FROM Table_2) AND smallint_column_2 = ALL
      (SELECT smallint_column_2 FROM Table_2);
```

with a construct like this:

```
SELECT * FROM Table_1
WHERE  smallint_column_1 * 100000 + smallint_column_2 = ALL
   (SELECT smallint_column_1 * 100000 + smallint_column_2
    FROM Table_2);
```

Put the fastest subquery at the deepest level. Because most DBMSs will process non-correlated subqueries by travelling from innermost statements to outermost statements, you're (to some extent) controlling the order of evaluation by choosing which expression will be inner and which will be outer.

Use scalar subqueries rather than Table subqueries. Because scalar subqueries are more restrictive, you are giving your DBMS more information when you use a construct that requires a scalar subquery. The DBMS might pass that extra information to its optimizer.

Consider alternatives to correlated subqueries. There are some SQL statements that work better (or look more natural) if you use joins, set functions, or Table operators.

Dialects

SQL-89 was very restrictive about subqueries. SQL-92 removed most of the restrictions and SQL3 changed very little. So most of the information in this chapter will apply for most of the DBMSs in use today. But it doesn't hurt to know what some of the historical restrictions are. Cautious programmers will avoid these situations:

- Row subqueries.
- Subqueries nested to a depth greater than 16 levels.
- Statements with more than 15 <Table reference>s (this is a maximum in the FIPS specification).
- Subqueries that contain `UNION`, `EXCEPT`, or `INTERSECT`.
- Scalar subqueries that contain `DISTINCT`, `GROUP BY`, or `HAVING`.
- Subqueries which do not appear on the right side of a comparison operator within a `WHERE` clause. This last restriction is the most significant because it used to be the case that "`WHERE` expression = `(SELECT` ...)" was legal syntax, but almost nothing else was.<$startrange>subqueries; queries: subqueries

32

Chapter 32

Searching with Set Operators

SQL supports three set operators: UNION, EXCEPT, and INTERSECT. We described their general effects in our discussion of set theory (see Chapter 2 "General Concepts"). Here's a quick recap, using two Tables: TABLE_1 contains these three, one-Column rows, {1,2,3} and TABLE_2 contains these three, one-Column rows, {1,3,5}.

The expression:

```
(Table_1) UNION (Table_2)
```

yields all non-duplicate rows from both TABLE_1 and TABLE_2, so the result is these four rows: {1,2,3,5}. The expression:

```
(Table_1) EXCEPT (Table_2)
```

yields all rows that are in TABLE_1 and are not also in TABLE_2, so the result is this row: {2}. The expression:

```
(Table_1) INTERSECT (Table_2)
```

yields all rows that are in TABLE_1 and are also in TABLE_2, so the result is these two rows: {1,3}

The result in all three cases is, of course, another Table; UNION and EXCEPT and INTERSECT take two Tables as input and produce one result Table as output (that's why some sources — particularly FIPS — refer to UNION and EXCEPT and INTERSECT as "Table operators" rather than "set operators") and so these constructs can also be used as a <Table reference> in an SQL statement.

<query expression>

In this chapter, we'll discuss both the implementation problems and the details for the three set operators. You'll notice that the list of implementation-specific restrictions is quite long, which reflects the difficulty that DBMS vendors have supporting set operators. Before we begin our discussion though, we want to emphasize that each of the set operators can be used to form what the SQL Standard calls a <query expression> — that is, an expression that results in a Table. Here is the full syntax required for a <query expression>:

```
<query expression> ::=
[ WITH [ RECURSIVE ] <with list> ] <query expression body>

   <with list> ::=
   <with list element> [ {,<with list element> }... ]

      <with list element> ::=
      <query name> [ (<Column name list>) ] AS (<query expression>)
         [ <search or cycle clause> ]

   <query expression body> ::=
   <non-join query expression> | <joined table>

      <non-join query expression> ::=
      <non-join query term> |
      <query expression> UNION [ ALL | DISTINCT ]
           [ <corresponding spec> ] <query term> |
        <query expression> EXCEPT [ ALL | DISTINCT  ]
           [ <corresponding spec> ] <query term>

           <query term> ::=
           <non-join query term> |
           <joined table>

           <non-join query term> ::=
           <non-join query primary> |
           <query term> INTERSECT [ ALL | DISTINCT  ]
              [ <corresponding spec> ] <query primary>

              <query primary> ::=
              <non-join query primary> |
              <joined table>
```

```
    <non-join query primary> ::=
    <simple table> |
    (<non-join query expression>)

        <simple table> ::=
        <query specification> |
        VALUES (<row value constructor>s) |
        TABLE <Table name>

<corresponding spec> ::=
CORRESPONDING [ BY (<Column name list>) ]

    <Column name list> ::=
    <Column name> [ {,<Column name>} ... ]

<search or cycle clause> ::=
<search clause> |
<cycle clause> |
<search clause> <cycle clause>

<search clause> ::=
SEARCH <recursive search order> SET <Column name>

    <recursive search order> ::=
    DEPTH FIRST BY <sort specification list> |
    BREADTH FIRST BY <sort specification list>

<cycle clause> ::=
CYCLE <cycle column list>
    SET <Column name> TO <cycle mark value>
    DEFAULT <non-cycle mark value> USING <Column name>

    <cycle column list> ::=
    <Column name> [ {,<Column name>}... ]

    <cycle mark value> ::= <value expression>

    <non-cycle mark value> ::= <value expression>
```

Although this syntax diagram looks extremely complicated, don't be too discouraged! Most SQL queries are fairly simple SELECT statements and those are mostly the types of examples we'll show you. And, in this chapter, we're just going to concentrate on the set operators anyway. However, a brief description of some of the terms in the diagram is warranted.

- UNION and EXCEPT may appear in a <non-join query expression> and INTERSECT may appear in a <non-join query term>. In none of the cases are the input Columns involved allowed to have a BLOB, CLOB, or NCLOB <data type>.
- A <query term> is either a <joined table> (see Chapter 30 "Searching with Joins") or a <non-join query term>.
- A <non-join query term> is either a <non-join query primary> or a <query term> that uses INTERSECT.
- You use a <query primary> to specify the second Table operand of an INTERSECT operation. A <query primary> is either a <joined table>, a parenthesized <non-join query expression>, a SELECT statement (i.e., SELECT ... FROM ... WHERE ...), a Table constructor, or TABLE <Table name> (which evaluates to SELECT * FROM <Table name>). If you want to restrict your code to Core SQL, don't use TABLE <Table name>.
- A Table constructor is the <keyword> VALUES followed by a comma- delimited, parenthesized list of rows or an expression that evaluates to a Table. Here's an example of the first case:

```
... VALUES (10,'hello',B'1011'),
           (20,'goodbye',B'1111'),
           (30,'bobby',B'0000') ...
```

  is a Table constructor that constructs a three-Column Table with three rows. (Each value inside the VALUES clause may be any expression that evaluates to a single value.) Here's another example, this time of the second case:

```
... VALUES (SELECT column_1, column_5 FROM Table_1 WHERE column_1=10) ...
```

  is a Table constructor that constructs a two-Column Table.

  If you want to restrict your code to Core SQL, don't use a Table constructor that involves a Table expression, don't use a Table constructor anywhere but in an INSERT statement, and make all your Table constructors contain exactly one row.

Set Operation Syntax

The required syntax for the simplest form of a set operation is as follows.

```
<query expression> {UNION | EXCEPT | INTERSECT} <query expression>
```

Here's an example of each:

```
SELECT boss_name, salary FROM Bosses
UNION
SELECT employee_name, salary FROM Employees;
```

```
SELECT boss_name, salary FROM Bosses
EXCEPT
SELECT employee_name, salary FROM Employees;

SELECT boss_name, salary FROM Bosses
INTERSECT
SELECT employee_name, salary FROM Employees;
```

Despite the complicated <query expression> syntax we showed you earlier, assume that <query expression> means "SELECT ..." or "VALUES ..." or "TABLE <Table name>" — we want deliberately to avoid some complications of the official syntax description. For now, it is enough to say that there are slight restrictions on the type of <query expression> that can be an argument for UNION or EXCEPT and slightly different restrictions for INTERSECT. These restrictions are obscure and have little or no practical effect.

In the previous examples, the first SELECT statement retrieves two Columns (BOSS_NAME, SALARY) and so does the second SELECT statement (EMPLOYEE_NAME, SALARY). This reflects a mandatory rule — each input Table must have the same number of Columns and each corresponding pair of Columns must have comparable <data type>s. This is because each pair of Columns will merge into a single Column of the result Table — that is, BOSS_NAME and EMPLOYEE_NAME will merge into one result Column and so will SALARY and SALARY. Usually, your DBMS decides which Column to merge with which Column by looking at ordinal position; it merges the first Columns from each input Table, then the second Columns, and so on. Merging by ordinal position is the simplest method, but there are alternative ways, which we'll discuss later. First, though, we'll add a bit more to our basic set operation syntax.

ALL | DISTINCT

The required syntax for a slightly more complicated form of a set operation is as follows.

```
<query expression>
{UNION | EXCEPT | INTERSECT}
[ ALL | DISTINCT ]
<query expression>
```

Although the default for all three set operations is duplicate elimination, you can instruct your DBMS otherwise. The optional <keyword> ALL after UNION, EXCEPT, or INTERSECT means "keep all duplicates," while the optional <keyword> DISTINCT means "eliminate duplicates." In SQL-92, the <keyword> DISTINCT was not valid syntax, but it has always been the default — that is, if you do not explicitly say ALL, then the DBMS assumes that you want to eliminate duplicates. Assume that TABLE_1 contains these five, one-Column rows: {0,1,2,2,3} and TABLE_2 contains these five, one-Column rows: {1,2,3,5,5}.

The expressions:

```
(Table_1) UNION (Table_2)
(Table_1) UNION DISTINCT (Table_2)
```

both yield all non-duplicate rows from TABLE_1 and TABLE_2: {0,1,2,3,5}. The expression:

```
(Table_1) UNION ALL (Table_2)
```

yields all rows from TABLE_1 and TABLE_2: {0,1,2,2,2,3,3,5,5}. The expressions:

```
(Table_1) EXCEPT (Table_2)
(Table_1) EXCEPT DISTINCT (Table_2)
```

both yield all non-duplicate rows that are in TABLE_1 and are not also in TABLE_2: {0}. The expression:

```
(Table_1) EXCEPT ALL (Table_2)
```

yields all rows that are in TABLE_1 and are not also in TABLE_2: {0,2}. (For EXCEPT ALL, if a row appears x times in the first Table and y times in the second Table, it will appear z times in the result Table — where z is $x - y$ or zero, whichever is greater). The expressions:

```
(Table_1) INTERSECT (Table_2)
(Table_1) INTERSECT DISTINCT (Table_2)
```

both yield all non-duplicate rows that are in TABLE_1 and are also in TABLE_2: {1,2,3}. The expression:

```
(Table_1) INTERSECT ALL (Table_2)
```

yields all rows that are in TABLE_1 and are also in TABLE_2: {1,2,3}. (For INTERSECT ALL, if a row appears x times in the first Table and y times in the second Table, it will appear z times in the result Table — where z is the lesser of x and y).

That is, when you use an expression like "SELECT ... <set operator> SELECT ...," the effect is the same as if you'd used "SELECT DISTINCT ... <set operator> SELECT DISTINCT ...." When you use an expression like "SELECT ... <set operator> ALL SELECT ...," then any duplicates are paired off against each other, one by one.

TRAP: The [ALL|DISTINCT] option also appears at the beginning of a SELECT expression (i.e., SELECT [ALL|DISTINCT] <select list> FROM <Table-reference> ...). But in that case, the default is ALL rather than DISTINCT. By contrast, after a set operator, the default is DISTINCT. There's an inconsistency here — maybe the original assumption was that when you SELECT you don't need DISTINCT, but when you UNION you do need DISTINCT.

UNION ALL is probably a faster operation than UNION DISTINCT but for theoretical reasons you shouldn't go out of your way to preserve duplicate rows. Use the ALL option only for those cases where duplicates don't matter, where duplicates won't happen anyway, or where the result of UNION ALL is only going to be used for summary-information purposes.

For the purposes of set operation, two NULLs are "duplicates" of each other. Now let's expand our set operation syntax a little more.

CORRESPONDING

The required syntax for the final form of a set operation is as follows.

```
<query expression>
{UNION | EXCEPT | INTERSECT}
[ ALL | DISTINCT ]
[ CORRESPONDING [ BY (<Column name list>) ] ]
<query expression>
```

In a well-designed database, when Tables have similar Columns, the Columns have similar names. For example, suppose two Tables, VILLAS and MANSIONS, are defined with these CREATE TABLE statements:

```
CREATE TABLE Villas (
   county char(20),
   acreage DECIMAL(4,2),
   price DECIMAL(8));

CREATE TABLE Mansions (
   owner char(20),
   acreage DECIMAL(4,2),
   house_rating INT,
   price DECIMAL(8));
```

Notice that two <Column name>s — ACREAGE and PRICE — are in both Tables, although the Columns they represent don't occupy the same ordinal positions. Now, if we want a list of properties which are both villas and mansions, we can use this simple intersection:

```
SELECT acreage, price FROM Villas
INTERSECT
SELECT acreage, price FROM Mansions;
```

But such a query is a lot of work. To formulate it, we must look at the definitions for each Table, figure out which Columns they have in common, and then list those Columns (in the right order) in our query. It would be far simpler to be able to say, "Select Columns with the same names." The optional CORRESPONDING clause for a set operation does just that. Here's an example that is equivalent to the last one:

```
SELECT * FROM Villas
INTERSECT CORRESPONDING
SELECT * FROM Mansions;
```

The <keyword> CORRESPONDING, used alone after a set operator, means "instead of going by Column position as in the 'simple' format, merge all those Columns which have the same name, regardless of their position." In this case, the Columns which have the same name in both Tables are ACREAGE and PRICE, so those are the Columns that will appear in the result Table.

Now suppose that we only wanted the ACREAGE Column in our result — we're not interested in the PRICE at all. Because CORRESPONDING, by itself, automatically merges every pair of Columns with the same name, we can't use it to form a quick query for the answer we want. Frankly, the easy solution is to return to the simple format and say:

```
SELECT acreage FROM Mansions
INTERSECT
SELECT acreage FROM Villas;
```

But let's pretend that we have some reason to avoid using a SELECT in this situation. There are alternatives, one of which is the expression "TABLE <Table-name>," so let's consider this expression:

```
TABLE Mansions
INTERSECT CORRESPONDING
TABLE Villas;
```

which gives us two Columns — ACREAGE and PRICE — and now let's consider the following expression:

```
TABLE Mansions
INTERSECT CORRESPONDING BY (acreage)
TABLE Villas;
```

which gives us one Column — ACREAGE. It's a contrived example, but if we assume that the query is not SELECT, then INTERSECT CORRESPONDING BY ... is the simplest way to use a set operator and merge specific same-name Columns.

The rules for this operation are:

1. If CORRESPONDING BY is used with a set operator, at least one <Column name> must be in the comma-delimited and parenthesized BY list and each of the <Column name>s in the list must identify a Column that appears in both input Tables. The number of Columns in the result Table will equal the number of Columns in the BY list.
2. If CORRESPONDING is used with a set operator, you may not specify a Column list. The number of Columns in the result Table will equal the number of Columns that both Tables have in common.
3. If you omit the CORRESPONDING clause entirely, the number of Columns in the result Table will equal the number of Columns that you explicitly specify in your query.

To sum it up, there are three ways to pick which Columns to merge with a set operation: (*a*) merge "all" Columns by ordinal position (the simple format), (*b*) merge "all Columns with the same name" (the CORRESPONDING format), and (*c*) merge "specified Columns with the same name" (the CORRESPONDING BY format).

Result Names and ORDER BY

When you're doing a set operation, if the <Column name>s of two merged Columns are the same, then the merged result Column has that name too. If the <Column name>s of two merged Columns are not the same, then, by default, the merged Column is given some unique temporary name by your DBMS. Why would anyone care what the name of a merged Column is? Well, if you want the rows in the result Table to come out in some specific order, you'll have to use an ORDER BY clause — which can only operate on the result Table and that means the names of the result Table's Columns must be known. An ORDER BY clause may optionally appear after a <query expression>; here is the required syntax:

```
<query expression> [ ORDER BY <sort specification list> ]

   <sort specification list> ::=
   <sort specification> [ {,<sort specification> }... ]

      <sort specification> ::=
      <sort key> [ COLLATE <Collation name> ] [ {ASC | DESC} ]

         <sort key> ::= scalar_expression
```

The ORDER BY clause provides your DBMS with a list of items to sort and the order in which to sort them; either ascending order (ASC, the default) or descending order (DESC). It must follow a <query expression> — this means it operates on the final Table that results from the evaluation of the query; it cannot operate on any interim result Tables at all. The <sort key> you specify can be any expression that evaluates to a single value that identifies a Column of the final result Table — this is almost always a <Column name> and thus our concern to know what name will result from a set operation.

Suppose, then, you want to specify a sort order for the result of our earlier examples:

```
SELECT boss_name, salary FROM Bosses
UNION
SELECT employee_name, salary FROM Employees;
```

In this case, it isn't possible to add an ORDER BY clause that specifies ORDER BY boss_name or ORDER BY employee_name at the end of the query — these names identify the original Columns, not the merged result Column. The name of the merged result Column is defined by the Standard to be implementation-dependent; that is, it will be a name provided by your DBMS, but what name will be provided doesn't even have to be documented; it's considered to be an internal thing.

In SQL-92, you can solve this dilemma with an ORDER BY clause that specifies ORDER BY 1 — this instructs the DBMS to sort by the first result Column, no name required. This, however, is not legal in SQL3, so you'll have to force your own names for the result Columns by providing an AS clause in each select list for corresponding Columns and then using that name in the ORDER BY clause. Here's an example:

```
SELECT boss_name AS sort_name, salary FROM Bosses
UNION
SELECT employee_name AS sort_name, salary FROM Employees
ORDER BY sort_name;
```

With this syntax, you're forcing the corresponding Columns in each input Table to have the same name. This name is thus the name given to the merged result Column and can therefore be used in an ORDER by clause to identify that result Column.

[Obscure Rule] The Collation of a merged Column with a character string <data type> will depend on the coercibility characteristics of the two input Columns and whether you add the optional `COLLATE` specification or not. If you want to restrict your code to Core SQL, don't add the `COLLATE` clause.

Result <data type>s and Compatibility

Consider this SQL statement:

```
SELECT 'A', 5.0 FROM Table_1
UNION
SELECT 'BB', 12 FROM Table_2;
```

The two queries that make up the `UNION` operator's Table operands are union compatible; each corresponding pair of Columns is comparable (that is, we can compare `'A'` with `'BB'` and we can compare `5.0` with `12`). The rules about the resultant merged Columns are:

1. The first result Column has a `CHAR(2)` <data type> (see "Rules of Aggregation" for the `CASE` expression on page 573 in Chapter 29 "Simple Search Conditions"), belongs to the same Character set as `'A'` (the result always belongs to the Character set of the first input Column) and has `COERCIBLE` coercibility.
2. The second result Column has a `DECIMAL` or `NUMERIC` <data type> with implementor-defined precision and a scale of 2 (again, see "Rules of Aggregation" for the `CASE` expression on page 573).

   Now consider this SQL statement:

```
SELECT 'A', 5.0 FROM Table_1
UNION
SELECT 12, 'BB' FROM Table_2;
```

This statement will fail; it's an error to try to merge Columns which are not union compatible.

Set Operation Examples

Earlier in this chapter, we defined two example Tables: `VILLAS` and `MANSIONS`. Let's suppose that they have these contents:

VILLAS

COUNTY	ACREAGE	PRICE
Lacombe	39.00	100000
Stettler	15.78	900000
Roseland	15.77	200000
Victoria	17.90	NULL
Victoria	17.90	NULL

MANSIONS

OWNER	ACREAGE	HOUSE_RATING	PRICE
Bodnar	15.77	NULL	200000
Melnyk	39.00	15	900000
Skoreyko	39.00	0	900000
Mudriy	NULL	NULL	NULL

Based on this data, here are some examples of SQL statements that use set operators and their results.

Example Statement:

```
   -- "self-union"
SELECT * FROM Villas
UNION DISTINCT
SELECT * FROM Villas
ORDER BY acreage DESC;
```

Result Table:

COUNTY	ACREAGE	PRICE
Lacombe	39.00	100000
Victoria	17.90	NULL
Stettler	15.78	900000
Roseland	15.77	200000

Example Statement:

```
   -- "NULL is the same as NULL"
SELECT price FROM Villas
EXCEPT ALL
SELECT price FROM Mansions;
```

Result Table:

PRICE
100000
NULL

Example Statement:

```
   -- "NULL is the same as NULL"
SELECT DISTINCT price FROM Villas
EXCEPT ALL
SELECT DISTINCT price FROM Mansions;
```

Result table:

PRICE
100000
NULL

Example Statement:

```
SELECT * FROM Villas
INTERSECT CORRESPONDING
SELECT * FROM Mansions;
```

Result table:

ACREAGE	PRICE
15.77	200000

Example Statement:

```
SELECT acreage, 'Villa' AS type
FROM Villas
UNION
SELECT acreage, 'Mansion' AS type
FROM Mansions;
```

Result table:

ACREAGE	TYPE
39.00	'Villa'
15.78	'Villa'
15.77	'Villa'
17.90	'Villa'
15.77	'Mansion'
39.00	'Mansion'
NULL	'Mansion'

Updatability

Like joined Tables, Tables merged with a set operator aren't updatable in SQL-92. Usually, this means that a View which is based on a query containing a set operator can't be the object of a `DELETE`, `INSERT`, or `UPDATE` statement.

But such Views might be updatable in SQL3. For example, if the set operator is `UNION ALL` and the original Tables are both updatable, then so is the result Table. This feature causes some complications because the DBMS has to track the original Tables. Most DBMSs support set operations by creating new temporary Tables, therefore a data-change operation would only affect the result Table and not the original Table.

Consider a situation where you want to change the rows that result from a UNION of two Tables. There are three possible situations:

1. You want to delete a row. In this case, if the row you want to DELETE was derived from the first input Table, then the DELETE operation will remove that row from the first input Table. If the row you want to DELETE was derived from the second input Table, then the DELETE operation will remove that row from the second input Table.
2. You want to update a row. Once again, if the row you want to UPDATE was derived from the first input Table, then the UPDATE operation will change that row in the first input Table. If the row you want to UPDATE was derived from the second input Table, then the UPDATE operation will change that row in the second input Table.
3. You want to insert a row. This isn't allowed, because your DBMS wouldn't know into which underlying Table the new row should be put.

Now consider a situation where you want to change the rows that result from an EXCEPT operation of two Tables. There are two possible situations:

1. You want to update a row. Because every row of the result is derived from a row of the first input Table, the UPDATE operation will change that row in the first input Table.
2. You want to delete a row *or* insert a row. Neither of these are allowed. In the first case, if you delete a row and that row was derived from a row that is duplicated in the first input Table, the row you "deleted" would still be in the result, causing confusion. In the second case, if you insert a row that also happens to be duplicated in the second input Table, the row you "inserted" wouldn't be part of the result, causing confusion.

Finally, consider a situation where you want to change the rows that result from an INTERSECT operation of two Tables. There are three possible situations:

1. You want to insert a row. If the first input Table doesn't contain a row with the same values, that row is inserted into the first input Table and if the second input Table doesn't contain a row with the same values, that row is inserted into the second input Table. However, if the first input Table already contains a row with the same values as the row you want to insert — but the result Table doesn't have a row derived from that row of the first input Table, then the new row is inserted into the first input Table. The same thing holds for the second input Table too; if the second input Table already contains a row with the same values as the row you want to insert — but the result Table doesn't have a row derived from that row of the second input Table, then the new row is inserted into the second input Table.
2. You want to update a row. If the row you want to UPDATE was derived from the first input Table, then the UPDATE operation will change that row in the first input Table. If the row you want to UPDATE was derived from the second input Table, then the UPDATE operation will change that row in the second input Table.
3. You want to delete a row. This isn't allowed, because your DBMS wouldn't know from which underlying Table the row should be deleted.

Recursive Unions

[Obscure Rule] applies for this entire section.

Suppose you make widgets, which are made of doohickeys and framistats, and framistats, in turn, are made of a certain number of screws, nails, and so on. You get a request: list all parts — that is, list all widgets, all doohickeys, all framistats, all screws, and all nails. This is a "bill of materials" problem. It's not a burning issue, but it's hard to solve with SQL-92, where the only way you can generate a list of parts is to use several queries to scan the PARTS Table — whenever your DBMS finds a part that's made up of other parts, it has to start another query to determine its components, and so on. SQL3 supports a set operation — the RECURSIVE UNION — to solve this problem; it follows a trail of rows for you. Let's go back to the full syntax required for a <query expression> that we showed you at the beginning of this chapter. The parts we haven't talked about yet are used to form a RECURSIVE UNION. Here's the relevant syntax:

```
<query expression> ::=
[ WITH [ RECURSIVE ] <with list> ] <query expression body>

   <with list> ::=
   <with list element> [ {,<with list element> }... ]

      <with list element> ::=
      <query name> [ (<Column name list>) ] AS (<query expression>)
         [ <search or cycle clause> ]

      <query expression body> ::=
      <non-join query expression> | <joined table>

      <search or cycle clause> ::=
      <search clause> | <cycle clause> | <search clause> <cycle clause>

         <search clause> ::=
         SEARCH <recursive search order> SET <Column name>

            <recursive search order> ::=
            DEPTH FIRST BY <sort specification list> |
            BREADTH FIRST BY <sort specification list>

         <cycle clause> ::=
         CYCLE <cycle column list>
           SET <Column name> TO <cycle mark value>
           DEFAULT <non-cycle mark value> USING <Column name>

            <cycle column list> ::=
            <Column name> [ {,<Column name>}... ]
```

```
<cycle mark value> ::= <value expression>

<non-cycle mark value> ::= <value expression>
```

The optional WITH clause for a <query expression> is made up of one or more elements, each of which is a named query that optionally includes names for the Columns that result from that query. (If you include the optional <Column name> list, you must provide a name for every result Column.) The definition of a WITH element may also include the optional <search or cycle clause>.

A WITH clause preceding a <query expression> provides a list of related element queries for a search. WITH by itself identifies a non-recursive set of element queries — this means that an element in the list may not contain the <query name> of an element that follows it in the list. WITH RECURSIVE, on the other hand, identifies a set of element queries that are potentially recursive — so an element can contain the <query name> of a following element.

If a WITH clause's elements cycle at least once — that is, if element one uses element two and element two uses element three and element three cycles back to use element one — and if at least one element is a <non-join query expression> formed with UNION, then the WITH clause is RECURSIVE; a potentially recursive WITH clause's element queries each depend on the query which follows them in the list — that is, the first element in the list is a query that contains the <query name> of the second element in the list (and so depends on that query), the second element is a query that contains the <query name> of the third element, and so on and a WITH RECURSIVE clause's element queries each depend on another element in a way that causes at least one cycle of each element query to be executed. A linearly recursive WITH clause is a clause where each element query has at most one reference to another query in the list.

The optional <Column name> subclause within the WITH clause allows you to specify names for the Columns returned by the query. (Note that the element query may not use an expression which would result in a result Column with a NO COLLATION coercibility attribute.) If any two Columns returned by a WITH element query have the same name or if the WITH query is potentially recursive, you must use the <Column name> subclause to uniquely name each Column of the result Table.

For each element query in a WITH clause, the element is a recursive query if it depends on another element query. (Such queries may not include set operators unless the second operand includes the name of the element query on which this element depends, nor may they invoke routines that affect the element query on which this element depends, nor may they include table subqueries that affect the element query on which this element depends, nor may they include OUTER JOIN specifications that affect a <Table reference> that names the element query on which this element depends, nor may they include a <query specification> that names the element query on which this element depends.) Each element query accumulates rows for the final result. An element's <query name> is the name used in an iteration of the entire <query expression> to identify the parents of any row being accumulated into the result. If each accumulated row has only one parent (that is, it results from a query that uses only one other query in the WITH list), the query is a linear RECURSIVE UNION. If accumulated rows have more than one parent (that is, they result from a query that uses more than one other query in the WITH list), the query is a nonlinear RECURSIVE UNION.

An expandable element query is a linearly recursive element query whose query contains UNION or UNION ALL. If a WITH clause element query is not expandable, the element definition may not include a <search or cycle clause>.

A WITH element query defined with a <search clause> can specify a search order of either SEARCH DEPTH FIRST BY or SEARCH BREADTH FIRST BY followed, in both cases, by a <sort key> and either ASC or DESC (the syntax for the <sort specification list> is the same as the syntax we showed you earlier for the ORDER BY clause's <sort specification list>). SEARCH DEPTH FIRST means "travel down the tree structure first" and SEARCH BREADTH FIRST means "travel across the tree structure first." The Column named in the SET subclause that follows must be a Column with an INTEGER <data type>; your DBMS will set that Column to a value that indicates when a row accumulated into the result was found.

A WITH element query defined with a <cycle clause> helps your DBMS determine whether a row that has already been accumulated is found a second time. This rarely happens in real life and so it probably means an error when it happens for a query. By adding a <cycle clause> to a WITH element definition, you can avoid getting into infinite loops by setting a limit on how long you want the search to go on. The <cycle column list> names the Columns affected by the <cycle clause>. The SET <Column name> and the USING <Column name> may not identify any of the Columns returned by the query, nor may they be the same Column. The <cycle mark value> and the <non-cycle mark value> must both be <character string literal>s that are one character long. They may not be the same value.

Dialects

Here are just some of the many restrictions that some DBMSs had placed on set operations in the past:

- IBM DB2 — the <data type>s of corresponding Columns must be exactly the same and be defined with exactly the same size.
- IBM SQL/DS — neither of the input <query expression>s may contain DISTINCT.
- Various — neither the input <query expression>s nor the result Table may be used with set functions, with GROUP BY or with HAVING.
- dBASE IV, SQL Server — all set operators are unsupported, period.

Those restrictions are history now. The ones which you are much more likely to encounter are the ones that are allowed for Entry-Level SQL-92:

- No derived Column list is allowed, which effectively means that you can't use <literal>s or expressions in queries that use set operators.
- Set operators are illegal inside subqueries, in INSERT ... SELECT and in View definitions.
- EXCEPT, INTERSECT, and CORRESPONDING are illegal.

Even if your DBMS supports SQL3, it might only be Core SQL. If you want to restrict your code to Core SQL, don't use WITH [RECURSIVE], the INTERSECT set operator, a CORRESPONDING clause with any set operator or any set operator with an explicit DISTINCT.

33

Chapter 33

Searching with Groups

This chapter deals with three optional points of a SELECT statement: the GROUP BY clause, the set functions {AVG, COUNT, MAX, MIN, SUM, EVERY, ANY, SOME, GROUPING}, and the HAVING clause. Often these things appear together; the common factor is summaries (or amalgams) of Columns — with groups, rather than with details. We group together where values are equal. For example, confronted with the detail list {Smith Smith Smith Jones Jones}, we could summarize it to be, "three Smiths, two Joneses." Such a summary is known in SQL as a *grouped Table*.

GROUP BY Clause

The GROUP BY clause is an optional portion of the SELECT statement. It defines a grouped Table. The required syntax for the GROUP BY clause is as follows.

```
GROUP BY <grouping specification>

   <grouping specification> ::=
   <grouping Column reference list> |
   ROLLUP (<grouping Column reference list>) |
   CUBE (<grouping Column reference list>) |
   GROUPING SETS (<grouping set list>) |
   () |
   <grouping set>,<grouping set list>
```

```
<grouping Column reference list> ::=
{<Column reference> [ COLLATE <Collation name> ]} [,...]

<grouping set list> ::=
<grouping set> [ {,<grouping set>}... ]

   <grouping set> ::=
   <grouping Column reference> |
   (<grouping column reference list>) |
   ROLLUP (<grouping Column reference list>) |
   CUBE (<grouping Column reference list>) |
   ()
```

GROUP BY defines a grouped Table; a set of groups of rows where each group consists of the rows in which all the values of the grouping Column(s) are equal (the group is the entire Table if you use the HAVING clause without a preceding GROUP BY clause). Here are three SELECT statements; each contains a GROUP BY clause:

```
SELECT   column_1 FROM Table_1
GROUP BY column_1;

SELECT   column_1 FROM Table_1
WHERE    column_1 BETWEEN 10 AND 50
GROUP BY column_1;

SELECT   column_1 FROM Table_1
WHERE    column_1 BETWEEN 10 AND 50
GROUP BY column_1 HAVING SUM(column_1)>12;
```

These examples illustrate that the GROUP BY clause contains a list of <Column reference>s (the grouping Columns) and that it comes at a certain place within the various optional or compulsory clauses of a SELECT statement. In each case, the grouping <Column reference> names a Column that belongs to a Table named in the SELECT ... FROM clause — the argument of the GROUP BY clause is a list of (optionally qualified) <Column name>s and only <Column name>s; SQL doesn't allow you to use <literal>s, Column expressions, or any operator/function except COLLATE in a GROUP BY clause. In addition, when a SELECT statement includes GROUP BY, the statement's select list may consist only of references to Columns that are single-valued per group — this means that the select list can't include a reference to an interim result Column that isn't also included in the GROUP BY clause unless that Column is an argument for one of the set functions (AVG, COUNT, MAX, MIN, SUM, EVERY, ANY, SOME; each of which reduce the collection of values from a Column to a single value). These are severe restrictions, but we'll show you ways to get around some of the restrictions.

The GROUP BY clause allows you to summarize SQL-data. For an example of how it works, let's look at some basic queries on one of the sample Tables we defined in Chapter 29 "Simple Search Conditions": the Payroll Table, which looks like this:

PAYROLL

EMPNUM	RATE	LOCATION	PAID	APPT
1	6.00	10TH FLOOR	1989-10-31	10:15:00
2	5.00	16TH FLOOR	1989-09-30	10:20:00
3	5.00	WAREHOUSE	1989-09-30	10:30:00
4	8.00	BASEMENT	1989-10-15	12:00:10
10	16.00	16TH FLOOR	1989-09-30	12:30:00
11	16.00	16TH FLOOR	1989-10-15	13:15:10
20	9.00	WAREHOUSE	1989-10-15	14:00:00
28	?	16TH FLOOR	1989-09-15	14:10:00
35	9.00	10TH FLOOR	1989-10-31	14:20:00
40	16.00	10TH FLOOR	1989-10-31	14:35:07

The simplest GROUP BY example on Payroll groups the location Column into its four different values. Here's the SELECT statement:

```
SELECT   location FROM Payroll
GROUP BY location;
```

To get the result for this SELECT statement, your DBMS will first evaluate the FROM clause to construct an interim result Table (in this case, the entire Payroll Table), then pass this interim result to the GROUP BY clause. When it evaluates the GROUP BY clause, it breaks the interim result into groups which have the same values in location (the grouping Column), then passes this interim result to the select list. When it evaluates the select list, your DBMS throws out all Columns which aren't named in the select list. The result, then, is:

LOCATION
10TH FLOOR
16TH FLOOR
WAREHOUSE
BASEMENT

A slightly more complicated example groups Payroll's location and rate Columns. Here's the SELECT statement:

```
SELECT   location, rate FROM Payroll
GROUP BY location, rate;
```

To get the result for this SELECT statement, your DBMS will follow the same steps we described for the last example — up until it reaches the interim result that contains groups which have the same values in location (the first grouping Column). At this point, instead of passing the result to the select list, the DBMS will now break the new interim result into groups which have the same values in location and rate (the second grouping Column). This interim result is then passed on to the select list for evaluation. The final result is (note that the NULL value in the rate Column is in a group of its own; for GROUP BY all NULLs form a single group):

LOCATION	RATE
10TH FLOOR	6.00
10TH FLOOR	9.00
10TH FLOOR	16.00
16TH FLOOR	5.00
16TH FLOOR	16.00
16TH FLOOR	?
WAREHOUSE	5.00
WAREHOUSE	9.00
BASEMENT	8.00

One last example — grouping with a WHERE clause. Here's a SELECT statement:

```
SELECT   location, rate FROM Payroll
WHERE    rate > 6.00
GROUP BY location, rate;
```

To get the result for this SELECT statement, your DBMS will get a copy of the Payroll Table (evaluate the FROM clause), remove any rows where the rate value is less than or equal to 6 (evaluate the WHERE clause), break the result into groups which have the same values in location and rate (evaluate the GROUP BY clause), and remove any Columns which aren't named in the select list. The result is:

LOCATION	RATE
10TH FLOOR	9.00
10TH FLOOR	16.00
16TH FLOOR	16.00
16TH FLOOR	?
WAREHOUSE	9.00
BASEMENT	8.00

Rules for Grouping Columns

In the GROUP BY clause:

- Each Column in a GROUP BY clause must unambiguously name a Column that belongs to a Table named in the SELECT statement's FROM clause. The name may be qualified, i.e., it may be a <Column reference>. Such a Column is called a grouping Column; its values will be grouped for the final result.

- The grouping Column <data type> may not be BLOB, CLOB, NCLOB, or ARRAY.
- If the grouping Column <data type> is CHAR or VARCHAR, then the <Column reference> may be accompanied by COLLATE <Collation name>. This addition was added to SQL with SQL-92 and may not be supported by all DBMSs. The idea is that you should be able to match for upper/lowercase, or use PAD SPACES when you're defining a group's values. Other than COLLATE, all SQL operators and functions are illegal in a GROUP BY clause.

In the select list:

- You must follow "The Single-Value Rule" — every Column named in the select list must also be a grouping Column, unless it is an argument for one of the set functions.
- The select list may include derived Columns — <literal>s, scalar functions, and <Column name>s within expressions (only the GROUP BY clause disallows expressions).

Here are some examples of grouped SELECT statements, legal and not (a is a Column of Table T):

```
SELECT a FROM T GROUP BY a;
   -- legal: grouping Column = select Column

SELECT a || a FROM T GROUP BY a;
   -- legal: a is grouped and it applies to both instances in select list

SELECT MAX(a) AS b FROM T GROUP BY a;
   -- legal: a need not be in select list

SELECT a+5 FROM T GROUP BY a;
   -- legal: expression in select list refers to grouping Column

SELECT 5 FROM T GROUP BY a;
   -- legal: the <literal> isn't a reference to a Column of T, so it doesn't
have to be a grouping Column: you'll get a bunch of "5"s

SELECT a*5 AS b FROM T GROUP BY b;
   -- illegal: a is not a grouping Column and b isn't evaluated until the select
list is; by then it's too late

SELECT a,max(a) FROM T;
   -- illegal: GROUP BY "implied," see set functions

SELECT a+5 FROM T GROUP BY a+5;
   -- illegal: expression in GROUP BY
```

TRAP: The superficial similarity of the `GROUP BY` clause and the `ORDER BY` clause often misleads people. The big difference is that grouping is done on the input (that is, the Tables named in the `FROM` clause), while ordering is done on the output (that is, the Columns named in the select list). So, although you can say "`ORDER BY` integer" (only in SQL-92 though) and "`ORDER BY` expression," it makes no sense to say "`GROUP BY` integer" or "`GROUP BY` expression." On the other hand, grouping Columns don't have to be in the select list, as sorted Columns must.

TRAP: The SQL Standard doesn't specify how many Columns can be grouped or what the size of a grouping Column may be (except that it can't be a large object string), but most DBMSs allow fairly small numbers and sizes. When people create Tables, they often allot hundreds of characters for `VARCHAR` Columns (like "address" or "comment"), thinking that there is plenty of room in the row. Later they find that their DBMS can't use those Columns in a `GROUP BY` clause, due to their size. The moral — Don't make Columns bigger than they have to be.

The Single-Value Rule

The rationale for this rule is as follows. Suppose you have a list of cities and countries. If this SQL statement were legal:

```
SELECT    city, country FROM Cities_And_Countries
GROUP BY country;
```

what value would come out in the `city` Column? There are plausible answers such as, "any city will do provided it's in the country," or "the DBMS should assume that we want to group by both country and city." The problem with those answers is that they try to compensate for a formal user error. What the user really needs to know is, "that does not compute."

The rule does not mean that all values must be distinct. We could multiply everything times zero, yielding zeros in every Column in the select list, and we would still be specifying "single-valued per group." The true meaning is that there must be, for each group, one (and only one) value that is appropriate as an answer for the query. Sometimes the DBMS doesn't realize this, as in an SQL statement like:

```
SELECT   capitalcity, country FROM Cities_And_Countries
GROUP BY country;
```

but if that's the case, we can easily tell the DBMS this is so by adding a grouping Column to the statement:

```
SELECT   capitalcity, country FROM Cities_And_Countries
GROUP BY country, capitalcity;
```

The single-value rule is sensible and it is Standard SQL. Don't be misled by a "textbook" describing the one DBMS which does not follow the Standard.

Grouping by Expressions

We said earlier that, while you can use "GROUP BY Column list" in your SELECT statements, you can't use "GROUP BY expression list." This means that these two SQL statements are both illegal:

```
SELECT   EXTRACT(MONTH FROM bdate) FROM Table_1
GROUP BY EXTRACT(MONTH FROM bdate);

SELECT   EXTRACT(MONTH FROM bdate) AS ebdate FROM Table_1
GROUP BY ebdate;
```

Looks like we can't group by MONTH; we have to group by the whole date. Bummer. Luckily, there is a way out if you have SQL-92 and some patience:

```
SELECT   ebdate
FROM     (SELECT EXTRACT(MONTH FROM bdate) AS ebdate FROM Table_1)
GROUP BY ebdate;
```

This example uses a Table subquery in the FROM clause and puts all the necessary calculations inside that Table subquery. The outer SELECT does a grouping of the result — which is now legal, since the ebdate Column is clearly identified as a Column belonging to the Table named in the FROM clause. If your DBMS doesn't support Table subqueries in the FROM clause, try making a View, or a temporary Table, with the same logic. Whatever you do will be slow because two Tables are being produced, one for the temporary Table and one for the grouping.

New Syntax

Until now, all of our examples have shown GROUP BY followed by one or more <Column reference>s. This was the only available option until SQL3, which adds this syntax:

```
GROUP BY ROLLUP(grouping Columns)
GROUP BY CUBE(grouping Columns)
GROUP BY ()
GROUP BY GROUPING SETS grouping Column
GROUP BY GROUPING SETS (grouping Columns)
GROUP BY GROUPING SETS ROLLUP(grouping Columns)
GROUP BY GROUPING SETS CUBE(grouping Columns)
GROUP BY GROUPING SETS()
GROUP BY (grouping Columns),<grouping set list>
GROUP BY ROLLUP(grouping Columns),<grouping set list>
GROUP BY CUBE(grouping Columns),<grouping set list>
GROUP BY (),<grouping set list>
```

GROUP BY GROUPING SETS effectively allows groups within groups — in one pass, it generates multiple aggregated groups that would otherwise require a set operator to put the different result sets together. For example:

```
SELECT    A.id,B.name,COUNT(*)
FROM      Table_1 AS A, Table_2 AS B
WHERE     A.number = B.number
GROUP BY GROUPING SETS (A.id,(A.id,B.name));
```

In this example, the GROUP BY clause determines the first requirement — groups of IDs — by grouping the A.id values from the Table_1 Table. It then determines the second requirement — number of IDs by id and name — by grouping the A.id values from Table_1 with the B.name values from Table_2.

The new grouping syntax like "GROUP BY (grouping Columns), <grouping set list>", also known as *concatenated grouping*, puts groups together.

A <grouping specification> of () (called *grand total* in the Standard) is equivalent to grouping the entire result Table; i.e., to the result returned by:

```
SELECT select list FROM Tables
WHERE  conditions
HAVING conditions
```

A <grouping specification> of ROLLUP means get one group out of all grouping Columns, by rolling each group into the next until only one remains. It is equivalent to the result returned by:

```
SELECT   select list FROM Tables
WHERE    conditions
GROUP BY GROUPING SETS (
  (ROLLUP col_1,ROLLUP col_2,...,ROLLUP col_n),
  (ROLLUP col_1,ROLLUP col_2,...,ROLLUP col_n-1),
  (ROLLUP col_1,ROLLUP col_2,...,ROLLUP col_n-2),
  ...
  (ROLLUP col_1),
  () )
HAVING   conditions
```

A <grouping specification> of CUBE means get one group out of all grouping Columns, by grouping all possible combinations of the grouping Columns. It is equivalent to the result returned by:

```
SELECT   select list FROM Tables
WHERE    conditions
GROUP BY GROUPING SETS (
  (CUBE col_1,CUBE col_2,...,CUBE col_n-2,CUBE col_n-1,CUBE col_n),
  (CUBE col_1,CUBE col_2,...,CUBE col_n-2,CUBE col_n-1),
  (CUBE col_1,CUBE col_2,...,CUBE col_n-2,CUBE col_n),
  (CUBE col_1,CUBE col_2,...,CUBE col_n-2),
   ...
  (CUBE col_1),
  (CUBE col_2,...,CUBE col_n-2,CUBE col_n-1,CUBE col_n),
  (CUBE col_2,...,CUBE col_n-2,CUBE col_n-1),
  (CUBE col_2,...,CUBE col_n-2,CUBE col_n),
  (CUBE col_2,...,CUBE col_n-2),
   ...
  (CUBE col_2),
   ...
  (CUBE col_3),
   ...
  (CUBE col_n),
  () )
HAVING   conditions
```

As an example of these new options, assume there is a Table, Table_1, that looks like this:

TABLE_1

COLUMN_1	COLUMN_2	COLUMN_3
1	A	.55
1	A	.55
1	B	1.00
1	B	1.35
2	A	6.00
2	A	1.77

Let's do an ordinary GROUP BY, with only <Column reference>s as grouping Columns, on Table_1:

```
SELECT   column_1,
         column_2,
         SUM(column_3) AS "SUM"
FROM     Table_1
GROUP BY column_1,column_2;
```

The result is:

COLUMN_1	COLUMN_2	"SUM"
1	A	1.10
1	B	2.35
2	A	7.77

Now let's do a GROUP BY with ROLLUP:

```
SELECT   column_1,
         column_2,
         SUM(column_3) AS "SUM"
FROM     Table_1
GROUP BY ROLLUP(column_1,column_2);
```

This time, the result is:

COLUMN_1	COLUMN_2	"SUM"
1	A	1.10
1	B	2.35
1	NULL	3.45
2	A	7.77
2	NULL	7.77
NULL	NULL	11.22

In addition to the same groups returned by the ordinary GROUP BY, GROUP BY ROLLUP gets a group of each group; the group of column_1 "1" values (with a NULL for the grouping of "A" and "B" in column_2), the group of column_1 "2" values (with a NULL for the grouping of "A" in column_2), and the group of column_1 "1" and "2" values (with a NULL for the grouping of "A" and "B" in column_2).

Finally, let's do a GROUP BY with CUBE:

```
SELECT   column_1,
         column_2,
         SUM(column_3) AS "SUM"
FROM     Table_1
GROUP BY CUBE(column_1,column_2);
```

This time, the result is:

COLUMN_1	COLUMN_2	"SUM"
1	A	1.10
1	B	2.35
1	NULL	3.45
2	A	7.77
2	NULL	7.77
NULL	A	8.87
NULL	B	2.35
NULL	NULL	11.22

In addition to the same groups returned by the GROUP BY ROLLUP, GROUP BY CUBE gets a group of each combination of groups; the group of column_1 "1" values, the group of column_1 "2" values, the group of column_2 "A" values (with a NULL for the grouping of "1" and "2" in column_1), and the group of column_2 "B" values (with a NULL for the grouping of "1" in column_1).

If you want to restrict your code to Core SQL, don't use ROLLUP or CUBE, and don't add a COLLATE clause to any grouping Column reference.

Set Functions

The SQL set functions — more commonly called *aggregate functions* — are AVG, COUNT, MAX, MIN, SUM, EVERY, ANY, SOME, GROUPING. Each one takes the collection of values from a Column and reduces the collection to a single value. The required syntax for a set function specification is as follows.

```
<set function specification> ::=
<general set function> |
COUNT(*) |
<grouping operation>

    <general set function> ::=
    <set function type> ([ {DISTINCT | ALL} ] Column expression)

      <set function type> ::=
      COUNT | MAX | MIN | SUM | AVG | EVERY | ANY | SOME

    <grouping operation> ::=
    GROUPING (<Column reference>)
```

The Column expression that follows a <general set function> can be a <Column reference>, a <literal>, a scalar function, or an arithmetic expression — in short, it can be any expression (other than a query or subquery or another set function) which evaluates to a Column, as long as that Column doesn't have a <data type> of BLOB, CLOB, or NCLOB. Each <general set function> operates on the entire collection of non-null values in its Column argument — grouping rules apply because grouping is implied — and can optionally be qualified with either DISTINCT or ALL. If you specify DISTINCT, your DBMS will eliminate any duplicate values from the Column before applying the set function. If you specify ALL, your DBMS will apply the set function to every non-null value in the Column. The default is ALL. When a set function eliminates NULLs, your DBMS will return the SQLSTATE warning 01003 "warning-null value eliminated in set function."

Here's an example Table; we'll use it for the explanations of the set functions that follow:

TABLE_1

COLUMN_1
10
20
10
20
30
NULL

The COUNT function has two forms; it can have an asterisk as an argument or a Column expression as an argument. It returns an integer.

- COUNT(*) returns the number of rows in the argument Table, rather than the number of values in any particular Column, so this SQL statement returns 6:

  ```
  SELECT COUNT(*) FROM Table_1;
  ```

- COUNT(Column) and COUNT(ALL Column) are equivalent; both return the number of non-null values in "Column," so these SQL statements both return 5:

  ```
  SELECT COUNT(column_1) FROM Table_1;
  SELECT COUNT(ALL column_1) FROM Table_1;
  ```

- COUNT(DISTINCT Column) returns the number of unique, non-null values in "Column," so this SQL statement returns 3:

  ```
  SELECT COUNT(DISTINCT column_1) FROM Table_1;
  ```

The MAX function returns the maximum value and can't be used with Columns that have a <data type> of ROW, REF, BLOB, CLOB, or NCLOB. The <data type> and size of the result will be the same as the <data type> and size of the Column expression itself.

- MAX(Column), MAX(ALL Column), and MAX(DISTINCT Column) are equivalent; all three return the largest of the non-null values in "Column," so these SQL statements all return 30:

  ```
  SELECT MAX(column_1) FROM Table_1;
  SELECT MAX(ALL column_1) FROM Table_1;
  SELECT MAX(DISTINCT column_1) FROM Table_1;
  ```

  It's rare to find explicit ALL or DISTINCT with MAX.

The MIN function returns the minimum value and can't be used with Columns that have a <data type> of ROW, REF, BLOB, CLOB, or NCLOB. The <data type> and size of the result will be the same as the <data type> and size of the Column expression itself.

- MIN(Column), MIN(ALL Column), and MIN(DISTINCT Column) are equivalent; all three return the smallest of the non-null values in "Column," so these SQL statements all return 10:

```
SELECT MIN(column_1) FROM Table_1;
SELECT MIN(ALL column_1) FROM Table_1;
SELECT MIN(DISTINCT column_1) FROM Table_1;
```

  As with MAX, it's rare to find explicit ALL or DISTINCT with MIN.

The SUM function returns a total and can't be used with a UDT. The <data type> of the Column expression must be numeric or INTERVAL; in the first case, the result <data type> will also be numeric, with the same scale as the expression, but (possibly) a larger precision. That's necessary — consider what would happen if you had a DECIMAL(2) Column containing two values: 51, 51. The result of SUM would be 102, which is DECIMAL(3), so the DBMS has to be able to increase the precision for the result. If you're not sure that your DBMS will give SUM a great enough precision, increase the precision of the Column expression using a CAST function. In the second case, the result <data type> will be INTERVAL with the same precision as the Column expression.

- SUM(Column) and SUM(ALL Column) are equivalent; both return the total of the non-null values in "Column," so these SQL statements both return 90:

```
SELECT SUM(column_1) FROM Table_1;
SELECT SUM(ALL column_1) FROM Table_1;
```

- SUM(DISTINCT Column) returns the total of the unique, non-null values in "Column," so this SQL statement returns 60:

```
SELECT SUM(DISTINCT column_1) FROM Table_1;
```

The AVG function returns an average and can't be used with a UDT. The <data type> of the Column expression must be numeric or INTERVAL; in the first case, the result <data type> will also be numeric, with scale and precision equal to or greater than the Column expression's scale and precision (most DBMSs increase the scale but leave the precision alone). In the second case, the result <data type> will be INTERVAL with the same precision as the Column expression.

- AVG(Column) and AVG(ALL Column) are equivalent; both return the average of the non-null values in "Column," so these SQL statements both return 18:

```
SELECT AVG(column_1) FROM Table_1;
SELECT AVG(ALL column_1) FROM Table_1;
```

- AVG(DISTINCT Column) returns the average of the unique, non-null values in "Column," so this SQL statement returns 20:

```
SELECT AVG(DISTINCT column_1) FROM Table_1;
```

The EVERY function, new to SQL with SQL3, returns a truth value and can only be used with Columns that have a <data type> of BOOLEAN.

- `EVERY(Column)`, `EVERY(ALL Column)`, and `EVERY(DISTINCT Column)` are equivalent; all three return `FALSE` if any of the values in "Column" are `FALSE` and all three return `TRUE` if no value in "Column" is `FALSE`. For these two Tables:

TABLE_1	TABLE_2
COLUMN_1	COLUMN_1
TRUE	TRUE
TRUE	TRUE
FALSE	UNKNOWN
FALSE	
UNKNOWN	

these SQL statements all return `FALSE`:

```
SELECT EVERY(column_1) FROM Table_1;
SELECT EVERY(ALL column_1) FROM Table_1;
SELECT EVERY(DISTINCT column_1) FROM Table_1;
```

And these SQL statements all return `TRUE`:

```
SELECT EVERY(column_1) FROM Table_2;
SELECT EVERY(ALL column_1) FROM Table_2;
SELECT EVERY(DISTINCT column_1) FROM Table_2;
```

The `ANY` function (and its synonym `SOME`), new to SQL with SQL3, returns a truth value and can only be used with Columns that have a <data type> of `BOOLEAN`.

- `ANY(Column)`, `ANY(ALL Column)`, and `ANY(DISTINCT Column)` are equivalent; all three return `TRUE` if any of the values in "Column" are `TRUE` and all three return `FALSE` if no value in "Column" is `TRUE`. For these two Tables:

TABLE_1	TABLE_2
COLUMN_1	COLUMN_1
TRUE	FALSE
TRUE	FALSE
FALSE	UNKNOWN
FALSE	
UNKNOWN	

these SQL statements all return `TRUE`:

```
SELECT ANY(column_1) FROM Table_1;
SELECT ANY(ALL column_1) FROM Table_1;
SELECT ANY(DISTINCT column_1) FROM Table_1;
```

And these SQL statements all return `FALSE`:

```
SELECT ANY(column_1) FROM Table_2;
SELECT ANY(ALL column_1) FROM Table_2;
SELECT ANY(DISTINCT column_1) FROM Table_2;
```

The GROUPING function, new to SQL with SQL3, operates on an argument that must be a <Column reference>, where the Column referred to is a grouping Column for the query. You use it in conjunction with the various grouping sets options of the GROUP BY clause. It returns either an integer or the value of some Column — the Standard is unclear on this point.

DISTINCT Set Functions

Because DISTINCT <set function> is usually a slow process, it's worthwhile to look for ways to avoid it. With MIN, MAX, EVERY, ANY, and SOME, DISTINCT means nothing, so there's no problem omitting it there. If the Column happens to be a primary key or unique key, then DISTINCT will have no effect because the values are all distinct anyway, so again, no problem omitting it there. (Although a unique key Column might have a million NULLs in it — that won't matter because the set functions ignore NULLs anyway). The only things you must be sure of, if you remove the <keyword> DISTINCT because the Column is primary or unique, are (*a*) that the PRIMARY KEY/UNIQUE Constraint is NOT DEFERRABLE and (*b*) that there is no chance that the database definition will ever change.

TIP: If you use ODBC, then you should check whether your DBMS supports the SQLRowCount function for result sets; if it does, then you won't have to use COUNT(*) to find out how many rows answer a query. This is particularly a time-saver if the query contains DISTINCT, because COUNT(DISTINCT ...) is a particularly slow function.

Set Functions and the "Ignore NULLs" Policy

All the set functions ignore NULLs (the COUNT(*) function looks like an exception but if you think of it as a shorthand for COUNT(1) you will realize that no NULLs are ever involved there). In other words, when we calculate SUM(x), we are not calculating the sum of all values of x, but the sum of all *known* values of x. This policy is the result of practical experience; some early SQL DBMSs didn't ignore NULLs, but now they all do.

Now, this is a little inconsistent, because in most arithmetic expressions that involve NULL, the result is NULL (e.g., 5 + NULL yields NULL). This leads to a TRAP: SUM(a)+SUM(b) is not the same as SUM(a+b)! Consider these two rows:

	a	b
row#1	5	NULL
row#2	5	5

Because the SUM of {5,5} is 10, and the SUM of {NULL,5} is 5, the result of SUM(a)+SUM(b) is 15. However, because (5+NULL) is NULL, and (5+5) is 10, and the SUM of {NULL,10} is 10, then SUM(a+b) is 10! So which answer is correct: 15 or 10? The cautious person would perhaps reply, "Both answers are wrong — the result should be NULL." However, we have already posited that in the context of set functions, we want to ignore NULLs. In this context, the best answer is the one that ignores the most NULLs — to wit: 15. Therefore, the correct expression to use is SUM(a)+SUM(b), not SUM(a+b). A clinching argument is that SUM(a)+SUM(b) involves fewer "add" operations than SUM(a+b), and is therefore less subject to the cumulative effects of rounding. Similar considerations apply for all set functions with expressions that contain + or - or || operators.

Because of the "ignore NULLs" policy, it should be rare for a set function to return NULL. The only cases are: for MIN or MAX or SUM or AVG or EVERY or ANY or SOME, if every one of the Column values is NULL or if the SELECT returns no rows at all, the function returns NULL (so, in fact, these functions could return NULL even if the Column is defined as NOT NULL, yielding another case where you shouldn't be fooled by a NOT NULL Constraint definition.) The COUNT function can never return NULL — if there are no rows returned, then the count is, naturally enough, zero.

Set Functions in Subqueries

Who makes more than the average salary? What is the cheapest book? That's the kind of question that requires a comparison with a subquery that contains a set function. In other words, you need a condition with this general format:

```
... WHERE <value> <comparison-operator> (SELECT <set function> ...)
```

For example:

```
SELECT ... FROM  ... WHERE ... = (SELECT MIN(price) FROM book);
```

This is one of the cases where it's much easier to use a subquery than a join.

If you try to do something more complex, you will probably run into some restrictions because set functions within subqueries are hard to implement. We'll give just one example of a restriction (from SQL-92) — if the set function's argument is an "outer reference" Column (i.e., the name of a Column in the outer enclosing query), then that must be the only <Column reference> within that argument and the set function has to appear either in a select list or within a subquery that belongs to a HAVING clause. For example, this complex query uses illegal syntax:

```
SELECT * FROM Table_1 WHERE 0 = (
  SELECT SUM(Table_1.column_1+Table_2.column_1)
  FROM Table_2);
```

It would be even more illegal if the set function appeared in the WHERE clause or if there was a third level of subquery nesting. Nobody can remember such a complex rule, and there are more like it, so the cautious programmer simply avoids trying anything fancy when using set functions within subqueries.

Retrieval with a Set Function

Here's some examples of set functions, using the sample database we defined in Chapter 29 "Simple Search Conditions." To find the total number of employees with payroll records (retrieve the number of records in a Table):

```
SELECT COUNT(*) AS pay_count FROM Payroll;
```

The result is:

PAY_COUNT
10

`COUNT(*)` counts all rows of a Table, regardless of `NULL`s.

To find the number of employees with known pay rates (retrieve the number of non-null values in a Column):

```
SELECT COUNT(rate) AS pay_count
FROM   Payroll;
```

The result is:

PAY_COUNT
9

`COUNT(column)` eliminates `NULL`s before counting a Column's values.

To find the number of pay rates (retrieve the number of unique values in a Column):

```
SELECT COUNT(DISTINCT rate) AS pay_count
FROM   Payroll;
```

The result is:

PAY_COUNT
5

The `DISTINCT` option eliminates duplicates before a set function is processed.

To find the sum of the pay rates by location (group a Table into like values combined with a set function):

```
SELECT   location,
         SUM(rate) AS sum_rate
FROM     Payroll
GROUP BY location;
```

The result is:

LOCATION	SUM_RATE
10TH FLOOR	31.00
16TH FLOOR	37.00
BASEMENT	8.00
WAREHOUSE	14.00

To find the number of employees in each department:

```
SELECT   COUNT(empnum) AS emp_count,
         dept
FROM     Employee
WHERE    dept<'D'
GROUP BY dept;
```

The result is:

EMP_COUNT	DEPT
2	A
4	B
1	C

If you want to restrict your code to Core SQL, don't use the set functions EVERY, ANY, SOME, or GROUPING, don't use a set function unless it operates only on a <Column reference> that refers to a Column belonging to a Table named in the FROM clause, and when counting, always use COUNT(*) — don't use COUNT(Column) or COUNT(ALL Column) at all.

HAVING Clause

What departments have four employees? In which branches is the smallest book's size less than 40mm? Those are two questions that require comparison of an absolute value with a set function and thus represent the most common situations where we'd find it useful to bring in a HAVING clause. The HAVING clause is an optional portion of the SELECT statement. It, too, defines a grouped Table. The required syntax for the HAVING clause is as follows.

```
HAVING <search condition>
```

The HAVING clause defines a grouped Table that contains only those groups for which its search condition is TRUE and usually follows a GROUP BY clause. HAVING operates on the interim result produced by the evaluation of the SELECT statement at that stage:

- If the statement is "SELECT ... FROM ... HAVING ...," HAVING operates on the entire FROM Table, treating it as a single group. (GROUP BY is implied, but the result has no grouping Columns.)
- If the statement is "SELECT ... FROM ... WHERE ... HAVING ...," HAVING operates on the rows of the FROM Table that are TRUE for the WHERE conditions, again, treating the interim result as a single group.
- If the statement is "SELECT ... FROM ... WHERE ... GROUP BY ... HAVING ...," HAVING operates on the interim groups returned by GROUP BY.

The HAVING clause's search condition may include ANDs, ORs, relational operators, scalar and arithmetic expressions, and so on — much like a WHERE clause's search condition. The difference between a WHERE condition and a HAVING condition is implied by the clause order. The DBMS evaluates WHERE *before* it does the grouping; it evaluates HAVING *after* it does the grouping — thus, WHERE filters rows and HAVING filters groups. It's usually more efficient to filter before grouping (because then there will be fewer rows to group), so it's best to put most simple conditions in the WHERE clause and use HAVING only for the following situations:

- If one of the condition's operands is a set function. Because a set function is not evaluated until you group, it is impossible to use one in a WHERE clause.
- If there is a quirk in a particular DBMS's optimizer. For one DBMS, GROUP BY a HAVING a = 7 works well because (since the grouping Column and the condition Column are the same) the two clauses can be evaluated simultaneously. For most DBMSs, putting a condition in the HAVING clause is a hint that you want to avoid using any indexes.

Operands in the HAVING clause are subject to the same restrictions as in the select list:

- Column expressions in both must be single-valued per group.
- Column references must be unambiguous.
- If a SELECT statement contains HAVING without a preceding GROUP BY clause, the select list can't include any references to Columns belonging to a Table named in the FROM clause unless those references are used with a set function.
- If HAVING includes a subquery, it can't include outer Column references unless those references are to grouping Columns or are used with a set function.

Let's look closely at an SQL statement which contains a HAVING clause:

```
SELECT   column_1,
         COUNT(column_2)
FROM     Table_1
GROUP BY column_1
HAVING   COUNT(column_1) >= 5;
```

In this SQL statement, the expression COUNT(column_2) is okay because, although column_2 is not a grouping Column, it appears within a set function. Suppose that Table_1 looks like this:

TABLE_1

COLUMN_1	COLUMN_2
1	0
1	1
1	2
2	3
2	4
2	5
2	6
2	7
2	8
2	9

Table_1 has 3 rows where column_1 is 1 and 7 rows where column_1 is 2. The column_1 = 1 group does not meet the HAVING clause's condition — the smallest acceptable count is 5.

However, the column_1 = 2 group does meet HAVING's condition and so the result of our SQL statement is:

COLUMN_1	COLUMN_2
2	7

Here is another way to get the same result, without using a HAVING clause:

```
SELECT column_1,
       c_count
FROM   (SELECT   column_1,
                 COUNT(column_2) AS c_count
       FROM      Table_1
       GROUP BY column_1)
WHERE  c_count >=5;
```

It is always possible to eliminate a HAVING clause and use a query expression in the FROM clause instead. But most programmers prefer to stick with HAVING because it is the traditional and familiar tool for solving this sort of problem.

HAVING without GROUP BY

This SQL statement means "if there are more than 3 a's in the whole Table, display how many a's there are":

```
SELECT COUNT(a) FROM Somethings
HAVING COUNT(a) > 5;
```

As is usual, because there is a set function in the SELECT statement, there is an implied GROUP BY. Therefore grouping rules apply; the select list in such an SQL statement may contain only single-valued Columns.

Retrieval using Grouping

Here's one more example of grouping, using the sample database we defined in Chapter 29 "Simple Search Conditions." To find the departments with less than two employees (group a Table, then eliminate all groups which do not fulfill a condition):

```
SELECT   dept FROM Employee
GROUP BY dept HAVING COUNT(*)<2;
```

The result is:

DEPT
C
D

Views of Groups

It's a straightforward exercise to make a View which is based on a grouping operation — the result is a grouped View. Here's an example:

```
CREATE VIEW Employee_Groups AS
  SELECT   department_id, COUNT(employee_id) AS count_employee_id
  FROM     Employees
  GROUP BY department_id;
```

Now, whoever uses the `Employee_Groups` View will see an ordinary Table with two Columns: `department_id` and `count_employee_id`. But the user's view window won't be totally transparent.

Problem 1 Consider what happens for this SQL statement:

```
SELECT * FROM Employee_Groups
WHERE  count_employee_id = 7 AND department_id = 'XX';
```

Remember (from Chapter 18 "SQL Tables and Views") that your DBMS may try to "transform" this query into a query on the underlying Base table. The best transform is:

```
SELECT   department_id, COUNT(employee_id) FROM Employees
WHERE    department_id = 'XX'
GROUP BY department_id HAVING COUNT(employee_id) = 7;
```

Observe that one, and only one, of the conditions of the original `WHERE` clause has been split out and put in a new `HAVING` clause. Based on timings, we believe that some DBMSs don't do this. We believe they put both conditions in the `HAVING` clause. That's much less efficient.

Problem 2 Consider what happens for this SQL statement:

```
SELECT MAX(count_employee_id) FROM Employee_Groups;
```

Your DBMS might attempt to transform this into:

```
SELECT   department_id, MAX(COUNT(employee_id)) FROM Employees
GROUP BY department_id;
```

that is, into a sensible question along the lines of, "which department has most employees." But `MAX(COUNT(employee_id))` is an illegal expression (you can't nest set functions) and the result will be some error message defined by your DBMS. This is legal; the SQL Standard doesn't demand that a DBMS should handle groups within groups or set functions within set functions.

TIP: That's why we named this View and its Column `Employee_Groups` and `count_employee_id` — the names tip off the user that a `COUNT` in a grouped View is involved. That lessens the confusion if the DBMS doesn't generate a clear error message.

Dialects

The older (pre-1992) DBMSs had these restrictions on grouping:

- Any set functions in the `HAVING` clause had to appear in the select list.
- `HAVING` was illegal if there was no `GROUP BY` clause.
- Groups within Views and subqueries worked only under a full moon (or some undefined equivalent!).

Nowadays, SQL DBMSs support grouping, set functions, and `HAVING` clauses in a manner pretty much as we have described here except for the new SQL3 features.

It's also fairly easy to find DBMSs which will accept non-standard syntax. Sybase ignores the Single-Value Rule so you can use any Column you like in the select list. Oracle includes basic statistical-analysis set functions; STDDEV (standard deviation) and VARIANCE. Several DBMSs allow "`GROUP BY` expression" or even "`GROUP BY` ordinal position," as if the `GROUP BY` clause is analogous to the `ORDER BY` clause.

34

Chapter 34

Sorting Search Results

In SQL, you can only sort search results returned by a Cursor. However, when you're using Direct SQL, you're always using an implied Cursor and so we'll describe the ORDER BY clause now.

ORDER BY Clause

The required syntax for the ORDER BY clause is as follows.

```
<query expression> [ ORDER BY <sort specification list> ]

   <sort specification list> ::=
   <sort specification> [ {,<sort specification> }... ]

      <sort specification> ::=
      <sort key> [ COLLATE <Collation name> ] [ {ASC | DESC} ]

         <sort key> ::= scalar_expression
```

An ORDER BY clause may optionally appear after a <query expression>; it specifies the order rows should have when returned from that query (if you omit the clause, your DBMS will return the rows in some random order). The query in question may, of course, be a VALUES statement, a TABLE statement, or (most commonly) a SELECT statement. (For now, we are ignoring the possibility that the SQL statement is DECLARE CURSOR because that is strictly a matter for "SQL in host programs;" see Chapter 39 "Embedded SQL Binding Style.")

The ORDER BY clause provides your DBMS with a list of items to sort and the order in which to sort them; either ascending order (ASC, the default) or descending order (DESC). It must follow a <query expression> because it operates on the final Table that results from the evaluation of the query; it cannot operate on any interim result Tables at all. The <sort key> you specify can be any expression that evaluates to a single value that identifies a Column of the final result Table — this is almost always a <Column name>. Here's a simple example:

```
SELECT   column_1
FROM     Table_1
ORDER BY column_1;
```

This SQL statement retrieves all column_1 values from Table_1, returning them in ascending order. The following SQL statement does exactly the same:

```
SELECT   column_1
FROM     Table_1
ORDER BY column_1 ASC;
```

This SQL statement also retrieves all column_1 values from Table_1 — but returns them in descending order:

```
SELECT   column_1
FROM     Table_1
ORDER BY column_1 DESC;
```

The optional sort <keyword>s ASC and DESC stand respectively for "ascending order" and "descending order." Some examples of ascending order are {1,2,3} and {A,B,C}; examples of descending order are {3,2,1} and {C,B,A}. If you omit the sort <keyword>, it defaults to ASC.

Note that, because ORDER BY may operate only on a final result, you can't put it in a subquery or before a set function — that is, these two SQL statements are illegal:

```
SELECT column_1
FROM   Table_1
WHERE  column_1 > ANY
       (SELECT   column_1
        FROM     Table_2
        ORDER BY column2);

SELECT   column_1
FROM     Table_1
ORDER BY column_1
UNION ALL
SELECT   column_1
FROM     Table_2;
```

An ORDER BY <sort key> is normally the name of a Column in the query's select list. It cannot be a <literal> — the SQL-92 option of putting an integer after ORDER BY to identify a Column by its ordinal position in the result Table is not allowed in SQL3. The <sort key> can, however, be an expression that evaluates to a Column of the result Table (even if that Column isn't in the select list). Because this is the case, it is useful to remember that such Column expressions may be given explicit names using "[AS <Column name>]" clauses. The "[AS <Column name>]" clause can also be useful for "unioned" SELECTs. For example:

```
SELECT   column_1 AS column_1_or_column_2
FROM     Table_1
UNION ALL
SELECT   column_2 AS column_1_or_column_2
FROM     Table_2
ORDER BY column_1_or_column_2;
```

Whatever way you identify the result Columns you want to sort, though, they may not have a <data type> of BLOB, CLOB, or NCLOB. For a <sort key> with a character string <data type>, you may also specify an explicit Collation for your DBMS to use when sorting that Column's values.

If ORDER BY contains multiple <sort key>s, the primary ordering is by the first <sort key>, the secondary ordering is by the second <sort key> and so on — this is called *major-to-minor ordering*. For example, here's an extract from a telephone book:

Dunbar L	11407 141 Ave	456-4478
Duncan J	9419 101A Ave	423-0541
Duncan J	14705 103 Ave	452-9565
Duncan J	4911 40 Ave	450-6289
Duncan L	9110 150 St	486-2075

As one would expect in a telephone book, the entries are sorted (*a*) by surname and then (*b*) by first initial. In SQL, this order would be accomplished with a SELECT statement like this one:

```
SELECT   surname, initial, address, phone
FROM     Clients
ORDER BY surname, initial;
```

Sorting NULLs

It isn't usually possible to make meaningful comparisons with null values, so the following comparison rules are applicable only in the context of an ORDER BY clause:

- A NULL is "equal" to a NULL for sorting purposes.
- [NON-PORTABLE] Either a NULL is greater than all non-null values or a NULL is less than all non-null values — it's non-standard because the SQL Standard requires implementors to define whether NULLs sort high or low. Most vendors say, "NULLs are greater than all

non-null values" — in this case, a Table with these rows: {7,5,-1,NULL} will end up in this order: {-1,5,7,NULL} if you ask for an ascending sort.

[OCELOT Implementation] The OCELOT DBMS that comes with this book sorts NULLs low; a NULL is less than all non-null values.

The Effect of DESC

We've already said that if you put the <keyword> DESC after a <sort key>, the ordering will be *reversed* for that <sort key>. Unfortunately, we have to belabor what appears to be an obvious and simple fact because some pundits have misstated it. The following statements, taken from SQL books available at your book store, are drivel:

- "DESC is a sticky flag, so if you say "ORDER BY a DESC, b" then both a and b will appear in descending order." If anyone knows how this myth got started, please write to us; we're curious.
- "If a vendor says that NULLs are greater than non-NULLs, then (for standard SQL) they should appear last, even if DESC is specified." In other words — taking the example we used in the last section — if you asked for an ascending sort of a Table with these rows: {7,5,-1,NULL}, you'd get {-1,5,7,NULL} and if you asked for a descending sort you'd get {7,5,-1,NULL}. In fact, standard SQL requires that the descending result be what a sane person would expect: {NULL,7,5,-1}.

Deprecated SQL-92 Syntax

The following examples taken from real working programs illustrate syntax that you should avoid or change for SQL3.

```
SELECT   E.dept FROM Employees E
WHERE    age < 21
ORDER BY E.dept;
```

Get rid of any <Column reference>s in an ORDER BY clause — the actual name of the Column in the select list is merely dept, despite appearances. Use an AS clause to give the Column another name if there is resulting ambiguity.

```
SELECT   balance, (balance - amount)
FROM     Accounts
ORDER BY 1, 2;
```

Get rid of any Column ordinal position references in an ORDER BY clause — using ordinals as Column numbers is frowned on by SQL-92 and banned by SQL3. Again, the solution is to use an AS clause, so the Columns have explicit names — for example:

```
SELECT   balance, (balance - amount) AS balance_minus_amount
FROM     Accounts
ORDER BY balance, balance_minus_amount;
```

SQL3 Features

The following three SQL statements, which are illegal in SQL-92, are legal in SQL3:

```
SELECT   column_1 FROM Table_1
ORDER BY column_2;
```

The <sort key> column_2 is not in the select list, but it does belong to Table_1 so this type of ORDER BY works, provided that the query does not contain DISTINCT, a grouped Table, a set function, or a set operator.

```
SELECT   column_1 + 5 FROM Table_1
ORDER BY column_1 + 5;
```

The <sort key> column_1 + 5 is an unnamed value expression, but this type of ORDER BY is legal because column_1 + 5 appears in the query's select list. Your DBMS will find it by comparing the expressions, rather than comparing <Column name>s.

```
SELECT   char_column FROM Table_1
ORDER BY char_column COLLATE Schema_1.Polish;
```

The COLLATE clause specified for the <sort key> overrides whatever default Collation char_column has.

Essentially, these SQL3 "features" let you write sloppy code. We advise that you stick with the SQL-92 rule that all <sort key>s must be names of Columns in the result select list. These three SQL statements, equivalent to the ones we've just shown you, are better code — and are legal in both SQL-92 and SQL3:

```
SELECT   column_1, column_2 FROM Table_1
ORDER BY column_2;

SELECT   column_1 + 5 AS column_1_plus_5 FROM Table_1
ORDER BY column_1_plus_5;

SELECT   column_1 COLLATE Schema_1.Polish AS colpolish FROM Table_1
ORDER BY colpolish;
```

Sorted Retrievals

Here's some examples of sorted retrievals, using the sample database we defined in Chapter 29 "Simple Search Conditions." To retrieve an alphabetical list of departments, either of these SQL statements will work:

```
SELECT dept FROM Department ORDER BY dept ASC;

SELECT dept FROM Department ORDER BY dept;
```

The result is:

DEPT
A
B
C
D
E

`ORDER BY` defaults to a sort in ascending order when no sort order is specified. To retrieve departments in descending order:

```
SELECT dept FROM Department ORDER BY dept DESC;
```

This time, the result is:

DEPT
E
D
C
B
A

To find an alphabetic list of employee names grouped by their departments sorted in descending order (retrieve multiple Columns with nested sort levels):

```
SELECT dept,surname FROM Employee ORDER BY dept DESC,surname;
```

The result is:

DEPT	SURNAME
E	FRANCIS
E	OLSEN
D	MORGAN
C	JONES
B	JONES
B	MARSH
B	TURNER
B	WARREN
A	KOO
A	SMITH

To find employee numbers and rates for employees with employee numbers less than 20 and to sort these by employee number within descending pay rate order, within descending location order:

```
SELECT   empnum,rate,location FROM Payroll WHERE empnum<20
ORDER BY location DESC,rate DESC,empnum;
```

The result is:

EMPNUM	RATE	LOCATION
3	5.00	WAREHOUSE
4	8.00	BASEMENT
10	16.00	16TH FLOOR
11	16.00	16TH FLOOR
2	5.00	16TH FLOOR
1	6.00	10TH FLOOR

To sort employee numbers in descending order within the daily pay rate:

```
SELECT   empnum,'Daily Rate=' AS comment, RATE*8 AS d_rate  FROM Payroll
ORDER BY d_rate,empnum DESC;
```

The result is:

EMPNUM	COMMENT	D_RATE
3	Daily Rate=	40.00
2	Daily Rate=	40.00
1	Daily Rate=	48.00
4	Daily Rate=	64.00
35	Daily Rate=	72.00
20	Daily Rate=	72.00
40	Daily Rate=	128.00
11	Daily Rate=	128.00
10	Daily Rate=	128.00
28	Daily Rate=	NULL

Dialects

All SQL DBMSs support the ORDER BY clause. Some of them even allow the "ORDER BY <expression>" syntax described previously as an SQL3 feature or some variant thereof — we expect they all will fairly soon.

35

Chapter 35

Changing SQL-data

The SQL-data change statements are INSERT, UPDATE, and DELETE. Many people call these the SQL "update" statements — which is okay, provided you don't mix up "update" (lowercase, meaning INSERT or UPDATE or DELETE) with UPDATE (uppercase, meaning only UPDATE). We prefer the term "data change statements" because it's unambiguous.

In this chapter, we'll discuss changes to SQL-data in all aspects including hidden changes; changes of Views; the syntax of INSERT, UPDATE, and DELETE; access (Privilege) rules; and the new SQL3 feature — changes to joined Tables. But we won't talk about four important and relevant matters because they merit chapters of their own:

Multiple data changes and transactions discussed in Chapter 36 "SQL Transactions."

Data changes and constraints discussed in Chapter 20 "SQL Constraints and Assertions."

Data changes and triggers discussed in Chapter 24 "SQL Triggers."

Data changes through Cursors discussed in Chapter 39 "Embedded SQL Binding Style" — in particular, data changes with "positioned" UPDATE/DELETE.

After reading this chapter, you'll know everything that there is to know about the SQL-data change statements taken in isolation. But we give you fair warning; we'll revisit some of these points when we put them in context later on.

The SQL-data Change Statements

In SQL, there are fundamentally only three conceivable data-change operations that can be performed at the row level: the addition of a new row, the editing of an existing row, and the removal of an existing row. So the only SQL statements that you'll ever need to change SQL-data are (respectively): INSERT, UPDATE, and DELETE. Before getting into the details of each individual statement, we'll note those features or restrictions which are common to two or more of them.

The "set at a time" rule. If multiple rows are involved in a data change operation, you must abandon "row at a time" thinking. For example, a WHERE clause is completely evaluated before a DELETE operation begins to remove rows and an UPDATE operation is not affected by a change to the last row for "uniqueness" purposes.

The "updatable Table" rule. Although the object of a data change statement can be a View (or a derived Table), ultimately the changes actually happen to one or more Base tables. Sometimes, though, an operation won't make sense if applied to the appropriate Base table and so the SQL-data change statement won't work.

The "read only" rule. SQL provides a statement that is used to prevent any data changes from happening. If you execute SET TRANSACTION READ ONLY, then all INSERT, UPDATE, and DELETE statements will fail; your DBMS will return the SQLSTATE error 25006 "invalid transaction state-read-only transaction."

The "default values" rule. Remember that any <Column definition> or Domain definition can include the clause "DEFAULT value." Your DBMS uses the value specified to provide a value for a Column that is implicitly the object of a data change operation. You can also use this value explicitly by specifying the <keyword> DEFAULT in an INSERT statement or an UPDATE statement — this has the effect of setting a Column to its default value. If you didn't use a DEFAULT clause when you defined a Column or Domain, that's okay — it still has a default value: NULL (provided, of course, that there isn't also a NOT NULL Constraint on the Column or Domain).

The "Column integrity" rule. At the same time that you defined a Column, you declared its <data type>. The <data type> limits the values that the Column can contain. For example, if it's a DATE, then you can't insert the character string 'Hello, world' into it. This limitation — that a Column's data must conform to its <data type> — is enforced on any assignment; it is an implicit Constraint on the Column. This implicit Constraint isn't like the explicit Constraints we talked about in Chapter 20 on constraints and assertions though. The big difference between them is that Column integrity is checked when the SQL-data change statement starts, while explicit Constraints are checked when the SQL-data change statement ends. In other words, your DBMS vets your INSERTs and UPDATEs; it won't let utter garbage through no matter how you insist.

The "no data" condition. Any SQL-data change statement can be a perfect success — and still affect zero rows. INSERT, UPDATE, and DELETE all depend to some extent on "search conditions," so it should be clear that sometimes there will be no rows to insert or update or delete.

In that case, the SQL-data change statement hasn't failed — it just hasn't found anything that fulfills your requirements for a change. In such cases, your DBMS will return the `SQLSTATE warning 02000 "no data."` (If you're a programmer who'll want to know the exact number of rows that any SQL-data change statement affects, see our discussion of the `SQLRowCount` function in Chapter 47 "SQL/CLI: Diagnostic Functions.")

The "data change object" condition. For each SQL-data change statement, there is a syntax diagram that has "<Table reference>" in a prominent place. This somewhat anticipates the conclusion of the chapter because a <Table reference> can include <Correlation name>s, parentheses, and various Table operators. As usual, we suggest that, until you've read through the entire chapter, you should interpret <Table reference> as <Table name>.

The "tentative" condition. Finally, you'll note that in the description of each SQL-data change statement, we use the word "tentatively" when telling you what it does. This is not a standard term; we use it merely to indicate that any new row is "on probation" — it's not too late to take your move back until `COMMIT` time.

INSERT Statement

The `INSERT` statement's job is to tentatively add new rows to a Table. If `INSERT` succeeds, there will be a number (zero or more) of new rows in your target Table. The required syntax for the `INSERT` statement is as follows.

```
INSERT INTO [ ONLY ] <Table name>
[ (<Column name> [ {,<Column name>} ... ]) ]
[ OVERRIDE SYSTEM GENERATED VALUES ]
<query expression> |

INSERT INTO [ ONLY ] <Table name> DEFAULT VALUES
```

The `INSERT` statement has two forms. The first evaluates a query to construct one or more rows to be inserted into a Table. The second constructs one row — containing default values for every Column — and inserts it into a Table. The <Table name> identifies your target Table; the Table that you want `INSERT` to add rows to. The target Table must be updatable — that is, it must either be a Base table or a View that is not a read-only Table. If <Table name> does not include a <Schema name> qualifier, your target Table must belong to the SQL-session default Schema. If your target Table is a typed Table, your `INSERT` statement may include the optional <keyword> `ONLY`.

To execute `INSERT`, your current <AuthorizationID> needs the `INSERT` Privilege on every Column directly affected by the insert operation — and, if an object Column is a derived Column (as it is in the case of a View), your current <AuthorizationID> also needs the `INSERT` Privilege on every underlying Table that makes up your target Table.

INSERT Column List

In the first form of `INSERT`, you can optionally specify a parenthesized object Column list, wherein you provide your DBMS with the unqualified names of the Columns that are the targets for each value returned by the <query expression>. Each Column named must belong to the Table named in the INTO clause; <Column name>s may not be repeated in the list but you may list the Columns in any order — the number of Columns in the list must match the number of result Columns returned by the query. INSERT places data into the Columns of the target Table in the order that you list them in the INSERT Column clause; the first value specified is assigned to the first Column named, the second value is assigned to the second Column named, and so on. Any Columns of the target Table that are omitted from the INSERT Column clause are assigned their default value. For example, these SQL statements create a new Table and insert one row of data into it:

```
CREATE TABLE Table_1 (
   column_1 INTEGER, column_2 CHARACTER(7), column_3 DATE);

INSERT INTO Table_1 (column_3, column_1)
VALUES (DATE '1996-12-31', 20);
```

If a Column in the Column list is a self-referencing Column, your INSERT statement must include the OVERRIDE SYSTEM GENERATED VALUES clause.

If you omit the Column list clause from an INSERT statement, your DBMS will assume you mean "all Columns in the Table, in their ordinal position order." In this case, INSERT places data into the Columns of the target Table in the implied order listed; the first value specified is assigned to the first Column of the target Table, the second value is assigned to the second Column of the target Table, and so on. For example, the following SQL statements create a new Table and insert one row of data into it:

```
CREATE TABLE Table_1 (
   column_1 INTEGER, column_2 CHARACTER(7), column_3 DATE);

INSERT INTO Table_1
VALUES (20, 'GOODBYE', DATE '1996-12-31');
```

<query expression>

The <query expression> that makes up the first form of INSERT is usually a SELECT statement, but it's also common to see the Table constructor "VALUES (value commalist)" here (usually with only a single row). In this latter case, you can use the specifications DEFAULT (for insert default value), NULL (for insert null value), ARRAY??(??) or ARRAY[] (for insert an empty array) within the "value commalist" to specify a value for a Column. The order and number of the values must correspond to the order and number of the Columns in the INSERT Column list. If you're using a <query expression>, the INSERT's <Table name> may not identify a Table that also appears in any FROM clause in that <query expression>. The <query expression> provides zero or more rows of data values when it is evaluated; its search conditions are effectively evaluated for each row before any rows are added to the target Table. Here's an example:

```
INSERT INTO Table_1 (column_1, column_3)
   SELECT column_1, column_3 FROM Table_2;
```

You can insert a null value into a Column either by placing the <keyword> NULL in the INSERT ... VALUES clause or by omitting a Column that has no defined default value from an explicit <Column name> clause. For example, given this Table definition:

```
CREATE TABLE Table_1 (
   column_1 INTEGER, column_2 CHARACTER(7), column_3 DATE);
```

these INSERT statements, which insert one row of data into Table_1 using <literal>s and/or the <keyword> NULL, are equivalent:

```
INSERT INTO Table_1 (column_2, column_3)
VALUES ('GOODBYE', DATE '1996-12-31');

INSERT INTO Table_1 (column_1, column_2, column_3)
VALUES (NULL, 'GOODBYE', DATE '1996-12-31');

INSERT INTO Table_1
VALUES (NULL, 'GOODBYE', DATE '1996-12-31');
```

NOTE: All three of these examples result in a new record in Table_1, with the specified values 'GOODBYE' in column_2, '1996-12-31' in column_3, and the null value in column_1.

- In the first example, the null value is implied because no explicit value is specified for column_1 (the Column was defined without a DEFAULT clause so its default value is NULL). It is necessary to provide a <Column name> clause list of the Columns you want to assign the values to if your INSERT statement contains fewer source values than the target Table has Columns.
- In the second and third examples, the null value is explicitly stated as the value to be assigned to Table_1.column_1 and therefore the <Column name> clause can be (but does not have to be) omitted. The explicit use of the <keyword> NULL over-rides the assignment of a default value to a Column that is omitted from a <Column name> clause. This, of course, assumes that the Column has not been defined with a NOT NULL Constraint.

You can insert a default value into a Column either by placing the <keyword> DEFAULT in the INSERT ... VALUES clause or by omitting a Column that has a defined default value from an explicit <Column name> clause. For example, given the following Table definition:

```
CREATE TABLE Table_1 (
   column_1 INTEGER DEFAULT 35,
   column_2 CHARACTER(7),
   column_3 DATE);
```

these INSERT statements, which insert one row of data into Table_1 using <literal>s and/or the <keyword> DEFAULT, are equivalent:

```
INSERT INTO Table_1 (column_2, column_3)
VALUES ('GOODBYE', DATE '1996-12-31');

INSERT INTO Table_1 (column_1, column_2, column_3)
VALUES (DEFAULT, 'GOODBYE', DATE '1996-12-31');

INSERT INTO Table_1
VALUES (DEFAULT, 'GOODBYE', DATE '1996-12-31');
```

NOTE: All three of these examples result in a new record in Table_1, with the specified values 'GOODBYE' in column_2, and '1996-12-31' in column_3, and the default value 35 in column_1.

- In the first example, the default value is implied because no explicit value is specified for column_1.
- In the second and third examples, the default value is explicitly stated as the value to be assigned to Table_1.column_1 and therefore the <Column name> clause can be (but does not have to be) omitted.

DEFAULT VALUES

You can write your INSERT statement with the <keyword>s DEFAULT VALUES instead of with a <query expression> if every Column belonging to your target Table is to get its default value for a single row. These two INSERT statements are thus equivalent:

```
INSERT INTO Table_1 (column_1,column_2,column_3)
VALUES (DEFAULT,DEFAULT,DEFAULT);

INSERT INTO Table_1 DEFAULT VALUES;
```

INSERT will fail if attempts are made to insert:

- a value which does not match a Column's <data type>;
- the null value into a Column defined with a NOT NULL Constraint;
- a duplicate value into a Column defined with a UNIQUE Constraint;
- a value not found in the referenced UNIQUE Column, into a Column defined as part of a FOREIGN KEY Constraint; or
- a value which does not fall into a Column's CHECK Constraint guidelines.

NOTE: If the access mode of the current SQL transaction is read-only and the target Table is not a temporary Table, an INSERT statement will fail; your DBMS will return the SQLSTATE error 25000 "invalid transaction state."

INSERT Examples

Here are some examples of INSERT statements. First, let's assume that two Tables (named Authors_1 and Authors_2) have these definitions:

```
CREATE TABLE Authors_1 (
   id INTEGER CONSTRAINT constraint_1 PRIMARY KEY,
   name VARCHAR(6) DEFAULT 'none');

CREATE TABLE Authors_2 (
   id INTEGER DEFAULT 12,
   name VARCHAR(6));
```

To add a single row to Authors_1, we have three choices:

```
-- INSERT with no INSERT Column list
INSERT INTO Authors_1
VALUES (1,'Jonson');

-- INSERT with INSERT Column list
INSERT INTO Authors_1 (id,name)
VALUES (1,'Jonson');

-- INSERT with INSERT Column list, reversed
INSERT INTO Authors_1 (name,id)
VALUES ('Jonson',1);
```

To add several rows at a time to Authors_1, we can do this:

```
INSERT INTO Authors_1 (id,name)
VALUES (2,'Smith'),
       (3,'Jones'),
       (4,'Martin'),
       (5,'Samuels'),
       (6,DEFAULT),
       (7,NULL);
```

The DEFAULT specification inserts the Column's default value (or NULL, if no default was defined). The NULL specification inserts a null value. At this point, Authors_1 looks like this:

AUTHORS_1

ID	NAME
1	Jonson
2	Smith
3	Jones
4	Martin
5	Samuels
6	none
7	NULL

To add all the rows in Authors_1 to Authors_2, we can do any of these:

```
INSERT INTO Authors_2
   SELECT id,name FROM Authors_1;

INSERT INTO Authors_2 (id,name)
   SELECT id,name FROM Authors_1;

INSERT INTO Authors_2 (name,id)
   SELECT name,id FROM Authors_1;

INSERT INTO Authors_2 (id,name)
   TABLE Authors_1;
```

To add an "all default values" row to Authors_2, try:

```
INSERT INTO Authors_2
VALUES (DEFAULT, DEFAULT);

INSERT INTO Authors_2 (id,name)
VALUES (DEFAULT, DEFAULT);

INSERT INTO Authors_2 (name,id)
VALUES (DEFAULT, DEFAULT);

INSERT INTO Authors_2 DEFAULT VALUES;
```

At this point, Authors_2 looks like the following (the first 7 rows come from Authors_1, the last row is the default row we just inserted):

AUTHORS_2

ID	NAME
1	Jonson
2	Smith
3	Jones
4	Martin
5	Samuels
6	none
7	NULL
12	NULL

INSERT **Physics**

Most DBMSs simply append newly inserted rows to the end of the target Table. But some (more sophisticated) DBMSs will put new rows wherever they can find space (there might be gaps left by earlier DELETE statements). And a few DBMSs will put new rows in order, according to the target Table's primary key (this is called *clustering*; variants of clustering are practiced by DB2 and Oracle).

A general recommendation — which we often ignore — is that the optional INSERT Column list should always be explicitly stated. That way, if someday the target Table is altered and a Column is dropped, the INSERT will fail and you'll be reminded that you have to change that particular operation.

If you want to restrict your code to Core SQL, don't use a <query expression> with EXCEPT, INTERSECT, or CORRESPONDING in an INSERT statement; don't use a <query expression> that names an underlying Table of your target Table in an INSERT statement; don't use the <query expression> TABLE <Table name> in an INSERT statement; if you use the <query expression VALUES (value commalist) in an INSERT statement, make sure it constructs only one new row; and don't use the DEFAULT VALUES form of the INSERT statement.

UPDATE **Statement**

The UPDATE statement's job is to tentatively edit existing rows in a Table. If UPDATE succeeds, there will be a number (zero or more) of changed rows in your target Table. The required syntax for the UPDATE statement is as follows.

```
UPDATE [ ONLY ] <Table name> SET
  <Column name>=scalar_expression
   [ {,<Column name>=scalar_expression} ... ] |
  ROW=row_expression
[ WHERE <search condition> ]
```

UPDATE works by changing one or more values in zero or more rows of the target Table, Column by Column. The <Table name> identifies your target Table; the Table that has the rows you want to UPDATE. The target Table must be updatable — that is, it must either be a Base table or a View that is not a read-only Table. If <Table name> does not include a <Schema name> qualifier, your target Table must belong to the SQL-session default Schema. If your target Table is a typed Table, your UPDATE statement may include the optional <keyword> ONLY.

There are two forms of UPDATE; the first lets you specify multiple Column changes that don't necessarily change every value in a row, the second lets you specify changes to every value in a row with a single SET clause. To execute UPDATE, your current <AuthorizationID> needs the UPDATE Privilege on every Column directly affected by the update operation — and, if an object Column is a derived Column (as it is in the case of a View), your current <AuthorizationID> also needs the UPDATE Privilege on every underlying Table that makes up your target Table — or, if your target Table is a View made with LEFT OUTER JOIN, RIGHT OUTER JOIN, FULL OUTER JOIN, or UNION JOIN, your current <AuthorizationID> also needs the INSERT Privilege on every underlying Table that makes up your target Table.

SET **Column**

In the first form of UPDATE — UPDATE <Table> SET <Column>=<value> — you must specify at least one Column change expression. The Column named must, of course, belong to your target Table; you can change multiple Columns of the same Table (in any order), but you can't change the same Column more than once in a single UPDATE statement. The scalar_expression you use to assign a new value to a Column may be any expression (except one that contains a set function) that evaluates to a single value that is assignable to that Column's <data type>, including the specifications DEFAULT (for change to default value), NULL (for change to null value), ARRAY??(??) or ARRAY[] (for change to an empty array). Most often, scalar_expression will be a <literal>. For example, using the Authors_1 and Authors_2 Tables from our discussion of the INSERT statement, we could do this:

```
UPDATE Authors_1 SET
   name='Finch'
   WHERE id=7;
```

This UPDATE statement changes the last row of Authors_1 from {7,NULL} to {7,'Finch'} — if you don't specify that a Column should be changed, the DBMS leaves it alone; it keeps its original value.

SET **ROW**

In the second form of UPDATE — UPDATE <Table> SET ROW=row_expression — you may specify only the one change expression; it will change the entire applicable row. The row_expression may be any expression that evaluates to a row of values, equal in number to, and <data type> compatible with, every Column in your target Table (usually, this is a <row value construc-

tor> but it could also be a <row subquery>). For example, we could change a whole row with either of the following two statements:

```
UPDATE Authors_1 SET
   ROW = ROW(9,'Allan')
WHERE id=7;

UPDATE Authors_1 SET
   id=9,
   name='Allan'
WHERE id=7;
```

As we've shown, you can add the optional WHERE clause in both forms of UPDATE to define the rows you want to change. If you omit the WHERE clause, your DBMS will assume that the condition is TRUE for all rows (and so UPDATE every row of the target Table). The WHERE clause's <search condition> can be any condition at all, as long as it doesn't invoke an SQL-invoked routine that possibly modifies SQL-data. The WHERE clause's search condition is effectively evaluated for each row of the target Table before any of the Table's rows are changed; each <subquery> in a WHERE clause's search condition is effectively executed for each row of the target Table and the results are then used to apply the search condition to the given row. Here's some examples:

```
-- to change all names to upper case
UPDATE Authors_1 SET
   name = UPPER(name);

-- to change all names to lower case
UPDATE Authors_1 SET
   name = LOWER(name);

-- to change all names to 'Johnson'
UPDATE Authors_1 SET
   name = 'Johnson';
```

UPDATE Examples

To change the last row in Authors_1 so that the id Column is the last id belonging to Authors_2 and the name Column is NULL:

```
UPDATE Authors_1 SET
   id   = (SELECT MAX(id) FROM Authors_2),
   name = NULL
WHERE id = 9;
```

To add 1 to the id Column and cast the id value to a character string, putting the result in the name Column:

```
UPDATE Authors_1 SET
   id   = id + 1,
   name = CAST(id AS VARCHAR(6))
WHERE id = 1;
```

This example is even sillier than it looks because real people very rarely change the value in a primary key Column — but we put it here to bring up an important fact. Consider the result of this statement, which is the row: {2,'1'}. Why isn't the result: {2,'2'}? Because the assignments in the SET clause happen all at once, rather than in a sequence — so the id value in the CAST(id AS VARCHAR(6)) expression is the original value (1), rather than the value we're changing it to (2). This "all at once" effect is typical of SQL. Because of it, Column value swaps are easy.

Let's try to do some updates which will cause errors. The first UPDATE statement in this set of examples will result in a "constraint violation" error, the next two will result in a "syntax" error:

```
UPDATE Authors_1 SET
   id = NULL;
-- fails because ID is a primary key and must thus be non-null

UPDATE Authors_1 SET
   name = DATE '1994-01-03';
-- fails because a date can't be assigned to a character string Column

UPDATE Authors_1 SET
   id = 1,
   id = 1;
-- fails because the same Column can't be changed more than once in a single
UPDATE statement
```

Here's an UPDATE statement that sets the Authors_1.name Column to a corresponding Authors_2.name value:

```
UPDATE Authors_1 SET
   name=(SELECT name FROM Authors_2 WHERE id<=7 and id=Authors_1.id);
```

This example will only work if Authors_2 has a row, with a matching id, for every applicable row in Authors_1. At this point, Authors_1 and Authors_2 look like this:

AUTHORS_1		**AUTHORS_2**	
ID	NAME	ID	NAME
1	Jonson	1	Jonson
2	Smith	2	Smith

AUTHORS_1

ID	NAME
3	Jones
4	Martin
5	Samuels
6	none
12	NULL

AUTHORS_2

ID	NAME
3	Jones
4	Martin
5	Samuels
6	none
7	NULL
12	NULL

UPDATE Physics

Most DBMSs fit a changed row in the same place as the old one — a good idea, because if UPDATEs always caused changes in row location, there would be much more disk activity (especially if there are indexes which point to the original row location). But your DBMS might shift rows if you change the primary key or if you change a variable size Column and it becomes longer. (In the latter case, there might not be enough room to fit the changed row in the original location.) These, of course, are "implementation-dependent" considerations, but we suggest that you hesitate slightly before you change primary key or variable size Columns.

Some general recommendations — try to group all updates for the same Table into the same UPDATE statement, do not substitute a DELETE plus an INSERT for an UPDATE, and keep in mind that UPDATE can be a relatively slow operation.

If you want to restrict your code to Core SQL, don't use a <search condition> that names an underlying Table of your target Table in an UPDATE statement.

DELETE Statement

The DELETE statement's job is to tentatively remove existing rows from a Table. If DELETE succeeds, there will be a fewer number (zero or more) of rows in your target Table. The required syntax for the DELETE statement is as follows.

```
DELETE FROM [ ONLY ] <Table name>
[ WHERE <search condition> ]
```

The rules for DELETE are analogous to the rules for UPDATE:

- The <Table name> must identify an updatable Table that belongs to the SQL-session default Schema if you don't provide an explicit <Schema name> qualifier.
- If the WHERE clause is omitted, the DBMS will assume that the condition is TRUE for all rows (and so DELETE every row).
- The WHERE clause's <search condition> can be any condition at all, as long as it doesn't invoke an SQL-invoked routine that possibly modifies SQL-data.
- The WHERE clause's search condition is effectively evaluated for each row of the target Table before any of the Table's rows are marked for deletion.

- Each <subquery> in a WHERE clause's search condition is effectively executed for each row of the target Table and the results are then used to apply the search condition to the given row.

To execute DELETE, your current <AuthorizationID> needs the DELETE Privilege on the target Table — and, if the target Table is a derived Table (as it is in the case of a View), your current <AuthorizationID> also needs the DELETE Privilege on every underlying Table that makes up your target Table.

DELETE Examples

Here's some examples of DELETE statements:

```
DELETE FROM Authors_1 WHERE name = name;
   -- deletes if name is not null

DELETE FROM Authors_1 WHERE name IS NOT NULL;
   -- deletes if name is not null

DELETE FROM Authors_1 WHERE name IS NULL;
   -- deletes if name is NULL

DELETE FROM Authors_2 WHERE id < 2;
   -- deletes some rows

DELETE FROM Authors_2;
   -- deletes all rows
```

DELETE Physics

With most DBMSs, a deleted row disappears from view in the Table but actually remains in the underlying file for a while. Consider: if row #1 is at file offset 0, row #2 is at file offset 100, and row#3 is at file offset 200 — and you delete row #1 — should your DBMS now move row #2 to file offset 0, move row #3 to file offset 100, change all indexes, and truncate the file? That would take a long time, so the typical response is to put a "record deleted" flag at file offset 0 instead.

There are some DBMSs which will eventually reclaim this space. Of course that's usually good — otherwise they wouldn't do it — but it could cause trouble if you use a non-standard "row id" address which is derived from a row's location. If row ids can change without warning, you've got trouble. With such DBMSs, it might be useful to put a row in limbo rather than delete it; set all Columns to NULL. Once that's done, the row effectively disappears because most searches are never TRUE for NULL Columns. But the row stays in position, reserved, and won't be reclaimed.

If you want to restrict your code to Core SQL, don't use a <search condition> that names an underlying Table of your target Table in a DELETE statement.

Data Change Operations

Generalizing shamelessly, we compare here the steps required to do an UPDATE with the step required to do a SELECT:

UPDATE	SELECT
Read row from file	Read row from file
Ensure new values are valid for <data type>	
Add to log	
Change indexes	
Check for Constraint violation	
Write row back to file	

The bottom line is: changes cost more than queries. Be consoled by the thought that updates are less frequent than reads (in a bank that we used to work for, we measured the ratio as 1 to 1,000). In fact, both programmers and users are willing to sacrifice a lot of extra trouble during data changes — constructing an index, say — if the result is a little less trouble during queries. The investment should not merely be to save speed but to save trouble. That is why there are many mechanisms for guaranteeing that the data is valid. The makers of SQL were well aware that updates need care and protection.

Bulk Changes

A *bulk change* is an operation that affects a significant percentage of the rows in a Table. Because all updates are slow, a fortiori, bulk changes are extremely slow. There are some DBMS-specific ways to reduce the pain:

- Use a vendor utility for multiple insertions (such as Oracle's SQLLOAD).
- Pass and retrieve arrays of rows with one call (ODBC's SQLBulkOperations).
- Access the underlying DBMS files directly (possible if the DBMS uses a non-proprietary file format such as comma-delimited, or .dbf).
- Drop indexes and re-create them after the update.

But none of those tricks are portable. We're more interested in ways to reduce data change time in standard SQL. Here are two ways that work for everybody, sometimes.

1. Reduce the row count

This suggestion is more than a bromide. A way to reduce the row count will suggest itself if you look hard at the SET clause. Here's an example:

```
UPDATE Table_1 SET
  column_1 = 'Jonson';
```

And here's an equivalent UPDATE statement that might be a bit faster:

```
UPDATE Table_1 SET
  column_1 = 'Jonson'
 WHERE column_1 <> 'Jonson' OR column_1 IS NULL;
```

The reasoning here is that if column_1 already has 'Jonson' in it, there's no point setting it to 'Jonson'. It's a mechanical process; just look at what's in the SET clause and put the reverse in the WHERE clause. Here's another example:

```
UPDATE Table_1 SET
  column_1 = column_1 * 1.1;
```

And here's an equivalent UPDATE statement that might be a bit faster:

```
UPDATE Table_1 SET
  column_1 = column_1 * 1.1 WHERE column_1 <> 0;
```

The reasoning here is that if column_1 is zero or NULL, then multiplication can't affect it. There are analogous observations for addition, division, and subtraction.

2. Do multiple updates in one pass

Think of year-end or month-end when you must: (*a*) pay 1% interest to clients with positive balances and (*b*) charge 2% interest to clients with negative balances. Here's how to do it in two passes:

```
UPDATE Clients SET
   balance = balance * 1.01
WHERE balance > 0;

UPDATE Clients SET
   balance = balance * 1.02
WHERE balance < 0;
```

And here's how to do it faster in one pass:

```
UPDATE Clients SET
  balance = CASE balance
              WHEN balance > 0 THEN balance * 1.01
              ELSE balance * 1.02
              WHERE balance <> 0
            END;
```

Often it's just a matter of anticipating what other jobs are likely to come up in the near future for the same data.

Dialects

Data change is a stable section of SQL. All vendors support it; few vendors offer any variations or extensions. The ones that you might run into are:

- Dropped `INTO` clause, for example: `INSERT Employees VALUES (...);` supported by Sybase.
- Multi-column `SET` clauses, for example: `UPDATE Employees SET (column1,column2) = (column3,column4)` supported by Oracle.
- TRUNCATE; to delete all rows but leave definition intact, supported by Oracle 7.

At the time of writing, we know of no vendor with complete support for the SQL3 "update a join" feature. Many have partial support, though. This is the sort of feature that attracts awed attention (it's hard to implement), but the important things are before that; it's best to look for a clean, simple implementation.

36

Chapter 36

SQL Transactions

"An SQL-transaction (transaction) is a sequence of executions of SQL-statements that is atomic with respect to recovery. That is to say: either the execution result is completely successful, or it has no effect on any SQL-schemas or SQL-data."

— The SQL Standard

A *transaction* is an ordered set of operations (of SQL statements). The effects of a transaction — the data changes and Catalog changes — are considered as an indivisible group. Either all the effects happen or none of them do. This all-or-nothing requirement is called *atomicity.* Atomicity is actually one of four requirements of an ideal transaction:

1. Atomic — the group of operations can't be broken up.
2. Consistent — at transaction beginning and end, the database is consistent.
3. Isolated — other transactions have no effect on this transaction.
4. Durable — once a change happens, it's persistent (i.e., permanent).

Taken from the initial letters, these four requirements are called the "ACID requirements."

There are one or more operations in a transaction. There are one or more transactions in an SQL-session. Transactions within an SQL-session do not overlap each other. The initiation of a transaction happens (generally speaking) with the first SQL data-access statement. The end of a transaction happens with one of the two — vitally important! — "transaction terminator" statements: `COMMIT` or `ROLLBACK`.

A logical grouping of operations — Maybe dBASE and Paradox programmers (who haven't encountered transactions before) will ask, "Why is Atomicity a transaction requirement?" We could answer, "It is analogous to the way that SQL deals with sets rather than individual rows and we prefer to deal with groups, it's policy." More cogently, we could answer, "If a set of operations are a logical unity, then they should also be a physical unity." Let us prove that with a much-used, conventional example: the bank transfer.

```
[[ logical start of transaction ]]
Withdraw $1000 from Joe's savings account.
Deposit $1000 to Joe's chequing account.
[[ logical end of transaction ]]
```

Now, suppose that some external event separated Joe's withdrawal from his deposit — a system crash or a tick of the clock so that the operations take place on two different days or a separate overlapping transaction on the same accounts. Any of these would cause us to end up with a bad "database state," because the data will show a withdrawal that shouldn't happen according to company rules or accounting principles — to say nothing of what Joe will think!

In SQL, such a state of affairs is theoretically impossible. First of all, if the system crashes and we bring it up again, we will not see any record of the withdrawal — that's what "atomic with respect to recovery" guarantees. Second, the clock does not tick — `CURRENT_TIME` and all other niladic datetime function values are frozen throughout the life of a transaction. And third, there can be no overlapping transaction — due to the principle of *Isolation*, which we'll examine in greater detail as part of multi-user and multi-tasking considerations in Chapter 37 "SQL Transaction Concurrency."

The point of the example is to show that the withdrawal and the deposit must succeed together or fail together. The transaction criterion is that all SQL statements within it must constitute a logical unit of work — that is, a sequence (ordered set) of operations (executions of SQL statements) that take the DBMS from a consistent state to a consistent state (possibly by changing nothing — a transaction can consist of a series of `SELECT` statements).

It's your job to figure out what operations fit together as a logical unit of work. It's the DBMS's job to ensure that the operations will all fail or all succeed, together.

Initiating Transactions

A transaction begins, if it hasn't already begun, when one of these SQL statements is executed:

- Any SQL-Schema statement: `ALTER`, `CREATE`, `DROP`, `GRANT`, `REVOKE`.
- The SQL-data statements `OPEN`, `CLOSE`, `FETCH`, `SELECT`, `INSERT`, `UPDATE`, `DELETE`, `FREE LOCATOR`, `HOLD LOCATOR`.
- One of the new SQL3 statements `START TRANSACTION`, `COMMIT AND CHAIN`, `ROLLBACK AND CHAIN`.
- The SQL-control statement `RETURN` if it causes the evaluation of a subquery when there is no current transaction.

It's usually a bad idea to start a transaction with an SQL-Schema statement and usually you'll find that the new SQL3 statements aren't implemented yet, so in practice, your DBMS initiates a transaction when you issue `INSERT`, `UPDATE`, `DELETE` or any variant of `SELECT`. Once a transaction is initiated, all subsequent SQL operations will be part of the same transaction until an SQL termination (COMMIT or ROLLBACK) happens.

Here's an example of an SQL-session showing transaction boundaries. It contains two transactions, illustrated by a series of SQL statements. (Technically, the SQL-session and transactions are executions of these statements, not the statements themselves.) Not every SQL statement shown is within a transaction — CONNECT, SET SESSION AUTHORIZATION, and DISCONNECT are not transaction-initiating statements. (Look for explanations of these statements in Chapter 38 "SQL Sessions.")

```
CONNECT TO 'TEST' USER 'TEST';
SET SESSION AUTHORIZATION 'TRANSFEROR';
  -- first transaction begins
  UPDATE chequing SET balance = balance - 1000.00 WHERE client = 'Joe';
  UPDATE saving SET balance = balance + 1000.00 WHERE client = 'Joe';
  COMMIT;
  -- first transaction ends
SET SESSION AUTHORIZATION 'REPORTER';
  -- second transaction begins
  SELECT balance FROM chequing WHERE client = 'Joe';
  COMMIT;
  -- second transaction ends
DISCONNECT ALL;
```

Terminating Transactions

There are two transaction-terminating statements: COMMIT and ROLLBACK. The first saves all changes while the second destroys all changes. Although they don't do exactly the same thing, they both have several similar effects on your SQL-data. We'll talk about these similarities first.

When COMMIT or ROLLBACK are executed, the transaction ends. There is no Privilege for COMMIT or ROLLBACK; any <AuthorizationID> can issue a COMMIT statement or a ROLLBACK statement; they are always legal.

[Obscure Rule] — we'll talk about Cursors in Chapter 39 "Embedded SQL Binding Style," prepared statements in Chapter 44 "SQL/CLI Statement Functions," and locks in Chapter 37 "SQL Transaction Concurrency."

- The effect of a COMMIT statement or a ROLLBACK statement on any open Cursors is that those Cursors are normally closed. This means that, if you've instructed your DBMS to retrieve some rows and are going through those rows with a FETCH statement, you'll have to instruct your DBMS to get those rows for you again — the rule is that COMMIT and ROLLBACK cause destruction of result sets. The exception to this rule is that some advanced DBMSs have an option, called the *holdable Cursor*, which allows Cursor work to go on after COMMIT, at considerable cost in performance. Even holdable Cursors are destroyed by ROLLBACK.
- The effect of a COMMIT statement or a ROLLBACK statement on prepared SQL statements is that they might become unprepared. This is one of the few "implementation-dependent"

behaviour characteristics which has real significance to programmers. It simply means that if you have prepared SQL statements, you might have to prepare them again.

- The effect of a COMMIT statement or a ROLLBACK statement on locks is that they are released.

Any information that you gained in the last transaction might have become untrue for the next transaction — transactions are supposed to be isolated from each other. So it's understandable that the transaction terminators cause Cursors to be closed, statements to be unprepared, and locks to be released. If you want to be sure of the exact behaviour of a particular DBMS, there's a CLI function — SQLGetInfo — that gives that information. But the easy way to write portable code is to assume the worst; always close all Cursors before COMMIT or ROLLBACK and always re-prepare all SQL statements after COMMIT or ROLLBACK.

COMMIT Statement

The COMMIT statement ends a transaction, saving any changes to SQL-data so that they become visible to subsequent transactions. The required syntax for the COMMIT statement is as follows.

```
COMMIT [ WORK ] [ AND [ NO ] CHAIN ]
```

COMMIT is the more important transaction terminator as well as the more interesting one. (Though some would use the word "troublesome" rather than "interesting" here.) The basic form of the COMMIT statement is its SQL-92 syntax; simply the <keyword> COMMIT (the <keyword> WORK is simply noise and can be omitted without changing the effect).

The optional AND CHAIN clause is a convenience for initiating a new transaction as soon as the old transaction terminates. If AND CHAIN is specified, then there is effectively nothing between the old and new transactions, although they remain separate. The characteristics of the new transaction will be the same as the characteristics of the old one — that is, the new transaction will have the same access mode, isolation level, and diagnostics area size (we'll discuss all of these shortly) as the transaction just terminated. The AND NO CHAIN option just tells your DBMS to end the transaction, i.e., these four SQL statements are equivalent:

```
COMMIT;
COMMIT WORK;
COMMIT AND NO CHAIN;
COMMIT WORK AND NO CHAIN;
```

All of them end a transaction without saving any transaction characteristics. The only other options, the equivalent statements:

```
COMMIT AND CHAIN;
COMMIT WORK AND CHAIN;
```

both tell your DBMS to end a transaction, but to save that transaction's characteristics for the next transaction. If you want to restrict your code to Core SQL, don't use AND CHAIN or AND NO CHAIN with COMMIT.

What's supposed to happen with COMMIT:

- SQL Cursors are closed, SQL statements are unprepared, and locks are released, as noted earlier. Any savepoints established in the current transaction are also destroyed.

- Any temporary Table whose definition includes `ON COMMIT DELETE ROWS` gets its rows deleted.
- All deferred Constraints are checked. Any Constraint that is found to be violated will cause a "failed `COMMIT`" — your DBMS will implicitly and automatically do a `ROLLBACK`.
- If all goes well, any changes to your SQL-data — whether they are changes to Objects or to data values — become "persistent" and thus visible to subsequent transactions.

Once a change is committed, you've reached the point of no turning back (or no rolling back, to carry on with SQL terms). The most important effects are that committed changes are no longer isolated (other transactions can "see" them now) and they are durable — if you turn all your computers off, then turn them back on again, then look at your data, you will still see the changes. If your computers are conventional, there's an easy explanation for that; the DBMS must write to disk files.

For once, the easy explanation is the true one but the mechanics aren't as easy as you might think. For one thing, during a transaction, your DBMS can't simply overwrite the information in the current database files because if it did, the "before" state of the database (before the transaction started) would become unknown. In that case, how could `ROLLBACK` happen? So instead of writing changes as they happen, your DBMS has to keep information about the before and after states as long as the transaction is going on. There are two ways to do this: with a backup copy and with a log file.

The backup copy solution is familiar to anyone who has ever made a `.BAK` file with a text editor. All the DBMS has to do is make a copy of the database files when the transaction starts, make changes to the copied files when SQL statements that change something are executed, and then, at `COMMIT` time, destroy the original files and rename the copies. (And if `ROLLBACK` happens instead, it simply destroys the copies.) Though the plan is simple, the backup copy solution has always suffered from the problem that database files can be large and therefore, in practice, a DBMS can only back up certain parts of certain files — which makes tracking the changes complex. And the complexities grow in SQL3, because "savepoints" — which we'll discuss shortly — require the existence of an indefinite number of backup copies. So this solution will probably be abandoned soon.

The log file solution is therefore what most serious DBMSs use today. Every change to the database is written to a log file in the form of a copy of the new row contents. For example, suppose that there is a Table called `Savings` containing three rows (Sam, Joe, Mary) with balances of ($1000, $2000, $3000) respectively. If you issue this SQL statement:

```
UPDATE Savings SET balance = balance + 1000.00 WHERE client = 'Joe';
```

a DBMS that uses log files will write a new row in the log file to reflect the required change; it won't make any changes (yet) in the original database file. It then has a situation that looks something like this:

`SAVINGS` **Table**		**LOG**			
CLIENT	BALANCE	ACTION	TABLE IDENTIFIER	CLIENT	BALANCE
Sam	1000.00	update	savings	Joe	3000.00
Joe	2000.00				
Mary	3000.00				

This is called a write-ahead log because the write to the log file occurs before the write to the database. Specifically, it's a by-row write-ahead log because the entries in the log are copies of rows. The plan now, for any later accesses during this transaction, is:

- If a `SELECT` happens, then the search must include a search of the log file as well as the main file. Any entries in the log will override the corresponding row in the `Savings` Table.
- If another `UPDATE` happens or an `INSERT` happens, a new entry will be inserted into the log file.
- If a `DELETE` happens, a new entry will be inserted in the log file too, this time with the action field set to delete.
- Most conveniently, if the system crashes, then the log is cleared.

There is a different log for each user and the file IO can get busy. One thing to emphasize about this system is that the log file is constantly growing; every data change operation requires additional disk space. And after each data change, the next selection will be a tiny bit slower, because there are more log-file records to look aside at. For efficiency reasons, some DBMSs offer options for batched operations; you can suppress log-file writing and write directly to the main database files and/or you can clear the log at the end of every transaction. If log-file writing is suppressed, performance improves but safety declines and transaction management becomes impossible.

Let us say that a `COMMIT` at last happens and it's time to "terminate the transaction while making all data changes persistent." The DBMS now has to issue an "OS commit," then read all the rows from the log file and put them in the database, then issue another "OS commit." We're using the phrase "OS commit" (operating-system commit) for what Microsoft usually calls "flushing of write buffers." The DBMS must ensure that the log file is physically written to the disk before the changes start and ensure that the database changes are physically written to the disk after the changes start. If it cannot ensure these things, then crash recovery may occasionally be impossible. Some operating systems will refuse to cooperate here because safety considerations get in the way of clever tricks like "write-ahead caching" and "elevator seeking." The DBMS won't detect OS chicanery, so you should run this experiment:

1. `UPDATE` a large number of rows (at least ten thousand).
2. Issue a `COMMIT`.
3. Run to the main fusebox and cut off power to all computers in the building. Make sure the cutoff happens before the `COMMIT` finishes.
4. Restore power and bring your system back up. Look around for temporary files, inconsistent data, or corrupt indexes. If you find them, then your OS is not cooperating with your DBMS, so be sure to always give both your DBMS and your OS plenty of time to write all changes. NOTE: Because this test usually fails, you should backup your database first!

Adding up all the operations, we can see that a secure DBMS data change plus `COMMIT` is quite a slow job. At a minimum — ignoring the effect on `SELECT`s — there is one write to a log file, one read of a log file, and one write to a DBMS file. If the OS cooperates, this is done with full flushing so these are physical uncached file IO operations. The temptation is to skip some of the onerous activity, in order to make the DBMS run faster. Because most magazine reviews include benchmarks of speed but not of security, the DBMS vendor is subject to this temptation too.

The Two-Phase COMMIT

In an ordinary situation, COMMIT is an instruction to the DBMS and it's been convenient to say that the DBMS is handling all the necessary operations (with the dubious help of the operating system, of course). That convenient assumption becomes untrue if we consider very large systems. To be precise, we have to take into account these possibilities:

- there are multiple DBMS servers;
- there is a DBMS server, and some other program which also needs to "commit."

In such environments, the COMMIT job must be handled by some higher authority — call it a *transaction manager* — whose job is to coordinate the various jobs which want the commit to happen. The transaction manager then becomes responsible for the guarantee that all transactions are atomic because it alone can ensure that all programs commit together or not at all.

The coordination requires that all COMMITs take place in two phases — first lining up the ducks, then shooting them. The transaction manager in Phase One will poll all the programs, asking, "Are you ready?" If any response is "no," or any response is missing, the system-wide commit fails. Meanwhile, all the polled programs are gearing up, refusing other requests for attention, and standing ready for the final order to fire. In Phase Two, the transaction manager issues a final instruction, system-wide, and the synchronized commit actually happens. In this scenario, there is one global transaction which encompasses several subordinate transactions. It will always be possible that the encompassing transaction can fail even though any given DBMS server is ready to proceed. In such a case — once again — you might get a ROLLBACK when you ask for a COMMIT.

And that is what two-phase commit is. It's strictly a problem for very large and secure environments, but it's reassuring to know there are mechanisms for coordinating different and heterogeneous servers.

SAVEPOINT Statement

The SAVEPOINT statement establishes a savepoint at the current point in the current transaction. The required syntax for the SAVEPOINT statement is as follows.

```
SAVEPOINT <savepoint name> | <simple target specification>
```

You can establish multiple savepoints for a single transaction (up to some maximum defined by your DBMS). You specify a savepoint either with a <simple target specification> that has an integer data type or with a <savepoint name>.

If you use a <simple target specification> your DBMS will make up an integer (greater than zero) and assign it to the target. For example, SAVEPOINT :x will get a value for x which you can use in subsequent savepoint-related statements.

The modern convention is to label with names rather than numbers, so we suggest that you concentrate on <savepoint name> which must be an unqualified <regular identifier> or <delimited identifier> and has a scope that includes the entire transaction in which you define it. An example of a savepoint specification using a savepoint name is:

```
SAVEPOINT point_we_may_wish_to_rollback_to;
```

Savepoint names must be unique within their transaction. If there is already a SAVEPOINT statement with the same name in the transaction, it will be overwritten.

If you want to restrict your code to Core SQL, don't use the SAVEPOINT statement.

ROLLBACK Statement

The ROLLBACK statement rolls back (ends) a transaction, destroying any changes to SQL-data so that they never become visible to subsequent transactions. The required syntax for the ROLLBACK statement is as follows.

```
ROLLBACK [ WORK ] [ AND [ NO ] CHAIN ]
[ TO SAVEPOINT {<savepoint name> | <simple target specification>} ]
```

The ROLLBACK statement will either end a transaction, destroying all data changes that happened during any of the transaction or it will just destroy any data changes that happened since you established a savepoint. The basic form of the ROLLBACK statement is its SQL-92 syntax; simply the <keyword> ROLLBACK (the <keyword> WORK is simply noise and can be omitted without changing the effect).

The optional AND CHAIN clause is a convenience for initiating a new transaction as soon as the old transaction terminates. If AND CHAIN is specified, then there is effectively nothing between the old and new transactions although they remain separate. The characteristics of the new transaction will be the same as the characteristics of the old one — that is, the new transaction will have the same access mode, isolation level, and diagnostics area size (we'll discuss all of these shortly) as the transaction just terminated. The AND NO CHAIN option just tells your DBMS to end the transaction — that is, these four SQL statements are equivalent:

```
ROLLBACK;
ROLLBACK WORK;
ROLLBACK AND NO CHAIN;
ROLLBACK WORK AND NO CHAIN;
```

All of them end a transaction without saving any transaction characteristics. The only other options, the equivalent statements:

```
ROLLBACK AND CHAIN;
ROLLBACK WORK AND CHAIN;
```

both tell your DBMS to end a transaction, but to save that transaction's characteristics for the next transaction.

ROLLBACK is much simpler than COMMIT; it may involve no more than a few deletions (of Cursors, locks, prepared SQL statements, and log-file entries). It's usually assumed that ROLLBACK can't fail, although such a thing is conceivable (for example, an encompassing transaction might reject an attempt to ROLLBACK because it's lining up for a COMMIT).

ROLLBACK cancels all effects of a transaction. It does not cancel effects on objects outside the DBMS's control (e.g., the values in host program variables or the settings made by some SQL/CLI function calls). But in general, it is a convenient statement for those situations when you say, "oops, this isn't working" or when you simply don't care whether your temporary work becomes permanent or not.

Here is a moot question. If all you've been doing is SELECTs, so that there have been no data changes, should you end the transaction with ROLLBACK or COMMIT? It shouldn't really matter because both ROLLBACK and COMMIT do the same transaction-terminating job. However, the popular conception is that ROLLBACK implies failure, so after a successful series of SELECT statements the convention is to end the transaction with COMMIT rather than ROLLBACK.

Some DBMSs support rollback of SQL-data change statements, but not of SQL-Schema statements. This means that if you use any of CREATE, ALTER, DROP, GRANT, REVOKE, you are implicitly committing at execution time. Therefore, this sequence of operations is ambiguous:

```
INSERT INTO Table_2 VALUES(5);
DROP TABLE Table_3 CASCADE;
ROLLBACK;
```

With a few DBMSs, the result of this sequence is that nothing permanent happens because of the ROLLBACK. With other DBMSs — the majority — the result will be that both the INSERT and the DROP will go through as separate transactions so the ROLLBACK will have no effect. Both results are valid according to the SQL Standard — this is just one of those implementation-defined things that you have to be wary of. The best policy is to assume that an SQL-Schema statement implies a new transaction and so cannot be rolled back.

ROLLBACK ... TO SAVEPOINT

The most beneficial new SQL3 feature, in transaction contexts, is the ability to limit how much will be rolled back by ROLLBACK. With savepoints, you can specify from what point the changes will be cancelled. In underlying terms, this means you can specify where to truncate the log file. First, though, you have to establish a savepoint somewhere in your transaction. You do it with the SAVEPOINT statement.

If you've established a savepoint for a transaction, you can roll all operations that have happened in that transaction back to that point with the ROLLBACK statement's optional TO SAVEPOINT clause. For example, to ROLLBACK to the savepoint established in the previous example, you would issue this SQL statement:

```
ROLLBACK TO SAVEPOINT point_we_may_wish_to_rollback_to;
```

This form of ROLLBACK is not a transaction terminator statement; it merely causes a restoration of state. A ROLLBACK statement that contains the AND CHAIN clause may not also contain a TO SAVEPOINT clause.

If you want to restrict your code to Core SQL, don't use AND CHAIN, AND NO CHAIN, or TO SAVEPOINT with ROLLBACK.

RELEASE SAVEPOINT Statement

The RELEASE SAVEPOINT statement destroys one or more savepoints in the current transaction. The required syntax for the RELEASE SAVEPOINT statement is as follows.

```
RELEASE SAVEPOINT <savepoint name> | <simple target specification>
```

The RELEASE SAVEPOINT statement removes the specified savepoint, as well as any subsequent savepoints you established for the current transaction. For example, this SQL statement:

```
RELEASE SAVEPOINT point_we_may_wish_to_rollback_to;
```

removes the savepoint we established earlier. If we had established any other savepoints after `point_we_may_wish_to_rollback_to`, those savepoints would also disappear.

If you want to restrict your code to Core SQL, don't use the `RELEASE SAVEPOINT` statement.

Using Savepoints

A savepoint may be thought of as a label of a moment between operations. For illustration, suppose a transaction that consists of these SQL statements:

```
INSERT INTO Table_1 (column_1) VALUES (5);
SAVEPOINT after_insert;
UPDATE Table_1 SET column_1 = 6;
SAVEPOINT after_update;
DELETE FROM Table_1;
```

At this point in the transaction, the SQL statement:

```
ROLLBACK TO SAVEPOINT after_update;
```

will cause the DBMS to cancel the effects of the `DELETE` statement, the SQL statement:

```
ROLLBACK TO SAVEPOINT after_insert;
```

will cause the DBMS to cancel the effects of both the `DELETE` statement and the `UPDATE` statement and the SQL statement:

```
ROLLBACK;
```

will cause the DBMS to cancel the effects of the entire transaction, as well as to end the transaction. When a transaction ends, all savepoints are destroyed.

The savepoint option is good for tentative branching. We can follow some line of DBMS activity and if it doesn't work we can go back a few steps, then pursue a different course. The option's also good for separating `ROLLBACK`'s two tasks, "transaction terminate" and "cancel," from each other. The incidental effects (such as closing of Cursors) happen regardless of whether `ROLLBACK` alone or `ROLLBACK TO SAVEPOINT` is used.

Transaction Tips

The following tips are viable only if the DBMS is alone, is following the SQL Standard's specifications, and uses logs as we have described them. But if not, there shouldn't be much harm done by at least considering them.

- `COMMIT` or `ROLLBACK` quickly after `INSERT`, `UPDATE`, or `DELETE`. A quick transaction end will flush the log and thus speed up most accesses.
- `COMMIT` or `ROLLBACK` slowly after `SELECT`. Transaction terminators tend to wipe out items that might be reusable (prepared statements, Cursors, and locks). It's convenient to get maximum use from these items before releasing them.
- Use temporary Tables. If you're making temporary data, no matter how much, the place to store temporary data is in temporary tables with `ON COMMIT DELETE ROWS`. Because there is no need to worry about recovering any data in such Tables, your DBMS might be able to optimize by doing direct writes to the database files without a log.

- SELECT first. Because SELECT can be slower after an UPDATE than before an UPDATE, it might help to get selections out of the way before doing data changes.
- Keep out non-database work. If there are lengthy calculations to do in your host program, they should happen outside the SQL transaction. Do them before the transaction initiator and after the transaction terminator. The same applies for the SQL statements that don't access SQL data such as the SQL-session SET statements.

A final piece of advice (which is not a tip but a concession to reality) is that you will occasionally have to break up logical units of work because they're too big. For example, if you're going through every row in a huge Table, adding 1 to a particular Column, you might want to break up the transaction so that there's a COMMIT after every few changes. This is only safe though because you can keep track of where you left off and you can write your own "rollback" (subtracting 1) if necessary. The primary rule should remain that the logical unit of work should be the physical unit (transaction) too. Departures from that rule are not the stuff of everyday programming work. Security (consistency) first, performance second.

See Also

All SQL operations have something to do with transactions. This chapter has singled out only the major points with particular attention to the COMMIT and the ROLLBACK statements. There is more relevant information in Chapter 20 "SQL Constraints and Assertions" (where we talk about deferred Constraints), in Chapter 37 "SQL Transaction Concurrency" (particularly with regard to the SET TRANSACTION statement), and throughout Chapters 39–52 on binding styles.

Dialects

SQL has supported transaction work since the early days (SQL-86). There are some packages which graft SQL-like statements onto non-SQL environments (dBASE III contained an example), but if you are using a true SQL DBMS then you at least can depend on the essentials of COMMIT [WORK] or ROLLBACK [WORK]. The main differences between DBMSs are in the following areas:

- What incidental items are destroyed by transaction termination.
- Whether SQL-Schema statements form transactions of their own.
- Whether CHAIN and SAVEPOINT features are supported (both of these are SQL3, neither is a Core SQL requirement, so support should not be expected).

Sybase has been refining "Log work" for several years. This was one of the first DBMSs to feature "savepoints." The log is visible as a table. There is an option for suspending logging.

The ODBC specification is that auto-commit should happen. This requirement can be turned off (to what Microsoft calls "manual commit" mode), but auto-commit is the default so ODBC programmers should either turn it off (which looks like a good idea!) or get used to the quirks that auto-commit brings on. Namely, in auto-commit mode every statement gets committed, so ROLLBACK is meaningless. However, execution of a SELECT statement is not followed by an automatic commit — ODBC's documentation is unclear about this, but it would make little sense to SELECT (which usually opens a Cursor) and immediately COMMIT (which usually closes all Cursors). Also — apparently — the ODBC function SQLCloseCursor implies a COMMIT. ODBC's "auto-commit" default mode is a departure from the SQL Standard, but we must understand that ODBC is designed to accommodate a wide variety of data sources.

37

Chapter 37

SQL Transaction Concurrency

Although there is never more than one current SQL transaction between your DBMS and your application program at any point in time, the operational problem — although perhaps we should call it a "challenge" or an "opportunity" — is that many DBMSs run in multi-tasking or multi-user scenarios. These may range from the fairly simple (e.g., an MS-Windows background task running in conjunction with a foreground task) to the fairly complex (e.g., a heterogeneous mix of computers connected over a network via TCP/IP). The problem/challenge/opportunity has grown larger in recent years, with the demand for "2457" (twenty-four hour by seven-day) accessibility and with the demand for DBMS servers that can operate on Internet hosts (especially with WindowsNT and Linux operating systems).

In SQL, the primary unit of work is the "transaction," as we saw in the previous chapter. The interesting difficulties lie with transaction concurrency, which we define as follows:

Concurrency. The running together of two transactions, which may access the same database rows during overlapping time periods. Such simultaneous accesses, called *collisions*, may result in errors or inconsistencies if not handled properly. The more overlapping that is possible, the greater the concurrency.

The proper handling of collisions requires some work on the part of the application programmer. It is possible to leave the whole matter in the hands of the DBMS, but that would almost certainly lead to performance which everyone would call unacceptable. Therefore, your requirement for this part of the job is to understand how errors or inconsistencies can arise during collisions, to use the somewhat paucous SQL options which can increase concurrency, and to help the DBMS* along with a variety of settings or application plans.

* Though we use the singular word "DBMS," we note once again that there may, in fact, be several cooperating agencies responsible for transaction management.

Isolation Phenomena

What sort of errors and inconsistencies can creep in during concurrent operations? Database groupies generally use four categories, which they call — in order by seriousness — Lost Update, Dirty Read, Non-Repeatable Read, and Phantom.

In the descriptions that follow, the conventions are that Txn#1 and Txn#2 are two concurrent transactions, that "change" has its usual sense of "an `INSERT` or `UPDATE` or `DELETE`," and "read" means "`FETCH`" or some close equivalent. The charts are timelines with time points, so that events shown lower down in the chart are taking place later in time.

LOST UPDATE

Txn#1	Txn#2
...	Read
Read	...
Change	...
...	Change
Commit	...
...	Commit

The "lost update" is the change made by Txn#1. Because Txn#2 makes a later change, it supersedes Txn#1's change. The result is as if Txn#1's change never happened.

DIRTY READ

Txn#1	Txn#2
Read	...
Change	...
...	Read
Rollback	...
...	Rollback

Here, the key is that Txn#2 "reads" after Txn#1 "changes" and so Txn#2 "sees" the new data that Txn#1 changed to. That change was ephemeral though; Txn#1 rolled back the change. So Txn#1's change really never happened, but Txn#2 based its work on that change anyway. The old name for the Dirty Read phenomenon is "uncommitted dependency."

NON-REPEATABLE READ

Txn#1	Txn#2
...	Read
Read	...
...	Change
Read	...
...	Commit
Commit	...

The supposition here is that Txn#1 will "read" the same row twice. The second time, though, the values in the row will be different. This is by no means as serious an inconsistency (usually) as Lost Update or Dirty Read, but it does certainly break the requirements of an ACID transaction.

PHANTOM

Txn#1	Txn#2
`SELECT * FROM t WHERE col=5;`	`...`
`...`	`INSERT INTO t(col) VALUES(5);`
`...`	`UPDATE t SET col=5 WHERE col=6;`
`SELECT * FROM t WHERE col=5;`	`...`

This now-you-don't-see-it-now-you-do phenomenon is one that often slips through, especially with older or dBASE-like DBMSs. The reason is that DBMSs might notice concurrent access to rows, but fail to notice concurrent access to the *paths* to those rows. Phantoms can affect transactions which contain at least two <search condition>s which in some way overlap or depend on one another. Phantoms are rare and are usually tolerable, but can cause surprise errors because even some good DBMSs let them through, unless you take explicit measures to signal "no phantoms please."

Pessimistic Concurrency: LOCKING

The most common and best-known way to eliminate some or all of the transaction concurrency phenomena is locking. Typically, a lock works like this:

Txn#1	Txn#2
"LOCK" the desired object	...
...	Wait: desired object is locked
Read and/or Change	...
Read and/or Change	...
Commit (which releases locks)	...
...	"LOCK" the desired object

Here, the Object being locked might be a Column, a row, a page, a Table, or the entire database. Incidentally, when a lock is on a Column, locks are said to be "finely granular" — when a lock is on a page or Table or database, locks are said to be "coarsely granular." DBMSs with coarse-granularity locking have less concurrency (because a lock on row#1 causes an unnecessary lock on other rows as well), but are efficient despite that because the coarser the granularity, the fewer locks exist, and therefore searching the list of locks is quicker. At this moment, it appears that the majority of important DBMSs support locking by row with some (non-standard) optional syntax that allows locking by Table.

A lock is much like a reservation in a restaurant. If you find that your desired seat has already been taken by someone who came before you, you must either wait or go elsewhere.

Usually an SQL DBMS supports at least two kinds of locks: "shared locks" and "exclusive locks." A *shared lock* exists because there is nothing wrong with letting two transactions read the same row; concurrency can only cause trouble if one transaction or the other is updating. Therefore, at retrieval time, a shared lock is made and this shared lock does not block other transactions from accessing the same row (with another retrieval). At change time, the shared lock is upgraded to an *exclusive lock* which blocks both reads and writes by other transactions. The use of different kinds of locks is something that distinguishes an SQL DBMS from a DBMS that depends on the operating system (operating systems like MS-DOS support exclusive locks only).

The famous irritant with a lock-based concurrency resolution mechanism is the "deadlock" (or deadly embrace) which goes like this:

Txn#1	**Txn#2**
Lock Row #1	...
...	Lock Row #2
Attempt to Lock Row #2 -- WAIT, because it's locked	...
...	Attempt to Lock Row #1 -- WAIT, because it's locked
WAIT	WAIT

Because Txn#1 is waiting for Txn#2 to release its lock, but Txn#2 is waiting for Txn#1 to release its lock, there can be no progress. The DBMS must detect situations like this and force one transaction or the other to "rollback" with an error.

Locking is reliable and popular. However, it is sometimes criticized for being based on an excessively pessimistic assumption; that something which you read could be something that you will change. The result is a profusion of "shared locks," the great majority of which turn out to be unnecessary because only a relatively small number of rows are actually updated.

Optimistic Concurrency: TIMESTAMPING

There are several ways to control concurrency without locking. The most common ones can be grouped together as the "optimistic assumption" ways and the most common of those ways is timestamping. With timestamping, there are no locks but there are two situations which cause transaction failure:

- If a younger transaction has "read" the row, then an attempt by an older transaction to "change" that row will fail.
- If a younger transaction has "changed" the row, then an attempt by an older transaction to "read" that row will fail.

The general effect of these rules is that concurrency is high, but failure is frequent. Indeed, it is quite possible that a transaction will fail many times. But what the heck, one can put the transaction in a loop and keep retrying until it goes through.

Some DBMSs enhance the concurrency further by actually "reading" a row which has been changed by another transaction and deciding whether the change is significant. For example, it often happens that the same Column is being updated so that it has the same value for both transactions. In that case, there may be no need to abort.

Most optimistic concurrency mechanisms are not particularly good for detecting Non-Repeatable Reads or Phantoms.

SET TRANSACTION Statement

By now, we've come to expect that SQL statements aren't used to specify methods. Instead, they state the requirements. That's the idea behind the SET TRANSACTION statement. It tells the DBMS — somewhat indirectly — what sort of concurrency phenomena are intolerable for the next transaction, but it does not say how they are to be prevented. That detail is left up to the DBMS itself — that is, the choice of concurrency protocol (locking, timestamping, or some other method) is implementation-dependent. The required syntax for the SET TRANSACTION statement is as follows.

```
SET [ LOCAL ] TRANSACTION <transaction mode> [ {,<transaction mode>}... ]

   <transaction mode> ::=
   <transaction access mode> |
   <isolation level> |
   <diagnostics size>

      <transaction access mode> ::=
      READ ONLY | READ WRITE

      <isolation level> ::=
      ISOLATION LEVEL
      {READ UNCOMMITTED | READ COMMITTED | REPEATABLE READ | SERIALIZABLE}

      <diagnostics size> ::=
      DIAGNOSTICS SIZE <number of conditions>

         <number of conditions> ::= <simple value specification>
```

The SET TRANSACTION statement sets certain characteristics for the next transaction. There are three options, any or all of which can be set by a single SET TRANSACTION statement.

The first transaction characteristic is its access mode; a transaction can either be a READ ONLY transaction or a READ WRITE transaction. The second transaction characteristic is its isolation level; a transaction can either allow READ UNCOMMITTED, READ COMMITTED, REPEATABLE READ, or SERIALIZABLE operations. The final transaction characteristic is the size of its diagnostics area; you set this to the number of conditions you want your DBMS to be able to provide you with information on (it must be at least one). The <diagnostics size> is a transaction characteristic which has nothing to do with concurrency, so we won't discuss it further here — look for it in our chapters on binding styles. That leaves us with the choice of specifying READ ONLY versus READ WRITE and the choice of specifying one of: READ UNCOMMITTED, READ COMMITTED, REPEATABLE READ, or SERIALIZABLE for a transaction. Here's some example SQL statements:

```
SET TRANSACTION
   READ WRITE
   ISOLATION LEVEL REPEATABLE READ;

SET TRANSACTION
   READ ONLY
   ISOLATION LEVEL READ UNCOMMITTED;
```

As the name suggests, SET TRANSACTION is only good for setting the characteristics of one transaction (though there are a few exceptions to this rule when we add the optional <keyword> LOCAL, an SQL3 feature). Unless you're using the SQL3 START TRANSACTION statement (which we'll discuss on page 699 of this chapter), the SET TRANSACTION statement should precede all other statements in a transaction. If you don't specify it, the default situation is:

```
SET TRANSACTION
   READ WRITE
   ISOLATION LEVEL SERIALIZABLE;
```

Access Mode

If the transaction's isolation level is READ UNCOMMITTED, then READ ONLY is the default (and only legal) access mode option. For all other isolation levels, either READ ONLY or READ WRITE are legal options and the default is READ WRITE.

The declaration READ ONLY tells the DBMS that all statements in the upcoming transaction will be "read" statements; they only read SQL data, they don't make any changes. The declaration READ WRITE tells the DBMS that there may be either "read" or "change" statements in the upcoming transaction.

NOTE: Changes to TEMPORARY Tables don't count as "changes" because TEMPORARY Tables aren't shared between different transactions anyway. So regardless of what you do with TEMPORARY Tables, as long as you make no changes to SQL-data or persistent

SQL Objects (e.g., Schemas, Tables, Domains, and so on), you can declare a transaction's access mode to be READ ONLY.

There are no guarantees that specifying READ ONLY will do any good at all, but it certainly won't hurt — and it might result in performance gains. Here's why. If your DBMS sees that all transactions are READ ONLY, then it doesn't have to set any locks at all — no isolation phenomena can arise when all jobs are doing nothing but reading. If only one transaction is READ ONLY, there is still a good strategy available; the DBMS can make a temporary copy of the Tables that you SELECT from (or at least of the rows in the result sets). Following that, all FETCH statements are operating on the temporary copy, instead of on the original Table, and therefore collisions are impossible. Typical application situations where READ ONLY is called for include: report writers, screen displayers, and file dumps. The option might have a particularly good effect if the transaction contains statements which contain set functions.

Isolation Level

The <isolation level> characteristic you specify in a SET TRANSACTION statement determines the degree of "isolation" of the upcoming transaction. This effectively means that the value you choose will tell your DBMS which concurrency phenomena are tolerable or intolerable for the transaction. It's up to the DBMS to decide how precisely it will follow your instruction — the Standard allows it to upgrade the specification (but never to downgrade it, you're always guaranteed at least the isolation level you've asked for). For example, your DBMS could take a READ UNCOMMITTED specification and set the next transaction's isolation level to SERIALIZABLE (a higher level of isolation) instead. But because your DBMS cannot downgrade the specification, there is no harm in setting the <isolation level> as precisely as possible.

READ UNCOMMITTED

READ UNCOMMITTED is the lowest level of transaction isolation. If you specify READ UNCOMMITTED, you are risking that the transaction — no matter what it is doing — might deliver a "wrong" answer. Because it is always unacceptable for the database itself to contain wrong data, it is illegal to execute any "change" statements during a READ UNCOMMITTED transaction. That is, READ UNCOMMITTED implies READ ONLY.

READ UNCOMMITTED means "allow reading of rows which have been written by other transactions, but not committed" — so Dirty Reads, Non-Repeatable Reads, and Phantoms are all possible with this type of transaction. However, Lost Update is not possible for the simple reason that, as already stated, changes of any kind are illegal. Lost Updates are, in fact, prevented in all the standard SQL isolation levels. The concurrency level is as high as it can be — in a locking situation, no locks would be issued and no locks would be checked for. We could say that, for this transaction, concurrency checking is turned off.

The READ UNCOMMITTED level is a good choice if (*a*) the transaction is usually slow, (*b*) errors are likely to be small, and (*c*) errors are likely to cancel each other out. The most certain example of such a situation is a single SELECT statement containing a set function such as COUNT(*). Any "report" where the user isn't likely to care about details, is also a good candidate. You tolerate a huge degree of error every time you use a search engine on the World Wide Web.

READ COMMITTED

READ COMMITTED is the next level of transaction isolation. READ COMMITTED means "allow reading of rows written by other transactions only after they have been committed" — so Non-Repeatable Reads or Phantoms are both possible with this type of transaction but Lost Update and Dirty Read are not. The READ COMMITTED level allows for a reasonably high level of concurrency — in a locking situation, shared locks must be made, but they can be released again before the transaction ends. For any "optimistic" concurrency resolution mechanism, READ COMMITTED is the favored level. Conventional wisdom says that concurrency based on optimistic assumptions gets very slow if the isolation level is high.

The READ COMMITTED level is always safe if there is only one SQL statement in the transaction. Logic tells us that there will be no Repeatable Read errors if there is only one "read."

REPEATABLE READ

REPEATABLE READ is the next level of transaction isolation. By specifying REPEATABLE READ, you are saying to your DBMS, "Don't tolerate Non-Repeatable Reads (or, for that matter, Dirty Reads or Lost Updates) for the next transaction." Phantoms continue to be tolerated. With REPEATABLE READ, the concurrency drops sharply. In a locking situation, the DBMS will be obliged to put a "shared lock" on every row it fetches and keep the lock throughout the transaction. From the DBMS's point of view, the difference between this level and the previous one is: with READ COMMITTED, the locks can be released before the transaction ends; with REPEATABLE READ they can't be.

The REPEATABLE READ level is what most programmers prefer for multi-statement transactions that involve "changes." Examples would be bank transfers or library book checkouts.

SERIALIZABLE

SERIALIZABLE is the highest level of transaction isolation. At the SERIALIZABLE isolation level, no concurrency phenomena — even Phantoms — can arise to plague the programmer. This is the lowest level for concurrency. Often the DBMS must respond by coarsening the granularity and locking whole Tables at once. Because the result is likely to be poor performance, this is usually not the isolation level that the DBMS vendor manuals suggest — they'll steer you to REPEATABLE READ. But SERIALIZABLE is the default isolation level in standard SQL and it's the only level that all standards-compliant vendors are guaranteed to support (theoretically, a vendor could ignore the lower levels and just "upgrade" all <isolation level> specifications to SERIALIZABLE).

Because the SERIALIZABLE level won't tolerate Phantoms, it's especially indicated for transactions which contain multiple SELECT statements or for when you don't know what the statements will be, as in dynamic SQL. It is the only level which assures safe, error-free transactions every time. If your application consists wholly of short (i.e., fast-executing) statements which affect only a few records at a time, don't get fancy — leave everything at the default SERIALIZABLE level. Nevertheless, we suspect that SERIALIZABLE is used somewhat more often than appropriate. The choice of isolation level is something you should at least give a moment's thought to, on a case-by-case basis.

The word SERIALIZABLE reflects the idea that, given two overlapping transactions — Txn#1 and Txn#2 — we can get the same results as we would get if the transactions were "serial" rather than "overlapping" — that is, if Txn#1 followed Txn#2 or Txn#2 followed

Txn#1 in time, the end result would be the same. This does not mean that the transactions are replayable though. The DBMS can only take responsibility for data stored in the database. It can not guarantee that a transaction's statements are replayable if the parameter values from the host (application) program change or if the SQL statements contain niladic functions such as CURRENT_DATE, CURRENT_TIME, CURRENT_TIMESTAMP, or CURRENT_USER.

SET LOCAL TRANSACTION

If your DBMS supports transactions that may affect more than one SQL-server, you can use the <keyword> LOCAL (new to SQL with SQL3) to set the transaction characteristics for the next local transaction. If you omit LOCAL, you're instructing your DBMS to set the transaction characteristics for the next transaction executed by the program, regardless of location. If LOCAL is specified, then you may not also specify the size of the transaction's diagnostics area.

Certain errors can arise when you try to use the SET TRANSACTION statement:

- If you try to issue it when a transaction has already begun, SET TRANSACTION will fail; your DBMS will return the SQLSTATE error 25001 "invalid transaction state-active SQL-transaction."
- If you issue it when there are holdable-Cursors still open from the previous transaction and the isolation level of that transaction is not the same as the isolation level you're specifying for the next transaction, SET TRANSACTION will fail; your DBMS will return the SQLSTATE error 25008 "invalid transaction state-held cursor requires same isolation level."
- If you issue SET LOCAL TRANSACTION and your DBMS doesn't support transactions that affect multiple SQL-servers, SET LOCAL TRANSACTION will fail; your DBMS will return the SQLSTATE error 0A001 "feature not supported-multiple server transactions."

If you want to restrict your code to Core SQL, don't use SET LOCAL TRANSACTION and don't set any transaction's isolation level to anything but SERIALIZABLE.

START TRANSACTION Statement

In SQL3, you don't need the SET TRANSACTION statement except for setting the characteristics of local transactions. Instead, you can use the START TRANSACTION statement to both initiate the start of a new transaction and to set that transaction's characteristics. The required syntax for the START TRANSACTION statement is as follows.

```
START TRANSACTION <transaction mode> [ {,<transaction mode>}...]

   <transaction mode> ::=
   <isolation level> |
   <transaction access mode> |
   <diagnostics size>
```

Each of the transaction characteristics — <isolation level>, <transaction access mode>, and <diagnostics size> — works the same and has the same options as those we discussed for the SET TRANSACTION statement. The only real difference between the two statements is that SET TRANSACTION is considered to be outside of a transaction; it defines the characteristics for the next transaction coming up — while START TRANSACTION is considered as the beginning of a transaction; it defines the characteristics of the transaction it begins.

One other thing of note: the characteristics of a transaction that you start with a START TRANSACTION statement are as specified in that statement — even if the specification is implicit because you leave out one or more of the transaction mode options. That is, even if one or more characteristics are omitted from START TRANSACTION, they will default to the appropriate values — they will not take on any non-default characteristics even if you issue a SET TRANSACTION statement that includes other specifications for those characteristics just before you begin the transaction.

If you want to restrict your code to Core SQL, don't use the START TRANSACTION statement.

Special Problems

The SQL-Schema change statements (CREATE, ALTER, DROP, GRANT, REVOKE) require drastic solutions to ensure concurrency. Typically, a DBMS must lock all the INFORMATION_SCHEMA descriptors. That means that SQL-Schema statements cannot run concurrently with anything else.

The INSERT statement is more concurrent than the UPDATE or DELETE statements. By definition, any "new" row is a not-yet-committed row and therefore is invisible to all other transactions (except transactions which are running at the READ UNCOMMITTED isolation level). INSERT will have problems in cases where the target Table includes a Column with a serial data type (which is non-standard) — in such cases, the DBMS cannot guarantee that the value will truly be serial unless the isolation level of all transactions is SERIALIZABLE.

It is fairly easy to lock a "row" in a Base table because there is usually some fixed physical file address which corresponds to the row. However, an "index key" in an index file is a slipperier thing. Index keys can move, as anyone who has studied B+trees can tell you. So, when you update a row, remember that you may be locking not only the row, but an entire page of an index.

Regardless of isolation level, none of the isolation phenomena should occur during: (*a*) implied reading of Schema definitions (i.e., while finding Objects during the "prepare" phase ... as opposed to "explicit" reading, which is what happens if you SELECT ... FROM INFORMATION_SCHEMA.<Table name>); (*b*) the processing of integrity Constraints (but not Triggers). The implication is that standard SQL DBMSs have to lock the whole database when preparing a statement and at the end of a statement's execution phase. This is a difficult requirement.

Transactions and Constraint Checking

There is one other SQL transaction management statement: SET CONSTRAINTS. We talked about SET CONSTRAINTS a bit in Chapter 20 "SQL Constraints and Assertions"; basically, it allows you to tell the DBMS when you want it to check any deferrable Constraints that were affected during a transaction. A transaction always begins with an initial default constraint mode for every Constraint that is used during the course of the transaction. A Constraint's initial constraint mode, specified when the Constraint was created, determines when the Constraint will be checked for violation of its rule; immediately at the end of each SQL statement executed or later on in the transaction. The SET CONSTRAINTS statement is used to specify a different constraint mode for one or more DEFERRABLE Constraints during the course of a transaction.

SET CONSTRAINTS Statement

The required syntax for the SET CONSTRAINTS statement is as follows.

```
SET CONSTRAINTS <Constraint name list> {DEFERRED | IMMEDIATE}

   <Constraint name list> ::=
   ALL |
   <Constraint name> [ {,<Constraint name>}... ]
```

Remember that all Constraints and Assertions are defined with a deferral mode of either NOT DEFERRABLE or DEFERRABLE. A deferral mode of NOT DEFERRABLE means that the Constraint must be checked for violation as soon as the SQL statement that affects it is executed — this type of Constraint can't be affected by the SET CONSTRAINTS statement and we'll ignore it here. A deferral mode of DEFERRABLE, on the other hand, allows you to specify when you want your DBMS to check the Constraint for violation — the choices are at statement end or at transaction end — and such Constraints may be affected by the SET CONSTRAINTS statement.

An integrity Constraint's constraint mode may change during the course of a transaction. If the Constraint is a NOT DEFERRABLE Constraint, its constraint mode is always IMMEDIATE. But if the Constraint is a DEFERRABLE Constraint, then its constraint mode at the beginning of a transaction will either be IMMEDIATE or DEFERRED, depending on the way you defined the Constraint — if you defined it as DEFERRABLE INITIALLY IMMEDIATE, the Constraint's constraint mode at transaction start will be IMMEDIATE and if you defined it as DEFERRABLE INITIALLY DEFERRED, the Constraint's constraint mode at transaction start will be DEFERRED. You can use the SET CONSTRAINTS statement to change these default constraint mode settings for one or more Constraints — but only for the duration of the transaction that you use it in. (You can actually issue SET CONSTRAINTS at two different times. If you issue it during a transaction, you're changing the constraint mode of only those Constraints that are affected during that same transaction. If you issue it when there is no current transaction, you're changing the constraint mode of only those Constraints that are affected during the very next transaction.)

The SQL statement:

```
SET CONSTRAINTS ALL IMMEDIATE;
```

has the effect of setting the constraint mode of every DEFERRABLE Constraint to IMMEDIATE. IMMEDIATE means that the Constraints must be checked for violation after the execution of every SQL statement — including after SET CONSTRAINTS. The SQL statement:

```
SET CONSTRAINTS ALL DEFERRED;
```

has the effect of setting the constraint mode of every DEFERRABLE Constraint to DEFERRED. DEFERRED means that the Constraints should not be checked for violation after the execution of every SQL statement but should instead be checked at some later time, but no later than the end of the current transaction. (COMMIT includes an implied SET CONSTRAINTS ALL IMMEDIATE statement so that all Constraints are checked at transaction end.)

If you provide a list of <Constraint name>s instead of using the <keyword> ALL, the constraint mode of only those Constraints is affected. For example, if you have these Constraints:

```
Constraint_1 DEFERRABLE INITIALLY IMMEDIATE
Constraint_2 DEFERRABLE INITIALLY IMMEDIATE
```

```
Constraint_3 DEFERRABLE INITIALLY IMMEDIATE
Constraint_4 DEFERRABLE INITIALLY DEFERRED
Constraint_5 DEFERRABLE INITIALLY DEFERRED
Constraint_6 DEFERRABLE INITIALLY DEFERRED
```

and you issue this SQL statement:

```
SET CONSTRAINTS Constraint_1,Constraint_3,Constraint_4 DEFERRED;
```

the result is that `Constraint_1`, `Constraint_3`, `Constraint_4`, `Constraint_5`, and `Constraint_6` will all have a constraint mode of `DEFERRED` and `Constraint_2` will continue to have a constraint mode of `IMMEDIATE`.

All Constraints with a constraint mode of `IMMEDIATE` are checked for violation at SQL statement end. Constraints with a constraint mode of deferred, on the other hand, are not checked until transaction end. This lets you do operations which temporarily put your data into an unsound state and can thus be very useful.

Dialects

Some DBMSs support locking, some support timestamping, some support both. Beyond that fundamental point of difference, there are many implementation-dependent features. For example, the granularity (by Column or row or page or Table or database), the number of distinct isolation levels that are actually supported (remember that pseudo-support is possible by simply upgrading to the next level), and whether to support SQL-92 or SQL3 syntax. Most DBMSs are still idiosyncratic with respect to support for the `SET TRANSACTION` statement.

IBM's DB2 and its imitators have explicit statements for locking Tables: `LOCK TABLE` <name> `IN {EXCLUSIVE|SHARED} MODE`. This reduces the total number of locks and actually enhances concurrency if your intention is to access every row in the Table.

ODBC specifies a variety of options which essentially are options for row identifiers used in scrolling. There are also CLI-specific commands for setting transaction isolation or other concurrency-related characteristics.

Oracle has Locks Display and other utilities that help administrators to monitor concurrency.

Goodies

The OCELOT DBMS that comes with this book supports concurrency. These are the specifications:

Concurrency resolution mechanism:	Locking
Maximum number of concurrent connections:	indefinite
Isolation levels actually supported:	`SERIALIZABLE`
Granularity:	database
Additional features:	none

For installation and configuration instructions, refer to the file OCELOT.TXT on the CD-ROM.

38

Chapter 38

SQL Sessions

An SQL-session spans the execution of one or more consecutive SQL statements by a single user. In order to execute any SQL statements, your DBMS has to establish an SQL-Connection (using the CONNECT statement) — the SQL-session thus initiated is then associated with that SQL-Connection. If you don't explicitly do a CONNECT statement on your own, your DBMS will effectively execute a default CONNECT statement to establish an SQL-Connection for you — this is known as the *default SQL-Connection.*

An SQL-Connection has two possible states: it is either current or dormant. Only one SQL-Connection (and its associated SQL-session) can be current at a time. An SQL-Connection is initially established by a CONNECT statement as the current SQL-Connection and it remains the current SQL-Connection unless and until another CONNECT statement or a SET CONNECTION statement puts it (and its associated SQL-session) into a dormant state by establishing another SQL-Connection as the current SQL-Connection. When would you use SET CONNECTION? Well, the SQL Standard says that your DBMS must support at least one SQL-Connection — but it may support more than one concurrent SQL-Connection. In the latter case, your application program may connect to more than one SQL-server, selecting the one it wants to use (the current or active SQL-Connection) with a SET CONNECTION statement.

An SQL-Connection ends either when you issue a DISCONNECT statement or in some implementation-defined way following the last call to an <externally-invoked procedure> within the last active SQL-client Module.

Every SQL-session has a user <AuthorizationID> to provide your DBMS with an <AuthorizationID> for Privilege checking during operations on SQL-data. You can specify this

<AuthorizationID> with the CONNECT statement or allow it to default to an <AuthorizationID> provided by your DBMS. You can also change the <AuthorizationID> during the SQL-session.

Every SQL-session also has a default local time zone offset to provide your DBMS with a time zone offset when a time or a timestamp value needs one. When you begin an SQL-session, your DBMS sets the default time zone offset to a value chosen by your vendor. You can change this to a more appropriate value with the SET TIME ZONE statement.

Every SQL-session has what the SQL Standard calls "enduring characteristics" — these all have initial default values at the beginning of an SQL-session, but you change any of them with the SET SESSION CHARACTERISTICS statement. SQL-sessions also have a "context" — characteristics of the SQL-session that your DBMS preserves when an SQL-session is made dormant so that it can restore the SQL-session properly when it is made current again. The context of an SQL-session includes the current SESSION_USER, the CURRENT_USER, the CURRENT_ROLE, the CURRENT_PATH, the identities of all temporary Tables, the current default time zone offset, the current constraint mode for all Constraints, the current transaction access mode, the position of all open Cursors, the current transaction isolation level, the current transaction diagnostics area limit, the value of all valid locators, and information of any active SQL-invoked routines.

SQL-Connections

You can establish an SQL-Connection either explicitly, by issuing a CONNECT statement; or implicitly, by invoking a procedure that works on SQL-data when there is no current SQL-session (in this case, your DBMS acts as if you explicitly issued CONNECT TO DEFAULT;). You can change the state of an SQL-Connection (from current to dormant and back again) with the SET CONNECTION statement. You can also end an SQL-Connection (and therefore its associated SQL-session) with the DISCONNECT statement. Here's how.

CONNECT Statement

The CONNECT statement explicitly establishes an SQL-Connection. The establishment of an SQL-Connection gives you access to the SQL-data on an SQL-server in your environment and thus starts an SQL-session. The required syntax for the CONNECT statement is as follows.

```
CONNECT TO
   DEFAULT |
   <SQL-server name> [ AS <Connection name> ] [ USER <AuthorizationID> ]
```

The CONNECT statement may not be executed during a transaction unless your DBMS supports transactions that affect multiple SQL-servers.

DEFAULT Connection

The SQL Standard does not require an explicit CONNECT statement to start an SQL-session. If the first SQL statement in an SQL-session is anything other than a CONNECT statement, your DBMS will first execute this SQL statement:

```
CONNECT TO DEFAULT;
```

to establish the default SQL-Connection before proceeding further. You can also issue an explicit CONNECT TO DEFAULT; statement if you want to deliberately establish your DBMS's default SQL-Connection. In either case, if the default SQL-Connection has already been established, (e.g., it was already the subject of a CONNECT statement or a SET CONNECTION statement and no DISCONNECT statement has been issued for it) CONNECT will fail; your DBMS will return the SQLSTATE error 08002 "connection exception-connection name in use."

[NON-PORTABLE] The effect of CONNECT TO DEFAULT; is non-standard because the SQL Standard requires implementors to define the default SQL-Connection and the default SQL-server. [OCELOT Implementation] The OCELOT DBMS that comes with this book treats the (explicit or implicit) SQL statement:

```
CONNECT TO DEFAULT;
```

as equivalent to this SQL statement:

```
CONNECT TO 'ocelot' AS 'ocelot' USER 'ocelot';
```

This CONNECT statement causes the OCELOT DBMS to establish a SQL-Connection to a default Cluster (or default SQL-server) called OCELOT, using a default <Connection name> of OCELOT and a default user <AuthorizationID> of OCELOT. If the default Cluster can't be found, the DBMS will create it.

<SQL-Server name> Clause

The other form of the CONNECT statement has three possible arguments, only one of which is mandatory. The syntax CONNECT TO <SQL-server name>; e.g.,

```
CONNECT TO 'some_server';
```

establishes an SQL-Connection to the SQL-server named. (Remember that the SQL-server is that portion of your environment that actually carries out the database operations.) <SQL-server name> is either a <character string literal>, a <host parameter name>, or an <SQL parameter reference> whose value represents a valid <SQL-server name>. The SQL Standard is deliberately vague about just what an SQL-server is and consequently leaves the method for determining its location and the communication protocol required to access it up to the DBMS.

AS Clause

The syntax CONNECT TO <SQL-server name> AS <Connection name>; e.g.,

```
CONNECT TO 'some_server' AS 'connection_1';
```

establishes an SQL-Connection named connection_1 to the SQL-server named. <Connection name> is a <simple value specification>, (e.g., a <character string literal>, <host parameter name>, or <SQL parameter reference>) whose value represents a valid <Connection name>. (If <Connection name> does not evaluate to a valid <Connection name>, CONNECT will fail; your DBMS will return the SQLSTATE error 2E000 "invalid connection name.")

[NON-PORTABLE] A <Connection name> must be a <regular identifier> or a <delimited identifier> that is no more than 128 octets in length, but the value of a valid <Connection name> is non-standard because the SQL Standard requires implementors to define what a valid <Connection name> may be and to which Character set <Connection name>s belong.

[OCELOT Implementation] The OCELOT DBMS that comes with this book defines a <Connection name> as any valid <regular identifier> or <delimited identifier> whose characters belong to the INFORMATION_SCHEMA.SQL_TEXT Character set.

If your CONNECT statement doesn't include the optional AS <Connection name> clause, the value of <Connection name> defaults to the value of <SQL-server name>. The following SQL statements are therefore equivalent (assuming that the default SQL-Connection is to an SQL-server named some_server):

```
CONNECT TO DEFAULT;
CONNECT TO 'some_server';
CONNECT TO 'some_server' AS 'some_server';
```

NOTE: The AS clause can only be omitted from the first CONNECT statement issued for a particular SQL-server. On the second and subsequent Connections, an explicit <Connection name> must be provided to your DBMS because <Connection name>s must be unique for the entire SQL-environment at any given time. You'll use the <Connection name> with the SET CONNECTION statement to switch between different SQL-Connections. If <Connection name> evaluates to a <Connection name> that is already in use — e.g., it was the subject of CONNECT TO or SET CONNECTION and DISCONNECT has not been issued for it — CONNECT TO will fail; the DBMS will return the SQLSTATE error 08002 "connection exception-connection name in use."

USER **Clause**

The syntax CONNECT TO <SQL-server name> USER <AuthorizationID>; e.g.,

```
CONNECT TO 'some_server' USER 'bob';
```

establishes an SQL-Connection, with an SQL-session <AuthorizationID> of bob, to the SQL-server named. <AuthorizationID> is a <simple value specification> — e.g., a <character string literal>, <host parameter name>, or <SQL parameter reference> — whose value represents a valid <AuthorizationID>. (If <AuthorizationID> does not evaluate to a valid user <AuthorizationID>, CONNECT will fail; your DBMS will return the SQLSTATE error 28000 "invalid authorization specification.")

If your CONNECT statement doesn't include the optional USER <AuthorizationID> clause, the value of the SQL-session user defaults to an <AuthorizationID> chosen by your DBMS. The following SQL statements are therefore equivalent (assuming that the default SQL-Connection is to an SQL-server named some_server):

```
CONNECT TO DEFAULT;
CONNECT TO 'some_server';
CONNECT TO 'some_server' AS 'some_server' USER 'default_user';
```

[NON-PORTABLE] The effect of omitting the optional USER clause from a CONNECT statement is non-standard because the SQL Standard requires implementors to define their own initial default SQL-session <AuthorizationID>. [OCELOT Implementation] The OCELOT DBMS that comes with this book has an initial default <AuthorizationID> of OCELOT.

CONNECT Examples

This SQL statement:

```
CONNECT TO 'some_server';
```

establishes an SQL-Connection to the SQL-server specified. The <Connection name> defaults to some_server; the SQL-session <AuthorizationID> is set to the DBMS's initial default <AuthorizationID>. This SQL statement:

```
CONNECT TO 'some_server' AS 'Connection_1';
```

establishes an SQL-Connection named Connection_1 to the SQL-server specified. The SQL-session <AuthorizationID> is set to the DBMS's initial default <AuthorizationID>. This SQL statement:

```
CONNECT TO 'some_server' USER 'bob';
```

establishes an SQL-Connection to the SQL-server specified. The <Connection name> defaults to some_server; the SQL-session <AuthorizationID> is set to bob. And this SQL statement:

```
CONNECT TO 'some_server' AS 'Connection_1' USER 'bob';
```

establishes an SQL-Connection named Connection_1 to the SQL-server specified. The SQL-session <AuthorizationID> is set to bob.

Executing the CONNECT statement has the effect that the SQL-Connection established becomes the current SQL-Connection and its associated SQL-session becomes the current SQL-session. The SQL-Connection and SQL-session that were current when you executed CONNECT (if any) become dormant with their context information preserved by the DBMS so that they can be properly restored later on. If the CONNECT statement fails, the current SQL-Connection and its associated SQL-session (if any) remain the current SQL-Connection and current SQL-session.

If CONNECT fails because your DBMS is unable to establish the SQL-Connection, you'll get the SQLSTATE error 08001 "connection exception-SQL-client unable to establish SQL-connection." If CONNECT fails because the SQL-server refuses to accept the SQL-Connection, you'll get the SQLSTATE error 08004 "connection exception-SQL-server rejected establishment of SQL-connection."

If you want to restrict your code to Core SQL, don't use the CONNECT statement.

SET CONNECTION Statement

[NON-PORTABLE] An SQL-compliant DBMS can either limit the number of concurrent SQL-Connections to one or it can support multiple concurrent SQL-Connections. [OCELOT Implementation] The OCELOT DBMS that comes with this book allows multiple concurrent SQL-Connections to be made; each begins a separate SQL-session for the <Cluster name> specified. Thus, OCELOT supports multi-user operations — one or more Users may connect to the same Cluster simultaneously — and OCELOT supports multi-tasking operations — the same user may connect to multiple Clusters simultaneously. Each such connection is a separate SQL-Connection (it must be identified by a unique <Connection name>) and is associated with a separate SQL-session.

The SET CONNECTION statement is used to select an SQL-Connection from all available SQL-Connections — it makes a dormant SQL-Connection current. As a consequence, any other SQL-Connection that was current then becomes dormant. The required syntax for the SET CONNECTION statement is as follows.

```
SET CONNECTION DEFAULT | <Connection name>
```

The SET CONNECTION statement activates a dormant SQL-Connection and makes it the current SQL-Connection. SET CONNECTION may not be executed during a transaction unless your DBMS supports transactions that affect multiple SQL-servers. The SQL statement:

```
SET CONNECTION DEFAULT;
```

will establish your DBMS's default SQL-Connection as the current SQL-Connection. If there is no current or dormant default SQL-Connection (that is, if CONNECT TO DEFAULT; wasn't previously issued during the SQL-session), SET CONNECTION will fail; your DBMS will return the SQLSTATE error 08003 "connection exception-connection does not exist."

The syntax SET CONNECTION <Connection name>; will establish the SQL-Connection specified as the current SQL-Connection. <Connection name> must be a <simple value specification> — e.g., a <character string literal>, <host parameter name>, or <SQL parameter reference> — whose value identifies the current, or a dormant, SQL-Connection. If <Connection name> does not evaluate to either the current or a dormant SQL-Connection, SET CONNECTION will fail; your DBMS will return the SQLSTATE error 08003 "connection exception-connection does not exist." For example, this SQL statement:

```
SET CONNECTION 'connection_2';
```

makes the SQL-Connection called connection_2 the current SQL-Connection and puts the previous (if any) SQL-Connection into a dormant state. If your DBMS is unable to activate connection_2, SET CONNECTION will fail and your DBMS will return the SQLSTATE error 08006 "connection exception-connection failure."

If you want to restrict your code to Core SQL, don't use the SET CONNECTION statement.

DISCONNECT Statement

An SQL-Connection can be closed whether it is the current SQL-Connection or a dormant SQL-Connection, but may not be closed while a transaction is on-going for its associated SQL-session. The required syntax for the DISCONNECT statement is as follows.

```
DISCONNECT <Connection name> | DEFAULT | CURRENT | ALL
```

The DISCONNECT statement terminates an inactive SQL-Connection. DISCONNECT may not be executed during a transaction — if you attempt to terminate an SQL-Connection that is processing a transaction, DISCONNECT will fail; your DBMS will return the SQLSTATE error 25000 "invalid transaction state."

You can disconnect a specific SQL-Connection by naming it (with DISCONNECT <Connection name>;), you can disconnect your DBMS's default SQL-Connection (with DISCONNECT DEFAULT;), you can disconnect the current SQL-Connection (with DISCONNECT CURRENT;) or you can disconnect the current and all dormant SQL-Connections at once (with DISCONNECT

ALL;). For example, this SQL statement closes an inactive SQL-Connection called connection_1, whether it is current or dormant;

```
DISCONNECT 'connection_1';
```

As usual, <Connection name> must be a <simple value specification> — e.g., a <character string literal>, <host parameter name>, or <SQL parameter reference> — whose value identifies the current, or a dormant, SQL-Connection. (If <Connection name> is not the name of either the current SQL-Connection or a dormant SQL-Connection, DISCONNECT will fail; your DBMS will return the SQLSTATE error 08003 "connection exception-connection does not exist.") If <Connection name> names the current SQL-Connection and DISCONNECT executes successfully, there will no longer be a current SQL-Connection until another CONNECT statement or SET CONNECTION statement establishes one. This SQL statement:

```
DISCONNECT DEFAULT;
```

terminates the DBMS's default SQL-Connection whether it is current or dormant. (If the DBMS's default SQL-Connection is neither the current SQL-Connection nor a dormant SQL-Connection, DISCONNECT will fail; your DBMS will return the SQLSTATE error 08003 "connection exception-connection does not exist.") If the default SQL-Connection is the current SQL-Connection and DISCONNECT executes successfully, there will no longer be a current SQL-Connection until another CONNECT statement or SET CONNECTION statement establishes one. This SQL statement:

```
DISCONNECT CURRENT;
```

terminates the current SQL-Connection. If there is no current SQL-Connection, DISCONNECT will fail; your DBMS will return the SQLSTATE error 08003 "connection exception-connection does not exist." If DISCONNECT executes successfully, there will no longer be a current SQL-Connection until another CONNECT statement or SET CONNECTION statement establishes one. This SQL statement:

```
DISCONNECT ALL;
```

closes the current, and all dormant, SQL-Connections. If there are no current or dormant SQL-Connections, DISCONNECT will fail; your DBMS will return the SQLSTATE error 08003 "connection exception-connection does not exist." If DISCONNECT executes successfully, there will no longer be any SQL-Connection (current or dormant) until another CONNECT statement or SET CONNECTION statement establishes one.

Any errors other than SQLSTATE 08003 or SQLSTATE 25000 that are detected by your DBMS while DISCONNECT is being executed will not cause DISCONNECT to fail. Instead, DISCONNECT will execute successfully and your DBMS will return the SQLSTATE warning 01002 "warning-disconnect error."

The SQL Standard suggests that DISCONNECT should be automatic when an SQL-session ends — but lets the DBMS decide when this has occurred. Recommendation: To be absolutely sure of correct results, always end your SQL-sessions with the explicit DISCONNECT statement:

```
DISCONNECT ALL;
```

If you want to restrict your code to Core SQL, don't use the DISCONNECT statement.

SQL-Session Management

SQL provides four statements that help you manage your SQL-session. Each one lets you specify a value for one or more SQL-session characteristics. The SQL-session management statements are SET SESSION CHARACTERISTICS, SET SESSION AUTHORIZATION, SET ROLE, and SET TIME ZONE.

SET SESSION CHARACTERISTICS Statement

The SET SESSION CHARACTERISTICS statement sets the value of one or more transaction characteristics for the current SQL-session. The required syntax for the SET SESSION CHARACTERISTICS statement is as follows.

```
SET SESSION CHARACTERISTICS AS
   <transaction mode> [ {,<transaction mode>}... ]

   <transaction mode> ::=
   <isolation level> |
   <transaction access mode> |
   <diagnostics size>
```

You can set the same characteristics for all the transactions in an entire SQL-session as you can for a single transaction. Each of the transaction characteristics — <isolation level>, <transaction access mode>, and <diagnostics size> — works the same and has the same options as those we discussed for the SET TRANSACTION statement in Chapter 37. The values you specify for any transaction characteristic in a SET SESSION CHARACTERISTICS statement are enduring values — should you cause the current SQL-session to go dormant and then reactivate it later, your DBMS will reset each characteristic to the value you specified the last time you issued SET SESSION CHARACTERISTICS for that SQL-session. Here's an example:

```
SET SESSION CHARACTERISTICS AS
   READ WRITE
   ISOLATION LEVEL REPEATABLE READ
   DIAGNOSTICS SIZE 5
```

If you want to restrict your code to Core SQL, don't use the SET SESSION CHARACTERISTICS statement.

SET SESSION AUTHORIZATION Statement

The SET SESSION AUTHORIZATION statement sets the session user <AuthorizationID> for the current SQL-session. The required syntax for the SET SESSION AUTHORIZATION statement is as follows.

```
SET SESSION AUTHORIZATION <value specification>
```

When you start an SQL-session, your DBMS sets the value of the session user <AuthorizationID> for the SQL-session to the <AuthorizationID> specified with the CONNECT statement. The session user <AuthorizationID> is the value returned by the SESSION_USER function and is usually also the value returned by the CURRENT_USER (or USER) function. Your DBMS uses the session <AuthorizationID> as a default <AuthorizationID> in cases where no explicit <AuthorizationID> overrides it — for example, whenever you run a Module that wasn't defined with an explicit AUTHORIZATION clause, your DBMS assumes the owner of the Module is the SQL-session <AuthorizationID>. The owner of any temporary Tables defined for the SQL-session is the SQL-session <AuthorizationID>.

[NON-PORTABLE] SET SESSION AUTHORIZATION may always be executed at the start of an SQL-session. Whether you can use the SET SESSION AUTHORIZATION statement at any other time is non-standard because the SQL Standard requires implementors to define whether the SQL-session <AuthorizationID> may be changed once an SQL-session has begun. [OCELOT Implementation] The OCELOT DBMS that comes with this book allows the SQL-session <AuthorizationID> to be changed at any time (except during a transaction).

You can change the value of the SQL-session <AuthorizationID> with the SET SESSION AUTHORIZATION statement; simply issue SET SESSION AUTHORIZATION followed by a <character string literal>, a character string <host parameter name> (with optional indicator), a character string <SQL parameter reference>, or a user function (either CURRENT_ROLE, CURRENT_USER, SESSION_USER, SYSTEM_USER, or USER). Whichever you use, the value represented by the <value specification> must be a valid user <AuthorizationID> — if it isn't, SET SESSION AUTHORIZATION will fail; your DBMS will return the SQLSTATE error 28000 "invalid authorization specification."

SET SESSION AUTHORIZATION can only be issued outside of a transaction. If you try to execute the statement and a transaction is currently active, SET SESSION AUTHORIZATION will fail; your DBMS will return the SQLSTATE error 25001 "invalid transaction state-active SQL-transaction."

For an example of SET SESSION AUTHORIZATION, assume that the session user <AuthorizationID> for your SQL-session is bob and you'd like to switch it to sam. Here's three different ways to do it:

```
SET SESSION AUTHORIZATION 'sam';

SET SESSION AUTHORIZATION :char_variable;
   -- assume the value of the host variable "char_variable" is SAM

SET SESSION AUTHORIZATION CURRENT_USER;
   -- assume the value of CURRENT_USER is SAM
```

If you want to restrict your code to Core SQL, don't use the SET SESSION AUTHORIZATION statement.

SET ROLE Statement

The SET ROLE statement sets the enabled Roles for the current SQL-session. The required syntax for the SET ROLE statement is as follows.

```
SET ROLE <value specification> | NONE
```

When you start an SQL-session, your DBMS sets the value of the current Role <AuthorizationID> for the SQL-session to the <AuthorizationID> specified with the CONNECT statement (or to NULL, if the CONNECT statement doesn't provide a <Role name>). The current Role <AuthorizationID> is the value returned by the CURRENT_ROLE function. Either one of CURRENT_USER or CURRENT_ROLE may be NULL at any time, but they may not both be NULL at the same time — the non-null identifier is the SQL-session's current <AuthorizationID>. That is, if CURRENT_ROLE is set to some <Role name>, then CURRENT_USER must be NULL and your DBMS will use the current Role for Privilege checking before processing any SQL statements in the SQL-session.

You can change the value of CURRENT_ROLE with the SET ROLE statement; simply issue SET ROLE followed by a <character string literal>, a character string <host parameter name> (with optional indicator), a character string <SQL parameter reference>, or a user function (either CURRENT_ROLE, SESSION_USER, SYSTEM_USER, or USER). Whichever you use, the value represented by the <value specification> must be a valid <Role name> and that name must identify a Role that has been granted either to PUBLIC or to the SQL-session <AuthorizationID> — if it isn't, SET ROLE will fail; your DBMS will return the SQLSTATE error 0P000 "invalid role specification." You can also change the value of CURRENT_ROLE to NULL by issuing SET ROLE followed by the <keyword> NONE.

SET ROLE can only be issued outside of a transaction. If you try to execute the statement and a transaction is currently active, SET ROLE will fail; your DBMS will return the SQLSTATE error 25001 "invalid transaction state-active SQL-transaction."

For an example of SET ROLE, assume that the current Role for your SQL-session is NULL and you'd like to switch it to Teller_Role. Here's two different ways to do it:

```
SET ROLE 'Teller_Role';

SET ROLE :char_variable;
   -- assume the value of the host variable "char_variable" is TELLER_ROLE
```

If you want to restrict your code to Core SQL, don't use the SET ROLE statement.

SET TIME ZONE Statement

[NON-PORTABLE] An SQL-session always begins with an initial default time zone offset that is non-standard because the SQL Standard requires implementors to define their own initial default time zone offset. [OCELOT Implementation] The OCELOT DBMS that comes with this book has an initial default time zone that represents UTC — its default time zone offset is INTERVAL +'00:00' HOUR TO MINUTE.

The SQL-session default time zone offset is used to specify the related time zone for all times and timestamps that don't include an explicit <time zone interval>. You can use the SET TIME ZONE statement to change the default time zone offset for the current SQL-session. The required syntax for the SET TIME ZONE statement is as follows.

```
SET TIME ZONE LOCAL | interval_expression
```

The SET TIME ZONE statement changes the current SQL-session's default time zone offset. It has two possible arguments: the <keyword> LOCAL or an expression that evaluates to some non-null INTERVAL HOUR TO MINUTE value between INTERVAL -'12:59' HOUR TO MINUTE and INTERVAL +'13:00' HOUR TO MINUTE. (If you specify an interval that is NULL or an interval that falls outside the proper range, SET TIME ZONE will fail; your DBMS will return the SQLSTATE error 22009 "data exception-invalid time zone displacement value.")

SET TIME ZONE can only be issued outside of a transaction. If you try to execute the statement and a transaction is currently active, SET TIME ZONE will fail; your DBMS will return the SQLSTATE error 25001 "invalid transaction state-active SQL-transaction."

The effect of this SQL statement:

```
SET TIME ZONE LOCAL;
```

is to set the time zone offset for the current SQL-session to your DBMS's initial default time zone offset.

The SQL syntax SET TIME ZONE interval_expression is used to set the time zone offset for the current SQL-session to the value that results when interval_expression is evaluated. For example, this SQL statement:

```
SET TIME ZONE INTERVAL -'03:00' HOUR TO MINUTE;
```

uses the <interval literal> INTERVAL -'03:00' HOUR TO MINUTE to set the time zone offset for the current SQL-session to minus three hours, i.e., UTC time plus 3 hours equals local time.

If you want to restrict your code to Core SQL, don't use the SET TIME ZONE statement.

39

Chapter 39

Embedded SQL Binding Style

SQL DBMSs communicate with SQL applications through a common programming language interface that is invoked through one of the SQL Standard-defined binding styles, or interface options. The programming language used is called a *host language*. An SQL DBMS must support the use of at least one host language, either for embedded SQL programming or for invoking external routines and/or procedures.

There are three main binding styles:

1. With *embedded SQL*, you can put SQL statements directly into "host programs" (programs written in Ada, C, COBOL, FORTRAN, MUMPS, Pascal, or PL/I) — making them part of the host program's source code. Because the host language's compiler won't recognize SQL statements as valid statements of its language, some sort of preprocessor is required to make this work.
2. With *SQL/CLI*, you can call an SQL DBMS's library from a host program. The SQL statements you want to execute are parameters of the call. Because SQL's modus operandi won't quite match the host language's, helper functions are required for the interface definition.
3. With the *Module language*, you can dispense with host programs and write entire Modules in SQL. You'll still have to call these Modules from one of the standard host languages though.

There is one other binding style — *Direct SQL* — which involves no host language. The entry of SQL statements on a keyboard, for example, is Direct SQL. Direct SQL is, under the covers, merely an implementation of a program written with one of the main three binding styles (Module, Embedded, or SQL/CLI).

Reflecting what we believe is their relative importance, this book contains one chapter on embedded SQL, then several chapters on SQL/CLI, and then one chapter on the Module binding style.

Because we believe that SQL/CLI will quickly become the SQL interface of choice, this chapter omits large amounts of detail, in favour of providing the necessary detail in our chapters on SQL/CLI. Still, this chapter is a good opportunity to introduce the basic concepts in a simple way. Embedded SQL is easy to read, so we have a trouble-free first viewing of the problems that a program writer must solve. Watch in particular for solutions of the "impedance mismatch" problem (getting SQL objects to link with host-language analogs), the "Weltanschauung" problem (handling one-row-at-a-time rather than whole-set-at-a-time), and the "control" problem (adjusting host program flow based on SQL execution information).

What is Embedded SQL?

Embedded SQL was once the predominant standard way to mix SQL statements with host languages. It lets you mix SQL statements directly into an application program written in some common computer programming language. It is especially associated with COBOL or PL/I programs and IBM's DB2 and big iron; however most of the big DBMS vendors support it on microcomputers too. Support is weak among small DBMS vendors and especially weak for computer host languages that aren't currently in vogue.

SQL can be embedded into many host languages, but support varies depending on the vendor and depending on the language. The following are the standard host languages (i.e., the ones mentioned in the SQL Standard). A DBMS that supports the embedded SQL binding style must support SQL embedded into at least one of these languages:

Ada: Standard. Weakly supported.

C: Standard. Well supported.

COBOL: Standard. Packages are sometimes supplied by the COBOL vendor. For example, Micro Focus offers XDB SQL as an optional add-on along with appropriate interfacing.

Fortran: Standard. Well supported, but interfacing is sometimes awkward.

MUMPS: Standard. Weakly supported.

Pascal: Standard. Not everybody supports Borland Delphi's special characteristics such as `Pchar` null-terminated string references.

PL/I: Standard. Weakly supported.

Here are some other host languages that have some importance but are not (yet) standard:

BASIC: Not supported by the SQL Standard. The vendor support which exists is usually restricted to a single dialect (such as Microsoft BASIC or PowerBASIC).

Java: Not supported by the SQL Standard. Probably Java will achieve recognition as an "official" host language for SQL, but most current efforts are for a CLI standard called JDBC.

For all of these languages, support is better via the SQL/CLI.

So, to begin with, you start with a host language, writing your code in the normal way. When you get to a point where a database operation needs to be carried out, use embedded SQL statements (rather than routines written in the host language; an executable SQL statement can be put into a program anywhere that an executable host language statement can be) to carry them out — the host code "calls" SQL statements. You can pass data between the host and SQL; SQL-data values go to variables in the host code, host program values go to SQL Columns or functions or some other appropriate database target. Before compiling your program, you'll need to go through a preprocessing step — hence the name: precompiler.

To make it all possible, you have to follow rigid conventions:

- Begin every SQL statement with the SQL prefix appropriate for the host language.
- End every SQL statement with the SQL terminator appropriate for the host language.
- Declare all host-language program variables which will be shared with SQL in a special `DECLARE` section.
- Declare additional program variables for error handling.

Precompilers

Most precompilers are standalone utility programs. A few are integrated with the compiler itself. Regardless of their startup method, all precompilers must do a certain series of operations which turn an embedded-SQL module into a module that the host compiler can compile. These are the operations which the sample Precompiler that comes with this book does for a C program:

1. Open the Input File (the file containing embedded SQL).
   Open the Output File (the file which the compiler needs).
2. Read a token from the Input File. At end: exit.
3. If the token is not `EXEC` or the next token is not SQL: write the token to the output file.
   Goto 2.
4. If the next tokens are `BEGIN DECLARE SECTION`:
   `/* The following tokens must be variable definitions */`
   Read and write the following tokens. While doing so, keep track of and store: variable name, variable size, variable type. Because this is supposed to be a C program, certain keywords are expected, such as `char` or `short`. Stop when the next tokens are `END DECLARE SECTION`.
   Goto 2.
5. If the next token is `CREATE` or `INSERT` or some other SQL <keyword> indicating that this is the beginning of an executable SQL statement:
   Write the words `SQLExecDirect(-1,`.

Read and write until "`;`" is seen. ("`;`" is the "terminator" of SQL in C.)
Write `,-3)`.
Goto 2.

NB: While reading and writing, a "host variable" token may be encountered of the form: <colon><host-variable-name>. The precompiler must convert this to whatever the appropriate form is for a pass-by-address parameter and output a statement like `SQLBindCol(...,&hostvariable);`.

If the precompiler finishes without severe errors, there is an output program. The output from the precompiler is the input for the compiler. From that, the compiler produces an object file. Then the linker comes into play. The linker will encounter some external references, for example the `SQLExecDirect` call that the precompiler produced. To resolve these references, the linker will look in a library — which is another essential part of the DBMS package for use with precompilers.

In theory, a precompiler could act differently provided it met the functional specification. We have described what we know best; this book's sample Precompiler.

SQL Prefixes and Terminators

The precompiler lacks the smarts to figure out the syntax of the host language program. After all, host language code can get pretty complex. All the precompiler can do is look for signals that say "embedded SQL starts here" or "embedded SQL ends here." Or, to use the formal terms, embedded SQL statements must have a prefix and a terminator. Usually the prefix is `EXEC SQL` and the terminator is a semicolon. There is a bit of variation among the standard host languages:

- For Ada, use: `EXEC SQL` ... `;`
- For C, use: `EXEC SQL` ... `;`
- For COBOL, use: `EXEC SQL` ... `END-EXEC`
- For Fortran, use: `EXEC SQL` ... <no end> (i.e., no explicit terminator)
- For MUMPS, use: `&SQL(` ... `)`
- For Pascal, use: `EXEC SQL` ... `;`
- For PL/I, use: `EXEC SQL` ... `;`

Our preferred languages for discussion are C and Pascal, so it's just as easy to say, "All SQL statements must be prefixed by `'EXEC SQL'` and terminated by `';'`." The case of the <keyword>s `EXEC SQL` (or the other prefixes) doesn't matter, but it is compulsory that they be together (rather than on separate lines). Everything between `EXEC SQL` and `;` must be legal

SQL — host language statements or comments have no place here. Aside from that, format is fairly free, as this example snippet shows:

```
...
{                               /* Braces around SQL statements are a good idea. */
EXEC sql
   CREATE DOMAIN d5 INTEGER;
   EXEC SQL
   CREATE DOMAIN                  /* This is a new-style comment not a C comment */
   d6 INTEGER
;
}
...
```

Host Variables

Embedded SQL statements can contain host language variables in the same places that any other scalar expression can be placed. The host variables allow you to pass data between the program and your SQL-data. In an SQL statement, a <host variable name> must be preceded by a colon to distinguish it from an SQL Object name. Host variables may not be qualified or subscripted and must return only scalar values.

An important and inevitable part of any embedded SQL program is the declare section — the variable declarations that appear between `EXEC SQL BEGIN DECLARE SECTION;` and `EXEC SQL END DECLARE SECTION;` as in:

```
EXEC SQL BEGIN DECLARE SECTION;
  int   x;
  char  y[5];
EXEC SQL END DECLARE SECTION;
```

In this example, `x` and `y` are host variables. They are defined according to the rules of the host language (in this case, C). But the definitions must be comprehensible to the precompiler too because the precompiler must know the data type, size, and name of each host variable. The trick, for making a variable that both the host and SQL can understand, is to keep the definition simple. Only a few data types are legal and tricks usually aren't — even simple tricks like enumerations or constants or macros will confuse the precompiler.

SQL <data type> and Host Variable Correspondence

Host variable data types must be compatible with the <data type> of the SQL-data values they'll be receiving or sending. The appropriate data type analogs for each host language, as defined by the SQL Standard, are as follows (`L` stands for length, `P` for precision, `S` for scale, `T` for time fractional seconds precision, `Q` for <interval qualifier>, and `N` for the implementation-defined size of a structured type reference; assume an 8-bit character set is in use):

For Ada:

SQL <data type>	Ada Data Type
SQLSTATE	SQL_STANDARD.SQLSTATE_TYPE
CHAR(L)	SQL_STANDARD.CHAR, with P'LENGTH of L
VARCHAR(L)	None
CLOB(L)	None
BIT(L)	SQL_STANDARD.BIT, with P'LENGTH of L
BIT VARYING(L)	None
BLOB(L)	None
BOOLEAN	SQL_STANDARD.BOOLEAN
SMALLINT	SQL_STANDARD.SMALLINT
INTEGER	SQL_STANDARD.INT
DECIMAL(P,S)	None
NUMERIC(P,S)	None
REAL	SQL_STANDARD.REAL
DOUBLE PRECISION	SQL_STANDARD.DOUBLE_PRECISION
FLOAT(P)	None
DATE	None
TIME(T)	None
TIMESTAMP(T)	None
INTERVAL(Q)	None
UDT	None
REF	SQL_STANDARD.CHAR, with P'LENGTH of N
ARRAY	None
ROW	None

For C:

SQL <data type>	C Data Type
SQLSTATE	char, with length 6
CHAR(L)	char, with length (L+1)
VARCHAR(L)	char, with length (L+1)

CLOB(L)	struct {
	long x_reserved
	unsigned long x_length
	char x_data[L];
	}

BIT(L)	char, with length L/8

SQL <data type>	C Data Type
BIT VARYING(L)	None
BLOB(L)	`struct { long x_reserved unsigned long x_length char x_data[L]; }`
BOOLEAN	pointer to long
SMALLINT	pointer to short
INTEGER	pointer to long
DECIMAL(P,S)	None
NUMERIC(P,S)	None
REAL	pointer to float
DOUBLE PRECISION	pointer to double
FLOAT(P)	None
DATE	None
TIME(T)	None
TIMESTAMP(T)	None
INTERVAL(Q)	None
UDT	None
REF	char, with length N
ARRAY	None
ROW	None

For COBOL:

SQL <data type>	COBOL Data Type
SQLSTATE	PICTURE X(5)
CHAR(L)	alphanumeric, with length L
VARCHAR(L)	None
CLOB(L)	01 XXXX. 49 XXXX-RESERVED PIC S9(9) USAGE IS BINARY. 49 XXXX-LENGTH PIC S9(9) USAGE IS BINARY. 49 XXXX-DATA PIC X(L).
BIT(L)	alphanumeric, with length L/8+1
BIT VARYING(L)	None
BLOB(L)	01 XXXX. 49 XXXX-RESERVED PIC S9(9) USAGE IS BINARY. 49 XXXX-LENGTH PIC S9(9) USAGE IS BINARY. 49 XXXX-DATA PIC X(L).
BOOLEAN	PICTURE X

SQL <data type>	COBOL Data Type
SMALLINT	PICTURE S9(SPI) USAGE BINARY, where SPI is implementation-defined
INTEGER	PICTURE S9(PI) USAGE BINARY, where PI is implementation-defined
DECIMAL(P,S)	None
NUMERIC(P,S)	USAGE DISPLAY SIGN LEADING SEPARATE, with PICTURE as specified (note 1)
REAL	None
DOUBLE PRECISION	None
FLOAT(P)	None
DATE	None
TIME(T)	None
TIMESTAMP(T)	None
INTERVAL(Q)	None
UDT	None
REF	alphanumeric with length N
ARRAY	None
ROW	None

NOTES: 1. If S=P, then a PICTURE with an 'S' followed by a 'V' followed by P '9's. If P>S>0, then a PICTURE with an 'S' followed by P-S '9's followed by a 'V' followed by S '9's. If S=0, then a PICTURE with an 'S' followed by P '9's optionally followed by a 'V'.

For Fortran:

SQL <data type>	Fortran Data Type
SQLSTATE	CHARACTER, with length 5
CHAR(L)	CHARACTER, with length L
VARCHAR(L)	None
CLOB(L)	CHARACTER XXXX(L+8) INTEGER*4 XXXX_RESERVED INTEGER*4 XXXX_LENGTH CHARACTER XXXX_DATA EQUIVALENCE(XXXX(5), XXXX_LENGTH) EQUIVALENCE(XXXX(9), XXXX_DATA)
BIT(L)	CHARACTER, with length L/8+1
BIT VARYING(L)	None

SQL <data type>	Fortran Data Type
BLOB(L)	CHARACTER XXXX(L+8) INTEGER*4 XXXX_RESERVED INTEGER*4 XXXX_LENGTH CHARACTER XXXX_DATA EQUIVALENCE(XXXX(5), XXXX_LENGTH) EQUIVALENCE(XXXX(9), XXXX_DATA)
BOOLEAN	LOGICAL
SMALLINT	None
INTEGER	INTEGER
DECIMAL(P,S)	None
NUMERIC(P,S)	None
REAL	REAL
DOUBLE PRECISION	DOUBLE PRECISION
FLOAT(P)	None
DATE	None
TIME(T)	None
TIMESTAMP(T)	None
INTERVAL(Q)	None
UDT	None
REF	CHARACTER with length N
ARRAY	None
ROW	None

For MUMPS:

SQL <data type>	MUMPS Data Type
SQLSTATE	character, with maximum length at least 5
CHAR(L)	None
VARCHAR(L)	character with maximum length L
CLOB(L)	None
BIT(L)	None
BIT VARYING(L)	None
BLOB(L)	None
BOOLEAN	None
SMALLINT	None
INTEGER	character
DECIMAL(P,S)	character
NUMERIC(P,S)	character

SQL <data type>	MUMPS Data Type
REAL	character
DOUBLE PRECISION	None
FLOAT(P)	None
DATE	None
TIME(T)	None
TIMESTAMP(T)	None
INTERVAL(Q)	None
UDT	None
REF	character
ARRAY	None
ROW	None

For Pascal:

SQL <data type>	Pascal Data Type
SQLSTATE	PACKED ARRAY [1..5] OF CHAR
CHARACTER(1)	CHAR
CHAR(L), L>1	PACKED ARRAY [1..L] OF CHAR
VARCHAR(L)	None
CLOB(L)	None
BIT(L)	PACKED ARRAY [L/8] OF CHAR
BIT VARYING(L)	None
BLOB(L)	None
BOOLEAN	BOOLEAN
SMALLINT	None
INTEGER	INTEGER
DECIMAL(P,S)	None
NUMERIC(P,S)	None
REAL	REAL
DOUBLE PRECISION	None
FLOAT(P)	None
DATE	None
TIME(T)	None
TIMESTAMP(T)	None
INTERVAL(Q)	None
UDT	None

SQL <data type>	Pascal Data Type
REF	PACKED ARRAY[1..N] OF CHAR
ARRAY	None
ROW	None

For PL/I:

SQL <data type>	PL/I Data Type
SQLSTATE	CHARACTER(5)
CHAR(L)	CHARACTER(L)
VARCHAR(L)	CHARACTER VARYING(L)
CLOB(L)	DCL level. lvchar 49 len1 FIXED BINARY (31) 49 len2 FIXED BINARY (31) 49 data CHAR (n)
BIT(L)	BIT(L)
BIT VARYING(L)	BIT VARYING(L)
BLOB(L)	DCL level. lvchar 49 len1 FIXED BINARY (31) 49 len2 FIXED BINARY (31) 49 data CHAR (n)
BOOLEAN	BIT(1)
SMALLINT	FIXED BINARY(SPI), where SPI is implementation-defined
INTEGER	FIXED BINARY(PI), where PI is implementation-defined
DECIMAL(P,S)	FIXED DECIMAL(P,S)
NUMERIC(P,S)	None
REAL	None
DOUBLE PRECISION	None
FLOAT(P)	FLOAT BINARY (P)
DATE	None
TIME(T)	None
TIMESTAMP(T)	None
INTERVAL(Q)	None
UDT	None
REF	CHARACTER VARYING(N)
ARRAY	None
ROW	None

Input and Output Variables

A host variable can be either an input host variable or an output host variable. (We always speak from the perspective of the DBMS so "input" means "input to the DBMS" and "output" means "output from the DBMS.")

Here is a set of embedded SQL and C statements; x and y appear as input host variables:

```
EXEC SQL CREATE TABLE Table_1 (
            column_1 INT, column_2 CHAR(4));

x = 1; strcpy(y,"1234");

EXEC SQL INSERT INTO Table_1
         VALUES (:x,:y);

EXEC SQL DELETE FROM Table_1
         WHERE column_2 = :y;

EXEC SQL UPDATE Table_1 SET
            column_2 = :x;           /* ERROR! */
```

In each case, it's easy to see the host variables — they're the names with colons in front. In the last SQL statement in the example, the use of :x is an error, because x is an "int" and column_2 has a CHAR <data type>. Usually the precompiler will catch that type of error — if it doesn't, there will be an error message at runtime. The subject of data type compatibility is a tortuous one but if you paid attention while reading our chapters on the various SQL predefined <data type>s, it should hold no terrors for you. Nevertheless, it is difficult to write language-independent embedded SQL code — inevitably, one has the host language's data type in mind when putting together the SQL code.

Indicator Variables

No host language can handle NULLs. So how can a host program receive an SQL output host variable with a NULL value? And how can a host program pass an input host variable with a NULL value? In both cases, the answer is that you have to pass two parameters by address; one to the data itself and one to a numeric variable containing a flag for "is NULL" or "is not NULL." This numeric variable is called an *indicator variable.*

Indicator variables are "signed numeric with scale zero." In practice, they are almost always 32-bit integers. They too should appear within a declare section. For example:

```
EXEC SQL BEGIN DECLARE SECTION;
var host : Integer; {Variable, intended for use as data}
var host_indicator : Longint; {Variable, intended for use as indicator}
EXEC SQL END DECLARE SECTION;
```

In an embedded SQL statement, indicators follow host variables. The required syntax is as follows.

```
:<host variable name> [ [ INDICATOR ] :<indicator name> ]
```

Here are two equivalent examples:

```
EXEC SQL INSERT INTO Table_1
          VALUES (:host INDICATOR :host_indicator);

EXEC SQL INSERT INTO Table_1
          VALUES (:host :host_indicator);
```

For input host variables — any indicator value less than zero means the value passed was NULL and any indicator value greater than or equal to zero means the value passed was a non-null value. For output host variables, the DBMS uses the specific indicator value –1 to mean the value passed was NULL and the specific value zero to mean the value passed was a non-null value. If the indicator variable value means NULL, then the host variable's contents are irrelevant.

Use of indicators is optional. There is no need for them if there is no chance that NULL values will occur. However, because "nullability" is a transient characteristic, many programmers use indicators as a matter of course after every host variable.

Here is an embedded SQL statement in which x appears as an output host variable:

```
EXEC SQL SELECT column_1 INTO :x FROM Table_1;
```

but it's not a particularly good example because it only works if you know in advance that there's a maximum of one row in Table_1. (Think: if there were two rows, there would be two values for column_1, but there's only one host variable for the output: x.) Because of the assumption that there will never be more than one row retrieved, this form of SELECT is referred to as a "singleton SELECT." A more flexible approach exists for getting output SELECT results, as output host variables, from SQL to the host language; the SQL Cursor.

Cursors

The most famous of the impedance-mismatch problems is that SQL operates on sets while host languages operate on set members. Therefore an SQL query — by which we almost always mean a SELECT statement — is returning more data than a host variable can store. It's not enough to reply, "use an array then." Although sometimes arrays are indeed helpful, we have to keep in mind that (*a*) the set might be gigantic and (*b*) there might be a two-way requirement (that is, rows which go out might also come back in). Either of these considerations make array definitions inappropriate for a general solution. The true and standard solution is the Cursor. With a Cursor, you can get only one row at a time — namely the row that the Cursor is "positioned on."

To understand the role of a Cursor, remember that your DBMS builds a result Table that contains all of the rows retrieved by an SQL query executed in an application program. Your DBMS uses a Cursor to make the rows of the result Table available to the program; the Cursor identifies, or points to, the current row of the result Table. When a Cursor is pointing to a row, it is said to be positioned on that row — and you can UPDATE or DELETE that row using the "positioned" forms of the UPDATE and DELETE statements.

To get it all working, you need to do four things: DECLARE a Cursor, OPEN the Cursor, FETCH (repeatedly) from the Cursor (manipulating the rows one by one), and CLOSE the Cursor. This Pascal program does all four things, in the form of a classic FETCH loop which is familiar to all SQL programmers.

```
{ Pascal program, using fetch loop }
var
EXEC SQL BEGIN DECLARE SECTION;
   sample_integer : Integer;
   sample_boolean : Boolean;
EXEC SQL END DECLARE SECTION;
j : Integer;

begin
  EXEC SQL CONNECT TO DEFAULT;
  EXEC SQL DECLARE sample_cursor CURSOR FOR
           SELECT * FROM sample_table;
  EXEC SQL OPEN sample_cursor;
  for j := 1 to 100 do begin
    EXEC SQL FETCH sample_cursor
             INTO :sample_integer, :sample_boolean;
    end;
  EXEC SQL CLOSE sample_cursor;
  EXEC SQL DISCONNECT DEFAULT;
end.
```

The DECLARE CURSOR statement defines the query (usually a SELECT statement) that will get the SQL-data you want. It is not an executable statement, it is only (as the name implies) declarative. The action begins with the OPEN statement. When OPEN happens, the SELECT actually takes place, so now the DBMS has a set of rows waiting to be fetched — these rows are called the current active set, or the result Table. The FETCH statement is the host program's way of asking the DBMS, "May I have the next record please?" In this example, we have assumed that the DBMS will always answer YES and put values into the host variables sample_integer and sample_boolean — realistically, of course, we should also check whether the FETCH, in fact, succeeds. This is a check which we'll perform in a later example. Anyway, once the loop is done, the CLOSE statement will throw out the set of rows that the OPEN statement produced, thus closing the Cursor.

Some of the things you can do with Cursors besides merely FETCH from them, include:

- DELETE and UPDATE rows at the current Cursor position.
- FETCH something other than the "next" row (this option is called the "SCROLL Cursor option").

DECLARE CURSOR Statement

The DECLARE CURSOR statement defines a Cursor. The required syntax for the DECLARE CURSOR statement is as follows.

```
DECLARE <Cursor name> [ <cursor sensitivity> ]
   [ SCROLL ] CURSOR [ WITH HOLD ] [ WITH RETURN ]
   FOR <cursor specification>

   <cursor sensitivity> ::=
   SENSITIVE |
   INSENSITIVE |
   ASENSITIVE

   <cursor specification> ::=
   <query expression> [ <order by clause> ]
   [ FOR {READ ONLY | UPDATE [ OF <Column name> list ]} ]
```

Each Cursor you define must have a unique name in the Module in which it's defined. Its <cursor specification> results in a Table when evaluated. An INSENSITIVE Cursor is a Cursor that effectively causes a separate copy of its result Table to be created; the Cursor accesses that copy, rather than the original result, so any changes made to the original result by other methods won't be visible to this Cursor. A SENSITIVE Cursor is a Cursor that works directly on its result Table; it makes no copy, so other changes made to the result Table will be visible to this Cursor. An ASENSITIVE Cursor may or may not make a copy of its result Table; whether other changes to its result Table will be visible is implementation-defined. The default is an ASENSITIVE Cursor.

Normally, you can access the Cursor's result Table, one row at a time, only in the order that your DBMS gets the rows. A SCROLL Cursor is a Cursor that can hop around in its result set. In the first case, then, only FETCH NEXT is allowed, while for a SCROLL Cursor, all forms of FETCH are allowed.

The optional updatability clause defaults to FOR READ ONLY if the Cursor's definition includes either INSENSITIVE, SCROLL, or an ORDER BY clause, or if the Cursor's result Table is not an updatable Table. If none of these are true, you can either specify FOR UPDATE OF followed by a list of the result Columns you want to update or the Cursor definition will default to that state.

FOR READ ONLY means the Cursor is not updatable — that is, UPDATE and DELETE operations won't be allowed on this Cursor. FOR UPDATE OF, permitted only on an updatable Cursor, means that the Columns specified may be the target of an UPDATE operation. If you include a Column list, only those Columns can be updated by the Cursor. If you omit the Column list, the effect is the same as if you included a list that names every Column of the result Table.

If DECLARE CURSOR includes the optional WITH HOLD clause, the Cursor is a holdable Cursor. This means that if the Cursor is open when a transaction is terminated with a COMMIT statement, it won't be closed — it will stay open into the next transaction. A holdable Cursor is always closed by ROLLBACK.

If your Cursor definition includes the optional WITH RETURN clause, the Cursor is called a *result set Cursor.* A result set Cursor that is declared in an SQL-invoked procedure returns a result set if it is open when the procedure ends.

Here's an example of DECLARE CURSOR based on the sample Tables we defined in Chapter 29 "Simple Search Conditions":

```
EXEC SQL DECLARE emps_cursor SCROLL CURSOR FOR
      SELECT   dept,empnum,surname,gname,address
      FROM     Employee WHERE dept <= 'C'
   FOR UPDATE OF surname,address;
```

This Cursor definition will allow you to get all the rows of the Employee Table where the dept value is A, B, or C. It will also allow you to UPDATE the values of the surname and address Columns of the retrieved rows.

If you want to restrict your code to Core SQL, don't declare a Cursor with either SENSITIVE, INSENSITIVE, or ASENSITIVE; don't declare a Cursor with SCROLL; don't declare a Cursor with WITH RETURN; and don't declare a Cursor with ORDER BY if you've declared it with FOR UPDATE with, or without, a Column list.

OPEN **Statement**

The OPEN statement opens a Cursor. The required syntax for the OPEN statement is as follows.

```
OPEN <Cursor name>
```

The OPEN statement processes the Cursor's query (it's an error if the Cursor is already open). In order to OPEN a Cursor then, your current <AuthorizationID> has to have all the Privileges required to process that query.

While it is open, a Cursor identifies a result Table, as well as a certain position within the rows of that Table; it can be on some row of the Table, before some row of the Table, or after the last row of the Table. Immediately after you execute OPEN, the Cursor is positioned before the first row of its result Table.

Here's an example of OPEN, based on the sample Cursor we defined in the last section:

```
EXEC SQL OPEN emps_cursor;
```

This SQL statement will evaluate the Cursor query:

```
SELECT   dept,empnum,surname,gname,address
FROM     Employee
WHERE    dept<='C'
```

and position the Cursor before the first row of the result Table.

FETCH Statement

The FETCH statement positions a Cursor on a specific row of its result Table, and retrieves that row's values into host variables. The required syntax for the FETCH statement is as follows.

```
FETCH [ [ <fetch orientation> ] FROM ] <Cursor name>
INTO <fetch target list>

   <fetch orientation> ::=
   NEXT |
   PRIOR |
   FIRST |
   LAST |
   {ABSOLUTE | RELATIVE} <simple value specification>

   <fetch target list> ::=
   <target specification> [ {,<target specification>}... ]
```

The FETCH orientation specification is one of the <keyword>s listed before the <Cursor name>; it defines which row of the Cursor's result Table FETCH will get next. FETCH NEXT (row), FETCH PRIOR (row), FETCH FIRST (row), and FETCH LAST (row) are self-explanatory. FETCH NEXT is the default and is the only legal option if the Cursor is not a SCROLL Cursor. For FETCH ABSOLUTE and FETCH RELATIVE, let *n* be the <simple value specification> (it must be a <literal>, SQL parameter, or host variable that represents an integer): FETCH ABSOLUTE *n* moves the Cursor to the *n*th row of its result Table (counting backward from the end if *n* is negative) and FETCH RELATIVE *n* moves the Cursor to the *n*th row from the current position (again, counting backward if *n* is negative). Assuming that the fetch orientation does identify a row of the result Table (e.g., that there is a NEXT row), then the Cursor is positioned on that row and the SQL-data values are retrieved from that row. If the fetch orientation has gone beyond the result Table — that is, if there is no NEXT row because FETCH already retrieved the final row — then the Cursor is positioned either after the last row or before the first row of the result Table (depending on which way the fetch orientation was moving) and no SQL-data is retrieved.

<Cursor name> is the name of the OPEN Cursor whose result Table you want to FETCH. The values retrieved from each row are placed into a list of host variables by FETCH. You provide your DBMS with the comma-delimited list of output host variables (and their optional indicators) in FETCH's INTO clause. The first value in the row that the Cursor is positioned on is assigned to the first host variable in the list, the second value is assigned to the second host variable, and so on (the number of Columns in the result Table and the number of host variables must, of course, match — as must their <data type>s).

Here's some examples of FETCH, based on the sample Cursor we opened in the last section:

```
EXEC SQL FETCH NEXT FROM emps_cursor
  INTO :dept,
       :empnum,
       :surname :surname_indicator,
       :gname :gname_indicator,
       :address :address_indicator;
```

This SQL statement will position the Cursor on the next row of the result Table (which happens to be the first row in this example) and assign the SQL-data values from each Column in that row to the corresponding host variables. Because we declared the Cursor as a SCROLL Cursor, we could use this FETCH statement instead:

```
EXEC SQL FETCH ABSOLUTE 4 FROM emps_cursor
  INTO :dept,
       :empnum,
       :surname :surname_indicator,
       :gname :gname_indicator,
       :address :address_indicator;
```

This SQL statement will position the Cursor on the fourth row of the result Table and assign the SQL-data values from each Column in that row to the corresponding host variables.

If you want to restrict your code to Core SQL, don't use FETCH with a <fetch orientation> — always let it default to FETCH NEXT.

Singleton SELECT Statement

If you know that a result Table will contain only one row of SQL-data, you don't need to declare a Cursor to get that result into your application program. Instead, you can use the form of the SELECT statement called the singleton SELECT — it puts the values found in a single row into a set of host variables. The required syntax for a singleton SELECT is as follows.

```
SELECT [ ALL | DISTINCT ] <select list>
INTO <target specification> [ {,<target specification>}... ]
<table expression>
```

The singleton SELECT statement can only be embedded in an application program. It can only retrieve one row of SQL-data. It is an error if more than one row might satisfy the query — you must use a Cursor to manipulate the data instead.

The singleton SELECT looks exactly like a regular SELECT statement except for the INTO clause that comes between the select list and the <table expression> (i.e., FROM ... WHERE ... etc.). The INTO clause works like the INTO clause in the FETCH statement; you provide your DBMS with a comma-delimited list of output host variables (and their optional indicators) therein and your DBMS places the first value in the result row into the first host variable in the list, the second value in the result row into the second host variable, and so on (the number of Columns in the result row and the number of host variables must, of course, match — as must their <data type>s).

Here's an example of a singleton SELECT based on the sample Tables we defined in Chapter 29 "Simple Search Conditions":

```
EXEC SQL SELECT dept,empnum,surname,gname,address
INTO   :dept,
       :empnum,
       :surname :surname_indicator,
       :gname :gname_indicator,
       :address :address_indicator
FROM   Employee
WHERE  empnum=10;
```

This SQL statement will evaluate the query:

```
SELECT dept,empnum,surname,gname,address
FROM   Employee
WHERE  empnum=10
```

and assign the SQL-data values from each Column in that row to the corresponding host variables.

INSERT Statement

A special form of the INSERT statement exists for use with a Cursor. The required syntax is as follows.

```
INSERT INTO <Cursor name> [ (<Column name> [ , ... ]) ]
{<query expression> | DEFAULT VALUES}
```

This form of the INSERT statement works exactly the same as the INSERT we described in Chapter 35 on SQL-data change statements except that you put a <Cursor name> instead of a <Table name> in the INTO clause. That is, the target of the INSERT operation is the Cursor's result Table. Here's an example:

```
EXEC SQL INSERT INTO emps_cursor
VALUES (:dept,
        :empnum,
        :surname :surname_indicator,
        :gname :gname_indicator,
        :address :address_indicator);
```

If you want to restrict your code to Core SQL, don't use this form of the INSERT statement.

Positioned UPDATE Statement

The positioned UPDATE statement lets you UPDATE the Cursor's current row. The required syntax for the positioned UPDATE statement is as follows.

```
UPDATE [ <Table name> ] SET
{<Column name>=scalar_expression [ {, ...} ] | ROW=row_expression}
WHERE CURRENT OF <Cursor name>
```

This form of the UPDATE statement works exactly the same as the UPDATE we described in Chapter 35 on SQL-data change statements except that you put "WHERE CURRENT OF <Cursor name>" after the SET assignments instead of the (optional) "WHERE condition" clause and that you can omit the <Table name> after UPDATE because the <Cursor name> in the WHERE clause identifies the UPDATE target Table anyway.

The Cursor must be open, must be an updatable Cursor, and must be positioned on a row of its result Table. That row (the current row) is the row that will be updated. Each Column that is a target of the SET clause must have been mentioned in the FOR UPDATE OF clause of the Cursor's definition. Any updated Column may not be named in the Cursor's ORDER BY clause.

Here's an example of a positioned UPDATE based on the sample Cursor we fetched with earlier:

```
EXEC SQL UPDATE Employee SET
  surname = :new_surname :new_surname_indicator,
  address = :new_address :new_address_indicator
WHERE CURRENT OF emps_cursor;
```

This SQL statement changes the values of the surname and address Columns in the current row of the Cursor's result Table. After the UPDATE, the Cursor remains on its current row. It won't move until another FETCH statement is executed.

If you want to restrict your code to Core SQL, don't omit the <Table name> from a positioned UPDATE statement, don't add an ORDER BY clause to your Cursor definition, and don't have an UPDATE target that is a host variable or SQL parameter.

Positioned DELETE Statement

The positioned delete statement lets you DELETE the Cursor's current row. The required syntax for the positioned DELETE statement is as follows.

```
DELETE [ FROM <Table name> ] WHERE CURRENT OF <Cursor name>
```

This form of the DELETE statement works exactly the same as the DELETE we described in Chapter 35 on the SQL-data change statements except that you use "WHERE CURRENT OF <Cursor name>" instead of the (optional) "WHERE condition" clause and that you can omit the FROM <Table name> clause after DELETE because the <Cursor name> in the WHERE clause identifies the DELETE target Table anyway.

The Cursor must be open, must be an updatable Cursor, and must be positioned on a row of its result Table. That row (the current row) is the row that will be deleted. Here's an example of a positioned DELETE based on the sample Cursor we fetched with earlier:

```
EXEC SQL DELETE FROM Employee WHERE CURRENT OF emps_cursor;
```

This SQL statement deletes the current row of the Cursor's result Table. After the DELETE, the Cursor is positioned before the row that follows the deleted row (or after the last row if the deleted row was the last row). It won't be positioned on another row until another FETCH statement is executed.

CLOSE Statement

The CLOSE statement closes a Cursor. The required syntax for the CLOSE statement is as follows.

```
CLOSE <Cursor name>
```

The CLOSE statement destroys the Cursor's result Table (it's an error if the Cursor isn't open). Closing a Cursor causes your DBMS to immediately check all Constraints that were affected by Cursor operations for violation and to execute any triggered actions that were deferred during the Cursor operations. Here's an example:

```
EXEC SQL CLOSE emps_cursor;
```

A Cursor is also closed by ROLLBACK and (unless it's a holdable Cursor) by COMMIT.

Embedded SQL Examples

Here is an example program which selects and fetches ten rows in Table T and displays the contents. This program watches for NULL values which it indicates by displaying a question mark rather than a number. (The use of "?" to mean "NULL" is conventional in displays and printouts but sometimes blanks are used instead.)

```
#include <stdio.h>                              /* Example CHAP39_1.C */
EXEC SQL BEGIN DECLARE SECTION;
    int x;
    int x_indicator;
EXEC SQL END DECLARE SECTION;
int i;
void main ()
{
   EXEC SQL CONNECT TO database_or_server USER Josephine;
   EXEC SQL DECLARE example_cursor CURSOR FOR SELECT col_1 FROM T;
   EXEC SQL OPEN example_cursor;
```

```
for (i=0; i<10; ++i) {
  EXEC SQL FETCH example_cursor INTO :x INDICATOR :x_indicator;
  if (x_indicator < 0) printf("?\n");
  else printf("%d\n",x); }
EXEC SQL CLOSE example_cursor;
EXEC SQL DISCONNECT database_or_server; }
```

Diagnostics

"I beseech you in the bowels of Christ, consider that you may be wrong."

—Cromwell

After any embedded SQL statement, you can add code to ask the DBMS, "Has anything gone wrong?" and if so, "What has gone wrong?". The DBMS's answers — *diagnostics* — are categorized and coded in a standard way, so you have some advance knowledge about what the possible scenarios are. The basic piece of diagnostic information is SQLSTATE.

Originally, the basic item of diagnostic information was an integer variable called sqlcode (or in Fortran: SQLCOD). After every SQL statement, the DBMS would put a value in sqlcode. If the value was less than zero, that meant "error." If the value was zero, that meant "success." If the value was greater than zero, that meant "success with additional information," that is, a warning. The most common warning was +100, which meant "no data." This was an easy system to follow and it was common practice to add lines like these after every SQL statement:

```
if (sqlcode < 0) {
  printf("Error!\n"); /*or some more sophisticated error-handling action*/
  exit(1); }
```

It is still common today to see sqlcode checking especially because all DBMS vendors still allow for it. However, the SQL-92 Standard "deprecated" use of sqlcode and the SQL3 Standard doesn't recognize it at all. SQLSTATE is the modern basic item of diagnostic information.

A big advantage of SQLSTATE is that the possible values are standardized for each error category, a level of agreement that was never achieved with the sqlcode values. SQLSTATE is a 5-character variable which you should define in the declare section. After every SQL statement, the DBMS will put a value (the status code) into SQLSTATE. The status code consists of digits or uppercase letters between A and Z. The first two letters or digits are the "class" (the general category), the next three letters or digits are the "subclass" (the specific category, if any). You can see a complete list of status codes, and descriptions thereof, in Chapter 47 "SQL/CLI: Diagnostic Functions." For now, content yourself with the knowledge of the most important classes:

- Class '00' is 'SUCCESS'. When you see this, everything's going fine.
- Class '01' is 'SUCCESS WITH INFO', or 'WARNING'. For example, perhaps some precision was lost during an arithmetic calculation. There is usually no cause to change the course of your program's flow, but displaying a message is often an appropriate action for your program to take.
- Class '02' is 'NO DATA'. Every FETCH loop should watch for this one because FETCH will cause 'NO DATA' if there is nothing more to fetch.

- All other classes are 'ERROR'. The SQL statement has failed. Check paranoidly. If SQLSTATE contains anything other than '00' or '01' or '02', you might have to take some corrective action or even abort the job.

  Let us now rewrite our FETCH loop program. This time we'll check SQLSTATE.

```
#include <stdio.h>                          /* Example CHAP39_2.C */
EXEC SQL BEGIN DECLARE SECTION;
int x;
int x_indicator;
char sqlstate[6]; /* SQLSTATE is 5 characters. Allow for '\0' too. */
EXEC SQL END DECLARE SECTION;
int i;
void main ()
{
  EXEC SQL CONNECT TO database_or_server USER Josephine;
  if (... != "00" && ... != "01")
    printf("Connection failed. sqlstate = %s.\n",sqlstate);
  EXEC SQL DECLARE example_cursor CURSOR FOR SELECT col_1 FROM T;
  /* There is no need to check for errors after a DECLARE statement. */
  EXEC SQL OPEN example_cursor;
  if (... != "00" && ... != "01")
    printf("OPEN failed. sqlstate = %s.\n",sqlstate);
    goto disconnect_database; }
  for (;;) {  /* This loop is not infinite. There are breaks. */
    EXEC SQL FETCH example_cursor INTO :x INDICATOR :x_indicator;
    if (... == "02") {
      /* The 'NO DATA' class just means there's no more to fetch. */
      break; }
    if (... == "01") printf("Warning: sqlstate=%s.\n",sqlstate);
    if (... != "00" && ... != "01" && ... != "02") {
      printf("FETCH failed. sqlstate = %s.\n",sqlstate);
      break; }
    if (x_indicator < 0) printf("?\n");
    else printf("%d\n",x); }
  EXEC SQL CLOSE example_cursor;
  /* Doubtless a CLOSE will always succeed, but let's check anyway. */
  if (... != "00") printf("After close, sqlstate=%s.\n",sqlstate);
 disconnect_database:
  EXEC SQL DISCONNECT database_or_server;
  /* We're ending the program, but let's check anyway. */
  if (... != "00")
    printf("After disconnect, sqlstate=%s.\n",sqlstate); }
```

If you find it tedious to check SQLSTATE after every single error, there is an SQL directive to automate the procedure — the WHENEVER statement.

WHENEVER Statement

The required syntax for the WHENEVER statement (omitting some details) is as follows.

```
WHENEVER <condition> {GOTO | GO TO} <target of goto>
```

or

```
WHENEVER <condition> CONTINUE
```

The WHENEVER <condition> is one of:

- SQLWARNING ... true if SQLSTATE contains the '01' status code class.
- NOT FOUND ... true for the SQLSTATE '02' class.
- SQLEXCEPTION ... true for any other SQLSTATE class. (The old SQL-92 name for this is SQLERROR.)
- SQLSTATE (list) ... an SQL3 innovation, rarely supported.
- CONSTRAINT (name) ... an SQL3 innovation, rarely supported.

The WHENEVER target is a label or address which would be legal as the argument of a GOTO statement in the host language. The WHENEVER directive is not an executable statement; it's a signal to the precompiler. The precompiler responds to it by generating appropriate "if ... goto ..." statements after every SQL statement.

> TIP: When you write a program for the first time, put EXEC SQL WHENEVER SQLEXCEPTION GOTO error_abort; at the start. After you've got the program working, edit it and put in error testing that's more specific.

Serious programs contain considerably more than basic SQLSTATE checks. To begin with, they have different reactions depending on the specific class and subclass in the status code. They also make use of SQL's GET DIAGNOSTICS statement. With GET DIAGNOSTICS, one can ask more about the context, get an implementation-defined error message, and perhaps retrieve several different diagnostics (it's possible, for instance, that the DBMS generated several warnings before it ultimately gave up and generated an error).

GET DIAGNOSTICS Statement

The GET DIAGNOSTICS statement gets exception or completion condition information from the diagnostics area. The required syntax for the GET DIAGNOSTICS statement is as follows.

```
GET DIAGNOSTICS
   {<statement information> | <condition information>}

   <statement information> ::=
   <statement information item> [ {,<statement information item>}... ]
```

```
<statement information item> ::=
<simple target specification> = <statement item name>

  <statement information item name> ::=
  NUMBER |
  MORE |
  COMMAND_FUNCTION |
  COMMAND_FUNCTION_CODE |
  ROW_COUNT |
  TRANSACTIONS_COMMITTED |
  TRANSACTIONS_ROLLED_BACK |
  TRANSACTION_ACTIVE

<condition information> ::=
EXCEPTION <condition number>
  <condition information item> [ {,<condition information item>}... ]

 <condition information item> ::=
 <simple target specification> = <condition item name>

   <condition information item name> ::=
   CONDITION_IDENTIFIER | CONDITION_NUMBER |
   RETURNED_SQLSTATE | CLASS_ORIGIN |
   SUBCLASS_ORIGIN | SERVER_NAME |
   CONNECTION_NAME | CONSTRAINT_CATALOG |
   CONSTRAINT_SCHEMA | CONSTRAINT_NAME |
   TRIGGER_CATALOG | TRIGGER_SCHEMA |
   TRIGGER_NAME | CATALOG_NAME |
   SCHEMA_NAME | TABLE_NAME |
   COLUMN_NAME | CURSOR_NAME |
   ROUTINE_CATALOG | ROUTINE_SCHEMA |
   ROUTINE_NAME | SPECIFIC_NAME |
   PARAMETER_NAME | MESSAGE_TEXT |
   MESSAGE_LENGTH | MESSAGE_OCTET_LENGTH

<condition number> ::= <simple value specification>
```

There are two forms of the GET DIAGNOSTICS statement. The first gets information about the overall execution of the immediately preceding SQL statement, while the second form gets more specific information about one or more specific errors. Here are some examples of GET DIAGNOSTICS:

```
GET DIAGNOSTICS :smallint_host_variable = ROW_COUNT;

GET DIAGNOSTICS :char_host_variable = DYNAMIC_FUNCTION;

GET DIAGNOSTICS EXCEPTION 1 :char_host_variable = SUBCLASS_ORIGIN;
```

Not wanting to bore you twice, we'll defer the detailed discussion of the diagnostics area's fields until Chapter 47 — when we talk about the SQL/CLI's SQLGetDiagRec and SQLGetDiagField functions.

Dynamic SQL

In the examples so far, we've assumed that we know some things in advance about the database and the SQL statements we're going to execute. For example, in our FETCH loop examples, we make the assumptions that the <Table name> is T, that T has a Column called col_1, that col_1 has a numeric <data type> and so on. A program which contains such assumptions is called a static SQL program because its SQL statements are changeless. Let us now suppose that we lack advance knowledge about the program. The classic supposition is, "What if the user types in a SELECT command on the keyboard?" We need to use a more flexible (and somewhat less efficient) tool set — the components of dynamic SQL.

Start with the basic supposition; that the user types in an SQL statement on the keyboard. There is a simple embedded SQL statement which parses and executes strings at runtime: EXECUTE IMMEDIATE. Here is an example:

```
gets(a_string);                              EXAMPLE A
for (i=0; i<1000; ++i) {
  EXEC SQL EXECUTE IMMEDIATE :a_string; }
```

In this example, a_string is a character string host variable. If it contains the string INSERT INTO T VALUES (5), then the above statement is equivalent to:

```
for (i=0; i<1000; ++i) {
  EXEC SQL INSERT INTO T VALUES (5); }
```

The good news about dynamic SQL is that you have an SQL interpreter available. That's remarkable when you compare SQL with a host language. You can't write equivalent code which will parse and execute a C statement from C or a Pascal statement from Pascal! The result is that your SQL code is more capable than your host language code. The bad news is that interpreters are slow. Faced with repetitive operations like the ones in our example above, we would rather replace "parse and execute many times" with "parse once, execute many times." Luckily, there are embedded SQL statements for that — PREPARE and EXECUTE. Here is a replacement example, which does the same thing but is maybe more efficient:

```
gets(a_string);                              EXAMPLE B
EXEC SQL PREPARE :a_string;
for (i=0; i<1000; ++i)  {
  EXEC SQL EXECUTE :a_string; }
```

NOTE: Some smart DBMSs can detect simple situations like the one in this example and optimize accordingly. For example, if you program with Oracle you will gain nothing by replacing Example A with Example B.

The ultimate in embedded-SQL complexity is a dynamically-executed query such as a SELECT statement. We can't define host variables and indicators in advance, because we don't know what the <data type>s of the result Columns are — or even how many Columns the query will return. The first time you see dynamic SQL query code, you may have trouble understanding it. But the second time, you'll have less trouble — because it will be the same. Most programmers use a boilerplate, so the program structure turns out to be similar in every program. In pseudocode, that structure looks like this:

```
if (the statement is a query) do begin:
  Execute the statement. || Variation: just prepare the statement.
  Ask the DBMS: "how many Columns were there?"
    Let the response be C.
  for (Column-number = 1 to C) do:
    Ask the DBMS: "for Column[Column-number], return data type etc."
    Using the DBMS's response, allocate appropriate RAM in host program.
    end.
  ...
  OPEN Cursor.
  Loop:
    FETCH. The fetch targets are the allocated areas in the host program.
    if (no-data) exit loop.
```

At this point, code varies depending on what we want to do with the dynamically-retrieved data. For instance we could display it:

```
    display data.
    Next.
  CLOSE Cursor.
  end.
```

Principally, you're asking the DBMS to DESCRIBE what it finds. The key statements for the purpose are:

- `ALLOCATE DESCRIPTOR` ... which tells the DBMS to allocate an area internally (i.e., within the DBMS) for storing the description.
- `DESCRIBE` <SQL statement name> <using descriptor> ... which fills the descriptor with information about the SQL statement.
- `GET DESCRIPTOR` ... which takes descriptor field values and puts them into host program variables.
- `DEALLOCATE DESCRIPTOR` ... which gets rid of what `ALLOCATE DESCRIPTOR` made.

As with `GET DIAGNOSTICS`, we'll defer the detailed discussion of the descriptor area's fields until Chapter 46 — when we talk about the SQL/CLI's `desc` functions.

Summary

An *embedded SQL host language program* is an application program that contains both host language programming statements and SQL statements. Embedded SQL programs may be written in any of the high-level languages — ADA, C, COBOL, FORTRAN, MUMPS, PASCAL, and PL/I — supported by the SQL Standard. Such programs use SQL instead of routines written in the host language to carry out database operations.

Embedded SQL statements are either static SQL statements or dynamic SQL statements. *Static SQL* is static in the sense that the embedded SQL statement is fully known and coded when your program is written. Executing the program does not change the SQL statement in any way. *Dynamic SQL* is so-called because the embedded SQL statement is not fully known when your program is written. Some part of it will be generated during the execution of the program.

SQL statements embedded in an application program must reference host variables to pass values between the program and SQL-data. *Host variables* are host language variables referenced in an embedded SQL statement. They must be declared within a "declare section" that is delimited by the `BEGIN DECLARE SECTION` and `END DECLARE SECTION` statements. The declare section must precede any use of the host variables. Because host variables must map to host language variables, they are not nullable unless they are coupled with an indicator variable.

An *indicator variable* is a host language variable that acts as an indicator for another host variable. The purpose of an indicator variable is to highlight null values and overflow conditions for the host variable it's coupled with. Embedded SQL application programs must prepare for passing null values by pairing an indicator with any host variable that might be assigned a null value.

SQL provides a *status host variable* — `SQLSTATE` — whose values indicate whether or not an SQL statement was successfully executed. All embedded SQL programs must contain at least one status host variable declaration.

The major problem in combining SQL with any host language is the inability of most other languages to handle multiple records at one time; one of the major SQL features. The SQL Object "Cursor" is provided by the SQL Standard to give the host languages a facility for dealing with a set of retrieved SQL-data records, one at a time.

An excellent summary of the embedded SQL specification appears in the SQL Standard. Part five says:

- Embedded SQL is "syntax for embedding SQL-statements in a compilation unit that otherwise conforms to the standard for a particular programming language (host language)."

- Embedded SQL specifies "how an equivalent compilation unit may be derived that conforms to the particular programming language standard. In that equivalent compilation unit, each embedded SQL-statement has been replaced by one or more statements in the host language, some of which invoke an SQL externally-invoked procedure that, when executed, has an effect equivalent [to] executing the SQL-statement."

Dialects

Embedded SQL is well specified by part five of the SQL Standard — ISO/IEC 9075-5: SQL/Bindings. The differences between SQL-92 and SQL3 in this area are minor, but you may find that older programs handle dynamic-SQL "descriptors" in a different way. Instead of declaring that descriptors are internal to the DBMS, old programs may allocate an area within the host program itself. This area, usually called SQLDA (SQL Dynamic Area) or something similar, is a structure like this:

```
#define  MV    64
struct sqlda {
  char sqldaid[8];          /* "SQLDA    " */
  long int sqldabc;         /* length of sqlda  */
  int sqln;                 /* max sqlvar occurrences = MV */
  int sqld;                 /* current sqlvar occurrences */
  struct sqlvar {           /* defined sqln times, occurs sqld times */
    int sqltype;            /* <data type> of Column  */
    int sqllen;             /* size of Column */
    char far *sqldata;      /* pointer -> host variable */
    int far *sqlind;        /* pointer -> indicator */
    struct sqlname {        /* string, up to 30 bytes long */
     int length;            /* 1-word size of name */
     char data[30]; } sqlname; } sqlvar[MV]; };
struct sqlda sqlda={"SQLDA",0,64,0};
```

The job of the DESCRIBE statement is to fill in the entire SQLDA. Then the host program can access the fields by simply referring to the structure's components.

As we mentioned, it is possible to integrate the precompiler with the compiler. Thus the process of precompiling and compiling appears to be a single step. IBM's DB2 is particularly noteworthy for this convenient feature.

Another convenience is the allowance of "SQL" keywords for data type descriptions within the declare section. This usually goes hand-in-hand with macros or typedefs within a header file supplied by the vendor. Thus, one could have:

```
EXEC SQL BEGIN DECLARE SECTION;
  SQLCHAR x(5);
  SQLINTEGER y;
EXEC SQL END DECLARE SECTION;
```

This enables programmers to use similar declarations for a variety of host languages. Because the same header file can be used in the SQL/CLI, it's easy to put together packages which use some embedded SQL modules and some SQL/CLI modules.

40

Chapter 40

SQL/CLI Binding Style

SQL DBMSs communicate with SQL applications through a common programming language interface that is invoked through one of the SQL Standard-defined binding styles, or interface options. There are three main approaches to writing complete programs with SQL:

1. With embedded SQL, you can put SQL statements directly into host programs. We described this binding style in Chapter 39.
2. With the Module binding style, you can dispense with host programs and write entire Modules in SQL. You'll still have to call these Modules from one of the standard host languages though. We'll describe this binding style last.
3. With SQL/CLI, you can call an SQL DBMS's library from a host program. The SQL statements you want to execute are parameters of the call. Because SQL's *modus operandi* won't quite match the host language's, helper functions are required for the interface definition. This binding style is the subject of the next several chapters.

The SQL/CLI, or Call-level Interface binding style, is defined in part three of the SQL Standard. In this chapter, we'll give you an introduction to this SQL binding style.

WARNING: The SQL/CLI chapters were written before the official release of the part of the SQL3 Standard that covers SQL/CLI. By the time you read this, some details in Chapters 40–52 may be false or obsolete. We therefore maintain an errata sheet on the web at:
`http://ourworld.compuserve.com/OCELOTSQL/errata.htm`
For current information on the released SQL Standard, check this web page.

Embedded SQL used to be the most important way of putting SQL statements into application programs. Nowadays, the CLI is the most important. Not because it's simpler — far from it! The CLI's real advantages are:

- There's no precompiler (this makes debugging easier).
- DLLs can be substituted (bringing the usual advantages of modularity).
- ODBC — the best-known SQL CLI — is very popular.

Onward, then, to the CLI essentials. CLI stands for *Call Level Interface*. You have probably heard of an API (Application Programming Interface) which is a non-SQL name for the same sort of thing. The CLI defines a set of public functions which can be called from a host language. Each function has a name, a parameter list, and a required algorithm (what the DBMS must do when you call it using this function).

CHAP40_1.C

Here's a short C program that uses the CLI (the prototypes and short code examples that follow throughout our description of the CLI are all in C):

```
#include "sqlcli.h"                                              /* [Note 1] */
SQLHENV       henv;                                              /* [Note 2] */
SQLHDBC       hdbc;
SQLHSTMT      hstmt;
void main ()
{
  SQLAllocHandle(SQL_HANDLE_ENV,NULL,&henv);                   /* [Note 3] */
  SQLAllocHandle(SQL_HANDLE_DBC,henv,&hdbc);
  SQLConnect(hdbc,....,SQL_NTS);
  SQLAllocHandle(SQL_HANDLE_HSTMT,hdbc,&hstmt);
  SQLExecDirect(hstmt,"CREATE TABLE World(hello INT)",SQL_NTS);
                                                               /* [Note 4] */
  SQLFreeHandle(SQL_HANDLE_STMT,hstmt);                        /* [Note 5] */
  SQLDisconnect(hdbc);
  SQLFreeHandle(SQL_HANDLE_DBC,hdbc);
  SQLFreeHandle(SQL_HANDLE_ENV,henv); }
```

This sample program has all the necessary CLI ingredients. It will take several pages to say how they all work, but the main points are noted in the code as follows:

[Note 1] Include the SQL/CLI header file. The standard name is "sqlcli.h" but you might see this statement — #include "sql.h" — instead. The header file has the prototypes of all the CLI functions and #defines for all the constants. The function names begin with SQL and the constant names begin with SQL_ — that's the convention in C programs. You can program standard SQL without following this convention, but it seems reasonable to follow it.

[Note 2] Variable declarations. The convention this time is: h stands for handle — so a henv is a handle of an env, a hdbc is a handle of a dbc, and a hstmt is a handle of a stmt. And now, because those abbreviated words will appear many times in the next 300 pages, we'd advise you to memorize them:

- env is an "allocated thing [resource] used for an environment."
- dbc is an "allocated thing [resource] used for a database connection."
- stmt is an "allocated thing [resource] used for a statement."

For the record, the Standard's usual names for env, dbc, and stmt are "allocated SQL-environment," "allocated SQL-connection," and "allocated SQL-statement," respectively. We will always use the abbreviations because they are what appear in sqlcli.h and in all programs. Besides, we believe it's crazy to call a stmt a statement — a stmt is a *resource*; a statement is a *string*. Let's not confuse the peanut with the shell. As it happens, the sqlcli.h header file has "typedef"s for SQLHENV and the other handles; they're all 32-bit integers. Other important typedefs are SQLINTEGER ("long int"), SQLSMALLINT ("short int"), SQLCHAR ("char"), and SQLRETURN ("short int," used for return codes only). Using, say, SQLINTEGER x in a program rather than "long int x", helps make it clear that "x" will see use in an SQL function.

[Note 3] Setup functions. The bare minimum procedure involves making an env, making a dbc, connecting using the dbc, and making a stmt. Notice the &s in the program code; these are "output" parameters ("output" from the DBMS point of view). They're passed by address because the DBMS fills in the values for them.

[Note 4] Meat. The only actual SQL-language statement in our program is a string argument for a CLI function call. This is the actual database work.

[Note 5] Tear-down functions. In a reverse of the setup procedure, we call functions for destroying a stmt, disconnecting using the dbc, destroying the dbc, and destroying the env. Notice that every function call used a handle — that's normal. Doubtless the DBMS is merely malloc'ing a bit of memory for each of our "allocated things," but we can't access the fields directly. Instead, we use a henv or a hdbc or a hstmt.

SQLCHAR, SQLINTEGER, and Other Typedefs

Here are the type definitions in the sqlcli.h header file. We use these names for declarations of C variables in all our examples.

```
typedef unsigned char  SQLCHAR;       /* 8-bit-octet strings */
typedef long int       SQLINTEGER;    /* 32-bit, signed */
typedef short int      SQLSMALLINT;   /* 16-bit, signed */
typedef float          SQLREAL;       /* see heading: IEEE */
typedef double         SQLDOUBLE;     /* see heading: IEEE */
typedef void*          SQLPOINTER;    /* pointer, untyped */
```

```
typedef long int       SQLHENV;       /* 32-bit env handle */
typedef long int       SQLHDBC;       /* 32-bit dbc handle */
typedef long int       SQLHSTMT;      /* 32-bit stmt handle */
typedef long int       SQLHDESC;      /* 32-bit desc handle */
```

NOTE: In the ODBC 3.0 header file, `SQLHENV` and `SQLHDBC` and `SQLHSTMT` and `SQLHDESC` are all `typedef void*` instead of `typedef long int`. In older versions of the ODBC header file, the names were `HENV`, `HDBC`, `HSTMT`, etc.

SQLRETURN

All CLI functions return a 16-bit value. We refer to this value as the `SQLRETURN` value because `sqlcli.h` contains this line:

```
typedef SQLSMALLINT SQLRETURN;
```

In standard SQL, there are only six possible `SQLRETURN` values:

-2	"invalid handle"
-1	"error"
0	"success"
1	"success with info"
99	"need data"
100	"no data"

Programs should check these values, but for space reasons, we leave `SQLRETURN` out of many of our examples.

Handle Relationships

A handle is a 32-bit integer which can be used as a unique identifier of a "resource." The following chart shows all the resources which have handles. The relationships between resources are either optional ("zero-to-many" — shown with double arrows) or mandatory (either "one-to-one" or "zero-to-one" — shown with single arrows).

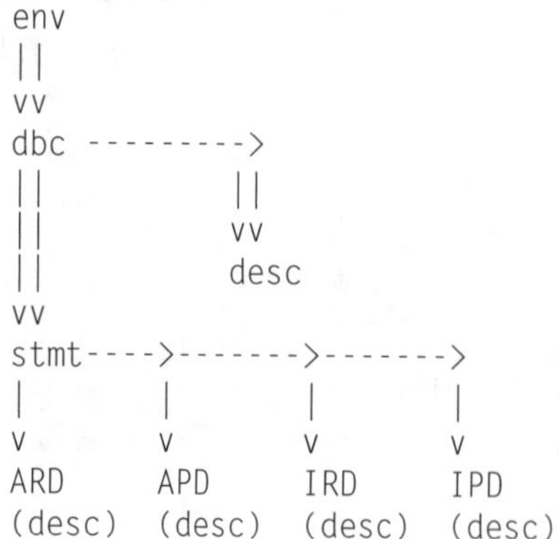

```
env
||
vv
dbc --------->
||          ||
||          vv
||          desc
vv
stmt---->------->------->
|       |       |       |
v       v       v       v
ARD     APD     IRD     IPD
(desc)  (desc)  (desc)  (desc)
```

How to Run Example Programs

This book contains several example programs that we use to illustrate the SQL/CLI. Each example program is also included on the CD that accompanies the book, numbered in order of appearance (e.g., the "example C program" shown earlier, "`CHAP40_1.C`"). To try out any of the example programs, follow these steps.

If you use Microsoft Windows 3.x:

- Copy these files from the CD to your working directory: `OCELOT16.DLL`, `OCELOT16.LIB`, `SQLCLI.H`, and the C program file.
- Using a standard-C package, compile and link. For example, this is a sequence for Borland C++ version 3.1 (with the MS-DOS command line):

```
path=c:\borlandc\bin;c:\borlandc\lib;c:\borlandc\include
bcc /I\borlandc\include /L\borlandc\lib /W /M /N /ml chap40_1.c ocelot16.lib
```

- Run the program from the MS-DOS command line.

If you use Microsoft Windows 95:

- Copy these files from the CD to your working directory: `OCELOT32.DLL`, `OCELOT32.LIB`, `SQLCLI.H`, and the C program file.
- Using a standard-C package, compile and link. For example, this is a sequence for Symantec C++ version 7.0 (with the MS-DOS command line):

```
path=c:\sc\bin;c:\sc\lib;c:\sc\include
sc /I\sc\include /WA /g /mn /s /L/M chap40_1.c kernel32.lib ocelot32.lib
```

- Run the program from the MS-DOS command line.

RECOMMENDATION: Add your own screen-display statements so you'll see the values of program variables when you run the program. If there's a CLI function that you want to get experience with, put it into your own program, link with the library supplied with this book, and run. As well as being good practice, this will help you learn what is NOT standard SQL because we deliberately kept out "implementation-defined" features when we wrote this DBMS.

"Standard SQL CLI" equals "Core ODBC API"

History: Microsoft published the ODBC 1.0 specification in 1992. It became popular. Soon there were supporting interfaces for all the major DBMSs that worked under Microsoft Windows. ODBC became a *de facto* standard specification for calling SQL from host programs without a precompiler. The ISO Standard CLI came out in 1995. The influence of ODBC on the standard CLI is apparent in almost every routine. Indeed, it sometimes is hard to understand the official Standard document without studying Microsoft's ODBC manual too. On its part, Microsoft made major changes in ODBC 3.0 (1998). They added several new functions and deprecated several old ones, in order to get closer to the SQL Standard. Microsoft's ODBC 3.0 manual makes the following claims:

"ODBC aligns with the following specifications and standards that deal with the Call-Level Interface (CLI). (ODBC's features are a superset of each of these standards.)

- The X/Open CAE Specification "Data Management: SQL Call-Level Interface (CLI)

- ISO/IEC 9075–3:1995 (E) Call-Level Interface (SQL/CLI)

As a result of this alignment, the following are true:

- An application written to the X/Open and ISO CLI specifications will work with an ODBC 3.0 driver or a standards-compliant driver when it is compiled with the ODBC 3.0 header files and linked with ODBC 3.0 libraries, and when it gains access to the driver through the ODBC 3.0 Driver Manager.
- A driver written to the X/Open and ISO CLI specifications will work with an ODBC 3.0 application or a standards-compliant application when it is compiled with the ODBC 3.0 header files and linked with ODBC 3.0 libraries, and when the application gains access to the driver through the ODBC 3.0 Driver Manager.

The Core interface conformance level encompasses all the features in the ISO CLI and all the non-optional features in the X/Open CLI. Optional features of the X/Open CLI appear in higher interface conformance levels. Because all ODBC 3.0 drivers are required to support the features in the Core interface conformance level, the following are true:

- An ODBC 3.0 driver will support all the features used by a standards-compliant application.
- An ODBC 3.0 application using only the features in ISO CLI and the non-optional features of the X/Open CLI will work with any standards-compliant driver."

Whoa! The SQL Standard CLI isn't quite as close to Core ODBC as Microsoft is suggesting. There are a few incompatibilities in names, there are two differences in prototype definitions (of `SQLColAttribute` and `SQLGetInfo`), and ODBC's default behaviour for "commits" is *sui generis*. But we'll note those bugs as we step on them. Once you know what they are, you'll be able to adjust.

Because this is a book on the SQL Standard, our chapters on the CLI won't show you the various extra features that appear in ODBC but not in the standard CLI. And we note only once — now — that any feature which is marked "SQL3" is a feature of the standard CLI but not necessarily of ODBC.

How each CLI Function will be Described

In these chapters, we will describe each CLI function separately. We've put them in order according to this rule — if we can't describe A without knowing about B, then B should come before A. This means that some tedious minor functions precede some important ones, but the advantage is that you can read from front to back. Better to slog, rather than jump around.

The structure of each CLI-function description is semi-rigid. You can expect to find these things, in this order:

1. Function prototype. This is the prototype as it appears in the header file, `sqlcli.h`. It gives a quick idea of the function's name and what <data type>s the parameters have. There is a comment beside each parameter indicating whether it's an "input" parameter (its value goes from the application to the DBMS) or an "output" parameter (its value goes from the DBMS to the application).
2. Job. A one-sentence description of what the function is for. This may be followed by an indication of whether the function is essential or not. Several functions are obsolete or redundant, so you can skip the details on your first pass through these chapters.

3. Algorithm. Exactly what does the DBMS do with this function? This section is in a sort of pseudocode. We're trying to make the instructions readable, but we won't spare you from mind-numbing (but necessary) details.
4. Notes. Whatever strikes us as worthy of remark about a function.
5. Example. A code snippet written in C. Usually the example will be an incomplete program, with "..." to indicate that we haven't repeated stuff which doesn't advance the story. Most commonly, we leave out the "setup" and "tear-down" phases illustrated in the example program shown at the beginning of this chapter.
6. ODBC. Anything that relates specifically to ODBC, but not to the standard CLI. If a standard CLI procedure doesn't exactly match the ODBC spec, it gets noted here. If ODBC has a truly significant feature that is not in the standard CLI, we mention it curtly.

Having said that, let's get on with the descriptions. Here's a quick list of the 62 standard CLI functions:

NAME	CATEGORY	FUNCTION
`SQLAllocConnect`	`dbc`	Obsolescent: Make a `dbc`
`SQLAllocEnv`	`env`	Obsolescent: Make an `env`
`SQLAllocHandle`	`dbc,env,stmt`	Essential: Make `env`, `dbc`, `stmt`, or `desc`
`SQLAllocStmt`	`stmt`	Obsolescent: Make a `stmt`
`SQLBindCol`	`desc`	Useful: Associate Column descriptor to `stmt`
`SQLBindParameter`	`desc`	Useful: Associate parameter to `stmt`
`SQLCancel`	D parameters	Minor: Stop unfinished statement execution
`SQLCloseCursor`	Cursors	Essential: Close cursor
`SQLColAttribute`	`desc`	Useful: Get info re result set structure
`SQLColumnPrivileges`	Catalog	Junk: Get metadata re Column privileges
`SQLColumns`	Catalog	Junk: Get metadata re Columns
`SQLConnect`	`dbc`	Essential: Connect to SQL-server/database
`SQLCopyDesc`	`desc`	Minor: Make copy of descriptor
`SQLDataSources`	general	Minor: List available servers
`SQLDescribeCol`	`desc`	Useful: Get info re result set structure
`SQLDisconnect`	`dbc`	Essential: Disconnect SQL-server/database
`SQLEndTran`	Statements	Essential: `Commit` or `Rollback`
`SQLError`	Diagnostics	Obsolete: Get diagnostics information
`SQLExecDirect`	Statements	Useful: Prepare + Execute a statement
`SQLExecute`	Statements	Essential: Execute a prepared statement
`SQLFetch`	Cursors	Useful: Bring in next result-set row
`SQLFetchScroll`	Cursors	Essential: Bring in any result-set row
`SQLForeignKeys`	Catalog	Junk: Get metadata re foreign keys
`SQLFreeConnect`	`dbc`	Obsolescent: Destroy `dbc`

NAME	CATEGORY	FUNCTION
SQLFreeEnv	env	Obsolescent: Destroy env
SQLFreeHandle	Handles	Essential: Destroy env, dbc, stmt, or desc
SQLFreeStmt	stmt	Obsolescent: Destroy stmt and other things
SQLGetConnectAttr	dbc	Useless: Get attribute of dbc
SQLGetCursorName	Cursors	Minor: Get Cursor name
SQLGetData	desc	Useful: Get value from result set
SQLGetDescField	desc	Essential: Get 1 desc field
SQLGetDescRec	desc	Useful: Get 7 desc fields
SQLGetDiagField	Diagnostics	Essential: Get diagnostics information
SQLGetDiagRec	Diagnostics	Useful: Get diagnostics information
SQLGetEnvAttr	env	Minor: Get attribute of env
SQLGetFunctions	general	Minor: List CLI functions supported
SQLGetInfo	general	Essential: Get attribute of dbc etc.
SQLGetLength	locator	Minor: Length of CLOB/BLOB
SQLGetParamData	desc	Minor: Get data from procedure parameters
SQLGetPosition	locator	Minor: Indicate substring start position
SQLGetStmtAttr	stmt	Essential: Get attribute of stmt
SQLGetSubstring	locator	Minor: Get portion of CLOB/BLOB
SQLGetTypeInfo	Catalog	Junk: Get metadata re data types
SQLMoreResults	Cursors	Minor: See if more result sets
SQLNumResultCols	desc	Useful: Get selected-Column count
SQLParamData	D parameters	Minor: For passing data piecemeal
SQLParameters	Catalog	Junk: Get metadata re parameters
SQLPrepare	Statements	Essential: Prepare a statement
SQLPrimaryKeys	Catalog	Junk: Get metadata re primary keys
SQLPutData	D parameters	Minor: For passing data piecemeal
SQLRoutinePrivileges	Catalog	Junk: Get metadata re Privileges
SQLRoutines	Catalog	Junk: Get metadata re routines
SQLRowCount	Diagnostics	Useful: Get affected-rows count
SQLSetConnectAttr	dbc	Useless: Change dbc attribute
SQLSetCursorName	Cursors	Essential: Change Cursor name
SQLSetDescField	desc	Essential: Change 1 desc field
SQLSetDescRec	desc	Useful: Change 7 desc fields
SQLSetEnvAttr	env	Useless: Change env attribute
SQLSetStmtAttr	stmt	Useful: Change stmt attribute
SQLSpecialColumns	Catalog	Junk: Get metadata re search Columns

NAME	CATEGORY	FUNCTION
SQLTablePrivileges	Catalog	Junk: Get metadata re Table Privileges
SQLTables	Catalog	Junk: Get metadata re Tables

And that concludes our brief introduction to the CLI. Before we begin describing each of the functions in this list in detail, we'll show you a sample function description, using a common CLI function subroutine — CharacterStringRetrieval.

CharacterStringRetrieval

Function Prototype:

```
void CharacterStringRetrieval (
  SQLCHAR *Target,                    /* CHAR* output */
  SQLCHAR *Source,                    /* CHAR* input */
  SQLINTEGER MaxTargetOctetLength,    /* 32-bit output */
  SQLINTEGER *SourceOctetLength       /* 32-bit output */
  );
```

Job: The common subroutine for Character String Retrieval appears in 24 CLI functions. You don't directly call it, but you see the effects. We thought this would be a good way to introduce the format we use for CLI function descriptions.

Algorithm:

```
If (MaxTargetOctetLength <= 0)
  return error: HY090 CLI-specific condition-invalid string length or buffer
length
If (SourceOctetLength is not a null pointer)
  /* We set *SourceOctetLength = the size of the source string, even if we don't
actually copy the entire source to target. */
  Set *ReturnedOctetLength = strlen (Value)
If (we don't use null-termination in this environment)
  /* In COBOL or FORTRAN you wouldn't expect null-termination, since strings
don't end with a '\0' in those languages. But we never take this path.*/
Else
  /* In C, and also in Pascal, strings end with '\0'. We'll assume null-termina-
tion then. But now you're aware that it's a characteristic of the host language
we're using, not a requirement of standard SQL. */
  If (we're using WideChar i.e. 16 bits per character)
    sizeof(null-terminator) = 2
  Else sizeof(null-terminator) = 1
```

```
  Set # of octets to copy = MaxTargetOctetLength-sizeof(null-terminator)
  If (# of octets to copy < 0)
    /* Put out '\0' if possible, but there's no room for copying */
  Else
    If (# of octets to copy > strlen(source))
      Set # of octets to copy = strlen(source)
      Copy:
        Set # of octets to copy=strlen(Source) - sizeof(null-terminator)
        From: Source
        To: Target
    Append null-terminator to Target.
If (strlen(Target) < strlen(Source))
  warning 01004 - string data, right truncation
```

Notes:

- The idea is simply to copy the `*Source` string to the `*Target` string, but there's a safeguard against overflowing `*Target` (that's why we pass `MaxTargetOctetLength`) and there's a place to store the original size (that's why we pass `*ReturnedOctetLength`).
- The `*Target` string will always be null-terminated, unless `TargetOctetLength=0`.
- There are variations of this routine where ...`OctetLength` is 16-bit.
- There is a slight variation of this routine for `BLOB` retrieval — it works the same way, but ignores anything to do with null terminators.
- `CharacterStringRetrieval(target,source,max,&sourcelength)` is expressible using the standard-C <string.h> function `strxfrm`: `sourcelength = strxfrm(target,source,max);`

Example:

```
/ * SPECIMEN ONLY — you don't really want to call this function */
#include "sqlcli.h"       /* includes definitions of SQL... stuff */
SQLCHAR target[100];      /* SQLCHAR is 8-bit ISO if Windows98 */
SQLINTEGER returnsize;    /* SQLINTEGER is always 32-bit signed */
...
CharacterStringRetrieval(target,"ABC",5,&returnsize);
/* Now target has: ABC\0 and returnsize = 5. */
...
CharacterStringRetrieval(target,"ABC",3,&returnsize);
/* Now target has: AB\0 and returnsize = 2. */
```

ODBC: In ODBC 1.0's documentation there was some contradictory information about the workings of Character String Retrieval, but everything is settled now.

41

Chapter 41

SQL/CLI: env Functions

In this chapter, we'll describe the first essential CLI resource — the env. For CLI programs, the env is the all-encompassing context area — all CLI programs begin by establishing an env. The env contains some information directly ("attributes" and "diagnostics"), but what's important is that an env contains zero or more dbcs (although there's no point in having an env without a dbc). Here's a closeup view of an env:

```
-------------------------
- [env Attributes]      -
- [env Diagnostics]     -
-------------------------
| |
| |
v v
... to dbcs
```

Null Termination

Traditionally, there have been three ways to define character strings:

1. They are fixed length. Example: a COBOL PIC X(5) variable.
2. They are variable length and a separate variable tells us the size. Example: the 16-bit octet-length — SIZE% — in a BASIC string var$ or the 8-bit octet-length which is the first byte of a Turbo Pascal string.

3. They are variable length and the end is marked by a termination code. Example: the 8-bit byte = '\0' which ends strings in C programs. This code, which in a wide-character string would be a 16-bit word 0x0000, is the null terminator. Inprise Pascal (Delphi) uses the same convention for PChar variables.

We've assumed that any DBMS which supports C/Pascal interfaces will go with null termination. That affects the CLI in only one way; you can receive null-terminated strings from the DBMS whenever Character String Retrieval is called for. Going the other way — passing null-terminated strings to the DBMS — is legal regardless of the setting of NULL TERMINATION. That's because you indicate null termination of input strings using SQL_NTS for "size."

Sixteen of the CLI functions accept an input-string parameter. In these functions, the parameter immediately following the input-string parameter is the *input-string length* — for example:

```
<function name> (... input_string, input_string_length);
```

The input length should be the number of octets in the input string, not including the null termination octet(s). However, you can pass SQL_NTS (-3) instead — this stands for "null terminated string" — and let the DBMS calculate the string size. Remember, though, that programs which pass SQL_NTS are many nanoseconds slower than programs which pass an absolute length.

There are six CLI functions for creating envs, dropping envs, getting env attributes, and setting env attributes. Their descriptions follow.

SQLAllocHandle(SQL_HANDLE_ENV,...)

Function Prototype:

```
SQLRETURN SQLAllocHandle(
  SQLSMALLINT HandleType,      /* 16-bit input = SQL_HANDLE_ENV */
  SQLINTEGER InputHandle,      /* 32-bit input */
  SQLINTEGER *OutputHandle     /* pointer to 32-bit output, a henv */
);
```

Job: Allocate an env.

- How to make an env

  Usually the first SQL-related instruction is the call to make an env:

```
#include "sqlcli.h"
 SQLHENV      henv;             /* declare a henv, name it: henv */
 SQLRETURN    sqlreturn;        /* code returned by SQL function */
 ...
   sqlreturn =
     SQLAllocHandle(SQL_HANDLE_ENV,SQL_NULL_HANDLE,&henv);
 ...
```

The first parameter (HandleType) is SQL_HANDLE_ENV.

The second parameter (InputHandle) doesn't matter here. As a style note — we follow a convention that "if the parameter value doesn't matter, then use a constant containing the word NULL or 00." This convention helps make it clear that the value we're passing has no significance.

The third parameter (*OutputHandle) must be an address of an environment handle. As explained before, we prefer to call an environment handle a "henv". But use a descriptive name for your program variable if you have one.

If the function succeeds, you have a new env. Keep the henv, you'll need it later for input to other functions.

- Testing for error returns

  [Obscure Rule] Error-testing is a bit unusual because the DBMS may put something into OutputHandle even if the function fails. This annotated code snippet shows the scenarios:

```
sqlreturn = SQLAllocHandle(SQL_ALLOC_ENV,SQL_HANDLE_NULL,&henv);
if (sqlreturn < 0) {
  /* There was an error so SQLAllocHandle returned a negative value. */
  if (sqlreturn == SQL_NULL_HANDLE) {      /* SQL_NULL_HANDLE=-2 */
    /* SQL_HANDLE_ENV is not a valid code -- an "impossible" error */ }
  else {
    /* sqlreturn must be SQL_ERROR (-1), the only other possibility */
    if (&henv==0)
      /* The problem is "invalid use of null pointer" -- the last parameter --
         OutputHandle -- was zero. This error too is "impossible". */
    if (henv<>SQL_NULL_HENV) {
      /* The DBMS has placed a "skeleton env handle" in henv. It's not good for
         much, but you can use henv to get an error message with the
         SQLGetDiagRec function. */ }
    else {
      /* The DBMS has placed zero in henv. There was an error, there is no
         skeleton env handle to get error messages with. You'll have to guess
         that there wasn't enough memory. */ } }
else {
  /* There was no error. */ }
```

There are several other possible errors/exception conditions that the SQLAllocHandle function might "raise." If they occur, the function will return a negative number: –2 (SQL_INVALID_HANDLE) or –1 (SQL_ERROR). For more detailed information, look up the SQLSTATE codes beginning with HY, HY001, or HY014 in Chapter 47 "SQL/CLI: Diagnostic Functions."

Algorithm:

```
If (HandleType == SQL_HANDLE_ENV) {
  The DBMS allocates an object in memory. The DBMS creates a 32-bit handle for
  this object, its unique identifier. The DBMS puts the handle in the memory
  location addressed by OutputHandle. }
```

Notes:

- This is one of several SQLAllocHandle variants. The HandleType input parameter may contain any one of:

(implementation-defined)	<1
SQL_HANDLE_ENV	1 /* handle of an env */
SQL_HANDLE_DBC	2 /* handle of a dbc */
SQL_HANDLE_HSTMT	3 /* handle of a stmt */
SQL_HANDLE_DESC	4 /* handle of a desc */
(implementation-defined)	>100

  In discussions of other CLI functions, we will usually ignore the "implementation-defined" possibilities.

ODBC: The SQLAllocHandle function is new in ODBC 3.0. Error information will not be available until you call the "connect" function.

SQLAllocEnv

Function Prototype:

```
SQLRETURN SQLAllocEnv(
  SQLHENV *henv              /* pointer to 32-bit output, a henv */
  );
```

Job: Make an env.

Algorithm:

```
sqlreturn = SQLAllocEnv(&henv);
```

is the same as

```
sqlreturn = SQLAllocHandle(SQL_HANDLE_ENV,SQL_NULL_HANDLE,&henv);
```

Notes:

- Implicit Calls

  In the algorithm description, the words "is the same as" mean that, in effect, the DBMS calls SQLAllocHandle when you call SQLAllocEnv. So you have called SQLAllocHandle indirectly, or — as the Standard puts it — "implicitly." For purposes of interpreting the somewhat legalistic Standard, it makes absolutely no difference whether you perform an operation explicitly or implicitly.

- Obsolescent Handle Functions

  SQLAllocEnv is one of six functions — SQLAllocEnv, SQLFreeEnv, SQLAllocConnect, SQLFreeConnect, SQLAllocStmt, SQLFreeStmt — which are nowadays, mostly redundant. They are a legacy of the days when there were only three kinds of resources: env, dbc, and stmt. Mostly, you will see them in programs written for early versions of ODBC. The Standard does not "deprecate" these functions, so we may assume that they will continue to be part of standard SQL for the indefinite future. However, their presence will make a program look old-fashioned. The only exception is SQLFreeStmt which has a few useful options.

Example:

```
#include "sqlcli.h"
SQLHENV      henv;
SQLRETURN    sqlreturn;
...
sqlreturn = SQLAllocEnv(&henv);
if (sqlreturn == SQL_ERROR) {
  printf("Error: could not make an env.\n");
  exit(1); }
```

ODBC: The SQLAllocEnv routine has been in ODBC since version 1.0. The ODBC 3.0 manual deprecates it, suggesting that users should switch to using SQLAllocHandle(SQL_HANDLE_ENV,...).

SQLGetEnvAttr

Function Prototype:

```
SQLRETURN  SQLGetEnvAttr(
  SQLHENV henv,                  /* 32-bit input */
  SQLINTEGER Attribute,          /* 32-bit input */
  SQLPOINTER Value,              /* ANY* pointer to output */
  SQLINTEGER BufferLength,       /* 32-bit input */
  SQLINTEGER *StringLength);     /* 32-bit pointer to output */
```

Job: Get an env attribute. At the moment, there is only one standard env attribute — a flag saying whether strings are null-terminated. The flag has this #define in sqlcli.h:

```
#define SQL_ATTR_OUTPUT_NTS 10001 /* NULL TERMINATION env attribute */
```

Algorithm:

```
If (henv is not a henv or env is a skeleton env)
  return with error: CLI-specific condition - invalid handle
Empty env's diagnostics area.
If (Attribute <> SQL_ATTR_OUTPUT_NTS)
  return with error: HY092 CLI-specific condition-invalid attribute identifier
Set *Value = env's NULL TERMINATION env attribute
/* This value is 1 (TRUE) if the DBMS uses null termination; it is 0 (FALSE) if
   not. */
```

Notes:

- The `BufferLength` and `StringLength` parameters are unused. They're there in case a future edition of the SQL Standard requires more information. Or, as with all functions, there is a chance that your particular DBMS stores attribute information that the Standard doesn't officially require.

Example:

```
#include "sqlcli.h"
SQLHENV    henv;
SQLINTEGER attribute;
...
SQLGetEnvAttr(henv,SQL_ATTR_OUTPUT_NTS,&attribute,00,00);
```

ODBC: The `SQLGetEnvAttr` function is new in ODBC 3.0. There are also a few other `env` options which are specific to ODBC.

SQLSetEnvAttr

Function Prototype:

```
SQLRETURN  SQLSetEnvAttr(
  SQLHENV henv,               /* 32-bit input -- env handle */
  SQLINTEGER Attribute,       /* 32-bit input */
  SQLPOINTER Value,           /* ANY* input */
  SQLINTEGER StringLength     /* 32-bit input */
  );
```

Job: Set an `env` attribute. At the moment there is only one standard `env` attribute — whether output strings are null-terminated — see the discussion of the `SQLGetEnvAttr` function on page 759 for detailed remarks on the subject of Null Termination. It is probably sufficient to know that you do not want to change this attribute if you program in C or Pascal.

Algorithm:

```
If (henv is not a henv) or (env is skeleton env)
   return with error: CLI-specific condition-invalid handle
Empty the env's diagnostics area.
If (there is a dbc in this env)
   /* You should call SQLSetEnvAttr before calling
      SQLAllocHandle(SQL_HANDLE_DBC,...) */
   return with error: HY011 CLI-specific condition-attribute cannot be set now
 If (Attribute <> SQL_ATTR_OUTPUT_NTS)
   return with error: HY092 CLI-specific condition-invalid attribute identifier
If (Attribute == SQL_ATTR_OUTPUT_NTS)
/* in sqlcli.h there is a line: "#define 10001 SQL_ATTR_OUTPUT_NTS" */
   If (Value == TRUE) then set env's NULL TERMINATION attribute = TRUE.
   Else If
      (Value == FALSE) then set NULL TERMINATION attribute = FALSE.
   Else return with error: HY024 CLI-specific condition-invalid attribute value
```

Notes:

- There might be some other implementation-defined env attributes. That is why there is a StringLength parameter — in case there is an implementation-defined attribute represented as a character string.

Example:

```
#include "sqlcli.h"
SQLHENV     henv;
SQLINTEGER  Value=1;
void main ()
{
  if (SQLAllocHandle(SQL_HANDLE_ENV,SQL_NULL_HANDLE,&henv)<0) {
    printf("Error: can't create the env\n");
    exit(1); }
  if (SQLSetEnvAttr(henv,SQL_ATTR_OUTPUT_NTS,(void*)Value,NULL)<0) {
    printf("Error: can't set the NULL TERMINATION env attribute\n");
    exit(1); }
  exit(0); }
```

ODBC: The SQLSetEnvAttr function is new in ODBC 3.0. It is impossible to change the NULL TERMINATION env attribute. There are other attributes. For example, to explicitly state that your application is written for ODBC version 3.0, say:

```
version = SQL_OV_ODBC3;          /* 00000003L */
SQLSetEnvAttr(henv,SQL_ATTR_ODBC_VERSION,&version,00);
```

SQLFreeHandle(SQL_HANDLE_ENV,...)

Function Prototype:

```
SQLRETURN SQLFreeHandle(
  SQLSMALLINT HandleType,    /* 16-bit input */
  SQLINTEGER Handle          /* 32-bit input (must be a henv) */
  );
```

Job: Destroy an env. This is the reverse of the SQLAllocHandle(SQL_HANDLE_ENV,...) function.

Algorithm:

```
If (Handle is not a henv)
  return error: CLI-specific condition-invalid handle
Empty the env's diagnostics area.
If (there is a dbc associated with the env)
  return error: HY010 CLI-specific condition-function sequence error
Deallocate env and anything associated with it, such as RAM.
The handle is now invalid.
```

Notes:

- This is usually the last function call in a CLI program.

Example:

```
#include "sqlcli.h"
SQLHENV     henv;
...
SQLFreeHandle(SQL_HANDLE_ENV,henv);
```

ODBC: The SQLFreeHandle function is new in ODBC 3.0.

SQLFreeEnv

Function Prototype:

```
SQLRETURN SQLFreeEnv(
  SQLHENV henv                    /* 32-bit input */
  );
```

Job: Destroy an env. This is the reverse of the SQLAllocEnv function. SQLFreeEnv is redundant.

Algorithm:

```
sqlreturn = SQLFreeEnv(henv);
```

is the same thing as

```
sqlreturn = SQLFreeHandle(SQL_HANDLE_ENV,henv);
```

Notes:

- The Standard does not say that the SQLFreeEnv function is deprecated. All DBMSs should support it.

Example:

```
#include "sqlcli.h"
SQLHENV     henv;
...
SQLAllocEnv(&henv);
...
SQLFreeEnv(henv);        /* henv is now an invalid handle */
...
```

ODBC: The SQLFreeEnv function has been in ODBC since version 1.0. The ODBC 3 manual deprecates it, suggesting that users should switch to using SQLFreeHandle(SQL_HANDLE_ENV,...).

And that's it for the env functions. In the next chapter, we'll take a look at the dbc functions.

42

Chapter 42

SQL/CLI: dbc Functions

In this chapter, we'll describe the second essential CLI resource — the dbc. For CLI programs, the dbc is at the level below env and above stmt. The env may contain multiple dbcs and the dbc may contain multiple stmts (the dbc may also contain multiple descs, but only of the "user" kind). Here's a closeup view of a dbc:

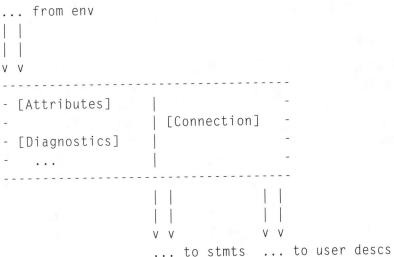

```
... from env
| |
| |
v v
-------------------------------------
- [Attributes]       |              -
-                    | [Connection] -
- [Diagnostics]      |              -
-    ...             |              -
-------------------------------------
                     | |          | |
                     | |          | |
                     v v          v v
                     ... to stmts  ... to user descs
```

There are eight CLI functions for creating dbcs, dropping dbcs, getting dbc attributes, setting dbc attributes, connecting, and disconnecting. Their descriptions follow.

SQLAllocHandle(SQL_HANDLE_DBC,...)

Function Prototype:

```
SQLRETURN SQLAllocHandle (
  SQLSMALLINT HandleType,     /* 16-bit input = SQL_HANDLE_DBC */
  SQLINTEGER InputHandle,     /* 32-bit input, must be a henv */
  SQLINTEGER *OutputHandle    /* pointer to 32-bit output, a hdbc */
  );
```

Job: Allocate a dbc.

Algorithm:

```
if (HandleType) == SQL_HANDLE_DBC) {
   The DBMS allocates a new dbc, and associates it with the env (the env's han-
dle is passed in InputHandle) and returns the handle of the new dbc into the
memory location addressed by OutputHandle. }
```

That is, If (HandleType == SQL_HANDLE_DBC), then the job is to allocate a new dbc.

Notes:

- The second parameter, InputHandle, must be a valid henv so this function call happens after SQLAllocHandle(SQL_ALLOC_ENV,...).
- Keep the hdbc, you'll need it later for SQLAllocHandle(SQL_HANDLE_STMT, ...), for SQLFreeHandle(SQL_HANDLE_DBC, ...) and for other functions.

Example:

```
#include "sqlcli.h"
SQLHENV      henv;              /* handle of an env */
SQLHDBC      hdbc;              /* handle of a dbc */
SQLRETURN    sqlreturn;         /* code returned by SQL function */
...
  sqlreturn = SQLAllocHandle(SQL_HANDLE_DBC,henv,&hdbc);
  ...
```

ODBC: The SQLAllocHandle function is new in ODBC 3.0. Error information will not be available until you call the "connect" function.

SQLAllocConnect

Function Prototype:

```
SQLRETURN SQLAllocConnect (
  SQLHENV henv,         /* 32-bit input, must be a henv */
  SQLHDBC *hdbc         /* pointer to 32-bit output, a hdbc */
  );
```

Job: Make a new dbc. SQLAllocConnect is obsolete.

Algorithm:

```
sqlreturn = SQLAllocConnect(henv,&hdbc);
```

is the same as:

```
sqlreturn = SQLAllocHandle(SQL_HANDLE_DBC,henv,&hdbc);
```

Example:

```
#include "sqlcli.h"
SQLHENV     henv;
SQLHDBC     hdbc;
SQLRETURN   sqlreturn;
...
if (SQLAllocEnv(&henv)>0) {
  if (SQLAllocConnect(henv,&hdbc)>0) {
     ... a hdbc exists } }
```

Notes:

- Although SQLAllocConnect is in the "obsolescent" category, it is still a standard function supported by all DBMSs.

ODBC: The SQLAllocConnect routine has been in ODBC since version 1.0. The ODBC 3.0 manual deprecates it, suggesting that users should switch to using SQLAllocHandle(SQL_HANDLE_DBC,...).

SQLConnect

Function Prototype:

```
SQLRETURN  SQLConnect(
  SQLHDBC hdbc,                  /* 32-bit input */
  SQLCHAR *ServerName,           /* CHAR* input */
  SQLSMALLINT NameLength1,       /* 16-bit input (ServerName length)*/
  SQLCHAR *UserName,             /* CHAR* input */
  SQLSMALLINT NameLength2,       /* 16-bit input (UserName length) */
  SQLCHAR *Authentication,       /* CHAR* input */
  SQLSMALLINT NameLength3        /* 16-bit input
                                    (Authentication length)*/
  );
```

Job: Establish an SQL-Connection for a dbc. The details of "how to connect" depend largely on the implementation. We describe two broad cases: a Single-Tier Scenario (everything on one computer) and a Two-Tier Scenario (Client on one computer, Server on another computer). One or the other will be fairly close to your specific implementation.

- Single-Tier scenario
  - Step 1. The client (which is effectively the same thing as "the DBMS") verifies that the parameters have valid data. Specifically, it must be true that: (*a*) The dbc exists. If it doesn't, the return is CLI-specific condition — invalid handle. Read up on the SQLAllocHandle function to see how to set up the handle. (*b*) There is no SQL transaction running on this Connection. (Actually some sophisticated systems allow this, but we assume the normal case.) If there is one, the return is 0A001 feature not supported — multiple transactions. It's okay if you have a transaction going on a different SQL-Connection — this just means you can't connect twice using the same dbc handle. Read up on SQLDisconnect if you're already connected. (*c*) The ServerName parameter is valid. This should be a string, with a maximum length of 128 octets (as usual the length is passed along with the string, NameLength1, and may be SQL_NTS). If it's not valid, the return is HY090 invalid string length or buffer length. If ServerName is a blank string, the DBMS assumes the <SQL-server name> is 'DEFAULT'. (*d*) The UserName is valid. The contents of this string will become the <AuthorizationID>, so the string should contain a valid identifier, such as: 'USER_1' or ' USER_1 ' (lead and trail spaces don't matter). (*e*) The authentication is valid. Usually a blank is acceptable: ''.
  - Step 2. The DBMS "opens" the database named ServerName. This may seem like a misuse of the parameter, but the fact is, we don't need to contact a server — but we do need to open a database. And it's fairly common that there will be more than one database on a computer, so names are necessary.
- Two-Tier scenario
  - Step 1. The client (the local task which your application is calling) verifies that the parameters have valid data. This step is local, the only likely difference is that the

client will not bother to verify the "authentication" parameter because that's usually the server's problem.

- Step 2. If ServerName = "DEFAULT":

```
If (User Name Length <> 0) invalid string or buffer length
If (Authentication Length <> 0) invalid string or buffer length
If (Somebody else already in as default) connection name in use
   Otherwise:
(Compare the effect of a "CONNECT TO DEFAULT;" statement.)
```

- Step 3. Using RDA, the client finds the server identified by the parameter ServerName and sends a message to the server containing the parameter values (UserName and Authentication). If the network's down or the server's not out there, then the return is: 08001 connection exception-SQL-client unable to establish SQL-session.
- Step 4. The server does its own validation of UserName and Authentication. One possibility is that the Authentication is designed to be a password and it doesn't match the UserName's password. In this case, the return is: 08004 connection exception-SQL-server rejected establishment of SQL-session. Notice the difference between this error and the one described in Step 3 — SQLSTATE is '08001' if the client can't talk to the server; SQLSTATE is '08004' if they can talk, but the server says no.
- Step 5. All having gone well, we now have a new SQL-session. If there was already an SQL-session in progress, it becomes dormant. The new SQL-session becomes the current SQL-session. The new SQL-session's session <AuthorizationID> becomes UserName — that is, if the UserName parameter is 'X' and you use the niladic function SESSION_USER in an SQL statement, you'll get 'X'.

Example:

```
/* CHAP42_1.C */
/* This is a program example. Connection is to the default database for the
DBMS that came with this book. For variety, we test sqlreturn each time. Tear-
down calls are omitted. */
#include "sqlcli.h"
SQLHENV    henv;
SQLHDBC    hdbc;
SQLRETURN  sqlreturn;
void main ()
{
 sqlreturn = SQLAllocHandle(SQL_HANDLE_ENV,SQL_NULL_HANDLE,&henv);
 if (sqlreturn == SQL_SUCCESS || sqlreturn == SQL_SUCCESS_WITH_INFO) {
   sqlreturn = SQLAllocHandle(SQL_HANDLE_DBC,henv,&hdbc);
   if (sqlreturn == SQL_SUCCESS ||
       sqlreturn == SQL_SUCCESS_WITH_INFO) {
```

```
    sqlreturn = SQLConnect(hdbc,
                (SQLCHAR*)"OCELOT",SQL_NTS,
                (SQLCHAR*)"OCELOT",SQL_NTS,
                (SQLCHAR*)"",SQL_NTS);
    if (sqlreturn == SQL_SUCCESS ||
        sqlreturn == SQL_SUCCESS_WITH_INFO) {
      printf("connected successfully.\n"); } } } }
```

ODBC: SQLConnect has been a supported function since ODBC 1.0. But there are other, non-standard, ODBC functions which can be used to connect. The alternatives take advantage of the Windows environment (by putting up dialog boxes etc.) and assume that Microsoft's Driver Manager software will take care of some details.

CONNECT versus SQLConnect

There is an SQL statement which we've already discussed:

```
CONNECT TO <SQL-server-name> [AS <Connection name>]
           USER <AuthorizationID>;
```

You are not supposed to execute this SQL statement using the CLI! The business of connecting is to be handled exclusively through the SQLConnect function. So if you write a program which accepts user commands in the form of SQL statements, you must intercept any that begin with "CONNECT ..." and call the SQLAllocConnect and SQLConnect functions for them. Unfortunately, this is difficult because there is an imperfect mapping between the arguments of the CONNECT statement and the parameters of SQLConnect.

Similar interceptions will be necessary for the three other SQL statements which must not be executed directly using the CLI: DISCONNECT, COMMIT, and ROLLBACK. For each of these statements there is an approximate CLI-function analogue: SQLDisconnect, SQLEndTran(...SQL_COMMIT), and SQLEndTran(...SQL_ROLLBACK).

SQLDisconnect

Function Prototype:

```
SQLRETURN SQLDisconnect(
  SQLHDBC hdbc                    /* 32-bit input */
  );
```

Job: End an SQL session which was started by calling the SQLConnect function. Analogous to the SQL DISCONNECT statement.

Algorithm:

```
If (hdbc parameter is not a handle of a dbc)
  return error: CLI-specific condition-invalid handle
Empty the diagnostics area associated with dbc.
If (there is no connection associated with dbc)
 /* i.e. we didn't call SQLConnect or we already called
    SQLDisconnect */
  return error: 08003 connection exception-connection does not exist
For (each stmt associated with the dbc)
   If (there is a deferred parameter number)
    return error: HY010 CLI-specific condition-function sequence error
If (a transaction is active)
  /* Before disconnecting you must end the transaction,
     try calling SQLEndTran */
  return error: 25001 invalid transaction state-active SQL-transaction
For (each stmt associated with the dbc)
  Free the stmt's descs (ARD, APD, IRD, IPD)
  Free the stmt
Free any descs which are directly associated with the dbc
If (Client/Server)
  Tell the server that this connection is over.
  If (server won't reply / server won't let go)
    /* This is only a warning, by now the disconnect is unstoppable */
    there will be a warning: 01002 warning-disconnect error
If (the connection we just disconnected was the current connection)
  There is now no current connection
```

Notes:

- A connected dbc takes up space and in a multi-user scenario there might be conflicts with other SQL-sessions using the same server. You should always call SQLDisconnect to end an SQL-session, although some single-tier DBMSs don't require it. After you call SQLDisconnect, you can either re-connect (see SQLConnect) or finish the tear-down process by freeing the dbc (see SQLFreeHandle(SQL_HANDLE_DBC...)).
- There is a side effect; a previously-dormant SQL-Connection might become current. That can only happen if the DBMS allows double-connections on the same dbc.

Example:

```
/* All function calls except SQLDisconnect are in skeletal form. */
#include "sqlcli.h"
SQLHENV henv;
SQLHDBC hdbc;
...
SQLAllocHandle(...);      /* SQLAllocHandle call for env */
SQLAllocHandle(...);      /* SQLAllocHandle call for dbc */
SQLConnect(hdbc,...);     /* connect: see previous example */
 /* we could now call SQLAllocHandle(SQL_HANDLE_STMT,...);
  and then perform various functions related to the stmt */
SQLDisconnect(hdbc);
SQLFreeHandle(hdbc,...); /* SQLFreeHandle call for dbc */
SQLFreeHandle(...); }    /* SQLFreeHandle call for env */
```

ODBC: The SQLDisconnect function has been around since ODBC 1.0. SQLDisconnect causes automatic dropping of all statements and descriptors open on the connection.

SQLGetConnectAttr

Function Prototype:

```
SQLRETURN  SQLGetConnectAttr(
  SQLHDBC hdbc,                   /* 32-bit input */
  SQLINTEGER Attribute,           /* 32-bit input */
  SQLPOINTER Value,               /* pointer to 32-bit output */
  SQLINTEGER BufferLength,        /* 32-bit input */
  SQLINTEGER *StringLength        /* pointer to 32-bit output */
  );
```

Job: Get the value of a dbc attribute. The standard implementation of the SQLGetConnectAttr function doesn't do anything important, but there might be non-standard, implementation-defined attributes that you can retrieve using SQLGetConnectAttr. The standard connection attribute has this #define in sqlcli.h:

```
#define SQL_ATTR_AUTO_IPD 10001
```

It is, of course, an integer and may not be set by SQLSetConnectAttr. SQL_ATTR_AUTO_IPD stands for SQL Attribute: Automatically Populate IPD. This is a flag integer with a value of either TRUE (1) or FALSE (0). SQL_ATTR_AUTO_IPD is the only standard attribute for a connection. If SQL_ATTR_AUTO_IPD is TRUE, the DBMS "populates" the IPD (implementation parameter descriptor) whenever you prepare an SQL statement. That means that there will be, automatically, one parameter descriptor for every parameter marker (symbolized by "?") inside your SQL statement. For example, if you execute this SQL statement:

```
INSERT INTO Table_1 VALUES (?);
```

there will be an automatic IPD. IPD contents are the subject of Chapter 46.

Algorithm:

```
If (hdbc is not a hdbc)
  return error: CLI-specific condition-invalid handle
Empty the dbc's diagnostics area.
If (Attribute <> SQL_ATTR_AUTO_IPD)
  return error: HY092 CLI-specific condition-invalid
  attribute identifier
If (Attribute = SQL_ATTR_AUTO_IPD)
  If (SQLConnect not done)
    return error: 08003 connection exception-connection does not exist
  Set *Value = value of dbc's SQL_ATTR_AUTO_IPD attribute
  field (0 or 1).
```

Notes:

- There might be several implementation-defined attributes for connections. The Standard allows for that. That's why BufferLength and *Stringlength — which aren't needed for SQL_ATTR_AUTO_IPD — are defined parameters. They're there in case someday it's necessary to return a character string value.
- Some things which we think of as "connection attributes" are not retrieved with SQLGetConnectAttr. They are:
  - The default time zone offset — get it by extracting the <time zone interval> from SQL's CURRENT_TIME function.
  - The default Catalog — get it by selecting from the INFORMATION_SCHEMA_CATALOG_NAME Table or by using SQLGetInfo with SQL_CATALOG_NAME.
  - The default Schema — get it by using SQLGetDiagField after any erroneous statement.
  - The default Character set — get it by using SQLGetDiagField after any erroneous statement.
  - The default Collation — get it by using SQLGetInfo with SQL_COLLATING_SEQUENCE.
  - The <Connection name> — get it by using SQLGetDiagField after any erroneous statement.
  - The <SQL-server name> — get it by using SQLGetInfo with SQL_DATA_SOURCE_NAME or SQLGetInfo with SQL_SERVER_NAME.
  - The SQL-session user — get it from SQL's SESSION_USER function or by using SQLGetInfo with SQL_USER_NAME.

- In the final version of the SQL/CLI there will be two more attributes — SQL_ATTR_SAVEPOINT_NAME and SQL_ATTR_SAVEPOINT_NUMBER.

Example:

```
#include "sqlcli.h"
SQLHDBC         hdbc;
SQLINTEGER      popid;
...
if (SQLGetConnectAttr(hdbc,SQL_ATTR_AUTO_IPD,&popid,00,NULL) < 0) {
  printf("Error.\n");
else {
  if (popid==1) printf("It's true.\n");
  if (popid==0) printf("It's false: DBMS isn't full SQL\n"; }
/* Going on from here: if popid is true, we can make SQL statements with param-
eters (?s). Then we can assign buffers/variables based on the IPD. Or we can
make sure our currently-assigned parameters are okay. If pop is false: we can
still use parameters, but we have to fill in IPD values "manually". */
```

ODBC: The SQLGetConnectAttr function is new to ODBC 3.0 but a very similar function (SQLGetConnectOption) existed in ODBC 2.0. ODBC allows for 16 possible Attributes. One is SQL_ATTR_AUTO_IPD. Most of the others are related to ODBC's optional features (timeout, trace file, network packet size, etc.).

SQLSetConnectAttr

Function Prototype:

```
SQLRETURN SQLSetConnectAttr(
  SQLHDBC hdbc,             /* 32-bit input -- SQL-connection handle */
  SQLINTEGER Attribute,     /* 32-bit input */
  SQLPOINTER Value,         /* pointer to *ANY input */
  SQLINTEGER StringLength   /* 32-bit input */
  );
```

Job: Set the value of a dbc attribute.

Algorithm:

```
If (hdbc is not really a handle of a dbc)
  return error: CLI-specific condition-invalid handle
Empty dbc's diagnostics area.
```

```
If (Attribute <> SQL_ATTR_AUTO_IPD)
  return error: HY092 CLI-specific condition-invalid
  attribute identifier
If (Attribute == SQL_ATTR_AUTO_IPD)
  /* the SQL_ATTR_AUTO_IPD attribute may not be set */
  return error: HY092 CLI-specific condition-invalid
  attribute identifier
```

Notes:

- This function is useless unless there are implementation-defined dbc attributes.
- In the final version of the SQL/CLI there will be two more attributes — SQL_ATTR_SAVEPOINT_NAME and SQL_ATTR_SAVEPOINT_NUMBER.
- Value might be a pointer; that's why we've used SQLPOINTER in the prototype. But it's usually an integer. C programmers, when passing an integer value here, will use casts such as (PTR) or (SQLPOINTER) or (void*).

Example:

```
#include "sqlcli.h"
SQLHDBC hdbc;
...
sqlreturn = SQLSetConnectAttr(hdbc,SQL_ATTR_AUTO_IPD,(void*)5,00);
if (sqlreturn == SQL_SUCCESS || sqlreturn == SQL_SUCCESS_WITH_INFO) {
  /* function call succeeded -- which it shouldn't */
else
  /* function call failed, as expected */
```

ODBC: The SQLSetConnectAttr function is new in ODBC 3.0 but ODBC 2.0 had a broadly similar function (SQLSetConnectOption). ODBC allows for 16 dbc attributes of various types, usually pointers.

SQLFreeHandle(SQL_HANDLE_DBC,...)

Function Prototype:

```
SQLRETURN SQLFreeHandle(     /* function returns SMALLINT */
    SQLSMALLINT HandleType,  /* 16-bit input, = SQL_HANDLE_DBC */
    SQLINTEGER Handle        /* 32-bit input, must be a hdbc */
    );
```

Job: Destroy a dbc.

Algorithm:

```
If (HandleType == SQL_HANDLE_DBC)
  If (Handle is not really a handle of a dbc)
     return error: CLI-specific condition-invalid handle
  Empty the dbc's diagnostics area.
  If (dbc is still connected)
  /* you must call SQLDisconnect before you can destroy a dbc */
    return error: HY010 CLI-specific condition-function
    sequence error
  Deallocate the connection and anything associated with it.
  The handle becomes invalid.
```

Notes:

- If SQLFreeHandle returns SQL_ERROR, then the handle is still live and you can get diagnostics.
- The name SQLFreeHandle is unfortunate. We are not "freeing a handle." We are destroying the resource to which the handle refers. In embedded SQL contexts, the preferred word for this process is "deallocate."
- Before you call SQLFreeHandle(SQL_HANDLE_DBC...), you must call SQLDisconnect. Therefore, by this time, there are no stmts or descs associated with the dbc.

Example: Typically, an SQL application ends with a flurry of freeings:

```
SQLDisconnect(hdbc);                     /* ends the SQL-session */
SQLFreeHandle(SQL_HANDLE_DBC,hdbc);
SQLFreeHandle(SQL_HANDLE_ENV,henv);  /* ends the application */
```

ODBC: The SQLFreeHandle function is new in ODBC 3.0. There will be some differences in behaviour if you use ODBC-specific features, such as tracing or environment sharing.

SQLFreeConnect

Function Prototype:

```
SQLRETURN SQLFreeConnect(
  SQLHDBC hdbc                          /* 32-bit input */
  );
```

Job: Destroy a dbc. This is the reverse of the SQLAllocConnect function. SQLFreeConnect is redundant.

Algorithm:

```
sqlreturn = SQLFreeConnect(hdbc);
```

is the same thing as

```
sqlreturn = SQLFreeHandle(SQL_HANDLE_DBC,hdbc);
```

Notes:

- The Standard does not say that the `SQLFreeConnect` function is deprecated. Nevertheless, `SQLFreeHandle(SQL_HANDLE_DBC,...)` is more modern.

Example:

```
#include "sqlcli.h"
SQLHENV      henv;
SQLHDBC      hdbc;
...
SQLAllocConnect(henv,&hdbc);
...
SQLFreeConnect(hdbc);
/* hdbc is now an invalid handle */
...
```

ODBC: The `SQLFreeConnect` function has been in ODBC since version 1.0. The ODBC 3.0 manual deprecates it, suggesting that users should switch to using `SQLFreeHandle(SQL_HANDLE_DBC...)`.

And that's it for the `dbc` functions. In the next chapter, we'll take a look at the `stmt` functions.

43

Chapter 43

SQL/CLI: stmt Functions

In this chapter, we'll describe the third essential CLI resource — the stmt. For CLI programs, the stmt is at the level below dbc and (usually) above desc. The dbc may contain multiple stmts and the stmt may contain four descs. Here's a closeup view of a stmt:

```
... from dbc
| |
| |
v v
------------------------------------
- [Attributes]                     -
-                                  -
- [Diagnostics]                    -
-                                  -
- [Cursor] [Result Set] [Statement] -
------------------------------------
|           |           |           |
|           |           |           |
v           v           v           v
... to IPD  ... to IRD  ... to APD  ... to ARD
```

There are six CLI functions for creating stmts, dropping stmts, getting stmt attributes, and setting stmt attributes. Their descriptions follow.

SQLAllocHandle(SQL_HANDLE_STMT,...)

Function Prototype:

```
SQLRETURN SQLAllocHandle (
  SQLSMALLINT HandleType,    /* 16-bit input = SQL_HANDLE_STMT */
  SQLINTEGER InputHandle,    /* 32-bit input, must be a hdbc */
  SQLINTEGER *OutputHandle   /* pointer to 32-bit output, a hstmt */
  );
```

Job: Allocate a stmt.

Algorithm:

```
If (HandleType == SQL_HANDLE_STMT) {
      If InputHandle is not a valid hdbc:
        return error: CLI-specific condition-invalid handle
      The dbc's diagnostics area is emptied.
      If hdbc is not "connected":
        Set *OutputHandle = 0
        return error: 08003 connection exception-connection
        does not exist
      If maximum number of stmts has already been made:
        Set *OutputHandle = 0
        return error: CLI-specific condition-limit on number of
        handles exceeded
      If (dbc's connection is not the current connection)
        Change current connection = dbc's connection
      If (memory-allocation failure while trying to
          allocate the new stmt)
        Set *OutputHandle = 0
        return error: CLI-specific condition-memory allocation error
      Make four descs: an IPD, an IRD, an APD, an ARD.
      (The four descs have some pre-set values, described
       in Chapter 46.)
      Set *OutputHandle = handle of new stmt. }
```

Notes:

- You cannot allocate a stmt until you have allocated a dbc and connected (with SQLConnect).
- The handle of the new stmt is "unique," which means that there is no other stmt in the env with the same value. This uniqueness would not be guaranteed if there were two envs, but that's usually impossible anyway.

- The Standard calls it the "handle of the allocated SQL-statement," but in all our examples we name it a hstmt, which is the general fashion.
- Keep the hstmt. You'll need it later for SQLFreeHandle(SQL_HANDLE_STMT...) and for quite a few other things. In fact, the majority of CLI functions (42 of the 62) take a hstmt as input.

Example:

```
#include "sqlcli.h"
...
SQLHDBC     hdbc;
SQLHSTMT    hstmt;
...
sqlreturn = SQLAllocHandle(SQL_HANDLE_STMT,hdbc,&hstmt);
```

ODBC: The SQLAllocHandle function is new in ODBC 3.0.

SQLAllocStmt

Function Prototype:

```
SQLRETURN SQLAllocStmt(
  SQLHDBC hdbc,              /* 32-bit input, must be a hdbc */
  SQLHSTMT *hstmt            /* pointer to 32-bit output, a hstmt */
  );
```

Job: Make a new stmt.

Algorithm:

```
SQLRETURN = SQLAllocStmt(hdbc,&hstmt);
```

is the same as

```
SQLRETURN = SQLAllocHandle(SQL_HANDLE_STMT,hdbc,&hstmt);
```

Notes:

- The Standard does not deprecate SQLAllocStmt. All DBMSs should continue to support it. It is, however, redundant.

Example:

```
#include "sqlcli.h"
...
SQLHDBC     hdbc;
SQLHSTMT    hstmt;
...
SQLAllocStmt(hdbc,&hstmt);
...
```

ODBC: The SQLAllocStmt function has been in ODBC since version 1.0. The ODBC 3.0 manual deprecates it, suggesting that users should switch to using SQLAllocHandle(SQL_HANDLE_STMT...).

SQLGetStmtAttr

Function Prototype:

```
SQLRETURN SQLGetStmtAttr(
    SQLHSTMT hstmt,              /* 32-bit input -- statement handle */
    SQLINTEGER Attribute,        /* 32-bit input */
    SQLPOINTER Value,            /* pointer to ANY* output */
    SQLINTEGER BufferLength,     /* 32-bit input */
    SQLINTEGER *StringLength);   /* pointer to 32-bit output */
```

Job: Retrieve one attribute of a stmt.

Algorithm:

```
If (Attribute == SQL_ATTR_APP_ROW_DESC)
  Set *Value = (SQLHDESC) stmt's ARD handle.
If (Attribute == SQL_ATTR_APP_PARAM_DESC)
  Set *Value = (SQLHDESC) stmt's APD handle.
If (Attribute == SQL_ATTR_IMP_ROW_DESC)
  Set *Value = (SQLHDESC) stmt's IRD handle.
If (Attribute == SQL_ATTR_IMP_PARAM_DESC)
  Set *Value = (SQLHDESC) stmt's IPD handle.
If (Attribute == SQL_ATTR_CURSOR_SCROLLABLE)
  If (DBMS supports scrollable Cursors)
    Set *Value = "Cursor scrollable" attribute (0 or 1) (false or true)
  Else
```

```
    return error: HYC00 CLI-specific condition-optional feature
    not implemented
If (Attribute == SQL_ATTR_CURSOR_SENSITIVITY)
  If (implementation supports sensitive Cursors)
    Set *Value = "Cursor sensitivity" attribute (0 or 1 or 2)
  Else
    return error: HYC00 CLI-specific condition-optional feature
    not implemented
If (Attribute == SQL_ATTR_METADATA_ID)
  Set *Value = "metadata ID" attribute (0 or 1)
If (Attribute == SQL_ATTR_CURSOR_HOLDABLE)
  If (implementation supports holdable Cursors)
    Set *Value = "Cursor holdable" attribute (0 or 1)
  Else
    return error: HYC00 CLI-specific condition-optional feature
    not implemented
If (Attribute == none of the above)
  return error: HY092 CLI-specific condition-invalid attribute
  identifier
```

Notes:

- Here is a list of the standard stmt attributes:

Value	#define in SQLCLI.H	Settable?	Data type	Remarks
–3	SQL_ATTR_CURSOR_HOLDABLE	yes	SQLINTEGER	ANSI SQL3 only 0=nonholdable 1=holdable
–2	SQL_ATTR_CURSOR_SENSITIVITY	yes	SQLINTEGER	0=asensitive 1=insensitive 2=sensitive
–1	SQL_ATTR_CURSOR_SCROLLABLE	yes	SQLINTEGER	ANSI SQL3 only 0=nonscrollable 1=scrollable
10010	SQL_ATTR_APP_ROW_DESC	yes	SQLHDESC	ARD
10011	SQL_ATTR_APP_PARAM_DESC	yes	SQLHDESC	APD
10012	SQL_ATTR_IMP_ROW_DESC	no	SQLHDESC	IRD
10013	SQL_ATTR_IMP_PARAM_DESC	no	SQLHDESC	IPD
10014	SQL_ATTR_METADATA_ID	yes	SQLINTEGER	SQL3 only 0=false 1=true

Other stmt attributes may be defined in particular implementations. (Reminder: SQLHDESC stands for "handle of a desc," a 32-bit value.)

- When you allocate a stmt (with SQLAllocHandle or SQLAllocStmt), the DBMS automatically sets up four descs: the ARD, the APD, the IRD, and the IPD. You can pick up the handles of these descs by calling SQLGetStmtAttr with SQL_ATTR_APP_ROW_DESC, SQL_ATTR_APP_PARAM_DESC, SQL_ATTR_IMP_ROW_DESC, and SQL_ATTR_IMP_PARAM_DESC, respectively; you'll need these because there are several CLI functions which use a desc handle as input.
- When you get a result set (by calling SQLExecDirect or SQLExecute for a query expression such as, "SELECT ..."), the DBMS implicitly declares a Cursor. What kind of Cursor? That depends on the "cursor" attributes:
  - SQL_ATTR_CURSOR_SCROLLABLE
    If 0 = "false" = SQL_NONSCROLLABLE; you can only fetch NEXT.
    If 1 = "true" = SQL_SCROLLABLE; you can fetch FIRST, NEXT, PRIOR, LAST, ABSOLUTE, and RELATIVE.
    The default is 0 but you can call SQLSetStmtAttr to change that.
  - SQL_ATTR_CURSOR_SENSITIVITY
    If 0 = SQL_ASENSITIVE = SQL_UNSPECIFIED; sensitivity isn't known.
    If 1 = SQL_INSENSITIVE; changes made elsewhere won't be seen here.
    If 2 = SQL_SENSITIVE; changes made elsewhere will be seen here.
    The default is 0, but you can call SQLSetStmtAttr to change that.
  - SQL_ATTR_CURSOR_HOLDABLE
    If 0 = "false" = SQL_NONHOLDABLE; Cursor disappears at transaction end.
    If 1 = "true" = SQL_HOLDABLE; Cursor remains at transaction end.
    The default is probably 0 (you'd have to call SQLGetInfo to be certain) but you can call SQLSetStmtAttr to change that.
- When you use a Catalog function (such as SQLColumns or SQLTables), the DBMS has to search the "metadata," that is, the INFORMATION_SCHEMA Views. The SQL_ATTR_METADATA_ID attribute indicates how searches are conducted with Catalog functions. We discuss this in more detail in Chapter 51 "SQL/CLI: Catalog Functions."
- The BufferLength and StringLength parameters aren't currently in use. They're there in case we ever have a statement attribute that contains a string value.

Example:

```
#include "sqlcli.h"
HSTMT hstmt;
HDESC hipd;
...
SQLGetStmtAttr(
      hstmt,                      /* handle of stmt */
      SQL_ATTR_IMP_PARAM_DESC,    /* we want the IPD handle */
      &hipd,                      /* put the handle here */
      00,                         /* "don't care" */
      NULL);                      /* "don't care" */
```

ODBC: The SQLGetStmtAttr function is new in ODBC 3.0 (in ODBC 2.0 there was a nearly equivalent function, SQLGetStmtOption).

SQLSetStmtAttr

Function Prototype:

```
SQLRETURN SQLSetStmtAttr(
  SQLHSTMT hstmt,             /* 32-bit input - statement handle */
  SQLINTEGER Attribute,       /* 32-bit input */
  SQLPOINTER Value,           /* pointer to ANY* input */
  SQLINTEGER StringLength     /* 32-bit input */
  );
```

Job: Set an attribute of the stmt — to change the DBMS's behaviour for Cursor control, to change the handle used for an application desc, or to change the search method for Catalog functions.

There are eight standard stmt attributes, listed in the previous section.

Algorithm:

```
If (Attribute is not one of the settable attributes)
  return error: HY092 CLI-specific condition-invalid attribute
  identifier
If (Attribute = SQL_ATTR_APD_HANDLE)
  If (Value is not the handle of a desc)
    return error: HY024 CLI-specific condition-invalid attribute value
  If (desc's SQL_ALLOC_TYPE field = 'AUTOMATIC')
    If (desc is not stmt's default/automatic APD)
      return error: HY017 CLI-specific condition-invalid use of
      automatically-allocated descriptor handle.
   Desc becomes associated with this stmt, as its APD, non-exclusively.
If (Attribute = SQL_ATTR_ARD_HANDLE)
  If (Value is not the handle of a desc)
    return error: HY024 CLI-specific condition-invalid attribute value
  If (desc's ALLOC_TYPE field = 'AUTOMATIC')
    If (desc is not stmt's default/automatic ARD)
      return error: HY017 CLI-specific condition-invalid use of
      automatically-allocated descriptor handle.
   Desc becomes associated with this stmt, as its ARD, non-exclusively.
If (Attribute = SQL_ATTR_CURSOR_SCROLLABLE)
  If (the DBMS does not support scrollable Cursors)
```

```
      return error: HYC00 CLI-specific condition-optional feature
      not implemented
    If (stmt already has an open Cursor)
      /* You can't change how a Cursor works while the Cursor is open */
      return error: HY011 CLI-specific condition-attribute cannot be
      set now
    If (Value is not SQL_SCROLLABLE (1) or SQL_NONSCROLLABLE (0))
      return error: HY011 CLI-specific condition-attribute cannot be
      set now
    Stmt's Cursor's "scrollable" attribute = Value.
  If (Attribute == SQL_ATTR_CURSOR_SENSITIVITY)
    If (the DBMS does not support sensitive Cursors)
      return error: HYC00 CLI-specific condition-optional feature
      not implemented
    If (there is already an open Cursor for stmt)
      return error: HY011 CLI-specific condition-attribute cannot be
      set now
    If (Value is not SQL_SENSITIVE (2) or SQL_INSENSITIVE (1)
        or UNSPECIFIED (0))
      return error: HY024 CLI-specific condition-invalid attribute value
    Stmt's Cursor's "sensitivity" attribute = Value.
  If (Attribute == SQL_ATTR_METADATA_ID)
    If (Value not TRUE or FALSE)
      return error: HY024 CLI-specific condition-invalid attribute value
    Set stmt's "metadata id" attribute = Value.
  If (Attribute == SQL_ATTR_CURSOR_HOLDABLE)
    If (the DBMS does not support holdable Cursors)
      return error: HYC00 CLI-specific condition-optional feature
      not implemented
    If (stmt already has an open Cursor)
      return error: HY011 CLI-specific condition-attribute cannot be
      set now
    If (Value is not SQL_HOLDABLE (1) or SQL_NONHOLDABLE (0))
      return error: HY024 CLI-specific condition-invalid attribute value
    Set stmt's Cursor's "holdable" attribute = Value.
```

Notes:

- The specification allows for implementation-defined attributes and for the possibility of future change. That's why the `StringLength` parameter exists, although it's not currently used.
- `SQL_ATTR_APP_ROW_DESC` and `SQL_ATTR_APP_PARAM_DESC` are listed as settable attributes, so you can change the `stmt`'s ARD and APD. (You can't change the `stmt`'s IRD and IPD.) The

Value parameter must point to the handle of a user desc. This option makes it possible to save or share application descs.

- SQL_ATTR_CURSOR_SCROLLABLE and SQL_ATTR_CURSOR_HOLDABLE are used to specify whether a stmt's Cursor is "scrollable" and/or "holdable."
- SQL_ATTR_METADATA_ID is an abbreviation for "the attribute for metadata identifiers," e.g., the names of Tables in INFORMATION_SCHEMA.
- For the third parameter, Value, you may have to pass (void*)hdesc, i.e., handle of a desc which has been cast to a pointer. That's because our C prototype is SQLPOINTER. The Standard merely says that this is an ANY parameter — that is, it could be any type.

Example: Change the settings of all settable stmt attributes. This example only shows what the syntax looks like for the various options. More realistic examples will appear in Chapters 45, "SQL/CLI: Cursor Functions," 46 "SQL/CLI: desc Functions," and 51 "SQL/CLI: Catalog Functions."

```
#include "sqlcli.h"
SQLHSTMT hstmt;
SQLHDESC hdesc1,hdesc2;
SQLINTEGER scrollable = SQL_SCROLLABLE;
SQLINTEGER sensitivity = SQL_INSENSITIVE;
SQLINTEGER metadata_id = SQL_FALSE;
SQLINTEGER holdable = SQL_NONHOLDABLE;
...
SQLSetStmtAttr(hstmt,SQL_ATTR_APP_ROW_DESC,hdesc1,00);
SQLSetStmtAttr(hstmt,SQL_ATTR_APP_PARAM_DESC,hdesc2,00);
SQLSetStmtAttr(hstmt,SQL_ATTR_CURSOR_SCROLLABLE,scrollable,00);
SQLSetStmtAttr(hstmt,SQL_ATTR_CURSOR_SENSITIVITY,sensitivity,00);
SQLSetStmtAttr(hstmt,SQL_ATTR_METADATA_ID,metadata_id,00);
SQLSetStmtAttr(hstmt,SQL_ATTR_CURSOR_HOLDABLE,holdable,00);
```

ODBC: The SQLSetStmtAttr function is new in ODBC 3.0 but there was a similar function in ODBC 2.0 (SQLSetStmtOption).

SQLFreeHandle(SQL_HANDLE_STMT,...)

Function Prototype:

```
SQLRETURN SQLFreeHandle(     /* function returns SMALLINT */
    SQLSMALLINT HandleType,  /* 16-bit input, = SQL_HANDLE_STMT */
    SQLINTEGER Handle        /* 32-bit input, must be a hstmt */
    );
```

Job: Destroy a stmt.

Algorithm:

```
If (HandleType == SQL_HANDLE_STMT)
  If (Handle is not a hstmt)
    return error: CLI-specific condition-invalid handle
  Empty the stmt's diagnostics area.
  The stmt's dbc becomes the "current dbc."
  If (there is a deferred parameter associated with stmt)
    return error: HY010 CLI-specific condition-function sequence error
  If (there is an open Cursor associated with the stmt)
    Throw away all information about the Cursor's result set
     Close the Cursor
  Deallocate the stmt's four automatic descs: ARD, APD, IRD, IPD.
  Deallocate stmt.
```

Notes:

- Correctly speaking, this function "frees the stmt"; it doesn't merely free the stmt's handle.
- The DBMS calls SQLFreeHandle(SQL_HANDLE_STMT...) implicitly, for all stmts in a dbc, as part of an SQLDisconnect operation.
- There is a mention here of a "current" dbc. If there are multiple dbcs, the DBMS will implicitly switch when necessary to the dbc whose handle is passed in the function call (or, as in this case, to the dbc associated with the stmt whose handle is passed in the function call). This switching is transparent. There is no need, when using the CLI, for any analogue of the basic SQL "SET CONNECTION ..." statement.
- Freeing a stmt causes an implicit "close Cursor" operation, but not an implicit "end transaction" operation.
- Quite often, programmers allocate a stmt only once and re-use the same stmt throughout the SQL-session. So SQLFreeHandle(SQL_HANDLE_STMT...) may be seen only infrequently.

Example:

```
#include "sqlcli.h"
SQLHDBC     hdbc;
SQLHSTMT    hstmt;
...
SQLAllocHandle(SQL_HANDLE_STMT,hdbc,&hstmt);
...
SQLFreeHandle(SQL_HANDLE_STMT,hstmt);
```

ODBC: The SQLFreeHandle function is new in ODBC 3.0.

SQLFreeStmt

Function Prototype:

```
SQLRETURN SQLFreeStmt(
  SQLHSTMT hstmt,              /* 32-bit input */
  SQLSMALLINT Option;          /* 16-bit input */
  );
```

Job: SQLFreeStmt has five different jobs, depending on the value of Option:

- If Option is 0, SQLFreeStmt's job is to close a Cursor.
- If Option is 1, SQLFreeStmt's job is to destroy a stmt.
- If Option is 2, SQLFreeStmt's job is to unbind Columns.
- If Option is 3, SQLFreeStmt's job is to unbind parameters.
- If Option is 4, SQLFreeStmt's job is to reallocate.

Algorithm:

```
If (Option == SQL_CLOSE (0))
  If (there is a Cursor)
    Cancel all information about the result set.
    Close the Cursor.
If (Option == SQL_DROP (1))
  /* SQLFreeStmt(...,SQL_DROP) is the reverse of SQLAllocStmt(...). */
  sqlreturn = SQLFreeStmt(hstmt,SQL_DROP);
  is the same as:
  sqlreturn = SQLFreeHandle(SQL_HANDLE_STMT,hstmt);
If (Option == SQL_UNBIND (2))
  /* This affects the application row descriptor (ARD). In
     effect, it cancels out any SQLBindCol calls made on stmt. */
  For (i=1; i<=ARD.SQL_DESC_COUNT;++i)
    Set ARD.IDA[i].SQL_DESC_DATA_POINTER = 0
If (Option == SQL_RESET_PARAMS (3))
  /* This affects the application parameter descriptor (APD). In
     effect, it cancels out any SQLBindParameter calls made on stmt. */
  For (i=1; i<=APD.SQL_DESC_COUNT;++i)
    Set APD.IDA[i].SQL_DESC_DATA_POINTER = 0
If (Option == SQL_REALLOCATE (4))
  Destroy the stmt's statement and Cursor parts
If (Option == none of the above)
  return error: HY092 CLI-specific condition-invalid attribute
  identifier
```

Notes:

- Regrettably, we are forced to mention a few details before their time for full discussion is come. For the immediate purpose, we hope it is enough to say that:
  - *Result sets* are temporary Tables which result from the execution of an SQL query.
  - *Cursors* are named interface objects through which result sets can be retrieved one row at a time.
  - *Bindings* are associations between a host program's host variables (i.e., pointers to data buffers and indicator variables) and their corresponding SQL Objects (Columns and/or parameter markers). Often Columns are bound with the `SQLBindCol` function while parameters are bound with the `SQLBindParameter` function.
- Because `SQLFreeHandle` is now the main function for freeing resources, the name `SQLFreeStmt` is now a misnomer — we don't use `SQLFreeStmt` for freeing `stmts` nowadays. However, it maintains a residue of usefulness. It's good for "partial `stmt` freeing"; freeing things associated with `stmts` that might be taking up space or whose continued existence might cause conflict with other operations.
- `SQLFreeStmt(...,SQL_CLOSE)` does exactly the same thing as the `SQLCloseCursor` function, except for one detail; if there is no Cursor currently open, then `SQLCloseCursor` returns an error, while `SQLFreeStmt(...,SQL_CLOSE)` does not return an error.
- `SQLFreeStmt(hstmt,SQL_DROP)` is now just another way of saying `SQLFreeHandle(SQL_HANDLE_STMT,hstmt)`.
- `SQLFreeStmt(...,SQL_UNBIND)` and `SQLFreeStmt(...,SQL_RESET_PARAMS)` are handy ways of "disassociating" the application's RAM from the DBMS, so that there won't be inadvertent access to memory that's no longer valid. Here's an example:

```
x=malloc(1024);                                  /* malloc an area */
SQLBindCol(...,x,...);          /* Add binding to the malloc'd area */
free(x);                      /* uh oh. x is no longer a valid pointer */
SQLFreeStmt(...,UNBIND Columns);           /* Chances of GPF reduced */
```

  However, only the "data pointer" field is cleared — not the "indicator pointer" field (this is probably an inadvertent omission from the Standard).
- `SQLFreeStmt(...,SQL_REALLOCATE)` can be used to clear parts of `stmts`:
  - The "statement" (a copy of the SQL statement string last prepared or executed for this `stmt`, including "select" source statements).
  - The "Cursor," including the Cursor's result set. These things take up space, so presumably `SQLFreeStmt(...,SQL_REALLOCATE)` is useful under low-memory conditions. But normally it's unnecessary — "statement" and "Cursor" are superseded in any case when an SQL statement is re-prepared/re-executed.

Example: Because SQLFreeStmt(...,SQL_DROP) is the reverse of SQLAllocStmt(...), we show both these obsolescent calls together.

```
#include "sqlcli.h"
SQLHDBC hdbc;
SQLHSTMT hstmt;
...
SQLAllocStmt(hdbc,&hstmt);          /* allocate a stmt */
SQLBindCol(hstmt,...);              /* bind a stmt Column */
SQLFreeStmt(hstmt,SQL_UNBIND);      /* unbind all stmt Columns */
...
SQLFreeStmt(hstmt,SQL_DROP);        /* free a stmt */
```

ODBC: The SQLFreeStmt function has been in ODBC since version 1.0. The ODBC 3.0 manual deprecates the use of SQLFreeStmt(...,SQL_DROP), suggesting that the user should switch to using SQLFreeHandle(SQL_HANDLE_STMT,...). The ODBC action for SQL_UNBIND is different; ARD.SQL_DESC_COUNT is set to 0. The ODBC action for SQL_RESET_PARAMS is different; APD.SQL_DESC_COUNT is set to 0. The SQL_REALLOCATE option is not supported.

And that's it for the stmt functions. In the next chapter, we'll take a look at the statement functions.

44

Chapter 44

SQL/CLI Statement Functions

Of the 62 CLI functions, only three actually handle what we know as "SQL statements." There are two steps in SQL statement handling: the "prepare" step and the "execute" step. You can do these steps separately, using the `SQLPrepare` and `SQLExecute` functions or you can roll them together and just use the `SQLExecDirect` function. The following flowchart shows the steps involved:

```
[[ SQL statement ]]
|
|       -
>    -    -
  -         -                 ---------------
 -   Is the   -               -               -
- statement  -  ---> no ---> - Return error  -
 -   valid?   -               - diagnostics   -
   -        -                 -               -
     -    -                   ---------------
       -
     |                                  PREPARE PHASE
     v
```

```
     yes
      |
      v
-----------------------------
- Make “Prepared statement” -
- associated with stmt      -
-----------------------------
    |
    v
------------------------------
- Execute prepared statement -        EXECUTE PHASE
------------------------------
    |
    v
      -
    -   -
  -       -
 -  Is the  -               --------
- statement - ---> no ---> - done -
 - a query? -               --------
  -       -
    -   -
      -
     |
     v
    yes
     |
     v
------------------------------------
- associate Cursor with result set -
------------------------------------
     |
     v
--------
- done -
--------
```

Preparable SQL Statements

Some SQL statements are not preparable. Here's the list of all possibilities showing whether the SQL statement can be prepared.

SQL STATEMENT	SQL STATEMENT CLASS	PREPARABLE?
ALTER	Schema	yes
CALL	control	yes
CLOSE	data	NO
COMMIT	transaction	NO [Note 2]
CONNECT	Connection	NO [Note 1]
CREATE	Schema	yes
DELETE	data change	yes
DISCONNECT	Connection	NO [Note 1]
DROP	Schema	yes
FETCH	data	NO
GET DIAGNOSTICS	diagnostics	NO
GRANT	Schema	yes
INSERT	data change	yes
OPEN	data	NO
RELEASE SAVEPOINT	transaction	NO [Note 2]
RETURN	control	yes
REVOKE	Schema	yes
ROLLBACK	transaction	NO [Note 2]
SAVEPOINT	transaction	NO [Note 2]
SELECT with no INTO	query	yes
SELECT with INTO	query	NO
SET CONNECTION	Connection	NO [Note 1]
SET CONSTRAINTS MODE	transaction	yes
SET LOCAL TIME ZONE	SQL-session	yes
SET ROLE	SQL-session	yes
SET SESSION	SQL-session	yes
SET TRANSACTION	transaction	yes
START TRANSACTION	transaction	yes
UPDATE	data change	yes

Notes: The "preparable statements" for embedded SQL are as above, except:

- [Note 1] Connection statements are "directly executable" with embedded SQL, but not preparable.
- [Note 2] COMMIT, ROLLBACK, RELEASE SAVEPOINT, and SAVEPOINT are "preparable" with embedded SQL.

There are some SQL statements which you may use in other contexts (such as embedded SQL or SQL/PSM), but their use is inappropriate with the CLI because their functionality is included in special function calls which require a henv or hdbc as the input handle — and the SQLPrepare function requires a hstmt. For such SQL statements, there will usually be an analogous CLI function. For example, CONNECT and DISCONNECT statements are not preparable, but there are SQLConnect and SQLDisconnect functions; GET DIAGNOSTICS is not preparable but there are SQLGetDiag... functions; COMMIT and ROLLBACK are not preparable but there is an SQLEndTran ("end transaction") function.

SQLPrepare

Function Prototype:

```
SQLRETURN SQLPrepare(
  SQLHSTMT hstmt,          /* 32-bit input */
  SQLCHAR *StatementText, /* pointer to CHAR* input = SQL statement */
  SQLINTEGER TextLength    /* 32-bit input */
  );
```

Job: Check an SQL statement for syntax or access errors. If all is well, make this string the "prepared SQL statement" associated with stmt. It is then ready to execute.

Algorithm:

```
If (there is an open Cursor associated with stmt)
  /* You must close Cursor before re-using the stmt */
  return error: 24000 - invalid Cursor state -
Get the string using StatementText and TextLength. This is a typical example of
a pass of a character string, except that TextLength is an integer rather than
a smallint. TextLength may be SQL_NTS.
If the TextLength value doesn't make sense:
  return error: HY090 CLI-specific condition-invalid string length
  or buffer length
If (the string contains "DELETE|UPDATE ... WHERE CURRENT OF ...")
  If (Cursor is not the name of a Cursor associated with another
      stmt of the same dbc)
    return error: 34000 invalid Cursor name
  /* Note the word "another" -- don't use positioned UPDATE|DELETE with
  the same stmt you executed the SELECT with */
```

```
If (statement violates a format rule, syntax rule, or access rule)
Or (statement is not a preparable statement)
Or (statement is a <simple comment>)
Or (statement has a ? parameter marker in an invalid position)
  return error: (exact error depends on the nature of the violation)
                (often 42000 Syntax error or access rule violation)
Determine the data types of the ? parameter markers.
/* An example of a ? in an invalid position is: SELECT -? FROM t; */
Destroy some things which are associated with stmt, left over from
the last time we called SQLPrepare for the same stmt:
     -- the "prepared statement", and
     -- the "Cursor" (if any).
/* Leftovers exist because stmts are re-usable objects. */
Note: destroying a Cursor can have a cascading effect: if there is
another prepared statement that references that Cursor (e.g. DELETE
FROM t WHERE CURRENT OF <Cursor name>), it too is destroyed.
Note: destroying a Cursor does not imply destroying the Cursor name.
Now we have "prepared." The statement is called a "prepared statement."
If (prepared statement is a SELECT)
 /* The prepared SELECT statement is called the "select source." */
 If (there is no Cursor name) (as set by SQLSetCursorName)
   Set Cursor name = an implementation-dependent identifier beginning
   with the letters SQL_CUR or SQLCUR.
```

Notes:

- You can process SQL statements in two separate phases using the `SQLPrepare` and `SQLExecute` functions. Usually, you would want to do the two phases separately if the SQL statement appeared in a loop — you'd call `SQLPrepare` before entering the loop and you'd call `SQLExecute` within the loop. That way, you'd only be preparing once but executing many times. If you used the alternative — `SQLExecDirect` — you'd be preparing and executing with every iteration of the loop.
- The prepare and execute phases of SQL resemble the compile and execute phases of most computer languages. If we were going to make a distinction between preparing and compiling, we would point out that: (*a*) preparing fails if an SQL statement refers to an inaccessible Table, but compiling does not fail if a file is unavailable at compile time; and (*b*) compiling results in executable code, but preparing results only in a descriptive "plan" which needs some interpretation at run time. Such, at least, is the state of SQL today. There are no true SQL compilers.

- If SQLPrepare finds an error, the stmt's state is unchanged. An SQL statement that was previously prepared continues to be "live." For example:

```
SQLPrepare(hstmt,"UPDATE t SET t_column = t_column + 1",SQL_NTS);
SQLExecute(hstmt);
SQLPrepare(hstmt,"SELCT * FROM t",SQL_NTS);     /* sic-"SELCT" */
SQLExecute(hstmt);
```

  The second SQLPrepare won't work because "SELCT" is bad SQL syntax — but what happens to the SQLExecute that follows it? Answer: it executes the "UPDATE t ..." statement a second time. Silly, eh? Well it wouldn't happen if we had made sure to check what the SQLPrepare call returned.
- Some DBMSs do nothing during SQLPrepare. They defer even syntax checking until SQLExecute time. You have to be ready for such non-standard behaviour; do not assume that an SQL statement is grammatical until it's been executed.
- There is no "UnPrepare" function. Instead, prepared statements are removed by:
  - Calling SQLPrepare again for the same stmt.
  - Calling SQLFreeStmt(...,SQL_REALLOCATE).
  - Cascade effects — for example, if the prepared statement depends on a Cursor which is destroyed.
  - (Usually) calling SQLEndTran, the "transaction-end" function which is used instead of COMMIT or ROLLBACK. It is best to assume that SQL statements need re-preparing after transaction end, though some DBMSs preserve prepared statements. You can find out what your DBMS does by calling the SQLGetInfo function. (In any case, if a Cursor is holdable, its result set survives if the termination is with COMMIT.)
- In standard SQL, the SQL statement does not have to end with a semicolon.

Example:

```
#include "sqlcli.h"
SQLHSTMT hstmt;
...
SQLPrepare(hstmt,"DELETE FROM t",SQL_NTS);
                                   /* Now we need to call SQLExecute. */
```

ODBC: The SQLPrepare function has been part of ODBC since ODBC version 1.0.

SQLExecute

Function Prototype:

```
SQLRETURN SQLExecute(
  SQLHSTMT hstmt                          /* 32-bit input */
  );
```

Job: Execute a prepared SQL statement. You must do an SQLPrepare first.

Algorithm:

```
If (SQLPrepare has not been performed for this stmt)
  return error: HY010 CLI-specific condition-function sequence error
If (there is an open Cursor associated with this stmt)
  /* This would happen if you don't close the Cursor after the last
     execution of a SELECT statement; see SQLCloseCursor */
  return error: 24000 Invalid Cursor state -
If (there are input parameters)
  Get parameter addresses and do appropriate "casting" (described in
  our chapter on SQL/CLI desc functions)
Execute the prepared statement. It is now the "executed statement."
If (the statement was SELECT)
  Set up a Cursor (described in our chapter on SQL/CLI Cursor
  functions)
  Change the row descriptors (described in our chapter on SQL/CLI
  desc functions)
If (there are output parameters)
  Get parameter addresses and do appropriate "casting"
Change the Diagnostics Area
```

Because there are many possible SQL statements, the range of possible problem conditions is wide — see especially the SQLSTATE errors in class 22000 (data exception) and class 23000 (integrity constraint violation) in Chapter 47 "SQL/CLI: Diagnostic Functions." Watch also for warnings and even "No data" conditions (for example, execution of UPDATE Table_1 SET column_1 = 0; will result in SQLSTATE 02000 "Data not found" if there are no rows in TABLE_1).

Notes:

- Calls to SQLExecute always follow calls to SQLPrepare (for the same stmt), but other function calls may intervene.

Example: In this example we prepare and execute two SQL statements. We use two different stmts, so that we can get all the preparing done before we start executing.

```
#include "sqlcli.h"
...
SQLHSTMT hstmt1, hstmt2;
...
SQLPrepare(hstmt1,"INSERT INTO t VALUES (1)",SQL_NTS);
SQLPrepare(hstmt2,"INSERT INTO t VALUES (2)",SQL_NTS);
...
SQLExecute(hstmt1);
SQLExecute(hstmt2);
```

ODBC: The SQLExecute function has been around since ODBC 1.0.

SQLExecDirect

Function Prototype:

```
SQLRETURN  SQLExecDirect(
  SQLHSTMT hstmt,             /* 32-bit input -- statement handle */
  SQLCHAR *StatementText,     /* CHAR* input */
  SQLINTEGER TextLength       /* 32-bit input */
  );
```

Job: Prepare and execute an SQL statement.

Algorithm:

```
SQLRETURN = SQLExecDirect(hstmt,"text",text-length);
```

is the same as

```
SQLRETURN = SQLPrepare(hstmt,"text",text-length);
if (sqlreturn <> SQL_ERROR && sqlreturn <> SQL_INVALID_HANDLE) {
   sqlreturn = SQLExecute(hstmt); }
```

Notes:

- Technically, SQLExecDirect is redundant: you can do the same thing by calling SQLPrepare and SQLExecute. But programmers prefer to use SQLExecDirect for SQL statements that will only be prepared and executed once.
- Because SQLExecDirect includes a "prepare" step, it follows that non-preparable SQL statements cannot be arguments of SQLExecDirect. Such statements include CONNECT, DISCONNECT, COMMIT, ROLLBACK — refer to the table of preparable and non-preparable SQL statements on page 795.
- Does the size of a string include the null terminator?
  - If you are passing a string's octet length: No. For example:

```
SQLExecDirect(hstmt,"abcd",4);
```

  - If you are passing (maximum) target octet length: Yes. For example:

```
char x[8];
...
SQLGetCursorName(hstmt,x,8,&strlen_or_ind);
```

  - If the DBMS is returning the (actual) target octet length: No. Using the previous example, if a null-terminated string "abcd\0" is returned, then strlen_or_ind will equal 4.
  - If the string is a BIT or BINARY string: No.

Example: Take a value at run time, incorporate it in an SQL statement. This is how you can pass a parameter value without using a `desc` function.

```
#include "sqlcli.h"
...
void measurement_update (float measurement, SQLHSTMT hstmt)
{
  int len;
  SQLCHAR statement[50];
  len = sprintf(statement, "UPDATE t SET measurement = %f",
                measurement);
  SQLExecDirect(hstmt, update_statement, len); }
```

CHAP44_1.C; Basic "Interactive SQL" Program: If you want to put together a program that accepts SQL statements from the keyboard and displays results on the screen, this is the skeletal arrangement:

```
#include "sqlcli.h"
...
SQLAllocHandle(); SQLAllocHandle(); SQLConnect(); SQLAllocHandle();
...
for (;;)
  printf("Type in an SQL statement, 0 user: \n");
  gets(user_statement);
  if (SQLExecDirect(StatementHandle,user_statement,SQL_NTS)>=0) {
    printf("OK\n"); }
  else {
    printf("Error\n"); }
...
SQLFreeHandle(); SQLDisconnect(); SQLFreeHandle(); SQLFreeHandle();
```

In this code, notice how `SQLExecDirect` is fundamental — it's the only CLI function that must be called for every iteration of the loop. In later examples, we'll show you other things that are necessary here (e.g., how to exit from the loop, what to do with errors, and how queries need special handling).

ODBC: The `SQLExecDirect` function has been around since ODBC 1.0.

SQLEndTran

Function Prototype:

```
SQLRETURN SQLEndTran(
  SQLSMALLINT HandleType,         /* 16-bit input */
  SQLINTEGER Handle,              /* 32-bit input */
  SQLSMALLINT CompletionType      /* 16-bit input */
  );
```

Job: End a transaction, either with `COMMIT` or with `ROLLBACK`. `SQLEndTran` is not a "statement" function but we believe that it fits in this chapter because it's used to `COMMIT` or `ROLLBACK` the results of SQL statements that have been processed with `SQLExecute` or `SQLExecDirect`.

Algorithm:

```
If (HandleType is not one of: SQL_HANDLE_ENV, SQL_HANDLE_DBC,
    SQL_HANDLE_STMT)
  return error: CLI-specific condition-invalid handle
If (HandleType == SQL_HANDLE_STMT)
  If (Handle is not a hstmt)
    return error: CLI-specific condition-invalid handle
  return error: HY092 CLI-specific condition-invalid attribute
  identifier
     The COMMIT/ROLLBACK will be done for the dbc associated with
     this stmt
If (HandleType == SQL_HANDLE_DBC)
  If (Handle is not a hdbc)
     return error: CLI-specific condition-invalid handle
  return error: HY092 CLI-specific condition-invalid attribute
  identifier
  The dbc's diagnostics area is emptied.
     The COMMIT/ROLLBACK will be done for the specified dbc
If (HandleType == SQL_HANDLE_DESC)
  If (Handle is not a hdesc)
           return error: CLI-specific condition-invalid handle
  return error: HY092 CLI-specific condition-invalid attribute identifier
     The COMMIT/ROLLBACK will be done for the dbc associated with
     this desc
If (HandleType == SQL_HANDLE_ENV)
  If (Handle is not a henv, or env is a skeleton env)
```

```
    return error: HY092 CLI-specific condition-invalid attribute
    identifier
     The COMMIT/ROLLBACK will be done for all dbcs associated with
     this env
If (CompletionType is not either COMMIT (0) or ROLLBACK (1))
  return error: HY012 CLI-specific condition-invalid transaction
  operation code
If (the current transaction is part of an encompassing transaction)
  If (transaction control is not controlled by this DBMS alone)
    return error: 2D000 Invalid transaction termination -
/* The rest of the algorithm might iterate several times if the
   Handle is a henv, and there are multiple active dbcs */
For (each stmt in the dbc)
  If (a deferred parameter number is associated with the stmt)
    return error: HY010 CLI-specific condition-function sequence error
For each stmt in the dbc:
  If (there is a non-holdable Cursor associated with the stmt)
    Close the Cursor and destroy its copy of the select source
    Remove any associated fetched row
If (CompletionType == SQL_COMMIT (0))
  Commit.
  /* The usual "commit" operations happen, as described in the
     Transactions chapter. For example: if a temporary Table was
     created with the ON COMMIT DELETE [ROWS] option, all its rows
     are deleted. Warning: checking of deferred Constraints might
     result in: 40002 Transaction rollback-integrity constraint
     violation */
  If (any other error prevents commitment now)
    /* For example, writing to disk causes a "disk full" error */
    return error: 40??? Transaction rollback-implementation-defined
    subclass value
If (CompletionType == SQL_ROLLBACK)
  Rollback.
  /* The usual "rollback" operations happen, as described in the
     Transactions chapter. */
The transaction is now terminated.
```

Notes:

- See the SQLSTATE error codes HY010, HY092, and 40002 in Chapter 47 "SQL/CLI: Diagnostic Functions." Pay particular attention to 40002, which implies that ROLLBACK occurred when you asked for COMMIT.

- Because COMMIT and ROLLBACK are non-preparable SQL statements, the correct way to end a transaction is to call SQLEndTran. Some DBMSs accept SQLExecDirect(hstmt,"COMMIT",SQL_NTS); anyway, but it's not legal according to the SQL Standard and you can't be sure exactly what will happen. In the final version of SQL/CLI, there will be more options — for rollback-to-savepoint and release-savepoint.
- There is no point in passing a hstmt or a hdesc to SQLEndTran — you just get an error message. These enhancements have been suggested and may be implemented somewhere: (*a*) if you pass a hstmt, COMMIT/ROLLBACK will occur for the dbc associated with the stmt; (*b*) if you pass a hdesc, COMMIT/ROLLBACK will occur for the dbc associated with the desc.
- When there is only one env and one dbc, the convention is to use the henv for this function:

```
SQLEndTran(SQL_HANDLE_ENV,henv,SQL_COMMIT);
```

- Look again at Chapter 36 "SQL Transactions" before you try to use SQLEndTran.

Example:

```
#include "sqlcli.h"
SQLHDBC hdbc;
SQLHSTMT hstmt;
...
SQLAllocHandle(SQL_HANDLE_STMT,hdbc,&hstmt);
/* Do an SQL statement using a stmt associated with dbc */
SQLExecDirect(hstmt,"INSERT INTO t1 SELECT * FROM t2",SQL_NTS);
/* Commit the statement results using the dbc */
SQLEndTran(SQL_HANDLE_DBC,hdbc,SQL_COMMIT);
```

ODBC: The SQLEndTran function was added in ODBC 3.0, but there was a nearly-equivalent function in ODBC 2.0 (SQLTransact). With ODBC, if the HandleType value is not SQL_HANDLE_ENV or SQL_HANDLE_DBC, the return is HY092 (invalid attribute/option identifier), rather than "invalid handle".

With ODBC, the default behaviour is "autocommit" (i.e., perform an automatic "commit" after every SQL statement), so SQLEndTran has nothing to do. *This is a major difference between ODBC and Standard SQL*. The suggested way to resolve it is to call an ODBC function which turns the "autocommit" flag off:

```
SQLSetConnectAttr(hdbc,SQL_ATTR_AUTOCOMMIT,(void*)SQL_AUTOCOMMIT_OFF,0);
```

And that's it for the statement functions. In the next chapter, we'll take a look at the Cursor functions.

45

Chapter 45

SQL/CLI: Cursor Functions

When you execute a query, you are implicitly opening a Cursor. For example, the function call:

```
SQLExecDirect(hstmt,"SELECT * FROM Table_1",SQL_NTS);
```

will open a Cursor.

The reason for Cursors is that a query returns a set of rows — a "result set," as it's usually referred to in CLI contexts. But it is not possible for the host language to deal with the whole result set at once — it must deal with one row at a time. The Cursor is the Object that indicates which row of the result set you're currently dealing with.

Cursor movement is just part of the story: "Get the stick, Rover," coos the hopeful master. Rover charges off, picks up the stick, and sits down. "No, I mean get the stick and *fetch it to me*!" addends the master. So Rover trots dutifully back to his caller and sits down again — still holding the stick in his teeth. "!@###~$!!," yells the master (we've amended the wording slightly as this is a family computer book). "I wanted you to get the stick, then fetch it, then *put it in my hands*!"

Well, you know, Rover is a lot like our faithful pal SQL. The execution of an SQL query (the subject of the last chapter) is analogous to a dog picking up a stick. Now, in this chapter, we've reached step 2 — fetch the stick. And — like Rover — that's as far as we go. Step 3, delivering the fetched stuff into your hands, must wait until you have a thorough grounding in the `desc` functions. So this chapter is short. The only thing we'll worry about now is the mechanics of opening, closing, fetching, and naming Cursors. The fun part — doing something with the contents — will come later.

The following diagram shows a result set; the result of an execution of a query statement which has returned three rows. The Cursor is represented by the symbol <<<. The diagram shows where the Cursor is (*a*) after the execution, (*b*) after one fetch, (*c*) after another fetch, (*d*) after another fetch, and (*e*) after another fetch.

(a)	*(b)*	*(c)*	*(d)*	*(e)*
<<<				
Row #1	Row #1 <<<	Row #1	Row #1	Row #1
Row #2	Row #2	Row #2 <<<	Row #2	Row #2
Row #3	Row #3	Row #3	Row #3 <<<	Row #3
				<<<

Notice that there are five possible positions of the Cursor because it is possible to be "before the first row" or "after the last row," as well as "on each row."

There are six CLI functions for creating Cursors, dropping Cursors, getting Cursor attributes, and fetching from Cursors. Their descriptions follow.

SQLFetch

Function Prototype:

```
SQLRETURN SQLFetch (
  SQLHSTMT hstmt                  /* input: 32-bit handle */
  );
```

Job: Get the next row of a Cursor's result set. (Assumption: using `hstmt`, you've already run a query which returned a result set.)

You can use `SQLFetch` for one-row-at-a-time processing of a result set. `SQLFetch` is appropriate for sequential processing because it always gets the "next" row. For random-access processing, use a different function — `SQLFetchScroll`.

Algorithm:

```
If (there is no executed statement for hstmt)
  return error: HY010 CLI-specific condition-function sequence error
If (there is no open Cursor)
  return error: 24000 Invalid Cursor state -
If (Cursor position is not already after the last row)
  Set Cursor position = next Cursor position, i.e. go forward
If (Cursor position is now after the last row)
  Return with: 02000 "Data Not found-No data"
Transfer the values in the select list to bound Columns, if any.
(Column-binding and transfer is the subject of the CLI desc chapter.)
```

For common errors, see our descriptions of `SQLSTATE` codes `HY010`, `24000`, and `02000` in Chapter 47 "SQL/CLI: Diagnostic Functions." Note that `SQLSTATE 02000` is not an exception condition — it is a completion condition. There are also possible errors — data exceptions — which can take place during transfers. There are also possible warnings, such as 01004 "string data right truncation."

Notes:

- SQLFetch only works if there is an open Cursor. A Cursor is automatically opened as a result of executing an SQL query statement. A Cursor can be explicitly closed using the CLI function SQLCloseCursor. Usually, though, a Cursor is closed as a result of calling the CLI function SQLEndTran.
- There is no such Cursor position as "two places after the last row." A Cursor which is "after the last row" does not move.

Example: Here's a fetch loop example:

```
#include "sqlcli.h"
...
SQLHSTMT  hstmt;
...
SQLExecDirect(hstmt,"SELECT * FROM Employees ORDER BY dept",SQL_NTS);
for (;;) {
  sqlreturn = SQLFetch(hstmt);
  if (sqlreturn <> SQL_SUCCESS && sqlreturn <> SQL_SUCCESS_WITH_INFO) {
    if (sqlreturn == SQL_NO_DATA) break;
    printf("Error!\n");
    break; }
  printf("*\n"); }
SQLCloseCursor(hstmt);       /* "Close Cursor" -- more details soon. */
...
```

Here's another example, functionally the same as the previous one, but the style is different — using names, macros, and indentation à la Microsoft:

```
#include "sql.h"             // "sqlcli.h" equivalent supplied with ODBC
SQLRETURN   rc;              // rc is an abbreviation for return code
#define SQL_SUCCEEDED(rc) (rc == SQL_SUCCESS ||
                           rc == SQL_SUCCESS_WITH_INFO)
/* sqlcli.h has this instead:
   #define SQL_SUCCEEDED(rc) (((rc)&(~1))==0) */
...
rc = SQLFetch(hstmt0);
while (SQL_SUCCEEDED(rc)) {
   ... rc = SQLFetch(hstmt0);
} // while
```

ODBC: All versions of ODBC support the SQLFetch function as described here, but ODBC version 3.0 has an optional feature; you can fetch multiple rows with one call. Logically, such a feature is unnecessary and it makes applications more complex. We assume Microsoft added the feature for performance reasons.

Fetch Loops

When dealing with a result set, the procedure is almost always to:

- make a result set, and
- begin a loop which calls SQLFetch for each row; stopping when there are no more rows. Here's what it looks like in pseudocode:

```
Make a result set.
LOOP:
  Call SQLFetch to get the next row.
  Check for no more rows. If this is the end of result set, exit loop.
  Check for errors.
  Do something with the result row (for example display the contents).
```

Let's explore these pseudocode statements in a little more detail.

- Make a result set.

  You create a result set when you execute an SQL "query." The "query" statements are the ones that begin with SELECT or VALUES or TABLE. For example, this CLI function call makes a result set associated with stmt:

```
sqlreturn = SQLExecDirect(hstmt,"SELECT column_1 FROM Table_1",SQL_NTS);
```

  (There is also a group of CLI functions, called the *Catalog functions*, which execute SQL queries implicitly. See Chapter 51 on that subject.)

- Call SQLFetch to get the next row.

```
sqlreturn = SQLFetch(hstmt);
```

- Check for end of result set.

  Eventually, the SQLFetch function will return SQL_NO_DATA. At that point, it is certain that the SQLSTATE class is '02'. SQL_NO_DATA is a completion condition — the function is completed. But there wasn't any row to fetch, so no data actually moved from bound Columns into host variables. The Cursor is now positioned "after the last row" and if you call SQLFetch again, it will remain there. This is a cue to break out of the fetch loop:

```
if (sqlreturn == SQL_NO_DATA) break;
```

- Check for errors.

SQLFetch functions rarely return SQL_ERROR, but we'll do some checking to be on the safe side:

```
if (sqlreturn == SQL_ERROR) {
  printf("Error!\n");
  break; }
```

The break; means that we exit the loop, just as if this were a "no data" return code. Alternatively, you could continue, in the hope that the Cursor has moved forward despite the error and the next row is okay.

- Do something with the result row.

  The data in the fetched row will go to host variables in the program. We do not show that here. We will revisit fetch loops later, after looking at desc functions. Until then, remember — Rover is still holding the stick.

SQLFetchScroll

Function Prototype:

```
SQLRETURN SQLFetchScroll(
  SQLHSTMT hstmt,                    /* 32-bit input. handle */
  SQLSMALLINT FetchOrientation,      /* 16-bit input. code */
  SQLINTEGER FetchOffset             /* 32-bit input. offset. */
  );
```

Job: Get a specified row of a Cursor's result set. (Assumption: using hstmt, you've already run a query which returned a result set.)

You can use SQLFetchScroll for one-row-at-a-time processing of a result set. SQLFetchScroll is appropriate for random-order processing because it always gets the "specified" row. For sequential processing, use a different function — SQLFetch.

Algorithm:

```
If (there is no executed statement for hstmt)
  return error: HY010 CLI-specific condition-function sequence error
If (there is no open Cursor)
  return error: 24000 Invalid Cursor state -
If (FetchOrientation is not a valid value)
  return error: HY106 CLI-specific condition-invalid fetch orientation
If (Cursor is not a scroll Cursor and
    FetchOrientation<>SQL_FETCH_NEXT)
  /* scroll Cursors must be explicitly designated with SQLSetStmtAttr */
  return error: HY106 CLI-specific condition-invalid fetch orientation
```

```
If (Cursor position is now after the last row)
  Return with: 02000 "Data Not found-No data"
Transfer the values in the select list to bound Columns, if any.
(Column-binding and transfer is the subject of the CLI desc chapter.)
```

Notes:

- SQLFetchScroll works pretty much the same way as SQLFetch, except for the way it positions the Cursor. There are six possible values of the FetchOrientation parameter:
  - If the value is 1, the #define in sqlcli.h is SQL_FETCH_NEXT and the requested action is "Fetch the next row of the result set," just as for SQLFetch. SQL_FETCH_NEXT is the only legal orientation if the Cursor is non-scrollable.
  - If the value is 2, the #define in sqlcli.h is SQL_FETCH_FIRST and the requested action is "Fetch the first row of the result set."
  - If the value is 3, the #define in sqlcli.h is SQL_FETCH_LAST and the requested action is "Fetch the last row of the result set."
  - If the value is 4, the #define in sqlcli.h is SQL_FETCH_PRIOR and the requested action is "Fetch the previous row of the result set."
  - If the value is 5, the #define in sqlcli.h is SQL_FETCH_ABSOLUTE and the requested action is "Fetch row#n of the result set" (where n = FetchOffset — see parameter list). The FetchOffset parameter can be negative, in which case the DBMS seeks relative to the end of the result set rather than relative to the beginning of the result set. If you pass FetchOrientation=SQL_ABSOLUTE and FetchOffset=0, you fetch the first row in the result set.
  - If the value is 6, the #define in sqlcli.h is SQL_FETCH_RELATIVE and the requested action is "Fetch row#n of the result set" (where n = current row# +FetchOffset). Once again, the FetchOffset parameter can be negative. If you pass FetchOrientation=SQL_RELATIVE and FetchOffset=0, you re-fetch the same row as last time.
- The ABSOLUTE and RELATIVE fetch orientations may be thought of as similar to the arguments for the C function lseek.
- By definition, the following function calls are the same:

```
SQLFetchScroll(...,NEXT,...)  = SQLFetchScroll(...,RELATIVE,+1)
                               or SQLFetch(...)
SQLFetchScroll(...,PRIOR,...) = SQLFetchScroll(...,RELATIVE,-1)
SQLFetchScroll(...,FIRST,...) = SQLFetchScroll(...,ABSOLUTE,+1)
SQLFetchScroll(...,LAST,...)  = SQLFetchScroll(...,ABSOLUTE,-1)
```

- If you want to do anything other than "Fetch next," the Cursor must be declared "scrollable" before the query is executed. Here's how:

```
SQLSetStmtAttr(hstmt,SQL_ATTR_CURSOR_SCROLLABLE,(void*)SQL_SCROLLABLE,00);
```

If you don't call this function, then queries executed on this stmt will be non-scrollable. A non-scrollable Cursor is useful only for SQLFetch and SQLFetchScroll(...SQL_FETCH_NEXT...). A non-scrollable Cursor is generally slightly more efficient than a scrollable Cursor.

- It might be convenient to use SQLFetchScroll for paged-display purposes. For example, start by displaying the first 20 rows on the screen. If the user presses a "next page" button, fetch the next 20 rows. If the user presses a "previous page" button, fetch the previous 20 rows. This process is easy to keep track of with SQLFetchScroll(...,ABSOLUTE,...) using a FetchOffset value to which you add or subtract 20, depending on the button pushing. (In multi-user environments, paged displays might require a different mechanism.)
- FetchOrientation only works within the bounds of the result set. For example, suppose that there are 3 rows in a result set. If you try to fetch row number 20 — using SQLFetchScroll(...,ABSOLUTE,20) — the function will fail with SQLSTATE 02000 "no data." The possible surprise lies in the fact that the Cursor is now positioned, not at some nonexistent "row#20," but just after the last row of the result set — so if you then call SQLFetchScroll(...,PRIOR,...), the DBMS will fetch row#3.
- SQLFetch and SQLFetchScroll calls can be interlaced.

Example:

```
#include "sqlcli.h"
SQLHSTMT hstmt;
...
SQLSetStmtAttr(hstmt,SQL_ATTR_CURSOR_SCROLLABLE,(void*)SQL_SCROLLABLE,00);
...
SQLExecDirect(hstmt,"SELECT column_1 FROM T ORDER BY column_1",SQL_NTS);
...
SQLFetchScroll(hstmt,SQL_FETCH_LAST,00);         /* get last row */
SQLFetchScroll(hstmt,SQL_FETCH_RELATIVE,-1);     /* now 2nd-last row */
```

ODBC: The ODBC function is pretty much as described above, except for details — for example, SQLFetchScroll(hstmt,SQL_ABSOLUTE,0) will cause the Cursor to be positioned before the first row (in standard SQL it would cause the Cursor to be positioned at the first row). The more important difference is that ODBC allows many extensions, such as multi-row retrieval and retrieval using "bookmarks" (which are a special sort of row address).

SQLCloseCursor

Function Prototype:

```
SQLRETURN SQLCloseCursor(
  SQLHSTMT hstmt                        /* 32-bit input */
  );
```

Job: Close a Cursor.

Algorithm:

```
If (there is no executed statement associated with stmt)
  return error: HY010 CLI-specific condition-function sequence error
If (there is no open Cursor associated with stmt)
  return error: 24000 Invalid Cursor state -
The open Cursor is "placed in the closed state".
The open Cursor's "copy of the select source is destroyed".
/* That means there is no more result set to fetch from. However, the IRD is
still there. */
```

Notes:

- You should close the Cursor when you are done processing a result set. Otherwise, you won't be able to re-use the `stmt`. `SQLPrepare` and `SQLExecute` will return with an error if there is an open Cursor.
- The DBMS automatically closes the Cursor when executing any of these CLI functions:
  - `SQLFreeStmt(...,SQL_CLOSE)`
  - `SQLEndTran` (but see description of "held Cursors" on page 818)
  - `SQLCancel`
  - `SQLFreeHandle(SQL_HANDLE_STMT,...)`
  - `SQLMoreResults`

  However, it is good style to call `SQLCloseCursor` explicitly, rather than depending on automatic behaviour.
- `SQLFreeStmt(...,SQL_CLOSE)` does exactly the same thing as the `SQLCloseCursor` function, except for one detail; if there is no Cursor currently open, then `SQLCloseCursor` returns an error, while `SQLFreeStmt(...,SQL_CLOSE)` does not return an error.

Example: This is a repetition of the earlier "fetch loop" example. Notice that `SQLCloseCursor` is called at the end of the loop.

```
#include "sqlcli.h"
...
SQLHSTMT  hstmt;
...
SQLExecDirect(hstmt,"SELECT * FROM Employees ORDER BY dept",SQL_NTS);
for (;;) {
  sqlreturn = SQLFetch(hstmt);
  if (sqlreturn <> SQL_SUCCESS && sqlreturn <> SQL_SUCCESS_WITH_INFO) {
    if (sqlreturn == SQL_NO_DATA) break;
    printf("Error!\n");
    break; }
  printf("*\n"); }
SQLCloseCursor(hstmt);       /* "Close Cursor" */
```

ODBC: The SQLCloseCursor function is new in ODBC 3.0; with earlier ODBC versions, the way to close Cursors was SQLFreeStmt(hstmt,SQL_CLOSE);. If ODBC's "autocommit" mode is in effect, then SQLCloseCursor causes a COMMIT. (In order for this to work, the DBMS must avoid performing an automatic commit immediately after execution of the SELECT statement which causes the Cursor to be opened.)

SQLGetCursorName

Function Prototype:

```
SQLRETURN SQLGetCursorName(
  SQLHSTMT hstmt,             /* 32-bit input Handle*/
  SQLCHAR *CursorName, /* CHAR * output: we'll put Cursor name here */
  SQLSMALLINT BufferLength, /* SMALLINT inputMax *Cursorname length */
  SQLSMALLINT *NameLength   /* SMALLINT * output returned name length*/
  );
```

Job: Retrieve the current <Cursor name> which is associated with hstmt.

Algorithm:

```
If (there is no Cursor name associated with hstmt)
  /* looks like SQLSetCursorName was never called, so the DBMS must generate an
implicit Cursor name */
  Set the Cursor name = 'SQL_CUR' (or 'SQLCUR') plus some
  implementation-defined characters (e.g.: 'SQL_CUR9999'). If the DBMS has to
  make up a name like this, it will ensure that no two statements use the same
  Cursor name.
Copy the value of the Cursor name to *CursorName. This is a standard case of
Character String Retrieval.
```

Notes:

- With embedded SQL, the <Cursor name> is important. With the CLI, the <Cursor name> is not important — we distinguish between statements using the hstmt value. The only time you actually need a <Cursor name> is when you have to use positioned UPDATE|DELETE statements (we'll discuss positioned UPDATE|DELETE statements later in this chapter; see page 816).
- The <Cursor name> exists independently of the Cursor itself. You can retrieve a <Cursor name> even if the Cursor is not open.
- An implicit <Cursor name> begins with the letters SQL_CUR or SQLCUR (e.g., SQL_CUR0001). In practice, implicit <Cursor name>s are not more than 18 characters long. A <Cursor name> is created implicitly (if it doesn't already exist) when either of these things happens: (*a*) SQLPrepare is called and the prepared statement is a query or (*b*) SQLGetCursorName is called. Once an implicit <Cursor name> is established, it remains until the stmt is freed or until a call to SQLSetCursorName changes it explicitly.

Example:

```
#include "sqlcli.h"
...
SQLHSTMT hstmt;
SQLCHAR Cursor_name[128+1];
SQLSMALLINT Cursor_name_length;
...
SQLGetCursorName(hstmt,Cursor_name,sizeof(Cursor_name), &Cursor_name_length);
```

ODBC: The SQLGetCursorName function has been around since ODBC 1.0. In ODBC, implicit <Cursor name>s always begin with SQL_CUR (not SQLCUR).

SQLSetCursorName

Function Prototype:

```
SQLRETURN SQLSetCursorName(
  SQLHSTMT hstmt,                /* 32-bit input */
  SQLCHAR *CursorName,           /* CHAR* input */
  SQLSMALLINT NameLength         /* 16-bit input */
  );
```

Job: Associate a <Cursor name> with a stmt.

Algorithm:

```
If (there is already an open Cursor associated with hstmt)
  return error: 24000-invalid Cursor state -
Get the value passed in *CursorName, with length = NameLength.
Trim lead or trail spaces.
Check that value conforms to the usual rules for <identifier>.
If (the value begins with the letters 'SQL_CUR' or 'SQLCUR')
  /* Only the DBMS can assign names that begin with 'SQL_CUR' or 'SQLCUR' */
  return error: 34000 invalid <Cursor name>
If (value = <Cursor name> of another stmt in the same dbc)
  /* <Cursor name>s must be unique */
  return error: 34000 invalid <Cursor name>
```

Notes:

- You only need to call SQLSetCursorName if you intend to execute "positioned UPDATE|DELETE" statements.

- It is a good idea to assign your own <Cursor name> rather than depending on an implicit <Cursor name>.
- The best time to call `SQLSetCursorName` is immediately after calling `SQLAllocHandle(SQL_HANDLE_STMT,...)`.
- The <Cursor name> is permanent. It exists until the `stmt` is freed or until superseded by another call to `SQLSetCursorName`. Opening and closing the Cursor has no effect on the name.

Example:

```
#include "sqlcli.h"
...
SQLHSTMT hstmt;
...
SQLAllocHandle(SQLHANDLE_STMT,hdbc,&hstmt);
SQLSetCursorName(hstmt,"Cursor_1",sizeof("Cursor_1"));
```

ODBC: The `SQLSetCursorName` function has been around since ODBC version 1.0. If the <Cursor name> already exists, ODBC requires that the `SQLSTATE` should be `3C000` "`Duplicate <Cursor name>`" instead of `34000`.

Embedded SQL versus CLI

Here is an embedded SQL example which uses a Cursor:

```
EXEC SQL DECLARE x CURSOR FOR SELECT * FROM A;
EXEC SQL DECLARE y CURSOR FOR SELECT * FROM B;
EXEC SQL OPEN x;
EXEC SQL FETCH x ... ;
EXEC SQL CLOSE x;
```

Here is a CLI example which does pretty well the same thing:

```
SQLAllocHandle(SQL_HANDLE_STMT,hdbc,&hstmt1);
SQLAllocHandle(SQL_HANDLE_STMT,hdbc,&hstmt2);
SQLExecDirect(hstmt1,"SELECT * FROM A",SQL_NTS);
SQLFetch(hstmt1);
SQLCloseCursor(hstmt1);
```

Comparing these two examples, you will notice two major differences:

1. In the CLI, there is no `OPEN` statement — Cursors are implicitly opened by execution of a `SELECT` statement.
2. In the CLI, there is no use of <Cursor name>s — different Cursors are associated with different `stmts`, so `hstmt` alone is sufficient for unique identification.

The CLI functions SQLGetCursorName and SQLSetCursorName are unimportant. CLI programmers only worry about <Cursor name>s if they have to use positioned UPDATE|DELETE statements.

Positioned UPDATE|DELETE Statements

In Chapter 39 on embedded SQL, we mentioned that there are two kinds of UPDATE and DELETE statements. The normal kind (called "searched UPDATE" and "searched DELETE") provide conditions for changing or removing rows in a WHERE clause — these statements are not our concern here. The Cursor-related kind (called "positioned UPDATE" and "positioned DELETE") are distinguished by the presence of a WHERE CURRENT OF <Cursor name> clause rather than a conditional WHERE clause. Here's an example of each:

```
EXEC SQL UPDATE Table_1 SET column_1 = 5 WHERE CURRENT OF Cursor_1;

EXEC SQL DELETE FROM Table_1 WHERE CURRENT OF Cursor_1;
```

The first example will update only one row in Table_1; the row that underlies the result-set row which is indicated by the current position of Cursor_1. The second example will delete only that single row of Table_1.

With the CLI, there is one complicating factor — the positioned UPDATE|DELETE statement must be executed using a different stmt than the stmt which is associated with Cursor_1. This is just a corollary of the reasonable rule that, "at any given time there may be only one statement associated with a stmt." Because there is already an active statement (the SELECT which caused the Cursor to be opened), the positioned UPDATE must go elsewhere. A general skeleton of a positioned UPDATE|DELETE operation, then, could be:

```
Allocate stmt_1
Allocate stmt_2
Get or set the <Cursor name> for stmt_1
Execute SELECT on stmt_1 (thus opening the Cursor)
Fetch on stmt_1 (thus positioning the Cursor)
Execute positioned UPDATE|DELETE on stmt_2, using the <Cursor name>
```

(If, later, the same row is re-fetched using SQLFetchScroll, then results are implementation-defined.)

Example: This program uses a positioned DELETE statement. Just by the way, we'll use "A delimited identifier" for our <Cursor name>. In real life the <Cursor name> would be a short <regular identifier> like X or Cursor_1 or SELECTION_WHERE_X_GT_0.

```
#include "sqlcli.h"
SQLHENV henv;
SQLHDBC hdbc;
SQLHSTMT hstmt_1,hstmt_2;
SQLRETURN sqlreturn;
void main () {
```

```
SQLAllocHandle(SQL_HANDLE_ENV,00,&henv);
SQLAllocHandle(SQL_HANDLE_DBC,henv,&hdbc);
SQLConnect(hdbc,"OCELOT",SQL_NTS,"OCELOT",SQL_NTS,NULL,00);
SQLAllocHandle(SQL_HANDLE_STMT,hdbc,&hstmt_1);
SQLAllocHandle(SQL_HANDLE_STMT,hdbc,&hstmt_2);
/* In C, the symbol \" can be used when the symbol " is in a string.
   The symbol \042 would have the same effect, since in the ANSI repertoire
   the code for quote-mark is octal 042. */
SQLSetCursorName(hstmt_1,"\"A delimited identifier\"",24);
SQLExecDirect(hstmt_1,"SELECT * FROM T",16);
for (;;) {
    sqlreturn = SQLFetch(hstmt_1);
    if (SQLFetch(hstmt_1)==SQL_NO_DATA) break;
   /* In C, the symbol \ is used for string continuation. */
  SQLExecDirect(hstmt_2,"DELETE FROM T WHERE CURRENT OF \
  \"A delimited identifier\"",SQL_NTS); }
SQLCloseCursor(hstmt_1);
SQLEndTran(SQL_HANDLE_DBC,hdbc,SQL_COMMIT);
SQLFreeHandle(SQL_HANDLE_STMT,hstmt_2);
SQLFreeHandle(SQL_HANDLE_STMT,hstmt_1);
SQLDisconnect(hdbc);
SQLFreeHandle(SQL_HANDLE_DBC,hdbc);
SQLFreeHandle(SQL_HANDLE_ENV,henv); }
```

Singleton SELECTs

In embedded SQL, there is a construct called the singleton SELECT. Here's an example:

```
EXEC SQL SELECT Column_1 INTO :host_variable FROM Table_1;
```

In the CLI, there is no equivalent of a singleton SELECT. All query results, even ones that consist of zero rows or one row, must be processed via the Cursor functions.

Sensitive Cursors

What happens if a Cursor is open on stmt_1 and a data change operation happens on stmt_2? We've already noted that "positioned UPDATE|DELETE statements" are possible, but here we're asking about effects in a more general way — that is, we're assuming that the SQL-data change statement is INSERT, UPDATE, or DELETE and that stmt_2 is associated either with the same dbc or with another dbc. For example, suppose you've executed this SQL statement:

```
SELECT * FROM Table_1;
```

and you are now fetching from the result. But — after the SELECT was processed and before your first FETCH, some UPDATE took place on one row of Table_1. When you FETCH that row, will you see the new values or the original values? There are three possible answers, which depend on an attribute of the stmt called the *Cursor sensitivity*. Here are the options:

1. If the attribute value is 0, the #define in sqlcli.h is SQL_UNDEFINED and the requested action is, "I don't care whether I see new or old values; leave it up to the implementation."
2. If the attribute value is 1, the #define in sqlcli.h is SQL_INSENSITIVE and the requested action is, "Show me the original values."
3. If the attribute value is 2, the #define in sqlcli.h is SQL_SENSITIVE and the requested action is, "Show me the changed values."

The default is SQL_UNDEFINED (which may be known as SQL_ASENSITIVE in ANSI SQL3). Your best option is to just leave this attribute setting alone and do what you can to avoid the situation. If you must specify one of the other settings, you can do so with a call to the SQLSetStmtAttr function, for example:

```
SQLSetStmtAttr(hstmt,SQL_ATTR_CURSOR_SENSITIVITY,(void*)SQL_INSENSITIVE,00);
```

You would probably want an insensitive Cursor if the fetched rows have to be consistent with each other. However, most DBMSs maintain insensitive Cursors by making a copy of the Table (that is, the rows in the result set are not necessarily identical to the rows of the Table from which you selected). Therefore, an insensitive Cursor is always a *read-only* Cursor. The SQLGetStmtAttr function can be used to check which Cursor sensitivity option is currently in effect. The SQLGetInfo function can be used to check whether a DBMS supports the Cursor sensitivity options. Many DBMSs support SQL_UNSPECIFIED only.

Holdable Cursors

Another stmt attribute that affects Cursor management is "holdability." This attribute, which can also be set with the SQLSetStmtAttr function, affects the question, "What happens to an open Cursor when we end a transaction with SQLEndTran(...SQL_COMMIT)?" Here are the two possible options:

1. If the attribute value is 0, the #define in sqlcli.h is SQL_NONHOLDABLE and the requested action is, "Close the Cursor."
2. If the attribute value is 1, the #define in sqlcli.h is SQL_HOLDABLE and the requested action is, "Leave the Cursor open into the next transaction."

The default is SQL_NONHOLDABLE. In fact, for most DBMSs, holdability is not yet an option (this is an SQL3 feature). It is difficult to maintain integrity and concurrency if Cursors stay open over transaction boundaries. Holdable Cursors are not supported in SQL-92, in ISO SQL3, or in ODBC.

SQLMoreResults

Function Prototype:

```
SQLRETURN SQLMoreResults(
  SQLHSTMT hstmt        /* 32-bit input */
  );
```

Job: Find out if there is another result set associated with the stmt. If so, position the Cursor at the start of the next result set (that is, before the first row of the next result set). This is an SQL3 function.

Only one SQL statement can produce multiple result sets:

CALL <procedure-name>

That's because a "procedure" might contain multiple SELECT statements. In such a case, result sets are returned in the order they were produced.

Algorithm:

```
If (there is no executed statement associated with stmt)
  return error: HY010 CLI-specific condition-function sequence error
If (the executed statement did not return any result sets)
  return error: HY010 CLI-specific condition-function sequence error
/* Presumably the first Cursor is already open and processed. */
Close the Cursor associated with stmt.
If (there are no more result sets)
  return warning: No data-no additional dynamic result sets returned
Open Cursor for the new result set /* with the same <Cursor name> */
Position Cursor before first row of the new result set
```

Notes:

- SQLMoreResults does an implicit "close Cursor" call.
- Result sets must be processed one at a time. You cannot process them in parallel (though that's a feature that's being considered for SQL4).
- Because earlier versions of the SQL Standard didn't support SQL procedures, there was no need for an SQLMoreResults function until SQL3.

Example:

```
#include "sqlcli.h"
SQLHSTMT hstmt;
...
SQLExecDirect(hstmt,"CALL proc()",SQL_NTS);
SQLFetch(hstmt);
...
SQLMoreResults(hstmt);
SQLFetch(hstmt);
```

ODBC: `SQLMoreResults` has been around since ODBC version 1.0. That has more to do with ODBC's non-standard "batching" feature than with support for procedures. However, Microsoft has always assumed that DBMSs support procedures.

And that's it for the Cursor functions. In the next chapter, we'll take a look at the "meat" of CLI — the `desc` functions.

46

Chapter 46

SQL/CLI: desc Functions

In this chapter, we'll describe the fourth essential CLI resource — the desc. We have much to say about:

- What is in a desc — fields of the header and the "item descriptor areas."
- How to make a desc or how to use an automatically-made desc.
- Similarities and differences of ARDs, APDs, IRDs, and IPDs.
- Functions which attack descs directly: SQLAllocHandle, SQLGetDescField, SQLSetDescField, SQLGetDescRec, SQLSetDescRec, SQLCopyDesc, and others.
- Functions which attack descs indirectly: SQLBindParameter, SQLBindCol, SQLColAttribute, SQLDescribeCol, and others.

Descriptor Areas

Here is a piece of CLI code:

```
SQLExecDirect(hstmt,"SELECT col_1,col_2 FROM T WHERE col_1=?", SQL_NTS);
SQLFetch(hstmt);
```

The SELECT statement in this example contains a question mark; it represents a parameter marker — that is, it means "there is an input parameter here." (An *input parameter* is a host variable value which travels from the application to the DBMS. For some CALL statements, a parameter may be an output parameter but the normal case is that parameters are input parameters.) The input will happen during SQLExecDirect.

The SELECT statement also contains a two-Column select list (col_1,col_2). The existence of a select list implies "there are output rows here." (An *output row* consists of one or more Columns in a result set whose values travel from the DBMS to the application.) The output will happen during SQLFetch.

What are the addresses of the host variables? How will NULL values be flagged? What is already known or can be specified about the characteristics of each value: <data type>, size, precision, scale, Character set, etc.? Descriptor areas — or descs — are available to handle such questions for both parameters and row Columns.

Automatic descs

There are four automatic descs; here's a brief description of each:

- IRD, or Implementation Row Descriptor. Its typical use — to find out what the DBMS knows about a result set. The IRD is filled in when you call SQLPrepare for a SELECT statement.
- ARD, or Application Row Descriptor. Its typical use — to tell the DBMS how to transfer a result set to the host. The important fields of the ARD must be filled in by the host program.
- IPD, or Implementation Parameter Descriptor. Its typical use — to provide information about the DBMS's view of parameters. The DBMS may be capable of "populating" the IPD fields; otherwise, the programmer must take some responsibility for this job.
- APD, or Application Parameter Descriptor. Its typical use — to tell the DBMS how to transfer an input parameter. (Parameters are marked in an SQL statement with "?" parameter markers.)

Here's a pseudo struc declaration for future reference in this chapter's examples.

```
desc struc {
  SQL_DESC_ALLOC_TYPE smallint,                      /* header fields ... */
  SQL_DESC_COUNT smallint,
  SQL_DESC_DYNAMIC_FUNCTION char[],
  SQL_DESC_DYNAMIC_FUNCTION_CODE integer,
  SQL_DESC_KEY_TYPE smallint,
  IDA struc occurs n times {
    SQL_DESC_CHARACTER_SET_CATALOG varchar[],  /* IDA[n] fields ... */
    SQL_DESC_CHARACTER_SET_SCHEMA varchar[],
    SQL_DESC_CHARACTER_SET_NAME varchar[],
    SQL_DESC_COLLATION_CATALOG varchar[],
    SQL_DESC_COLLATION_SCHEMA varchar[],
    SQL_DESC_COLLATION_NAME varchar[],
    SQL_DESC_DATA_POINTER void*,
    SQL_DESC_DATETIME_INTERVAL_CODE smallint,
    SQL_DESC_DATETIME_INTERVAL_PRECISION smallint,
    SQL_DESC_INDICATOR_POINTER integer*,
```

```
    SQL_DESC_KEY_MEMBER smallint,
    SQL_DESC_LENGTH integer,
    SQL_DESC_NAME varchar[],
    SQL_DESC_NULLABLE smallint,
    SQL_DESC_OCTET_LENGTH integer,
    SQL_DESC_OCTET_LENGTH_POINTER integer*,
    SQL_DESC_PARAMETER_ORDINAL_POSITION smallint,
    SQL_DESC_PARAMETER_SPECIFIC_CATALOG varchar[],
    SQL_DESC_PARAMETER_SPECIFIC_SCHEMA varchar[],
    SQL_DESC_PARAMETER_SPECIFIC_NAME varchar[],
    SQL_DESC_PRECISION smallint,
    SQL_DESC_SCALE smallint,
    SQL_DESC_TYPE smallint,
    SQL_DESC_UDT_CATALOG varchar[],
    SQL_DESC_UDT_SCHEMA varchar[],
    SQL_DESC_UDT_NAME varchar[],
    SQL_DESC_UNNAMED smallint
    }
  }
APD = desc;
IPD = desc;
ARD = desc;
IRD = desc;
```

Throughout this chapter, we'll replace long-winded references using program-like conventions. For example, it is often necessary to make statements like this, "Within the Application Parameter Descriptor, in the *n*th occurrence of the Item Descriptor Area, set the SCALE attribute to 5." We will make such statements the following way:

```
"Set APD.IDA[n].SQL_DESC_SCALE = 5"
```

For a programmer, the second statement is shorter, clearer, and better. We'll use such statements as convenient conventions, without implying that all DBMSs store desc information with this structure.

The desc Fields

On first reading, we suggest that you skip quickly through this section. But bookmark this page — you'll have to refer to the desc field descriptions many times.

The first entries in a descriptor area are the desc "header" fields. Then come the fields of the desc "item descriptor area" (IDA), which is multiple-occurrence. In our discussions of each group, entries are in alphabetical order. Each entry begins with a field identifier (the code used for identification), a <data type>, and an indicator of the field's importance, e.g.,

```
SQL_DESC_ALLOC_TYPE 1099          Type: SMALLINT. Importance: Low.
```

This description should be read as follows: the SQL descriptor field is identified by the code SQL_DESC_ALLOC_TYPE, which is a number. The sqlcli.h line for this field is:

```
#define SQL_DESC_ALLOC_TYPE 1099
```

This book uses SQL_DESC_ALLOC_TYPE as both a field identifier and a field name. The field's <data type> is SMALLINT (short signed integer). Relatively speaking, the field is of low importance (this is our subjective estimate).

Each field entry contains some text description, accompanied by examples if the field is of high importance. Finally, each entry ends with a small chart. For example:

	May be gotten by ...	May be set by ...
ARD	user	SQLGetData, user
IRD	SQLGetData[P], user[P]	SQLPrepare
APD	SQLExecute, user	SQLGetDescField
IPD	SQLExecute, user	SQLPrepare[I], user

This chart should be read as follows: when this field is in the ARD, it may be gotten by the user (presumably with the SQLGetDescField function) and it may be set by the SQLGetData function or by the user (presumably with the SQLSetDescField function). And so on for the IRD, APD, and IPD. In the chart, the symbol [I] means, "this function is applicable only when the AUTO POPULATE flag is on" — which usually it isn't, as you may recall from the discussion of SQLSetEnvAttr. The symbol [P] means, "this function is legal only if the statement is prepared." The chart does not show functions which are, in functional effect, containers of other functions. For example, many fields may be affected by SQLExecDirect, but we won't show that; we only show SQLPrepare and/or SQLExecute. If either "May be gotten by" or "May be set by" is blank for a particular automatic desc, that means the field is not affected by any "get" or "set" function (as appropriate) for that desc.

The desc Header Fields

There are five desc header fields: SQL_DESC_ALLOC_TYPE, SQL_DESC_COUNT, SQL_DESC_DYNAMIC_FUNCTION, SQL_DESC_DYNAMIC_FUNCTION_CODE, and SQL_DESC_KEY_TYPE. Their descriptions follow.

SQL_DESC_ALLOC_TYPE

SQL_DESC_ALLOC_TYPE 1099

Type: SMALLINT. **Importance:** Low.

Possible values: SQL_DESC_ALLOC_AUTO (1) or SQL_DESC_ALLOC_USER (2). The value is set permanently when the desc is created. Those descs made implicitly by a call to SQLAllocHandle(SQL_HANDLE_STMT,...) are automatic descs; they will have SQL_DESC_ALLOC_AUTO in this field. Those descs made explicitly by a call to SQLAllocHandle(SQL_HANDLE_DESC,...) are user descs; they will have SQL_DESC_ALLOC_USER in this field.

	May be gotten by ...	May be set by ...
ARD	SQLFreeHandle, user	SQLAllocHandle
IRD	SQLFreeHandle, user[P]	SQLAllocHandle
APD	SQLFreeHandle, user	SQLAllocHandle
IPD	SQLFreeHandle, user	SQLAllocHandle

SQL_DESC_COUNT

SQL_DESC_COUNT 1001

Type: SMALLINT. **Importance:** High

Provides the number of item descriptor areas in the desc. Conceptually, there is a correspondence between the value in SQL_DESC_COUNT and the number of actual items — the "number of parameters" (for IPDs and APDs) or "the number of Columns" (for IRDs and ARDs). However, this correspondence is not automatically true. You have to make it so.

Initially, the field value is 0. The SQLPrepare function will set IRD.SQL_DESC_COUNT = <the number of Columns in the select list>. If "populate IPD" is true, the SQLPrepare function will set IPD.SQL_DESC_COUNT = <the number of parameter markers in SQL statement>.

If you call a function which effectively creates a new IDA, then the COUNT field value may go up. For example, if ARD.SQL_DESC_COUNT=0 and you call SQLBindCol for COLUMN_1, then ARD.SQL_DESC_COUNT is set to 1.

In ODBC, the value goes down if you "unbind" the last IDA (by setting desc.IDA[n].SQL_DATA_POINTER=0).

	May be gotten by ...	May be set by ...
ARD	SQLGetData, SQLGetDescRec, user	SQLBindCol, SQLSetDescRec, user
IRD	SQLGetDescRec[P], user[P], SQLNumResultCols[P]	SQLPrepare
APD	SQLExecute, SQLGetDescRec, SQLGetParamData, SQLParamData, user	SQLBindParameter, SQLSetDescRec, user
IPD	SQLExecute, SQLGetDescRec, user	SQLBindParameter, SQLPrepare[I], SQLSetDescRec, user

SQL_DESC_DYNAMIC_FUNCTION

SQL_DESC_DYNAMIC_FUNCTION 1031

Type: VARCHAR. **Importance:** Low.

This is an SQL3 field only; it's not in ODBC. It provides an SQL_TEXT string containing a copy of the prepared statement. For example, after:

```
SQLPrepare(hstmt,"INSERT INTO Table_1 VALUES (5)",SQL_NTS);
```

IRD.SQL_DESC_DYNAMIC_FUNCTION will contain 'INSERT'. You can get the same information with the SQLGetDiagField function.

	May be gotten by ...	May be set by ...
ARD		
IRD	user	SQLPrepare
APD		
IPD	user	SQLPrepare

SQL_DESC_DYNAMIC_FUNCTION_CODE

SQL_DESC_DYNAMIC_FUNCTION_CODE 1032

Data type: INTEGER. **Importance:** Low.

This is an SQL3 field only; it's not in ODBC. It provides a numeric code for the prepared statement. For example, after:

```
SQLPrepare(hstmt,"INSERT INTO Table_1 VALUES (5)",SQL_NTS);
```

IRD.SQL_DESC_DYNAMIC_FUNCTION_CODE will contain 50 (you can find the list of possible codes in Chapter 47 "SQL/CLI: Diagnostic Functions"). You can get the same information with the SQLGetDiagField function.

	May be gotten by ...	May be set by ...
ARD		
IRD	user	SQLPrepare
APD		
IPD	user	SQLPrepare

SQL_DESC_KEY_TYPE

SQL_DESC_KEY_TYPE 1029

Type: SMALLINT. **Importance:** Low.

This is an SQL3 field only; it's not in ODBC. If a SELECT statement's select list contains all the Columns of the Table's primary key, the value is 2. If it contains all the Columns of one of the Table's preferred candidate keys, the value is 1. Otherwise, the value is 0. For example, suppose that TABLE_1 has two Columns, COL_1 and COL_2, and that TABLE_1's primary key is (COL_1). In that case:

```
SQLPrepare(hstmt,"SELECT * FROM Table_1",SQL_NTS);
```

will set IRD.SQL_DESC_KEY_TYPE = 1, and

```
SQLPrepare(hstmt,"SELECT COUNT(*) FROM Table_1",SQL_NTS);
```

will set IRD.SQL_DESC_KEY_TYPE = 0.

	May be gotten by ...	May be set by ...
ARD		
IRD	user	SQLPrepare
APD		
IPD		

The desc Item Descriptor Area (IDA) Fields

There are 28 desc IDA fields:

SQL_DESC_CHARACTER_SET_CATALOG	SQL_DESC_CHARACTER_SET_SCHEMA
SQL_DESC_CHARACTER_SET_NAME	SQL_DESC_COLLATION_CATALOG
SQL_DESC_COLLATION_SCHEMA	SQL_DESC_COLLATION_NAME
SQL_DESC_DATA_POINTER	SQL_DESC_DATETIME_INTERVAL_CODE
SQL_DESC_DATETIME_INTERVAL_PRECI-SION	SQL_DESC_INDICATOR_POINTER
SQL_DESC_KEY_MEMBER	SQL_DESC_LENGTH
SQL_DESC_NAME	SQL_DESC_NULLABLE
SQL_DESC_OCTET_LENGTH	SQL_DESC_OCTET_LENGTH_POINTER
SQL_DESC_PARAMETER_MODE	SQL_DESC_PARAMETER_ORDINAL_POSITION
SQL_DESC_PARAMETER_SPECIFIC_CATALOG	SQL_DESC_PARAMETER_SPECIFIC_SCHEMA
SQL_DESC_PARAMETER_SPECIFIC_NAME	SQL_DESC_PRECISION
SQL_DESC_SCALE	SQL_DESC_TYPE
SQL_DESC_UDT_CATALOG	SQL_DESC_UDT_SCHEMA
SQL_DESC_UDT_NAME	SQL_DESC_UNNAMED

These fields are also known as the "Item Fields," the "fields of the Descriptor Record" (an ODBC term), and as the "detail records." Their descriptions follow.

Character Set Fields

SQL_DESC_CHARACTER_SET_CATALOG 1019

Type: VARCHAR. **Importance:** Low.

SQL_DESC_CHARACTER_SET_SCHEMA 1020

Type: VARCHAR. **Importance:** Low.

SQL_DESC_CHARACTER_SET_NAME 1021

Type: VARCHAR. **Importance:** Low.

These three fields are SQL3 fields only; they're not in ODBC. Together, they make up the qualified name of a Character set and are meaningful only if the item's <data type> is CHAR, VARCHAR, or CLOB. Some example values are: 'OCELOT', 'INFORMATION_SCHEMA', and 'ISO8BIT' (for the three fields, respectively).

	May be gotten by ...	May be set by ...
ARD	SQLGetData, user	user
IRD	SQLGetData, user	SQLPrepare
APD	SQLExecute, user	user
IPD	SQLExecute, user	SQLPrepare[I], user

Collation Fields

SQL_DESC_COLLATION_CATALOG 1016

Type: VARCHAR. **Importance:** Low.

SQL_DESC_COLLATION_SCHEMA 1017

Type: VARCHAR. **Importance:** Low.

SQL_DESC_COLLATION_NAME 1018

Type: VARCHAR. **Importance:** Low.

These three fields are ANSI SQL3 fields only; they're not in ISO SQL3 or ODBC. Together, they make up the qualified name of a Collation and are meaningful only if the item's <data type> is CHAR, VARCHAR, or CLOB.

For a select list, a standard DBMS may set these fields to a <Collation name> — for example, 'OCELOT', 'INFORMATION_SCHEMA', and 'POLISH' (for the three fields, respectively). You can change the fields, but it does not matter — the DBMS never reads them.

	May be gotten by ...	May be set by ...
ARD	user	user
IRD	user	SQLPrepare
APD	user	user
IPD	user	SQLPrepare[I], user

SQL_DESC_DATA_POINTER

SQL_DESC_DATA_POINTER 1010

Type: POINTER. **Importance:** High.

Provides the address of a host variable. Meaningful in the APD (where it points to an input parameter) or in the ARD (where it points to a target for the result-set Column).

The initial value is 0. When this field is set to a non-zero value, the item is considered to be "bound" — a "bound parameter," a "bound target." Application programmers must ensure that the address is valid.

This field is reset to 0 if a change is made to a non-pointer field in the same IDA using the SQLSetDescField function. For example: if, using SQLSetDescField, you set IPD.IDA[4].SQL_DESC_DATETIME_INTERVAL_CODE = 1, the side effect is that IPD.IDA[4].SQL_DESC_DATA_POINTER = 0. Moral: change this field last.

In ODBC, the name is SQL_DESC_DATA_PTR.

	May be gotten by ...	May be set by ...
ARD	SQLGetData, SQLFreeStmt, user	SQLSetDescRec, user
IRD		
APD	SQLExecute, SQLFreeStmt, user	SQLBindParameter, SQLSetDescRec, user
IPD		SQLSetDescRec, user

SQL_DESC_DATETIME_INTERVAL_CODE

SQL_DESC_DATETIME_INTERVAL_CODE 1007

Type: SMALLINT. **Importance:** Medium.

This field will only be meaningful if the SQL_DESC_TYPE field is 9 (SQL_DATETIME) or 10 (SQL_INTERVAL). It will contain a datetime subtype (a number between 1 and 5) or an interval subtype (a number between 1 and 13). For example, if SQL_DESC_TYPE = 9 and SQL_DESC_DATETIME_INTERVAL_CODE = 5, then the item's precise <data type> is known to be TIMESTAMP WITH TIME ZONE. If you change the SQL_DESC_TYPE field to 9 or 10, you must change SQL_DESC_DATETIME_INTERVAL_CODE too.

	May be gotten by ...	May be set by ...
ARD	user	SQLSetDescRec, user
IRD	SQLGetData, SQLDescribeCol, user	SQLPrepare
APD	SQLExecute, user	SQLSetDescRec, user
IPD	SQLExecute, user	SQLBindParameter, SQLSetDescRec, SQLPrepare[I], user

SQL_DESC_DATETIME_INTERVAL_PRECISION

SQL_DESC_DATETIME_INTERVAL_PRECISION 1014

Type: SMALLINT. **Importance:** Medium.

This field will only be meaningful if the SQL_DESC_TYPE field is 9 (SQL_DATETIME) or 10 (SQL_INTERVAL). This is the precision of the leading datetime field — not the fractional-seconds precision. For example, a DATE value has three fields: YEAR, MONTH, and DAY. The first ("leading") datetime field in a DATE is YEAR, which always has four positions: yyyy. Therefore, desc.IDA[n].SQL_DESC_DATETIME_INTERVAL_PRECISION = 4.

In ODBC, SQL_DESC_DATETIME_INTERVAL_PRECISION is 26 rather than 1014 and <data type> is INTEGER rather than SMALLINT.

	May be gotten by ...	May be set by ...
ARD	user	user
IRD	SQLGetData, SQLDescribeCol, user	SQLPrepare
APD	SQLExecute, user	user
IPD	SQLExecute, user	SQLBindParameter, SQLPrepare[I], user

SQL_DESC_INDICATOR_POINTER

SQL_DESC_INDICATOR_POINTER 1009

Type: POINTER TO INTEGER. **Importance:** Medium

Provides the address of an indicator. This field is used together with SQL_DESC_DATA_POINTER. For example, suppose that you set ARD.IDA[n].SQL_DESC_INDICATOR_POINTER = &indicator (where &indicator means, "the address of a variable named indicator in the host program"). If SQLGetData retrieves a null value for the *n*th Column in the select list, indicator is set to SQL_NULL_DATA (-1). The field's initial value is 0.

In ODBC, the name is SQL_DESC_INDICATOR_PTR.

	May be gotten by ...	May be set by ...
ARD	SQLGetData, user	SQLBindCol, SQLSetDescRec, user
IRD		
APD	user	SQLBindParameter, SQLSetDesc, user
IPD		

SQL_DESC_KEY_MEMBER

SQL_DESC_KEY_MEMBER 1030

Type: INTEGER. **Importance:** Low.

This field is in SQL3 only; it's not in ODBC. If a fetched item is from a Column of the selected Table's primary key or a preferred candidate key, then the value is 1 (true); otherwise, it's 0 (false). For example:

```
SQLPrepare(hstmt,"SELECT 5 FROM t",SQL_NTS);
```

will set IRD.IDA[1].SQL_DESC_KEY_MEMBER = 0. (See also the header field SQL_DESC_KEY_TYPE.)

	May be gotten by ...	May be set by ...
ARD		
IRD	user	SQLPrepare
APD		
IPD		

SQL_DESC_LENGTH

SQL_DESC_LENGTH 1003

Data type: INTEGER. **Importance:** Medium.

For all character string <data type>s, this is the defined length in characters — for example, it equals 12 for a Column defined as VARCHAR(12). For all bit string <data type>s, this is the defined length in bits. For all temporal <data type>s, this is the defined length in positions — for example, it equals 10 for a Column defined as a DATE (because 2000-01-01 is 10 positions). For a BLOB <data type>, this is the defined length in octets. In ANSI SQL, SQL_DESC_LENGTH may be changed with the SQLSetDescField function. In ISO SQL, it may not be.

	May be gotten by ...	May be set by ...
ARD	user	user
IRD	SQLGetData, SQLDescribeCol, user	SQLPrepare
APD	SQLExecute, user	user
IPD	SQLExecute, user	SQLPrepare[I], user

SQL_DESC_NAME

SQL_DESC_NAME 1011

Type: VARCHAR. **Importance:** Low.

This provides the derived Column name if there's a select list. For example, after:

```
SQLPrepare(hstmt,"SELECT col_1 FROM Table_1",SQL_NTS);
```

the DBMS sets IRD.IDA[n].SQL_DESC_NAME = "Col_1". In ANSI SQL, SQL_DESC_NAME may be changed with the SQLSetDescField function. In ISO SQL, it may not be. In ODBC, named parameters are supported.

	May be gotten by ...	May be set by ...
ARD	user	user
IRD	SQLDescribeCol, user	SQLPrepare
APD	user	user
IPD	user	user

SQL_DESC_NULLABLE

SQL_DESC_NULLABLE 1008

Type: SMALLINT. **Importance:** Medium.

This field is 1 (true) (SQL_NULLABLE) if the value might be NULL; otherwise it's 0 (false) (SQL_NO_NULLS). For a populated IPD, SQL_DESC_NULLABLE is 1. In ANSI SQL, SQL_DESC_NULLABLE may be changed with the SQLSetDescField function. In ISO SQL, it may not be. In ODBC, the value might also be 2 (SQL_NULLABLE_UNKNOWN).

	May be gotten by ...	May be set by ...
ARD	user	user
IRD	SQLDescribeCol, user	SQLPrepare
APD	user	user
IPD	user	SQLPrepare[I], user

SQL_DESC_OCTET_LENGTH

SQL_DESC_OCTET_LENGTH 1013

Type: INTEGER. **Importance:** Medium.

For any character string, bit string, or BLOB <data type>, this is the item's maximum length in octets.

This field matters for "output"; if a CHAR Column is fetched, the number of octets transferred will be <= SQL_DESC_OCTET_LENGTH. For example, if you intend to fetch into a C host variable defined as "char[20]", then you should set ARD.IDA[n].SQL_DESC_OCTET_LENGTH = 20. For "input" (SQL_PARAM_MODE_IN parameters), SQL_DESC_OCTET_LENGTH is not relevant. When the DBMS inputs parameters, it uses the length pointed to by the SQL_DESC_OCTET_LENGTH_POINTER field.

Despite some contradictions in other documents, we believe that datetime or interval transfers are not affected by the value in this field.

	May be gotten by ...	May be set by ...
ARD	SQLGetDescRec, user	SQLBindCol, SQLSetDescRec
IRD	SQLGetDescRec, user	SQLPrepare, SQLSetDescRec
APD	SQLGetDescRec, user	SQLBindParameter, SQLSetDescRec
IPD	SQLGetDescRec, user	SQLBindParameter, SQLPrepare[I], SQLSetDescRec, user

SQL_DESC_OCTET_LENGTH_POINTER

SQL_DESC_OCTET_LENGTH_POINTER 1004

Data type: POINTER TO INTEGER. **Importance:** Medium.

This field provides the address of a length in octets. Its initial value is 0 (ARD/APD). For VARCHAR or BIT VARYING or BLOB <data type>s, this length is the actual length, which may be less than the defined length. For other character string and bit string <data type>s, the actual and maximum lengths are the same because size is fixed. The size of the \0 terminator is not included in the octet length. For other <data type>s, the value is implementation-defined.

This field and the SQL_DESC_INDICATOR_POINTER field may point to the same place. In ISO SQL, IPD.IDA[n].SQL_DESC_LENGTH may be changed with the SQLSetDescField function. In ANSI SQL, it may not be. In ODBC, the name is SQL_DESC_OCTET_LENGTH_PTR.

[Obscure Rule] The rules change if SQL_DESC_OCTET_LENGTH_POINTER and SQL_DESC_INDICATOR_POINTER contain the same address value (this is actually imprecise; the rules don't really change, but octet length is always set after indicator and we stop if indicator == SQL_NULL_DATA).

If they're separate:

```
On Output (taking SQLFetch for our example):
If fetched value IS NULL:
  SQLFetch sets *SQL_DESC_INDICATOR_POINTER = SQL_NULL_DATA (-1)
  SQLFetch does not set *SQL_DESC_OCTET_LENGTH_POINTER
If fetched value IS NOT NULL:
  SQLFetch sets *SQL_DESC_INDICATOR_POINTER = 0
  SQLFetch sets *SQL_DESC_OCTET_LENGTH_POINTER = string size in octets
On Input:
  *SQL_DESC_INDICATOR_POINTER should be either 0 or -1.
  *SQL_DESC_OCTET_LENGTH_POINTER can be SQL_NTS, SQL_DATA_AT_EXEC or length.
```

If they're the same:

```
On Output (taking SQLFetch for our example):
If fetched value IS NULL:
  SQLFetch sets *SQL_DESC_INDICATOR_POINTER = SQL_NULL_DATA (-1)
If fetched value IS NOT NULL:
  SQLFetch sets *SQL_DESC_INDICATOR_POINTER = 0
/* We've proposed a change to the ISO committee; the following is an assumption
   that they'll adopt it: */
    () if CHAR or BLOB:
          *SQL_DESC_OCTET_LENGTH_POINTER = length
    () otherwise:
          "implementation-dependent", but assume it's like ODBC:
          *SQL_DESC_OCTET_LENGTH_POINTER = length
          ... This overrides the setting of
              *SQL_DESC_INDICATOR_POINTER=0.
          ... So "strlen_or_ind" is a misnomer; it's "strlen_and_ind"
If (CHAR or BLOB)
  If (truncation would occur):
```

```
    SQLFetch sets *SQL_DESC_INDICATOR_POINTER = length
  If (truncation would not occur):
    SQLFetch sets *SQL_DESC_INDICATOR_POINTER = 0
On Input:
  *SQL_DESC_INDICATOR_POINTER may be 0,-1,SQL_NTS,SQL_DATA_AT_EXEC, or length.
```

The rules are a little confusing, but that's the price we have to pay for backward compatibility — some of the older CLI functions allow for only one pointer variable which serves for both "indicator" and "string length" information.

	May be gotten by ...	May be set by ...
ARD	user	SQLBindCol, SQLSetDescRec, user
IRD		
APD	SQLExecute, user	SQLBindParameter, SQLSetDescRec, user
IPD		

SQL_DESC_PARAMETER_MODE

SQL_DESC_PARAMETER_MODE 1021

Data type: SMALLINT. **Importance:** Low.

This field is in SQL3 only; it's not in ODBC. Its possible values are: 1 (SQL_PARAM_MODE_IN), 2 (SQL_PARAM_MODE_INOUT), and 4 (SQL_PARAM_MODE_OUT). If the "populate IPD" flag is true and the SQL statement is "CALL ...", and the first parameter of the called routine is input, the DBMS sets IPD.IDA[1].SQL_DESC_PARAMETER_MODE=1.

In ANSI SQL, users may only change this field in the IPD (with the SQLSetDescField function). In ISO SQL, users may change this field in the IPD, the APD, and the ARD. In ODBC, a field named IPD.IDA[n].SQL_DESC_PARAMETER_TYPE can be set to SQL_PARAM_INPUT, SQL_PARAM_INOUT, or SQL_PARAM_OUTPUT. The default value is SQL_PARAM_INPUT.

	May be gotten by ...	May be set by ...
ARD		
IRD	user	
APD	SQLExecute	SQLBindParameter
IPD		SQLPrepare[I], user

SQL_DESC_PARAMETER_ORDINAL_POSITION

SQL_DESC_PARAMETER_ORDINAL_POSITION 1022

Type: SMALLINT. **Importance:** Low.

This field is in SQL3 only; it's not in ODBC. It provides an ordinal number, for SQL routine parameters. If this item corresponds to the first parameter in an SQL "CALL ..." statement, the

DBMS sets `IPD.IDA[n].SQL_DESC_PARAMETER_ORDINAL_POSITION=1`. `SQLPrepare` sets IPD if "populate IPD" is true.

In ANSI SQL, users may only change this field in the IPD (with the `SQLSetDescField` function). In ISO SQL, users may change this field in the IPD, the APD, and the ARD.

	May be gotten by ...	May be set by ...
ARD		
IRD	user	
APD		
IPD		SQLPrepare[I], user

Parameter Fields

`SQL_DESC_PARAMETER_SPECIFIC_CATALOG 1023`

Type: `VARCHAR`. **Importance:** Low.

`SQL_DESC_PARAMETER_SPECIFIC_SCHEMA 1024`

Type: `VARCHAR`. **Importance:** Low.

`SQL_DESC_PARAMETER_SPECIFIC_NAME 1025`

Type: `VARCHAR`. **Importance:** Low.

These three fields are SQL3 fields only; they're not in ODBC. Together, they make up the qualified name of a parameter in an SQL "`CALL ...`" statement. `SQLPrepare` sets IPD if "populate IPD" is true.

In ANSI SQL, users may only change these fields in the IPD (with the `SQLSetDescField` function). In ISO SQL, users may change these fields in the IPD, the APD, and the ARD.

	May be gotten by ...	May be set by ...
ARD		
IRD	user	
APD		
IPD		SQLPrepare[I], user

SQL_DESC_PRECISION

`SQL_DESC_PRECISION 1005`

Type: `SMALLINT`. **Importance:** Medium.

For all numeric <data type>s, this is a precision — i.e., for `DECIMAL` and `NUMERIC`, it's the number of digits both before and after the decimal point; for `INTEGER` and `SMALLINT`, it's the fixed implementation-defined number of decimal or binary digits; for `REAL`, `FLOAT`, and `DOUBLE PRECISION`, it's the number of bits or digits in the mantissa. For all temporal <data type>s, this is the fractional seconds precision — that is, the number of digits after the decimal point in the

SECOND datetime component. The default value in each case is what you'd get if you used the <data type> with its default value in a CREATE TABLE statement.

	May be gotten by ...	May be set by ...
ARD	SQLGetData, user	SQLSetDescRec, user
IRD	SQLGetData, SQLDescribeCol, user	SQLPrepare
APD	user	SQLSetDescRec
IPD	SQLExecute, user	SQLBindParameter, SQLSetDescRec, SQLPrepare[I], user

SQL_DESC_SCALE

SQL_DESC_SCALE 1006

Type: SMALLINT. **Importance:** Medium.

For DECIMAL or NUMERIC <data type>s, SQL_DESC_SCALE is the number of digits after the decimal point. The default value is zero — that is, if you change the SQL_DESC_TYPE to SQL_DECIMAL or SQL_NUMERIC, then the value in SQL_DESC_SCALE is implicitly set to 0. For SMALLINT or INTEGER <data type>s, the DBMS will set IRD.IDA[n].SQL_DESC_SCALE = 0 during SQLPrepare and ignore the field on all other occasions. For all other <data type>s, the value of SQL_DESC_SCALE is irrelevant. The field's initial value is 0.

	May be gotten by ...	May be set by ...
ARD	SQLGetData, user	SQLSetDescRec, user
IRD	SQLGetData, SQLDescribeCol, user[P]	SQLPrepare
APD	user	SQLSetDescRec, user
IPD	SQLExecute, user	SQLBindParameter, SQLSetDescRec, SQLPrepare[I], user

SQL_DESC_TYPE

SQL_DESC_TYPE 1002

Type: SMALLINT. **Importance:** High.

This field provides the item's <data type>. Its possible values are:

1	(SQL_CHAR)	15	(SQL_BIT_VARYING)
2	(SQL_NUMERIC)	16	(SQL_BOOLEAN)
3	(SQL_DECIMAL)	17	(SQL_UDT)
4	(SQL_INTEGER)	18	(SQL_UDT_LOCATOR)
5	(SQL_SMALLINT)	19	(SQL_ROW_TYPE)
6	(SQL_FLOAT)	20	(SQL_REF)
7	(SQL_REAL)	30	(SQL_BLOB)
8	(SQL_DOUBLE)	31	(SQL_BLOB_LOCATOR)
9	(SQL_DATETIME)	40	(SQL_CLOB)
10	(SQL_INTERVAL)	41	(SQL_CLOB_LOCATOR)
12	(SQL_VARCHAR)	50	(SQL_ARRAY)
14	(SQL_BIT)	51	(SQL_ARRAY_LOCATOR)

For datetime and interval items, the subtype is in the SQL_DESC_DATETIME_INTERVAL_CODE field.

You may set ARD.IDA[n].SQL_DESC_TYPE = SQL_C_DEFAULT. By setting SQL_DESC_TYPE with SQLSetDescField, *you cause all other fields of the IDA to be reset to implementation-dependent values*. Moral: Always set SQL_DESC_TYPE first.

	May be gotten by ...	May be set by ...
ARD	SQLGetData, user	SQLBindCol, SQLSetDescRec, user
IRD	SQLGetData, SQLDescribeCol, user	SQLPrepare
APD	user	SQLBindParameter, SQLSetDescRec, user
IPD	SQLExecute, user	SQLBindParameter, SQLSetDescRec, SQLPrepare[I], user

UDT Fields

SQL_DESC_UDT_CATALOG 1026

Type: VARCHAR. **Importance:** Low.

SQL_DESC_UDT_SCHEMA 1027

Type: VARCHAR. **Importance:** Low.

SQL_DESC_UDT_NAME 1028

Type: VARCHAR. **Importance:** Low.

These three fields are SQL3 fields only; they're not in ODBC. Together, they make up the qualified name of the item's user-defined type, if it has one.

	May be gotten by ...	May be set by ...
ARD	user	user
IRD	SQLGetData, user	SQLPrepare
APD	SQLExecute, user	user
IPD	SQLExecute, user	user

SQL_DESC_UNNAMED

SQL_DESC_UNNAMED 1012

Type: SMALLINT. **Importance:** Low.

This field has two possible values: 1 (true) (SQL_UNNAMED) or 0 (false) (SQL_NAMED).

In the IRD; if the select list contains an initially-unnamed Column, then the DBMS makes up a name, returns the made-up name to the SQL_DESC_NAME field, and sets the SQL_DESC_UNNAMED field to SQL_UNNAMED. For example, after:

```
SQLPrepare(hstmt,"SELECT 5+1 FROM Table_1",SQL_NTS);
```

the DBMS might set IRD.IDA[n].SQL_DESC_NAME = "expr1" (this is the value an Access clone would give) and then set IRD.IDA[n].SQL_DESC_UNNAMED = 1 (SQL_UNNAMED).

In the IPD; if "auto-populate" happens, then the DBMS sets IPD.IDA[n].SQL_DESC_UNNAMED = 1 (SQL_UNNAMED).

In ANSI SQL, users may change this field (with the SQLSetDescField function). In ISO SQL, they may not.

	May be gotten by ...	May be set by ...
ARD	user	user
IRD	user	SQLPrepare
APD	user	user
IPD	user	SQLPrepare[I], user

The desc Functions

We are now ready to describe the individual desc functions. There is a good deal of redundancy here because several functions are available that do the same thing. If you're a beginner, we suggest that you pay particular attention to SQLSetDescField and SQLGetDescField because it is possible to do nearly everything with those two low-level functions alone.

There are 14 desc functions. Their descriptions follow.

SQLAllocHandle(SQL_HANDLE_DESC,...)

Function Prototype:

```
SQLRETURN SQLAllocHandle(
  SQLSMALLINT HandleType,     /* 16-bit input = SQL_HANDLE_DESC */
  SQLINTEGER InputHandle,     /* 32-bit input, must be a hdbc */
  SQLINTEGER *OutputHandle    /* 32-bit output, a hdesc */
  );
```

Job: Allocate a user desc. (Note: User descs are unimportant. We start off with this function for symmetry reasons.)

Algorithm:

```
If (HandleType == SQL_HANDLE_DESC)
If (InputHandle is not a valid handle of a dbc)
  return error: CLI-specific condition-invalid handle
Empty the dbc's diagnostics area.
If (dbc is not connected)
  Set *OutputHandle = 0
  return error: connection exception-connection does not exist
If (the maximum number of descs has already been allocated)
  Set *OutputHandle = 0
  /* The maximum number of descs is implementation-defined */
  return error: HY014 CLI-specific condition-limit on number of handles
  exceeded
If (there's not enough memory)
  Set *OutputHandle = 0
  return error: HY001 CLI-specific condition-memory allocation error
Allocate a new desc, associated with the dbc.
Set desc.SQL_ALLOC_TYPE = 2 i.e. SQL_DESC_ALLOC_USER.
/* Thus this desc is marked as a user desc, not an automatic desc. */
*OutputHandle = handle of new desc.
```

Notes:

- In early prototypes of the CLI there were separate calls for different resource types (see SQLAllocEnv, SQLAllocConnect, SQLAllocStmt). Eventually people realized that the number of handle types might grow indefinitely, so SQLAllocHandle was defined as a generalized "allocate handle" function for all current and future resource types.
- Call this function after you have allocated a dbc and after you have connected because the InputHandle parameter is a hdbc.

- This function is only for user descs. There are two kinds of descs: automatic descs and user descs. The DBMS implicitly sets up 4 automatic descs (ARD, APD, IRD, IPD) when SQLAllocHandle(SQL_HANDLE_STMT,...) is called and associates them with the stmt. You explicitly set up user descs with SQLAllocHandle(SQL_HANDLE_DESC,...) and they are associated with the dbc.
- Using another function (SQLSetStmtAttr), you can replace one of the automatic descs with a user desc. Such descs can be shared among multiple stmts.
- Using another function (SQLCopyDesc), you can save the contents of an automatic desc in a user desc for backup purposes.

Example:

```
#include "sqlcli.h"
...
SQLHDBC hdbc;
SQLHDESC hdesc;
...
SQLConnect(hdbc,...);
...
SQLAllocHandle(SQL_HANDLE_DESC,hdbc,&hdesc);
```

ODBC: The SQLAllocHandle function is new in ODBC 3.0; in ODBC 2.0 the desc resource could not be explicitly allocated.

SQLFreeHandle(SQL_HANDLE_DESC,...)

Function Prototype:

```
SQLRETURN SQLFreeHandle(       /* function returns SMALLINT */
   SQLSMALLINT HandleType,     /* 16-bit input, = SQL_HANDLE_DESC */
   SQLINTEGER Handle           /* 32-bit input, must be a hdesc */
   );
```

Job: Destroy a user desc. (Remember that the SQLFreeHandle function can be used to destroy any resource: an env, a dbc, a stmt, or a desc. We are treating the four variants as four separate functions. In this section, our sole concern is desc.)

Algorithm:

```
If (HandleType == SQL_HANDLE_DESC)
  If (Handle is not really a handle of a desc)
    return error: CLI-specific condition-invalid handle
Empty the desc's diagnostics area.
The desc's dbc becomes the "current dbc".
```

```
If (there is a deferred parameter number)
  return error: HY010 CLI-specific condition-function sequence error
If (desc.SQL_DESC_ALLOC_TYPE == SQL_DESC_ALLOC_AUTO)
  /* You can't free any of the four descs (ARD IRD APD IPD) that were
     automatically allocated when you made a stmt. They stay around till you
     free the stmt. You can only free a "user"desc -- a desc which you
     allocated explicitly with SQLAllocHandle. */
  return error: HY017 CLI-specific condition-invalid use of
  automatically-allocated descriptor
/* The following cancels the effects of any SQLSetStmtAttr calls which
   might have made the user desc into an ARD or APD, in place of the
   automatic ARD or APD desc. */
For (each stmt associated with dbc)
  If (stmt is associated with the desc)
   If (the desc is currently the stmt's ARD)
    Re-associate stmt with the automatically-allocated ARD
     If (the desc is currently the stmt's APD)
    Re-associate stmt with the automatically-allocated APD
Deallocate desc.
The handle becomes invalid.
```

Notes:

- If SQLFreeHandle returns SQL_ERROR, then the handle is still live and you can get diagnostics.
- This function is the reverse of the SQLAllocHandle(SQL_HANDLE_DESC,...) function. Only user descs are destructible with SQLFreeHandle(SQL_HANDLE_DESC,...).
- The SQLDisconnect function will automatically destroy all descs associated with a dbc. So technically you don't need to call SQLFreeHandle(SQL_HANDLE_DESC...) if you are about to disconnect.

Example:

```
#include "sqlcli.h"
SQLHDESC hdesc;
...
SQLFreeHandle(SQL_HANDLE_DESC,hdesc);
```

ODBC: SQLFreeHandle(SQL_HANDLE_DESC,...) is new in ODBC 3.0.

SQLGetDescField

Function Prototype:

```
SQLRETURN SQLGetDescField (
  SQLHDESC hdesc,                   /* 32-bit input */
  SQLSMALLINT RecordNumber,         /* 16-bit input */
  SQLSMALLINT FieldIdentifier,      /* 16-bit input */
  SQLPOINTER Value,                 /* VOID* output */
  SQLINTEGER BufferLength,          /* 32-bit input */
  SQLINTEGER *StringLength          /* 32-bit output */
  );
```

Job: Get one field from a desc.

Algorithm:

```
If (FieldIdentifier<> one of the FieldIdentifier codes in "The Desc Fields")
  return error: HY091 CLI-specific condition-invalid descriptor field
  identifier.
If (FieldIdentifier is the code for one of the IDA fields)
  /* The RecordNumber parameter would be irrelevant for a "header field", but
     IDA is multiple-occurrence so we need a valid index for IDA fields */
  If (RecordNumber < 1)
  return error: '07009': Dynamic SQL error-invalid descriptor index.
  If (RecordNumber > SQL_DESC_COUNT)
    /* Example: if the desc is an IRD, and the only SQL statement so far is
       INSERT, then SQL_DESC_COUNT is zero. If now you pass SQL_DESC_TYPE as the
       FieldIdentifier parameter and 5 as the RecordNumber parameter, then the
       DBMS returns with return code = SQL_NO_DATA. */
    Return with warning: '02000': No data.
If (FieldIdentifier is only applicable for a Prepared Statement, and there is
no Prepared Statement)
  /* Example: if the desc is an IRD, and no SQLPrepare or SQLExecDirect
     has happened for the stmt associated with the desc, then a request for
     SQL_DESC_TYPE would make no sense. */
  Return error: HY007 CLI-specific condition-associated statement is not
  prepared.
If (FieldIdentifier is not applicable for this type of desc)
 /* Example: if the desc is an IPD, then a request for
    SQL_DESC_INDICATOR_POINTER would make no sense. */
  Return with error HY091 CLI-specific condition-invalid descriptor field
  identifier.
If (the field is in its initially-undefined state)
```

```
    /* Example: if the desc is an IPD, and the DBMS doesn't
       "automatically populate" the IPD, then most fields stay in their
       "undefined" state. */
    Return with error HY091 CLI-specific condition-invalid descriptor
    field identifier.
  Retrieve the value of the field indicated by the FieldIdentifier parameter, and
  put it in the place pointed to by the Value parameter. Notice that the value
  might be a smallint, or it might be an integer, or it might be a character
  string. In the latter case, the rules of Character String Retrieval apply.
```

Notes:

- SQLGetDescField is a fundamental desc routine. There are several other routines which are, conceptually, wrappers for one or more SQLGetDescField calls. For example, the SQL-ColAttribute function will implicitly call SQLGetDescField after finding the IRD; SQLGet-DescRec will retrieve seven desc fields at once (name, type, subtype, length, precision, scale, and nullable).
- In our descriptions of the desc fields, the charts of the functions that affect each field use the word "user" to identify those cases where SQLGetDescField may be called to retrieve a single value after explicitly passing the field's numeric identifier.
- The first SQLGetDescField parameter is a hdesc. To get this handle, save the handle when you call SQLAllocHandle (if it's a user desc) and call SQLGetStmtAttr (if it's an automatic desc).
- The second parameter — FieldIdentifier — is unnecessary for a header field. For an IDA, it's an index to the multiple-occurrence structure and should contain a value between 1 and "count."

Example: Assume you have just called:

```
SQLExecDirect(hstmt,"SELECT * FROM Table_1",SQL_NTS);
```

Because SQLExecDirect implies a SQLPrepare phase, the DBMS has filled in some of the IRD fields, as follows:

```
------------------------------------------------------------------
-
-------------------
--SQL_DESC_COUNT -
- -----------------     << picture of IRD after "SELECT * FROM Table_1" >>
- | 00003        |
- -----------------
-
-------------------------------------------------------------
- - SQL_DESC_NAME | SQL_DESC_PRECISION | SQL_DESC_TYPE | ... |
-------------------------------------------------------------
-   1-'Col_1'     | 00005              | 00002         | ... |
-   2-'Col_2'     | 00004              | 00003         | ... |
-   3-'Col_3'     | ??                 | 00001         | ... |
-   ------------------------------------------------------------
-
------------------------------------------------------------------
```

For space reasons, we've shown only a few fields in this diagram. But there's enough to make it clear that (*a*) the DBMS found three Columns in the result set (as indicated by SQL_DESC_COUNT = 3), (*b*) the first Column is named COL_1, its <data type> is NUMERIC (as indicated by SQL_DESC_TYPE = 2) and its precision is 5, (*c*) the second Column is named COL_2, its <data type> is DECIMAL (as indicated by SQL_DESC_TYPE = 3) and its precision is 4, and (*d*) the third Column is named COL_3, its <data type> is CHAR (as indicated by SQL_DESC_TYPE = 1) and its precision is unset because CHAR Columns have no precision (they have a length instead).

Here are some SQLGetDescField calls — and what will be put into the Value variable:

```
SQLGetDescField(hdesc,00,SQL_DESC_COUNT,&value,00,NULL);
```

— gets 3

```
SQLGetDescField(hdesc,1,SQL_DESC_TYPE,&value,00,NULL);
```

— gets 2

```
SQLGetDescField(hdesc,3,SQL_DESC_PRECISION,&value,00,NULL);
```

— gets 4

And here is a larger code snippet that finds out the hdesc value (a necessary preliminary!), then displays the name of every Column in TABLE_1:

```
#include "sqlcli.h"
...
SQLHSTMT hstmt;                          /* handle of stmt */
SQLHDESC hdesc;                          /* handle of IRD */
SQLSMALLINT i,col_count;                 /* used for a loop counter */
SQLCHAR col_name[128+1];
...
SQLExecDirect(hstmt,"SELECT * FROM Table_1",SQL_NTS);
SQLGetStmtAttr(hstmt,SQL_ATTR_IMP_ROW_DESC,&hdesc,00,NULL);
SQLGetDescField(hdesc,00,SQL_DESC_COUNT,&col_count,00,NULL);
printf("The Columns of Table_1 are:\n");
for (i=1; i<=col_count; ++i) {
  SQLGetDescField(hdesc,i,SQL_DESC_NAME,col_name, sizeof(col_name),NULL);
  printf("%s\n",col_name); }
...
```

ODBC: The SQLGetDescField function is new in ODBC 3.5. There are some implementation-defined additional fields. The expected behaviour is somewhat different if you ask for a field which has no defined value; a standard-conformant DBMS would return SQL_ERROR, an ODBC-conformant DBMS would return SQL_SUCCESS and an undefined value.

SQLSetDescField

Function Prototype:

```
SQLRETURN SQLSetDescField(
  SQLHDESC hdesc,                  /* 32-bit input */
  SQLSMALLINT RecordNumber,        /* 16-bit input */
  SQLSMALLINT FieldIdentifier,     /* 16-bit input */
  SQLPOINTER Value,                /* ANY* input */
  SQLINTEGER BufferLength          /* 32-bit input */
  );
```

Job: Assign a value to one field in a desc.

Algorithm:

```
If (desc is associated with a "deferred parameter")
  return error: HY010 CLI-specific condition-function sequence error
If (desc is an IRD)
  /* This error will appear only for ISO SQL3: */
  return error: HY016 CLI-specific condition-cannot modify an
  implementation row descriptor
If (FieldIdentifier is not a code used in "The Desc Fields" list)
  return error: HY091 CLI-specific condition-invalid descriptor field
  identifier
If (this field cannot be set by the user)
  return error: HY091 CLI-specific condition-invalid descriptor field
  identifier
If (FieldIdentifier == SQL_DESC_COUNT)
    Set desc.SQL_DESC_COUNT = Value
If (this is an IDA field i.e. not a header field)
 If (RecordNumber < 1)
   return error: 07009 Dynamic SQL error-invalid descriptor index
 /* We have: a particular field in a particular IDA of a desc identified by
   FieldIdentifier/RecordNumber/hdesc respectively).
   We have: a new value for that field (in Value/BufferLength). */
If (FieldIdentifier == SQL_DESC_OCTET_LENGTH_POINTER)
 Set desc.IDA[RecordNumber].SQL_DESC_OCTET_LENGTH_POINTER = Value
If (FieldIdentifier == SQL_DESC_INDICATOR_POINTER)
 Set desc.IDA[RecordNumber].SQL_DESC_INDICATOR_POINTER = Value
If (FieldIdentifier == SQL_DESC_CHARACTER_SET_CATALOG
   (or SCHEMA) (or NAME))
```

```
  /* Value points to a string, BufferLength is string size, possibly
     BufferLength == SQL_NTS */
  Trim lead and trail spaces from the string.
  Ensure that the string is a valid identifier.
  /* Valid identifiers may include introducers. */
  Copy string to desc.IDA[RecordNumber].SQL_DESC_CHARACTER_SET_CATALOG
  (or SCHEMA) (or NAME)
 If (RecordNumber > desc.SQL_DESC_COUNT)
  /* Change SQL_DESC_COUNT so it equals the maximum IDA index number */
  Set desc.SQL_DESC_COUNT = RecordNumber
 If (FieldIdentifier <> SQL_DESC_COUNT)
  If (FieldIdentifier not SQL_DESC_OCTET_LENGTH_POINTER|
      SQL_DESC_DATA_POINTER|INDICATOR_POINTER)
    Set desc.IDA[RecordNumber].SQL_DESC_DATA_POINTER = 0
 If (FieldIdentifier == SQL_DESC_DATA_POINTER)
  Set desc.IDA[RecordNumber].SQL_DESC_DATA_POINTER = Value
  If (Value <> 0)
    /* The "Consistency check" is described later in this chapter.
       Basically, it just checks that field values aren't absurd. */
    If ("Consistency check" failure)
     /* SQL_DESC_DATA_POINTER field might be changed despite the error */
     return error: HY021 CLI-specific condition-inconsistent descriptor
     information
 If (FieldIdentifier == SQL_DESC_TYPE)
  If (Value is not a valid data type, for example SQL_NUMERIC)
    return error: HY004 CLI-specific condition-invalid data type
  Set desc.IDA[RecordNumber].SQL_DESC_TYPE = Value
  /* See the "Default values" chart in this section */
     Set other fields to their "default values"
    If (FieldIdentifier == SQL_DATETIME_INTERVAL_CODE)
  If (desc.IDA[RecordNumber].SQL_DESC_TYPE is datetime (9))
    If (Value=1 or 2 or 4: i.e.: date or time or time with time zone)
      Set desc.IDA[RecordNumber].SQL_DESC_PRECISION = 0
    If (Value=3 or 5: i.e.: timestamp or timestamp with time zone)
     Set desc.IDA[RecordNumber].SQL_DESC_PRECISION = 6
    Set other fields to implementation-dependent values
  If (desc.ida[RecordNumber].SQL_DESC_TYPE is interval)
    Set desc.IDA[RecordNumber].SQL_DESC_DATETIME_INTERVAL_PRECISION = 2
    If (Value is for an interval that ends with SECOND)
```

```
    Set desc.IDA[RecordNumber].SQL_DESC_PRECISION = 6
  Else
   Set desc.ida[RecordNumber].SQL_DESC_PRECISION = 0
/* For other FieldIdentifier values, there is no standard procedure.
  A reasonable assumption is that the DBMS would simply copy
  Value to the field indicated by FieldIdentifier. */
```

Notes:

- Sometimes `Value` is a pointer; sometimes it's an integer; sometimes it's a smallint; depending on `FieldIdentifier`.
- If you must change multiple fields in one IDA, do them in this order:
  - Change the `SQL_DESC_TYPE` field first.
  - Change the `SQL_DESC_DATETIME_INTERVAL_CODE` field second.
  - Change the other fields (except for `SQL_DESC_DATA_POINTER`) in any order.
  - Change the `SQL_DESC_DATA_POINTER` field last.

  If you don't set fields in this order, you'll get errors. It's deliberate.
- If an error happens, the value of the field may be changed anyway.
- If you change a header field, you should pass `RecordNumber = 0` (otherwise, in theory, you could inadvertently change the `SQL_DESC_COUNT` field).
- The <data type> of `Value` should correspond to the <data type> of the field being changed. For example, if changing the `SQL_DESC_SCALE` field, `Value` should contain a `SMALLINT` value. For a list of the <data type> correspondences between the SQL predefined <data type>s and host variables, see Chapter 39 "Embedded SQL Binding Style." Because there are some differences between embedded SQL and the SQL/CLI, here is a concise summary for the SQL/C <data type> correspondences, with some adjustments and notes that are specific to SQL/CLI:

SQL	C	Notes
ARRAY	-	
ARRAY LOCATOR	long	
BIT (length)	char[length/8]	Assumes 8-bit chars, rounded up
BIT VARYING(length)	-	You can cast to BIT
BLOB (length)	char[length]	Assumes 8-bit chars
BLOB(length)	long	
BOOLEAN	long	Standard is not explicit here
CHAR or CLOB	char[length+1]	
CLOB(length)	long	
DATE	-	ODBC defines a struc for this
DECIMAL(p,s)	-	Cast to char or (rarely) to float

SQL	C	Notes
DOUBLE PRECISION	double	
FLOAT(p)	-	if p<=23:float, if p>23:double
INTEGER	long	
INTERVAL(q)	-	
NUMERIC(p,s)	-	Cast to char or (rarely) to float
REAL	float	
REF	char[L]	L is implementation-defined
SMALLINT	short	
TIME(t)	-	ODBC defines a struc for this
TIMESTAMP(t)	-	ODBC defines a struc for this
UDT	-	
UDT LOCATOR	long	

Note: The symbol "-" means there is no official correspondence according to the Standard, but some DBMSs will try to do an implicit cast.

Note: In a similar list for Delphi, we would find that SQL's REAL corresponds to Delphi's Float (not Delphi's Real), and that SQL's CHAR corresponds to Delphi's Pchar (not Delphi's packed array of char).

- The SQLSetDescField function can only set one field at a time. Therefore, it is a "fundamental" function. There are other functions which can be used to change multiple fields (SQLSetDescRec, SQLBindParameter, and SQLBindCol).
- Default Values — A change to SQL_DESC_TYPE will cause other IDA fields to be reset to their "default values." This chart shows the changes. Any fields not shown are reset to implementation-dependent values.

If SQL_DESC_TYPE is changed to ...	... Then these fields change too
SQL_CHAR, SQL_VARCHAR, SQL_CLOB	SQL_DESC_CATALOG etc.: default set SQL_LENGTH: maximum length [Note 1]
SQL_BIT, SQL_BIT_VARYING, SQL_BLOB	SQL_LENGTH: maximum length
SQL_DATETIME	SQL_PRECISION: 0
SQL_INTERVAL	SQL_DATETIME_INTERVAL_PRECISION: 2
SQL_DECIMAL, SQL_NUMERIC	SQL_PRECISION: maximum precision [Note 2] SQL_SCALE: 0
SQL_FLOAT	SQL_PRECISION: default precision [Note 2]

[Note 1] The "maximum length" is not the usual default value for a CHAR <data type>. If you say CREATE TABLE Table_1 (col_1 CHAR);, the default length is 1. That is why, in ODBC, if you set SQL_DESC_TYPE to SQL_CHAR, the SQL_LENGTH field changes to 1. But in standard SQL, it becomes a character string <data type>'s "maximum possible length," which is an implementation-defined size.

[Note 2] The "default precision" of SQL_DECIMAL, SQL_NUMERIC, and SQL_FLOAT <data type>s is implementation-defined.

- The Standard has omitted mention of all other <data type>s in relation to SQLSetDescField and ends with a note that says an error will be returned for any type not shown in the chart. In effect, this means that all <data types> other than SQL_CHAR, SQL_VARCHAR, SQL_CLOB, SQL_BIT, SQL_BIT_VARYING, SQL_BLOB, SQL_DATETIME, SQL_INTERVAL, SQL_DECIMAL, SQL_NUMERIC, and SQL_FLOAT are technically illegal here. The wise programmer will assume that these matters will be resolved by the DBMS vendor — not being able to use SQL_INTEGER, for example, seems too severe a restriction to be followed.
- Consistency check — While you're changing descriptor fields, you might cause temporary inconstancy. Here's how:
  - [Step 1] You change SQL_DESC_TYPE to SQL_DECIMAL. Changing the <data type> triggers a wholesale resetting of all other IDA fields to default values. For example, the SQL_DESC_PRECISION field becomes 1 (an implementation-defined default), the SQL_DESC_SCALE field becomes 0, and the SQL_DESC_DATA_POINTER becomes a null pointer.
  - [Step 2] You change SQL_DESC_SCALE to 5. Now the scale is greater than the precision. That is inconsistent — a DECIMAL(1,5) definition is illegal. But don't worry — the DBMS won't reject your change.
  - [Step 3] You change SQL_DESC_PRECISION to 6. Now the fields are consistent again.
  - [Step 4] You change SQL_DESC_DATA_POINTER to a host-variable address. Changing the data pointer triggers a consistency check. The rationale for delaying the consistency check until you change the data pointer is that temporary inconsistencies are inevitable if you change one field at a time, but it doesn't matter as long as the data pointer is a null pointer. When you set the data pointer, you "bind the Column" to the host variable. At that point, the DBMS cannot allow any further inconsistency. If you've read our chapters about the various SQL predefined <data type>s, you'll find that the consistency check is merely an enforcement of the rules you already know. And there are no **GOTCHAs because the DBMS only checks what's relevant. It looks for these things:
    - SQL_DESC_PRECISION, SQL_DESC_SCALE, SQL_DESC_LENGTH, SQL_DESC_DATETIME_INTERVAL_CODE, and SQL_DESC_DATETIME_INTERVAL_PRECISION must be valid if it's possible to specify precision, scale, length and/or specific datetime or interval leading-field precision when you're defining a Column of the given <data type>. For example, FLOAT(precision) is legal in definitions, therefore SQL_DESC_PRECISION must have a valid value if SQL_DESC_TYPE = SQL_FLOAT. On the other hand, precision is not specifiable for REAL Columns, so there is no check of SQL_DESC_PRECISION if SQL_DESC_TYPE = SQL_REAL. If SQL_DESC_TYPE is NUMERIC or DECIMAL, then scale and precision must be valid for the <data type> (e.g., scale cannot be greater than precision). Warning: this description is of the

SQL Standard "Consistency Check" definition. The ODBC "Consistency Check" is more picky.

- For IDAs within application descriptors (ARDs or APDs), `SQL_DESC_TYPE` must be a <data type> that's representable in the host language. In our charts of <data type> correspondences (see Chapter 39 on embedded SQL), we showed you that the SQL `INTEGER` <data type> translates directly to a C data type — long. Easy times. Now what about the `NUMERIC` <data type>? Well, you'd have to `CAST` it to something that C can handle; either a floating-point or a character-string. Casting is easy — just change the <data type> as we described in each <data type> chapter.
- If the DBMS detects an inconsistency during execution of `SQLSetDescField` or `SQLSetDescRec`, the `SQLSTATE` error return is `HY021` "`CLI-specific condition-inconsistent descriptor information.`"

TIP: Even though you never need an `SQL_DESC_DATA_POINTER` value in an IPD IDA, set it anyway. That will force a consistency check. It's better to check for inconsistency in advance, rather than waiting for the consistency error to happen when you try to execute the statement.

- The DBMS may also detect inconsistency during execution of `SQLBindParameter` or `SQLBindCol`, but usually there is a final Consistency Check during `SQLExecute`. If the DBMS detects an inconsistency during execution of `SQLExecute`, the `SQLSTATE` error return is either `07001` "`Dynamic SQL error-using clause does not match dynamic parameters`" or `07002` "`Dynamic SQL error-using clause does not match target specifications.`" (There appears to be an error in the Standard; this is what we believe is the intended meaning.)

Example: You have an SQL statement which uses an integer input parameter. You want to tell the DBMS about it by setting certain fields of the APD. Assume that the "auto-populate IPD" flag is off, so you'll have to set some fields in the IPD too. Here's how.

```
#include "sqlcli.h"
SQLHSTMT hstmt;
SQLHDESC hapd,hipd;  /* hapd="handle of APD"; hipd="handle of IPD" */
SQLINTEGER input_variable;   /* this has the value we pass */
...
SQLPrepare(hstmt,"INSERT INTO Table_1 VALUES (?)",SQL_NTS);
SQLGetStmtAttr(hstmt, SQL_ATTR_APP_PARAM_DESC, &hapd, 00, NULL);
SQLSetDescField(hapd,1,SQL_DESC_TYPE,(void*)SQL_INTEGER,00);
SQLSetDescField(hapd,1,SQL_DESC_DATA_POINTER,&input_variable,00);
SQLGetStmtAttr(hstmt, SQL_ATTR_IMP_PARAM_DESC, &hipd, 00, NULL);
```

```
SQLSetDescField(hipd,1,SQL_DESC_TYPE,(void*)SQL_INTEGER,00);
SQLSetDescField(hipd,1,SQL_DESC_DATA_POINTER,&input_variable,00);
input_variable = 55;
SQLExecute(hstmt);
...
```

The following is a picture of the APD after the `SQLSetDescField` calls are done:

```
- ---------------------- ------------------
--SQL_DESC_ALLOC_TYPE- - SQL_DESC_COUNT -
- ---------------------- -----------------
- | 00001               | | 00001        |
- ---------------------- -----------------
-
-----------------------------------------------------
-- SQL_DESC_DATA_POINTER | SQL_DESC_TYPE | ........ |
-----------------------------------------------------
-  1-&input_variable     | 00004         | ........ |
- ---------------------------------------------------
```

We will revisit "parameter passing" again after discussing the `SQLBindCol` function.

SQLGetDescRec

Function Prototype:

```
SQLRETURN SQLGetDescRec(
  SQLHDESC hdesc,               /* 32-bit input */
  SQLSMALLINT RecordNumber,     /* 16-bit input */
  SQLCHAR *Name,                /* CHAR* output */
  SQLSMALLINT BufferLength,     /* 16-bit input */
  SQLSMALLINT *NameLength,      /* CHAR* output */
  SQLSMALLINT *Type,            /* 16-bit output */
  SQLSMALLINT *SubType,         /* 16-bit output */
  SQLINTEGER *Length,           /* 32-bit output */
  SQLSMALLINT *Precision,       /* 16-bit output */
  SQLSMALLINT *Scale,           /* 16-bit output */
  SQLSMALLINT *Nullable         /* 16-bit output */
  );
```

Job: Retrieve the values of several fields from one Item Descriptor Area of a `desc`.

Algorithm:

```
/* hdesc refers to a desc. */
/* RecordNumber n refers to IDA[n] within the desc. */
If (RecordNumber < 1)
 return error: 07009 dynamic SQL error-invalid descriptor index
If (RecordNumber > desc.SQL_DESC_COUNT)
 return warning: 02000 no data -
If (desc is an IRD and associated statement is not prepared)
 return error: HY007 CLI-specific condition-associated statement is not
 prepared
/* Retrieve into *Name,*Type,*Subtype,etc. ... If any parameter is a null
   pointer (0000:0000), just ignore it. */
Set *Name = desc.IDA[RecordNumber].SQL_DESC_NAME (use the
usual Character String Retrieval method).
Set *NameLength = desc.IDA[RecordNumber].SQL_DESC_NAME.
Set *Type = desc.IDA[RecordNumber].SQL_DESC_TYPE
Set *SubType = desc.IDA[RecordNumber].SQL_DESC_DATETIME_INTERVAL_CODE
Set *Length = desc.IDA[RecordNumber].SQL_DESC_OCTET_LENGTH
Set *Precision = desc.IDA[RecordNumber].SQL_DESC_PRECISION.
Set *Scale = desc.IDA[RecordNumber].SQL_DESC_SCALE.
Set *Nullable = desc.IDA[RecordNumber].SQL_DESC_NULLABLE field.
```

Notes:

- In effect, calling SQLGetDescRec is equivalent to calling SQLGetDescField several times, with different field identifiers: SQL_DESC_NAME, SQL_DESC_TYPE, SQL_DESC_DATETIME_INTERVAL_CODE, SQL_DESC_OCTET_LENGTH, SQL_DESC_PRECISION, SQL_DESC_SCALE, and SQL_DESC_NULLABLE.
- Regarding the value of *Length, the Standard actually says it should be set to "the length (in octets or positions, as appropriate)" ...which is ambiguous. We have taken the ODBC specification as our guide here — it says *Length should be set to SQL_DESC_OCTET_LENGTH.
- For fields which are "not applicable," pass null parameters. For example, the SQL_DESC_NAME field is usually meaningless within an ARD or an APD. So for *Name, BufferLength, and *Namelength, pass null if you're retrieving from an ARD or APD. By passing null pointers, you can limit the values you get to fill only the fields you really want.
- SQLGetDescRec's BufferLength parameter is defined as SMALLINT (16-bit). SQLGetDescField's BufferLength parameter is defined as INTEGER (32-bit). However, the apparent inconsistency causes no problems; the length of a Name string is typically only a few octets.

Example: The following code snippet is an exact copy of the example used for the SQLGetDescField function with only one line changed.

```
SQLGetDescField(hdesc,i,SQL_DESC_NAME,col_name,sizeof(col_name),NULL);
```

is replaced by a call to SQLGetDescRec which gets only the name.

```
#include "sqlcli.h"
...
SQLHSTMT hstmt;                     /* handle of stmt */
SQLHDESC hdesc;                     /* handle of IRD */
SQLSMALLINT i,col_count;            /* used for a loop counter */
SQLCHAR col_name[128+1];
...
SQLExecDirect(hstmt,"SELECT * FROM Table_1",SQL_NTS);
SQLGetStmtAttr(hstmt,SQL_ATTR_IMP_ROW_DESC,&hdesc,00,NULL);
SQLGetDescField(hdesc,00,SQL_DESC_COUNT,&col_count,00,NULL);
printf("The Columns of Table Table_1 are:\n");
for (i=1; i<=col_count; ++i) {
  SQLGetDescRec(hdesc,i,col_name,sizeof(col_name),
                NULL,NULL,NULL,NULL,NULL,NULL,NULL);
  printf("%s\n",col_name); }
...
```

ODBC: The SQLGetDescRec function is new in ODBC 3.5. (In ODBC 2.0, the desc fields were always retrieved via other functions such as SQLDescribeCol.) SQLGetDescRec is apparently short for "Get Descriptor Record." "Descriptor record" is ODBC jargon; "Item Descriptor Area" (IDA) is the standard term. The fact that the name is SQLGetDescRec, rather than SQLGetIDA, illustrates the influence of ODBC over the Standard.

SQLSetDescRec

Function Prototype:

```
SQLRETURN SQLSetDescRec(
  SQLHDESC hdesc,             /* 32-bit input */
  SQLSMALLINT RecordNumber,   /* 16-bit input */
  SQLSMALLINT Type,           /* 16-bit input */
  SQLSMALLINT SubType,        /* 16-bit input */
  SQLINTEGER Length,          /* 32-bit input */
  SQLSMALLINT Precision,      /* 16-bit input */
  SQLSMALLINT Scale,          /* 16-bit input */
```

```
  SQLPOINTER Data,            /* ANY* input */
  SQLINTEGER *StringLength,   /* 32-bit output */
  SQLINTEGER *Indicator       /* 32-bit output */
  );
```

Job: Set the values for several fields in one Item Descriptor Area of a desc.

Algorithm:

```
If (desc is associated with a "deferred parameter")
   return error: HY010 CLI-specific condition-function sequence error
If (RecordNumber < 1)
   return error: 07009 dynamic SQL error-invalid descriptor index
If (desc is an IRD)
   /* This error will appear only for ISO SQL3: */
   return error: HY016 CLI-specific condition-cannot modify an
   implementation row descriptor
  Set desc.IDA[RecordNumber].SQL_DESC_TYPE = Type
  Set desc.IDA[RecordNumber].SQL_DESC_PRECISION = Precision
  Set desc.IDA[RecordNumber].SQL_DESC_SCALE = Scale
  Set desc.IDA[RecordNumber].SQL_DESC_DATETIME_INTERVAL_CODE = SubType
If (desc is an IPD)
   /* for IPD: this is the length in characters / bits / positions */
 Set desc.IDA[RecordNumber].SQL_DESC_LENGTH=Length
Else
 /* for APD or ARD: this is the length in octets */
 Set desc.IDA[RecordNumber].SQL_DESC_OCTET_LENGTH=Length
If (StringLength is not a null pointer)
 Set desc.IDA[RecordNumber].SQL_DESC_OCTET_LENGTH_POINTER=StringLength
 Set desc.IDA[RecordNumber].SQL_DESC_DATA_POINTER = Data
If (Indicator is not a null pointer)
 Set desc.IDA[RecordNumber].SQL_DESC_INDICATOR_POINTER=Indicator
If (Data is not a null pointer)
 If ("Consistency Check" fails)
   return error: HY021 CLI-specific condition-inconsistent descriptor
   information
If (RecordNumber > desc.SQL_DESC_COUNT)
 Set desc.SQL_DESC_COUNT = RecordNumber
/* If any errors occur, then desc.SQL_DESC_COUNT will not be changed,
   but the other fields mentioned in this description may be. */
```

Notes:

- In effect, calling SQLSetDescRec is equivalent to calling SQLSetDescField several times with different field identifiers: SQL_DESC_TYPE, SQL_DESC_PRECISION, SQL_DESC_SCALE, SQL_DESC_DATETIME_INTERVAL_CODE, SQL_DESC_LENGTH or SQL_DESC_OCTET_LENGTH, SQL_DESC_OCTET_LENGTH_POINTER, SQL_DESC_DATA_POINTER, and SQL_DESC_INDICATOR_POINTER.
- Using SQLSetDescRec on an ARD is somewhat similar to using SQLBindCol on the stmt which contains the ARD.
- Using SQLSetDescRec on an APD is somewhat similar to using SQLBindParameter on the stmt which contains the APD.
- The parameters of SQLSetDescRec do not correspond to the parameters of SQLGetDescRec. For example, there is no way to set the SQL_DESC_NAME field.
- Because of the peculiar algorithm logic, it is impossible to set SQL_DESC_OCTET_LENGTH_POINTER or SQL_DESC_INDICATOR_POINTER to null values.
- A Consistency Check always happens. Therefore, if there are other fields that you want to set, you should call SQLSetDescField before you call SQLSetDescRec.
- If you are changing an IPD, StringLength and Indicator should be null pointers.

Example: This is an efficient way to execute an SQL statement many times varying only the input parameter (represented in the statement by "?"). The code will insert 50 rows, with values between 1 and 50. We have deliberately varied some names and parameter declarations, to show a style preferred by other programmers.

```
#include "sqlcli.h"
SQLHSTMT hstmt;
SQLHDESC hdesc1,hdesc2; /* hdesc1 is APD, hdesc2 is IPD */
SQLINTEGER i;           /* the loop counter, and the input value */
...
/* prepare the statement -- outside the loop */
SQLPrepare(hstmt, "INSERT INTO Table_1 VALUES (?)", SQL_NTS);
/* Associate i with APD */
SQLGetStmtAttr(hstmt,SQL_ATTR_APP_PARAM_DESC,&hdesc1, 0L,(SQLINTEGER *)NULL);
SQLSetDescRec(
   hdesc1,1,SQL_INTEGER,0,0L,0,0,(SQLPOINTER)&i,(SQLINTEGER *)NULL,
   (SQLINTEGER *)NULL);
/* Associate parameter marker with IPD */
SQLGetStmtAttr(hstmt,SQL_ATTR_IMP_PARAM_DESC,&hdesc2,
               0L,(SQLINTEGER *)NULL);
SQLSetDescRec(
   hdesc2,1,SQL_INTEGER,0,0L,0,0,(SQLPOINTER)NULL,(SQLINTEGER *)NULL,
   (SQLINTEGER *)NULL);
for (i=1; i<50; ++i)
   {
```

```
    /* execute the statement -- inside the loop */
    SQLExecute(hstmt);
    }
...
```

WARNING: This code is "efficient" because it calls SQLPrepare and the SQLSetDescRec functions only once for an SQL statement that is executed 50 times. Usually, taking code out of loops is the right thing to do. But, for at least one DBMS, it's better to bind i (as a deferred parameter) after the call to SQLExecute.

ODBC: SQLSetDescRec is new in ODBC 3.0. You can set SQL_DESC_OCTET_LENGTH_POINTER or SQL_DESC_INDICATOR_POINTER to null by passing null pointers in the StringLength or Indicator parameters. In standard SQL, the DBMS ignores null pointers in those parameters.

SQLCopyDesc

Function Prototype:

```
SQLRETURN SQLCopyDesc(
  SQLHDESC source_hdesc,      /* 32-bit input */
  SQLHDESC target_hdesc       /* 32-bit input */
  );
```

Job: Copy a source desc to a target desc.

Algorithm:

```
If (source_hdesc is not a hdesc)
  return error: CLI-specific condition-invalid handle
If (target_hdesc is not a hdesc)
  return error: CLI-specific condition-invalid handle
    The target desc's diagnostics area is emptied.
    If (source_desc is associated with a "deferred parameter")
     return error: HY010 CLI-specific condition-function
     sequence error
    If (target_desc is associated with a "deferred parameter")
     return error: HY010 CLI-specific condition-function sequence error
    If (Target Desc is an IRD)
     return error: HY016 CLI-specific condition-cannot modify an
     implementation row descriptor.
```

```
    If (Source Desc is an IRD)
      If (associated statement not prepared)
        return error: HY007 CLI-specific condition-associated statement is not
        prepared)
Copy the contents of every field in source desc to target desc — with the
exception of the SQL_DESC_ALLOC_TYPE field. SQL_DESC_ALLOC_TYPE keeps its orig-
inal value.
```

Notes:

- There are other ways to copy an entire desc. For example, you could call the SQLGetDescField and SQLSetDescField functions repeatedly. But SQLCopyDesc is the easy way.
- If you're thinking of copying stmt #1's APD to stmt #2's APD, there's an alternative; you can allocate a user desc and share it. Here's how:
  - Make a user desc:

```
SQLAllocHandle(SQL_HANDLE_DESC,hdbc,&hdesc_user);
```

  - Say that stmt #1's APD is the user desc:

```
SQLSetStmtAttr(hstmt1,SQL_ATTR_APP_ROW_DESC,(void*)hdesc_user,00);
```

  - Fill in the fields of stmt #1's APD (using SQLSetDescRec, etc.)
  - Say that stmt #2's APD is the user desc:

```
SQLSetStmtAttr(hstmt2,SQL_ATTR_APP_ROW_DESC,(void*)hdesc_user,00);
```

  Now there's no need to copy, because stmt #2's APD is stmt #1's APD.
- One possible use of SQLCopyDesc is to copy an IRD to an ARD. The point is the IRD and the ARD fields are supposed to be similar; the IRD is set up automatically, so after the copy, the ARD will have the values that the DBMS thinks should be there. If you want to change these values slightly, you can fine-tune using SQLSetDescField.
- Another possible use of SQLCopyDesc is to save desc information — if, for example, you have a small number of queries that are executed repeatedly using the same stmt. Here's how:
  - Allocate a user descriptor with

```
SQLAllocHandle(SQL_HANDLE_DESC,...).
```

  - Copy an automatic desc to the user desc with SQLCopyDesc.
  - Change the automatic desc for some temporary purpose.
  - Copy the user desc back to the automatic desc, with SQLCopyDesc. This is like "pushing" all the desc fields to a stack, making changes, then "popping" to restore the original values.
- Some DBMSs will perform a consistency check on the target desc's IDAs if any target_desc.IDA[n].SQL_DESC_DATA_POINTER is not a null pointer.
- The copy is possible even if the source and target descs are in different connections.

Example: This shows how to copy values from one Table to another. The trick works like this:

- Step 1: Prepare a `SELECT` statement from the source Table. This yields the IRD of the source. Bind the result set with `SQLSetDescRec`. This yields the ARD of the source.
- Step 2: Prepare an `INSERT` statement on the target Table. This yields the IPD of the target.
- Step 3: Copy the source RDs to the target PDs.

The trick would work for any pair of Tables, provided Columns have compatible <data type>s.

```
#include "sqlcli.h"
SQLCHAR   szCol_1[6];/* sz is "string, zero terminated" */
SQLINTEGER cbCol_1;  /* col_1's indicator */
SQLHSTMT     hstmt_source, hstmt_target;
SQLHDESC     hard_source, hird_source; /* source's ARD+IRD handles */
SQLHDESC     hapd_target, hipd_target; /* target's APD+IPD handles */
...
 /* Get the handles of each desc that we'll use */
 /* SELECT from the source. */
 SQLExecDirect(hstmt_source,"SELECT col_1 FROM Sources",SQL_NTS);
 SQLGetStmtAttr(hstmt_source,SQL_ATTR_APP_ROW_DESC, &hard_source,0,NULL);
 SQLGetStmtAttr(hstmt_target,SQL_ATTR_APP_PARAM_DESC, &hapd_target,0,NULL);
 /* Bind source Column #1. This changes the source's ARD. */
 SQLSetDescRec(
   hard_source,1,SQL_CHAR,NULL,NULL,NULL,NULL,szCol_1, &6,&cbCol_1);
 /* Copy source's ARD to target's APD */
 SQLCopyDesc(hard_source,hapd_target);
 /* Copy source's IRD to target's IPD */
 SQLGetStmtAttr(
   hstmt_source,SQL_ATTR_IMP_ROW_DESC,&hird_source,0,NULL);
 SQLGetStmtAttr(hstmt_target,SQL_ATTR_IMP_PARAM_DESC, &hipd_target,0,NULL);
 SQLCopyDesc(hird_source, hipd_target);
 /* Prepare to INSERT in the target. */
 /* Once again, we assume "auto-populate IPD" is not true. If it were true,
   SQLPrepare would overwrite what we've just copied to the IPD. */
 SQLPrepare(hstmt_target,"INSERT INTO Targets VALUES (?)", SQL_NTS);
 /* Fetch loop */
 for (;;) {
   sqlreturn = SQLFetchScroll(hstmt0, SQL_FETCH_NEXT, 00);
   if (sqlreturn <> SQL_SUCCESS &&
       sqlreturn <> SQL_SUCCESS_WITH_INFO) break;
```

```
   /* According to the row descriptors of the SELECT: we fetched into
      szCol_1 and cbCol_1. According to the parameter descriptors of INSERT:
      we'll get our values from szCol_1 and cbCol_1. Thus the fetch's "output"
      is the insert's "input". */
   SQLExecute(hstmt_target); }
SQLCloseCursor(hstmt_source);
...
```

ODBC: The `SQLCopyDesc` function arrived with ODBC 3.0. ODBC's Driver Manager will handle copying if the source and target handles are associated with different drivers.

SQLBindCol

Function Prototype:

```
SQLRETURN SQLBindCol(
  SQLHSTMT hstmt,                  /* 32-bit input */
  SQLSMALLINT ColumnNumber,        /* 16-bit input */
  SQLSMALLINT BufferType,          /* 16-bit input */
  SQLPOINTER Data,                 /* ANY* input */
  SQLINTEGER BufferLength,         /* 32-bit input */
  SQLINTEGER *StrLen_or_Ind        /* 32-bit pointer to output */
  );
```

Job: Bind a Column to a host variable by setting fields in the ARD.

Algorithm:

```
If (ColumnNumber < 1)
  return error: 07009 Dynamic SQL error-invalid descriptor index
If (BufferType <> SQL_C_DEFAULT and BufferType is not a valid type code)
  /* A "valid type code" could be one of: 1 (SQL_CHAR), 2 (SQL_NUMERIC),
     3 (SQL_DECIMAL), 4 (SQL_INTEGER), 5 (SQL_SMALLINT), 6 (SQL_FLOAT),
     7 (SQL_REAL), 8 (SQL_DOUBLE), 18 (SQL_UDT_LOCATOR), 20 (SQL_REF),
     30 (SQL_BLOB), 31 (SQL_BLOB_LOCATOR), 40 (SQL_CLOB),
     41 (SQL_CLOB_LOCATOR), etc. But no host language has corresponding
     <data type>s for all of those; see the data type correspondences
     lists in our chapter on embedded SQL. */
  return error: HY003 CLI-specific condition-invalid data type in
  application descriptor
If (BufferLength <= 0)
  return error: HY090 CLI-specific condition-invalid string length or buffer
length
Set ARD.IDA[ColumnNumber].SQL_DESC_TYPE = BufferType
```

```
Set ARD.IDA[ColumnNumber].SQL_DESC_OCTET_LENGTH = BufferLength
Set ARD.IDA[ColumnNumber].SQL_DESC_LENGTH = maximum for this data type
Set ARD.IDA[ColumnNumber].SQL_DESC_DATA_POINTER = Data
Set ARD.IDA[ColumnNumber].SQL_DESC_OCTET_LENGTH_POINTER = StrLen_or_Ind
Set ARD.IDA[ColumnNumber].SQL_DESC_INDICATOR_POINTER = StrLen_or_Ind
If (ColumnNumber > ARD.SQL_DESC_COUNT)
 Set ARD.SQL_DESC_COUNT = ColumnNumber
/* If an error occurs: the DBMS leaves SQL_DESC_COUNT unchanged, but may set IDA
fields to implementation-dependent values. */
```

Notes:

- Technically, a host variable is "bound" when it is associated with a host-variable address. Because SQLBindCol causes a setting of ARD.IDA[ColumnNumber].SQL_DESC_DATA_POINTER, we can describe it thus, "SQLBindCol performs a binding of an output host variable for a result-set Column; specifically the result-set Column indicated by the ColumnNumber parameter."
- Technically, this host variable is called a "target specification." SQLBindCol is for values that flow out from the DBMS to a host variable.
- The usual idea is that what you set up with SQLBindCol will later be used by SQLFetch or SQLFetchScroll. Alternatively, you could bind after fetching, using the SQLGetData function.
- You need a valid hstmt, but you don't need a result set yet. That is, you can SELECT either before or after you call SQLBindCol.
- Calling SQLBindCol for a stmt is conceptually similar to calling SQLSetDescRec for the stmt's ARD. In fact, everything that you can do with SQLBindCol and more, can be done with SQLSetDescRec. However, SQLBindCol is seen far more often than SQLSetDescRec.

WARNING: You are passing addresses. The DBMS will write to those addresses. So there are two easy ways to cause GPFs:

• Pass the address of a local variable, exit from the procedure that the local variable is defined in, then call SQLFetch.

• Pass a buffer that is too small to hold the result. For CHAR and BIT <data type>s, there is a guard against this (you pass BufferLength to tell the DBMS when it must stop). For numeric <data type>s, there is also a guard against this (if you say that BufferType is SQL_SMALLINT, the DBMS won't move a 32-bit value to it). But if you enter the wrong value for DataType... Ka-Boom! As a safeguard, some programmers deliberately "unbind" when they finish fetching — see the description of SQLFreeStmt(...,SQL_UNBIND) on page 790.

- SQLBindCol does not set every defined field in the ARD. You might have to follow up with a call to SQLSetDescField if for some reason you have to change a low importance field, like SQL_DESC_DATETIME_INTERVAL_PRECISION.

- The value of BufferLength is irrelevant for non-string <data type>s. Nevertheless, you must always pass a value greater than zero.

Example:

```
/* This example shows a retrieval of a CHAR string. */
#include "sqlcli.h"
SQLHSTMT hstmt;
SQLCHAR value[128];
SQLINTEGER value_indicator;
...
SQLBindCol(hstmt,1,SQL_CHAR,value,sizeof(value),&value_indicator);
SQLExecDirect(stmt,"SELECT 'ABCDE' FROM t",SQL_NTS);
SQLFetch(hstmt);
/* At this point, value has "ABCDE\0", value_indicator has zero. */
...
```

```
/* This example shows a retrieval of a floating-point variable. The C
   data type is float, but we use SQL_REAL. We'd like to pass NULL as
   the BufferLength parameter -- it's irrelevant -- but we can't. */
#include "sqlcli.h"
#include <math.h>
SQLHSTMT hstmt;
SQLREAL value;  /* sqlcli.h has "typedef float SQLREAL" */
SQLINTEGER value_indicator;
...
SQLBindCol(hstmt,1,SQL_REAL,&value,sizeof(value),&value_indicator);
SQLExecDirect(stmt,"SELECT 1.5E5 FROM t",SQL_NTS);
SQLFetch(hstmt);
/* At this point, value has 1.5E5, value_indicator has zero. */
...
```

```
/* This example shows a retrieval of two Columns from the first row of
   TABLE_1. It displays their values, or displays "NULL". */
#include "sqlcli.h"
SQLINTEGER col_1;
SQLCHAR   col_2[128];
SQLINTEGER col_1_ind,col_2_ind;
SQLHSTMT  hstmt;
SQLHDESC  hdesc;
...
SQLBindCol(hstmt,1,SQL_INTEGER,&col_1,sizeof(col_1),&col_1_ind);
```

```
SQLBindCol(hstmt,2,SQL_CHAR,col_2,sizeof(col_2),&col_2_ind);
SQLExecDirect(hstmt,"SELECT col_1,col_2 FROM Table_1",SQL_NTS);
SQLFetch(hstmt);
if (col_1_ind == SQL_NULL_DATA) printf("NULL\n");
else printf("%ld.\n",col_1);
if (col_2_ind == SQL_NULL_DATA) printf("NULL\n");
else printf("%s.\n",col_2);
...
```

Here is a picture of the ARD after the SQLSetDescField call is done:

```
- ----------------------- ------------------
--SQL_DESC_ALLOC_TYPE- - SQL_DESC_COUNT -
- ----------------------- -----------------
- | 00001               | | 00002        |
------------------------------------------
-
------------------------------------------------------
-- SQL_DESC_DATA_POINTER | SQL_DESC_TYPE | ........ |
------------------------------------------------------
-  1-&col_1              | 00004         | ........ |
------------------------------------------------------
-  2-col_2 (address)     | 00001         | ........ |
------------------------------------------------------
```

Here is a picture of the IRD after the SQLExecDirect call is done:

```
- ----------------------- ------------------
--SQL_DESC_ALLOC_TYPE- - SQL_DESC_COUNT -
- ----------------------- -----------------
- | 00001               | | 00002        |
- ----------------------------------------
-
-----------------------------------------------------
-- SQL_DESC_NAME        | SQL_DESC_TYPE | ........ |
-----------------------------------------------------
-  1-'Col_1'            | 00005         | ........ |
-  --------------------------------------------------
-  2-'Col_2'            | 00001         | ........ |
-----------------------------------------------------
```

[Obscure Rule] In this example, COL_1 is actually a SMALLINT (SQL_DESC_TYPE = 5), but it's being transferred to an INTEGER (SQL_DESC_TYPE = 4). That is not a problem — the DBMS will automatically "CAST (<smallint Column value> TO INTEGER)." In fact, the DBMS will automatically cast from the IRD type to the ARD type. If the cast is syntactically impossible, an SQLSTATE error appears: 07006 "Dynamic SQL error-restricted data type attribute violation."

ODBC: SQLBindCol always triggers a consistency check. The value of BufferLength must be >= 0 (standard SQL says the value of BufferLength must be > 0). The difference looks trivial, but the majority of ODBC application programs would collapse tomorrow if a DBMS vendor decided to enforce the standard SQL rule.

SQL_C_DEFAULT

There is a lazy way to bind numbers. Instead of passing a real <data type>, pass 99 (SQL_C_DEFAULT). Here is an example using SQLBindCol — notice that the third parameter is SQL_C_DEFAULT, so after SQLBindCol, the value in ARD.IDA[n].SQL_DESC_TYPE == SQL_C_DEFAULT. When SQLFetch occurs, it handles the default request like this:

- Set ARD.IDA[n].SQL_DESC_TYPE = IRD.IDA[n].SQL_DESC_TYPE.
- Set ARD.IDA[n].SQL_DESC_PRECISION = IRD.IDA[n].SQL_DESC_PRECISION.
- Set ARD.IDA[n].SQL_DESC_SCALE = IRD.IDA[n].SQL_DESC_SCALE. (These are temporary settings. SQLFetch never makes permanent changes to any desc fields.) Now there is enough information to continue the fetch:

```
#include "sqlcli.h"
SQLHSTMT hstmt;
SQLSMALLINT col_1;
...
SQLExecDirect(hstmt,"SELECT col_1 FROM Table_1",SQL_NTS);
SQLBindCol(hstmt,1,SQL_C_DEFAULT,&col_1,1,NULL);
SQLFetch(hstmt);
```

And now, a few words of urgent warning:

- The only fields involved are type, precision, and scale — not length or octet length.
- There is no check for possible overflow of the target output.
- The ODBC specification does not agree with the Standard about what the default <data type> codes should be.

Retrieving Column Values

Column retrieval involves executing a SELECT statement, then fetching from the result set to variables defined in your host program. The Columns in the select list must be "bound" to the host-variable addresses. The problems you must solve — with the DBMS's help — are:

- The impedance mismatch between SQL <data type>s and host language types.
- Telling the DBMS where to put the data.
- Telling the DBMS how null values should be signalled to the host.
- Ensuring that the DBMS does not go beyond the host-variable buffers.

There are two solutions to these problems:

1. Call SQLBindCol, SQLSetDescField, or SQLSetDescRec, then fetch using SQLFetch or SQLFetchScroll.
2. Fetch using SQLFetch or SQLFetchScroll, then call SQLGetData.

The most popular option is to call SQLBindCol, then SQLFetch.

There are two descs involved here — the IRD (which the DBMS sets up when the SELECT statement is executed) and the ARD (which the host program sets up at any time before the fetch). The programmer's job, then, can be seen as making sure that the ARD matches the IRD and setting up appropriate buffers for the DBMS to fetch data into.

Fetch Loops Revisited

Once more into the "fetch," dear friends! Now that you know about binding, you can fetch INTO something. Here is a program that does so. Most functions are shown in skeletal form. There is a test for truncation.

```
#include "sqlcli.h"
SQLHENV      henv;
SQLHDBC      hdbc;
SQLHSTMT     hstmt;
SQLCHAR    char_string[128];
SQLINTEGER char_string_ind;
SQLRETURN  sqlreturn;
void main ()
{
 SQLAllocHandle(SQL_HANDLE_ENV,NULL,&henv);
 SQLAllocHandle(SQL_HANDLE_DBC,henv,&hdbc);
 SQLConnect(hdbc,...,SQL_NTS);
 SQLAllocHandle(SQL_HANDLE_HSTMT,hdbc,&hstmt);
 SQLExecDirect(hstmt,"SELECT ...",SQL_NTS);
 SQLBindCol(
    hstmt,1,SQL_CHAR,char_string,sizeof(char_string), &char_string_ind);
 for (;;) {
   sqlreturn = SQLFetch(hstmt);
   if (sqlreturn == SQL_NO_DATA) break;
   if (sqlreturn == SQL_ERROR) {
    printf("Error ... aborting\n");
    break; }
   if (sqlreturn == SQL_SUCCESS_WITH_WARNING) {
    /* We could call SQLGetDiagnostics to find out if sqlstate ==
       '01004' (string data right truncation), diagnostics is a later chapter.
       Instead, we'll see if the DBMS had more data than it sent. */
    if (char_string_ind >= sizeof(char_string) printf("[Truncated!]\n"); }
   if (char_string_ind==SQL_NULL_DATA) printf("NULL\n");
```

```
  else printf("%s.\n",char_string); }
 SQLCloseCursor(hstmt);
 SQLFreeHandle(SQL_HANDLE_STMT,hstmt);
 SQLDisconnect(hdbc);
 SQLFreeHandle(SQL_HANDLE_DBC,hdbc);
 SQLFreeHandle(SQL_HANDLE_ENV,henv);
}
```

SQLGetData

Function Prototype:

```
SQLRETURN SQLGetData(
  SQLHSTMT hstmt,               /* 32-bit input */
  SQLSMALLINT ColumnNumber,     /* 16-bit input -- index to IDA */
  SQLSMALLINT TargetType,       /* 16-bit input. Concise. */
  SQLPOINTER TargetValue,       /* VOID* output */
  SQLINTEGER BufferLength,      /* 32-bit input */
  SQLINTEGER *StrLen_or_Ind     /* 32-bit output */
  );
```

Job: Get a value from one Column of a result set. Call `SQLGetData` after calling `SQLFetch` or `SQLFetchScroll`.

Algorithm:

```
If (there is no fetched row associated with stmt)
 /* Looks like somebody forgot to call SQLFetch or SQLFetchScroll */
 return error: HY010 CLI-specific condition-function sequence error
If (the fetched row is "empty")
 /* Looks like somebody DELETEd the row */
 return warning: 02000 No data
If (ColumnNumber < 1 or ColumnNumber > IRD.SQL_DESC_COUNT)
 /*  IRD.SQL_DESC_COUNT is the number of Columns in the select list */
 return error: 07009 Dynamic SQL error-invalid descriptor index
If (ARD.IDA[ColumnNumber].SQL_DESC_DATA_POINTER <> 0)
 /* It's illegal to call SQLGetdata for a "bound" Column */
 return error: 07009 dynamic SQL error-invalid descriptor index
/* Following check is implementation-defined -- it depends whether the DBMS
   supports SQLGetData extensions -- see SQLGetInfo */
If (ARD.IDA[x].SQL_DESC_DATA_POINTER==0 for any IDA before ColumnNumber)
 return error: 07009 dynamic SQL error-invalid descriptor index
```

```
/* Following check is implementation-defined -- it depends whether the DBMS
   supports SQLGetData Extensions -- see SQLGetInfo */
If (ARD.IDA[x].SQL_DESC_DATA_POINTER<>0 for any IDA after ColumnNumber)
 return error: 07009 dynamic SQL error-invalid descriptor index
/* The rest of the SQLGetData algorithm is the same as the algorithm for
   fetching a "bound" Column -- see SQLBindCol for details. */
```

Notes:

- SQLGetData does not make permanent changes to the ARD. But it can be thought of as a function which makes a temporary binding for a specified Column in a result set and transfers the Column value to the bound target variable.
- It looks like there are two possible strategies for retrieving data — with SQLBindCol or with SQLGetData. Let's compare the two.

  The SQLBindCol strategy:

```
SQLExecDirect(...,"SELECT ...",...);
 SQLBindCol(...,1,&var_1,...);
 for (;;) {
  if (SQLFetch(...)==100) break; }
```

  The SQLGetData strategy:

```
SQLExecDirect(...,"SELECT ...",...);
for (;;) {
   if (SQLFetch(...)==100) break;
   SQLGetData(...,1,...,&var_1,...); }
```

  Look hard at where the loop is. The SQLBindCol strategy is apparently more efficient, because the binding happens only once. If you use SQLGetData, you'll have to use it for every iteration of the SQLFetch loop. On the other hand, maybe that's exactly what you want to do. There are times when you have to be flexible and change some factor (such as the variable's address) while inside the loop. Then SQLGetData is the choice.
- Suppose you bind Column #1 (using SQLBindCol), then you fetch, then you get Column #2 (using SQLGetData). That's legal. But it might not be legal to skip Columns, to get Columns out of order, or to get Columns twice. The ability to get Columns in any order is called the "SQLGetData Extensions" feature. You can check whether your DBMS supports it (you'll see how when we describe the SQLGetInfo function). But usually there's nothing difficult about getting Columns in ascending Column-number order.
- *StrLen_or_Ind points to a 32-bit integer, not a 16-bit integer. Thus the final three parameters — *TargetValue, BufferLength, *StrLen_or_Ind — do not form a typical example of Character String Retrieval parameters.
- Because SQLGetData cannot take advantage of the full set of ARD fields, it only gets used for simple situations.

Example:

```
#include "sqlcli.h"
#define CHAR_LENGTH 1000
SQLHSTMT hstmt;
SQLRETURN sqlreturn;
SQLINTEGER sIntegerColumn;
SQLINTEGER IntegerIndicator;
SQLCHAR szCharColumn[CHAR_LENGTH];
SQLINTEGER IntegerIndicator;
...
SQLExecDirect(hstmt,"SELECT col_1,col_2 FROM Table_1",SQL_NTS);
for (;;) {
  sqlreturn = SQLFetch(hstmt);
  if (sqlreturn != SQL_SUCCESS && sqlreturn != SQL_SUCCESS_WITH_INFO) {
   break; }
  SQLGetData(hstmt,1,SQL_INTEGER,&sIntegerColumn,00,&IntegerIndicator);
  if (IntegerIndicator != SQL_NULL_DATA) {
   if (sIntegerColumn > 0) {
    SQLGetData(hstmt,2,SQL_CHAR,szCharColumn,CHAR_LENGTH, &CharIndicator);
    if (CharIndicator == SQL_NULL_DATA) strcpy(szCharColumn,"");
    printf("%s.\n",szCharColumn); } } }
SQLCloseCursor(hstmt);
...
```

ODBC: `SQLGetData` has been around since ODBC version 1.0. `SQLGetData` can be used, with char or bit <data type>s, to get data in pieces. This is done by calling `SQLGetData` with `BufferLength = 1000` (to ask for the first 1,000 octets), calling again — for the same Column number with `BufferLength = 1000` (to ask for the next 1,000 octets), and so on. In the days of 16-bit operating systems, this was a useful feature.

SQLBindParameter

Function Prototype:

```
SQLRETURN SQLBindParameter (
  SQLHSTMT hstmt,                  /* 32-bit input */
  SQLSMALLINT ParameterNumber,     /* 16-bit input: must be > 0 */
  SQLSMALLINT InputOutputMode,     /* 16-bit input: must be one of:
                                      1 SQL_PARAM_MODE_IN,
                                      2 SQL_PARAM_MODE_INOUT,
                                      4 SQL_PARAM_MODE_OUT */
  SQLSMALLINT ValueType,           /* 16-bit input ... for the APD
                                      must be in table of host/SQL
                                      <data type> correspondences */
  SQLSMALLINT ParameterType,       /* 16-bit input ... for the IPD
                                      must be in table of concise
                                      types */
  SQLINTEGER Columnsize,           /* 32-bit input */
  SQLSMALLINT DecimalDigits,       /* 16-bit input */
  SQLPOINTER ParameterValue,       /* DEF */
  SQLINTEGER BufferLength,         /* 32-bit input */
  SQLINTEGER *StrLen_or_Ind        /* DEF */
  );
```

Job: Describe one "dynamic parameter specification" (in the IPD) and its host variable (in the APD). SQLBindParameter is useful if you pass parameters from the application to the DBMS. Such parameters are marked by parameter markers (question marks) in SQL statements.

Algorithm: The algorithm is too complex to show in the usual manner. For this function, we will have to make heavy use of texts and charts. What happens —

- If the function fails and returns -1 (SQL_ERROR): see 07009, HY015, and HY090 in Chapter 47 "SQL/CLI: Diagnostic Functions." (Note: If errors happen, some of the IPD and APD fields may be garbaged, although SQL_DESC_COUNT won't change.)
- If the function succeeds, some IPD and APD fields are set. The precise setting depends on a combination of factors, but in general we can say that:
  - hstmt designates which stmt. The affected descs are the stmt's IPD and APD.
  - ParameterNumber designates the item descriptor area within a desc. If ParameterNumber is n, then the affected IDAs are IPD.IDA[n] and APD.IDA[n].
  - ParameterType, Columnsize, and DecimalDigits affect IPD.IDA[n].
  - ValueType, BufferLength, ParameterValue, and Strlen_Or_Ind affect APD.IDA[n].
  - If ParameterNumber is greater than an APD or IPD's SQL_DESC_COUNT field, then that SQL_DESC_COUNT field gets the value in ParameterNumber.

- Sometimes passed values are ignored.
- Values should be consistent, but some DBMSs won't perform a consistency check until SQLExecute happens.

In the charts which follow, we show the effects on particular APD or IPD fields. Notice that the usual effect is that the field simply receives the value of a parameter that you pass, but that sometimes special calculations are necessary. Particularly complex are "datetime" and "interval" settings.

SQLBindParameter Effect on APD Fields

Field	Gets
SQL_DESC_PARAMETER_MODE	InputOutputMode
SQL_DESC_TYPE	ValueType
SQL_DESC_OCTET_LENGTH	BufferLength
SQL_DESC_DATA_POINTER	ParameterValue (an address)
SQL_DESC_INDICATOR_POINTER	StrLen_or_Ind (an address)
SQL_DESC_OCTET_LENGTH_POINTER	StrLen_or_Ind (an address)

For example, if you call SQLBindParameter with ParameterNumber=2, InputOutputMode = SQL_PARAM_MODE_OUT, ValueType=1 (the code for CHAR <data type>), BufferLength=5, ParameterValue = address of x_char_buffer and Strlen_Or_Ind = address of x_char_buffer_indicator, the result is that, in the APD.IDA[2] (i.e., the second item descriptor area in the application parameter desc), the settings are as follows: SQL_DESC_PARAMETER_MODE = SQL_PARAM_MODE_OUT, SQL_DESC_TYPE = 1, SQL_DESC_OCTET_LENGTH = BufferLength, SQL_DESC_DATA_POINTER = x_char_buffer address, SQL_DESC_INDICATOR_POINTER = x_char_buffer_indicator address, and SQL_DESC_OCTET_LENGTH_POINTER = x_char_buffer_indicator address.

SQLBindParameter Effect on IPD.IDA Fields for Numeric <data type>s

Field	Gets ...
SQL_DESC_TYPE	ParameterType
SQL_DESC_PRECISION	Columnsize
SQL_DESC_SCALE	DecimalDigits

This chart shows the effect on IPD.IDA[n] fields if the value of the passed ParameterType is 2 or 3 or 4 or 5 or 6 or 7 or 8 (SQL_NUMERIC or SQL_DECIMAL or SQL_INTEGER or SQL_SMALLINT or SQL_FLOAT or SQL_REAL or SQL_DOUBLE). For example, if you call SQLBindParameter with ParameterNumber = 1, ParameterType = 3, Columnsize=5, and DecimalDigits=4, the result is that, in the IPD.IDA[1] (i.e., the first item descriptor area in the Implementation Parameter Desc), the settings are as follows: SQL_DESC_TYPE=3, SQL_DESC_PRECISION=5, and SQL_DESC_SCALE=4.

SQLBindParameter Effect on IPD.IDA Fields for Datetime <data type>s

Field	Gets for ...		
	91 (date)	92 (time)	93 (timestamp)
SQL_DESC_TYPE	9	9	9
SQL_DESC_DATETIME_INTERVAL_CODE	1	2	3
SQL_DESC_LENGTH (in positions)	Columnsize	Columnsize	Columnsize
SQL_DESC_PRECISION (frac-sec)	0	DecimalDigits	DecimalDigits

This chart shows the effect on IPD.IDA[n] fields if the value of the passed ParameterType is 91 or 92 or 93 (date or time or timestamp). SQL_DESC_LENGTH is the length in "positions." SQL_DESC_PRECISION is the "fractional-seconds" precision. For example, if you call SQLBindParameter with ParameterNumber = 5, ParameterType=92, Columnsize=8, and DecimalDigits=0, the result is that, in the IPD.IDA[5] (i.e., the fifth item descriptor area in the Implementation Parameter Desc), the settings are as follows: SQL_DESC_TYPE=9, SQL_DESC_DATETIME_INTERVAL_CODE=2, SQL_DESC_LENGTH=8, and SQL_DESC_PRECISION=0.

SQLBindParameter Effect on IPD.IDA Fields for Interval Year/Month <data type>s

Field	Gets for ...	
	101 (year)	102 (month)
SQL_DESC_TYPE	10	10
SQL_DESC_DATETIME_INTERVAL_CODE	1	2
SQL_DESC_LENGTH (in positions)	Columnsize	Columnsize
SQL_DESC_PRECISION (frac-sec)	0	0
SQL_DESC_DATETIME_INTERVAL_PRECISION (lead)	Columnsize-1	Columnsize-1

Field	Gets for ...
	107 (year to month)
SQL_DESC_TYPE	10
SQL_DESC_DATETIME_INTERVAL_CODE	7
SQL_DESC_LENGTH (in positions)	Columnsize
SQL_DESC_PRECISION (frac-sec)	0
SQL_DESC_DATETIME_INTERVAL_PRECISION	Columnsize-4

The charts show the effect on IPD.IDA[n] fields if the value of the passed ParameterType is 101 or 102 or 107 (interval year or interval month or interval year-to-month). SQL_DESC_LENGTH is the length in "positions." SQL_DESC_PRECISION is the "fractional-seconds" precision.

SQL_DESC_DATETIME_INTERVAL_PRECISION is the "leading field" precision. For example, if you call SQLBindParameter with ParameterNumber = 2, ParameterType=107, Columnsize=8, and DecimalDigits=0, the result is that, in the IPD.IDA[2] (i.e., the second item descriptor area in the Implementation Parameter Desc), the settings are as follows: SQL_DESC_TYPE=10, SQL_DESC_DATETIME_INTERVAL_CODE=7, SQL_DESC_LENGTH=8, SQL_DESC_PRECISION=0, and SQL_DESC_DATETIME_INTERVAL_PRECISION=(8 - 4)=4.

SQLBindParameter Effect on IPD.IDA Fields for Interval Day/Time <data type>s with No SECONDs

Field	Gets for ...	
	103 (day)	104 (hour)
SQL_DESC_TYPE	10	10
SQL_DESC_DATETIME_INTERVAL_CODE	3	4
SQL_DESC_LENGTH (in positions)	Columnsize	Columnsize
SQL_DESC_PRECISION (frac-sec)	0	0
SQL_DESC_DATETIME_INTERVAL_PRECISION (lead)	Columnsize-1	Columnsize-1

Field	Gets for ...		
	105 (minute)	108 (day to hour)	109 (day to minute)
SQL_DESC_TYPE	10	10	10
SQL_DESC_DATETIME_INTERVAL_CODE	5	8	9
SQL_DESC_LENGTH (in positions)	Columnsize	Columnsize	Columnsize
SQL_DESC_PRECISION (frac-sec)	0	0	0
SQL_DESC_DATETIME_INTERVAL_PRECISION	Columnsize-1	Columnsize-4	Columnsize-7

Field	Gets for ...
	111 (hour to minute)
SQL_DESC_TYPE	10
SQL_DESC_DATETIME_INTERVAL_CODE	11
SQL_DESC_LENGTH (in positions)	Columnsize
SQL_DESC_PRECISION (frac-sec)	0
SQL_DESC_DATETIME_INTERVAL_PRECISION	Columnsize-4

The charts show the effect on IPD.IDA[n] fields if the value of the passed ParameterType is 103 or 104 or 105 or 108 or 109 or 111 (interval day or interval hour or interval minute or interval day to hour or interval day to minute or interval hour to minute). SQL_DESC_LENGTH is the length in "positions." SQL_DESC_PRECISION is the "fractional-seconds" precision.

SQL_DESC_DATETIME_INTERVAL_PRECISION is the "leading field" precision. For example, if you call SQLBindParameter with ParameterNumber = 2, ParameterType=104, Columnsize=3, and DecimalDigits=0, the result is that, in the IPD.IDA[2] (i.e., the second item descriptor area in the Implementation Parameter Desc), the settings are as follows: SQL_DESC_TYPE=10, SQL_DESC_DATETIME_INTERVAL_CODE=4, SQL_DESC_LENGTH=3, SQL_DESC_PRECISION=0, and SQL_DESC_DATETIME_INTERVAL_PRECISION=(3 - 1)=2.

SQLBindParameter Effect on IPD.IDA Fields for Interval Day/Time <data type>s with SECONDs:

Field	Gets for ...
	106 (second)
SQL_DESC_TYPE	10
SQL_DESC_DATETIME_INTERVAL_CODE	6
SQL_DESC_LENGTH (in positions)	Columnsize
SQL_DESC_PRECISION (frac-sec)	DecimalDigits
SQL_DESC_DATETIME_INTERVAL_PRECISION (lead)	Columnsize-DecimalDigits-2 or Columnsize-1

Field	Gets for ...
	110 (day to second)
SQL_DESC_TYPE	10
SQL_DESC_DATETIME_INTERVAL_CODE	10
SQL_DESC_LENGTH (in positions)	Columnsize
SQL_DESC_PRECISION (frac-sec)	DecimalDigits
SQL_DESC_DATETIME_INTERVAL_PRECISION	Columnsize-DecimalDigits-11 or Columnsize-10

Field	Gets for ...
	112 (hour to second)
SQL_DESC_TYPE	10
SQL_DESC_DATETIME_INTERVAL_CODE	12
SQL_DESC_LENGTH (in positions)	Columnsize
SQL_DESC_PRECISION (frac-sec)	DecimalDigits
SQL_DESC_DATETIME_INTERVAL_PRECISION	Columnsize-DecimalDigits-8 or Columnsize-7

Field	Gets for ...
	113 (minute to second)
SQL_DESC_TYPE	10
SQL_DESC_DATETIME_INTERVAL_CODE	13
SQL_DESC_LENGTH (in positions)	Columnsize

Field	Gets for ...
	113 (minute to second)
SQL_DESC_PRECISION (frac-sec)	DecimalDigits
SQL_DESC_DATETIME_INTERVAL_PRECISION	Columnsize-DecimalDigits-5 or Columnsize-4

The charts show the effect on IPD.IDA[n] fields if the value of the passed ParameterType is 106 or 110 or 112 or 113 (interval second or interval day-to-second or interval hour-to-second or interval minute-to-second). SQL_DESC_LENGTH is the length in "positions." SQL_DESC_PRECISION is the "fractional-seconds" precision. SQL_DESC_DATETIME_INTERVAL_PRECISION is the "leading field" precision. The Column size must include one position for a "." if there is a fractional-seconds amount — that is, INTERVAL '+5.00' SECOND has a length of 5 (Columnsize=5) and a fractional seconds precision of 2 (DecimalDigits=2), so the precision of the leading field is (Columnsize - DecimalDigits - 2) = (5 - 2 - 2) = 1. For example, if you call SQLBindParameter with ParameterNumber = 1, ParameterType=110, Columnsize=12, and DecimalDigits=0, the result is that, in the IPD.IDA[1] (i.e., the first item descriptor area in the Implementation Parameter Desc), the settings are as follows: SQL_DESC_TYPE=10, SQL_DESC_DATETIME_INTERVAL_CODE=10, SQL_DESC_LENGTH=12, SQL_DESC_PRECISION=0, and SQL_DESC_DATETIME_INTERVAL_PRECISION=(12 - 10)=2.

SQLBindParameter Effect on IPD.IDA Fields for Other <data type>s

Field	Gets ...
SQL_DESC_TYPE	ParameterType
SQL_DESC_LENGTH (in chars or bits)	Columnsize

The chart shows the effect on IPD.IDA[n] fields if the value of the passed ParameterType is 1 or 12 or 14 or 15 or 30 or 40 (CHAR or CHAR VARYING or BIT or BIT VARYING or BLOB or CLOB). For example, if you call SQLBindParameter with ParameterNumber = 8, ParameterType = 1, and Columnsize = 50, the result is that, in the IPD.IDA[8] (i.e., the eighth item descriptor area in the Implementation Parameter Desc), the settings are as follows: SQL_DESC_TYPE = 1 and SQL_DESC_LENGTH = 50.

Notes:

- ValueType might be SQL_C_DEFAULT.
- *StrLen_or_Ind might be SQL_DATA_AT_EXEC.
- *StrLen_or_Ind might be SQL_DATA_NULL.
- Datetime codings are an occasional source of confusion because the specification was changed a few years ago. Make sure, especially, that ParameterType is one of the "Concise Codes" for datetimes.
- The DBMS does not have to perform a consistency check at this time. Contrast SQLSetDescField and SQLSetDescRec, which require a consistency check as soon as SQL_DATA_POINTER contents change to a non-zero value.

- Beware if you prepare before you bind. For example:

```
SQLPrepare(hstmt,"UPDATE Table_1 SET int_column =?+5",SQL_NTS);
SQLBindParameter(hstmt,...);
SQLExecute(hstmt);
...
```

This sequence is okay according to standard SQL rules. But a DBMS exists which evaluates input parameters while processing SQLPrepare, instead of waiting and evaluating parameters while processing SQLExecute. In that case, the above example won't work. Or — even worse — it will appear to work because SQLPrepare picks up an input parameter that you made for a completely different statement! It's difficult to fix this problem by changing the order of the statements, but you could at least get rid of leftover bound parameters by calling SQL-FreeStmt(...SQL_RESET_PARAMS).

Example:

```
...
SQLHSTMT hstmt;
SQLCHAR c[6];
...
SQLBindParameter(
   hstmt,1,SQL_PARAM_MODE_IN,SQL_C_CHAR, SQL_CHAR,5, 00,c,00,NULL);
SQLExecDirect(hstmt,"UPDATE Table_1 SET col_1 = ?",-3);
```

This example shows how to bind a character parameter. Here, SQLExecDirect contains an SQL statement with a single parameter marker (? is a parameter marker). Before executing the SQL statement, we must bind that parameter. Let's look at the SQLBindParameter arguments, in order:

- [hstmt] is the stmt handle — same as in the SQLExecDirect function.
- [1] is ParameterNumber — it's 1 because we're binding parameter number 1.
- [SQL_PARAM_MODE_INPUT] is InputOutputMode — this is "input" (from host to DBMS).
- [SQL_C_CHAR] is ValueType — SQL_C_CHAR = 1, i.e., the input is a host char field.
- [SQL_CHAR] is ParameterType — SQL_CHAR = 1, i.e., the input is an SQL CHAR field.
- [5] is Columnsize — the input is 5 characters long.
- [00] is DecimalDigits — the value here doesn't matter because we're dealing with a char field.
- [c] is ParameterValue — what we're actually passing here is the address of c.
- [00] is BufferLength — the value here doesn't matter. (Note: Many programmers would pass [6] here, i.e., the number of octets in c. We deplore this misleading practice. If the parameter mode is SQL_PARAM_MODE_IN, the "octet length" is not determined by what is passed for BufferLength.)

- [NULL] is *StrLen_or_Ind — in this case, we won't supply an indicator pointer.

```
...
SQLHSTMT hstmt;
SQLCHAR date [] = "1994-01-31";
...
SQLBindParameter(
   hstmt,1,SQL_PARAM_MODE_IN,SQL_C_CHAR,SQL_TYPE_DATE, 10,0,date,11,0);
SQLExecDirect(
   hstmt,"SELECT * FROM Table_1 WHERE date_field = ?",SQL_NTS);
```

This example shows how to bind a date parameter. This is much like the previous example, but this time ParameterType is SQL_TYPE_DATE. (Note: ParameterType is SQL_TYPE_DATE (91) — not SQL_DATE (9). Columnsize is 10 because the number of positions in a date is 10: 'yyyy-mm-dd'.) In such bindings, there is an implicit CAST to DATE. One of the strengths of SQLBindParameter is that it makes implicit casts easy. So here's what most programmers do:

- Store everything in the host program as character strings.
- Pass ValueType = SQL_C_CHAR for every SQLBindParameter call.
- Set ParameterType = desired SQL <data type>, forcing the DBMS to perform appropriate conversions.

```
...
SQLHSTMT    hstmt;
SQLINTEGER  i;                 /* sqlcli.h has "typedef long SQLINTEGER" */
SQLINTEGER  i_indicator;
...
SQLPrepare(hstmt,"INSERT INTO Table_1 VALUES (?)",SQL_NTS);
SQLBindParameter(
      hstmt,                   /* hstmt = "handle of stmt" */
      1,                       /* ParameterNumber = "parameter #1" */
      SQL_PARAM_MODE_IN,       /* InputOutputType = "in" */
      SQL_C_LONG,       /* ValueType = "long int" (as seen from C) */
      SQL_INTEGER,      /* ParameterType = "int" (as seen from SQL) */
      00,               /* Columnsize "don't care" */
      00,               /* DecimalDigits "don't care" */
      &i,               /* ParameterValue "address of input data" */
      00,               /* BufferLength "don't care" */
      &i_indicator);    /* *StrLen_or_Ind "address of indicator" */
i_indicator=SQL_NULL_DATA;    /* sqlcli.h has "#define SQL_NULL_DATA -1" */
SQLExecute(hstmt);
```

This example shows how to bind a nullable integer parameter. Here, the value of i does not matter because the indicator variable's value is –1. Ultimately, what gets inserted is a NULL value.

```
#include   "sqlcli.h"
#include    <math.h>
#include    <stdio.h>
input_string char[20];
SQLHENV     henv;
SQLHDBC     hdbc;
SQLHSTMT    hstmt;
SQLSMALLINT experiment_no;
SQLREAL   measurement;
void main () {
 SQLAllocHandle(SQL_HANDLE_ENV,00,&henv);
 SQLAllocHandle(SQL_HANDLE_DBC,henv,&hdbc);
 SQLConnect(hdbc,"Exp",SQL_NTS,...);
 SQLAllocHandle(SQL_HANDLE_HSTMT,hdbc,&hstmt);
 SQLExecDirect(
   hstmt,"CREATE TABLE Experiments(no INT,measurement REAL)",SQL_NTS);
 SQLPrepare(hstmt,"INSERT INTO Experiments VALUES (?,?)",SQL_NTS);
 SQLBindParameter(
   hstmt,1,SQL_PARAM_MODE_IN,SQL_C_SHORT,SQL_SMALLINT,0,0,
   &experiment_no,0,0);
SQLBindParameter(
   hstmt,2,SQL_PARAM_MODE_IN,SQL_C_FLOAT,SQL_REAL,24,0,
   &measurement,0,0);
 for (experiment_no=0; experiment_no<10; ++experiment_no) {
   printf("Enter measurement:\n");
   gets(input_string);
   measurement=atof(input_string);
   SQLExecute(hstmt); }
 SQLEndTran(SQL_HANDLE_DBC,hdbc,SQL_COMMIT);
 SQLFreeHandle(SQL_HANDLE_STMT,hstmt);
 SQLDisconnect(hdbc);
 SQLFreeHandle(SQL_HANDLE_DBC,hdbc);
 SQLFreeHandle(SQL_HANDLE_ENV,henv);
}
```

This example shows how to bind two parameters in a loop; it contains calls to SQLPrepare and SQLBindParameter before the loop starts. Note that, for the Columnsize of the measurement parameter, we used 24. In fact, the precision of a REAL is implementation-defined; for some DBMSs, the appropriate value here is 7.

ODBC: The SQLBindParameter function is new in ODBC 3.0. An ODBC 2.0 function named SQLSetParam was pretty well the same except that it had no InputOutputMode parameter. ODBC uses the abbreviation SQL_PARAM_INPUT rather than SQL_PARAM_MODE_IN. ODBC, in addition to the actions described for standard SQL, will change ARD.IDA[n].SQL_DESC_SCALE and ARD.IDA[n].SQL_DESC_PRECISION to "default" values if ARD.IDA[n].SQL_DESC_TYPE becomes SQL_NUMERIC.

Who Should Populate the IPD?

We've had to repeat, tiresomely, the phrase, "if your DBMS supports auto-population of the IPD ..." because this is a major factor of the CLI that's implementation-defined. Let's have a last look at what it means.

If the DBMS supports auto-population of the IPD, then:

- You can find this out by calling SQLGetConnectAttr.
- You can't change the setting by calling SQLSetConnectAttr.
- The IPD IDA fields will be populated by SQLPrepare.

The action is analogous to what SQLPrepare does to an IRD (for a SELECT statement), so what's the problem? Why don't all DBMSs support auto-population? After all, in an SQL statement like this:

```
UPDATE Table_1 SET col_1 = 5.1E4 + ?
```

the DBMS must know the definition of the parameter (represented by ?) because it "knows" the <data type> of both Table_1.col_1 and of the <literal>. Well, to answer that, we must remind you that a DBMS is often two quite different programs: the client (driver) and the server (data source). Now, it's true that the server can figure out what a parameter must be. But the client knows nothing about Table_1.col_1 unless the server tells it. As Microsoft puts it, "... most data sources do not provide a way for the driver to discover parameter metadata." What it comes down to then is, "Yes, the DBMS should populate the IPD." But it won't, so you should. Luckily, because you're setting up the host variables anyway, you usually have all the information you need to set up the IPD at the time you write your application.

SQLColAttribute

Function Prototype:

```
SQLRETURN SQLColAttribute(
  SQLHSTMT hstmt,                   /* 32-bit input */
  SQLSMALLINT ColumnNumber,         /* 16-bit input, base 1, = Column #
                                       in result data corresponds to
                                       IRD.IDA[n] */
  SQLSMALLINT FieldIdentifier,      /* 16-bit input */
  SQLCHAR *CharacterAttribute,      /* to char[L], where L = max
                                       VARCHAR length. field value
                                       ret'd to here if CHAR,
                                       else ignored */
  SQLSMALLINT BufferLength,         /* 16-bit input =
                                       sizeof(CharacterAttribute)
                                       ignored if non-CHAR */
  SQLSMALLINT *StringLength,        /* 16-bit output */
  SQLINTEGER *NumericAttribute      /* 32-bit output */
  );
```

Job: Get one field value from an IRD.

Algorithm:

```
If (it's an "ITEM")
 /* There must be an open Cursor */
If (FieldIdentifier is ..._CATALOG or ..._SCHEMA or ..._NAME)
 /* The return is a character string, it goes to CharacterAttribute */
 SQLGetDescField (<descriptor handle>,ColumnNumber,FieldIdentifier,
                  CharacterAttribute,BufferLength,&StringLength);
Else If (FieldIdentifier is ..._TYPE)
 /* The return is an integer, it goes to NumericAttribute */
 If (datetime)
   NumericAttribute = "concise code value"
 If (interval)
   NumericAttribute = "concise code value"
 Else
   NumericAttribute = <data type>
Else
 SQLGetDescField(
   <descriptor handle>,ColumnNumber,FieldIdentifier,&NumericAttribute,
   BufferLength,&StringLength);
```

Notes:

- SQLColAttribute stands for "[get] Column Attribute." The word "attribute" here means "a field in the Implementation Row Descriptor (IRD)."
- The IRD is populated by preparing or executing a SELECT statement. For example, when displaying on the screen, it is useful to know the <Column name> and the <data type>. Those are two of the pieces of information that SQLColAttribute will provide you.
- All of the information that SQLColAttribute returns can also be found via the SQLGetDescField function.
- With some DBMSs, it is a bad idea to retrieve IRD fields after SQLPrepare but before SQLExecute. The reason, once again, is that the driver may not have an easy time querying the data source for such "metadata" information. In this case, the driver may actually execute a dummy SQL statement merely in order to find out what fields the data source returns. Such a process is inefficient. Therefore, it is commonly recommended that the IRD-information functions — SQLColAttribute, SQLDescribeCol, and sometimes SQLGetDescField or SQLGetDescRec — should be deferred until the SQL statement is executed. If the SQLExecute function call is in a loop, then you should set flags appropriately so that the IRD-information function is only called once.

Example:

```
#include "sqlcli.h"
...
name  char[10];
SQLSMALLINT name_length;
SQLRETURN sqlreturn;
...
SQLExecDirect(hstmt,"SELECT x AS column_name FROM Table_1",SQL_NTS);
...
/* We'd like to know the name. */
sqlreturn=SQLColAttribute (
     hstmt,
     1,                    /* the Column number */
     SQL_DESC_NAME,        /* the field identifier, = 1011 */
     name,                 /* this is where the name will go */
     10,                   /* BufferLength -- too small! */
     &name_length,
     00);                  /* NumericAttribute doesn't matter */
     /* The result is: sqlreturn==SQL_SUCCESS_WITH_INFO, and if we now got the
        diagnostics we would see sqlstate='01004' (truncation). The value in
        name is "column_NA\0". The value in name_length is 11. */
```

ODBC: SQLColAttribute arrived with ODBC 3.0. In ODBC 2.x there was a similar function, SQLColAttributes, which is now deprecated. Syntactically, ODBC 3.0's SQLColAttribute function is nearly standard CLI. But ODBC supports only 14 of the standard FieldIdentifier values (1001 through 1013 and 1099). ODBC also has 15 non-standard values in the "implementation-defined" range, for items like "the name of the Base table" or "whether the Column is case sensitive." In standard SQL, the fields of an IRD are still valid even after a Cursor is closed — but this is not the case with ODBC. In earlier versions, ODBC and the standard CLI had different type specifications for the BufferLength and StringLength parameters. These differences have now been resolved.

SQLDescribeCol

Function Prototype:

```
SQLRETURN SQLDescribeCol(
  SQLHSTMT hstmt,                 /* 32-bit input */
  SQLSMALLINT ColumnNumber,       /* 16-bit input */
  SQLCHAR *ColumnName,            /* CHAR* output */
  SQLSMALLINT BufferLength,       /* 16-bit input */
  SQLSMALLINT *NameLength,        /* 16-bit output */
  SQLSMALLINT *DataType,          /* 16-bit output */
  SQLINTEGER *Columnsize,         /* 32-bit output */
  SQLSMALLINT *DecimalDigits,     /* 16-bit output */
  SQLSMALLINT *Nullable);         /* 16-bit output */
```

Job: Get the following information about one Column in a result set: the <Column name>, the <data type>, the Column size, the scale, and whether the Column might contain nulls.

Algorithm:

```
If (no statement was prepared with hstmt)
 return error: HY010 CLI-specific condition-function sequence error
Find the IRD for hstmt.
If (IRD.SQL_DESC_COUNT == 0)
 /* there are no "result set" Columns so last statement must have been a
    non-query */
 return error: 07005 Dynamic SQL error-prepared statement not a
 Cursor specification
If (ColumnNumber < 1)
  /* in some non-standard implementations, ColumnNumber can be 0 */
  return error: 07009 dynamic SQL error-invalid descriptor index
If (ColumnNumber > IRD.SQL_DESC_COUNT)
  return error: 07009 dynamic SQL error-invalid descriptor index
    /* Use the Character String Retrieval routine for the following: */
    Copy IRD.IDA[ColumnNumber].SQL_DESC_NAME to ColumnName,NameLength
```

```
Switch (IRD.IDA[ColumnNumber].SQL_DESC_TYPE)
 case: == SQL_DATETIME
  /* if type = 9 and subtype = 1, return 91. and so on */
  Set *DataType = 91, 92, 93, 94 or 95, depending on whether
  IRD.IDA[ColumnNumber].SQL_DESC_DATETIME_INTERVAL_CODE is 1, 2,
  3, 4 or 5, respectively.
 case: == SQL_INTERVAL
  /* if type = 10 and subtype = 1, return 101, and so on */
  Set *DataType = 101, 102, 103, 104, 105, 106, 107, 108, 109, 110,
  111, 112 or 113, depending on whether IRD.IDA[ColumnNumber].SQL_
  DESC_DATETIME_INTERVAL_CODE is 1, 2, 3, 4, 5, 6, 7, 8, 9, 10, 11,
  12 or 13, respectively. */
 default:
  Set *DataType = IRD.IDA[ColumnNumber].SQL_DESC_TYPE
Switch (IRD.IDA[ColumnNumber].SQL_DESC_TYPE)
 case: == any "char" <data type> code
  Set *Columnsize = IRD.IDA[ColumnNumber].SQL_DESC_OCTET_LENGTH
 case: == any "numeric" <data type> code
  Set *Columnsize = the maximum length in decimal digits
 case: == any "bit" or "datetime" or "interval" <data type> code
  Set *Columnsize = IRD.IDA[ColumnNumber].SQL_DESC_LENGTH
Switch (IRD.IDA[ColumnNumber].SQL_DESC_TYPE)
 case: == any "exact numeric" <data type> code
  Set *DecimalDigits = IRD.IDA[ColumnNumber].SQL_DESC_SCALE
 case: == any "datetime" or "interval" <data type> code
  Set *DecimalDigits = IRD.IDA[ColumnNumber].SQL_DESC_PRECISION
 default:
  Set *DecimalDigits = some implementation-dependent value
Set *Nullable = IRD.IDA[ColumnNumber].SQL_DESC_NULLABLE
```

Notes:

- Most of the information that SQLDescribeCol returns can also be found via the SQLGet-DescField function, or via the SQLColAttribute function. So SQLDescribeCol is a redundancy. It continues to be popular because it's a handy wrapper; the information that SQLDescribeCol returns is what's commonly needed for simple applications.
- The SQL Standard does not provide for the possibility that people may wish to pass null pointers for unwanted parameters.
- Sometimes SQLDescribeCol is called in order to provide information for a reporting program. In that case, ColumnName and NameLength are used for the report-Column headers, DataType is used to determine whether right justification is needed, ColumnLength+2 is the maximum Column width, DecimalDigits helps COBOL programs decide what the

totallers' PICs are, and Nullable, if true, may cause creation of a separate "null?" Column.

- Sometimes SQLDescribeCol is called in order to provide information that can be used by SQLBindCol. In that case, DataType can be passed directly, ColumnLength can be passed directly, ColumnLength can be used to decide how big a buffer must be malloc'd, DecimalDigits can be passed directly, and Nullable can be used to decide whether an indicator is necessary. However, such a scheme cannot be carried out without some advance checking. For example, not all <data type>s can be passed directly — some must be CAST to a "char" with length equal to ColumnLength (usually).
- The source field for Columnsize will depend on the <data type>. The following table shows the effects of the calculation in the "Algorithm" section:

<data type>	field	example definition	example Columnsize
CHAR, VARCHAR, BLOB	SQL_DESC_OCTET_LENGTH	CHAR(18)	18
DECIMAL, NUMERIC	SQL_DESC_PRECISION	DECIMAL(5,3)	5
SMALLINT	SQL_DESC_PRECISION [1]	SMALLINT	5
INTEGER	SQL_DESC_PRECISION [1]	INTEGER	10
FLOAT	SQL_DESC_PRECISION [1]	FLOAT(53)	15
REAL	SQL_DESC_PRECISION [1]	REAL	7
DOUBLE PRECISION	SQL_DESC_PRECISION [1]	DOUBLE PRECISION	15
BIT, BIT VARYING	SQL_DESC_LENGTH	BIT(6)	6
DATE, TIME, TIMESTAMP	SQL_DESC_LENGTH	DATE	10
INTERVAL	SQL_DESC_LENGTH	INTERVAL SECOND(1)	4 [2]

Note 1: This <data type> usually has a binary-radix precision, so the value in SQL_DESC_PRECISION is in bits. When this is the case, the DBMS converts to the number of decimal digits that would be needed to represent the <data type>'s largest literal (not including space for sign, decimal point, or exponent).

Note 2: The INTERVAL example is based on an assumption that the leading field precision is 2; the specified fractional precision is 1, so a typical <literal> would be INTERVAL '-33.5' SECOND.

- Old-timers may recognize that the fields retrieved by SQLDescribeCol are analogous to the fields of IBM DB2's SQLDA (SQL descriptor area) used for embedded SQL DESCRIBE statements in days of yore.

Example:

```
#include "sqlcli.h"
#include stdlib.h
SQLHSTMT hstmt;
SQLCHAR column_name[128+1];
```

```
SQLSMALLINT column_name_length;
SQLSMALLINT data_type;
SQLINTEGER column_size;
SQLSMALLINT decimal_digits;
SQLSMALLINT nullable;
SQLCHAR *lpBuffer;
...
SQLExecDirect(hstmt,"SELECT col_1 FROM Table_1",SQL_NTS);
...
SQLDescribeCol(
     hstmt,                     /* handle of stmt */
     1,                         /* Column number */
     column_name,               /* where to put Column name */
     sizeof(column_name),       /* = 128+1 ... allow for \0 */
     &column_name_length,       /* where to put name length */
     &data_type,                /* where to put <data type> */
     &column_size,              /* where to put Column size */
     &decimal_digits,           /* where to put scale/frac precision */
     &nullable);                /* where to put null/not-null flag */
/* Allocate a buffer that we will fetch into. */
switch (data_type) {
  case SQL_BIT:              lpBuffer = malloc(column_size/8+1);
  case SQL_REAL:             lpBuffer = malloc(column_size+6+1);
  case SQL_DOUBLE_PRECISION: lpBuffer = malloc(column_size+7+1);
  case SQL_CHAR:             lpBuffer = malloc(column_size+1);
  case SQL_DECIMAL:          lpBuffer = malloc(column_size+2+1);
  case SQL_INTEGER:          lpBuffer = malloc(column_size+1+1);
  ...
  }
```

ODBC: The SQLDescribeCol function has been around since ODBC 1.0. The differences between the ODBC and Standard specifications are only minor. Unlike Standard-conformant drivers, ODBC drivers can accept 0 for a Column number, can return a blank string in ColumnName, can return SQL_NULLABLE_UNKNOWN in Nullable, and return SQL_DESC_OCTET_LENGTH for ColumnLength of datetime, interval, or bit <data type>s.

SQLNumResultCols

Function Prototype:

```
SQLRETURN SQLNumResultCols(
  SQLHSTMT hstmt,                   /* 32-bit input */
  SQLSMALLINT *ColumnCount          /* pointer to 16-bit output */
  );
```

Job: Find out how many Columns are in a result set.

Algorithm:

```
If (there is no prepared statement associated with StatementHandle)
return error: HY010 CLI-specific condition-function sequence error
Set *ColumnCount = IRD.SQL_DESC_COUNT
```

Notes:

- All this function does is retrieve the "count" field in the IRD, which is zero if the last prepared/executed SQL statement was a non-query, or — if the last prepared/executed SQL statement was a query — is the number of Columns in the select list.
- SQLNumResultCols(hstmt,&column_count) is effectively the same as:

```
SQLGetStmtAttr(hstmt,SQL_ATTR_IMP_ROW_DESC,&hdesc,00,NULL);
SQLGetDescField(hdesc,00,SQL_DESC_COUNT,&column_count,00,NULL);
```

- Some applications call SQLNumResultCols in order to find out whether the last executed statement was a query. If it was something else — INSERT, for instance — then *ColumnCount would be 0. This is a reliable test, but SQL3 programmers can use desc.SQL_DESC_DYNAMIC_FUNCTION_CODE for a slightly more precise answer.

Example:

```
#include "sqlcli.h"
SQLSMALLINT column_count;
...
SQLPrepare(hstmt,...);
if (SQLNumResultCols(hstmt,&column_count)<0) {
 ... invalid handle, statement not prepared, etc. }
if (column_count==0) {
 ... it wasn't a query expression }
 if (column_count>0) {
 ... now we know how many Columns we must bind }
```

ODBC: The SQLNumResultCols function has been around since ODBC 1.0.

SQLGetParamData

Function Prototype:

```
SQLRETURN SQLGetParamData(
  SQLHSTMT StatementHandle,          /* 32-bit input */
  SQLSMALLINT ParameterNumber,       /* 16-bit input */
  SQLSMALLINT TargetType,            /* 16-bit input */
  SQLPOINTER TargetValue,            /* ANY* output */
  SQLINTEGER BufferLength,           /* 32-bit input */
  SQLINTEGER *StrLen_or_Ind          /* 32-bit output */
  );
```

Job: Get the value of an unbound <output parameter>. `SQLGetParamData` is rare. You only need it if all these things are true:

- You have executed an SQL statement which begins with the word `CALL`.
- The called procedure has "output parameters" (direction of flow is from DBMS to host-language buffers).
- You did not bind the output parameters in advance with `SQLBindParameter`, `SQLSetDescRec`, or `SQLSetDescField`.

Algorithm:

```
If the last statement for hstmt was not a CALL statement:
  return error: HY010 CLI-specific condition-function sequence error
If the parameter referred to by ParameterNumber doesn't exist, or was bound as
"input" parameter, or (implementation-defined restriction) has already been
transferred:
  return error: 07009 dynamic SQL error-invalid descriptor index
Transfer data from DBMS internal buffers to variables in the host-language pro-
gram. The algorithm is the same as the SQLGetData algorithm; the only important
difference is that the desc is an APD rather than an ARD.
```

Notes:

- It is implementation-defined whether the parameters must be accessed in ascending parameter-number order. You can call `SQLGetInfo(...SQL_GETPARAMDATA_EXTENSIONS...)` to find out whether your DBMS supports getting any parameter in any order.
- The "source" is already described in the IPD; you only need to pass a description of the "target."
- The possible values of `TargetType` are:

SQL_C_CHARACTER	1
SQL_C_INTEGER	4
SQL_C_SMALLINT	5
SQL_C_REAL	7

SQL_C_DOUBLE	8
SQL_C_DEFAULT	99 (use IPD <data type>, precision, scale)
SQL_APD_TYPE	-99 (APD specifies <data type> already)

We recommend against using SQL_C_DEFAULT because "type, precision, scale" is often insufficient information.

Example:

Scenario: You have a procedure named Withdraw. It takes five parameters. The first three parameters are input parameters. The fourth parameter is an output parameter which is pre-bound with SQLBindParameter. The fifth parameter is an output parameter which you will pick up with SQLGetParamData.

```
SQLCHAR       amount[10];
SQLINTEGER    teller_id;
SQLINTEGER    customer_id;
SQLCHAR       message1[101];
SQLCHAR       message2[101];
SQLINTEGER    message2_indicator;
...
SQLBindParameter(
 hstmt,1,SQL_PARAM_MODE_IN,SQL_C_CHAR,SQL_DECIMAL,6,2, amount,0,NULL);
SQLBindParameter(
 hstmt,2,SQL_PARAM_MODE_IN,SQL_C_LONG,SQL_INTEGER,0,0, &teller_id,0,NULL);
SQLBindParameter(
 hstmt,3,SQL_PARAM_MODE_IN,SQL_C_LONG,SQL_INTEGER,0,0, &customer_id,0,NULL);
SQLBindParameter(
 hstmt,4,SQL_PARAM_MODE_OUT,SQL_CHAR,SQL_C_CHAR,100,0,x message1,0,NULL);
strcpy(amount,"15.33");
teller_id = 44;
customer_id = 90182;
SQLExecDirect(hstmt,"CALL Withdraw (?,?,?,?,?)",24);
SQLGetParamData(hstmt,5,
       SQL_C_DEFAULT,                /* TargetType */
       message2,                     /* TargetValue */
       100,                          /* BufferLength */
       &message2_indicator);         /* *StrLen_or_Ind */
```

A possible result from this code would be: message2 contains the null-terminated string "abc" and message2_indicator contains 3.

ODBC: The SQLGetParamData function is not part of ODBC 3.0.

And that's it for the desc functions. In the next chapter, we'll take a look at the diagnostic functions.

47

Chapter 47

SQL/CLI: Diagnostic Functions

What if something goes wrong? Every env and dbc and stmt and desc has a structure called the Diagnostics Area. The DBMS fills it with information about what happened during the last function call. The diagnostics area has one "header" and zero or more "status records." The following partial illustration shows only the most important fields:

```
----------------------------------------
- SQL_DIAG_RETURNCODE | SQL_DIAG_NUMBER -
- --------------------+-----------------
- -             -1    | 00003           |
----------------------------------------
-     -------------------------------------------------------------------
-   - SQL_DIAG_SQLSTATE | SQL_DIAG_MESSAGE_TEXT                 | ... |
--------------------------------------------------------------------
- 1 - 23000    | Integrity Constraint Violation - constraint <X> | ... |
- 2 - 01003    | Warning - null value eliminated in set function | ... |
- 3 - 01008    | Warning - implicit zero-bit padding             | ... |
--------------------------------------------------------------------
```

This diagram shows the diagnostics area of a stmt, just after this function call:

```
sqlreturn = SQLExecDirect(
   hstmt,"UPDATE T SET a=(SELECT MAX(b) FROM X),c=X'5'",SQL_NTS);
```

Looking at the header, we can see that the function failed because the SQL_DIAG_RETURN-CODE field is –1, which is SQL_ERROR (sqlreturn will also equal –1). Also, from the fact that the header's SQL_DIAG_NUMBER field is 3, we can see that there are three status records.

Looking at the status records, we can see that three different things went wrong during the execution of the SQL statement. Two of them were merely warnings ("completion conditions"). The DBMS probably encountered these conditions while it was setting up for the UPDATE, but it kept on going. Then it hit a showstopper; an "exception condition." Although this "integrity Constraint violation" error was the third condition encountered, it is the first in order among the status records because an error's priority is higher than a warning's priority.

The SQL_DIAG_SQLSTATE field contains a code for a reasonably precise categorization of the condition. This code is called the *status code*, or SQLSTATE value (because the DBMS always puts the status code in the SQL_DIAG_SQLSTATE field). You can see what the SQLSTATE codes mean by looking at the chart of codes at the end of this chapter.

The SQL_DIAG_MESSAGE_TEXT field might be the sort of text you'd like to send to the user's screen for this condition. Unlike the status code, the message text is implementation-dependent; it's not standardized. It might be internationalized; that is, it might not be in English. So there is a lot more information here than a mere "failed" return code. And there are many more fields than the ones in the picture, which can help you get an even more precise diagnosis of "why didn't the SQLExecDirect function work." In order to retrieve the diagnostics-area information into your application program, you need to use one of these CLI functions:

- SQLGetDiagField — you'll need this function to get any field from any part of the diagnostics area, one field at a time.
- SQLGetDiagRec — with this function, you can pick up several of the most popular fields, including SQL_DIAG_SQLSTATE and SQL_DIAG_MESSAGE_TEXT.
- SQLError — you'll want to know about this slightly obsolescent function because it appears frequently in legacy code.
- SQLRowCount — this isn't exactly a diagnostics function, but it does get a value from a particular diagnostics-area field: SQL_DIAG_ROW_COUNT.

The descriptions of these four functions follow.

SQLGetDiagField

Function Prototype:

```
SQLRETURN SQLGetDiagField(
  SQLSMALLINT HandleType,       /* 16-bit input */
  SQLINTEGER Handle,            /* 32-bit input */
  SQLSMALLINT RecordNumber,     /* 16-bit input */
  SQLSMALLINT DiagIdentifier,   /* 16-bit input */
  SQLPOINTER DiagInfo,          /* ANY* output */
  SQLSMALLINT BufferLength,     /* 16-bit input */
  SQLSMALLINT *StringLength     /* 16-bit output */
  );
```

Job: Get one piece of information from a diagnostics area; for example, the SQLSTATE of a warning that was posted for the last function call.

There are 37 variations of SQLGetDiagField, depending on the diagnostics field whose value you want to examine. Here's an example and short description of each variation; each uses these shorthands:

- The words "last call" mean, "the last function called using this handle, other than SQLGetDiagField or SQLGetDiagRec or SQLError." The principle (anti-Heisenbergian) here is that the act of observation must not affect the thing observed, so the diagnostics routines don't themselves post diagnostics information.
- The punctuation ...., at the beginning of each function example's parameter list means, "assume there is a valid handle type and handle here." The HandleType parameter must be SQL_HANDLE_ENV, SQL_HANDLE_DBC, SQL_HANDLE_STMT, or SQL_HANDLE_DESC. The corresponding Handle parameter must be a henv or hdbc or hstmt or hdesc. Where the only acceptable value is a hstmt, the parameter list starts with SQL_HANDLE_STMT,hstmt.
- The name used for the DiagInfo parameter gives an indication of the <data type> that SQLGetDiagField returns: smallint, integer, or character string.
- The word NULL in a function's argument list means, "doesn't matter." None of the diagnostics fields contain NULL in the SQL sense.
- The four-digit number at the beginning of each paragraph is the code for the DiagIdentifier parameter. We have done the same thing here that we did in Chapter 46 on the desc functions; namely, treating the name of the sqlcli.h code constant as the name of the field.

Diagnostics Fields — Header

The nine "Header" fields in a diagnostics area occur only once. It does not matter what you pass for the RecordNumber parameter.

0001

```
SQLGetDiagField(
        ........,00,SQL_DIAG_RETURNCODE,&smallint,00,NULL);
```

This field gives you the last call's return code: SQL_SUCCESS, SQL_ERROR, SQL_SUCCESS_WITH_INFO, SQL_NEED_DATA, or SQL_NO_DATA. You need to call this if you failed to save the return code in an sqlreturn variable.

0002

```
SQLGetDiagField(........,00,SQL_DIAG_NUMBER,&integer,00,NULL);
```

This field gives you the number of Status Records (exception or completion conditions) that the DBMS generated for the last call. The value will be zero if the return code is SQL_SUCCESS and will probably (but not certainly) be zero if the return code is SQL_NO_DATA.

0003

```
SQLGetDiagField(
    SQL_HANDLE_STMT,hstmt,00,SQL_DIAG_ROW_COUNT,&integer,00,NULL);
```

If the last call was SQLExecDirect or SQLExecute for an UPDATE, DELETE, or INSERT statement, this field gives you the number of rows affected. Read about the SQLRowCount function which returns the same information. You must call this function immediately after calling SQLExecDirect or SQLExecute.

0007

```
SQLGetDiagField(
     SQL_HANDLE_STMT,hstmt,00,SQL_DIAG_DYNAMIC_FUNCTION,
     charstring,sizeof(charstring),&charstring_size);
```

If the last call was SQLExecDirect or SQLExecute, this field gives you a string that describes the type of SQL statement executed. Usually this is the first two or three <keyword>s in the statement. The official list of SQL statements and their function codes is shown at the end of this section.

0012

```
SQLGetDiagField(
     SQL_HANDLE_STMT,hstmt,00,SQL_DIAG_DYNAMIC_FUNCTION_CODE,
     &integer,00,NULL);
```

If the last call was SQLExecDirect or SQLExecute, this field gives you the code value for the type of SQL statement executed; see the codes in the "SQL_DIAG_DYNAMIC_FUNCTION Codes" listings, beginning on page 891. If you allow users to type in SQL statements, it's handy to call SQLPrepare and then call this function, so you know what kind of SQL statement it is before you call SQLExecute. (This won't work with ODBC.)

0013

```
SQLGetDiagField(
        SQL_HANDLE_STMT,hstmt,00,SQL_DIAG_MORE,&integer,00,NULL);
```

The return value for this field is either 1 "true" or 0 "false"; if there are more status records than would fit in the diagnostics area, you get a "true" code here. You may or may not be able to change the maximum size of the diagnostics area with the SET TRANSACTION ... DIAGNOSTICS SIZE statement.

0034

```
SQLGetDiagField(
    ........,00,SQL_DIAG_TRANSACTIONS_COMMITTED,&integer,00,NULL);
```

This field gives you the number of transactions committed.

0035

```
SQLGetDiagField(
    ........,00,SQL_DIAG_TRANSACTIONS_ROLLED_BACK, &integer,00,NULL);
```

This field gives you the number of transactions rolled back.

0036

```
SQLGetDiagField(
    ........,00,SQL_DIAG_TRANSACTION_ACTIVE,&integer,00,NULL);
```

This field gives you a 1 "true" if a transaction is currently active. (A transaction is active if a Cursor is open or the DBMS is waiting for a deferred parameter.)

SQL_DIAG_DYNAMIC_FUNCTION Codes

If the last call was SQLExecDirect or SQLExecute, SQLGetDiagField's SQL_DIAG_DYNAMIC_FUNCTION gives you a string that describes the type of SQL statement executed. As we said earlier, this is usually the first two or three <keyword>s in the SQL statement. Here's the official list of SQL statements and their function codes (note that not all these SQL statements are executable in a CLI context; we have given a full list here so as to avoid repetition elsewhere).

List of SQL Statements and Codes in SQL-92, but not in CLI

DYNAMIC_FUNCTION	DYNAMIC_FUNCTION_CODE	
(string)	**(number)**	**(sqlcli.h definition)**
ALLOCATE CURSOR	1	not defined
ALLOCATE DESCRIPTOR	2	not defined
CREATE TRANSLATION	79	not defined
DEALLOCATE DESCRIPTOR	15	not defined
DEALLOCATE PREPARE	16	not defined
DESCRIBE	20	not defined
DYNAMIC CLOSE	37	not defined
DYNAMIC DELETE CURSOR: (positioned)	38	not defined
DYNAMIC FETCH	39	not defined
DYNAMIC OPEN	40	not defined
DYNAMIC UPDATE CURSOR: (positioned)	42	not defined
EXECUTE	44	not defined
EXECUTE IMMEDIATE	43	not defined
FETCH	45	not defined
GET DESCRIPTOR	47	not defined
PREPARE	56	not defined
SELECT (multiple row)	21	not defined
SET CURRENT_PATH	69	not defined
SET DESCRIPTOR	70	not defined

List of Additional SQL Statements and Codes in SQL-92 and CLI

DYNAMIC_FUNCTION	DYNAMIC_FUNCTION_CODE	
(string)	**(number)**	**(**sqlcli.h **definition)**
'' (empty string)	0	<unknown statement type>
ALTER DOMAIN	3	SQL_DIAG_ALTER_DOMAIN
ALTER TABLE	4	SQL_DIAG_ALTER_TABLE
CLOSE CURSOR	9	SQL_DIAG_CLOSE_CURSOR
COMMIT WORK	11	SQL_DIAG_COMMIT
CONNECT	13	SQL_DIAG_CONNECT
CREATE ASSERTION	6	SQL_DIAG_CREATE_ASSERTION
CREATE CHARACTER SET	8	SQL_DIAG_CREATE_CHARACTER_SET
CREATE COLLATION	10	SQL_DIAG_CREATE_COLLATION
CREATE DOMAIN	23	SQL_DIAG_CREATE_DOMAIN
CREATE SCHEMA	64	SQL_DIAG_CREATE_SCHEMA
CREATE TABLE	77	SQL_DIAG_CREATE_TABLE
CREATE VIEW	84	SQL_DIAG_CREATE_VIEW
DECLARE CURSOR	101	SQL_DIAG_DECLARE_CURSOR
DELETE CURSOR	18	SQL_DIAG_DELETE_CURSOR
DELETE WHERE	19	SQL_DIAG_DELETE_WHERE
DISCONNECT	22	SQL_DIAG_DISCONNECT
DROP ASSERTION	24	SQL_DIAG_DROP_ASSERTION
DROP CHARACTER SET	25	SQL_DIAG_DROP_CHARACTER_SET
DROP COLLATION	26	SQL_DIAG_DROP_COLLATION
DROP DOMAIN	27	SQL_DIAG_DROP_DOMAIN
DROP SCHEMA	31	SQL_DIAG_DROP_SCHEMA
DROP TABLE	32	SQL_DIAG_DROP_TABLE
DROP TRANSLATION	33	SQL_DIAG_DROP_TRANSLATION
DROP VIEW	36	SQL_DIAG_DROP_VIEW
DYNAMIC DELETE CURSOR: (preparable, positioned)	54	SQL_DIAG_DYNAMIC_DELETE_CURSOR
DYNAMIC UPDATE CURSOR: (preparable, positioned)	55	SQL_DIAG_DYNAMIC_UPDATE_CURSOR
GRANT	48	SQL_DIAG_GRANT
INSERT	50	SQL_DIAG_INSERT
OPEN	53	SQL_DIAG_OPEN
REVOKE	59	SQL_DIAG_REVOKE
ROLLBACK WORK	62	SQL_DIAG_ROLLBACK

DYNAMIC_FUNCTION	DYNAMIC_FUNCTION_CODE	
(string)	**(number)**	**(sqlcli.h definition)**
SELECT (single row)	65	SQL_DIAG_SELECT
SELECT (dynamic single row)	41	SQL_DIAG_SELECT
SELECT CURSOR (dynamic multiple row)	85	SQL_DIAG_SELECT_CURSOR
SET CATALOG	66	SQL_DIAG_SET_CATALOG
SET CONNECTION	67	SQL_DIAG_SET_CONNECTION
SET CONSTRAINT	68	SQL_DIAG_SET_CONSTRAINT
SET NAMES	72	SQL_DIAG_SET_NAMES
SET TIME ZONE	71	SQL_DIAG_SET_TIME_ZONE
SET SESSION AUTHORIZATION	76	SQL_DIAG_SET_SESSION_AUTHORIZATION
SET SCHEMA	74	SQL_DIAG_SET_SCHEMA
SET TRANSACTION	75	SQL_DIAG_SET_TRANSACTION
UPDATE CURSOR (positioned)	81	SQL_DIAG_UPDATE_CURSOR
UPDATE WHERE	82	SQL_DIAG_UPDATE_WHERE

List of Additional SQL Statements and Codes in SQL3, but not in CLI

DYNAMIC_FUNCTION	DYNAMIC_FUNCTION_CODE	
(string)	**(number)**	**(sqlcli.h definition)**
ALTER MODULE	95	not defined
ALTER ROUTINE	17	not defined
ALTER TYPE	60	not defined
ASSIGNMENT	5	not defined
BEGIN END	12	not defined
CASE	86	not defined
CREATE MODULE	51	not defined
CREATE ORDERING	114	not defined
CREATE TRANSFORM	117	not defined
DECLARE VARIABLE	96	not defined
DROP MODULE	28	not defined
FOR	46	not defined
FREE LOCATOR	98	not defined
HANDLER	87	not defined
HOLD LOCATOR	99	not defined

DYNAMIC_FUNCTION	DYNAMIC_FUNCTION_CODE	
(string)	**(number)**	**(sqlcli.h definition)**
IF	88	not defined
LEAVE	89	not defined
LOOP	90	not defined
RESIGNAL	91	not defined
SET TRANSFORM GROUP	118	not defined
SIGNAL	92	not defined
TEMPORARY TABLE	93	not defined
WHILE	97	not defined

List of Additional SQL Statements and Codes in SQL3 and CLI

DYNAMIC_FUNCTION	DYNAMIC_FUNCTION_CODE	
(string)	**(number)**	**(sqlcli.h definition)**
CALL	7	SQL_DIAG_CALL
CREATE ROLE	61	SQL_DIAG_CREATE_ROLE
CREATE ROUTINE	14	SQL_DIAG_CREATE_ROUTINE
CREATE TRIGGER	80	SQL_DIAG_CREATE_TRIGGER
CREATE TYPE	83	SQL_DIAG_CREATE_TYPE
DROP ROLE	29	SQL_DIAG_DROP_ROLE
DROP ROUTINE	30	SQL_DIAG_DROP_ROUTINE
DROP TRANSFORM	116	SQL_DIAG_DROP_TRANSFORM
DROP TRIGGER	34	SQL_DIAG_DROP_TRIGGER
DROP ORDERING	115	SQL_DIAG_DROP_ORDERING
DROP TYPE	35	SQL_DIAG_DROP_TYPE
GRANT ROLE	49	SQL_DIAG_GRANT_ROLE
RELEASE SAVEPOINT	57	SQL_DIAG_RELEASE_SAVEPOINT
RETURN	58	SQL_DIAG_RETURN
REVOKE ROLE	60	SQL_DIAG_REVOKE_ROLE
SAVEPOINT	63	SQL_DIAG_SAVEPOINT
SET ROLE	73	SQL_DIAG_SET_ROLE
SET SESSION CHARACTERISTICS	109	SQL_DIAG_SET_SESSION_CHARACTERISTICS
START TRANSACTION	111	SQL_DIAG_START_TRANSACTION

Note: In some contexts, the names DYNAMIC_FUNCTION and DYNAMIC_FUNCTION_CODE are COMMAND_FUNCTION and COMMAND_FUNCTION_CODE, respectively.

Diagnostics Fields — Status Records

The 28 "status records" in a diagnostics area can occur multiple times. You must pass a record number between 1 and SQL_DIAG_NUMBER (or you can pass any positive number and see whether SQLGetDiagField returns SQL_NO_DATA). Other terms for Status Record are: Descriptor Record (preferred by Microsoft) and Condition Information Item (preferred by the SQL Standard in non-CLI contexts). Strings are returned according to the rules of Character String Retrieval.

< 0

A status record with a number less than zero identifies an implementation-defined diagnostics field.

0004

```
SQLGetDiagField(
    .......,n,SQL_DIAG_SQLSTATE,charstring,sizeof(charstring),
    &charstring_size);
```

This field gives you a 5-character status code — remember to allow 6 characters because of the null terminator. SQLSTATE is the most important diagnostics field. You'll find the complete list of SQLSTATE values (often called simply *status codes*) at the end of this chapter. Quite often, the SQLSTATE class determines whether the other diagnostics fields have meaningful values.

0005

```
SQLGetDiagField(.......,n,SQL_DIAG_NATIVE,&integer,00,NULL);
```

This field gives you an integer which has an implementation-defined numeric code for the error type. If your DBMS has been around for a few years, this will be the same as the SQLCODE value. It was once standard for DBMSs to return SQLCODE and sometimes (for instance with IBM's DB2) the SQLCODE is more informative than the SQLSTATE value. But there is no standardized interpretation for the codes, except that values less than zero are "errors," equal to zero is "success," greater than zero are "warnings," and specifically +100 is "warning-no data." Alternate name: SQL_DIAG_NATIVE_CODE.

0006

```
SQLGetDiagField(
    .......,n,SQL_DIAG_MESSAGE_TEXT,charstring,sizeof(charstring),
    &charstring_size);
```

This field gives you an error message — sometimes merely an explanation of the SQLSTATE meaning, but the better DBMSs have context-sensitive tips. Useful for displays. Often, due to an ODBC requirement, messages start with bracketed information about the server and driver.

0008

```
SQLGetDiagField(
    .......,n,SQL_DIAG_CLASS_ORIGIN,charstring,sizeof(charstring),
    &charstring_size);
```

This field gives you the naming authority responsible for the definition of the class (the first two letters of SQLSTATE). Example: 'ISO 9075' would mean that the condition is documented in ISO/IEC 9075:1999 and is therefore "standard."

0009

```
SQLGetDiagField(
    ........,n,SQL_DIAG_SUBCLASS_ORIGIN,charstring,
    sizeof(charstring),&charstring_size);
```

This field gives you the naming authority responsible for the definition of the subclass (the last three letters of SQLSTATE). Example: 'ODBC 3.0' would mean that the condition is documented in Microsoft's ODBC manual version 3.0 but is not in any ISO specification, and is therefore "not standard."

0010

```
SQLGetDiagField(
    ........,n,SQL_DIAG_CONNECTION_NAME,charstring,
    sizeof(charstring),&charstring_size);
```

This field gives you the <Connection name>. With the CLI, this field is of minor importance because the primary identifier for an SQL-Connection is the hdbc.

0011

```
SQLGetDiagField(
    ........,n,SQL_DIAG_SERVER_NAME,charstring,
    sizeof(charstring),&charstring_size);
```

If the last SQL statement was a failed CONNECT, DISCONNECT, or SET CONNECTION, this field gives you the server which returned the error. Otherwise, you get the same information that you'd get by calling SQLGetInfo(...,SQL_DATA_SOURCE_NAME,...).

0014

```
SQLGetDiagField(........,n,SQL_DIAG_CONDITION_NUMBER,&integer,00,NULL);
```

This field gives you the number of the Status Record (the terms "condition number" and "status record number" are synonymous). This will be the same thing as the RecordNumber parameter, so you won't find out anything new here.

0015

```
SQLGetDiagField(
    ........,n,SQL_DIAG_CONSTRAINT_CATALOG,charstring,
    sizeof(charstring), &charstring_size);
```

0016

```
SQLGetDiagField(
    ........,n,SQL_DIAG_CONSTRAINT_SCHEMA,charstring,
    sizeof(charstring), &charstring_size);
```

0017

```
SQLGetDiagField(
    ........,n,SQL_DIAG_CONSTRAINT_NAME,charstring,
    sizeof(charstring), &charstring_size);
```

If SQLSTATE is '23000' (integrity constraint violation) or '27000' (triggered data change violation) or '40002' (transaction rollback-integrity constraint violation), then fields 0015, 0016, and 0017 give you the Catalog, Schema, and name of the violated Constraint.

0018

```
SQLGetDiagField(
    ........,n,SQL_DIAG_CATALOG_NAME,charstring,sizeof(charstring),
    &charstring_size);
```

0019

```
SQLGetDiagField(
    ........,n,SQL_DIAG_SCHEMA_NAME,charstring,sizeof(charstring),
    &charstring_size);
```

0020

```
SQLGetDiagField(
    ........,n,SQL_DIAG_TABLE_NAME,charstring,sizeof(charstring),
    &charstring_size);
```

0021

```
SQLGetDiagField(
    ........,n,SQL_DIAG_COLUMN_NAME,charstring,sizeof(charstring),
    &charstring_size);
```

Fields 0018, 0019, 0020, and 0021 give you the Catalog, Schema, and Table identifiers, plus the Column identifier if applicable, for what "caused" the problem. If SQLSTATE = '23000' or '27000' or '40002', these fields will identify the Table with which the violated Constraint is associated (assuming there is one such Table). If SQLSTATE = '42000', this is the Object that couldn't be found or on which you lack Privileges (the Standard contains some ambiguities here, but it seems that these fields may be blank for access violations). If SQLSTATE = '44000', this is the View that has a violated WITH CHECK OPTION. If SQLSTATE = '09000' or '40004', this is the Table with the Trigger that can't be executed. If SQLSTATE is any other value, results are implementation-dependent.

0022

```
SQLGetDiagField(
    ........,n,SQL_DIAG_CURSOR_NAME,charstring,sizeof(charstring),
    &charstring_size);
```

If SQLSTATE = '01001' or '24000', this field gives you the identifier of a Cursor. If SQLSTATE is anything else, results are implementation-dependent.

0023

```
SQLGetDiagField(
    ........,n,SQL_DIAG_MESSAGE_LENGTH,&integer,00,NULL);
```

This field gives you the character length of the implementation-defined message string. You can get the same information using SQL_DIAG_MESSAGE_TEXT. By the way, the C include file sqlcli.h says "#define SQL_MAXIMUM_MESSAGE_LENGTH 512" so the suggestion is that you allow 512 bytes for the message — but it's only a suggestion. It might be interesting to compare SQL_MAXIMUM_MESSAGE_LENGTH with what SQLGetDiagField returns for SQL_DIAG_MESSAGE_LENGTH.

0024

```
SQLGetDiagField(
    ........,n,SQL_DIAG_MESSAGE_OCTET_LENGTH,&integer,00,NULL);
```

This field gives you the octet length of the implementation-defined message string. This will be the same as the message length in characters if the Character set is 8-bit.

0025

```
SQLGetDiagField(
    ........,n,SQL_DIAG_CONDITION_NAME,&charstring,
    sizeof(charstring), &charstring_size);
```

This field gives you the name of an unhandled user-defined exception. Alternate name: SQL_DIAG_CONDITIONS_IDENTIFIER.

0026

```
SQLGetDiagField(
    ........,n,SQL_DIAG_PARAMETER_NAME,charstring,
    sizeof(charstring), &charstring_size);
```

This field gives you the name of a parameter — presumably the parameter which contained bad (input) data. Because named parameters are not a universal feature, most DBMSs will not return anything here.

0027

```
SQLGetDiagField(
    ........,n,SQL_DIAG_ROUTINE_CATALOG,charstring,
    sizeof(charstring), &charstring_size);
```

0028

```
SQLGetDiagField(
    ........,n,SQL_DIAG_ROUTINE_SCHEMA,charstring,
    sizeof(charstring), &charstring_size);
```

0029

```
SQLGetDiagField(
    ........,n,SQL_DIAG_ROUTINE_NAME,charstring,sizeof(charstring),
    &charstring_size);
```

0030

```
SQLGetDiagField(
    ........,n,SQL_DIAG_SPECIFIC_NAME,charstring,
    sizeof(charstring), &charstring_size);
```

If the SQLSTATE error class is '38' (external routine exception) or '39' (external routine invocation exception), fields 0027, 0028, and 0029 give you the full identifier of the routine that "caused" the error, while field 0030 gives you the routine's specific name.

0031

```
SQLGetDiagField(
    ........,n,SQL_DIAG_TRIGGER_CATALOG,charstring,
    sizeof(charstring), &charstring_size);
```

0032

```
SQLGetDiagField(
    ........,n,SQL_DIAG_TRIGGER_SCHEMA,charstring,
    sizeof(charstring), &charstring_size);
```

0033

```
SQLGetDiagField(
    ........,n,SQL_DIAG_TRIGGER_NAME,charstring,sizeof(charstring),
    &charstring_size);
```

If SQLSTATE = '40004' or '09000', fields 0031, 0032, and 0033 give you the full identifier of the Trigger that "caused" the problem.

Algorithm:

```
If (HandleType <> SQL_HANDLE_STMT, SQL_HANDLE_ENV, SQL_HANDLE_DBC,
    or SQL_HANDLE_DESC)
   return error: CLI-specific condition-invalid handle
If (handle isn't really the type indicated by HandleType)
   return error: CLI-specific condition-invalid handle
If (DiagIdentifier isn't a valid code)
   return error: HY024 CLI-specific condition-invalid attribute value
If (FieldIdentifier is for one of the Status Record fields)
   If (RecordNumber < 1)
     return error: 35000 invalid condition number -
   If (RecordNumber > actual number of status records)
     return warning: 01000 no data -
If (FieldIdentifier is for one of the Header fields)
```

```
If (FieldIdentifier == SQL_DIAG_ROW_COUNT)
  If (last call was not SQLExecute or SQLExecDirect)
    return error: HY092 CLI-specific condition-invalid attribute
    identifier
    Otherwise: return a diagnostics-area field, as already
    described.
```

Notes:

- Status Records are sorted according to the severity of the error class:
  - Highest: Errors that cause rollback (class '40').
  - Lower: Ordinary errors (everything except '40' or '01' or '02').
  - Lower: No-data warning (class '02').
  - Lowest: Mere warning (class '01').

Thus, the first Status Record is the most important. If the return code is SQL_ERROR, you can be sure that the first Status Record describes an error condition.

- The SQLSTATEs associated with the possible SQLGetDiagField errors are only mentioned for documentary reasons. The SQLGetDiagField function does not itself post any diagnostics. The way you check for errors is — look at the return code, then start guessing. These tips may be useful:

```
If (SQLGetDiagField returns SQL_SUCCESS_WITH_INFO)
   Probably the DiagInfo buffer is too small.
   Compare BufferLength (the maximum size of the DiagInfo buffer)
   to StringLength (the actual size of the string to be returned).
   If BufferLength is smaller, there's your problem.
If (SQLGetDiagField returns SQL_INVALID_HANDLE)
   Sure, check that the handle is valid. But this problem can also
   occur if SQLHandleType is not SQL_HANDLE_..., so check that too.
If (SQLGetDiagField returns SQL_ERROR)
   Check HandleType+DiagIdentifier. If the handle isn't a hstmt, then
   you can't ask for SQL_ROW_COUNT.
   Check RecordNumber. If you're looking for a header field, then it
   doesn't matter what you pass in RecordNumber. If you're looking for
   a status field, then RecordNumber must be >= 1.
   Check DiagIdentifier. If you use constants defined in sqlcli.h: the
   value here should be a constant beginning with SQL_DIAG_... -- but
   that's not enough. Also, make sure it's one of the values listed
   above.
   Check BufferLength. If you're looking for a numeric field, then it
   doesn't matter what you pass in BufferLength. If you're looking for
   a string field, then BufferLength must be >= 1.
If (SQLGetDiagField returns SQL_NO_DATA)
   This always means that the value you passed in RecordNumber is
   greater than the value in the diagnostics area's NUMBER field.
   For example: you passed 1 but there are zero status records.
```

- Some header fields always have valid information, even if the last call didn't end with an error or warning. For example, you can find out the last executed SQL statement and how many rows it affected, even if the number of Status Records is zero.
- The great majority of diagnostics are only applicable to stmts. You will only need to get a dbc's diagnostics area fields if the last call used a dbc handle, which usually means if the last call was connect, disconnect, endtran, or some variants of allochandle and freehandle. As for envs and descs, they too have diagnostics areas but use of SQLGetDiagField with henvs and hdescs is esoteric.

Example:

```
#include "sqlcli.h"
...
SQLHSTMT     hstmt;
SQLINTEGER   diag_number;          /* gets # of status records */
SQLINTEGER   row_number;
SQLCHAR      sqlstate[5+1];        /* gets SQLSTATE */
SQLCHAR      catalog[128+1];       /* gets a catalog name */
SQLSMALLINT  catalog_octet_length;/* size of catalog name */
SQLCHAR      schema[128+1];        /* gets a schema name */
SQLSMALLINT  schema_octet_length; /* size of schema name */
SQLCHAR      name[128+1];          /* gets an object name */
SQLSMALLINT  name_octet_length;   /* size of name */
...
/* Make a one-Column Table, with a CHECK Constraint. */
SQLExecDirect(
  hstmt,"CREATE TABLE Ts(col_1 INT,CHECK (col_1=7))",SQL_NTS);
/* Try to violate the CHECK Constraint. */
SQLExecDirect(hstmt,"INSERT INTO Ts VALUES(15)",SQL_NTS);
/* Find out how many status records are in the diagnostics area. */
SQLGetDiagField(
   SQL_HANDLE_STMT,00,SQL_DIAG_COUNT,&diag_count,00,NULL);
/* Loop: For each status record ... */
for (row_number=1; row_number<=diag_number; ++row_number) {
  /* Get SQLSTATE. */
  SQLGetDiagField(
    SQL_HANDLE_HSTMT,hstmt,row_number,SQL_DIAG_SQLSTATE,
    sizeof(sqlstate), sqlstate,NULL);
  /* The first two octets of SQLSTATE are the error class. */
  /* if class = '23' integrity constraint violation: what constraint? */
  if (memcmp(sqlstate,"23",2)==0) {
    /* Get Catalog . Schema . name of the Constraint */
```

```
    SQLGetDiagField(
       SQL_HANDLE_STMT,hstmt,row_number,
       SQL_DIAG_CONSTRAINT_CATALOG,catalog, sizeof(catalog),
       &catalog_size);
    SQLGetDiagField(
       SQL_HANDLE_STMT,hstmt,row_number,SQL_DIAG_CONSTRAINT_SCHEMA,
       schema,sizeof(schema),&schema_size);
    SQLGetDiagField(
       SQL_HANDLE_STMT,hstmt,row_number,SQL_DIAG_CONSTRAINT_NAME,
       name,sizeof(name),&name_size);
} }
```

ODBC: The SQLGetDiagField function is new in ODBC 3.0 (older ODBC versions had only SQLError for getting diagnostics fields). In addition to all the standard options, ODBC has an additional useful-looking one — SQL_DIAG_CURSOR_ROW_COUNT —for getting the number of rows in an open Cursor. (ODBC also gives row and Column number within the result set.) ODBC, unlike standard SQL, sorts status records by row number.

SQLGetDiagRec

Function Prototype:

```
SQLRETURN  SQLGetDiagRec(
  SQLSMALLINT HandleType,          /* 16-bit input */
  SQLINTEGER Handle,               /* 32-bit input */
  SQLSMALLINT RecordNumber,        /* 16-bit input */
  SQLCHAR *Sqlstate,               /* CHAR* output */
  SQLINTEGER *NativeError,         /* 32-bit output */
  SQLCHAR *MessageText,            /* CHAR* output */
  SQLSMALLINT BufferLength,        /* 16-bit input */
  SQLSMALLINT *TextLength);        /* 16-bit output */
```

Job: Get SQLSTATE, sqlcode, and error-message from one status record.

Algorithm:

```
If (HandleType <> SQL_HANDLE_ENV | SQL_HANDLE_DBC | SQL_HANDLE_STMT
    | SQL_HANDLE_DESC)
Or (what handle references isn't the type that HandleType indicates)
   return error: CLI-specific condition-invalid handle
If (RecordNumber < 1)
   return error: 35000 invalid condition number -
If (RecordNumber > number of status records in diagnostics area)
```

```
   /* SQLGetDiagRec returns +100, but doesn't make its own diagnostics */
   /* In ODBC, some output parameters would be changed anyway. */
   return error: no data -
If (SqlState is not a null pointer)
   Set *SQLState = status record [RecordNumber] . SQL_DIAG_SQLSTATE
If (NativeError is not a null pointer)
   Set *NativeError =
       status record [RecordNumber] . SQL_DIAG_NATIVE_ERROR
If (MessageText is not a null pointer)
   /* ... The message text is copied in the usual Character String
      Retrieval way. */
   Set *MessageText =
       status record [RecordNumber ]. SQL_DIAG_MESSAGE_TEXT
```

For description of the SQL_DIAG_SQLSTATE, SQL_DIAG_NATIVE_ERROR, and SQL_DIAG_MESSAGE_TEXT fields, see the SQLGetDiagField descriptions beginning on page 888.

Notes:

- The assumption behind SQLGetDiagRec is that, when you want diagnostics information, you specifically want SQL_DIAG_SQLSTATE, SQL_NATIVE_ERROR, and SQL_DIAG_MESSAGE_TEXT (both contents and length). If the assumption is wrong and you want only some of these fields, or you want other fields, then you might find that SQLGetDiagField is all you need. We observed similar assumptions at work when we looked at the desc functions, SQLGetDescField and SQLGetDescRec.
- Calls to SQLGetDiagRec are frequent after a CLI function returns an error. That is:

```
if (SQLfunction(...) < 0)  SQLGetDiagRec(...);
```

is the normal way of calling.

Example: This example shows that SQLGetDiagRec and SQLGetDiagField may be similar. The first call retrieves dbc's SQLSTATE using SQLGetDiagField — we pass NULL for the final 4 parameters because we don't care about them.

```
#include "sqlcli.h"
SQLCHAR sqlstate[6];
 ...
   SQLGetDiagField(SQL_HANDLE_DBC,hdbc,1,sqlstate, sizeof(sqlstate),NULL);
   SQLGetDiagRec(SQL_HANDLE_DBC,hdbc,1,sqlstate,NULL,NULL,00,NULL);
```

This example shows the minimalist error-handling procedure for applications that are written in a hurry; if anything goes wrong, print a message and stop the program. The symbol SQLFunc... means "any CLI function." The "if (sqlreturn < 0)" test uses an assumption (true at the moment) that SQL_SUCCESS and SQL_SUCCESS_WITH_INFO and SQL_NO_DATA — the non-problems — are all greater than or equal to zero; SQL_INVALID_HANDLE and SQL_NEED_DATA and SQL_ERROR — the problems — are less than zero.

```
#include "sqlcli.h"
SQLCHAR sqlstate[5+1];
SQLCHAR sqlmessage[SQL_MAX_MESSAGE_LENGTH+1];
SQLRETURN sqlreturn;
...
sqlreturn = SQLFunc(...);
if (sqlreturn < 0) {
  printf("Error: \n");
  if (sqlreturn==SQL_INVALID_HANDLE) {
    /* For the SQL_INVALID_HANDLE return code, there are no associated
       status records. So we have to make up and display our own
       error. */
    printf("Invalid handle.\n"); }
  if (sqlreturn==SQL_NEED_DATA) {
    /* This is shown for completeness; "need data" needs discussion later */
    printf("Need data.\n"); }
  if (sqlreturn==SQL_ERROR) {
    if (SQLGetDiagRec(...,...,1,sqlstate,NULL,sqlmessage,00,NULL)
       == SQL_NO_DATA) {
      /* Read the SQLAllocEnv description for special notes about
         handling errors from that function. For all other CLI functions, there
         will be at least one status record, so you won't get here. */
      printf("(No status rows).\n"); }
    else {
      printf("SQLSTATE=%s.\n",sqlstate);
      printf("MESSAGE_TEXT=%s.\n",sqlmessage); }
    exit(1); }
```

This example displays warning or error messages after an execution.

```
#include "sqlcli.h"
SQLCHAR  sqlstate[6], sqlmessage[SQL_MAX_MESSAGE_LENGTH+1];
SQLINTEGER sqlnative, sqlmore;
SQLSMALLINT sqlrecordnumber, sqlmessagelength;
SQLHSTMT hstmt;
SQLRETURN sqlreturn1, sqlreturn2;
...
sqlreturn1 = SQLExecDirect(hstmt,"SQL statement goes here",SQL_NTS);
if (sqlreturn1 == SQL_ERROR || sqlreturn1 == SQL_SUCCESS_WITH_INFO) {
  for (sqlrecordnumber=1;;++sqlrecordnumber) {
```

```
    sqlreturn2=SQLGetDiagRec(
               SQL_HANDLE_STMT,hstmt,sqlrecordnumber,sqlstate,
               &sqlnative, sql_message,sizeof(sql_message),
               &sql_message_length);
  if (sqlreturn2 == SQL_NO_DATA || sqlreturn2 < 0) break;
  printf("SQLExecDirect returned: %d\n",sqlreturn1);
  printf("Status code = %s\n",sqlstate);
  printf("Native code or sqlcode = %ld\n",sqlnative);
  printf("Error/Warning message = %s.\n",sqlmessage);
  if (sqlmessagelength>sizeof(sqlmessage)
    printf("May be truncated.\n"); }
SQLGetDiagField(SQL_HANDLE_STMT,hstmt,1,SQL_DIAG_MORE,
    &sqlmore,00,NULL);
if (sqlmore) {
  printf("Not all Error/Warning conditions have been displayed!\n"); }
```

ODBC: The SQLGetDiagRec function is new in ODBC 3.0; applications for earlier ODBC versions use SQLError, which is similar. ODBC example programs often use the names SqlState, Msg, and rc where we have tended to use SQLSTATE, sqlmessage, and sqlreturn.

SQLError

Function Prototype:

```
SQLRETURN  SQLError(
  SQLHENV henv,                /* 32-bit input */
  SQLHDBC hdbc,                /* 32-bit input */
  SQLHSTMT hstmt,              /* 32-bit input */
  SQLCHAR *Sqlstate,           /* pointer to char* output -- char[5+1] */
  SQLINTEGER *NativeError,     /* pointer to 32-bit output */
  SQLCHAR *MessageText,        /* pointer to char* output */
  SQLSMALLINT BufferLength,    /* 16-bit input */
  SQLSMALLINT *TextLength      /* pointer to 16-bit output */
  );
```

Job: Return "diagnostics" — i.e., the completion conditions (warnings) and exception conditions (errors) that are associated with the env or dbc or stmt.

Although all standard DBMSs will support it and although it is an official SQL3 function, SQLError is obsolete. The modern way to get diagnostics is with SQLGetDiagRec or SQLGetDiagField.

Algorithm:

```
/* The diagnostics come from a stmt or (if hstmt is 0) from a dbc or
   (if hdbc is also 0) from an env. SQLError does not get diagnostics
   from all three resources at once, or from a desc. */
If (hstmt <> 0)
  Set Handle = hstmt
Else
  /* hstmt == 0 */
  If (hdbc <> 0)
    Set Handle = hdbc
  Else
    /* hstmt == 0 and hdbc == 0 */
    If (henv <> 0)
      Set Handle = henv
    Else
      /* hstmt == 0 and hdbc == 0 and henv == 0 */
      return error: CLI-specific condition-invalid handle
/* Now Handle == handle of stmt or dbc or env */
/* The diagnostics, if any, were created by the last CLI function
   that was called using Handle. */
For (each status record generated by the last CLI function)
  If (we have already called SQLError and gotten this status record)
    continue
  If (there are no more status records)
    return SQL_NO_DATA (+100)
    /* ... a DBMS that follows the ODBC requirements would set
    sqlstate = '00000', NativeError = +100, before returning
    SQL_NO_DATA. This is a signal to the application program that it
    should break out of a loop. */
  Else
    break
/* We are now looking at a status record which was generated by a
   previous function call using the (passed) Handle. The following
   is the same as if we called:
     SQLGetDiagRec (<handle type>, <Handle>, <# of status record>,
     Sqlstate,NativeError, MessageText, BufferLength, TextLength) */
Return status record's SQL_DIAG_SQLSTATE value to Sqlstate.
Return status record's SQL_DIAG_MESSAGE_TEXT value to MessageText
(the return happens in the usual way for Character String Retrieval).
Return status record's SQL_DIAG_NATIVE value, presumably SQLCODE, to
NativeError.
```

Notes: The last five parameters of SQLError are the same as the last five parameters of SQLGetDiagRec. The effective difference is that, with SQLGetDiagRec, you pass a RecordNumber parameter, while with SQLError you depend on the DBMS to keep an internal counter — SQLError will always retrieve the next status record.

Example:

```
#include "sqlcli.h"
...
SQLCHAR sqlstate[6];           /* not 5: 6!! Allow for \0 at the end! */
SQLINTEGER sqlnative;           /* this is a "long int" */
SQLHSTMT hstmt;
...
sqlreturn=SQLExecDirect(hstmt,"INSERT VALUES",SQL_NTS);
/* The above is illegal SQL so the return code will be negative */
if (sqlreturn==SQL_ERROR) goto error_handler_for_stmt;
...
error_handler_for_stmt:
/* **TRAP: sometimes errors happen for dbc or env functions too, each
   type of handle needs a separate error-handling procedure. */
SQLError(0,0,hstmt,sqlstate,&sqlnative,NULL,00,NULL);
/* sqlstate is probably '42000' */
/* sqlnative is probably less than zero */
...
```

ODBC: The SQLError function has been around since ODBC 1.0. In ODBC 3.0, it is labelled "deprecated" and ODBC's driver manager will map it to SQLGetDiagRec.

SQLRowCount

Function Prototype:

```
SQLRETURN SQLRowCount(
  SQLHSTMT hstmt,            /* 32-bit input -- statement handle */
  SQLINTEGER *RowCount       /* 32-bit output */
  );
```

Job: Find out how many rows were inserted or updated or deleted during the execution of the last SQLExecute or SQLExecDirect call.

Algorithm:

```
If (hstmt does not refer to an executed statement)
   return error: HY010 CLI-specific condition-function sequence error
Set *RowCount = stmt's diagnostics area's SQL_DIAG_ROW_COUNT value.
```

Notes:

- The row count is the number of rows affected when you call SQLExecute or SQLExecDirect and the SQL statement you're executing begins with INSERT or UPDATE or DELETE (the SQL-data change statements).
- Only directly affected rows matter. If you delete one primary key row and there are 10 foreign key rows that are also deleted because the FOREIGN KEY Constraint definition includes ON DELETE CASCADE, then a total of 11 rows are deleted — 1 directly, 10 indirectly — so the SQLRowCount function returns 1.
- Only "searched UPDATE" and "searched DELETE" statements matter. The UPDATE ... WHERE CURRENT OF <Cursor> and DELETE ... WHERE CURRENT OF <Cursor> statements have no effect on row count.
- With some DBMSs, SQLRowCount will contain the number of rows returned by the last SELECT statement. That's very useful if you want to display the results on the screen along with a Windows scrollbar. If your DBMS won't give you that, there are other options: (*a*) use a SELECT COUNT(*) statement (may be unreliable in a multi-user environment, may fail if selection is of a grouped View), (*b*) call SQLGetDiagField with the SQL_DIAG_CURSOR_ROW_COUNT option (non-standard, works only with ODBC), or (*c*) call SQLFetchScroll until the return is SQL_NO_DATA.
- You can get the same result by calling:

```
SQLGetDiagField(SQL_HANDLE_STMT,hstmt,00,SQL_DIAG_ROW_COUNT,
                &RowCount,00,NULL);
```

  but SQLGetDiagField only returns results for "the last function," which means (for instance) that if you've fetched since you executed the UPDATE statement, SQLGetDiagField can't tell you anything. SQLRowCount, which returns results for "the last SQLExecute or SQLExecDirect function," is better.
- If the number of changed rows is zero, then SQLExecute and SQLExecDirect both return SQL_NO_DATA (not SQL_SUCCESS or SQL_SUCCESS_WITH_INFO).

Example:

```
#include "sqlcli.h"
SQLINTEGER row_count;
...
if (SQLExecDirect(hstmt,"INSERT INTO Table_1 VALUES (1)",SQL_NTS)>=0) {
  if (SQLRowCount(hstmt,&row_count)>=0) {
    /* The value of row_count is 1. */ } }
```

ODBC: The SQLRowCount function has been around since ODBC 1.0.

And that's it for the diagnostic functions. Now let's take a look at the Standard's SQLSTATE codes.

SQLSTATE Codes

The SQL status parameter SQLSTATE is a 5-character string value with 2 parts: the first 2 characters represent a class value, the following 3 characters represent a subclass value. SQLSTATE codes are limited to digits and simple Latin uppercase letters.

Class values that begin with 0, 1, 2, 3, 4, A, B, C, D, E, F, G, or H are called *standard-defined classes* and identify status conditions defined in either the SQL Standard or some other international standard. Subclass values associated with standard-defined classes that also begin with one of those 13 characters are called *standard-defined subclasses* and also identify status conditions defined in either the SQL Standard or some other international standard, while subclass values associated with standard-defined classes that begin with 5, 6, 7, 8, 9, I, J, K, L, M, N, O, P, Q, R, S, T, U, V, W, X, Y, or Z are called *implementation-defined subclasses* and identify status conditions defined by DBMS vendors.

Class values that begin with 5, 6, 7, 8, 9, I, J, K, L, M, N, O, P, Q, R, S, T, U, V, W, X, Y, or Z are called *implementation-defined classes* and identify exception conditions defined by DBMS vendors. All subclass values except '000' (no subclass) associated with implementation-defined classes are implementation-defined subclasses. An implementation-defined completion condition is identified by returning an implementation-defined subclass together with one of the SUCCESSFUL COMPLETION, WARNING, or NO DATA classes.

If a subclass value is not specified for a condition, then either subclass '000' or an implementation-defined subclass is returned.

If multiple conditions are returned, then your DBMS decides which condition is the one that will be returned in the SQLSTATE parameter. (Any number of condition values, in addition to SQLSTATE, may be returned in the diagnostics area.)

Using the CLI, you can retrieve SQLSTATE with one of the diagnostics functions (SQLGetDiagField, SQLGetDiagRec, or SQLError). Using embedded SQL, you can retrieve SQLSTATE with GET DIAGNOSTICS, or you can let the DBMS fill it in automatically. Because the status codes are reasonably standard, application programmers can anticipate what SQLSTATE values may crop up and they can write appropriate error-testing or descriptive routines. The rest of this chapter contains detailed descriptions for all SQLSTATEs which are defined in the SQL Standard, as well as summary information about some SQLSTATEs which are used in common application environments, such as ODBC.

We suggest you examine the list of SQLSTATE codes and decide which warnings and errors you must take specific action for. Make a case statement which will be executed after each SQL operation. If you are programming for ODBC 3.x, don't worry about the obsolete ODBC 2.0 entries in the list — Microsoft's driver manager will translate them to the current standardized value. If you use the list in conjunction with some vendor manual, you will probably notice that our descriptions are more specific and detailed; however, you should prefer the vendor's description in case of outright contradiction. For casual users, the DBMS's in-context error-message displays, accompanied by a pointer to the offending SQL statement, will suffice. But that is an "after-the-fact" proposition. If your job is to program for errors that haven't happened yet, you need a complete list with some examples and explanations for every entry.

Here is an example of a tiny C program (runnable in a DOS box) with one embedded SQL statement, followed by a case statement that checks for an error:

```
EXEC SQL INCLUDE SQLCA; /* so error message defined here? */
EXEC SQL BEGIN DECLARE SECTION;
char sqlcode[6]; /* Notice we allow 6 characters, there's a \0 too */
EXEC SQL END DECLARE SECTION;
void main () {
  EXEC SQL DROP TABLE x RESTRICT;
  portability(sqlstate);              /* Perhaps change the class */
  switch (sqlstate) {
     case '.....':                    /* Okay */
     case '.....':                    /* Table not found */
     case '.....':                    /* Another table depends */
     default:                         /* All other errors */
     } }
/* In a portable program you won't know what subclasses were added by
   each vendor, so change all implementation-defined subclasses
   to '000'. NIST uses a similar technique for its compliance-test
   programs. */
void portability (char sqlstate[])
{
   if (sqlstate[2]>='I' || (sqlstate[2]>='4' && sqlstate[0]<='9') {
     /* The third character of sqlstate, which is the first byte of
        subclass, is a letter >= 'I' or is a digit >= '4' --
        implementation-defined. */
     sqlstate[2]=sqlstate[3]=sqlstate[4]='0'; } }    /* subclass = '000' */
```

SUCCESSFUL COMPLETION SQLSTATEs

The following SQLSTATE codes identify a successful completion condition.

00000 successful completion

The "successful completion" class identifies "completion conditions" (as opposed to "exception conditions," which are errors). In the case of SQLSTATE 00000, the last SQL operation sailed through without a problem. The 00000 status code is invisible to CLI programs because the Standard says if the return code = SQL_SUCCESS, then no status records are generated.

WARNING SQLSTATEs

The following SQLSTATE codes identify a successful completion condition with a warning.

`01000 warning`

The "warning" class identifies completion conditions that were processed with some type of warning. They are usually associated with some DBMS-specific informational message, which you can retrieve with `SQLGetDiagRec` or `GET DIAGNOSTICS`. In the CLI, the existence of a warning diagnostic is signalled by the `SQLRETURN` value `SQL_SUCCESS_WITH_INFO (1)`. `SQLSTATE 01000` is the miscellaneous-warning category. For completion conditions that fit in the warning class, but don't fit in one of the subclasses listed below (such as `01001`), this is what you'll get. Suggestion for this `SQLSTATE` — get the message with `SQLGetDiagRec`, display the message, and continue.

`01001 warning-cursor operation conflict`

This `SQLSTATE` was included in the SQL-92 Standard by mistake; the corrigendum bulletin #3 says it should only be an SQL3 `SQLSTATE`. The NIST tests expect DBMSs to return `SQLSTATE=01001` if you `DELETE` with and without a Cursor in the same transaction.

`01002 warning-disconnect error`

There was an error during execution of the CLI function `SQLDisconnect`, but you won't be able to see the details because the `SQLDisconnect` succeeded.

`01003 warning-null value eliminated in set function`

The set function had to ignore a `NULL` when working on its argument. For example, the `SUM` of 5 and `NULL` is 5 (not `NULL`), but `01003` warns you that the result may be inaccurate because `NULL` usually means "unknown."

`01004 warning-string data, right truncation`

Happens when you try to squeeze a 5-character (or bit) value into a 4-character (or bit) space (remember that "string" can be either character or bit string). The truncation should happen for data outbound from the database to a host variable, for example in the statement "`SELECT ... INTO :x`". It should not happen for data inbound to the database — that would be not a warning but an error (`22001`).

`01005 warning-insufficient data item descriptor areas`

Every descriptor area has multiple IDAs. You need one IDA per Column of a result set or one per parameter. Either reduce the number of Columns in the select list or reduce the number of ?s in the SQL statement as a whole.

`01006 warning-privilege not revoked`

There is no Privilege descriptor for a combination of: this grantor, this grantee, this action. The DBMS does not return an error if a Privilege revocation fails — instead, it revokes whatever Privileges it can and returns this warning. If an equivalent Privilege was granted by a different grantor, it continues to exist, but warning `01006` does not appear.

`01007 warning-privilege not granted`

Probably the grantor doesn't hold a Privilege `WITH GRANT OPTION`. For example, Susan has the `UPDATE` Privilege on `TABLE_1` (without grant option) and the `INSERT` Privilege on `TABLE_1` (`WITH GRANT OPTION`). She says, "`GRANT SELECT, INSERT, UPDATE ON Table_1 TO Joe;`". Result: Joe gets the `INSERT` Privilege, but not the `SELECT` or `UPDATE` Privileges, hence this warning (some DBMSs will generate the warning twice because two Privileges are ungranted). Warning `01007` also appears if the grantor has zero Privileges `WITH GRANT OPTION` and says "`GRANT ALL`

PRIVILEGES ...". On the other hand, if the grantor holds zero Privileges period, the result is error 42000 instead of warning 01007.

01008 warning-implicit zero-bit padding
Suppose you insert B'1' — a one-bit binary <literal> — into a two-bit Column. The second bit will be a 0 and the DBMS will return this warning.

01009 warning-search condition too long for information schema
Suppose you say "CREATE TABLE ... CHECK (<condition>)", and the length of <condition> is larger than what can be stored in the INFORMATION_SCHEMA View, CHECK_CONSTRAINTS, in its CHECK_CLAUSE Column. The Table will still be created — this warning only means you won't be able to see the entire information about the Table when you look at INFORMATION_SCHEMA. See also 0100A and 0100B.

0100A warning-query expression too long for information schema
This is the same as warning 01009 except that instead of a search condition (as in a CHECK clause), you're using a query (usually SELECT). Thus, if you say "CREATE VIEW ..." with a very long query, the size of Column VIEW_DEFINITION in View VIEWS in INFORMATION_SCHEMA is a limiting factor.

0100B warning-default value too long for information schema
This is the same as warning 01009 except that instead of a search condition (as in a CHECK clause), you're using a default value.

0100C warning-dynamic result sets returned

0100D warning-additional result sets returned

0100E warning-attempt to return too many result sets

0100F warning-fewer locators than dynamic result sets

0102F warning-array data, right truncation

01Hxx warning-external routine warning
The author of the external routine chooses the subclass value of xx.

01S00 warning-invalid connection string attribute (ODBC 2+3)
The ODBC function SQLBrowseConnect or SQLDriverConnect requires a parameter string with a certain format. Connection happens anyway.

01S01 warning-error in row (ODBC 3)
With ODBC 3.x, this warning happens only for SQLExtendedFetch or SQLFetchScroll. Although an "error" has happened, this is only a warning because other rows might have been returned without error.

01S02 warning-option value changed (ODBC 3)
You used an ODBC function to change an option (e.g., SQLSetEnvAttr). This warns you that the change occurred.

01S06 warning-attempt to fetch before the result set returned the first rowset (ODBC 3)

It would be clearer to use this wording, "attempt to fetch before the first row in the result set." This error would be returned if your last fetch was of the first row in the result set and now you attempt to fetch PRIOR.

01S07 warning-fractional truncation (ODBC 3)

You'll get this error if, for example, you assigned the value 5.432 to a Column whose definition is DECIMAL(3,2) — that is, the scale of the target is 2 and the scale of the source is 3, so only 5.4 is stored. A problem with the non-fractional part would result in another SQLSTATE: 22003.

01S08 warning-error saving file DSN (ODBC 3)

A warning from SQLDriverConnect. The Connection succeeds but the file indicated by the FILEDSN keyword was not saved.

01S09 warning-invalid keyword (ODBC 3)

A warning from SQLDriverConnect. The Connection succeeds but the SAVEFILE keyword was ignored.

NO DATA SQLSTATEs

The following SQLSTATE codes identify a successful completion condition where no data has been found that matches the given criteria.

02000 no data

The "data not found" class identifies completion conditions that were processed without any data that matched the given criteria being found. If the status code is class 02, then the return code will be SQL_NO_DATA. Most programs do not look for status records if the return code is SQL_NO_DATA, but there is a slight chance that a warning exists. The DBMS does not make a status record for SQLSTATE 02000, but it might make status records for implementation-defined subclasses within class 02. SQLSTATE 02000 goes together with sqlcode = +100 and return code = SQL_NO_DATA. There are several scenarios which lead to SQLSTATE 02000:

- Fetches — if the Cursor position is now past the last row or before the first row in the result set — e.g., due to a SQLFetchScroll(...,SQL_PRIOR,...) call when Cursor was on first row of the result set.
- Updates — zero rows were affected by an INSERT, UPDATE, or DELETE statement.
- Diagnostics — no status record corresponds to the RecordNumber parameter.
- desc functions — no item descriptor area corresponds to the RecordNumber parameter
- In general — whenever you ask for data and there is no data.

In the CLI, the DBMS does not generate status records for SQLSTATE=02000. The only way to check for "no data" is to look at the return code.

02001 no data-no additional result sets returned

It is possible for a CALL statement to produce multiple result sets but in this case there are no more. 02001 is possible if the function is SQLMoreResults.

ERROR SQLSTATEs

The following SQLSTATE codes identify an exception condition; something is preventing an SQL statement from being successfully completed.

03000 SQL statement not yet complete

The "SQL statement not yet complete" class identifies exception conditions that relate to incomplete processing of SQL statements.

07000 dynamic SQL error

The "dynamic SQL error" class identifies exception conditions that relate to dynamic SQL processing errors.

07001 dynamic SQL error-using clause does not match dynamic parameters

You might encounter this error if you set the length of a descriptor, then EXECUTE ... USING <descriptor>. Often this exception results from consistency-check failure during SQLExecute: see SQLSTATE HY021. In ODBC, the name for this subclass is "wrong number of parameters."

07002 dynamic SQL error-using clause does not match target specifications

Often this exception results from consistency-check failure during SQLExecute: see SQLSTATE HY021. Sometimes this exception results from an incorrect number of parameters — but see also: SQLSTATE 07008. In ODBC, the name for this subclass is "COUNT field incorrect."

07003 dynamic SQL error-cursor specification cannot be executed

07004 dynamic SQL error-using clause required for dynamic parameters

You cannot simply EXECUTE an SQL statement that has dynamic parameters — you also need to use a USING clause. See also: SQLSTATE 07007.

07005 dynamic SQL error-prepared statement not a cursor-specification

This results from an attempt to use ODBC function SQLColAttribute or SQLDescribeCol for an SQL statement that returned no result set or from using DECLARE CURSOR followed by a prepare or execute of an SQL statement that does not return a result set.

07006 dynamic SQL error-restricted data type attribute violation

You are using a parameter whose value does not match the <data type>; the DBMS cannot even try to CAST to the correct <data type> because the source and target are too different. For example, you have a host variable defined as SQLINTEGER, you have a Column containing a TIMESTAMP, and you try to fetch that Column into the host variable. With CLI, this might mean that you forgot to re-bind the parameters when you prepared a new SQL statement.

07007 dynamic SQL error-using clause required for result fields

You cannot simply EXECUTE an SQL statement which has result fields — you also need to use a USING clause. See also: SQLSTATE 07004.

07008 dynamic SQL error-invalid descriptor count

Using the embedded SQL ALLOCATE DESCRIPTOR statement, you allocated a 5-item descriptor. Now you are trying to use the sixth item in that descriptor. See also: SQLSTATE 07009.

07009 dynamic SQL error-invalid descriptor index

You are using a CLI descriptor function (such as SQLBindCol or SQLBindParameter) and the Column number is less than 1 or greater than the maximum number of Columns. Or you are using the embedded SQL `ALLOCATE DESCRIPTOR` statement with a size which is less than 1 or greater than an implementation-defined maximum. See also: `SQLSTATE 07008`.

`07S01 dynamic SQL error-invalid use of default parameter`
You used `SQLBindParameter` with `SQL_DEFAULT_PARAMETER`, but now it turns out that the parameter does not have a default value.

`08000 connection exception`
The "connection exception" class identifies exception conditions that relate to SQL-Connections.

`08001 connection exception-SQL-client unable to establish SQL-connection`
The client could not get in touch with the server — perhaps there is no such server or perhaps the network is busy.

`08002 connection exception-connection name in use`
The name of an SQL-Connection must be unique. With standard SQL, this would happen if you said "`CONNECT` ... `AS 'X'` ..." twice (only one `X` at a time, please).

`08003 connection exception-connection does not exist`
You are trying to use a connection-related function (such as `SQLGetConnectAttr`) but the SQL-Connection is not open. Or you said "`DISCONNECT 'X'`" and either `X` was never connected or has already been disconnected. If the call is `SQLAllocHandle(SQL_HANDLE_STMT,...)`, `&hstmt` is set to zero. You can get diagnostics from the `hdbc`.

`08004 connection exception-SQL-server rejected establishment of SQL-connection`
You'll get this error if, for example, the `SQLConnect` function was unsuccessful. The server might not like the password or it might already be handling the maximum number of clients.

`08006 connection exception-connection failure`
This occurs for a `SET CONNECTION` statement where the argument is presumably a dormant Connection. The failure might be due to a server failure that occurred while the Connection was dormant. The `SET CONNECTION` might be implicit — for example, a `DISCONNECT` statement might result in an attempt to re-establish the last dormant Connection.

`08007 connection exception-transaction resolution unknown`
While you were trying to `COMMIT`, you were cut off. This is a bad one because you are not told whether the transaction finished successfully or not. The ODBC manual calls this error, "Connection failure during transaction" and implies that it can happen for `ROLLBACK` too.

`08S01 connection exception-communication link failure` (ODBC 2+3)
This can happen during execution of pretty well any ODBC function. Perhaps there was a hiccup on a phone line.

`09000 triggered action exception`
The "triggered action exception" class identifies exception conditions that relate to Triggers.

`0A000 feature not supported`
The "feature not supported" class identifies exception conditions that relate to features you're trying to use, but that your DBMS hasn't implemented. The Standard does not specify

what will cause this SQLSTATE, possibly because the expectation is that all features will be supported. If the feature is ODBC-related, see also: SQLSTATE IM001, HYC00.

0A001 feature not supported-multiple server transactions
The meaning is "a single transaction cannot be performed on multiple servers." Such a feature is sophisticated and rare.

0B000 invalid transaction initiation
The "invalid transaction initiation" class identifies exception conditions that relate to beginning a transaction.

0D000 invalid target type specification
The "invalid target type specification" class identifies exception conditions that relate to specifying a target for data.

0E000 invalid schema name list specification
The "invalid schema name list specification" class identifies exception conditions that relate to specifying Schema paths.

0F000 locator exception
The "locator exception" class identifies exception conditions that relate to locators: BLOB and CLOB <data type>s and their values.

0F001 locator exception-invalid specification
This will be returned if a value passed for a BLOB or CLOB is invalid.

0F002 locator exception-update attempted with non-updatable locator

0F003 locator exception-location does not represent specified object

0F004 locator exception-unknown native value

0G000 reference to null table value

0H000 invalid SQLSTATE value

0K000 resignal when handler not active

0K002 resignal when handler not active-modifying SQL-data not permitted

0K003 resignal when handler not active-prohibited SQL-statement attempted

0K005 resignal when handler not active-function executed no return statement

0L000 invalid grantor

0N000 most specific type mismatch in invocation of type-preserving function

0P000 invalid role specification

0Q000 source result set not created by current SQL-server

0R000 cursor already allocated to result set or procedure

20000 case not found for case statement

21000 cardinality violation

Suggested error message: "subquery contained more than one row." For example, suppose you have a Table T, with a Column S1 and two rows. In both rows, Column S1 has the value 5. Then either "SELECT (SELECT s1 FROM T) FROM ..." (scalar subquery) or "... WHERE 5 = (SELECT s1 FROM T)" (row subquery) violate cardinality. Another possibility, applicable to embedded SQL only, is that you are using a singleton-SELECT statement format but there are two rows returned. Some cardinality violations, e.g., OVERLAPS operand with degree greater than 2, cause SQLSTATE=42000 instead of SQLSTATE=21000.

21S01 cardinality violation-insert value list does not match column list (ODBC 2+3)

For example, the statement "INSERT INTO T (a,b) VALUES (1,2,3)" is trying to insert three values into two Columns.

21S02 cardinality violation-degree of derived table does not match column list (ODBC 2+3)

For example, the SQL statement "CREATE VIEW (a,b) AS SELECT a,b,c FROM T;" is creating a 2-Column View for a 3-Column select.

22000 data exception

The "data exception" class identifies exception conditions that relate to data errors.

22001 data exception-string data, right truncation

Suppose you try to insert a 5-character string into a Column defined as CHAR(4) or suppose you use the expression "CAST (12345 AS CHAR(4))". No truncation actually occurs because the SQL statement fails. See also: SQLSTATE 01004.

22002 data exception-null value, no indicator parameter

Suggested error message: "NULL seen, host program passed no indicator." For example, you used SQLBindCol but passed no parameter for an indicator value to be returned to. This is not an error unless you fetch a NULL.

22003 data exception-numeric value out of range

Suggested error message: "the numeric value <> is too big to fit in the target <>." Often this is the result of an arithmetic overflow — for example, "UPDATE ... SET SMALLINT_COLUMN = 9999999999" or you're trying to retrieve a value of 5 billion into a host variable defined in Pascal as "Word." Fractional truncation won't cause this error, see SQLSTATE 01S07.

22004 data exception-null value not allowed

22005 data exception-error in assignment

This error appears for GET DESCRIPTOR and SET DESCRIPTOR statements where the <data type> and size indicated in the descriptor does not match the value.

22006 data exception-invalid interval format

For example, a year-month interval should contain only a year integer, a '-' separator, and a month integer. See also: SQLSTATE 22015.

22007 data exception-invalid datetime format

Suggested message: "For the <data type> <>, <> is not a valid value." This error only occurs if there is an explicit or implicit CAST to a datetime (date or time or timestamp). See also: SQLSTATE 22008, 22018.

22008 data exception-datetime field overflow
Suggested message: "For the data type <>, <> is not a valid value." One thing to look for — arithmetic which causes the DAY field of a date to be greater than the last day of the month — for example DATE '1994-03-31' + INTERVAL '01' MONTH. See also: SQLSTATE 22007.

22009 data exception-invalid time zone displacement value
Suggested message: "The time zone displacement value <> is outside the range –12:59 to 13:00." This could happen for SET LOCAL TIME ZONE INTERVAL '22:00' HOUR TO MINUTE;.

2200A data exception-null value in reference target

2200B data exception-escape character conflict

2200C data exception-invalid use of escape character

2200D data exception-invalid escape octet

22010 data exception-invalid indicator parameter value
The value of the indicator variable is less than zero but is not equal to –1 (SQL_NULL_DATA).

22011 data exception-substring error
Suggested message: "The maximum length of SUBSTRING parameter is <>." For example, "... SUBSTRING (string_column FROM 5 FOR 100) ..." when the length of STRING_COLUMN is only 1.

22012 data exception-division by zero
For example, "... column_name / ? ...," where ? is a parameter marker and the value of the parameter at run time is 0. If the Column contains NULL, then the result is NULL — the Standard makes it clear that dividing NULL by zero is not an error.

22014 data exception-invalid update value

22015 data exception-interval field overflow
Suggested message: "The <> field contains <>, the maximum is <>." For example, "... DATE '1993-01-01' + INTERVAL '1000' YEAR ..." (this is a tricky one — the default size of all interval fields including year fields is only 2 digits). See also: SQLSTATE 22006.

22018 data exception-invalid character value for cast
Suggested message: "The character <> cannot be used when CASTing to data type <>." For example, if you try to cast '1994/10/10' to a date, it won't work because the separator is '/' (the correct separator is '-').

22019 data exception-invalid escape character
Suggested message: "The LIKE escape value <> is longer than 1 character." The expression "... LIKE '...' ESCAPE 'AB' ..." would return this error.

2201B data exception-invalid regular expression

2201C data exception-null row not permitted in table

22020 data exception-invalid limit value

22021 data exception-character not in repertoire

Suggested message: "The character <> is not in the repertoire of Character set <>." For example, the Character set SQL_CHARACTER does not contain the tilde (~), so this <literal> is not allowed: "... _SQL_CHARACTER '~' ...".

22022 data exception-indicator overflow

Suggested message: "indicator is too small for size value <>." This could happen if you use embedded SQL and you define the indicator as a C "short int" or Pascal "Word." If you use SQL/CLI, then the message won't happen because all indicators must be 32-bit.

22023 data exception-invalid parameter value

22024 data exception-unterminated C string

Suggested message: "the C parameter string starting with <> is too long." For example, an SQL statement uses a ? parameter for a string but at runtime it is seen that the C char-string does not have a terminating '\0'. The DBMS can only detect this error if it knows what the maximum string size is, i.e., only in embedded SQL. Usually this problem will appear as a too-long or improperly-formatted string, so several other SQLSTATE error returns are possible — for example, SQLSTATE 22019.

22025 data exception-invalid escape sequence

Suggested message: "LIKE pattern <> has invalid escape sequence <>." If you use an escape character, it must be followed in the pattern by _ or % or another escape character. If you use "... LIKE 'X%@' ESCAPE '@' ...," you'll get this error.

22026 data exception-string data, length mismatch

With ODBC this error should only occur for SQL_LONGVARCHAR or SQL_LONGVARBINARY strings. For standard SQL, this error should only occur for bit strings.

22027 data exception-trim error

Suggested message: "the TRIM string <> is longer than 1 character." For example, "... TRIM('AB' FROM '...') ..." results in this error.

22028 data exception-row already exists

2202C data exception-sublist error

2202D data exception-null instance used in mutator function

2202E data exception-array element error

2202F data exception-array data, right truncation

23000 integrity constraint violation

The "integrity constraint violation" class identifies exception conditions that relate to Constraint violations. Suggested message for SQLSTATE 23000: "Attempted violation of constraint <>." For example, Table T has a PRIMARY KEY Constraint and you attempt to insert two rows into T, both with precisely the same values in all Columns. For SQL-92, this SQLSTATE applies to attempted violations of any kind of Constraint, including NOT NULLs and FOREIGN KEY Constraints. The message can also occur if the total length of a foreign key Column list is exceeded. See also: SQLSTATE 40002.

23001 integrity constraint violation-restrict violation

`24000 invalid cursor state`

The "invalid cursor state" class identifies exception conditions that relate to Cursors. For `SQLSTATE 24000`, the Cursor-related operation can't happen because some preliminary function hasn't been called or hasn't been completed — for example:

- `OPEN` <Cursor>, then immediately try to `OPEN` <Cursor> again.
- `FETCH` without opening the Cursor.
- `OPEN` <Cursor>, forget to `FETCH`, then `DELETE` ... `WHERE CURRENT OF` <Cursor>.

For CLI programs, the DBMS returns `SQLSTATE=24000` if you try to `FETCH` and there is no result set (for example, because the previous SQL statement was `INSERT`). However, if there was no previous SQL statement at all, then the return is not `24000` but `HY010` (CLI-specific error-function sequence error).

`25000 invalid transaction state`

The "invalid transaction state" class identifies exception conditions that relate to transactions. For `SQLSTATE 25000`, you are most likely trying to execute an SQL statement that can only be executed at transaction start — for example, you are issuing a `SET SESSION AUTHORIZATION` statement after selecting something. Alternatively, you specified `SET TRANSACTION READ ONLY` and now you are saying `UPDATE`, `DROP`, etc. Finally, it is possible you are saying `INSERT` after a `FETCH`.

`25001 invalid transaction state-active SQL-transaction`

`START TRANSACTION` or `DISCONNECT` or `SET SESSION AUTHORIZATION` or `SET ROLE` statements cannot be issued if a transaction has already been started.

`25002 invalid transaction state-branch transaction already active`

`SET TRANSACTION LOCAL` ..., which applies only in multiple-server contexts, is illegal if a local transaction is already happening.

`25003 invalid transaction state-inappropriate access mode for branch transaction`

`25004 invalid transaction state-inappropriate isolation level for branch transaction`

`25005 invalid transaction state-no active SQL-transaction for branch transaction`

`25006 invalid transaction state-read-only SQL-transaction`

`25007 invalid transaction state-schema and data statement mixing not supported`

Some DBMSs do not allow SQL-Schema statements (such as `CREATE`) to be mixed with SQL-data statements (such as `INSERT`) in the same transaction.

`25008 invalid transaction state-held cursor requires same isolation level`

The `SET TRANSACTION` statement cannot be used to change isolation level if there is a held Cursor made with a different isolation level left over from the last transaction.

`25S01 invalid transaction state-transaction state unknown` (ODBC 3)

The attempt to end the transaction (with `SQLEndTran`) failed for at least one of the environment's Connections.

`25S02 invalid transaction state-transaction is still active` (ODBC 3)
The attempt to end the transaction (with `SQLEndTran`) failed; the transaction did not end (that is, the transaction is not rolled back).

`25S03 invalid transaction state-transaction is rolled back` (ODBC 3)
The attempt to end the transaction (with `SQLEndTran`) failed; the transaction is rolled back (that is, the transaction ended).

`26000 invalid SQL statement name`
Probable cause — you failed to `PREPARE` an SQL statement and now you are trying to `EXECUTE` it.

`27000 triggered data change violation`
With SQL-92, you can cause this error with interlocked `FOREIGN KEY` Constraints that `CASCADE ON UPDATE`, so that when you `UPDATE` row#1 in `TABLE_1`, it causes an `UPDATE` to row#2 in `TABLE_2`, which in turn causes an `UPDATE` to row#1 in `TABLE_1` — and that's an error because the Standard doesn't allow this kind of looping. With SQL3, this error can also happen for Triggers. See also: `SQLSTATE 09000`, `40004`.

`28000 invalid authorization specification`
This error is caused by an invalid <AuthorizationID>. For example, "`SET SESSION AUTHORIZATION 'PUBLIC'`" is illegal because `'PUBLIC'` has a special significance in SQL. It's implementation-defined whether this can happen due to an entry of the wrong password.

`2A000 direct SQL syntax error access or rule violation`
This error does not appear in ordinary programs.

`2B000 dependent privilege descriptors still exist`
You used "`REVOKE GRANT OPTION FOR`" but not `CASCADE`.

`2C000 invalid character set name`
Presumably an invalid <Character set name> would be one that begins with a digit, contains a non-Latin letter, etc.

`2D000 invalid transaction termination`
Has to do with savepoints and atomicity of transactions. Should not be a matter of concern until SQL3 gets going.

`2E000 invalid connection name`
For a `CONNECT` statement, the argument must be a valid <identifier>.

`2F000 SQL routine exception`
An SQL routine is a procedure or function which is written in SQL. `SQLSTATE` class `2F` identifies exception conditions that relate to SQL routines. (Exceptions for non-SQL routines are class `38`.)

`2F002 SQL routine exception-modifying SQL-data not permitted`
The probable cause of this error is that the `CREATE PROCEDURE` or `CREATE FUNCTION` statement contained the clause `CONTAINS SQL` or `READS SQL`, but the function contains an SQL statement which can modify the database (for example, an `UPDATE` statement). The corresponding external-routine exception is `38002`.

`2F003 SQL routine exception-prohibited SQL-statement attempted`

The prohibited procedural SQL statements are the SQL-transaction statements (START TRANSACTION, SET TRANSACTION, SET CONSTRAINTS, CREATE SAVEPOINT, RELEASE SAVEPOINT, COMMIT, ROLLBACK) or the SQL-Connection statements (CONNECT, SET CONNECTION, DISCONNECT) or the SQL-Schema statements (CREATE, DROP, ALTER, GRANT, REVOKE). The corresponding external-routine exception is 38003.

`2F004 SQL routine exception-reading SQL-data not permitted`

The probable cause of this error is that the CREATE PROCEDURE or CREATE FUNCTION statement contains the clause CONTAINS SQL, but the function contains an SQL statement which reads the database (for example, a SELECT statement). The corresponding SQL-routine exception is 38004.

`2F005 SQL routine exception-function executed no return statement`

`30000 invalid SQL statement`

`31000 invalid target specification value`

`33000 invalid SQL descriptor name`

If, in embedded SQL, you use "EXECUTE ... USING DESCRIPTOR 'X';", a descriptor named X must exist.

`34000 invalid cursor name`

If the function is SQLSetCursorName, then the problem is that a <Cursor name> must be a unique, valid <identifier>. If the function is SQLPrepare or SQLExecDirect, the SQL statement is "UPDATE ... WHERE CURRENT OF <Cursor>" or "DELETE ... WHERE CURRENT OF <Cursor>" and <Cursor> is not the name of an open Cursor.

`35000 invalid condition number`

With embedded SQL, you get this by saying "GET DIAGNOSTICS EXCEPTION 0". With the CLI, you get this by calling SQLGetDiagRec or SQLGetDiagField with a RecordNumber parameter less than 1. If RecordNumber is greater than the number of status records, you don't get this error. Instead, you get an SQL_NO_DATA return code.

`36000 cursor sensitivity exception`

The "cursor sensitivity exception" class identifies exception conditions that relate to Cursors and their sensitivity attribute.

`36001 cursor sensitivity exception-request rejected`

An attempt was made to open a sensitive Cursor, but the DBMS cannot guarantee that data changes will be visible throughout the transaction.

`36002 cursor sensitivity exception-request failed`

For example, an attempt was made to execute a positioned DELETE statement, but there is a sensitive Cursor open and (for some implementation-dependent reason) the effects of the DELETE cannot be made visible via that Cursor.

`37000 dynamic SQL syntax error or access rule violation`

The SQL-92 Standard originally mentioned this SQLSTATE, but according to a later correction (corrigendum bulletin #3) we should use SQLSTATE = 42000 instead. That is what all ODBC 3.x drivers do.

`38000 external routine exception`

An external routine is a procedure or function which is written in a language other than SQL. `SQLSTATE` class `38` identifies exception conditions that relate to external routines. (Exceptions from SQL routines are class `2F`.)

`38001 external routine exception-containing SQL not permitted`

The probable cause is that the `CREATE PROCEDURE` or `CREATE FUNCTION` statement contained the clause: `NO SQL`, but the routine contains an SQL statement.

`38002 external routine exception-modifying SQL-data not permitted`

The probable cause is that the `CREATE PROCEDURE` or `CREATE FUNCTION` statement contained the clause: `NO SQL` or `CONTAINS SQL` or `READS SQL`, but the function contains an SQL statement which can modify the database (for example, an `UPDATE` statement).

`38003 external routine exception-prohibited SQL-statement attempted`

The prohibited procedural SQL statements are the SQL-transaction statements (`START TRANSACTION`, `SET TRANSACTION`, `SET CONSTRAINTS`, `CREATE SAVEPOINT`, `RELEASE SAVEPOINT`, `COMMIT`, `ROLLBACK`) or the SQL-Connection statements (`CONNECT`, `SET CONNECTION`, `DISCONNECT`) or the SQL-Schema statements (`CREATE`, `DROP`, `ALTER`, `GRANT`, `REVOKE`).

`38004 external routine exception-reading SQL-data not permitted`

The probable cause is that the `CREATE PROCEDURE` or `CREATE FUNCTION` statement contained the clause: `NO SQL` or `CONTAINS SQL`, but the function contains an SQL statement which reads the database (for example, a `SELECT` statement).

`39000 external routine invocation exception`

`39001 external routine invocation exception-invalid sqlstate returned`

`39004 external routine invocation exception-null value not allowed`

`3B000 savepoint exception`

`3B001 savepoint exception-invalid specification`

`3B002 savepoint exception-too many`

`3C000 ambiguous cursor name`

A more appropriate wording is: duplicate <Cursor name>. In ODBC, you can get this by calling `SQLSetCursorName` with an argument that is the name of an already-open Cursor.

`3D000 invalid catalog name`

Presumably a <Catalog name> could be invalid if it is used as a qualifier or as the argument of `SET CATALOG` and does not refer to an existing Catalog or is not a valid <identifier>. However, all those situations are equally covered by `SQLSTATE=42000` (syntax error or access violation). For `SQLSetConnectAttr`, the problem is with a `SQL_ATTR_CURRENT_CATALOG` specification.

`3F000 invalid schema name`

Presumably a <Schema name> could be invalid if it is used as a qualifier or as the argument of `SET SCHEMA` and does not refer to an existing Schema or is not a valid <identifier>. However, all those situations are equally covered by `SQLSTATE=42000` (syntax error or access violation).

`3G000 invalid UDT instance`

`40000 transaction rollback`

`40001 transaction rollback-serialization failure`

Two SQL jobs are running simultaneously and a concurrency problem arose. For example, using a locking protocol, there was a deadlock or using a timestamp protocol, a younger job has read the Object.

`40002 transaction rollback-integrity constraint violation`

This occurs for `COMMIT` if there were deferred Constraints (deferred Constraints aren't checked until `COMMIT` time unless `SET CONSTRAINTS IMMEDIATE` is executed). So, you asked for `COMMIT` and what you got was `ROLLBACK`. See also: `SQLSTATE 23000`.

`40003 transaction rollback-statement completion unknown`

The SQL-Connection was lost during execution of an SQL statement.

`40004 transaction rollback-triggered action exception`

This occurs for `COMMIT` if there was a deferred Constraint — presumably a `FOREIGN KEY` Constraint unless Triggers are supported by the DBMS — and there was an attempt to violate the Constraint. See also: `SQLSTATE 09000, 27000`.

`42000 syntax error or access rule violation`

The favourite exception. Syntax errors include not just grammar or spelling errors, but "bind problems" such as failure to find an Object. Access violations are due to lack of Privileges. A high security DBMS will try to hide from the user whether the problem is "you don't have access to `X`" as opposed to "`X` isn't there" — that's why these two different categories are lumped together in one `SQLSTATE` (thus, users can't discover what the <Table name>s are by trying out all the possibilities).

TRAP: It's easy to think that a syntax violation will always be caught during the prepare stage. Not so. Many DBMSs don't bind until the execution stage. You have to check after both `SQLPrepare` and `SQLExecute` and perhaps even after `SQLFetch` (because a DBMS may evaluate expressions in the select list at `FETCH` time or a Column might have been dropped since the Cursor was opened).

`42S01 syntax error or access rule violation-base table or view already exists` (ODBC 3)

This is caused by something like "`CREATE TABLE T ...`" when there's already a Table named T.

`42S02 syntax error or access rule violation-base table or view not found` (ODBC 3)

This is caused by something like "`SELECT * FROM T;`" when there's no Table named T.

`42S11 syntax error or access rule violation-index already exists` (ODBC 3)

This is caused by something like "`CREATE INDEX I ON T(c);`" when there's already an index named I.

`42S12 syntax error or access rule violation-index not found` (ODBC 3)

This is caused by something like "`DROP INDEX I;`" when there's no index named I.

`42S21 syntax error or access rule violation-column already exists` (ODBC 3)
This is caused by something like "`ALTER TABLE T ADD COLUMN c ...`" when Column C already exists.

`42S22 syntax error or access rule violation-column not found` (ODBC 3)
This is caused by something like "`SELECT c FROM T;`" when Table T has no Column named C.

`44000 with check option violation`
This is caused by something like "`CREATE VIEW V AS SELECT x FROM T WHERE x=5 WITH CHECK OPTION;`" then "`UPDATE V SET x = 6;`". The View's `WITH CHECK OPTION` clause is violated by the attempted `UPDATE`, which fails.

`45000 unhandled user-defined exception`

`70100 operation aborted` (ODBC 2)
Possible because tasks or threads can be destroyed in some operating systems, but don't expect to see this.

`H1zzz SQL Multimedia part 1`

`H2zzz SQL Multimedia part 2`

`H3zzz SQL Multimedia part 3`

`H4zzz SQL Multimedia part 4`

`H5zzz SQL Multimedia part 5`

`H6zzz SQL Multimedia part 6`

`H7zzz SQL Multimedia part 7`

`H8zzz SQL Multimedia part 8`

`H9zzz SQL Multimedia part 9`

`HAzzz SQL Multimedia part 10`

`HBzzz SQL Multimedia part 11`

`HCzzz SQL Multimedia part 12`

`HDzzz SQL Multimedia part 13`

`HEzzz SQL Multimedia part 14`

`HFzzz SQL Multimedia part 15`

`HY000 CLI-specific condition-invalid handle`
`      CLI-specific condition-dynamic parameter value needed`
There is no status record for the invalid-handle exception. The return from the CLI function is –2 (`SQL_INVALID_HANDLE`), so the only test for invalid-handle is:

```
if (sqlreturn == SQL_INVALID_HANDLE) ...
```

The "invalid handle" exception occurs if (*a*) the passed hstmt or hdbc or henv or hdesc is not a handle of any resource at all or (*b*) the passed handle refers to the wrong type of resource, for example you passed a hdesc but a hdbc was expected in this context.

There is no status record for the need-data exception either. The return from the CLI function is +99 (SQL_NEED_DATA), so the only test for need-data is:

```
if (sqlreturn == SQL_NEED_DATA) ...
```

This exception is associated with deferred parameters.

`HY001 CLI-specific condition-memory allocation error`
Probable cause: a malloc failure. One possible solution is to close all other windows. If SQLAllocHandle(SQL_HANDLE_ENV ,...): the DBMS returns 0 to &henv. Because there is no valid handle, you can't get diagnostics. If SQLAllocHandle(SQL_HANDLE_DBC ,...): the DBMS returns 0 to &hdbc. You can get diagnostics using the henv.

`HY003 CLI-specific condition-invalid data type in application descriptor`
Actually, the invalid <data type> is not in an application descriptor, but in the parameter of a CLI function (SQLBindCol, SQLBindParameter, SQLGetData, SQLGetParamData).

`HY004 CLI-specific condition-invalid data type`
The SQLGetTypeInfo function requires a DataType parameter whose value is either SQL_ALL_TYPES or one of the "concise type" codes. If the DataType parameter has an invalid value, you get this error. SQLSetDescField and SQLBindParameter parameters must also contain "concise type" codes.

`HY007 CLI-specific condition-associated statement is not prepared`
A function (for example SQLGetDescField) requires a descriptor field, but the SQL statement has not been prepared so no description exists.

`HY008 CLI-specific condition-operation cancelled`
Many functions can operate asynchronously. Such operations can be cancelled using the SQLCancel function. That's what happened to this one.

`HY009 CLI-specific condition-invalid use of null pointer`
One of the parameters for a function is a pointer (address). The passed pointer (address) is 0000:0000, which isn't acceptable. Some DBMSs will return this error if they detect that the host language can't handle pointers.

`HY010 CLI-specific condition-function sequence error`
Some functions won't work unless some other function has successfully executed. For example, it's impossible to "fetch" if you've never connected or selected. Or, an asynchronously executing function has not finished. Or, the last SQLExecute or SQLExecDirect call returned SQL_NEED_DATA (meaning the SQL statement has not finished executing) and you're trying to free the stmt. See also: SQLSTATE 24000.

`HY011 CLI-specific condition-attribute cannot be set now`
Some settings cannot be changed in the middle of a transaction. For example, you can't call the function SQLSetConnectAttr to change SQL_ATTR_TXN_ISOLATION, after you've already done some inserts.

HY012 CLI-specific condition-invalid transaction operation code

For the function SQLEndTran, the only possible arguments are SQL_COMMIT, SQL_ROLLBACK, or a savepoint option.

HY013 CLI-specific condition-memory management error

Many functions can return this. Usually the reason is "low memory conditions."

HY014 CLI-specific condition-Limit on number of handles exceeded

This can come from a routine that allocates a handle (env, dbc, stmt, desc) such as SQLAllocHandle. The maximum number of handles is implementation-defined for each type.

- If SQLAllocHandle(SQL_HANDLE_ENV,NULL,&henv): the DBMS puts a handle in &henv despite the error; however, the handle is just a skeleton — you won't be able to use it to allocate a connection handle.
- If SQLAllocHandle(SQL_HANDLE_DBC,henv,&hdbc): the DBMS puts 0 in &hdbc (SQL_NULL_HDBC). You can get diagnostics using the henv.
- If SQLAllocHandle(SQL_HANDLE_STMT,hdbc,&hstmt): the DBMS puts 0 in &hstmt (SQL_NULL_HSTMT). You can get diagnostics using the hdbc.
- If SQLAllocHandle(SQL_HANDLE_DESC,hdbc,&hdesc): the DBMS puts 0 in &hdesc (SQL_NULL_HDESC). You can get diagnostics using the hdbc.

HY015 CLI-specific condition-no cursor name available

Obsolete — happens only for ODBC 2.x drivers, when you call SQLGetCursorName.

HY016 CLI-specific condition-cannot modify an implementation row descriptor

The target of a function (for example SQLCopyDesc) was an IRD, which can't be changed.

HY017 CLI-specific condition-invalid use of an automatically allocated descriptor handle

An attempt was made to free or change a descriptor which was not made by the application program.

HY018 CLI-specific condition-Server declined cancel request

The ODBC function SQLCancel was called; it's up to the data source to decide whether this can be processed. For example, the data source might not be responding to the driver manager's requests.

HY019 CLI-specific condition-non-character and non-binary data sent in pieces

The function SQLPutData was called twice for the same parameter or Column; this is only allowed for character and binary data.

HY020 CLI-specific condition-attempt to concatenate a null value

The function SQLPutData was called twice for the same parameter or Column; in one of the calls, the passed value was NULL.

HY021 CLI-specific condition-Inconsistent descriptor information

The fields of a desc have failed the consistency check. For example, the SQL_DESC_SCALE value is greater than the SQL_DESC_PRECISION value (for a DECIMAL field) or the SQL_DESC_TYPE value is SQL_DATETIME but the SQL_DESC_INTERVAL_CODE value is 6 (only 1 to 5 would be legal). This error happens only for the function calls SQLSetDescField and SQLSetDescRec. For other functions, inconsistency causes SQLSTATE 07001 or 07002.

HY024 CLI-specific condition-invalid attribute value
One of the "attribute" functions was called (SQLGetEnvAttr, SQLSetEnvAttr, SQLGetConnectAttr, SQLSetConnectAttr, SQLGetStmtAttr, SQLSetStmtAttr). The numeric value for the attribute parameter for this function is not defined.

HY055 CLI-specific condition-non-string data cannot be used with string routine

HY090 CLI-specific condition-invalid string length or buffer length
You called any CLI function that passes a string value. The size parameter for this string value was less than or equal to zero, and was not equal to –3 (SQL_NTS).

HY091 CLI-specific condition-invalid descriptor field identifier
A descriptor is a structure with information about a selected Column (in a result set); a field in that descriptor is usually identified by a numeric code; the number you used was out of bounds. For example, you can't call SQLColAttribute with a field identifier parameter = 0.

HY092 CLI-specific condition-invalid attribute/option identifier
You called any CLI function that passes an option number (for example SQLGetConnectAttr). The value you passed was not one of the defined values.

HY095 CLI-specific condition-Function type out of range (ODBC 3)
The SQLGetFunctions function was called, with a FunctionId parameter, the value of which is not defined for ODBC. This SQLSTATE is not mentioned in the SQL3 Standard.

HY096 CLI-specific condition-invalid information type

HY097 CLI-specific condition-column type out of range

HY098 CLI-specific condition-scope out of range

HY099 CLI-specific condition-nullable out of range

HY103 CLI-specific condition-invalid retrieval code (ODBC 3)
The ODBC function SQLDataSources or SQLDrivers was called, with a Direction parameter, the value of which does not equal SQL_FETCH_FIRST, SQL_FETCH_NEXT, etc.

HY104 CLI-specific condition-invalid precision or scale value
The maximum precision or scale for some <data type>s is up to the data source (i.e., sometimes the driver can't handle big things), so the SQLBindParameter function gets this return. Try querying the data source to find out what its maxima are.

HY105 CLI-specific condition-invalid parameter mode
The function call (e.g., SQLBindParameter) contains an InputOutputMode parameter, the value of which is not one of: SQL_PARAM_MODE_IN, SQL_PARAM_MODE_OUT, SQL_PARAM_MODE_INOUT.

HY106 CLI-specific condition-invalid fetch orientation
Only certain fetch "orientations" are allowed (e.g., NEXT, FIRST, LAST, PRIOR, ABSOLUTE, RELATIVE). The value you passed wasn't one of them, for the function SQLFetchScroll. Or, if the

Cursor isn't a `SCROLL` Cursor, the only legal orientation is `NEXT`. ODBC variations — this could also happen for `SQLExtendedFetch` and the name for this `SQLSTATE` is: Fetch type out of range.

`HY107 CLI-specific condition-Row value out of range`

One of the ODBC "fetch" or "set position" functions was called (e.g., `SQLFetch`) and the Cursor is "key set driven," but the row involved isn't in the key set's range.

`HY109 CLI-specific condition-invalid cursor position`

A row could not be fetched probably because it has been deleted or because it is now locked.

`HY110 CLI-specific condition-invalid driver completion` (ODBC 3)

The ODBC function `SQLDriverConnect` contains a `DriverCompletion` parameter, the value of which is not defined for ODBC. This `SQLSTATE` is not mentioned in the SQL Standard.

`HY111 CLI-specific condition-invalid bookmark value` (ODBC 3)

The ODBC function `SQLExtendedFetch` or `SQLFetchScroll` was called, with a `FetchOrientation` parameter, the value of which was not defined for ODBC or was a null pointer. This `SQLSTATE` is not mentioned in the SQL Standard.

`HYC00 CLI-specific condition-optional feature not implemented` (ODBC 3)

Many of the ODBC functions have optional features. It is unlikely that any driver will support every optional feature. When the driver doesn't, this is the error you'll get. See also: `SQLSTATE 0A000` (which applies to unimplemented features outside the CLI) and `SQLSTATE IM001` (which applies to unsupported ODBC functions rather than features). The ODBC manual refers to `HYC00` as "particularly significant."

`HYT00 CLI-specific condition-timeout expired` (ODBC 3)

You can specify a timeout value in milliseconds (with the `SQLSetStmtAttr` ODBC function call). If the timeout value that you set goes by and the statement is unfinished, this return happens.

`HYT01 CLI-specific condition-connection timeout expired` (ODBC 3)

This is similar to `HYT00`, but it applies to the connection rather than to the statement.

`HZzzz Remote Database Access`

The Remote Database Access standard, ISO/IEC 9579-2, defines several subclass code values which may be passed on via SQL, but are not defined within SQL. These will all be in the class `HZ`.

`IM001 driver does not support this function` (ODBC 2+3)

There are a lot of ODBC functions. Some drivers don't support them all, especially because ODBC 3.x is still new (and Microsoft keeps changing it). So this error comes from the driver. Compare `SQLSTATE HYC00`.

`IM002 Data source name not found and no default driver specified` (ODBC 2+3)

This happens when you're connecting with ODBC and there's no DSN registered.

`IM003 specified driver could not be loaded` (ODBC 2+3)
Possibly the driver's DLL is missing or is not in the directory that the driver manager is searching.

`IM004 driver's SQLAllocHandle on SQL_HANDLE_ENV failed` (ODBC 2+3)
Usually this would indicate low memory or that the maximum number of handles is exceeded or a problem with function sequence.

`IM005 driver's SQLAllocHandle on SQL_HANDLE_DBC failed` (ODBC 2+3)
Usually this would indicate low memory or that the maximum number of handles is exceeded or a problem with function sequence.

`IM006 driver's SQLSetConnectAttr failed` (ODBC 2+3)
A connection error (during `SQLBrowseConnect` or `SQLConnect` or `SQLDriverConnect`).

`IM007 no data source or driver specified; dialog prohibited` (ODBC 2+3)
An error return from the ODBC function call `SQLDriverConnect`.

`IM008 dialog failed` (ODBC 2+3)
The `SQLDriverConnect` function puts up a dialog box; presumably the user did not end with "OK".

`IM009 unable to load translation DLL` (ODBC 2+3)
A failure during connect or during `SQLSetConnectAttr` probably due to a missing DLL, which may indicate an installation error.

`IM010 data source name too long` (ODBC 3)
The ODBC connection functions (`SQLBrowseConnect` or `SQLConnect` or `SQLDriverConnect`) have a maximum size for the name of the data source (DSN). You've exceeded it.

`IM011 driver name too long` (ODBC 3)
The `SQLBrowseConnect` and `SQLDriverConnect` functions have a maximum size for the name of the driver. You've exceeded it.

`IM012 driver keyword syntax error` (ODBC 3)
The `SQLBrowseConnect` or `SQLDriverConnect` functions require data in a fixed format.

`IM013 trace file error` (ODBC 3)
Couldn't perform an operation on the trace file, perhaps a failure to write because of a disk-full situation.

`IM014 invalid name of file DSN` (ODBC 3)
The `SQLDriverConnect` function requires a valid identifier.

`IM015 corrupt file data source` (ODBC 3)
The `SQLDriverConnect` function can't read the file.

And that's it for CLI diagnostics. In the next chapter, we'll take a look at some general functions.

48

Chapter 48

SQL/CLI: General Functions

In this chapter, we discuss `SQLDataSources`, `SQLGetFunctions`, and `SQLGetInfo`. We call these the "general" functions because they are used primarily in applications which are not tied to a specific DBMS or a specific database. Generalized applications need to find out what is available, as part of a long initialization process. Here are the descriptions of the three general functions.

SQLDataSources

Function Prototype:

```
SQLRETURN SQLDataSources(
  SQLHENV henv,                  /* 32-bit input */
  SQLSMALLINT Direction,         /* 16-bit input, =
                                    SQL_FETCH_FIRST or SQL_FETCH_NEXT */
  SQLCHAR *ServerName,           /* pointer to char* output */
  SQLSMALLINT BufferLength1,     /* 16-bit input */
  SQLSMALLINT *NameLength1,      /* pointer to 16-bit output */
  SQLCHAR *Description,          /* pointer to char* output */
  SQLSMALLINT BufferLength2,     /* 16-bit input */
  SQLSMALLINT *NameLength2       /* pointer to 16-bit output */
  );
```

Job: Return names of data sources — that is, servers or databases.

Algorithm:

```
If (henv is not really an env handle or env is skeleton)
  return error: CLI-specific condition-invalid handle
Empty the diagnostics area associated with henv.
If (Direction is not SQL_FIRST (2)or SQL_NEXT (1))
  return error: HY103 CLI-specific condition-invalid retrieval code
If (Direction == SQL_FIRST (2))
  /* Cursor position is for first row of "Data Sources" Table */
If (Direction is SQL_NEXT (1))
  /* Cursor position is for next row of "Data Sources" Table
     (it's 1st row if we've never called SQLDataSources before)
     (it's 1st row if last call to SQLDataSources returned "no data")
   */
If (Cursor position is now past end)
  return with warning: 02000 no data -
"Fetch" into ServerName and Description parameters
/* The usual Character Set Retrieval rules apply. */
```

Notes:

- The SQL Standard is firm about the meaning of the term "data source" — the `SQLDataSources` function is supposed to return names of SQL-servers. For some single-tier desktop DBMSs (which are not based on a client-server architecture), it is more reasonable to expect that the names returned here will be names of databases. In any case, the name is something you can use in an `SQLConnect` call.

- You would use this function for browsing ("What servers can I connect to?") or for checking availability ("Is server X up yet?"). In many commercial installations, the application is tightly linked to a particular server, so calling SQLDataSources has no point — either you can call SQLConnect and succeed or you cannot. There is a big implementation-defined question here, namely, how does anybody know what servers are out there? That depends on how the system is configured, but — sometimes — there is a query to see what names are established on the network or a directory search for Catalog files.
- In theory, the maximum length of ServerName should be the implementation-defined maximum length of a VARCHAR string. In practice, the maximum length of ServerName is 128 characters.
- This is one of the very few functions for which the input handle is a henv. You can call SQLDataSources before allocating a dbc or connecting. There might be several data sources associated with an env.
- Imagine that there is a Table "Data Sources" containing two CHAR Columns: "servername" (or "databasename") and "description". The SQLDataSources function will FETCH a single row from this Table. SQLDataSources would have been implemented as a Catalog function — that is, it would have returned a result set — if it were not for the inconvenient fact that we want to retrieve data sources information before we connect.

Example: This example displays a list of available servers; assume that the "Data Sources" Table looks like this:

"Data Sources"

"servername"	"description"
Wally	A server on the organization's main computer
Sammy	A local server used for test purposes

```
#include "sqlcli.h"
 SQLHENV henv;
 SQLCHAR name[128+1], description[1024];
 SQLSMALLINT name_length, description_length;
 SQLRETURN sqlreturn;
 ...
 SQLAllocHandle(SQL_HANDLE_ENV,00,&henv);
```

```
for (;;) {
  sqlreturn = SQLDataSources(
    henv,                          /* henv parameter */
    SQL_FETCH_NEXT,                /* Direction */
    name,                          /* *ServerName */
    sizeof(name),                  /* BufferLength1 */
    &name_length,                  /* *NameLength1 */
    description,                   /* *Description */
    sizeof(description),           /* BufferLength2 */
    &description_length            /* NameLength2 */
    );
  if (sqlreturn == SQL_NO_DATA) break;
 printf("ServerName = %s. Description = %s.\n",name,description); }
SQLFreeHandle(SQL_HANDLE_ENV,henv);
```

ODBC: This function has been available since ODBC 1.0. The Driver Manager handles the call, by checking the registry of data sources which have been installed using the ODBC installation program. In fact, SQLDataSources is very much an ODBC sort of call because it is difficult to see how one could find a server list without using some sort of non-standard "Driver Manager."

TIP: With Windows 3.x, the ODBC driver information is stored in an .INI file which you can query directly with GetPrivateProfileString. With Windows95, the ODBC driver information is stored in the registry.

SQLGetFunctions

Function Prototype:

```
SQLRETURN  SQLGetFunctions(
  SQLHDBC hdbc,                  /* 32-bit input */
  SQLSMALLINT FunctionId,        /* 32-bit input */
  SQLSMALLINT *Supported         /* pointer to 16-bit output */
  );
```

Job: Find out whether a specified CLI function is supported. The legal list of FunctionID values, as defined (with #define) in sqlcli.h, follows — function codes are in alphabetical order; the version of standard SQL, or ODBC, which requires support of the function is noted after the function's numeric code:

FunctionID **Values**

#define SQL_API_SQLALLOCCONNECT	1	SQL-92
#define SQL_API_SQLALLOCENV	2	SQL-92

FunctionID Values

#define SQL_API_SQLALLOCHANDLE	1001	SQL-92
#define SQL_API_SQLALLOCHANDLESTD	74	X/Open
#define SQL_API_SQLALLOCSTMT	3	SQL-92
#define SQL_API_SQLBINDCOL	4	SQL-92
#define SQL_API_SQLBINDPARAM	1002	ODBC 3
#define SQL_API_SQLBINDPARAMETER	72	SQL-92
#define SQL_API_SQLBROWSECONNECT	55	ODBC 3
#define SQL_API_SQLBULKOPERATIONS	24	ODBC 3
#define SQL_API_SQLCANCEL	5	SQL-92
#define SQL_API_SQLCLOSECURSOR	1003	SQL-92
#define SQL_API_SQLCOLATTRIBUTE	6	SQL-92
#define SQL_API_SQLCOLATTRIBUTES	6	ODBC 2
#define SQL_API_SQLCOLUMNPRIVILEGES	56	SQL-92
#define SQL_API_SQLCOLUMNS	40	SQL3
#define SQL_API_SQLCONNECT	7	SQL-92
#define SQL_API_SQLCOPYDESC	1004	SQL-92
#define SQL_API_SQLDATASOURCES	57	SQL-92
#define SQL_API_SQLDESCRIBECOL	8	SQL-92
#define SQL_API_SQLDESCRIBEPARAM	58	ODBC 3
#define SQL_API_SQLDISCONNECT	9	SQL-92
#define SQL_API_SQLDRIVERCONNECT	41	ODBC 3
#define SQL_API_SQLDRIVERS	71	ODBC 3
#define SQL_API_SQLENDTRAN	1005	SQL-92
#define SQL_API_SQLERROR	10	SQL-92
#define SQL_API_SQLEXECDIRECT	11	SQL-92
#define SQL_API_SQLEXECUTE	12	SQL-92
#define SQL_API_SQLEXTENDEDFETCH	59	ODBC 3
#define SQL_API_SQLFETCH	13	SQL-92
#define SQL_API_SQLFETCHSCROLL	1021	SQL-92
#define SQL_API_SQLFOREIGNKEYS	60	SQL-92
#define SQL_API_SQLFREECONNECT	14	SQL-92
#define SQL_API_SQLFREEENV	15	SQL-92
#define SQL_API_SQLFREEHANDLE	1006	SQL-92
#define SQL_API_SQLFREELOCATOR	1031	SQL3
#define SQL_API_SQLFREESTMT	16	SQL-92
#define SQL_API_SQLGETCONNECTATTR	1007	SQL-92
#define SQL_API_SQLGETCONNECTOPTION	42	ODBC 2
#define SQL_API_SQLGETCURSORNAME	17	SQL-92

FunctionID Values

#define SQL_API_SQLGETDATA	43	SQL-92
#define SQL_API_SQLGETDESCFIELD	1008	SQL-92
#define SQL_API_SQLGETDESCREC	1009	SQL-92
#define SQL_API_SQLGETDIAGFIELD	1010	SQL-92
#define SQL_API_SQLGETDIAGREC	1011	SQL-92
#define SQL_API_SQLGETENVATTR	1012	SQL-92
#define SQL_API_SQLGETFUNCTIONS	44	SQL-92
#define SQL_API_SQLGETINFO	45	SQL-92
#define SQL_API_SQLGETLENGTH	1022	SQL-92
#define SQL_API_SQLGETPARAMDATA	1025	SQL-92
#define SQL_API_SQLGETPOSITION	1023	SQL-92
#define SQL_API_SQLGETSTMTATTR	1014	SQL-92
#define SQL_API_SQLGETSTMTOPTIONS	46	ODBC 2
#define SQL_API_SQLGETSUBSTRING	1024	SQL3
#define SQL_API_SQLGETTYPEINFO	47	SQL-92
#define SQL_API_SQLMORERESULTS	61	SQL-92
#define SQL_API_SQLNATIVESQL	62	ODBC 3
#define SQL_API_SQLNUMPARAMS	63	ODBC 3
#define SQL_API_SQLNUMRESULTCOLS	18	SQL-92
#define SQL_API_SQLPARAMDATA	48	SQL-92
#define SQL_API_SQLPARAMETERS	2002	SQL-92
#define SQL_API_SQLPARAMOPTIONS	64	ODBC 3
#define SQL_API_SQLPREPARE	19	SQL-92
#define SQL_API_SQLPRIMARYKEYS	65	SQL-92
#define SQL_API_SQLPROCEDURECOLUMNS	66	ODBC 3
#define SQL_API_SQLPROCEDURES	67	ODBC 3
#define SQL_API_SQLPUTDATA	49	SQL-92
#define SQL_API_SQLROUTINEPRIVILEGES	1026	SQL3
#define SQL_API_SQLROUTINES	2003	SQL3
#define SQL_API_SQLROWCOUNT	20	SQL-92
#define SQL_API_SQLSETCONNECTATTR	1016	SQL-92
#define SQL_API_SQLSETCONNECTOPTION	50	ODBC 2
#define SQL_API_SQLSETCURSORNAME	21	SQL-92
#define SQL_API_SQLSETDESCFIELD	1017	SQL-92
#define SQL_API_SQLSETDESCREC	1018	SQL-92
#define SQL_API_SQLSETENVATTR	1019	SQL-92
#define SQL_API_SQLSETPARAM	2	ODBC 2
#define SQL_API_SQLSETPOS	68	ODBC 2

FunctionID Values

#define SQL_API_SQLSETSCROLLOPTIONS	69	ODBC 2
#define SQL_API_SQLSETSTMTATTR	1020	SQL-92
#define SQL_API_SQLSETSTMTOPTION	51	ODBC 2
#define SQL_API_SQLSPECIALCOLUMNS	52	SQL3
#define SQL_API_SQLSTATISTICS	53	X/Open
#define SQL_API_SQLTABLEPRIVILEGES	70	SQL-92
#define SQL_API_SQLTABLES	54	SQL3
#define SQL_API_SQLTRANSACT	23	ODBC 2

Algorithm:

```
If (hdbc is not really a handle of a dbc)
  return error: CLI-specific condition-invalid handle
Empty the dbc's diagnostics area.
If (no connection opened on hdbc)
  return error: 08003 connection exception-connection does not exist
If (the function identified by FunctionId is supported)
  Set *Supported = 1 (true);
Else
  Set *Supported = 0 (false).
```

Notes:

- SQL_API_SQLCOLATTRIBUTE and SQL_API_SQLCOLATTRIBUTES have the same value: 6. This error is no longer important because SQLColAttributes was only an ODBC 2.0 function.
- Calling SQLGetFunctions(...,SQL_API_SQLGETFUNCTION,...) looks a little like asking a person, "Are you awake?", i.e., the answer is either "yes" or you get no answer at all. But in some contexts, it's a perfectly reasonable question. For instance, all versions of ODBC include a Driver Manager — a DLL layer separate from the DBMS itself (the "driver" and the "data source"). In an ODBC context, you're really asking the Driver Manager a question about the driver and that's a question you can expect either a "yes" or a "no" answer for.
- It's clear from the FunctionID value chart that some CLI functions are old, some are new, some are implementation-specific, some are standard. That's why it makes sense to call SQLGetFunctions right after connecting and branch to an appropriate path depending on which functions are supported. The SQLGetInfo function is useful for the same sort of purpose.
- If you are using MS-Windows and you are calling the DBMS directly, the question you really want to ask is, "Is the function name exported?"

Example: Although Microsoft's documentation marks the ODBC function `SQLStatistics()` as "ISO 92," it's not an ISO Standard function. So before using it, we will ask whether our DBMS supports it. Here's how.

```
#include "sqlcli.h"
/* In case SQL_API_STATISTICS isn't in sqlcli.h, we define it here. */
#define SQL_API_SQLSTATISTICS 53
SQLHENV henv;
SQLHDBC hdbc;
SQLSMALLINT supported;
void main ()
{
  SQLAllocHandle(SQL_HANDLE_ENV,...);
  SQLAllocConnect(SQL_HANDLE_DBC,...);
  SQLConnect(hdbc,...);
  if (SQLGetFunctions(hdbc,SQL_API_SQLSTATISTICS,&supported)<0) {
    printf("SQLGetFunctions failed.\n"); }
  else {
    if (!supported) {
      printf("SQLStatistics is not supported.\n"); }
    else {
      printf("SQLStatistics is supported.\n");
  SQLDisconnect(...);
  SQLFreeHandle(SQL_HANDLE_DBC,...);
  SQLFreeHandle(SQL_HANDLE_ENV,...);
```

ODBC: The `SQLGetFunctions` function has been around since ODBC version 1.0. The third parameter, `*Supported`, can be a pointer to an array.

SQLGetInfo

Function Prototype:

```
SQLRETURN  SQLGetInfo(
  SQLHDBC hdbc,                  /* 32-bit input */
  SQLSMALLINT InfoType,          /* 16-bit input */
  SQLPOINTER InfoValue,          /* pointer to ANY* output */
  SQLSMALLINT BufferLength,      /* 16-bit input */
  SQLSMALLINT *StringLength      /* pointer to 16-bit output */
  );
```

Job: Ask whether a DBMS supports a specified feature and if it does, which of several possible syntax variations the DBMS uses.

The SQLGetInfo function's InfoType parameter has 47 possible values which we'll describe in the following paragraphs. Each paragraph begins with a value (the InfoType value), a name (the #define of this value in sqlcli.h), and the <data type> of the value that SQLGetInfo returns, followed by a few remarks.

- 24 SQL_ACCESSIBLE_ROUTINES — CHAR(1) The result is 'Y' if routines metadata — such as the rows in INFORMATION_SCHEMA.ROUTINES — is accessible only to users who hold EXECUTE Privileges on routines; otherwise the result is 'N'. In ODBC, this code does not exist; 24 is the code for SQL_CURSOR_ROLLBACK_BEHAVIOR.
- 19 SQL_ACCESSIBLE_TABLES — CHAR(1) The result is 'Y' if Tables metadata — such as the rows in INFORMATION_SCHEMA.TABLES — is accessible only to users who hold SELECT Privileges on Tables; otherwise the result is 'N'. A standard DBMS should return 'N' because access to INFORMATION_SCHEMA Views is possible if you hold any Privilege, not just the SELECT Privilege. This code determines the operation of the CLI Catalog functions: SQLColumnPrivileges, SQLColumns, SQLForeignKeys, SQLPrimaryKeys, SQLResultSetStructure, SQLSpecialColumns, SQLTablePrivileges, SQLTables. In ODBC, this code exists but the meaning is different.
- 86 SQL_ALTER_TABLE — INTEGER The return is a bit map; one bit on for each ALTER TABLE clause the DBMS supports:
    - If ALTER TABLE ... ADD COLUMN:

  0001 hex (SQL_AT_ADD_COLUMN)
    - If ALTER TABLE ... DROP COLUMN:

  0002 hex (SQL_AT_DROP_COLUMN)
    - If ALTER TABLE ... ALTER COLUMN:

  0004 hex (SQL_AT_ALTER_COLUMN)
    - If ALTER TABLE ... ADD CONSTRAINT:

  0008 hex (SQL_AT_ADD_CONSTRAINT)
    - If ALTER TABLE ... DROP CONSTRAINT:

  0010 hex (SQL_AT_DROP_CONSTRAINT)

  Any SQL-92 DBMS must return 001b hex (all bits except ALTER COLUMN on). Any SQL3 DBMS must return 001f hex (all bits on). In ODBC, this code exists but the meaning is different.
- 10003 SQL_CATALOG_NAME — CHAR(1) The return is 'Y' if the DBMS supports <Catalog name>s (as qualifiers, presumably); 'N' if not. Any SQL-92 DBMS must return 'Y'.
- 10004 SQL_COLLATING_SEQUENCE — CHAR(254) The return is the <identifier> of "the default Collation of [the server]" — which is ambiguous. Probably it's the <identifier> of the default Collation of the dbc's default Character set — which is useless. If you want the Schema's Character set, SELECT from INFORMATION_SCHEMA.SCHEMATA. If you want the Collation of a Base table's Column, SELECT from INFORMATION_SCHEMA.COLUMNS. If you want the Collation of a result set Column, call the SQLGetDescField function. In ODBC, the designation for this code is SQL_COLLATION_SEQ and "ISO 8859-1" or "EBCDIC" are possible returns.
- 23 SQL_CURSOR_COMMIT_BEHAVIOR — SMALLINT The return is a bit map, with one bit on, determined by what actions the DBMS takes when COMMIT happens:

- [close Cursor, delete prepared statements] DELETE:

0000 hex (SQL_CB_DELETE)

- [close Cursor, keep prepared statements] CLOSE:

0001 hex (SQL_CB_CLOSE)

- [keep Cursor open, keep prepared statements] PRESERVE:

0002 hex (SQL_CB_PRESERVE)

A standard SQL DBMS should return 0000 hex (SQL_CB_DELETE).

- 10001 SQL_CURSOR_SENSITIVITY — INTEGER The return is a bit map, with zero or more bits on, determined by the DBMS's behaviour when rows are updated outside the Cursor:
  - [don't see rows updated during same transaction]:

  0001 hex (SQL_INSENSITIVE)

  - [see rows updated during same transaction]:

  0002 hex (SQL_SENSITIVE)

  - [can't tell whether we see them or not]:

  0000 hex (SQL_UNSPECIFIED) or 0000 hex (SQL_ASENSITIVE)
- 2 SQL_DATA_SOURCE_NAME — CHAR(128) The return is the name of a data source (in client/server terms; a server name). This is the name that was passed in the SQLConnect call.
- 25 SQL_DATA_SOURCE_READ_ONLY — CHAR(1) The return is 'Y' if the data source (in client/server terms; the server) cannot allow data to be "modified" — an undefined word. Presumably, the meaning is: every transaction begins with the implicit statement SET TRANSACTION READ ONLY.
- 17 SQL_DBMS_NAME — CHAR(254) The return is the name of the DBMS. It's implementation-defined, but one can assume that there will be a vendor name here. The sqlcli.h file does not contain SQL_DBMS_NAME.
- 18 SQL_DBMS_VERSION — CHAR(254) The return is the version number of the DBMS, in a rigid format: nn.nn.nnnn[optional description], where n is any decimal digit. Examples: "00.00.0000", "01.02.03 Vendor X's Version #1 Release #2 Patch #3". In ODBC, the name is SQL_DBMS_VER.
- 26 SQL_DEFAULT_TRANSACTION_ISOLATION — INTEGER The return is a bitmask, with one bit on for the default transaction isolation level — that is, what the transaction isolation level is if you can't execute SET TRANSACTION ISOLATION LEVEL {READ COMMITTED | READ UNCOMMITTED | REPEATABLE READ | SERIALIZABLE}. The possible values are:

  0001 hex (SQL_TXN_READ_UNCOMMITTED)
  0002 hex (SQL_TXN_READ_COMMITTED)
  0004 hex (SQL_TXN_REPEATABLE_READ)
  0008 hex (SQL_TXN_SERIALIZABLE)

  A standard DBMS should return SQL_TXN_SERIALIZABLE.
- 10002 SQL_DESCRIBE_PARAMETER — CHAR(1) The return is 'Y' if the DBMS is capable of "describing dynamic parameters" — which is ambiguous. Apparently, the return has nothing to do with the DBMS's ability to support "auto-populate of IPD" or the non-standard SQLDescribeParameter function. Apparently, all DBMSs which support the embedded SQL DESCRIBE INPUT statement should return 'Y'; otherwise they should return 'N'.

- 8 SQL_FETCH_DIRECTION — INTEGER The return is a bitmask, with zero or more bits on, depending on the options one can use with the SQLFetchScroll function. The possible values are:

  0001 hex (SQL_FD_FETCH_NEXT)
  0002 hex (SQL_FD_FETCH_FIRST)
  0004 hex (SQL_FD_FETCH_LAST)
  0008 hex (SQL_FD_FETCH_PRIOR)
  0010 hex (SQL_FD_FETCH_ABSOLUTE)
  0020 hex (SQL_FD_FETCH_RELATIVE)

  A standard DBMS should return 003f hex — that is, all bits on.

- 81 SQL_GETDATA_EXTENSIONS — INTEGER The return is a bitmask, with zero or more bits on, depending on the DBMS's ability to handle out-of-order SQLGetData calls. Minimally, a DBMS allows SQLGetData only for Columns that were not bound with SQLBindCol and only in sequence (that is, after getting information for Column n, you can only get information for Column n+1). The possible options are:

  - [if you can call SQLGetData for bound Columns]:

  0001 hex (SQL_GD_ANY_COLUMN)

  - [if you can call SQLGetData in any order]:

  0002 hex (SQL_GD_ANY_ORDER)

- 20000 SQL_GETPARAMDATA_EXTENSIONS — INTEGER The return is a bitmask, with zero or more bits on, depending on the DBMS's ability to handle out-of-order SQLGetParamData calls. Minimally, a DBMS allows SQLGetParamData only for Columns that were not bound and only in sequence (that is, after getting information for parameter n, you can only get information for parameter n+1). The possible options are:

  - [if you can call SQLGetParamData for bound Columns]:

  0001 hex (SQL_GPD_ANY_COLUMN)

  - [if you can call SQLGetParamData in any order]:

  0002 hex (SQL_GPD_ANY_ORDER)

  Compare this with SQL_GETDATA_EXTENSIONS.

- 28 SQL_IDENTIFIER_CASE — SMALLINT Returns a number between 1 and 4, depending how the DBMS stores <regular identifier>s. The possible options are:

  - [change to uppercase]:

  1 (SQL_IC_UPPER)

  - [change to lowercase]:

  2 (SQL_IC_LOWER)

  - [don't change case]:

  3 (SQL_IC_SENSITIVE)

  - [don't change case, but do case-insensitive searches]:

  4 (SQL_IC_MIXED)

  A standard DBMS should always return SQL_IC_UPPER because only <delimited identifier>s are stored in mixed case.

- 73 SQL_INTEGRITY — CHAR(1) The return is 'Y' if the DBMS supports basic integrity Constraints: NOT NULL, UNIQUE, PRIMARY KEY, FOREIGN KEY ... NO ACTION, CHECK, and Column defaults. Otherwise the return is 'N'. A standard DBMS should return 'Y'. In ODBC, code 73 is SQL_OPT_IEF and the return is 'Y' if the DBMS supports the optional integrity enhancement facility of SQL-89.
- 34 SQL_MAXIMUM_CATALOG_NAME_LENGTH — SMALLINT The return is the length, in characters, of the largest possible <Catalog name>, without qualifiers or introducers. Expect 18 for an SQL-89 DBMS, 128 for a later DBMS.
- 30 SQL_MAXIMUM_COLUMN_NAME_LENGTH — SMALLINT The return is the length, in characters, of the largest possible <Column name>, without qualifiers or introducers. Expect 18 for an SQL-89 DBMS, 128 for a later DBMS.
- 97 SQL_MAXIMUM_COLUMNS_IN_GROUP_BY — SMALLINT The return is the largest number of Columns that a GROUP BY clause can hold (zero if that's unknown or unlimited). Expect 6 for a DBMS that meets the FIPS 127-2 entry-level spec and 15 for a DBMS that meets the FIPS 127-2 intermediate-level spec.
- 99 SQL_MAXIMUM_COLUMNS_IN_ORDER_BY — SMALLINT The return is the largest number of Columns that an ORDER BY clause can hold (zero if that's unknown or unlimited). Expect 6 for a DBMS that meets the FIPS 127-2 entry-level spec and 15 for a DBMS that meets the FIPS 127-2 intermediate-level spec.
- 100 SQL_MAXIMUM_COLUMNS_IN_SELECT — SMALLINT The return is the largest number of Columns that a select list can hold (zero if that's unknown or unlimited). Expect 100 for a DBMS that meets the FIPS 127-2 entry-level spec and 250 for a DBMS that meets the FIPS 127-2 intermediate-level spec.
- 101 SQL_MAXIMUM_COLUMNS_IN_TABLE — SMALLINT The return is the largest number of Columns that a Base table can hold (zero if that's unknown or unlimited). Expect 100 for a DBMS that meets the FIPS 127-2 entry-level spec and 250 for a DBMS that meets the FIPS 127-2 intermediate-level spec.
- 1 SQL_MAXIMUM_CONCURRENT_ACTIVITIES — SMALLINT The return is the largest number of stmts that can be active at the same time. With some implementations, it might be possible to allocate two stmts, i.e., call SQLAllocHandle(SQL_HANDLE_STMT,...) twice, but impossible to "select" with both hstmt#1 and hstmt#2. The return is zero if maximum concurrent activities is unknown. (A stmt is "active" if it is associated with an open Cursor or a deferred parameter.)
- 31 SQL_MAXIMUM_CURSOR_NAME_LENGTH — SMALLINT The return is the length, in characters, of the largest possible <Cursor name>, without qualifiers or introducers. Expect 18 for an SQL-89 DBMS and 128 for a later DBMS.
- 0 SQL_MAXIMUM_DRIVER_CONNECTIONS — SMALLINT The return is the maximum number of connections between one driver and one server, or the maximum number of connections period, or zero if the maximum is not fixed.
- 10005 SQL_MAXIMUM_IDENTIFIER_LENGTH — SMALLINT The return is the length, in characters, of the largest possible <identifier> for any kind of Object. This value won't be greater than any of the SQL_MAXIMUM_..._NAME_LENGTH values. Expect 18 for an SQL-89 DBMS and 128 for a later DBMS.

- 32 SQL_MAXIMUM_SCHEMA_NAME_LENGTH — SMALLINT The return is the length, in characters, of the largest possible <Schema name>, without qualifiers or introducers. Expect 18 for an SQL-89 DBMS and 128 for a later DBMS.
- 20001 SQL_MAXIMUM_STMT_OCTETS_DATA — SMALLINT The return is the maximum number of octets that can exist in an SQL-data statement (such as INSERT) or zero if there's no fixed limit.
- 20002 SQL_MAXIMUM_STMT_OCTETS_SCHEMA — SMALLINT The return is the maximum number of octets that can exist in an SQL-Schema statement (such as CREATE SCHEMA) or zero if there's no fixed limit.
- 35 SQL_MAXIMUM_TABLE_NAME_LENGTH — SMALLINT The return is the length, in characters, of the largest possible <Table name>, without qualifiers or introducers. Expect 18 for an SQL-89 DBMS and 128 for a later DBMS. But don't be surprised if it's smaller; many implementations treat <Table name> as "file name" and are therefore subject to whatever constraints the operating system imposes.
- 106 SQL_MAXIMUM_TABLES_IN_SELECT — SMALLINT The return is the maximum number of <Table name>s which may appear in a query's FROM clause, i.e., after SELECT ... FROM. This will be less than or equal to the maximum number of joins and will be less than or equal to the maximum number of <Table reference>s in an SQL statement as a whole, after Views are expanded. A FIPS entry-level DBMS would return 15 for the maximum number of <Table reference>s in an SQL statement and a FIPS intermediate-level DBMS would return 50.
- 107 SQL_MAXIMUM_USER_NAME_LENGTH — SMALLINT The return is the length, in characters, of the largest possible <AuthorizationID>, without introducers or qualifiers. The value is the same as the contents of SESSION_USER. Expect 18 from an SQL-89 or FIPS 127-2 entry level DBMS, expect 128 from a more powerful DBMS — unless the DBMS gets <AuthorizationID>s from an outside source, such as the operating system's login name. In that case, the limit ultimately depends on what the operating system says.
- 85 SQL_NULL_COLLATION — SMALLINT Returns a number between 1 and 2, depending on the placement of NULL values in sort sequences (ORDER BY). The possible options are:
  - [treat NULLs as "greater than" all other values]:

  1 (SQL_NC_HIGH)
  - [treat NULLs as "less than" all other values]:

  2 (SQL_NC_LOW)
- 90 SQL_ORDER_BY_COLUMNS_IN_SELECT — CHAR(1) Returns 'Y' if the DBMS allows only those ORDER BY Columns which also appear in the select list; otherwise 'N'. For example: SELECT column_1 FROM Table_1 ORDER BY column_2; is illegal in SQL-92 (so an SQL-92 DBMS would return 'Y'), but is legal in SQL3.
- 115 SQL_OUTER_JOIN_CAPABILITIES — INTEGER (Not CHAR(1), there was an error in early versions of the SQL Standard.) The return is a bitmask, with zero or more bits on, depending on the outer join variations that the DBMS supports. The possible options are:
  - [simple LEFT OUTER JOIN]:

  0001 hex (SQL_OUTER_JOIN_LEFT)

- [simple RIGHT OUTER JOIN]:

0002 hex (SQL_OUTER_JOIN_RIGHT)

- [FULL OUTER JOIN works]:

0004 hex (SQL_OUTER_JOIN_FULL)

- [outer joins may be nested]:

0008 hex (SQL_OUTER_JOIN_NESTED)

- [ON-clause Columns needn't be in Table order]:

0010 hex (SQL_OUTER_JOIN_NOT_ORDERED)

- [inner Table can be INNER JOIN]:

0020 hex (SQL_OUTER_JOIN_INNER)

- [ON predicate needn't be "=" comparison]:

0040 hex (SQL_OUTER_JOIN_ALL_COMPARISON_OPS)

- 20003 SQL_REF_LENGTH — SMALLINT The return is the length, in octets, of a <reference type>.
- 43 SQL_SCROLL_CONCURRENCY — INTEGER The return is a bitmask, with zero or more bits on, depending on the DBMS's ability to handle concurrency (multi-user) problems while dealing with scroll Cursors. The possible options are:
  - [read-only scrollable Cursors are okay]:

0001 hex (SQL_SCCO_READ_ONLY)

  - [updatable scrollable Cursors are okay in conjunction with lowest locking level]:

0002 hex (SQL_SCCO_LOCK)

  - [updatable scrollable Cursors are okay in conjunction with optimistic concurrency — row identifiers or timestamps]:

0004 hex (SQL_SCCO_OPT_ROWVER)

  - [updatable scrollable Cursors are okay in conjunction with optimistic concurrency — comparing values]:

0008 hex (SQL_SCCO_OPT_VALUES)

- 14 SQL_SEARCH_PATTERN_ESCAPE — CHAR(1) The return is the fixed escape character which can be used for pattern matching in some of the CLI Catalog functions (e.g., SQLTables). Conceptually, if the search-pattern-escape is '~', then the metadata search conducted for such functions implicitly contains a clause "... LIKE ... ESCAPE '~' ...." In ODBC, the DBMS may return ' ' if search-pattern escape is not supported for Catalog functions.
- 13 SQL_SERVER_NAME — CHAR(128) The return is a character string; the implementation-defined character string which is the "actual name" of a server. This often will be the same as the string returned for SQL_DATA_SOURCE_NAME, but some implementations make a distinction between "data source" and "server."
- 94 SQL_SPECIAL_CHARACTERS — CHAR(254) The return is a character string containing all characters "other than uppercase letters, lowercase letters, digits, and underscore" which can appear in <regular identifier>s.

  - Note 1: this definition has nothing to do with the SQL Standard's definition for special characters.
  - Note 2: this definition is not the same as the definition ODBC uses.
  - Note 3: an SQL standard DBMS will return a blank string here. If you want to use strange non-alphabetic characters in names, use <delimited identifier>s.
- 46 SQL_TRANSACTION_CAPABLE — SMALLINT The return is a number indicating what sort of SQL statements the DBMS allows within a transaction. The possible options are:
  - [transactions are not supported at all]:

  0 (SQL_TC_NONE)
  - [DML only, DDL causes error]:

  1 (SQL_TC_DML)
  - [DML okay, DDL okay]:

  2 (SQL_TC_ALL)
  - [DML okay, DDL causes COMMIT]:

  3 (SQL_TC_COMMIT)
  - [DML okay, DDL is ignored]:

  4 (SQL_TC_IGNORE)

  DML stands for "data manipulation language" (SELECT, INSERT, etc.); DDL stands for "data definition language" (ALTER, DROP, GRANT, CREATE, REVOKE). This addresses one of the implementation-defined questions in standard SQL, "Is a DDL statement just like any other or does it have to be in a transaction of its own?" Because many DBMSs will automatically COMMIT before and after a DDL statement, you can expect the most common return to be SQL_TC_COMMIT. No standard SQL DBMS will return SQL_TC_NONE. In ODBC, the code name is SQL_TXN_CAPABLE.
- 72 SQL_TRANSACTION_ISOLATION_OPTION — INTEGER The return is a bitmask, with zero or more bits on, depending on the isolation levels the DBMS supports. The possible options are:
  - [supports READ UNCOMMITTED level]:

  0001 hex (SQL_TRANSACTION_READ_UNCOMMITTED)
  - [supports READ COMMITTED level]:

  0002 hex (SQL_TRANSACTION_READ_COMMITTED)
  - [supports REPEATABLE READ level]:

  0004 hex (SQL_TRANSACTION_REPEATABLE_READ)
  - [supports SERIALIZABLE level]:

  0008 hex (SQL_TRANSACTION_SERIALIZABLE)

  Standard SQL DBMSs will at least return SQL_TRANSACTION_SERIALIZABLE because SERIALIZABLE must be the default isolation level. Standard SQL DBMSs will allow all four options in SET TRANSACTION statements, but it's implementation-defined whether a DBMS can, in fact, go to a higher level. For instance, the DBMS may respond to a SET TRANSACTION ISOLATION LEVEL REPEATABLE READ; request by setting the isolation level to SERIALIZABLE, a higher level. In ODBC, the code name is SQL_TXN_ISOLATION_OPTION.

- 47 SQL_USER_NAME — CHAR(128) The return is a character string which is the same value as CURRENT_USER.

Algorithm:

```
If (hdbc is not a handle of a dbc)
  return error: CLI-specific condition-invalid handle
If (dbc is not connected)
  return error: 08003 connection exception-connection does not exist
Empty the dbc's diagnostics area.
If (InfoType not a valid code)
  return error: HY096 CLI-specific condition-invalid information type
```

Notes:

- You want to write a portable DBMS application? Then you have to keep asking yourself, "Does every DBMS support the feature(s) you're using, in the way you use them?" Hint: the answer is no. We've come a long way in the last few years and the support for "standard SQL" is a lot better than it once was. But there are always DBMSs behind the curve and always applications that push the envelope. The SQLGetInfo function is designed to provide information for the most common questions and unresolved issues.
- Many SQLGetInfo variants ask about non-standard features or non-standard behaviour. If you know that your DBMS is completely standard, then you shouldn't have to ask these questions.
- SQLGetInfo is currently undergoing revision. Until the dust settles, you should ignore the options that are new in SQL3. Get the information directly from one of the INFORMATION_SCHEMA Tables — SQL_FEATURES, SQL_IMPLEMENTATION_INFO, SQL_SIZING, or SQL_SIZING_PROFILES.

Example: In this code snippet we will use the four main types of SQLGetInfo returns: to a smallint, to a bitmask, to a CHAR(1) string, and to a long string. We assume that SQLConnect has happened already.

```
#include "sqlcli.h"
...
SQLSMALLINT max_columns;
char  y_or_n      ## [2]:
;
SQLSMALLINT fd;
CHAR  server_name ## [129]:
;
SQLINTEGER server_name_size;
...
SQLGetInfo(hdbc,SQL_ORDER_BY_COLUMNS_IN_SELECT,y_or_n,2,NULL);
```

```
if (y_or_n  ## [0]:
=='Y')
  /* order-by Columns must be in the select list */;
SQLGetInfo(hdbc,SQL_MAXIMUM_COLUMNS_IN_TABLE,&max_columns,00,NULL);
if (max_columns > 10)
  /* more than 10 Columns are allowed in a select list * */
SQLGetInfo(hdbc,SQL_FETCH_DIRECTION,&fdirection,00,NULL);
if ( fetchdirection & FD_FETCH_ABSOLUTE)
  /* SQLFetchScroll can be done with FETCH ABSOLUTE */;
SQLGetInfo(hdbc,SQL_SERVER_NAME,server_name,129,&server_name_size);
if (server_name_size>0) {
  /* server_name has the name of a server, null-terminated. */;
```

ODBC: The `SQLGetInfo` function has been around since ODBC 1.0.

Compare the ODBC prototype for `SQLGetInfo` with the standard SQL-92 prototype:

```
ODBC                                   Standard SQL
   SQLRETURN  SQLGetInfo(                  SQLRETURN SQLGetInfo(
     SQLHDBC hdbc,                           SQLHDBC hdbc,
     SQLSMALLINT InfoType,                   SQLSMALLINT InfoType,
     SQLPOINTER InfoValue,                   SQLPOINTER InfoValue,
     SQLSMALLINT BufferLength,               SQLINTEGER BufferLength,
     SQLSMALLINT *StringLength               SQLINTEGER *StringLength
     );                                      );
```

The types are incompatible! It's because of these incompatibilities that the last two parameter types were changed in SQL3.

And that's it for the CLI general functions. In the next chapter, we'll take a look at the deferred parameter functions.

49

Chapter 49

SQL/CLI: Deferred Parameter Functions

This short chapter describes an option for passing input parameters after execution begins.

[Obscure Rule] applies for the whole thing.

The concept behind deferred parameters is illustrated by these two flow charts:

```
Processing immediate parameters    Processing Deferred parameters
--------------------               --------------
- SQLBindParameter -               - SQLExecute -
--------------------               --------------
         |                               |
----------------                        / \
-SQLExecute   -                        /   \
----------------                      /need \ yes ----------------
                                     / data? \___ - SQLParamData -
                                     \       /    - +            -
                                      \     /     - SQLPutData   -
                                        |         ----------------
                                        | no
                                   --------------------------
                                   - SQLExecute (continued) -
                                   --------------------------
```

Briefly stated — in the immediate-parameter situation all necessary information is supplied before SQL statement execution begins; in the deferred-parameter situation the execution is interrupted and the host supplies the missing information by calling SQLParamData and SQLPutData.

Programmers can survive with immediate parameters alone. Indeed, in all the previous chapters, we have assumed that deferred parameters won't happen — had we allowed for them, we would have had to do some things differently.

The reasons for use of deferred parameters are:

- Long strings can be passed a piece at a time. This was an important thing in the days of 16-bit operating systems, when the maximum string size was effectively limited by the segment size.
- Microsoft uses deferred parameters in ODBC examples and test programs.

These are the days of 32-bit operating systems. Passing large buffers is no longer a problem. However, deferred parameters are still part of the standard SQL CLI. You might see them in legacy code or in some exotic applications (for example, packet transfers). You will not see deferred parameters in embedded SQL or PSM applications.

How to Pass Deferred Parameters

The mechanism for passing deferred parameters involves a package of signals and functions:

- Setting the last parameter = SQL_DATA_AT_EXEC (-2). Technically:

```
Set *(APD.IDA[n].SQL_DESC_OCTET_LENGTH_POINTER) = -2
```

For example:

```
#include "sqlcli.h"
SQLHSTMT hstmt;
SQLHDESC hdesc;
SQLINTEGER dp = SQL_DATA_AT_EXEC;
...
SQLGetStmtAttr(hstmt,SQL_ATTR_IMP_PARAM_DESC,&hdesc,00,NULL);
SQLSetDescField(hdesc,1,SQL_DESC_OCTET_LENGTH_POINTER,&dp,00);
```

- Looking for SQL_NEED_DATA after SQLExecute or SQLExecDirect — for example:

```
sqlreturn = SQLExecute(hstmt);
if (sqlreturn == SQL_NEED_DATA) /* deferred parameter seen ... */
```

- Looping — calling SQLParamData for each parameter and calling SQLPutData for each piece of data in each parameter.

The two CLI functions needed for deferred parameter support are SQLParamData and SQLPutData; their descriptions follow. We'll also describe SQLCancel in this chapter (see page 955) — it might be used to cancel functions which are waiting for deferred parameters (hence its inclusion here), but might have unrelated uses as well.

SQLParamData

Function Prototype:

```
SQLRETURN SQLParamData(
  SQLHSTMT hstmt,                 /* 32-bit input */
  SQLPOINTER Value               /* pointer to ANY* output */
  );
```

Job: Check whether a deferred parameter value is needed. If so, interrupt; if not, continue with previously-interrupted statement execution.

Algorithm:

```
If (no deferred parameter number is associated with stmt)
  return error: HY010 CLI-specific condition-function sequence error
/* A "deferred parameter" is an APD.IDA for which DEFERRED is true.
   DEFERRED is true if: *(APD.IDA[n].SQL_DESC_OCTET_POINTER) ==
   SQL_DATA_AT_EXEC, i.e. -2. */
If there is a deferred parameter, but no deferred parameter value:
  /* i.e.: if we have not already gotten the value in a prior call to
     SQLParamData */
  If (APD.IDA[n].SQL_DESC_DATA_POINTER is not a null pointer)
    return error: HY010 CLI-specific condition-function sequence error
  Set data-pointer value = Value (temporarily, for SQLPutData to see)
  return exception: HY(no subclass) CLI-specific condition-dynamic
  parameter value needed
/* Since there are no [more] deferred parameter values, execution can proceed
 . Restart the SQLExecute or SQLExecDirect process which was
   interrupted when deferred parameters were encountered. */
```

Notes:

- `SQLParamData` is needed if `SQLExecute` or `SQLExecDirect` returns `SQL_NEED_DATA (+99)`. In its turn, `SQLParamData` causes a further generation of `SQL_NEED_DATA` (if there are more parameters to process) or else it finishes off the execution that began with `SQLExecute` or `SQLExecDirect`.
- If `SQL_NEED_DATA` has been returned, the deferred parameter must be dealt with. You will get an error if you attempt to call any of these functions — `SQLCopyDesc`, `SQLFreeHandle`, `SQLEndTran`, `SQLDisconnect`, `SQLGetDescField`, `SQLGetDescRec`, `SQLSetDescField`, `SQLSetDescRec` — using the same `hstmt` or using a `hdesc` associated with the deferred parameter. A `stmt` with a deferred parameter is considered to be "active." An active `stmt` may be cancelled (with the `SQLCancel` function), but the only recommended action is to call `SQLParamData`.

- SQL_NEED_DATA is a positive value (+99). Therefore, if you use deferred parameters, you must not use the blithe code we've used in our examples so far:

```
if (sqlreturn < 0) /* error */
if (sqlreturn >= 0) /* all's well, must be warning or success */
```

As we said earlier, some of your operating assumptions must change if this option is used.

- Do not confuse SQLParamData with SQLGetParamData.

Example: See next section, on SQLPutData.

ODBC: SQLParamData has been around since ODBC 1.0.

SQLPutData

Function Prototype:

```
SQLRETURN SQLPutData (
  SQLHSTMT hstmt,             /* 32-bit input */
  SQLPOINTER Data,            /* pointer to ANY* input */
  SQLINTEGER StrLen_Or_Ind     /* pointer to indicator|octet-length */
  );
```

Algorithm:

```
If (there is no deferred parameter associated with stmt)
  return error: HY010 CLI-specific condition-function sequence error
If (there is no SQL_DESC_DATA_POINTER value)
  /* the data-pointer value should have been supplied by SQLBindParameter */
  return error: HY010 CLI-specific condition-function sequence error
  /* At this point, we have enough data (via the current APD fields plus the
Data and StrLen_Or_Ind parameters) to complete the input parameter description.
For details of what input-parameter description process looks like, see SQL-
BindParameter. */
```

Notes:

- SQLPutData is used only in association with SQLParamData.
- SQLPutData can be used repeatedly if (for a long character or binary string) the data must be supplied in pieces.
- Nullness trumps deferrability. If there's an indicator and it's -1 (SQL_NULL_DATA), then the parameter passed is NULL — there is no deferring.

Example: In the following example, we will pass CHAR(4) parameters in four separate pieces, one character at a time. This is absurdly small — usually pieces are at least 2 kilobytes

— but it illustrates the method nicely. Try to imagine that the data is input from some large file or pipeline. The algorithm works like this:

- Application initializes in the usual way.
- Application prepares an INSERT statement.
- Application calls SQLBindParameter for two SQL_DATA_AT_EXEC parameters. The application identifies the parameters as #1 and #2 — later, those values will be retrieved by SQLParamData. Thus the values identify which parameter is being processed.
- Application calls SQLExecute for the prepared INSERT statement. DBMS returns SQL_NEED_DATA because SQL_DATA_AT_EXEC parameters exist.
- Application calls SQLParamData. DBMS returns SQL_NEED_DATA because SQL_DATA_AT_EXEC parameters exist. DBMS also fills in the parameter number — #1 — from SQLBindParameter pass. Loop:
  - Application calls SQLPutData for the next piece.
  - Loop ends when the application has no more pieces.
- Application calls SQLParamData again. DBMS returns SQL_SUCCESS because there are no more parameters to process.
- Application cleans up in the usual way.

```
#include <stdio.h>
#include <string.h>
#include "sqlcli.h"
#define MAX_DATA_LENGTH 1
void main () {
SQLHENV     henv;
SQLHDBC     hdbc;
SQLHSTMT    hstmt;
SQLRETURN   rc;
SQLCHAR     OutData[1];
SQLCHAR     InData[]="abcd";
SQLSMALLINT Param1 = 1, Param2 = 2;
SQLINTEGER  Param1Length, Param2Length;
SQLPOINTER  pToken;
int         offset;
  SQLAllocHandle(SQL_HANDLE_ENV,SQL_NULL_HANDLE,&henv);
  SQLAllocHandle(SQL_HANDLE_DBC,henv,&hdbc);
  rc=SQLConnect(hdbc,"OCELOT",SQL_NTS,"OCELOT",SQL_NTS,"",SQL_NTS);
  SQLAllocHandle(SQL_HANDLE_STMT,hdbc,&hstmt);
```

```
  rc=SQLExecDirect(
    hstmt,
    "CREATE TABLE Tests(big_col_1 CHAR(4), big_col_2 CHAR(4))",
    SQL_NTS);
  rc=SQLPrepare(
    hstmt,
    "INSERT INTO Tests(big_col_1,big_col_2) VALUES(?,?)",
    SQL_NTS);
  /* There are two Columns. There are two ?s. There will be two
     parameters. Bind them with SQLBindParameter. Don't pass a
     buffer address (which is what you would usually do). Instead,
     pass 1 and 2 (Param1 contains 1 and Param2 contains 2.) */
  SQLBindParameter(
    hstmt,1,SQL_PARAM_MODE_IN,SQL_CHAR,SQL_CHAR,4,0,&Param1,
    MAX_DATA_LENGTH,&Param1Length);
  SQLBindParameter(
    hstmt,2,SQL_PARAM_MODE_IN,SQL_CHAR,SQL_CHAR,4,0,&Param2,
    MAX_DATA_LENGTH,&Param2Length);
  /* Set Param1Length and Param2Length = SQL_DATA_AT_EXEC;
     the DBMS will see this because we passed addresses of
     Param1Length and Param2Length. */
  Param1Length = Param2Length = SQL_DATA_AT_EXEC;
  rc=SQLExecute(hstmt);
/* For data-at-execution parameters, call SQLParamData to get the */
/* parameter number set by SQLBindParameter. Call InitUserData.   */
/* Call GetUserData and SQLPutData repeatedly to get and put all  */
/* data for the parameter. Call SQLParamData to finish processing */
/* this parameter and start processing the next parameter.        */
  while (rc == SQL_NEED_DATA) {
    rc = SQLParamData(hstmt,&pToken);
    if (rc == SQL_NEED_DATA) {
      for (offset=0;offset<=3;++offset) {      /* "Initialize" */
        OutData[0] = InData[offset];           /* "Get" */
        SQLPutData(hstmt,OutData,1); } } }     /* "Put" */
  SQLEndTran(SQL_HANDLE_DBC,hdbc,SQL_COMMIT);  /* commit */
  SQLFreeHandle(SQL_HANDLE_STMT,hstmt);        /* cleanup + exit */
  SQLDisconnect(hdbc);
  SQLFreeHandle(SQL_HANDLE_DBC,hdbc);
  SQLFreeHandle(SQL_HANDLE_ENV,henv); }
```

ODBC: `SQLPutData` has been around since ODBC 1.0.

SQLCancel

Function Prototype:

```
SQLRETURN SQLCancel(
  SQLHSTMT hstmt                          /* 32-bit input */
  );
```

Job: (Try to) stop a currently-executing function. There are two things that "currently-executing" might mean:

- Scenario #1: The `hstmt` is associated with a deferred parameter.
- Scenario #2: A routine associated with the `stmt` might be running "concurrently." For example, in an MS-Windows environment, you might call a CLI function in one thread but now you're in another thread, and the function is still running. You know what the `stmt` handle is and you want to stop the function.

Algorithm: For Scenario #1:

```
Clear the diagnostics area.
Disassociate the statement source and parameter number from the stmt.
```

It is now possible to call `SQLEndTran`, `SQLDisconnect`, `SQLFreeHandle`, etc. — otherwise, you would have to fill in the deferred-parameter values. See the description of deferred parameters.

For Scenario #2:

```
The server receives the request to cancel.
The server tries to cancel.
If (cancel fails)
  /* Reasons for failure might be: communication problem, or the
     function is doing a "commit" (which can't be interrupted). */
  return error: HY018: CLI-Specific condition-Server declined the cancellation
request
If (cancel succeeds)
  The server returns: okay.
```

The cancelled routine can leave diagnostics behind, if it was running asynchronously. (However, in ODBC, a routine which was cancelled from another thread will leave no diagnostics behind.)

Notes:

- A "successful completion" of this function doesn't mean much; it only means that the server has seen and accepted the request to cancel. More significant is the return that the cancelled function returns: `HY008 CLI-specific condition-operation cancelled`.
- We believe that `SQLCancel` is used most frequently for the situation described as Scenario #1. For the situation described as Scenario #2, there is heavy dependence on

operating-system features so it is not possible to specify exactly how SQLCancel works in standard SQL.

- The cancelled routine might have already done some diagnostics and the diagnostics area is not cleared. Other than that, a cancelled routine leaves no effect.

Example: This example shows the use of SQLCancel against an active process with deferred parameters.

```
#include "sqlcli.h"
SQLHSTMT hstmt;
...
if (SQLExecute(hstmt) == SQL_NEED_DATA) {
  SQLCancel(hstmt); }
```

This example shows the use of SQLCancel against an asynchronous process on another thread. It works like this — suppose you are shutting down and there is some asynch/other-thread function that you've given up on. To make sure you are cancelling, you have to ask two things, "Did SQLCancel work?" (that tells you that the server accepts the request to cancel), and "Did the cancelled function fail?" (that tells you that the server succeeded in cancelling).

```
/* Start asynch/other-thread/waiting function */
...
Call <function> again, using the same hstmt.
If (SQL_STILL_EXECUTING) {
  Call SQLCancel.
  If ("00000" i.e. "successful completion") {
    /* !! Do not assume the routine is cancelled !! */
    Call <function> again.
    If (SQL_STILL_EXECUTING) {
      /* Cancellation request has not yet succeeded. Wait. */
      /* loop here */
    If (SQL_ERROR and "HY008" i.e. "operation cancelled") {
      /* The cancellation is complete. The statement is over. */
    If (anything else) {
      /* Probably the function finished normally, i.e. the */
      /* SQLCancel arrived too late. The statement is over. */
```

ODBC: The SQLCancel function has been around since ODBC 1.0. In ODBC 2.x, SQLCancel(hstmt) was precisely the same as SQLFreeStmt(hstmt,SQL_CLOSE) if there was no asynch running. That is no longer so! If you want to close a Cursor, with ODBC 3.x or with the standard CLI, you must use SQLCloseCursor (hstmt).

And that's it for the CLI deferred parameter functions. In the next chapter, we'll take a look at the locator functions.

50

Chapter 50

SQL/CLI: Locator Functions

In this chapter, we'll describe the CLI locator functions — `SQLGetLength`, `SQLGetPosition`, and `SQLGetSubString`. These functions are used with locators of `BLOB`s and `CLOB`s. They are new in SQL3; as far as we know, no DBMS supports them. Our description is, therefore, fairly brief.

What is a Locator?

When you assign the value of a `BLOB`, `CLOB`, `NCLOB`, `UDT`, or `ARRAY` to an embedded host language variable or a host language parameter, your DBMS generates and assigns a locator to the target, to uniquely identify a value of the corresponding type. The locator is a 4-octet, non-zero integer (that is, locators are 32-bit `INT`s) and exists only until the current transaction ends (unless it is held).

Locators have certain properties.

- A locator may be either valid or invalid.
- A locator may be a holdable locator.

When a locator is initially created, it is marked valid and (if applicable) not holdable. You have to execute a `HOLD LOCATOR` statement before the end of the transaction in which a locator is created if you want that locator to be holdable. A non-holdable locator remains valid until the end of the transaction in which it was generated, unless it is explicitly made invalid by a

FREE LOCATOR statement or a ROLLBACK WITH SAVEPOINT statement. A holdable locator may remain valid beyond the end of the transaction in which it was generated; it becomes invalid when you execute a FREE LOCATOR statement, a ROLLBACK WITH SAVEPOINT statement, or if the transaction in which it is generated (or any subsequent transaction) is rolled back. All locators are made invalid when the current SQL-session ends.

The following items can have the "data type" LOCATOR: a host variable, a host parameter, an SQL parameter in an external routine, and a value returned by an external function. To specify an item as a locator, add the <keyword>s AS LOCATOR to the specification. According to the SQL Standard, this then allows the passing of very large data values "without transferring the entire value to and from the SQL-agent." That is, if you're dealing with an image, why do this:

- DBMS reads into DBMS memory, then
- DBMS transfers to host language memory, then
- host language writes copy?

The procedure could do it without transfers, with a locator.

Standard SQL provides two statements for use with locators. Brief descriptions of each follow.

FREE LOCATOR Statement

The FREE LOCATOR statement removes the association between a locator variable or parameter and the value represented by that locator. The required syntax for the FREE LOCATOR statement is as follows.

```
FREE LOCATOR :host_parameter_name [ {,:host_parameter_name}... ]
```

The FREE LOCATOR statement frees one or more locators — that is, it marks the locators identified by the <host parameter name>s as invalid.

If you want to restrict your code to Core SQL, don't use the FREE LOCATOR statement.

HOLD LOCATOR Statement

The HOLD LOCATOR statement marks a locator variable or parameter as a holdable locator. The required syntax for the HOLD LOCATOR statement is as follows.

```
HOLD LOCATOR :host_parameter_name [ {,:host_parameter_name}... ]
```

The HOLD LOCATOR statement lets you change the status of one or more locators from non-holdable to holdable. The difference between the two has to do with when a locator becomes invalid; a non-holdable locator remains valid until the end of the transaction in which it was generated (unless it is explicitly made invalid), while a holdable locator may remain valid beyond the end of the transaction in which it was generated. All locators are made invalid when the current SQL-session ends.

If you want to restrict your code to Core SQL, don't use the HOLD LOCATOR statement.

The rest of this chapter describes the three CLI locator functions.

SQLGetLength

Function Prototype:

```
SQLRETURN  SQLGetLength(
  SQLHSTMT hstmt,                 /* 32-bit input */
  SQLSMALLINT LocatorType,        /* 16-bit input */
  SQLINTEGER Locator,             /* 32-bit input */
  SQLINTEGER *StringLength,       /* pointer to 32-bit output */
  SQLINTEGER *IndicatorValue      /* pointer to 32-bit output */
  );
```

Job: Return the length of the value represented by a `BLOB`, `CLOB`, or `NCLOB` locator.

Algorithm:

```
If (there is a prepared statement associated with hstmt)
  return error: HY010 CLI-specific condition-function sequence error
If (LocatorType is not SQL_BLOB_LOCATOR or SQL_CLOB_LOCATOR)
  return error: CLI-specific condition-invalid argument value
If (Locator does not refer to a Locator)
  return error: 0F001 locator exception-invalid specification
If (LocatorType==SQL_BLOB_LOCATOR and Locator doesn't refer to a BLOB)
Or (LocatorType==SQL_CLOB_LOCATOR and Locator doesn't refer to a CLOB)
  return error: dynamic SQL error-restricted data type attribute
  violation
Case:
If (the Large Object's value is NULL)
   If (IndicatorValue is a null pointer)
     return error: data exception-null value, no indicator parameter
     Set *IndicatorValue = SQL_NULL_DATA i.e. -1
  Else
   If (IndicatorValue is not a null pointer)
     Set *IndicatorValue = 0
   If (LocatorType == SQL_BLOB_LOCATOR)
     Set *StringLength = length of BLOB, in octets
   If (LocatorType==SQL_CLOB_LOCATOR)
     Set *StringLength = length of CLOB, in characters
```

Notes:

- The octet length and the character length will be the same value only if 8-bit Character sets are in use.

Example:

```
#include "sqlcli.h"
...
SQLINTEGER  lob;                  /* large object locator */
SQLINTEGER  len;                  /* length */
SQLINTEGER  ind;                  /* indicator */
...
SQLGetLength(hstmt,SQL_CLOB_LOCATOR,lob,&len,&ind);
```

ODBC: Because this is an SQL3 function, it is not in ODBC 3.0.

SQLGetPosition

Function Prototype:

```
SQLRETURN SQLGetPosition(
  SQLHSTMT hstmt,                   /* 32-bit input */
  SQLSMALLINT LocatorType,          /* 16-bit input */
  SQLINTEGER SourceLocator,         /* 32-bit input */
  SQLINTEGER SearchLocator,         /* 32-bit input */
  SQLCHAR *SearchLiteral,           /* pointer to *ANY */
  SQLINTEGER SearchLiteralLength,   /* 32-bit input */
  SQLINTEGER FromPosition,          /* 32-bit input */
  SQLINTEGER *LocatedAt,            /* pointer to 32-bit integer */
  SQLINTEGER *IndicatorValue        /* pointer to 32-bit integer */
  );
```

Job: Return the position of a passed string within a `BLOB`, `CLOB`, or `NCLOB`.

Algorithm:

```
If (stmt is associated with a prepared or executed statement)
  return error: HY010 CLI-specific condition-function sequence error
    If (LocatorType is not SQL_BLOB_LOCATOR or SQL_CLOB_LOCATOR)
  return error: CLI-specific condition-invalid argument value
If (Locator does not refer to a Locator)
  return error: 0F001 locator exception-invalid specification
If (LocatorType==SQL_BLOB_LOCATOR and Locator doesn't refer to a BLOB)
Or (LocatorType==SQL_CLOB_LOCATOR and Locator doesn't refer to a CLOB)
  return error: dynamic SQL error-restricted data type attribute
  violation
If (the Large Object's value is NULL)
  If (IndicatorValue is a null pointer)
    return error: data exception-null value, no indicator parameter
  Set *IndicatorValue = SQL_NULL_DATA i.e. -1
Else
  If (IndicatorValue is not a null pointer)
    Set *IndicatorValue = 0;
Set *LocatedAt = position of string within the BLOB or CLOB or NCLOB.
```

ODBC: Because this is an SQL3 function, it is not in ODBC 3.0.

SQLGetSubString

Function Prototype:

```
SQLRETURN  SQLGetSubString(
  SQLHSTMT hstmt,                      /* 32-bit input */
  SQLSMALLINT LocatorType,              /* 16-bit input */
  SQLINTEGER SourceLocator,             /* 32-bit input */
  SQLINTEGER FromPosition,              /* 32-bit input */
  SQLINTEGER ForLength,                 /* 32-bit input */
  SQLSMALLINT TargetType,               /* 16-bit input */
  SQLPOINTER TargetValue                /* pointer to output */
  SQLINTEGER BufferLength,              /* 32-bit input */
  SQLINTEGER *StringLength,             /* pointer to integer output */
  SQLINTEGER *IndicatorValue);          /* pointer to integer output */
```

Job: Extract a portion of a BLOB, CLOB, or NCLOB, returning the result as a string or, alternatively, as a new BLOB, CLOB, or NCLOB.

Algorithm:

```
if (stmt is associated with a prepared or executed statement)
  return error: HY010 CLI-specific condition-function sequence error
If (LocatorType is not SQL_BLOB_LOCATOR or SQL_CLOB_LOCATOR)
  return error: CLI-specific condition-invalid argument value
If (Locator does not refer to a Locator)
  return error: 0F001 locator exception-invalid specification
If (LocatorType==SQL_BLOB_LOCATOR and Locator doesn't refer to a BLOB)
Or (LocatorType==SQL_CLOB_LOCATOR and Locator doesn't refer to a CLOB)
  return error: dynamic SQL error-restricted data type attribute
  violation
If (the Large Object's value is NULL)
  If (IndicatorValue is a null pointer)
    return error: data exception-null value, no indicator parameter
  Set *IndicatorValue = SQL_NULL_DATA i.e. -1
Else
  If (IndicatorValue is not a null pointer)
    Set *IndicatorValue = 0;
Transfer the substring from the BLOB, CLOB, or NCLOB to TargetValue,
using a procedure analogous to Character Retrieval Procedure.
```

ODBC: Because this is an SQL3 function, it is not in ODBC 3.0.

And that's it for the CLI locator functions. In the next (and final) chapter on the CLI, we'll take a look at the Catalog functions.

51

Chapter 51

SQL/CLI: Catalog Functions

The CLI Catalog functions are so called because they involve implicit searches of the metadata — what in pre-SQL-92 days was known as the *system catalog*. Nowadays, the metadata is in INFORMATION_SCHEMA. The functions and the INFORMATION_SCHEMA Views which provide most of the information for them are:

Function	**Related** INFORMATION_SCHEMA **View(s)**
SQLColumnPrivileges	COLUMN_PRIVILEGES
SQLColumns	COLUMNS
SQLForeignKeys	KEY_COLUMN_USAGE, REFERENTIAL_CONSTRAINTS, TABLE_CONSTRAINTS
SQLGetTypeInfo	
SQLParameters	PARAMETERS
SQLPrimaryKeys	KEY_COLUMN_USAGE, TABLE_CONSTRAINTS
SQLRoutinePrivileges	ROUTINE_PRIVILEGES
SQLRoutines	ROUTINES
SQLSpecialColumns	COLUMNS
SQLTablePrivileges	TABLES, TABLE_PRIVILEGES
SQLTables	TABLES

You should study Catalog functions if:

- your problem matches the limited range of ad-hoc solutions offered here,
- they're the standard in your shop,
- you're maintaining an old ODBC program,
- your DBMS doesn't support INFORMATION_SCHEMA, or
- you want to see what extremely long SELECT statements look like.

Otherwise, study the description of the INFORMATION_SCHEMA in Chapter 16 "SQL Catalogs" and use the simple mechanisms you already know. It's cleaner to SELECT from a View in INFORMATION_SCHEMA.

Some Necessary Preliminaries

Calling a Catalog function is equivalent to calling SQLExecDirect with an argument containing a SELECT statement. That means that data is returned in a result set. You may traverse the rows in the result set using SQLFetch or SQLFetchScroll. You should call SQLCloseCursor when there is nothing more to fetch.

For most Catalog functions, you pass (character string) input parameters to specify which rows should be selected for the result set. There are several rules concerning these input parameters. There is no use trying to figure out what the rationale is behind these rules. You'll simply have to learn them if you want Catalog functions to work reliably. Here they are:

- Accessible tables. You may recall that there is an option to the SQLGetInfo function, namely SQL_ACCESSIBLE_TABLES, which returns as follows:
  - 'Y': the DBMS only returns information about Tables to users who have SELECT Privileges on the Tables.
  - 'N': the DBMS returns information about Tables based on some other implementation-defined criterion.

  In fact, all standard DBMSs should return 'N' because information is available to users who have any Privileges on the Tables, not necessarily just SELECT Privileges. In all that follows, we will just assume that the INFORMATION_SCHEMA rows are the rows that would be available in standard SQL.
- Catalogs. Not every DBMS supports Catalogs. For the cases where we say that a <Catalog name> is retrieved, it is possible that the actual retrieval will be NULL. Once again, this is a case where NULL means "not applicable."
- Length. All input-string parameters are accompanied by a SMALLINT parameter — the "length." This length should be the number of octets in the input string. The special value SQL_NTS is permissible. The special value 0 (zero) is permissible and a zero-length string means "don't care" — for example, if you pass a zero-length string for a parameter named *SchemaName, the DBMS will accept all <Schema name>s in the Catalog.
- Metadata ID. You may recall that there is an option to the SQLGetStmtAttr function, namely SQL_ATTR_METADATA_ID, which returns either TRUE or FALSE.
  - If Metadata ID is TRUE:
    - If there is such a thing as a <Catalog name> (which is the case in all standard DBMSs), then you must not pass a null pointer for any Catalog function parameter which is labelled *CatalogName. Passing a null

pointer will result in the error: `HY009 CLI-specific condition-invalid use of null pointer`.

    - You must not pass a null pointer for any Catalog function parameter which is labelled `*SchemaName`. Passing a null pointer will result in the error: `HY009 CLI-specific condition-invalid use of null pointer`.
    - You may pass a string which begins and ends with quotes, as is the custom for <delimited identifier>s. If you do pass a quoted string, the quotes are stripped and the string is not converted to uppercase. If you don't pass a quoted string, the string is converted to uppercase.
- If Metadata ID is `FALSE`:
    - You may pass a null pointer for any string parameter. Doing so is equivalent to passing a string with zero length.
    - The string may be treated as a search pattern; that is, wild cards are allowed as they are in `LIKE` predicates. If you need to find out what the value is for the escape character, call `SQLGetInfo(hdbc,SQL_SEARCH_PATTERN_ESCAPE,...)`.

TIP: You'll only have to learn one set of rules if Metadata ID is always `TRUE`. Therefore, as soon as you allocate a `stmt`, execute this function:

```
SQLSetStmtAttr(hstmt,SQL_ATTR_METADATA_ID,(void*)1,00);
```

and leave it that way. Henceforward, we'll forget about the possibility that Metadata ID could be `FALSE`.

In ODBC, searching is different in significant ways; quotes are not stripped, <identifier>s are always converted to uppercase, regardless of the value of Metadata ID. If quotes are not present, then trail spaces are trimmed. The character used for <delimited identifier>s may be something other than a quote mark.

TIP: There's no way to remove the incompatibilities between standard SQL and ODBC here, but they won't matter if you follow two policies. One: avoid <delimited identifier>s. Two: pass all string values in uppercase.

SQLColumnPrivileges

Function Prototype:

```
SQLRETURN SQLColumnPrivileges(
  SQLHSTMT hstmt,                /* 32-bit input */
  SQLCHAR *CatalogName,          /* pointer to CHAR* input */
  SQLSMALLINT NameLength1,       /* 16-bit input */
  SQLCHAR *SchemaName,           /* pointer to CHAR* input */
  SQLSMALLINT NameLength2,       /* 16-bit input */
  SQLCHAR *TableName,            /* pointer to CHAR* input */
  SQLSMALLINT NameLength3,       /* 16-bit input */
  SQLCHAR *ColumnName,           /* pointer to CHAR* input */
  SQLSMALLINT NameLength4        /* 16-bit input */
  );
```

Job: Get metadata concerning Column Privileges.

Algorithm:

```
Execute the following SELECT statement and return a result set.
SELECT
  TABLE_CATALOG AS table_cat,      /* VARCHAR(128) */
  TABLE_SCHEMA AS table_schem,     /* VARCHAR(128) NOT NULL */
  TABLE_NAME,                      /* VARCHAR(128) NOT NULL */
  COLUMN_NAME,                     /* VARCHAR(128) NOT NULL */
   GRANTOR,                        /* VARCHAR(128) */
   GRANTEE,                        /* VARCHAR(128) NOT NULL */
   PRIVILEGE_TYPE AS privilege,    /* VARCHAR(128) NOT NULL */
   IS_GRANTABLE                    /* VARCHAR(3) */
FROM INFORMATION_SCHEMA.COLUMN_PRIVILEGES
WHERE
   CATALOG_NAME = ?               /* use CatalogName parameter */
   AND SCHEMA_NAME = ?            /* use SchemaName parameter */
   AND TABLE_NAME = ?             /* use TableName parameter */
   AND COLUMN_NAME = ?            /* use ColumnName parameter */
ORDER BY table_cat,table_schem,TABLE_NAME,COLUMN_NAME,privilege;
```

Notes:

- The algorithm's SELECT statement does not reflect some minor matters. See "Some Necessary Preliminaries" on page 964.

Example:

```
#include "sqlcli.h"
SQLHSTMT hstmt;
SQLCHAR CatalogName[128+1],SchemaName[128+1],TableName[128+1];
SQLCHAR ColumnName[128+1];
SQLRETURN sqlreturn;
...
sqlreturn = SQLColumnPrivileges(
  hstmt,CatalogName,SQL_NTS,SchemaName,SQL_NTS,TableName,
  SQL_NTS,ColumnName,SQL_NTS);
```

ODBC: `SQLColumnPrivileges` has been around since ODBC 1.0. However, searching is significantly different; see "Some Necessary Preliminaries" on page 964.

SQLColumns

Function Prototype:

```
SQLRETURN SQLColumns(
  SQLHSTMT hstmt,                 /* 32-bit input */
  SQLCHAR *CatalogName,           /* pointer to CHAR* input */
  SQLSMALLINT NameLength1,        /* 32-bit input */
  SQLCHAR *SchemaName,            /* pointer to CHAR* input */
  SQLSMALLINT NameLength2,        /* 32-bit input */
  SQLCHAR *TableName,             /* pointer to CHAR* input */
  SQLSMALLINT NameLength3,        /* 32-bit input */
  SQLCHAR *ColumnName,            /* pointer to CHAR* input */
  SQLSMALLINT NameLength4         /* 16-bit input */
  );
```

Job: Get metadata concerning Columns.

Algorithm:

```
Execute the following SELECT statement and return a result set.
SELECT
TABLE_CATALOG AS table_cat,          /* VARCHAR(128) */
TABLE_SCHEMA  AS table_schem,        /* VARCHAR(128) NOT NULL */
TABLE_NAME,                          /* VARCHAR(128) NOT NULL */
COLUMN_NAME,                         /* VARCHAR(128) NOT NULL */
```

```
CASE DATA_TYPE
  WHEN 'CHARACTER' THEN 1
  WHEN 'NUMERIC' THEN 2
  WHEN 'DECIMAL' THEN 3
  WHEN 'INTEGER' THEN 4
  WHEN 'SMALLINT' THEN 5
  WHEN 'FLOAT' THEN 6
  WHEN 'REAL' THEN 7
  WHEN 'DOUBLE PRECISION' THEN 8
  WHEN 'VARCHAR' THEN 12
  WHEN 'BIT' THEN 14
  WHEN 'BIT VARYING' THEN 15
  WHEN 'REF' THEN 20
  WHEN 'DATE' THEN 91
  WHEN 'TIME' THEN 92
  WHEN 'TIMESTAMP' THEN 93
  WHEN 'TIME WITH TIME ZONE' THEN 94
  WHEN 'TIMESTAMP WITH TIME ZONE' THEN 95
  WHEN 'INTERVAL' THEN
    CASE INTERVAL_TYPE
      WHEN 'YEAR' THEN 101
      WHEN 'MONTH' THEN 102
      WHEN 'DAY' THEN 103
      WHEN 'HOUR' THEN 104
      WHEN 'MINUTE' THEN 105
      WHEN 'SECOND' THEN 106
      WHEN 'YEAR TO MONTH' THEN 107
      WHEN 'DAY TO HOUR' THEN 108
      WHEN 'DAY TO MINUTE' THEN 109
      WHEN 'DAY TO SECOND' THEN 110
      WHEN 'HOUR TO MINUTE' THEN 111
      WHEN 'HOUR TO SECOND' THEN 112
      WHEN 'MINUTE TO SECOND' THEN 113
      END
  END AS DATA_TYPE,                          /* SMALLINT */
DATA_TYPE     AS TYPE_NAME,                  /* VARCHAR(128) NOT NULL */
```

```
CASE
  WHEN DATA_TYPE = 'CHARACTER'
    OR DATA_TYPE = 'VARCHAR'
    OR DATA_TYPE = 'CLOB'
    OR DATA_TYPE = 'BLOB'
    OR DATA_TYPE = 'BIT'
    OR DATA_TYPE = 'BIT VARYING'
    THEN CHARACTER_MAXIMUM_LENGTH
  WHEN DATA_TYPE = 'NUMERIC'
    OR DATA_TYPE = 'DECIMAL'
    OR DATA_TYPE = 'SMALLINT'
    OR DATA_TYPE = 'INTEGER'
    OR DATA_TYPE = 'REAL'
    OR DATA_TYPE = 'FLOAT'
    OR DATA_TYPE = 'DOUBLE PRECISION'
    THEN NUMERIC_PRECISION
  WHEN DATA_TYPE = 'DATE' THEN 10
  WHEN DATA_TYPE = 'TIME' THEN
    CASE
      WHEN DATETIME_PRECISION > 0 THEN 9+DATETIME_PRECISION
      ELSE 8
      END
    END
  WHEN DATA_TYPE = 'TIMESTAMP' THEN
    CASE
      WHEN DATETIME_PRECISION > 0 THEN 20+DATETIME_PRECISION
      ELSE 19
      END
    END
  WHEN DATA_TYPE = 'TIME WITH TIME ZONE' THEN
    CASE
      WHEN DATETIME_PRECISION > 0 THEN 15+DATETIME_PRECISION
      ELSE 14
      END
    END
```

```
   WHEN DATA_TYPE = 'TIMESTAMP WITH TIME ZONE' THEN
     CASE
       WHEN DATETIME_PRECISION > 0 THEN 26+DATETIME_PRECISION
       ELSE 25
       END
     END
   END AS COLUMN_SIZE,                               /* INTEGER */
 CHARACTER_OCTET_LENGTH AS BUFFER_LENGTH,            /* INTEGER */
 CASE
   WHEN DATA_TYPE = 'DATE'
     OR DATA_TYPE = 'TIME'
     OR DATA_TYPE = 'TIMESTAMP'
     OR DATA_TYPE = 'TIME WITH TIME ZONE'
     OR DATA_TYPE = 'TIMESTAMP WITH TIME ZONE'
     THEN DATETIME_PRECISION
   WHEN DATA_TYPE = 'NUMERIC'
     OR DATA_TYPE = 'DECIMAL'
     OR DATA_TYPE = 'SMALLINT'
     OR DATA_TYPE = 'INTEGER'
     THEN NUMERIC_SCALE
   ELSE NULL
   END AS DECIMAL_DIGITS,                        /* SMALLINT */
 NUMERIC_PRECISION_RADIX AS num_prec_radix,      /* SMALLINT */
 CASE
   WHEN IS_NULLABLE='NO' THEN 0
   ELSE 1
   END AS  nullable,                            /* SMALLINT NOT NULL */
 '' AS remarks,                                 /* VARCHAR(254) */
 COLUMN_DEFAULT AS COLUMN_DEF,                  /* VARCHAR(254) */
 CASE DATA_TYPE
   WHEN 'CHARACTER' THEN 1
   WHEN 'NUMERIC' THEN 2
   WHEN 'DECIMAL' THEN 3
   WHEN 'INTEGER' THEN 4
   WHEN 'SMALLINT' THEN 5
   WHEN 'FLOAT' THEN 6
   WHEN 'REAL' THEN 7
   WHEN 'DOUBLE PRECISION' THEN 8
   WHEN 'VARCHAR' THEN 12
```

```
  WHEN 'BIT' THEN 14
  WHEN 'BIT VARYING' THEN 15
  WHEN 'REF' THEN 20
  WHEN 'DATE' THEN 9
  WHEN 'TIME' THEN 9
  WHEN 'TIMESTAMP' THEN 9
  WHEN 'TIME WITH TIME ZONE' THEN 9
  WHEN 'TIMESTAMP WITH TIME ZONE' THEN 9
  WHEN 'INTERVAL' THEN 10
  END AS sql_data_type,                          /* SMALLINT */
CASE DATA_TYPE
  WHEN 'DATE' THEN 1
  WHEN 'TIME' THEN 2
  WHEN 'TIMESTAMP' THEN 3
  WHEN 'TIME WITH TIME ZONE' THEN 4
  WHEN 'TIMESTAMP WITH TIME ZONE' THEN 5
  WHEN 'INTERVAL' THEN
    CASE INTERVAL_TYPE
      WHEN 'YEAR' THEN 1
      WHEN 'MONTH' THEN 2
      WHEN 'DAY' THEN 3
      WHEN 'HOUR' THEN 4
      WHEN 'MINUTE' THEN 5
      WHEN 'SECOND' THEN 6
      WHEN 'YEAR TO MONTH' THEN 7
      WHEN 'DAY TO HOUR' THEN 8
      WHEN 'DAY TO MINUTE' THEN 9
      WHEN 'DAY TO SECOND' THEN 10
      WHEN 'HOUR TO MINUTE' THEN 11
      WHEN 'HOUR TO SECOND' THEN 12
      WHEN 'MINUTE TO SECOND' THEN 13
      END
   ELSE NULL AS sql_datetime_sub,              /* INTEGER */
  CHARACTER_OCTET_LENGTH AS char_octet_length,/* INTEGER */
  ORDINAL_POSITION,                            /* INTEGER NOT NULL */
  IS_NULLABLE,                                 /* VARCHAR(254) */
  CHARACTER_SET_CATALOG AS char_set_cat,       /* VARCHAR(128) */
  CHARACTER_SET_SCHEMA  AS char_set_schem,     /* VARCHAR(128) */
  CHARACTER_SET_NAME    AS char_set_name,      /* VARCHAR(128) */
```

```
 COLLATION_CATALOG     AS collation_cat,      /* VARCHAR(128) */
 COLLATION_SCHEMA      AS collation_schem,    /* VARCHAR(128) */
 COLLATION_NAME,                              /* VARCHAR(128) */
 USER_DEFINED_TYPE_CATALOG AS udt_cat,        /* VARCHAR(128) */
 USER_DEFINED_TYPE_SCHEMA AS udt_schem,       /* VARCHAR(128) */
 USER_DEFINED_TYPE_NAME AS udt_name           /* VARCHAR(128) */
FROM INFORMATION_SCHEMA.COLUMNS
WHERE
      CATALOG_NAME = ?                /* From CatalogName parameter */
      AND SCHEMA_NAME = ?             /* From SchemaName parameter */
      AND TABLE_NAME = ?              /* From TableName parameter */
      AND COLUMN_NAME = ?             /* From ColumnName parameter */
ORDER BY table_cat,table_schem,TABLE_NAME,ORDINAL_POSITION;
```

Notes:

- The algorithm's SELECT statement does not reflect some minor matters. See "Some Necessary Preliminaries" on page 964.
- Some of the newer SQL3 <data type>s, for instance BOOLEAN, are not yet representable by a numeric DATA_TYPE code.
- TYPE_NAME is implementation-defined. This field is supposed to accommodate DBMSs which use non-standard <data type> names.
- COLUMN_SIZE is implementation-defined when the <data type> is SMALLINT, INTEGER, REAL, FLOAT, or DOUBLE PRECISION. For the algorithm, we assumed that the DBMS will return NUMERIC_PRECISION.
- The algorithm does not show all the calculations required for INTERVAL <data type>s. Put simply, the rule is that COLUMN_SIZE is the number of positions.
- BUFFER_LENGTH is implementation-defined. The intent is that the value should be the number of octets transferred during SQLFetch or SQLFetchScroll, so for character string <data type>s the source would be the CHARACTER_OCTET_LENGTH Column in INFORMATION_SCHEMA.COLUMNS.
- REMARKS is implementation-defined.
- SQL_DATA_TYPE is not defined at all. The algorithm shows what we believe was the intention.
- For SQL_DATETIME_SUB, the Standard contains errors. The algorithm shows what we believe was the intention.
- SQL_DATA_TYPE, CHAR_OCTET_LENGTH, ORDINAL_POSITION, and IS_NULLABLE are not defined in the Standard. The algorithm shows what we believe was the intention.
- The Columns udt_cat, udt_schem, and udt_name are strictly SQL3 (for user-defined types). To run the query with an SQL-92 DBMS, remove the references to those fields.

Example: Given <Table name> T, make an SQL statement which selects all the Columns in T without using the "*" shorthand. For example, if T has two Columns — COLUMN_1 and COLUMN_2 — the output string will be:

```
SELECT COLUMN_1,COLUMN_2 FROM T;
```

Use this only with <regular identifier>s.

```
#include "sqlcli.h"
SQLHSTMT hstmt;
SQLCHAR select_statement[1024];
SQLCHAR column_name[128+1];
...
sqlreturn = SQLColumns(
  hstmt,"OCELOT",SQL_NTS,"OCELOT",SQL_NTS,"T",SQL_NTS,NULL,0);
/* Take column_name from the fourth Column in the result: COLUMN_NAME. */
SQLBindCol(hstmt,4,SQL_CHAR,column_name,128+1,NULL);
strcpy(select_statement,"SELECT ");
for (;;) {
  sqlreturn = SQLFetch(hstmt);
  if (sqlreturn == SQL_NO_DATA) break;
  strcat(select_statement,column_name);
  strcat(select_statement,","); }
SQLCloseCursor(hstmt);
select_statement[strlen(select_statement)-1]='\0'; /* cut last "," */
strcat(select_statement," FROM T");
SQLExecDirect(hstmt,select_statement,SQL_NTS);
```

ODBC: SQLColumns has been around since ODBC 1.0. The final three Columns (udt_cat, udt_schem, udt_name) do not appear in ODBC.

SQLForeignKeys

Function Prototype:

```
SQLRETURN SQLForeignKeys(
  SQLHSTMT hstmt,              /* 32-bit input */
  SQLCHAR *PKCatalogName,      /* pointer to CHAR * input */
  SQLSMALLINT NameLength1,     /* 16-bit input */
  SQLCHAR *PKSchemaName,       /* pointer to CHAR * input */
  SQLSMALLINT NameLength2,     /* 16-bit input */
  SQLCHAR *PKTableName,        /* pointer to CHAR * input */
  SQLSMALLINT NameLength3,     /* 16-bit input */
  SQLCHAR *FKCatalogName,      /* pointer to CHAR * input */
  SQLSMALLINT NameLength4,     /* 16-bit input */
  SQLCHAR *FKSchemaName,       /* pointer to CHAR * input */
  SQLSMALLINT NameLength5,     /* 16-bit input */
  SQLCHAR *FKTableName,        /* pointer to CHAR * input */
  SQLSMALLINT NameLength6      /* 16-bit input */
  );
```

Job: Depending on the input parameters,SQLForeignKeys will either (*a*) return a result set with information about a referenced Table, (*b*) return a result set with information about a referencing Table, or (*c*) both (*a*) and (*b*). By definition, every foreign key is associated with one referencing Table, one referenced Table, and one primary or unique key. The returned result set will contain information about them too.

Algorithm: To visualize how the DBMS gets the result set and what it will contain, assume that the DBMS makes a View and then SELECTs from it. We are trying, in the following CREATE VIEW statement, to make it clear what each <Column name> will be (that's why there are AS clauses) and what each Column <data type> will be (that's why there are /* comments */). The View we're creating is a join of three INFORMATION_SCHEMA Views: KEY_COLUMN_USAGE, REFERENTIAL_CONSTRAINTS, and TABLE_CONSTRAINTS.

```
CREATE VIEW TEMPORARY_VIEW AS SELECT
   UK.TABLE_CATALOG     AS UK_table_cat,    /* VARCHAR(128) */
   UK.TABLE_SCHEMA      AS UK_table_schem,  /* VARCHAR(128) NOT NULL */
   UK.TABLE_NAME        AS UK_TABLE_NAME,   /* VARCHAR(128) NOT NULL */
   UK.COLUMN_NAME       AS UK_COLUMN_NAME,  /* VARCHAR(128) NOT NULL */
   FK.TABLE_CATALOG     AS FK_table_cat,    /* VARCHAR(128) */
   FK.TABLE_SCHEMA      AS FK_table_schem,  /* VARCHAR(128) NOT NULL */
   FK.TABLE_NAME        AS FK_TABLE_NAME,   /* VARCHAR(128) NOT NULL */
   FK.COLUMN_NAME       AS FK_COLUMN_NAME,  /* VARCHAR(128) NOT NULL */
   CO.ORDINAL_POSITION AS ORDINAL_POSITION,   /* SMALLINT NOT NULL */
```

```
CASE FK.UPDATE_RULE
  WHEN 'CASCADE'     0
  WHEN 'SET NULL'    2
  WHEN 'NO ACTION'   3
  WHEN 'SET DEFAULT' 4
  END              AS UPDATE_RULE,     /* SMALLINT */
CASE FK.DELETE_RULE
  WHEN 'CASCADE'     0
  WHEN 'SET NULL'    2
  WHEN 'NO ACTION'   3
  WHEN 'SET DEFAULT' 4
  END              AS DELETE_RULE,     /* SMALLINT */
FK.CONSTRAINT_NAME   AS FK_NAME,          /* VARCHAR(128) */
UK.CONSTRAINT_NAME   AS UK_NAME,          /* VARCHAR(128) */
CASE UK.CONSTRAINT_TYPE
  WHEN 'PRIMARY KEY' 'PRIMARY'
  WHEN 'UNIQUE KEY'  'UNIQUE '
  END              AS UNIQUE_OR_PRIMARY /* CHAR(7) */
FROM INFORMATION_SCHEMA.KEY_COLUMN_USAGE AS CO,
     INFORMATION_SCHEMA.REFERENTIAL_CONSTRAINTS AS FK,
     INFORMATION_SCHEMA.TABLE_CONSTRAINTS AS UK
WHERE
      CO.CONSTRAINT_NAME = FK.CONSTRAINT_NAME        /* see note */
      AND
      FK.UNIQUE_CONSTRAINT_NAME = UK.CONSTRAINT_NAME
                                                     /* see note */
```

Incidentally, the Standard needs 15 pages to express the above — this is a tribute to the expressive power of the SELECT statement. To get our result set, we will SELECT from this View. For the sake of an example, assume there are three Tables, with these definitions:

```
CREATE TABLE T1 (
   t1_col_1 ... PRIMARY KEY);

CREATE TABLE T2 (
   t2_col_1 ... PRIMARY KEY,
   t2_col_2 ... REFERENCES T1);

CREATE TABLE T3 (
   t3_col_1 ... REFERENCES T1,
   t3_col_2 ... REFERENCES T2);
```

In the following, we use the words "is passed" to mean "is not a null pointer and does not contain all spaces."

[1] If the *PKTableName parameter is passed, search the temporary View, looking for primary key:

```
SELECT * FROM TEMPORARY_VIEW
WHERE UK_TABLE_NAME = ?    /* ? is for the *PKTableName parameter */
AND UK_SCHEMA_NAME = ?     /* included if *PKSchemaName is passed */
AND UK_CATALOG_NAME = ?    /* included if *PKCatalogName is passed */
ORDER BY FK_table_cat,FK_table_schem,FK_TABLE_NAME,ORDINAL_POSITION;
```

What this means is: if you pass *PKTableName = 'T2', you get a result set with information about every FOREIGN KEY Constraint that references T2. Given the above example Tables, the result of this call:

```
SQLForeignKeys(
    hstmt,NULL,0,NULL,0,"T2",2,NULL,0,NULL,0,NULL,0);
```

is:

UK_TABLE_NAME	UK_COLUMN_NAME	FK_TABLE_NAME	FK_COLUMN_NAME
T2	T2_COL_1	T3	T3_COL_1

[2] If the *FKTableName parameter is passed, search the temporary View looking for foreign key:

```
SELECT * FROM TEMPORARY_VIEW
WHERE FK_TABLE_NAME = ?       /* ? is for the *FKTableName parameter */
AND FK_SCHEMA_NAME = ?        /* included if FKSchemaName is passed */
AND FK_CATALOG_NAME = ?       /* included if FKCatalogName is passed */
ORDER BY FK_table_cat,FK_table_schem,FK_TABLE_NAME,ORDINAL_POSITION;
```

What this means is: if you pass *FKTableName = 'T2', you get a result set with information about all the foreign keys defined in T2. Given the above example Tables, the result of this call:

```
SQLForeignKeys(
    hstmt,NULL,0,NULL,0,NULL,0,NULL,0,NULL,0,"T2",2);
```

is:

UK_TABLE_NAME	UK_COLUMN_NAME	FK_TABLE_NAME	FK_COLUMN_NAME
T1	T1_COL_1	T2	T2_COL_1

[3] If both the *PKTableName and *FKTableName parameters are passed, then search the temporary View looking for both primary and foreign key:

```
SELECT * FROM TEMPORARY_VIEW
WHERE UK_TABLE_NAME = ?    /* ? is for the *PKTableName parameter */
AND UK_SCHEMA_NAME = ?     /* included if *PKSchemaName is passed */
AND UK_CATALOG_NAME = ?    /* included if *PKCatalogName is passed */
AND FK_TABLE_NAME = ?          /* ? is for the *FKTableName parameter */
AND FK_SCHEMA_NAME = ?         /* included if FKSchemaName is passed */
AND FK_CATALOG_NAME = ?        /* included if FKCatalogName is passed */
ORDER BY FK_table_cat,FK_table_schem,FK_TABLE_NAME,ORDINAL_POSITION;
```

What this means is: if you pass *PKTableName = 'T1' and *FKTableName = 'T3', you get a result set with information about one of the foreign keys that's in T3. Given the above example Tables, the result of this call:

```
SQLForeignKeys(
    hstmt,NULL,0,NULL,0,"T1",2,NULL,0,NULL,0,"T3",2);
```

is:

UK_TABLE_NAME	UK_COLUMN_NAME	FK_TABLE_NAME	FK_COLUMN_NAME
T1	T1_COL_1	T3	T3_COL_1

Notes:

- The above SELECT statements do not reflect some minor matters. See "Some Necessary Preliminaries" on page 964.
- For readability, this example only shows the joins on "name" Columns — it omits the joins on "Schema" and "Catalog" Columns.

Example: This function call might put several rows in the result set because we are asking for "any Catalog," "any Schema."

```
#include "sqlcli.h"
SQLHSTMT hstmt;
SQLRETURN sqlreturn;
...
sqlreturn = SQLForeignKeys(hstmt,
          "",0,       /* Primary Catalog */
          "",0,       /* Primary Schema */
          "T",SQL_NTS, /* Primary Table  */
          "",0,       /* Foreign Catalog*/
          "",0,       /* Foreign Schema */
          "",0);      /* Foreign Table  */
```

ODBC: The SQLForeignKeys function has been around since ODBC 1.0. Most of the <Column name>s are different in ODBC. That's partly because ODBC only recognizes references to primary keys, it doesn't expect that foreign keys could reference unique keys.

SQLGetTypeInfo

Function Prototype:

```
SQLRETURN SQLGetTypeInfo(
  SQLHSTMT hstmt,                    /* 32-bit input */
  SQLSMALLINT DataType               /* 16-bit input */
  );
```

Job: Return a result set with one row for each <data type> that the DBMS supports. It is possible to select a particular <data type>.

Algorithm: The SQL Standard asks us to pretend that there is a TYPE_INFO Table containing information about the <data type>: its name, whether there is a scale, the SQL <data type> code, and so on. To help the pretense, we have actually made an INFORMATION_SCHEMA View which is defined according to the Standard's specification. Please see "INFORMATION_SCHEMA.TYPE_INFO" on page 332 of Chapter 16 "SQL Catalogs" for a complete description.

Assuming that such a View exists, the DBMS algorithm is simple:

```
If (
  DataType==SQL_ALL_TYPES i.e. 0) then in effect this search happens:
       SELECT *
       FROM   INFORMATION_SCHEMA.TYPE_INFO;
```

If the DataType parameter contains a value other than SQL_ALL_TYPES (0), then, in effect, this search happens:

```
       SELECT *
       FROM   INFORMATION_SCHEMA.TYPE_INFO
       WHERE  DATA_TYPE = ?;
```

where the parameter marker ? stands for "the value of the DataType parameter."

Notes:

- Much of the information returned by SQLGetTypeInfo is stuff you already know, because it's standard. What you should worry about is the parts labelled "implementation-defined." For example, the maximum size of a CHAR Column varies from DBMS to DBMS. Unfortunately, the TYPE_INFO View lacks a few items which might be useful — such as the Character set.
- A typical application — if you allow the user to create Tables, it's handy to call SQLGetTypeInfo and display list boxes (showing the localized <data type> names) or explanatory notes based on implementation-defined maxima.

Example: This Column will display "10," because the third Column in INFORMATION_SCHEMA.TYPE_INFO is COLUMN_SIZE and the Column size for a DATE <data type> is always 10 positions. The value of SQL_TYPE_DATE is 91.

```
#include "sqlcli.h"
SQLHSTMT hstmt;
SQLINTEGER column_size;
...
SQLGetTypeInfo(hstmt,SQL_TYPE_DATE);
SQLBindCol(hstmt,3,SQL_INTEGER,&column_size,00,NULL);
SQLFetch(hstmt);
SQLCloseCursor(hstmt);
printf("column size = %d\n",column_size);
```

ODBC: SQLGetTypeInfo has been around since ODBC 1.0, but many of the Columns are new in ODBC 3.0. The implicit SELECT statements contain the clause ORDER BY DATA_TYPE.

SQLParameters

Function Prototype:

```
SQLRETURN SQLParameters (
  SQLHSTMT      hstmt,                /* 32-bit input */
  SQLCHAR       *CatalogName,         /* CHAR* input */
  SQLSMALLINT   NameLength1,          /* 16-bit input */
  SQLCHAR       *SchemaName,          /* CHAR* input */
  SQLSMALLINT   NameLength2,          /* 16-bit input */
  SQLCHAR       *RoutineName,         /* CHAR* input */
  SQLSMALLINT   NameLength3,          /* 16-bit input */
  SQLCHAR       *ParameterName,       /* CHAR* input */
  SQLSMALLINT   NameLength4           /* 16-bit input */
  );
```

Job: Get metadata concerning parameters.

Algorithm:

```
Execute the following SELECT statement and return a result set.
SELECT
   SPECIFIC_CATALOG AS routine_cat,   /* VARCHAR(128) */
   SPECIFIC_SCHEMA AS routine_schem, /* VARCHAR(128) NOT NULL */
   SPECIFIC_NAME AS routine_name,     /* VARCHAR(128) NOT NULL */
   PARAMETER_NAME,                    /* VARCHAR(128) NOT NULL */
```

```
    PARAMETER_MODE,                         /* VARCHAR(254) NOT NULL */
    (see notes) AS DATA_TYPE,               /* INTEGER NOT NULL */
    DATA_TYPE AS TYPE_NAME,                 /* VARCHAR(128) NOT NULL */
    (see notes) AS PARAMETER_SIZE,                  /* INTEGER */
    (see notes) AS BUFFER_LENGTH,                   /* INTEGER */
    (see notes) AS DECIMAL_DIGITS,                  /* SMALLINT */
    NUMERIC_PRECISION_RADIX AS num_prec_radix,      /* SMALLINT */
    (see notes) AS sql_datetime_sub,                /* SMALLINT */
    CHARACTER_OCTET_LENGTH AS char_octet_length,    /* INTEGER */
    ORDINAL_POSITION,                           /* INTEGER NOT NULL */
    CHARACTER_SET_CATALOG AS char_set_cat,      /* VARCHAR(128) */
    CHARACTER_SET_SCHEMA AS char_set_schem,     /* VARCHAR(128) */
    CHARACTER_SET_NAME AS char_set_name,        /* VARCHAR(128) */
    COLLATION_CATALOG AS collation_cat,         /* VARCHAR(128) */
    COLLATION_SCHEMA AS collation_schem,        /* VARCHAR(128) */
    COLLATION_NAME,                             /* VARCHAR(128) */
    USER_DEFINED_TYPE_CATALOG AS udt_cat,       /* VARCHAR(128) */
    USER_DEFINED_TYPE_SCHEMA AS udt_schem,      /* VARCHAR(128) */
    USER_DEFINED_TYPE_NAME AS udt_name,         /* VARCHAR(128) */
    <implementation-defined> AS REMARKS         /* VARCHAR(254) */
  FROM INFORMATION_SCHEMA.PARAMETERS
  WHERE
    CATALOG_NAME LIKE ?
    AND SCHEMA_NAME LIKE ?
    AND ROUTINE_NAME LIKE ?
    AND PARAMETER_NAME LIKE ?
  ORDER BY routine_cat,routine_schem,routine_name,PARAMETER_NAME;
... where the four ? parameters are CatalogName, SchemaName, RoutineName, and
ParameterName, in that order.
```

Notes:

- The algorithm's SELECT statement does not reflect some minor matters. See "Some Necessary Preliminaries" on page 964.
- For the result set's DATA_TYPE, BUFFER_LENGTH, DECIMAL_DIGITS, and SQL_DATA_TYPE Columns, the DBMS uses the same calculations that it uses for the SQLColumns function — see the long CASE expressions in "SQLColumns" on page 967.
- The value in TYPE_NAME is implementation-defined; in our implementation, we defined that it's the same as PARAMETERS.DATA_TYPE.
- The value in the result set's PARAMETER_SIZE Column is the same as the value in the BUFFER_SIZE Column. (Although PARAMETER_SIZE and BUFFER_SIZE depend on several

implementation-defined rules, we believe that any practical DBMS will employ the same rules for both Columns.)

- The DBMS will only return rows for routines on which you have EXECUTE Privileges.

Example:

```
/* This shows every parameter in routine X. */
#include "sqlcli.h"
...
SQLParameters(hstmt,"",0,"",0,"X",1,"",0);
...
```

ODBC: There is no ODBC equivalent of SQLParameters.

SQLPrimaryKeys

Function Prototype:

```
SQLRETURN SQLPrimaryKeys(
  SQLHSTMT hstmt,              /* 32-bit input */
  SQLCHAR *CatalogName,        /* pointer to CHAR* input */
  SQLSMALLINT NameLength1,     /* 16-bit input */
  SQLCHAR *SchemaName,         /* pointer to CHAR* input */
  SQLSMALLINT NameLength2,     /* 16-bit input */
  SQLCHAR *TableName,          /* pointer to CHAR* input */
  SQLSMALLINT NameLength3      /* 16-bit input */
  );
```

Job: Given a <Table name>, return a list of the Columns in the Table's primary key. The return is a result set.

Algorithm:

```
If values are passed in the CatalogName and SchemaName and TableName parame-
ters, the main rule is that this query is effectively executed:
SELECT
      K.TABLE_CATALOG AS table_cat,
      K.TABLE_SCHEMA AS table_schem,
      K.TABLE_NAME,
      K.COLUMN_NAME,
      K.ORDINAL_POSITION,
      K.CONSTRAINT_NAME AS pk_name
      FROM INFORMATION_SCHEMA.KEY_COLUMN_USAGE AS K,
```

```
          INFORMATION_SCHEMA.TABLE_CONSTRAINTS AS P
      WHERE K.CONSTRAINT_CATALOG = P.CONSTRAINT_CATALOG
      AND   K.CONSTRAINT_SCHEMA = P.CONSTRAINT_SCHEMA
      AND   K.CONSTRAINT_NAME = P.CONSTRAINT_NAME
      AND   K.TABLE_CATALOG = ?
      AND   K.TABLE_SCHEMA = ?
      AND   K.TABLE_NAME = ?
      AND   P.CONSTRAINT_TYPE = 'PRIMARY KEY'
      ORDER BY table_cat,table_schem,TABLE_NAME,ORDINAL_POSITION;
... where the three ? parameter markers are for CatalogName, SchemaName, and
TableName, respectively.
```

Notes:

- The only returned rows are for PRIMARY KEY Constraints. If there is a UNIQUE Constraint — even a UNIQUE Constraint that is referenced by a foreign key — SQLPrimaryKeys will not see it.

Example:

```
/* The result set will contain all primary keys from Tables in Schema OCELOT in
   Catalog OCELOT. */
#include "sqlcli.h"
SQLHSTMT hstmt;
...
SQLPrimaryKeys(
  hstmt,"OCELOT",sizeof("OCELOT"),"OCELOT",sizeof("OCELOT"),"",0);
```

ODBC: The SQLPrimaryKeys function has been around since ODBC 1.0. The name of the fifth returned Column is KEY_SEQ instead of ORDINAL_POSITION.

SQLRoutinePrivileges

Function Prototype:

```
SQLRETURN SQLRoutinePrivileges(
  SQLHSTMT hstmt,             /* 32-bit input */
  SQLCHAR *CatalogName,       /* pointer to CHAR* input */
  SQLSMALLINT NameLength1,    /* 16-bit input */
  SQLCHAR *SchemaName,        /* pointer to CHAR* input */
  SQLSMALLINT NameLength2,    /* 16-bit input */
  SQLCHAR *RoutineName,       /* pointer to CHAR* input */
  SQLSMALLINT NameLength3     /* 16-bit input */
  );
```

Job: Get information about Privileges on routines.

Algorithm:

```
Produce a result set using this query:
SELECT
  ROUTINE_CATALOG AS routine_cat,    /* VARCHAR(128) */
  ROUTINE_SCHEMA AS routine_schem,   /* VARCHAR(128) NOT NULL */
  ROUTINE_NAME AS routine_name,      /* VARCHAR(128) NOT NULL */
  SPECIFIC_NAME AS specific_name,    /* VARCHAR(128) NOT NULL */
  GRANTOR AS GRANTOR,                /* VARCHAR(128) */
  GRANTEE AS GRANTEE,                /* VARCHAR(128) NOT NULL */
  PRIVILEGE_TYPE AS privilege,       /* VARCHAR(128) NOT NULL */
  IS_GRANTABLE AS IS_GRANTABLE       /* VARCHAR(3) */
FROM INFORMATION_SCHEMA.ROUTINE_PRIVILEGES
WHERE ROUTINE_CATALOG = ?
AND   ROUTINE_SCHEMA = ?
AND   ROUTINE_NAME = ?
ORDER BY routine_name,routine_cat,routine_schem;
... where the three ? parameter markers are replaced by the string values in,
respectively, the CatalogName and SchemaName and RoutineName parameters.
```

Notes:

- In SQL-92, there is no such thing as a routine. Therefore `SQLRoutinePrivileges` is supported only by SQL3 DBMSs.
- The value in the `RoutineName` parameter is matched against `ROUTINE_NAME`, not `SPECIFIC_NAME`.

Example:

```
#include "sqlcli.h"
SQLHSTMT hstmt;
...
/* any Catalog, any Schema, any name */
SQLRoutinePrivileges(hstmt,"",0,"",0,"",0);
...
/* Catalog A, any Schema, any name */
SQLRoutinePrivileges(hstmt,"A",1,"",0,"",0);
...
/* Catalog A,Schema B, any name */
SQLRoutinePrivileges(hstmt,"A",1,"B",1,"",0);
...
/* Catalog A,Schema B,name C */
SQLRoutinePrivileges(hstmt,"A",1,"B",1,"C",1);
```

ODBC: `SQLRoutinePrivileges` is not in ODBC 3.0.

SQLRoutines

Function Prototype:

```
SQLRETURN SQLRoutines(
  SQLHSTMT hstmt,                 /* 32-bit input */
  SQLCHAR *CatalogName,           /* pointer to CHAR* input */
  SQLSMALLINT NameLength1,        /* 16-bit input */
  SQLCHAR *SchemaName,            /* pointer to CHAR* input */
  SQLSMALLINT NameLength2,        /* 16-bit input */
  SQLCHAR *RoutineName,           /* pointer to CHAR* input */
  SQLSMALLINT NameLength3,        /* 16-bit input */
  SQLCHAR *RoutineType,           /* pointer to CHAR* input */
  SQLSMALLINT NameLength4         /* 16-bit input */
  );
```

Job: Retrieve information about functions and procedures.

Algorithm:

```
Produce a result set using this query:
SELECT
  ROUTINE_CATALOG AS routine_cat,    /* VARCHAR(128) */
  ROUTINE_SCHEMA AS routine_schem,   /* VARCHAR(128) NOT NULL */
  ROUTINE_NAME,                      /* VARCHAR(128) NOT NULL */
  SPECIFIC_NAME,                     /* VARCHAR(128) NOT NULL */
  ROUTINE_TYPE,                      /* VARCHAR(254) NOT NULL */
  DATA_TYPE,                         /* INTEGER */
  TYPE_NAME,                         /* VARCHAR(128) */
  PARAMETER_SIZE,                    /* INTEGER */
  DECIMAL_DIGITS,                    /* SMALLINT */
  NUM_PREC_RADIX,                    /* SMALLINT */
  SQL_DATA_TYPE,                     /* SMALLINT */
  SQL_DATETIME_SUB,                  /* SMALLINT */
  CHAR_OCTET_LENGTH,                 /* INTEGER */
  CHAR_SET_CAT,                      /* VARCHAR(128) */
  CHAR_SET_SCHEM,                    /* VARCHAR(128) */
  CHAR_SET_NAME,                     /* VARCHAR(128) */
  COLLATION_CATALOG AS collation_cat,/* VARCHAR(128) */
```

```
  COLLATION_SCHEMA AS collation_schem,/* VARCHAR(128) */
  COLLATION_NAME,                    /* VARCHAR(128) */
  UDT_CATALOG AS udt_cat,            /* VARCHAR(128) */
  UDT_SCHEMA AS udt_schem,           /* VARCHAR(128) */
  UDT_NAME,                          /* VARCHAR(254) */
  LANGUAGE,                          /* VARCHAR(128) */
  IS_DETERMINISTIC,                  /* VARCHAR(254) */
  SQL_DATA_ACCESS,                   /* VARCHAR(254) */
  MAX_DYNAMIC_RESULT_SETS,           /* INTEGER */
  REMARKS                            /* VARCHAR(254) */
FROM INFORMATION_SCHEMA.ROUTINES
WHERE ROUTINE_CATALOG = ?
AND   ROUTINE_SCHEMA = ?
AND   ROUTINE_NAME = ?
AND   ROUTINE_TYPE = ?
ORDER BY ROUTINE_NAME,routine_cat,routine_schem;
... where the three ? parameter markers stand for the values passed in the Cat-
alogName, SchemaName, RoutineName, and RoutineType parameters.
```

Notes:

- We have made liberal use of "<name>" as a shorthand in the select list in the algorithm. The meaning, in each case, is, "the input for this value, and the attendant calculations, are the same as for the Column of the same name in the result set of SQLColumns."
- REMARKS is implementation-defined.
- [Obscure Rule] There are three variants of SQLRoutines which are so different, they should be regarded as different functions. These variants are easily recognized by the arguments: one argument is always % and the others are always "" (blank strings). The variants always return result sets with five Columns.
  - The first variant is:

```
SQLRoutines(hstmt,"%",1,"",0,"",0,"",0);
```

This is effectively equivalent to:

```
SELECT DISTINCT ROUTINE_CATALOG AS routine_cat,
                CAST(NULL AS VARCHAR(128)),
                CAST(NULL AS VARCHAR(128)),
                CAST(NULL AS VARCHAR(254)),
                CAST(NULL AS VARCHAR(254))
FROM INFORMATION_SCHEMA.ROUTINES;
```

  - The second variant is:

```
SQLRoutines(hstmt,"",0,"%",1,"",0,"",0);
```

This is effectively equivalent to:

```
SELECT DISTINCT CAST(NULL AS VARCHAR(128)),
                ROUTINE_SCHEMA AS ROUTINE_SCHEM,
                CAST(NULL AS VARCHAR(128)),
                CAST(NULL AS VARCHAR(254)),
                CAST(NULL AS VARCHAR(254))
FROM INFORMATION_SCHEMA.ROUTINES;
```

- The third variant is:

```
SQLRoutines(hstmt,"",0,"",0,"",0,"%",1);
```

This is effectively equivalent to:

```
SELECT DISTINCT CAST(NULL AS VARCHAR(128)),
                CAST(NULL AS VARCHAR(128)),
                CAST(NULL AS VARCHAR(128)),
                ROUTINE_TYPE,
                CAST(NULL AS VARCHAR(254))
FROM INFORMATION_SCHEMA.ROUTINES;
```

Example:

```
#include "sqlcli.h"
SQLHSTMT hstmt;
...
SQLRoutines(hstmt,
    "CATALOG_1",sizeof("CATALOG_1"),
    "SCHEMA_1",sizeof("SCHEMA_1"),
    "ROUTINE_1",sizeof("ROUTINE_1"),
    "",0);
```

ODBC: `SQLRoutines` is not in ODBC 3.0.

SQLSpecialColumns

Function Prototype:

```
SQLRETURN SQLSpecialColumns(
  SQLHSTMT hstmt,               /* 32-bit input */
  SQLSMALLINT IdentifierType,   /* 16-bit input */
  SQLCHAR *CatalogName,         /* CHAR* input */
  SQLSMALLINT NameLength1,      /* 16-bit input */
  SQLCHAR *SchemaName,          /* CHAR* input */
```

```
  SQLSMALLINT NameLength2,        /* 16-bit input */
  SQLCHAR *TableName,             /* CHAR* input */
  SQLSMALLINT NameLength3,        /* 16-bit input */
  SQLSMALLINT Scope,              /* 16-bit input */
  SQLSMALLINT Nullable            /* 16-bit input */
  );
```

Job: Show the Columns that can be used for uniquely identifying a row in a given Table.

Algorithm:

```
If (IdentifierType <> SQL_BEST_ROWID)
  return error: HY097 CLI-specific condition-column type out of range
If (Scope not SCOPE_CURRENT_ROW or SCOPE_TRANSACTION or SCOPE_SESSION)
  return error: HY098 CLI-specific condition-scope type out of range
If (Nullable not SQL_NO_NULLS or NULLABLE)
  return error: HY099 CLI-specific condition-nullable type out of range
Produce a result set using this query:
SELECT
SCOPE,                          /* SMALLINT */
COLUMN_NAME,                    /* VARCHAR(128) NOT NULL */
... AS DATA_TYPE,               /* SMALLINT NOT NULL */
... AS TYPE_NAME,               /* VARCHAR(128) NOT NULL */
... AS COLUMN_SIZE,             /* INTEGER */
... AS BUFFER_LENGTH,           /* INTEGER */
... AS DECIMAL_DIGITS,          /* INTEGER */
... AS pseudocolumn             /* INTEGER */
FROM INFORMATION_SCHEMA.COLUMNS
WHERE <column "is special" i.e. "is the best rowid">
AND   scope = ?
AND   catalog_name = ?
AND   schema_name = ?
AND   table_name = ?
AND  NOT EXISTS <any nullable Column in the set of Columns>
ORDER BY SCOPE;
... where the four ? parameters are Scope, CatalogName, SchemaName, and Table-
Name, in that order.
```

Notes:

- We have used ... in the algorithm's select list as a shorthand. The meaning of this shorthand is that the same inputs and calculations should be used as were used in the lengthy `CASE` expressions for the `SQLColumns` function.
- Don't worry about the outré select list in the algorithm. The only thing that you really need is the <Column name> and the scope. All the rest can be found using straightforward selections from `INFORMATION_SCHEMA` Views.
- It's implementation-defined which Columns make the "best rowid" and have a particular "scope".
- The Special Column Type can be:
  - 1 `SQL_BEST_ROWID`
- The Scope of Row Id can be:
  - 0 `SQL_SCOPE_CURRENT_ROW` (valid while Cursor is positioned on that row — the ODBC name is `SQL_SCOPE_CURROW`)
  - 1 `SQL_SCOPE_TRANSACTION` (valid until transaction ends)
  - 2 `SQL_SCOPE_SESSION` (valid until SQL-session ends)
- How does the DBMS pick what Columns are special?
  - First choice: the "rowid."
  - Second choice: a single Column which is defined as `UNIQUE` or `PRIMARY KEY`.
  - Third choice: a combination of Columns which make up a `UNIQUE` or `PRIMARY KEY`.
  - Fourth choice: a "serial number" Column.
  - Fifth choice: a "timestamp" Column (the Sybase way).

  Columns lose points if nullable; gain points if short, numeric, constrained.
- What's a pseudo-column? Perhaps it's called the ROWID (Oracle), perhaps it's Ingres's TID. Sometimes a TIMESTAMP is also a pseudo-column but that's not relevant here. For purposes of illustration, we have had to pretend that pseudo-columns exist in the `COLUMNS` View.
- The Pseudo Column Flag can be:
  - 0 `SQL_PSEUDO_UNKNOWN`
  - 1 `SQL_PSEUDO_NOT_PSEUDO`
  - 2 `SQL_PSEUDO_PSEUDO`
- Many DBMSs support "rowid" as a unique identifier. The rowid is often directly translatable to a physical address in the Table's underlying file, so searches by rowid tend to be fast. Some disadvantages of rowid — addresses can change; format differs between DBMSs.
- What good is the `SQLSpecialColumns` function? Assume there's a Table that you're navigating one screenload at a time. You want to allow the user to edit each row or even delete it. But you don't want to lock all the rows in the result set. By finding and storing the Column values that constitute the unique identifiers of the result set rows, you can do these things with separate selections. The big problem is concurrency. If you want to do your own multi-user scheming, this is the function for you.
- Our description ignores some obvious and minor errors in the SQL Standard.

- If speed is not a major concern and portability is a major concern, do not use SQLSpecialColumns with its heavily implementation-dependent assumptions. Instead, find out what the unique key Columns are by searching the INFORMATION_SCHEMA.KEY_COLUMN_USAGE View.
- It is often a bad idea to pass SQL_NO_NULLS in the Nullable parameter. By insisting that nullable Columns are unacceptable, you are interfering with the DBMS's algorithm for choosing the "best" rowid.
- There might be no rows returned. But if you define every Table with a primary or unique key, SQLSpecialColumns can't fail.
- Because calculation happens à la SQLColumns, the COLUMN_SIZE for BIT and BIT VARYING <data type>s is a length in bits.

Example:

```
#include "sqlcli.h"
SQLHSTMT hstmt;
...
SQLSpecialColumns(
    hstmt,                          /* hstmt */
    SQL_BEST_ROWID,                 /* IdentifierType */
    "OCELOT",sizeof("OCELOT"),      /* CatalogName,NameLength1 */
    "OCELOT",sizeof("OCELOT"),      /* SchemaName,NameLength2 */
    "T",sizeof("T"),                /* TableName,NameLength3 */
    SQL_SCOPE_TRANSACTION,          /* Scope */
    SQL_PSEUDO_UNKNOWN);            /* Nullable */
```

ODBC: The SQLSpecialColumns function has been in ODBC since version 1.0. Perhaps because it depends on non-standard features, SQLSpecialColumns wasn't in the SQL-92 CLI (but was in X/Open). Besides the "best rowid" option, one can ask about Columns which are automatically changed whenever there is an update (e.g., Sybase's TIMESTAMP Column).

SQLTablePrivileges

Function Prototype:

```
SQLRETURN SQLTablePrivileges(
  SQLHSTMT      hstmt,            /* 32-bit input */
  SQLCHAR       *CatalogName,     /* CHAR* input */
  SQLSMALLINT   NameLength1,      /* 16-bit input */
  SQLCHAR       *SchemaName,      /* CHAR* input */
  SQLSMALLINT   NameLength2,      /* 16-bit input */
  SQLCHAR       *TableName,       /* CHAR* input */
  SQLSMALLINT   NameLength3       /* 16-bit input */
  );
```

Job: Show what Privileges the user holds, given <Table name>(s).

Algorithm:

```
Produce a result set using this query:
SELECT
  TABLE_CATALOG AS table_cat,    /* VARCHAR(128) */
  TABLE_SCHEMA AS  table_schem,  /* VARCHAR(128) NOT NULL */
  TABLE_NAME,                    /* VARCHAR(128) NOT NULL */
  GRANTOR,                       /* VARCHAR(128) */
  GRANTEE,                       /* VARCHAR(128) NOT NULL */
  PRIVILEGE_TYPE AS privilege,   /* VARCHAR(128) NOT NULL */
  IS_GRANTABLE                   /* VARCHAR(3) */
FROM INFORMATION_SCHEMA.TABLE_PRIVILEGES
WHERE
  CATALOG_NAME LIKE ?
  AND SCHEMA_NAME LIKE ?
  AND TABLE_NAME LIKE ?
ORDER BY table_cat,table_schem,TABLE_NAME,privilege;
... where the three ? parameters are CatalogName, SchemaName, TableName, in
that order.
```

Notes:

- The algorithm's SELECT statement does not reflect some minor matters. See "Some Necessary Preliminaries" on page 964.
- If you lack the UPDATE Privilege on a Table T, that does not prove that this SQL statement:

```
UPDATE T SET column_1 = 5;
```

is illegal for you. You might have a Column UPDATE Privilege on column_1 only (Column Privileges are discovered by calling SQLColumnPrivileges or selecting from INFORMATION_SCHEMA.COLUMN_PRIVILEGES). You might hold a Role or an implementation-defined "super user" Privilege. So the only guaranteed proof is — try it and see.

```
x=SQLExecDirect(hstmt,"UPDATE T SET column_1=5 WHERE 1=2", SQL_NTS);
if (x<0) {
  SQLGetDiagField(...<sqlstate>)
  if ('42000')
    /* UPDATE failed. SQLSTATE='42000' access/syntax error.
       Most likely the problem is that you lack Privileges. */
  else
    /* UPDATE failed but for some other reason. Test is no good. */ }
else {
  /* UPDATE succeeded, so you have the right Privileges. */  }
```

The key for this tip is to use an always-FALSE condition in the WHERE clause — do not try setting the Column to itself and do not depend on ROLLBACK.

Example:

```
/* This shows every Table you have Privileges on. */
#include "sqlcli.h"
...
SQLTablePrivileges(hstmt,"",0,"",0,"",0);
...
```

ODBC: The SQLTablePrivileges function has been around since ODBC version 1.0.

SQLTables

Function Prototype:

```
                                 /* not in SQL-92, but in SQL3 */
SQLRETURN SQLTables(
  SQLHSTMT hstmt,                /* 32-bit input */
  SQLCHAR *CatalogName,          /* CHAR* input */
  SQLSMALLINT NameLength1,       /* 16-bit input */
  SQLCHAR *SchemaName,           /* CHAR* input */
  SQLSMALLINT NameLength2,       /* 16-bit input */
  SQLCHAR *TableName,            /* CHAR* input */
  SQLSMALLINT NameLength3,       /* 16-bit input */
  SQLCHAR *TableType,            /* CHAR* input */
  SQLSMALLINT NameLength4        /* 16-bit input */
  );
```

Job: Show information about specified Table(s).

Algorithm:

```
For a moment let us ignore the *TableType parameter. Now, the SQLTables func-
tion is effectively the same as this query:
SELECT
  TABLE_CATALOG AS table_cat,          /* VARCHAR(128) */
  TABLE_SCHEMA AS table_schem,         /* VARCHAR(128) */
  TABLE_NAME,                          /* VARCHAR(128) */
  CASE TABLE_TYPE
    WHEN 'VIEW' THEN
      CASE TABLE_SCHEMA
        WHEN 'INFORMATION_SCHEMA' THEN
          'SYSTEM TABLE'
        ELSE
          'VIEW'
        END
    WHEN 'BASE TABLE' THEN
      'TABLE'
    ELSE
      TABLE_TYPE
    END
    AS TABLE_TYPE,                         /* VARCHAR(254) */
  CAST('' AS VARCHAR(254)) AS remarks      /* VARCHAR(254) */
FROM INFORMATION_SCHEMA.TABLES
WHERE TABLE_CATALOG = ?
AND   TABLE_SCHEMA = ?
AND   TABLE_NAME = ?;
... where the three ? parameters are filled in by CatalogName, SchemaName, and
TableName in that order — but see notes regarding TABLE_TYPE.
```

Notes:

- The `*TableType` parameter is a wrinkle which is hard to show in an SQL statement but it's reasonably straightforward. The idea is that there are five general categories of Tables: the `INFORMATION_SCHEMA` Views (`'SYSTEM TABLE'`), all other Views (`'VIEW'`), ordinary Base tables (`'TABLE'`), and the two kinds of temporary Tables (`'GLOBAL TEMPORARY'` or `'LOCAL TEMPORARY'`). To restrict to the categories you want, pass a commalist in `*TableType` — for example, `'SYSTEM TABLE','VIEW'`. Or pass `SYSTEM TABLE,VIEW` (the quote marks are optional). Or pass nothing (if you pass a blank string, the DBMS returns Tables in all categories).

- The algorithm's SELECT statement does not reflect some minor matters. See "Some Necessary Preliminaries" on page 964.
- The REMARKS Column is supposed to contain an implementation-defined description of the Table. For IBM's DB2, this would be the value that you enter with a COMMENT statement.
- Many Windows applications have a "File" menu item and within that an "Open..." menu item, for putting a dialog box on the screen. Your database application doesn't have files — it has Tables — but the dialog box should look similar.
- SQLTables was not available in SQL-92; it is new to SQL with SQL3.
- [Obscure Rule] There are three variants of SQLTables which are so different, they should be regarded as different functions. These variants are easily recognized by the arguments: one argument is always % and the others are always "" (blank strings). The variants always return result sets with five Columns.
  - The first variant is:

```
SQLTables(hstmt,"%",1,"",0,"",0,"",0);
```

This is effectively equivalent to:

```
SELECT DISTINCT TABLE_CATALOG AS table_cat,
                CAST(NULL AS VARCHAR(128)),
                CAST(NULL AS VARCHAR(128)),
                CAST(NULL AS VARCHAR(254)),
                CAST(NULL AS VARCHAR(254))
FROM INFORMATION_SCHEMA.TABLES;
```

  - The second variant is:

```
SQLTables(hstmt,"",0,"%",1,"",0,"",0);
```

This is effectively equivalent to:

```
SELECT DISTINCT CAST(NULL AS VARCHAR(128)),
                TABLE_SCHEMA AS table_schem,
                CAST(NULL AS VARCHAR(128)),
                CAST(NULL AS VARCHAR(254)),
                CAST(NULL AS VARCHAR(254))
FROM INFORMATION_SCHEMA.TABLES;
```

  - The third variant is:

```
SQLTables(hstmt,"",0,"",0,"",0,"%",1);
```

This is effectively equivalent to:

```
SELECT DISTINCT CAST(NULL AS VARCHAR(128)),
                CAST(NULL AS VARCHAR(128)),
                CAST(NULL AS VARCHAR(128)),
                CASE TABLE_TYPE
```

```
            WHEN 'VIEW' THEN
              CASE TABLE_SCHEMA
              WHEN 'INFORMATION_SCHEMA' THEN
                 'SYSTEM TABLE'
               ELSE 'VIEW'
               END
              WHEN 'BASE TABLE' THEN 'TABLE'
              ELSE TABLE_TYPE
              END
          AS TABLE_TYPE,
         CAST(NULL AS VARCHAR(254))
FROM INFORMATION_SCHEMA.TABLES;
```

There are no Privilege checks; with variant SQLTables functions, you can find Tables that you have no Privileges on. Compare the variant SQLRoutines functions.

Example:

```
#include "sqlcli.h"
SQLHSTMT hstmt;
...
/* In CATALOG_1, in SCHEMA_1, find Table T, which may be either a Base
   table or a View. */
SQLTables(
  hstmt,"CATALOG_1",SQL_NTS,"SCHEMA_1",SQL_NTS,"T",SQL_NTS, "",SQL_NTS);
/* The following example is derived from an example supplied by Microsoft for
   SQL Server 6.0. Notice these subtleties:
   (a) the catalog and schema parameters are passed with NULL,0 -- passing
   NULL,0 is legal only if METADATA is FALSE, if METADATA were TRUE the
   parameters would have to be passed as "",0
   (b) "q%" is a search pattern i.e. we are looking for <Table name>s which
   begin with the letter q -- again, this is only legal if METADATA ID is
   FALSE
   (c) the search should be case sensitive (Microsoft suggests the opposite, so
   some caution is necessary here)
   (d) the search will only find Base tables -- not Views. */
SQLTables(hstmt,NULL,0,NULL,0,TEXT("q%"),SQL_NTS,
TEXT("'TABLE'"),SQL_NTS);
```

ODBC: The SQLTables function has been around since ODBC version 1.0. In ODBC, the result set is guaranteed to be in order by table_cat, table_schem, TABLE_NAME ... — this order is not specified in the Standard but it will probably be the case.

The End

The description of SQL/CLI is — at long last — finished. Here's a summary of some of the good and the bad and the ugly points that we've talked about in the past several chapters:

- The impedance-mismatch problem is solved. It's considerably easier, for the vendor especially, to supply a library of functions rather than to allow mixing of host language code with SQL code. Because most programmers are well acquainted with the concept of a function library, there are no strong objections to the practice.
- The CLI's functionality is analogous to that of "dynamic SQL" in the embedded SQL specification. The absence of "static SQL" does entail that there will have to be some parsing and binding at runtime which, in theory, could have been done once and for all when the program was produced.
- A considerable debt is owed by the programming community to SAG, X/Open, and Microsoft. Before the CLI came along, SQL was a much smaller deal. The use of the CLI has opened up the power of database programming to a much wider audience than the embedded SQL and PSM styles were ever likely to produce. Particularly, this is true for shrink-wrapped software.
- The CLI contains many redundancies.
- The CLI specifications often appear to be influenced by ideas which run counter to the general spirit of SQL.
- The CLI is much more complex than it would have been if a single design team had started with standard SQL-92 as a base.

52

Chapter 52

Module Binding Style

SQL DBMSs communicate with SQL applications through a common programming language interface that is invoked through one of the SQL Standard-defined binding styles, or interface options. There are three main approaches to writing complete programs with SQL:

1. With embedded SQL, you can put SQL statements directly into host programs. We described this binding style in Chapter 39.
2. With SQL/CLI, you can call an SQL DBMS's library from a host program. This binding style was the subject of the last twelve chapters.
3. With the Module language, you can dispense with host programs and write entire Modules in SQL. You'll still have to call these Modules from one of the standard host languages though. The Module language binding style is the subject of this chapter.

Because we believe that SQL/CLI will quickly become the SQL interface of choice, this chapter omits large amounts of detail, in favour of providing the necessary detail in our chapters on SQL/CLI.

NOTE: The SQL Standard actually describes three kinds of SQL Module, each of which has certain characteristics and contains various kinds of Module Objects (principally, routines). An SQL-client Module contains only externally-invoked procedures, an SQL-session Module contains only SQL statements prepared in that SQL-session, and an SQL-server Module — the SQL/PSM type — is a Schema Object that contains only SQL-invoked routines.

SQL-client Modules

SQL-client Modules are programming modules that contain externally-invoked procedures — that is, SQL procedures that are invoked by a host language. Generally speaking, this methodology is really the basic SQL binding style; all of the binding styles — direct SQL, embedded SQL, CLI, or SQL-client Modules — at least conceptually, involve a program module. Before SQL/PSM came on the scene, SQL "module language" was the only way to identify SQL Modules. But now, with the advent of SQL/PSM and (far better) of SQL/CLI, we believe this method of utilizing SQL will rapidly become obsolete and so we give only a brief description here.

An SQL-client Module is an Object — a programming module — that you define with SQL's module language; a subset of SQL that allows you to write database routines in pure SQL. It contains SQL statements that will operate on your SQL-data and you link it (in some implementation-defined way) with modules of code in one or more of the Standard's host languages. The database routines are called *externally-invoked procedures* because they are invoked by the host language program to which you link the Module to which they belong.

MODULE Statement

The MODULE statement defines an SQL-client Module. The required syntax for the MODULE statement is as follows.

```
<SQL-client Module definition> ::=
MODULE [ <SQL-client Module name> ]
[ NAMES ARE <Character set name> ]
  LANGUAGE {ADA | C |COBOL | FORTRAN | MUMPS | PASCAL | PLI | SQL}
  <Module authorization clause>
  [ PATH <Schema name> {,<Schema name>}... ]
  [ TRANSFORM GROUP {<group name> |
    {<group name> FOR TYPE <UDT name>} , ...} ]
  [ DECLARE TABLE statement(s) ]
  <Module contents>...

      <Module authorization clause> ::=
      SCHEMA <Schema name> |
      AUTHORIZATION <AuthorizationID> |
      SCHEMA <Schema name> AUTHORIZATION <AuthorizationID>

      <Module contents> ::=
      DECLARE CURSOR statement(s) |
      PROCEDURE statement(s)
```

An SQL-client Module doesn't have to be named (unless the Module's LANGUAGE clause specifies ADA, in which case you must give the Module a valid Ada library unit name); your SQL-environment can contain multiple unnamed SQL-client Modules. If you do name an

SQL-client Module, though, you must give it a unique name (for all SQL-client Modules) in your SQL-environment. An <SQL-client Module name> is a <regular identifier> or a <delimited identifier>.

The optional NAMES ARE clause provides the name of the Module's default Character set — the Character set that your DBMS will use for any character strings in the Module that don't include an explicit Character set specification. If you omit this clause, the Module's default Character set is chosen by your DBMS and must contain at least every <SQL language character>.

The LANGUAGE clause provides the name of the host language that will invoke the routines this Module contains.

The Module authorization clause provides either the Module's default Schema, the Module's <AuthorizationID>, or both (at least one must be included).

- SCHEMA <Schema name> provides an explicit <Schema name> — this will be the default <Schema name> qualifier for any Objects referred to in the Module without explicit qualifiers. If you omit this clause, the default <Schema name> defaults to the value in the AUTHORIZATION clause.
- AUTHORIZATION <AuthorizationID> provides an explicit <AuthorizationID> to be the owner of the Module — this will be the <AuthorizationID> whose Privileges will be checked when the Module's SQL statements are executed. If you omit this clause, your DBMS will treat the SQL-session <AuthorizationID> as the Module's owner at runtime.

The optional PATH clause provides a list of <Schema name>s that will be used as the Module's default path — that is, the qualifying <Schema name>s that will be used for any unqualified <Routine name>s in this Module. You can name zero or more Schemas in this clause (your DBMS will pick the one that matches the unqualified routine best at runtime); each Schema in the list must belong to the same Catalog to which this Module's default Schema belongs. If you omit this clause, it will default to a list of Schemas, containing at least this Module's default Schema, chosen by your DBMS.

The optional TRANSFORM GROUP clause provides a <group name> for each UDT parameter that has no locator; see Chapter 27 "User-Defined Types."

You can declare zero or more temporary Tables for the Module. Each will be visible only to the Module you declare them in.

The <Module contents> clause is the meat of the Module — it contains the SQL statements that do the work you need done on your SQL-data. You can declare zero or more Cursors here (see Chapter 39 on embedded SQL), as well as one or more externally-invoked procedures (with the PROCEDURE statement, see the following section).

If you want to restrict your code to Core SQL, don't use the NAMES ARE clause, the PATH clause, the TRANSFORM GROUP clause, or any DECLARE TABLE statements in a MODULE statement.

PROCEDURE Statement

The PROCEDURE statement defines an externally-invoked procedure. The required syntax for the PROCEDURE statement is as follows.

```
PROCEDURE <procedure name>
{(<host parameter declaration> [ {, <host param dec>}... ] ) |
<host parameter declaration>...};
SQL procedure statement;

    <host parameter declaration> ::=
    :<host parameter name> <data type> [ AS LOCATOR ] |
    SQLSTATE
```

An externally-invoked procedure is an SQL procedure that is called from a host language program. It belongs to an SQL-client Module and must have a <procedure name> that is unique (for all procedures) within that Module. A <procedure name> is a <regular identifier> or a <delimited identifier> and should conform to the host language you'll be calling it from.

Each procedure has to contain a list of one or more parameter declarations, terminated with a semicolon — SQLSTATE is always mandatory. Your list should be enclosed in parentheses, with each parameter declaration separated from the next by a comma (though our syntax diagram shows that both the parentheses and the commas are currently optional, this is a deprecated feature in the Standard, so avoid it). Other than SQLSTATE, each parameter has a name (preceded by a colon), a <data type> and — if it is a BLOB, CLOB, NCLOB, UDT, or ARRAY — an optional AS LOCATOR indicator. A call of an externally-invoked procedure has to supply the same number of arguments as the parameter declarations in the procedure.

Each procedure has to contain exactly one SQL procedure statement terminated with a semicolon. This is the SQL statement that gets executed when the procedure is called. An SQL procedure statement is any executable SQL statement — this includes all the SQL-Schema statements, the SQL-data statements, the SQL-control statements, the SQL-transaction statements, the SQL-Connection statements, the SQL-session statements, and the SQL diagnostics statement.

If you are calling the procedure from:

Ada — use only these <data type>s in your <host parameter declaration>s: CHARACTER, BIT, SMALLINT, INTEGER, REAL, DOUBLE PRECISION; declare SQLSTATE's base type as SQL_STANDARD.SQLSTATE_TYPE; and identify the procedure by its <procedure name>, as if it was declared within an Ada library unit specification that has a name equal to the name of the SQL-client Module that contains the procedure.

C — use only these <data type>s in your <host parameter declaration>s: CHARACTER, CHARACTER VARYING, BIT, INTEGER, SMALLINT, REAL, DOUBLE PRECISION; and declare SQLSTATE as a C char with length 6.

COBOL — use only these <data type>s in your <host parameter declaration>s: CHARACTER, BIT, NUMERIC, INTEGER, SMALLINT; and declare SQLSTATE as a COBOL PICTURE X(5).

Fortran — use only these <data type>s in your <host parameter declaration>s: CHARACTER, BIT, INTEGER, REAL, DOUBLE PRECISION; and declare SQLSTATE as a Fortran CHARACTER with length 5.

MUMPS — use only these <data type>s in your <host parameter declaration>s: CHARACTER VARYING, INTEGER, DECIMAL, REAL; and declare SQLSTATE as a MUMPS character with maximum length greater than or equal to 5.

Pascal — use only these <data type>s in your <host parameter declaration>s: CHARACTER, BIT, INTEGER, REAL; and declare SQLSTATE as a Pascal PACKED ARRAY [1..5] OF CHAR.

PL/I — use only these <data type>s in your <host parameter declaration>s: CHARACTER, CHARACTER VARYING, BIT, BIT VARYING, DECIMAL, INTEGER, SMALLINT, FLOAT; and declare SQLSTATE as a PL/I CHARACTER(5).

For a list of the correspondences between SQL <data type>s and host data types, see "Host Variables" on page 719 in Chapter 39 on embedded SQL.

Here's an example of an SQL-client Module:

```
MODULE module_1
    NAMES ARE ASCII_FULL
    LANGUAGE C
    SCHEMA catalog_1.schema_1 AUTHORIZATION bob
    DECLARE LOCAL TEMPORARY TABLE Table_1 (
       COLUMN_1 INTEGER, COLUMN_2 CHARACTER VARYING(25))
       ON COMMIT DELETE ROWS;
    PROCEDURE proc_1 (
       :var_1 INTEGER, :var_2 CHARACTER VARYING(25));
       INSERT INTO Table_1 (column_1, column_2)
          VALUES (:var_1, :var_2);
    PROCEDURE proc_2 (
       :var_1 INTEGER);
       UPDATE Table_2 SET
          column_3 = column_3*:var_1 WHERE column_3 IN
            (SELECT column_1 FROM Table_1);
```

53

Chapter 53

Style

Here is one SQL operation, written in two contrasting styles. Notice the different names, spacing, indentation, and choice of optional keywords:

[CASUAL]

```
SELECT * FROM T WHERE C1>5 ORDER BY 1 ASC;
```

[FORMAL]

```
SELECT   package_id, special_handling_code, buy_date
FROM     Packages
WHERE    package_id > 1.0
ORDER BY package_id;
```

Casual style is better for notes, examples, blackboard discussions, and prototypes. We use it in this book whenever we enclose an SQL statement in an illustrative sentence, as when we say that `SELECT * FROM T WHERE C1>5 ORDER BY 1 ASC` is an example of casual style. We don't wear suits on beaches and we believe that casual style is appropriate for our purposes. On the other hand, a serious program demands some formality. There is one good reason and one bad reason.

- Appearance — Okay, this is the bad reason. Formal style persuades others, perhaps even yourself, that you used some sort of organization and design.

- Coherence — You can read statements more easily if you know in advance the shape, order, and vocabulary. More time is spent "reading" code than "writing" it, so you will save time by investing time at the start.

Besides, maybe you do wear suits on beaches.

A True Story

There once was a clever DBMS named O_____ (tm). The people who program O_____ were mulling in their tall building in Redwood Shores, CA one day. "Sometimes we have to run the same SQL statements twice," they mulled. "So why should we parse the same statement again when we already know what the Access Plan is from the first time we ran it?" And they came up with a clever plan. They put the first SQL statement in a cache! Then, when the second SQL statement came along, they had a clever way of telling that it was really something they'd done before (maybe with a parameter or two different but that doesn't affect the story). And they just re-used the same Access Plan and saved oodles of time. They even used this clever plan for Views — which was great. Except that their way of comparing the new SQL statement with the cached SQL statement was, well, simple. What they did was: they compared every byte in the cached statement with every byte in the new statement. That's it. No lower-to-upper conversions, no lead-space trimming, nothing but a `REP CMPSB` (that's `strcmp` to you C fans).

What happened next? Well, in all the good-doobie programming shops, where everybody wrote every detail according to the same style rules ... why, the programs ran faster. But in all the other programming shops, where freedom and creativity ruled, nothing happened.

The moral of the story: choose a common style, then *stick to your style*.

Authority

To get the rules of good SQL style for you, we culled them from actual rules of large programmer shops or by just looking at what rules are implicit in code written by experts (for example, the sample code in vendors' manuals). Where we had to note inconsistencies — and there are several — we've made no attempt to clean them up. Where we are aware of minority views, we've reported them. And where we saw opportunities to improve things by adding some new reasonable rule, we didn't — on the grounds that anything which is really reasonable would already be common practice.

Having said that we are following common practice, we must also say that no single person or organization actually obeys all these prescriptions. About half of the world's database programmers obey about half of the style rules, sometimes.

We've organized the style rules into two general classes: layout rules and naming rules. Within the classes, the rules are in no particular order. The numbers are arbitrary.

Layout Rules

1. Capitals

Write SQL <keyword>s in uppercase. Write <Table name>s with an initial capital, small letters after that; when a <Table name> has two parts, use an initial capital for each part. Write <Column name>s in lowercase. For example:

```
CREATE TABLE Widgets (
    width SMALLINT);
UPDATE Temporary_Personnel SET
    discharge_date = CURRENT_DATE;
```

Names of other, non-Column Objects should also have an initial capital. For example:

```
GRANT UPDATE
    ON Widgets
    TO Sandra, Maria;
```

Exception: If a name is an acronym — e.g., NATO or SQL or NIST — use all capital letters.

Alternative: Some write everything in lowercase — it's easier to remember. And we've seen examples written entirely in uppercase — but not recent examples. You should remember that <regular identifiers> are stored in uppercase, but it's been a long time since any DBMS insisted that Object names must be entered in uppercase in the first place.

2. Spaces

Put a single space after every SQL <token> — that is, after every <keyword> and after <identifier>s and after operators such as * or + or =. For example:

```
SELECT width * 5 ...
```

Exception: There need be no spaces after scalar or set function names or within parentheses. For example:

```
SELECT MAX(width) ...
```

Exception: There should be no space before comma (,) or semicolon (;). There should, however, be a space after the comma. For example:

```
SELECT width, length ...
... DECIMAL (7, 2) ...
```

Exception: There should be no space at the end of a line.

Exception: In a qualified name, there should be no space before or after the period (.).

Alternative: Some would omit spaces around comparison operators or arithmetic operators. For example:

```
... (a=b) OR (b=c) ...
```

3. Line Breaks

[Skip this rule if you use SQL/CLI or direct SQL]

There are alternate rules for "when to switch to a new line," usually called "breaking." The common rule is to break on every clause-start <keyword>. In a SELECT statement, the clause-start <keyword>s are: SELECT itself, FROM, ON, WHERE, GROUP, HAVING, ORDER; the Boolean operators AND / OR are usually considered to be equivalent to clause-start <keyword>s. Additionally, some prescribe a break after every full expression. For example:

```
SELECT    width,
          length+5
          FROM  Widgets,
                Foobars
          WHERE width > 5
          AND   length >= 5
          ORDER BY  width;
```

Others will place multiple items on a line if there aren't too many to fit. For example:

```
SELECT    width, length + 5
FROM      Widgets, Foobars
WHERE     width > 5
AND       length >= 5
ORDER BY width;
```

Notice the indentation at the start of each line — or lack thereof! It is rare to find, say, a SELECT statement starting on Column #1 but all subsequent clauses starting on Column #3. In any case, to accomplish the lined-up effect, one uses spaces rather than tab characters. The indentation seen in the above SELECT statements is to Column position 10 to accommodate ORDER BY; with non-SELECT statements indent is random.

Exception: One group prefers to right-justify the main <keyword>s. For example:

```
SELECT width,  length + 5
    FROM Widgets, Foobars
          WHERE width > 5
          AND length >= 5
          ORDER BY width;
```

There is a universal rule in all languages — if it's nested, indent. So further indentation will be necessary for subqueries. For example:

```
SELECT width, length, width + 10
       FROM  Widgets
       WHERE width <> 7
       AND   length =
          (SELECT expression
                  FROM t);
```

Notice the position of the `(` preceding the word `SELECT`.

Alternative: Put the `(` at the end of the previous line. However, placing a closing `)` on the same line as the end of the statement is normal — even though this differs from the way many C programmers use `{}` braces and differs from the way many Pascal programmers write begin ... end blocks.

Alternative: Put the initial <keyword> of a major clause on a line of its own, as is done with `WHERE` and `AND` in this example:

```
SELECT  length
  FROM  widgets
  WHERE
     (rowid = 5)
     AND
     (specialty = 'FUN');
```

Note also the different indentation of the conditional clauses.

Alternative: Put `OR`ed conditions on the same line but break for `AND`. For example:

```
SELECT   length
  FROM   widgets
  WHERE  (rowid = 5 OR rowid = 6 OR rowid = 7)
     AND  width > 1;
```

Alternative: Add line breaks for each level of a nested function. For example:

```
SELECT SUBSTRING(
   UPPER(title)
   FROM 1 TO 5)
   FROM Books;
```

Make a new line for `UNION`. Treat `AND NOT` as a single operator.

3a. Continuation Lines

When room is unavailable on a line, break if possible at a comma or equal sign or other operator <keyword>. If there are too many <Column name>s to fit in one line, break thus:

```
SELECT Column_1, Column_2, Column_3, Column_4, Column_5,
       Column_6, Column_7, Column_8, Column_9, Column_10 ...
```

Alternative: There is a minority view that commas should be shifted. For example:

```
SELECT Column_1, Column_2, Column_3, Column_4, Column_5
      ,Column_6, Column_7, Column_8, Column_9, Column_10 ...
```

3b. Indenting CREATEs

In a CREATE TABLE statement, every new Column goes on a new line. When it helps, you may indent so that each part of the <Column definition> is at the same position on the line — but nobody does that all the time. Here's an example:

```
CREATE TABLE Transactions
   (transactionid  INTEGER        NOT NULL,
    amount         DECIMAL(7, 2),
    partid         INTEGER,
    comments       VARCHAR(3000));
```

Usually CREATE TABLE statements will also have Constraint clauses. We have split them out here, adding the Constraints in later ALTER TABLE statements. Constraints are, in fact, separate from Tables but if you find that splitting up the Table definition into separate statements is unacceptable, you're not alone. The other part of this illustration shows our preference for giving names to everything, including Constraints — see Rule 16. Here's an example:

```
ALTER Table Transactions
ADD CONSTRAINT transaction_primary_key
PRIMARY KEY (transactionid);

ALTER Table Transactions
ADD CONSTRAINT transaction_references_inventory
FOREIGN KEY partid REFERENCES Inventory(partid)
ON UPDATE CASCADE
ON DELETE CASCADE;
```

3c. Indenting INSERTs

Here is an INSERT statement formed according to the same rules as discussed. Notice that the SELECT in the example is not indented like a subquery would be.

```
INSERT  INTO Recreation_players
        (playerno, name, town, phoneno)
SELECT  playerno, name, town, phoneno
FROM    Players
WHERE   leagueno IS NULL;
```

For streams of INSERT statements, one relaxes the rules to squeeze to one line. For example:

```
INSERT INTO Personnel VALUES (1, 2, 3, 'Maximum');
INSERT INTO Personnel VALUES (7, 4, 166, 'Minimum');
INSERT INTO Personnel VALUES (15, -6, 0, NULL);
```

It might appear nice to line up the values in this example, but that's not what people do.

3d. Indenting UPDATEs

If we apply the rules consistently, then an UPDATE statement should look like this:

```
UPDATE Contacts
SET    first_grade = 'A', second_grade = 'B', third_grade = 'C';
```

Alternative: The more common style is to break for each assignment. For example:

```
UPDATE Contacts
SET    first_grade = 'A',
       second_grade = 'B',
       third_grade = 'C';
```

4. Statement End

End statements with a semicolon without a preceding space. For example:

```
COMMIT;
```

Exception: Where the semicolon is inappropriate, omit it (for example, in COBOL shops or where the vendor won't accept it).

5. Comments

A simple comment begins with a double minus sign (--) and ends at the next line. Unfortunately, if an SQL statement comes from keyboard input, then the dialog manager will strip the line breaks. And, OSs disagree whether a line break is one character (LF) or two (CR+LF).

Because of the danger that presents to the parser, many eschew all comments in the SQL statement and put them in the host language code. For example:

```
/* Here is a C comment preceding an embedded SQL statement */
        EXEC SQL
        SELECT width, length
        FROM   Widgets;
/* Here is a C comment following an embedded SQL statement */
```

The problem disappears if your DBMS supports SQL3, which allows C-like comments — i.e., comments that begin with /* and end with */. Although C-like comments are far from universal, they are the preferred style among Microsoft SQL Server users. Occasionally, they are even used for section headings, thus:

```
/***********************************
    The Table creations
    ***********************************/
    CREATE Table ...
    CREATE Table ...
/***********************************
    The procedure definitions
    ***********************************/
    CREATE PROCEDURE ...
    CREATE PROCEDURE ...
```

Speaking of comments, Weinberg (The Psychology of Computer Programming) suggested that code and comments should be written in separate columns. This would make it easier to focus on the code when debugging (if a program has bugs then the comments are probably lies).

6. Qualifiers

When an SQL statement contains references to more than one Table, use <Column reference>s rather than <Column name>s. This is particularly true for joins. For example:

```
SELECT Widgets.length, Foobars.width
FROM   Widgets, Foobars
WHERE  Widgets.length = Foobars.width;
```

Not only does the qualification of a <Column reference> help the reader see which Table a Column belongs to, it guards against later breakage of the code (if, for instance, a new Column named `width` is someday added to `Widgets`). Sometimes the qualification may have to include Schema and <Catalog name>s too. If qualification starts to get at all lengthy, use <Correlation name>s.

7. Shorthands

7a. Shorthands for Lists

Do not use "SELECT * ..." to mean "SELECT all Columns ...". List the Columns you want by name. For example:

```
SELECT length, width
FROM   Widgets;
```

Exception: In the set function COUNT(*), the asterisk is necessary and in "EXISTS (SELECT * ..." the asterisk is preferred.

Do not use an INSERT statement without a Column list. List the Columns you want by name. For example:

```
INSERT INTO Widgets
    (length, width)
  VALUES (1, 2);
```

Exception: Streams of INSERT statements contain no Column list, see rule 3c.

Do not use GRANT ALL PRIVILEGES or REVOKE ALL PRIVILEGES for a Privilege list. List the Privileges you want by name. For example:

```
GRANT SELECT, UPDATE
ON TABLE Widgets
TO Sandra, Joan;
```

7b. Shorthands for Expressions

Usually, expression shorthands involve learning new syntax. For example, COALESCE(a,b) is short for CASE WHEN a IS NOT NULL THEN a ELSE b END. But we'd guess that some people would have to look up COALESCE to find out what it means. On the other hand, they might be able to puzzle out the longer CASE expression because they've seen similar constructs in most other computer languages. The consensus seems to be to use the longer expression, rather than the shorthand — unless the shorthand itself is a common and well-understood construct.

8. Short Forms

For <data type>s, use short forms — CHAR rather than CHARACTER, VARCHAR rather than CHARACTER VARYING, INT rather than INTEGER, BLOB rather than BINARY LARGE OBJECT.

Speaking of shortness — though this has nothing to do with Rule 8 — a too-long name is Parts_Which_Have_No_Serial_Numbers.

9. Redundancy

9a. Noise <keyword>s

Where a <keyword> is optional and eliminating it would cause no change in meaning, eliminate it. One example:

```
GRANT UPDATE, INSERT
ON    Widgets ...
```

instead of:

```
GRANT UPDATE, INSERT
ON TABLE Widgets ...
```

Another example:

```
SELECT   width
FROM     Widgets
ORDER BY width;
```

instead of:

```
SELECT   width
FROM     Widgets
ORDER BY width ASC;
```

Another example:

```
COMMIT;
```

instead of:

```
COMMIT WORK;
```

Another example:

```
SELECT width
FROM   Widgets;
```

instead of:

```
SELECT ALL width
FROM       Widgets;
```

Remember Shannon and information theory; when a word adds nothing to the meaning, it is not information. It is noise.

Exception: It's never bad to add unnecessary parentheses if there is any chance that a reader might not guess what the precedence of operators might be. For example:

```
SELECT (width * 5) + 4
FROM   Widgets;
```

Exception: Although UNION DISTINCT is not in common use, it is clear that SQL3's designers believe that explicitly saying DISTINCT is good.

9b. Superfluous Clauses

Most SQL programmers are willing to say the same thing twice "to make the meaning clearer." We give two examples of this bad but normal practice. The first shows a superfluous NOT NULL clause:

```
CREATE TABLE Widgets
   (width      INT         NOT NULL,
    CONSTRAINT widget_pkey PRIMARY KEY(width));
```

In SQL-92 and SQL3, a primary key is automatically NOT NULL.

The second example shows a superfluous predicate:

```
SELECT width
FROM   Widgets
WHERE  spoffo BETWEEN 'A' AND 'AZZZ'
AND    spoffo LIKE 'A%';
```

The BETWEEN clause is unnecessary. It's probably there for "optimization" reasons which are outside the scope of this chapter.

9c. Explicitizing

You don't need to start any program with the SQL statement:

```
CONNECT TO DEFAULT;
```

because the DBMS would CONNECT TO DEFAULT anyway. So should you bother? According to one DBMS expert, "yes." In general, if some critical process is *implicit* (performed automatically as default behaviour), you might do good by making it *explicit* (specified in the instruction). You're making your intentions clear not only to the reader, but also to the DBMS, so this act is more than a mere comment. In this view, the first SQL executed statement should be CONNECT.

10. Literals

Enter <exact numeric literal>s using maximum scale but without lead zeros and without leading + signs. For example:

```
UPDATE Widgets
SET    maximality = 10.00;
```

Exception: When using <literal>s in arithmetic expressions, use the scale you want to the result to have. (Note: If you want to be emphatic about what specific numeric <data type> you are using, consider using CAST.)

Even if a search of a character string Column is probably case-insensitive, use both upper- and lowercase as you would if you were inserting. For example:

```
SELECT     surname
FROM       Widgets
WHERE      surname = 'Smith';
```

Do not put trailing spaces in <character string literal>s unless they are necessary for comparisons with PAD SPACE Collations.

For binary items, use X'....' rather than B'....' notation. For example:

```
INSERT INTO Widgets (bobbet)
VALUES (X'427A');
```

11. Specify Character Sets

We can't call this "common practice" because we haven't seen much of _introducer use, but it would be consistent with the preceding to say that if a character string has, or will have, non-Latin letters and the default Character set is not obvious, specify the Character set.

12. Statement Splitting

Most SQL programmers are willing to write very long SQL statements. There is some practical justification for this tendency: (*a*) if any form of "auto-commit" is in effect, then splitting up SQL statements could leave the database in an inconsistent state and (*b*) most DBMSs optimize at the statement level, so putting everything in one statement might provide useful information to the optimizer.

Alternative: A minority view (which we espouse) holds that separate thoughts belong in separate sentences, as in any ordinary language. For example, we've suggested before that it's a good idea to add Constraints later (with ALTER TABLE), rather than mix all Constraints with <Column definition>s in the original CREATE TABLE statement.

13. Impossibilities

Consider this example of a CASE expression:

```
CASE Column_of_doom
WHEN > 5 THEN '>5'
WHEN <= 5 THEN '<=5'
END
```

It's hard to be sure, but it looks like the writers didn't ask, "What if Column_of_doom is NULL?". There should be an explicit ELSE clause here to allow for that. Defensive programmers code for the "default" or "otherwise" case, even if the case can't possibly happen.

14. Precise Comparisons

Comparisons with > and < operators are sometimes vaguer than they need be. For example:

```
name > 'X'     /* what if somebody is named 'X'? */
position < 1  /* you mean position <= 0? */
```

By rephrasing the comparison with a >= or <= operator, you can sometimes catch such problems.

15. Distributing NOTs.

"Neither a borrower nor a lender be." — Polonius

Instead of saying "be not a borrower or a lender," Polonius said, "neither a borrower nor a lender be" — using a separate negation word for each negated thing. This was an application of one of DeMorgan's Rules:

```
NOT (A OR B)  can be changed to NOT(A) AND NOT(B)
NOT (A AND B) can be changed to NOT(A) OR NOT(B)
```

Because the changed form is closer to the way that people actually talk, it is easier to read.

Naming Rules

Everyone says that onomatopoeia is the oldest profession. Or, at least, they would say that, if they knew that onomatopoeia originally meant "the making of names," and that Adam's first job was to name all the beasts in the Garden of Eden.

16. Give everything a name

The DBMS often lets you skip giving an Object a name; it just assigns a default name. But this default name is arbitrary. And besides, no two DBMSs use the same rules for default names. So, give explicit names to expressions in select lists. For example:

```
SELECT (length + width) AS length_and_width
FROM   Widgets;
```

Consider giving explicit names to Constraints in CREATE TABLE, ALTER TABLE, CREATE DOMAIN, and ALTER DOMAIN statements. If you don't, how will you drop the Constraints later? And how will you interpret the diagnostics which include <Constraint name>s? Here's an example:

```
CREATE TABLE Widgets
   (length     INT,
    CONSTRAINT Widgets_Length_Checker CHECK (length > 0));
```

Exception: Usually one does not give names to simple Column Constraints like NOT NULL or PRIMARY KEY.

Actually, naming is just one prominent example of a case where the DBMS will assign some "implementation-dependent" value if you don't specify one yourself. In all such cases, it's probably safer to specify.

17. When a name has two parts, separate the parts with the underscore character (_)

For example: `ytd_sales` `initial_extent`

Alternative: For <Table name>s especially, you can keep the parts unseparated but capitalize the second word. For example: `OrderItems` `DepartmentNumbers`

18. Avoid names that might be reserved words in some SQL dialect

The way to do this is to use names that refer to objects in the real world that you're modelling with your database. You can be fairly sure that names like `CandyStores`, `book_title`, or `swather` are not names that the DBMS needs for its own purposes. If you must be absolutely sure, you can take further measures — but there are problems with all of them.

- You can use the list of <keyword>s in Chapter 2 "General Concepts." This list includes reserved words used in major SQL dialects, as well as reserved words used in all standard SQL variations at the time of printing. It's better to look it up here rather than depend on a vendor's manual. But it's impossible to keep such a list up to date.
- You can check by passing to your DBMS an SQL statement containing the <identifier> and looking for an error message. For example, try to execute something like "`CREATE TABLE` <word> `(`<word> `INT);`". If the SQL statement works, <word> is not a reserved word. However, this won't tell you if some other DBMS reserves that word or if the next version of your DBMS will reserve it.
- You can put underscores (_) in names. This is unpopular. The SQL Standards committee doesn't intend to add <keyword>s containing underscores in any future SQL version. However, there are some exceptions: words that begin with `CURRENT_` or `SESSION_` or `SYSTEM_` or words that end with `_LENGTH`. Underscores have special meanings when used with introducers, with `LIKE` predicates, and with `SIMILAR` predicates. The SQL Standards committee will also avoid <keyword>s containing digits in all future versions. So try `Mussels4`. But first read Rule 25.
- You can enclose all names with quotes (`""`). But <delimited identifier>s cause their own problems; see Rule 19.

19. Avoid <delimited identifier>s

The troubles with them are, first, that double quote marks are false signals to many people who are used to thinking that quote marks appear around strings instead of names. Second, there's case sensitivity — `"X"` is not the same as `"x"`. Third, quote marks are ugly.

Exception: <Table name>s might require <delimited identifier>s because some DBMSs use files for Tables. File names include special characters, `.` or `/` or `\` or `:` , that are illegal in regular <identifier>s.

Exception: Microsoft Access programmers often use <delimited identifier>s for <Table name>s (Access is a non-standard SQL which uses `[]`s instead of `""`s to mark the delimitation).

Exception: Applications which generate SQL statements, such as user interfaces, might automatically enclose all <identifier>s inside " "s.

Exception: Of course, if you use SQL <special character>s in your names, you must use <delimited identifier>s.

With all these exceptions, you might decide to take the minority line and use <delimited identifier>s regularly. If you do, at least avoid names that have lead or trailing spaces. Some DBMSs' processes include an automatic `TRIM`.

20. Names of Tables are plural; names of all other Objects are singular

Thus, in the `INFORMATION_SCHEMA`, we have a View named `SCHEMATA` and the Columns of this View are: `CATALOG_NAME`, `SCHEMA_NAME`, and so on. Often a plural is a collective noun, for example: `INVENTORY`. Admittedly, this means that <Table name>s will be longer (at least in English), but it's a subtle signal that distinguishes <Table name>s from other <identifier>s.

Alternative: The dissenting minority points out that the English phrases for many tabular items are singular: "`ADDRESS BOOK`" (not "`ADDRESSES BOOK`"), "`PHONE BOOK`", "`INVESTMENT PORTFOLIO`", "`RESTAURANT LIST`", etc.

21. Use words in your national language

The fact that SQL <keyword>s look like English is irrelevant. For example, this sample SQL statement appeared in an article in a Polish magazine:

```
UPDATE studenci SET nazwisko='Kowalski';
```

This does mean that names will sometimes include characters outside the regular English alphabet. Obviously, the effect on portability is unfortunate but if your DBMS doesn't support accented characters in names, then it doubtless won't properly support them in data values either, so why would you use such a DBMS anyway? Precisely because you don't know what a `nazwisko` is, you can see that a Pole would have trouble understanding the word that you use instead of `nazwisko`.

22. Don't worry about how <Column name>s appear when a Table is displayed on the screen

That's something that changes anyway (use `AS` clauses). Instead, worry about how names appear if you print out a program. Remember — The goal is long-term comprehension so ephemeral considerations such as screen-display deserve low priority.

23. Names should be descriptive, but not too descriptive

Minimally, you should avoid algebra like `UPDATE k SET k1=4` — where no one could possibly guess what `k` and `k1` are supposed to represent. Medianly, you should avoid non-specific descriptors like `PHONE_NUMBER` — where no one can be sure whether the referent is a home or office or general contact telephone number. But stop there! Avoid names like `SOLDIERS_IN_THE_ARMY` because (presumably) all the soldiers in the database are in the army; the "in the army" bit is only helpful if you also have soldiers in the navy and you have to distinguish between them. This part of the rule — avoid making accidents part of the identification — is analogous to one of the normalization rules.

24. If two Columns from different Tables are based on the same Domain, they should have the same name

In fact, they should have the Domain's name. For example:

```
CREATE DOMAIN surname VARCHAR(25);
CREATE TABLE Students (surname surname, ...);
CREATE TABLE Professors (surname surname, ...);
```

This rule would apply even if your DBMS doesn't support explicit creation of Domains or if you use SQL3's user-defined type feature — you're still using the concept of Domains.

Exception: This rule does not apply for two Columns in the same Table.

Incidentally, when <Column name>s are the same, `NATURAL JOIN` is easier. That's usually a blessing, but some caution is required — you certainly don't want to cause a join over two Columns which have the same name by accident.

25. Digits are a bad sign

Too often we use digits as arbitrary distinguishers — e.g., `Lines_1` / `Lines_2` — when there is some intrinsic difference between `Lines_1` and `Lines_2` that could be expressed in the names, for example, `Lines_Freshwater` and `Lines_Longitude`. Particularly bad are the digits `'0'` and `'1'` which look too much like the letters `'O'` and `'l'`.

26. Try to stop a name at 18 characters; the maximum length allowed in SQL-89

Mainly, it's hard to remember a long name. For example, do you remember if the name mentioned in rule 8 was `Parts_Which_Have_No_Serial_Numbers`? Or was it `Parts_Which_Have_No_Serialnumber`?

27. Repeat the <Table name> in the <Column name> ... not

Firstly, you'd end up violating rule 24. Secondly, if you make a View of the Table, you'll have to either violate this rule or make View <Column name>s not equal to Table <Column name>s. For example, the `INFORMATION_SCHEMA` View called `GRANTS` has a Column called `IS_GRANTABLE` instead of `GRANT_IS_GRANTABLE`. Remember, if you really need to make it clear what Table the Column is in, you can use a <Column reference>: `GRANTS.IS_GRANTABLE`.

Exception: A Column which is part of the primary key of the Table could include the <Table name> in the singular. For example, the `INFORMATION_SCHEMA` View called `SCHEMATA` has a Column called `SCHEMA_NAME` — and any foreign keys that reference `SCHEMATA` would be Columns called `SCHEMA_NAME` too (assuming that Views could have such Constraints). There are several conflicting conventions for foreign keys. In any case, though, it is not part of your mandate to ensure that all <Column name>s in the database must be unique.

28. Depend on a dialect ... not

This can be subtle, e.g., `UCASE` is a function name that some people seem to think is standard SQL (in fact it's ODBC). Write with lowest common denominator syntax when you can, but test it first with an SQL3 parser to make sure you're not going to violate a rule when you upgrade.

29. Sometimes <Correlation name>s (or aliases) are simply necessary because the actual <Table name> is unwieldy, containing qualifiers or lengthy path names

In Oracle, use of <Correlation name>s actually helps the optimizer. But should you always use <Correlation name>s? No, they're most appropriate in SELECT statements where <Column name>s must be qualified.

30. Abbreviations

Legacy SQL code has frequent abbreviations: PROV for PROVINCE, DEPT for DEPARTMENT, LEN for LENGTH, FNAME for FIRST_NAME, and so on. Judging from trends in other computer languages, this taste will become obsolete. At this moment it's still a matter of taste. A few abbreviated prefixes/suffixes are used for some common Domains: _id for single-Column candidate key (e.g., author_id, program_id), _no for ordinal number (e.g., player_no, receipt_no), qty_ for quantity (e.g., qty_of_goods_sold), avg_ for average (e.g., avg_qty_of_goods_sold), min_ for minimum (e.g., min_weight), max_ for maximum (e.g., max_length), and sum_ for total (e.g., sum_balance). Notice that some of the prefixes are derived from SQL <keyword>s.

- Examples of <Domain name>s/<Column name>s. Some names that we have seen in use in databases for banking/libraries/retail shops/government include: firstname, lastname or surname, street, houseno, aptno or unitno or suiteno, city, state or province, country, phoneno or email, sex, birth_date, account_id, balance, account_open_date, account_close_date, transaction_code, author_firstname, author_lastname, title, callno, isbn, year_published, checkout_date, loan_type, amount, itemno, transaction_time, transaction_code.

  Certainly, we've seen many other names too, in many styles. We picked ones that generally fit the criteria that we've described heretofore.

31. Host language conventions

There is certainly an argument that this C code snippet looks fine:

```
EXEC SQL
INSERT INTO Recordings (szRecording)
VALUES (:szRecording);
```

The point here is that the C host variable szRecording associates with the SQL Column szRecording. Hence the same name. In general, we could say that SQL Object names are often influenced by conventions used in the most common host language, such as C in this case. We don't condemn this practice, we just ignore it because our concern is SQL conventions rather than host language conventions.

One detail about the szRecording in the preceding example; it's in a Polish notation, that is, the sz in the name indicates the data type (string zero). We will concern ourselves solely with the question, "Is it good SQL to embed <data type> information in names, for example szrecording or name_char or (more subtly) namestring?" The answer, judging as usual from what seems to be common practice, is yes that's okay, but nobody is doing so systematically. Sometimes we do see <Column name>s that end in _date or num[eric], but we don't see consistency.

For the narrower concept — Domains — we have Rule 24.

32. User names

If you have control over user names, prefer first names: Ralph, Mike, Lucien. Where necessary add the first letter of the last name: JeanC, RalphK, LucienB. This convention appears to derive from names on the Internet.

Often there is no choice in this regard because the operating system feeds user names to the DBMS.

33. Comma lists

Whenever a list is disordered, people wonder why. For example, these SQL statements look a trifle curious:

```
SELECT firstname, travel_allowance, surname
FROM   SalesPersons;

SELECT *
FROM   States
WHERE  state_abbreviation IN('WY','MI','AK','CO');
```

If there is some hidden order, add a note explaining what it is. Otherwise, change to a natural or alphabetical order.

Examples of Statements in Formal Style

Here are some actual SQL statement examples. We have not edited them to fit all the rules in this chapter.

```
ALTER Table Countries
ADD   gnp   DECIMAL(8, 2);

COMMIT;

CONNECT TO 'c:\db';

CREATE TABLE players
    (playerno  SMALLINT  NOT NULL  PRIMARY KEY,
     name      CHAR(15)  NOT NULL              ,
     leagueno  SMALLINT                         DEFAULT 99);

ALTER Table players
ADD Constraint check_playerno
CHECK (playerno BETWEEN 00 AND 99);

CREATE   VIEW ages (playerno, age) AS
SELECT   playerno, 1986 - YEAR_OF_BIRTH
```

```
FROM     Players;

DELETE FROM Order_Items
WHERE partid IN (
      SELECT partid
      FROM   Inventory
      WHERE  description LIKE 'd%');

GRANT   SELECT, UPDATE
ON      Jackets
TO      Carol, Kathleen;

INSERT INTO Gradings (gradeno, inspectorid, description)
VALUES (3, ?, 'Prime');

INSERT INTO Temporary_Workers (workerid, name, town, phoneno)
SELECT   workerid, name, town, phoneno
FROM     Workers
WHERE    benefit IS NULL;

SELECT   title
FROM     Videos
WHERE    out_date > DATE '1994-07-06'
GROUP BY title
HAVING   COUNT(*) > 1
ORDER BY title;

SELECT   accountid, balance
FROM     Accounts
WHERE    (town = 'Amesville'
OR       balance < 0)
AND NOT  (town = 'Amityville'
AND      balance < 0);

SELECT  NAME, TOWN
FROM    PLAYERS
WHERE   TOWN IN ('Inglewood', 'Stratford')

SELECT  first_name, last_name
```

```
FROM     Students
WHERE    studentno IN
        (SELECT      studentno
         FROM        Delinquent_Students
         WHERE       excuse IN ('sick','unhappy','deprived')) UNION
SELECT   first_name, last_name
FROM     Teachers
WHERE    teacher_status = 'sick';

SELECT  Realtors.name AS realtor_name, Vendors.name AS vendor_name
FROM    Members_Of_Real_Estate_Board Realtors, Sellers_Of_Farm_Land Vendors
WHERE   Realtors.name = Vendors.contact_name;

UPDATE   Addresses
SET      street               = ?,
         houseno              = ?,
         town                 = ?,
         state_or_province    = ?,
         zip_or_postal_code   = ?,
         country              = ?
WHERE    CURRENT OF Selection;

SELECT  title, release, censorrtg, runtime
  FROM  title
 WHERE  runtime BETWEEN 120 AND 231
 ORDER  BY release DESC
```

Host Language Programs

Some programmers keep SQL statements apart from host language statements, in separate procedures (or even separate modules). Others allow mixing, as in this (embedded Pascal SQL) example:

```
EXEC SQL SELECT COUNT(*) INTO :counter FROM Specifiers;
if (counter=0) Writeln('Empty Table!');
if (counter>0) begin
  EXEC SQL UPDATE Specifiers SET process_count = process_count + 1;
end;
```

The following style notes apply to either SQL/CLI or to embedded SQL.

34. Host language variable names should be similar to corresponding SQL <Column name>s but not identical

35. Put comments in the host program (not inside the SQL statement) using the host program's comment style

36. Employ assertions

Here we use the word "assertion" in the non-SQL sense; a conditional statement that you'd like to have in the debug version but not in the production version.

SQL is interpretive, so all "asserting" has to take place at runtime. In programs, the best method is to add executable SQL statements with `#if/#endif` host language directives.

WARNING: Some SQL precompilers ignore `#if` and `#endif`. For example, this assertion example checks that Column `PROGRAMS.SUMMARY` has matching definitions in both C and SQL. The format of the `SQLExecDirect` call is not a common style; you should take it merely as a suggestion.

```
...
#define SUMMARY_LENGTH [500]
SQLCHAR summary[SUMMARY_LENGTH+1];
#if DEBUG_ON
SQLINTEGER character_maximum_length;
  #endif
  ...
/* assertion start */
#if DEBUG_ON
  character_maximum_length = 0;
SQLExecDirect(hstmt,"SELECT CHARACTER_MAXIMUM_LENGTH\
                     FROM   INFORMATION_SCHEMA.COLUMNS\
                     WHERE  TABLE_NAME = 'PROGRAMS'\
                     AND    COLUMN_NAME = 'SUMMARY'",
              SQL_NTS);
SQLFetch(hstmt);
SQLGetData(hstmt,1,SQL_INTEGER,&character_maximum_length,NULL,NULL);
if (character_maximum_length <> SUMMARY_LENGTH) exit(1);
if (SQLFetch(hstmt) != SQL_NO_DATA) exit(1);
#endif
 /* assertion end -- if you survive to here, things are all right */
 SQLExecDirect(hstmt,"SELECT summary FROM Programs",SQL_NTS);
```

The following style notes apply only to SQL/CLI.

37. Use conventional names

For example, resource handles are `henv`, `hdbc`, `hstmt`, and `hdesc`. When there is more than one `stmt`, use ordinals: `hstmt1`, `hstmt2`, and so on.

38. Declare variables with constants or macros supplied in `sqlcli.h`

For example:

```
#include "sqlcli.h"
#define NAMELEN 50
...
SQLCHAR name[NAMELEN];
SQLCHAR create[] = "CREATE TABLE NameID (\
                    id INT,name CHAR(50))";
...
```

39. If an SQL statement contains constants which are also used in the host program, check or edit the statement at runtime

For example, add this to the last example:

```
...
sprintf(create,"CREATE TABLE NameID(id INT,name CHAR(%d))",NAMELEN);
...
```

40. When testing a function's return values, programmers use various styles

For example:

```
if (SQL_ERROR == SQLAllocStmt (hdbc,&hstmt)) goto error;
if (sqlreturn = (SQLExecute(hstmt)) < 0) {
  printf("sqlreturn = %ld\n",sqlreturn);
  exit(1); }
```

Summary

Whatever you write, may later be read.

Whatever style you choose for serious programs, stick with it consistently.

Index

B

G

M

O

Q

R

S

T

U

What's on the CD-ROM?

SQL-99 Complete, Really is accompanied by the companion CD-ROM which contains much more than the programming code, including the following HTML files:

- Appendix A — Remote Database Access
- Appendix B — SQL Taxonomy
- Appendix C — Non-portable SQL Features
- Appendix D — Incompatibilities with SQL-92
- Appendix E — SQL Web Sites
- Appendix F — Glossary

  The entries in this glossary include the computer-related words, names, acronyms, abbreviations, SQL keywords, and official terms used in the book, as well as those that are common in the SQL/database industry.
- Appendix G — Errata

The CD-ROM also includes a Windows .DLL demonstration SQL DBMS. The current supported environment is Microsoft™ Windows95 with available RAM of at least 2 MB.

For more information on the CD-ROM's contents, DBMS installation, and usage documentation, read `OCELOT.TXT` on the CD-ROM.
